The Making of the French Episcopate 1589–1661

The Making of the French Episcopate 1589–1661

Joseph Bergin

1996
Yale University Press
New Haven & London

Copyright © 1996 Yale University

All rights reserved. This book may not be reproduced, in whole or in part, in any form (beyond that permitted by Sections 107 and 108 of the U.S. Copyright Law and except by reviewers for the public press), without written permission from the publishers.

Set in Garamond by Best-set Typesetters Co., Hong Kong and printed by St Edmundsbury Press Ltd., Bury St Edmunds, Suffolk

Library of Congress Cataloging-in-Publication Data

Bergin, Joseph, 1948–
    The making of the French episcopate, 1589–1661 / Joseph Bergin.
      p.   cm.
    Includes bibliographical references and index.
    ISBN 0-300-06751-8 (cloth)
    1. Catholic Church—France—Bishops. 2. France—Church history—16th century. 3. France—Church history—17th century. 4. France—History—16th century. 5. France—History—17th century. I. Title.
BX1529.B457 1996
262'.12—dc20
                                                                       96-18336
                                                                             CIP

CONTENTS

Preface vii
List of Maps x
Abbreviations xi

I THE FRENCH CHURCH AND ITS BISHOPS

CHAPTER 1 3
A Peculiar Institution?

CHAPTER 2 44
Making Bishops

CHAPTER 3 90
Le Temporel: Wealth and Revenues

CHAPTER 4 138
Bishops, Pensions and Pensioners

II PROFILES OF THE EPISCOPATE

CHAPTER 5 167
Origins

CHAPTER 6 208
Educating Bishops

CHAPTER 7 245
Before the Call: Clerical Status and Pre-Episcopal Activities

CHAPTER 8 293
Dioceses and Bishops: Patterns of Episcopal Tenure

III THE CROWN AND THE EPISCOPATE

CHAPTER 9 335
The Episcopate and the Wars of Religion

CHAPTER 10 365
Henri IV and the Stabilisation of the Episcopate

CHAPTER 11 416
Consolidation and Contradiction 1610–30

CHAPTER 12 460
A Turning Point?

CHAPTER 13 494
The Mazarin Years 1643–61

Conclusions and Comparisons 542

IV BIOGRAPHICAL DICTIONARY 559

Bibliography 721
Index 739

PREFACE

THE IDEA OF writing a full-scale study of the group, at once both large and small, that has governed the French church throughout its history can hardly count as evidence of excessive originality. Other historians have, as the following pages show, tried their hand at just such a subject. Inevitably they have focused their attention on particular periods or problems relating to the composition or activities of the episcopate, with the perhaps paradoxical result that a newcomer to the field enjoys considerable latitude as to the approach he may wish to adopt. In my own case, previous studies in the field of the Catholic (or Counter) Reformation made me curious about the great mass of bishops who are *not* cited in the available literature on the subject. Research on Richelieu, Mazarin and the Guises had a similar effect. Put at its simplest, I was anxious to know more about the lesser known *chers collègues* of the likes of du Perron, La Rochefoucauld, Richelieu and Mazarin. But given the impossibility of discovering – let alone accounting for – what they did during their episcopal careers, it seemed at least worth establishing who these men actually were and how it was that they reached their elevated status of bishops.

But even such an apparently narrowly-focused enquiry turned out to be full of unexpected questions and problems, as the initial assumptions about the nature of both the subject and the research it would entail had to be modified. And above all, it became a study in social, political and ecclesiastical history extending far beyond the bounds of conventional religious history. Indeed, it is my hope that this book may help to show how far these often separated furrows ploughed by historians are, ultimately, just part of a larger field, the headlands and shape of which are too often lost from view. For these reasons alone, the decision to include an extensive biographical dictionary in this volume seemed in the end both logical and necessary.

Needless to say, a book of this size has taken some considerable time to research and bring to completion. Having originally contemplated working on a particular aspect of the subject as a graduate student, but shied away from it on the assumption that the sources simply did not exist, I returned to it over a decade ago and commenced work in the Vatican archives during a period of sabbatical leave. Further research was then interrupted until another spell of leave in 1991–2, when much of the research in French archives was done. Shorter stints of research followed, especially in provincial archives, in 1993 and 1994. I owe a particular debt to my department for enabling me to take leave and to the University of Manchester for supplying research and travel funds over the years. Above all, by making me a Research Fellow for the year 1993–4, it enabled me to do the bulk of the writing of the book, something which would have been virtually impossible in the normal course of one or even several academic years. Financial support for my research was also forthcoming from the British Academy, which also provided a publication subvention to meet the costs arising mainly from the biographical dictionary. As I measure the extent of the support received, I think it would be unpardonable not to thank the referees, sometimes anonymous, who have taken the time and trouble to put my case as persuasively as possible. Such time-consuming work is all too easy to overlook, but in the contemporary academic world, it is essential. In my own case, their willingness to perform this task means a great deal, and has spared me several further years of sweating over a hot stove!

It will be no less obvious that I have run up a large number of less quantifiable debts to both individual scholars and institutions while I have been working on what seemed an interminable project. Over several years Laurence Brockliss, Joan Davies, Robert Descimon, Daniel Dessert, Mark Greengrass and Sharon Kettering were unfailingly generous in supplying me with references and material derived from their own research. Similar generosity was shown by Françoise Bayard, William Beik, Pierre Blet, Richard Bonney, James Collins, Christian Jouhaud, Wolfgang Kaiser, Nicole Lemaître, Olivier Poncet, Orest Ranum, Ellery Schalk and Marc Venard. My thanks are also due to the many archivists and librarians who dealt with my queries either by post or *in situ* during my visits to their *dépôts*. And to those whom I may have forgotten to mention, I can only offer my apologies.

Later, as the book began to take shape, I received invaluable assistance from friends closer to home. Mike Hannah worked hard to computerise the data I had accumulated on aspects of the bishops' biographies. Large sections of the manuscript were read – and much improved – by Mark Greengrass, Nigel Griffin, and Gordon Kinder. Bruce Taylor undertook the worst of all chores, that of reading the proofs, and spotted a considerable number of mistakes and inconsistencies which always seem to escape the vigilance of any author. Without the hard work and patience of Mary Carruthers, my long-suffering editor, the final lap of the journey would have been much more fraught. To her, and to John Nicoll at Yale, my debts only seem to accumulate – *les paierai-je?*

As to my own family, they must by now be tired of being told how much neglect they have suffered during the writing of this book. But my regret at the neglect is no less acute for all that and I am looking forward to making up for it.

Manchester
May 1996

LIST OF MAPS

1	*French dioceses, 1600*	xii
2	*Revenues of French dioceses, ca 1600–20*	114
3	*Revenues of French dioceses, 1641*	118
4	*Geographical origins of French bishops*	171
5	*All bishops per diocese, 1589–1661*	311
6	*Bishops nominated per diocese, 1589–1661*	313
7	*Dioceses attracting reigning bishops*	314
8	*Dioceses losing bishops*	315

ABBREVIATIONS

Anselme	Père Anselme, *Histoire généalogique de la maison royale de France* etc
AAE	Archives des Affaires Etrangères
AAE, France	AAE, Mémoires et Documents, France
AAE, CP	AAE, Correspondance Politique
AC	Archives Communales
Acta Camerarii	ASV, Fondo Consistoriale, Acta Camerarii
Acta Misc	ASV, Fondo Consistoriale, Acta Miscellanea
AD	Archives Départementales
AN	Archives Nationales
ANG	*Acta Nuntiaturae Gallicae*
Arch Chantilly	Archives du château de Chantilly
ASV	Archivio Segreto Vaticano
Barb lat	MS Barberini latini
BAV	Bibliotheca Apostolica Vaticana
BI	Bibliothèque de l'Institut de France
BL	British Library
BN	Bibliothèque Nationale
DBF	*Dictionnaire de biographie française*
DBI	*Dizionario biografico degli Italiani.*
DDC	*Dictionnaire de droit canonique*
DGS	*Dictionnaire du grand siècle*
DHGE	*Dictionnaire d'histoire et de géographie ecclésiastiques*
Doss bleus	Dossiers bleus
Gallia	*Gallia Christiana*
Gallia Chr Nov	*Gallia Christiana Novissima*
MC	Archives Nationales, Minutier Central
Misc Arm	ASV, Miscellanea Armarium
MS Fr	Manuscrit français
MS lat	Manuscrit latin
MS Naf	Manuscrit, nouvelles acquisitions françaises
N Fr	ASV, Nunziatura di Francia
PC	ASV, Processus Consistoriales
P Or	Pièces Originales.

1 *French dioceses, 1600*

I
THE FRENCH CHURCH AND ITS BISHOPS

CHAPTER 1

A Peculiar Institution?

THE OFTEN REMARKABLE strides taken in recent decades by research into the religious history of early modern France have illuminated whole corners of a past which previously seemed condemned to remain unknown because unknowable. The results of that research have become part of the staple diet of historians of early modern Europe generally. But because research often advances unevenly – resembling a skirmishing party concentrating on a particular target more than a full-bodied army attempting to sweep all before it – gaps in knowledge remain, and with the passage of time ideas about particular subjects which once seemed satisfactory come to appear rather dated and substandard.

There can be little doubt that the French episcopate of the seventeenth century is one such subject. This is not to say that historical judgements about it are lacking. What emerges most strikingly from even a cursory review of the historical literature is the sheer range of such judgements. Often contradictory generalisations about the character of the episcopate have gained currency over the years. Indeed, it is precisely the currency of such general, but poorly informed, images of the French episcopate of the *ancien régime* which has become so problematic and so unhelpful to those interested in the subject.

To a considerable extent, these views are based on a limited body of anecdotal evidence, itself garnered from a wide spectrum of letters or memoirs of the time. Diarists and letter-writers from Pierre de l'Estoile to Mme de Sévigné commented on the doings of bishops, frequently attributing to them attitudes and activities that as often as not were based on little more than gossip or personal prejudice. The *locus classicus* for such comment is the widely read and oft-repeated *Historiettes* of Tallemant des Réaux, that titillating mixture of malice and fact. Accordingly, historical accounts of the seventeenth-century episcopate have varied considerably over the years, depending on the extent to which historians preferred to accept negative or positive comments by contemporaries upon France's bishops, and thus to construct examples of 'good' or 'bad' bishops.

What is remarkable about these accounts is the largely unchanging range of evidence and exemplars on which they are based. Negative accounts tend to dwell upon underage child bishops like Henri IV's illegitimate son, Henri de Bourbon-Verneuil who was given the opulent see of Metz at the age of four; on alleged 'atheists' like Beaumanoir de Lavardin, bishop of Le Mans, or on libertines like *Monsieur le Coadjuteur* himself, the second Cardinal de Retz, the epitome of the intriguing, womanising, and worldly bishop who owed his succession to the see of Paris entirely to family influence and pressure. A few lesser known but comparable cases added both spice and variety to hostile or pessimistic views of the episcopate. The approach adopted by historians holding a more optimistic view of an episcopate which had put the disasters of the sixteenth century behind it and was making strenuous attempts to conform to Tridentine expectations of bishops, was not fundamentally different: their picture of this serious-minded episcopate is also built up around exemplary invididuals. This is particularly the case when it comes to the quest for French bishops who either consciously modelled their careers on that of Carlo Borromeo, the great reforming archbishop of Milan (1565–84), or who were regarded by their contemporaries or by immediate posterity as French versions of Borromeo. This quest for a genealogy of the 'good bishop' could lead down unexpected paths. If there was an exemplar of the human and religious qualities which were held to constitute the ideal bishop, it was another man who did not belong to the French church, but whose example and authority was regarded as important in shaping a whole generation of bishops – François de Sales, bishop of Geneva-Annecy (d. 1620).[1] Lesser, or at least less celebrated, examples abound of bishops whose biographies were promptly written up and circulated as part of an attempt to promote a Tridentine model of what bishops should be; the same message was also to be found in printed versions of funeral sermons delivered in honour of particular bishops. That these could be more than mere homage to the individual concerned is clear from the work of Antoine Godeau (1605–72), bishop of Vence and Grasse, a founding member of the Académie Française, and a widely read spiritual author.[2] His sermons were highly prized reworkings of the *bonus pastor* theme, and his lives of Saint Paul, Saint Augustine and Carlo Borromeo were followed by his *Eloge des évêques français qui se sont rendus les plus illustres*, the early editions of which included only three highly individual bishops from the seventeenth century – de Sales, Jean-Baptiste Gault of Marseille, and Alain de Solminihac of Cahors. Subsequent editions are themselves evidence of a tradition that was being constantly reworked, since they

---

1 See Giuseppe Alberigo, 'Carlo Borromeo come modello di vescovo nella chiesa post-tridentina', *Rivista Storica Italiana*, 79 (1967), 1031–52; Antoine Degert, 'Saint Charles Borromée et le clergé français', *Bulletin de Littérature Ecclésiastique*, 4th series, 4 (1912), 145–59, 193–213; Raymond Darricau, 'La Posterità spirituale di San Carlo Borromeo in Francia nei secoli xvii–xix', *La Scuola Cattolica*, 112 (1984), 733–64.
2 There is no full modern account of Godeau's work and influence. The study by Georges Doublet, *Godeau évêque de Grasse et de Vence 1605–1672*, 2 vols (Paris 1911–12) is incomplete.

added new names to Godeau's initial pantheon; that of 1802 added no fewer than twelve, including Godeau himself, from the pre-Louis XIV seventeenth-century church! Whether the view taken of the French episcopate was positive or negative, it remained focused on just a handful of individuals, leaving the hundreds of remaining bishops in limbo.

However, sermons, hagiography, and related literature did not eliminate historical research as a source of facts and ideas about the episcopate. Indeed, not a few seventeenth-century bishops were themselves historians and antiquarians, often interested in establishing accurate succession-lists of bishops for their own dioceses. A few even engaged in this research themselves. Jean Plantavit, bishop of Lodève (1625–46) compiled a *Chronologia* of his predecessors, and even added an invaluable chapter which narrates the curious circumstances in which he himself became bishop.[3] His immediate successor at Lodève, François Bosquet, was a more learned scholar, though he saw no point in attempting to rewrite Plantavit's work. Among many other endeavours, he concentrated on preparing a history of the Avignon popes, which Colbert's famous scholar-librarian, Etienne Baluze, later revised and published, before himself writing a history of the bishops of Tulle, his native town.[4] Such scholarly activities were not isolated, and it seems probable that some of the numerous other diocesan histories published during the century were sponsored by reigning bishops. It may be supposed that such scholarly endeavours were not wholly disinterested, at least on the part of their episcopal sponsors, for whom the ensuing diocesan histories were primarily episcopal histories. Beyond that, these works reflect an important change in the French church which this study wishes to suggest but which it cannot fully investigate – namely, the growing assertion, or re-assertion, of episcopal dominance within the affairs of the seventeenth-century French church.

But arguably the historiographical enterprise which did most to reflect the new-found importance of episcopal office in the post-Tridentine church was the famous *Gallia Christiana*, the first edition of which was published as early as 1626 by Claude Robert, former tutor to an archbishop of Bourges: the *Gallia* was less a history of the French church than an attempt to provide a comprehensive and systematic series of lists and biographical sketches of the incumbents of France's bishoprics, as well as of its abbeys, priories, cathedral dignities and so on. Similar historical enterprises were undertaken in other countries at the time, but it says much for the historiography of the French church that the *Gallia Christiana*, possibly because of its accessibility, still remains by far the most influential source of information about the French upper clergy until the seventeenth century.[5]

Yet it would be disingenuous to allege that the historiography of the

---

3 Jean Plantavit, *Chronologia praesulum Lodovensium* (Aramontii 1634). This work was dedicated to Richelieu who is addressed as 'Potentissimum totius Imperij Gallici Administrum'.
4 Etienne Baluze, *Vitae paporum Avennionensium* (Paris 1693).
5 For a very brief account, see Denys Hay, *Annalists and Historians: Western Historiography from the Seventh to the Eighteenth Century* (London 1977), 163–6.

French episcopate has remained stuck precisely where successive editions of either Godeau's *Eloge des évêques illustres* or the *Gallia Christiana* left it. Revised initially by the Sainte-Marthe brothers in 1656, the *Gallia* was considerably expanded by the Maurists during the eighteenth century, and republished in 1863 with a final volume by its last editor. It also served as a model for Henri Fisquet's *France Pontificale*, published in twenty-one volumes between 1864 and 1873, as well as for P A Jean's more limited compilation, *Archevêques et évêques de France depuis 1682*, which appeared in 1891. At the turn of the century, an attempt at an entirely new version, the *Gallia Christiana Novissima*, was launched, but it only reached seven volumes and was confined to the dioceses of Provence. It was then abandoned, though not before it had hinted at what could be achieved by careful research in those ecclesiastical archives which had survived the havoc wreaked by the French Revolution. Quite independently, two far more summary listings of the bishops not just of France but of the whole of Christendom also appeared (or began appearing) in the late nineteenth and early twentieth century – P B Gams's rather sketchy *Series Episcoporum* and the *Hierarchia Catholica medii et recentioris aevi*, much the better documented of the two publications, and based on first-hand sources from the papal archives. The stamina of such a scholarly tradition is noteworthy, and it may not yet be entirely dead, as is evidenced by the publication as recently as 1974 of an exhaustive, if extremely laconic, listing of all French bishops since 1592 in the form of an *épiscopologe* tucked away in the obscure columns of the as yet incomplete *Dictionnaire d'histoire et de géographie ecclésiastiques*.[6] It may well be that the survival of this tradition owes something to the lack of a comprehensive dictionary of French biography. But whatever the intentions that lay behind these successive enterprises, they at least make it feasible to envisage a systematic study of the French episcopate in a given historical period; limited though they may be as works of scholarship, they serve as an irreplaceable point of departure for any attempt to advance into uncharted terrain.

Despite this kind of scholarship, it took some considerable time for French ecclesiastical history to emerge from the largely confessional or hagiographical ghetto in which it found itself confined for much of the nineteenth and early twentieth century. This was due to several factors rather than to any single one of them. Its rehabilitation owed a great deal to a generation (if not a school) of historians who were primarily interested in the changing face of popular religious practice, especially in the eighteenth century. Subsequently, their work and that of their successors gradually led in

---

6   DHGE, xviii, article 'France', cols 161–526. The *épiscopologe* lists in alphabetical order all French bishops since 1592, regardless of where they served. For each one of them, it attempts to list, in standardised form, ten biographical details, beginning with the date and place of birth, the dates of their first nomination to a diocese, confirmation by Rome, and of their consecration, followed by the place of consecration and names of the bishops who performed the ceremony, and ending with the dates of resignation, transfers to other dioceses and, finally, death.

several new directions, including the social history of the clergy generally, the religious culture of social élites, and questions of authority and power within a given church or diocese. The earliest of these studies were devoted to the eighteenth or even nineteenth centuries, while those concerned with the seventeenth rarely ventured into the first half of the century.[7] Yet these changes did not transform the historiographical landscape instantly, and Paul Broutin's influential two-volume study of *La Réforme pastorale au xviie siècle* was still largely conceived in terms of individual biographies, especially of bishops, and was based essentially on early biographical – and often virtually hagiographical – sources.[8] The French discovery of prosopography – though it would not be called that for some considerable time – occurred at about the same time, though at that point it had very little to do with ecclesiastical history. Initially, it was identified with the work of the François Bluche on the magistrates of the sovereign courts of Paris, and was also concerned with problems of ennoblement. However, once accepted, prosopography soon proved how fertile it could be. In the past twenty years, it has produced a lengthening shelf of studies, albeit of varying quality, and its methods have proved especially suited to the study of well-defined professional or social groups: magistrates of particular courts, merchant élites, provincial governors and intendants, municipal oligarchies, financiers, cathedral and other canons and, last but not least, bishops.

It was perhaps this slow and, in some respects, unpredictable shift in historians' interests which enabled one recent historian to preface a brief study of the social origins of the bishops of early seventeenth-century France by saying that every French historian had come to know a bishop or two. Of course, to many historians of the so-called *grand siècle* still faced with a wide range of objects of study, two or so bishops may seem quite enough. But to historians of the church as well as of politics in the widest sense, whether it be national or local politics, it is still far too few. Indeed, for all the work done on French religious history to date, one of the problems with the historiography of the French church in an age of Counter-Reformation or of Catholic reform arises from the reluctance of historians to know more than 'a bishop or two'. As already suggested, both negative and positive assessments of the church in seventeenth-century France continue to be based on assumptions about the upper clergy, assumptions which when examined often turn out to include just a few well-known cases of bishops who were either models

---

7   Gabriel le Bras, *Introduction à l'histoire de la pratique religieuse*, 2 vols (Paris 1942); *idem.*, *Etudes de sociologie religieuse*, 2 vols (Paris 1955–6). Most of the contents of the second of these collections were written in the 1930s and 1940s, and include essays on the second half of the seventeenth century and the eighteenth. For some of the subsequent early studies dealing with the seventeenth century, see Thérèse-Jean Schmitt, *L'Organisation ecclésiastique et la pratique religieuse dans l'archidiaconé d'Autun de 1650 à 1750* (Autun 1957); Louis Pérouas, *Le Diocèse de la Rochelle 1648–1724: Sociologie et pastorale* (Paris 1964).

8   Paul Broutin, *La Réforme pastorale en France au xviie siècle: Recherches sur la tradition pastorale après le Concile de Trente*, 2 vols (Tournai 1956).

of what a Counter-Reformation bishop in the tradition of Borromeo or de Sales should be or, on the contrary, were 'scoundrels and schemers' in the mould of, say, the Cardinal de Retz.

There is, therefore, every reason for attempting to modify and improve upon such crude *images d'Epinal*. A number of scholars have already helped to lay the foundations and map out the way forward. A brief review of the most significant of them will suggest something of both their scale and substance, as well as their methodological implications. The first, and indeed the only one, of these studies was comparative in format. Its author, Norman Ravitch, was essentially concerned with establishing how far the French and the English episcopate were dominated by nobles in the age of Louis XIV and his successor, a period he labelled 'the age of aristocracy'.[9] In the case of France, his analysis showed that by the eighteenth century, episcopal office was an aristocratic near-monopoly from which commoners and even recently ennobled families were virtually excluded. For her part, Marilyn Edelstein focused on the use to which François I put the vast store of church patronage which the Concordat of Bologna formally confided to him, and concluded that, as far as recruitment to the episcopate was concerned, the king allowed the old nobility to take the lion's share, as indeed had his predecessor Louis XII.[10]

This concern with the social origin and status of France's bishops over several centuries was also to surface in Michel Péronnet's vast thesis on the early modern French episcopate as a whole. It was more wide-ranging in both its time-scale and the issues it addressed than anything that had preceded it, and was considerably more ambitious in its scope than that of either Ravitch or Edelstein: its point of departure was the generation of bishops in office at the outbreak of the French revolution, *la génération de 1789* as he put it – a corporate élite which dominated the French church and its dealings with the crown, as evidenced particularly by its activities during the general assemblies of the clergy. To understand how the bishops came to possess such remarkable power and collective self-assurance, Péronnet embarked on a full-scale analysis of the bishops seated since the Concordat of Bologna had been negotiated between François I and Clement VII in 1516 – in all, twelve generations and no fewer than 1,416 individuals. He, too, attached considerable importance to their social background, and particularly to the extent to which episcopacy and aristocracy were intertwined from one generation to the next. But he was not satisfied with a socio-historical explanation of the rise of a powerful episcopal bench. He looked to other factors also, and in particular to the educational background and pre-episcopal careers of the individuals

---

9 Norman Ravitch, *Sword and Mitre: Government and Episcopacy in France and England in the Age of Aristocracy* (The Hague 1966).
10 Marilyn Edelstein, 'The Social Origins of the Episcopacy in the Reign of Francis I', *French Historical Studies*, 8 (1974), 377–92; idem, 'Les Origines sociales de l'épiscopat sous Louis XII et François I', *Revue d'Histoire Moderne et Contemporaine*, 20 (1978), 239–47.

concerned, concluding that the net effect of all this was what he called the 'regularisation' of an episcopate, whose growing homogeneity was the main source of its power and confidence. Inevitably, given the main focus of his work, much of what Péronnet had to say about the sixteenth and seventeenth centuries was fairly sketchy and hurried, but he clearly appreciated the need to engage in systematic prosopographical research if the French episcopate of the period were to acquire a credible profile. To date, his is the most complete framework available for the analysis of the episcopate of any age.[11]

More recently still, Frederic Baumgartner scrutinised the episcopate from Henri II to Henri IV, from 1547 to 1610 – a period of acute difficulty, as we shall see, for France's bishops. His point of departure was different again: in an earlier study on the political thought of the Catholic League, he had encountered bishops who, surprisingly, were not quite on the side of the fence that one might have expected them to be during the crisis of royal succession after the murder of Henri III. Consequently, the principal focus of Baumgartner's study was the predicament of the French bishops during the wars of religion, and in particular their political and ecclesiastical activities. It culminated in the crucial part an active minority of them played in the conversion of Henri IV to Catholicism. On the other hand, Baumgartner's efforts to discover and assess the religious role of bishops within their dioceses only yielded meagre results, partly because of the difficulty of ascertaining exactly what that consisted of in a period of extreme turmoil, but also because of the value of the conclusions which could be drawn from such evidence as does survive. For the rest, Baumgartner's analysis of the mechanisms of episcopal nomination and succession, the changing face of royal patronage, and the social background of the bishops themselves, tended largely to follow Péronnet's categories and methods. Lastly, his analysis of the bishops who took office under Henri IV was too brief to convey a genuine sense of the sheer confusion and complexity of what was happening at the time.[12]

I

As a subject of historical study, the French episcopate between the Reformation and the Revolution is thus not *terra incognita*. But the widely differing emphasis of each of the major studies just reviewed indicates that no single approach to the subject has acquired the kind of canonical status which it would be difficult to jettison without serious justification. Yet if the analysis which is proposed in the present study is to carry conviction, it is essential at

11 Michel Péronnet, *Les Evêques de l'ancienne France*, 2 vols (Lille 1978). This is a photocopied reproduction of the typescript of Péronnet's *thèse d'état*, presented in 1976. Much of the material contained in its appendices is illegible or so poorly reproduced as to be unusable.
12 Frederic J Baumgartner, *Change and Continuity in the French Episcopate: The Bishops and the Wars of Religion 1547–1610* (Durham, North Carolina 1986).

the outset to offer an explanation of each successive term in its title. Apart altogether from defining its scope, this will also reveal the difficulties that await the historian of this subject, not least by presenting the sources on which it is based. But rather than reducing this exercise to a dry treatise on method, we may use it as an opportunity to explore some of the long-term structures and often peculiar features of the French church.

To begin with, it will be evident from the historiographical review that for the crucial seventy or so years following the wars of religion, during which the French episcopate gradually acquired many of the characteristics that it would retain until the Revolution, there has been no systematic study which would correspond to the research undertaken on other social, political, or religious groups, or which can be compared to the studies written on the bishops of both earlier and later periods. This lacuna has always made it difficult for historians to form a clear idea of the episcopate of the early generations of the Catholic Reformation, and of the nature of their contribution to both religious and political life at the time. In chronological terms, the present exploration begins with the highly confused situation at the closing stages of the wars of religion, at a time when one Most Christian King, assassinated as a tyrant who had allegedly abandoned the church and Catholicism, was succeeded by a Most Christian King who was Protestant and the acknowledged leader of the Protestant party and church. It ends with the death of Mazarin and the emergence of a Most Christian King whose long personal rule would witness the consolidation of so many of the political, institutional, and religious changes initiated under his two predecessors.

The time-scale of this study thus has a unity which may not be immediately obvious. It might have made more sense to limit it to the reigns of Henri IV and Louis XIII, on the grounds that when the latter died in 1643 some important changes with regard to the appointment of bishops were imminent, and that the long ministry of Mazarin was not typical, for obvious reasons, of the reign of Louis XIV as a whole. But it might just as easily be argued that the present study should have gone even further and included the half-century of Louis XIV's personal rule, thereby presenting a fuller picture of the changing character of the French episcopate over more than a century. Desirable though that might be, there would have been a number of practical difficulties which, taken together, might well have prevented it from ever being completed – except perhaps by a whole team of researchers. Moreover, the following pages will endeavour to show that the most enduring and crucial changes to the character of the episcopate had been effected by the time of Mazarin's death, though the cardinal's own behaviour partially obscures this, and that there were few significant changes during Louis XIV's personal rule. As it stands, the time-scale covers nearly three-quarters of a century, which is certainly long enough to measure both the long-term effect of such changes as did occur, and the more long-standing characteristics of the episcopal bench.

Establishing the chronological limits of a study like this is, however, not the most difficult problem. We have already seen that previous studies of the French episcopate have not followed any single methodological format. Admittedly, most of them have shared an interest in questions like the social origins of bishops, but each one then proceeded to focus on particular aspects of the subject. Such diversity of approach is probably inevitable, given the virtual impossibility of embracing in a single study every question of interest to historians about the episcopate of a given generation. Any new attempt to take up the subject thus enjoys a certain latitude when it comes to method or approach. Moreover, every study is defined as much by its self-imposed limits as by its ambitions, and it would be misleading to conceal the fact. If there are negative as well as positive reasons for the present book's taking the shape that it has, they concern substance as much as method, and it will help if we clarify them at the outset.

The first consideration was how to define the scope of the project in such a way that the final outcome had a certain internal coherence to it, and that this objective (coherence being always a relative notion) was not frustrated by the virtually limitless extension of the subject matter itself. But this coherence had to be based on more than just convenience, expediency, or questions of form and presentation. As the title indicates, the conclusion eventually reached was that to concentrate on the making of the episcopate was likely to prove the most tenable approach to the subject, but more importantly still, that it would yield the most sustainable and credible results. This option has not, as we shall frequently see, eliminated difficult problems with documentation and interpretation on almost every issue discussed. Yet it would be foolish to deny that this choice of approach limits the focus of what has been attempted, and some readers may well feel they have been deprived of what they would most wish to know – namely, what bishops did and were once they had become bishops. Yet a study which attempted to weigh and judge the administrative and pastoral record of several hundred reigning bishops scattered across no fewer than 113 dioceses, is itself open to even more serious objections. The most obvious of these is that of superficiality, which has become all the more inescapable now that a number of detailed studies of individual dioceses and their bishops have been published for the period covered in this book. What they have shown is the huge variety of the dioceses of France and, therefore, of the circumstances to which any given bishop had to adjust before attempting to pursue a chosen course of action. Religious and pastoral traditions varied from region to region, and new approaches to problems of government and reform were not always feasible or welcomed, as is evident simply from the research undertaken into the revived practice of pastoral visitations in the sixteenth and especially seventeenth centuries.[13]

---

13 See Bernard Plongeron, 'Charles Borromée, example et modèle: son influence en France (xvie–xixe siècles)', in *San Carlo Borromeo e il suo tempo* (Rome 1986), i. 493–525.

Any attempt to measure national episcopal activities or to reach conclusions applicable to the French church as a whole would thus be premature and highly questionable. For the foreseeable future, it is likely that the study of what bishops did *qua* bishops will continue to be done, and properly so, at diocesan or provincial, rather than national level. Even were a genuinely nationwide study possible, it would still need to account for all the influences and pressures which could determine the behaviour of bishops once installed in their dioceses, influences which might have had very little to do with their pre-episcopal careers or experience.

On the other hand, what a study like the one proposed in the following pages can seek to achieve is to present as wide-ranging a profile as possible of those who became bishops between the final phase of the wars of religion and the beginning of the personal government of Louis XIV. This entails an extended prosopographical analysis of the 351 bishops who were nominated to French dioceses between the accession of Henri IV in 1589 and the death of Mazarin in 1661. It is the need to define the *corps épiscopal* in precise numerical terms which is the first imperative, and this in turn confers on the terminal dates of the study an importance which they do not otherwise possess. In spite of that, we shall see later that this total figure is by no means a 'given', and that it could only be arrived at after a series of assumptions were made about the minimum requirements for someone to be considered a bishop.

The temptation to assume that any *ancien régime* élite was born and not made is a powerful one, but it should be resisted, not least because it tends to disguise changes over what was, after all, a very long time-span. The present study, while not ignoring the obvious advantages enjoyed by ambitious clerics who could boast distinguished birth, wealth, and influential connections, allows from the outset for the possibility that access to the episcopate fluctuated from generation to generation, and that the changes in its social composition may provide some of the answers to questions about the bishops' behaviour as diocesans, as well as in their relations with the crown. But this study also attempts to look beyond the sometimes limiting framework imposed by the search for the social origins of the bishops, and considers, to the extent the often rather laconic sources permit, the relative importance of their geographical and professional origins for the character of the episcopate as a whole.

For similar reasons, it seemed no less essential to investigate the kind of educational experience they had before setting their sights on high church office. It is a subject that is rendered extremely slippery by both the paucity of first-hand sources and, in particular, by the often misleading terminology used by contemporaries to describe the achievements of those who had pursued university studies. The educational profile of the episcopate presented here must, therefore, be rather tentative, and because of that it should not be mistaken for a complete intellectual or cultural profile; that would require extensive research and could form the subject of an entire study in its own right.

The question of how future bishops occupied themselves in the years between the completion of their studies and their episcopal nomination also deserves close scrutiny. Like education, its contribution to the success of those who became bishops is problematic. For a large number of those whose principal title to the mitre was their pedigree and their family's services, past and present, this chapter of their curriculum vitae is often rather slight. Others could point to a wide range of experience, pastoral and administrative. But since episcopal promotion was never explicitly subjected to the test of experience, the latter is not a sure guide to the manner in which bishoprics were bestowed on individuals. Yet a study of pre-episcopal careers can at least suggest some insights into the calibre and experience of those who were called upon to govern France's dioceses. It cannot, needless to say, claim to predict how these men would conduct themselves, individually or collectively, once raised to the episcopate; though the fact, for example, that incoming bishops were increasingly middle-aged by the 1640s and 1650s itself suggests that radical shifts in their outlook and behaviour, once they had become bishops, were unlikely.

It may be conceded that the greater the number of vantage-points from which a subject is examined, the more it may fragment into discrete elements. Yet without prejudging the conclusions that will emerge later in this study, the preceding comments would seem to imply that there was no single route to the episcopate. To understand why this might be the case, we also need to carry the analysis forward into the realm of royal patronage, a subject which will occupy a substantial section of this book. This may seem a fairly straightforward matter, but that is far from being the case. If its importance is not in doubt, it can hardly be said that there is a tried-and-tested methodology for dealing with it which does full justice to all of its aspects – a situation which may seem paradoxical in view of the extent to which recent historiography has used concepts of patronage as a means towards re-orienting the political (and social) history of early modern France. With the exception of a handful of detailed studies, the historiography of the French church has largely escaped such influences, partly because its principal centres of interest – religious reform, popular religion, and so on – do not lend themselves well to such treatment. Individual studies have demonstrated that nepotism and wider family interests were at least as prevalent among the lower clergy as they have always been suspected of being among the higher ranks, with much of the evidence for such behavioural patterns being provided by what might be called the 'corporate' clergy, and especially the cathedral chapters. But studies of this kind, often confined to a particular institution or locality, offer only limited guidance on how to tackle a subject as 'nation wide' in scope as that of the episcopate. Now, for reasons that will become clear in the next chapter, it is fair to say that the nomination of bishops in France was highly 'patronage-driven' throughout this period, despite different attempts to apply to it rules of both procedure and principle. In the event, nominations were only partly subjected to bureaucratic forms, and even these were relatively limited in scope, which is a major reason why the attempt to follow the vagaries of the crown's use of its jealously guarded privilege of nominating bishops, and to understand the forces which attempted to influence its choices, raises so many problems.

In the context of the present study, it should be noted that the term 'patronage' itself has at least two principal meanings. The narrower (and older) of them refers to the offices (or other 'graces') which were at the crown's disposal, and which were the objects of competition; this might be described as patronage-as-largesse. This conception has increasingly been overtaken by a more broadly conceived one which historians (and other social scientists) use in order to describe a style of government and decision-making which is primarily concerned with personal and group interests rather than with matters of policy or principle. In this perspective, in which patronage is the dynamic element of the whole political process, and no longer just the benefits which are being competed for, it might be labelled patronage-as-process.[14] Both meanings of the term will figure in the following pages, and in contexts which should prevent unnecessary confusion between them.

The fact that patronage-as-process has, as already suggested, been increasingly adopted as an all-encompassing tool for analysing the workings of the early-modern French monarchy, means that it can easily spark unrealistic expectations. For the most part, histories of patronage begin by attempting to reconstitute the often multi-layered networks, formal and informal, of patrons and clients, and then try to follow them as they compete with other networks for office, favour, and advantage. To date, most such studies have tended to be sharply focused – on ministerial or socio-professional groups, localities or provinces – and this, of course, provides the kind of stable framework that makes detailed analysis feasible. But, inevitably, such intense concentration upon a particular subject makes it virtually impossible to take equal account of other elements of the picture or offer a complete history of the patronage mechanism in question. Arguably, this might be less of a problem if it was clear that there was anything like a single, overarching 'system' of patronage which, if only we could pull together all its disparate elements, would somehow reveal the underlying 'logic' by which the realm was governed and patronage in the traditional sense of largesse was dispensed. But, judging by the present state of research, no early modern state achieved that high level of integration, formal and informal, and indeed the pervasiveness of patronage

---

14 See the discussions in Robert R Harding, *Anatomy of a Power Elite: the Provincial Governors of Early Modern France* (New Haven and London 1978), Sharon Kettering, *Patrons Brokers and Clients in Seventeenth-Century France* (Oxford 1986); and Kristen B Neuschel, *Word of Honor: Interpreting Noble Culture in Sixteenth-Century France* (Ithaca, N.Y. 1989).

and clientage has been presented as one consequence of the inadequate integration of the governing institutions of seventeenth century France.[15] Even if it is conceded that generic patronage was the glue which kept the polity together, it does not follow that patronage should be viewed in the singular, as an integrated entity: more like a kaleidoscope than a mosaic, its constituent elements were not firmly fixed in relation to each other.

In this regard, it is no exaggeration to say that the French episcopate poses greater problems for historians concerned with patronage than most subjects. It was a body dispersed throughout every corner of the realm, and it consisted of men drawn from every part of that realm. Between 1589 and 1661 a total of 351 bishops were nominated to 113 dioceses. Clearly, the range of 'interests' concerned when dioceses became vacant was potentially enormous. Looked at in this way, those joining the episcopal bench needed to pass through what amounted to the eye of a needle – and that needle took the form of attracting the attention and winning the approval of the king, his ministers and entourage generally. Some candidates managed to do so directly and personally; others were members of families with known court and ministerial connections. But the majority could only attract royal benevolence by proxy, through ties of friendship, kinship, or clientage. Each episcopal nomination thus has its own history, involving a varying number of *dramatis personae*. Existing studies would suggest that an analysis of episcopal patronage should begin with an attempt to reconstitute the networks into which individual bishops fitted. Such an approach would entail examining not only the local, provincial, and central connections of these men, as would be required in the case of non-ecclesiastical figures, but also their specifically ecclesiastical affiliations. Potentially inexhaustible, this kind of patronage history 'from the bottom up' would be more tractable if all of the bishops of our period were equally well known. Yet such is emphatically not the case, and for every Gondi, Grimaldi, or Guise who wore the mitre, there were large numbers of contemporaries whose backgrounds, both familial and personal, remain highly obscure; even bishops of distinguished family origins are often among the least known (and knowable) *as individuals*, and it has to be assumed that their entry into the episcopate came about because of their family connections to the crown. Here is one of many areas of investigation in which 'knowing a bishop or two' causes particular problems: by assuming an episcopate that was highly homogeneous, it minimises the problems that lurk beneath the surface.

The difficulties of reconstituting the patronage networks of France's incoming bishops might not be insuperable in themselves were they not compounded by a problem of a very different order. It is a problem we encounter in the study of royal patronage generally, and concerns not just positions in the church: that is the lack of adequate documentation. The

---

15 Kettering, *Patrons, Brokers and Clients*, ch 6.

problem arises principally for two reasons. The first is a familiar one to early modern historians – the paucity of papers, official and private, belonging to ministers, courtiers, bishops and other individuals involved in the political process. The second, which we shall encounter again later in this study, is the less familiar but no less significant one of the meagre range of documentation which the nomination of bishops generated in the first place. In practical terms what this means is that the vast majority of nominations remain enveloped in virtual silence, and can only be approached indirectly by the historian. The material available for the analysis of episcopal patronage is thus extremely uneven. Obviously, cases which are well documented may be used, firstly in order to uncover how particular bishops obtained the mitre, and secondly to suggest some broader patterns which might apply to other bishops. But this kind of approach requires a fair amount of caution, and we must recognise that, in numerous instances, information, both direct or indirect, on the circumstances of a promotion is simply non-existent.

As a consequence, the history of episcopal patronage proposed in this study is one that will focus on the role of the crown. There are obvious advantages in adopting what may seem at first sight a rather conventional approach. It provides a consistent thread to the analysis, which might otherwise fragment into numerous discrete items, and, because all bishops ultimately owed their good fortune to the crown, it forms the best single vantage-point from which to observe the shaping and reshaping of the episcopate for nearly three quarters of a century. Despite the different types of pressure brought to bear upon it, the crown steadfastly refused to surrender its rights to choose bishops. Yet in adopting this approach, we should be aware of its limitations and try to counteract them. It certainly does not mean that the 'patronage' perspective on the episcopate can simply be replaced by a 'policy' perspective, which would carry with it the assumption that royal policy and its variations over time were the only subject for study. As we shall see, the crown's ability to control episcopal nominations did indeed vary over time, but this variation was not just a matter of having a clear 'policy' at some times, or not having one at others. The idea that the crown could define and pursue a policy that was somehow independent of considerations of favour and reward, whether to social groups, families, or individuals, in return for, or in expectation of, service and loyalty does not fit seventeenth-century realities very convincingly. Judging by the conclusions of earlier studies, it seems best to regard the crown as being situated at the centre of what could be called a parallelogram of forces which, taken together, account for the success and failure of those in search of office, episcopal or otherwise. If, in subsequent chapters, names like Henri IV, Louis XIII, Richelieu and Mazarin are regularly used in connection with royal episcopal patronage, it is to some extent as collective nouns, and does not assume, unless the contrary is clear from the context, direct personal responsibility for the individual choices in question.

This is not to say that the choosing of bishops was a process in which anonymous actors pulled all the strings from behind the stage set, or that no one individual took the initiative or bore responsibility for a given nomination. Abundant evidence to the contrary will appear in due course. As in other spheres of government, all decisions were formally the king's decisions, which makes precise measurement of royal initiative in individual cases hard to gauge, especially when those involved in a process like selecting bishops were often content to remain in the shadows. Rarely do we find any contemporary comment upon this, least of all from the highest levels of government. The closest we get to an acknowledgement of the problem came in 1657 when Anne of Austria apparently suffered an attack of moral scruples after the nomination of one of Mazarin's closest clients, Zongo Ondedei, to the see of Fréjus. Rome was delaying confirmation of him because of rumours of his unsuitability, some of which appeared to derive from comments by Anne herself. For obvious reasons Rome took them seriously enough to instruct the nuncio to elicit a letter of recommendation for Ondedei from Anne, explicitly stating that he was worthy of becoming a bishop.[16] This only made her dilemma more acute, and she finally sent her confessor to the nuncio in secret. The confessor let it be understood that she would not oppose Ondedei's confirmation, but went on to point out that, although all bishops were nominated with her participation and consent, that could not be construed as meaning she was personally vouching for their suitability; she was in no position to do so, and there was now a council of persons equipped to do just that.[17] Such an admission was highly unusual, and could only be made in private. Moreover, the fact that it dates from the 1650s rather than, say, the 1590s or the 1620s, is itself an indication of the kinds of changes in attitude, and the ambiguities surrounding them, which later chapters will trace in more detail.

With these contrasting considerations in mind, the most fruitful approach to episcopal nominations appears to be one which not only uses the crown as a focus for analysis, but which does so in a way which attempts to keep the 'patronage' and the 'policy' perspectives running in tandem, and which also takes account of the frequent overlapping between them. Over the period covered in this study, the balance between the two might shift either way; understanding the reasons for this will be an important theme running through the following pages. The uneven, sometimes haphazard state of the sources available for such a study militates against a thematic treatment of episcopal patronage. What is available, however, lends itself more effectively

---

16 ASV, N Fr 111a, fos 7, 14, 20, 25v, 27v-8r, Rome to nuncio, 5 Mar, 14 May, 16 July, 1 Oct, 26 Nov, 1657 respectively. *Ibid*, fos 111, 113–14, 225, 244, Piccolomini to Rome, 6 Apr, 13 Apr, 26 Oct, 7 Dec 1657 respectively.
17 *Ibid*, fo 246, Piccolomini to secretary of state, 21 Dec 1657, quoting the confessor's exact words in Latin, as if to ensure there could be no further ambiguity about the queen's position. The reference to a council of suitable persons is, of course, to the *conseil de conscience*, first instituted in 1643.

to a broadly chronological approach which, although it can lead to repetition or to the exclusion of some common patterns, facilitates a close analysis of the points of change over an extended period.

II

Mention has been made more than once of the problems of documentation which lie in the way of any attempt at a wide-ranging history of the French episcopate. That other historians have already encountered them partly obviates the need for an extended commentary on the problem here, and in any case it seems advisable to reserve such discussion for specific instances where the problem arises. Yet a few observations of general relevance may be made at this point.

Probably the most common historical image of France is that of a precociously and enduringly centralised state. Most people, historians included, would probably extend that image to the French church, attributing the presence of such centralisation to the structures of the Catholic church generally, or to the nature of the relationship between church and state under the *ancien régime*. In practice, however, the stereotype does not satisfactorily fit historical reality. As so often in French history, there seems to be a vast disproportion between the size of the governmental machine and its capacity to generate, let alone preserve, working archives which reflect what it actually did rather than what it claimed the power to do. The historian attempting to study France's bishops is just as likely to be struck by the fragmented character of the church, even despite the royal prerogative of appointing bishops and the emergence of a strong sense of collective self-awareness among the episcopate. This impression is strongly reinforced by the experience of searching for the sources on which to base an historical account of the episcopate. What might be called the 'central archives' of the French church owe their existence almost entirely to the emergence of the general assemblies after 1560 and their contributions to the royal finances. As a result, the archives in question deal almost entirely with the deliberations of these assemblies and the financial records of their relations with the monarchy and the financial groups they deal with; the official papers of the *agents-généraux*, who were entrusted with handling the clergy's business between meetings of the assemblies, survive only for the eighteenth century, but their range is limited by the nature of their responsibilities.

It might be expected that the crown, given that it enjoyed the right to nominate bishops for papal confirmation, would have kept records capable of compensating for the limited character of the church's own archives. But here, too, the results are distinctly disappointing. Direct archival evidence of crown activities has not survived, and there is, for example, nothing remotely comparable to the archives of the Spanish crown's *Patronato Real* – probably because they never existed in the first place. Even in the one area where one might have expected some incentive to collect information, namely in relation to diocesan revenues and the calculation of pensions payable from them, there is virtually total silence. It is not even clear whether the successive secretaries of state who drew up the royal *brevets* nominating individual bishops ever kept complete minutes or registers of these documents; if they did, they have not survived. This may seem a trivial point, but it has important consequences for the present study. In the cases of dozens of bishops, especially under Henri IV and Louis XIII, we do not know when they were actually nominated by the king; in those instances in which not merely the precise date but even the month or the year of such nominations remain unknown, the task of scrutinising the circumstances in which the bishops were appointed is rendered so much more arduous. For the same reason, it also becomes difficult to measure and understand delays either in filling vacant sees or in securing papal confirmation once a royal nomination had been made – and sometimes both. For a study like this one, the lack of such precision is a regrettable drawback.

On the other hand, there is some surviving evidence to show that the crown was not always as well informed as might be expected as to the precise identity of at least some of its bishops. Occasionally, royal letters presenting episcopal nominees to the pope left blanks where christian names should have appeared, and the names of their recently-deceased predecessors were not always accurately rendered either! A nominee to the see of Toulon in 1638, the abbé de Loyac, had his nomination cancelled *in extremis* when it was learned that his eyesight was too poor.[18] Even if such ignorance was by no means the norm, and information was actually sought by royal ministers or advisers on candidates for the episcopate, there is no sign for our period that files or dossiers were compiled in relation to them. Thus, nothing like the lists of candidates for vacant dioceses such as were kept by the secretary of the Castilian *Patronato Real* have ever come to light in France for the period before Louis XIV instituted the *feuille des bénéfices*. Indeed, the only uniform source which survives for the vast majority of bishops appointed from the early 1610s onwards, the formal inquiry *de vita et moribus* into newly-nominated bishops, is to be found not in France, but in the archives of the papal consistory, during whose regular meetings candidates for bishoprics were proposed, examined, and confirmed. These papal dossiers have their own deficiencies as a historical source, as we shall see later, but their location in

---

18 *Lettres, instructions diplomatiques et papiers d'état de Richelieu*, ed D L M Avenel, 8 vols (Paris 1853–77), vi. 228, instructions for Chavigny, secretary of state, 1 Nov 1638; *Lettres de Chapelain*, ed Philippe Tamizey de Larroque, 2 vols (Paris 1880–3), i. 307–8, Chapelain to Antoine Godeau, 28 Oct 1638: 'M de Loyac, évesque prétendu de Toulon, a remis le brevet qu'il en avoit du Roy, qui le luy a osté sur ce qu'il a fort mauvaise veue'. It was around this time that reports of the incapacity (owing to loss of sight) of Joachim d'Estaing bishop of Clermont probably began to reach the court.

Rome rather than in France, is itself worthy of note. The inquiry itself was virtually always conducted in France on behalf, not of the king, but of the pope. This does not necessarily mean that the papacy was always better informed than the crown about new bishops, simply that the material available for the study of them was compiled with Roman rather than French exigencies in mind.

As a result, the historian must seek out the evidence on which to construct a general view of the episcopate wherever it can be found, in central and provincial sources, both manuscript and printed. The results are bound to be uneven, reflecting in part the personal histories, but also the social and even intellectual backgrounds, of France's bishops in the period under study. The undertaking is thus an uncertain one, and if it escapes the danger of presenting potentially arbitrary findings, that is due in some part to the fact that, unlike some subjects of prosopographical enquiry, the French episcopate was at any given time a finite body of known individuals.

III

Important as these issues are, there are others of a rather different order which also need to be considered because of their substantive implications for what is to follow. At first sight, they may appear too self-evident to require more than cursory comment, but, as so often, familiar terms can readily disguise unfamiliar realities. Three questions in particular merit attention. Who was a *bishop* in the late sixteenth and seventeenth centuries? What was it that *made* a man a bishop? Finally, what do we mean by the *French church*?

The first question is no doubt easier to deal with than the second, but the answer is obviously crucial for the definition of the body of individuals to be embraced by this study. It is here that the approach of the historian may well differ from that of the theologian or the canon lawyer, both of whom try to apply timeless criteria, ignoring the fact that at certain periods of history – of which sixteenth- and early seventeenth-century France is one – reality did not neatly conform to expectation. It is for this reason that the existing lists of who was, or was not, bishop of a given diocese in this period, need careful scrutiny. For example, the bishops figuring in the successive volumes of the *Hierarchia Catholica* are those who received formal papal confirmation and whose provisions have left their trace in the papal archives. One of the papacy's prime concerns was to maintain a clear and known line of succession to bishoprics, and it took great care in formal acts of provision to state whom an incoming bishop was succeeding, and for what reason (death, resignation, heresy, exchange, deposition). Irregular successions of the kind that still occurred under Henri IV and, to a lesser extent, Louis XIII, created embarrassing problems, and the surviving record tends to disguise or massage them.

The most recent listing of all French bishops in office since 1592 adopts a different approach again, by simply omitting all mention of those who may have secured their papal provisions but who, for whatever reason, failed or refused to have themselves consecrated.[19] This method is more restrictive than that of the *Hierarchia Catholica* and, if translated into a diocese-by-diocese listing, would leave some significant gaps for the sixteenth and early seventeenth centuries. In the last analysis, the problem is one of determining who was actually regarded as a bishop at a given time – and in accordance with which set of standards. Clearly, the growth of episcopal pluralism in the sixteenth century meant that the link between a bishop and an individual diocese was attenuated, especially where dioceses were subject to rapid exchange or transfer among those benefiting from this practice. In some cases, sixteenth-century French bishoprics were granted not so much to bishops as to administrators, as also happened to some of the dioceses of the Holy Roman Empire. In that case, the link was even more tenuous, and was distinctly more financial and temporal than it was spiritual.

These somewhat abstract considerations may be usefully illustrated by a number of examples, some of them involving both distinguished individuals and dioceses. In 1594, Henri IV nominated Philippe du Bec, the royalist bishop of Nantes, as archbishop of Reims, the first non-Guise (or non-Guise-dependent) archbishop since early in the century. But around the same time and as part of a political and financial settlement with the young duc de Guise, he agreed to allow a brother of the duc to be 'designated' as du Bec's successor. The last of the Guise cardinals, Louis de Lorraine (1575–1621), duly became du Bec's coadjutor in 1602 and then, when the latter died in 1605, his successor. But there is no record in papal archives of Guise's provisions as archbishop. Nor did the cardinal ever take the trouble to have himself ordained a priest, let alone consecrated as a bishop, not least because he was probably secretly married to a former mistress of Henri IV, Charlotte des Essarts, by whom he had several children, one of whom would become bishop of Condom in the late 1650s. Failure to have himself consecrated means that he could not be included in any corpus of bishops defined by the criterion of consecration. He could thus be excluded from the Reims episcopate for two different sets of reason. From 1622 to 1629, the cardinal was briefly followed as archbishop of Reims by an exiled English Benedictine, William Gifford, but he in turn was succeeded by the last Guise archbishop of Reims, the fourteen-year old Henri de Lorraine, who abdicated in 1640 in order to succeed to his father's title of duc de Guise. Needless to say, young Guise was neither ordained nor consecrated, and his title to Reims also went unrecorded in Rome. Yet, in both his case and that of his uncle, papal records show that their respective successors were explicitly given their provisions as a result respectively of the death and abdication of Guise archbishops whose

---

19 *DHGE*, xviii, cols 161–526.

own provisions were inexistent! Other sources make it clear, however, that the papacy of the day recognised both Guises as enjoying a valid claim to the see of Reims and regarded them as its ruling archbishops; at no time was any effort made to dislodge them or appoint someone else. This contrasts with the experience of the young Henri de Savoie-Nemours, who was nominated to Reims during the Fronde, but who then failed to secure provisions or have himself consecrated. When he finally surrendered his claim to Reims in 1657, the new archbishop, Cardinal Antonio Barberini, was given his provisions to the see, not as a consequence of the resignation of Nemours, but of the death in 1651 of the previous archbishop, Léonor d'Etampes de Valençay.

How is this long chain of succession to be evaluated, and which of those involved is to be included among the corpus of bishops under study here? On a strict canon-law interpretation, Reims might be considered to have had only three archbishops between 1594 and 1657, their tenure amounting to a mere twenty-two years out of a total of sixty-three. A more historical view, not wedded to such criteria, would hold that there were five archbishops in all, three of whom were consecrated, and then proceed to explore the significance of this pattern of succession and changes to it over time. But the two approaches, the legal and the historical, would at least agree to exclude one of those concerned, Savoie-Nemours, who never appears to have taken possession of Reims or administered it in any capacity between 1651 and 1657.

Other instances can be found to put the experience of Reims in perspective. In late 1616, Sébastien Galigaï, brother-in-law of Marie de' Medici's favourite, Concini, was nominated archbishop of Tours and duly obtained papal confirmation. But the Concini régime was destroyed in April 1617 before Galigaï could have himself consecrated or take possession of Tours; indeed, he judged it politic not to insist on his right to Tours and promptly resigned his claim to it altogether. It should come as no surprise that cases can also be found of bishops who died after receiving their formal papal provisions but before they were consecrated or took possession of their diocese. Perhaps the best-known example of this was Eustache Gault, confirmed as bishop of Marseille in January 1640, only to die unconsecrated just two months later; he was immediately succeeded by his younger brother, Jean-Baptiste, who governed Marseille briefly in 1642–3. Should the historian regard all three of these men as bishops, or simply defer to the letter of canon law in determining who was or who was not a bishop? Here too, a historical perspective would surely see only one of the Gault brothers, Jean-Baptiste, as having effectively been a bishop.

In making a historical judgement about such problems, the attitudes of contemporaries should also be taken into account. In the case of the Guises, for example, there is no doubt that contemporaries regarded them, whether consecrated or not, as archbishops of Reims, and official correspondence unhesitatingly refers to them as such; they openly held and administered the diocese for many years. The same could be said of Cardinal La Valette, son of the duc d'Epernon, unconsecrated archbishop of Toulouse between 1613 and 1627, as it could of other more obscure figures holding more obscure dioceses. At the same time, however, it is worth noting that contemporary attitudes were slowly changing, and that what was not looked at askance early in the century was becoming both more rare and more unacceptable by mid-century. Antonio Barberini, for example, was nominated to Poitiers in 1651 but had not received his provisions before he accepted Reims in 1657. For all his status as cardinal, it is clear that he was never regarded as bishop of Poitiers by contemporaries, and the *Hierarchia Catholica* omits any formal reference to him in connection with Poitiers.[20] Likewise, Henri de Savoie-Nemours does not seem to have been referred to as *Monsieur de Reims* in the way his Guise predecessors undoubtedly were. This increasing rigour is itself a historical development which can be attributed to a variety of factors, among them the gradual disappearance of the episcopal pluralism and related practices of the previous century.

The question of who is to count as a bishop also arises in relation to coadjutor-bishops, whom we shall frequently encounter in these pages. The term itself suggests an assistant bishop, whose purpose it was to serve a ruling bishop who was old, infirm, or for some reason unable to govern his diocese properly. In practice, the primary purpose in appointing a coadjutor was usually to ensure the future succession to a given diocese, and contemporaries were, perhaps not surprisingly, in the habit of referring to coadjutorships as *survivances*. Of course, not all coadjutors actually survived long enough to come into their full inheritance, and that fact might appear to exclude those falling into that category from consideration in this study. But that, too, seems unnecessarily narrow a view. The real distinction lies elsewhere: it is, perhaps paradoxically, between those who did and those who did not have themselves consecrated bishops. Although that distinction appears to contradict the point just made in relation to ruling bishops, contemporary practices and attitudes point strongly to its validity. Those coadjutors who at least proceeded to consecration could, and often did, play significant roles both in diocesan affairs as well as in those of the French clergy as a whole. To deny a place among the episcopate to those of them – only a few in number, it should be said – who were unfortunate enough to die before they could take full personal possession of a diocese seems, at least on historical grounds, excessively legalistic. By way of example, one has only to point to the considerable administrative and pastoral duties performed on his uncle's behalf by the young Retz as coadjutor of Paris before the events of the Fronde swept him into political life; his well-known hold on the *curés* of Paris, which historians

---

20 *Hierarchia Catholica*, iv. 280. The editor simply notes that he was nominated to Poitiers by the king, but that the pope refused to grant his provisions.

of the Fronde unfailingly underline, was entirely due to the fact that he was a consecrated and active coadjutor to his indolent uncle. By the time the latter died in 1654, Retz was a prisoner who would never again set foot in his diocese. No one, least of all a historian of the episcopate, would wish to ignore the pre-Fronde Retz and focus simply on the post-Fronde cardinal and archbishop who was forced to resign Paris after years of exile.

An example of a long-serving coadjutor who failed to become a full, ruling bishop was Henri Boivin, coadjutor of Avranches between 1616 and 1639, and whose death came less than a year before that of his aged uncle, François Péricard. Boivin had been consecrated a bishop in May 1617, and it was because of long-standing Péricard family service to the Guises that Boivin administered the see of Reims on behalf of the young, unconsecrated archbishop, Henri de Lorraine-Guise between 1634 and his death.[21] Yet another variation is represented by Pierre de Bertier, who became coadjutor of Montauban in 1634, where the ageing bishop, Anne de Murviel, wanted nothing to do with him and made life so impossible for him that, until Murviel's death in 1651, Bertier was forced to direct his energies elsewhere, distinguishing himself as a preacher as well as in the affairs of the French clergy.

By contrast, there is a category of coadjutor who does not really qualify for inclusion in the ranks of the episcopate – those who, having obtained their provisions from Rome, failed to proceed to consecration, and finally either died or resigned before the designated see fell vacant. Dreux Hennequin became coadjutor of Soissons in 1612 in succession to his uncle Jérôme, but promptly resigned his title on his uncle's death in 1619 because, when the moment of choice came, he preferred to remain in his career of *conseiller-clerc* in the parlement of Paris. In 1634, Jacques Ribier obtained a similar right to succeed his uncle Pierre du Vair as bishop of Vence in Provence, but even before receiving his papal provisions as coadjutor in 1636 formally renounced any future claim to the Vence succession. It was, incidentally, this renunciation, not revealed until after du Vair's death in 1638, that enabled Richelieu to grant Vence to Antoine Godeau, bishop of the equally tiny neighbouring diocese of Grasse.[22] Neither Hennequin nor Ribier was ever consecrated, and for that reason neither can be regarded as having committed himself unequivocally to an episcopal career; when the time came for them to make a final choice, both renounced such a career. But most coadjutors did not fall into this category. The majority were consecrated as bishops, enjoyed limited revenues and rights to exercise their episcopal functions while their predecessors lived, and in due course assumed all the normal rights and duties of episcopal office. There is, therefore, every reason to regard them as an integral part of the French episcopate from the time they obtained their

---

21 *DHGE*, xviii. col 199–200, Boivin notice.
22 Doublet, *Godeau évêque de Grasse et de Vence*, i. 219–21, quoting archival sources.

coadjutorships, and not simply from the moment they succeeded their predecessors.

Finally, brief mention should be made of a further category of bishop still be found in seventeenth-century France. Suffragan bishops – not to be confused with bishops who were suffragans of an archdiocese – were occasionally taken on by ruling bishops to perform essentially religious functions within their dioceses. They were paid a limited pension for their services, and had no claim on the bishop or the diocese beyond that, nor could they exercise any episcopal function outside the diocese to which they were assigned. In the imperial *Reichskirche*, they were widely used by the often unconsecrated prince-bishops, and their limited status meant that they represented no threat to the dynastic interests of the great families who dominated the remaining Catholic bishoprics after the Reformation. Metz, which still technically belonged to the *Reichskirche* although its bishop was nominated by the king of France, had a succession of suffragan bishops in the seventeenth century, two of whom, Nicolas Coëffetau and Etienne Puget, were later nominated to Marseille.[23] Up to fifty French dioceses had experience of this kind of bishop during the sixteenth century, but it is clear that they were in steady decline by the opening of the seventeenth.[24] Lyon seems to have had a continuous line of serving suffragans down to 1630, when Richelieu's brother terminated the tradition.[25] The blind bishop of Clermont, Joachim d'Estaing, employed at least two suffragans in the 1630s and 1640s, and angrily defied family and ministerial pressure to take a coadjutor by pointing to their presence.[26] It is also likely that the French episcopate's official view of the dignity of episcopal office was also a factor in eliminating suffragan bishops. Reformers concerned with the state of particular dioceses governed by ageing bishops were certainly not averse to recommending suffragans as a temporary solution where conditions seem to suggest that nominating a coadjutor would be a slow and possibly fractious affair.[27] But in other respects their status seemed too inferior for them to govern a diocese effectively. A circular issued in the name of the Assembly of Clergy in 1658 to all bishops asking them not to consecrate

---

23 Of the two, only Puget effectively became bishop of Marseille. Coëffetau received papal approval in 1622, but like Eustache Gault in 1640, died before he took possession of his see.
24 *Hierarchia Catholica*, iii. Appendix 1, pp. 324–3.
25 *Ibid*, iv. Appendix 2, pp. 383–4.
26 AD Puy-de-Dome, 1 G 175 (unnumbered bundle), contract between Estaing and André de Sauzéa, for duties as suffragan, 13 Dec 1635; *ibid*, receipt from Sauzéa for his travelling and other expenses in Clermont, 25 Sept 1643; ASV, PC 48, fos 703–17, for the royal letter of nomination of Jean de Mallevaud as suffragan bishop, 7 July 1648, and the inquiry *de vita et moribus*, 7 Sept 1648. Estaing gives his reasons for not taking a coadjutor in his notarized procuration to take Mallevaud as suffragan: *ibid*, fo 713; he repeats them more stridently in a letter to Cardinal Barberini: BAV, Barb lat 7958, fo 2, 2 Dec 1647 (?). The Clermont cathedral chapter had petitioned Louis XIII to ensure Estaing would take a coadjutor around 1639: AAE, France 830, fo 191, undated.
27 BSG, MS 3238, fos 343–4, record of meeting held by Cardinal La Rochefoucauld and others on 1 Sept 1619 to discuss problematic dioceses like Nîmes, Viviers and Coutances.

the abbé de Montigny, who had recently obtained papal provisions as a bishop *in partibus infidelium*, and reminding them of a resolution of the most recent assembly against allowing such ordinations, showed that collective attitudes had probably hardened. Because of their alleged uselessness or lack of means of support, these bishops, it was argued, 'avilissent la dignité du Ministère' and were a threat to the rights of the Gallican church.[28] Whatever their value to the bishops who employed them, it is clear that both they and their contemporaries regarded suffragan bishops as little more than glorified vicars-general; unlike coadjutors, their status never enabled them to play any real role in the affairs of the French church. Contemporary evidence points overwhelmingly in one direction: that suffragan bishops were not to be regarded as forming part of the episcopate.

Limited as it may seem, it will be clear from this attempt to define the contours of the episcopate that late sixteenth- and seventeenth-century French bishops were a more diverse group of men than either canon law or contemporary models of the ideal bishop would lead us to suspect; and this will become even more apparent after their social, educational and professional backgrounds have been explored in later chapters. Much would be done during the period covered by this study to eliminate irregularities that were increasingly unacceptable – bishops holding more than one diocese or who refused to have themselves consecrated, for example – but a uniform episcopate corresponding closely to canonical norms did not fully appear until the age of Louis XIV.

In any event, it is for these reasons that the figures proposed by historians for the total number of French bishops who held office at any time between François I and Louis XIV have always varied. Yet no study attempting to provide even a limited analysis of the evolution of the episcopate can avoid the obligation to establish as precisely as possible the numerical size of the episcopate under consideration; this is even more necessary in a prosopographical study. One further consideration needs to be added to those already discussed in order to specify the *corpus episcoporum* of this volume. It concerns the actual selection of bishops, a problem which will be discussed at greater length later. It should suffice here to note that the dominant voice in this process was that of the crown, with the papacy playing a secondary though not negligible role. When considering the episcopate from Henri IV to the death of Mazarin, all those successfully nominated by the crown for papal approval between August 1589, the formal beginning of Henri IV's reign, and March 1661, have been included. They even include one or two bishops originally nominated by Henri III just before his assassination and whose nominations were duly confirmed by Henri IV, who in doing so adopted them as his own nominees when he might well have chosen to ignore them or make different choices. Equally, one or two of Henri III's last

---

28   ASV, N Fr 114, fo 345, circular of 4 Oct 1658.

nominees obtained their provisions after August 1589, but where this occurred without any recourse to his successor, they have been treated as pre-Henri IV bishops. Obviously, Henri IV was not really in a position to secure papal provisions for his nominees for several years after 1589, and it might be argued that this study should have taken as its point of departure either the king's conversion to Catholicism in 1593 or his absolution by the pope in 1595. But, as we shall see in due course, this would be far more arbitrary, as the king did make numerous nominations, some of them successful, before 1593 or 1595. The death of Mazarin in early March 1661 may seem an equally arbitrary date. But without wishing to exaggerate the political and other changes which followed the cardinal's death, there are sound reasons for maintaining this final date. In fact, it was in the weeks before his death that Mazarin made the largest single batch of episcopal nominations of the entire period since 1589. However, as these bishops did not obtain their papal provisions until mid-1661, historians might easily be tempted to classify them as post-Mazarin promotions and therefore as representing the first signs of Louis XIV's approach to episcopal nominations. Mazarin's action, coming when he was ailing quickly, meant that when he died not a single French diocese was vacant in the sense of not having an 'évêque nommé', an extremely unusual situation which shows just how determined he was to reward certain families and individuals rather than leave matters to his untried royal godson.[29] Moreover, Mazarin's move also serves to underscore the point that it was crown initiative (irrespective of how freely royal choices were actually made) which was the crucial factor in the making of the episcopate, and this is the essential reason why the date of the royal nomination rather than of the papal confirmation has been taken as the criterion for determining the overall size of the episcopal bench.

It is on the basis of these assumptions and these calculations that a total figure of 351 has been arrived at for new members of the French episcopate between 1589 and 1661.

IV

At first sight, the term 'French church' seems as self-explanatory as the expression 'bishop'. But that, too, is simply not the case. No attempt to understand the role or the evolution of the episcopate within the French church can expect to make much sense unless it attempts to convey at the outset some of the complexity of the institutional framework in which the

---

29 The position of two dioceses, Lombez and Rieux, both near Toulouse, remains uncertain. Their bishops died in late 1657, but their successors did not receive their papal provisions until 1662, and no sure dates are available for their nominations. They may have been nominated during Mazarin's ministry, but they may also have had to seek royal confirmation after his death in 1661.

episcopate moved and acted. Not that this is the only source of peculiarity in the history of the French episcopate, as we shall discover in the following pages. Of course, the French church was not unique, and much of what we shall be observing had its parallels in other parts of Europe. But that does not of itself guarantee ready familiarity with early modern churches, French or otherwise. Above all, in attempting to comprehend some of the characteristic, defining elements of the French church, it is necessary to put aside modern notions of institutional rationality.

To some extent, the general outline and structure of that church appears straightforward enough. For virtually the entire period covered by this study, it was divided into a total of 113 dioceses, fourteen (fifteen after 1622) of which were archbishoprics enjoying metropolitan status and prerogatives. Leaving its geographical compass temporarily to one side, these numbers alone suffice to make the French church by far the largest single 'national' church in early modern Europe – over twice as large as that of the Spanish kingdoms with their fifty-five or so dioceses. Admittedly, the Italian peninsula contained nearly three times as many dioceses as France, but its political fragmentation means that such a statistic has little significance. The English and Welsh churches, on the other hand, had a modest total of twenty-seven dioceses.

But the French church was not merely a large collection of dioceses housed under a single political or organisational 'roof'. Since the early Middle Ages, it had always been closely related to the French monarchy in a number of ways, while both monarchy and church found in the loosely-defined 'liberties of the Gallican church' a fruitful source of ideas about their autonomy from the papacy and their relation to each other. In addition, the growth of a system of regular assemblies of clergy, especially after 1560, and the church's contribution to the finances of the monarchy did much to stimulate and define the church's sense of its own identity; it could never be said, for example, of French bishops as it was of their Spanish *confrères*, that 'the meeting of two bishops is a phenomenon'.[30] One important result was that, for most purposes, the French church came to be viewed in terms of the 'Clergé de France' rather than simply by the territorial limits of the French monarchy – the 'Clergé de France' consisting essentially of those dioceses which participated in the regular assemblies of clergy and were subject to their financial decisions. This, as we shall see, has a direct bearing on how the total size of the French episcopate at any one time is to be computed. As for the assemblies themselves, their importance as a vehicle for the exercise of episcopal power within the French church, and as an avenue to episcopal office itself would grow steadily over the years, particularly under Louis XIII and his successors, and will be reviewed in later chapters. It may, however, be suggested at this

---

30 William J Callahan, *Church, Politics and Society in Spain, 1750–1874* (Cambridge, Mass. 1984), 8.

point that, as the only estate of the realm with the right to meet regularly in assembly, the French clergy in general, and the bishops in particular, enjoyed considerable advantages over other groups in society in competing for power and prestige as well as in defending their principles and privileges.

The French church, and its episcopate in particular, were not created in a day, but some periods of its history were especially significant as they effectively laid down patterns which would remain relatively stable for over a millenium. The earliest part of Roman Gaul to be evangelised were the southern provinces which were included in *Gallia Narbonnensis*. This region, which corresponded roughly to the later provinces of Provence and Languedoc, with extensions westwards into Gascony and the Garonne valley, and northwards into the Dauphiné, was also the most urbanised part of Gaul. The religious and ecclesiastical structures which Christianity brought with it were essentially those of the already christianised and urbanised areas of the eastern parts of the Empire, Italy, North Africa, and Mediterranean Spain. In particular, ecclesiastical, as distinct from secular, 'dioceses' were originally urban units which hesitantly reached out into their immediate rural hinterland, which was not converted to Christianity quite so readily. Consequently, where towns were numerous, dioceses were thus bound to be equally numerous and small in scale. With each diocese based on a Roman *civitas*, there were almost as many episcopal sees in fourth-century Gaul as there were to be in seventeenth century France.

This early pattern of development also accounts for the fact that well over half of all the bishoprics in the seventeenth-century French church were located to the south of the line between Bordeaux and Grenoble – and this does not include the sees included in the papal enclave of Avignon. Parishes, of course, were much slower to form than dioceses, partly owing to the time-lag between urban and rural conversion, and when they did take shape in later centuries, many of these southern dioceses naturally embraced only a modest number of parishes. With a total of sixteen parishes, the see of Vence in Provence had the smallest number of parishes of any in France before the Revolution. The neighbouring see of Grasse, which at various times was merged with that of Vence – notably between 1592 and 1601, and between 1638 and 1653 – had only twenty-five parishes. The coastal diocese of Agde near Béziers in Languedoc had but twenty-six. In this region, too, even the major sees, such as Toulouse, Narbonne, Arles, Aix, and Embrun, all of which enjoyed archiepiscopal rank, were not much larger than their dependent, suffragan dioceses which together made up their 'provinces'. All of these dioceses were in any case considerably smaller than those immediately to the north of them such as Agen with 384 parishes, Cahors with 785, and Rodez with 475.

Many of these cities of Roman Gaul declined or stagnated in subsequent centuries and, for all the importance of episcopal seats in sustaining some sort of urban presence in early medieval Europe, it was almost inevitable that some of them would fail to expand when urban growth returned in the later medieval and early modern period. Indeed, in many such cases, it was only the continuing presence of a bishop, a cathedral chapter, and an episcopal administration which prevented such places from sinking into total oblivion, or distinguished them from the smaller towns of the diocese in question. When the ecclesiastical and political map of France was about to be redrawn in 1790, and dioceses were about to be suppressed, many of these towns protested bitterly that such action was tantamount to signing their death-warrant.[31] Even today, the historian needs to peer closely at relatively detailed maps in order to locate towns as small and scattered as Rieux, Lectoure, Lombez, Saint-Papoul, Vabres, Saint-Pons, Conserans and Mirepoix (all within striking distance of Toulouse) on the one hand, and those of Senez, Digne, Sisteron, Riez, Apt, and Saint-Paul-Trois-Châteaux in Upper Provence on the other; in most of them, only an old and occasionally impressive cathedral comes as an unexpected surprise to the unsuspecting visitor.

By contrast, the provinces of central and northern France present a number of different characteristics. Their original conversion to Christianity was slower. In social and economic terms, the contrasts with the southern provinces were striking. Urbanisation had never been as extensive, and many of those towns which did exist there also suffered and declined after the later years of the Roman Empire. With the exception of two or three scattered clusters of relatively small dioceses, these of central and northern France were territorially very extensive, particularly in the number of parishes they contained. Only dioceses like Mâcon and Chalon-sur-Saône, Meaux and Senlis, Avranches and Dol stand out for their modest size. By contrast, sees like Limoges, Clermont, Bourges, Chartres, Sens and Rouen were truly enormous. Even in the seventeenth century, it took a week to traverse the elongated diocese of Chartres on foot, while Rouen, with approximately 1,338 parishes, had the largest number of parishes of any French diocese. To some degree, the large number of parishes in northern France, particularly in Normandy, Picardy, and around Paris probably reflected a much more dense and compact parochial network, for even the largest dioceses there were visibly smaller territorially than some of the central dioceses. For example, the diocese of Meaux, one of the smallest in northern France, nevertheless had 223 parishes in the mid-seventeenth century, while Paris *extra muros* had 417. In this regard, northern France resembled the parish networks of southern England.[32] It also seems that it was the dioceses of central France like Poitiers, Limoges and Bourges which were the largest in purely territorial terms: not only were their parishes numerous, but they were also larger in size than those of northern France. It should be said that no accurate figure for the total number

---

31 See Ted W Margadant, *Urban Rivalries in the French Revolution* (Princeton 1992), 64–6, 122–5, 224–5.
32 See Christopher Haigh, *English Reformations* (Oxford 1993), 5, 297, n 6.

of parishes in the early modern French church has yet been provided by historians, but there is good reason to believe that they amounted to about 30,000 at most.[33] This total, like so much else in the early modern church, was shared out in a highly haphazard and uneven manner between the individual dioceses of the day.

Clearly, to be governable at all, large or middling-size dioceses needed to be subdivided in some way, not least because several of the towns which served as episcopal 'capitals' were themselves situated on or near the actual peripheries of the dioceses in question. Over the centuries a complicated network of *archiprêtrés*, *archidiaconés* or *doyennés* evolved, and with them a hierarchy of diocesan ecclesiastical dignitaries, many of whom, incidentally, would become bishops under Henri IV and his successors. On the other hand, such administrative subdivision could do nothing whatever to remove another abiding anomaly of French ecclesiastical geography – the presence within many dioceses, especially in Brittany and Normandy, of enclaves which belonged to other dioceses. Although these were the subject of regular complaint by bishops, especially by those intent on tightening their grip on their dioceses, they, too, survived until the Revolution; they may have been a nuisance, but they were tolerated, partly no doubt because, though numerous, they were not especially large in size.

Once the episcopal map of France had been completed – at least in the sense that there were no major territorial 'gaps' inside its perimeter – it remained remarkably resistant to further alteration. Indeed, only one attempt of any significance to redraw diocesan boundaries and create new bishoprics was made during the later medieval and early modern period – that of Pope John XXII in the early fourteenth century. Sixteen new dioceses, all but two of them in southern France, were established in 1317. They were partly designed to combat the religious challenge of Catharism, but they were also intended to augment the episcopal patronage available in southern France during the days of the French-dominated Avignon papacy. For the most part, the dioceses subdivided by John XXII were not especially large before 1317, while the emergence of the new dioceses of Saint-Flour, Tulle, and Sarlat did very little to compress the sprawling dioceses of Clermont, Limoges and Périgueux out of which they were carved. Only the western sees of Maillezais and Luçon, both extracted from the enormous diocese of Poitiers, achieved something along those lines. The other bishoprics of the centre and north of the kingdom were entirely untouched by the papacy's efforts, no doubt because the French crown's control there was firmer and it was unwilling to countenance papally-directed diocesan subdivision.

---

33 None of the available sources yield an accurate figure, since virtually all are known to either duplicate or leave out parishes from diocese to diocese. The figures in the *Répertoire des visites pastorales de la France, première série*, 4 vols (Paris 1977–85) indicate that the number of parishes per diocese was not constant. I am indebted to James B Collins for supplying me with figures in a private communication based on his own research.

In the two centuries that followed, the French monarchy rather than the papacy gradually emerged as the key force in determining the evolution of the French episcopal bench; in doing so, it extended its influence into the southern dioceses – in spite of a theoretically elective episcopate after the Pragmatic Sanction of Bourges of 1438. The fact that the Cathar challenge had led to the establishment of new dioceses was evidence of some understanding of the possibility of altering the episcopal map in response to a religious crisis, and the need to do so. Yet, perhaps surprisingly, no such sense of urgency appears to have surfaced during the next major religious crisis – that of the Protestant Reformation in the sixteenth century. By then, of course, the French monarchy had formally acquired the right to appoint to vacant French bishoprics, but it still seemed more intent on consolidating and enforcing a prerogative which was not always popular or well accepted, than it was on adding to its fund of episcopal patronage by creating new dioceses. Moreover, the one attempt made at this time to reshape bishoprics – that of Philip II in the Netherlands after 1559 – produced a sufficiently explosive reaction there to dispel any inclination that might have existed in France to follow his example. In any event, from the late 1550s onwards, both the crown and the papacy found it sufficiently difficult to contain Protestant pressure, and they wholly lacked the political control required for so complex and protracted a business as creating new dioceses. It is ironic in the circumstances that the only new diocese added to the French church at this juncture was that of Boulogne, carved out of the existing diocese of Thérouanne as a direct consequence of Philip II's reorganisation of the bishoprics of the Netherlands.

The subsequent experience of the wars of religion themselves did little to stimulate any urgent desire to reshape the inherited geography of the French church. To some extent, the sheer difficulty of restoring the material fabric of the church after the havoc of the religious wars saw to that, and decisively defined the church's immediate priorities from the 1590s onwards. Several dioceses, especially in the south and south-west, were occupied by Huguenots and were in varying degrees inaccessible to their bishops, while numerous others were without functioning cathedrals or episcopal residences until well into the middle decades of the following century.

Yet the continuing vitality of Protestantism in seventeenth-century France raised the question of the adequacy of existing diocesan arrangements. The church's response was cautious in the extreme, and the focus was on specific cases rather than on general adjustments. A prime example of the aspiration for an independent bishopric is that of the Burgundian provincial capital, Dijon, where municipal pride was offended by its subjection to the very large diocese of Langres. Dijon was the only provincial 'capital' and seat of a parlement not to have a bishop as well. The Catholic League which dominated the city in the last years of the wars of religion petitioned Rome for a diocese

A Peculiar Institution? 33

for the city, and the king's council later lent support.³⁴ Sébastien Zamet, bishop of Langres from 1615 to 1655, was persuaded to support the city's pleas in the late 1620s, and in February 1630 the king's council again cleared the way for negotiations to begin to secure the establishment by the papacy of a new diocese. But in the end, it was the powerful opposition of the canons of Zamet's own cathedral who brought everything to a halt; such opposition was bound to be noticed in Rome, but it would probably not have been decisive if the crown had come up with compelling reasons of its own for supporting Dijon's case.³⁵ It was not until 1730 that Dijon finally became the seat of a bishopric.

Elsewhere, different considerations were at stake. For example, it appears that there was some suggestion in 1624 of subdividing the large diocese of Poitiers, which also included a big Protestant population, though the discussion does not seem to have amounted to very much.³⁶ But La Rochelle, as the undeclared capital of French Protestantism, was regarded as a uniquely difficult and particular challenge. The fall of the city in October 1628 revived discussion of how best to deal with this former bastion of opposition which Richelieu, the *dévots*, and Louis XIII were all keen to retrieve for Catholicism. The outcome is particularly instructive, bearing in mind that this was a moment when crusading Catholicism was at the height of its influence. In his declaration of November 1628, immediately after the city's capture, Louis XIII announced his intention of requesting the pope to found a diocese in the city. But from the outset the objective was not so much to create a wholly new diocese as to relocate and rename the older diocese of Maillezais. Some initial steps were taken to remove the see from Maillezais. Names of suitable candidates for the newly located bishopric were canvased, and neighbouring bishops likely to be affected by the change appeared ready to cooperate.³⁷ But once again, whatever plans were in train were shelved, possibly because the crown was unable to accommodate the intended change with other episcopal appointments being made around the same time.³⁸ A second, more obscure

---

34 Noël Valois, ed, *Inventaire des arrêts du conseil d'état (règne de Henri IV)*, 2 vols (Paris 1886), i. 251, no 3789, decree of 3 July 1597.
35 Père Anselme, *Histoire généalogique et chronologique de la maison royale de France et des grands officiers de la Couronne*, 9 vols (Paris 1726–30), ii. 236.
36 Marcelle Formon, 'Henri-Louis Chasteigner de la Rocheposay, évêque de Poitiers (1612–51)', *Bulletin de la Société des Antiquaires de l'Ouest*, 4th ser, 3 (1955), 169.
37 Alain de Solminihac, *Lettres et documents*, ed Eugène Sol (Cahors 1930), 1–2. The dating of these letters exchanged between Barrault, bishop of Bazas, and Solminihac, future bishop of Cahors, may be open to question.
38 Pierre Grillon, ed, *Papiers de Richelieu. Section politique intérieure. Correspondance et papiers d'état*, 6 vols (Paris 1975, in progress), iv. pp 61–2, queen mother to Richelieu, 29 Jan 1629. The bishop of Nantes had suggested to her that the bishopric of Maillezais be returned to its earlier status as an abbey, and that a diocese be founded in La Rochelle, with Nicolas Grillié, her almoner, as bishop. Marie asked Richelieu to support this move with Louis XIII, especially as the archbishop of Bordeaux apparently agreed to it.

attempt was made after the king's death in 1643, and again a royal nomination was made 'par anticipation'.[39] This time, it seems that the incumbent bishop of neighbouring Saintes objected to the prospect of losing part of his diocese without adequate compensation.[40] Even the idea of moving the see of Maillezais to some other town also aroused strong objections: the bourgeois of Fontenay-le-Comte, where the bishop often resided, had no desire to become the formal seat of the diocese, on the grounds that the immigration it would bring about would raise prices of goods and food![41] In fact, it was only after Henri de Béthune, the bishop of Maillezais appointed in 1629, himself became archbishop of Bordeaux in 1646 that the way was at last open to remove the see of Maillezais to La Rochelle, a move duly completed by 1648. The new diocese also included two *archiprêtrés* and a few parishes near the city of La Rochelle itself which had hitherto been part of the diocese of Saintes. On this occasion, potential opposition was obviated by the decision to offer the new diocese to the bishop of Saintes himself. Change had thus taken twenty years, yet the result of this redrawing of boundaries was a diocese as elongated and misshapen as many of its historic counterparts, and with an episcopal town as geographically marginal as any in France at the time.[42] Indeed, the next initiative comparable to that concerning La Rochelle did not occur until 1694, though this time it did bring about the subdivision rather than the transfer of a diocese: the equally misshapen diocese of Nîmes was cut in half, in the hope that the tenacious Protestant presence in the area would be more satisfactorily dealt with if there was also a bishopric based at Alès. These examples should make it abundantly clear that reshaping the diocesan map of France was not to be undertaken lightly; it threatened numerous interests, individual and collective, few of whom were prepared to make the sacrifice required for a new diocese to be properly endowed with revenue.

If the subdivision of bishoprics was thus not a key concern of the seventeenth-century French church, the amalgamation of small dioceses was scarcely more so. However, a few changes were made, and their vicissitudes are also worthy of attention. The sees of Valence and Die had effectively been merged in the fifteenth century, and remained united without serious problems for generations thereafter, only to be divorced for no evident reason during the 1690s. The experience of France's two smallest dioceses was rather more complex. A first attempt to join together the tiny Provençal sees of Grasse and Vence was made during the 1590s. It foundered in the face of local resistance, neither diocese being willing to surrender its separate identity. But

---

39 Pérouas, *Le Diocèse de la Rochelle 1648–1724*, 129.
40 BN, MS Baluze 175, fos 120, 126, Bishop Raoul of Saintes to Mazarin, 20 Apr and 29 June 1643 respectively.
41 See A L Bertrand, *La Vie de Messire Henri de Béthune, archévêque de Bordeaux 1604–80*, 2 vols (Paris 1902), i. 145–6.
42 Pérouas, *La Rochelle*, 75.

it failed above all because the merger, brought about in 1592, came about through Savoyard influence in Provence, and because the beneficiary of the union, Guillaume le Blanc (who was already bishop of Vence) had joined the Catholic League against Henri IV. Henri's triumph was bad news for Le Blanc, who never gained 'peaceful possession' of Grasse, and the two dioceses were formally divorced after his death in 1601.[43] Yet a second attempt at union was made by Richelieu in the late 1630s, when he secured Grasse for his protégé, Antoine Godeau. The mediocrity of Grasse's endowment seems to have troubled Richelieu more than it did Godeau, but the willingness of the Bishop of Vence's (Pierre du Vair) nephew and intended successor to renounce his rights to Vence facilitated Richelieu's desire to improve Godeau's position.[44] In subsequent years, Godeau does not appear to have encountered hostility as acute as that which greeted Le Blanc a generation earlier, but by the end of the Fronde he had made an enemy of Mazarin who either promoted, or at least did nothing to prevent, a new 'disunion' of Grasse and Vence in 1653.[45] Surprisingly, perhaps, it was Vence that Godeau chose to retain, and he continued to suprise contemporaries, as he had since his original acceptance of Grasse in 1636, by remaining a resident bishop in this remote, miniscule, and impoverished diocese until his death in 1672. Other bishops occasionally put forward merger suggestions of their own, such as that made by Robert Cupif concerning the small Breton dioceses of Dol and Saint-Pol-de-Léon during the Fronde. Although the dioceses were relatively small, his plan stood little chance of success; Cupif was a highly unpopular outsider who had sparked strong local opposition to his previous attempts to govern Saint-Pol.[46]

The limited, episodic character of attempts to subdivide or merge dioceses was one reason why the size and number of French bishoprics remained remarkably stable during the sixteenth and seventeenth centuries. Clearly, the French monarchy evinced no great desire to imitate John XXII and to expand its fund of episcopal patronage by creating new dioceses. This may seem surprising in an age when the crown was usually anxious to augment all available sources of patronage, and often did so by subdividing existing areas of secular administration. Louis XIV may have made a few changes to the map, and in doing so imposed his wishes on both the papacy and the French clergy, but his changes were largely *ad hoc*, and were not seen as heralding anything more wide-ranging or systematic. The conservatism of the monarchy is doubtless explicable in terms of the difficulty of obtaining both

---

43 Georges Doublet, 'Guillaume le Blanc, évêque de Grasse et de Vence', *Annales du Midi*, 13 (1901), 177–98, 346–65; *DBF*, vi. 583–4.
44 See Doublet, *Godeau*, i. 219–21.
45 See René Pillorget, *Les Mouvements insurrectionnels de Provence entre 1596 et 1715* (Paris 1975), 515–18, on the continuing local opposition to a union of the two sees, with the inhabitants of one diocese fearing their bishop would abandon them for the other.
46 *DHGE*, xiii. cols 1112–13.

clerical and papal agreement to such changes, to the complexities of the changes themselves, and to the problems of endowing new bishoprics.

V

Yet, however stable the map of existing French dioceses proved to be, it would be misleading to assume that there was no change and conclude that this was a church with totally static boundaries. The fact remains that the overall size of the French church was primarily determined by the territorial expansion of the French monarchy. The 113 dioceses of the early seventeenth century had grown to 130 by 1789. But it should also be realised that church and monarchy were not perfectly in step as far as the practical consequences of this expansion were concerned. The resulting discrepancies also have a direct bearing on how the 'French church' is to be defined, and consequently on the size and evolution of the French episcopate during the period under study.

It was mainly, but not exclusively, along its long and constantly evolving eastern frontier that the ecclesiastical and political map of France was subject to most change and variation. Indeed, the ecclesiastical map inherited from earlier centuries fitted less and less well with the increasingly 'national' organisation of the French church – and that of others, too – during the sixteenth and seventeenth centuries. If the French church added the new diocese of Boulogne to its number in 1567, it was, as we saw, primarily because Philip II was determined to reorganise the church in the Netherlands by increasing the number of its dioceses from five to seventeen. Apart from his stated intention of combating heresy there, one of Philip's other purposes was to create archbishoprics at Cambrai and Malines, and in doing so to remove these dioceses, especially Cambrai, from their historic subordination to the French archbishopric of Reims. No further changes occurred in this region until the personal rule of Louis XIV, when the initiative shifted decisively in favour of France, with the sees of Saint-Omer, Arras and Cambrai being added to the French church soon after the conquest of the provinces in which they were situated. As early as 1650, the retired bishop of Belley, Jean-Pierre Camus, was nominated by Mazarin to the see of Arras, which was already occupied by French forces, but he died shortly afterwards, and it was not until the late 1660s that a French bishop was finally installed there.[47]

Meanwhile, further to the east, the greatest ambiguity surrounded the status of the so-called *trois-évêchés* of Metz, Toul and Verdun, none of which was genuinely incorporated into the French church for a century or more after they had been seized by Henri II in 1552. Subject to varying degrees of

---

47 *Hierarchia Catholica*, iv. 100, 'Atrebaten', nn. 7–8; *DBF*, vii. cols 1013–14.

political control by the French monarchy, they remained ecclesiastically part of the Holy Roman Empire, suffragans of the archbishop of Trier, and subject to the Germanic Concordat of 1448. In practice, however, the position of the individual bishoprics differed sharply. Verdun escaped French influence altogether for as long as there was an independent duchy of Lorraine, whose dukes generally ensured that the bishopric was held by a family member.[48] The see of Toul seemed at times to be far more susceptible to French pressure, but local resistance as well as unflinching opposition from the papacy effectively prevented the French monarchy before Louis XIV from successfully nominating its candidates for the bishopric. Louis XIII and Richelieu made a determined effort to do so when Toul fell vacant in 1637, and Henri Arnauld, brother of the *grand* Arnauld and future bishop of Angers, was nominated by Louis XIII only to abandon his hopes three years later after experiencing the full force of papal opposition to French claims over Toul.[49] It was only in 1664 that Louis XIV obtained a special papal indult enabling him to nominate bishops of Toul in future. At Metz, the diocese most fully under French control, the situation was again different. Held for most of the sixteenth century by Guise-Lorraine family members, this strategically important and immensely well-endowed see was given from the reign of Henri IV onwards to French royal nominees, the best known of whom was Henri de Bourbon-Verneuil, bastard son of Henri IV. The king secured the see in advance for his son at an early age, and he held it until he was forced to resign and marry nearly forty years later by Louis XIV.[50] Yet despite this royal control, the see of Metz and its unconsecrated incumbent – and *a fortiori* those of Toul and Verdun – were not regarded under Henri IV and Louis XIII as forming part of the 'Clergé de France'. Of the three, Metz should perhaps not be entirely forgotten, as it served to some extent as a 'school' for bishops, attracting a series of French suffragan-bishops who over the years administered the diocese on behalf of the unconsecrated Bourbon-Verneuil, some of whom later came to occupy French dioceses in their own right.

By contrast, no such obstacles were encountered with the smaller and less important see of Belley, which was incorporated without difficulty into the French church after Henri IV had acquired the provinces in which it was situated from Savoy by the Treaty of Lyon in 1601. Indeed, the first French royal nominee to Belley, the celebrated Jean-Pierre Camus, was to play an important part as preacher, writer and polemicist in the affairs of the French

---

48 See Leo Just, 'Das Staatskirchentum der Herzöge von Lotharingen-Bar von 1445 bis 1633', *Archiv für Mittelrheinische Kirchengeschichte*, 5 (1953), 223–63; also Michel Pernot, 'Un acteur de la Réforme catholique en Lorraine: Jean des Porcelets de Maillane évêque de Toul (1608–1624)', in René Taveneaux, ed, *Saint Pierre Fourier et son temps* (Nancy 1992), 73–84.

49 Isabelle Bonnot, *Hérétique ou saint? Henry Arnauld évêque janséniste d'Angers au xviie siècle* (Paris 1983), 98–100.

50 During most of the sixteenth century, Metz was held by a succession of members of the Lorraine family, of whom several were Guises.

church under Louis XIII, and thus helped to smooth the process of integration of his diocese into the French church. If there was pressure to redraw the ecclesiastical map of the Alpine region, it came essentially from the dukes of Savoy, who pursued a policy of territorial consolidation and were as allergic as any Gallican to the idea that parts of their lands might be subject to foreign bishops or archbishops. Several French dioceses such as Grenoble and Embrun included lands in Savoy, while some Savoyard dioceses were themselves subject to the archbishops of Vienne and Embrun. But, although French bishops here often had to consent to delegate their powers of jurisdiction over their Savoyard territories, the efforts of successive dukes to incorporate them into their own dioceses or to found new dioceses remained fruitless until the creation of Chambéry in 1779.[51]

Further south, the papal enclave of Avignon and its suffragans retained their separate status under Henri IV and his successors. The ecclesiastical province of Avignon had been carved out of that of Arles as recently as 1474 by Sixtus IV for his favourite nephew, demonstrating that it was not impossible to change existing structures provided there was sufficient determination. The papacy directly filled the bishoprics of Avignon, Carpentras and Vaison, often with reliable bishops of Italian rather than of local extraction.[52] However, the neighbouring see of Orange was in a more uncertain position, both because of its dominant Protestant population and the fact that Orange belonged to the Protestant house of Nassau-Orange. On the other hand, it was a suffragan diocese of the French ecclesiastical 'province' of Arles. For that reason, its experience is an interesting one. From 1572 until 1646, the see was held by three members of the Tulles family from Villefranche near Avignon, who were gradually drawn into the purview and service of the French crown. The last of them, Jean-Vincent de Tulles, was even transferred by Mazarin to the French see of Lavaur in 1646. His immediate successor in Orange, Hyacinthe Serroni, a Roman like Mazarin and a Dominican like Mazarin's brother, was also extremely active in French service during the later phase of the Franco-Spanish conflict. He, too, would be rewarded by Mazarin in early 1661 with a transfer to the see of Mende. It was as individuals in the service of Mazarin that Tulles and Serroni finally found a place among the French episcopate. During all this time, the see of Orange itself officially remained outside the French church, and the monarchy acquired no formal right to determine the choice of bishops there. But although that right still lay with the pope, it was increasingly accepted by all parties that in practice candidates needed – and knew that they needed – the clear support of the king of France

---

51 See Achille Erba, *La Chiesa sabauda tra Cinque e Seicento: Ortodossia tridentina, gallicanesimo savoiardo e assolutismo ducale (1580–1630)* (Rome 1979), chs 1–2; René Favier, *Les Villes du Dauphiné aux xviie et xviiie siècles* (Grenoble 1993), 84–5.
52 Marc Venard, *Réforme protestante, réforme catholique dans la province d'Avignon au xvie siècle* (Paris 1993), 114–15.

if they were to be successful, not least because royal cooperation was also essential to episcopal efforts to restore Catholicism in Orange.[53]

The contours of the French church on its southern, especially Pyrenean, perimeter were not without some original traits of their own. First, the two Béarn bishoprics of Oloron and Lescar had historically never been part of the French church. They were not included in the provisions of the Concordat of Bologna, and their bishops continued during the sixteenth century to be appointed ostensibly by the Pope 'at the supplication' of the kings of Navarre, princes of Béarn, who ensured that the sees were dominated by members of the ruling Foix-Albret family. In fact, with the imposition of the Reformation there under Henri IV's mother, Jeanne d'Albret, the bishops were either openly Protestant, like Gérard Roussel, or only managed to hold on to their title by adopting an ambiguous religious position. When Henri IV added the French throne to that of Navarre, some change was likely, if only because the restoration of Catholicism in Béarn was one of the conditions of his absolution by Clement VIII in 1595. That restoration was delayed for twenty-five years, although Henri IV showed his intentions by nominating indisputably Catholic bishops to Oloron and Lescar in the late 1590s. For the next two decades, the predicament of the two bishops – unable to reside in their dioceses or enjoy their revenues – greatly exercised the French clergy, prodding them to maintain pressure on the crown for the restoration of Catholicism in Béarn. Strictly speaking, the two dioceses were only part of the French church after 1620 but, in virtually every other respect, the process of integration was complete before that date, and may safely be dated back to the episcopal nominations of Henri IV. Elsewhere along the Franco-Spanish frontier, it was from Spain that the pressure for change came. It has recently been argued that 'a cornerstone of Philip II's policy was his determination to make the authority of his Church coincide with national frontiers', and his efforts to reshape dioceses were emphatically not confined to the Netherlands: in the face of strong and protracted opposition, he engineered some significant transfers and creations of dioceses in his Spanish kingdoms. With papal approval, he saw to it that Spanish areas subject to the French dioceses of Bayonne and Comminges were removed and made subject to Spanish episcopal jurisdiction. The diocese of Elne, historically part of the province of Narbonne, was removed and made subject to Tarragona in 1564. Elne itself was later removed to the larger city of Perpignan, and it was as the diocese of Perpignan that it was restored to Narbonne and the French church in 1678, as a consequence of the French conquest of Roussillon.[54]

The main potential of the French church for change and future expansion

53 Pierre Hurtebise, 'La Famille de Tulle et le siège épiscopal d'Orange', *Archivum Historiae Pontificiae*, 25 (1987), 411–30.
54 Henry Kamen, *The Phoenix and the Flame: Catalonia and the Counter-Reformation* (New Haven and London 1993), 73–7. The quotation is at p 75.

may have lain on its peripheries, but this was never a simple matter of direct and instant integration of previously non-French dioceses. Little pressure for the incorporation of such dioceses seems to have been exercised by the French church itself. Contrary to what might perhaps be expected, it was not the French but the Spanish crown, especially under Philip II, which was the more determined to force the pace of ecclesiastical change to its advantage, and to do so along lines designed to make both the Flanders and the Spanish churches as free as possible of all vestiges of external subordination. By comparison, relatively little was done before Louis XIV to extend the frontiers of the French church. In the meantime, both crown and church were content to live with cases like those of Metz and Orange, half-way houses in which the discreet exercise of royal patronage could prepare the way for subsequent integration.

VI

The early seventeenth-century French church was also something rather more than an undifferentiated collection of 113 dioceses. Like other churches, it possessed its own internal organisation, and bishops were distinguished by a range of different titles and positions. Until 1622, when Paris became an archbishopric, the church was divided into fourteen provinces, each headed by an archbishop. Once again, the size and distribution of these provinces was anything but uniform. Eight of the provinces lay south of the Bordeaux-Vienne line, though admittedly most of the dioceses belonging to the large Bordeaux province were in fact north of that line. By far the smallest in every respect was the province of Arles, with just two French suffragans, Marseille and Toulon, but Embrun, with Digne, Senez and Glandèves, was scarcely much bigger. Historically, the largest province of all was Bourges, which included dioceses as far south as Albi, Cahors, Mende and Rodez. Not far behind was the vast province of Tours, which included all of the dioceses in the provinces of Maine, Anjou and Brittany. Tours remained unquestionably the largest single province after Bourges was reduced in size with the creation of the new province of Albi in 1676. Only one French diocese appears to have escaped the 'provincial' net altogether: Le Puy claimed to be directly subject to the papacy.

This distribution of French dioceses into provinces was almost as old as the dioceses themselves, and there had been no change to the map since John XXII had established the province of Toulouse in 1317. Only the status of Paris, historically a suffragan of the archbishop of Sens, came to seem somewhat anomalous during the sixteenth and early seventeenth century, due in part to the crown's more permanent residence in Paris and the emergence of the clerical assemblies which usually met there. An ideal opportunity to raise it to archiepiscopal status arose in 1622 when the sees of Paris and Sens simultaneously fell vacant: in normal times, the difficulties of forcing change upon an incumbent archbishop, especially when it meant the reduction of his province by the removal of several suffragan dioceses, were usually enough to inhibit such attempts at innovation. In 1622, however, Louis XIII was prepared to accept the need for a change in the status of Paris. The new archbishop of Sens, Octave de Bellegarde, was promoted from the southern diocese of Comminges in the Pyrenees, thanks mainly to the influence of his cousin, the duc de Bellegarde, who was then high in the king's favour. But his nomination was made conditional upon his acceptance of the creation of a new province of Paris which would remove Orléans, Chartres, Meaux and Senlis from the province of Sens.[55] The immediate beneficiary of the change was Jean-François de Gondi, the third and least distinguished of the four members of his family to hold Paris in succession. Yet despite his nomination to Sens, Bellegarde proved reluctant to accept the change, and the king eventually allowed his provisions as archbishop to be despatched without him formally renouncing any of Sens's claims to jurisdiction over Paris.[56] The Paris-Sens dispute rumbled on for decades but, with Paris sure of royal support, there was little that Bellegarde or his successors could do to inhibit the gradual emergence of Paris as the leading see – or at least of its archbishop as the leading ecclesiastical figure – of the realm, though, in the event, that was retarded by continuing Gondi possession of Paris until Cardinal de Retz's reluctant resignation in 1660. The Paris-Sens dispute was not finally buried until 1664.[57]

By contrast, the creation of the province of Albi under Louis XIV in 1676 proved infinitely less troublesome, though it is worth noting that it, too, was only undertaken while the sees of Bourges and Albi were both vacant. The justification for the new province was the inability of the archbishop of Bourges to deal with the Protestant problem in the southern dioceses of his province, but it is doubtful if anyone believed this, let alone imagined that it was the most obvious or effective way of tackling the Protestant challenge.[58]

Among the select contingent of French archbishops, a number claimed to be rather more than mere titular heads of provinces, and consistently asserted rights to primatial status. Bourges claimed to be primate of Aquitaine, Reims of 'Germany' and Lyon of the Gauls, and so on. But by 1600 there was little

---

55 See G Audollent, *La Création de l'archevêché de Paris* (Paris 1922).
56 BAV, Barb lat 7941, fo 5, Louis XIII to pope, 27 Aug 1623. AD Yonne, G 2, unfoliated bundle of documents on this dispute, with copy of Louis' earlier letter to the French ambassador in Rome, 22 Sept 1622.
57 AD Yonne, G 2, Michel le Tellier, secretary of state, to Louis-Henri de Gondrin, archbishop of Sens, conveying the king's refusal to reconsider the status of Paris. See Cynthia A Goulden, 'Changes in the Episcopal Structure of the Church of France in the Seventeenth Century as an Aspect of Bourbon State-building', *Bulletin of the Institute of Historical Research*, 48 (1975), 214–29.
58 Goulden, 'Changes in Episcopal Structure', 226.

real substance to these grandiose titles, since the archbishops enjoying them proved no more successful than archbishops with no such claims in exercising effective authority over their suffragan bishops. The fact is that archiepiscopal authority generally was structurally weak in a church in which the Gallican view of episcopal autonomy, regardless of actual title or rank, was universally shared by all bishops, whatever their other convictions. Archbishops could only exercise limited authority as courts of appeal or as arbiters of disputes involving their suffragans. Indeed, if they aimed at effective leadership, they were better advised to act in concert with suffragans, rather than over their heads. Rarely was there more scope for such informal authority than in the later sixteenth and seventeenth century with the appearance of regular assemblies of clergy, whose members were elected by provincial assemblies, and in which voting was also by province. Formal provincial councils also met in the later sixteenth and early seventeenth centuries, partly in order to apply the decrees of the Council of Trent to French conditions, although none met after the Council of Bordeaux in 1624. Yet other sources of 'provincial' solidarity were present, all of them important: the role of the bishops in provincial estates like those of Burgundy, Languedoc, Brittany or Dauphiné was perhaps the most prominent of them. In some of these estates, such as Languedoc, the bishops were the dominant and most active group, and one reason why a see like Narbonne was so desirable was that its archbishop was titular president of the estates of Languedoc.

It needs to be added, of course, that archbishops were not alone in claiming a measure of distinction and separateness. A large number of bishops – perhaps even a majority – still claimed that 'feudal' titles of one kind or another, most commonly that of count or baron, were attached to their diocese, albeit with relatively slight justification in some cases. Real or imaginary, such titles were a reminder of how far episcopal rank was assimilated historically to aristocratic status and power, and how important seigneurial jurisdiction generally remained as a source of both power and revenue to bishops. The bishop of Viviers entitled himself 'conte de Viviers, prince de Donzère et de Chasteauneuf sur Rosne'.[59] The bishop of Mende, for example, claimed to be count of Gévaudan, but the assertiveness of Bishop Sylvestre de Marsillac in this regard was evidently too much for his cathedral chapter who besought him not to omit his real title of 'bishop of Mende' from official documents![60] If many of these titles were hollow unless significant endowments accompanied them, six northern dioceses came with titles which did have highly desirable attributes attached to them. Reims, Langres, and Châlons-sur-Marne carried a duchy and a peerage, and Beauvais, Laon, and Noyon a county and a peerage. All six entitled their holder to be seated in the

---

59 'Lettres et actes inédits de Msgr de l'Hostel évêque de Viviers', ed E J Hurault, *Revue du Vivarais* (1931), 2–3.
60 See Jean Orcibal, *Jean Duvergier de Hauranne, abbé de Saint-Cyran et son temps* (Louvain 1948), 11, n 5.

parlement of Paris. These advantages were real and considerable, and partly explain the attractivness of the dioceses, despite the fact that some were only modestly endowed with income. Louis XIV extended the number of such dioceses by specially creating the ducal peerage of Saint-Cloud for the archbishop of Paris.[61]

In the final analysis, it is the tenacity and antiquity of existing boundaries and structures which leaves the strongest impression, making change troublesome and laborious at the best of times. Redrawing diocesan boundaries always involved a large number of interests, and not merely those of the bishops who were directly concerned. Compensation, symbolic and material, needed to be made available if cooperation was to be secured, and in this regard ecclesiastical change was not fundamentally different from similar changes in secular royal administration. But with the church itself reluctant to initiate change, and the crown usually lacking the (mainly financial) incentive to make the kind of changes from which it benefited in royal administration, the marginal character of change is easy to understand. If reform was seen to be necessary and urgent in the French church after the wars of religion, it was essentially the moral and spiritual reform of individuals and communities rather than the reshaping of their church that was envisaged. It is not difficult to imagine that such assumptions had a subtle influence on the manner in which both church and crown approached the business of making bishops.

---

61 Jean-Pierre Labatut, *Les Ducs et pairs de France au xviie siècle* (Paris 1972), 70.

CHAPTER 2

Making Bishops

THE CLERGY, AT whose collective apex stood the episcopate, was regarded throughout medieval and most of early modern Europe as the first of the three orders of society. The precedence which they enjoyed over the other two orders was only one of several features which distinguished them from the rest of society. Among these, the most fundamental was the fact that no member of the clergy was born as one: in Catholic Europe at least, the clerical estate only endured from one generation to the next because it was 'colonised' in varying degrees by members of the other two estates; the methods by which social groups perpetuated their place among the clergy had to take account of the basic fact of clerical celibacy. There would be no point in expanding here on the myriad ways by which families obtained places within the clerical hierarchy for their sons and daughters. But even when allowance is made for the deals and horse-trading which occurred where church offices were changing hands, it should be remembered that these offices were neither venal nor hereditary. For that reason, retaining them over more than one generation was far from assured, and required considerable foresight and application.

The prestige and authority invested in church offices was one obvious reason for their attractiveness to all ranks of society, and that attractiveness was substantially enhanced by the way in which the church's considerable material endowments were attached to individual offices and functions within the church. The term 'benefice' itself illustrates this point: officially, it referred to the material reward attached to the performance of an office or function in the church, which was therefore reserved in principle for those carrying out the duties of their office. *Beneficium propter officium* – the reward to him who performs the duty – was the epigrammatic way of expressing the official understanding of the relationship between function and reward. But it is doubtful if this strict interpretation was ever faithfully represented in reality, and throughout French society it was the term 'benefice', with its connotation of material reward, which loomed largest in attitudes to positions in the church. Despite strenuous attempts to reverse this pattern by placing the emphasis on function and duty, when individual church positions, bishoprics included, fell vacant in the seventeenth century, those with an interest in their fate appear to have immediately thought — if we can judge by their letters and comments — of the financial value of the vacant office as much as of the office itself.

For all those — individuals, families or social groups — sufficiently well placed to envisage careers in the church and to acquire benefices, a bishopric was historically the most attractive of all offices. On the purely religious plane, the bishop was credited with two forms of power. The first, known as the power of orders and derived directly from his consecration as a bishop, conferred on him a sacerdotal character that was more complete than that of ordinary priests; the power of orders entitled him, and him alone, to ordain other priests, and thus to perpetuate the clergy. The bishop's other power was that of jurisdiction, which enabled him to legislate for, and govern, his diocese. The precise relationship between the two, one religious the other jurisdictional, was endlessly debated, as were the origins of episcopal power generally. If, for example, the two powers were wholly separate, then the power of jurisdiction could be exercised by an unconsecrated bishop, thus raising the possibility of a rather different type of episcopate. It was this distinction which enabled many sixteenth-century bishops to govern their dioceses without being consecrated, and though they could obviously not perform certain religious duties reserved to bishops, contemporaries did not refuse, as we saw in the previous chapter, to acknowledge them as bishops for all that. Such tolerance declined sharply in the seventeenth century in the face of pressure from the post-Tridentine papacy and from reformers within the French church, pressure which emphasised the pastoral as well as the administrative responsibilities of bishops.

Episcopal office was attractive not simply because the highest material rewards were attached to it — in practice, many dioceses were relatively modestly-endowed by comparison with wealthy abbeys and priories — but because of the combination of authority, status, leadership, esteem, and wealth which it conferred. The manner in which such ingredients were combined accounted for the relative attractiveness, or the lack of it, of individual French bishoprics, but other factors such as geographical location, the size of a diocese, its proximity to or distance from court, or from family seats, could also powerfully influence those in search of episcopal office. Not all dioceses were equal, but no diocese was ever quite so unattractive as to remain vacant for lack of candidates; even the smallest and remotest diocese was a potential gateway to the wider world of the French church, which brought with it the possibility of promotion and transfer to a better diocese. Of course, some dioceses might be regarded by court-oriented families and ecclesiastics as too distant and beyond the pale of civilisation, but local families or candidates of more modest background were hardly touched by such disdain. No study of the making of the episcopate in any age can afford to ignore such distinctions, which at the very least suggest that an episcopate that was highly homogeneous, socially or otherwise, was more difficult to achieve than might be imagined.

The manner in which the French episcopal bench was chosen was subject to important variations during the later Middle Ages and sixteenth century, and the French church remained highly ambivalent about them until the seventeenth century. An extended historical commentary on the subject is not possible here, but a number of its aspects need some clarification. Sixteenth- and seventeenth-century critics (some of them bishops) of the system whereby bishops were nominated by the king of France, publicly and repeatedly appealed for a return to a system of episcopal elections by the canons of cathedral chapters. In making such criticisms they painted a rosy and nostalgic portrait of a church once governed by an elected episcopate. In fact, it was only in the course of the eleventh-century investiture controversy that protest against long-standing political control of episcopal nominations had first erupted, leading to demands for free episcopal elections. The classic procedure subsequently laid down was for bishops to be elected by the canons of the diocesan cathedral gathered together as an electoral college, albeit with earlier notions of wider clerical and lay participation (or at least approval) conveniently removed.

However, inherited attitudes and social pressures were far more than mere cobwebs waiting to be blown away by inventive reformers and canon lawyers. Change did occur, but it was piecemeal and unpredictable. To begin with, the term 'elect' could be construed in more than one sense, and could just as readily mean 'selection' (and thus the avoidance of contested elections) as 'election' in our sense, and the signs are that such views still held sway in some early modern political elections.[1] Moreover, clear electoral procedures acceptable to all concerned with episcopal successions were themselves much slower to emerge, and when they did, they were rarely sufficient to deter those wishing to overturn one election by another: after all, if contested papal elections were possible, then similar divisions and schisms could be reproduced lower down the scale for episcopal elections; cathedral chapters were no more harmonious than the college of cardinals, especially when rival candidates emerged from among their members. Nor was an episcopal election ever quite final, since even 'elected' bishops still needed to be confirmed, either by their archbishop, the secular ruler or, later, the pope; that, too, could be the ideal opportunity for external intervention in elections, especially when it was not difficult to make allegations that the proper forms had not been observed. Thus inconclusive, disputed elections leading to litigation and even violence served to discredit episcopal elections over time, and to invite outside parties to claim a part in the selection of bishops. The papacy did so in many parts of Europe from the twelfth and thirteenth century onwards, arguing that it

---

1 For a study of early modern elections in a different context, but which reveals contemporary understandings of what they entailed, see Mark A Kishlansky, *Parliamentary Selection: Social and Political Choice in Early Modern England* (Cambridge 1986).

had both an overriding right and duty to provide churches with suitable pastors. Financial needs, but also political relations with Europe's rulers, provided the papacy with an added reason for wanting well-disposed episcopates.

The Avignon papacy was particularly well placed to intervene directly in southern and central France during the fourteenth century.[2] The French monarchy, too, was not slow to see advantages in securing elections favourable to its interests, which of course were often hard to distinguish from the ambitions of its own servants and their families, and their search for ecclesiastical preferment.[3] Yet the French clergy, led by the bishops and especially the chapters, remained strongly attached to episcopal elections as an ideal to be restored, and they were still demanding this up to the Estates General of 1614. For the French clergy, episcopal elections symbolised the 'oneness' of bishop and cathedral chapter which together both 'represented' and governed the diocesan church. The last successful episcopal election on record was that of a bishop of Vannes in 1590, but this was in Brittany and during the Catholic League, two facts which did nothing to advance the cause of elections.

This attachment to the principle of ecclesiastical elections was not confined to the clergy, and successive Estates General meeting during the wars of religion also demanded their restoration, though, typically, the different estates held differing views on who could participate in such elections; the memory of ancient traditions was manifestly not dead.[4]

But historical reality, as already suggested, fitted only approximately into this vision of harmony inherited from an idealised early church. Furthermore, the subsequent historiography of church-state and king-papacy relations was unduly influenced by the bitter ideological exchanges over church-state relations from the later Middle Ages down to the reign of Louis XIV. It is apparent that since at least the time of Philip the Fair, the French church and its leading figures were willing enough in practice to accept royal intervention in the selection of bishops and other church dignitaries; papal intervention appeared to them more capricious, and always liable to favour outsiders, especially Italians, at the expense of Frenchmen; by comparison, French bishops drawn broadly from the royal entourage seemed to offer much better guarantees of royal support and protection of the church's privileges.[5] This lack of enthusiasm for papal intervention did not change fundamentally in succeeding centuries, when forceful monarchs were usually in a position to

---

2 See Jean Guademet, *Eglise et société en Occident au moyen âge* (London 1984), chs xvi-xvii.
3 For an excellent evocation of these elections and their context in one southern French diocese, see Nicole Lemaître, *Le Rouergue flamboyant: le clergé et les fidèles du diocèse de Rodez 1417–1563* (Paris 1988), 19ff, 217ff.
4 Gaston Zeller, *Les Institutions de la France au xvie siècle* (Paris 1948), 349; Roger Doucet, *Les Institutions de la France au xvie siècle*, 2 vols (Paris 1948), ii. 698–9.
5 See Joseph R Strayer, *The Reign of Philip the Fair* (Princeton 1980), 240–1.

ensure that royal candidates were 'elected', by the use of force if necessary. During the Avignon papacy and later, especially during the Great Schism with its 'withdrawals of obedience' from rival popes, the crown strengthened its position still further and the papacy lost the initiative for good. In theory, the Pragmatic Sanction of 1438, which came into being towards the end of the conciliar crisis following the Council of Basle, removed both the crown and the papacy from the picture, by formally restoring episcopal elections. Despite a few subsequent attempts to amend the terms of the Sanction, which had been essentially anti-papal in its inspiration, the crown continued to extend its sway and to secure episcopal preference for its servants and supporters. The measure of its success may be gauged from one simple statistic: it has been calculated that between 1483 and 1515, 79 out of the 109 dioceses which then made up the French church were held by royal councillors or members of their families.[6]

Nevertheless, this should not be interpreted as a one-directional, one-dimensional process, since the crown's freedom and ability to impose candidates of its choice differed from province to province, and it could not succeed without enlisting local support or neutralising local resistance. Here as elsewhere, the truth of the remark, 'the king can do anything he wishes, but not everything he wishes', was fully demonstrated. The diocese of Rodez was one of many which experienced its share, though not an especially large one, of disputed elections in the fifteenth and early sixteenth centuries, and their historian concludes that 'the failure of the Gallican system can probably be attributed to the lack of clear electoral rules after the Pragmatic Sanction had been set aside in favour of a short-sighted political realism which benefited both the king and the pope'.[7] Local candidates, supported by their families and networks of allies and patrons, would continue to dominate numerous bishoprics, but that could no longer be ensured by local power alone. For all its limitations, the crown was increasingly able to place outsider bishops in dioceses remote from their backgrounds and interests, one consequence of which was that at least some of them were tempted, particularly in the sixteenth century, either not to reside in their dioceses at all or to exchange them for a more attractive see as soon as the opportunity arose. The outcome was an episcopate that was more transient and less local in recruitment.

I

It is not surprising, in the light of such developments, that much has been written about the Concordat of Bologna of 1516 which put the nomination of

6 Marilyn Edelstein, 'Les Origines sociales de l'épiscopat sous Louis XII et François I', *Revue d'Histoire Moderne et Contemporaine*, 20 (1978), 239–47.
7 Lemaître, *Rouergue flamboyant*, 223. The Gallican system referred to here refers not merely to episcopal elections but to minimal dependence on Rome generally.

bishops on a new footing *de jure*. Yet both its scope and innovatory character have often been either misunderstood or over-estimated. Arguably, it was its articles dealing with appeals from French courts to Rome which contributed most decisively to the practical realisation of Gallican church structures in subsequent generations; most of its long-forgotten clauses were concerned with revising existing rules or practices over the collation of the vast mass of lesser church benefices. At the most obvious level of abolishing episcopal (and abbatial) elections outright and reserving the right to nominate bishops to the king, it consciously jettisoned the electoral principle of the Pragmatic Sanction and codified what had increasingly been actual practice – namely, resort to royal patronage from below, or direct royal intervention from above. It also brought the papacy back into the equation by giving it the right to confirm or reject the king's nominees to all 'consistorial' benefices (so called because subject to confirmation in the papal consistory); it even permitted the pope to appoint his own candidates directly if two successive royal nominees proved unsuitable, and it has been argued that the sixteenth-century French monarchs were extremely anxious to avoid such papal intervention.[8] Finally, the papacy also benefited financially from the restoration of the annates payable by holders of consistorial benefices but abolished by the Pragmatic Sanction. The view that the concordat was a carve-up of the benefice system between king and pope was widely held by the University of Paris, magistrates in the parlement of Paris, and by the clergy themselves, and it was duly opposed by them with varying degrees of conviction.[9]

It is also important to realise that the Concordat of Bologna was negotiated at a time when the question of church reform was being discussed by a general council of the church; regardless of the posturing of both Louis XII and François I, the wording of the article covering episcopal nominations speaks to these intentions. However much it might be ignored or interpreted in the following decades, it was a permanent reminder of royal promises and obligations, leaving the door open for pressure to be applied at a later date on the crown to honour them. The actual text is laconic enough, but it is doubly interesting from our perspective in that it did at least attempt to specify *who* was to be regarded as a suitable candidate for the episcopate:

> in the event of a vacancy, the king of France of the time will be required to present and nominate to us or our successors, within six months beginning from the date of the said vacancy, an earnest (*gravis* in latin) master or licentiate in theology, or a doctor or licentiate in both or one of the laws,

---

[8] Frederic J Baumgartner, *Change and Continuity in the French Church. The Bishops and the Wars of Religion* (Durham, NC 1986), 12.

[9] Roger Doucet, *Etude sur le gouvernement de François I dans ses rapports avec le parlement de Paris*, 2 vols (Paris 1921–6), is the fullest study. See also the revisions in R J Knecht, *Renaissance Prince and Patron. The Reign of Francis I* (Cambridge 1994), 90–103.

from a famous university and after rigorous examination, who is in his twenty-seventh year, and who is in other respects suitable'.[10]

There was nothing automatic about this formula, which had only been agreed upon after negotiation. For example, it was originally proposed that nobles be exempted from its educational requirement, and it was apparently at French insistence that such exemption was finally restricted to ecclesiastics from the royal family itself 'and to other high-ranking persons' (*personis sublimibus*), as well as to members of religious orders whose constitutions prevented them from taking university degrees. Indeed, the French argument on this point was, ostensibly at least, that the king wished to avoid being too hard pressed for church benefices by unqualified nobles, who should instead be motivated into studying at university and taking actual degrees.[11] The fact that French nominees were to be in their twenty-seventh year was a special concession to the French church, since the norm for bishops elsewhere in Europe was that they be aged thirty.

This is, for our purposes, the core of the concordat, but some of its anomalies and silences should also be noted, since it is too readily assumed that it addressed and coherently resolved all matters of importance in relation to the episcopate. For one thing, since it was a revision and supersession of the Pragmatic Sanction, the concordat's terms were only applicable to 'the kingdom of France, Dauphiné and the county of Die and Valentinois', but not to provinces, notably Provence or Brittany, which were not part of the French monarchy in 1438. It was agreed in 1516 that the pope would, however, confer similar rights of nomination there on the king by a special personal indult. This created difficulties later in the century, when the papacy sometimes proved slow to grant such indults. Indeed it became part of the argument as to how the French church should be defined, with the Gallicans arguing that the same law should prevail in all provinces regardless of the date of their union with France, while the papacy and its supporters claimed that all post-1438 acquisitions were *pays d'obédience* where church appointments could only be made by virtue of a papal indult. This remained the papal position with regard to Brittany and Provence until 1586 when the indult granted to Henri III effectively buried their exceptional status.[12] In the light of this, it is not difficult to see why the Trois-Evêchés and, later, frontier bishoprics acquired during the seventeenth century, were not regarded as being automatically incorporated into the French church, and why even Louis

---

10 Jules Thomas, *Le Concordat de 1516. Ses origines, son histoire au xvie siècle*, 3 vols (Paris 1910), ii. 64, for original Latin text. Similar stipulations had been contained in the Pragmatic Sanction of 1349: see Knecht, *Renaissance Prince*, 102.
11 Thomas, *Concordat de 1516*, i. 353.
12 *Lettres du cardinal d'Ossat*, ed Amelot de la Houssaye, 5 vols (Amsterdam 1718), ii. 40–3, Ossat to Villeroy, secretary of state, 22 Feb 1596, for a masterly and extensive discussion of the Breton question, based on Ossat's experience of the Roman curia. See also Doucet, *Institutions*, ii. 680–1.

XIV still needed special indults to nominate his candidates to the dioceses in question.¹³

Moreover, the concordat made no mention of the custom whereby if a bishop died in or near Rome, the pope was entitled to nominate his successor without waiting for a royal nomination. Needless to say, in the sixteenth century, when French cardinals and bishops were either frequently resident or briefly present in Rome, and when some of them held impressive collections of wealthy benefices, the French crown was as reluctant as its Spanish counterpart to see so much valuable patronage escape its grasp altogether; while the papacy, having made so many concessions to Europe's Catholic monarchs, fought tenaciously to preserve such marginal, though highly symbolic, expressions of its own patronage power. Frequent tussles thus ensued, with the French crown insisting that French bishops travelling to, or living in, Rome be granted a papal brief called *de non vacando in curia*, which in effect gave them exemption from these Roman conditions.

By the time of Henri IV and Louis XIII, these confrontations had become rare enough, but the papacy was still prepared to make its point if an occasion arose.¹⁴ One did in 1626, for example, when Archbishop Marquemont of Lyon died; though he had resided in Rome for long periods, and had only returned there in 1624, he had either neglected to seek or failed to obtain a brief *de non vacando*. Urban VIII was determined to make a direct appointment to Lyon, and having first proposed the bishop of Poitiers, he finally chose the authoritarian, ultramontane Charles Miron, bishop of Angers. But Louis XIII's advisers were naturally reluctant to accept this exercise in papal unilateralism, which might also set a dangerous precedent if allowed to pass. After intensive negotiations by the nuncio, a compromise was reached which ostensibly reversed the post-Bologna norm: the pope's man, Miron, would indeed become archbishop, but with the prior consent of the king of France! Officially, however, the pope absolutely declined to allow any public trace of royal intervention to appear, refusing to insert the phrase 'at the request of the king' in the provisions, or to grant any pensions off Lyon requested by Louis XIII. Experience taught that any such formulae inserted in provisions would be seized upon later as precedents with which to counter papal prerogatives. One would thus never guess from the tenor of the pope's formal brief to Miron, asserting that his appointment was entirely on the pope's initiative (*motu proprio*), that there had been extensive consultation, and that Urban VIII had frankly accepted that in the case of these vacancies he could simply not

---

13 Raymond Darricau, 'Comment les souverains pontifes et les rois de France concevaient la nomination aux bénéfices devenus vacants par la mort de leur titulaires en cour de Rome', in *Miscellanea in onore di Martino Giusti* (Vatican City 1978), i. 184–6; R Darricau, 'Louis XIV et le Saint-Siège. Les indults de nomination aux bénéfices consistoriaux (1643–1670)', *Bulletin de Littérature Ecclésiastique* 66 (1965), 17–34, 107–31.

14 *Lettres du cardinal d'Ossat*, iv. 303–5, Ossat to Villeroy, 13 Mar 1601, for Clement VIII's views on Carcassonne, whose bishop, Annibale Rucellaï, had died in Rome.

appoint a bishop who did not have royal approval.¹⁵ The only other known case in this period came in 1648 when Cardinal Michele Mazarin, brother of the chief minister, also suddenly died in Rome. Innocent X, a bitter enemy of Mazarin, was also determined to exercise his prerogative, and consistently refused to accept the French nominee to Aix, Jérôme Grimaldi, despite the fact that he was a former nuncio to France and a cardinal. This time, there was much diplomacy but no agreement, and Aix remained vacant until 1655 when the new pope, Alexander VII, conceded defeat and accepted Grimaldi.¹⁶

The concordat also stipulated that the king of France would submit his choices for the episcopate to the pope, but it said nothing, as one might expect, of how such choices were to be made in the first place. How far might the king effectively 'delegate' his prerogative to others, whose choices he simply ratified so that they could be formally nominated for confirmation in Rome? Might not the king himself consequently become simply someone who rubber-stamped other people's choices, rather like the post-1516 popes in respect of royal nominations? Such delegation, were it to be accepted, could take more than one form, and indeed several were to appear during the following century, which it may not be amiss to discuss here.

The most public delegation of the royal prerogative came in the shape of the apanages granted to members of the royal family, or of dower lands assigned to royal spouses or widows. Within the areas covered by royal apanages, it was customary for their holders to appoint to offices and church benefices, great and small, and for a long time few exceptions were made to this blanket concession. Henri III's brother received the duchy of Anjou in apanage in 1576, and though there was no explicit mention of bishoprics or abbeys in the clauses of the grant, it was assumed by all concerned that Anjou was entitled to 'present' his choice of bishops there for royal confirmation.¹⁷ By the terms of her marriage contract of 1572, Henri IV's first wife, Marguerite de Valois, was granted dower lands in south-west France which included the dioceses of Agen and Condom. Henri IV confirmed this grant in 1594 though he was estranged from her by then, and in subsequent years she showed how much she valued the privileges it had conferred on her.¹⁸ Following in the same tradition, Marie de' Medici's dower rights were even more extensive, as they included presentation rights to Clermont and Saint-Flour in the Auvergne, and to the seven Breton dioceses (not to mention an impressive

---

15   ASV, N Fr 66, fos 155–9, 163, 166–7, 275–6, 279–83, letters from Bernadino Spada, papal nuncio, on the Lyon question, Oct–Dec 1626. See Darricau, 'Comment les souverains pontifes et les rois de France concevaient la nomination aux bénéfices devenus vacants par la mort de leur titulaires en cour de Rome', 177–81.
16   *DHGE*, xxii, cols 245–9.
17   See Mack P Holt, *The Duke of Anjou and the Politique Struggle during the Wars of Religion* (Cambridge 1989), 70–2. Professor Holt kindly confirmed this interpretation in private correspondence, for which I thank him.
18   AD Haute-Garonne, B 1909, fos 274–5, patents of 2 Oct 1594 registered by the parlement of Toulouse.

number of abbeys and lesser benefices, even including parishes, as well as in Normandy, the Bourbonnais and elsewhere).[19] As regent of France for several years, and after that until the royal coup of April 1617, Marie was obviously well placed to exercise her dower rights as she saw fit. But with her exile to Blois, and especially her flight and revolt of 1619–20, objections were raised at court to her continuing enjoyment of such presentation rights. It was argued that such power was dangerous, as it would enable her to oblige those in search of ecclesiastical advancement to espouse her political interests also, to the detriment of those of the crown.[20] But Marie held firm, and insisted in the ensuing settlement with the court that these presentation rights be fully confirmed. They formed the core of her active role as a patron of prospective bishops during the 1620s.[21]

But a lesson may well have been learned from this experience, for when the question of marrying and endowing Gaston d'Orléans arose in 1626, considerable care was taken to define the terms of his privileges as an *apanagiste*; past settlements and precedents were collected and examined, and presentation rights to the bishoprics within his apanage (which included Chartres and Orléans) were, for the first time, explicitly excluded from its terms.[22] No further occasion for such grants arose under Louis XIII or during the Mazarin ministry, but the fact that Anne of Austria's dower settlement did not include episcopal presentation rights, shows that the generosity of Henri III and Henri IV was clearly a thing of the past.

Of course, the practical consequences of such alienations of direct royal power to nominate bishops may not always have been precisely those intended by the legislation. Marie de' Medici's advisers warned her to exercise constant vigilance in defence of hers. The drafting, probably around 1620, of a full list of such benefices, right down to the lowliest *cure* or *chapellenie* in the Forez or the Haute Marche, was a response to just such a need. Sébastien Bouthillier, future bishop of Aire, warned her from Rome that a number of benefices in her gift had been filled without consulting her and that the nominees tried to obtain provisions in the curia.[23] Louis XIII himself was not beyond trying to pre-empt her choices by indicating the names of those whose interests he had at heart and asking her to oblige him accordingly.[24] Even before the first Cardinal de Retz was pronounced dead in August 1622, the king wrote to

---

19 They are listed in BI, MS Godefroy 320, fos 257–60.
20 AAE, France 772, fo 157v, abbé Tantucci to Richelieu, 13 July 1617, reporting the objections by 'ceulx du conseil'.
21 *Ibid*, fo 115, queen mother's demands to present to bishoprics and other benefices, 16 Aug 1619; fo 132, *brevet* confirming her dower rights over presentation to benefices, 24 Sept 1619.
22 BN, MS Fr 3668, fo 128, undated memorandum on terms of Gaston's apanage.
23 AAE, CP Rome 23, fos 36–7, letter to Claude Bouthillier, 1 June 1621.
24 AAE, France 775, fos 71–4, Louis de Marillac to Richelieu, Sept (?) 1621; *Lettres de la main de Louis XIII*, ed E Griselle, 2 vols (Paris 1914), i. 143–4, letter to queen mother, Aug-Sept 1621. Both letters deal with the Breton benefices of the late bishop of Marseille, Arthur d'Espinay de Saint-Luc, which the king had disposed of before realising that the presentation rights belonged to his mother, and which he asked her to confirm retrospectively.

Marie asking her to ensure that two of Retz's abbeys go to one of his nephews.[25] When she granted one of them as requested but made no mention of the other, the king, no doubt strongly prompted by the Gondi family, thanked her but politely asked her to oblige him in respect of the other abbey, promising to reward her servants on another occasion.[26] This seems to have worked, and whatever the pressure Marie was under from her own entourage over the abbey in question, she was subtly reminded that her fount of patronage was smaller than that of the king, and that a promise of later reward from him was worth keeping in reserve.

The experiences of Gaston d'Orléans were, as already suggested, quite different to those of his mother. Although formally denied presentation rights to the sees of Chartres and Orléans, contemporaries were not convinced that was the last word on the matter – and neither was Gaston himself. When Orléans became vacant in August 1630, at a time when relations within the royal family were extremely tense, Louis XIII turned to Richelieu for suggestions as to whom he should nominate. Richelieu uncharacteristically declined to provide any name, and instead recommended that the king take due care and time over such serious matters, as haste over episcopal nominations was to be avoided at all costs. But Louis XIII ignored this advice and swiftly appointed Nicolas de Netz to Orléans. Within days, Gaston was furiously complaining of the speed of the decision; he did not actually claim any right of presentation, but he repeatedly protested that his legitimate interest in the diocese of Orléans had been ignored.[27] For his part, Netz seems genuinely to have believed that Gaston had some formal say in the filling of the vacancy.[28] In 1641, Gaston tried to prevent Richelieu's confessor from succeeding as bishop of Chartres, but given Gaston's semi-disgrace and the identity of the chosen candidate, it is hardly surprising that he did not get very far.[29]

These were not the only ways in which the royal prerogative to choose bishops could be delegated or alienated. Even where formal arrangements to this effect did not exist, courtiers, favourites, ministers or other individuals competed to present persons of their choosing to the ruler for royal nomination. Doing so was entirely consistent with contemporaries' understanding of what the king's 'grace' meant in practice, and in certain instances the initiative might come from the king himself, taking the form of an invitation to present a candidate to him for his approval. Most of the time, this was done

25 BN, MS 500 Colbert 98, fo 168v-9r, letter of 10 Aug. Retz died a few days later.
26 *Ibid*, fo 169v-70r, undated letter.
27 See my essay 'Richelieu and his bishops?', in Joseph Bergin and Laurence Brockliss (eds) *Richelieu and his Age* (Oxford 1992), 194 and references.
28 BSG, MS 3249, fo 202, Netz to Cardinal La Rochefoucauld, 19 Aug 1630, 'Le Roy m'ayant fait l'honneur de me nommer à l'Evesché d'Orléans lorsque j'y pensois le moins croyant que la nomination en appartenoit à Monsieur frère du Roy à cause de son appenage'.
29 Pierre Blet, 'Vincent de Paul et l'épiscopat français', in *Vincent de Paul. Actes du colloque international d'études vincentiennes* (Rome 1983), 88–9.

verbally and informally, and has thus left very few traces. There was nothing exceptional about it – kings regularly did the same for royal offices in the provinces – but during the reigns of Charles IX and Henri III matters went a step further with the granting of signed royal letters addressed to the particular individuals who were to present their candidates. Such a development tended to formalise the delegation of the royal prerogative, and to provide the beneficiaries with the basis for a precedent which could be invoked later, one which, if accepted by the crown, would have led to the quasi-permanent right of individuals or families to determine who became bishop of a particular diocese. We can only speculate on what might have happened to the Richelieu family had they not been able to invoke such a claim to the diocese of Luçon under Henri IV. Further evidence of this will appear later, but it would be a mistake to assume that such attitudes were quickly swept away with the recovery of the crown after the religious wars. One example of what it meant may suffice here. In 1626, Louis XIII's favourite of the day, François de Baradat, obtained the see of Noyon – not especially rich, but with a peerage attached to it – for his brother Henri. In 1651, the bishop was anxious to retire, claiming that war damage in Noyon was so bad that the diocese was no longer capable to sustaining his 'dignité épiscopale', and he opened negotiations with Gaston d'Orléans's *éminence grise*, La Rivière, future bishop of Langres. But Baradat's elder brother was furious at such independence and, indeed, presumption. He argued that all those years ago, Louis XIII had really given Noyon to *him* as a reward for his services, and that his brother 'should keep Noyon in his family for as long as it had individuals capable of holding it, and that he hoped the king would be good enough to allow him to keep it'.[30] Baradat had not, it seems, received any written patent from Louis XIII, but this did not much concern him: as far as he was concerned, his episcopal brother merely held Noyon in trust for him and the next generation of the family, and could not, therefore, dispose of it independently to a third party. In the event, Bishop Baradat's talks collapsed and he remained at Noyon until his death in 1659. It may not have taken the Fronde to revive such patrimonial attitudes towards dioceses, but the circumstances of the Fronde no doubt facilitated the bluntness with which they were articulated.

The stipulations of the Concordat of Bologna referred only to vacant sees, and required the king to nominate a bishop within a six-month period. But this, as we shall see presently, hardly begins to convey the complex reality of the making of bishops. If dioceses only changed hands as a result of the death of reigning bishops, as classical canon law assumed to be the norm, then matters would have been relatively straightforward. But this was certainly not the case, least of all in the sixteenth and early seventeenth century, when

---

30   BN, MS Fr 25025, fo 420, 14 May 1651: 'le devoit laisser dans la maison tant qu'il y auroit des personnes capables de le tenir et que le Roi auroit la bonté de le luy conserver'.

bishoprics often changed hands by means of resignations, exchanges, coadjutorships, regressions and so on. The concordat codified the prerogatives of crown and papacy but, like most documents of its kind, it was an adjustment to a long-standing range of practices, not a revolution which would clear them away forever. The most obvious victim of the concordat, episcopal elections, had been all but dead for quite some time. While the granting of formal powers of nomination to the king served to concentrate further the attention of candidates and their supporters on the court, it did nothing to abolish centuries-old practices and attitudes towards church benefices. It is clear that no one, king and pope included, imagined that practices such as resigning bishoprics in favour of nominated successors (*resignatio in favorem*), of obtaining as a coadjutor someone (usually a member of one's own family) who would later succeed automatically as bishop on the death of the incumbent, of exchanging a diocese with another bishop (called *permutation*), or of recovering a bishopric if, having resigned it to someone else, that bishop predeceased the person who had resigned it to him, had been definitively set aside by the concordat – if only because it made no mention of them. It was, for example, generally accepted that cardinals wishing to resign their dioceses should have the freedom to select personally their successors. The king's patronage powers under the concordat were thus held to be enveloped, broadly speaking, in a spectrum of practices long acknowledged by, and enshrined in canon law. It was this array of precedents which offered so much scope for independent action to those in search of bishoprics and other major benefices. Admittedly, these practices were customs rather than rights, always subject to approval or veto by the crown, and as such not binding upon the king of the day. But they could only be modified or set aside altogether in the course of time by a deliberate, sustained royal policy of ignoring or marginalising them. But so long as they survived, most of the initiatives concerning bishoprics normally came from either reigning bishops, ecclesiastics in search of a diocese, and families and patrons of clerical hopefuls, rather than from the crown itself.

Finally, although the Concordat of Bologna attempted to specify what it was that made candidates suitable for episcopal office, neither then nor in the succeeding generations did the crown establish a clearly structured mechanism, a special commission or a branch of the royal council, to handle episcopal nominations, reviewing candidates' suitability and making recommendations to the king. Even when changes were made, they, too, were adjustments, not revolutionary departures. As a consequence, French episcopal nominations would continue to be primarily patronage-driven for a very long time.[31]

---

31 For a comparison with the situation in Castile, see Helen E Rawlings, 'The Secularisation of Castilian Episcopal Office under the Habsburgs, c. 1516–1700', *Journal of Ecclesiastical History* 38 (1987), 53–79.

II

While clearly of the first importance, the royal action of nominating someone to a bishopric was, in fact, only one of a long sequence of steps, all of which were a necessary part of the making of a bishop. As nominations could be revoked or declined along the way, there was no absolute guarantee of a successful outcome. For example, Antoine de Pluvinel's brother-in-law found his hopes of becoming bishop of Grenoble cruelly dashed in 1607: Henri IV cancelled his nomination at the last possible moment, when Rome had formally accepted him and was preparing to grant him his provisions.[32] Such drastic interventions were unusual, but they show how much latitude the crown enjoyed when it found pressing reasons to change course over particular nominations. Because the individual experience of obtaining the mitre is frequently lost from view both in general accounts of the episcopate and in the pious platitudes of too many episcopal biographies, the remainder of this chapter is devoted to exploring the protracted business of becoming a fully-confirmed bishop, and what it typically involved. The exposition which follows is based primarily on actual historical facts rather than on canon-law rules, many of which appear quite incidental or were in the process of adaptation during this period. Of course, the effect may be to suggest that there was a typical route to the episcopate, but the case-studies devoted to individual successions which complete the chapter, should amply suffice to offset any such impression of uniformity.

Statistically, it is clear that most episcopal vacancies arose through the death of incumbent bishops. This was the simplest eventuality, at least in the sense that it paved the way for a direct royal nomination; in principle, successions of this kind were the most 'open' of all. But even here individual success or failure could depend on a number of elements. If a bishop died at court, in Paris, or a major city, the news travelled rapidly and was, usually at least, reliable; but if a bishop died in a remote diocese, things could be different. In general, news that bishops had died, were at death's door, or were beyond all hope of recovery, travelled no less fast, but often turned out to be unfounded, or at the least premature. Dozens of examples of news of such 'vacancies' could be compiled for the period studied here. Indeed, it may be wondered whether some of these rumours were not wishful thinking, or were deliberately spread by those with their eyes trained on individual dioceses with a view to 'bouncing' the king and his entourage into making a nomination. The crown was aware of this temptation, and made periodic efforts to counteract it: in regulations for the secretaries of state approved in 1617, it was stipulated that they should not deliver any *brevet de nomination* to bishoprics before receiving confirmation of the death of the previous

---

32 *Recueil de lettres missives de Henri IV*, ed X Berger de Xivrey and J Gaudet, 9 vols (Paris 1843–76), vii. 259–60, Henri IV to Cardinal Givry, 31 May 1607. BN, MS Fr 18002, fo 161, Halincourt, ambassador in Rome, to Henri IV, 2 May 1607.

bishop.[33] But whatever the motives of those involved, there can be little doubt as to the contemporary perception that speed of response was a major factor in becoming a bishop.

This perception may in turn have been sharpened by the lack of any formal machinery for the handling of episcopal vacancies, and in particular for assessing the claims of different candidates. Had such a procedure existed and been widely known, it would have made precipitation pointless. But as matters stood, the immediate objective was to mobilise as much support as possible and as quickly as possible, and to lobby royal favourites, ministers, and any other influential figures at court. Yet speed did not count for everything during the period we are considering. Royal nominations could be, and were, frequently delayed for a variety of reasons which defy simple classification. It was said of François I that he made a point of showing his liberality by granting royal patronage to the first person who petitioned him, but such anecdotal evidence can be stretched too far. The crown could, and did, resist pressure from court factions or families. In the mid-1630s, the Provençal *savant* Peiresc reported to a Roman correspondent who was anxious to become a bishop that it was now customary to leave dioceses vacant for up to three months so as to have the time to choose a suitable candidate.[34] Sometimes delays exceeded the six months allowed by the Concordat of Bologna, but there is no sign that the papacy ever attempted to exercise its right to nominate directly in these cases. In fact, it was much more likely to blame individuals nominated by the crown for their slowness in seeking their papal provisions than to blame the crown for its delays.

Where bishoprics changed hands through resignations, exchanges or coadjutorships, the situation was naturally rather different. There was no actual vacancy at any point during the procedure. In such cases, the initiative was normally taken by incumbent bishops who, even after they had formally signed an act of resignation of their diocese before a notary, still retained their freedom of action until the crown formally approved of their intentions; if it did not approve of their choice of successor, the bishops remained fully in possession of their existing diocese, and could always attempt a similar move at some later date. But normally the crown would not wish to oppose a bishop who desired to retire outright because of age or ill-health. As with bishops seeking coadjutors, it was far more likely to object to the successor whom they had in mind, for the simple reason that it did not wish to see valuable church patronage siphoned off by incumbent bishops and their supporters. In 1653, the elderly bishop of Digne in Provence sought permission to take a coadjutor, but he was advised by the secretary of state, Brienne, that the king – meaning Mazarin, presumably – would not approve his designated

---

33 Orest Ranum, *Richelieu and the Councillors of Louis XIII* (Oxford 1963), 186.
34 *Lettres de Peiresc*, ed Philippe Tamizey de Larroque, 8 vols (Paris 1888–98), iv. 161, Peiresc to Jean-Jacques Bouchard, 1 Aug 1636.

successor; however, Brienne assured the bishop the he would succeed if he were to negotiate with the abbé Janson, and concluded that 'His Majesty would be extremely pleased and will gladly take steps to grant you those things which would be advantageous to you'.[35] Such direct evidence of crown-inspired choices of coadjutors or successors to bishops still in office is rare enough in this period: thus, at any rate, did Toussaint de Janson, successively bishop of Digne, Marseille and Beauvais, future cardinal, ambassador, and grand almoner of France, begin his rise to prominence as humble coadjutor of Digne in 1655.

III

For those who succeeded in obtaining royal approval, their immediate reward took the form of a *brevet de nomination*, a short document countersigned and issued by the secretary of state whose turn it was to act as secretary in attendance on the king (*en quartier*). In the case of a politically influential secretary of state, like Villeroy or Puysieux under Henri IV and Louis XIII, this mundane secretarial role could, of course, conceal a secretary's own part in actually securing a particular nomination. Attempts were made, especially under Louis XIII, to curb the scope for abuse by the secretaries where matters of royal patronage were concerned, but it is highly doubtful whether a secretary's routine personal attendance on the king was normally significant in decisions to fill vacant dioceses.[36] *Brevets de nomination*, which have not survived in large numbers, were highly formulaic documents which did not change much during the period, and they commonly offer only the most fleeting of justifications for the grant of a bishopric to a given candidate. Most of the time, they referred vaguely to the 'qualities, capacity and good life' of the candidate, but until the 1620s it was not unknown for them to declare that a bishopric was given as a favour to (*en faveur de*) someone else, to whom either the king or the incoming bishop was beholden, and who was thereby clearly identified as the real beneficiary of the king's largesse.

But obtaining a *brevet* was not the end of things for a would-be bishop, who might have to endure a further period of waiting and uncertainty. *Brevets* could be revoked, so that the grant of one did not mean that lobbying and competition for a vacant diocese immediately ceased. This was all the more true when the *brevet* was given to a third party (as often happened during the sixteenth century) who would then attempt to find an ecclesiastic whom he would 'present' to the king once he had negotiated with him over the terms

---

35   BN, MS Fr 20661, fo 169, Brienne to Bishop of Digne, 7 Mar 1653: 'Sa Majesté en sera fort aise et se disposera volontiers à vous accorder les choses qui pourront estre à vostre avantage'.
36   Ranum, *Richelieu and the Councillors of Louis XIII*, Appendix A, 186–9, for the text of one such attempt, the *règlement* of June 1617. Other attempts can be traced in R Mousnier, *Les Règlements du conseil du roi sous Louis XIII* (Paris 1949).

of the episcopal succession. But even when given directly to the individual selected for a diocese, a *brevet* should in practice be regarded as a negotiable claim to a diocese, not the certainty that the grantee was assured of becoming a bishop. Unfortunately it is impossible to know how often *brevets* were either revoked or declined, but indirect evidence of revocations and dashed expectations can sometimes be detected, not least in the grant of pensions off vacant bishoprics. For example, in April 1610, Charles Prévost, having been nominated as coadjutor of Coutances, made arrangements with a view to obtaining his provisions from Rome. But nothing further is known about him or his nomination, and the contract for the provisions was cancelled without explanation in December 1612. The bishop of Coutances was eighty-four years old at that time, and presumably needed a younger man as coadjutor; if, as seems possible, he acted independently in seeking a coadjutor, he almost certainly offended the Matignon family which dominated the diocese and wanted it for a family member when it became vacant again. At any rate, the aged bishop was left to soldier on alone until his death in 1620.[37] Charles Talon, brother of the famous Omer, *avocat-général* in the Paris parlement, was nominated to Saint-Pol-de-Léon in 1635 after the previous holder, René de Rieux, had been deposed for rebellion by assisting Marie de' Medici in her flight into exile in 1631.[38] But it seems as if Talon sensed the dangers of such an appointment and he quietly returned his *brevet* before obtaining his papal provisions; the next appointee, Robert Cupif, was much less perspicacious and would pay a heavy price for his ambition. His isolation within the episcopate was such that by the late 1650s he was even prepared to accept the position of bishop of Killala in Cromwellian Ireland, a fate from which he was only saved by death.[39]

But the more normal sequel to a *brevet* was the issue of a formal letter of nomination signed by the king and addressed directly to the pope. Without this, no future bishop could even begin to take steps towards obtaining his papal provisions. The papal curia always refused to acknowledge simple *brevets* as representing a valid title to a benefice. Considering them to be private documents, it rejected the occasional effort of French ecclesiastics to obtain provisions on the strength of them.[40] No clearer witness of the *brevet*'s provisional character or limited value could be asked for. But even letters of nomination were not irrevocable, as we saw in the case of Grenoble, and there are other instances from the reigns of Henri IV and Louis XIII where the crown cancelled nominations, even after those concerned had initiated the search for provisions in Rome. As far as we can tell, letters of nomination were

---

37 AN, MC, XII, 41, acts of 17 Apr 1610 and 24 Dec 1612.
38 BN, MS lat 17026, fo 59, Louis XIII to Ambassador Noailles and Cardinal Antonio Barberini, 31 July 1635.
39 *Dictionnaire historique, géographique, et biographique du Maine-et-Loire*, ed C Port, 3 vols (Paris-Angers 1876–8), i. 871.
40 *Lettres du cardinal d'Ossat*, iv. 448, Ossat to Henri IV, 26 Jan 1601.

usually drafted and signed virtually simultaneously with, or within days of, the *brevet*. But sometimes the delay might be longer than that, suggesting either royal indecision or second thoughts, lobbying by other candidates and their patrons, or the successful candidate's search for royal support for the grant of papal provisions partly or wholly exempt from the payment of annates.

For most of the sixteenth century, the despatch of letters of nomination to Rome would have sufficed to initiate moves leading to papal confirmation of bishops. But this, too, had begun to change with the gradual introduction of a formal *processus* or enquiry into the life and behaviour (*de vita et moribus*) of royal nominees to the episcopate. Sometimes called in French the *enquête d'idonéité*, its purpose was to establish the suitability of royal nominees for office. Medieval papal rulings about such an enquiry had long been ignored, but with the formal concession by Renaissance popes (especially in the early sixteenth century) of nomination rights to many of Europe's rulers, the need for such an enquiry was increasingly felt. The Council of Trent added its voice to this demand, though it refused to lay down a general procedure that would be applied for all national churches, preferring to leave it instead to each church to organise its own enquiries. This was evidently unsatisfactory, and in 1591 Gregory XIV issued new instructions which principally empowered the nuncio, or if he was absent or unable to act, a local bishop, to conduct the enquiry. In 1627, Urban VIII again revised the procedures, and for the first time a fixed questionnaire consisting of thirteen questions about the nominee and thirteen in a separate enquiry about the vacant diocese, was laid down as the basis of the enquiry. There was to be no further alteration to the procedure until the nineteenth century.[41]

Despite the French crown's dislike of the Council of Trent's decrees and papal legislation generally, it appears that at least some such enquiries were conducted under Henri III and Henri IV, sometimes by the nuncios, but usually by archbishops or bishops of the province in which the vacant diocese was situated. These particular enquiries have not survived except in highly condensed form in Rome, where they were used to present royal nominees for approval in consistory. Suspicion of their veracity had long been present, and in 1610 a French ecclesiastic denounced them directly to the pope as misleading fabrications and urged a tightening up of procedures.[42] In fact, the papacy seems to have begun to act by then anyway, and to urge that the enquiries be

---

41 For a succinct account of the institution, see Louis Jadin, 'Procès d'information pour la nomination des évêques et abbés des Pays-Bas, de Liège, et de Franche-Comté d'après les archives de la congrégation consistoriale', *Bulletin de l'Institut Historique Belge de Rome* 6 (1928), 5–27.

42 Claude d'Angennes, bishop of Noyon, claimed in 1585 to the papal nuncio that the pope was being misled by these enquiries: see L Serbat, *Les Assemblées du clergé de France: origines, organisation, développement 1561–1615* (Paris 1906), 387, nuncio to Rome, 25 Nov 1585; ASV, Lettere di Vescovi 19, fo 69, Olivier du Bois to Paul V, 9 Oct 1610.

normally conducted by the nuncio who might in certain circumstances delegate some, but not all, of the work to a local bishop.[43] During the following decades, the nuncio played an increasingly visible part in these enquiries but those conducted by local bishops were still generally acceptable. During the crisis of Franco-papal relations of 1639–40, the parlement of Paris challenged papal activities and declared that the nuncio was engaging in an unacceptable exercise of papal jurisdiction by conducting such enquiries in France. But the papacy held firm, while Richelieu did not wish to make an issue of this particular question. In any case the papacy claimed that the enquiry was not an act of jurisdiction at all, but simply the collection of information to which the pope was perfectly entitled before confirming a royal nominee.[44]

The enquiry itself consisted of a series of depositions in answer to standardised questions about the royal nominees. Those giving evidence were not supposed to be relatives or enemies of the candidate, although in practice distant kin did sometimes appear among them. In general, friends, teachers and mentors, past and present, tended to predominate. Their evidence was, as would be expected, highly favourable to the nominee, not least because the enquiry itself, coming as it did *after* rather than before a royal nomination, inevitably tended to demonstrate that the king's choice had been suitable in the first place! Nor was the procedure adversarial in character: there was no confrontation of witnesses, and it is not at all clear how far nuncios undertook independent investigations of dubious or conflicting statements, despite provision to that end in papal legislation. If they did so and uncovered unflattering details about newly nominated bishops, they may have communicated such information separately from the normal channels to the curia, for there is virtually no trace of it in their correspondence. A rare exception, it would appear, to this came in 1622 when the nuncio, Ottavio Corsini, informed the papal secretary of state that he had conducted the enquiry into Dominique de Vic, son of the late keeper of the seals and coadjutor-designate to the archbishop of Auch, but added that he had himself learnt that de Vic had kept, and possibly still kept, a mistress.[45] De Vic's progress was not halted by this embarrassing revelation, which was not divulged, though he may have been rebuked privately by the nuncio.

Most of the enquiries *de vita et moribus* were done within days, or at least a few weeks, of the royal nomination. But some, particularly during the 1610s, were done before the official dates of nomination, which suggests that decisions about episcopal successions were occasionally taken in advance of actual

---

43 In July 1606, the papal nuncio writing in support of Philippe Cospeau, stated in a matter of fact way that the enquiry into Cospeau had been 'fatto avanti di me'. ASV, Fondo Borghese II, 248, fo 297, letter to papal secretary of state.

44 Pierre Blet, 'Le Concordat de Bologne et la réforme tridentine', *Gregorianum*, 45 (1964), 272–6.

45 BAV, Barb lat 8057, fo 238, Ottavio Corsini, nuncio, to Cardinal Ludovisi, 4 July 1622.

vacancies. The nominee himself did not take part in the enquiry, though he must have played some part in suggesting the names of those who could testify for him. Indeed witnesses regarded it as an honour to do so, and they often included reigning bishops whose detailed knowledge of the candidate's biography was often very thin. However, the new bishop did have to present himself before the nuncio or presiding prelate to formally take and sign the Council of Trent's profession of faith which was obligatory for all those taking up church office. The signed profession of faith formed part of the dossier then forwarded to Rome, where it was scrutinised with increasing rigour as the century wore on.

The 'administrative' rôle played by the papal nuncios in the making of bishops inevitably raises the wider, and much more important, question of how much influence they could exercise in the actual choice of bishops. The temptation to assume that they helped to obtain bishoprics for certain individuals but vetoed promotion for others is strong, yet there is probably little basis for it. The role of particular nuncios (and a papal legate, in particular) will be noted in later chapters, so that only a few general points need be made here. Overall, it seems that successive nuncios played relatively little part in episcopal nominations, even though for many decades their standing instructions required them to keep a careful eye on such matters. Historians hoping that their correspondence would provide an ideal source for the analysis of the competition for bishoprics and the patronage networks involved in such competition, are likely to be severely disappointed. What is remarkable is how few mentions there are of such matters in normal circumstances, with nuncios usually confining themselves to transmitting recommendations on behalf of some newly nominated bishop who appeared particularly deserving of favourable financial treatment by the curia; these recommendations were often made in what seems a highly guarded, even formulaic manner, and would usually not otherwise include any comment on the nomination process itself. The implication is clear enough – that, for all their involvement with the formal processes that followed a royal nomination, nuncios did not wish to play a regular part in such nominations. Beyond that, it seems that they were most likely to intervene whenever a candidate with a reputation for holding strong Gallican and, later in the century, Jansenist views was put forward. Such intervention was not without its dangers; it could lead to considerable resentment at court, and it stood a better chance of success if it preceded the formal nomination of a candidate by the king; once a nomination was made and had become public knowledge, the nuncio's scope for action was rather limited, and he was probably best advised to pass on his objections to a candidate to Rome, where a higher authority could take whatever action it thought appropriate to the case. Nuncios may have had more influence in other parts of Catholic Europe, but it is a fantasy to imagine that in seventeenth-century France, they were in any position to play the role of 'bishop-maker'.

The search for papal provisions began in France, since the preparatory arrangements which it required could be complex. The royal letter of nomination was itself addressed directly to the pope, but in actual fact it, and other letters of recommendation to the papal secretary of state, the cardinal protector of France, and other curial figures, were initially sent to a 'solicitor' specialising in negotiating provisions to benefices in the Curia, whose first task was to pass on the letters to the French ambassador in Rome. The ambassador himself received a formal royal letter, and sometimes separate instructions or recommendations in individual cases, and it was not until he formally presented the royal letters to the pope that the process of obtaining papal confirmation could actually begin.

However, obtaining papal confirmation was not as simple as this might imply, and several more mundane preparatory steps had to taken, which were largely the responsibility of the incoming bishop himself. Most of the actual negotiation and paperwork in Rome was done not by the ambassador or his subordinates, but by 'solicitors' specialising in such work in the curia. It was therefore essential for candidates to make the arrangements and provide the documentation that would enable these men to move into action. In turn, the solicitors worked under the instructions of other specialists known as *banquiers expéditionnaires en cour de Rome*, whose title on its own suggests that their role was to obtain and despatch papal provisions, and to pay the funds which these required. Paris, Lyon, Toulouse and possibly a few other French cities had a number of these *banquiers* who specialised in the financial aspects of the French church's relations with the Roman curia, especially in transferring the funds which obtaining provisions for benefices always entailed. These expenses were partly administrative costs, and together they constituted an impressive list of fees payable to the papal officials involved in the preparation and despatch of bulls, fees to the cardinals actually presenting and proposing candidates in consistory, postal and foreign-exchange costs, and so on. Taken on their own, the fees could amount to a tidy sum, and were the consequence of a development in the papal curia with which seventeenth-century Frenchmen were themselves familiar – the multiplication of officials and the fees which they charged thanks to the venality of office practised by the papacy.

Normally, newly nominated French bishops would, therefore, seek out a Paris-based *banquier* as being in a better position than his provincial counterparts to secure their provisions and transfer the often large sums of money involved. This latter consideration could lead them to select the *banquier* who could offer them the best terms. In 1645, Henri de Béthune of Maillezais was promoted to the archbishopric of Bordeaux, which of course required a whole new set of papal provisions, not merely to Bordeaux itself, but for the abbey of Mauléon he already held and wished to retain. He thus obtained a detailed quotation of expected costs from four separate Parisian *banquiers*, benefice by benefice, leading to an agreement in January 1647 with the keenest of the bidders.⁴⁶ This may not have been unusual, and it is not hard to understand Béthune's approach when it emerges that he expected to pay 26,960 *livres* in all. The immediate upshot of such preliminary exploration was a notarised contract with a *banquier*: an estimated figure for the cost of papal provisions was agreed upon, with clauses stipulating how much the bishop should pay in advance, and what would happen should expenses be either higher or lower than anticipated. In the case of Archbishop Béthune, the final bill for a total of thirteen bulls came to 22,000 *livres*, just under 5,000 less than he had originally anticipated: the bulls for Bordeaux cost him 12,507 *livres*, with most of the balance being consumed in the costs incurred by the *banquier* and Béthune's own agent in Rome.⁴⁷

The main reason, of course, for the high sums payable to the curia was the tax known as the annates which, as the name suggests, was supposed to represent one year of revenue from the benefices that were changing hands. This was no longer true by the seventeenth century.⁴⁸ Ever since their introduction during the Middle Ages, the annates had been unpopular, and both the Council of Basle and the Pragmatic Sanction of 1438 had outlawed such payments (and the related loss of specie from the kingdom) to the curia. But one consequence of the concordat of 1516 was their reintroduction, although no mention whatever was made of them in the concordat itself; this was a separate concession by François I which made the concordat palatable to the papacy.⁴⁹ An attempt to suppress them again in 1560 proved shortlived.⁵⁰ Paying annates in full was as unpopular among seventeenth-century French bishops as it no doubt was among lesser clerics. The question surfaced again in late 1639 and 1640 during the crisis of Franco-papal relations, when the lead was taken by a number of bishops who held several unsuccessful discussions about the annates. Their aim was not the abolition but the moderation of the tax, and they strongly, albeit misleadingly, protested that French benefices were substantially over-taxed by comparison with those of Spain.⁵¹ Another reason for this discontent was that the assessments of benefices for papal tax purposes were long out of date, having been made centuries earlier and not subsequently brought up to date, so that the original assessments remained enshrined in the tax-registers of the Apostolic Chamber which used the figures as a crude multiplier (or divider) when computing the annates owed by a given bishopric.

46 AD Gironde, G 260, bundle of unnumbered papers relating to Béthune's affairs, with detailed memoranda on the costs of provisions in Rome.
47 AN, MC, XCVI 48, procuration to *banquier*, 7 Jan 1647, with final settlement of account, dated 25 July 1648, added.
48 Thomas, *Concordat de 1516*, i. 104ff, 340–1.
49 Pierre Blet, 'Concordat' in *Dictionnaire du grand siècle*, ed F Bluche (Paris 1992), 380.
50 Baumgartner, *Change and Continuity*, 15–16.
51 See Joseph Bergin, *Cardinal de La Rochefoucauld. Leadership and Reform in the French Church* (New Haven and London 1987), 81–2, and sources quoted there, especially from the correspondence of the nuncio, Ranuccio Scotti.

It was probably this archaic practice as much as the actual burdensomeness of the tax which irked bishops and other clerics. Certainly, the curia's figures, expressed in florins, bear relatively little relation, on a diocese-by-diocese comparison, to the known hierarchy of diocesan revenues in the seventeenth century. Just to take two examples, Coutances and Dax, both estimated in 1648 to be worth 18,000 *livres* a year, were 'taxed' on the basis of 2,500 and 500 florins respectively. It is unfortunately impossible to know how many dioceses may have been turned down on such grounds by candidates for episcopal office, but stray references to financial difficulties suggest that it happened during the seventeenth century.[52]

Clearly, mobilising the means with which to pay the annates was of major concern for a newly appointed bishop about to negotiate a contract with a *banquier expéditionnaire*. It was here that revenue from benefices already held proved especially invaluable, as they could provide ready cash or the collateral with which to borrow money. Incoming bishops were not entitled to pledge the revenues from their future dioceses as a method of raising cash; whether that was always observed in practice is impossible to discover, but there may have been practical as well as canon-law reasons for this impediment: the fact, for example, that success in Rome was not guaranteed might well deter potential lenders from providing funds against such poor surety. Not surprisingly, this is the reason why royal nominees without any personal patrimony or benefices always aroused such comment from contemporaries, who were unused to seeing such individuals promoted to the episcopate. When the respected preacher and university teacher, Philippe Cospeau, became bishop of Aire in 1606, his lack of means was widely remarked upon, as was, needless to say, the generosity of the duc d'Epernon, who had secured Aire for Cospeau, in paying the sums owed by the new incumbent.[53] Over thirty years later, Richelieu emulated Epernon's example by providing 6,000 *livres* towards the costs of Jean de Lingendes's provisions to the diocese of Sarlat, since the preacher-bishop had no private means or benefices.[54] On the other hand, he had felt no obligation to do the same for the similarly unbeneficed Antoine Godeau in 1636, since Godeau, though a Richelieu protégé, enjoyed considerable personal means as an only son related to wealthy merchant families in Paris. It does not seem as if Mazarin was ever minded to repeat Richelieu's generosity, even though a few of his nominees were men without obvious sources of funds.[55]

---

52 Vincent de Paul, *Correspondance, Entretiens, Documents*, ed. Pierre Coste, 14 vols (Paris, 1922–5), ii. no 700, de Paul to Joseph Dehorgny in Rome, 3 Feb 1644: 'Monsieur de Boulogne ne veut point de son évêché par l'impuissance qu'il a de payer 23 mil livres qu'on lui demande à Rome. *Si quid potes, adjuva illum*'.

53 BN, MS lat 17021, fo 81; ASV, Fondo Borghese II, 248, fo 297, nuncio to secretary of state, 15 July 1606.

54 BN, MS Fr 15610, p 601, Henri Arnauld to president Barillon, 20 May 1640.

55 They include François Faure and Dominique Ithier, both of whom became bishop of Glandevès in Provence in the 1650s, and who had taken serious political risks on Mazarin's behalf during the Fronde.

Most episcopal appointees did not have an Epernon or a Richelieu waiting to pay their bills. Some undoubtedly relied on their families to provide temporary credit until such time as they could begin actually drawing their diocesan revenues. In 1640, the monk Charles de Saint-Paul (the name by which Charles Vialart was known in the reformed congregation of Cistercians, the Feuillants, of which he was superior-general) was appointed bishop of Avranches, but his monastic vow of poverty meant that he possessed no personal resources. To finance his papal provisions, he turned to his wealthy and devout mother, Jeanne Hennequin, widow of a former president in the *grand conseil* and *maître des requêtes*, who lent him 10,000 *livres* for that purpose.[56]

Another solution to the cost of becoming a bishop was, not surprisingly, to seek to obtain a reduction, either total or partial, of the annates payable to the curia. That outcome was, as far as we can tell, avidly sought by virtually everyone nominated by successive kings of France in the period under review, but it was formidably difficult to achieve. The way to success began with the obtaining of letters of recommendation from the king himself, but also from members of the royal family, ministers, cardinals, and anyone else who could conceivably convince the pope and his court of the virtues of financial magnanimity towards the candidate in question. Royal letters to the pope and influential cardinals would press the claims of indigent episcopal nominees whose merit the king had so clearly and wisely recognised, and whom the papacy should now play its part in promoting to the bench; the element of self-congratulation was barely concealed in such appeals. In October 1602, the Benedictine Jean Garnier, a royal almoner and preacher who had been nominated to Montpellier, promised to deliver to a *banquier expéditionnaire* 'letters of nomination and favour from the king and several other lords who write in support of Garnier for the said gratis'.[57] Antoine Revol, nephew of a former secretary of state and incoming bishop of Dol in Brittany, also promised to obtain similar letters from Henri IV, Villeroy (then principal secretary of state) and 'other lords' in February 1603.[58] But the king and his entourage were at least as likely, and possibly more so, to make identical appeals on behalf of high born or well connected nominees. In this instance, the petition had nothing to do with the lack of means: annates could easily be paid in full by a prince of the blood or a minister's son, but now it was their lineage or their closeness to the royal personage which was expected to incline the curia to generosity; the honour of the king and those who were socially or politically close to him was directly involved. Such an appeal was infinitely more difficult to resist in Rome, where high-level support could also be drummed up by the French ambassador. When it came, the ensuing grant of provisions without the payment of the annates

---

56 AN, MC, LXXIII, 358, contract of 6 July 1640.
57 AN, MC, XII, 34, contract of 1 Oct 1602: 'lettres de nomination et de faveur du Roy, que de plusieurs autres seigneurs qui escripvent en faveur dudit sieur Garnier pour lesdits gratis'.
58 *Ibid*, 35, contract of 25 Feb 1603.

proved to be a perfect opportunity to remind the king of France of the pope's paternal concern and support for him, those close to him, and his kingdom.

But the really high born or truly indigent were a small minority among the episcopate, whose other members did not see why they should pay the full rate of their annates. Hence their appeals to patrons to obtain an assortment of royal, ministerial and other *lettres de faveur* pleading for leniency towards them, appeals which might endure for several weeks or longer after the initial royal nomination and before any practical steps were taken to seek one's papal provisions.[59] This quest for official patronage could take time, as it might well involve waiting until a suitable opportunity for making one's case at court arose; it was, incidentally, an important reason for the slowness in the granting of papal provisions, which should not be regarded as resulting merely from the inertia of the papal bureaucracy.[60]

For its part, the papacy knew perfectly well that such demands would be made on behalf of incoming bishops, and it seems to have evolved a subtle method of measuring the relative substance of the requests for annate reductions. In particular, it took very little account of 'lettres de cabinet' bearing the royal signature, but which in fact did not express actual royal support for a candidate's claims; such form-letters were regarded as emanating from the serving secretaries of state who were held to be subject to pressure or open to bribery by interested parties. Discounting such forms of recommendation, papal officials insisted that more unmistakable proof of the king's support be provided. The multiplication of letters of support from the king and his entourage was thus stimulated by the falling value of simple face-value recommendations. Once again, the inference is obvious enough: newly chosen bishops habitually needed patrons and supporters to help them obtain the best possible financial settlement with the curia. Precedents, of course, could also be useful, but were limited. Both Richelieu and Mazarin, for example, made it a point of honour that when they obtained dioceses for their *maîtres de chambre*, they should receive their provisions free of charge, as this was said to be a privilege enjoyed by cardinals. The papacy was rarely in a mood to encourage the creation of precedents of any kind, because it feared (or at least argued that it did) that other rulers, especially of Spain, would demand similar concessions for their subjects. Bishops might, therefore, have to fall back on their own ingenuity in pursuit of their objective. The famous Bishop Caulet, on being nominated to Pamiers, one of the well-endowed southern dioceses, showed considerable astuteness and initiative in arguing his case for exemption from the annates by sending Rome a

---

59 BN, MS Fr 18011, fo 291, Archbishop Marquemont to Louis XIII, 3 Nov 1617.
60 Solminihac, *Lettres et documents*, 360, Solminihac to Vincent de Paul, 20 Aug 1647, denouncing the tardiness of the new bishop of Périgueux whose brother was intriguing for such support to the detriment of his diocese.

copy of his predecessor's report of several years earlier on the state of the diocese.[61]

By the time the political, bureaucratic, and administrative formalities necessitated by an episcopal nomination were completed in France, there was a substantial dossier ready to be sent to Rome by the *banquier* engaged by each bishop-designate. The more prominent items in it, consisting of the letters of nomination and recommendation, were to be turned over to the French ambassador, who alone was judged suitable to present them personally to the pope and the curial dignitaries to whom they were addressed. Once the preliminary presentation and recommendation of a candidate had been made, the subsequent role of the ambassador was less predetermined: much would depend on the specific circumstances of individual nominations, on candidates' (or their families') relations with ambassadors, or on objections to candidates arising in Rome — in other words, on the ebb and flow of Franco-papal relations concerning the episcopate generally. As we saw, the humbler *démarches* and dealings with curial officials were left to the solicitor engaged by the French *banquier*: it was he who transmitted the main dossier to the consistorial congregation, the body responsible for preparing the work of the papal consistory of cardinals, who would be called on to examine royal nominations to the episcopate. The congregation, which dated from the reforms instituted by Sixtus V in the late 1580s, scrutinised each dossier, and as the seventeenth century wore on, it became increasingly stringent and legalistic in its interpretation of the rules. This is particularly noticeable in the case of the profession of faith taken by the candidates, or the omission of certain details from the enquiry. Likewise, if a reduction of annates was requested, the assertions contained in the enquiry about the diocese and its revenues were looked at closely, and if the enquiry was held to be inadequate, supplementary evidence was called for. The text of Bishop Puget of Marseille's enquiry was lost by a curial official in 1644, and he flatly refused to do anything about despatching Puget's provisions until he had received a second copy of the document from the papal nuncio's secretary in France.[62]

Whatever the delays and queries, the Roman procedure culminated in the two meetings of the consistory where a candidate was first proposed and then canonically 'instituted' as a bishop. After that, it was a question of obtaining the drafting and 'expedition' of the necessary papal bulls. These could be more or less numerous — and thus more or less expensive — depending on how many benefices were involved. In respect of the bishop's new diocese alone, there would normally be nine bulls in all, addressed to different persons or institutions; but if, as happened in most cases, the bishop held other benefices which he was intent on retaining, he needed new bulls for them, too, since strictly

---

61 ASV, N Fr 92, fo 69v, Caulet to Cecchini, papal datarius, 4 Nov 1644. The report *ad limina*, as it was called, was rarely sent by French bishops to Rome, despite papal insistence. The Pamiers report is in *ibid*, fos 68v-9v.
62 AAE, CP Rome 84, fos 48v-9r, Ambassador Saint-Chamond to Brienne, 18 July 1644.

speaking they were canonically 'incompatible' with holding episcopal office. To cite the case of the much-beneficed Archbishop Béthune again: when he was confirmed to Bordeaux in 1647, no fewer than thirteen bulls in all were issued.

Another option that incoming bishops could try was to travel to Rome in person and plead their own case. The desire to obtain exemption, in whole or in part, from paying annates was not necessarily the only reason for travelling to Rome to seek one's provisions, and it is not possible to say how many of those who did make the journey benefited from it by obtaining their bulls quickly and at reduced cost. Perhaps the best known case of a bishop whose presence in Rome broke a log-jam over his confirmation was that of the young Richelieu, who was confirmed very quickly after his arrival there. However, the evidence strongly suggests that he did not achieve this single-handed, and that he had organised strong support from the ambassador and Villeroy, the ambassador's powerful father, beforehand.[63] In retrospect, the number of candidates who did go to Rome seems surprisingly limited. If we can assume that the bishops-designate who went there stayed on to have themselves consecrated, as seems almost certain, then they numbered no more than thirty-six in all; of that number, at least one-third were either Italians or French clerics who were already resident in Rome anyway.[64] Of the twenty-one bishops-designate who actually travelled from France to Rome, most did so in the decade or more after the ending of the civil wars, when claims to often long-vacant dioceses were complicated and Rome was uncertain how to respond to some royal nominations, as in the case of Richelieu; this was followed somewhat later by a sprinkling of younger clerics during the 1610s, most of whom went there in search of their provisions as coadjutor-bishops. But from the early 1620s onwards, it seems as if the pull of Rome evaporated altogether, and all French bishops subsequently consecrated in Rome were resident there or elsewhere in Italy. By that juncture, the problems experienced previously over episcopal tenure and nominations had largely abated, and incoming bishops evidently felt that the exertion and the cost of the return journey to Rome were no longer particularly worthwhile. This, incidentally, should not be taken to mean that French bishops became strangers to Rome, since many are known to have travelled to Italy and even lived in Rome well before becoming bishops.

IV

The arrival of a bishop's provisions in France triggered a new round of obligations and rituals. In certain instances, especially in the early decades of

---

63 See Joseph Bergin, *The Rise of Richelieu* (New Haven and London 1991), 72–3.
64 It seems almost inconceivable that a new bishop would leave Rome and wait until returning to France before being consecrated. Only one French bishop who travelled to Italy in this period is known to have been consecrated outside Rome – Gilles de Souvré of Comminges, whose consecration took place in Ravenna: *DHGE*, xviii. cols 495–6, no 2777.

this period, the provisions were not delivered to the new bishop personally, but were first turned over to the individual – a favourite, a minister for example – who had been instrumental in obtaining the bishop's promotion; there followed an unofficial, but highly symbolic, encounter during which the patron presented the bulls to the new bishop, thereby publicly advertising his influence over and claims on him. In 1608, the bulls for Montpellier were sent expressly to no less a figure than the Huguenot, Sully, who having secured the see for Pierre Fenouillet, boasted that in this instance the king had been better advised by a Huguenot than he would have been by a Catholic concerning a Huguenot-dominated diocese.[65] Thirty years later, Richelieu posted off the provisions for Saint-Papoul to his uncle, Amador de la Porte, so that he could personally present them to the new bishop, his friend Bernard Despruetz, though there was no suggestion that La Porte was Despruets's patron to the same degree.[66]

The new bishop was also required to take the oath of fidelity to the king, a permanent reminder of the place occupied by bishops in the 'feudal' hierarchy, essentially because of the temporalities attached to their sees. The oath could be taken by proxy, but that never became the norm. For their own different reasons both kings and bishops were anxious to publicly display the bonds the oath created between them; bishops who were unable, especially in the 1610s, to come to court in person to take the oath made a point of apologising for not doing so.[67] For new bishops, about to embark on a career which had inevitable political connotations, the opportunity for a personal encounter with the sovereign and his entourage was not to be missed. The oath itself was often administered during the royal mass at court, usually after the reading of the gospel, especially under Louis XIV. There was no written text of the oath until the 1620s, when the grand almoner of France, who bore overall responsibility for the religious life of the court, attempted to draft a formula which was initially less than popular.[68]

It was normally as an immediate consequence of the oath that the king issued letters-patent granting the *mainlevée des saisies*, i.e. lifting the sequestration of episcopal temporalities which had been triggered by the death or resignation of the previous incumbent. But for the *mainlevée* actually to take effect, it had to be formally authorised by the *chambre des comptes*, doughty guardian of the royal domain and regalian rights generally, and it would only do this after it had registered the royal letters-patent and the oath of fidelity

---

65 BN, MS Fr 18003, fo 275, Ambassador Brèves to Villeroy, 13 Sept 1608, recounting his efforts to obtain Fenouillet's bulls *gratis* from the pope. BN, MS lat 17026, fo 155, extract from Sully's *Mémoires*.
66 *Lettres, instructions diplomatiques et papiers d'état de Richelieu*, ed D L M Avenel, 8 vols (Paris 1853–76), v. 992, Richelieu to La Porte [1636].
67 BN, MS Clairambault 377, fo 657, Louis de la Baume de Suze, bishop of Viviers, to Pontchartrain, secretary of state, 10 Apr 1621, pleading rebel movements in his diocese as his reason for not coming to court in person.
68 See Pierre Blet, 'Fidèle au pape, fidèle au roi', in *Hommage à Roland Mousnier* (Paris 1981), 317, for the text of the oath as administered in 1671 to Etienne le Camus of Grenoble.

taken by the bishop.[69] This was potentially the most litigious item of business facing a new bishop, as the officials of the *chambre* were always likely to object to one element or another of the procedure.

But the overriding reason for registering the oath – and therefore for conflict – was that doing so formally terminated the *régale*, which was to be the centre of the celebrated Gallican dispute that began in 1673 when Louis XIV insisted that *every* diocese in the French church (and not just those of the north, centre and parts of the south, as hitherto) was subject to this inalienable and imprescriptible regalian right. In dioceses where it traditionally applied, the *régale* opened when, through death or retirement, the see fell vacant. There were two dimensions to it. In its spiritual dimension, the *régale* enabled the crown to appoint to benefices in the bishop's gift which became available during the vacancy; in its temporal dimension, it reserved the revenues of the diocese to the crown, and entrusted the management of them to a specially appointed administrator (an *économe*). However, theory and practice diverged widely. Since the time of Charles IX the revenues had been turned over to the Sainte Chapelle in Paris, which in turn remitted half of the returns to the *chambre des comptes*. In 1641 Richelieu removed them altogether from the Sainte Chapelle, which received suitable indemnity for this loss and, against the stubborn resistance of the *chambre des comptes*, he insisted that the revenues of a vacant diocese be remitted in due course by the *économe* to the incoming bishop.[70]

Despite the heated *regnum*-versus-*sacerdotium* polemics to which it gave rise, the *actual* importance of the *régale* to newly appointed bishops remains largely unknown. Perhaps for just that reason, what emerges from the surviving records differs from the traditional accounts. These records make it clear that most incoming bishops whose dioceses were subject to the *régale* did not wait until taking their oath of fidelity before opening negotiations with the Sainte Chapelle, and that at least some did so within weeks of their initial nomination by the king. The purpose of the negotiations was to reach an accord whereby the bishop-designate, or his representatives, would agree to pay a stipulated sum to the Sainte Chapelle which, in return, would cede the revenues during the period of the *régale* to him. Quite how the calculations were made is difficult to say, but it seems that the canons of the Sainte Chapelle, however anxious they might be to defend their rights in principle, were not especially keen to have to deal directly with the *économes* appointed to manage diocesan revenues. If that deduction is accurate, it would help

69 AN, P 725, vols i-ii; P 726, vols i-iii, archives of the *chambre des comptes* containing episcopal oaths of fidelity, letters-patent ordering the end of the sequestrations and the ensuing decrees of the *chambre*. These papers have survived in surprising numbers, though they do not specify reasons for refusals to register certain oaths of fidelity. The *chambre* demanded that bishops perform the feudal *foy et homage*, and supply an *aveu et dénombrement* of lands they held of the king.

70 See Pierre Blet, *Les Assemblées du clergé et Louis XIV de 1670 à 1693* (Rome 1972), esp 117–24, for a succinct historical account.

explain why the financial cost to incoming bishops of 'buying out' the canons was far from exorbitant. Guillaume de Laubespine acquired rights to the revenues of Orléans in 1598 on the basis of 550 *écus* for a year.[71] Similar rights in Laon cost Louis Séguier just 200 *écus*.[72] The canons accepted 700 *écus* for the revenues of Saint-Flour between June 1597 and June 1599.[73] Much later, in 1624, Jacques de Neuchèze, newly nominated to Chalon-sur-Saône, agreed to pay for the *régale* on the basis of 200 *livres* a month for the first six-months of its duration, and 150 per month thereafter; Neuchèze duly paid 2,100 *livres* for one year of *régale*.[74] Even if episcopal revenues were lower than usual during vacancies, such figures represent only a proportion of the annual income of the diocese concerned. Some bishops, on the other hand, proved less prompt to settle their accounts or objected to the imposition of the *régale* in the first place, which led to litigation and sequestrations of episcopal temporalities. Claude de la Madeleine was nominated to Autun sometime in 1612 or 1613, but he was not given his provisions until 1620 and not consecrated until September 1621. The Sainte Chapelle insisted the *régale* ran without interruption from his predecessor's death in December 1611, and when a settlement was finally reached in 1624, the total bill came to 18,800 *livres*.[75] The sum may seem a large one but, in fact, if calculated in the light of the examples given above, it comes to just over 1,500 *livres* per year. Since Autun traditionally claimed to be exempt from the *régale*, it can be assumed that Bishop La Madeleine was entitled to its revenues for those intervening years, and could afford the sums eventually demanded of him. This, in turn, should help to explain why Richelieu was able to terminate such arrangements altogether in 1641 by compensating the Sainte Chapelle with the revenues of just two abbeys.

For the new bishop, however, the most important event was undoubtedly the *sacre*, the ceremony of consecration which made him a bishop in the fullest sense of the word. The time-lag between the papal confirmation and consecration could vary considerably, but the trend throughout the period was towards relatively speedy consecration; even so, delays were common enough, even on the part of bishops whose reputation might lead one to expect a greater sense of urgency on their part. On the whole, it was coadjutor-bishops, especially if young and destined to succeed an uncle or family member, who were in the least hurry to be consecrated; assured of future tenure, their sense of urgency was understandably diminished. From the 1620s onwards, the papacy itself proved increasingly unwilling to permit underaged bishops to be consecrated until they had reached the minimum age required by the Concordat of Bologna. Of course, a proportion of newly confirmed bishops

71 AN, MC, VIII 417, 13 July 1598.
72 *Ibid*, 418, 16 Jan 1599.
73 *Ibid*, 419, 10 July 1599.
74 AN, MC, VI 309, acts of 1 June 1624 and 4 Jan 1625.
75 *Ibid*, 15 June 1624.

were not in priestly orders at all, and had first to take these orders; that also took time, even when they obtained a special papal dispensation to do so outside the normal times of the year, and to ignore the normal intervals (the interstices as they were called) between the different orders. Only then could consecration follow. For many bishops it often proved to be an ideal occasion publicly to acknowledge the patronage or friendship of existing bishops, three of whom were required to perform a consecration. The surviving information on consecrations can often help us to piece together relationships within the episcopal bench. But it is not infallible, since new bishops were not always at liberty to make this kind of gesture. It might happen, for example, that the archbishop of the ecclesiastical province to which they belonged would insist on acting as principal consecrator, as if to underline the ascribed hierarchical rather than the personal relationship between them; it is not difficult to see that such insistence was hard for incoming bishops to ignore. Yet a few examples may well provide an insight into the possibilities that did exist. It is not suprising that the Breton *ligueur* Georges d'Aradon, elected bishop of Vannes in 1590 by the chapter, should have been consecrated by the pro-League papal legate, Cardinal Sega, whose co-consecrators were the exiled archbishop of Glasgow, James Beaton, and Guillaume Rose, the militant bishop of Senlis. Another *ligueur*, Génébrard of Aix, was also consecrated by Beaton and Rose in 1592. It also comes as no surprise that a considerable number of bishops who had uncles or other family members already in the episcopate, were usually consecrated by them; in these cases, consecrations, particularly when they occurred in the cathedral of the older family bishop, were as much a celebration of family as of episcopal solidarity.

The 'geography' of episcopal consecrations in this period is also of considerable interest. Information exists on the places of consecration of 293 out of the 351 bishops, though it should be remembered that a handful of the remaining bishops were not consecrated at all[76]. The information that does exist is more complete for the end than for the beginning of the period, which inevitably skews the kinds of conclusions which can be drawn from it. As it stands, however, it shows that the consecrations of bishops nominated between the 1590s and 1610s tended to be fairly widely dispersed throughout France. Between a quarter and two-fifths of them took place in Paris, while of the remainder a steady proportion took place in provincial cathedrals. But from the 1620s onwards, there is a notable change. Paris and its environs claimed over half in the 1620s alone, and reaching a peak of 80 per cent during the 1630s, a decade which, in any case, saw a higher number of Parisians entering the episcopate than ever before. Although the capital's share dropped again in the 1640s, it was host to three out of every four consecrations during the last decade of Mazarin's ministry. Provincial cathedrals, including even those of Toulouse or Lyon, seem to have been the

---

76 *DHGE*, xviii, art 'France'. The information is derived from the *épiscopologe* at cols 161–526.

principal losers, with smaller churches in the provinces hosting almost as many consecrations after the 1620s. There were, as we shall see, particular reasons – family origins, educational history, and so on – for the attraction of a Paris consecration, but even they do not fully explain the city's predominance by the middle of the century. It seems reasonable to suggest that the episcopate was, like the aristocracy from which it was in part drawn, gradually being pulled into a process of centralisation which was only partly political in nature.[77]

The choice of church for a consecration may also prove an illuminating guide to the kind of episcopate we are dealing with in this study. In the provinces, consecrations in cathedral churches were normally the result of having the diocesan bishop (or archbishop) as the principal consecrator, although other churches were occasionally used also. But in larger cities, and especially in Paris, it was arguably the use of non-cathedral churches, especially but not exclusively those of religious orders, which is more interesting. As might be expected, members of religious orders honoured their order's churches by being consecrated in them. In all other cases, however, the new bishop's choice of church was no accident, as it enabled him to associate the church and its clergy, whether secular or regular, in the honour of his elevation, while advertising to a broader public the bishop's personal and even spiritual affiliation with them. It will come as no surprise that Henri Arnauld was consecrated at Port Royal, the Fouquet brothers at the Jesuit church of Saint-Louis in Paris, or university professors and doctors of theology in the chapels of the Sorbonne or the college of Navarre.

Always considerable affairs, episcopal consecrations appear to have become more and more baroque in their splendour, particularly in Paris, as the century wore on. Only a relatively small number of bishops, about fifteen in all, were consecrated in out-of-the-way churches, which probably had family or personal significance for them. But in general, the days when a bishop like Anne de Murviel of Montauban would have himself consecrated almost privately in the chapel of his family's château by a cardinal – François de Sourdis – did not last very long, and were probably never common. A desire for highly public consecrations may also explain the attraction of the churches of the religious orders for such events, especially as parish churches, at least in seventeenth-century Paris, lagged far behind them in their ability to rebuild and redecorate.[78] Indeed, if we examine the consecrations which took place in the city and its environs, it appears that of the thirty or more churches involved, no more than three were parochial. Ten of the churches were used only once for this purpose, which suggests particular connections between them and the bishops in question. The chapel of the *évêché* of Paris was

---

77 See Robert R Harding, *Anatomy of a Power Elite* (New Haven and London 1978), ch. 12, 'Social Centralization'.
78 I owe this point to Neil McGregor who has shown this for the Jesuit and Minim churches compared with the parish church of Saint-Paul in the Marais.

regularly used throughout the period, but increasingly it was the religious orders which attracted these ceremonies. Among the latter, the great abbeys of Sainte-Geneviève, Saint-Victor and Saint-Germain-des-Prés were particularly prominent in the opening decades of the period, but they were gradually overtaken by the churches of the newer religious orders. Apart from the Dominicans, it was the churches of the Feuillants, the Carmelites (inside and near Paris), and the Visitation order which were among the most attractive, while those of the Oratory or Vincent de Paul's Congregation of the Mission did not begin to appear until mid-way through the period. The popularity of churches attached to female religious houses such as the Carmelites and the Visitation is also noteworthy. But it was the Jesuit church of Saint-Louis which, with the gradual return of the Jesuits to Paris under Henri IV and Louis XIII, eventually emerged as the church most highly used for consecrations. Its attractiveness only becomes fully apparent during the 1650s, which account for nine of the seventeen bishops consecrated there. This, of course, reflects the entry into the episcopate of an increasing number of graduates of Jesuit schools, particularly of the college of Clermont in Paris. A similar identification with an *alma mater* is evident in the ten consecrations which took place in the chapels of the colleges of the Sorbonne and Navarre. Here, too, half of the total is accounted for by the 1650s, a fact which, as we shall see in a later chapter, reflects the growing number of their theology graduates joining the episcopate.

For all their patronage of sometimes austere religious houses, new bishops were not usually hair-shirted ascetics, and most were not averse to selecting a time and a date for their consecration which would ensure an impressive turnout. The attendance of the king or queen and at least some of the court was especially valued, and could be expected for sons of the aristocracy in particular. But long-serving royal almoners might also be similarly honoured as a mark of recognition for their services. It was for this reason that Anne of Austria, Philippe d'Orléans, the duc de Vendôme, Marshal de l'Hôpital and members of Anne's entourage attended the consecration of Louis de Bernage, bishop of Grasse, in early 1654.[79] Consecration during a general assembly of the French clergy was also prized: it provided an ideal occasion for reaffirming episcopal solidarity, and the sermon at the consecration mass, especially when delivered by bishops who were well-known preachers, was a perfect moment to broadcast the ideals of episcopal office. Antoine Godeau's 'learned and apostolic sermon' at the consecration of Bernard de Marmiesse of Conserans on 'the holiness and duties of the episcopate', was said to have deeply impressed the large congregation, many of them bishops, assembled at the Hôtel-Dieu of Pontoise in December 1656.[80] When Gilbert de Choiseul was

---

79 BN, MS lat 17025 (ii), fo 121.
80 *Ibid*, fo 136: 'docte et apostolique prédication... la sainteté et les devoirs de l'épiscopat'.

consecrated bishop of Comminges in Paris in April 1646, thirty-five bishops attended the ceremony, as Choiseul, a doctor of the Sorbonne as well as an aristocrat, was highly regarded by them and by the court.[81] Both Marmiesse and Choiseul were consecrated while general assemblies of the clergy were in session, which accounts for the quality of the attendance, episcopal and otherwise. The affiliations or activities of the new bishop's family would also determine the kind of attendance at his consecration. For example, when Denis de la Barde, nephew of Claude Bouthillier, *surintendant des finances*, was consecrated in July 1642, the *intendants des finances* and many other 'persons of rank' were present.[82]

Indeed, from the 1630s onwards, Paris consecrations were regularly reported in Théophraste Renaudot's *Gazette*, and consecrations were increasingly followed by collations or even banquets for invited guests. Bishop Choiseul entertained his *confrères* and other guests at the hôtel de Vitry on the evening of his *sacre*.[83] Perhaps the greatest 'society' consecration of all during this period was that of Anne de Lévis, archbishop of Bourges, in May 1651, during the Fronde. Son of the duc de Ventadour who founded the ultra-*dévot Compagnie du Saint-Sacrement*, and Marguerite de Montmorency, he was accompanied from his residence to the consecration by the princes of Condé and Conty. Anne of Austria, Philippe d'Orléans, princes of the blood and a large number of peers were in attendance, 'who were all later splendidly entertained after the Queen had taken communion from the hands of the new Archbishop'.[84]

Once consecrated, there was, in principle, no further impediment to bishops exercising their powers to govern their dioceses. They would already have taken formal possession of their cathedral church; this was a canonically obligatory and symbolic step which signified their 'union' with the diocese in question, but that first *prise de possession* was usually done by proxy. When they had completed final formalities and, should they have been consecrated in Paris, paid their respects to assorted ministers, courtiers and others, it remained only for bishops to depart for their dioceses and take up residence there. This, too, required due solemnity and was accomplished by means of a solemn entry and personal *prise de possession* which represented the consummation of their spiritual marriage to their diocesan church.

Reformers in every generation were apt to deplore the slowness of royal nominees in pressing on to become consecrated bishops. But, though there were abuses, there were also delays which had nothing to do with an alleged lack of urgency among candidates. It should be clear from the preceding pages that becoming a bishop was not a simple affair. Vacancies of up to a year and

---

81 ASV, N Fr 93, fo 149, *avvisi* of 13 Apr 1646.
82 BN, MS lat 17024, fo 176, 7 July 1642.
83 BN, MS lat 17025, fo 107.
84 BN, MS lat 17024, fo 160: 'qui furent tous ensuitte traitez splendidement après que la Reine eut communié par les mains du nouvel archévêque'.

beyond were extremely common, and should not be regarded as *prima facie* evidence of insouciance on the part of the incoming bishops. In any case, as previously suggested, it would be misleading to assume that all episcopal successions were essentially the same. The number of exceptions to the prevailing general pattern is significant. In order to grasp the continuing diversity of means by which bishops were made in seventeenth-century France, it will be useful at this point to turn from the general and towards the particular, and to do so by means of a small sample of case-studies.

V

Two confidentiaires

There is relatively little in the formal record to draw attention to the bishops who succeeded each other at Saint-Flour under Henri IV.[85] Pierre de la Baume, a former tutor to Henri III's younger brother the duc d'Alençon, had been bishop of Saint-Flour in Upper Auvergne for twenty-three years when he died in 1595. A relative, possibly a brother of his, Prosper de la Baume, tried to present himself as his successor, but with what title remains unknown, and in any case he soon vanished. It is likely that Saint-Flour was one of many dioceses which experienced a power vacuum in the 1590s, and that Henri IV, whom Clement VIII was about to absolve and officially acknowledge as king in 1595, had little control over events there.

This situation played into the hands of Henri de Noailles, comte d'Ayen, whose family seat was in the Auvergne and the Limousin, and who had himself supported Henri IV against the League. The Noailles family had already provided high-ranking members of the church in the person of François and Gilles, uncles of Henri, who were successively bishops of Dax (1556–97), but above all leading diplomats in royal service. Gilles, who was never consecrated, decided to resign Dax and received permission to do so in 1595;[86] two years later, Henri IV allowed his nephew and principal heir, the comte d'Ayen, to present to him his choice of successor not just for Dax, but for Saint-Flour as well. Having no sons or relatives of the proper age to present to the king, Ayen seems to have made a strategic decision. Family influence in Dax was probably limited at this juncture, despite his two uncles' long tenure there, so he presented to Henri IV the son of a prominent Bordeaux parlementaire family, Jean-Jacques du Sault, as his nominee for bishop. Quite how the choice was made and on what conditions remains unknown. Saint-Flour was a different matter, and Noailles was already moving to establish himself as the leading political figure in the region – which Henri

85 *Hierarchia Catholica*, iv. 189, 'S Flori'. The papacy also believed that Noailles was twenty-seven years old by 1609, when in fact he was only twenty.
86 A Degert, *Histoire des évêques de Dax* (Paris 1903), 297–8.

IV would later publicly underscore by nominating him royal governor and lieutenant-general in the Upper Auvergne.[87] Accordingly, in August 1597, Noailles also presented to Henri IV his choice for Saint-Flour, Raymond Rouchon, a priest from Cusance in Cahors diocese, not particularly far from lands held by the Noailles family. Rouchon's background is otherwise wholly unknown, but there were still *bourgeois* inhabitants of Cusance by that name in the later seventeenth and eighteenth centuries.[88] Rouchon himself was cited variously as a doctor in theology and in law,[89] but the only evidence – undated, alas – which survives suggests that he was a bachelor in theology from the nearby University of Cahors; his papal bulls refer to him as a 'master of theology', an ambiguous guide to his academic achievements, which were hardly outstanding.[90] Meanwhile, Noailles had already obtained the gift of the revenues of Saint-Flour from the king, and he proceeded to organise the leases of its temporalities. He also insisted on striking a hard bargain with the Sainte Chapelle over the *régale*, instructing his agent in Paris that 100 *écus* a year seemed to him quite enough to pay for it.[91] Rouchon's nomination was accepted by both the king and the pope, and his bulls were dated March 1599. He appears to have been consecrated and taken his oath of fidelity in Toulouse in February 1600.[92]

There had been little hurry at any point since La Baume's death in 1595. Rouchon, who does not appear to have taken up residence in Saint-Flour itself but to have remained in Quercy, was probably elderly by the time of his elevation, and thus could not be counted on to retain Saint-Flour for very long. Noailles still needed to ensure the diocese would not escape him if Rouchon were to die suddenly. Thus in December 1601, at Noailles's residence, Rouchon signed the necessary resignation document, with the explicit condition that he resigned in favour of comte de Noailles's son, Charles, or whoever else the comte chose to propose to king and pope, and with a request for an annual pension of just 400 *écus* for himself.[93] Whether Noailles made any use of this deed is unknown, but Rouchon's death in July 1602 automatically invalidated it. From Noailles's point of view, the major problem was that his second son, Charles, in whose favour Rouchon had resigned, was still only twelve years old, and clearly unacceptable in Rome. Yet it is a sign of Noailles's increased confidence – he was governor of Upper Auvergne by now

---

87 Robert J Kalas, 'Wealth, Power and Place in Sixteenth-Century France: The Rise of the Selves and Noailles Families' (Unpublished PhD thesis, New York University 1982), esp 365–7.
88 AD Lot, B 1299, Jean Rouchon of Cusance, 1661; B 1334, Toinette Rouchon and nephew, Antoine, *bourgeois* of Cusance, 1764.
89 BN, MS lat 17025, fo 84, Rouchon is cited as doctor in law and royal almoner in a procuration for the *prise de possession* of Saint-Flour cathedral, 29 Mar 1599.
90 AD Lot, F 492, no 2, undated copy of diploma issued by chancellor of University of Cahors.
91 J-B Poulbrière, 'Une poignée de documents sur la Haute Auvergne', *Bulletin Historique et Scientifique de l'Auvergne*, 8 (1888), 142, n 1, letter to agent in Paris, 31 Oct. 1598.
92 BN, Doss bleus 383, doss 15343, fos 1–3.
93 BN, MS lat 17025, fo 84, 14 Dec 1601.

– that instead of looking for a second Rouchon figure, he appears to have chosen to 'present' his son to Henri IV, and with success, for within months the boy was styling himself, or was being so styled by his father, as 'the nominated bishop of Saint-Flour'.[94] The bishopric remained officially vacant until September 1609, when the young Noailles received his bulls, but it was probably several years later before he could have himself consecrated.

It was in 1575 that Henri III allowed André de Bourdeille and his brother, the celebrated chronicler Pierre, abbé de Brantôme, to present to him their choice for bishop of Périgueux. Leaders of a powerful local noble family, they selected their cousin François de Bourdeille, then a monk of Saint-Denis, but proceeded to keep most of the revenues of the bishopric for themselves. In 1594, André's son, Henri, who was by then *sénéchal* and governor of Périgord, obtained confirmation from Henri IV of this *droit de présentation* should the bishop of Périgueux ever wish to resign. The king cited the family's services, past and present, as the reason for the grant but, as the text of his patent suggests, he probably had no real idea of what, if anything, they planned to do. The patent was thus a form of insurance for Bourdeille and 1594 was a good moment to extract this kind of concession from a hard-pressed Henri IV. But given Bishop Bourdeille's advanced age – he was seventy-seven years old in 1594 – action would be needed sooner or later. It was not until November 1599, though, that an acceptable successor was found and the terms of an agreement were signed. Jean Martin, a canon and experienced official of Périgueux cathedral who was also vicar-general of François de Bourdeille, agreed to become coadjutor to the ageing bishop, but under conditions which made him a mere caretaker for the Bourdeille family. The terms of the agreement are unambiguous, clearly showing the patrimonial convictions of a noble family like the Bourdeille. Martin explicity agreed that he would hold Périgueux 'on behalf of and for the benefit of the said vicomte de Bourdeille, without any claim on any part of the fruits, profits and emoluments of the said see'. Not only that, but Martin allowed Bourdeille to appoint to benefices in the bishop's gift; he also promised to resign to whomsoever the Bourdeille family designated and whenever they wished him to do so and finally, like Rouchon, he accepted a pension of a mere 400 *écus* a year and a farm belonging to the bishopric.[95] In the event, Martin never served as coadjutor to his predecessor, who was probably persuaded subsequently to resign Périgueux outright to Martin, as is clearly implied by the reference to Bourdeille's 'cession' in the official consistorial record.[96]

94 Poulbrière, 'Une poignée de documents', docs no. xxvii^bis-xxviii, documents dated 4 Jan 1603 and 27 Nov 1604.
95 A Dujarric-Descombes, 'Résignation de François de Bourdeille-Montancey évêque de Périgueux (1599)', *Bulletin de la Société Historique et Archéologique du Périgord*, 15 (1888) 394–402, for the text of Henri IV's 1594 grant and the *contrat de confidence* of November 1599: 'pour et au profit dudit sieur vicomte de Bourdeille, sans qu'il puisse prétendre, ni demander aucune chose en tous les fruits, profits et emolumens dépandant dudit évêché'.
96 *Hierarchia Catholica*, iv. 277, 'Petragoricen'.

No royal *brevet* has survived for either Rouchon or Martin's nomination, but there can be no doubt that each document would have made it perfectly clear the two bishops were nominated *en faveur* of Noailles and Bourdeille respectively. Nor do we know what kind of agreement, if indeed any, was formally signed between Noailles and Rouchon, or whether Rouchon made undertakings similar to those of Jean Martin. But everything about his brief episcopate shows that he was bound hand and foot by Noailles, for whom he was evidently more of a domestic retainer than a conventional clerical client with a minimum of personal autonomy. He did what he was told at all times, and after his demise Charles de Noailles easily obtained the Saint-Flour diocese, which he governed without interruption until he moved to Rodez as late as 1646! By contrast, Martin's status as a *confidentiaire* at Périgueux was spelled out in all its abject detail before a notary, but the intriguing fact is that by background and previous career he was neither a retainer nor a glorified chaplain of the Bourdeille family. He was relatively young in 1599, held senior offices in both the cathedral and diocese of Périgueux, and had even served as secretary to the First Estate at the 1588 Estates General, which made him somewhat more than a local figure.[97] Why he was willing to become bishop on these terms is hard to say, and he left no clue as to his reasons. He may well have accepted Bourdeille's conditions so as to ensure Périgueux did not remain vacant (as Saint-Flour did after 1602), or in the hope that a divided Bourdeille family might not be able to mistreat him. It was perhaps because he was of more considerable stature, both within and beyond his diocese, that, unlike Rouchon, Martin was not called upon to resign during the following decade. Indeed, when he died in office in January 1612, he was not succeeded by a Bourdeille nominee, and it was apparently his successor who persuaded Louis XIII to revoke the presentation privilege made to the Bourdeille family by Henri III and Henri IV.[98] The Bourdeille family's efforts to convert Périgueux into a quasi-patrimonial see were undermined, and the next generation had to be satisfied with an admittedly substantial pension off its revenues.[99]

VI

An Italian connection

Guillaume du Vair was an unmarried sexagenarian in minor orders when he was nominated by Louis XIII to Lisieux in August 1617, less than a year after

---

97 ASV, Misc Arm XII, 145, fo 370.
98 Dujarric-Descombes, 'Résignation de Bourdeille', 400–1, for Brantôme's angry comments about the manner in which the Martin succession was handled and his personal interest ignored in 1599.
99 *Hierarchia Catholica*, iv. 277, 'Petragoricen', n 3.

he had been removed by the favourite Concini from high office as keeper of the seals. To assist him in his new office, which he had probably not previously envisaged holding, least of all at that age, he was particularly fortunate to have the services of a devoted nephew, Guillaume Aleaume, son of du Vair's sister Antoinette. These services were all the more valuable in that Aleaume had been himself a bishop since 1615 of the small upland diocese of Riez in Provence, at the opposite end of the kingdom. Aleaume owed his original elevation in large part to his uncle's influence at court, so when du Vair requested his assistance in Lisieux in 1618, Aleaume was hardly in a position to refuse, even though he had a diocese of his own to run. He effectively abandoned Riez for Lisieux, which he administered until du Vair's death in August 1621. But sometime before his death, du Vair, who had recovered his keepership of the seals in the meantime, decided to attach his nephew permanently to Lisieux by obtaining royal permission to take him as his coadjutor, and the necessary papers were sent to Rome.

As in many other similar instances, du Vair's death supervened before anything had been settled, and opened up unexpected possibilities, as the secretary of state for foreign affairs, Puysieux, quickly realised. Puysieux, like so many of his predecessors in that post, was particularly concerned with ensuring that France had influential friends in Rome. The opportunity to reward and oblige one such friend in 1621 was simply too good to be missed, especially as it promised to reinforce Puysieux's personal control of French diplomacy. The papal nuncio in France from 1616 to 1621, the well known Cardinal Guido di Bentivoglio, had just returned to Rome where Puysieux hoped he would become a leading pro-French figure. Pensions and other gratifications had always been an essential part of party-building activities, French or otherwise, in the curia. Puysieux was now prepared to offer Riez to Bentivoglio, which in turn would enable him to cut substantially the size of the pension from the treasury originally promised to the cardinal. He boasted to Bentivoglio that he had been able to seize the initiative and persuade Louis XIII and his favourite Luynes to agree to his plan precisely because nobody but himself remembered anything about the Lisieux coadjutorship originally intended for Aleaume! Thus when Aleaume came to court to renegotiate his claim to Lisieux, he was told that he must resign Riez, as he could not expect to be allowed to hold two dioceses.[100] He readily accepted the offer, but insisted that he would only resign Riez after he had received his provisions to Lisieux.[101] He was not ready to act on the strength of promises, even in writing, and as an incumbent bishop he could not be obliged to resign Riez against his will. Puysieux and Bentivoglio accepted

---

100 ASV, *fondo* Pio 88, fos 25v-6r, Puysieux to Bentivoglio, Montauban 22 Sept 1621. Aleaume's claim to Lisieux, based on his uncle's resignation, was now void, since acts of resignation were automatically invalidated by death.
101 BI, MS Godefroy 269, fo 68, Michel de Marillac to Monsieur [. . .], 24 May 1622.

these terms.¹⁰² At no time, apparently, was it suggested that Aleaume simply return to Riez and leave the wealthier and more prestigious see of Lisieux to Bentivoglio, since by then, Aleaume's claim on Lisieux was evidently regarded as too strong to ignored, even in order to cultivate a leading Roman cardinal like Bentivoglio. Aleaume's provisions to Lisieux were issued first, in March 1622, and Bentivoglio's to Riez the following July. Puysieux, the insider, suggested to Bentivoglio that Riez, which he valued at 14–15,000 *livres* a year, was preferable to a pension of 18,000 *livres* from the treasury, especially as the balance would be made up by a separate pension. Bentivoglio wanted both Riez and the full treasury pension, no doubt having no more faith than most Roman cardinals in the prompt or full payment of pensions from France.¹⁰³ He kept Riez for less than three years, resigning it to the Minim, Lopis de la Fare, in mid-1625.¹⁰⁴

This was the last instance in the period under study of a widespread sixteenth-century practice, that of attracting leading Italian churchmen residing in Rome into the service of French interests there by making French dioceses available to them in lieu of pensions. Bentivoglio never set foot in Riez, and almost certainly never intended to do so, but he did reserve a pension of 5,000 *livres* for himself when resigning it.¹⁰⁵ Another former nuncio, Jérôme Grimaldi, would become archbishop of Aix in the 1650s, but he proceeded to reside there continuously for thirty years and become a major figure in Provence.¹⁰⁶ Mazarin attempted to give the see of Montpellier to Cardinal d'Este in 1655, but this attempt to repeat the Bentivoglio-Riez move failed, and the cardinal had to be satisfied with an abbey and a pension instead.¹⁰⁷ Not even the post-Fronde Mazarin enjoyed the freedom to dispose of French bishoprics for purposes which were by then regarded as inappropriate – the maintenance of non-resident political clients. As we shall see later, the use of pensions, sometimes payable by French bishoprics, had been increasingly used in Rome as an alternative since the reign of Henri IV; the practice was more acceptable than continuing to nominate absentee foreign bishops, though it inevitably led to clashes between the French bishops concerned and their high-status Italian pensioners.

---

102 BN, MS Fr 18017, fo 245, Bentivoglio to Luynes, 19 Oct 1621; ASV, *fondo* Pio 88, fo 35v, Puysieux to Bentivoglio, 18 Nov 1621.
103 ASV, *fondo* Pio 88, fo 37, Puysieux to Bentivoglio, 20 Nov 1621.
104 *Gallia Chr Nov* (Riez), cols 429–30, royal *brevet* confirming Bentivoglio's resignation, 28 Apr 1625. Peiresc, *Lettres*, vii. 585, n. 1, Peiresc to Bentivoglio, 15 Jan 1626.
105 ASV, PC 21, fo 335, Louis XIII to Urban VIII, letter of nomination of La Fare in place of Bentivoglio, with stipulation of pension, 28 Apr 1625.
106 *DHGE*, xxii, cols 245–9, for an extensive notice.
107 ASV, N Fr 109, fo 288, *avvisi* of 16 July 1655. Este had previously had his eye on the coadjutorship of Narbonne: N Fr 107, fo 362v, 3 Oct 1653. AAE, France 896, fo 92, Mazarin to Colbert, 11 July 1655 informing of Este's renunciation and asking him to turn over the *brevet* to François Bosquet of Lodève.

VII

The search for a coadjutor

When Octave de Bellegarde moved from the southern diocese of Conserans to become archbishop of Sens in 1622, his uncle and patron, Roger, duc de Bellegarde, *grand écuyer de France* and close companion of Louis XIII, was apparently allowed to propose a successor of his choice for Conserans. But as Bellegarde only made this assertion years later, we do not know on which grounds he singled out a Carthusian monk resident in Paris, Bruno Ruade, and presented him to Louis XIII. Ruade apparently declined the honour at first, but the king circumvented him by persuading the abbot-general of the Carthusians to compel Ruade to accept it.[108] He duly complied, using the time-honoured language of monastic obedience and religious sacrifice, and duly went off to live in his remote Pyrenean diocese, where he apparently had an uneventful episcopate, although like other bishops he did come into conflict with holders of alienated church property.[109] By the late 1630s, however, he was old and seriously infirm. Conserans was not a large diocese, but it was worth 15,000 *livres* a year, which made its bishop comfortable rather than opulent.

At any rate, it is hardly surprising that the ageing Ruade attracted the attention of ambitious ecclesiastics, their families and patrons. Roger de Bellegarde, too, was still alive in the late 1630s, although his support for Marie de' Medici against Richelieu in 1630–1 meant that his days of favour were long since past. But as he and his family had dominated Conserans, directly and indirectly, since Henri III's time, he was not content now to leave matters to others. So in 1639 he recommended yet another of his clerical nephews to Richelieu for the coadjutorship of Conserans, and also tried to precipitate a decision by warning the Cardinal that Bishop Ruade had opened discussions with a lawyer at the Toulouse parlement, Pierre Marmiesse, with a view to taking his son as his coadjutor.[110] But Richelieu seems to have paid no attention to Bellegarde's petition. Marmiesse had indeed been assiduously cultivating Ruade for several years and would claim that in 1639 Ruade had sent him 'the resignation of his bishopric in my favour'. But Marmiesse appears to have done nothing about the matter since his son Bernard, who at that time was a twenty-year old theology student at the Sorbonne, would have been unacceptable to the crown on age grounds alone.

---

108 *Recueil de lettres du Révérendissime Père Dom B Ruade Chartreux Evesque de Conserans touchant sa promotion à sondit Evesché* (Paris 1623). This edifying collection includes the letters exchanged between the king, Ruade and the General of the Carthusians, but makes no mention of any other factors in the nomination. Bruno was only Ruade's name in religion; he had been christened Philibert.
109 AD Haute-Garonne, E 292, unfol, 'Contre des gentilshommes qui troublent Monsieur l'Evesque de Conserans dans la jouissance des dismes', 1630.
110 AAE, France 834, fo 59, Bellegarde to Bouthillier de Chavigny, 11 Sept 1639.

It was not until March 1642 that Marmiesse began using the good offices of Henri de Senneterre with Bouthillier de Chavigny, secretary of state and confidant of Richelieu, to press his son's case and to denounce the pressures to which the ageing Ruade, isolated by his allegedly venal servants in his diocesan residence, was being subjected.[111] Marmiesse had good reason to worry by then, since other suitors had emerged and their claims were being pressed on Ruade, notably those of the widowed Pierre de Marca, the celebrated Gallican magistrate and former president of the parlement in Pau, who enjoyed the patronage of chancellor Séguier in particular. It is doubtful if Marca had any prior personal connection with Ruade, but as one of Cinq-Mars's judges in 1641, his standing in the eyes of Louis XIII and his ministers was hardly in any doubt.[112] Marca was determined to become a bishop by then, and was willing to start at Conserans. Ruade, who was by now so paralysed that he was unable even to sign his name, was persuaded to take steps towards obtaining him as his coadjutor, and a formal resignation for the benefit of Marca was drawn up by a notary in May 1642, only days before France's Cardinal-Minister completed his testament, which he too was unable to sign, not so far away in Narbonne.[113]

Ruade's decision caused some fury, and Seneterre denounced it to Chavigny as a forgery which Marca had purchased from the bishop's servants.[114] Then, in September 1642, the Marmiesse family brought Ruade to live in Toulouse where they redoubled their efforts to obtain the resignation of Conserans. He finally obliged them in October 1642, by resigning for the benefit of Bernard de Marmiesse, who was by now a Sorbonne doctor of theology and well known to members of Richelieu's circle.[115] But Marca was not inactive either, and he obtained his *brevet* and letters of nomination for Rome only weeks after Richelieu's death, in late December 1642. Knowing this, Marmiesse promptly forwarded the text of Ruade's *second* resignation to Rome in order to block Marca's demand for his provisions. Marca appealed to the royal council to support his nomination, as a result of which the intendant in Languedoc, François Bosquet, was commissioned to investigate the circumstances of Ruade's resignation.[116] As it happens, Bosquet was, like his patron Marca, also in search of episcopal office by now, but he prudently refrained from showing his ambitions in this case. His long report led to a further decree of council in April 1643 which fully supported Marca, and this support was continued by the regency régime of Anne of Austria and

---

111 AAE, France 1632, fos 71–2, Marmiesse to Chavigny, 25 Mar 1642; fo 73, Senneterre to Chavigny, 27 Mar. Senneterre was a regular correspondent of Chavigny.
112 The most informative study of Marca is that by V Dubarat in his edition of Marca's *Histoire de Béarn* (Paris-Pau 1894), vol i, which prints numerous *pièces justificatives*.
113 AAE, France 1632, fo 88, text of Ruade's resignation.
114 *Ibid*, fo 100, letter to Chavigny 15 June 1642.
115 *Ibid*, fo 73, Senneterre pointed this out to Chavigny in Mar 1642.
116 AD Haute-Garonne, E 292, unfol, for Bosquet's *procès-verbal* of his investigation.

Mazarin.¹¹⁷ But Rome was in no hurry whatever to oblige Marca, and the Marmiesse counter-campaign proved a perfect reason for prevarication. Marca's Gallicanism, though fundamentally moderate, had been too publicly expressed during the crisis of 1639–40, and this was not forgotten in Rome. With his book of 1639 on the liberties of the Gallican church, the *De Concordia*, placed on the Index in 1642, his prospects of immediate episcopal status were not bright.

The death of Ruade in February 1645 automatically invalidated his resignation, and meant that new letters of nomination had to be obtained by Marca. He was by then serving as a royal intendant in occupied Catalonia, so that he was less likely to be dropped as the crown's choice for Conserans. In any case, the Marmiesse interest had faded from view by now: they doubtless realised the pointlessness of continuing the fight in the face of such clear determination, and that it might jeopardise their son's episcopal prospects for good.¹¹⁸ But the new pope was as unrelenting towards Marca as his predecessor: Marca had to wait another three years for his provisions, during which interval he virtually abandoned his Gallican views of 1639.¹¹⁹

For all his unending complaints, Marca's tenacity and services were to be handsomely rewarded: he went on to become archbishop of Toulouse in 1652 and was nominated to succeed Retz in Paris just before his death in 1662.¹²⁰ Nor was all lost for the young Bernard Marmiesse: he recovered from his initial defeat, and then enormously boosted his episcopal prospects by serving for a term as *agent-général* of the French clergy. What no one might have anticipated around 1642 was that years later he would become Marca's immediate successor at Conserans in 1653!

VIII

Finding the highest bidder?

Two bishops, Christophe de Lestang and his nephew Vital, both clients of the house of Joyeuse, held the see of Carcassonne without interruption between 1603 and 1652. Vital initially served as coadjutor to his uncle between 1615 and 1621, and when he died in September 1652, in the later stages of the

---

117   Marca, *Histoire de Béarn*, i. ccci, for text of the decree which recapitulates previous developments.
118   *Ibid*, i. lxxxv, Bosquet to Séguier, 23 Mar 1643; p. lxxxvi, Bosquet to Marca 25 Mar 1643. Bosquet claimed that as soon as they realised that Mazarin took a personal interest in Marca's succession, the Marmiesses abandoned the fight, but that may be somewhat premature.
119   *Ibid*, i. cxvi-cxxii. See also Marca's correspondence during these years over Conserans, and the humiliation to which the papacy was subjecting him over his views, in *Lettres inédites de Pierre de Marca au chancelier Séguier*, ed P Tamizey de Larroque (Paris 1881), 24–43.
120   Marca became a major figure in French ecclesiastical politics during the 1650s, especially in the Jansenist and Retz affairs, in which he acted as Mazarin's principal agent. This accounts for his move to Toulouse and then Paris.

Fronde, candidates for this small, but rich diocese were not hard to find. The king's confessor thought it should go to François Servien, brother of Abel, a former secretary of state who would become finance minister a few months later, especially as the abbé Servien had earlier been proposed for Fréjus when it was rumoured to be vacant. Mazarin's client, Claude Auvry, bishop of Avranches, also thought Servien should get Carcassonne, adding that 'in truth his services speak for themselves'.[121] Servien was indeed nominated to the diocese, but less than a year later, before any papal provisions had been despatched, he and his brother switched their attention to the opposite end of the realm, where their family had had office-holding connections since the beginning of the century – the financially and geographically more attractive see of Bayeux. This had become vacant with the death of Edouard Molé, eldest son of the first president of the Paris parlement, and the refusal, after almost a year and a half of hesitation, by his brother, François Molé, of the succession.[122]

But not untypically for these years, nothing was decided for nearly nine months. Servien was not formally nominated to Bayeux until May 1654, when he also agreed to give up his claim on Carcassonne, which quickly attracted the interest of those with episcopal ambitions. Colbert, who had become intendant of Mazarin's personal affairs in 1651, was a willing intermediary between his master and those in search of favours of all kinds. By June 1654, he had begun to organise what can only be described as an auction of the diocese of Carcassonne. It had evidently been made clear by Mazarin that serious contenders would need to be willing to surrender the equivalent of a very large slice of the revenues of the diocese in benefices or in pensions payable off Carcassonne. For several weeks, Colbert reported with increasing frequency to Mazarin whose replies were equally frequent and usually rapid, giving a vivid sense of the atmosphere of competition for a bishopric. The bishop of Dol was keen on moving to Carcassonne, but frankly confessed to Colbert that he lacked the means required of candidates and 'did not have the means in order to offer the necessary recompense'.[123] Three weeks later, Colbert was asking Mazarin whether he should not break off negotiations with another candidate, the abbé Jean-Philippe de Bertier, who had also made an offer, so that he could agree terms with François Fouquet, bishop of Agde, and brother of the other finance minister. Mazarin replied that a deal with Fouquet was preferable, but on certain conditions which he wished Colbert to convey to him before finalising anything.[124] Days later, Colbert informed Mazarin that another candidate, the abbé de Sorèze, was now

---

121   AAE, France 885, fos 190–1, Charles Paulin to Mazarin 15 Oct 1652, 'veritablement ses services parlent d'eux mesme'; fo 311, Auvry to Mazarin 29 Oct.
122   AAE, France 892, fo 315, Auvry to Mazarin 4 Sept 1653.
123   BN, MS Baluze 176, fo 39, Colbert to Mazarin, 18 June 1654: 'ne la pouvoit pas recompenser de ce qui estoit necessaire'.
124   *Ibid*, fo 77, letter of 6 July, reply of 11 July.

offering to surrender an abbey worth 12,000 *livres* a year as well as a pension of 14,000 a year off Carcassonne. Mazarin still evidently wished to hear from Fouquet, although he thought Sorèze's offer a serious one; it would be acceptable on condition that he was also a 'capable candidate'; moreover, Sorèze's financial offer would also enable the king to satisfy those to whom he had promised pensions.[125] But the chase was far from over, and other interested parties manifested themselves: Colbert reported within a few days that Fouquet of Agde had just suggested a grand scheme involving himself, the bishop of Saint-Flour, Sorèze, and another son of Mathieu Molé, keeper of the seals, all exchanging benefices and pensions – with Fouquet set to emerge as the clear winner! The hard-nosed Colbert could not resist adding a caustic comment: 'This is where endeavour gets us. Your Eminence should consider whether this can be done; as for myself, I cannot believe it will'. Bertier and Sorèze were still in the lists however, the former offering to surrender his abbey and 12,000 *livres* of pension off Carcassonne, the latter his abbey and 14,000 *livres* in pensions. Colbert opined that while both men seemed deserving candidates, it seemed to him that 'without doubt the first has the advantage of birth and, as I believe, in merit'.[126] Mazarin now seemed to prefer Bertier, but Molé had not quite given up and Mazarin awaited his response.[127] As Mazarin hinted, the nomination to Carcassonne had become part of a larger effort to satisfy those promised pensions during the Fronde. The correspondence tails off abruptly at this juncture, but the eventual outcome was very different from that which Mazarin and Colbert had expected, as politico-ecclesiastical considerations of a different order took a hand. First of all, François Fouquet, like Servien before him, switched his attention from Carcassonne to the coadjutorship of Narbonne, a far more attractive prize than either Bayeux or Carcassonne.[128] Why the other candidates dropped out is less obvious, but in May 1655, Louis de la Vallette, illegitimate son of the first duc d'Epernon and bishop of neighbouring Mirepoix since 1629, was nominated to Carcassonne. His difficulties with the Huguenot population of Mirepoix were such that he was anxious to move elsewhere, though that alone hardly explains why the crown was ready to oblige him; it may be suggested that Mazarin was anxious to reward and cultivate the powerful Epernon interest generally.[129] No less interestingly, La Valette fared rather better than might be expected from Colbert's accounts of his negotiations the previous year: he was required to pay three pensions worth just 7,500 *livres*. It seems

---

125   *Ibid*, fo 86, letter of 13 July, reply of 15 July.
126   *Ibid*, fo 92, letter of 18 July, reply 24 July: 'Voilà a quoy aboutist l'industrie. Vostre Eminence verra si cela se peut, pour moy, je n'en crois rien'. For Colbert's view of Bertier: 'sans doute le premier passe en naissance et comme je crois en mérite'.
127   *Ibid*, fo 109, letter of 28 July.
128   AAE, France 894, fo 400, Nicolas Fouquet to Mazarin, 8 Nov 1655, asking for his approval of the arrangements for Narbonne agreed by the archbishop and Bishop Fouquet of Agde.
129   ASV, N Fr 109, fo 163, *avvisi* of 14 May 1655.

highly likely that his episcopal rank and social status (his illegitimacy apart) protected him from the kind of exploitation that previous candidates could have expected and, indeed, were prepared to put up with.

IX

For all their peculiarities, these case-studies reveal some common features of contemporary attitudes and behaviour where episcopal nominations between the 1590s and the 1650s were concerned. Changes in both attitudes and behaviour could and did occur over time, and the appointment of *confidentiaires* like Rouchon and Martin would be unthinkable from at least the 1620s onwards. Non-resident bishops would remain a constant feature of the *ancien régime* church, but the awarding of dioceses to men who manifestly had no intention of residing in them at all ceased. But beyond that, views of what was possible or acceptable when appointing bishops were, as the evidence presented here does more than hint, resistant to irrevocable, once-for-all changes. Likewise, the case-studies show just how often the real initiative might lie with individuals and families seeking advancement, and that the king and his entourage often merely reacted to external pressures on them. Royal freedom of action was not itself a constant and, as later chapters will show, was a function of broader political circumstances. Lastly, episcopal successions frequently entailed hard-nosed bargaining, the shape of which would vary according to the type of succession at issue. The Carcassonne case of the 1650s may not be typical, even of 'open' successions, but it shows how far such wheeling and dealing could go, especially if the crown itself became directly involved in raising the odds. But even where this was not the case, aspiring candidates knew that realising their ambitions might well involve protracted negotiations and elaborate arrangements, all of which helped to ensure that those with the best social, ecclesiastical, and political connections had a decided advantage over their rivals.

As the case-studies also show, among the many calculations which contenders for bishoprics had to make, the financial one was far from being the least important. The two chapters that follow will examine the world of the episcopate from a perspective that is much less familiar to historians than it was to seventeenth-century bishops – that of the financial value of bishoprics, the charges upon their revenues, and the pensions which ensured that the destination of vacant dioceses was of interest to more than just the individual who received royal and papal approval.

CHAPTER 3

Le Temporel: *Wealth and Revenues*

IN THE PRECEDING discussion of the making of bishops, relatively little mention was made of the one prerequisite which mattered more than all the others put together, namely the existence of vacant dioceses. The point may seem too obvious to need saying, but it will readily be conceded that many an episcopal career must have turned on the haphazard, unexpected manner in which dioceses became available at particular moments. Even coadjutor-bishops were nominally appointed to 'vacant' dioceses 'in the lands of the infidel' (*in partibus infidelium*), regardless of which particular French diocese they were destined to govern in due course. The making of the episcopate during the generations with which this book is concerned cannot, therefore, be divorced from the diocesan network which played an important part in its evolution.

Of the different elements which comprise this connection of bishops and dioceses, one in particular has rarely received more than cursory acknowledgement by historians. It is what contemporaries, bishops included, referred to simply as *le temporel*, an expression which stands for the complex array of endowments, rights, and privileges that generated the income which enabled bishops to discharge their obligations and live in accordance with the standards expected of them. Historical neglect of the material and financial dimension of episcopal office is in sharp contrast with both objective realities and contemporary behaviour. The objective reality of *le temporel* is evident in the accumulated endowments of the French church which, despite episodic but partial attempts at spoliation, remained impressively intact until they were sold off as *biens nationaux* in the early stages of the Revolution. Its subjective pervasiveness was, as we saw in the previous chapter, no less marked, especially in the minds and behaviour of those who, at whatever level of the clerical hierarchy, competed so fiercely for actual possession of these endowments. It can be seen most clearly in the fact that the word benefice, which strictly speaking meant the material reward attached to the performance of a spiritual function, should have become so universally used to designate the office and the function themselves, so leading to the kind of conflation and abuse that church reformers in every generation would deplore.

The language of benefice-holding and the criticisms made of contemporary practice, would figure prominently in any full-scale analysis of the temporalities attached to French dioceses, irrespective of the period in question. But even an abridged attempt at such a study would be out of place in a book which is not directly concerned with the manner in which bishops, once made, actually administered their dioceses. If, however, the present chapter is devoted to issues related to episcopal temporalities, it is primarily with the intention of explaining some of the ways in which dioceses might be attractive or unattractive to would-be or even reigning bishops. In order to do this, an attempt will be made to present a sketch of the financial hierarchy of France's dioceses. But, as this hierarchy was not necessarily a static one, it is also necessary to attempt an analysis of episcopal finances, for, without it, the broader picture of the progression or stagnation of the revenues of a given diocese cannot be grasped. Such an analysis, especially if it is concentrated on a limited number of case-studies, may also help to highlight both the problems and opportunities which could determine whether the revenues of a diocese would progress, stagnate or even decline over a century.

I

The most immediate impression to arise from even a cursory look at the sources concerned with episcopal vacancies and successions is how freely contemporaries commented upon the financial value of bishoprics. This was as characteristic of those directly involved in the choice of new bishops as it was of the observers and gossips who reported on such matters. Even when bargaining over vacant sees did not take the forms described in the preceding chapter, it is clear from the unapologetic, matter-of-fact way in which assertions about the financial value of bishoprics were made, that contemporaries felt no need to be reticent about such matters, nor that they were infringing the rules of *bienséance* in making their evaluations so openly. This can only mean that the financial returns of episcopal office were regarded by all parties – from the king downwards – as a legitimate part of normal interest in, or competition for, that office. This was all the more likely since so many of the clerics in search of bishoprics were already holders of benefices *in commendam*, and thus in the habit of thinking of ecclesiastical office in financial terms.[1]

There were any number of perfectly good reasons for this continual circulation of information, the accuracy of which, of course, cannot always be taken

---

1 For an example, see Retz's description of the diocese of Agde, which was briefly offered to him in 1643: 'Agde... qui n'a que vingt-deux paroisses et qui vaut plus de trente mille livres de rente', *Oeuvres*, ed Marie-Thérèse Hipp and Michel Pernot (Paris 1984), 169.

for granted. Bishoprics might change hands through transfers and promotions, which raised questions about financial profit and loss to those involved; bishops might retire and retain for themselves a greater or smaller proportion of the revenues in the form of a pension; incoming coadjutor-bishops also had to be assigned a fixed pension off the revenues for the duration of their coadjutorship; finally, and most frequently of all, pensions were also assigned to third parties when dioceses fell vacant, always the most convenient time to impose such obligations. In such a context, it is hardly surprising that Richelieu's fellow ministers Effiat or Bouthillier could write to inform him that a particular diocese, then vacant, was worth so much *per annum*; they probably did so in the knowledge that he and the king wished to reward a particular individual with a suitably endowed diocese, or to impose a pension on it.[2] Mazarin was even more tolerant of such behaviour, and talk of revenues, pensions and financial settlements involving bishoprics and other benefices abounds in his surviving papers.

At the opposite end of the spectrum, witnesses giving evidence as part of the canonical inquisition required by the papacy into vacant dioceses were routinely asked to indicate the annual revenue and charges of those dioceses; few witnesses declined to quote a figure, but while many of them were either guesswork or based on hearsay, some witnesses claimed to have been given credible figures by episcopal officials or the lease-holders of the temporalities in question. It was partly on the basis of these figures that Rome fixed the sums payable in annates by incoming bishops – a matter which was anything but uncontroversial in the early decades of the seventeenth century. Moreover, by this juncture contemporaries were also aware of historical variations in episcopal revenues, an awareness admittedly sharpened by the obligation to pay annates to the papacy. It was frequently argued, for example, that the annates imposed on French benefices were too high. The curia's *libri taxationum* having been compiled centuries earlier, it was claimed that they took little or no account of the fact that since then many dioceses had suffered financial decline, especially through the material destruction of the religious wars, the usurpation of lands, and the enforced sales of church property in order to fund the crown's struggle with the Huguenots. It was also argued that certain northern French bishoprics like Coutances or Saint Malo had lost out during the Reformation in England, with the confiscation of temporalities they had held there since the Middle Ages.[3] Occasionally, more specific cases were argued: in 1648, for example, it was alleged that the small Breton

---

2   For example, see *Les Papiers de Richelieu (Politique intérieure: Correspondance et papiers d'état)*, ed Pierre Grillon, 6 vols (Paris 1975, in progress), iv. 106–7, Effiat to Richelieu, about the rumoured vacancy of Lodève, which he understood was worth 17–18,000 *livres* a year; *ibid*, 556, Bouthillier to Richelieu, 19 Aug 1629, reporting that Dol was vacant and worth 14–15,000 *livres* a year.
3   BN, MS Fr 17364, p 377, Louis XIII to marquis de Coeuvres, French ambassador in Rome, ca 1620, repeating this assertion about Coutances and requesting a reduction in the cost of papal provisions for the new bishop.

see of Dol had been wealthier when it had been an archbishopric, while in more recent times damage from flooding by the sea had further reduced its revenues.[4]

Bishops themselves were foremost among those who kept an eye on dioceses and their financial standing. Examples of this interest are legion. In 1653 Bishop Claude Auvry of Coutances considered that of the vacant sees of Bayeux and Carcassonne, the latter was the more valuable by about 1,000 *livres* yearly, 'which I know because of the leases of these two benefices'.[5] Not many could claim such accurate sources of information, but Auvry's contemporary, Bishop Dony d'Attichy of Riez, bluntly asked Mazarin in 1652 how many of his fellow bishops could boast of having raised their revenues by a third, as he had; when he arrived at Riez in 1628, they had amounted to just 12,000 *livres* a year.[6] In a very different register, René du Louet, bishop of Quimper, asserted in 1650 that his diocese was 'easily the poorest in France', although a bishop whose entire career was spent in western Brittany may be forgiven for not realising that there were dioceses elsewhere – in Provence, for example – that were less well-endowed than even Quimper.[7] But while du Louet was merely arguing that he badly needed a coadjutor-bishop, Auvry and Dony were angling to secure a transfer to another, better endowed diocese; and when bishoprics became available, men like them had to conduct discreet financial enquiries before entering the competition for them. Whenever there were linked transfers of reigning bishops from one diocese to another, it was common practice for the parties to demand accurate information about annual revenues so as to prevent any loss to themselves as a result of an exchange.

Sometimes, such a financial 'également' involved the exchange of other benefices or the creation of lifetime pensions. Possibly the most revealing and elaborate instance of this occurred in 1629 when Henri de Sourdis, having left his first diocese of Maillezais to succeed his brother at Bordeaux, agreed to surrender Maillezais to Henri de Béthune, Sully's nephew, who held the title to Bayonne at the time. The exchange may not be a typical one, but its details offer a fascinating illustration of the kind of bargaining in which bishops were prepared to engage. Because Bordeaux, for all its archiepiscopal rank, was less attractive financially than Maillezais, then one of France's richest bishoprics with a lease-value of 35,000 *livres*, Béthune was obliged to indemnify Sourdis for his loss in giving up Maillezais. The immediate results of their negotiations were laid out in Louis XIII's letter to Rome where, conveniently,

---

4 ASV, PC 52, fos 30–2, evidence of Thomas Boulain, canon and cantor of Dol cathedral, before papal nuncio, 3 Dec 1648.
5 AAE, France 892, fo 315, letter to Mazarin 4 Sept 1653: 'en ayant la connaissance par les baulx de ces deux bénéfices'.
6 AAE, France 886, fo 358, undated letter to Mazarin, probably 1652.
7 ASV, PC 48, fo 790, 4 May 1650, *procuration* for the purpose of taking a coadjutor bishop: 'le plus pauvre de France sans difficulté'.

Béthune's father was then ambassador. Not only did Béthune have to transfer three of his abbeys to Sourdis, but he agreed to pay him a substantial pension of 12,600 *livres* a year from the revenues of Maillezais.[8] The price was a high one, considerably more than the difference in revenue – about 10,000 *livres* – between Bordeaux and Maillezais.[9] In this case – but possibly also in others which are not so well documented – agreeing to end the Sourdis family's long tenure of a wealthy diocese like Maillezais may have carried its own premium. But this was not all, since, in a subsequent agreement which had tacit royal approval, Béthune also surrendered his title to Bayonne to Sourdis who, in return, agreed to reduce his Maillezais pension by 5,000 *livres*; Sourdis then used the Bayonne vacancy to effect a further exchange of benefices with the new bishop there, Raymond de Montaigne. The scale of these exchanges may have been unusual, and the extensive patronage and goodwill enjoyed by both Sourdis and Béthune at court were clearly essential to the outcome; large numbers of far less ambitious schemes failed during this period because of the absence of such connections. For one thing, bishops drawn from aristocratic, ministerial, or otherwise favoured groups were perfectly placed to accumulate other benefices, held *in commendam*, and were thus more likely to be able to indulge in such complex transfers of this kind. But above all, it is their determination to strike a hard bargain in favourable circumstances which emerges most plainly. As happened in this particular case, that did not prevent litigation breaking out a few years later, with Béthune demanding that the entire agreement be annulled on the grounds that Sourdis's assurances about some of Maillezais's revenues were misleading![10]

Numerous other variations on the theme of contemporary attention to the financial value of bishoprics could be adduced to underscore the general point being made here. It is therefore particularly ironic that despite the circulation of so many facts and figures – inflated or deflated depending upon the purposes for which they were intended – reliable, accurate information for episcopal revenues was – and remains – far from easy to obtain. Indeed, it is not clear to what extent the crown, whose decisions could have serious financial implications for bishops, both old and new, itself possessed up-to-date information on these revenues. Certainly, there is no surviving evidence capable of proving that its sources of information were necessarily any better than those of, say, a bishop like Claude Auvry, with his extensive personal contacts. Had the crown been well informed, it seems highly unlikely that

---

8 *Archives Historiques de la Gironde*, 14 (1884–5), 67–8, letter to Philippe de Béthune, 23 Mar 1629.
9 AD Gironde, G 245, Bordeaux was leased at 15,515 *livres* in 1615 but receipts in 1630 totalled 26,400, so at the time of the exchange its value may have been around 24–25,000 *livres*.
10 AD Gironde, G 257, *Factum pour Messire Henry de Béthune*, which recapitulates the terms of the concordats of 21 Mar and 23 Nov 1629 concerning Maillezais and Bayonne respectively, and outlines Béthune's difficulties since then at Maillezais over disputed sources of income from offices which Sourdis had assured him were at the bishop's disposition.

someone as well-placed as Hugues de Lionne, the former secretary to Anne of Austria and to the *conseil de conscience* who became a *ministre d'état* in 1659, would have confessed in late 1660 that he had no trustworthy figures for the revenues of Gap in Dauphiné, of which his own father, Artus de Lionne, was then bishop! Lionne did not feel he could trust his father's intendant, whom he suspected of pursuing his own interests, to supply him correct information. The matter was urgent in late 1660, since his aged father finally seemed ready to resign the diocese, and his son desperately needed a trustworthy *état au vrai* so that he could negotiate with the numerous candidates for the succession to Gap.[11]

In this case – and no doubt in many others of a similar kind – it might be asked why Lionne did not turn for information to either the *chambre des comptes* or the Sainte Chapelle, which between them were responsible for administration of the *régale*. But neither body seems to have required detailed statements of the value of vacant bishoprics before concluding agreements about the sums of money payable to them for the *régale*. As we saw in the previous chapter, the sums payable in respect of the *régale* before 1641 were probably too small to have spurred either of them to keep a close check on episcopal revenues; the payments they demanded certainly look too rounded-up to be the result of detailed investigation. At any rate, no trace of such records have been found among their surviving archives. Thus, for all its presumed vigilance with regard to church temporalities, it seems as if the French crown was nothing like as well-informed as its counterparts elsewhere – or, possibly, as some of its own subjects! Certainly, it had nothing resembling the Spanish *Cámara de Castilla*, one of whose functions was to provide up-to-date information on diocesan values in order to recalculate with each vacancy the value of pensions imposed on dioceses, since the pensions were not supposed to exceed one-third of the revenues in question.[12] Here, too, the Spanish monarchy's *tutelle* over the church seems to have been, at least in institutional and financial terms, far more exacting, and its *patronato real* more solidly based. Studies of the episcopal revenues of Tudor England and Wales convey a similarly strong impression of central control based on often quite detailed information.[13]

Comparisons like these do not augur well for the prospects of a thorough study of French episcopal temporalities in general, or their revenues in particular. But the point of making the above comparisons at all is as much

---

11 'Lettres inédites de Hugues de Lionne', ed Ulysse Chevallier, *Bulletin de la Société d'Archéologie et de Statistique de la Drôme*, 12 (1878), 126–8, letter to Humbert de Lionne, 31 Dec 1660.

12 See Christian Hermann, *L'Eglise d'Espagne sous le patronage royal (1476–1834)* (Madrid 1988), esp ch 7, whose impressive figures contrast sharply with the French experience. See also Ivan Cloulas, 'La Monarchie catholique et les revenus épiscopaux: les pensions sur les mitres de Castille pendant le règne de Philippe II 1556–1598', *Mélanges de la Casa de Velázquez*, 4 (1968), 107–42.

13 See Felicity Heal, *Of Prelates and Princes. A Study of the Economic and Social Position of the Tudor Episcopate* (Cambridge 1980).

substantive as methodological. In their own way, they provide perhaps unfamiliar evidence of the enduring autonomy of the French church which, although compelled to contribute taxes (*décimes* and *dons gratuits*) to the crown, nevertheless succeeded in maintaining administrative control over its own internal taxation machinery, and by the same token over the sources of its wealth. Regrettable though it obviously is, this lack of uniform, easily tabulated information about ecclesiastical income turns out to be a function of the French church's capacity to keep its secrets to itself. Even when historians turn to local archives, the outcome is no different: the most striking fact about their sometimes enormous mass of documentation concerning episcopal temporalities is how rare it is to find tabulations of episcopal income and expenditure among them – or even data which could be readily translated into totals of this kind. The episcopal official who painstakingly compiled a detailed table of the temporalities of Toulouse and their revenues for every year between 1648 and 1673 never thought it worth his while to add them up and determine the overall totals![14]

This is not to say that no attempts were made to produce tables of episcopal income during the seventeenth century. The first publication of such 'statistics' came with the appearance in 1648 of the *Pouillé royal contenant les bénéfices appartenans à la nomination ou collation du Roy*, attributed to the Jesuit Pierre Labbé, and apparently based on the unpublished declarations made by the clergy themselves to their General Assembly of 1641.[15] A comparison of the two documents shows that similarities greatly outweigh differences in their figures, but Labbé's work is disfigured by numerous inaccuracies, some of which are merely typographical, and it therefore needs to be approached with caution. The next attempt at such a compendium was the *Recueil des bénéfices de France*, published in 1690, but its date renders it of little use for our purposes.[16] Before that, admittedly, the Colbertian drive to collect useful statistics of all kinds had seen provincial intendants attempting evaluations of episcopal and other ecclesiastical revenues, especially in the reports commissioned by Colbert himself in the mid-1660s; it was this tradition which produced the well known 'memoirs for the instruction of the duc de Bourgogne' (Louis XIV's grandson) in the late 1690s.[17] Most of these figures,

---

14   AD Haute-Garonne, 1 G 726, 'Estat des fermes de l'archévesché depuis 1648 jusqu'en 1673'.
15   I have used the copy in the BN (with the call number: Ld1 8). The 1641 declarations are in AAE, France 841, fos 1–117.
16   Georges d'Avenel, *Richelieu et la monarchie absolue*, 3 vols (Paris 1884–90), iii. 456–7, for a list of the figures for France's bishoprics. D'Avenel himself argued that the figures should be doubled, or even tripled in some cases, in order to obtain true values. The multiplier seems rather crude, and is in any case totally erroneous where values can be checked against original sources.
17   For Colbert's initiatives, see *L'Intendance de Champagne à la fin du xviie siècle*, ed Jean-Pierre Brancourt (Paris 1983), 8–15. Few of the surviving reports have been published, although quite a few have survived. See for example, *La Bretagne en 1665 d'après le rapport de Colbert de Croissy*, eds Jean Kerhervé, François Roudaut and Jean Tanguy (Brest 1978).

with the exception of those produced during the 1660s or early 1670s, also come too late for our purposes, though they may be used as a pointer to longer-term trends in episcopal revenues. For all its approximate nature, incapable of satisfying demands for statistical precision, data of this kind can nevertheless be utilised by historians. It can be considered as being in the 'public domain' of the time; to the extent that it circulated alongside other figures and evaluations, it can be said to have played a part in shaping the opinions, and thus the preferences, of those with a personal interest in France's bishoprics.

II

A national league-table of episcopal revenues, however it is presented, is always likely to read like an accountant's balance-sheet – i.e. not readily intelligible to the uninitiated. Before attempting to present such figures for discussion, it may be worthwhile examining the principal sources of those revenues, with a view to explaining the behaviour of contemporaries, bishops included, as well as the trends experienced by those revenues during the first half of the seventeenth century. As with the geography and institutional shape of the dioceses, the sources of episcopal income changed relatively little over the centuries, but this did nothing to ensure that they would be homogeneous from one end of the realm to another. For our present purposes, it will suffice to examine a number of key sources of income, since the lack of information for a large number of dioceses renders any attempt at a nationwide typology quite meaningless. How many bishops, in France or elsewhere, could double their income every leap-year by virtue of the right to appropriate the proceeds of the parish chests (*fabriques*) throughout his diocese, as the bishop of Aire, in deepest Gascony, was entitled to do?[18] In the absence of any serious investigation of nationwide patterns of church wealth in pre-Revolutionary France, this is one of the many questions which must remain unanswerable for the present.

Seigneurial property was as common a component of episcopal temporalities as it was of the patrimony of nobles or office-holders throughout early modern France. The expression 'seigneurial property' does not begin to account for the bewildering complexity of the rights and revenues which come under that heading. The ownership of landed estates was only one of the many forms it took. It has often been noted, for example, that forests and woodland constituted a prized element of such possessions, and it is clear that ecclesiastical properties still included valuable assets of this kind down to the Revolution. This appears to have been particularly so in northern and

---

18 Pierre Duval, *Description de l'évêché d'Aire en Gascogne* (np, 1651), 6. The *fabrique* was the equivalent of the churchwarden's chest.

north-eastern France, but it may have occurred in other parts of the country also. In a diocese like Châlons-sur-Marne, the annual tree-felling – the *coupe ordinaire* – produced a substantial proportion of the bishop's revenues in the first half of the seventeenth century.[19] *Coupes extraordinaires*, for which royal permission was required, could produce sizable windfalls in cash, and were for that reason a standing temptation for hard-up benefice-holders who were merely temporary masters of the properties.[20] The revenues of the bishops of Meaux were reported to have fallen by over a quarter by the later seventeenth century because the stands of great timber (*futaie*) had been dilapidated by such fellings and had been replaced with less lucrative coppice (*taillis*).[21] Similarly the neighbouring bishop of Senlis argued in 1669 that most of his revenue came from the episcopal woods, and that it could be raised further by careful management, and specifically by lengthening the interval between the major tree-felling operations.[22]

Whatever form it took, it is clear that in the majority of bishoprics for which evidence is available, seigneurial property generally was the principal source of revenue. It was common for one or more major *seigneuries* to constitute a kind of financial backbone in particular dioceses. This is especially true in northern and central France, though one experienced observer described the barony of Aubagne, belonging to the bishops of Marseille, as 'one of the most delightful places in the province'.[23] Geographical concentration of their temporalities also seems to have been crucial to the financial well-being of bishoprics, as contemporaries themselves sensed when itemising them. Those of Montauban were in four major clusters, which a senior parlementaire from Toulouse described as being 'solid properties with guaranteed revenues which in peacetime are in no danger of collapsing'.[24] In the later seventeenth century, the two *comtés* of Dieppe and Aliermont provided half of the net income of the wealthy archbishop of Rouen.[25] At neighbouring Lisieux, it was the *comté* of the same name which was the largest single source of income in

19 AD Marne, G 306–45, annual accounts 1596–1631, 1639–49, 1654–5.
20 AD Saône-et-Loire, G 87, letters-patent of 1650, authorising bishop of Mâcon to cut timber to the value of 20,000 *livres* in order to purchase the previous bishop's personal residence or build a new one for the bishopric of Mâcon, since the previous residence was uninhabitable and abandoned.
21 A M de Boislisle, ed, *Mémoires des intendants pour le duc de Bourgogne: la généralité de Paris* (Paris 1881), 77.
22 AN, E 435, fo 155, decree of the council of finance, 9 Dec 1669. The revenues of Senlis had risen from a paltry 3,000 *livres* around 1610 to over 20,000 *livres* by the 1650s, a spectacular result for such a small diocese.
23 *Lettres de Peiresc*, ed Philippe Tamizey de Larroque, 8 vols (Paris 1888–98), vii. 580, Peiresc to Cardinal Bentivolgio, 19 Apr 1622: 'un des lieux les plus delicieux de la province'.
24 *Papiers de Richelieu*, iv. 636, Gilles le Masuyer to Richelieu, 9 Oct 1629: '(de) très bons fonds et de revenu asseuré qui ne peut périr en temps de paix'.
25 Guy Lemarchand, *La Fin du féodalisme dans le pays de Caux. Conjoncture économique et démographique, et structure sociale dans une région de grande culture, de la crise du xviie siècle à la stabilisation de la Révolution (1648–1795)* (Paris 1989), 177.

mid-century, followed by three lesser *seigneuries*.²⁶ Most of the bishop of Poitiers's revenue derived from six *seigneuries*, which included the favourite episcopal residence, the manor of Dissay. With the temporalities also massively concentrated 'aux portes de Poitiers', and with so many of the local nobility figuring among the bishop's vassals, it was not surprising that Charles Colbert should conclude that the bishop of Poitiers, with about 40,000 *livres* of revenue a year, enjoyed a measure of authority which not even the provincial governor of the day could rival.²⁷ Further to the east, the bishop of Clermont held four major *seigneuries*; the most important of these, Mozun, was leased for 6,210 *livres* in 1651, when it accounted on its own for nearly a third of his revenue; the seven remaining *terres et seigneuries* grossed 8,365 *livres* a year between them. A marginal note against the return for Mozun reveals far more about its importance than any statement of its lease value ever could: 'the estate of Mozun is very extensive and one of the most seigneurial of the whole kingdom; a host of nobles owe hommage to it. It is a stronghold which in wartime makes the entire province tremble.'²⁸ The last remark was hardly innocent in 1651, when the diocese was vacant, and the crown feared that the vicomte d'Estaing, brother of the recently deceased bishop, would be in a perfect position to make trouble if the see was not given to another member of his family.²⁹ In a country which continued to experience considerable internal disorder until Louis XIV's personal rule, this kind of seigneurial *place forte* was hardly a luxury. But even when disorder was not a problem, *seigneuries* like Aubagne, Mozun, or Dissay sometimes served as alternatives to the city or town which was the official seat of the bishopric, but with which relations might be fractious, and in which episcopal authority or freedom of movement might be curtailed. Consequently, it was logical for bishops during the wars of religion (and in some cases, later) to try to hold on to these major *seigneuries* at all costs; if left with no real choice in the matter, the best option was probably to sacrifice only those which, as the bishop of Le Puy seems to have realised, were either the least valuable or were the most vulnerable by virtue of being too distant from the epicentre of episcopal power.³⁰

It was, of course, the same logic which made local families covet episcopal

26 H de Formeville, *Histoire de l'ancien évêché-comté de Lisieux*, 2 vols (Lisieux 1873), i. cccclxi-iv, 'état au vrai des revenus de l'Evêché pour l'année 1659'.
27 BN, MS 500 Colbert 278, fo 9. Colbert's figure for the bishop's revenues was almost certainly an exaggeration.
28 AD Puy-de-Dôme, 1 G 153, pièce 4: 'la terre de Mozun est de grande estendue et des plus seigneurialles du Royaume, quantité de gentilshommes en relèvent. C'est une place forte qui dans la guerre faict trembler toutte la province.' Over twenty years previously, Effiat had written to Richelieu when Bishop d'Estaing was rumoured dead: 'il y a des places d'importance, y ayant deux maisons bien fortes qui appartiennent à l'évesque': *Papiers de Richelieu*, iii. 42, letter of Jan 1628.
29 BN, MS Fr 25025, fo 309v, 21 Oct 1650.
30 AD Haute-Loire, G 775, undated memorandum (but eighteenth century?) on *rentes* payable to bishop by holders of certain peripheral properties.

seigneuries. Where they were successful in acquiring them, their well-known determination to retain them thereafter sometimes constituted a powerful incentive to them to influence the choice of future bishops for the diocese. The Matignon family acquired the major barony of Saint-Lô in the Coutances diocese from Bishop Artus de Cossé in the 1570s, and their retention of it was subsequently facilitated by having docile clients or family members as bishop there until the 1640s.[31] But it is a mistake to think that all sales (*aliénations*) of this kind were confined to the period of the civil wars. René de Rieux acquired the marquisate of Ouessant in northern Brittany from the elderly Bishop of Saint-Pol-de-Léon around 1610, and went to great lengths to justify his acquisition as being mainly to the bishop's benefit![32] But ensuring that his own son, also called René de Rieux, would be the next bishop of Saint-Pol meant there would be no serious challenge to the transaction from a discontented bishop. The Rieux family would probably have had episcopal ambitions for its younger sons regardless of such transactions, but the latter certainly gave those ambitions added point. During the years in which he was nominally bishop of Agde, the future comte d'Alais compounded the sixteenth-century sale of the bishopric's principal barony by disposing of others as late as 1616; the result, it was claimed in 1626, was a substantial decline in Agde's revenues.[33] Possibly the largest of these exercises in spoliation occurred in Bourges around 1620 when the prince of Condé, governor of Berry, secularised two abbeys and other church properties, ostensibly in order to endow a Jesuit college, but in effect further impoverishing the archbishopric of Bourges. Condé's behaviour was strongly criticised at the time, but to little effect, since he, too, ensured that successive archbishops would be clients with very little influence or distinction.[34] It would take a detailed diocese-by-diocese analysis to determine the extent of such *aliénations*, and their possible influence in later generations on the choice of bishops for the dioceses most affected by them.

By the 1620s, however, many bishops had begun to reverse that trend and, taking advantage of favourable royal legislation, were determined to repurchase *seigneuries* sold off in previous generations. With revenues from existing temporalities already rising by then, owing to improved economic

---

31 René Toustain de Billy, *Histoire ecclésiastique du diocèse de Coutances*, ed A Héron, 3 vols (Rouen 1874–86), iii, 186.

32 BAV, Barb lat 7956, fo 48, Jean de Bonsi to Cardinal Borghese, 3 Dec 1612. The fact that Rieux used Ouessant as his principal title thereafter is rather better evidence of who benefited. According to Pourcelet, Rieux already had the *réserve* of Saint-Pol before Neufville died.

33 ASV, PC 24, fo 487, evidence of Fulcran de Barrez, later bishop of Agde, 1 June 1625. The beneficiaries are not mentioned, but they were probably close to the Alais's Montmorency affinity.

34 BN, MS Fr 17364, pp 672, 682, Louis XIII to pope and Sillery, French ambassador in Rome, n.d., outlining Condé's changing plans for incorporated benefices in Bourges. See also *Lettres de Peiresc*, vii. 572, Peiresc to Cardinal Bentivoglio, 14 Dec 1621, 'Il se plait maintenant à Bourges plus que jamais depuis qu'il y a mis un nouvel archevesque à sa dévotion comme vous aurez sceu.'

conditions, such an objective was increasingly possible, especially as the properties could be repurchased at the original sale price. Unfortunately, this subject has been far less studied than the *aliénations* of the previous century, doubtless because the latter were sponsored by the crown and were closely tied into its financial history. But it is fair to argue that the recovery in episcopal revenues during this period was bolstered by the effects of repurchases where they were effected. It even became common practice for leases of episcopal properties to contain a special clause excluding the revenues arising from the redemption of *biens aliénés* while a lease was in force. Obviously, the determination of bishops to pursue such policies of redemption, and the rate of success varied enormously. Between 1620 and the early 1640s, the bishop of Rodez resold some of these properties in order to raise money to rebuild the episcopal palace burnt down by his opponents in 1589.[35] Successive bishops of Lisieux, for example, seem to have obtained letters-patent allowing them to do the same at various times from the 1610s to the 1650s, but this offers no guide as to what they did in reality.[36] Sometimes, it was those bishops who acquired a reputation for being 'saints prélats' who proved most adamant in their determination to recover lost temporalities, and the opposition they provoked locally may owe as much to such considerations as to their religious policies. During his early years at Cahors, the energetic Alain de Solminihac recovered three *seigneuries*, a mill, and a number of small *rentes*, as well as winning a series of lawsuits guaranteeing his rights, fiscal and honorific, as count of Cahors; he also defeated the cathedral chapter's efforts to oblige him to assume sole responsibility for repairs to the cathedral.[37] In this, and possibly other cases, the additional revenue generated may not have been more a few thousand *livres* at most, but the bishop's victories were a clear warning to all that he was capable of protecting his rights, and with them his revenues. As late as 1663, it was observed that the properties of the Provençal diocese of Glandèves usurped in the previous century could only be recovered from the powerful local noble family which held them if the bishops were themselves 'personnes d'authorité'; episcopal rank alone would not provide the necessary authority, and social status and good political connections seemed indispensable.[38] In the light of these examples, it can safely be said that not all bishops were equally well placed to repurchase alienated properties, and that this fact may partly account for the uneven rise in episcopal revenues from one diocese to the next during this period.

---

35 AD Aveyron, 1 G 79, 'mémoire sur le temporel aliéné de Rodez', n.d. [mid-1640s?].
36 Formeville, *Histoire de l'ancien évêché-comté de Lisieux*, i. p. cccclii-iii.
37 Alain de Solminihac, *Lettres et documents*, ed Eugène Sol (Cahors 1930), 202–7, 'Mémoire résumant les procès engagés par Msgr Alain pour recouvrer des biens aliénés et des honneurs abandonnés', n.d., but dealing with the years up to 1643 approximately.
38 BN, MS 500 Colbert 180, fos 254–400, 'roolle des archévêchés, évêchés ... de Provence, 1663', at fo 385. Glandevès was one of the middle-ranking dioceses of Provence with regard to annual revenue, and some of its temporalities were located in Savoyard lands.

Alongside *seigneuries*, great and small, episcopal temporalities invariably included a host of smaller properties – land and houses, mills, and tolls etc – whose annual returns might be tiny. But it was rights of jurisdiction which were an essential, and at times a lucrative, part of seigneurial authority. Such rights could, of course, exist separately from land. Bishops like those of Beauvais were full *seigneurs* of their episcopal town, and it was their court and officials who were the dominant authority in municipal affairs. Elsewhere, as in Albi, Le Puy or Digne, bishop and king were joint *seigneurs*, an arrangement which sometimes tended to erode episcopal authority.[39] Despite this, the bishop of Le Puy's authority was very considerable outside of his official seat: he was *comte* of Velay, and *seigneur direct* in sixteen of the *mandements* into which his diocese was subdivided.[40] The profits of jurisdiction usually took the form of seal or registry fees, fines, confiscations, transfer fees on property (*champarts, lods et ventes*) and so on, but despite their proliferation, their contribution to episcopal revenues as such was usually fairly limited. The bishop of Le Puy, because of his extensive jurisdictional rights, was probably unusual in that, in 1661, 12 per cent of his income was drawn from the receipts of ten *greffes*, his *officialité*, and the *cour commune* of the town of Le Puy itself.[41] And although the profits of jurisdiction were reduced by administrative costs, bishops were in no hurry to abandon seigneurial rights, owing to their non-monetary advantages of power, patronage, and control over communities. The archbishops of Lyon lost the valuable *justice temporelle* of the city during the sixteenth century, but they were indemnified with an annuity of 2,000 *livres* payable from royal tax-funds.[42] The bishops of Clermont lost the *comté* of Clermont to Catherine de' Medici in the 1560s, but received no indemnity for the ensuing loss of status, jurisdiction and revenue. Losses on such a scale were rarely forgotten in subsequent generations.

The extent to which church tithes contributed to seventeenth-century episcopal incomes also remains poorly understood. They were, of course, originally designated for the upkeep of parish clergy but over the centuries they had largely fallen into the hands of the upper clergy, chapters of clergy, or monastic orders. The huge geographical variations in the rates of tithe make systematic study and generalisation extremely hazardous. From the *grèves des décimables* during the wars of religion to the rural anticlericalism of the eighteenth century, tithes were never popular, not least because the clergy frequently attempted to extend them to new forms of cultivation. Surviving

---

39 Georges Frêche, *Toulouse et le région Mid-Pyrénées au siècle des Lumières* (Paris 1974), 481; Bernard Rivet, *Une Ville au xvie siècle: Le Puy en Velay* (Le Puy 1988), 175.
40 Rivet, *Le Puy*, 176.
41 AD Haute-Loire, G 107, no 7, 'Estat du revenu de l'évesché du Puy de l'année 1661'. This document was drawn up because of the departure of Henri de Maupas to Evreux, and it was necessary to make a pro-rata assessment of his share of the revenues for the year.
42 AD Rhône, 1 G 290, leases and accounts 1586–1740; *ibid*, 10 G 1458, nos 4–13, leases 1629–1718. The leases regularly refer to the indemnity of 2,000 *livres* payable from the *recettes générales*.

leases of episcopal properties are rarely specific enough to pin down, even approximately, the proportion of revenue derived from tithes, which in any case are frequently impossible to distinguish from normal seigneurial dues in areas where the bishop was also the *seigneur*.[43] Perhaps the best-known general distinction is the one made between the the clergy of the south, who depended heavily on tithes, and those of the north, who could count on other forms of endowment. The frontiers between the two areas remain rather vague, but it does seems as if dioceses like Albi and Montauban on the northern edge of Languedoc drew most of their income from tithes, while Gascon dioceses like Auch claimed to have few if any alternative sources of revenue to the tithe.[44] Indeed, if there is a wider geographical unity in this respect, it is one which places the southern French dioceses alongside those of northern (Old) Castile, some of which drew over 90 per cent of their income from tithes.[45]

This kind of geographical contrast may easily lead one to assume that southern dioceses were poor by comparison with their northern counterparts. Apart from noting the inevitable exceptions to such a broad geographical generalisation – Provençal bishoprics, for example, drew only modest sustenance from the tithe[46] – it is only necessary to say at this point that the generalisation itself is highly dubious in relation to episcopal revenues. As we shall see, an impressive number of southern dioceses were surprisingly rich given their modest size, but especially when compared to the often larger and, on paper, more prestigious northern sees. For some French bishops, at least, though tithes might be a source of trouble, they were not synonymous with indigence.

This sketch of the main sources of episcopal revenues would not be complete without some mention of *le spirituel*, whose contribution is rarely mentioned in existing studies of the subject. Because receipts from this source were of their nature 'casual', they were frequently excepted from the terms of leases, and handled separately by the bishop's intendant or secretary; this, in turn, means that traces of them are few and haphazard. But it would be mistaken to ignore them altogether for that reason. In general, it would seem that they were in decline after the fifteenth and sixteenth centuries, when proceeds from different kinds of chancery fees, dispensations, visitations or synodal charges, were apparently lucrative. Indeed, if they are familiar to historians at all, it is probably as the fiscal 'abuses' indulged in by the

43 John McManners, 'Tithe in Eighteenth-Century France: a Focus for Rural Anticlericalism', in Derek Beales and Geoffrey Best eds, *History, Society and the Churches* (Cambridge 1985), 147–68.
44 *Ibid.* See also Jean Rives, 'Les Refus de dîmes dans la ville d'Auch à la veille de la Révolution', *Actes du 96ᵉ Congrès National des Sociétés Savantes* (Toulouse 1971), ii. 237–57.
45 Maximiliano Barrio Gozalo, 'Perfil socio-económico de una élite de poder: les obispos de Castilla la Vieja 1600–1840', *Anthologica Annua*, 28–29 (1981–2), 105.
46 René Pillorget, *Les Mouvements insurrectionnels de Provence entre 1596 et 1715* (Paris 1975), 80–1.

pre-Reformation church, and which were to some extent either reduced or reformed in subsequent generations.[47] In the late 1540s, for example, the bishop of Le Puy charged 1,618 *livres* for four sets of ordinations in just one year, while his seal yielded 555 *livres*.[48] But the decline in revenues from this source was neither universal nor precipitous. In 1651 at Clermont, the fees arising from the bishop's secretariat and little seal were conservatively calculated at approximately 3,000 *livres* a year because, it was observed, Clermont was an enormous diocese with numerous clergy and ecclesiastical institutions; the same two sources yielded 5,000 *livres* over a half-century later.[49] But at Autun, the combined impact of reform and litigation (*arrêts et edits*) was seen as financially disastrous by the second half of the seventeenth century, when it was estimated that overall revenues had fallen by over 10,000 *livres* to around 7,000 *livres* since 1516. The loss was entirely attributed to the collapse of two items – fees from the little seal and from dispensations to clergy in respect of their obligation of residence: where they had once netted 8,000 and 2,000 *livres* respectively, they now grossed a mere 160 *livres* between them.[50] A reformed and resident clergy could spell serious trouble for episcopal finances.

Apart from those just mentioned, there were relatively few obvious ways of increasing episcopal temporalities after the wars of religion. The great ages of lay generosity were well and truly gone, and there was probably no great difference, leaving aside the effect of the redemptions, between the map of diocesan temporalities of around 1600 and those of 1789. Yet a happy few dioceses did benefit from the incorporation of monastic houses into their holdings, and, in some instances, their contribution to episcopal revenues was considerable. Without the abbey of Saint-Rémy, the revenues of Reims simply bore no relation to the archbishop's rank as first peer of the realm, and so long as Reims was in Guise hands (down to 1640) Saint-Rémy was always joined to it. But Saint-Rémy had always attracted aristocratic pretenders (Bouillon and the Este-Nemours in addition to the Guise themselves), and it became definitively detached from the archbishopric after 1640. Reims was eventually compensated under Louis XIV by the incorporation of a lesser abbey, Saint-Thierry, whose temporalities nevertheless boosted its revenues by around 12,000 *livres*.[51] The abbey of Saint-Jean had been attached to the see of Sens before 1602,[52] while Louis XIV added that of Mont-Saint-Martin in 1664 as an inducement to persuade the archbishop finally to abandon his

47 See P Imbart de la Tour, *Origines de la Réforme*, vol 2 (2nd ed, Paris 1946), 244ff.
48 Rivet, *Le Puy*, 177. Those ordained had to obtain letters of ordination from the bishop's secretariat, for which they paid a set fee.
49 AD Puy-de-Dôme, 1 G 153, no 4, *état du revenu*, 1651; *ibid*, no 7, *état du revenu*, 1719.
50 AD Saône-et-Loire, G 431, *inventaire des titres*, n.d. but in seventeenth-century hand.
51 Joseph Bergin, 'The Decline and Fall of the House of Guise as an Ecclesiastical Dynasty', *Historical Journal* 34 (1982), 234–55; *Intendance de Champagne*, ed Brancourt, 113. The incorporation was completed in 1696 on the initiative of Louis XIV.
52 AD Yonne, G 453, general lease of revenues, 19 Oct 1602.

refusal to recognise Paris's status as an archbishopric.[53] As for Paris itself, which rose from being a rich to being the richest French diocese in the second half of the century, it benefited from the incorporation of abbeys like Saint-Maur-les-Fossés and Saint-Magloire in the previous century.

Other cases of such augmentation occurred in the seventeenth century, but they were probably few in number and slight in value.[54] The fact is that it took considerable influence at court to obtain such largesse and then to defend it against opposition and the inevitable court cases. It is no exaggeration to say that it was bishops with powerful connections rather than dioceses with inadequate revenues who were the principal beneficiaries, and that where such incorporations occurred, they usually accentuated rather than redressed existing imbalances in the financial standing of bishoprics.

III

With revenues that were so diverse and geographically dispersed, the management of a bishop's *temporel* was not a simple affair, and it required more than mere technical expertise on the part of their intendants. It is only possible to comment on a few aspects of the problem here. For one thing, the management of temporalities was always a major source of episcopal patronage, with numerous officials, receivers, bailiffs, and lesser servants to be appointed, or reappointed, by incoming bishops; unlike some of the bishop's 'spiritual' officials, these were virtually all local men who probably served more than one bishop. Sometimes members of bishops' own families took a hand in the task, either as intendants or as lessees of prominent episcopal properties.[55] Managing temporalities also required an active display of episcopal authority, especially in the decades following the religious wars, as well as personal intervention in the pursuit of lawsuits, the negotiation of leases and contracts, the reception of homage from vassals, and so on. As the 'diary' of Bishop Turicella of Marseille for the 1610s shows, this constituted a demanding, but indispensable, round of obligations, journeys, and activities.[56] There can be little doubt that the gradual emergence of a more

---

53 Cynthia A Goulden, 'Changes in the Episcopal Structure of the Church of France in the Seventeenth Century as an Aspect of Bourbon State-building', *Bulletin of the Institute of Historical Research*, 48 (1975), 217.

54 Michel Péronnet, *Les Evêques de l'ancienne France*, 2 vols (Lille 1978), i. 591.

55 In 1629, it was alleged that the most valuable cluster of Montauban's temporalities were leased by the Bishop's nephew: *Papiers de Richelieu*, iv. 636, Gilles le Masuyer to Richelieu, 9 Oct 1629. The temporalities of Lavaur were managed during the 1620s and 1630s by a nephew of the bishop, Claude du Vergier: A Vidal, 'Du Vergier évêque de Lavaur et les siens', *Reuve Historique du Tarn*, 17 (1900), 73–86.

56 AD Bouches du Rhône, 5 G 683, *livre de raison* of Jacopo Turicella, 1611–17, probably kept by a secretary, which shows his movements and commitments in a very matter-of-fact, but cumulatively revealing manner.

consistently residential and long-serving episcopate in this period also reinforced the calibre and vigilance of financial administration. But equally it was one of the main reasons why even residing bishops found themselves compelled to spend time in Paris, at court, or in cities with sovereign courts; the greater their vigilance in temporal matters, the more likely they were to be engaged in lawsuits which could only be won by assiduous lobbying. At any rate, it seems likely that such vigilance, rather than economic trends *per se*, was responsible for some notable rises in episcopal revenues. As we saw, Bishop Dony of Riez claimed to have raised his from 12,000 to 18,000 *livres* between 1628 and 1652.[57] The revenues of Senlis fell by the end of the *ligueur* Guillaume Rose's episcopate to about 3,000 *livres*, having stood at 7,500 *livres* some twenty years earlier; by 1651, they were declared to be about 20,000 *livres*, an improvement that was attributed mostly to the efforts of Nicolas Sanguin, bishop since 1622.[58] Of course, residence on its own was no guarantee of good management, and elderly bishops in particular were vulnerable to a range of 'monopolles' practised by officials, *fermiers*, and even family members anxious to extract from them leases or items of episcopal property on advantageous terms. Nevertheless, in the early decades of the century at least, observers were convinced that a resident bishop's revenues would *always* be higher than those of a non-resident.[59]

The particular methods employed for the administration of the various episcopal properties could make a considerable difference to revenue levels. With the exception of a small handful of properties – usually favourite estates or places of residence – most seem to have been held under leases of varying duration, frequently in multiples of three years. Long emphyteutic leases had probably become rare by the seventeenth century, and both papal and royal legislation attempted to outlaw the practice where church property was concerned.[60] But it would be simplistic to imagine that the practice of

---

57 AAE, France 886, fo 358, undated letter to Mazarin, probably 1652. Jacques Mauclerc, vicar-general of Riez under Doni, and Antoine Godeau, bishop of the neighbouring diocese of Grasse, both confirmed this claim: ASV PC 52, fo 82, Godeau's evidence to papal nuncio on state of Riez diocese, 29 May 1652; PC 53, fo 489–90, Mauclerc's evidence, 27 May 1652.

58 ASV, PC 53, fo 797v-800, evidence of Antoine Loysel, about state of Senlis diocese, June 1651, on resignation of Nicolas Sanguin; AD Oise, G 637, lease of 17 Feb 1603 and 23 Nov 1605, both for sum of 3,000 *livres*. At the outset of Guillaume Rose's reign, Senlis had been leased for 7,500 *livres*. If Loysel's evidence is accurate, then Sanguin's efforts were not surpassed by his successors, since the bishop's revenues were leased for 20,000 *livres* in the early eighteenth century: *ibid*, G 637, contract of 27 Apr 1707.

59 *Lettres de Peiresc*, vii. 580, Peiresc to Cardinal Bentivolgio, 19 Apr 1622: 'Vostre evesché de Riez bien mesnagé vauldra 12,000 libvres de rente à un prélat qui reside sur les lieux, mais à n'y residant pas il s'en manquera quelque chose, et de faict Mr de Lisieux d'à present n'a jamais faict bail plus hault de xi mil livres.' 'Mr de Lisieux' was Guillaume Aleaume, bishop of Riez from 1614 to 1621, when he succeeded his uncle Guillaume du Vair at Lisieux. Peiresc had been du Vair's secretary.

60 See E Lormeau, *Des Menses épiscopales en France. Etude historique et juridique* (Alençon 1905), 58–9. Decrees of the Council of Trent and legislation under Charles IX took a similar line in banning long leases of church property.

subleasing was uniform across the kingdom. In some parts of France, leases on ecclesiastical lands remained in the hands of the same families for decades on end; such entrenched local interests were often accused of conspiring to keep lease values artificially low.[61] But the quasi-alienation of episcopal temporalities which was extremely common in seventeenth- and eighteenth-century England and which often saw properties leased for as little as one-tenth of their real value, was much less frequent throughout France.[62] The bishops of Montauban in the 1650s seem not only to have renewed individual leases by competitive auction each year, but to have done so in such a way that the solvency of each individual *fermier* had to be underwritten by the remaining *fermiers* in a given district.[63] Some southern bishops also found it convenient to lease their temporalities not as individual items but in groups defined by the territorial units, such as the *claveries* of Gascony or the *mandements* of Languedoc, into which their dioceses were administratively subdivided.[64]

But perhaps the biggest decision of all was whether to consolidate and 'centralise' leases of individual properties into a general lease, in a manner analogous to the *fermes générales* of royal taxes or large noble estates. As only a relatively limited number of such arrangements have come to light, generalisations about them can be no more than tentative in character. But as with tax-farming, the principal advantage of a general lease to the bishops was the possibility of shifting not only financial risk, but also the burden and the costs of administration onto other shoulders, and in such a way that a steady, budgetable income, payable at regular intervals by *fermiers* with considerable private means, could be relied upon; the *fermiers* could also be required to pay *décimes* and other fixed costs of bishops, and so only remit to them the net revenue from the lease.

Broadly speaking, the organisation of a *ferme générale* can be regarded as a sign of confidence among the contracting parties in their ability to exercise adequate control over the individual units of the episcopal *temporel*, as well as over their sub-lessees or administrators. Insofar as can be judged, this had become the normal method of episcopal administration by the second half of the seventeenth century. Before that, however, the picture seems altogether more varied and confused. After the wars of religion, the state of many dioceses probably made the establishment of a *ferme générale* too risky or

---

61 The temporalities of Senlis were leased, without interruption, it seems, by Pierre and Jean Truyart between 1584 and the early 1620s: AD Oise, G 637, unnumbered bundle of financial documents, including leases of 1584, 1603, 1605, 1619.
62 See Christopher Clay, ' "The Greed of Whig Bishops": Church Landlords and their Lessees 1660–1760', *Past and Present*, 87 (1980), 128–57, esp 134ff.
63 AD Tarn-et-Garonne, G 47, opening bids and final valuations of leases of properties in Gascon districts (*claveries*), 1652; *ibid*, G 48, fos 549–56, 'état des bénéfices . . . mis aux enchères', 1658.
64 In addition to Montauban (see previous note), the temporalities of Mende were leased by *mandement*: see AD Lozère, G 651, leases made during the 1670s.

uncertain, unless bishops were willing to accept a low income in return. As in tax-farming, *fermiers* sometimes took on too much and defaulted, leaving episcopal finances more confused than ever. In addition, individual bishops seem to have been wary of turning over their *temporel* to a *fermier général*, but one can only speculate about individual motivation in such matters. It appears, for example, that after twenty-five years' experience of a *ferme générale*, Bishop Joachim d'Estaing of Clermont reverted to a form of direct management during the 1640s; he himself dealt with the sub-farmers, whom he may have retained on an *ad hoc* basis for years after their leases had technically expired. Yet when Estaing died in 1651, it was argued that a new round of leases would actually *raise* his successor's income appreciably![65] Elsewhere, the bishop of Le Puy attempted a *ferme générale* in 1629, but it never seems to have come into operation.[66] His successor tried again in 1646, with more success.[67] Interestingly, both bishops of Le Puy seem to have insisted on maintaining their right to negotiate and sign sub-leases rather than turn over this prerogative, and its profits, to their *fermiers généraux*. There was thus nothing irreversible about the appearance of a *ferme générale* for the administration of episcopal revenues. Such arrangements may have become more numerous across France under Louis XIV, but there were still many bishops who did not wish to surrender direct administrative control of their temporalities.

IV

The preceding discussion should make it possible to understand why providing a satisfactory national table of episcopal revenues for our period faces serious difficulties. The problem is not simply one of a lack of figures for particular dioceses, which is regrettable enough, but how to interpret those figures which have survived so randomly. The extant *états* and *comptes* represent a rather wide range of evidence, the original purpose and nature of which are often hard to determine. Some give actual annual revenues; others are no more than receivers' lists of individual properties and undated, miscellaneous receipts from them.[68] Others still are a combination of actual and lease values for particular years, but in several instances it is not even possible to establish whether the figures include or exclude the standing charges payable from the annual revenues. A considerable number include revenues, probably substantial in some cases, payable in kind, but because they are expressed in local systems of measurement, translation into monetary values is simply

65 AD Puy-de-Dôme, 1 G 153, 'estat du revenu annuel, 1651': 'Nota qu'il y a douze ans qu'il n'a esté faict des fermes desdites terres, Mons l'Evesque en ayant jouy de ses mains, et qu'asseurement les fermes s'en feroient presentement plus avantageuses.'
66 AD Haute-Loire, G 23, fo 13, text of lease for four years, 20 May 1629, and its annulment on 18 Jan 1633.
67 *Ibid*, fo 97, reference to *ferme générale* signed on 23 Aug 1646.
68 For examples of this: AD Côtes d'Armor, 1 G 386–90, *comptes* of see of Quimper for various years between 1614 and 1641; AD Aube, G 329, 330, 462–3, miscellaneous *états* of revenues of Troyes 1602–6, 1615–16, 1639, 1677–8.

impossible. Such a heterogeneous assortment cannot form the basis of a critical, diocese-by-diocese listing of episcopal revenues. In the case of some dioceses, however, fairly continuous sets of figures have survived and, as in the previous chapter, they will provide the opportunity for a limited number of case-studies, the purpose of which is to explore in greater depth the factors which account for the financial vicissitudes of seventeenth-century bishoprics generally.

It is for these reasons that the following table is based mainly on three sets of sources which have one thing at least in common – with a few exceptions, they cover all of the dioceses of France! This is a more precious attribute than it might seem at first, since it can help to establish preliminary orders of magnitude, however crude or fragile they may be. The sources are also sufficiently dispersed chronologically to suggest something of the movement of episcopal revenues over the period as a whole. The first set of figures comes from the register of an otherwise obscure *banquier expéditionnaire en cour de Rome* named Pourcelet who, like those bankers alluded to in the previous chapter, specialised in the transmission of papers and money to Rome with a view to obtaining provisions for those nominated to benefices in France. Pourcelet was one of several such *banquiers* operating in Paris, and he clearly handled only a percentage of the dioceses being filled during the first two and a half decades of the seventeenth century, the period covered by his register. Yet he made entries in his register for every diocese and its consistorial benefices, though in several cases the information may be somewhat out of date because nominations went back to Henri III's reign; in the case of some dioceses, he clearly updated his information about revenues when he was able to do so. Thus, two columns have been provided in the table to take account of his updated figures (P1, P2). In general, it can be said that while his information was uneven and a few of his returns puzzling, as a professional benefice-watcher, Pourcelet was better placed than virtually any of his contemporaries to know what the financial value of France's bishoprics was.

The second source is the series of revenue declarations made by bishops and other benefice-holders to the 1641 Assembly of Clergy when it was revising the assessments for the *décimes* payable to the crown (AG 1641). The next column is taken from the figures of the 1648 *Pouillé Royal* which, as noted earlier, usually approximates closely to the 1641 assembly's figures (PR 1648). Finally, an admittedly mixed series of figures from the late 1650s to the mid-1670s has been added with a view to completing the chronological scope of the table, and to point to subsequent developments. The figures in this column are based partly on the extant reports on a number of provinces or *généralités* compiled by the intendants for Colbert, partly on evidence provided by episcopal and Roman archives. As far as can be judged, most of the figures in question are based on serious efforts made at the time to ascertain the size and nature of episcopal revenues. At any rate, taken as a whole, these successive sets of figures can be regarded as crudely representative of contemporary knowledge of the financial value of France's bishoprics.

Episcopal revenues by diocese

Diocese	P1	P2	AG 1641	PR 1648	1650–70s
Agde	14,000	20,000	25,000	25,000	35,000
Agen	12,000	16,000	25,000	25,000	27,000
Aire	15,000	20,000	18,000	18,000	18,000
Aix	16,000	18,000	25,000	—	30,000
Albi	60,000	—	45,000	100,000	———
Alet	15,000	—	18,000	16,000	16,000
Amiens	10,000	—	16,000	20,000	———
Angers	8,000	—	16,000	20,000	14,000
Angoulême	8,000	10,000	10,000	10,000	———
Apt	4,000	—	8,000	8,000	8,000
Arles	15,000	20,000	30,000	30,000	36,000
Auch	60,000	—	90,000	90,000	65,140
Autun	10,000	—	14,000	20,000	17,731
Auxerre	18,000	—	24,000	30,000	———
Avranches	8,000	—	12,000	20,000	7,000
Bayeux	15,000	—	36,000	36,000	35,000
Bayonne	12,000	—	14,000	15,000	———
Bazas	10,000	—	10,000	10,000	———
Beauvais	30,000	40,000	40,000	30,000	43,000
Belley	4,000	5,000	—	—	4,000
Béziers	15,000	—	18,000	22,000	30,000
Bordeaux	16,000	—	30,000	30,000	37,500
Boulogne	6,000	—	9,000	9,000	6,000
Bourges	8,000	—	9,000	10,000	9,000
Cahors	12,000	30,000	10,000	10,000	25,000
Carcassonne	15,000	—	30,000	30,000	25,000
Castres	20,000	—	25,000	25,000	25,000
Châlons/Marne	10,000	—	14,000	16,000	21,000
Chalon/Saône	4,000	—	8,000	8,000	8,000
Chartres	20,000	—	18,000	18,000	20,000
Clermont	10,000	—	14,000	15,000	19,500
Comminges	30,000	50,000	36,000	36,000	36,000
Condom	18,000	—	30,000	30,000	30,000
Conserans	16,000	—	18,000	18,000	14,000
Coutances	12,000	—	12,000	18,000	24,000
Dax	6,000	—	18,000	18,000	9,000??
Digne	6,000	—	8,000	8,000	12,000
Dol	6,000	10,000	22,000	22,000	18,000
Embrun	12,000	15,000	12,000	12,000	———

Le Temporel: *Wealth and Revenues* 111

Episcopal revenues by diocese (Cont)

Diocese	P1	P2	AG 1641	PR 1648	1650–70s
Evreux	12,000	—	13,000	16,000	12,000
Fréjus	15,000	—	22,000	22,000	21,850
Gap	7,000	—	9,000	9,000	—
Glandèves	4,000	—	8,000	8,000	14,000
Grasse	4,000	—	7,000	8,000	4,500
Grenoble	10,000	12,000	15,000	15,000	—
Langres	15,000	—	25,000	25,000	—
Laon	7,000	8,000	9,000	9,000	6,000
Maillezais/ La Rochelle	10,000	18,000	40,000	40,000	40,000
Lavaur	15,000	20,000	22,000	22,000	22,000
Lectoure	12,000	—	20,000	20,000	16,000
Le Mans	16,000	—	25,000	25,000	—
Le Puy	6,000	12,000	20,000	20,000	—
Lescar	10,000	—	20,000	10,000	14,000
Limoges	15,000	—	30,000	30,000	—
Lisieux	18,000	34,000	33,000	33,000	37,000
Lodève	10,000	—	10,000	10,000	15,000
Lombez	18,000	20,000	—	—	20,000
Luçon	8,000	—	16,000	16,000	20,000
Lyon	10,000	—	30,000	30,000	31,000
Mâcon	5,000	—	7,000	8,000	8,000
Marseille	18,000	—	16,000	20,000	20,000
Meaux	8,000	—	22,000	22,000	20,000
Mende	15,000	—	30,000	30,000	40,000
Mirepoix	15,000	—	20,000	20,000	25,000
Montauban	15,000	20,000	20,000	20,000	—
Montpellier	8,000	10,000	18,000	16,000	20,000
Nantes	10,000	—	22,000	22,000	24,000
Narbonne	30,000	—	50,000	50,000	—
Nevers	6,000	—	7,000	7,000	8,000
Nîmes	7,000	8,000	12,000	12,000	6,000
Noyon	8,000	—	8,000	8,000	8,000
Oloron	10,000	11,250	15,000	10,000	12,000
Orléans	10,000	—	16,000	20,000	—
Pamiers	12,000	22,000	12,500	15,000	—
Paris	30,000	—	66,000	90,000	—
Périgueux	10,000	—	18,000	10,000	15,000
Poitiers	15,000	—	24,000	24,000	40,000?

112 *The Making of the French Episcopate 1589–1661*

Episcopal revenues by diocese (Cont)

Diocese	P1	P2	AG 1641	PR 1648	1650–70s
Quimper	4,000	5,000	7,000	12,000	15,000
Reims	20,000	—	22,000	30,000	27,000
Rennes	8,000	9,000	18,000	16,000	19,000
Riez	8,000	—	—	15,000	18,000
Rieux	12,000	—	12,000	12,000	14,000
Rodez	15,000	20,000	40,000	20,000	26,000?
Rouen	25,000	—	50,000	50,000	——
St-Brieuc	6,000	8,000	14,000	14,000	12,000
St-Flour	7,000	—	9,000	9,000	——
St-Malo	18,000	—	24,000	40,000	30,000
St-Papoul	6,000	18,000	10,000	10,000	12,000
St-Paul/3 Chât[x]	—	—	10,000	10,000	10,000
St-Pol-de-Léon	4,000	—	8,000	8,000	15,000
St-Pons	5,000	12,000	8,000	8,000	16,000
Saintes	10,000	—	14,000	14,000	——
Sarlat	6,000	—	15,000	15,000	10,000?
Séez	7,000	—	9,000	16,000	——
Senez	5,000	—	7,000	7,000	12,000
Senlis	8,000	—	18,000	28,000	20,000
Sens	15,000	—	27,000	27,000	——
Sisteron	6,000	9,000	12,000	12,000	15,000
Soissons	6,000	8,000	8,000	8,000	8,000
Tarbes	12,000	—	8,000	8,000	——
Toulon	8,000	—	9,000	9,000	9,000
Toulouse	30,000	—	40,000	40,000	53,000
Tours	10,000	—	16,000	16,000	18,000
Tréguier	6,000	—	11,000	12,000	15,000
Troyes	6,000	—	—	9,000	——
Tulle	6,000	—	8,000	8,000	8,000
Uzès	7,000	8,000	18,000	16,000	20,000
Vabres	8,000	—	9,000	9,000	——
Valence-Die	10,000	12,000	20,000	20,000	16,000
Vannes	5,000	8,000	8,000	14,000	17,000
Vence	4,500	—	5,000	6,000	6,500
Vienne	12,000	—	12,000	12,000	15,000
Viviers	10,000	—	25,000	25,000	——

This table, as already suggested, can only be expected to help to establish relatively broad orders of magnitude. All the values expressed in it are nominal rather than real, and as such, it takes no account of inflation. The attempt to deflate the figures in order to make allowance for the erosion of nominal values would probably render them even more arbitrary, as it could

Le Temporel: *Wealth and Revenues*   113

only be done by comparing them to the changes in, say, Parisian grain prices for the same period. In any case, the purpose of the figures is not so much to determine the purchasing power of episcopal revenues as to compare the relative wealth of the dioceses themselves.

In general, it is during the opening decades of the period that, as might be expected, figures for episcopal revenues are most difficult to find. The data provided by the banker Pourcelet stretch between roughly the 1590s and mid-1620s, with the bulk of his figures being probably closer to the years 1600 to 1610 than to the 1620s; for all their imperfections, his entries can be taken as reflecting in a crude way the condition of France's dioceses in the decade or so immediately after the wars of religion (see Map 2). A rapid classification of his figures for 112 (out of 113) dioceses will lay the basis for comparison with later figures.[69] Thus, only twenty-one of the dioceses in the first column yielded an annual income of over 15,000 *livres*. Nine were in northern France, twelve in the south, and of the latter all but two were in the south-west. The historic hierarchy of episcopal wealth is undoubtedly reflected in Pourcelet's figures, with Auch and Albi easily ahead of all other dioceses, north or south. Paris had not yet emerged as the richest diocese of France, and at this point it had to share its rank of *proxime accessit* with Beauvais and Rouen in the north, but also with Toulouse, Narbonne and Comminges in the south-west; but by 1625, as other sources show, its revenues had begun to reach 60,000 *livres* a year.[70] A glance at Pourcelet's figures also shows how spectacularly successful an episcopal pluralist Cardinal Joyeuse, who effectively held Narbonne, Toulouse and Rouen simultaneously post-1604, actually was! When transposed onto a map, the figures make it clear that the most significant cluster of these wealthy dioceses, one-third of the overall total, was to be found in Upper Languedoc and the Gascony-Pyrenees region, with Auch, Toulouse and Albi as its backbone. During the sixteenth century, the wealth of Comminges and Conserans, neighbouring dioceses in the Pyrenees, had also been well-known, as had that of Condom, but the endowment of small sees like Castres and Lombez would probably have been less widely so. It may come as a surprise that none of the great dioceses of the centre figure among Pourcelet's wealthiest sees. In normal times, as is clear from other sources, sees like Lyon and Maillezais would certainly have belonged in such company, but Pourcelet's low returns for them at the beginning of the century do seem to reflect accurately a very substantial, albeit temporary, fall in their revenues.[71] By the 1620s at the

---

69 BN, MS Fr 4328, fos 1–74. He entered no figure for the see of Saint-Paul-Trois-Châteaux.
70 AN, MC, LXXVIII, 221, 23 Feb 1625, lease at 60,000 *livres* a year, commencing on 1 Jan 1625.
71 For Lyon: AD Rhône, 1 G 290, fos 1–2, lease in 1587 for 16,000 *livres* a year; AN, MC, LXXVIII, 158, leased at 12,600 *livres*, 26 April 1600. The revenues of Maillezais were given as 8,300 *livres* in 1587 and 13,000 *livres* in 1613: AD Gironde, 245, for leases and 'états des fermes' of Maillezais.

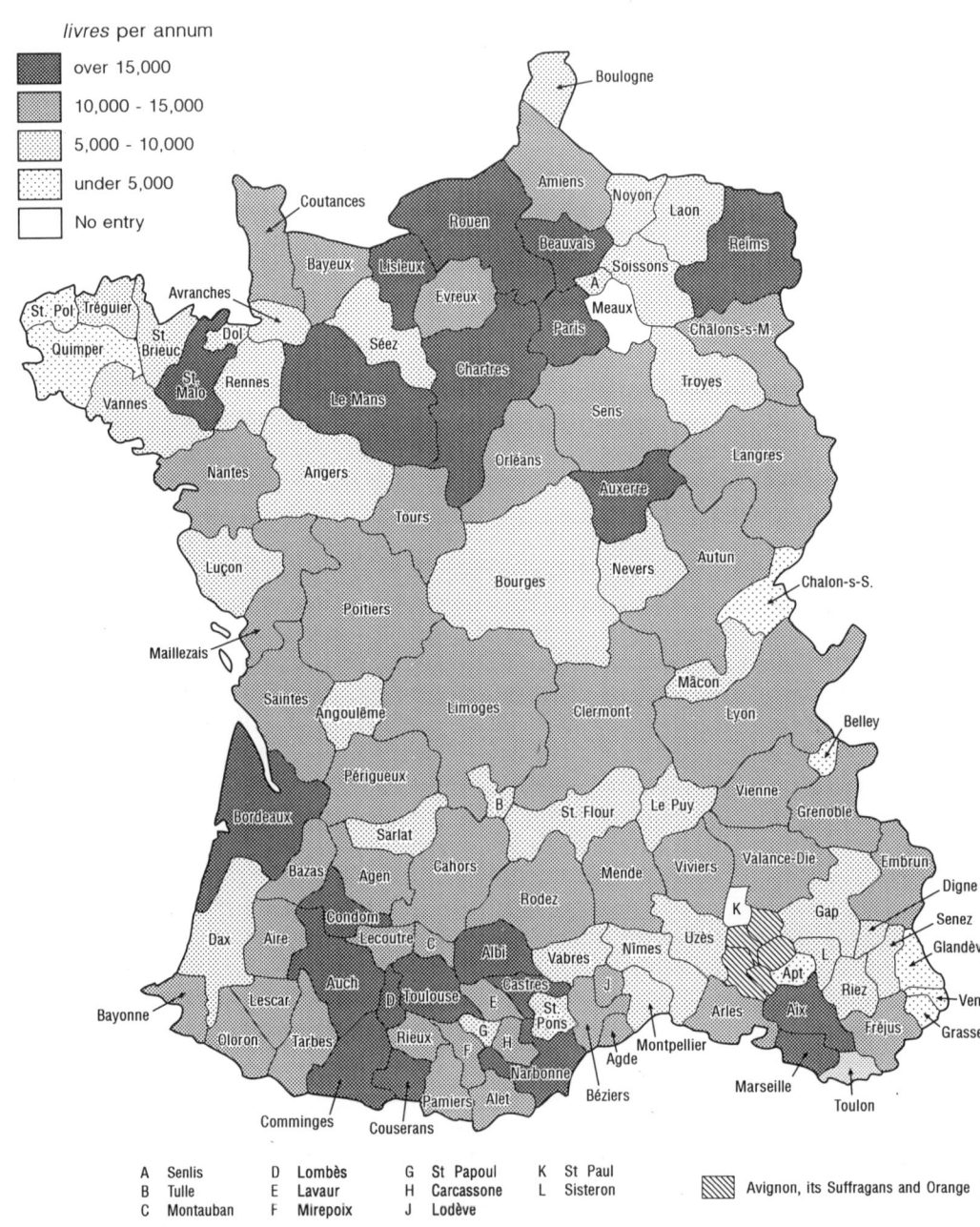

2 *Revenues of French dioceses, ca 1600–20*

latest, both had recovered from their financial problems, and were already edging close to their maximum values for the century as a whole. As for the top tier of northern dioceses registered by Pourcelet, they clustered around Paris and Rouen, extending westward to embrace Chartres and Le Mans. Three somewhat isolated dioceses on the extremities of northern France also belonged to this group – Saint-Malo, Reims and Auxerre.

The largest category is that of dioceses with revenues between 10,000 and 15,000 *livres* a year. It is here, perhaps, that the tentative nature of Pourcelet's data is most apparent, with no fewer than seventeen and eighteen dioceses being listed as worth 15,000 *livres* and 10,000 *livres* respectively. The majority of the dioceses just to the north and south of the Bordeaux-Lyon line fit into this category. Of the Breton dioceses, only Nantes belongs in it, and from Provence those of Arles and Fréjus.[72]

With the third category of dioceses between 5,000 and 10,000 *livres* we begin to approach those with either temporary (thanks to the religious wars) or structural problems of under-endowment. Totalling thirty-seven dioceses, it is the second largest grouping. It embraces most of the dioceses of Brittany (5), Provence (6), and the north-east (7). Of the south-western dioceses, only Dax belongs in this group, while the six Languedoc dioceses were, like Uzès, Nîmes and Montpellier, located mostly in the eastern half of the province, where it is probable that war damage and the usurpations of church property account for the paucity of revenue. But perhaps the most surprising impression is that of seeing large dioceses like Angers, Bourges, Rennes and Troyes in the same company as their much smaller and less well-known fellows. Troyes was the most southerly of a cluster of six Champagne-Picardy dioceses which were seriously under-endowed when their historical reputations and status are considered.

As for the final and smallest category of dioceses (eight in all) worth less than 5,000 *livres* in the early seventeenth century, they were concentrated essentially in Brittany and upper and eastern Provence, with Belley and Chalon-sur-Saône, also on the eastern perimeter of the realm, completing the list. The neighbouring dioceses of Vence and Grasse in Provence were always regarded as the poorest in France, which was reason enough for wishing to amalgamate them; equally, as we saw, the failure to do so for more than short periods of time, forcefully demonstrates the strength of resistance to change from above.

The second column of figures derived from Pourcelet's register only covers thirty-five, or less than one-third of all dioceses, and for that reason it is too limited to require extended comment. It can be assumed that these figures were entered, on average, between ten and twenty years after the first set. It

---

72 Pourcelet gave a return of 10,000 *livres* for Nantes (BN, MS Fr 4328, fo 28r). It was leased in 1604 at 8,500 *livres*, so taking account of reserved sources of income, his figure was reasonably accurate.

is not surprising therefore that in every case, they show a rise in episcopal revenues in the generation following the accession of Henri IV. With a few exceptions, the rises in question seem basically consistent with the kinds of figures available for later in the century.

The next major set of figures is taken from the declarations made by French benefice-holders to the Assembly of Clergy in 1641. The data taken from the so-called *Pouillé Royal* of 1648 are, as already pointed out, sufficiently similar in most cases not to need further comment.[73] Comparison between Pourcelet's figures and those of 1641 is not without its problems. There is, inevitably, always some danger with a fiscally oriented set of figures, which is what those of 1641 were, especially when they are based on declarations, not on informed assessments. But although we know little about the conventions governing the declarations, it may be assumed that the assembled clergy were making some attempt to ensure relative fairness, if only because self-interest dictated that no one escape too lightly at others' expense. Some of the figures appear to be inconsistent but, as with those of Pourcelet, that may reflect some short-term developments of which we remain ignorant. Cahors, for example, was valued at 10,000 *livres*, when its revenues were normally at least twice that figure.

At any rate, the time-lag between these figures and Pourcelet's is probably over thirty years for the majority of dioceses, long enough for the after-effects of damage or usurpations occasioned by the wars of religion to abate. Adopting a roughly similar classification to that for Pourcelet's returns, it emerges that there were nineteen dioceses (two less than in the equivalent category in the previous section) with over 30,000 *livres* per annum in 1641. Nine of those included among the twenty-one richest dioceses in the opening decades of the century were no longer in the top group by the early 1640s, though there is no return at all for one of them, Lombez, to the west of Toulouse. Perhaps the most surprising 'defections' are those of Chartres and Reims: the first is explicable in terms of a prolonged stagnation which saw its revenues actually fall from 20,000 to 18,000 *livres*; as for Reims, Guise mismanagement, a *de facto* vacancy of two years before 1641, the loss of the abbey of Saint Rémy, and the effects of war between them more than account for its problems. In the longer term, the relative decline of Chartres was confirmed, while Reims would eventually regain its position among France's richer dioceses. These 'losses' among northern dioceses were only partly made up for by the appearance of Bayeux, whose presence gave a certain geographical compactness to the five dioceses there belonging to this top category. Eight new dioceses established themselves among France's richest in the decades before 1641, but as we noted above, some of them such as Lyon, Maillezais, and Bayeux, should probably have been among them for some time, and contemporaries would not have been surprised at their recovery. Marseille dropped

---

73 See above, p 96.

back, to be replaced by neighbouring Arles. Excepting Maillezais, Limoges was the only one of the great central dioceses to find a place among this well-endowed élite. The remaining three newcomers (Carcassonne, Mende and Rodez) further strengthen the impression of the relative prosperity of France's southern dioceses towards mid-century. The figures suggest a change, however, in the southern hierarchies of wealth, with Auch now well out in front of Albi, Narbonne and Toulouse, though it may be doubted whether the relative positions of Albi and Auch were really as fixed as the declarations imply.[74] At any rate, eleven of France's nineteen richest dioceses lay south of the Bordeaux-Lyon line, a proportion identical to that derived from Pourcelet's figures.

The second and largest category includes forty dioceses whose revenues ranged between 16,000 and 30,000 *livres*. Slightly more than half of them were worth 20,000 *livres* or less, so the upper reaches of this band were less densely populated. As is evident from the accompanying map (3), the biggest geographical contingent among them consists of the large central and northern dioceses astride the Loire, with extensions eastwards to include Sens, Auxerre and Langres, and south-westwards to Poitiers and Luçon. But, as for the previous category, the largest contingent was to be found in the southern, especially Languedoc, dioceses. All but five of the province's twenty-two dioceses were by now either in this category or in the one above it.[75]

The third category ranging between 15,000 and 9,000 *livres* was only slightly smaller than the second, and indeed between them they comprised over two-thirds of all French dioceses. The range of revenues within this category was probably the most even, though this would have been little consolation to those congregated in its lower range! In geographical terms, it was widely dispersed, but with clusters of dioceses in the west (especially Brittany), the south-central, and eastern Alpine-Provence regions, and with a few eastern Languedoc dioceses (Vabres, Alet, Nîmes) finding themselves in company uncharacteristic of the province's dioceses. The presence among them of a diocese like Cahors, widely held to be one of France's wealthier dioceses, is puzzling, as is that of Evreux and Coutances in Normandy, but it may be due to short-term factors around 1641 which await a further explanation.

The final category of dioceses, the seventeen with less than 8,000 *livres* a year, is a relatively large one, comprising over one-seventh of the country's bishoprics. It is perhaps the category which changed least over time and from which it was inherently the most difficult to escape. With the exception of its Breton contingent of three, virtually all of its dioceses were again located along the eastern marches of the kingdom. It may come as a surprise to find

---

74   The entry of 100,000 *livres* for Albi in the *Pouillé Royal* is clearly an exaggeration, and the 90,000 for Auch may also be, but probably to a lesser degree.
75   The five were Rieux, Vabres, Alet, Nîmes and Lombez, though there is no return in 1641 for the last diocese.

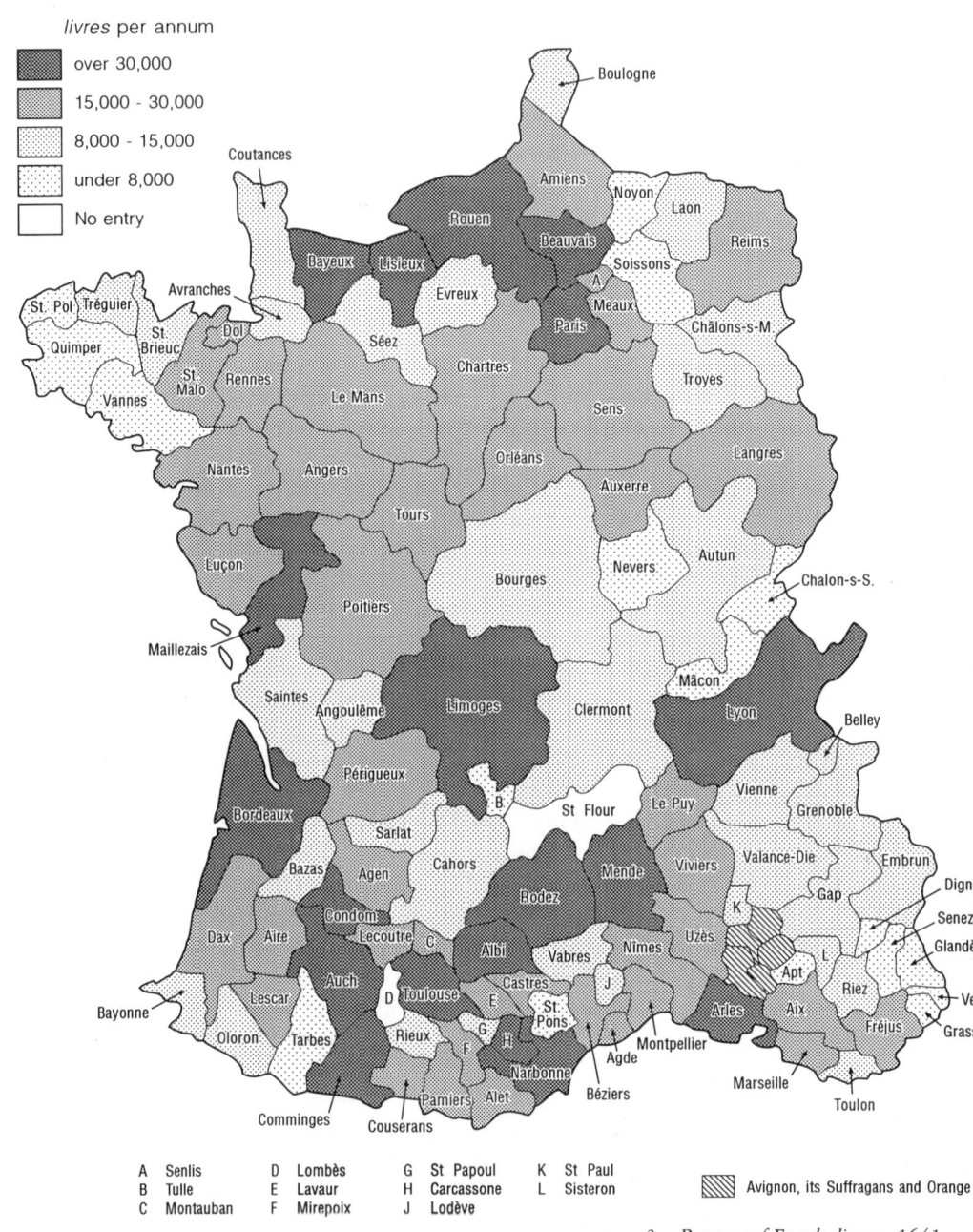

3 *Revenues of French dioceses, 1641*

among them dioceses like Soissons and Noyon, but their endowment was historically quite meagre, and neighbouring sees like Laon and Troyes were only marginally better off throughout the century as a whole. Further south, Chalon-sur-Saône, Mâcon and Nevers were also among France's poorest dioceses, situated in a region where, with the exception of Lyon, dioceses were not particularly well endowed. The remainder of the poor relations were to be found in eastern and upper Provence where, in contrast to Languedoc, to be a small diocese did not necessarily mean to be a rich one.

Despite its incompleteness and heterogeneous make-up, the final column of figures from the late 1650s to the early 1670s, largely confirms the patterns just described. In purely nominal terms, the revenues of most dioceses continued to rise, but moderately rather than spectacularly. A few more dioceses, such as Béziers, Mende, Saint-Malo, and Poitiers, had now joined those enjoying annual revenues of 30,000 *livres* or more, and which now accounted for about one-fifth of all dioceses. But the largest proportion, around 60 per cent, of bishoprics yielded revenues ranging between 10,000 and 24,000 *livres* a year. The poorest dioceses, with less than 10,000 *livres*, were approximately as numerous as the richest with over 30,000 *livres*. The overall pattern had not changed much over sixty or so years. Archbishoprics like Bourges, Embrun, Vienne and Tours remained at best among the modestly, or even poorly endowed, sees. In 1649, papers were despatched to Rome to show that the poorest of the four, Bourges, with an income of 9,000 *livres*, was unable to meet its normal expenses.[76] As for the poorest dioceses, the geographical position on the eastern edge of the kingdom of Boulogne, Laon, Noyon and Soissons compounded their difficulties when war came from the 1630s onwards, since these dioceses continued to suffer damage from troops until peace finally came in 1659. But war probably also affected better-off dioceses, such as Reims and Châlons-sur-Marne. In the mid-1650s it was claimed that Langres, which had been previously among France's wealthier dioceses, had seen its revenues fall through war damage to a mere 10–12,000 *livres*.[77]

Limited though this analysis may be, it will be evident that there was no simple correlation within the French church between the endowment of a bishopric on the one hand, and its size, location or hierarchical rank on the other. It is clear that the largest number of well-endowed dioceses was to be found in southern France, below a line running from, say, Bordeaux to Grenoble, and that this was not merely because half of all France's dioceses were located here. Yet it would be potentially misleading to conclude that

---

76 ASV, PC 48, fos 354–5, *état* of revenues and *charges*, included as a separate statement in evidence to the nuncio, Nov 1649. The new archbishop, Anne de Ventadour, was better placed than his predecessors to bear the costs of being archbishop.

77 ASV, PC 52, fos 652–3, evidence to papal nuncio on state of diocese, Mar 1655. This kind of evidence is not without an element of special pleading, but the overall impact of war can hardly be doubted.

this meant southern dioceses were more attractive to candidates for the mitre than those elsewhere in France, since so many other factors could determine candidates' preferences. Northern France was not devoid of wealthy dioceses, with a number of Norman dioceses consistently among the best endowed. It is hardly surprising that Hugues de Lionne should have thought of Bayeux in 1659 as a *pays gras*, not least because he was probably comparing it with the relatively poor dioceses of Dauphiné and Provence.[78] But Rouen and Lisieux also held their own well, as did Beauvais and Paris. Indeed, the most spectacular rise in revenues recorded by any bishop in the seventeenth century is by Paris which, from being among the leading half-dozen at the outset, had become the richest by the age of Louis XIV.[79] Pourcelet returned a value of 30,000 *livres* for Paris around 1600, but two leases in 1618 and 1625, for 42,000 and 60,000 *livres* respectively, are remarkable evidence of its take-off under subsequent Gondi stewardship.[80] By the 1670s or 1680s, the revenues were in the region of 80,000 *livres*.[81] How this was done, since it is not clear that important new sources of revenue were added during the period, remains another mystery awaiting its historian. Under vigilant management and with the benefits of peace, Reims, too, would return to its earlier perch among the best endowed dioceses under Louis XIV. Even a tiny diocese like Senlis could, as we saw, improve its financial attractiveness by sustained and careful management. When Cardinal La Rochefoucauld exchanged Clermont for Senlis in 1610, he insisted on a pension off Clermont in order to compensate for the considerable loss of income sustained by the move;[82] had his successor wished to make a similar exchange in the early 1650s, the arrangements would have been very different, since Senlis had at least caught up with Clermont by then. The comparison between these two middle-, or even low-ranking, dioceses may serve as a pointer to the kinds of financial readjustments that were possible during this period, and which would help to alter the attractiveness of dioceses to those anxious for episcopal office.

V

Inevitably the preceding analysis remained limited in scope, restricted by the statistics on which it was based. But it is possible to move beyond generali-

---

78 Lionne's father was at that time bishop of Gap.
79 Strasbourg, once it had become incorporated into the French church, became the richest French bishopric, allegedly shoring up the position of the Rohan family, whose members held it without interruption after 1704.
80 AN, MC, LXXVIII, 207, 19 June 1618, nine-year lease to run from 24 June 1618; LXXVIII, 221, 23 Feb 1625, nine-year lease to run from 1 Jan 1625. No explanation was given for the curtailment of the preceding lease, but the difference in value of the two leases may explain why Archbishop Gondi wished to cancel the first lease and raise its value. Neither lease included profits from seigneurial rights such as *quint et requint*, *droits de relief* and *rachat*, *aubaine*, confiscations, as well as vacant offices, the seal and secretariat of the archdiocese etc.
81 BN, MS 500 Colbert 157, fo 86, no date.
82 *Hierarchia Catholica*, iv. 153, 'Claramontan', n 2.

sations on the French church as a whole and, by turning to case-studies of a small number of dioceses for which something like adequate documentation survives, to obtain a more direct insight into the vagaries of episcopal revenues. In particular, it may be worthwhile comparing the experience of two northern with those of two southern dioceses, although it has to be admitted that the surviving evidence is not always comparable in nature, and therefore direct point-by-point comparisons are not always possible.

Until the incorporation of the Lorraine dioceses of Verdun and Toul in the eighteenth-century, Châlons-sur-Marne was a frontier diocese. It was not especially large by comparison with neighbours like Langres or Reims. Like them, however, it had a peerage attached to it, and the prestigious title of *comte et pair* was always likely to attract ambitious clerics. Held by sons of great nobles under François I and Henri II, it subsequently came into the hands of a family which achieved prominence as secretaries of state during the same period – the Clausse – three generations of whom occupied it without interruption from 1571 until 1640. This long tenure gave way to that of a successor with a less meteoric, but extremely respected robe background, Félix Vialart, perhaps the best-known of all Châlons's bishops during the early modern period.

Towards the end of the religious wars, when Bishop Clausse was a *ligueur* and the town was royalist (mainly out of a desire to shake off Guise dominance), the annual accounts of the bishop's receiver show that the revenues of the diocese fluctuated at slightly less than 10,000 *livres* a year, not taking into account quantities of grain included in the annual receipts.[83] It was only very slowly that they moved above the 10,000 *livres* mark, which means that Pourcelet's return of 10,000 *livres*, possibly inscribed in his register when Henri Clausse became coadjutor to his uncle in 1608, was roughly accurate, and reflected Châlons's position among the less well-off dioceses at that particular time.[84] Yet in nominal terms, there is no doubting the steady rise in episcopal income during the 1610s and the 1620s (the accounts being lost for the period 1620–6). The main sources of income were the lands managed under leases, tree-felling, sales of wine and grain, and the inevitable litany of lesser items. The proceeds of the annual tree-cutting accounted for between 30 and 45 per cent of the receipts during the 1600s and the 1610s. There are few signs of 'alienated' lands of any value being recovered, but the traditional dues payable by the artisans of the town of Châlons, which the bishop had surrendered in 1565 in return for a *rente* of 600 *livres* a year, were recovered through a decree of the parlement of Paris in 1606.[85] It took several years to enforce the ruling, but when it was, the *rentes des métiers* as they were called, netted the bishop a not insignificant 2,000 *livres* a year.

---

83 AD Marne, G 307, accounts for mid-June 1597 to mid-June 1598.
84 *Ibid*, G 312, receipts for 1605–6: 10,923 *livres*; G 314, receipts for 1607–8: 10,405 *livres*.
85 *Ibid*, G 315, accounts for 1608–9, with mention of the recovery by Bishop Clausse of the *rentes des métiers*.

By the time revenue figures appear again from 1626 onwards, albeit only for about six years, a number of interesting changes are noticeable. Henri Clausse had finally succeeded his long-serving uncle in 1624. From 1625 onwards there was a six-year *ferme générale* of the temporalities at an annual value of 12,500 *livres*, but there were significant exclusions (some of them *seigneuries*) from it, which meant that it provided no more than half of the revenues in some years, and in others less than that.[86] Unfortunately it is impossible to say how smoothly the lease ran its course, or whether it was renewed after its expiry in 1631. In addition, a number of *rentes* payable by the crown and worth about 1,450 *livres* a year, made their appearance for the first time in 1626. It seems as if they were originally personal investments made by either Bishop Henri Clausse or his uncle, but they were by now part of the bishopric's permanent endowment.[87] As for the revenues themselves for these years, at first sight they register a sharp rise in relation to the opening decades of the century; in reality, however, it was much less so than the totals in the accounts suggest. The year which comes closest to an accurate value of the episcopal revenues was 1628–9, when the total was 17,100 *livres*, with that of 1627–8 being roughly similar, if we remove a number of extraneous items from the year's final total of 20,369 *livres*.[88]

A decade later, by 1640, the gross receipts in the bishop's accounts had apparently jumped again to no less than 47,812 *livres* (admittedly for a sixteen-month period), but these figures merely show that episcopal finances and the revenues of the bishopric were not one and the same thing. Of that total, 15,000 *livres* was money borrowed by the bishop.[89] The same pattern is evident in the returns for 1643, which amounted to 45,696 *livres*, but 9,000 *livres* of that came from the late Bishop Clausse's estate and were earmarked for repairs to the bishop's residence.[90] Moreover, both of these accounts included income from personal property and other benefices belonging to Bishop Vialart. A declaration of revenues prepared in June 1640 provides a more realistic perspective, one which may of course be understating the value of the bishopric, but the distortion was probably not excessive. The actual annual income was given as 17,482 *livres*, with 7,200 *livres* coming from timber sales alone. Tithe returns had fallen by 3,500 *livres* to 1,500 *livres* because of war damage in Lorraine. The fixed costs of the see stood at 2,040

---

86 *Ibid*, G 252, notarised declaration by *fermiers* in respect of the lease, 3 June 1625.
87 *Ibid*, G 329, accounts for June 1626–June 1627. The largest of these *rentes*, worth 1,200 *livres* a year, was payable by the Paris *hôtel de ville* from the proceeds of the clerical *décimes*.
88 *Ibid*, G 331, Dec 1628–Dec 1629. For the previous year's total of 20,369 *livres*, an entry of 3,330 *livres* may be subtracted: G 330, 11 Dec 1627 to 25 Dec 1628. The accounts for these years included items of personal property and other benefices held by Bishop Clausse, so that these need to be identified and excluded from the episcopal returns.
89 *Ibid*, G 334, accounts for the period between May 1639 and Sept 1640.
90 *Ibid*, G 337, three sets of accounts for 1643, only one of which was mentioned in the printed inventory of the G series.

livres, leaving a net revenue at just over 15,440 *livres*.[91] Now this figure is not wildly different from that of 14,000 *livres* declared to the Assembly of Clergy the following year, from that of 15,000 *livres* 'at most' suggested by witnesses giving evidence in the 1641 enquiry into the vacant diocese, or from that of the 16,000 *livres* to be found in the *Pouillé Royal* of 1648.

By then there was a new bishop, Félix Vialart. He showed no inclination to resort to a *ferme générale*, and instead appointed a trusted priest as his principal receiver. The austere Vialart, who would often be viewed as a virtual Jansenist by some contemporaries, may well have held strict views on the proper way to administer church property. At any rate, by 1645, total annual receipts had fallen back sharply from the inflated figures of 1640 and 1643 to something nearer to earlier levels, and ranged between 20,498 and 28,310 *livres* from 1645 to 1649 inclusive.[92] Borrowings have already been mentioned, and in 1646, the receiver employed the term *deniers extraordinaires* for the first time to indicate this and analogous sources of income. Moreover, each year sums varying betwen 3,000 and 5,000 *livres* were entered as receipts, when they are actually sums due by the receivers from earlier years. It seems fair to say, therefore, that real revenues were probably not much in excess of 20,000 to 24,000 *livres* at most per year. This hypothesis seems to be borne out by the performance of key sources of revenue during these years. The stability of the value of properties granted in leases is unmistakable. The *ferme générale* of 1625–31 was, it will be recalled, valued at 12,500 *livres*, but in the 1640s, when there is no sign of a general lease, the properties held in individual leases were bringing in remarkably similar and unvarying amounts of money – 11,134 *livres* in 1646, 12,675 *livres* in 1647, 12,897 *livres* in 1648, 12,264 *livres* in 1649. The sale of timber from the *coupes ordinaires* varied rather more than this, and contributed a substantial proportion of the overall income, with annual figures fluctuating between 5,000 and 7,460 *livres*; sales of grain and wine grossed sums varying from 900 to 2,119 *livres* during the same years.[93]

There is, unfortunately, no way of measuring the effects of the Fronde and the resumption of war thereafter on Châlons, but it was probably limited. A sole surviving account for 1655 shows that revenues (minus *deniers extraordinaires* and arrears) amounted to about 21,000 *livres*, which would tally fairly closely with a detailed breakdown of the bishopric's leases compiled a year or so previously, and which valued them at 18,500 *livres*.[94] Ten years

91 *Ibid*, G 253, declaration dated 26 June 1640. The purpose of this statement is not indicated, but it may have been for submission to the Assembly of Clergy of 1641.
92 *Ibid*, G 339–43, accounts for the years 1645 to 1649.
93 Figures derived from AD Marne, G 339–43 inclusive, annual accounts for the years 1645 to 1649.
94 *Ibid*, G 345, account for 1655; *ibid*, G 253, 'Estat des biens qui font le domaine de l'Evesché de Chaalons et les noms de ceux qui les tiennent', n.d. but ca late 1653. Leases never accounted for the totality of revenues, either 'spiritual' or 'temporal', so the difference would have been made up from sources excluded from leases.

later, in 1664, receipts from leases totalled 20,614 *livres*. By 1680 however, the year of Vialart's death, a *ferme générale* was again in operation, and was valued at 30,500 *livres*. Vialart had obviously managed to raise revenues substantially since the 1650s, but the improvement could not be sustained in the adverse economic climate of the 1680s, and a new *ferme générale* was negotiated in 1684 for 24,500 *livres* a year.[95]

In purely nominal terms, therefore, the bishop of Châlons's revenues had at least doubled in over three-quarters of a century. Its relative ranking also improved, though it continued to rank among the middling sees as far as revenues were concerned. Even prolonged episcopal tenure could not of itself produce spectacular financial results. Ultimately, it was Châlons's peerage rather than its revenues which continued to make it attractive to bishops of high social standing: after Vialart's death in 1680 it was held by two Noailles brothers, followed in 1719 by a Saulx-Tavannes.

The condition of the neighbouring see of Reims forms a sharp contrast in many respects. Its prestige was in keeping with its archiepiscopal and primatial status, its peerage, and its historic associations with the French monarchy thanks to the coronation of generations of kings there. Its archbishops had always been leading ecclesiastical figures and, with members of the Guise family ensconced there throughout the sixteenth century, political figures, too. The point is not irrelevant, since Reims's 'temporal' fortunes were closely tied to the identity of those who held the title of archbishop.[96] For two brief periods between 1594 and 1605 and again from 1622 to 1628, it slipped from Guise hands. On each occasion the status of the abbey of Saint-Rémy, whose revenues exceeded that of the see of Reims itself, was disputed, with the Guises claiming it was separate from Reims, though they had been instrumental in having it formally attached to the archbishopric in 1555! After 1594 another powerful interest, the Protestant duc de Bouillon, demanded it for his son, and only returned it to the archbishop in 1601; but in doing so, he reserved such a massive pension on it that it was apparently worth only 600 *livres* a year to the archbishop.[97] The Guise family managed to retain the abbey in 1622 when William Gifford became archbishop of Reims. Separation occurred again in 1641, after the last Guise archbishop was deposed, but this time it was their relatives, the Savoie-Nemours, who gained possession of Saint-Rémy. Indeed, it probably did much to ensure that when Archbishop Etampes died in 1651, it was Saint-Rémy's abbot *in commendam*,

---

95 *Ibid*, G 253, 'recette des baux suivant le compte de 1664'; *ibid*, 'estat des biens et charges, 1680'; G 252, 18 Feb 1684, six-year lease by Bishop Noailles at 24,500 *livres* a year.

96 What follows is largely drawn from my earlier articles, 'The Decline and Fall of the House of Guise as an Ecclesiastical Dynasty', *Historical Journal*, 25 (1982), 781–803; 'The Guises and their Benefices 1588–1641', *English Historical Review*, 99 (1984), 34–58. Unless otherwise cited, all references are to material contained in these articles.

97 AD Marne, 2 G 161, no 18, lease of 28 Feb 1601. The pension of 8,000 *livres* was payable to Bouillon's son, and to make sure nothing would go awry, the *fermier* of Saint-Rémy was a Bouillon dependent, Charles Deshayes, *procureur général* at Sedan.

Henri de Savoie-Nemours, duc d'Aumale, who was nominated the next archbishop of Reims. Even when he subsequently resigned his title to Cardinal Antonio Barberini in 1657, Aumale retained control of Saint-Rémy. Thus, possession of Saint-Rémy, which in turn depended heavily on the politics of ecclesiastical patronage, meant that 'Reims' signified different things at different times, and that its value to an archbishop could vary considerably.

But this was not the only factor affecting the financial standing of Reims. Guise mismanagement was a characteristic feature of the first four decades of the century. It began, in all likelihood, with a legacy of debts and obligations from the League years, and was compounded by the chronic inability of the last two Guise archbishops to live within their means. The outcome was a long list of grants, temporary or long term, of parts of Reims's temporalities in order to satisfy servants, clients, and financial officials, all of whom were creditors in varying degrees. This was certainly not conducive to the kind of management that would improve its revenues, though between 1607 and 1614, a special royal commissioner worked hard to revoke illegal grants and recover other alienated items. It was particularly ironic that the Guises should claim in 1626 that only a Guise archbishop could effectively defend Reims's temporalities against predators and usurpers.[98]

Fermes générales were the norm throughout these early decades of the century. They enable us to plot the overall trend of Reims's revenues, though it should be noted that the *fermiers généraux* were almost invariably major creditors, which put them in a very strong bargaining position when terms were negotiated. For example, it was they who enjoyed the important, and probably profitable, right to renegotiate sub-leases on their own terms during the duration of their *fermes*. Here, a *ferme générale* was more a mechanism for the management of debt and credit needs than for the improvement of the bishopric's financial condition, though a generally favourable economic context did enable revenues to recover significantly. A first lease of Reims and Saint-Rémy in 1605 was valued at just 14,200 *livres* net; ten years later, thanks probably to the royal commissioner's work, their combined value was 35,828 *livres*, with Reims itself being valued at 23,677 *livres*. Both valuations were probably excessively high, as is evident from the fact that Reims was leased on its own by its new archbishop in 1623 for just 14,575 *livres* net. Ten years later again, in 1633, the revenues of Reims were evaluated at 20,655 *livres* in the final year of a *bail général*.[99] But by the mid-1630s, the young archbishop, Henri de Guise, admitted to being virtually bankrupt, and was later accused of dilapidating the valuable forests of Reims in order to raise ready cash. When he fled to Sedan and joined a revolt against Louis XIII in 1640, Reims and his other benefices were sequestrated and administered by a

---

98   ASV, Acta Camerarii 16, fos 190v-1r, records of consistory of 14 June 1627.
99   AD Marne, 2 G 32, 'estat du revenu' for 1633.

royal commissioner who seems to have spent considerable time and resources in putting them back on a normal footing. He valued Reims at 18,000 *livres*, and it was in fact declared at 22,000 *livres* to the 1641 assembly of clergy.

The real beneficiary of the commissioner's labours was the incoming archbishop, Léonor d'Etampes, formerly bishop of Chartres and a close associate of Richelieu until his disgrace in 1642. Though celebrated for his personal profligacy, Etampes was also an efficient administrator. There was plenty of scope for his talents, coming after long periods of relative neglect, and it was doubtless not hard to improve on the Guise record. In 1643 and subsequent years, according to a later account, his receiver reported record receipts from Reims (Saint-Rémy being in other hands), varying between 31,000 and 32,000 *livres*, minus about 3,500 *livres* for fixed costs – a change, albeit temporary, in fortunes that was reflected in the entry of 30,000 *livres* in the *Pouillé Royal* of 1648.[100] There is no direct evidence of how such returns were achieved, but it is probable that Etampes acted energetically to raise subleases and to recover properties alienated or granted on excessively easy terms. But the effort was not sustainable, as the subsequent fall in the value of subleases suggests, and continuing war damage clearly did not help. By the mid-1650s the overall returns had slipped back to just under 18,500 *livres* net.[101] Cardinal Barberini, his successor, signed a new *ferme générale* in 1657 at 19,000 *livres* a year, with excluded items valued at an additional 3,400 *livres*.[102] The return of peace, here too, undoubtedly helped Barberini's officials to do better, and by 1664 they declared the revenues to stand at 22,487 with another 4,200 *livres* to be added.[103] It was, incidentally, in the same year that the intendant Larcher reported Reims to be worth 24,000 *livres*.[104] But it would take the long-serving Charles-Maurice le Tellier (1671–1710) to apply his family's remarkable administrative skills to the ecclesiastical sphere, and he lost no time in doing so after Barberini's death in 1671. By 1673, he had already raised the revenues to just over 35,000 *livres* net; fifty years later, the lease of Reims (not taking into account the abbey of Saint-Thierry which was by then joined to it) was worth over about 45,000 *livres*.[105] If still not one of

100   *Ibid*, 2 G 32, no 9, 'Estat des despandances et revenu de l'archevesché de Reims dressé par ordre de Son Eminence en 1664'. Antonio Barberini was archbishop of Reims at this time.
101   *Ibid*, 2 G 32, no 8, 'Estat du revenu de Reims', 1657: total 18,473 *livres*.
102   *Ibid*, 2 G 32, undated memorandum: 'le bail faict par Monsgr le Cardinal à M Auger porte qu'il doibt rendre par an outre les charges 19,000 livres . . . il ne doubt point avoir le greffe du bailliage, celuy de l'officialité ny le gros registre, et les sceaux du secretariat et vicariat estimés 3,400 *livres* . . . '
103   *Ibid*, 2 G 32, no 9, 'Estat des despandances et revenu de l'archevesché de Reims dressé par ordre de Son Eminence en 1664.'
104   *L'Intendance de Champagne à la fin du xviie siècle*, ed Brancourt, 115.
105   AD Marne, 2 G 31, lease of Reims and Saint-Thierry for 60,000 *livres* (1722), for 65,000 *livres* (1741). The revenues of Saint-Thierry probably varied between 12,000 to 15,000 *livres*. The figure suggested for Reims would thus correlate closely with that of 46,100 *livres* to be found in the records of the royal *économats*, as given in Norman Ravitch, *Sword and Mitre: Government and Episcopacy in France and England in the Age of Aristocracy* (The Hague 1966), p 220.

France's richest sees, the revenues of Reims were no longer as out of line with its status as had been the case a century earlier.

The southern archdiocese of Toulouse appears to have experienced as many ups-and-downs as Reims, but in a rather different time-scale. Unusually, the evidence here consists almost totally of a profusion of raw data, but with virtually no contemporary commentary on the problems encountered or the strategies used in managing its revenues. For that reason, it may be best to present the data in tabular form before attempting to evaluate their significance.

Revenues of archbishopric of Toulouse 1595–1675

1595: 34,100	1648: 52,283
1597: 39,992	1649: 56,330
1598: 49,643	1650: 59,581
1599: 42,949	1651: 73,120
1600: no return	1652: 82,125
1601: 21,391	1653: 67,600
...	1654: 68,670
1605: 58,495	1655: 43,166
1608: 51,397	1656: 50,988
1609: 51,777	1657: 38,330
1610: 50,027	1658: 36,232
1612: 34,996	1659: 46,311
1613: 19,799	1660: 43,736
1615: 23,669	1661: 41,605
1616: 29,703	1662: 58,533
1617: 34,475	1663: 53,053
1618: 44,041	1664: 62,290
1619: 48,702	1665: 45,280
1620: 54,184	1666: 52,968
1621: 43,986	1667: 44,447
1622: 58,437	1668: 30,895
1623: 46,069	1669: 41,260
1624: 44,479	1670: 47,100
1625: 42,063	1671: 44,875
1626: no return	1672: 45,158
1627: 44,875	1673: 38,490
1628: 56,344	1674: 40,695
1629: 49,273	1675: 42,774

Despite the scarcity of non-quantitative evidence with which to interpret these figures, a few observations about them are in order. The first point is how high the revenues were in the late 1590s, despite the damage that the final struggles of the League in the diocese must have caused. The control exercised by Cardinal Joyeuse and his allies in and around Toulouse probably explains a trend which defies the experience of numerous other dioceses at this juncture. Toulouse in the 1590s was unmistakably among the three or four richest dioceses of France, and the figures for the later years of Henri IV's reign show that its returns kept on rising. The first steep drop in the returns were in fact the result of an episcopal succession which, between 1612 and 1616, saw the retiring archbishop, Cardinal Joyeuse, reserve most of the revenues for himself. The resignation of his successor, Cardinal La Valette, in 1627 had the same effect, since he left his successor, Charles de Montchal, with an annual pension of just 8,000 *livres*; La Valette may also have retained administrative control of the temporalities for a time, possibly turning them over to Montchal's stewardship only in 1629. It is particularly regrettable that no figures at all survive for the decade before and following La Valette's death in 1639. But the fact that for the first half of his episcopate, Montchal was financially dependent on La Valette and his powerful father, Epernon, governor of neighbouring Guyenne, suggests that he was hardly in a position to play the role of the aristocratic churchman that is often attributed to him. However, the figures show his last years (1648–51) were evidently years of abundance when Toulouse's revenues were probably as high as those of any French diocese.

Montchal's successor, Pierre de Marca, could certainly afford to pay the pensions totalling 12,000 *livres* which Mazarin imposed on Toulouse when nominating him as archbishop and about which Marca protested so bitterly. But the all-time record for revenue, that of 82,125 *livres* for 1652, proved impossible to sustain, and was cut to less than half within a few years. Ironically it is the abundant, uninterrupted data – which is so scarce for France's other dioceses – covering the following two decades which is the most difficult to explain satisfactorily. The returns from no fewer than seventy-four individual properties give no indication of how they were administered; if they were leased separately, then the leases appear to have been renewed each year and were, therefore, highly sensitive to local economic fluctuations. This effect would be compounded if the temporalities in question consisted largely of tithes payable in kind, which would be subject to sudden price changes or variations in the quality of harvest. At any rate, the returns show clearly that the rising values of previous years were halted in all but a few cases; those that continued to rise did so only marginally, and the gains were easily wiped out by the often substantial reductions in returns from other properties. Verfeil was the most substantial *seigneurie* belonging to the archbishop, and may be representative of the general trend, despite its unexplained absence from the accounts for the years from 1655 to 1661. It rose in value from 5,300 in 1649 to 9,400 *livres* in the bumper year of 1652, falling back to 8,000 *livres* in 1654. In the decade after 1662, however, when it appears again, its highest return was 5,900 *livres*, with figures in the region of 4,900 to 5,500 *livres* being far more common.[106] By the time Marca abandoned Toulouse for Paris in 1661, it was moving into an age of reduced opulence, even if its overall revenues were unmistakably high enough to make many a reigning bishop envious.

The last of the four cases to be considered here is that of an average diocese with few claims to distinction, Le Puy-en-Velay. Some of its characteristics have already been mentioned in passing, notably the fact that the bishop enjoyed extensive seigneurial and judicial powers in numerous areas of his diocese. As in many other dioceses, the most important sources of revenue were five to six *seigneuries* (with their judicial *greffes*) based in or around the most important towns of this overwhelmingly rural, upland diocese. But otherwise, its temporalities were far more modest than in some of the dioceses we have already seen: Le Puy's most valuable *seigneurie*, Monistrol, was leased for 1,570 *livres* in 1584, and was worth just 2,200 *livres* in 1661. A similar comparison of the returns from just five *seigneuries* between the same dates shows that an aggregate return of 4,130 *livres* for 1584 had risen to 6,378 *livres* by 1661, having been marginally higher at 6,620 *livres* in 1652. Leaving aside comparisons with other dioceses, these figures nevertheless signify a nominal 54 per cent increase for these properties during the period as a whole.

Unfortunately, similar precision is impossible with regard to the overall value of Le Puy to its bishop at any of these dates, and comparison has to be rather more speculative. Some surviving sixteenth-century figures show that, overall, episcopal revenues were remarkably stable, standing at 6,400 *livres* around 1530, 6,200 in 1548, and 6,666 in the early 1550s.[107] The wars of religion, and the accompanying *aliénations* of church properties, took their toll in an area with a strong Protestant presence, making the figure of 6,000 *livres* given by the banker Pourcelet, probably around the time of Jacques de Serres's nomination in the late 1590s, seem quite a plausible total for the revenues of the bishopric under Henri IV. By contrast, Pourcelet's second entry, made possibly when Serres's nephew became coadjutor in the mid-1610s, was for 12,000 *livres*, but this seems too high.[108] More mysterious still is the basis for the 1641 declaration, reproduced by the *Pouillé Royal*, which put the revenues at 20,000 *livres*, a figure not actually reached until about a century later.

The bishops of Le Puy between 1597 and 1640 were Jacques de Serres and his nephew Juste, members of a family that held important posts in the estates

---

106 AD Haute-Garonne, 1 G 726, 'Estat des affermes de l'archevesché depuis 1648, sans compter les lods et ventes.'
107 AD Haute-Loire, G 109, no 15, lease of 1 June 1551. A number of items – *lods et ventes*, fines and confiscations, a number of *greffes*, and visitation fees – were excluded from the lease, which were probably worth between 500 and 1,000 *livres* a year. See Rivet, *Une Ville au xvie siècle: Le Puy-en-Velay*, 176.
108 BN, MS Fr 4328, fo 41r.

of Velay and later as royal judges in the province.[109] But there is little evidence to suggest that either bishop was possessed of especial managerial skills or energy. Admittedly, Jacques de Serres was required to pay an annual pension of 4,000 *livres* to an otherwise unknown priest from Le Puy (who was apparently a *prête-nom* for César d'Aumont, baron de Chappes, a military nobleman), an obligation which probably meant that Serres was left with much less than the two-thirds of the revenues which the papacy had attempted to reserve for him.[110] Such a burden might be regarded as an incentive for a bishop to make administrative and financial changes in order to augment his income, but it is just as probable that it denied him some of the means he would need in order to undertake such changes in the first place.[111] Meanwhile, individual elements of the episcopal domain were regularly leased, overwhelmingly in money rather than in kind, though leases often specified minor dues in kind, such as chickens, grain, cheese, trout and partridges. In fact, very few sources of episcopal income were not leased out, and those which were collected directly were essentially items of 'casual' revenue probably worth no more than 1,000 *livres* a year.[112] As far as can be judged, most leases ran their course. Moreover, those which were terminated early and then replaced by new contracts, a phenomenon which was common enough during the 1630s, show few signs of a conscious drive to raise episcopal revenues.[113]

This is not to say that Juste de Serres was necessarily indolent or uninterested in financial questions, since the estates of Velay, which the bishop presided over *ex officio*, were, like those of Languedoc and other *pays d'états*, closely concerned with fiscal affairs. Indeed, in 1634, the bishop formed a partnership with his *bailli* in order to bid for the *équivalent* tax in Velay when the Languedoc estates came to auction it; the bishop's share in this private venture was to be two-thirds of the investment and the profits.[114] It may be, therefore, that he preferred to seek other ways of finding additional revenue. But he did organise and negotiate terms for a four-year *ferme générale* of the revenues of his bishopric in 1629, valued at 10,000 *livres* a year, but for reasons unknown it never took

109 The principal heir of Bishop Juste de Serres was 'noble Pierre de Serres, seigneur et baron d'Arlempe, juge et lieutenant général au pais de Vivarez et Valentinois' (G 22, fo 40, quittance of 2 Dec 1641).
110 *Hierarchia Catholica*, iv. 85, 'Anicien', n 2. The pensioner was Jean Bouillon, an obscure figure. The identity of the true beneficiary of the pension is to be found in Pourcelet's register, BN, MS Fr 4328, fo 41r. There was, apparently, another pension since the previous bishop's time.
111 Witnesses giving evidence in 1615 before the papal nuncio claimed, with some understandable exaggeration, that the bishop of Le Puy had very little revenue to live off: ASV, PC 13, fos 718–23.
112 AD Haute-Loire, G 776, incomplete (?) register of leases for the years 1597 to 1618; G 110, register of leases for 1619 to 1622.
113 *Ibid*, G 22, fos 509–79, leases for 1627–8; G 777, leases for 1630–9.
114 *Ibid*, G 22, fos 269–70, contract of 8 Mar 1634.

effect.[115] Preparations were made and conditions set out for a second attempt in 1633, but things may have got no further than that.[116]

It was left to his successor, Henri Maupas du Tour, successfully to negotiate and implement the first *ferme générale* of the period.[117] Commenced in 1646, its duration is not known, but its annual value, 10,500 *livres*, shows plainly enough that the bishopric's revenues had barely progressed in nearly two decades. Despite this, it seems certain that Maupas, who as both a newcomer and a northerner was probably disposed to question long-standing arrangements, wanted to achieve more than to simplify the management of his revenues through a *ferme générale*. He disposed of one piece of property in return for an annuity worth nearly twice its previous lease value.[118] A 'memorandum on the increased revenues which can be derived from the temporalities of Le Puy', which appears to date from some point during his episcopate, optimistically claimed that revenues could be augmented by up to 10,000 *livres* through a range of measures from renewing *terriers* and leases to charging the inhabitants for firewood, and obliging seigneurial 'subjects' to perform labour services; the biggest gains of all would be derived from replacing the flat-rate payment (*abonnement*) of tithes with a strict collection of a fixed percentage of actual harvests (*paiement à la gerbe*). But as was pointed out in the memorandum, changes like this were bound to be fiercely resisted by peasants defending customary practice, and lawsuits would be inevitable.[119] Maupas may have made a start of some kind, since in 1658 receipts for *corvées* in one of the principal *seigneuries* appear in the accounts for the first time.[120]

If this signalled an attempt to increase revenues in accordance with the analysis prepared for the bishop, then it was to prove short-lived, at least as far as Maupas was concerned: in July 1661, only months after Mazarin's death, he was transferred to the Norman see of Evreux. Yet even this event provides testimony of how exact – and exacting – seventeenth-century benefice-holders could be. Because of his transfer, Maupas was entitled to a proportion of the revenues of Le Puy for 1661 which was calculated at precisely seven months and eighteen and a half days, and this in turn necessitated an accurate set of accounts for the year. The total revenue for the year was given as 13,801 *livres*,

115 *Ibid*, G 23, fo 13, notarial act of 18 Jan 1633 cancelling the *ferme générale*, the actual text of which has not been found.
116 *Ibid*, G 107, no 9, 'Pactes et conditions soubs lesquelles Msgr... pretend affermer generallement les revenus temporelz de son Evesché et Conté'. One of these clauses gives the starting date as St John's Day 1633. This document shows numerous corrections and annotations, and is not proof that a lease was ever actually signed.
117 *Ibid*, G 23, fo 66, 25 July 1646, reference to general lease signed on 23 Apr 1646.
118 *Ibid*, G 775, undated memorandum, probably early eighteenth century.
119 *Ibid*, G 107, no 9. Bishop Juste de Serres had made an initial attempt to change tithe arrangements and won an initial lawsuit, only to find the case proceeded to the parlement of Paris where 'la chose est demeurée indécise.'
120 *Ibid*, G 113, fo 1, 'estat des revenus de l'evesché du Puy pour 6 années la première commençant à la feste de St Jean Baptiste 1658'.

and the pension of 3,000 *livres* reserved for Maupas on leaving Le Puy, corresponded approximately to the increase in revenue that his twenty-year episcopate had witnessed.[121]

Reviewing the financial history of these four dioceses, it is easier to identify differences than similarities. Yet a number of general points can be made. In all but one case, it is likely that episcopal revenues were abnormally low at the end of the religious wars, but that they benefited from the improved economic conditions of the following decades. Yet that did not necessarily lead to spectacular rises in revenues. Moreover, the extent to which individual dioceses began experiencing economic adversity in the 1630s or later was almost certainly not uniform. Diligent management by resident bishops could also make a difference in both good and bad times, but it does seem that by the 1640s or 1650s it became especially difficult to sustain, let alone improve on, the rise in revenues achieved in previous decades. This was in spite of the fact that French bishops do not appear to have been impeded in their attempts to raise their incomes by leasing practices that would prevent them from seeking to extract realistic rents or, unlike their English counterparts, to have had to avoid falling foul of potentially dangerous lessees drawn from the ranks of the nobility and aristocracy.[122] Unpredictable personal factors, such as the turnover of bishops, could also take a hand, leading to changes in financial administration, changes which the surviving documentation does not always adequately reveal. In the end, the most fruitful comparisons may not be between dioceses at all, but between episcopal temporalities and those of chapters and abbeys. It was their uninterrupted institutional continuity which enabled the latter to achieve often spectacular results in managing their temporalities, as has been demonstrated for some of the Languedoc chapters.[123] Even the most determined bishops were frequently absent from their dioceses or otherwise too busy to give the same proverbial attention to maximizing their revenues. Such absences would also characterise the eighteenth-century episcopate, but it seems that by then a sufficient measure of routine administrative control of temporalities had been achieved for personal residence to matter less, at least as far as revenues were concerned, than had been the case in earlier generations.

VI

It may well be objected that figures for episcopal revenues and efforts to increase them are largely meaningless unless expenditure is also taken into account. As might be expected, expenditure was also enormously varied. There is no doubt that bishops were expected to bring honour and respect to

---

121   *Ibid*, G 107, no 7, 'Estat du revenu de l'evesché du Puy de l'année 1661'.
122   Christopher Clay, ' "The Greed of Whig Bishops": Church Landlords and their Lessees 1660–1760', *Past and Present*, 87 (1980), esp 129–30, 135–7.
123   See E Le Roy Ladurie, *Les Paysans de Langudoc*, 2 vols (The Hague 1966), esp ii. 974–5, graph 18, for the rise in the revenues of the chapters of Béziers, Narbonne and Montpellier.

their rank in both church and society by maintaining a suitable household, but also through charitable works, generous hospitality, and other appropriate activities. Many did so, even on a lavish scale, while some were positively spendthrift. But as so often, it is the extreme cases, whether of magnificence or miserliness, which have long been cited by contemporaries and historians. How far is it possible to analyse and quantify the financial obligations of France's bishoprics?

The subject is both daunting and complex, and the potentially infinite variations in the financial behaviour of France's bishops could easily discourage anything beyond superficial curiosity. All that can be attempted here is a preliminary sketch towards an answer. The most useful starting-point for an investigation is to distinguish between the financial commitments which bishops could not avoid in their dioceses and the remaining elements of expenditure which were a matter of personal taste or policy. The first category, that of obligatory expenditure, can in turn be subdivided into essentially two groups – fixed costs (the *charges ordinaires*, as they were called) and the *décimes* payable to the crown. Each group is best analysed separately.

Like so many *ancien régime* terms, that of the *charges ordinaires* can easily mislead. It would be seriously mistaken to imagine that they somehow constituted the normal costs of governing a diocese. For that reason alone, probably no two dioceses had an identical list of *charges ordinaires*, since in every instance they had evolved over the centuries, with both their number and financial value depending on factors such as the relations between bishops and cathedral chapters, the distribution of the clerical tithe, acquisitions of property by bishops, the evolution of hospices or other charitable institutions, and so on.

Briefly, the *charges ordinaires* were the dues, payable either in money or in kind, to an array of individuals and institutions from the cathedral chapter and parish priests to religious houses and officials, hospices, and so on. From the rather patchy sources that are available, it is evident that episcopal practice varied hugely over time, with some bishops intent on reducing the *charges* to a strict minimum, while others allowed them to inflate in numbers, if not necessarily in financial value. For example, successive archbishops of Toulouse consistently limited their *charges ordinaires* to a small number of headings – alms, the hiring of preachers for Advent and Lent, repairs to buildings, salaries to officials, and legal fees – and these seem to have remained remarkably unchanged throughout the years studied here.[124] When evidence was given to the papal nuncio in 1652 that the *charges* of Toulouse amounted to around 13,000 *livres* a year, this was incorrect, as no more than 3,500 *livres* were spent in this way.[125] On the other hand, the most obvious feature of the *charges ordinaires* of Beauvais in the same years is the profusion

---

124   The list of *charges ordinaires* is identical for 1608 (AD Haute-Garonne, 1 G 280) and both 1652 and 1662 (1 G 718).
125   ASV, PC 53, fos 1051–4, enquiry of 6 Nov 1652. The remainder of the 13,000 *livres* went in paying *décimes* to the crown.

of items payable in money and kind. Yet the proportion of episcopal revenues represented by the *charges ordinaires* of Toulouse was more considerable than at Beauvais. On the other hand, nearly 15 per cent of the bishop of Glandèves's income in 1663 went on a single item – the daily allocations to the canons of the cathedral chapter, a charge which did not exist at all in either Toulouse or Beauvais.[126]

It also seems as if some of these expenses had been defined by agreement or arbitration in the past, and subsequently tended to become fixed 'pensions' which did not necessarily coincide any more with the expenses they were originally intended to cover. As pointed out above, nothing could be more mistaken than to imagine the *charges ordinaires* as constituting what might be regarded as the 'core' expenses of a bishop and his administration. In many cases for which evidence survives, many such 'core' expenses are not included at all among the *charges ordinaires* or only partly so, as when the salaries of episcopal office-holders figure among them. When Augustin Potier, the new bishop of Beauvais, leased his temporalities in 1617 for 30,000 *livres* a year, the *charges ordinaires* including salaries to office-holders amounted to around 2,980 *livres* in cash and further payments in kind, in other words the *charges* accounted for about 10 per cent of the annual revenue.[127] The same pattern applies to the see of Châlons-sur-Marne where the *charges ordinaires* oscillated between a mere 977 and 927 *livres* during the first two decades of the century; although they rose somewhat during the 1620s and 1630s, they were still as low as 1,199 *livres* in 1654. Even when paired with the salaries of officials, the combined totals rarely exceeded the 3,635 *livres* disbursed in 1629–30.[128]

This kind of pattern is repeated in several other known cases, with the *charges* amounting to far less in many instances. It is thus reasonable to suggest that in most dioceses the *charges ordinaires* did not exceed one-tenth of episcopal revenues. More extensive comparison is hindered by the very nature of administrative arrangements themselves. It was common practice when temporalities were administered through a *ferme générale*, for the *fermiers* to be made responsible for the payment of all the *charges ordinaires* and the royal *décimes*, but in most cases the contracts simply required them to pay in accordance with existing practice, without specifying the details or sums involved.[129] For all their obligatory character, therefore, the extent to which the *charges ordinaires* contributed to a bishop's costs might be, at best, modest, at worst insignificant.

126 BN, MS 500 Colbert 180, fo 385.
127 AN, MC, LXXXVI 195, lease of 28 Jan 1617, with accompanying 'estat des réserves, charges, redebvances, pensions, augmentations des curez et autres charges nouvelles'.
128 Figures taken from AD Marne, G 309–45, receipts and expenditure accounts 1602–55.
129 In some surviving contracts, the *charges* were laid out in an appendix which formed part of the lease itself; elsewhere, especially when the *fermiers* were renewing a lease, the contract simply stated that the *fermiers* were aware of their obligations and undertook to discharge them.

Particular items in a bishop's list of *charges ordinaires* could become a source of endemic conflict and litigation. Perhaps the best known of these concerns the relative liabilities of bishops and cathedral chapters for the repair and upkeep of the cathedral church itself. With many chapters insisting the cathedral church was under their direct jurisdiction and that it did not really 'belong' to the bishop at all, it is even less surprising that bishops were reluctant to pay more than an absolute minimum towards its upkeep. In the generation or two following the wars of religion, large numbers of French cathedrals were in states of disrepair varying from the extreme to the moderate. Frequently, episcopal residences were in no better state, as many had suffered at the hands of Huguenots or even Catholics during the wars; repairing and rebuilding them was, of course, primarily the bishops' responsibility. It may even be that particular dioceses were unattractive to candidates for the episcopate because of the physical destruction of cathedrals, residences and temporalities generally, especially in the early decades of the century. But the history of the rebuilding of cathedrals, and who paid for them, remains to be written. Individual bishops did contribute generously – but not necessarily because of any unavoidable obligation.[130] Judging by the successive enquiries conducted on behalf of the papacy, which are perhaps not a very accurate yardstick, the progress of rebuilding and repair was sluggish enough. By the late 1620s, the papacy was sufficiently impatient at this slow pace of restoration that it began imposing financial obligations on bishops to pay a specified annual sum over and above what their *charges ordinaires* laid down.[131] The effectiveness of this tactic may be doubted, as it had to be repeated more than once during episcopal successions in some dioceses. Elsewhere, several bishops – Albi, Sarlat, Cahors, and Montauban – in a region which had suffered much damage, protested against papally imposed obligations in the early 1640s, and obtained a discharge from them from the *grand conseil*.[132] These bishops were for the most part keen supporters of religious reform, and some of them probably contributed significantly to the rebuilding process, but from the evidence to hand, it seems as if they were in no mood to allow any

130 For example, in 1656 François Fouquet of Agde was reported as having built a seminary and a hospice at Agde out of his own pocket, and as having restored many places devastated by the wars, but no mention was made of either the cathedral or episcopal residence, despite the fact that in 1643 the papacy had required him to spend 4,000 *livres* on repairs to the cathedral: ASV, PC 55, fos 200v-5v, evidence of the archbishop of Arles, and the bishops of Viviers, Le Puy and Lodève.

131 The papacy's demands, based on the evidence presented in the diocesan enquiries, can be found briefly summarised in the notes relating to French episcopal promotions in *Hierarchia Catholica*, iv.

132 AN, V⁶ 170, decree of 19 Dec. 1642. What seems to have angered the bishops most was the fact that the syndics of the clergy of their dioceses were trying to use the parlements of Toulouse and Bordeaux to force them to pay the sums, varying from 1,000 to 4,000 *livres* a year, imposed by the papacy. The papacy was also trying to require them to found *monts-de-piété*.

back-door additions to be made to their financial obligations in their dioceses.

VII

By contrast, the fiscal obligations of bishops were inherently less susceptible to such tight control. Apart from the obligation to pay annates for their provisions and in contrast to their Spanish counterparts, French bishops entirely escaped the fiscal maw of the papacy.[133] But the demands of the monarchy were a different matter, and the *décimes* were anything but static after their systematic reintroduction in 1561. By 1615 the annual contribution had stabilised at 1.3 million *livres*. However, in 1621 the crown succeeded in extracting the first *don gratuit*, which under Richelieu and Mazarin would yield far more than the *décimes*.[134] It was in 1641 that the crown's financial demands rose most sharply, leading the Assembly of Clergy to revise the assessments which had been in use since 1516. Comparing the revenues declared for each bishopric on that occasion with the *décimes* for which bishops were assessed provides a covenient basis for judgement.[135] The possible margin of error in the revenue figures may be disregarded here, since the issue is the assessment made in response to the declared figures.[136] In the event, comparisons are possible for 106 out of the total of 113 dioceses. It appears that for five dioceses, the *décimes* represented 30 per cent or more of their annual income; for twenty dioceses between 20 and 29 per cent, while not far short of half (forty-nine in all) of them paid between 10 and 19 per cent of their revenues in *décimes*. Over a quarter were fortunate to pay less than 10 per cent to the crown. Boulogne, a poor diocese admittedly, was one of the least-taxed, but that was because most of its sources of revenue were 'hors du royaume'.[137] The map of episcopal *décimes* is also instructive. The great majority of the most heavily taxed dioceses were in southern France: only seven of the twenty-five dioceses paying over 20 per cent of their declared income in this way were located in northern or central France, while approximately 40 per cent of all the *décimes* paid by French bishops in 1641 was accounted for by the bishops of Languedoc and the south-west alone. Even when the superior endowment of many southern dioceses is taken into account this suggests that the southerners' complaint against the injustice of the *décimes'* assessment had at least some foundation in fact. But even here

---

133 See Christian Hermann, *L'Eglise d'Espagne sous le patronage royal* (1476–1834) (Madrid 1988), ch 8 (d).
134 See Pierre Blet, *Le Clergé de France et monarchie*, 2 vols (Rome 1959), i, part II; Claude Michaud, *L'Eglise et l'argent sous l'ancien régime* (Paris 1991).
135 The *décimes* assessments of 1641 are taken from BN, MS Fr 20737–9 which were once part of Charles-Maurice Le Tellier's papers.
136 The figures for revenue are based on AAE, France 841, fos 7–117.
137 BN, MS Fr 20737, fo 130.

there was no real consistency in what we would regard as over- or under-assessment. For example, the wealthy diocese of Toulouse paid less than any of its neighbours, some of whose revenues were less than half those of Toulouse.

As abridgements of episcopal revenues, both the *charges ordinaires* and the *décimes* were characterised by enormous variation. In the most extreme cases, they could between them account for nearly half of a bishop's income; at a minimum they were unlikely to take less than one-fifth. It is not difficult to see why bishops were so anxious to prevent them from expanding further. Conflicts between bishops and local ecclesiastical institutions over questions like cathedral repairs or annuities payable to hospices or religious houses also arose in part from a wish to keep the *charges ordinaires* under control, and they frequently won bishops a reputation for miserliness. The same concern may be less obvious in the case of the *décimes*, which sprang from royal fiscal needs. But as is well known, successive Assemblies of Clergy fought resolutely to keep royal demands in check. And it may also be that the assessments made both at the assemblies and in the diocesan *bureaux des décimes* were biased in favour of the bishops who dominated their proceedings.

At any rate, it was thanks in part to efforts of this kind that the financial position of France's bishops improved in relative terms as the seventeenth century progressed. With fuller and more accurate information on both revenues and *charges* it would doubtless be possible to devise a league-table of France's dioceses, from the richest and most attractive to the poorest. But even that would not take account of the individuals who entered the episcopate from one generation to the next. The fact is that the more the episcopate was dominated by sons of the nobility, the more likely its members were to possess other benefices *in commendam* before and during their tenure of office, and that these benefices were at times more valuable financially than their dioceses. And this factor, which probably did more than any other to distinguish the French episcopate from its European counterparts, almost certainly exerted a considerable influence on the attitudes of French clerics in search of the rank of bishop.

CHAPTER 4

Bishops, Pensions and Pensioners

IN CONSIDERING BOTH the making of bishops and the question of the attractiveness, financial or otherwise, of particular bishoprics, it would be mistaken to imagine that selecting a bishop was simply a matter of finding the most acceptable 'fit' between a particular candidate for the mitre and a vacant diocese. In a large number of cases, a range of what can only be called 'interests' combined to determine not merely who would obtain a particular bishopric, but under which conditions. The imposition of pensions on the revenues of bishoprics was among the most widely used ways of enlarging royal ecclesiastical patronage in both its patronage-as-process and patronage-as-benefits dimensions. It achieved the second objective by increasing the number of those entitled to share in the revenues attached to the sees in question. For that reason also, no discussion of episcopal income and expenditure would be complete without taking account of these pensions, which were far more arbitrary in their impact on episcopal finances since they were not subject to the same degree of control as the *charges ordinaires* or the *décimes*. As we shall see, they also varied enormously during the period under discussion, but unlike most of the other claims on episcopal revenues, it was not in response to economic change or local exigencies.

A study of the pensions imposed by the crown, with papal approval, on bishoprics may not seem either promising or important, but perhaps more than any of the issues discussed so far, it serves to connect the subject of episcopal revenues to the wider issues of patronage and control which will be raised in later chapters. At the most basic level, pensions, granted for life, were a pointed reminder that episcopal revenues were not exclusively reserved for bishops, even if at different times both individual bishops and dioceses might escape having to pay them. Moreover, the changing characteristics of episcopal pensions are in some respects a microcosm of the changing fortunes – and not merely economic – of the episcopate generally in its relations with the upper levels of French society, and above all with the crown. They were one of the most important means by which church wealth could be diverted, not to the royal treasury, but into the pockets of clerics and families whose identities changed over the years. In short, they can be seen as one of the classic options available to a monarchy whose ability to tap directly into clerical wealth was as limited as its capacity to tax the wealth of the better-off in French society generally. Royal episcopal patronage was not limited merely to nominating bishops who then went on to become lords of their dioceses. Indeed, as we shall discover, in certain circumstances this perspective can be turned on its head: the grant of one or more pensions might be the strongest indication of who was the real master of the diocese in question. Where that is the case, the history of pensions becomes essential to understanding the nature of both royal patronage and episcopal tenure.

Sixteenth-century – or even earlier – precedents in regard to episcopal pensions have not been satisfactorily elucidated by existing studies. There are several reasons for this state of affairs. One of the most banal is that, quite simply, pensions were not always fully recorded, even in the papal archives most directly concerned with episcopal appointments. Although the quality of the records had improved considerably by the seventeenth century, gaps remain, while even improved sources cannot alter the fact that comparison with earlier generations is extremely hazardous.[1] A more fundamental reason for the lack of clarity is that for centuries, church law had shown considerable suspicion towards the imposition of pensions on benefices. That suspicion was not based simply on material considerations, but on the assumption that individuals would hardly agree spontaneously to sacrifice part of their rights without the application of undue pressure or coercive force. This was the principal reason why pensions were virtually always imposed when sees were vacant, since it was at that point that candidates for the succession could be effectively pressed into consenting to them. It may be added that similarly strong suspicion centred on resignations, which often entailed the establishment of pensions, because of a fear of simony, an offence which involved the buying or selling of ecclesiastical preferment.[2]

This concern with the notionally 'free' character of pensions could extend further still. It was the main reason for strong opposition to the idea that pensions might be redeemed through buying out the pensioner with a capital sum set at several times (five or seven, for example) the annual value of the pension. Created voluntarily, a pension should only cease by voluntary resignation or death. In reality, it seems that redemption was sometimes informally practised: in 1638, Bishop Godeau was warned that his pension off

---

1 *Hierarchica Catholica*, iii-iv is the most widely available source of information on pensions; the material it contain is taken from the overlapping, but neither complete nor systematic, subseries which together make up the archives of the papal consistory. A fully accurate listing of all pensions would require exhaustive research on the minutes of the bulls of provision in the Vatican Archives.
2 See *Dictionnaire de droit canonique*, ed R Naz (Paris 1935–65), ii. cols 407–49, 'Bénéfices en Occident'; *ibid*, vi. cols 1346–53, 'pensions ecclésiastiques'; Jean Bernhard, Charles Lefebvre, Francis Rapp, *L'Epoque de la Réforme et du concile de Trente* (*Histoire du droit et des institutions de l'église en Occident*, xiv) (Paris 1989), 327ff.

Cahors might suddenly be terminated if the bishop of Cahors followed the recent example of another bishop in buying out his pensioner with a lump sum worth five times the pension's annual value.³ However, Rome, which ultimately controlled the whole process of creating pensions, was anxious to preserve the legal forms, even though it was not consistent in upholding them in other parts of Europe.⁴ Thus, when the crown imposed a pension of 4,000 *livres* on Grenoble in 1607, and declared it redeemable for the sum of 12,000 *livres*, Rome simply rejected the arrangement as it stood on the grounds of manifest simony.⁵ More generally, this was also the reason why the approval of resignations – and, by extension, of pensions – was reserved to the pope, since only he could nullify the standing suspicion of simony which they carried with them. Because of these elaborate institutional precautions, pensions themselves came to be treated virtually as benefices, requiring a royal *brevet de nomination*, papal provisions, and the payment of annate-like fees to the curia. Incoming or sitting bishops had to give explicit consent to new pensions before a notary, and their procuration was despatched to Rome, along with the other papers necessary for their confirmation in consistory.⁶

It seems that pensions began to increase dramatically throughout Europe from about the late fifteenth century onwards. It was apparently the curia, and its cardinals in particular, who showed the way, and in their search for the means to sustain a more expensive lifestyle they did not confine their attention simply to Italian churches.⁷ The cumulative effect of this development was to trigger, firstly criticism and, then, attempts at regulation and reform, both at Trent and later; the objective was not so much to abolish pensions

3 BN, MS Naf 1885, fo 250, Jean Chapelain to Godeau, 26 Feb 1638. The other bishop referred to by Chapelain was La Fayette of Limoges. Such private acts of redemption are an additional reason why calculating the total year-on-year value of pensions off bishoprics is impractical. I would like to thank Christian Jouhaud for this reference.

4 See Dante Ughetti, *François d'Amboise (1550–1619)* (Rome 1974), 413–14, two notarial acts, 8 Jan. 1609, in which Jean Bertaut, bishop of Séez, redeemed a pension of 600 *livres* payable to Thomas de Franchini, intendant of the royal fountains, for the sum of 3,000 *livres*. See also BN, MS Naf 1885, fos 250–1, Jean Chapelain to Antoine Godeau, 26 Feb 1638, for a reference to the redemption of a pension by the bishop of Limoges at five times its annual value. For the situation in the Venetian Republic, where the curia's interests were of a different order, see Antonio Menniti Ippolito, *Politica e carriere ecclesiastiche nel secolo xvii. I vescovi veneti fra Roma e Venezia* (Bologna 1993), esp 74–92.

5 BN, MS Fr 18002, fo 161, Halincourt, French ambassador in Rome, to Henri IV, 2 May 1607. The papacy was not opposed to a pension per se, but to the conditions attached to it, which raised questions about its voluntary character.

6 During the period covered by this book, perhaps the majority of these acts of consent and procuration were drawn up before apostolic rather than royal notaries, and no trace exists of their archives, particularly in Paris where the most active apostolic notaries were to be found.

7 See Mario Rosa 'Curia Romana e pensioni ecclesiastiche: fiscalità pontificia nel Mezzogiorno (secoli xvi-xviii)', *Quaderni Storici*, 42 (1979), 1015–55; Barbara McClung Hallmann, *Italian Cardinals, Reform and the Church as Property 1492–1563* (Los Angeles 1985), esp ch 1; Christian Hermann, *L'Eglise d'Espagne sous le patronage royal (1476–1834)* (Madrid 1988), ch 8.

outright but to impose an upper limit on their value in relation to the revenues of the benefices subjected to them.[8] Needless to say, once it had taken root, the practice of imposing pensions tended to develop its own momentum, and therefore to draw continuing, hostile comment. Writing shortly after the crisis of Venice's relations with Rome in 1606–7, Paolo Sarpi went as far as to denounce the imposition of pensions as nothing less than an alternative method for the papal curia to remain the *dominus beneficiorum*, despite the measures taken by Trent to reform the workings of the benefice system generally.[9] It does not appear as if any such criticism was levelled at the French monarchy over the pensions it imposed on bishoprics, though there was extreme unease in some clerical circles about what it seemed willing to tolerate, in the reign of Henri IV in particular. But the question implied in Sarpi's anticurial outburst may be rephrased and pruned of its polemical intent – how far did the crown use pensions as part of its control of high-level benefices, or in order to acquire such control?

I

Sixteenth-century France was not unfamiliar with pensions on bishoprics; some of them were regarded as uncontentious, especially where retiring bishops retained a share of a see's revenues for their old age. But it was probably the practice of episcopal pluralism, especially during the first three-quarters of the century, which did most to stimulate the growth in pensions. With both French bishops and absentee Italian cardinals frequently exchanging or resigning dioceses in rapid succession, the practice of 'reserving' a major part, or all, of their revenues, with the exception of a modest stipend for the incoming bishop, became familiar from at least the reign of François I onwards. Taken to extremes, it clearly subverted the normal bishop-diocese-pensioner relationship, and threatened to reduce serving bishops to the status of poorly endowed pensioners, dependent on opulent and well connected patrons who remained the real 'lords' of their bishoprics. Episcopal pluralism might have been on the wane by the 1570s, but as has been noted, one immediate side-effect was that those who had previously held several bishoprics at the same time now reserved very substantial pensions for themselves on resigning them, and individual dioceses could owe several such pensions to senior ecclesiastical figures.[10] Moreover, it seems likely that the rapid turnover of bishops in certain dioceses in mid-century had something to

8 Adrien Clergeac, *La Curie et les bénéfices consistoriaux. Etude sur les communs et menus services 1300–1600* (Paris 1911), 109.
9 Rosa, 'Curia romana e pensioni', 1015–17, quoting from Sarpi's *Trattato delle materie beneficiarie*, written around 1608–9.
10 Frederic J Baumgartner, *Change and Continuity in the French Episcopate. The Bishops and the Wars of Religion* (Durham, NC 1986), 64–5.

do with the precarious status of new bishops who were not really masters of their dioceses, and who may, as a result, have quickly moved elsewhere or turned their backs on an episcopal career altogether. The easier it was to hand around bishoprics and pensions in this way, usually within families or clientèles, the more obvious became their purely 'maintenance' functions to those concerned. For the most part, it appears that these kinds of favours were largely confined to cardinals and other leading bishops with good political connections and, consequently, to the relatively wealthy dioceses which passed through their hands.

Furthermore, it would seem that for much of the sixteenth century, the crown played a largely permissive, if not quite passive, role where pensions were concerned, except perhaps in its dealings with Italian and curial prelates, whom it wished to cultivate for political reasons. There is little evidence that it was particularly concerned with either limiting or controlling the phenomenon, perhaps because the main practitioners were drawn from the upper ranks of the upper clergy. Here, too, comparison with developments in churches in other countries is enlightening. In areas of southern Italy where the papacy still retained extensive patronage rights, Mario Rosa discovered that from the mid-sixteenth century onwards, not only was the number of bishoprics subject to pensions continually expanding, but the percentage of their revenues being diverted in this way gradually rose from one-tenth to one-quarter; it was to climb considerably higher in the next century, despite the papacy's own rules on pensions, with curia-based clergy as the main beneficiaries.[11] The Spanish kings had for centuries successfully invoked their status as a crusading force against Islam to win more extensive fiscal rights over the churches of the peninsula than their French counterparts. But it was the papacy which, from the late fifteenth century onwards, was instrumental in imposing pensions on Spanish benefices, bishoprics included. From 1523 onwards, in addition to nominating bishops for papal approval, Charles V and his successors were entitled to propose pensions of up to one-third of the revenues of the bishoprics in question. With the exception of a small number of dioceses that remained effectively exempt on the grounds of their inadequate revenues, all the remaining forty Spanish dioceses of the day were subjected to pensions between 1520 and 1564. The Spanish crown's systematic approach is even more evident in that it required bishops who were exempt from pensions nevertheless formally to acknowledge the crown's right to levy a pension on their sees. More to the point, it also obliged episcopal administrators to send the accounts of bishoprics for the five years preceding a vacancy, so as to enable royal officials to calculate as accurately as possible the total value of the pensions to be imposed on the diocese and, if appropriate, to add to the value of existing pensions. Some dioceses saw one-third

---

11 Rosa, 'Curia romana e pensioni', 1037–48; idem, 'Diocesi e vescovi del Mezzogiorno durante il viceregno spagnolo: Capitanata, Terra di Bari e Terra d'Otranto dal 1545 al 1714', in *Studi in onore di Gabriele Pepe* (Naples 1970), 531–80, at p 535.

of their revenues diverted into pensions, others one-quarter; tables listing bishoprics by pensionable category were even published in the late sixteenth or early seventeenth century, though in practice there was greater flexibility between the categories than official lists would suggest.[12]

The contemporary French monarchy, on the other hand, does not appear even to have considered such a systematic extension of its patronage to all dioceses, let alone to make the detailed administrative arrangements this would have required. In any case, it may have felt under less pressure, for a time at least, than its Spanish counterpart to look to pensions as an attractive source of additional largesse, since it had at its disposal over twice the amount of episcopal patronage, not forgetting the far greater, and still growing, number of abbeys and priories tenable *in commendam* which were also in its gift.

In some ways, the experiences of the wars of religion may have further highlighted the attractiveness of pensions to seekers after church patronage, and to Italian clerics in particular. With church property suddenly vulnerable to attack and usurpation, with revenues falling and difficult to collect, a fixed pension payable by a named benefice, especially a bishopric, could seem all the more attractive. The appeal of pensions was further enhanced by the fact that a given place of payment could be stipulated, Lyon being popular with Italians for obvious reasons. What made pensions even more attractive to allcomers was the fact that they were wholly free from the *charges ordinaires* and *décimes* for which bishops and benefice-holders generally were liable. The pensioner's only real worry was, therefore, to ensure that the holder of the benefice in question would honour his obligation to pay on a regular basis. Of course, *mauvais payeurs* were not uncommon in the period we are considering, and litigation over pensions between members of the French clergy was not uncommon.[13]

Rather more serious than this was another shift set in train by the wars of religion – the granting of pensions off bishoprics to laymen. The practice was slow to emerge into the open, because it was held to be a serious departure from normal church practice. But in view of the demands of the nobility and the indulgence of the crown towards them under Charles IX and Henri III, it is hardly surprising that the question should have come to preoccupy the clergy. The Assembly of Clergy held at Melun in 1579–80 was the first to attempt a systematic condemnation of these abuses, proposing that newly

---

12 Hermann, *Eglise d'Espagne sous le patronage royal*, ch 8; Ivan Cloulas, 'La Monarchie catholique et les revenus épiscopaux: les pensions sur les mitres de Castille pendant le règne de Philippe II', *Mélanges de la Casa de Velázquez*, 4 (1968), 107–42.

13 BN, MS Naf 1885, fos 250–1, Jean Chapelain to Antoine Godeau, 26 Feb 1638, for a fascinating discussion of the pros and cons of pensions versus simple benefices, which was occasioned by the grant of a pension of 2,000 livres off the revenues of Cahors by Louis XIII to Godeau. Chapelain's own preference was for benefices, but only, it appears, if they were 'proches de soy'.

appointed bishops should take an oath before their cathedral chapter declaring that not only had they not engaged in simony to obtain their see, but that they were not required to pay pensions to laymen. The assembly's general preoccupations were given added point by a specific complaint recorded in its deliberations, one which illustrates the problems facing individual bishops at this point. The bishop of Marseille admitted that he had given his consent a few years earlier to a pension off its revenues for the comte de Tende-Savoie, governor of Provence, but claimed that he had only done so in order to be sure of obtaining his papal provisions. By 1579 Tende was dead, and in law his pension should have died with him, but his widow was now demanding that the pension be paid to her in her husband's place. The extorting of pensions by powerful laymen in this way must have appeared bad enough to the clerical deputies, but the prospect of converting them into permanent liens on episcopal revenues was doubtless even more serious. The assembled clergy promised to assist Marseille and take up the matter directly with the king, though to what effect remains unknown.[14] Twenty years later, despite Sixtus V's stern but ineffective condemnation of simony and related abuses (and which was directed largely at French practices), the 1598 Assembly of Clergy still found it necessary to insert a remarkably similar article in its *cahier* against the giving of pensions to laymen.[15]

Pensions like those paid to the comte de Tende were essentially private obligations, and not what contemporaries referred to as pensions legally registered 'en cour de Rome'; yet under Henri III, as the clergy complained, they were routinely enforced by the royal council when disputes about them arose. The scale of the phenomenon under the last Valois is for this reason inherently hard to discern, all the more so as Charles IX and Henri III also made outright gifts of episcopal titles and revenues to laymen who were subsequently in a position to impose exacting financial terms on incoming bishops; where this happened, pensions in the strict sense were unnecessary.[16] The elusiveness of these arrangements, which overlap considerably, was also a function of their flexibility. For example, Silvio de Santacroce succeeded his uncle, Cardinal Prospero de Santacroce, as archbishop of Arles in 1574, and as was common for cardinals Prospero retained all but 1,000 ducats of the revenues on resigning in his nephew's favour. But by 1583, Prospero had ceded his entitlement to Charles IX's bastard son, the duc d'Angoulême, governor of Provence and grand prior of France in the order of Malta; this transfer is one of the few of its kind that is known to have obtained papal approval, no doubt because of Angoulême's personal status as a cleric.[17] When

---

14 *Collection des procès-verbaux des assemblées générales du clergé de France*, ed A Duranthon, 9 vols (Paris 1767–8), i. 133–5, 222.
15 *Ibid*, i. 161ff, article XIV.
16 See ch 9.
17 As a knight of Malta, Angoulême was technically a cleric entitled to hold church benefices *sine cura animarum*.

he died in 1586, Henri III transferred Angoulême's rights to a military commander with a very keen interest in church patronage, Louis Bertons, sieur de Crillon, though there is no evidence that this transfer was ever approved by Rome.[18] In the circumstances, this probably troubled neither Crillon nor the king unduly: here it was the layman who was the master of the bishopric, and the bishop who was the pensioner.

II

If the experience of the first cohort of bishops seated under Henri IV is any yardstick, the demand from both clerics and laymen for pensions continued to intensify in the closing decades of the sixteenth century. No doubt the final and most acute phase of the civil wars, which saw the virtual disappearance of royal power for several years after the events of 1588, played straight into their hands. For his part Henri IV, because of his need to satisfy allies, make friends, and rebuild royal patronage, proved more than ready to entertain such demands. A well-known letter to Sully from mid-1594 shows the king himself suggesting a pension of 12,000 *livres* off the revenues of Rouen, payable by whoever became the new archbishop; its purpose was to satisfy the different parties claiming a share of the estate of Cardinal Bourbon-Vendôme, but above all the former *ligueurs* now offering their recognition, at a price, of Henri as rightful king.[19] If no pension actually materialised in this instance, it was because the original plans of the king and his future minister were abandoned, and the king's own half-brother, Charles de Bourbon, became archbishop of Rouen; no doubt it was thought unseemly for a dignitary of his blood and rank to have to pay a pension to anyone. There is no reason to imagine that what the king was prepared in principle to do in the case of a see as distinguished as Rouen, he was unwilling to countenance for lesser dioceses. It should be added that both the pope and Mayenne, leader of the Catholic League, were equally willing to create pensions when they could do so during the last years of the League.[20] In the event, they enjoyed very few opportunities to do so, and it was therefore through the agency of Henri IV that most of the new pensions payable by bishoprics were established.[21]

18 *Gallia Chr Nov*, iii. 932–3.
19 *Recueil de lettres missives de Henri IV*, ed X Berger de Xivrey and J Gaudet, 9 vols (Paris 1843–76), iv. 205–6, to Rosny, early Aug 1594.
20 For example, when Luigi Alamanni, the Italian ligueur who had fled from Mâcon in the 1590s, resigned the see in 1599, the pope reserved the right to award pensions to him and other unnamed persons. This is the only example of such papal activity after 1593. *Hierarchia Catholica*, iv. 235, 'Matisconensis', n 2.
21 As far as can be determined, they included Aix and Fréjus. See *Hierarchia Catholica*, iv, under 'Aquen' and 'Forojuliensis'.

Moreover, demands for pensions had become more open and less furtive than previously, and in several instances it seems that episcopal nominations could only be made in the 1590s and 1600s if candidates were prepared to come to terms with demands for pensions. The great aristocracy led the way, and were eagerly imitated by less well-known figures. The great Gascon see of Auch, vacant since 1586, only began the return to normality in May 1597 when the Nemours family which controlled it finally agreed to renounce their claim in return for a huge pension of 24,000 *livres* payable to the duc de Nemours himself, even should he marry.[22] Henri III's former favourite, the duc d'Epernon, was in much less of a hurry to let go of the see of Aire, also in Gascony, which had also been given to him by Henri IV in 1594; he even wrote to Clement VIII in 1599 excusing himself and explaining his plans, especially for a son he was grooming for the church.[23] It was not until 1606 that he finally abandoned this tactic, and allowed Philippe Cospeau, who would become one of the most admired French bishops of his generation, to become bishop of Aire.[24] However, Epernon's son, the future Cardinal La Valette, was not left empty-handed as a result of this gesture, and he collected a proportionately larger pension of 6,000 *livres* a year from Cospeau and his successors than had Nemours off Auch.

A final but arguably more versatile example is that of Crillon, a Montmorency client whom Henri IV also generously favoured. In addition to holding the revenues of Arles since 1586, as we saw, Crillon also received grants at various times of those of Saint-Papoul, Fréjus, Senez, and Toulon, which between them constituted the largest clutch of 'titles' held by a single individual in this period. As early as 1595, we find him taking steps to ensure a smooth succession at Arles by negotiating terms directly with the nephew of the ageing archbishop, should he wish to retire. In return, Crillon promised to surrender his existing entitlement to the revenues and to be satisfied with a pension of 4,000 *livres*.[25] He was, it seems, in far less of a hurry to regularise the status of Saint-Papoul, Senez and Toulon, all of which had been vacant for several years, or of Fréjus, which had a papally appointed bishop since 1592. It was only in 1599 that a partly incapacitated relative of Crillon's obtained provisions to Toulon.[26] Fréjus had to pay a pension of 5,000 *livres* to another Crillon relative, and Senez one of 500 *livres*. As for Saint-Papoul, nothing is known about the conditions of the nomination of the obscure and short-lived Jean de Raymond there in 1601,

22 See ch 10, p 388.
23 ASV, Fondo Borghese I, 636, fo 443, letter of 12 Jan 1599.
24 ASV, Fondo Borghese II, 248, fo 297, Maffeo Barberini, nuncio, to Cardinal Borghese, 15 July 1606: 'Mons d'Espernon il quale si è fatto coscienza che da un suo figlio non capace fusse detento il detto Vescovado.'
25 *Gallia Chr Nov*, iii: Arles, 935, 'articles paiches (sic) et accords faicts' between Crillon and Horatio Montano, Avignon 15 Nov 1595.
26 *Hierarchia Catholica*, iv. 339 'Tolonensis', n 2.

but it seems unlikely that Raymond was treated by Crillon differently from his *confrères*.[27]

Clearly, not all of those with an interest in episcopal patronage could equal Crillon's virtuosity. But even if it was unusual, his record points to the need to examine the overall pattern of episcopal pensions under Henri IV. The Béarnais's reign, as we shall see presently, may not have set an unvarying precedent for following decades, but it offers an unrivalled point of comparison for both the past and the future. This kind of analysis is not without its tedious features, and needs to be prefaced by a few general observations.

To begin with, it should be realized that an attempt accurately to quantify the financial weight of pensions over time or indeed at any date in our period is frustrated by an inescapable attribute of pensions – being life-grants, their duration depended on mortality rates among pensioners. And as many of the pensioners throughout our period were individuals of whom little if anything is known beyond their names, it is obviously impossible to plot year-on-year variations in episcopal pensions.[28] Nor can the extent to which individual pensions were redeemed be satisfactorily plotted. Needless to say, the range of possible experiences was considerable. A limited number of bishops proved extremely lucky, and none more so than those originally designated as coadjutors to elderly bishops who, in a number of cases, died even before their coadjutors had been consecrated. For example, Pierre Paparin of Gap reserved half of the revenues when resigning it to his relative, Charles-Salomon du Serre in 1600, but he was dead before the succession had been completed, which left the new bishop free to enjoy the revenues to the full for the next thirty-seven years.[29] Men like du Serre came quickly into their 'inheritance', and because they had been initially designated as coadjutors they escaped having to pay pensions to third parties. Other bishops were much less fortunate, and it was not uncommon for them to be outlived by their pensioners, so that their successors also inherited one or more pensions – *pensions anciennes*, as they were referred to – along with the mitre. Perhaps the most extreme case of this experience was that of the see of Tréguier in Brittany. In 1619 it was offered to François de la Fayette, first almoner to Anne of Austria, but although he declined the offer of such a remote diocese, he seized the chance to obtain a pension of 2,000 *livres* from its revenues. He went on to become bishop of Limoges in 1627, and he outlived several bishops of

---

27 H Espitalier, 'Les Evêques de Fréjus du xiiie à la fin du xviiie siècle', *Bulletin de la Société d'Etudes Scientifiques et Archéologiques de la ville de Draguignan*, 22 (1898–9), 5; *Hierarchia Catholica*, iv. 189 'Forojuliensis', n 3.

28 This is largely because the main source of information is the archives of the papal consistory, conveniently presented in *Hierarchia Catholica*, iv. Unless otherwise noted, details on pensions are drawn from this repertoire.

29 *Gallia Chr Nov*, i. 520; *Hierarchia Catholica*, iv. 358.

Tréguier, collecting his pension until his death in 1676![30] Most of the pensions fell somewhere between the extremes represented by the experiences of Gap and Tréguier.

Returning now to the position under Henri IV, we find that out of France's 113 dioceses, there were eighteen to which the king never had an opportunity to make any kind of nomination, and thus to settle pensions on them. On the other hand, he made up to two or three episcopal nominations to a number of dioceses, but he did not consistently impose, or refrain from imposing, pensions on the dioceses concerned. At least ten of the dioceses to which he did nominate were almost certainly too poor (admittedly a relative category) to support a pension. In addition, there were eleven coadjutorial nominations, and sixteen cases of bishops retiring outright. Pensions for coadjutors and retiring bishops fell perfectly within the canonical definitions of 'evident necessity', and thus were in no real sense an exercise in financial patronage by the king; indeed, once he had agreed in principle to a resignation or a coadjutorship, the financial arrangements were left essentially to the individuals concerned. Finally, there were five cases of bishops transferring from one diocese to another and retaining a pension from the revenues of their first diocese; this too, was usually a matter for negotiation between the bishops, and not for unilateral imposition by the crown. Now what these last three categories have in common is that they normally precluded the creation of additional pensions for third parties. There was only one resignation, that of Arles in the late 1590s where, as noted above, an additional pension was created for Crillon, but this was only because he was returning control of the revenues to the archbishop.

Of the remaining sixty-six nominations made by Henri IV which afforded the crown a 'normal' opportunity to create pensions, it seems that the king did so on thirty-four occasions, or just over one in every two instances. Leaving coadjutor-bishops aside (they were normally active bishops entitled to a small share in the revenues of a diocese), this means that fifty-three dioceses, or slightly less than half of the total number in France, were required to pay pensions at some point *during* the reign. Inadequate evidence for earlier reigns and indeed for Henri IV's own, means that guesswork is unavoidable if we are to arrive at an overall total. But allowing for pensions that were still being paid since Charles IX's or Henri III's reigns, the real proportion of dioceses subject to pensions was obviously higher than that, possibly somewhere in the region of two-thirds. Of course, this figure would undoubtedly have been higher still were it not for the fact that a number of dioceses were held *en confidence* or something very close to it, and which made the awarding of pensions entirely superfluous.

Closer analysis of the individual pensions yields some interesting results,

---

30   ASV, PC 16, fo 269, letter of nomination to Tréguier, 6 May 1619. See J Aulagne, *La Réforme catholique du xvie siècle dans le diocèse de Limoges* (Paris 1905), 136–7.

despite the paucity of information in many cases. Of the thirty-four pensions which Henri IV is known to have granted, fourteen were clearly to the benefit of those who might be roughly called the masters of the dioceses at the time. Like the examples already seen, such as Nemours, Epernon, and Crillon, these men were nobles of considerable rank and power. In these and other cases, pensions were the *quid pro quo* for their consent to the return of normal episcopal tenure to the dioceses in question. In 1603 Constable Montmorency extracted a pension, nominally payable to one of his chaplains, of 9,000 *livres* off Carcassonne, which he had long dominated, before its incoming bishop could really contemplate taking over the diocese.[31] Montmorency's son-in-law, Ventadour, is known to have controlled the Languedoc see of Lodève for many years, and it is impossible to imagine that the nominal holder of a pension of 6,000 *livres* created in 1606, François de Silly, an obscure cleric from Agde diocese, was acting on behalf of anyone else but Ventadour. Only one of these fourteen cases has a peculiar twist to it: the master of Narbonne diocese was none other than Cardinal Joyeuse, who retained a pension estimated at about 24,000 *livres* when he resigned it in 1600.

The term 'masters of the dioceses' used to describe these individuals may seem excessive and, in the event, their dominance of the dioceses in question was sometimes short-lived. But while it lasted, there was no mistaking their attitude. The archbishop of Auch, for example, seems to have experienced difficulty meeting his annual payments of 24,000 *livres* to the duc de Nemours, who responded by having the revenues sequestrated and initiating lawsuits against him. The outcome of one such action, in early 1604, was nothing less than a blunt injunction from the *conseil privé* to Auch to pay what he owed Nemours – otherwise he should consider resigning his office to a successor to be designated by Nemours.[32] It should be added, however, that such rigour was not the preserve of predatory laymen: Philippe du Bec, archbishop of Reims, threatened his own nephew, Jean, bishop of Saint-Malo, with a similar fate if he did not pay him the pension he owed him off Saint-Malo's revenues![33] In the event, the bishops of Auch and Saint-Malo did not resign, though the warning perhaps sufficed to bring them into line. Auch even managed soon afterwards to have his pension reduced by a quarter and to have it transferred from Nemours to other beneficiaries.[34] That bishops in these situations were not entirely helpless is evident from a successful counter-attack by another incoming bishop. Jean de Bertier, bishop of Rieux from

---

31 Arch Chantilly, L/lxiii, fo 8, contract between Christophe de Lestang, Montmorency and his son-in-law, the comte d'Auvergne, for succession at Carcassonne. I would like to thank Mark Greengrass for this reference.
32 AN, V⁶ 1178, fo 42, 28 Oct 1603, Archbishop summoned before the council; V⁶ 7, decree of 7 Jan 1604.
33 AN, V⁶ 1175, fo 368, decree of 2 Apr 1602 (Dumont, no 5196); AN V⁶ 1177, fo 249, 10 Mar 1603.
34 AN, MC, VIII, 564, two acts of 4 Oct 1604, signed by Nemours as well as by Sully, Sillery and Jeannin, acting on behalf of Henri IV, arranging for the transfer of the pension.

1602 onwards, demonstrated that he had better connections – or at least that he knew how to use them better – than Monsieur de Clermont, a prominent Languedoc military noble, who had earlier managed to secure a promise of a pension off Rieux when it became vacant. Bertier took the matter to law and succeeded in persuading the king's council to cancel the concession.[35] Further evidence of similar conflicts has not so far come to light, but it may be doubted whether, even in the peculiarly difficult years of Henri IV's reign, the crown would really have followed the *conseil privé* in allowing bishops to be, in effect, removed from office because of failure to meet their obligations to demanding and powerful pensioners. Yet the fact that such action should have been envisaged at all by leading royal magistrates is indicative of how fragile episcopal tenure had become in certain circumstances.

The second category of pension-holder embraces those five cases where incoming bishops were required to pay pensions to members of their own families. It is closely related to the first, but differs from it in that it does not *necessarily* involve family control of the diocese in question. The closeness of the two categories is evident in the experience of the Richelieu family, masters since the 1580s of the diocese of Luçon. When the future cardinal became bishop there in 1606, it was on condition that he pay a pension to his eldest brother, Henri. Two further examples, each at a different end of the spectrum, will further illustrate what this might entail. In 1602, Antoine Bologne was nominated to the see of Digne in Upper Provence, a see which was in no sense dominated by his socially undistinguished relatives. It was his brother, Etienne, a well-respected royal almoner, who was instrumental in obtaining the diocese, and who might well have accepted the nomination for himself. But he passed it on to his brother, and in return for his good offices, secured a pension of 1,500 *livres* for himself.[36] The other example concerns Auxerre, which had had the celebrated Jacques Amyot as its bishop until 1593. A six-year vacancy followed during which a number of would-be successors manifested themselves, but to no avail. The reason was that Henri IV had already made a gift of the see to Pierre de Donadieu, a military noble from south-west France who was then governor of Angers. He possessed neither land nor influence in Burgundy, as far as we can tell, but he was as anxious to take as much advantage of royal bounty as anyone else. It seems that his exigencies deterred more than one candidate, including one of his own brothers, from pursuing the nomination to Auxerre, until in 1598 another brother, François the younger, finally accepted it, on condition of paying a pension of 3,000 *livres* to François the elder, who had previously turned it down![37] Ten years later, although Pierre had already died childless,

---

35 N Valois, *Inventaire des arrêts du conseil (Henri IV)* (Paris 1886–93), no 7006, decree of 30 Mar 1602.
36 *DBF*, vi. 885.
37 Abbé Lebeuf, *Mémoires concernant l'histoire civile et ecclésiastique d'Auxerre et de son ancien diocèse* (new ed, Paris 1848–55), ii. 197–201. The fact that the pension was payable not to Pierre but to François the elder, may have been a response to clerical criticism of pensions payable to laymen.

the family remained sufficiently well regarded by the crown for François the elder to become bishop of Saint-Papoul, in Languedoc, with the obligation of paying his episcopal brother at Auxerre a pension of 3,000 *livres*! Such cross-subsidisation through pensions within a single family was extremely unusual, but it underlines the capacity of influential families in the age of Henri IV to conduct their affairs *entre eux*.

The remaining categories of pensioners were, with one exception, smaller. Three pensioners appear to have been former claimants for the see in question who had renounced, or had been persuaded to renounce, their title in return for a pension. Three more seem to have obtained pensions as a reward for personal services to the crown. The final category contains nine pensioners, but it is purely residual, in that the basis on which the pensions were granted remains impossible to determine.

Both for Henri IV's reign and later, any possibility of putting together a comprehensive sociology of episcopal pensioners founders on the laconic character of the available information. In the case of the Carcassonne and Lodève pensions mentioned above, independent evidence enables us to connect the nominal to the real beneficiaries. But in many other cases, no such information has come to light, and it is simply impossible to say who lies behind the names of the obscure 'clerics' who are so commonly cited in French and Roman sources as recipients of sometimes considerable pensions.

With such a large number of bishops having to pay pensions, the identity of those who were fortunate enough to escape such an imposition is of no less interest. Thirty-seven dioceses in all were so favoured under Henri IV. In attempting to explain their good fortune, we may subdivide them into a number of categories – based on poverty, service, local power – some of which overlap with each other. As already hinted, it seems that about ten dioceses were almost certainly too poorly endowed to bear the weight of a pension, even though one of them, Noyon, had a peerage attached to it, and another, Bourges, was an archbishopric; the temporalities of the two Béarn sees of Oloron and Lescar were in Huguenot hands for many years, and their bishops had to be subsidised from funds provided by the Assemblies of Clergy.

In the case of at least thirteen other dioceses, local political power, either through previous tenure of the see or the patronage of incoming bishops, would seem to account for the absence of pensions; here too, some of the dominant families, such as the Matignon, Bourdeille or Lavardin, were also allies and supporters of Henri IV during the League and thus in a position to resist the award of pensions to outsiders. Reims, it is interesting to note, was not subject to a pension under Henri IV, although he nominated to it twice. His first nominee, Philippe du Bec, long-serving bishop of Nantes, was one of the king's strongest supporters against the Catholic League, so the award of a pension to a third party would hardly have been a sign of royal generosity; the king's second nominee, Louis de Lorraine-Guise, was from a family whose long dominance of Reims was more than sufficient to discourage anyone hoping to extract a pension from Reims.

The final and largest category, that of royal servants and supporters, accounts for at least seventeen of the Henrician bishops not obliged to pay pensions to others. The list includes names like Gondi, Sourdis, Beaune, La Guesle, du Perron, Hurault de Cheverny, Angennes, and several others that are less well-known. Henri IV filled the see of Bayeux three times, and although it passed for one of the best-endowed in northern France, none of his nominees had pensioners thrust upon them. When it is realised that the bishops were René de Daillon du Lude, Cardinal d'Ossat and Jacques d'Angennes, it is not difficult to see why this should have been so: either they personally or their families were among the king's staunchest allies and servants. Likewise, one would not expect someone like the Cardinal de Sourdis to have to pay a pension off Bordeaux, nor Cardinal Joyeuse off Rouen. There was, in some ways, a certain symmetry between the imposition of pensions in some dioceses, and not in others: the forces which were strong enough to extract pensions in one place were precisely those which prevented them from being imposed in others. If Henri IV was not always willing or able to reward supporters and servants as much as some of them expected, his readiness to shield them from pensions at a time of often low and insecure revenues was not without either its connotation of royal esteem or financial value.

The granting of pensions may have remained far more haphazard and selective than in Spain, but for several reasons, pensions off bishoprics were more contentious in Henrician France. Since the 1570s, as we saw, the assembled clergy had been highly critical of pensions for laymen. Their apprehension was shared by the papacy, but with many dioceses unfilled by the end of the religious wars, it was ready to take a more pragmatic line than the French clergy, and to disregard, for a time at least, its own previous attempts to insist that only *bona fide* clerics wearing clerical dress and reciting the office and breviary could hold pensions.[38] If the duc de Nemours surrendered the see of Auch in 1597 in return for a pension, it was largely through the efforts of the papal legate, Cardinal Medici. But the arrangement met some forthright criticism from French church leaders at the time, precisely because Nemours was empowered to keep the pension even were he to marry; their fear was that if laymen like Nemours could claim pensions, then this would perpetuate a *de facto* secularisation of church revenues.

In general terms, the papacy shared the same worries and objectives as the French clergy, and in approving new pensions off bishoprics, it regularly insisted that the beneficiaries be at least clerics and wear clerical dress. But for the years of Henri IV's reign at least, the papacy appears to have worried less about pensions *per se* than about the continuing usurpation and retention of major benefices by the lay aristocracy. The evidence for that concern does not

---

[38] *DDC*, vi. col. 1347, art. 'pension ecclésiastique'. The evidence for papal concern is to be found in the correspondence of the papal nuncios of the years 1578–86: *ANG*, vols v, vii, viii, eds, I Cloulas, R Toupin, P Blet (Rome 1962–70).

refer exclusively to bishoprics, probably because the papacy took the view that lay control of monastic benefices tenable *in commendam* had become so extensive as inevitably to affect attitudes in France, especially among the nobility, to episcopal office, too. Those concerns surfaced most clearly following a report in 1606 from the nuncio, Maffeo Barberini, on the abuse of major benefices during the wars by leading families, some of whom were still reluctant to change their ways. In particular, he singled out the Constable, Montmorency, who, though now suitably penitent, protested that the restitution of 100,000 *écus*' worth of church revenues that he acknowledged he had usurped during the wars, was absolutely impossible for him.[39] Most of that money probably derived from the sees of Carcassonne, Agde, Lodève, Castres, and perhaps others, which he had held at various times between the 1570s and the 1590s. Barberini's report seems to have been commissioned as a part of negotiations between Rome and the French crown over the continuing predicament of bishoprics and other major benefices; though we know nothing about the course of these talks, it may well be that the Montmorency case, involving the leading noble and royal servant of the kingdom, had the effect of raising unresolved general questions.[40] The outcome was that, over ten years after Henri's absolution and Cardinal Medici's arrival in France, Paul V offered to concede substantial pensions off benefices to laymen if only they would at least transfer direct control of them to ecclesiastics; and as a positive incentive for them to do so, he also promised to despatch all the necessary provisions entirely free of charge.[41] Initially, the pope was so nervous about this offer that he refused to put the decision in writing, and when he finally did so, in July 1606, he insisted that Henri IV keep it as secret as possible – the curia's fear was that the Spaniards and other Catholic rulers would quickly demand similar concessions for themselves.[42] The pope's request was apparently respected. Three years later, a new French ambassador in Rome confessed he only knew of the brief by hearsay, and no one in Rome either could or would tell him its contents, allegedly for fear of ecclesiastical sanctions.[43]

The extent to which lay holders of French benefices availed of the concession in subsequent years is extremely difficult to determine, since the curia was clearly anxious to leave as few traces of it as possible. At the time it was

---

39 BAV, Barb lat 8683, fo 11, Barberini to Borghese, 2 May 1606, referring to an earlier report (possibly that cited in following note); ASV, Fondo Borghese II, 248, fo 213, Barberini to Borghese, 30 May 1606.
40 ASV, Fondo Borghese III, 127E, fo 27, 'exemplar' of Montmorency's petition (in latin) to pope, undated. This may be the document enclosed with Barberini's letter of 4 Apr 1606: ASV, Fondo Borghese II, 248, fo 129.
41 ASV, Misc Arm XLV, 2 (Epistolae ad principes), fos 231–2, brief dated 8 July 1606. Copies in BAV, Barb lat 8684, fo 22, and BN, MS Fr 18001, fo 198.
42 BN, MS Fr 18001, fos 191v-2, Halincourt, French ambassador in Rome, to Villeroy, 27 June 1606. BAV, Barb lat 9684, fo 21, Cardinal Borghese to Maffeo Barberini, 9 Jan 1607.
43 BN, MS Fr 18004, fos 9v-10r, Savary de Brèves to marquis de Puysieux, 8 Jan 1609.

being negotiated, Barberini claimed that Montmorency was only imitating what others had been doing before him. At any rate, the pope's decision was not forgotten. In 1611, Montmorency himself urged it as grounds for the non-payment of fees in Rome by Crillon for his pensions off Arles and Fréjus.[44] In 1614, another of the Constable's relatives, Montmorency-Fosseux, who had occupied the see of Mende, among other places during the wars, and who still held benefices without proper title, applied for a similar pardon and penance from Rome: he received an unusual certificate from the French ambassador in Rome informing him that the Pope had absolved him for his actions, and would allow him to continue collecting the revenues of his benefices on condition that he allowed them to return to ecclesiastical possession and administration. The ambassador concluded by pointing out that Paul V had only made this concession verbally, 'being unwilling to allow any written statement of it to be made so as to avoid concessions which others might wish to obtain in similar cases'.[45]

Papal policy over pensions may appear to the modern eye to be a matter of saving form at the expense of substance, since the stipulation that actual holders of pensions had to be clerics *vivant cléricalement* did not necessarily prevent them from also being mere *prête-noms* acting for others. But questions of substance were by no means foreign to the papacy's attitudes. For one thing, it was plainly worried throughout Henri IV's reign about the potentially excessive value of pensions in relation to disposable revenues. There is no evidence to suggest that the crown took much care to limit the value of pensions under Henri III or Henri IV. As a result, it was left to the papacy to police the demands for pensions, and the provisions for new bishops repeatedly attempted to impose upper limits on pensions, limits which, in absence of reliable knowledge about revenues, were necessarily approximate. There is, on the other hand, no evidence of the papacy rejecting royal requests for pensions.

In view of practice in Spain and perhaps elsewhere, it might be expected that the papacy would try to ensure that pensions did not exceed more than one-third of the revenues, but only three efforts to do so have been recorded for the reign of Henri IV. Instead, Rome's normal practice was to specify that the pension requested should only be paid in full provided a minimum sum remained at the disposal of the incoming bishop. Even allowing for its ignorance about episcopal revenues, what is most evident is that the proportions between revenues and pensions were of a kind which later generations

---

44 BAV, Barb lat 7985, fo 2, letter to Cardinal Borghese, Feb 1611, requesting Borghese to assist in obtaining exempton for Crillon, for whom he had 'une si particulière affection', from payment 'suyvant le contract par Elle (= Sa Saintété) passé avec le Roy'. The contract in question clearly refers to the 1606 brief.

45 AD Yonne, G 1630, certificate dated 28 Oct 1614: 'ne voullant qu'il en soit pour ce faict aucune expédition affin d'éviter aux conséquences qu'autres vouldroient attirer en cas semblables.'

would regard as wildly unacceptable. Once again, the experience of the young Richelieu was not untypical: he was obliged, as we saw, to pay a pension of 4,000 *livres* to his eldest brother, but in its bulls of provision, the papacy insisted that this should only be on condition that 3,000 *livres* of disposable revenue were left over for the bishop. As we saw, Cospeau of Aire owed a pension of 6,000 *livres* to Epernon, while the minimum set for his own upkeep was a mere 1,000 *livres*. Ratios like these clearly ignored any idea that pensions should not exceed a limited percentage of revenues. Moreover, in the examples just cited, there is a hint that, in dealing with these problems, the curia reasoned, at least partly, in terms of the social status and consequent lifestyle of the incoming bishop rather than of the objective needs of bishops and their dioceses. A La Rochefoucauld, bishop of Angoulême, might have to pay 7,000 *livres* in pensions, but (like Richelieu) a minimum of 3,000 *livres* was earmarked for his upkeep, a good deal more than for a man like Cospeau, his exact contemporary in the episcopate, who could evidently make do with less. In the end, this kind of approach, which allowed powerful families and individuals to retain the greater part of episcopal revenues, was itself an acknowledgement of the enormous pressure on both the crown and the episcopate.[46]

III

Ignoring its unusual features, there is no doubt that the reign of Henri IV saw more bishops than in the past paying pensions. There are few signs that the pace of pension awards slowed towards the latter years of the reign when it might be thought that the king was under less pressure to make such gifts. The first decade or so of Louis XIII's reign seems at first sight to present a sharp contrast with far fewer pensions in evidence until the early to mid-1620s. It would, however, be wrong to regard this change as constituting a reaction to developments during the previous reign. There are several reasons for the change. The first is the large numbers of coadjutor-bishops nominated during these years; as we saw above, such nominations usually precluded pensions for third parties. But, as is clear from a limited number of cases from the early 1610s, and again in the 1630s and 1650s, this was not an absolute deterrent; indeed, in some cases, arrangements were made in advance for the payment of pensions to begin once the coadjutor had succeeded to the bishopric. In five out of the six known instances of this practice, it seems as if these were acts of episcopal rather than royal patronage, and were to the benefit of family and clients of the bishops concerned. But the great majority of incoming coadjutors did not have to face this prospect. However, some

---

46 The details in this paragraph are taken from the entries for French dioceses in *Hierarchia Catholica*, iv.

coadjutors were clearly more equal than others: where most normally expected a modest pension from the bishop's revenues for their upkeep, some could and did obtain more than such a modest *portion congrue*. Constable Montmorency's nephew, Paul de Fay-Peyraud, obtained half of the revenues of Uzès on becoming coadjutor in 1613, the first step towards regaining formal possession of a diocese his family had long dominated.[47]

As far as the other nominations during the early years of Louis XIII's reign are concerned, it is clear that many pensioners from Henri IV's time or even earlier were still alive, and this correspondingly reduced the scope for new pensions.[48] But two related developments form an interesting contrast with the recent past, and also point to later trends. The first is the clericalisation of the pensioners, something which had long been demanded by Rome, and which by the 1610s was the rule rather than the exception. One of the last lay pensioners off a bishopric was Claude de Bourdeille, *comte* de Montrésor, who received 6,000 *livres* for life off Périgueux in 1612.[49] If this seems like a return to the later sixteenth century, it should at least be remembered that until 1612 Périgueux was held *en confidence* in the interests of the Bourdeille family. Montrésor's pension, although substantial, nevertheless represented quite a surrender of family control over Périgueux. Because of its genesis, it is not entirely suprising that Montrésor's was also the biggest single new pension to be exacted until the mid-1620s. The duchess of Guise, niece and heiress of Cardinal Joyeuse, did not really see why her uncle's pension of 30,000 *livres* off Narbonne should die with him, and in August 1615 she obtained the reversion to both the archiepiscopal title and the pension for her second son. But nine months later, after requiring Archbishop Vervins to accept the principle of a continuing pension, she and her husband promised him that they would not insist upon actual payment.[50]

These pensions were unusual for the 1610s. What is significant is that large pensions for great nobles were already dying out, a fact which is reflected in the disappearance from the Roman records of conditions designed to ensure that incoming bishops would enjoy a minimum revenue. Combined pressure on the crown by both the clergy and the papacy gradually bore fruit, and it may be that the crown itself was not averse to seeing lay control of episcopal power and temporalities reduced in this way. The attitude of the Guises,

---

47 *Hierarchia Catholica*, iv. 200, 'Helenopolitan', n 1.
48 This is made clear in the papal records which use the term 'salvis antiquis pensionbus' to refer to the continuation of existing pensions under the new episcopate.
49 *Hierarchia Catholica*, iv. 277, 'Petragoricen', n 3. The pension was payable in full on condition that the new bishop disposed of 3,000 *livres* for himself.
50 AAE, France 1632, fo 178, two deeds dated 27 June 1616 in which the Guises and Vervins signed a private agreement, authenticated before a notary on the same day, on the terms of the pension and reversion. The agreement, being private, expressly allowed the Guises to override it should they so wish and have the pension formally 'created' in the Roman curia, which would make payment legally binding on the archbishop.

insisting in principle on the reversion of a major see and its pension but drawing back from actual payment, conveys something of the changes then under way. The outcome could hardly be described as a return to the *status quo ante* Charles IX, but there were some similarities to an earlier age. It was cardinals who still managed to do best, as if nothing had changed since the previous century, and who were almost totally free to make arrangements that suited them and their ambitions. Not only were they never required to pay pensions to others, but only they could still 'reserve' all but a fraction the revenues of a bishopric on resigning it to a successor of their own rather than anyone else's choosing. Cardinal Joyeuse, as we saw, did precisely that when resigning Toulouse in 1613, and was imitated by his successor, Cardinal La Valette, when he resigned it in 1627. It was not until his death in 1639 that his successor, Charles de Montchal, would enjoy more than a fraction of the revenues of this wealthy see. Richelieu, to his credit, did not go quite so far in resigning Luçon in 1623 – his pension represented about one-third of its revenues – but it became clear over a decade later that he remained the real master of the diocese.[51]

Alongside the clericalisation of pensioners and the reduction in the monetary value of individual pensions should be set a related development which, slowly at first, saw bishops themselves become the beneficiaries of pensions payable by their fellows. The example of the Donadieu brothers, bishops of Auxerre and Saint-Papoul, paying each other pensions of identical value under Henri IV is but a peculiar, if early, example of this. It is apparent that as the practice developed in subsequent decades, it was at least in part an attempt to compensate bishops for inadequately endowed sees or the loss of revenue incurred by moving to sees that were more desirable in other respects. The award of pensions in such instances tells us something about the relative financial value of one diocese to another. A peripheral see like Bayonne was less attractive than the archbishopric of Tours, even though Bayonne was held from the late 1590s onwards by Bertrand Deschaux, who himself originated from the region. The fact that he was first almoner to Louis XIII made him even more disposed to move to Tours, when it was offered to him in 1617. However, Tours was less well endowed than Bayonne, but instead of the new bishop of Bayonne having to pay a pension to Deschaux, it fell to the new bishop of Chartres to pay 3,000 *livres* a year to his recently installed neighbour at Tours. Within a few years, however, Chartres in turn had made good his loss, taking a pension off both Luçon and Comminges when they became available in 1623–4. Likewise, Victor Bouthillier, about to become bishop of Boulogne in 1626, claimed 1,000 *livres* a year off Pamiers, which was vacant at the same moment. Without bishops ever becoming a majority of pensioners, the following decades witnessed a significant number of pensions

---

51 In 1635, he persuaded his successor, Emery de Bragelongne, to resign Luçon so that Richelieu could give it to Pierre Nivelle, abbot-general of Cîteaux, whose place the cardinal himself wished to take.

being awarded to them, active or retired. The more instances of such cross-pensioning there were, the more they created financial ties among bishops.

A small number of pensions awarded during the 1610s and 1620s show that considerations other than simply the upkeep of clerics from well connected families were occasionally taken into account. Respected preachers of repute like the Dominicans Nicolas Coëffetau and Noël Deslandes, both of whom became bishops in later years, received pensions during the 1610s. It seems likely that the pensions were designed to sustain their religious activities rather than as prizes for well received sermons.

Despite the shifts just described, it is clear that by the mid-1620s the imposition of pensions had resumed on a more 'normal' basis – by which is meant simply that pensions were the rule rather than the exception when new bishops were appointed. This was related to increased opportunity, firstly because far fewer coadjutors were being nominated by then and, secondly, because older pensions were inevitably lapsing through death. Of the forty-one new bishops nominated between 1623 and 1630 inclusively, only fourteen escaped having to pay pensions, most of them because of their low revenues. Eight more escaped new pensions only because their bishoprics were still paying old pensions. As in previous decades, new pensioners included men who, like Mathieu de Morgues and Augustin de Thou, son of the historian, had initially been nominated to dioceses, only subsequently to withdraw and settle for a pension instead. Likewise, members of families with an interest, historic or recent, in particular dioceses figure among the pensioners of these years – two Hennequin for Soissons, a Ventadour for Lodève, a Béthune for Bayonne, a Neufville for Lyon, two La Mothe-Houdancourt brothers for Mende.

IV

In the light of such trends, several of which seem rather *ad hoc* in character, it comes as a considerable surprise to encounter a development which is altogether more systematic, namely the virtual disappearance of new pensions on bishoprics from the early 1630s onwards. By far the smallest number of pensions for the entire period is recorded between the years 1631 and 1651, when only sixteeen out of eighty-nine new bishops were required to pay them. This statistic would be noteworthy on its own, but the full extent of the change becomes clearer on close analysis of the purpose and destination of the pensions that were actually established. Nearly all of them were overwhelmingly of a conventional, non-patronage kind – four were for retiring bishops, five for bishops transferring to other sees, while two were for inadequately endowed bishops. Three further episcopal successions produced pensions because of the necessity to satisfy or even 'buy out' particular family interests with a view to facilitating particular nominations. The final two pensions, dating from 1648 and 1650 respectively, were exercises in political patronage which the events of the Fronde were always likely to revive, but which were kept in check for a few years yet.

Now, such a collapse in the number and range of pensions is too striking to be no more than the result of a prolonged fit of absent-mindedness. What lay behind it? It is unusual in such matters for any direct evidence of contemporary intentions to have survived, but there is one tantalising reference to this change of direction, though it does not quite go as far as to provide an explanation of it. Writing to Rome in mid-1636 to nominate a new bishop of Cahors, Louis XIII himself apologised for his decision to impose a relatively modest pension of 2,000 *livres* off Cahors for Antoine Godeau, whom he had just nominated to Grasse, a poorly endowed bishopric in Provence. This pension was, he confessed, 'contrary to the resolution which I took to discharge from now on the pensions on the bishoprics of my kingdom rather than to add new ones'; if he had broken his promise in this instance, the king added, it was purely 'in order to provide Godeau with the means of supporting himself in a state appropriate to his dignity as a bishop'.[52] At first glance, the king's statement suggests that his resolution was of recent origin, as evidenced in the expression 'from now on', yet the embarrassed tone of his justification of Godeau's pension also hints that the decision was not so recent that it was not already known about in Rome and thus needed defending. Judging by the actual record, the decision could have been taken at any time during the early 1630s. Only five pensions were imposed between 1631 and 1636, three of which were for incoming, retiring, or transferring bishops, while the two others involved family arrangements in which the Richelieu ministry had a direct interest.[53] Richelieu himself even allowed his own pension of 5,000 *livres*, which he had reserved on resigning Luçon in 1623, to be suppressed on the nomination of a new bishop in 1635; the gesture may have served his other purposes, nevertheless it was consistent with current policy.[54]

The wider context and underlying reasons for the royal decision will emerge in a later chapter, but the king's letter quoted above gives a first, indirect clue to them.[55] A slow-working reaction to the practices of the late sixteenth century had been taking shape; the *dévot* movement in the broadest sense was anxious to restore an active episcopate, and laid considerable stress

52   BN, MS lat 17025, fo 13, Louis XIII to Cardinal of Savoy, 17 June 1636: 'contre le dessein que j'ay fait de décharger dorénavant les Eveschez de mon Royaume des pensions qui sont sur eux que d'en establir de nouvelles . . . pour luy (Godeau) donner moien de s'entretenir en un estat convenable à la dignité d'Evesque.' The king made the same point in his accompanying letter to the French ambassador (*ibid*, fo 14), and no doubt to the pope, but this letter has been lost.
53   The coadjutorships of Montauban (for Pierre de Bertier, but supported by Richelieu over several years) and of Gap (for Artus de Lionne, brother in law of the secretary of state for war, Servien).
54   See Joseph Bergin, *Richelieu, Power and the Pursuit of Wealth* (New Haven and London 1985), 211–12.
55   See ch 12.

on the office and dignity of bishop. The Richelieu ministry, and the king himself, had become increasingly receptive to this pressure, regardless of political differences with some *dévots* themselves, and in the 1630s the crown possessed sufficient freedom of manoeuvre and willingness to respond to it. No less important is the fact that the change of outlook survived the demise of king and minister, because *dévot* influence remained strong during the minority of Louis XIV. Indeed, only two pensions, both for transferring bishops, were created between 1638 and 1646 inclusively, which was by far the leanest period for those on the lookout for pensions.

And yet the temptation for a regency government faced with mounting financial and political difficulties to return to earlier methods must have been severe. The clearest suggestion of this pressure, but at the same time of a continuing determination to hold fast to Louis XIII's promise, is the fact that while a number of incoming bishops in the mid-1640s were required to pay pensions to third parties, it was stipulated that they should be payable from the revenues of their non-episcopal benefices![56] When Artus de Lionne turned down the offer of a transfer from Gap to Embrun in 1648, he traded his claim to the archbishopric with Georges d'Aubusson de la Feuillade, the new incumbent, but instead of retaining a pension, which would have been virtually automatic in an earlier age, Lionne settled for an abbey currently held by la Feuillade.[57] This was, of course, benefice-trading of a familiar, hard-headed kind, but the most interesting feature of it is that it was capable of making room for a change of attitude towards bishoprics themselves.

Yet it would be no less of a surprise to learn that Louis XIII's self-denying ordinance was irreversible, even after twenty years. What is perhaps more unexpected is that it was observed for as long as it was. The Fronde ultimately shattered the consensus, though it did not do so overnight. The consensus underlying such self-denial was probably always fragile, and what the crown, with strong support, might enforce in one set of circumstances, could be reversed in others, when countervailing pressures strengthened sufficiently. As previously noted, only two pensions were awarded before 1652 that were reminiscent of earlier decades, in that they were destined for individuals or families whose political support the Mazarin régime did not wish to forego. Significantly, both pensions figure in the official Roman record as being 'for persons to be specified', habitually a good index of political patronage. In the first case, that of Sisteron in Provence, the beneficiary, Nicolas de Valavoire, was from a family of Mazarin clients, and was to become bishop of nearby Riez by the end of the Fronde;[58] in the second, that of Beauvais, a substantial

---

56 Gilbert de Choiseul, incoming bishop of Comminges (1644), Louis de la Rochefoucauld (Lectoure 1646), Léonor de Matignon (Lisieux, 1646) and Jacques le Noël du Perron (Evreux, 1646) are the four known examples of this.
57 ASV, PC 49, fo 8, evidence of Bishop Danès of Toulon, on Aubusson de la Feuillade's nomination to Embrun.
58 *Lettres du cardinal Mazarin pendant son ministère*, ed A Chéruel and G d'Avenel, 9 vols (Paris 1872–1906), ii. 902, letter to Michele Mazarin, 27 May 1647.

pension of 10,000 *livres* was awarded in 1650 to a member of the Potier family, whose political influence, especially in the parlement, was of major concern to Mazarin at the height of the Fronde.[59]

By contrast, what followed from 1652 onwards, when a large number of episcopal nominations were made, could be seen as an emphatic, because belated, release from self-restraint, an opening of the sluice-gates. The result was an unmistakable reversal of the patterns of the previous two decades. Of the forty-three nominations between 1652 and 1661, only thirteen new bishops were spared having to pay pensions. Of the latter, nine escaped either because of their low revenues or because it was coadjutors who were being nominated, while a tenth case involved the exchange of benefices. Bishops who were retiring or changing sees continued to benefit from pensions, while a few who were in particular favour with the Mazarin régime saw their political fidelity rewarded with pensions of a purely grace-and-favour kind. Antoine Godeau, who was definitely not in favour by 1653, was nevertheless compensated for losing the diocese of Grasse which he had held conjointly with Vence for over a decade; he was probably the only bishop of his generation for whom the total value of his pensions off other dioceses actually exceeded his episcopal revenues! These examples apart, bishops ceased to constitute a majority of those benefiting from crown largesse after the Fronde.

Both the numbers and the size of these post-Fronde pensions are reminiscent in some ways of the age of Henri IV. The comparison is not an idle one, because the largest of these pensions were granted to individuals from families or groups with considerable status and power. Not all were drawn from old noble families, as tended to be the case a half-century previously, and indeed the largest pensions now went to ministerial families. As we saw in a previous chapter, the eventual successor to Edouard Molé, who only lived to hold Bayeux for a few years (1647 to 1652), was François Servien, brother of the finance minister, but the initial successor was Molé's younger brother, François, who seems to have been reluctant to enter the episcopate; the upshot was that Servien's nomination to Bayeux came with a substantial compensatory pension of 8,000 *livres* to Mathieu Molé, another son of the keeper of the seals.[60] A similar sense of ministerial groups making their own arrangements is spectacularly evident among the Fouquet brothers. The eldest, François, left Agde to become coadjutor of Narbonne in 1656, while reserving all but 6,000 *livres* a year of the revenues of Agde for himself until he succeeded in full to Narbonne; at that point, it was agreed that Agde's revenues would revert to his successor there, his younger brother, Louis, while François himself would commence paying a massive pension of 25,000 *livres* from Narbonne to a third brother, the abbot Basile; for good measure, Louis would be also required to pay Basile a separate pension of 15,000 *livres* once he

---

59 *Ibid*, iv, 625, Mazarin to Michel Le Tellier, 24 June 1650.
60 ASV, PC 51, fo 512, letter of nomination of François Servien to Bayeux, reserving pension for Molé, *chevalier* of Order of Malta, 23 May 1654. See below, ch 13.

was fully in possession of Agde's revenues.[61] Such an arrangement may seem to suggest high levels of fraternal affection among the Fouquet brothers, but it more likely points to who the real power-broker among them actually was.

However, the majority, if not the most valuable, of the new post-Fronde pensions were held by obscure tonsured clerics, individuals whose names provide no means for determining just how they came to be in receipt of such largesse at all, unless, as we may suspect, they served as convenient *prête-noms* for more powerful men. Yet names like Brûlart, Grammont, Albret, Esparbès, Créqui, and Pardailhan also figure among the pensioners of the 1650s, a pointed reminder of both their continuing bargaining power and Mazarin's political debts to at least some of them.

Not all of the pensions awarded were nearly as substantial as those off Beauvais or Bayeux, and a notable feature of the post-Fronde pensions is how numerous rather than how valuable they could be. This does not mean that the cumulative value of pensions was negligible, since in some cases, it may have amounted to around 40 per cent of the revenues of given dioceses.[62] The variation in pensions during these years strongly suggests that each case was decided *ad hominem*, and that there was little attempt to tailor pensions to diocesan revenues; the result, almost inevitably, was an inflation in the overall size and value of pensions. The fragmentation of the pensions imposed on dioceses also says something of the number of debts, political as much as financial, that Mazarin had contracted during the Fronde. It may also be that Mazarin's own personal affairs had something to do with the proliferation of pensions. He had awarded an unknown number of them off his own personal benefices in the lead up to and during the Fronde, and by the end of the conflict, Colbert, who had taken control of the cardinal's personal finances in 1650–1, was constantly urging him to get rid of them by all available means. The results suggest that Colbert was being listened to,[63] though Colbert saw no contradiction in vigorously opposing the creation of a pension off Luçon when Mazarin was about to nominate his brother, Nicolas, as bishop in 1660, arguing that such an act would signify a severe loss of face for him and his family![64]

---

61 ASV, PC 55, fo 214, letter of nomination to coadjutorship of Narbonne, 9 Jan 1656; PC 54, fo 84, letter of nomination to Agde, 31 Oct 1656. See also *Hierarchia Catholica*, iv. 72, 252. For more information of this set of deals, see Xavier Azéma, *Un Prélat janséniste. Louis Foucquet évêque et comte d'Agde 1656–1702* (Paris 1963), 17ff.

62 Two pensions off Riez in 1652 amounted to 7,000 *livres*, while the revenues were estimated at about 17,000 *livres* (PC 53, fos 474–5, 488–92); three pensions, two of them new, off Aire in 1659 amounted to 6,000 *livres*, the revenues to an estimated 18,000 *livres* (PC 57, fos 268, 281–3).

63 The subject recurs so often in Colbert's letters to Mazarin that individual references are superfluous. See *Lettres, instructions et mémoires de Colbert* ed Pierre Clement (Paris 1863–70), vol i, but also numerous unpublished letters in AAE, France 875 and subsequent volumes.

64 *Ibid*, i. 445–6, letter to Mazarin, 8 Apr 1660.

As we shall see later, candidates for bishoprics in the 1650s had to be prepared to offer pensions if they were to stand a reasonable chance of success. Nor did it matter very much what the political record of a given nominee or his family might be. Pierre de Marca, archbishop of Toulouse in 1652, owed five pensions totalling 12,000 *livres*, Michel Tubeuf three totalling 8,000 *livres* off Saint-Pons and, finally, Hyacinthe Serroni, no fewer than seven totalling 9,800 *livres* off Mende.[65] What all three of these bishops – and some others – had in common was that they were close political allies of Mazarin. Past practice would suggest that it was precisely those enjoying such favour who would be spared the indignity of having to pay pensions. In the years after the Fronde, however, once the decision to resort to pensions on a wide scale was taken, even political allies in the episcopate were not spared; quite the contrary, they could expect to be called upon to shoulder a sometimes considerable financial burden. Clearly, this unpleasant message was badly understood by some of them. Marca, in particular, could not accept that his substantial political services should have had this outcome, and he constantly but vainly assailed Mazarin with requests that his pensions be transferred to others, fellow bishops not excluded.[66] Even what look like attempts to present evidence to the papal nuncio to the effect that the revenues of given dioceses were insufficient to sustain pensions, achieved nothing.[67] Perhaps the change is best symbolised in the experience of the second member of the Ventadour family to enter the episcopate, Louis-Hercule, in the 1650s. Where his elders had collected episcopal revenues in one form or another for decades in Languedoc, the new bishop of Mirepoix owed two pensions worth 5,000 *livres* to two of the most obscure clerical pensioners of the decade.[68]

V

Between Henri IV's accession and Mazarin's death, a total of sixteen French dioceses never had to pay pensions. Of the sixteen in question, nine were too poor, four were protected by a combination of status and influential incumbents, and the last three by influential noble families who intervened to good effect at the moment when episcopal nominations were actually made. Until 1652, the total of exempt dioceses had stood at twenty-five, a figure which would be higher still if pensions, sometimes of very short duration indeed, paid to retiring bishops were taken out of the equation. It may also be noted here that the French monarchy in this period never created – and perhaps

---

65 ASV, PC 53, fos 407–410 (Saint-Pons); *ibid*, fo 1040 (Toulouse); PC 59 fos 299–301 (Mende).
66 BN, MS Baluze 331, fos 3, 5, Mazarin to Marca, 4 Aug 1652 and 17 Mar 1653 respectively; Paule Jansen, *Le Cardinal Mazarin et le mouvement janséniste français 1653–1659* (Paris 1967), 44, n 49, citing letters from Marca to Mazarin of 8 July 1654 and 10 June 1656.
67 See ASV, PC 53, fos 394–405 (Saint-Pons).
68 ASV, PC 52, fo 967, letter of nomination, 16 June 1655.

never even considered creating – institutional rather than personal pensions off episcopal revenues.[69] Given that they would have tended to become permanent in character, institutional pensions, attributed to religious orders or to some other religious enterprise, would no doubt have met fierce resistance from the clergy as a whole; as they showed in other contexts, the clergy preferred to keep control of their revenues and to distribute their funds via the assemblies of clergy.[70] Pensions remained personal at all times, and therefore particularly sensitive to changes in patterns of royal patronage. And these changes were considerable, particularly at the beginning and end of the period studied in this book, when the crown's acute financial needs ensured that it was more than ready to use pensions in order to discharge its obligations to individuals and families.

Paradoxically, given the gradual erosion of *de facto* exemptions, the number of dioceses not paying pensions around 1661 was still relatively high at sixty-four, well over half the total; this was higher than under Henri IV, but it was largely the result of the policy operated during the 1630s and 1640s. Thus the map of France's dioceses by 1661 in respect of pensions remained as haphazard as it was at any time in the period we have been considering. To that extent, the vicissitudes of episcopal pensions may stand as a kind of metaphor for the evolution of the episcopate generally.

---

69 See Hermann, *L'Eglise d'Espagne sous le patronage royal*, 173–80, for the rather different situation which obtained in the Spanish church, especially post-1660, when institutional pensions grew considerably.
70 This was especially true of the funds devoted to the upkeep of Protestant pastors who converted to Catholicism, and the *caisse des conversions* generally.

II
Profiles of the Episcopate

CHAPTER 5

Origins

IN SEEKING TO explain the success of particular individuals who, by becoming bishops, joined what was one of the smallest of early modern French élites, clerical or lay, the historian is inevitably drawn to consider the question of their origins. In the case of bishops, the question is made all the more intriguing by the fact that episcopal office was held by celibate clerics who, unlike other élite groups in French society, were unable to transmit their offices to direct male heirs. The potential for variation in their social background was, accordingly, much greater, though the extent of such variation in practice would be determined by wider factors to be considered in later chapters.

Prosopographical studies of élite groups, both clerical and secular, in early modern France have multiplied in recent decades, sometimes with highly contrasting results. In virtually all of them, the temptation to explain success primarily in terms of social origins, whether it be for individuals, groups or institutions, has proved overwhelming. However, such an approach has not proved immune to the law of diminishing returns. Historians have recognised for some time that there are worrying problems with any attempt at precise social classification in this period of French history, with the result that a study such as the present one would rest on highly uncertain foundations if it confined itself simply to looking at the social status of bishops. This is one of the principal reasons why the results of the studies just mentioned have frequently proved to be inconclusive, which in turn makes it essential for the historian to take a broader, less predetermined view of what enabled individuals to reach the top of the ladder of success.

I

It is for these reasons that the question of the origins of the bishops will not be considered purely in relation to their *social* origins, however interesting and important these turn out to be. The first of the other factors to be considered is that of the bishops' geographical origins. Enquiries of this kind have been undertaken for other groups, for example the financiers who dominated the *affaires du roi* during the post-Fronde years.[1] Such studies have an inbuilt focus to them since they deal with individuals and families necessarily converging on the court and the capital. If those seeking to become bishops had increasingly to do likewise, and pass through the eye of a needle to achieve their ambition, it was invariably as part of a return journey which saw them disperse again to dioceses often extremely remote from court and capital. For that reason, the significance of geographical origins could not be the same as for groups whose final destination was Paris or Versailles.

It should not be thought, however, that the case for considering questions of geography derives from purely negative considerations. The particular geographical structure of France's dioceses, seen in an earlier chapter, would certainly seem justification enough for an attempt to discover where, literally, bishops actually came from. It may be suspected at the outset that some provinces were more accustomed than others to having native-born bishops, but how true is any such assumption? Were there provinces or cities which discernibly contributed disproportionate numbers of bishops? How significant a presence were foreigners among the episcopate in the generations after the wars of religion? Put differently, we may ask how 'French' the episcopate was during the period examined here. Finally, it should be said that the question of the geographical *origins* of bishops is not complete in itself, but should be considered in connection with that of the geographical *destinations* of bishops; if the two elements are considered, questions of geography begin to take on features which relate them to such wider questions as social status and patronage, to name but two.

Before proceeding to look more closely at these problems, a few general points need to be made on the question of episcopal origins in general. Historians of this period will hardly be surprised by the lack of information about quite a few bishops — a problem which is largely, though not exclusively, a consequence of their social origins. This deficiency is partly offset by the church's practice of noting the diocese of origin of all clerics taking orders, and of carefully preserving this particular 'identity' in formal records thereafter. But useful as this is, it should be pointed out that it may conceal pitfalls for the unwary, since the diocese of origin given in such records may only refer to the diocese in which an individual was born, and leave the question of where his family was from, and actually resided, entirely uncertain. The more obscure the individual, the more difficult this problem is to resolve. René Le Clerc, bishop of Glandèves in Provence (1627–51), may serve as a case in point. Thanks to ecclesiastical records, Beauvais is known to have been his place of birth, but attempts to trace a family of that name to Beauvais proved fruitless; the Le Clerc were in fact Parisian and of bourgeois background, and

---

[1] See Julian Dent, *Crisis in Finance. Crown, Financiers and Society in Seventeenth-Century France* (Newton Abbot 1973).

the Beauvais connection was probably due to the tenure by his father of a financial office there around 1590, when the bishop was born. Nor is Le Clerc's an isolated example, since a number of somewhat better known seventeenth-century bishops of Parisian residence, if not extraction, were born in provincial cities during the later years of the religious wars, because their families had temporarily left the city either for their own safety or to continue in royal service or other activities. Nicolas de Netz, bishop of Orléans (1630–46) was the son of a offical of the *cour des aides* temporarily resident in royalist Tours during the final years of the League; Jacques Camus, bishop of Séez (1614–50) was another, born in Bordeaux in 1584 when his father was a royal commissioner active in Guyenne. These difficulties can be far greater with provincial families. Pierre Scarron, bishop of Grenoble (1620–88) was born in Agen during the same year as Jacques Camus, though the reasons for Scarron's parents' movements are wholly unknown; at any rate, his birth there is probably Agen's only connection with a prominent Lyon merchant bourgeois family.

Bishops who were both obscure and members of religious orders are probably the most elusive of all, since the records usually prefer to expatiate on their religious affiliations to the exclusion of other biographical facts. Gérard Robin, of the Order of Augustinian Hermits, was briefly bishop of Lodève (1606–11), and is generally thought to have sprung from an otherwise unknown Languedoc family; in fact, he was of modest Savoyard origins, and it was only through his order that he moved to Languedoc, where he resided in the convent at La Voulte in the decade before he became a bishop.[2] With bishops from the other end of the social and ecclesiastical scale, discrepancies arising from place of birth are immediately obvious and require virtually no background knowledge to begin with. It is, for example, highly unlikely that bishops like Henri de Béthune or the Neufville-Villeroy brothers (all recorded as 'clerics of the diocese of Rome') would ever be classified as Italians because they happened to be born in Rome where their respective fathers were briefly France's ambassadors; nor is there any danger of Cardinal du Perron being listed as Swiss because his father was a Protestant in exile in Bern where du Perron was born in 1556.

More intractable but more significant because it applies to many more cases, is the discrepancy between the place of origin of both families and individuals, and their subsequent places of stable residence. This, too, is largely to be explained in terms of social mobility and political or professional activities, especially where the latter is the key factor. The range of such experience, it need hardly be said, is considerable, and historians need to be sensitive to its gradations. As with issues of social status, the most difficult problem is how to allow for changes over time. The same family may have

---

2 'Lettres et actes inédits de Monseigneur de l'Hostel évêque de Viviers', ed E J Hurault, *Revue du Vivarais* (1931), 15.

definitively changed not merely their place of normal residence – which might not be particularly important in itself – but the location of their wealth, influence, and power in a matter of a generation or two. In such cases, their geographical origins in the strict sense may no longer offer much of a clue to their actual geographical identity, though they might well help to explain why certain bishoprics proved attractive to them. But for every family which made a clear-cut break from their places of origin, how many others remained for a considerable time in the grey transitional category or, as in the case of the better-off nobility, deliberately retained a diversity of geographical spread through landholding, offices and family alliances! In such cases, there is a certain arbitrariness in defining their family seat as, say, Paris or Bordeaux or Poitiers, since it will inevitably fail to reveal other geographical attachments that remained only slightly less important for the families in question. A few instances of this variety have already been suggested, albeit indirectly, in the previous paragraph. The Camus family so prominent in Parisian parlementaire and financial circles by the second half of the sixteenth century first achieved wealth and prominence as merchants and municipal officers in Lyon. They had moved there from Auxonne in the early sixteenth century, a fact which might help to account for the fact that their most famous son, Jean-Pierre, was attracted by the diocese of Belley, which bordered on Lyon, in 1608. Even more distinguished were the Bellièvre, an even older Lyon family who reached the pinnacle of political achievement under Pomponne, *surintendant des finances* under Henri III and Chancellor of France under Henri IV. By the time the chancellor's sons became archbishops of Lyon under Henri IV, the main focus of the family's interests and power had naturally switched to Paris and the court, but their extensive Lyon connections were still largely intact; to return there with the title of archbishop must have been a source of immense satisfaction to a family which had long served Lyon's former archbishops in humbler capacities and indeed owed a great deal in earlier generations to ecclesiastical patronage.

With the Villeroy-Neufville family, everthing seems to move in the opposite direction, since their political and social ascent began with Parisian roots, but was consolidated when they established themselves, initially through intermarriage, as governors of the Lyonnais under Henri IV. By the time Camille de Neufville, grandson of Bellièvre's fellow-minister Villeroy, became archbishop of Lyon in 1653, the family's identification with Lyon was unmistakable, since the new prelate combined his episcopal office with that of governor. Yet because of the family's continuing social rise into the aristocracy, culminating in a peerage and a marshal's baton, identifying them as simply new-born Lyonnais seems less than satisfactory. It was precisely the combination of central and provincial interests which enabled Neufville to claim Lyon in 1653 despite opposition to his candidature, just as the family's court presence had assisted his younger brother, Ferdinand, to succeed Harlay de Sancy, their uncle, as bishop of Saint-Malo in the mid-1640s. A bishop like

Richelieu might publicly declare himself to be a Parisian, but there is no doubt that his family's real roots were in Poitou, which comprised the cardinal's bishopric of Luçon. Henri III's favourite, Epernon, father of two bishops, began his career as a classic, landless 'cadet de Gascogne'; but having made his fortune at court, he gradually established his family's principal base at Cadillac on the Garonne, prior to obtaining the governorship of Guyenne, a province with which Epernon family power became widely associated.

It will be evident, then, that any discussion of the geographical background needs to take account of these and other instances of mobility and multiple geographical roots. However, with considerable numbers of bishops originating in obscure provincial towns, little would be gained by grouping them together by their precise place of origin. It seems preferable to do so under two different headings, that of diocese and of province, since they correspond better to *ancien régime* realities. At first sight, provinces might seem the more useful and recognisable of the two headings, but in fact this becomes far less compelling on closer analysis. With the exception of clearly defined provinces like Brittany, Burgundy or Languedoc, provincial boundaries and identities fluctuated considerably throughout much of the rest of France. As a result, the 351 bishops seated during the period have been represented on a diocesan map, though in some cases the diocese to which a given bishop's family belonged requires some fine distinctions (see Map 4).

The first point to be made about the distribution is that thirty-four dioceses, or just thirty per cent of the total, never produced a bishop in this period. These dioceses are for the most part to be found in regions with large numbers of small dioceses, such as Provence and Languedoc, so that their 'failure' is hardly surprising in itself. Yet it was not always the smallest of these dioceses which were left empty-handed: not a single bishop originated from the larger Languedoc dioceses like Alet, Le Puy, Viviers, Albi, Nîmes or Mende, although the neighbouring diocese of Rodez produced seven on its own. In Provence, Vence and Grasse, France's smallest dioceses, produced three bishops between them, but their larger neighbours of Glandèves, Riez and Digne none at all. It may be that 'failures' such as these owe something to the uneven distribution of powerful families, noble or otherwise, in the provinces concerned. Turning to other parts of France, it may also come as a surprise to find some well-known northern dioceses falling into the same category. Curiously, Orléans and Auxerre, which produced no bishops, stand alone among their neighbours on all sides, though Orléans was the original *foyer* of bishops with names like Laubespine, Malier and Sévin. Further to the north, we find dioceses like Senlis, Boulogne, Laon and Châlons-sur-Marne faring no better, with their neighbours Amiens, Soissons, Noyon and Meaux only registering one bishop each. In Brittany, finally, only Dol, admittedly the smallest diocese there, failed to produce a bishop.

With 30 per cent of France's dioceses failing to produce a single bishop, we

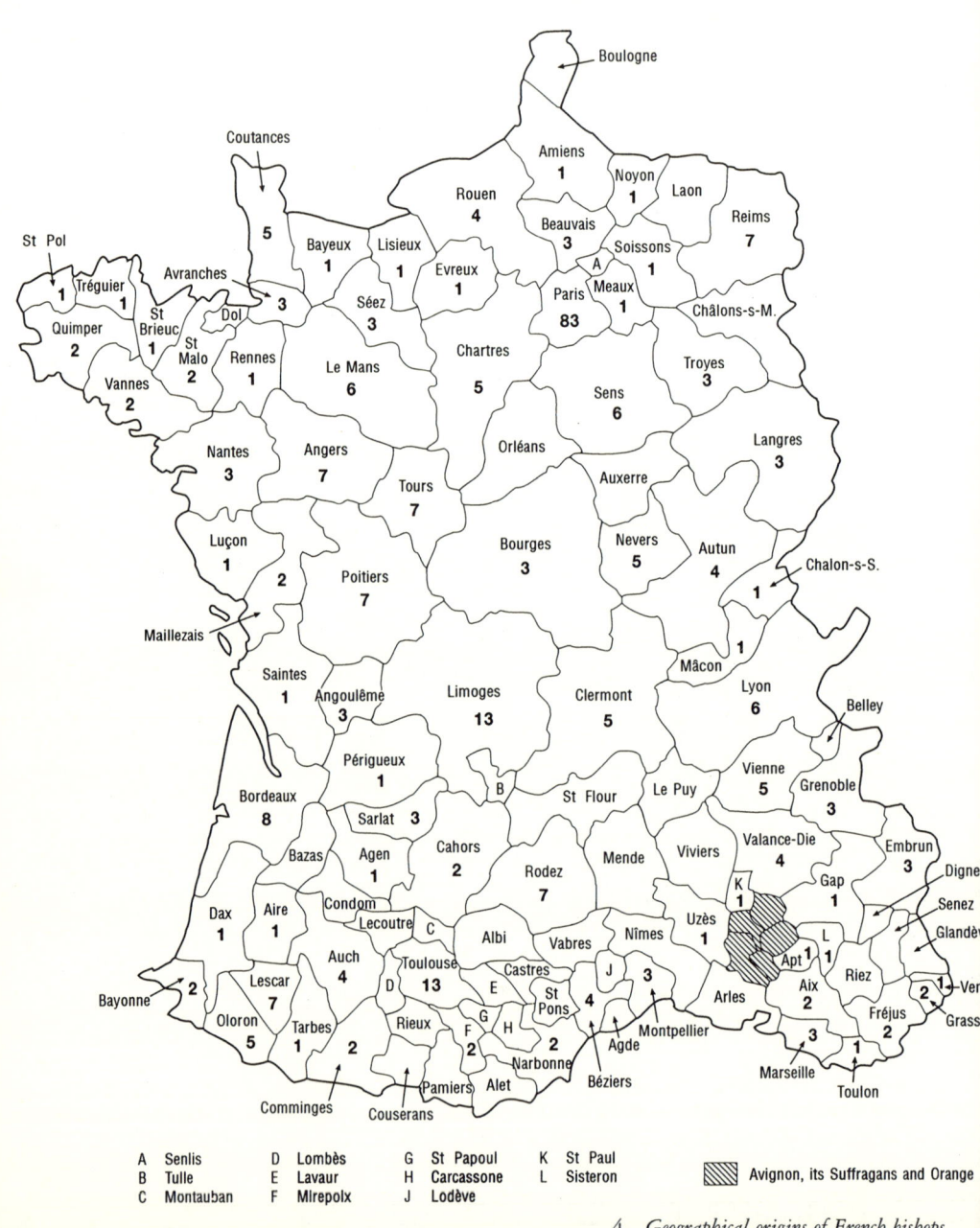

4 *Geographical origins of French bishops*

can turn our attention to the remainder. If we take the figure of three as a crude, purely arithmetical average of the number of bishops to hold office per diocese during this period, we may begin by identifying those dioceses producing between one and three bishops. This category includes no fewer than fifty-five dioceses, close on half the total. Inevitably they appear more randomly scattered on the map than those dioceses producing no bishops at all. However, eight out of the thirteen dioceses accounting for three bishops were located in central and northern France, while twenty-three out of the forty-two with one or two to their credit were concentrated south of the Bordeaux-Grenoble line.

The patterns reviewed so far point to one provisional, but highly important, result. Taken together, it emerges that eighty-nine dioceses only managed to produce ninety-five bishops between them. The remaining twenty-four dioceses (not much more than a fifth of the total) produced no fewer than 227 bishops, or slightly under two-thirds of the entire episcopate for the period. This huge disparity naturally requires some attention, but given what we known about *ancien régime* France, we should not expect even the happy few dioceses concerned to have shared the spoils evenly. Returning to the map, we can begin by focusing attention on the final category which consists of those dioceses producing an above-average number of bishops, i.e. four or more. Perhaps the most noticeable concentration of such dioceses is to be found in, and either side of, the Loire valley, Orléans excepted; this cluster of dioceses extends southwards into Poitou, the Limousin and even the Auvergne, and northwards into Maine and the Chartrain. The contributions of some of these dioceses may have been proportionately higher in the previous century or more, but it is evident that the ability to tap into royal church patronage had not been allowed to decay in provinces which, forming as they did a large part of the historic core of the French monarchy, still possessed a numerous nobility and enterprising urban and landed élites. By contrast, it is surprising to see that provinces like Normandy and Brittany did much less well, with only five out of sixteen dioceses producing three or more bishops. Rouen, a major city and France's largest diocese, only contributed four, which was one fewer than the more rural and remote see of Coutances.

However, even those northern dioceses like Reims or Sens (with seven and six bishops respectively) which fared particularly well by national standards, were simply dwarfed by Paris, whose contribution was no fewer than eighty-four bishops. By any measurement, this is an impressive total – not far short of a quarter of all the bishops of this period. It is the great variety among the Paris-born bishops which should be underlined here. When the geographical origins and movements of families as celebrated as the Harlays remain uncertain, it is not surprising to learn that establishing how long others had been settled in Paris can be problematic! Allowing for that, it seems that only a minority of those entering the episcopate were sons of first-generation Parisians, and that this phenomenon was more characteristic of the opening

Table 5.1 Parisians entering the episcopate

Decade	Total	Parisians	%
1589–1600	56	9	16
1601–10	54	8	14.8
1611–20	53	11	20.7
1621–30	57	15	26.3
1631–40	39	12	30.7
1641–50	41	16	39
1651–61	51	13	25.5

decades of our period, and especially under Henri IV; in general, these bishops were drawn from families who moved straight into high political or even ministerial positions in the royal government without a Parisian apprenticeship. For the majority of Parisians, however, two or more generations of residence and often intense activity in Paris, whether it be in business or the tenure of office, combined with insertion into kinship and patronage networks, seems to have been the norm. They ranged from modest merchant families like the Hardivilliers originating in Picardy or small towns in the Ile de France, to men like Guillaume du Vair, whose long pre-episcopal career spanning nearly forty years began and culminated in Paris as keeper of the seals. That Paris should provide nearly a quarter of the episcopate is manifest evidence of the advantages it possessed in relation to other cities and regions of France, and of the 'social centralisation' which developed alongside, and sometimes independently of, political centralisation.[3]

Moreover, the evidence shows that these advantages were on the increase as the period progressed (Table 5.1). Where Paris provided nine bishops in the 1590s and eight in the following decade, this rose to fifteen in the 1620s, twelve in the 1630s, sixteen in the 1640s and thirteen in the last decade of the Mazarin régime. With episcopal nominations fluctuating considerably over time, round numbers alone are an inadequate guide. But as a percentage of bishops nominated during the same decades, the trend is equally clear, ranging from between 15 and 20 per cent between the 1590s and 1610s, but rising to almost 40 per cent in the 1640s, before falling back to 25 per cent in the 1650s for the first time since the 1610s. It is not necessary to subscribe to the view that France was a highly centralised absolutist monarchy to realise that Paris acted as a magnet for a variety of social and professional groups who then found themselves well placed to benefit from royal largesse where bishoprics were concerned. As noted earlier, it is hardly surprising that even neighbouring provinces and dioceses should fare poorly in comparison with

---

[3] See the discussion in Robert R Harding, *Anatomy of a Power Elite* (New Haven and London 1978), esp ch 12.

its prodigious output, the outcome of which was to create a 'desert effect' where the provision of bishops by dioceses in northern and north-eastern France was concerned.

In the light of this trend, it might be expected that certain provincial 'capitals' were well-placed to emulate the success of Paris on an appropriately smaller scale. The obvious imitators would be those cities with parlements and other sovereign courts, on the grounds that they were the most likely to attract both nobles and aspiring bourgeois. Yet the record shows little uniformity of experience. That Rouen remained in the huge shadow of Paris is not altogether surprising, but the failure of Dijon and Rennes to produce more than one bishop apiece is far more so, especially in the case of Rennes, situated in a province with a partly non-French speaking population and a strong sense of provincial identity. The same applies to Aix-en-Provence and Grenoble, which, despite having a parlement and, in the case of Aix, a university, only contributed two and three bishops respectively; this hardly rates as a major achievement when less favoured neighbours like Arles, Grasse, or Fréjus could contribute two each. By contrast, with no such advantages, the Lyon-Vienne tandem managed a total of eleven bishops, a sign of sources of vitality and ambition not fastened to law or office-holding. But it was Toulouse, embedded in a dense urban and ecclesiastical network in Languedoc, which came second to Paris, with thirteen bishops known to have originated there. It resembled Paris also in that its success created a kind of desert in the dioceses surrounding it; the Languedoc diocese which came closest to Toulouse was Béziers, but its total of four bishops only shows how far behind it lagged. Bordeaux was the only other provincial capital to provide a significant contingent of bishops, eight in all.

Yet the success of at least some of these prominent cities-cum-dioceses in providing a respectable cohort of bishops, should not obscure that of others which figure less often in the historical geography of France's élites, or lead to the assumption that the episcopate was overwhelmingly urban – or even 'big-city' – in origin. Some dioceses, like Poitiers, Limoges and Rodez have already been mentioned, but the total of thirteen bishops contributed by the Béarn-Navarre dioceses of Lescar and Oloron may come as a greater surprise. One reason for their success is that two out of every three of them became bishops in their dioceses of origin, and that service to the Bourbon-Albret family stood them in extraordinarily good stead, even after Henri IV's reign.

Patterns like this particular one raise the broader question of the significance of the geographical origins of France's bishops. To what extent was the French episcopate drawn from families based in the dioceses they governed? Perhaps the most useful way of dealing with the problem is to return to the map and try to establish the geographical *destinations* of the bishops in relation to their dioceses of origin. Of the 351 bishops in all for the period, only forty-four became bishops of their native dioceses; a second group totalling

Table 5.2 *Geographical destination of incoming bishops*

Decade	Same diocese	Neighb diocese	Same province	Other	Total
1589–1600	10	17	7	21	55
1601–10	11	9	7	27	54
1611–20	8	14	6	25	53
1621–30	7	9	5	37	57
1631–40	2	5	0	32	39
1641–50	2	7	2	30	41
1651–61	4	9	3	35	51
Total	44	70	30	207	351

seventy became bishops of neighbouring dioceses contiguous with their own, while thirty became bishops of dioceses in the same province as their diocese of origin. But for the remaining 207 (58.9 per cent), becoming a bishop could mean geographical mobility on a significant scale, taking them to parts of the realm with which the majority were probably not particularly familiar.

These observations can be further substantiated by considering the geographical destinations of bishops on a decade-by-decade basis and using the same categories as in the previous paragraph. The accompanying table shows how sharply the numbers of bishops governing their native dioceses dropped from levels of around 20 per cent under Henri IV to relative insignificance by the 1630s and 1640s; a roughly comparable trend is observable for the two other categories, with the 1630s again appearing as the crucial decade. The slight resurgence in respect of all three categories in the 1650s shows that nothing was irreversible, but it should be seen primarily in terms of Mazarin's attempts to reward or acquire the fidelity of families of mainly provincial nobles. At any rate, the steady rise in the percentage of outsider bishops from just 37 per cent of the total in the 1590s to 68 per cent in the 1650s, with a record of 82 per cent in the 1630s, is the most eloquent statistic to emerge from these calculations. The 1630s and 1640s were, it will be recalled, the decades when more Paris-born bishops than ever before entered the episcopate, but the phenomenon was not limited simply to their growing presence.

Moroever, if one observes carefully the pattern of episcopal transfers and exchanges of dioceses during this period, there is precious little evidence of any powerful desire on the part of bishops to move to their native dioceses or to one close to it. In a handful of cases, probably no more than five in all, there are signs of such motivation at work, but in the vast majority of transfers, the desire for a better placed, better endowed, or more prestigious diocese is beyond dispute. It is not difficult to understand why Jean d'Olce was ready to abandon the impoverished see of Boulogne for his native Bayonne when the opportunity arose in 1643, though it seems that his personal preference was actually for Agde in Languedoc.⁴ When Orléans was rumoured vacant in 1641, the bishop of Maillezais's brother conveyed to Richelieu 'the intense desire that we in our family have always had to have my brother, the bishop of Maillezais, closer to us'. But the prospect of such a move did not make him forget that Orléans was also poorly endowed, and he was hard headed enough to demand that the move should not disadvantage his brother financially. In fact, it is just as likely that the Béthune family, whose geographical horizons cannot have been purely Paris-centred, were hoping to use their bishop to improve their position at court, and he would not have been the first bishop of Orléans to have served that purpose.⁵ The Matignon family was powerfully entrenched in lower Normandy, its lands straddling the boundaries of Coutances and Bayeux, so that for Léonor de Matignon to move from Coutances to the more prominent and wealthy see of Lisieux in 1646 made perfect sense. Above all, it might seem that for many of the Parisian bishops scattered throughout the provinces moving closer to Paris was a major spur to their ambition, but even here it is extremely difficult to find unequivocal evidence. Dominique Séguier, brother of the chancellor, left Auxerre for Meaux in 1637 primarily because of his court obligations as the king's first almoner, and his role as a councillor of state. The social, political, and other attractions of Paris were felt no less strongly by bishops whose geographical roots were far removed from the city.

More and more dioceses might become accustomed to outsider bishops by the mid-seventeenth century, but it may still be worth asking if there were not certain provinces or regions which escaped this trend and continued to be governed by a predominantly indigenous episcopate. This would possibly be expected in the more distant provinces with strong political traditions such as Brittany, Languedoc or Provence, to name only the more obvious cases. What is unexpected is that the results for all three provinces are broadly similar: in the case of both Languedoc and Brittany, the proportion of native-born bishops was identical at 29.7 per cent; but it was Provence which came out on top, with 38.8 per cent. This probably had much to do with the poverty and remoteness of some of its dioceses which made them undesirable in the minds of contemporaries to all but natives of Provence; it is not surprising therefore that it also had the highest number of dioceses – four in all – with a totally Provence-born episcopate. In western Brittany, where linguistic differences made it desirable for bishops to speak Breton, only Quimper enjoyed an

---

4   He was given a *brevet de nomination* to Agde, but then withdrew when the better connected François Fouquet, who had been bishop of Bayonne since 1637, wished to move to a more attractive see: ASV, PC 42, fo 157, letter of nomination of Dolce 'cy devant par nous nommé à l'Evesché d'Agde', to see of Bayonne, now vacant on Fouquet's resignation to Dolce, 23 June 1643.

5   AAE, France 840, fos 55–6, petition from Philippe de Béthune-Charost, 26 May 1641: 'le désir extreme que nous avons tousiours eu dans nostre maison de voir mon frère de Maillezais plus près de nous'.

unbroken succession of local bishops. In fact, one has to look elsewhere if one is to find sustained success in keeping outsiders at bay: in the two Béarnais dioceses of Lescar and Oloron, all ten bishops during this period were local men.

The process of 'de-territorialising' the episcopate, as it has been called, by which the link between local families (usually noble families or their surrogates) was broken, is mirrored in different ways in these figures. It is a process which cannot be given a birth certificate, and was probably as old as the ability of the crown and the papacy since the Middle Ages to obtain episcopal office for their respective servants and clients. It was, in all likelihood, also an irregular process, but even under Henri IV it was sufficiently advanced for less than one bishop in five to govern his native diocese; and from the 1620s, it accelerated sharply, paving the way for the pattern which, despite yet another reverse in the 1650s, has been taken as characteristic of the personal rule of Louis XIV.[6] The evidence presented here suggests that the geographical origins and mobility were much less circumscribed than the thesis of a 'territorial' episcopate suggests. Ever since the Middle Ages, clerical mobility had been considerable, whether it was on account of universities frequented or the never-ending search for suitable benefices. Those clerics who aspired to episcopal rank were less likely than most other social groups to be deterred by the prospect of holding office in unfamiliar parts of the kingdom.

So far this discussion of bishops' geographical origins has focused exclusively on the territory covered by the pre-Louis XIV French church. But the picture would not be complete without considering those who can be brought together under the convenient, but sometimes problematic, label of 'foreigners'. In this period, the term almost invariably conjures up images of Italians, no doubt because of their high-profile presence in France's affairs during the late fifteenth and sixteenth century. They remained the dominant contingent among bishops of non-French origin in the seventeenth century, but their presence must be placed in context. A total of just twenty-one bishops during this period were of foreign origin. In addition to Italians in the broad sense, this figure includes three other indisputably foreign nationals who made distinctive contributions to the French church: Jacopo Suarez (1552–1614), a Portuguese Franciscan who accompanied the Portuguese pretender Don Antonio to France in the mid-1580s and whose indefatigable preaching and disputations won him a diocese thirty years later; William Gifford (1554–1629), an English émigré who became a Benedictine monk while in France and ended his enormously varied career as archbishop of Reims; and finally, Philippe Cospeau (1571–1646), one of the most influential and long-serving bishops of his generation, born in Mons in the Spanish Netherlands. But of the remaining non-French bishops, a clear majority consisted of Italians from various parts of the peninsula, mainly from Florence

---

6 Michel Péronnet, *Les Evêques de l'ancienne France*, 2 vols (Lille 1978), ii. 623ff, esp 637.

and Rome. The great sixteenth-century immigration had ended, and only the entourages of figures like Marie de' Medici, Concini and Mazarin provided a much-reduced flow of newcomers in our period.⁷ Despite their exalted connections, the latter did not fare spectacularly well when it came to episcopal preferment. The days of François I and Catherine de' Medici, when the crown generously rewarded Italian servants and allies, were unmistakably over.⁸ Marie de' Medici's confessor became bishop of Marseille in 1605, but he was the only one to attain the honour; Concini obtained the archbishopric of Tours for his brother-in-law, Sébastien Galigaï-Dori, in early 1617, but the *maréchal's* assassination instantly dashed his hopes of enjoying such a prestigious title.⁹ It was Mazarin who came closest to reviving earlier practices. His brother Michele was briefly archbishop of Aix-en-Provence, where his successor was another Italian, Cardinal Grimaldi, a Mazarin client and former nuncio to France with whom Mazarin eventually fell out. Arguably, it was the grant of Poitiers, and then of Reims, to Cardinal Antonio Barberini in the 1650s which most resembled the earlier forms of overtly political patronage of high-ranking but non-resident Italian clergy with a firm eye on Franco-papal relations. Mazarin seems to have been ready to contemplate other acts of this kind, as is evidenced by the short-lived attempt to grant Montpellier to Cardinal d'Este in 1652.¹⁰

But by this juncture, France's ambitions in Italy and its relations with Italian states, the papal curia included, were very different from those of a century earlier, and Mazarin may have been pursuing his own personal ambitions in his use of episcopal patronage. Two additional points can serve to put this change in sharper perspective. The last example of a bishopric being offered to an absentee Italian cardinal before the 1650s dates from the early 1620s, when (as we saw in a previous chapter) the eminent Cardinal Bentivoglio, a highly pro-French former nuncio, was offered the rather obscure Provençal diocese of Riez rather than a more distinguished see, which a sixteenth-century predecessor might rightly have expected.¹¹ The second is the crown's switch away from bishoprics (and, to a lesser extent, other benefices) towards pensions in money as a method for building and nurturing a clientèle in Rome after Henri IV's time. When Bentivoglio resigned Riez after just three years and kept a pension off its revenues, he was only doing what had probably been intended by all concerned from the outset. Other

---

7   See Jean-François Dubost, *Les Italiens en France aux xvi⁰ et xvii⁰ siècles* (Thesis, 2 vols, Université de Paris-I, 1992). I would like to thank the author for allowing me to read his thesis, from which the following material about Italian prelates is partly derived.
8   Péronnet, *Evêques de l'ancienne France*, i. 490.
9   Sébastien Galigaï-Dori's papal provisions were dated 16 Dec 1616, but he had not been consecrated nor taken possession of the see of Tours before the coup of April 1617; he was soon 'persuaded' to resign the see outright, and was left in peace thereafter.
10 ASV, PC 52, fo 1051, letter of nomination of François Bosquet to Montpellier, vacant through the resignation of Cardinal d'Este, 10 July 1655.
11 See above, ch 2, p 82.

changes within the French church and episcopate also made it highly unlikely that Mazarin could distribute French bishoprics to Italian absentees on a significant scale.

The total number of Italian bishops in this period would, of course, be higher still were the label extended to those who were the sons of Italian families settled in France, even for a single generation. There is little reason to treat bishops like the second Gondi bishop of Paris, Henri (1596–1622) or Louis Dony, nephew of Michel de Marillac and bishop of Riez after 1628, as if they were Italian emigrés like their parents. Allowing for the different time-scales of their arrival and settlement in France, both bishops (and their siblings) seem to have been perfectly integrated into French society. A counter-example may help to put this point into its proper perspective. The one Italian family to have entered the French episcopate but which remained unmistakably Italian throughout the period we are concerned with was the Florentine senatorial family of Bonsi. It produced six successive bishops of Béziers after 1576, and accounts for five out of the thirteen Italian bishops to take office in France between 1589 and 1661. Throughout the entire period, the family itself remained permanently resident in Florence. Future bishops of Béziers were virtually all born, reared, and educated there, and only then were they despatched to the French court or to Béziers itself to prepare the way for an episcopal career – a unique record which depended on assiduous cultivation of royal and ministerial patronage.[12]

With Italians still maintaining a presence in the episcopate, it would be surprising if bishops originating from less distant dominions were not also to be found in its ranks. This brings us to a final, but much more problematic, group of bishops who number eleven in all. The first question to be asked about them is whether they should be regarded as foreign at all. Were the answer to be framed in purely legal terms, it would probably be a negative one, since the bishops in question originated in regions which the French monarchy had long regarded as French and its inhabitants as *regnicoles* – 'natural subjects' of the king of France. In practice, however, this principle may not have been fully respected, even by the crown itself.[13] At any rate, the areas concerned include Savoy, Piedmont, Avignon, and the Comtat Venaissin – the south-eastern marches of the kingdom. The five bishops originating in Savoy and Piedmont were subjects of the duke of Savoy, the six from Avignon and the Comtat subjects of the pope. The difference between the two groups may not seem significant, but there are good grounds for viewing the Savoyard-Piedmontese as foreign in origin, and those from the

---

12 See the biographical notices on the five bishops of Béziers by Bernard Barbiche, in *DBI*, xii. 375–6, 381–2, 388–95, 397–8.
13 For example, Pierre Fenouillet, a native of Savoy, was naturalised in March 1608, a few months after Henri IV had nominated him to the see of Montpellier; the intention presumably was to ensure there would be no difficulties later as to his status and his rights to hold French church benefices. BN, MS Fr 33047, p 547, Mar 1608.

Comtat-Avignon as French in all but name: the former were subjects of a prince with a territorially coherent state, while the latter lived in an enclave within France whose ruler was a permanent absentee. On the basis of such a distinction, the total number of Italian bishops in the episcopate in this period comes to eighteen, and foreign bishops to twenty-one, which amounts to just under 6 per cent of the entire episcopate.

The Savoyard-Piedmontese and Avignon-Comtat bishops, with a few exceptions, do at least have one trait in common, and that is the largely 'ordinary' way in which they entered the episcopate; to that extent, their careers form a marked contrast with the Italians just described, and for whom high placed patronage at court was the crucial factor. Their pre-episcopal careers were spent in France in a variety of activities, so that their progressive integration into French ecclesiastical and patronage structures made them seem even less like outsiders than would otherwise have been the case. All without exception obtained southern dioceses, mainly in Provence and Languedoc. The two Niçois, Clement and Octave Isnard, only had to move a few miles from home in order to become bishops of Glandèves on the eastern rim of Provence.[14] This kind of limited geographical range suggests something no less important about these bishops. Lacking the social status and connections, especially at court, of the Italian bishops, their aspirations were more limited, and they owed their advancement less to their achievements than to the patrons who effectively promoted them. It is clear, for example, that Avignon and the Comtat Venaissin were a fertile recruiting-ground for ecclesiastical clients of French aristocratic families such as the Joyeuse, Montmorency, and Ventadour throughout the sixteenth century. Four out of the five Avignonnais who entered the French episcopate in this period owed their elevation virtually entirely to such powerful patronage.

The chronological dimension of their presence gives added point to this contention. It is no accident that three-quarters of these bishops were seated under Henri IV, when this kind of patronage was at its most effective, for reasons that we shall examine later. Two of them took advantage of the confusion of the League years to obtain bishoprics in southern France, and were then lucky to survive the defeat of the League. Only one name stands out from the entire group, and his trajectory may help to substantiate *a contrario* the hypotheses offered here. Pierre Fenouillet was a native of Annecy who became a protégé of François de Sales, bishop of Geneva (but *de facto* of Annecy) and arguably the non-French bishop who exercised most influence over French churchmen and religious life in the early seventeenth century. After a period of activity in nearby Gap around 1600–4, Fenouillet went on to establish his reputation as an eminent preacher in Paris, possibly with the

---

14 The first of the Isnard bishops owed his entry to Glandèves to Savoyard influence in the area during the last phase of the religious wars in the early 1590s.

duc de Nemours as his first patron. His success was such that even Sully was attracted to him, and he initially obtained a promise from Henri IV to give Fenouillet the diocese of Poitiers should it become vacant. But when the bishop of Montpellier died in 1607, king and minister changed their plans, and entrusted this important Languedoc diocese to a man who seemed to possess the right talents for the post. Clearly, Fenouillet had escaped the local constraints of his early career, and was only prevented by particular circumstances from holding a major northern diocese. If he did in the end hold a Languedoc diocese like others in this category of bishop, it was as an outsider whose career had moved along patronage grooves that were different from theirs.

Moreover, Fenouillet's long reign at Montpellier from 1608 to 1652 ensured that he spanned the successive generations of bishops with non-French origins. The latter began to decline sharply from the mid-1610s onwards. Indeed, with the exception of the Bonsi dynasty at Béziers which was in many ways *sui generis*, only three non-French bishops were nominated between 1612 and 1646. The episcopate of Louis XIII and Richelieu was almost totally French-born. Indeed, by the early 1630s, Fenouillet and Philippe Cospeau of Nantes were, along with the inevitable Bonsi incumbent of Béziers, the only non-French bishops still in office. However, by the time Fenouillet, the last survivor of that episcopal generation, died in 1652, the seemingly inevitable elimination of foreign-born bishops had been halted, for a time at least, by Mazarin. He was instrumental in bringing the last of the Avignonnais, Jean-Vincent de Tulles, who was already bishop of Orange and a faithful client of his, into the French episcopate via the see of Lavaur; he repeated this success only weeks before his death by moving another Italian client, the Dominican Serroni, from the see of Orange to that of Mende. It was Mazarin who also brought the only other near-foreign bishop into the episcopate, in 1649. Charles d'Anglure de Bourlemont's family lands and loyalties straddled the France-Lorraine divide, while his own career was as much Italian as French, since through his mother he was related to Urban VIII and spent many of his pre-episcopal years in Rome. With the Barberinis as relatives and patrons, it was almost inevitable that any movement by Bourlemont in the direction of France would be through Mazarin, a former Barberini client himself.[15] By 1661, when Mazarin died, the number of foreign-born bishops in office had risen to five, and all, including the Bonsis, were in varying degrees personal clients of Mazarin. All of them were Italians, which might suggest that the traditions of previous generations were still as strong as ever. But the fact that there were only five of them makes it clear that Mazarin's

---

15   The Bourlemont branch of the Anglure family was resident in the diocese of Toul, on the eastern marches of Champagne, and its past history showed it tended regularly to switch its activities between the courts of Paris and Nancy, but it has not been included here with those families of non-French origin. See Laurent Bourquin, *Noblesse seconde et pouvoir en Champagne aux xvie et xviie siècles* (Paris 1994), 7 n 2, 39–40.

efforts proved only a brief interruption along the road to an episcopate that was wholly French in origin.

II

One of the most abiding images of the *ancien régime* episcopate is that of a socially exclusive group of men, populated almost entirely by sons of the nobility, great and small but especially the great. In fact, it is an image which owes much to eighteenth-century sources, culminating in the generation of bishops of 1789. By then the closeness of the alliance between throne and altar seemed perfectly mirrored in a self-confident, aristocratic episcopate containing a large number of courtiers and politicians, many of whom would refuse to embrace the impending political revolution or take the constitutional oath of 1791.[16] In the ensuing polemics about the church and the Revolution and the long shadow they have cast over historical writing, it was hardly surprising that the terms 'upper clergy', 'aristocracy', and 'reactionary' tended to be used almost interchangeably.

However, to extrapolate from the generation of 1789 and apply even historically valid judgements about it to previous centuries is to run a series of risks. The first is that of imposing potentially misleading forms of continuity, the second that of ignoring or distorting short-term developments which may contain important clues to the specific character of the episcopate of a given generation or set of generations.

Where the social origins of bishops are concerned, the risks are all the greater owing to the problems inherent in finding a satisfactory method of defining the structure of early modern French society. Historians familiar with the sixteenth and first half of the seventeenth century will be aware that any attempt to establish a tight classification of French social structures for this period is tantamount to inviting the ground to move under one's feet.[17] Although this is not the place to reopen debates over the nature of its social structures which have long divided historians, a few general points need to be made. In practical terms, the much discussed proposition that France was a society of orders or estates has not contributed a great deal to our

16 The most detailed recent studies include Nigel Aston, *The End of an Elite. The French Bishops and the Coming of the Revolution 1786–90* (Oxford 1992), which deals mostly with bishops in politics, but has astute comments on their standing in other respects; Timothy Tackett, *Religion, Revolution and Regional Culture in Eighteenth-Century France. The Ecclesiastical Oath of 1789* (Princeton 1986), places the bishops' response to the changes of the Revolution in a wider perspective; Péronnet, *Evêques de l'ancienne France*, focuses primarily on the bishops in office in 1789, with a detailed analysis of their social background and activities, especially in the Assemblies of Clergy under Louis XVI.

17 See the essays on this and related subjects in M L Bush, ed, *Social Classes and Social Orders in Europe since 1500* (London 1992), esp those by Peter Burke and William Doyle.

understanding of the social structure of the age and how it actually functioned.[18] It is perhaps only now that the inherent limitations of a highly idealised vision of social order, especially as set out in the work of its principal theorist, Charles Loyseau, writing at the beginning of the seventeenth century, are being recognised for what they are.[19]

Now, in any discussion of early modern social structure, much depends on the place and identity of the nobility. As is well known, the late fifteenth and sixteenth centuries were, by *ancien régime* standards, periods of rapid social mobility, when access to noble rank was easier than would be the case from the mid-seventeenth century onwards. This is not to deny that for those with money and influence, entry into the ranks of the nobility was still relatively smooth down to 1789, but the means of acquiring nobility had been severely reduced and streamlined by comparison with earlier centuries. Levels of tolerance and resentment of upward mobility, especially where it was rapid, also rose and fell from generation to generation, leaving historians with the difficult problem of how to gauge the extent to which those acquiring noble status for the first time were accepted by existing nobles.[20]

Since it is less the seventeenth-century bishops than their sixteenth- and even fifteenth-century families which are the subject of analysis at this point, we should avoid applying retrospectively to a less self-consciously structured society the kinds of classification which only came into vogue under Louis XIV, especially as a result of the successive *recherches de noblesse*. For that reason, it has seemed best to begin with a relatively simple structure which broadly distinguishes between nobles and non-nobles, since it makes it easier to engage in more detailed analysis of individual cases, both typical and unusual. This approach may seem to shy away from the complexities of early-modern social history, but for all the energy and ingenuity expended on the issue of nobility in France, it has never proved possible to demonstrate the existence of several *types* of nobility, and in particular that of a clearly distinct *noblesse d'épée* or *noblesse de robe*. What has been shown is that there were several routes towards nobility, but that in the end those taking them aspired to a status which was ultimately the same for all, however long it might take to reach it; and as this process was recommenced in – and by – each generation, the point was never quite reached when the nobility was a harmonious, unified social

---

18   Among modern historians, its most vehement champion was Roland Mousnier, whose extensive writings on the subject are summarised in his *Institutions of France under the Absolute Monarchy*, 2 vols (Chicago 1979–84).

19   See Howell A Lloyd, 'The Political Thought of Charles Loyseau', *European Studies Review*, 11 (1981), 53–82. Unpublished research by Robert Descimon also points to other ambiguities in Loyseau's arguments.

20   From the enormous bibliography on the subject, we may cite George Huppert, *Les Bourgeois Gentilshommes. An Essay on the Definition of Elites in Renaissance France* (Chicago 1977); Guy Chaussinand-Nogaret, ed, *Histoire des élites en France, du xvie au xxe siècle* (Paris 1991), esp the contributions of Arlette Jouanna and Jean-Marie Constant.

entity. It is with such caveats in mind that terms like old nobility, and *noblesses d'épée, de robe*, or *de cloche* are used in the following pages.

Moreover, as with the geographical origins of bishops, the study of their social origins requires attention to changes in status over a century or more, wherever the available sources allow, irrespective of the form of social classification adopted. Since it is not being argued here that it was the social status of individuals that was decisive in their success or failure to become bishops, we may examine the social background of the episcopate in a framework which enables us to connect their family's status to other factors, such as educational attainment, ecclesiastical activities, patronage, and so on.

The question of the social origins of France's bishops in the sixteenth and early seventeenth centuries has already attracted the attention of historians, and a brief account of their findings is indispensable if what follows is to fit into a wider time-scale. In a detailed study of the bishops chosen by François I during the generation following the Concordat of Bologna, Marilyn Edelstein found that the episcopate was overwhelmingly (95 per cent) of noble extraction. Of the 144 French-born bishops appointed during the reign, fifteen were impossible to identify, six were commoners, and the remaining 123 were of noble rank. Although arguing that nothing like a distinctive *noblesse de robe* had evolved at that juncture, Edelstein identified twenty-one bishops who owed their nobility to 'administrative' service to the crown, while conceding that the nobility generally at this time was a service nobility, active not merely in military affairs but also in 'civil' administration of various kinds. She also found that the parlementaire and financial milieux were unable to claim more than a few bishoprics under François I and that, like the handful of commoner bishops, they had to be satisfied with lesser dioceses.[21] In a subsequent brief study, Edelstein compared the episcopates of the reigns of François I and that of his predecessor Louis XII, in order to test the assumption that the pattern uncovered for the former's reign might be abnormal, given that François I was the first monarch to enjoy undisputed nomination rights to French bishoprics. Her conclusion was that even under the previous régime, when bishops were at least in theory elective, the outcome was not markedly different. The main difference was that François I appeared more generous towards the older nobility than his predecessor, and that the richest pickings clearly went to sons of princely families like the Bourbon, Vendôme, Lorraine, as well as major Italian cardinals.[22] If similar patterns were to be uncovered for even earlier periods, then it would be

---

21 Marilyn M Edelstein, 'The Social Origins of the Episcopacy in the Reign of Francis I', *French Historical Studies*, 8 (1974), 377–92. This article is based on her unpublished dissertation 'The Recruitment of the Episcopacy under the Concordat of Bologna in the Reign of Francis I' (Columbia University 1972).

22 Marilyn M Edelstein, 'Les Origines sociales de l'épiscopat sous Louis XII et François I', *Revue d'Histoire Moderne et Contemporaine*, 24 (1977), 239–47.

evident that we are dealing with a much longer tradition in which the nobility, whatever its origins and activities, manifestly dominated the ranks of the episcopate.

Beginning where Edelstein left off, but adopting the somewhat different social categories used by Michel Péronnet in his rapid survey of early modern French bishops, Frederic Baumgartner found that this pattern was to change quite markedly under the last three Valois rulers. Sons of the *noblesse de race*, defined as those whose nobility was old and based essentially on military service during earlier centuries, now accounted for only one of every two bishops; a separate category of *anoblis*, whose nobility, as the term suggests, was fairly recent and was based either on letters of nobility or ennoblement through offices, accounted for just 14 per cent of the total, with commoners also growing in numbers and representing 10 per cent of the total. The balance was made up of foreigners and those of undetermined social origins. These trends were, according to Baumgartner, further exacerbated under Henri IV, when the contribution of the *noblesse de race* fell even further to just 40 per cent. By then the *anoblis* stood at 23 per cent and commoners at 15 per cent, their highest scores respectively for the entire period between 1547 and 1610.[23] Finally, in a brief study focusing on the 108 bishops in office during the Estates General of 1614, Michael Hayden concluded that 63 per cent of them were 'noble', 32 per cent were commoners, and the rest were either of foreign or unknown extraction; these proportions he explained as being largely due to the policies of Henri IV who had nominated a large contingent of commoner bishops during the years around 1600.[24]

Even when allowing for differences between the historians over definitions and types of nobility, it is clear that the crisis of the wars of religion significantly trimmed the quasi-monopoly on episcopal office enjoyed by the nobility in the age of François I. For the four subsequent reigns taken together, old and new nobles accounted for 64 per cent of all bishops. The lowest point came under Charles IX, when it stood at just 59 per cent of the total, but rising to 68 per cent under his successor, Henri III. The figure of 63 per cent advanced by Hayden for the episcopate of 1614, which was largely the creation of Henri IV, begins to look plausible when seen in this longer perspective, one in which approximately two out of every three bishops were nobles of one kind or another. How far were these proportions respected or altered in the generations between 1589 and 1661?

In order to maintain a minimum of symmetry with the studies discussed above, the accompanying table (Table 5.3) classifies bishops on a reign-by-reign basis, with the Mazarin ministry labelled 'Early Louis XIV' for conven-

23 Frederic J Baumgartner, *Change and Continuity in the French Episcopate* (Durham, North Carolina 1986), esp ch 3 and Appendix 2–3. There are several errors of dating and identification in these Appendices.
24 J Michael Hayden, 'The Social Origins of the French Episcopacy at the Beginning of the Seventeenth Century', *French Historical Studies*, 10 (1977), 27–38.

Table 5.3   Social origins of bishops by reign

Period	Noms	Nobles	Commoners	Unknown	Foreign
Henri IV	108	61 (56.48)	33 (30.55)	5 (4.62)	9 (8.33)
Louis XIII	154	95 (61.68)	46 (29.87)	7 (3.89)	7 (4.54)
Early Louis XIV	89	66 (74.15)	14 (15.73)	3 (3.37)	6 (8.74)
Totals	351	222 (63.24)	93 (26.49)	15 (4.27)	21 (5.98)

Figures in brackets represent percentages

ience. There can be little dispute as to its overall significance – the gradual return of the nobility to a dominant position within the episcopate. Of course, that position was nothing like what it had been under François I and, as we shall see, the kinds of nobles it involved had also changed. In addition, the table seems to imply that the recovery was sustained and constant, and the percentage of nobles during the Mazarin ministry would be even more impressive, at over 76 per cent, if non French-born bishops of noble origin were included. Looking at the overall total for the period from 1589 to 1661 as a whole, it is remarkably close, at 63.2 percent, to the figure of 64 per cent which Baumgartner found for the years 1547 to 1610. On the face of it, there is only one conclusion that can be drawn from these comparisons, namely that for over a hundred years – from 1547 to 1661 – the overall proportion of nobles in the episcopate (just under two out of every three) varied by no more than a percentage point or two.

Valid though it might be, such a conclusion would not tell the full story. For all its brevity, Table 5.3 shows that the relative strengths of nobles and commoners among the episcopate were not stable over time, and suggests that closer analysis, based on shorter time-scales, is required if we are not to miss some interesting variations. A breakdown of the figures on a decade-by-decade basis may seem a trifle mechanical, but it has at least the merit of ensuring that the data are not subject to conscious or unconscious manipulation (Table 5.4). At any rate, what it shows is that the recovery of the nobility's place within the episcopate was a process with clearly discernible *temps forts* and *temps faibles*.

The record of Henri IV's reign appears rather more clearly in this analysis. While the overall percentage of nobles of all origins remains seven points lower than that suggested by Baumgartner for the same period, it is a percentage that was rising in the final phase of Henri's reign. Even so, this recovery was as nothing compared to the surge for the opening decade of Louis XIII's reign, which witnessed the highest proportion of nobles entering the episcopate since at least Henri II's time. The figures for the 1640s and 1650s were remarkably close to this level, showing that such proportions of noble bishops were neither intrinsically accidental nor unsustainable. But once again, the evidence shows that this was not a linear progression, and indeed that it was interrupted by a sharp fall, beginning in the 1620s and accelerating to reach levels familiar from Henri IV's reign by the 1630s.

The presence of commoners in the episcopate does not require extensive general comment at this point, since it is so closely tied to the fluctuations in the percentage of nobles. Though the percentages of socially unknowns is relatively small for the period as a whole, it is likely that more intensive research into this category of bishop would have the effect of increasing rather than lowering the number of those who should be regarded as commoners. As they stand, however, the proposed totals for commoner bishops are eloquent enough. Baumgartner estimated that they accounted for 10 per cent of all bishops seated between 1547 and 1589, but this aggregate disguises the fact that the percentage had risen steadily from just 4 per cent under Henri II to 15 under Henri III. For the period studied here, however, the aggregate is significantly higher than anything seen previously, standing at no less than 26.5 per cent, with the reigns of Henri IV and Louis XIII showing a remarkable consistency at around 30 per cent of the total (Table 5.3). But once again, closer scrutiny shows some significant patterns. A decade-by-decade analysis similar to that attempted for the nobility shows that the twin peaks of commoner presence came in the 1590s and 1630s, when over one new bishop in three was a commoner (Table 5.4). The 1600s and the 1620s prove to be the most 'representative' decades, since the percentage of commoner bishops nominated in each decade was extremely close to that for the period as a whole. By this reckoning also, the aggregate for Henri IV's reign as a whole would stand just less than two points below that suggested by Hayden (32 per cent) for the Henrician bishops still in office in 1614. But the most remarkable statistic concerns the proportion of commoners entering the episcopate during the 1630s, at the height of the ministry of Cardinal Richelieu, whose

Table 5.4 Social origins of bishops by decade

Decade	Noms	Nobles	Commoners	Unknown	Foreign
1589–1600	57	31 (54.38)	20 (35.08)	2 (3.50)	4 (7.0)
1600–10	54	32 (58.82)	14 (27.45)	3 (5.88)	5 (9.25)
1611–20	52	37 (71.15)	12 (23.07)	1 (1.92)	2 (3.84)
1621–30	57	34 (59.64)	16 (28.07)	3 (5.26)	4 (7.0)
1631–40	39	21 (53.84)	15 (38.46)	3 (7.69)	0
1641–50	41	31 (75.6)	7 (17.07)	1 (2.43)	2 (4.87)
1651–61	51	36 (70.5)	9 (17.64)	2 (3.92)	4 (7.84)
Totals	351	222 (63.2)	93 (26.49)	15 (4.27)	21 (5.98)

Figures in brackets represent percentages

views, at least as they are expressed in the *Testament Politique*, have always been assumed to be distinctly favourable to an episcopate comprised largely of nobles! It was only in 1640s that commoner bishops began to constitute a relatively marginal group among the new bishops, and the fall in their numbers seems sharp enough by comparison with the previous two decades as to suggest a virtual noble reaction. Even if this should prove to be the case, it should not be forgotten that the proportion of commoners nominated in the 1640s and 1650s (17.07 and 17.64 per cent respectively) still managed to remain above the maxima for the previous century.

Why such swings, which would not be visible at all in a reign-by-reign analysis, should have occurred will be the subject of detailed discussion later, but at the very least they indicate that relations between the crown and different social groups were far from static; the nobility, old and new, may have had considerable advantages when it came to competition for high church office, but clearly these did not yield consistent results. Certainly, as the experience of Pierre Fenouillet discussed earlier shows, social outsiders of different kinds remained serious contenders for episcopal office throughout the entire period under study, and they obviously managed to combine personal talents and patronage in a manner which compensated for their initial lack of social capital. Here, too, there are some surprises in store. For example, although the proportion of commoner bishops reached record levels in the 1590s and the 1630s, other changes occurring in episcopal patronage between these decades would ensure that the entry of a large number of commoners into the episcopate would not mean the same thing in each case.

It will be readily admitted that a binary social division as simple as noble and non-noble needs additional exegesis if it is to convey a genuine sense of bishops social background. Sons of royal princes and of *secretaires du roi* both enjoyed the benefit of noble privileges, but they could hardly have been more different in other respects. Nor does this apply merely to the nobility. Non-nobles could also differ hugely. Sébastien Zamet, bishop and duke of Langres, was the son of France's richest financier who was a gambling companion of Henri IV; his successor at Langres, Louis Barbier, was the son of a man who was at best a *commissaire de l'artillerie*, and Barbier was notoriously sensitive about his true origins. Thus, insofar as the available sources permit, it is essential to move beyond general social categories to examine the different forms of social status of France's bishops. Doing so also requires extending both the chronological and social ends of the spectrum, especially where the presence of the nobility is concerned.

The late medieval French church had its share – although the phenomenon has not been properly studied – of sons of royal and princely families in episcopal office, and they could usually count on holding first-ranking sees. This tradition was reinforced under François I, when the Bourbons and Vendômes, in particular, were especially well provided for. They maintained this kind of presence in subsequent generations, even to the point of producing a rival 'king' to Henri IV in the person of Cardinal Bourbon (1523–90), archbishop of Rouen, in 1589–90.[25] His nephew, Cardinal Bourbon-Vendôme, opted not to pursue his claim to the throne, but only survived him by four years, when a third Charles de Bourbon, this time Henri IV's own illegitimate half-brother, succeeded for a time to the see of Rouen.[26] Now with such precedents, it might be expected that some of the new king's numerous illegitimate offspring would have eventually perpetuated this particular tradition and established themselves in the upper reaches of the French church. In fact, only one did so, and even then his position was almost wholly marginal by comparison with that of his family predecessors. If Henri de Bourbon-Verneuil has any claim to fame, it is probably because he is habitually cited in historical accounts of the Henrician church as an illustration of the continuing abuse of episcopal patronage.[27] It was only in 1612, after Henri IV's death, that he was finally installed as bishop of Metz after sustained royal pressure on the chapter there since 1608. However, Metz was a special case, one whose political and military importance to the crown, as we have seen, eclipsed all other considerations. Moreover, the manner of Henri de Bourbon-Verneuil's long reign at Metz had far less in common with his French *confrères* than with the elected prince-bishops of the *Reichskirche*, to which Metz still technically belonged.[28] For the fifty years he held Metz, Verneuil was an unconsecrated absentee, a characteristic he shared with the only Valois family member to hold episcopal office during the period. Louis de Valois, son of Charles IX's illegitimate son, the duc d'Auvergne, held the see of Agde for a few years (1618–22) before abandoning it for a secular career under the name by which he is better known, the comte d'Alais. However, his brief episcopal experience owed less to his royal origins than to the ambitions of his Montmorency mother and relatives.[29]

These unusual cases apart, episcopal office failed to attract a single member, legitimate or illegitimate, of the extended royal family in this period. Only the Condé family, which had returned to Catholicism through Henri IV's

25 Frederic J Baumgartner, 'The Case for Charles X', *Sixteenth-Century Journal*, 4 (1973), 87–98.
26 Michael Wolfe, *The Conversion of Henri IV. Politics, Power and Religious Belief in Early Modern France* (Cambridge, Mass. 1993), particularly for Cardinal Bourbon-Vendôme.
27 The notoriety of the case was rendered all the greater by Henri IV's own alleged remark to the effect that he could count on easy absolution for his sins from a child-bishop.
28 Maarten Ultee, *The Abbey of St Germain des Prés in the Seventeenth Century* (New Haven and London 1981), 178–9.
29 Reared at Chantilly under the ultimate authority of Constable Montmorency, his grandfather, he was groomed like Henri de Bourbon-Verneuil, for episcopal office from an early age. Moves were afoot from 1608 onwards, when he was thirteen, to ensure he would succeed as bishop of Agde: Arch Chantilly, L/xcii, fo 25, Bishop du Puy of Agde to Montmorency, 7 June 1608. My thanks to Joan Davies for this and many other references relating to Montmorency interests. For Alais's career as governor of Provence, Sharon Kettering, *Judicial Politics and Urban Revolt in Seventeenth-Century France. The Parlement of Aix 1629–1659* (Princeton 1978), 129ff.

deliberate choice, seems to have been briefly tempted by that prospect. However, when in 1631 the princess of Condé requested the see of Auxerre, in her husband's new governorship of Burgundy, for their two-year old son, the prince of Conty, she received a polite rejection from Richelieu: such an idea was, he said, 'a proposition, which, as you well know, the king could not put into effect'.[30] The Condés were doubtless fully aware of earlier precedents, but failed to realise that underaged, blue-blooded children were no longer automatic candidates for the mitre, even if they could still aspire to the red hat.[31]

Among the lesser mortals who comprised the upper echelons of the French nobility, princely families of foreign extraction enjoyed a certain, albeit often disputed, pre-eminence. Six of the eight families of this rank to be found in seventeenth-century France had been active there in the previous century, but only one of them continued to provide bishops.[32] As far as the sixteenth-century church was concerned, the dominant and certainly the best-known figures of such rank were the three generations of Guise cardinals, whose accumulation of bishoprics and role in episcopal patronage generally was pervasive, though it remains poorly understood; the great archiepiscopal sees of Reims and Sens were increasingly central to their position in the church as the century wore on. However, in the two generations which followed the Blois murders of 1588, their ecclesiastical representatives were mediocre figures – each perfectly fitted Retz's description of himself as 'the least ecclesiastically-minded person in the world' – and although they continued to dominate the primatial see of Reims down to 1640, they exercised no real influence or patronage within the French church.[33] This tale of decline is neatly encapsulated in the fact that the last of their representatives to hold a bishopric, Charles-Louis (bishop of Condom 1659–68), was himself an illegitimate son of the last Guise cardinal; yet, of the three seventeenth-century Guise bishops, he was the one who least resembled his most recent family predecessors and who most resembled the kind of bishop of which both church and crown now approved.

The sixteenth-century church had, on the other hand, seen a considerable number of bishops drawn from the upper reaches of the powerful, titled aristocracy. Their power and influence in the church was doubtless enhanced by the fact that some of them simultaneously held several dioceses in one form of tenure or another; that, taken together with the fact that many of them

---

30 *Les Papiers de Richelieu. Politique intérieure: Correspondance et papiers d'état*, ed Pierre Grillon, 6 vols (Paris 1975, in progress), vi. 594–5, letter of 21 Sept 1631: 'une proposition que, vous sçavez bien, le roi ne peut effectuer'.
31 Conti succeeded Richelieu as abbot-general of Cluny in 1643, when he was fourteen, and was a candidate for the red hat during the Fronde.
32 Jean-Pierre Labatut, *Les Ducs et pairs de France au xvii* siècle* (Paris 1972), 74.
33 See Joseph Bergin, 'The Decline and Fall of the House of Guise as an Ecclesiastical Dynasty', *Historical Journal*, 25 (1983), 781–803. Retz's original expression was 'l'esprit le moins ecclésiastique qui fût au monde'.

were also cardinals, helped to heighten the aristocratic, even princely, character of France's leading bishops. That character was given additional lustre by the number of Italian cardinals from families like the Farnese, the Este, and the Trivulzio who held French bishoprics during the same period. Among these French prelates, we find illustrious names like Montmorency-Châtillon, Albret, Foix, Grammont, Luxembourg, Armagnac, Tournon, and Lenoncourt. But few of them were left by the time of Henri III. In some cases, this was due to their families adopting Calvinism (Albret), subdividing into Catholic and Protestant branches (for example, the Montmorency-Châtillon), or simply dying out altogether (Armagnac, Luxembourg). Other high-ranking families, such as the La Marck-Bouillon, Rohan or La Trémouille, might well have formed part of this episcopal élite, but they, too, were debarred by having adopted Protestantism. It also seems likely that the high mortality rates among such families occasioned first by the Italian and then the religious wars deprived them of younger sons to place in the church. At any rate, in subsequent decades, few natural successors to them appeared, and any attempt to match their success was probably rendered nugatory by the gradual suppression of episcopal pluralism in the decades following Trent. Had that not been so, rising families like the Joyeuse and Nogaret de la Valette might well have succeeded in emulating them, especially in the conditions of Henri III's reign, but they also lacked a sufficient number of family members capable of holding major episcopal titles at the moment, itself relatively brief, of their greatest influence. Perhaps the most surprising of all aristocratic absences from the highest circles of the French church was that of the Montmorency family, the disastrous experience of their Châtillon cousins excepted. The second Constable Montmorency did apparently have ecclesiastical ambitions for his illegitimate sons, one of whom answered to the title of 'Monsieur de Carcassonne' in the 1580s, but despite his power and favour in the latter years of his life, Montmorency was not the most adroit in promoting family interests.[34] To the extent that Montmorency's ambitions did come to anything, it was through related families like the Ventadour, the Budos, Fay-Peyraud and, as we saw, the Valois-Auvergne, in the first half of the seventeenth century.

The gradual disappearance by the early seventeenth century, of bishops of royal, princely, and high aristocratic pedigree – as indeed of their Italian counterparts – was bound to alter the character of the episcopate in more ways than one. If it did not preclude the renewed domination of the episcopate by the nobility from the 1640s onwards, the nobility in question was one which was increasingly reaching downwards to include those ennobled by office rather than upwards towards the highest circles of the aristocracy. It may even seem that the isthmus had been repaired and the clock turned back a century

---

[34] I am indebted to Joan Davies for several discussions of this subject, which her forthcoming book will investigate thoroughly.

or more by the later years of Louis XIV's reign, when the leading ecclesiastics would bear names like Bouillon, Noailles, Forbin, Estrées, and Rohan-Soubise, and when the red hat was not thought appropriate for Archbishop Harlay of Paris, nor the son of a financier like Bossuet, for all his outstanding abilities, thought suitable for Paris itself. But most of these new *grands d'église* were the beneficiaries of family mobility during the intervening generations and Louis XIV's own policies. Meanwhile, the ability of Richelieu and Mazarin to dominate the affairs of the French clergy, despite their less than elevated social origins, probably owed somewhat less than is usually imagined to their undoubted power and talents, and somewhat more to the altered social structure of the episcopate.

These considerations lead naturally to an analysis of the nobility which was actually present in the episcopate between Henri IV and Mazarin. As indicated earlier, the French nobility was a house with many mansions, and because it was in a state of constant evolution, no one set of criteria – rank, antiquity, mode of ennoblement etc – can fully account for its 'constitution' at any particular juncture. But since we are concerned here with the ancestry of the 222 bishops of noble extraction rather than with bishops themselves, it is justifiable to approach the subject in terms of modes of entry to the nobility rather than of putative types of nobility *per se*. It should for that reason be noted here that in order to assign bishops and their families to one group or another, it is the status of the family around the time of the bishop's birth which has been taken into account. In other words, it is the actual social rank of their fathers when the bishops were born which serves as the social *terminus ad quem*, and which has determined whether they should be regarded as being of noble or non-noble birth. For example, Guillaume Fouquet de la Varenne, bishop of Angers 1616–21, was son of Guillaume Fouquet, a companion of Henri IV. But for all the efforts made to disguise the facts, his origins were distinctly commoner, and it was only many years after the bishop's birth that the king ennobled his father.[35] By this reckoning, the bishop of Angers was born into a commoner family. Other examples could be cited of bishops born into families which had acquired ennobling offices, but had not held them long enough to be regarded as effectively ennobled by them.

Of the 130 bishops who, *faute de mieux*, can be loosely grouped together under the heading of 'old' nobility, the largest contingent, numbering no fewer than 107 bishops in all, was drawn from families whose nobility can be traced back to 1500 and earlier. The date employed here may well suggest a high level of accuracy in tracing the pedigree of the families in question, but no historian of later medieval or sixteenth-century France will be surprised at how much approximation is involved in these calculations. The ease with which non-noble families stepped into the shoes of declining or extinct noble families, sometimes bearing the same surname, both before and after 1500 is

---

35 See *DBF*, xiv. cols 722–3; Daniel Dessert, *Fouquet* (Paris 1987), 18.

the principal reason for this uncertainty.[36] Thus, to label them either a *noblesse de race* or a *noblesse d'épée* will always be partially misleading, since in many cases their *race* was neither particularly ancient nor eminent, while their *épée* status was, as often as not, something that followed rather than preceded their aggregation to the nobility. This was commonly based on a combination of factors such as the possession of fiefs, intermarriage with noble families, exemption from the *taille* and, not least, acceptance by local nobles. For the same reason, it makes even less sense to attempt to identify their nobility as either military or non-military in origin. What they have in common is arguably something more negative, but which they were happy enough to boast about in later centuries – the fact that their status was *not* derived from specific patents or confirmations of nobility and, above all, that they could not find any precise origin for it. In the circumstances, the purely descriptive label of 'old' nobility seems the one that best fits them, provided we do not subscribe to the nobility's own myths of their ancient origins.

To the 107 bishops who can be credited with pre-1500 noble origins of this type, we may add eight more, the time-scale of whose nobility remains unclear; their status as nobles by the time they became bishops is not in dispute, and it is likely that in at least some cases their nobility only became indisputable in the course of the sixteenth century. This leads on to the final two subgroups to be considered here – those who joined the ranks of the nobility 'par agrégation' during the sixteenth century. The first contains eight bishops drawn from four families of Italian origin which settled definitively in France during the sixteenth century and who belong in different ways to this group. The Dony and Litolfi-Moroni were regarded as nobles in Italy, where definitions of nobility were not the same as in France, and it seems that this was readily accepted when they were naturalised in France. In any case, subsequent intermarriage with French nobles smoothed their social integration.[37] By contrast, the Gondis and the Delbène, each of whom produced three bishops in our period, can be regarded as achieving noble status in France itself during the sixteenth century, after long careers in banking and finance; this is particularly clear in the case of the Gondis, thanks to a marshal's baton and a peerage for Albert de Gondi, duc de Retz (1522–1602).

The remaining subgroup is comprised of seven bishops drawn from French families which only acceded to similar noble status during the sixteenth century through military activities or fief-holding. They include, for example,

---

36 Numerous studies have revealed the extent to which ennoblement was a tacit social process. See E Perroy, 'Social Mobility among the French *noblesse* in the later Middle Ages', *Past and Present*, 21 (1962), 25–38; Huppert, *Les Bourgeois gentilshommes*.

37 BN, MS Fr 33047, p 475, naturalisation of Octavien Doni, son of Jacques (sic) 'noble florentin', Nov 1575; *ibid*, p 485, naturalisation of Constance de Litolfi, 'noble mantouan', Sept 1600. Doni married Michel de Marillac's sister, Litolfi the heiress of a Norman noble family.

Jean d'Estrades, bishop of Condom 1648–58, whose brother, Geoffroy comte d'Estrades, was a prominent diplomat and marshal of France before and after the Fronde. Like many families, the d'Estrades claimed to be *noblesse chevaleresque* with medieval origins, but in fact, they were bourgeois and (non-noble) office-holders of Agen before the generation of the bishop's grandfather. It was service under marshal Bellegarde during the religious wars that launched them on the road to noble status; Tallemant des Réaux's mid-seventeenth-century comment that they were *dubiae nobilitatis* should not be taken to mean that their nobility was a fiction, but that it was far less antique than they would have wished, given their recent achievements.[38] Another such family is that of Jean de Miossens-Sansons, bishop of Oloron 1652–8, whose origins were deliberately confused by his family in order to attach themselves to a branch of the Amanieu d'Albret family which held as one of its titles the comté of Miossens; the confusion was further facilitated by a marriage alliance with the Albret-Miossens, but it only took place in the bishop's own lifetime! In reality, the Miossens family is almost impossible to trace with any certainty before the mid-sixteenth century. In this case, too, what we are witnessing is a rather late insertion into the Béarnais nobility, helped by fief ownership, military service, and intermarriage in an age when such mobility was not yet restrained by royal policy.[39] The phenomenon was widespread in sixteenth-century France, but if only four bishops attained noble status in this fashion, it was probably because those taking this route needed patrons like Albret or Bellegarde if they were not to remain mired in the relative anonymity that characterised those who had been tacitly ennobled in this way.

We may now turn to the remaining bishops of noble origin, who numbered ninety-two in all. For different reasons, this contingent is if anything more heterogeneous than those we have just seen, but it has a positive rather than negative common feature in that its nobility is in principle traceable to a specific act of ennoblement, or to a continuous period of tenure of ennobling offices of one kind or another. Social pressures and royal policy between them ensured that the spectrum of those embraced by such a general heading was extensive. As a result, a certain amount of subdivision is necessary if the scale and meaning of the process is to emerge in any detail. Perhaps the most marginal subgroup consists of those who were ennobled by royal letters. They account for only seven bishops in all, with no fewer than three from a branch of the Villars family ennobled by Henri III in 1586. But they also include Artus de Lionne, bishop of Gap and father of Louis XIV's foreign minister, and Henri Arnauld, bishop of Angers, whose father was also ennobled by Henri III in 1577. With only five families involved, it would be easy to pass over this statistically insignificant group without further comment. Letters of

---

38 Gédéon Tallemant des Réaux, *Historiettes*, ed Antoine Adam, 2 vols (Paris 1960–1), ii. 663.
39 Charles de Beaumont, *Pièces inédites tirées des archives de la maison de Miossens-Sansons* (Pau 1885).

ennoblement were not held in high esteem in sixteenth- and seventeenth-century France, since they were sold for cash, and their worth was undermined by the fact that the crown itself regularly revoked them. Yet families like the Villars, Lionne, Arnauld, Maupeou and Serres were obviously of sufficient resourcefulness and eminence to survive these sudden reverses, retain their new noble status without obvious taint, and pursue their social and political ascent with considerable success. Three other bishops, however, have not been included among the nobility here, because the ennoblement they obtained was ostensibly no more than a confirmation of nobility which had allegedly been lost in recent generations owing to family misfortunes of one kind or another, and the confirmation occurred well into the careers of the bishops in question. A classic example of this tactic concerns Jean de Lingendes (bishop of Sarlat 1642–7, Mâcon 1651–65) who along with his brothers served Anne of Austria for many years; in return she obligingly issued them a long patent confirming and *restoring* their alleged old noble status in 1646, blithely ignoring the fact that the bishop's father was a *bourgeois* of Moulins.[40] The family of Etienne le Meingre (bishop of Grasse 1604–24) went even further: they obtained a similar confirmation of nobility from Henri IV, when they claimed descent from the early fifteenth-century marshal Boucicault; in reality they were descended from a local fisherman, a fraud which was only discovered and punished during the *recherches de noblesse* under Louis XIV.[41]

As might be expected, the great majority of families we are concerned with at present were ennobled by offices. The general features of this development and its broad political significance have been repeatedly discussed by historians, especially in recent decades. But as soon as one moves from generalisation to detailed analysis of ennoblement, it becomes apparent that to designate all those whose nobility was acquired *par charges* as belonging to an undifferentiated *noblesse de robe* is not particularly illuminating. Neither the reality nor the idea of a distinctive *noblesse de robe* can be applied to sixteenth- or early seventeenth-century France with any great conviction; to do so would be to lump together a number of avenues to nobility which had their own peculiar features and which, more to the point here, can delineate more precisely the kinds of office-based nobility enjoyed by the families of bishops.[42]

---

40 BN, MS Fr 4139, fos 314–18.
41 François-Paul Blanc, *Origines des familles provençales maintenues dans le second ordre sous le règne de Louis XIV. Dictionnaire généalogique* (Unpublished law dissertation, Aix-en-Provence 1971), 129–30. The letters of confirmation, partly quoted here, fabricate an explanation of their *dérogeance* and reasons from recent history (service during the religious wars) why they should be restored.
42 François Bluche and Pierre Durye, *Anoblissement par charges avant 1789*, 2 vols (in *Les Cahiers Nobles*, vols 23–4, n.p., 1962).

Historically, it was municipal offices, particularly those of mayor or alderman (both known by a great variety of names throughout France), which were the earliest *charges anoblissantes*. Moreover, this *noblesse de cloche* as it became known, was not something which had to be laboriously consolidated over two or more generations before it became transmissible to subsequent generations: a *capitoul* of Toulouse, a *consul* of Lyon, or a mayor or *échevin* of Poitiers or Angers was ennobled to the first degree (or generation) after a single term (usually a year) in office, whereas a presidency or councillorship in a sovereign court had to be held continually for at least two generations. But since only thirteen French cities possessed such an enviable privilege in the sixteenth century, it is not altogether surprising that, despite the widely scattered geographical origins of bishops, the families of only seventeen bishops entered the nobility by this route.[43] Of course, to some of these families, municipal office and the nobility it conferred was merely a social and professional *terminus a quo*, from which they rose into far more eminent positions; their subsequent experiences show just how office-based social mobility could be. The Bellièvre family's nobility may have originated with consular office in Lyon, but by the end of the sixteenth century, their status had risen infinitely higher than that, thanks to a presidency in the Grenoble parlement and the dignity of chancellor of France: within little more than a generation, *noblesse de cloche* had been subsumed into the parlementaire and ministerial *grande robe*. The Bouthillier family are usually held to have been ennobled under François I through municipal office in their native Angoulême, as were their neighbours the Nesmond family, but a generation or more later, Denis and Jean Bouthillier were practising as barristers in Paris. Although the practice of law did not of itself entail a loss of noble status, their nobility cannot have been especially evident to clients, acquaintances or colleagues, and the fact that they used the term 'noble homme' to describe their social status, amounts to nothing less than a confession of commoner status. However, in the next generation, two of Denis Bouthillier's sons became bishops, while the eldest, Claude, removed any doubts about their social ascension into the nobility by becoming successively secretary of state and *surintendant des finances*: by definition, ministerial office, involving as it did direct personal service to the king, could not but ennoble anyone who held it, however humble his social origins might be. The nobility of Mathieu Thoreau, the last bishop to be nominated by Mazarin in early 1661, was based on the mayoralty of Poitiers held by his father in 1621, since the office of *trésorier de France* that he and his son also held had not yet generated transmissible noble status. Within the opposite ends of the spectrum of ennoblement represented by these cases, we find many other families whose progress was far less spectacular, partly because of their geographical mobility.

---

43 *Ibid*, i. 25–37, for the towns concerned and the officials entitled to claim noble status.

With the exception of those ennobled for direct personal service to the king, instant ennoblement tended to be derided throughout the *ancien régime*, but such disparagement was as nothing compared to the scorn reserved for those purchasing positions of *secrétaire du roi* and associated offices in the different branches of the royal chancery. Not even the fact that these increasingly expensive sinecures were actually older than other forms of ennoblement by royal office could prevent them from being labelled *savonnettes à vilain*, as they mainly attracted financiers anxious to enjoy noble privileges without the purificatory delay imposed by 'normal' offices, and to escape the opprobrium which contemporary attitudes about their allegedly abject social origins usually entailed.

Fourteen bishops owed their nobility originally to this decried but perfectly legal source, and most of the ennoblements in question can be traced to the sixteenth century. Few of the bishops whose fathers had been *secrétaires du roi* acceded rapidly to the episcopate, and gaps of thirty to forty years between the two events are not uncommon – time enough for the bishops' own generation to move into less questionable avenues to social respectability. Bishops drawn from families ennobled by offices of *secrétaire du roi* were either originally from, or had converged on, Paris in the course of the sixteenth century, since it was there that most of these offices were available until Colbert's time.[44] Considering how high the Neufville de Villeroy family rose under Louis XIV – two highly attractive bishoprics followed by a marshal's baton and a peerage – it is worth noting that their nobility dates from around 1507, when the grandfather of Henri III's and Henri IV's minister was a *secrétaire du roi*. But few of the remaining Parisian families ennobled in this way exhibited comparable staying power or distinction. The Bertier family was originally ennobled by municipal office in Toulouse in the fifteenth century, while succeeding generations held offices of *secrétaire du roi* throughout the first half of the sixteenth century. But they resisted the temptation to uproot themselves geographically or seek higher status and office in Paris, as they might well have done. This decision may well seem to have imposed a long wait, as far as the episcopate was concerned, on a family with its fair share of clerics in each generation. But by the time their turn came, their powerful position in the Toulouse parlement and extensive family connections were enough for them to hold the see of Rieux for nearly a century.[45] Furthermore, when in the early 1630s one of them was awarded the coadjutorship of Montauban, the choice was widely welcomed on the grounds that his family and relatives were sufficiently powerful in the region to enable

---

44 David D Bien, 'Manufacturing Nobles: The Chancelleries in France to 1789', *Journal of Modern History*, 61 (1989), 449–50.
45 See J B Dubédat, *Histoire du parlement de Toulouse*, 2 vols (Paris 1885), esp vol ii; William Beik, *Absolutism and Society in Seventeenth-Century France* (Cambridge 1984). Extensive archives, preserved in the Pinsaguel branch of the family, remain, and their testaments and marriage contracts show the extent of their social relations: AD Haute-Garonne, 6J series.

the Catholicisation of this former Huguenot stronghold to proceed with greater effectiveness.[46]

However, the majority of bishops' families ennobled by office achieved their status by following a more conventional route, one which required at least two generations of tenure of an ennobling office before the noble privileges which its incumbents enjoyed personally could be transmitted to their descendants. As has been pointed out, this kind of nobility was gradual and purely customary until 1600, when Henri IV's well-known edict regulating the *taille* gave it tangible, statutory foundations for the first time; this, along with further legislative developments during the seventeenth century, was what made it far more common in the seventeenth and eighteenth centuries to think in terms of a specific *noblesse de robe*.[47] By Louis XIV's time, ennoblement by any means other than office-holding had virtually been eliminated. For the period we are concerned with here, this route to nobility mainly meant holding office in the sovereign courts – parlements, *chambres des comptes, cours des aides, bureaux des finances* – since it was only later during the seventeenth and eighteenth century that lesser courts gradually obtained similar privileges.

It seems that fifty-five bishops in all owed their nobility to this form of office-holding. The total may seem a rather modest one – almost exactly a quarter of all bishops from noble families – but it should be remembered that it refers to the origins of their nobility rather than to later developments within their families or within families ennobled by other means. Only three may be regarded as having been ennobled directly by holding ministerial office – Clausse, Laubespine, and Vic; in each of the three cases, ennoblement occurred during the sixteenth century. All but ten of the remaining fifty-two owed their status to office in the parlements. Among the latter, the lion's share went to Paris, which accounted for twenty-three in all, while Dijon could only muster one (Frémiot) and Rennes two (Champion and Caset). Bordeaux and Toulouse managed only four and five respectively, though with successive members of the Daffis family – which produced three bishops in our period – alternately holding office in both parlements, it is a moot point as to which parlement should be credited with ennobling them.

With only twenty bishops from families ennobled by the provincial parlements, it is hardly necessary to labour the point that these parlements played only a modest role in supplying recruits to the episcopate, even in the provinces where they were located; that role improves slightly if we were to add to the total those not yet noble bishops whose families were active in the parlements. The prominence of Paris, on the other hand, confirms the importance of both the city and its parlement as a recruiting ground for

---

46 ASV, PC 34, fos 405–32, dossier *de vita et moribus*, early 1634, for Pierre de Bertier.
47 Bluche and Durye, *Anoblissement par charges*, ii. 15–18, for a concise statement of the legal position.

Table 5.5 Origins of bishops' nobility

Decade	Old	Ennobled	Cloche	SR	Charges	Total
1590s	19	0	3	0	9	31
1600s	20		4	1	7	32
1610s	19	2	4	1	11	37
1620s	22	0	2	1	9	34
1630s	11	1	0	3	6	21
1640s	17	1	1	5	7	31
1650s	22	2	3	3	6	36
Total	130	6	17	14	55	222

ecclesiastical as well as administrative élites; this becomes even clearer when it is realised that some of the families, such as Le Clerc de Lesseville or Habert, whose nobility was derived initially from ennoblement or offices of *secrétaire du roi*, subsequently went on to make careers over several generations in the parlement there.[48]

This analysis should make it possible to grasp one of the major differences between the episcopate of François I and that of a century later. Not only was the total percentage of nobles in its ranks smaller by Louis XIII's time, but the nobility in question was more diverse in origin. However, the comparison as it stands is rather a static one. How far is it possible to follow the evolution during our period of the episcopate in respect of the origins of those who were noble? The accompanying table (5.5) offers a breakdown of the nobility among the episcopate in accordance with the descriptive labels proposed earlier in the chapter.

In discussing the above data and its significance, relatively little needs to be said about the three numerically small categories (ennobled, cloche, SR), except perhaps to reiterate the point made above about the slowness of sons of families ennobled through offices of *secrétaire du roi* to enter the episcopate. Their presence only becomes noteworthy from the 1630s onwards. This would seem to leave the field to the old nobility and those progressively ennobled *par charges* in the classic manner. But it is also worth repeating that they are not to be viewed as rivals locked into some kind of struggle for episcopal office, not least because in some provinces at least robe families often had their roots in older noble families.[49] What is evident from the table in any case, is that old noble families consistently provided the largest contingent of new bishops, and that the numbers did not vary a great deal between the 1590s and the 1620s inclusive. The 1630s did register a sharp fall in their

---

48 See François Bluche, *Les Magistrats du parlement de Paris au xviiie siècle* (Paris 1960), s.v. Lesseville, Habert.
49 See Jonathan Dewald, *The Formation of a Provincial Nobility. The Parlement of Rouen 1499–1610* (Princeton 1980), for the most valuable contribution.

numbers, but recovery was under way by the 1640s and was fully confirmed by the 1650s. As for those ennobled by office, it is noteworthy that those whose ennoblement was gradual rather than immediate also did best between the 1590s and the 1620s, and registered the single highest score during the 1610s when ministerial and *robe* families were well placed to push their interests with some success in a period of ministerial and political instability. By contrast, their fortunes sagged during the 1630s and remained that way into the 1650s. With commoners becoming more rare among the episcopate during the 1640s and 1650s, it might be expected that sons of ennobled office-holders would take their places, but it was sons of old nobles and of families ennobled by offices of *secrétaires du roi*, who claimed more episcopal prizes than at any time in the past. The fact that eight of the fifteen bishops from the latter category were seated during the 1640s and 1650s will hardly come as a surprise in view of what is known about the influence of financial circles during the Mazarin ministry before, and especially after, the Fronde.

In the longer perspective, stretching from the age of François I to that of Louis XVI, it would seem that the bishops seated between Henri IV's accession and Mazarin's death were, along with those of Charles IX and Henri III, among the most socially diverse. The episcopal generation of 1789 included only one undisputed commoner out of a total that now stood at 130 bishops, of whom 60 per cent could prove nobility antedating the year 1400, and 70 per cent antedating 1560.[50] Obviously, this kind of episcopate had not been conjured up overnight. The high levels of noble tenure of bishoprics evident from the 1640s onwards were confirmed and enhanced in subsequent decades. During the mid-years of Louis XIV's personal rule, from 1682 to 1700, bishops of noble stock already accounted for over 91 per cent of the bishops whose social origins are known; at the same time, as the proportions just cited suggest, bishops from recently ennobled families were also becoming fewer and fewer.[51] From the evidence of the present study, it seems fair to trace the beginnings of this noble reconquest to the post-Fronde years. The days when nearly one out of every three to four bishops could be non-noble would gradually become remote, even unthinkable.

III

The study of the nobility and of ennoblement, particularly in the sixteenth and early seventeenth centuries, underlines the extent to which bishops'

---

50 Michel Péronnet, 'Quelques réflexions sur les critères d'analyse d'un groupe social: la noblesse dans une durée séculaire', in *L'Anoblissement en France xve-xviiie siècles. Théories et réalités* (Bordeaux n.d. [1985]), 148–9, 152.
51 Norman Ravitch, *Sword and Mitre: Government and Episcopacy in France and England in the Age of Aristocracy* (The Hague 1966), 69–70.

families were in continual evolution, making the social distinctions devised by historians often resemble lines drawn in the sand. While many may have felt called to the episcopate, the few who were actually chosen clearly did not owe their success to their social rank alone. Other factors, some of which will be treated in later chapters, have also to be taken into account. However, one particular factor merits some consideration here, since it so often seems to be a natural extension of social status, namely the professional origins of the bishops. Of course, the term 'professional origins' has an unmistakably modern ring to it, reflecting an age in which social identity and rank are increasingly viewed in terms of well-defined professional activities. It goes without saying that its applicability to a society in which the dominant social ideal was one which encouraged people to live without exercising any profession at all, can only be problematic.[52] Equally problematic is the fact that certain offices, many of which were anything but sinecures, were filled not on the basis of merit or achievement, but on the social status of their incumbents. On these contrasting grounds alone, the relevance of professional activities to success in achieving high office in the church or elsewhere would seem limited at best. But these objections would deter a sociologist more than a historian of early modern society. What a study of the bishops' professional origins may enable us to do is to discover how far professional activities enabled sons of particular families to gain an advantage over others in the quest for episcopal office, by building upon, or compensating for the lack of, social status.

In fact the subject is potentially limitless in its scope. Ideally it would be necessary to analyse the professional origins of bishops on both the paternal and maternal sides of their families, and pursue the subject into the generation of their grandparents. And since we are dealing with non-venal, non-hereditary offices held by celibate ecclesiastics, it should also direct attention to their uncles, paternal and maternal. In practice, this could only be undertaken and achieve worthwhile results through exhaustive genealogical research, but even then it is virtually certain that the gaps in our information would be sufficiently enormous to inhibit satisfactory analysis. Even an attempt to study the activities of just the paternal grandfathers of the bishops has proved impractical owing to the fact that reliable information was available in too few cases. The problems facing the historian can readily be inferred from the scope of what follows, which is limited to a discussion of the evidence that is available for just the fathers of the bishops.

Information is available on the activities of the fathers of 243 (75 per cent) out of the 323 French-born bishops. As far as can be judged, both information and the lack of it is fairly randomly distributed across the social spectrum; it does not appear to be purely a function of modest social origins. In some

---

52 See the discussion in David A Bell, *Lawyers and Citizens. The Making of a Political Elite in Old Régime France* (Oxford 1994), 15–18.

respects, the more modest a bishop's social origins, the more contemporaries were likely to have enquired about his father's occupation, though caution is in order before taking their statements at face-value. Just as frequently virtually nothing can be discovered about the activities of the heads of families of long-established nobility, among whom it was not unknown for leading members to pass their entire lives *sans charges*; for others, it may simply be that information about the *charges* they held has not been recorded.[53] The intendants' reports under Louis XIV, particularly to Colbert in the 1660s, show how common it was for provincial *gentilshommes* to live on their estates in this way, despite pressure to serve the crown, especially in the royal armies. On the other hand, as already noted, notions like career and profession only very roughly fit the experience of those members of the old nobility for whom information is available. The higher up the social hierarchy families and individuals were located, the more likely they were to divide their time between several activities, some of which were exercised at the same time. Some of these men moved so imperceptibly from one rôle to another that registering their most notable activity – for example, those of ambassador or marshal of France – does not fully account for their professional rank.

Since no single method of classification of offices and activities is wholly satisfactory, it may be best to adopt one which fits best with a central theme of this book, the acquisition of office through proximity – which does not always imply physical proximity – to the royal power in its various manifestations. The following table brings together the activities, professions and offices held by fathers of bishops in three groups (Table 5.6).

The obvious starting-point for an analysis of this data, the court, is paradoxically among the most poorly documented and elusive. Most existing accounts of the *société de cour* fail dismally to give any real sense of what holding office entailed and how many people were normally active there at any particular time; in particular, it is virtually impossible to establish a distinction between those habitually employed at court and the much larger group of those, overwhelmingly nobles, who qualify as 'courtiers' by occasional attendance there.[54] The problem will return later when the activities of royal almoners who became bishops are discussed.[55] In the accompanying table, only nine members of the nobility have been assigned court office, purely because no other *charge* is known to have been held by them, or because

---

53 See Manfred Orléa, *La Noblesse aux états généraux de 1576 et de 1588* (Paris 1980), 138, makes this point about Louis de Brichantau, grandfather of the Brichantau brothers, Benajamin and Philibert, who were successively bishops of Laon. His observations would seem to apply to many other established noble families.
54 See Jean-François Solnon, *La Cour de France* (Paris 1987) is the most recent and ample study, but it is primarily a cultural history of the court, emphasising its civilising role.
55 The surviving records do not fully record even those individuals who were attached to the court by formal office-holding there: Jacqueline Boucher, 'L'Evolution de la maison du roi: des derniers Valois aux premiers Bourbons', *XVII Siècle* no 136 (1982), 359–79, esp 359–61.

Table 5.6 Professions of bishops' fathers

Group 1	
Court office	9
Ambassador	11
Marshal of France	6
Military command	10
Unspecified military office	20
Naval posts	2
Provincial governor	14
Provincial lt-gen	8
Urban governor	13
Prévôt/Sénéchal/bailli	4
Group 2	
Minister	8
Conseiller d'état	3
Maître des Requêtes	8
President of Parlement	16
Avocat- or Proc-General, Parlement	4
Conseiller of Parlement	13
Offices in other sovereign courts	15
Financiers/financial officials	18
Lesser royal office-holders	8
Urban magistrates	2
Greffier/syndic of Estates	3
Group 3	
Barrister	12
Procureur	1
Notary	4
Marchand-bourgeois	17
Doctor	5
Teacher	2
Others	7

their court office was the culmination of their careers. The difficulties are evident in the career of François de Richelieu, father of the two cardinals. His court office of *grand prévôt de l'hôtel et de France*, attained in 1578, was without doubt the high point of his career, which since the mid-1560s had seen him gradually rise through the ranks of the Montpensier *gendarmerie* regiment to the rank of captain; that part of his career was probably typical of many of the nobles entered in the above table as simply *militaires*. Thirteen individuals have also been entered as ambassadors, but high-level diplomacy in this period required a combination of social status, independent financial means, and powerful political connections – in other words, it was reserved mainly for wealthy nobles who already had a firm foothold at court. Only ambassadors to the Swiss Leagues occasionally departed from this pattern, possibly because France's relations with the Swiss were mainly about money and mercenaries.[56]

The headings which seem to apply to the largest segment of the nobility we are concerned with, are those of military officerships and various types of governorship. Between them they account for the fathers of seventy-five bishops. Posts like provincial governor or lieutenant-general, of governor of a town or a fortress or, to a lesser extent, of *sénéchal* or *bailli*, were primarily military functions, though any suggestion of a line tightly drawn around their military activities should be dismissed. Such posts were undoubtedly held by a number of those who have been entered as marshals of France, military commanders, or military officers without any particular qualification. In addition, court positions and political influence there also came their way, so that it was the *cumul* of functions, or more precisely of sources of power, central and local, military and political, rather than the primacy of any one of them in particular, which (as in more recent French history) accounts for their success in promoting family ambitions, inside and outside the church. The full range of possible combinations was, to say the least, extensive, and of course the greater it was the more it would provide a framework for the development of ties of clientage within the nobility. At the top of the pyramid, we might place the duc de Guise who was murdered in 1588: he was *grand maître de France*, the most prestigious office at court, governor of Champagne, and frequently commander of the royal army.[57] Over a generation later and much nearer the bottom of the pyramid, we could point to Jean Faure, from Sainte Quiterie in the Angoumois and possibly (but not certainly) of modest noble extraction, whose only known activity was that of governor of the town of Mirebeau, between Poitiers and Loudun. Somewhere in between these two extremes we might locate the Provençal noble Pierre Valavoire, a captain in the governor of the province's regiment and himself governor of the town of Sisteron; his service, his ties to important local families, and the governor's patronage all helped to bring him to Mazarin's attention in the 1640s, and finally to obtain a diocese (Riez in Provence) for his son, Nicolas, in 1652.[58]

---

56 E Rott, *Histoire de la représentation de la France auprès des cantons suisses, de leurs alliés et de leurs confédérés*, 10 vols (Berne 1900–35), esp vols 2–3. Successive ambassadors in the later sixteenth and seventeenth century were linked closely, sometimes by marriage, to the *trésoriers des ligues suisses*.

57 The office of *grand maître* made its holder titular head of the king's own household. For that reason, it should not be compared with offices like that of Admiral or Constable of France, which were of a somewhat different order, and were *grandes dignités de la Couronne*.

58 Sharon Kettering, *Patrons, Brokers and Clients in Seventeenth-Century France* (Oxford 1986), 92–3.

In all, therefore, ninety-seven bishops (30 per cent of all French-born bishops, and nearly 40 per cent of those among them for whom information is available) were born to fathers engaged at one time or another in diplomatic, military and gubernatorial activities. All but a handful of them were drawn from noble families, especially those of old noble stock.

The second set of professional activities may be equally wide-ranging internally, but they correspond more closely to what we might regard as continuous professional activity – political, legal, financial and municipal office. It also embraces far more individuals who were of non-noble background but whose families would almost always attain noble status a generation or so later. It accounts for the fathers of ninety-eight bishops. A substantial proportion of them may also be compared to the military-gubernatorial nobility, in that their offices, ranging from those of minister or secretary of state through *maîtres des requêtes* to presidents of parlements, ensured that they were men of considerable influence and connections. This can be seen most clearly in the fact that over two-thirds of them, or sixty-seven of the ninety-eight, were members of sovereign courts or held higher office. This bias in favour of highly placed office-holders becomes even more pronounced if we add the six bishops who were sons of major financial figures, since some of them, such as *intendants des finances* or *trésoriers de l'Epargne*, could enjoy influence and connections that were if anything superior to those even of presidents of the Paris parlement. Only about a quarter of the bishops in this category were sons of minor, mostly provincial, office-holders.

It is, inevitably, towards the bottom end of the professional hierarchy that we find most of the bishops who were sons of commoners. The symmetry is not perfect, especially for the sixteenth century, when commoners could be found in a large number of offices which, by Louis XIV's time, would be mostly out of bounds to them. Not surprisingly, it has proved possible to discover only forty-eight bishops whose fathers' occupations belong to this general category. The largest contingent is that of the *marchand-bourgeois*, but even here there is some imprecision, since the term itself, so typical of *ancien régime* society, allows for considerable variation between *rentier* and commercial lifestyles. The practice of the law in one form or another – notary, *procureur* and *avocat* – which was in almost every case a preliminary to the acquisition of an office of magistrate, constitutes the other main contingent. It is perhaps more unexpected to learn that five bishops were sons of medical doctors, not an especially respected profession, and one in which physicians despised surgeons! However, three of the five were sons of court doctors in the service of the king. It was to Henri IV's generosity that four out of five owed their episcopal rank. Two of them, Gaspard and Honoré du Laurens became archbishops of Arles and Embrun respectively, thanks not to their father, a doctor, but to their brother, who was physician (*médécin ordinaire*) to Henri IV. The father of the du Perron brothers was also a doctor, but as he later became a Protestant pastor, he never came near to serving the crown; however, the future cardinal made up for this initial drawback by winning the powerful patronage of the marshal Matignon who introduced him to the intellectuals and courtiers around Henri III.

The remaining professions in this group have been perhaps arbitrarily gathered together as 'others', but their rather residual character is no reason to pass over them without comment. They are a reminder of the arbitrariness of any categorisation of rank and occupation in early modern France. Not all bishops whose fathers belong in this category were obliged to accept insignificant dioceses. Léonard Destrappes was the son of an apothecary from Nevers, but held the archbishopric of Auch, one of France's wealthiest sees, from 1598 to 1630. The father of Charles de Montchal, archbishop of Toulouse, also began his career as an apothecary only to end it as *bailli* of his native Annonay, a position not normally held by commoners like him. This group includes fathers of bishops who were teachers (Fenouillet and Bertaut, the poet-bishop of Séez). We have already encountered Etienne le Meingre of Grasse, son of a fisherman, and Denis Cohon of Nîmes, son of a candlemaker. No doubt the fathers of some other bishops, for whom no information at all is available, would answer to similar occupations.

It would probably be mistaken, however, to imagine that the seventy-nine bishops in all whose fathers' occupations remain unknown, were somehow scions of families of humble status and professional activities. Bishops of such background were always likely to elicit comment in a society which disliked rapid mobility generally, and which readily cast aspersions on the origins of those deemed to have risen too far and too quickly; if their numbers were considerable, they would not have escaped notice by contemporaries. Yet for all its limited scope, the present chapter should have conveyed something of the diversity of the episcopate in the period under study. This diversity comes across most clearly in the geographical and even the social origins of the bishops, and is not contradicted by the more limited evidence of parental professional activities. To the extent that bishops were made rather than born, it is essential to turn our attention to some of the most important elements of their own pre-episcopal experiences in order to understand better the kind of *cursus honorum* which culminated in episcopal office.

CHAPTER 6

Educating Bishops

IN THE GREEK from which it was derived, the word bishop (*episkopos*) meant 'overseer', and in the Roman and post-Roman West in particular, the role of bishops as the ruling élite of the expanding church became firmly established. The very fact that they also took over some of the activities and characteristics of the civil administrators of the late Empire – some distinguished bishops having previously been imperial officials themselves – led to a fusion of roles which only further emphasised their capacity as rulers in both church and society. Their position was reinforced for centuries to come by the church's economic power as a landowner and *seigneur*, the effect of which was to place most of France's bishops among the leading fief-holders and men of the realm.

Within this inextricable compound of roles and powers, there was an equally long-standing tradition which saw bishops in a rather different light – as teachers and instructors of their flock. This was particularly pronounced in the early church, some of whose greatest figures, later officially proclaimed doctors of the church, were bishops like Ambrose, Chrysostom or Augustine. In more recent times, this tradition has been self-consciously modernised and has seen bishops of nearly every confession being granted the courtesy title of 'doctor'. During the intervening centuries, this feature of episcopal office may have been less conspicuous, partly for reasons just suggested, but also because of the rise of the universities and the gradual emergence of papal claims to doctrinal supremacy, if not yet infallibility. Yet the overall responsibility of bishops for the religious behaviour and, indirectly, beliefs of their people, had not been seriously questioned. In the sixteenth and seventeenth centuries, the impact of the Reformation drew attention to it even more urgently, and led to widespread concern at the incapacity of many bishops, French or otherwise, for this particular task. The need to define and preserve Catholic practices was suddenly greater than ever, and the long history of the Council of Trent, sociologically one of the most 'episcopal' of all councils, brought this dimension of the episcopal tradition back into sharp focus. While the Council may have failed to reach consensus on the origins and extent of episcopal authority, there can be no doubt that in its aftermath there was growing emphasis on the responsibilities of bishops, especially on their duty to preach the truth, and on the need for new synodal statutes, pastoral instructions, and changes to liturgical and penitential practice. The post-tridentine Catholic was to be a believer who was familiar with the tenets of his faith, not merely someone who went to church and participated in its rituals.

This had several effects. One was to focus attention again on the traditional ideal of the *bonus pastor*. Like the mirror-of-princes literature which it so strongly resembles, this form of thinking tended to be rather static, its attention fixed on ideals which were often abstracted from reality and presented discretely, with relatively little thought as to how they were to be attained in practice. From Gerson onwards, there were few marked developments in this ideal, merely a greater sense of urgency about the need for bishops to conform to a minimum set of expectations. Perhaps for that very reason, the lives of model bishops like Carlo Borromeo of Milan or François de Sales of Geneva came to assume even greater significance to successive generations trying to put some flesh on an elusive, disembodied ideal. They also had the attraction of depicting bishops who were not distant administrators of dioceses, but who were prepared to sacrifice themselves by becoming personally involved in the work of religious reform.[1]

If there could be no doubting the desired end, what were the means towards that end? In particular, what kind of education was best suited for a bishop? Perhaps not surprisingly, the *bonus pastor* literature offered little concrete discussion of how individuals might be prepared intellectually for their lofty calling; discussion was, after all, about bishops who were already in office, not about those who might one day join their ranks. But this lacuna was the result of more than just genre rigidities. In particular, it probably had much to do with the broad character of a bishop's office: he was expected before all else to govern his diocese, and if he was also the doctor of his flock, this did not mean he was somehow regarded as a professor of divinity. Secondly, there was a widely held view that good birth could provide many of the qualities required in a bishop, one which made sons of noble families seem the most naturally suited for the office. Although the weaknesses of this view were also realised, suspicion of bishops of modest background was a commonplace in medieval literature, since all but an exceptional few were thought to possess neither the *auctoritas* nor the detachment from material things which the office required.[2]

But it is equally clear that from at least the twelfth or thirteenth century onwards, considerations of this kind could not resolve all questions about the intellectual standards expected of bishops. With hindsight, it would be easy

---

1 See Hubert Jedin, *L'Evêque dans la tradition pastorale du xvie siècle*, ed Paul Broutin (Brussels 1953).
2 See Alexander Murray, *Reason and Society in the Middle Ages* (Oxford 1978), ch 13.

to regard this merely as a problem about the extent to which bishops frequented universities and took degrees there. It may have taken on this guise by the seventeenth century, but it would be mistaken to think it had always done so; the idea of an episcopate whose members were university graduates was not always self-evident; it was slow to take root and was never fully achieved in early modern France. Before that, for much of the later Middle Ages, the ideal was the subtly different one of a 'lettered' episcopate, which might have been to university, but which might also have acquired its letters by other means. Such a flexible view fitted well with the continuing presence – and, at times, dominance – of the nobility among the episcopate, since in many parts of Europe until the sixteenth century and even beyond, the sons of the nobility either did not attend university or if they did, declined to take degrees which, after all, were primarily sought by sons of their social inferiors. The pretensions of graduates to noble status because of their academic achievements – to be a *Doktoradel* – cannot have impressed those whose nobility was hereditary! For all the later medieval church's concern with the demands of graduates for preferential treatment in the granting of benefices, it is no accident that bishoprics were virtually the only rank in the church to escape attempts to reserve them in whole or in part for university graduates. Both church and crown needed, and made extensive use of, able graduates, and both parties were perfectly ready to promote them to high office in the church. But, as Bernard Guenée has pointed out, those who had received a university degree and had demonstrated superior intellectual ability, required many other qualities if they were to become bishops in the later medieval church at all; unless they were nobles, few of them entered the episcopate early in their careers or were ever called to govern prominent dioceses.[3] There continued to be criticism of 'unlettered' bishops, but it tended to ebb and flow, depending on the extent to which the ranks of the episcopate were open to graduates or were dominated by sons of the nobility whose letters were not the result of attending university.[4]

In this respect, the Concordat of Bologna, whose less-familiar clauses had so much to say about the prerogatives of graduates where church benefices were concerned, represents a significant moment. It is usually seen merely as having abolished episcopal elections, and granting the king of France the formal right to nominate episcopal candidates for approval by the papacy. But both parties to the concordat were, in principle at least, agreed that this right could not be unfettered, and that royal choices had to be somehow guided by criteria of what constituted an acceptable candidate. And since the concordat actually obliged the pope to confirm suitable royal candidates, and not to reject them on frivolous or specious grounds, it was essential to spell out what the term 'suitable' meant; failure to do so might wreck the concordat by

---

3 Bernard Guenée, *Between Church and State* (Chicago 1991), 12ff.
4 Murray, *Reason and Society*, 292ff.

leading to endless disagreement over the choice of bishops. For that reason, it is worth looking briefly at the changes made before a final text of the concordat was agreed, as they afford a rare glimpse into the thinking of the *dramatis personae* of episcopal patronage rather than of writers of edifying treatises on episcopal virtues; unusually for this kind of undertaking, it also reveals some of their second thoughts and the exceptions to the general rule that they were prepared to consider. At Bologna itself, pope and king agreed that when a bishopric fell vacant, the king would nominate 'a graduate or a noble, who was in at least his twenty-seventh year, and who was suitable in other respects'; further on, it was specified that 'the king may however nominate individuals who are not so qualified, but only if they are of royal extraction'.[5] Yet a subsequent instruction given to the French ambassador sent to finalise the actual clauses of the concordat reads as follows:

> The words 'or a noble' should be removed. For the good of the church and in order to free the king from the demands of nobles in favour of individuals not sufficiently qualified, as well as to encourage the nobility to study, it is better for the church, the nobility, and the security of the king's conscience that those nominated to bishoprics, whether nobles or not, should be qualified as the Concordat requires . . . the king wishes the pope to understand that no nobles, apart from those of royal blood, are to be exempted from this.[6]

In its ultimate form, the concordat was much more precise than this, and stipulated that candidates for bishoprics should, in addition to being men of good reputation and capacity, have acquired a doctorate or licentiate in theology or in canon and civil law (*in utroque jure*, as it was called), or in *either* canon or civil law, from a famous university and after proper examination (*cum rigore examinis*), and be otherwise suitable. But just as the suitability clause gained in specificity, the scope of the exemption clause also widened, as the vague language of the text itself makes clear: 'Yet those related by blood to the king and other high-ranking individuals (*personae sublimes*) . . . shall, for legitimate and reasonable causes to be expressed in their nominations and papal provisions, be provided to bishoprics by us and the pope'.[7]

The message conveyed by the concordat was thus more than a little discordant, but it was not fundamentally altered in subsequent generations. The Council of Trent's debates which have most attracted historians' attention were those about episcopal authority in relation to the papacy, and this has often led to a neglect of less dramatic questions debated there. The council was slow to put forward its own demands in relation to the education required

---

5   Jules Thomas, *Le Concordat de 1516. Ses origines, son histoire au xvie siècle*, 3 vols (Paris 1910), i. 335.
6   *Ibid*, i. 421.
7   *Ibid*, ii. 69, for the Latin and French texts. Members of religious orders prevented from taking degrees by their orders' constitutions were also included in this category.

of bishops. It began in 1547 with a highly general proposal which required bishops to possess, among other things, learning (*scientia*) and other virtues. But it was not until 1562, in one of its last sessions, that it passed a resolution which required them to possess the knowledge necessary for the discharge of the duties of their office; more to the point, they should also have *legitimately* obtained the degree of master, doctor, or licentiate in theology or canon law; if a candidate was not a graduate, he should be officially certified by an academy as being capable of teaching others.[8] The council's thinking was a blend of tradition and innovation: it would prefer to see bishops who were graduates and who had taken their examinations like every other graduate, but it retained the notion of a lettered episcopate which was not necessarily university educated. One reason for this is that Trent, like the concordat before it, wished to make allowance for members of religious orders whose constitutions did not permit them to take degrees.

Within France, where the council's decrees were never promulgated with royal approval, there was little impetus to add to, or clarify, the terms of the concordat. Attempts to reform the episcopate by legislation tended to arise from the demands of the Estates General from 1560 onwards, but these demands mainly focused on the abuses in royal nominations and the desirability of returning to a system of elections. As with the abolition of the venality of office within the secular sphere, this was the panacea which would remove all ills and provide a worthy episcopate, making it unnecessary to consider the intellectual *parcours* required of its members.

It was already being said in sixteenth-century France that no country had better laws than the French, but also that no one observed them less. The fact that the concordat contained a clause requiring bishops to be university graduates, is usually taken as an expression of the views of François I himself on the need for the nobility to educate their sons. But that inference seems poorly grounded, and is rather flattering to the king when compared with the blunt reply attributed to his contemporary, Charles V, when the Franche-Comté nobility complained of being left out in the cold by the low-born Cardinal Granvelle: 'What do you want me to tell you – that you are ignorant, without learning and education? Give your children an education, and I will have them serve me; otherwise do not expect me to make them public servants, but only soldiers, cavalrymen or domestic servants in my household.'[9] It seems more likely that the insistence placed on formal educational qualifications by the concordat was inspired by men like Chancellor Duprat,

---

8 See Jean Bernhard, Charles Lefebvre, Francis Rapp, *L'Epoque de la réforme et du concile de Trente* (*Histoire du droit det des institutions de l'église en occident*, xiv) (Paris 1989), part III, ch 3, for an analysis of the council's concern with reforming the nomination to, and tenure of benefices generally; Pierre Blet, 'Le Concordat de Bologne et la réforme tridentine', *Gregorianum*, 45 (1964), 246–8.

9 Quoted in Richard L Kagan, *Students and Society in Early Modern Spain* (Baltimore 1974), xxi, n 7.

who were themselves graduates, but that it was not they who subsequently played the leading roles in the selection of bishops. To the extent that there was royal prompting and that it was heeded at all, it took the form of leading families turning to humanist models of education and learning, rather than to the universities. François I, as a patron of this new learning, promoted some distinguished humanist scholars to the episcopate, irrespective of whether they held university degrees, and his successors continued to favour 'men of letters' – for example, Pierre Danès, Jacques Amyot the translator of Plutarch, and Pontus de Thyard, the poet – albeit on a lesser scale.[10] Moreover, insofar as it can be studied at all, the education of the sixteenth-century episcopate shows few signs that François I and his successors paid close attention to the relevant clauses in the concordat. In his study of the episcopate from 1547 to 1589, Baumgartner could only establish that 84 out of 262 bishops held university degrees.[11] The dominance of the nobility in the episcopate, especially under François I and Henri II, suggests that the exemption clause in the concordat was liberally used by them and their successors. Judging by the surviving evidence, it does not seem that they were even required formally to quote that clause in their letters of nomination, as the concordat demanded. Nor do occasional references to the question give a clear impression of official attitudes, either at court or in Rome. For example, when the young François de la Rochefoucauld became bishop of Clermont in 1585, it was entered in the record of the papal consistory, presumably on the basis of a statement supplied from France, that 'he was well versed in the humanities, philosophy and sacred letters'; but he was not a university graduate, since 'in France distinguished men (*viri illustres*) were not accustomed to taking degrees; it was enough for them to possess these and other virtues, and to be well-deserving in other respects'.[12]

This reluctance was beginning to change by the late sixteenth century, but there was still some way to go before sons of equally eminent families would undertake arduous theology studies leading all the way to the doctorate. Yet by 1685 it had become virtually unthinkable that an excuse such as La Rochefoucauld's could be made in mitigation. There is no simple explanation for the change in attitudes which occurred in the intervening century, and it certainly cannot be restricted to the narrow confines of ecclesiastical careerism. But the latter did make a contribution to the change, although it may seem somewhat indirect. As already noted, the question of the education of candidates for the mitre may not have exercised Assemblies of Clergy or the Estates General, but some less spectacular developments were already

---

10 Frederic J Baumgartner, 'Humanism and Heterodoxy in the French Episcopacy under Francis I', *Proceedings of the Western Society for French History*, 8 (1980), 57–68.
11 Frederic J Baumgartner, *Change and Continuity in the French Episcopate* (Durham, North Carolina 1986), Table IV, pp 244–5.
12 ASV, Acta Miscellanea 95, fo 489. See also Joseph Bergin, *Cardinal de La Rochefoucauld. Leadership and Reform in the French Church* (New Haven and London 1987), 17.

occurring which would change the wider context in which such candidates had to function. For example, it gradually became impossible for non-graduates to hold parishes in walled towns, while in a city like Paris – but possibly elsewhere, too – only doctors in theology could realistically expect to obtain a parish. A royal decree of 1606 extended this obligation, by insisting that all cathedral canons, dignitaries of collegiate churches, and important officials serving in the diocesan administration hold a law or a theology degree.[13] Similar requirements were appearing for other professional groups, such as lawyers. Now even if they were only codifying existing developments, the appearance of these conditions also intensified the trends in question; in due course, they meant that even the theology faculties welcomed larger contingents than hitherto of clergy in search of degrees. Admittedly, bishops were nowhere mentioned in these ordinances, but their enforcement in respect of those clergy who were the key figures in diocesan institutions and thus in closest contact with bishops, could not but have a certain capillary-action effect upon the episcopate itself. And, as we shall see in the next chapter, an increasing number of bishops in this period had themselves been active in diocesan administration at one level or another, or been canons and dignitaries of cathedral and other chapters; in the competition to obtain such sub-episcopal positions, the possession of a degree was increasingly necessary. To put it another way, it may be suggested that the need or the stimulus for future bishops to obtain university degrees may not have come in the first instance from the prospect of a mitre itself, but rather from that of the many other desirable ecclesiastical posts which individuals might wish to compete for.

Moreover, this is almost certainly one area where the social diversity of the episcopate discussed in the previous chapter had a significant impact: the accessibility of the episcopate to sons of commoners and recently ennobled families, a high proportion of whom had taken university degrees, probably injected its own momentum into the move towards a university educated episcopate. By the time noble families, old and new, began to dominate the episcopate again in the 1640s and 1650s, they had shown sufficient adaptability to realise that a formal university education crowned by a degree was essential if they were to achieve their ambitions.

This in turn was part of a wider change in attitudes among the nobility, not least among those of *épée* background; at a time when warfare itself increasingly demanded academic study (mathematics, ballistics and geography), it was even less likely that families would deny a full and suitable education to sons destined for the church, for which some degree of learning had always been held necessary. Evidence for their educational attainments and attitudes is notoriously hard to interpret, often taking the form of

13 See Dominique Julia and Jacques Revel, eds, *Histoire sociale des populations étudiantes*, ii (Paris 1989), 204–5; LWB Brockliss, *French Higher Education in the Seventeenth and Eighteenth Centuries. A Cultural History* (Oxford 1987), 5.

reminiscence.¹⁴ In all likelihood, it is mistaken to look for any kind of coherent view among them at any time before the middle of the seventeenth century at the earliest. For the sixteenth century, we can point to the incomprehension of a military commander like Monluc that young men could endure the routine and tedium of study at an age when they should be active.¹⁵ On the other hand, there is the counsel of a no less distinguished contemporary, the Huguenot La Noue who, having strongly regretted that 'church offices are no longer given in consideration of learning, but to those who are best at cultivating cardinals and bishops, or the king's favourites', went on to urge the nobility to embrace education in order to be able to compete more effectively for office and power, as well as resist the corruption and enervation which the passage of time inflicts on social groups.¹⁶ Over a half-century after La Noue, in 1656, another military noble, the commandeur de Jars, summed up developments since his own youth as follows: 'In my time, one made gentlemen study only to join the church; even they were mostly satisfied with just the Latin needed for their breviary. Those destined for the court or the army went to the academy. They learned to ride, to dance, arms, to play the lute, to leap, and that was all.'¹⁷

The sixteenth-century papacy, despite coming to believe that it had perhaps surrendered too much to the king of France at Bologna, was either unwilling or unable to invoke the terms of Bologna or Trent when it came to considering French episcopal nominations. No doubt, political considerations played a part in this, while from mid-century onwards the question of the Catholicism of France's bishops, whether already in office or just nominated for approval, loomed much larger in Rome. Fears that bishops might actually be Huguenots or the straw men of powerful nobles pushed the question of whether they possessed the proper educational standards into the background. But it could resurface in unexpected circumstances. Whenever there was suspicion that royal nominees were no more than caretakers (*confidentiaires*), especially under Henri III, they were commonly reported as being ignorant, as if to clinch the argument that they had no personal claim to episcopal office; an individual's social obscurity was rendered suspicious if he had no countervailing educational distinction. In 1604, Henri IV's choice of bishop of Troyes, René Breslay, was rumoured 'de n'avoir point estudié', and when the suspicion was relayed to Rome by the nuncio, the curia was sufficiently concerned to ask him to investigate the truth of the matter; he subsequently confirmed that while Breslay was virtuous and a good Catholic, he was indeed

---

14 Mark Motley, *Becoming a French Aristocrat. The Education of the Court Nobility 1580–1715* (Princeton 1990), for a study which, admittedly, focuses on the aristocracy, but also discusses wider noble attitudes.
15 Blaise de Monluc, *Commentaires*, ed P Courteault (Paris 1964), 345.
16 François de la Noue, *Discours politiques et militaires*, ed F E Sutcliffe (Geneva 1967), Discours V, 133–4, 148–9.
17 See Jonathan Dewald, *Aristocratic Experience and the Origins of Modern Culture: France 1570–1715* (Berkeley and London 1993), 79ff. The quotation is on p 81.

ignorant, had not studied, and showed no sign of any learning. Despite what was evidently a circumstantial report, the pope welcomed Breslay's nomination. It seems likely that he was relieved that Breslay was different from the previous nominee to Troyes, the king's own confessor, René Benoist, whom Clement VIII consistently refused to accept because *his* learning was held to be too wayward![18]

Yet the papacy was anxious to raise the intellectual calibre of the French episcopate, whose condition it could at least evaluate within a wider European framework. In 1591, when Gregory XIV defined the questions to be put to witnesses in the de *vita et moribus* enquiries, he closely followed Trent's demand that incoming bishops have a doctorate or licentiate in theology or canon law or, failing that, a certificate from a university declaring them capable of teaching others. Like Trent, which insisted that the degrees should have been legitimately obtained, Gregory insisted on careful scrutiny of the genuineness of the degrees which candidates claimed to possess. Ideally, the dossier to be transmitted to Rome should contain copies of their degree diplomas and a statement from the chancellor of the university where they had studied.[19] Urban VIII maintained these dispositions virtually untouched when he reformed the enquiry process in the late 1620s.

Writing the history of the education of seventeenth-century French bishops would have been greatly facilitated had these rules, especially about the provision of documentary evidence of degrees taken or universities attended, been properly observed! The fact that they were only slowly and partially implemented in France should not be read as evidence that the papacy was no longer concerned with the problem. There is, admittedly, no specific evidence that anyone was ever denied his episcopal provisions because he was not a university graduate, but from the 1620s, the papacy became less willing to treat requests for dispensations lightly. Before candidates for the mitre were formally proposed in consistory, individual dossiers were closely scrutinised; educational considerations were not the only ones to be taken into account, but the fact that the records now mention specific dispensations being granted to bishops because they had not taken a degree may be read as an expression of a hardening of the papacy's attitudes.[20] It is open to question as to how far the formal granting of dispensations was either intended or experienced as a personal rebuke by the bishops concerned. There is, however, some evidence that it may have had a measure of success in that, from the 1630s onwards there are several cases of royal nominees hurrying to take their

---

18 *ANG (Correspondance du nonce del Buffalo)*, iv. ed Bernard Barbiche (Rome 1964), 656, 677, 689, 710, letters of Jan–May 1604.

19 Louis Jadin, 'Procès d'information pour la nomination des évêques et abbés des Pays-Bas, de Liége et de Franche-Comté d'après les Archives de la Congrégation Consistoriale', *Bulletin de l'Institut Historique Belge de Rome*, 6 (1928), 15–18.

20 Bishops concerned included some famous figures among the episcopate, such as Alain de Solminihac of Cahors. Others were Emeric Marc de la Ferté of Le Mans (1639) and Eustache Gault, who did not live to take up his see of Marseille (1640).

degrees between the time of their nomination and the despatch of their dossiers to Rome; for the first time, too, a few of them even provided copies of their diplomas or a summary list of dates for their matriculation and degrees.[21] Of course, it still fell far short of what Gregory XIV had demanded in 1591 and which bishops in other countries, such as Spain, were regularly providing, but in its modest way, it is evidence that a change of attitude was slowly taking place in those looking for episcopal office.

I

These general considerations, to which we shall return later, provide a context in which to begin an examination of the actual educational cursus of the bishops. It is in many respects the most elusive element of their *curriculum vitae*, one which requires a considerable amount of qualification and extrapolation; yet it contributes in several ways towards an understanding not merely of the educational world through which they passed, but also of the ways in which it played a part in fashioning the milieu from which bishops were themselves drawn.

The earliest educational experience of future bishops is, as might be expected, that for which there is least information. Except in the biographies of well-known bishops, it is only rarely evoked, even by long-standing friends of new bishops in their depositions on their behalf before the papal nuncio. Despite the paucity of evidence, it is fair to assume that such pre-college schooling was heavily influenced by the bishops' social backgrounds, with those who could afford private, household education for their sons anxious to avoid mixing with sons of lower social groups in local schools from an early age. Sons of less prosperous or less distinguished families had to make do with the elementary schools, largely in the towns. Not many future bishops would have had the experience of Jean Bertaut or Pierre Fenouillet, whose fathers were themselves college teachers and who took personal charge of their sons' early education. Bertaut, moreover, began his own career as tutor to the Matignon family in lower Normandy, before moving into similar service for the Valois-Angoulême children under Henri III.[22] In this way, what might otherwise have been an obscure continuation of family tradition took a sharp new turn, leading Bertaut to the court of Henri III and Henri IV, and culminating in elevation to the see of Séez in 1606.

Sons of distinguished and wealthy, especially noble, families would have begun their schooling at home, under the direction of men employed by their

---

21   Examples include Etienne Pavillon of Alet: ASV, PC 37, fos 476–8, letters for baccalaureate and licentiate in canon law, 4 June 1637, and certificate of authenticity by archbishop's vicar-general. Pavillon's letter of nomination to Alet was dated 2 June.

22   Georges Grente, *Jean Bertaut, abbé d'Aunay, premier aumônier de la reine, évêque de Séez* (Paris 1903), 14–20.

families as tutors or chaplains; it was at this stage that they learned the rudiments of Latin which was so essential for future clerics. As large numbers of bishops were drawn from families which already had a foothold in the world of benefice-holding, it is equally probable that many future bishops were in practice confided from an early date to the care of their ecclesiastical uncles, paternal or maternal; this was even more likely to happen when the latter were themselves active bishops, who were expected to groom younger relatives for careers in the church.[23] Examples include Pierre III de Villars (archbishop of Vienne 1612–62) who was placed under the direction of his uncle, Nicolas de Villars, bishop of Agen, and Louis de Bassompierre, who was brought up mainly by his uncle, Charles de Balsac, bishop of Noyon.[24] At a much lower level of the social scale, we find the same kind of pattern: Denis Cohon (bishop of Nîmes and Dol), son of a candle-maker from Craon, was fortunate to have a uncle who was successively canon of Le Mans and of Chartres, and who first educated and then endowed him with his benefices.[25] Whatever the precise arrangements, the chances are that most of the tutors were themselves clerics; being under their direction was the future bishops first initiation into the clerical society which their families had chosen for them; the more ambitious families were for their sons' success in the church, the more important it was for the latter to be tutored in the proper *bonne conduite*, in which religious practices and virtues counted for as much as formal educational attainments. Very little is known about these tutors in general or in particular. Few future bishops can have been as well provided for as, say, Chasteignier de la Rocheposay (bishop of Poitiers) who had Tilenus and then Scaliger as mentors and tutors from an early age, or André Frémiot (Bourges), whose earliest tutor, Claude Robert, produced the original edition of *Gallia Christiana*, the first comprehensive attempt at a history of France's bishops.[26] In the case of Jean de Belleau, we know that his first tutor was also secretary to his episcopal uncle and predecessor at Meaux, Jean de Vieuxpont, which suggests an education entailing considerable familiarity with diocesan affairs from an early age.[27] Finally, it may be added that it was not unknown for future bishops to have been themselves private tutors, though it will probably never be established how many of those who owed their episcopal careers to their service of aristocratic families, actually served those families as tutors. But it is known that Louis Barbier, bishop of Langres, was first brought into the household of Gaston d'Orléans as a preceptor by another bishop, Pierre Habert of Cahors while he was one of Gaston's

23 See Motley, *Becoming a French Aristocrat*, 119–20.
24 Bassompierre was an illegitimate son of the Marshal Bassompierre and Charlotte de Balsac d'Entragues, and this may explain why he was entrusted to his episcopal uncle.
25 R Sauzet, *Contre-réforme et réforme catholique en bas Languedoc. Le diocèse de Nîmes au xviie siècle* (Louvain-Paris 1979), 217–18.
26 *DBF*, viii. 731; Michaud, *Biographie Universelle*, xv. 140
27 ASV, PC 13, fo 549.

almoners.[28] Gilles Boutault, bishop of Aire and Evreux, served as tutor and travelling companion to Gilles de Souvré, bishop of Comminges and Auxerre.[29] In these, and perhaps other cases, too, a tutorship eventually led to patronage by powerful 'employers', whose influence was decisive for their later careers.

It would be mistaken to apply our twentieth-century distinctions between types and stages of schooling rigidly to early modern France. In particular the age at which boys were sent to college, or later to university, varied, and often very considerable age disparities between students at every level seem to have been common. Moreover, boys entering college, especially as boarders, were frequently accompanied by their tutors, who were still sometimes completing their own studies, and who continued to 'govern' them and take overall responsibility for their academic progress.[30] The term 'college' was, like the term 'school' generally, also more protean than it would become later, serving as it did pupils ranging from the age of eight or nine to twenty and beyond.

Thanks to urban growth and religious polarisation, sixteenth- and seventeenth-century France witnessed an impressive expansion of the existing network of colleges. Gradually, most medium-sized towns acquired a college, whether through their own efforts or, especially by the early seventeenth century, through appeals to religious societies like the Jesuits, the Oratory or the Doctrinaires. The cursus and curriculum of the classic *collèges de plein exercise*, as they were called, also took their definitive shape during the same period. The model provided by the best-known colleges was one of at least six classes devoted to the humanities, with two additional years at the end for philosophy, but there were variations to this pattern, and not all colleges possessed the full range of classes. Modern distinctions between 'secondary' schools and universities were still blurred, both in terms of institutions and curriculum. For one thing, universities like Paris, Toulouse, Bourges and no doubt others, were themselves essentially collections of colleges – some of them belonging to religious orders – where most of the actual teaching was conducted. And these colleges straddled what subsequently became the secondary school/university divide, teaching humanities and philosophy as well as the higher 'university' sciences such as law and theology. It was thus entirely possible, for example, for men like Richelieu and his contemporaries to enter the College of Navarre in the University of Paris at the age of nine or ten, and stay there for the remainder of their studies, progressing all the way from the first humanities class to the doctorate in theology, if they so wished.

28 AN, Z¹a 515, *états* of household of Gaston d'Orléans, 1627, 1641.
29 ASV, PC 24, fo 662r, evidence of Gilles de Souvré, Apr 1626.
30 Roger Chartier, Marie-Madeleine Compère, Dominique Julia, *L'Education en France, du xviᵉ au xviiiᵉ siècle* (Paris 1976), 172.

With these remarks in mind, it is possible to approach this crucial period of the bishops' educational experience directly. Information has survived which enables us to identify the colleges frequented by 150 of the 351 (42.7 per cent) bishops under consideration. In the case of fifty-three others, it seems extremely likely that they went to college in their native cities – Paris, Toulouse, Bordeaux, and Lyon. It should be said that the principal source of this evidence is the papal enquiries, and that in a large number of cases, it consists of no more than a simple mention of a bishop having attended a particular college, and rarely mentions either dates or duration of stay. Such evidence, clearly, is not of the quality which college registers themselves might supply, but very few of these have survived from the sixteenth and early seventeenth centuries. Yet, as this evidence comes from bishops' former fellow-students or professors, and sometimes both, there is no reason to suppose that it was fabricated to impress the nuncio or Roman officials. Because of its provenance, the information only begins to accumulate for bishops nominated from the 1610s onwards, and even then there are some surprising gaps. Witnesses who had not been professors or fellow-students of new bishops simply did not comment on their pre-university education, doubtless out of ignorance of the facts. Our ignorance as to the colleges frequented by the likes of François Servien, Gilbert de Clérambault, or Charles de la Vieuville derives from this lack of comment, not from any suggestion of the social obscurity of the bishops themselves.

For the 108 bishops nominated by Henri IV, the harvest is distinctly meagre; the information relates to just eighteen bishops in all, too few to permit extended comment. Eight of them were taught humanities by the religious orders which they entered at an early age, while the educational cursus of the remaining ten has only been recorded because they are sufficiently known for one reason or another – for example, Richelieu, Pierre Fenouillet, Jean-Jacques de Barrault, or Jean Bertaut.

The educational profile of bishops nominated from the 1610s onwards shows a marked improvement, with information available on the colleges attended by 132 out of 243 (54.3 per cent) bishops. Inevitably both the size of the sample and the geographical origins of episcopal families means that finding distinct patterns of college attendance remains problematic. But some observations are nevertheless in order. Despite the perils of arguing from silence, it seems likely that a majority of the bishops took their humanities and philosophy courses in just one college. Yet even the limited information at our disposal also suggests that a significant minority attended not just one, but two or even three colleges during their career, and that the *peregrinatio academica* was not something confined to those attending university. But, whereas the reasons why the university students moved from place to place – a desire to attend the lectures of famous masters, academic or cultural tourism, and so on – have been frequently recorded, much less is known about the scale of movement from college to college. It may be the lack of senior classes in certain colleges which forced their pupils to move on. Where there was no such difficulty, the change of college obviously had much less to do with the personal preferences of the pupils as with those of their parents. As far as we can judge from our evidence, pupils tended to move from smaller, peripheral colleges to those in large cities or with a higher reputation. Paris was not the only pole of attraction, and college pupils were just as likely to move from Auch or Agen to Toulouse, from Caen to Rouen, or even from Dijon to Lyon. Religious orders, especially the mendicants, were in the habit of moving their members from one house to another, and educational considerations played a part in this practice.

But college attendance patterns had as much to do with types of college as with mere geography. Perhaps the most striking fact is that eighty-three of the 150 bishops for which we have information attended a Jesuit college at some point during their studies; that total, to which eighteen colleges contributed, would doubtless be higher still if it was clear precisely which of the different colleges in Toulouse, Bordeaux and elsewhere other bishops attended. The numbers of bishops contributed by these Jesuit colleges was not, however, evenly distributed, and well over half were produced by a trio of schools. Quite a number of bishops attended more than one Jesuit college, and movement from one to another seems to have been both easy and natural, facilitated by a common curriculum and teaching methods. Despite opposition, not least from the University of Paris, the Jesuits were readmitted by Henri IV to the huge jurisdictional area covered by the parlement of Paris in 1603, and it was not long before the number of colleges run by them began to increase; the expulsion of 1595 had not affected their colleges in the southern provinces. The College of Clermont in Paris began teaching again in 1618, but it was never allowed to become attached to the University of Paris.

No less important in its impact was Henri IV's and Louis XIII's personal patronage of the show-case Jesuit college of La Flèche, which opened its doors in 1607, and to which Henri urged the nobility to send their sons 'pour le bien du public'. Despite its peculiar location between Le Mans and Angers, the king's promptings were taken seriously, especially by the court-based nobility, but also by ambitious provincial families. The way was shown by men like the duc d'Epernon, whose son, the future Cardinal La Valette, was one of the college's earliest students, while René de Rieux, of ancient Breton noble stock, forsook his college in the University of Paris for La Flèche around the same time. The Florentine family of Bonsi, whose sons usually went to college either in Florence or the Jesuit college in Béziers (under the supervision of their uncle, the Bishop of Béziers), also began sending them to La Flèche as part of an effort to strengthen their existing ties with the court. Ministers and other leading royal officials – Zamet, Dony d'Attichy, de Vic, Séguier, for example – also directed their sons there. The desire to please the crown and cultivate good connections was undoubtedly a part of the calculations, all the more so as Henri IV had resumed, in 1608, his predecessor's practice of choosing as his confessor a Jesuit whose influence over the choice of bishops might also need to be taken into account. Within a few years, former students of La Flèche began entering the episcopate, and at least twenty-one of the bishops nominated after 1607 had studied there for a time. As far as is known, the first La Flèche graduate to enter the episcopate was Jean de Barrault, who was confirmed as bishop of Bazas in 1611, though he actually had his *brevet de nomination* in his pocket even before he entered La Flèche! Alumni of La Flèche benefited considerably from royal largesse during the 1610s, a decade in which many relatively young men were nominated to bishoprics, often as coadjutors with succession rights, and who had in many cases only recently finished their studies. The college's part in forming future bishops was thus quickly confirmed, ensuring that it would remain attractive to succeeding generations of aspiring clerics.

But it should not be assumed that La Flèche ever became an unofficial *petit séminaire* for France's bishops. It seems that by mid-century its star burned much less brightly, and that the initial reasons for frequenting it – royal patronage, fashion – were by now less compelling, while other colleges remained attractive. Nor was the network of Jesuit colleges ever quite as hierarchical in our period as such an assumption requires. An older college like that of Tournon, though equally eccentric in its location, continued to have pupils of distinguished origin, some of whom moved there from places like Lyon or Dijon, and then on to La Flèche or Paris. 'It was an academy frequented by the finest youth and nobility of France', was how one alumnus described it in 1605.[31] Jean-François de Gondi, the first archbishop of Paris, studied at Tournon around 1605 along with Claude de Rébé, a future archbishop of Narbonne, who had previously been to the Jesuit college at Lyon. Yet a generation later, the idea of sending the future Cardinal de Retz to Tournon does not seem to have been considered; its intake of students and perhaps its reputation had dropped markedly in the interval, and the future bishops passing through Tournon were relatively few in number and essentially natives of the Dauphiné-Lyonnais area.[32]

The college of Clermont in Paris had emerged as an alternative attraction once teaching resumed there in 1618. It was attended by at least nineteen of the bishops seated in our period, as compared to twenty-one for La Flèche; and only one of these bishops had studied at Clermont before it was closed down in 1595. Leaving aside the particular case of Henri de Lorraine-Guise, the first of its new generation of alumni to become a bishop was no less a figure than François d'Adhémar de Grignan, archbishop of Arles and a founder of the *Compagnie du Saint-Sacrement*, who received the see of Saint-Paul-Trois-

---

31 Quoted in Marie-Madeleine Compère and Dominique Julia, *Les Collèges français, 16e–18e siècles. Répertoire i: France du Midi* (Paris, 1984), 700. 'C'était une académie peuplée d'aussi belle jeunesse et noblesse qui fut en France.'
32 *Ibid*, 701–2.

Châteaux in 1630. Eighteen of his fellow-students followed in Grignan's footsteps over the next thirty years, so the college's advantages for those seeking episcopal office were hardly to be doubted. Apart from Grignan's younger brother, who succeeded him at Saint-Paul, they included sons of distinguished families who themselves became leading figures in the episcopate – the Fouquet brothers, Cardinal d'Estrées, Gilbert de Choiseul, Anne de Ventadour, Retz himself, Camille and Ferdinand de Neufville de Villeroy, and several others – with the future Cardinal d'Estrées becoming the first alumnus to enter the Académie Française in 1658. Their number might have been higher still were it not for the college's main disadvantage – the fact that it never secured affiliation to the University of Paris. Admittedly, this mattered only to those intent on studying theology in the University of Paris itself, for if they studied the philosophy course at Clermont, they could not matriculate or take the MA degree required by the university before being allowed to take its theology examinations. Those who did subsequently take Paris theology degrees had to curtail their stay in Clermont so as to complete their philosophy elsewhere. Those who remained at Clermont to study philosophy and even theology could not take a Paris theology degree, and as a result usually settled for a law degree from Paris or elsewhere. Those episcopal alumni like Jean d'Olce, bishop of Boulogne and Bayonne, who left Clermont and took no degree at all, were left to explain their choice as a case of *force majeure*.

In the circumstances, it is hardly surprising that the colleges of the University of Paris continued to attract students, some of whom indeed moved from Jesuit colleges like La Flèche to complete their philosophy course. Seventeen of the forty bishops known to have frequented two colleges or more finished up in Paris. A total of fifty-five bishops are known to have attended one of the many colleges affiliated to the university, but many more native Parisians among the bishops probably did so, too. Despite the attractions of La Flèche, Clermont or other places, the university's colleges were well able to hold their own, and the native Parisians who frequented them were joined by a substantial number of sons of the court nobility, for whom a college like Navarre or Harcourt was just as attractive.

The overall social composition of student bodies in early modern French colleges is impossible to determine in virtually every case. But it was no secret that some of the Paris colleges, Navarre in particular, enjoyed the favours of noble families. Jesuit colleges like Tournon, La Flèche and Clermont also attracted considerable numbers of nobles old and new, or members of the political or financial élites about to join their ranks. It is probably not a coincidence, therefore, that thirty-six out of the forty-five known alumni of these three colleges were of noble status; only five were clearly non-noble, while the status of another four cannot be determined. The proportion of non-noble bishops passing through the colleges of the University of Paris was undoubtedly higher, since they included many Parisian-born bishops about whose schooling, as distinct from their social origins, nothing is known. Whatever might be said of the nobility's traditional reluctance to take university degrees, there seems to be little reason to think that they neglected to send their offspring dedicated to the church to some of the best colleges of the day.

This in turn leads to another important consideration. Attendance at college and *a fortiori* at university, could be an expensive affair when they were not located in or near one's native town. Dewald has shown that lower and middling noble families from Normandy simply could not afford the costs of sending a son to a good college at, say, Caen or Rouen, let alone to Paris or Orléans, which were more expensive. Moreover, these costs rose steadily during the sixteenth century, and may have continued to do so thereafter. As a result, Dewald argues, such families stood little chance of competing in the marketplace for royal offices when their prices rose steadily if they could not afford to educate their sons to the standards required.[33] The costs of boarding at La Flèche or Clermont in the seventeenth century were also high.[34] *Mutatis mutandis*, the same argument could be applied to those destined for ecclesiastical office, which although not for sale, had at least always required letters. Even though there was a tradition of providing places in schools and universities for poor scholars, these were probably few enough by the seventeenth century. From this perspective, too, the advantages were distinctly on the side of families with wealth and connections, and with a foothold in the church hierarchy. Sons of nobles in particular were those most likely to have acquired church benefices *in commendam* at an early age, either from the older generation of their family or through continuing family influence. The revenue provided by these benefices was ideal when it came to defraying the often considerable costs of schooling at the colleges which were frequented by young men of similar background and which would improve individual chances of further advancement in the church.

II

The appeal of the colleges was both social and intellectual, and as they grew in numbers during the seventeenth century, the competition between them for students became ever more intense. Colleges like Clermont and La Flèche might be the best known, attracting an élite student-body because of their social cachet and intellectual distinction, but it is clear that the college of Guyenne in Bordeaux or of Bourbon in Rouen were also highly regarded and well frequented. Nor is it surprising that the universities began to fear them

---

33   Jonathan Dewald, *The Formation of a Provincial Nobility. The Magistrates of the Parlement of Rouen (1499–1610)* (Princeton 1980), 133–5.
34   Chartier, Compère, Julia, *Education en France*, 180.

as educational challengers which might take over whole areas long the preserve of the universities themselves; this fear was widespread, and explains why, especially in the seventeenth century, so many universities opposed the colleges' attempts to grant their own higher degrees or even to become affiliated to universities.

While attendance at a college by those destined for careers in the church was not a matter for debate or hesitation – even those aspiring to no more than possession of a parish began to do so in the seventeenth century – attitudes towards university education were more complex. This was partly for social reasons, and partly because, as we saw, being lettered and having been to university were not held to be synonymous. Indeed, it was not so much attending university which was problematic, as the actual taking of a degree; the latter was not an automatic climax to university studies, and it might not be taken if it was not actually needed to satisfy a particular or immediate ambition; the disparity between studies pursued and degrees taken was far wider at the beginning of the early modern period than it has ever been since then.

This general point is important because insofar as there has been any overall view of the educational record of the episcopate in our period, it is one that is largely confined to the question of the university degrees obtained by its members; more specifically, it perceives a shift in emphasis from law to theology. The shift was not sudden or massive, but was rather a tendency, the cumulative impact of which took about a century to become manifest. The main purpose of the interpretation is not simply to count and categorise degrees, but the more ambitious one of deriving episcopal 'types' from the kind of degrees taken: the bishop with a law degree was more likely to be an administrator, while his colleague with a theology degree would be more attuned to pastoral and spiritual concerns. The result, it is argued, was a contrast in episcopal styles, one which might, among other things, account for the haphazard progress of reform within the patchwork of dioceses which made up the French church. On the other hand, if the trend was towards bishops' taking theology degrees, it would follow that an increasing measure of homogeneity was being achieved; and with an educationally more unified episcopate, the French church could be seen as more uniformly moving towards a pastoral style of rule.[35]

This interpretation can easily lead to assumptions of a *post hoc propter hoc* kind. In particular, it makes the character of episcopal action depend on the kind of higher studies pursued by those entering the episcopate, almost to the exclusion of other factors which might have influenced them along the way. For the present, however, little would be gained by an attempt to confront the interpretation with arguments of a general kind. Only when a detailed assessment of what is known of the bishops' highest educational attainments

---

35 Michel Péronnet, *Les Evêques dans l'ancienne France*, 2 vols (Lille 1978), i. 456ff.

has been attempted, and interpreted in the light of contemporary attitudes and traditions, will it be possible to address the wider questions.

Nevertheless, because of the expectations which such a generalisation can prompt, it would be as well to establish from the outset what can and cannot be expected from the kinds of data which are available for this study. For one thing, the university matriculation registers which have been so well preserved in certain parts of Europe – England, Spain, and the Holy Roman Empire for example – and which have been the basis of some pioneering modern studies, have not survived to anything like the same degree in France.[36] The prosopography of university attendance and studies has been severely hampered by extensive archival losses which, despite important recent gains in our understanding, make the task of fitting the final educational experience of bishops into a clearly-defined context exceptionally difficult. One result is that even the limited body of material which does survive is often enigmatic, and has to be treated with caution. To take one example, the rector's book of the University of Paris, which exists up to the mid-1630s, might initially seem to list the names of all those matriculating or taking their MA degrees, but even that is not wholly certain, as the main reason for signing the rector's book – without which, for instance, one could not proceed to take a theology degree – was to claim the privileges attached to membership of the University; it is, therefore, no real guide to previous studies, and although it suggests something of students' intentions at the time of signing, it is not a reliable guide to subsequent achievements either.[37] Here and there, lists of graduands have survived for certain universities but, as a recent systematic survey has shown, the gaps for our period in both law and theology are enormous – there is virtually nothing, for example, for the law faculties of Paris, Orléans, Angers, Bourges, which served most of northern France; nor does the position seem much better for the southern universities, only some of which had active teaching, as distinct from diploma-granting, faculties. In theology, the situation is equally bleak for the larger teaching faculties with, for example, only the list of names of those taking the licentiate in Paris surviving without interruption for the entire period studied here.[38]

Consequently, nearly all of the figures and calculations made hitherto have had to be based on other, more subjective sources. By far the most important

---

36 For England, Lawrence Stone 'The Educational Revolution in England 1560 to 1640', *Past and Present*, 28 (1964), 41–80; *idem*, ed, *The University in Society*, 2 vols (London 1974); for the Empire, Richard C Schwinges, *Deutsche Universitätsbücher im 14 und 15 Jahrhundert. Studien zur Sozialgeschichte des Alten Reiches* (Stuttgart 1986); for Spain, Kagan, *Students and Society in Early Modern Spain* (quoted above, n 9).
37 BN, MS lat 9953–8, for the period 1519–1633.
38 Julia and Revel, *Histoire sociale des populations étudiantes*, ii, esp the contributions of Julia and Revel, 'Les Etudiants et leurs études dans la France moderne', p 397ff, 'annexe statistique', and of L W B Brockliss, 'Patterns of Attendance at the University of Paris 1400–1800' (a revised version of an article originally published in *Historical Journal*, 21 (1978), 503–44.

of these has been, and remains, the information supplied to Rome by, or on behalf of, incoming bishops, information which was summarised, along with other biographical details for use in consistory, and which has been reproduced in the volumes of the semi-official *Hierarchia Catholica*. In their published form, the data can easily seem to resemble the objective evidence of university registers themselves, but this impression can be highly misleading. Where they survive, the original depositions on which the published data are based are both more and less revealing than the data would lead us to expect. Moreover, where comparison with actual university sources is possible, it is apparent that in the evidence presented to the papal nuncios, there was a pronounced tendency to inflate the status of degrees taken by future bishops – all part of an effort to impress on Rome the seriousness with which requirements for bishops were taken in France, and to raise the standing of the candidate in its eyes. As the Council of Trent's decree requiring bishops to possess legitimately acquired degrees suggests, suspicions about fraud in this matter did genuinely exist, but it does not seem that French bishops were attempting to fabricate an educational cursus that had no foundation in fact; the reasons why the inflation of degrees might occur, without necessarily involving any intention to deceive, will become clearer later in this chapter. At the same time, the available evidence often reveals far more about the bishops' educational experience than the simple enumeration of degrees taken by individuals could ever do. This is bound to alter the historian's angle of approach to the entire subject, placing less emphasis on the statistics of degrees taken than on the range of studies undertaken, and where and with whom they were conducted.

Despite its shortcomings, the evidence as it stands points to 295 out of 351 (84 per cent) bishops holding a degree of some kind. In some ways, because of its magnitude, this statistic raises expectations that cannot be met, in that it presumes a range of information about their studies - places of study, as well as the dates and universities where degrees were taken - which simply does not exist in many cases. This would be less of a problem if it could be assumed that students graduated from the university at which they had studied. Though this was probably true for the great majority of university students generally, it does not take account of the tradition of students moving from university to university, not merely in the course of their studies, but also of studying at one (or more) university and then moving to another in order to take their degrees. Occasionally, such movement could be the result of university organisation itself: for example, until 1679 the University of Paris only granted degrees in canon law, which was not necessarily disadvantageous to clerics, but which obliged all those seeking the more widely required degree in both civil and canon law (*in utroque jure*) to repair to other universities in order to acquire it.

Given these problems, it is perhaps surprising that our sources provide information, albeit usually laconic in nature, about the universities

Table 6.1 Universities attended by bishops

Aix	3	Paris	124
Angers	6	Poitiers	3
Avignon	5	Pont-Mousson	2
Bordeaux	10	Toulouse	25
Bourges	4	Valence	2
Cahors	3	Foreign	25
Orléans	11		

These figures take account of the second university attended by a number of bishops when that is known.

frequented by 198 bishops (56 per cent of the total, 67 per cent of those known to have taken a degree). The information itself is unevenly spread across the period, and only becomes plentiful, if not completely satisfactory, for the bishops nominated from the 1610s, but especially the later 1620s, onwards. Allowing for this, a number of general points can be made. The majority of bishops appear to have continued their studies in the same city where they had attended college, provided it had a university. Only twenty-five bishops appear to have attended more than one university, but that is probably a considerable understatement arising from the nature of the evidence.

Of much greater interest, as will be evident from the above table, is the extent to which the University of Paris attracted future bishops, far more of whom frequented it than all of the other universities combined. Only Toulouse made any kind of showing as a competitor, and even then the contest was a hugely uneven one. Virtually all the other universities had to settle for rather low single figures. The attraction of Paris had always been powerful, particularly for clerics, but the extent to which it remained so in our period is striking. Perhaps it owed something to the fact that, in contrast to the map of France's colleges, that of the universities in our period was unchanged. The appeal of Paris was less marked among the bishops nominated before the late 1620s, whose university studies, as far as we can judge, still continued to reflect broadly their geographical origins. But from the 1630s onwards, when gaps in our information are far fewer than previously, the preponderance of Paris-educated bishops is overwhelming. This, in turn, can partly be explained by the large numbers of Parisians joining the episcopate in this and the following decade. But that is only part of the picture since it is remarkable how many future bishops, who in a previous generation might have studied at Toulouse, Bordeaux or Avignon, succumbed instead to the attraction of Paris. Moreover, all of the bishops nominated in these middle decades who attended two universities included Paris in their cursus. The well-known noble families, old and new, whose sons entered the episcopate in such numbers around mid-century, contributed in no small measure to this trend, and it may well be that their gradual acceptance of full university education – complete with degrees at the end of it – for their sons was prompted by the knowledge that the university's proximity to the highest political and ecclesiastical circles of the realm, could itself be an advantage.

A few examples here will help to show what this might entail. Bernard Daffis, son of a president in the Bordeaux parlement whose family was equally at home in Toulouse, went to university in Toulouse and Bordeaux under Henri IV, succeding his uncle as bishop of Lombez under Louis XIII. While Jean Daffis, his nephew and successor as bishop of Lombez in the late 1620s, attended college at both La Flèche and Paris, he followed family traditions by returning to Bordeaux to complete his law and theology studies. By that juncture, a new generation of *parlementaires* from Toulouse and Bordeaux were beginning to take matters a step further. The young Pierre de Bertier, whose episcopal uncles had both studied law in Toulouse, was sent off to display his abilities in Paris in the 1620s, emerging with distinction as a doctor of theology in 1632. Bernard Marmiesse, the son of another Toulouse magistrate, did exactly the same a decade later. The Fénélon family had traditionally been content to send their numerous clerics to Bordeaux, or even Cahors, but the last family member to be bishop of Sarlat took the road to Paris and returned from there with a degree in canon law, prior to succeeding to Sarlat in 1659. In these and cases like them, families were concerned with more than giving their sons a good university education: they were also measuring the extent to which a stay at the University of Paris would enhance their prospects in the church for later years. Meanwhile, as the table indicates, Toulouse and Bordeaux, but also Aix and Avignon, were steadily loosing their attraction for clerics destined for high office in the church.

By the standards of later medieval and early modern Europe, an episcopate in which roughly five out of six bishops (84 per cent) held a university degree can hardly be regarded as ignorant. The figure is significantly higher than that recorded for the sixteenth-century episcopate. The difference should not, however, be seized upon as evidence of a sudden educational revolution, as it is in part the result of the more systematic recording of the relevant information. Of the fifty-six bishops who constitute the remaining 16 per cent of the episcopate, over half (twenty-nine) belong to the 'unknowns' category for whom it has not been possible to determine whether they did or did not take a degree; it seems likely, however, that up to half of them had obtained a degree. In only twenty-seven of the fifty-six cases can it be said with certainty that bishops did not possess a degree of any kind. Moreover, it will be evident from the tables (6.2, 6.3) that both of these 'negative' categories were in marked decline during our period, as the trend towards a fully graduate episcopate acquired ever greater momentum. For example, only four bishops nominated after 1630 were non-graduates: three of these were former pupils of the college of Clermont who, because they had completed their philosophy course there, were unable to take theology degrees at the University of Paris.

Only one of the four, François de Rouxel de Médavy, was a noble who could be regarded as representative of older noble attitudes towards university education.

The fact that it was between the 1590s and later 1620s that the bulk of non-graduate bishops, numbering twenty-three, were nominated, is itself indicative of broader developments in our period. A breakdown of this group is revealing in more than one respect. Seven of them were members of religious orders in which degrees were not taken; we might also add the name of Alphonse de Richelieu, who would probably have taken a degree had he not left the University of Paris in order to join the austere Carthusian order. But nearly half (ten) of these twenty-three bishops were made up of sons of the higher nobility who still regarded university degrees as somewhat beneath their dignity; with names like Sourdis, Guise, Valois, Matignon and Béthune to boast of, this is not altogether surprising. Four more bishops of noble extraction may be considered alongside them, in that the call to the episcopate came either too early or too unexpectedly for them to have taken, or even need to take, a degree. This leaves but two isolated cases, which provide fascinating contrasts of a different order. The first is that of Cardinal du Perron, whose erudition and oratorical skills mesmerised his contemporaries well before he became a bishop, and who may be regarded as a late example of the lettered but non-graduate cleric. The other case was that of René Breslay, bishop of Troyes, the man whose lack of letters had no obvious excuse of birth or clerical status, which makes it all the more possible to see why stories circulating about his ignorance were taken as seriously as they were in 1604.

If, historically, attending university was one thing and taking a degree another, particularly for sons of the nobility, we should not be unduly surprised by some features of the educational profile of the bishops to which we may now turn our attention. To begin with, bishops with more than one degree were a small band, fewer than those with no degree at all. Only thirteen are recorded as having done so in our period, though there is some doubt possible in two or three cases. It is also open to dispute as to whether taking a doctorate in canon law in Paris, followed by a doctorate in civil law in Toulouse (Hector Douvrier), or taking a doctorate in Protestant theology at Montpellier, followed years later – after conversion to Catholicism – by a doctorate in theology in Rome (Jean Plantavit), should be regarded as obtaining two distinct degrees. The normal pattern, visible in the eleven other cases, was to proceed from a law degree to one in theology; to progress from a licentiate or doctorate in canon law, taken mostly at Paris, to a baccalaureate or licentiate in theology, was the most common sequence. If Raymond de Montaigne was the most precocious of France's bishops, his fellow-Bordelais, Jean II de Daffis, was probably the most highly qualified academically, possessing a doctorate in both theology and in canon and civil law from

Bordeaux.³⁹ One of the most unusual French bishops from this perspective must be Eustache Le Clerc de Lesseville, bishop of Coutances in 1658: one of the youngest ever rectors of the University of Paris, he was a doctor in theology and fellow of the Sorbonne, but he also held the licentiate in canon and civil law without which he could not have served as a clerical councillor in the Paris parlement after 1645.⁴⁰ It is for these reasons, and for others which will become clear later, that bishops with degrees in law and theology are considered in the following pages as theologians rather than as lawyers.

From the evidence to hand, it does not seem that many French bishops extended the range of the *peregrinatio academica* to include attendance at universities outside of France. As far as can be established, only nineteen bishops possessed degrees from foreign universities, two of them from Pont à Mousson in Lorraine, a university with close ties to Reims. All the remaining seventeen degrees were from Italian universities, where the taking of degrees while on the academic version of the grand tour was a long-established tradition. However, with eight of these degrees being taken by native-born Italians, the extent of French participation in the custom was distinctly limited. Of the remaining nine, three (Donadieu of Auxerre, Frémiot, and Barrault, all nominees of Henri IV) seem to have actually gone to Italy mainly in order to obtain their confirmation by Rome as bishops, and took degrees during their stay in Italy. A further four (Ruade, Auvry, Daillon du Lude and Bourlemont) took their degrees in Rome because they were intent on careers, or at least residing, there at the time, though Ruade soon changed his mind and joined the Carthusians instead! If the French episcopate was becoming increasingly French by birth, it was no less clearly becoming increasingly French by educational experience. It is thus time to turn our attention to the majority who neither had two degrees nor been to a foreign university.

The simplest presentation of the evidence on a reign-by-reign basis gives an initial, if fairly undifferentiated, view of the numbers of bishops with degrees in law and theology (Table 6.2). As explained above, in this and the following table, bishops who took a theology as well as a law degree have been entered as theologians. The general evolution of the relations between degrees in theology and law appears clear enough from Table 6.2. With more and more bishops holding degrees, the proportion of lawyers dropped by Louis XIII's reign to half, but then remained remarkably stable for half a century. The challenge from theology appears as a steady and cumulative rather than an all-conquering one. A more detailed, decade-by-decade table is needed – as

---

39 ASV, PC 25, fos 320–44, early 1628.
40 BN, MS lat 9958, fo 130.

Table 6.2 Degrees taken by bishops (by reign)

Reign	Bishops	Law	%	Theology	%
Henri IV	108	65	60.1	26	24
Louis XIII	154	77	50	45	29.2
Mazarin	89	45	50.5	37	41.5
Totals	351	187	53.2	108	36.7

Table 6.3 Degrees taken by bishops (by decade)

Decade	Bishops	Law	%	Theology	%
1590s	57	37	64.9	11	19.2
1601–10	54	29	53.7	17	31.5
1611–20	52	34	65.3	8	15.3
1621–30	57	23	40.3	17	29.8
1631–40	39	18	46.1	16	41.0
1641–50	41	22	53.6	15	36.5
1651–61	51	24	47.0	24	47.0
Totals	351	187	53.2	108	36.7

in the previous chapter – in order to pinpoint more accurately the nature and the chronology of the shifts occurring (Table 6.3).

At first sight, the evidence presented by this table appears to undermine the kind of steady, linear progression which the previous one exhibited. Despite this, it does help to reveal some important variations in the proportion of theology graduates among the episcopate, even though this proportion does not translate as a triumphant rising curve. Indeed, the percentage of theology graduates registered for the second part of Henri IV's reign would not be surpassed until the 1630s, when *dévot* influence was at its height. Perhaps the most tantalising statistic of all here is the dead heat for the final decade of Mazarin's ministry, when theologians were for the first time as numerous as lawyers among new bishops. It laid the foundations for the triumph of theology over law during the personal rule of Louis XIV, though in the present state of knowledge there are grounds for some skepticism about the figures occasionally quoted for that period.

But rather than confining our analysis to a commentary on statistical trends, it would be more enlightening to look closely at the worlds of contemporary law and theology studies. It is essential to study the similarities and differences between them if we are to understand the educational choices made by future bishops, and thus to understand why the balance between lawyers and theologians in the episcopate was such a shifting, uncertain one.

There were only three university faculties providing both teaching and degrees in higher subjects during the *ancien régime*, and of these we may quickly eliminate the medical faculty. Though a few of our bishops were sons of surgeons and physicians, only one, Honoré du Laurens (Embrun 1601–12), briefly studied medicine before switching to law; he did not, it seems, take a medical degree. As we have already seen, both Bologna and Trent bracketed law and theology studies together as qualifications deemed equally suitable for future bishops, and in this they were not departing from established tradition. But this equality of expectation does not begin to suggest the actual differences between the two courses of study. Even though generalisations valid for France as a whole are risky, there is little doubt that law was by far the easier option of the two: the course of study itself was far shorter, and as it did not require students to have taken the MA, it could be started at an earlier age than could theology; moreover, the examinations themselves were less rigorous, and the venality of some faculties in this regard was a subject of too much criticism at the time to be a fiction. The generalised social pressure, particularly from the owners of venal-hereditary offices, to make law degrees easier for their sons to obtain was obviously intense, and that pressure was increased rather than mitigated by the extending of the obligation to have such a degree to other legal practitioners like barristers and *procureurs*. Furthermore, the hierarchy of law degrees itself did not amount to much: the baccalaureate and licentiate were regularly taken on the same date by candidates, and the doctorate seems to have been an empty, if at times expensive, formality for those who wanted the title of doctor. With so little difference between a baccalaureate and a doctorate in law, it is not difficult to see why contemporaries were, as mentioned earlier, prone to inflate the status of degrees taken by individuals, and equally why historians need not become too exercised by that habit. In the circumstances, it may be wondered why individuals were content with a baccalaureate in canon law, as was the learned Chasteignier de la Rocheposay, bishop of Poitiers, who seems to have taken it purely for the sake of form. Only three other bishops in all appear to have been content with the baccalaureate in law, which may be regarded as constituting the absolute minimum of exposure to legal science. One of these bishops, Alain de Solminihac, bishop of Cahors, was among of the most energetic reforming bishops of his age, but he suffered the indignity of seeing the curia refusing to recognise his law degree from Cahors as genuine, when he was made bishop in 1636. By contrast, Raymond de Montaigne, nephew of the essayist and future bishop of Bayonne, caused a sensation when he took the doctorate in law at Bordeaux when still only fourteen years of age. However, he was held to be a prodigy and was thus untypical of law students generally. In an age when individuals could obtain special dispensations in order to become councillors in the parlements at the age of twenty, it is evident that the obligatory licentiate in civil and canon law was not excessively difficult to obtain.

Table 6.4 Types of law degrees taken by bishops

Decade	utroque	canon law
1590s	25	13
1600–10	17	13
1611–20	20	14
1621–30	15	11
1631–40	8	11
1641–50	6	16
1651–61	12	14

If we turn to look more closely at the kinds of law degree taken by our bishops, it is clear that a majority, 102 out of 195 opted for the classic course in canon and civil law, and furthermore that the majority of these graduates went all the way as far as the doctorate itself.[41] This choice was natural enough, in that it was the most widely available law degree, and that where a law degree was required for either ecclesiastical or secular office, it tended to be that in canon and civil law. That over half of those holding this degree had obtained the doctorate is itself a reflection of their social background, in the sense that the costs of the doctoral examination were obviously not a deterrent to them. Nor should it come as a surprise that a substantial minority of future bishops – ninety-one in all – held degrees in canon law.[42] It was an option which was self-evidently attractive to those destined for clerical careers from the outset, and along with theology it was a choice of degree that had a conscious career-professional element to it.

Moreover, the above table (6.4) suggests something of the extent to which the future bishops' law studies were evolving in a more clerical direction, showing as it does that those nominated from the 1630s onwards had increasingly opted to study canon law alone, rather than the previously dominant combination of canon and civil law. As we shall see later, it is a development which can also be related to attitudes towards the study of theology at university. However, one important factor which also influenced this trend towards the taking of canon law degrees needs to be noted before drawing too hasty conclusions. The fact is that until the reforms of Louis XIV in 1679, the University of Paris only awarded degrees in canon law. All of those – and among Parisians their numbers must have been considerable – seeking a degree in civil law or *in utroque jure* had to repair elsewhere to do so, which accounts for their recourse to universities at Orléans, Angers and some further afield. How many law students actually went there to study by the later

41 The figure of 195 includes *all* law degrees known to have been taken by bishops, including those who later took theology degrees.
42 The two remaining bishops were Jacques Danès of Toulon, who apparently took a doctorate in civil law only, and Hector Douvrier who took a double doctorate in canon and, later, civil law.

sixteenth and seventeenth centuries as distinct from a brief visit in order to take their degrees is debatable.[43] But clerics studying law in Paris were less affected by the university's concentration on canon law, and were under far less pressure than their lay counterparts to seek another degree at another university; the fact that up to half, if not more in reality, of all the canon law degrees were taken in Paris suggests that considerations of convenience as much as of career helped to determine their choices.

Thus, in an age when law students were an overwhelming majority of university students generally, the attraction of a relatively short course of study and none-too-exacting examinations scarcely needs further emphasis. But it should not be imagined that there were no specific reasons for taking this path, or that educational decisions were either purely mercenary or opportunist. To begin with, a substantial number of the bishops were not initially destined for church careers at all, and only took orders after making their way as royal office-holders, whether civil or military; the Fouquet brothers, François and Louis, are examples of bishops with extremely short lay careers, while a former provincial intendant like François de Villemontée represents the opposite extreme. The same incentive to study law would apply to those future bishops whose earliest aspirations were not the episcopate itself but, as already noted, clerical careers for which a legal qualification was still regarded as more appropriate than a theological one. Finally, for men nominated bishops in unexpected circumstances or before they had finished their studies – which was not uncommon, especially in the first decades studied here – a law degree was the one which could be acquired rapidly without the prolonged effort demanded by theology. But most surprising of all is how many bishops had actually studied theology for a number of years, but who withdrew before taking the baccalaureate examinations, and proceeded instead to take law degrees. Thus, with so many reasons for studying law, it was bound to take powerful counter-pressure or motivation to ensure that lawyers would not dominate the ranks of the episcopate even more than they did.

III

By any standard, theology studies could be long and arduous, and in Paris at any rate, the term 'with rigorous examination' was not a euphemism. The reformed statutes of the University of Paris (1600) required five years of study before candidates could present themselves for the baccalaureate, a term reduced to three years after 1618. Nor could students apply to take the baccalaureate examinations before completing their philosophy course and taking their MA degree. With the *tentativa* (a three-hour oral defence of a thesis which was the final stage of the baccalaureate), the first cycle of study

---

43 Julia and Revel, 'Etudiants et leurs études', *Histoire sociale des populations étudiantes*, ii, 110–12.

(*primum cursus*) was completed, and candidates could begin preparation for the series of disputations and defences which were indispensable before they could formally take the licentiate. This should not be construed to mean that the baccalaureate itself was an insignificant affair, merely that the examinations which followed for the licentiate, of which the twelve-hour defence known as the *Sorbonica* was the most famous, were themselves a considerable endurance test. In 1609, no fewer than seventeen students in Paris failed their baccalaureate examinations, but not even an appeal to the parlement succeeded in reversing the results![44] The contrast with the venality of the contemporary law faculty at Orléans could hardly be more pointed.[45] Preparation for the licentiate was supposed to last a further five years in Paris, and although dispensations were sometimes granted, they were much rarer than for the corresponding examinations in law. By contrast, the gap between the licentiate and the doctorate in theology was, in purely academic terms at least, relatively insignificant; the impediments to taking it were of a different order, mainly but not wholly financial.

The theology course at Paris was not imitated to the letter by all French universities, but its statutes had historically tended to be a model which others followed to a greater or lesser extent. Smaller institutions like Valence, Aix and Cahors were probably far less exigent with candidates, but although their student body was growing in the seventeenth century, they contributed very few of the theology graduates entering the episcopate during our period. It was the more prominent faculties, led by Paris, which claimed the lion's share.[46]

Before turning to the evidence available on the bishops' theological studies, a further comparative point may be made. Because the hierarchy of degrees was far more significant in theology than in law, given the interstices between the successive *épreuves* and the many obligations which theology faculties, especially that of Paris, imposed on bachelors preparing for the licentiate and doctorate, the temptation to inflate subsequently the status of the degrees obtained by incoming bishops was especially strong; this complexity, in turn made it all the more difficult, both for contemporaries and for historians, to detect the extent of the inflation. Only seventeen of our bishops were described at the time as being bachelors of theology; the remaining ninety-one theology graduates were held to be licentiates or doctors, a distinction which was easily blurred by the continuing use of the older term 'master of theology' to describe both categories indiscriminately. Where it is possible to verify claims, the effect is often to bring degrees down a grade, and sometimes

---

44 Yves Poutet, 'Les Docteurs de Sorbonne et leurs options théologiques au xviie siècle', *Divus Thomas*, 81 (1978), 217, n 6.

45 Brockliss, *French Higher Education*, 77–9; Julia and Revel, 'Etudiants et leurs études', *Histoire sociale des populations étudiantes*, ii, 110–13.

46 See the statistical appendixes for the different theology faculties in Julia and Revel, 'Etudiants et leurs études, *Histoire sociale des populations étudiantes*, ii, 433–58.

two, but there is no real hope of being able to discover the full extent of the exaggeration. The uncertainty surrounding the baccalaureate was understandable, given that its status as a genuine degree was open to question. For example, the duc d'Epernon's son, Louis de la Valette, was a student of theology in Paris in 1612–13, when he was chosen to be Cardinal Joyeuse's successor at Toulouse. He had recently defended his philosophy theses, and two witnesses who knew him in Paris believed that he had also just taken the baccalaureate in theology.[47] This was evidently meant to embellish the young man's record – *noblesse exige* – but, as in other comparable cases, it should not be regarded as deliberate deceit on their part. As it happens, there is no sign that La Valette ever became a bachelor, or even intended to become one, and in any case his elevation to the see of Toulouse made it doubly unlikely that he ever would. Other cases later in the century suggest that several bishops had done everything required of them in order to be admitted to take the baccalaureate; as a result, they too passed for bachelors, but they did not, understandably, broadcast the fact that they had actually stopped short of taking their degree! A similar but academically less significant inflation of degrees is observable in relation to the licentiate and the doctorate in theology. Members of the episcopate who often pass for doctors in theology, such as Léonor d'Etampes, Philippe Cospeau or even Richelieu, did not proceed beyond the baccalaureate in the first and last case, or the licentiate in that of Cospeau.

From our evidence, it seems that the dominance of Paris was even more marked in theology than in law, though it is possible that the evidence contains an inbuilt bias, the result of there being more information extant about Paris theology graduates. As the accompanying table shows, the overall superiority of Paris is unmistakable; with information to hand for the universities at which eighty-eight of the 108 theology graduates took their degrees, Paris claimed no fewer than fifty-six. Toulouse came a very poor second with just seven known graduates, followed by Avignon with four. Cahors, surprisingly, produced three episcopal graduates in theology, all of them of purely local origins. Apart from Bernard Daffis, Bordeaux only contributed one theology graduate, Jean de Salies who became bishop of Oloron in the late 1650s. Yet as the decade-by-decade breakdown of the figures makes clear, Paris had not always been so dominant. Among the bishops nominated between the 1590s and the 1620s, when the number of theologians among the episcopate was relatively low, known graduates of the Paris faculty were in a minority, albeit a growing one. Thereafter, the rising proportion of theology graduates on the bench worked greatly in its favour, with virtually two out of every three theology graduates among the bishops taking their degrees in Paris in the following three decades. With an increasing number of bishops attending college in Paris, and remaining there to continue their

---

47 ASV, PC 13, fos 35–50, evidence given to *inquisitio*, July 1613.

Table 6.5 Universities at which bishops took theology degrees

Univ	1590s	1600s	1610s	1620	1630s	1640s	1650s
Paris	3	7	5	7	11	10	13
Toulouse	0	1	0	1	3	0	2
Bordeaux	0	0	0	1	0	0	1
Angers	0	0	0	1	0	0	0
Bourges	0	0	0	0	1	0	1
Valence	0	0	0	1	0	0	1
Avignon	1	0	1	0	1	0	1
Cahors	1	0	0	1	0	0	1
Aix	1	0	0	0	0	1	0
P-Mousson	0	0	0	1	0	1	0
Foreign	2	2	0	2	0	2	1
Unknown	3	7	2	2	0	1	3
Totals	11	17	8	17	16	15	24

studies after completing their humanities, it would be surprising if the number of its theology graduates entering the episcopate did not reflect that development.

There is little doubt that the length and rigour of the theology course in Paris ensured that fewer bishops held theology degrees, whether from Paris or elsewhere, than might be expected. Consequently, among the bishops who had been Paris theology students and who were determined to take a degree in the subject, there must have been some temptation to decamp to a provincial university in order to do so; but for reasons which can only be dimly guessed at, the temptation appears to have been largely resisted, with the future Cardinal de Forbin-Janson apparently alone in succumbing to it by moving to Valence in order to take his doctorate.

The real question facing most theology students was whether or not to persevere with theology and proceed to the baccalaureate and beyond. Judging by the evidence presented to the papal nuncios from the 1610s onwards, it seems that the response of a number of future bishops was to take the less demanding option of withdrawing from the course in order to take a law degree, especially the licentiate or doctorate in canon law in the Paris law faculty. Unfortunately, the loss of that faculty's registers makes it impossible to test the accuracy of each known instance of this, but the fact that the individual changes of course were usually attested either by doctors or professors of the Paris theology faculty or by former fellow-students of the bishops concerned, lends them *prima facie* credibility.

For these reasons, only an approximate tally of these theology students taking law degrees, sometimes at rather short notice, can be attempted, but the results are not without interest. Twenty-five such cases, stretching from the 1610s to the 1650s, have come to light, all but six of them from 1630 onwards. In most cases, it is impossible to determine how far they had progressed in their theology studies, but individuals like Archbishop Gondrin of Sens, Charles de Rosmadec of Vannes, or François Péricard of Angoulême had spent between four and five years at the Sorbonne before opting to take a canon law degree; Edouard Molé, son of the first president of the parlement, had been declared *admissible* for the baccalaureate examinations in theology before he, too, followed suit. Henri de Laval-Boisdauphin of Saint-Pol-de-Léon had even defended his theology theses, but was apparently distracted by other unspecified business from completing the baccalaureate; whatever it was, the business in question did not prevent him from taking a degree in civil and canon law![48] All of these cases involve bishops nominated in the late 1640s and early 1650s and who had been contemporaries as students in the Paris theology faculty; the fact that they all chose the same degree prompts the suggestion that their decisions were not reached in isolation, and may even reflect wider uncertainty among the students of the faculty.

Allowing for the pressure to inflate the scholastic achievements of new bishops, it is clear that this category of law graduate cannot really have had much more than a rather elementary knowledge of law, but had spent anything from two to four years studying theology, usually at the Sorbonne. This pattern of behaviour was not confined to Paris theology students, since arguably the most extreme exemplars of it were two distinguished members of the Oratory, Jean-Baptiste Gault and Guillaume Le Boux; both were widely known as preachers with extensive pastoral experience, yet both obtained law degrees in mid-career, and in the case of Le Boux during the weeks which followed his nomination to Dax in October 1658.[49] In the case of Gault, the motive was probably the need to have a degree in order to hold office in the diocese of Bordeaux, in that of Le Boux the sense that a bishop without a degree was (by the late 1650s) an anomaly. Finally, we may also include in this particular sub-set of bishops with law degrees those who had pursued sometimes lengthy theology studies with the Jesuits, especially at the College of Clermont, a choice which made it impossible for them to take a theology degree in Paris.[50]

Mention of the Jesuits raises the question of the educational cursus of bishops who were members of religious orders. As we saw, the Concordat and the Council of Trent both acknowledged their peculiar position by making provision for those orders which did not allow their members to take degrees.

---

48 ASV, PC 49, fo 458, evidence of François Hallier, doctor of theology, Paris, Apr 1651.
49 ASV, PC 57, fo 433v-4r, evidence of Charles Dorron, superior of Paris house, Oratory, 16 Dec 1658.
50 They include Philibert de Beaumanoir de Lavardin of Le Mans, Anne de Lévis de Ventadour of Bourges, François de Visdelou, coadjutor of Quimper, and Laurent de Chéry, coadjutor of Nevers, all nominated in the late 1640s and 1650s.

Although the number of regulars in the episcopate was limited during our period, comprising just over 12 per cent, their experiences should not be ignored. Where future bishops joined their ranks at an early age, they obtained virtually their entire education, from college upwards, in their orders' own *studia*. It was in this way that bishops of extremely modest background like Louis Vigne of Uzès (Carmelite) and Louis Vervins of Narbonne (Dominican) under Henri IV, or Noël Deslandes (Dominican) of Tréguier or Guillaume Le Boux (Oratory) of Dax under Louis XIII and Mazarin respectively, were enabled to obtain an education and the opportunity to become more widely known, especially as preachers. Just over two-thirds of the regulars were holders of degrees, largely, as one might expect, in theology. In the case of most orders, the custom was to take university degrees in the normal way, like other secular clerics. But mendicant orders like the Franciscans or Dominicans, who usually ran their own specific educational institutions although they were formally affiliated to the universities where they were situated, also granted their own degrees on occasion, especially during assemblies of the orders' ruling bodies; a few, probably not more than three or so, of the nineteen theology degrees held by members of orders appear to have been 'internal' degrees of this kind, the circumstances or quality of which it is impossible to judge.[51] On the other hand, the Carthusians and the Minims, for example, did not take degrees at all. Of the two Carthusians in the episcopate, one (Philibert Ruade) had actually taken a law and a theology degree before joining the order, while the other (Alphonse de Richelieu) joined it just as he seemed to be proceeding towards a degree at the University of Paris. The case of the Minims is also interesting, particularly because they developed a strong tradition of non university-based scholarship and enquiry in seventeenth-century France.[52] The first of the five members to enter the episcopate in our period, Gaspar Dinet, bishop of Mâcon (1600–19), was an able diplomat and preacher whom Henri IV valued, and who refused the generalship of his order in 1597. Two others were best known as preachers who held senior positions within their order in France. But undoubtedly the most learned of them was Michel de Marillac's nephew, Louis Dony d'Attichy, bishop of Riez and later of Autun, who joined the order after studying for a time at La Flèche and Navarre, learned Greek and Hebrew, and had written the history of his order before his twenty-fourth year.

IV

The diversity of educational experience among the bishops of our period is thus not without its unexpected features, several of which need more investi-

---

51 For example, Hyacinthe Serroni, bishop of Orange and then Mende, was awarded the doctorate by the Dominican general chapter of 1644: A Touron, *Hommes illustres de l'ordre de Saint Dominique*, 6 vols (Paris 1743–9), v. 600.
52 See P J S Whitmore, *The Order of Minims in Seventeenth-Century France* (The Hague 1967).

gation than has been possible here. Nevertheless, what we have seen is sufficient to prompt a number of reflections which may help to relate the issues discussed in this chapter to other questions of broad significance for the character of the French episcopate of this period.

If we focus our attention on the bishops' overall educational cursus, and not merely on the specific question of whether or not they possessed degrees, there can be little doubt but they were an increasingly well-educated group. Certainly, criticism of ignorant, ill-educated bishops appears to have declined quite sharply in the seventeenth century by comparison with its predecessor, though that is admittedly a highly subjective yardstick. Following the full course of study in the new *collèges de plein exercise* gave them a solid grounding in the humanities and philosophy (assuming that they stayed on to take the two-year philosophy course at the end). The growth of this college-based curriculum had the effect of largely emptying the arts faculties of many universities, and in colleges run by the Jesuits – and later by the Oratory or the Doctrinaires – there can be little doubt that teaching standards were at least as high as in university arts faculties.[53]

What was begun in the colleges could be continued in the universities. But although universities were far older than colleges, responses towards what they had to offer were far more mixed. Since the later Middle Ages, most of them had been dominated by their law faculties, which had been gradually turned into degree factories in reply to ever-rising social demand. Within the ranks of the graduate clergy, lawyers had always been in the majority as there was always a far wider demand for their services; theology graduates were in far less demand among the secular than they were among the regular clergy. That this should continue to be the case among sixteenth- and seventeenth-century bishops with degrees is only to be expected. By contrast, in many universities, the teaching of theology was a marginal activity and, in places like Valence, Avignon and perhaps elsewhere, it was scattered through the houses of the religious orders which were only very loosely federated under the umbrella of their theology faculty. And since their students were drawn largely from the religious orders themselves, it is hardly surprising that so many secular clergy, future bishops included, intent on studying theology should have turned instead to Paris, whose reputation in the field was historically the highest of any university in Europe. But as only MA graduates of the University of Paris could take the theology course there, the choice of Paris was not merely a demanding one, it was also a long-term one. Even for the stout-hearted the prospect of up to eight years of study after philosophy and before the licentiate must have been a daunting one which in normal circumstances only a limited number of students would contemplate undertaking. Moreover, theology degrees were widely regarded as appropriate only for those wishing to teach the subject or interested in a particular range of church offfices, which meant that they were largely taken, at least in Paris, by sons of

---

53 See Brockliss, 'Patterns of Attendance', 489–93; Brockliss, *French Higher Education*, 20ff.

middling officials, bourgeois, and even artisans. To persuade clergy of more prominent social origins and with ambitions for higher positions in the church not merely to study theology, but to join in the fray of the theology faculty, with its disputations, its regular assemblies, and its politics, was no mean feat; it was in certain respects a minor cultural revolution, and it is not surprising that it did not take place overnight.[54]

The evidence presented in the preceding pages enables us to observe this rather uncertain process at a critical stage, with lawyers still maintaining their dominant position within the episcopate, but with more and more of its future members accepting the need to follow a theology course, even though many of them did not persevere long enough to claim the *bonnet du docteur*. To explain this gradual change, which would gather pace later in the seventeenth century, in terms of a single set of causes would be simplistic. Some have already been suggested and need not be repeated here. The papacy was certainly anxious to see that France's bishops were university graduates, but it could make its views felt only in a discreet manner; nor is there any positive evidence that it had a conscious preference for theology rather than law graduates. The real changes in attitude had to come from inside France itself, and they will be looked at in more detail in later chapters. But it is clear that the broad stream of reforming impulses that is usually labelled the *dévot* movement helped to create an environment in which demands for a better educated episcopate could be pressed more effectively. Our evidence shows that it was from the 1630s onwards that bishops who had taken their theology degrees in the 1610s and especially the 1620s began to figure more prominently as beneficiaries of royal patronage. The fact that the king's leading minister, Richelieu, was himself a theology graduate and provisor of the Sorbonne with a large ecclesiastical clientèle was not without effect on those seeking high office in the church; those who realised how extensive his influence over ecclesiastical patronage was and that he sought advice from a range of influential clerical figures on appointments were not slow to sense that educational attainments would enhance their chances of favourable treatment.[55]

In this respect, it was the willingness of sons of the nobility, old and new, to read the signals and undertake theology studies, even if in many cases they did not necessarily complete them, which made the crucial difference, and gradually set a pattern for fellow-nobles to follow. With characteristic lack of modesty, Retz claimed in his *Mémoires* that he was the first scion of the upper nobility to take the theology licentiate in the late 1630s.[56] But from our

---

54 Brockliss, *French Higher Education*, ch 5. I should like to thank Laurence Brockliss for his advice on this and other issues dealt with in this chapter.
55 For a study of Richelieu's dealings with the faculty of theology, see Laurence Brockliss, 'Richelieu, Education and the State', in Joseph Bergin and Laurence Brockliss, eds, *Richelieu and his Age* (Oxford 1992), 239–40, 252–61.
56 Jean-François-Paul de Gondi, Cardinal de Retz, *Mémoires*, ed Marie-Thérèse Hipp and Michel Pernot (Paris 1984), 136.

present perspective, the interesting feature of Retz's achievement is that in obtaining the coveted first place in the licentiate examinations, he defeated another noble, Henri de La Mothe-Houdancourt, who also happened to be Richelieu's candidate and cousin. No doubt, these men would not have been denied episcopal office had they not taken their degrees in theology, but their willingness to do so was not lost on those of their contemporaries who were also being groomed for the episcopate. Neither then nor later was the French crown seriously contemplating granting bishoprics according to rankings in Paris theology examinations, and La Mothe-Houdancourt soon had his revenge on Retz by being nominated to Rennes in 1640, two years after the licentiate; Retz was rewarded for his temerity by having to wait until Richelieu was dead before taking his doctorate and obtaining the coadjutorship of Paris. Robert Constantin, whose provocative Gallican theses of 1640 had been dedicated to Richelieu himself, evidently expected his doctorate to put him in a favourable position to obtain a bishopric, but the cardinal's death dashed his hopes.[57]

With Mazarin replacing Richelieu in 1642–3, the direct personal interest of the chief minister in these matters may have declined, but the *dévots* gathered around the new *conseil de conscience* were more than willing to maintain the pressure; even those among them, like Vincent de Paul or Jean-Jacques Olier, who preferred zeal to learning in the clergy, were well-disposed to university graduates entering the episcopate. In many other ways, too, attitudes were subtly changing. For example, public defences of theses, whether in philosophy or theology, by sons of well-known families, drew large and well-reported attendances. Even the semi-official *Gazette* conveyed an unambiguous message through the language it used to report on a number of episcopal nominations. The first instance of this concerned the coadjutorship of Montauban in 1634, to which Louis XIII nominated Pierre de Bertier, 'who is thereby rewarded for the first place which he achieved in his licentiate'.[58] A decade later the elevation of Gilbert de Choiseul-Praslin to the episcopate elicited the comment that 'His Majesty's choice demonstrates that He esteems this family's learning as much as He does its worth'.[59]

Yet it would be one-sided to focus excessively on this aspect of the educational experience of the bishops merely because it seems to herald later developments. The educational diversity which characterises the pre-Louis XIV episcopate needs to be viewed in its own terms. In the light of what we

---

57 Brockliss, 'Richelieu, Education and the State', 261, for the conflict aroused by his theses; Pierre Blet, 'Vincent de Paul et l'épiscopat de France', in *Actes du colloque international d'études vincentiennes* (Rome 1983), 89, for the nuncio's report on Constantin's and his patrons' manoeuvres in 1643 to obtain the see of Tréguier in Brittany via the resignation of the sitting bishop.

58 BN, MS lat 17027, fo 149, 13 Jan 1634: 'qui voit par là recompensée la première place qu'il eust de sa licence'.

59 BN, MS lat 17025, fo 107, 4 June 1644: 'ce choix de Sa Majesté ... fait connoistre qu'Elle n'estime pas moins le sçavoir que la valeur de cette maison'.

have seen, any attempt to make distinctions between the different kinds of bishops — especially between 'pastors' and 'administrators' — on the basis of distinctions law and theology studies, would lack a solid basis in fact. This could, in any case, only be demonstrated by research into how the bishops actually ran their dioceses, and the 'administrator' bishop may simply have been a bishop governing a diocese with an efficient, well-run administrative machine. Nor could the bishops' reaction to the Jansenist crisis, for example, be predicted from their university studies alone, since lawyers and theologians were equally numerous in both camps. Even when theology graduates became the largest contingent among France's bishops, they scarcely numbered a single theologian of real distinction.

The educational diversity of the pre-Louis XIV episcopate also reflects the continuing diversity of the bishops' social background. The sixteenth-century French church may not have had its equivalent of Oxbridge or the Roman *Collegium Germanicum*, in which the future upper clergy of England and the Empire studied and networked together to such impressive and enduring effect, but as the seventeenth-century progressed, it was moving steadily in that direction, with the emergence of Paris as the dominant place of study.[60] The phenomenon was not confined to university attendance, but probably began at college level. Prolonged schooling in Paris — or even Toulouse or Bordeaux, for that matter — was expensive, and ironically, the growing trend towards the study of theology among future bishops exacerbated this further, since it made the years of study appreciably longer; it required a considerable financial sacrifice from families, or that the students themselves possessed church benefices capable of paying for their upkeep. Either way, it was a development favouring the socially advantaged. And once the nobility had taken the crucial step of accepting that its sons might take degrees in theology, the effect was to make them even stronger competitors for high office in the church. With only two full university professors becoming bishops in this period, it is fair to say that giving mitres to the educated was less important than educating the social élite to compete successfully for the rewards to which it naturally aspired.

---

60 For the English episcopate, see Kenneth Fincham, *Prelate as Pastor. The Episcopate of James I* (Oxford 1990), 16–20; on the case of the Empire, over a much longer period, see Peter Schmidt, *Das Collegium Germanicum in Rome und die Germaniker* (Tübingen 1984).

CHAPTER 7

Before the Call.
Clerical Status and
Pre-Episcopal Activities

IF THERE IS an established image of the *ancien régime* episcopate, it is one in which younger sons of almost exclusively noble families were groomed for the mitre from an early age. With the stakes so high, nothing could be left to chance along the way, so that from the college through university and beyond, each stage of their pre-episcopal existence was an act of careful calculation. Future bishops were consequently cast in an ecclesiastical mould from beginning to end, even if it failed to prevent the appearance of some unintended specimens represented by the likes of a Retz or a Talleyrand. From an early age they were well endowed with benefices held *in commendam*, a tangible sign that their families were sufficiently well connected to tap into royal ecclesiastical patronage. Later, when they had taken their degrees and perhaps spent some time at Saint-Sulpice seminary, the same connections would secure them an almonership in one of the royal households or a position as grand vicar to a reigning bishop, since these posts were recognised as offering the best prospects of joining the episcopate in due course. A *cursus honorum* existed which those aspiring to the episcopate were fully conscious of – so much so, indeed, that it seemed designed to facilitate the elevation of those 'pre-destined' for the episcopate rather than to reward those who had provided unscripted proof of ability and experience, but whose social origins precluded any such 'pre-destination'.[1]

This is not the place to reopen discussion of an essentially eighteenth-century vision of the upper clergy. Even if it seems generally accurate for the episcopal 'generation of 1789', it would be unwise to imagine from the outset that it also applied *mutatis mutandis* to their predecessors of the centuries of the Reformation and Catholic Reformation. This is not merely because the

---

1 See Michel Péronnet, *Les Evêques de l'ancienne France*, 2 vols (Lille 1978), i. ch 2, 'en attendant la mitre'. See also Nigel Aston, *The End of an Elite. The French Bishops and the Coming of the Revolution 1786–90* (Oxford 1992), 9, who refers to 'restless *grands vicaires* unable to understand why there could be any delay in their advancement'. This is not to imply that all posts of *grand vicaire* were sinecures, but the fact that they were growing in numbers in the eighteenth century meant that some at least were.

contraction of opportunity which historians have suggested as characteristic of the pre-Revolutionary decades was itself peculiar to a given period, but also because the notion of a clearly delineated cursus or clerical mould was itself slow to take shape, and had not really done so before the eighteenth century.[2] It manifestly does not begin to account for the sheer diversity of activities – whether ecclesiastical or non-ecclesiastical – pursued by the future bishops of our period. Thus, for both empirical and conceptual reasons, it is advisable to approach the subject of this chapter with as few preconceived ideas as possible drawn from later experience about what was or was not an appropriate career for future bishops in early Bourbon France. That in turn requires some preliminary discussion of clerical attitudes and behaviour, the purpose of which is to enable us to understand rather better a number of features of the episcopate which would seem incongruous to later generations. Their implications for pre-episcopal careers will also emerge in due course.

To begin with, inherited medieval notions of clergy and cleric still held sway in the sixteenth and even seventeenth centuries, and only gradually changed as a consequence of both social and religious pressures during the two centuries after the Council of Trent. It was traditional for individuals notionally destined for an ecclesiastical career to become clerics at an early age, frequently before they were of age to begin their studies at college; doing so was no impediment to a secular career or even marriage in later life, and indeed it seems that before the eighteenth century, the great majority of these tonsured clerics did not proceed to take priestly orders.[3] It was the tonsure, received as early as eight or nine years of age, which formally conferred clerical status and, crucially, enabled clerics legally to hold church benefices. It did not commit them to take full priestly orders at any point in their careers. General rules concerning orders were, if anything, negative rather than positive in character, in that they only specified that orders such as the priesthood itself could *not* be taken before a certain age had been reached. The Concordat of Bologna, it will be recalled, required French bishops to be in their twenty-seventh year before being granted their provisions. The papacy issued exemptions to this rule in our period, though in doing so it increasingly insisted that actual consecration as a bishop could not take place until the candidate had reached the required age.

Likewise, canon law normally required those becoming bishops to be in 'major' orders (*in sacris*) for at least six months before their confirmation; dispensations from this, too, were not uncommon, and they could be required by men who were well above the minimum age for becoming a bishop. The record of no less a figure than Mazarin in constantly deferring the taking of

---

2 For a brief but spirited introduction, see Bernard Plongeron, *La Vie quotidienne du clergé français au xviiie siècle* (Paris 1974), esp part I, ch 3, part 2, ch 1.

3 See Joseph Bergin, 'Between Estate and Profession: The Catholic Parish Clergy of Early Modern Western Europe', in M L Bush ed, *Social Orders and Social Classes in Europe since 1500* (London 1992), 68–9, 79.

full orders, even after becoming a cardinal, is perhaps the best-known instance of a practice that was common among the clerics of early modern Europe.[4] The vast majority of the bishops studied here were tonsured at an early age, but it is probably fair to say that thereafter their behaviour was not markedly different from that of other clerics who never aspired to episcopal rank; it was not until the eighteenth century and the spread of seminaries that clerics were to take orders, the priesthood included, according to a far more regimented time-scale. If we are looking for a less exceptional example than Mazarin – who in any case never became a bishop – of the latitude enjoyed by clerics, it might be Pierre Habert, bishop of Cahors. Evidently a tonsured cleric from an early age, he became a lay *conseiller* in the Paris parlement in 1599, and later a *maître des requêtes* in 1611. From 1605 onwards he was regularly elected a deputy to the assemblies of the clergy, and he also served various *grands* like the Guises and the prince de Conty, in administering their benefices for them. Although first almoner to Gaston d'Orléans, he was still not a priest when nominated coadjutor-bishop of Cahors in 1622. Nor in the five years of his coadjutorship did he trouble to have himself consecrated a bishop, and only did so when he succeeded to Cahors in 1627.

In his slowness to take full priestly orders and thus to commit himself openly and irrevocably to a fully ecclesiastical career, Habert was by no means exceptional for his time. Indeed, if there was any pressure on him, it came from his father and then only in 1621 as he was making his will, which included a legacy specifically intended to persuade his son to become a priest.[5] It is quite likely that the only perceptible pressure on clerics to take orders came from their own families. There is no sign that Habert was under any pressure from Rome or elsewhere in the church to do so. Yet it seems clear that his clerical identity was not in doubt to his contemporaries, down to the notaries who described him as a 'noble et scientifique personne'.[6] Habert's hesitations and his different activities also underline how far the lack of distinction between secular and ecclesiastical activities could go.

This in turn raises questions about the extent to which bishops in our period conformed to contemporary ecclesiastical expectations. The first point to note is there were considerable gradations in clerical status, since orders ranged all the way from the tonsure which made a cleric of an individual to the priesthood itself. Along the way, the minor orders, which were not of

---

4 Madeleine Laurain-Portemer, 'Le Statut de Mazarin dans l'église. Aperçus sur le haut clergé de la contre-réforme', *Bibliothèque de l'Ecole des Chartes*, 127 (1969), 355–419, 128 (1970), 5–80 [reprinted in her *Etudes Mazarines*, i (Paris 1981)].

5 Yvonne Labbé, 'Une Famille de noblesse de robe: les Habert de Montmort seigneurs du Mesnil-Saint-Denis 1543–1720', *Paris et Ile-de-France*, 39 (1988), 26, 39–40.

6 AN, G8, 87, unnumbered file of procurations for the assembly of 1612. Notaries had a wide variety of ways of referring to clerics, especially if they were holders of benefices or other offices. 'Vénérable et discrete personne' was among the most common, but the label 'noble et scientifique personne' given to Habert conveys the notion of someone of greater-than-average status and attainments.

much significance in themselves but which gave some indication of a wish to persevere in the clerical path, had to be taken; only then could the major orders, as they were collectively called, of subdeacon, deacon, and priest be envisaged. The crucial point of no return was the subdiaconate, which was the first definitive step towards the priesthood; it was only taken by those intent on becoming priests, which explains why none of the orders preceding it had anything like the same significance. Thus the subdiaconate sufficed for those taking it to be considered 'in orders' (*in sacris*). There was a minimum age at which the various orders could be taken, as well as specified intervals (interstices, as they were called) between taking each individual order. Thus, the minimum age for the major orders had varied from seventeen for the subdiaconate, nineteen for the diaconate, and twenty-four for the priesthood. Trent raised the stakes still higher, by setting the minimum age for the subdiaconate at twenty-four, with the diaconate and priesthood following at an interval of a year each.[7] But as previously, exemptions could be obtained from Rome, and in any case the Tridentine rules were slow to be observed in France.

It will be clear from this discussion that taking the major orders was not something which clerics could envisage until well after they had completed their university studies, with the exception of those taking the licentiate in theology, in an age when neither seminaries nor analogous forms of preparation for full priestly orders had yet come into existence. Moreover, with new bishops needing only to be twenty-six years of age, it is not altogether surprising that many of the youngest French bishops were either not yet *in sacris*, or had only taken major orders shortly before their nomination to a diocese. Other factors, as we shall see presently, also helped to ensure that the clerical status of the future bishops would be a complex one.

We may now turn to an analysis of the clerical status of France's incoming bishops. An initial breakdown of the information available shows that approximately two-thirds of all bishops were in priestly orders by the time of their elevation (Table 7.1). The remaining one-third, accounting for 120 bishops in all, ranged from those who were mere tonsured clerics to deacons and subdeacons, *via* those with no orders at all or whose orders are unknown. Bishops whose orders are not known, it should be said, are not to be assimilated to those with no orders at all, since they are known to have been tonsured at some point years before their promotion; what is unknown is whether or not they took further orders in later years. Were our information complete, there would be no such group, and its eleven members would be redistributed among the others, priests included. At any rate, forty-five bishops were mere clerics or in minor orders, the minimum required for membership of the clerical estate. The fifty-six who were deacons and

---

7 Jean Bernhard, Charles Lefebvre and Francis Rapp, *L'Epoque de la réforme et du concile de Trente* (*Histoire du droit et des institutions de l'église en Occident*, xiv) (Paris 1989), 364–5.

Table 7.1 Clerical status of bishops at nomination

Priests	231	Clerics	38
Deacons	18	Orders Unknown	10
Subdeacons	38	No orders	9
Minor orders	7		

subdeacons should, as will be clear from the discussion above, be regarded as a transitional category, having more in common with those who were already priests than with those in minor orders or none at all; their accession to the priesthood was only a matter of time, not of principle.

Curiously, but not unusually for this period, it is the second smallest group, the nine bishops with no orders at all, who raise the most interesting but difficult questions. All but one of them was nominated by Henri IV, a fact which on its own may suggest something of the manner in which dioceses were filled during his reign. It includes figures as distinguished as Cardinals du Perron and Sourdis and the Béarnais Bertrand Deschaux, none of whom had been destined for an ecclesiastical career; the suddenness of their change of career meant that they did not even have the tonsure or minor orders at the time of their nominations. In fact, cases like these cannot be properly understood in ignorance of the sources on which the different categories used here are actually based. Until the 1610s, information on the clerical status of bishops is extremely thin and haphazard; the fact that it has not been possible to establish when someone like Cardinal d'Ossat took orders, or which orders he had taken before his nomination, is a telling example of the problems posed by the sources, and that the problem arises for the celebrated as much as for the obscure.[8] Above all, what information exists is drawn from Roman sources, which presumably reflect the status of individuals at the moment of papal confirmation rather than of royal nomination, though how up-to-date Rome's knowledge was in these matters is impossible to determine. At any rate, with often prolonged delays between nomination and confirmation – when anything from six months to two years and more was common, especially under Henri IV – it cannot simply be assumed that an individual bishop's status did *not* change in the intervening period. Cardinal Sourdis, after all, was already a cardinal before being confirmed as archbishop of Bordeaux in 1599, but he had been nominated as early as 1596 or early 1597 when he was still known as the comte de la Chapelle. Bertrand Deschaux was first nominated to Bayonne in 1595 or possibly earlier, so that it was no great achievement to have had himself tonsured less than a year before he was

---

8 Antoine Degert, *Le Cardinal d'Ossat. Evêque de Rennes et de Bayeux 1537–1604. Sa vie, ses négociations à Rome* (Paris 1894), 38. He was tonsured in 1556 (p 5), but the only source, which Degert accepts without any corroborating proof, for the view that he took orders in 1587 is de Thou's *History*!

confirmed by Rome in March 1599![9] The uncertainty over dates of episcopal nominations and the orders taken during the often long delays before Rome granted provisions means that the number of those nominated without orders under Henri IV was probably higher than the eight recorded here.

Some further examples should illustrate the nature of the problem. The twenty-year-old René Potier, son of a distinguished parlementaire and royalist, had already been nominated to the former *ligueur* stronghold of Beauvais when, in September 1594, he took minor orders. Papal confirmation followed in November 1596 when he was duly recorded as a cleric; he was ordained a priest on 23 February 1597, and consecrated bishop of Beauvais the following day, having obtained the necessary papal permissions and dispensations.[10] Etienne Polverel of Alet was drafted in to succeed his brother who died suddenly just after receiving his provisions in 1603. The younger Polverel was then actually a serving soldier, but in the four years that elapsed before obtaining his provisions in 1607, this earlier career had been erased: he now had a law degree, and was recorded as a priest when presented for confirmation by the papal consistory.[11] Jacques d'Angennes, who became bishop of Bayeux in 1606, was probably in a similar condition to Polverel when nominated by the king in 1604 or 1605, but he was recorded as an acolyte (one of the minor orders) when he was confirmed in 1606.[12]

Bishops who were seculars at the moment of nomination may have been a numerically insignificant minority, but since being a cleric at this time itself required so little, it is surprising that *any* seculars, let alone eight of them, should have obtained nominations at all. In the case of Polverel (and the acolyte Angennes) it was the imperative of keeping a royal gift in the family when elder brothers died or refused to accept it, which triggered such an unforeseen change of career. The last known case came in 1621, and involved the most enduring of all episcopal dynasties of the period – the Bonsi of Béziers. Cardinal Jean de Bonsi retired to Rome around 1615, having ensured that his nephew Dominique was already installed in Béziers as his coadjutor and successor.[13] But he died suddenly in late April 1621, which threw his uncle into a desperate panic. The only family member who seemed to him capable of ensuring the succession was Thomas, comte de Vaillan, Dominique's brother, but he was a courtier with neither a degree nor orders. The cardinal frantically mobilised all his connections to secure Béziers for the young man, then aged nineteen, who seemed so reluctant to accept it that he attempted to run away and join the Jesuits instead! Overwrought by the

---

9 AN, Z^{1}o 240, 16 June 1598.
10 ASV, Misc Arm XII 144, fo 198; AN Z^{1}o 240, 21 Sept 1594, 23 Feb 1597.
11 ASV, Acta Misc 97, fo 608.
12 AN, Z^{1}o 241, 21 Jan 1605, tonsure; ASV, Misc Arm XII 144, fo 206; *Hierarchia Catholica*, iv. 108, *Belvacen*, n 4.
13 BN, MS Clairambault 368, fo 153, Dominique Bonsi to Louis XIII, 5 Sept 1616, announcing his arrival in France to replace his uncle at Béziers, and awaiting the king's commands.

Table 7.2 *Orders taken by bishops before nomination*

Orders	Henri IV	Louis XIII	Mazarin	Totals
Priests	53	97	81	231
Deacons	7	11	0	18
Subdeacons	16	20	2	38
Minor orders	6	1	0	7
Clerics	12	22	4	38
Orders unknown	6	2	2	10
No orders	8	1	0	9
Totals	108	154	89	351

extreme stress, the cardinal himself then died in early July, having done just enough to obtain royal approval of his nephew who was in the end persuaded to accept the mitre: both his age and lack of orders meant that Thomas de Bonsi was only consecrated bishop in April 1626.[14]

It will be evident, if only from the dates of the cases just seen, that the question of bishops' clerical status is one that also needs to be examined in chronological perspective. To what extent did the kind of diversity we have just observed remain characteristic of France's bishops throughout the period? As in previous chapters, it seems best to present the data in two tables, reign-by-reign and decade-by-decade.

The first of the tables does more than suggest the long-term trend (Table 7.2). Overall, the proportion of future bishops who were *in sacris* by the time of nomination moved firmly from just seven out of ten under Henri IV to over nine out of ten during the Mazarin régime. Subdividing this expanding group also produces interesting comparisons. Slightly over half of those becoming bishops during Henri IV's reign were not priests, even by the time the papacy moved to confirm their nomination. Under Louis XIII, the proportion of priests among the new bishops rose from 49 to 63 per cent. Yet during the two reigns, subdeacons and deacons constituted a substantial minority of bishops *in sacris* when nominated; as a proportion of those *in sacris* they fell marginally – from just over 21 per cent under Henri IV to 19.5 per cent under Louis XIII. It was only during the Mazarin ministry that a decisive change manifests itself: eighty-three of the eighty-nine new bishops were *in sacris*, and of them no fewer than eighty-one were priests.

In sum, and as might be expected, it was the reign of Henri IV which produced the most heterogeneous crop of future bishops, viewed in terms of

14 See the voluminous correspondence about the Béziers succession in BN, MS Fr 18016, fos 85–293 *passim*, which contain numerous frantic letters from Bonsi to Louis XIII and Puysieux. Cardinal Sourdis and others let it be known that they would not be averse to obtaining a share of the Bonsi family benefices in France – something which Bonsi probably suspected and which would have exacerbated his anxiety.

Table 7.3 Orders taken by bishops before nomination

Decade	Pr	D	S-D	Min	Cl	Unkn	None	Totals
1590s	27	5	6	3	5	3	7	56
1601–10	28	2	11	3	7	3	1	55
1611–20	16	8	14	0	14	0	0	52
1621–30	43	3	4	0	5	1	1	57
1631–40	34	0	1	1	2	1	0	39
1641–50	38	0	1	0	1	1	0	41
1651–61	45	0	1	0	4	1	0	51
Totals	231	18	38	7	38	10	9	351

Pr = Priest; D = Deacon; S-D = Subdeacon; Min = Minor orders; Cl = Clerics; Unkn = Orders Unknown; None = No orders

their clerical status: it accounts for the largest contingent of those in minor orders, those with no orders at all, or those whose orders were unknown. These three categories dropped noticeably without altogether disappearing during the longer reign of Louis XIII. The *coup de grâce* only finally appears during the Mazarin ministry, when only four bishops, all politically well connected, were still simple clerics.

A decade-by-decade analysis offers a further refinement of this general pattern, enabling us to pinpoint more accurately swings or points of change within the rather broad tripartite chronology just outlined (Table 7.3). It confirms the observation that it was the decades of Henri IV's reign which provided the widest range of clerical types among incoming bishops. The only major difference between the 1590s and 1600s lies in the sharp fall in the number of bishops appointed while still laymen in the full sense. By contrast, the proportion of priests among the new bishops was remarkably stable across the two decades, though the overall proportion of bishops *in sacris* rose from approximately two-thirds to three-quarters.

With increasingly reliable information to hand for the bishops of the Louis XIII and Mazarin years (exemplified by the fall in the numbers from the category of unknowns), the trends emerging from a decade-by-decade study are bound to be more revealing. As already seen in relation to the social origins and the academic attainments of the bishops, the 1610s represent something of a regression, even in relation to the reign of Henri IV, with the sole exception of bishops who had previously not taken any orders at all. The proportion of future bishops *in sacris* actually fell for the only time during the entire period, although it did not return to the level recorded for the 1590s. The most obvious evidence of this reverse is to be seen in the fall in the number of priests being nominated bishops; indeed the figure easily represents the lowest percentage of priests entering the episcopate for any decade of the entire period. That priests were only marginally more numerous than mere clerics – sixteen against fifteen – during the 1610s itself suggests something of the changed political climate of the early years of Louis XIII's reign, during which noble families and incumbent bishops took full advantage of the crown's weakness and need to build support by securing the appoinment of young bishops, especially coadjutors; it was they who accounted for most of the clerics and subdeacons who between them comprised over half of all the bishops nominated during this decade. No less spectacular is the swing in the opposite direction registered in the 1620s, when three out of every four new bishops were priests, and those *in sacris* seven out of eight. The signs are, as a later chapter will demonstrate, that by the late 1610s a reaction had already set in against the uses of royal episcopal patronage since Henri IV's death, and that the record of the 1620s should not be credited simply to the arrival of Richelieu in office in the middle years of the decade. He was only one *dévot* among many, and *dévot* concern about the choice of bishops was being expressed for several years before his ministerial elevation. At any rate, the 1620s proved a real turning point, and in the following three decades the elimination of non-sacerdotal figures among the new bishops proceeded apace. Sustained throughout the 1630s, it reached its peak during the 1640s, only to drop back slightly in the last decade of Mazarin's ministry.

The variations in the totals observed for the three decades after 1630 are insignificant compared to those for the previous generation, since by now virtually nine out of every ten new bishops were ordained priests, and thereby fully committed to ecclesiastical careers. Leaving aside three bishops whose exact orders are unknown, it appears that only eleven of the 131 bishops nominated after 1631 were not in priestly orders. These are the exceptions which may be taken to prove the rule that was emerging so powerfully during this generation, and their identities are of particular interest. Subdeacons were the closest to full priestly orders, but only one of them was nominated in each decade from the 1630s onwards, and in many ways there was something emblematic about each of them. The first was Richelieu's own relative, Henri de La Mothe-Houdancourt, nominated in 1639; he was followed by the future Cardinal de Retz in 1643, at the very beginning of the regency, while Dominique de Ligny, nephew of Chancellor Séguier, completed the trio in the late 1650s. Only one bishop nominated in these thirty years was in minor orders – Jacques Danès, a former provincial intendant who, as witnesses testified to the papal nuncio, had made it publicly known that he was preparing to have himself ordained a priest; he did so shortly after his nomination and well before his confirmation in Rome.[15] With the six clerics nominated between 1630 and 1661 including men like Pierre de Marca,

---

15 ASV, PC 38, fo 702, attestation by Archbishop Gondi of Paris that Danès had taken the orders of subdeacon, deacon and priest *extra tempora*, i.e. outside of the normal times of the year for ordinations. See *ibid*, fos 707–9, evidence of Jacques Lescot, later bishop of Chartres, and Antoine de Bréda, *curé* of Saint-André-des-Arts, 23 Dec 1638.

Louis Barbier, Zongo Ondedei and Louis Fouquet, it is impossible to avoid the inference, one which applies to the other cases discussed above, that exceptions could be made for individuals enjoying political favour as a result of their own services or their families' powerful connections. But even these nominations, by being so few in number, served to underline the vagaries of royal, ministerial and court favour generally, and to point episcopal hopefuls firmly in the direction of taking full priestly orders before seriously envisaging the honours of the mitre.

With men *in sacris* gradually establishing a virtual monopoly on episcopal office, the question arises of how long they had been in orders before their nomination as bishops. Obviously, the fact that the priesthood could only be received at the age of twenty-four ensured that, in many cases, the maximum period in orders before the episcopate would not be a particularly long one. In practice, however, the minimum age offers no real guide to contemporary behaviour, and it was not uncommon for clerics to defer moving from the subdiaconate to the priesthood for many years.[16] The reasons for deferral cannot be fathomed in most cases. Yet there is good reason to believe that, from the 1620s onwards, those clergy who were influenced by the spiritual teaching of Bérulle and his influential disciples, such as Saint-Cyran, Condren, de Paul, and Olier, may have been slow to take priestly orders, not out of calculation, but out of a heightened sense of the gravity of what they were proposing to do.[17] At the same time, however, it would be naive to assume that the decision to be ordained a priest could ever be totally divorced from career prospects, especially that of the episcopate itself.

Unfortunately, these and other related questions are unlikely ever to be answered satisfactorily. In the absence of all but extremely fragmentary and dispersed ordination records, a systematic attempt to calculate the length of time future bishops had been in orders is simply impossible. The best that can be proposed is a somewhat impressionistic survey covering the bishops nominated between the late 1620s, when information from other sources becomes relatively plentiful, and the death of Mazarin. Before the late 1620s, too little is known about bishops who were in sacerdotal orders at the time of their nomination for any worthwhile conclusions to be drawn. However, for the period from 1629 to 1661 information is available for 103 out of the 129 men who were priests on becoming bishops. The principal weakness of this information lies in its subjective nature, since it was provided as evidence by witnesses before the papal nuncios in response to a question, introduced in

---

16 E.g. Bishop Doni d'Attichy of Riez was ordained subdeacon in 1609, but only became a deacon in 1620, and a priest in 1622. Six years later he was nominated to Riez: ASV, PC 26, fos 228v-9r, certificates of ordination.

17 See Michel Dupuy, *Bérulle et le sacredoce* (Paris 1969), and from a novel perspective, Jean Simard, *Une iconographie du clergé français au xviie siècle: les dévotions de l'école française et les sources de l'imagerie religieuse en France et au Québec* (Laval, Québec 1976).

1628 in the revised questionnaire concerning royal nominees to the episcopate, asking if, and for how long, they were in orders. Where future bishops had clearly been priests for a long time, witnesses' memories, and therefore their answers, proved rather approximate, but for the most part the evidence was given by men who knew the bishops well, having attended their first mass, seen their letters of ordination, or made their own enquiries on the matter.

With these caveats in mind, it is possible to suggest some general figures for the bishops nominated between 1629 and 1661. The figures concern 103 of the 129 priests who became bishops during this period, compared with a mere 21 out of 102 for the preceding forty years. The provenance of the figures should make it abundantly clear why precise calculations of averages or of trends would be rather meaningless. The only presentation capable of reflecting contemporary attitudes, as well as the evidence itself, is that suggested in the following table (Table 7.4).

As remarked earlier, church law required that incoming bishops should be *in sacris* for at least six months before their nomination. This alone would suffice to draw attention to the eleven individuals who did not fulfil that particular condition between 1629 and 1661.[18] The group cannot be said to be entirely homogeneous, but a combination of factors account for its size. Virtually all of those belonging to it were sons of well-placed noble families, and some of them were obviously being groomed to succeed relatives in the episcopate. Significantly, six out of the eleven were nominated during the post-Fronde years, when, with Mazarin's sanction, sons of the old nobility were becoming more numerous in the episcopate. Moreover, five of them were also under thirty years old, a fact which makes the lack of priestly orders easier to understand. Five of the eleven were actually proceeding to the priesthood while the process of nomination was itself under way; it was this which enabled witnesses to inform the nuncio that a particular bishop was, literally, a priest for only a few days (*a paucis diebus*).[19] If one were looking for an outsider among these men it would have to be Antoine Godeau, the poet who had originally been destined for the bar, and who was probably as surprised as were his contemporaries when Richelieu obtained the see of Grasse for him in 1636; apart from ministerial favour, the only trait he had in common with his ten socially more distinguished colleagues was his relative 'youth' – he was thirty-one years old.

This haste to take priestly orders shortly before or during the period of nomination becomes more manifest when viewed alongside the figures for those who had been ordained priests for more than six months before their

18 They are: François de Grignan, Godeau, Gondrin, Ferdinand de Neufville, Batholomé Delbène, Forbin-Janson, Cosnac, Sariac, Clérambault, Pierre de Bonsi, Clermont-Tonnerre.
19 E.g. Bernard Sariac, nominated bishop of Aire in late June 1657 was ordained priest three weeks later, which enabled witnesses at his *inquisitio* to testify that he was a priest since the previous Sunday: ASV, PC 57, fos 277v-8v, 19 July 1657.

Table 7.4 Duration of priestly orders before episcopal nomination 1629–61

Under 6 months	11
Over 6 months	1
Over a year	4
Over 2 years	5
Over 3 years	6
Over 4 years	8
Over 5 years	23
Over 10 years	29
Over 20 years	16
Total	103

nomination as bishops.[20] The evidence provided by the table in this regard is not without interest. In particular it shows that no more than ten bishops, in addition to the eleven just seen, had taken orders within less than two years of their selection. By contrast, the numbers of bishops who were priests for over five, ten, and even twenty years seems impressively large, accounting for well over half of the total with which we are concerned here. That in itself is of considerable significance, since it points to an episcopate which increasingly consisted not merely of men in priestly orders but who, whatever their ultimate ambitions, had not taken those orders purely with a view towards a rapid entry into the episcopate. Obviously, the longer individuals had been priests, the more true this is likely to be. If there is one group of bishops who may be regarded as the opposite of the eleven discussed in the previous paragraph, it is the sixteen who had been priests for over twenty years. Only one of those in orders for over twenty years, François de Salignac, could have realistically expected episcopal rank at the time when he became a priest during the 1630s, and indeed for many years it looked as if his family would never again hold their quasi-patrimonial see of Sarlat after it had escaped from their grasp in 1639. All of the other bishops under consideration had relatively little capital, socially or ecclesiastically, to their credit at the time of ordination.[21] Four were members of religious orders, and another four were bounded by the horizons of a particular diocese.[22] But for men with names like Lionne, Tubeuf or Boylesve, it is clear that the subsequent rise to promise of other family members was the *sine qua non* of their own elevation to the

---

20 Jean Dolce, nominated to Boulogne in August (?) 1632 had, according to witnesses, being ordained a priest just over six months earlier.
21 In addition to Salignanc, they include: Barrez, Bretel, Lionne, Deslandes, Desprutez, Raconis, Hardivilliers, Charles Vialart, Du Louet, Arnauld, Boislève, Tubeuf, Ruffier, Salies, Serroni.
22 Hyacinthe Serroni is himself something of an exception, as he had been bishop of Orange since 1647, transferring to Mende in 1661.

mitre, generating prospects that would have been fanciful in previous decades. By contrast, Henri Arnauld's family seemed on a decidedly downward trajectory from the mid-1620s onwards, when Richelieu blocked further advancement for them. But although Arnauld waited many years for a diocese to come his way, and was frustrated in his ambition to obtain the see of Toul in the later 1630s, he was probably the most talked-of bishop-to-be of the period covered in this book. When he was given Angers in 1649, twenty-five years after he had become a priest, contemporaries regarded his elevation as both thoroughly deserved and long overdue.[23] Yet it was not Arnauld who held the record for the longest interval between the priesthood and the episcopate: that belonged to an English exile of the previous generation, William Gifford, who was nominated to Reims in 1622, forty years after his ordination!

I

This discussion of bishops' clerical status at the moment of their nomination offers a valuable, if unusual, vantage point from which to observe the diversity that was still characteristic of them before Louis XIV. Clearly the pressure for an episcopate that was already *in sacris*, which began to assert itself particularly strongly from the 1620s onwards, had triumphed almost entirely by mid-century. That change was an important one, with obvious implications for the kinds of activity in which future bishops engaged before their promotion. But if a measure of homogeneity took so long to take shape on a matter as apparently basic as that of clerical orders, we should not expect to find it in greater abundance when it comes to the pre-episcopal careers of the same bishops. At one extreme, we find young bishops, of whom Richelieu himself, nominated to Luçon in 1602 while still well under twenty and a student at the University of Paris, is as good an example as any; over fifty years later, even the youngest bishops were in their mid- or late-twenties rather than in their teens, and those of them studying theology had still barely taken their degrees when the episcopate beckoned. At the other extreme, we find a man like William Gifford, who has just been mentioned. After several years in Rome as secretary to his fellow-exile, Cardinal William Allen, he moved to Douai and Lille, where he was dean of the chapter of Saint-Pierre. Secretly expelled from Lille, he settled in France under Henri IV, becoming a Benedictine monk in 1609. That did not prevent him from becoming dean of the Saint-Malo chapter in 1611 and six years later a suffragan bishop temporarily entrusted with administering the see of Reims. His advanced age meant that he was not expected to govern Reims for long after his nomination as

---

23 Isabelle Bonnot, *Hérétique ou saint? Henry Arnauld, évêque janséniste d'Angers au xvii*ᵉ *siècle* (Paris 1984), ch 1.

archbishop in 1622, and so it proved: his five-year reign there was the shortest episode in a highly varied career.[24]

Extreme cases, even more than hard cases, make bad law, and it can justifiably be objected that neither Richelieu nor Gifford were representative of the French episcopate generally. But they reflect the very wide spectrum of pre-episcopal career histories which were themselves the result of a combination of factors such as social origins, family traditions, patronage, age and so on. It would be naive to imagine that there was some kind of representative *curriculum vitae* to which future bishops attempted to conform. For a sizeable minority of them, the episcopate itself was their first real opportunity for action; for many others who were in their thirties or forties, it has proved impossible to trace any pre-episcopal activity. This may, of course, be the result of inadequate documentation, but it should not lead to the assumption that entering the episcopate in middle age (by seventeenth-century standards at least) carried with it a presumption of experience, pastoral or otherwise.

Indeed, in attempting to make sense of pre-episcopal biographies generally, the most problematic notion is arguably that of 'career'. For one thing, it suggests a certain continuity of activity and purpose sustained over a sufficiently long period of time for an individual to be readily identified with it. Relatively few of our bishops would be recognizable in such terms. Not only did many of them change their spheres of action over time, but they frequently engaged in more than one at a time. For similar reasons, the term 'career' may also suggest that it was because of a particular type or range of activities that individuals eventually became bishops. This, too, would be misleading as a generalisation, even though in individual cases it can be shown that a particular activity did have such an outcome. The French monarchy never embraced the principle that merit should be the basis of entry to the episcopate, and in practice merit, however defined, was a factor which had to be fitted around other considerations, and not the reverse, when it came to filling vacant dioceses. It is possible to go further and argue that, from the crown's point of view, specific 'services rendus' rather than a worthy *curriculum vitae* were far more deserving of reward.[25] Contemporaries, whether clergy or otherwise, would probably not have agreed on a single definition of merit appropriate for the episcopate. Insofar as it is possible to pin down their thinking at all, their ideal – which clearly reflects the weight of tradition – was one of a variable alliance of 'mérite' and 'naissance'. Meanwhile, for those

---

24 Alain Lottin, *Lille citadelle de la contre-réforme? (1598–1668)* (Westhoek 1984), 76, 339 n 13.
25 The clearest and most conscious example of this arose in 1643 when the see of Pamiers was given to Jacques de Montrouge, a royal almoner, in preference to François Bosquet, the intendant in Languedoc, to whom it was pointed out that Montrouge's services to Anne of Austria, in which he allegedly risked his life, were so vital as to brook no argument on other grounds: BN, MS Fr 15720, fo 331v, Charles de Montchal, archbishop of Toulouse, to François Bosquet, 21 July 1643.

consciously in search of a bishopric, it was far more advisable to position oneself advantageously through patronage ties and offices, than to accumulate a record of experience, pastoral or administrative. As we shall see, a handful of men who had been parish priests became bishops under Henri IV and his successors, but it was not *because* they had been parish priests; far more almoners in one or other royal household at court became bishops, and it was no secret that most almonerships were virtual sinecures entailing scarcely any real duties. There was, after all, little that a Guise, a Souvré, or a Gondi could actually *do* to demonstrate that they really had the necessary qualities to be a bishop, so that when royal letters of nomination referred to the services to church and crown of their forebears as the reason for promoting them, they were simply stating the truth of the matter. It is essential at the outset to allow for there being many roads to the episcopate, and that the temptation to seek a royal road may not be the best method of approach to the subject. Consequently, if the term career is used in the following pages, it is in a purely descriptive sense – as a convenient shorthand for the sum total of the activities engaged in by bishops before being raised to the episcopate.

Before turning to look in detail at these pre-episcopal activities, it may be worth pausing to consider briefly a phenomenon which, if only indirectly connected to what is to follow, will nevertheless help to underline the peculiarities of the episcopate. The presence of elder sons in its ranks, as among the clergy generally, is not a subject much explored by historians, no doubt because they were probably a small minority among the clergy generally. Ten examples have been found of eldest sons becoming bishops between 1589 and 1661, but this is likely to be too low a figure, given our limited knowledge of so many of the families in question. More surprisingly, two of these bishops – Octave de Bellegarde and Antoine Godeau – were in fact *only* sons! The best-known of the eldest sons was Cardinal Sourdis, cousin of Gabrielle d'Estrées, for whom Henri IV sought the red hat while he was still a layman, albeit wearing clerical garb.[26] Sourdis's notoriously violent temper and manners, not least in his dealings with his own family members, was probably exacerbated by his consciousness of his position as head of his family.[27] A generation later, in the mid-1630s, François Fouquet quickly abandoned his original career of *conseiller* in the Paris parlement, in order to enter the church. But most of the other eldest sons appear to have taken orders without a period in a secular career. In the case of Edouard Molé, there was no sign of a change of direction, let alone of haste. He was in his mid-thirties

---

26 ASV, Fondo Borghese I, 646, fo 112, Cardinal Medici, papal legate, to Cardinal Aldobrandini, 20 Jan 1597.
27 A typical instance is to be found in a letter to Marie de Medici, regent of France, in which he refers, with considerable distrust, to the manoeuvres of 'ceux de ma maison dont ie suis le chef pour la naissance et premier à servir Vostre Majesté, ma fortune n'estant point proportionné au rang que ie tiens': BN, MS Clairambault 364, fo 99, 28 Apr 1614.

when nominated to Bayeux in 1647, and yet both Mazarin and Molé's father recognised that he needed serious tutoring by Vincent de Paul if he was to become a competent bishop.

Not dissimilar were the occasions when younger sons succeeded their elder brothers, but still took orders. This generally manifests the power of family authority over individual preference. Albert de Bellièvre was succeeded by his brother Claude as archbishop of Lyon in 1604, leaving the *third* and only remaining son, Nicolas, to continue the family line. When Pierre Polverel of Alet died suddenly in Rome in 1603 before being consecrated bishop, his uncle, Bishop Christophe de Lestang of Carcassonne, insisted that his only remaining brother, Etienne, then a soldier, take the cloth and succeed him at Alet – thus effectively killing off the direct family line altogether.[28] In 1621, it was Cardinal Bonsi who decided that his nephew, Thomas, then a laymen, should succeed to the see of Béziers, and not his brother, Clement, who was at the time a canon of Saint Peter's in Rome.[29] It should also be noted that family imperatives obliged two bishops to quit episcopal office altogether and embrace secular careers in this period. This was all the easier in that neither Louis de Valois, comte d'Alais, who was bishop of Agde from 1618 to 1622, nor Henri de Guise, who was archbishop of Reims from 1628 to 1641, was ever a priest or a consecrated bishop.

On the other hand, some changes of direction were clearly personal rather than familial in origin. The future Cardinal Sourdis broke off his engagement to Chancellor Cheverny's daughter to follow a career in the church.[30] With twenty children, Antoine Arnauld did not lack offspring to provide for. But his son Henri, the future bishop of Angers, was initially trained in law, which he unwillingly practised until his father's death in 1619, when he promptly entered the church.[31] Likewise, Louis Fouquet, who made a promising début in the early 1650s as a *conseiller* in the parlement and then as a diplomatic agent for Mazarin, willingly embraced an ecclesiastical career in order to become bishop of Agde in succession to his brother, François.[32] In some, though not all, cases like these, it would seem as if the prospect of rapid advancement at the highest level in the church was a powerful incentive to change course, which in turn may well have facilitated families' acceptance of

---

28 G Clement-Simon, 'Célébrités de la ville de Brive: les Lestang, les Maynard de Lestang, les Polverel', *Bulletin de la Société historique et archéologique de la Corrèze*, 14 (1892), 598.

29 BN, MS Fr 18016, fo 109, letter to Puysieux, secretary of state, 29 May 1621, in which he explains his decision. Thomas Bonsi's reign in Béziers was short, and he was duly succeeded by his brother Clement.

30 Bernard Peyrous, *La Réforme catholique à Bordeaux 1600–1719*, 2 vols (Bordeaux 1995) i. 110–14.

31 Bonnot, *Hérétique ou saint?*, 94–6.

32 X Azéma, *Un prélat janséniste, Louis Fouquet, évêque et comte d'Agde (1656–1702)* (Paris 1963), 17–19.

such changes.³³ They scarcely needed the example of the Mazarin family, whose two sons became *hommes d'église* and cardinals, to convince them of the possibilities which high church office could offer.

II

Developments like these, when viewed alongside the fact that a number of bishops were either not in orders or had only taken minor orders before their nomination, should make it easier to understand why seventeenth-century France should also have had bishops whose previous careers were essentially secular in character. Their numbers were certainly large enough to merit some attention.

A total of at least forty-six bishops, accounting for over 13 per cent of the episcopate, belong in that category. It can be subdivided for our purposes into two subgroups, the smaller of which includes thirteen men for whom secular careers were originally intended or even embarked upon, but which were rapidly curtailed and which in no case involved marriage. As some of those concerned, like Thomas de Bonsi or Henri Arnauld, have been mentioned above, it is unnecessary to examine them any further here. The larger group includes thirty-three bishops. The secular careers of some of them were rather brief, but where this was the case it was due to the death of their wives; sixteen of the thirty-three bishops in this group were married and proceeded to take orders on becoming widowers. In one single instance, that of the intendant François de Villemontée, who became bishop of Saint-Malo in 1659, the bishop's wife was still alive; she reputedly accompanied him on his formal *entrée* to the city, even though their well-known *malheurs domestiques* had led to a perpetual separation and the taking of a vow of chastity on her part nearly a decade earlier.³⁴ Eleven of these men became bishops in the peculiar circumstances of Henri IV's reign, but it should not be imagined that once normality had returned, the episcopate was closed to men with secular backgrounds. The phenomeon was a persistent one throughout the entire period, falling off during the 1610s and 1620s (two per decade), but reappearing strongly from the 1630s onwards (seventeen for the years 1631–61). Eight of them were former military men, but they had not, it seems, served long enough to have risen to any kind of eminence in the military hierarchy. This, no doubt, may have been a factor, however indeterminate, in their

---

33 See from the *Reichskirche*, the example of a princely family of Schönborn, closely allied to Louis XIV's France: Stefan Kremer, *Herkunft und Werdegang geistlicher Führungsschichten in den Reichsbistümern zwischen Westfälischen Frieden und Säkularisationn* (Freiburg-im-Breisgau 1992), 39, n 41.

34 F Saulnier, 'Un prélat au xviiᵉ siècle. François de Villemontée évêque de Saint-Malo, sa femme et ses enfants', *Bulletin et Mémoires de la Société Archéologique de l'Ile-et-Vilaine*, 32 (1903), 107–38.

change of direction, but it also means that too little is known of their preecclesiastical careers for the historian to get near enough to them in order to analyse that most cherished of seventeenth-century *topoi* as it applies to them – their 'conversion'. Three of these 'seculars' were literary figures, admittedly a rather 'soft' category, but it could not be said that Cardinal du Perron, Jean Bertaut or Antoine Godeau brought anything but distinction to the French episcopate.

By far the biggest cohort of bishops of a secular background, numbering twenty-two out of the thirty-three, consisted of men who had served as royal magistrates and officials, ranging from a keeper of the seals like Guillaume du Vair, to a *grand maître* in the *eaux et forêts* administration like Dominique de Ligny. Not only were they the largest group, but their presence in the episcopate was well sustained, especially from the 1630s onwards, when they accounted for fourteen of the seventeen bishops with secular careers behind them. All but five of the twenty-two had at one time or another been *conseillers* in a parlement, especially in Paris, though not necessarily at the outset of their careers. However, most of these parlementaires did not remain content with a post as *conseiller*, but went on to become *maîtres des requêtes*, presidents of sovereign courts, and *conseillers d'état*, with four of them serving as provincial intendants along the way. Certainly, the profile of those becoming bishops from the 1630s onwards is unmistakably that of laymen-turned-clerics who had rendered substantial political and administrative service to the crown over many years. It was, of course, no disadvantage that a few of them – such as Ligny, Lionne, Brandon or Louis Fouquet – were relatives of ministers, which further enhanced the patronage links that all of them had formed with the ministers and council under Richelieu and Mazarin. Here, if anywhere, we encounter the quintessential 'political' bishop, though the term is not meant to convey either servility or the image of individuals being suddenly 'parachuted' into the episcopate as a direct reward for their services. This did happen in a limited number of cases, but mainly under Henri IV. Judging by the length of time they had been in orders before their nomination, there is no obvious difference between the behaviour of most of these bishops and that of their colleagues who had been designated for clerical careers from the outset; the longer they had been in orders, the more likely they were to have abandoned their secular careers or offices. An unusual exception is Raymond de Montaigne, who had become a priest in 1622 after his wife's death, but who continued to serve as president of the Saintes *présidial* court thereafter. Indeed, it was only on the very eve of his consecration as bishop of Bayonne, in mid-1630, that he was forced to resign by the bishops who had arrived to perform the consecration ceremony and who threatened to ride away in their carriages if he did not do so![35] Much more typical was Artus de Lionne, who

---

35 See Charles Dangibeaud, *Le Présidial de Saintes. Raymond de Montaigne lieutenant-général et président (1568–1637)* (Paris 1881), 50–2, doc. no xxxv, notarised statement concerning this affair by Montaigne, with his objections to resigning, 14 July 1630.

had begun his career as a *conseiller* in the Grenoble parlement but who had been a priest for twenty years before he was chosen for the coadjutorship of Gap in 1634; the presence of his brother-in-law, Abel Servien, in the ministry at this juncture doubtless helped bring to fruition his quest for a diocese which dated from at least the late 1620s.[36] Even the behaviour of the most political prelate of the age, the Gallican jurist Pierre de Marca, was not untypical of future bishops. He had actually been tonsured at the age of fourteen, in 1608, so that when his wife died in 1631 he imperceptibly slipped back into the clerical estate, while continuing to serve the crown as an intendant and a *conseiller d'état* before and after his initial nomination as bishop of Conserans in late 1642. It was Rome's opposition to his promotion which delayed his taking major orders until 1648 – a relatively clear case of 'wait and see'.[37] In the case of his fellow intendant, François de Villemontée, the delay in confirming him as bishop of Saint-Malo may have been engineered by the crown because his services as a provincial intendant in Picardy, the last remaining theatre of war with Spain, were still needed in 1657–8.[38]

Overall, however, it is clear that the number of those transferring rapidly from secular service to the crown into the higher reaches of the church was extremely limited, and in no way comparable with the pattern recorded for the Castilian bishops of either the sixteenth or seventeenth century.[39] In France, increasingly it was as if such individuals had to pass through a period of ecclesiastical initiation and retreat before they could envisage episcopal office.

III

This brings us back to the great majority – six out of every seven – of France's bishops in this period who followed the classic pattern of younger sons destined from an early age for the clergy. It is doubtful that any single method of classification would satisfactorily account for their experiences, and it seems best to concentrate upon the most salient forms of pre-episcopal activity,

---

36 Pierre Grillon, ed, *Les Papiers de Richelieu: Politique intérieure. Correspondance et papiers d'état*, 6 vols (Paris 1975 – in progress), iv. 197, Marillac to Richelieu, 5 Apr 1629, reporting that Lionne was claiming the see of Maillezais as his. AAE, CP Rome 81, fo 573, Servien to Richelieu, n.d. (but 1636 or early 1637, since after Servien's disgrace and before Bishop du Serre's death in May 1637) relating problems Lionne was having over the Gap coadjutorship because of the old bishop's vulnerability to pressure from other sources. It should also be noted that Lionne's son, Hugues, Louis XIV's future minister, was Servien's principal *commis* in the war ministry.
37 Pierre de Marca, *Histoire de Béarn*, ed V Dubarat, i (Pau 1894), p. lvi, doc cclxxxv.
38 AD Ile-et-Vilaine, G 54, letters-patent renewing *économat* of Saint-Malo on these grounds, 20 July 1657.
39 See Helen Rawlings, 'The Secularisation of Castilian Episcopal Office under the Habsburgs, c. 1516–1700', *Journal of Ecclesiastical History*, 38 (1987), 63, table 5.

while noting possible significant variations and deviations from them. In practical terms, this will mean trying to assemble a collective portrait which progressively moves from the simple to the complex. It is thus not a taste for paradox that has the following discussion of careers and activities begin with those bishops with no known experience or with experience of a specific kind, and only then move on to consider those whose activities were more multiform and hence more difficult to characterise! It will become abundantly clear en route how many of these activities were essentially patronage-driven, even if the element of patronage was to some extent present in nearly all of them.

The first category of bishop to be considered is that for which no record of any activity, other than that of holding benefices *in commendam*, can be discovered. This is hardly an exact science, but at a conservative count it includes seventy-three bishops, or just over one-fifth of the episcopate. The largest subgroup among them was made up of approximately thirty bishops who were in their mid-twenties or under at the time of nomination, bishops of whom the young Richelieu, as suggested earlier, may be regarded as a typical case. Admittedly the notion of a 'young' bishop is itself not an especially precise one, but the basis of the calculation made here is the Concordat of Bologna's insistence that French bishops be at least twenty-six (rather than thirty, as applied to the rest of Europe) at the time of nomination. In reality, of course, twenty-six was not especially young by seventeenth-century standards, but the reason for setting it in the first place was evidently to allow individuals a number of years after completing their studies in order to find an outlet for their energy and ambition, or at the very least to acquire a minimum of the *gravitas*, if not experience, which was desirable in a bishop. It should not be imagined, however, that the lack of any obvious activity or office was confined to young bishops. Indeed, a number of bishops nominated before the age of twenty-six had either practised law or held some church office, while others, who became bishops in their late twenties or early thirties, had in some cases only just completed their licentiate or doctorate in theology. The thirty-two-year-old François de Clermont-Tonnerre went straight to the see of Noyon in early 1661 only a few months after taking his doctorate.

What the overwhelming majority of these seventy-three bishops had in common, however, was noble ancestry of some distinction, allied in some cases to ministerial office. This will hardly come as a surprise in respect of those sufficiently well placed to obtain a royal nomination while under the official minimum age. Many of these bishops were, especially between the 1590s and 1620s, for all practical purposes designated by their families to succeed reigning bishops from their own families, or to recover bishoprics once held by family members; the age at which they did so depended upon episcopal longevity and political circumstances. Because of their social origins, they had at least one other feature in common: virtually all

Table 7.5 Bishops drawn from religious orders

Old Orders		Mendicant/New Orders	
OSB	12	OFM	7
O Cist	3	OP	5
OSA/OSEA	3	Minims	5
O Carthus	2	Carmelite	1
		Oratory	3
		Récollet	1
		SJ	1
Totals	20		23

of them held benefices *in commendam*, a question to which we shall return later.

The category of bishop which exhibits the highest degree of uniformity, at least at an institutional level, is that of members of the religious orders. This is not to say that their activities could not be diverse, especially in an age when even Capuchin friars were widely used by Europe's rulers to conduct sensitive diplomatic missions. The presence of the regulars among the French episcopate has never attracted much attention, and the impression given by the historiography is that it was patchy and of no great moment. Yet with a total of forty-three bishops – just over 12 per cent of the total – that presence was far from negligible. It is also clear that a small number of other bishops had at one time or another been members of an order, but had, as far as can be ascertained, ceased to be so before becoming bishops.[40] As it stands, the composition and changes over time to the group of regulars who became bishops have general implications for the character of the French episcopate.

The first point of note, as Table 7.5 shows, is the internal balance of this group of bishops. Of the forty-three individuals in question, twenty were members of the old 'monastic' orders in the broad sense, with the remainder drawn from the old mendicant orders and a few more recent creations. The extent to which the balance shifted between the 1590s and the 1650s is also of interest for what it may reveal of the fortunes of the orders in a changing political and religious climate.

To begin with, the number of bishops drawn from the old monastic orders may come as something of a surprise, given that so many of their monasteries had become tenable *in commendam* in the course of the sixteenth century, a

---

40 Victor Bouthillier had been a member of Bérulle's Oratory from 1617 to 1621, while Antoine Revol (bishop of Dol 1603–29) may have been a canon-regular of Saint-Ruf, but he is nowhere mentioned as such in the Roman documents concerning his confirmation to Dol: Dom Taillandier, *Histoire ecclésiastique et civile de Bretagne* (Paris 1750), ii. 'Catalogue historique des évêques et abbés de Bretagne', lxvi.

development which probably had a considerable effect on the relationship between the crown, the episcopate, and the orders themselves. This form of tenure meant that even the most distinguished of France's abbeys – from Saint-Denis to Bec or even Cluny - were given to sons of great noble families who were not professed members of the orders in question. The main consequence was that only a rather limited number of 'regular' abbots or priors of monasteries stood a serious chance of emerging from within these orders as influential ecclesiastical figures, and who might legitimately aspire to episcopal office. Yet it would be mistaken to conclude that those of them who did enter the episcopate were necessarily well-known or distinguished. Only eight of the twenty bishops may be so regarded, three of them because they had held major positions within their orders, the five others because of their intellectual, preaching, or other activities. The remaining twelve bishops owed their elevation to particular circumstances – local, family or political – rather than personal distinction, and to that extent their promotions were not intrinsically different in character to that of non-regular bishops. In the case of bishops like the Benedictines Gaspar du Laurens and Juste de Serres, or the Augustinian canon regular Alain de Solminihac, their entry into the religious life followed rather than preceded the gift of an abbey *in commendam*, a highly unusual occurrence in the French church as far as can be judged. And only in the case of Solminihac did becoming a professed religious give rise to activities (that of a reformer of his order) which manifestly enhanced his claims to episcopal preferment.

The largest subgroup among the bishops drawn from the old orders were the Benedictines (OSB), who have often been seen as having close ties with the French monarchy. No fewer than nine of the twelve Benedictine bishops were nominated under Henri IV, which may suggest a conscious attempt to build upon such traditional ties. The odd man out among them was, paradoxically, the most famous of them, Gilbert Génébrard, who although a professor at the Collège Royal for many years, turned *ligueur* and owed his brief tenure of the archbishopric of Aix to Mayenne and the pope. Most of the remainder can be identified in different ways with Henri IV, usually through family members or through patronage links of other kinds.

The record of the mendicants and the new orders forms a number of interesting contrasts with what we have just seen. Historically, their principal roles involved preaching and teaching, especially among the Franciscans (OFM) and the Dominicans (OP). This, along with fewer endowments, a less elaborate lifestyle than that of the monastic orders, and the frequency of movement from one convent to another, had long ensured that their social origins would be more modest than those of their monastic counterparts. Their route to the episcopate was thus likely to be different from that of the monastic clergy. They were also unusual in that the numbers of foreigners or first-generation Frenchmen among their members entering the episcopate was also much greater than the general average. The fact that the Franciscan 'family' of orders – the 'observant' and 'conventual' Franciscans, the Minims and Récollets – provided no fewer than thirteen of the twenty-three bishops in this category probably reflects the large number of houses and members they had in France rather than any inherent preference for the order as against other mendicants. In any case, among the Franciscans elevated to the episcopate, it was preaching rather than other activities which did most to bring them to the attention of the crown, and at least five of them held posts of either royal almoners or preachers. Only one, Guillaume Hugues, was singled out primarily for his skills as a diplomat and politician, and even then it was only thanks to the insistence of the French ambassador in Rome, who saw Hugues at first hand while he was minister-general of the Franciscan Conventuals (or the Cordeliers as they were known in France); the last two members of the order to be promoted, François Faure and Dominique Ithier, were not merely experienced preachers, but they had openly preached loyalty to the crown during the Fronde. By contrast, the small number of Dominicans in the episcopate may come as a surprise, given their activities as preachers and guardians of orthodoxy, but their influence may have declined now that the post of king's confessor which they had held for much of the later Middle Ages had passed into other hands. Indeed it was only thanks to Mazarin that they reached the modest figure of five bishops in this period, since he was responsible for the elevation of his own brother, Michele, to Aix in 1644, and later of his brother's Dominican *compagnon*, Hyacinthe Serroni, bishop of Orange, to Mende in 1661.[41]

But it is the presence of a former Jesuit and three members of the Oratory which adds an unexpected twist to the mendicant presence in the episcopate. The Jesuit constitutions forbade its members to accept bishoprics and other church offices, and this condition was fully observed in France; had the order's rules been different, its members would surely have been rewarded with episcopal office. Henri IV had offered the see of Aix to the man who was later to become his confessor, Pierre Coton, but he declined the royal gift. In the 1630s, Richelieu firmly opposed the nomination of the well-known preacher, André Valladier, though it is true that he had left the Jesuits many years previously.[42] Quite why or when the idea that Louis-Hercule de Ventadour, who had become a Jesuit in the 1630s, should become a bishop was first mooted remains unclear, but by the end of the Fronde, when sons of the aristocracy were again figuring prominently in the episcopate, the pope and the Jesuit superior-general were bombarded with pressing letters from Louis XIV and the French court for Ventadour's release from the order's ban, but to

---

41 Philippe Gourreau de la Proustière, *Mémoires*, ed Béatrix de Buffevent (Paris 1990), 159.
42 *Lettres, instructions diplomatiques et papiers d'état de Richelieu*, ed D L M Avenel, 8 vols (Paris 1853–76), iv. 711, Richelieu to Cardinal La Vallette, 20 Apr 1635.

no avail.[43] It was only after suggestions were made that he should transfer to a military order that he was finally allowed by the pope to be professed as a monk of Cluny with the intention that he would not still be a Jesuit on his accession to the diocese of Mirepoix in 1655.[44]

In sharp contrast to the Jesuits, Bérulle's Oratory, as a loosely structured congregation of secular priests, imposed no such formal restrictions on its members, and towards the very end of his life Bérulle himself was prepared to accept the archbishopric of Tours when it was rumoured vacant.[45] His successor, Charles de Condren, turned down the see of Reims, preferring to coach and advise a younger generation of clerics, some of whom became bishops.[46] The latter included members of the Oratory itself, Achille de Harlay-Sancy and the Gault brothers; thereafter, perhaps because of fears of their Jansenist associations, Oratorians failed to enter the episcopate in the numbers that might otherwise have been expected. Only one of its members, Guillaume Le Boux, was nominated during the entire Mazarin régime, and he owed his promotion to his talents as a preacher, which he had also deployed in support of the crown in its dispute with Cardinal de Retz in the mid-1650s.[47]

Well before that juncture, it had become clear that the presence of the monastic orders among the episcopate had fallen off sharply. Under Henri IV they had produced eleven bishops, as against seven for the mendicants, new and old. A rough equilibrium obtained from the 1610s to the 1630s, but only one bishop of monastic background, the Cistercian Claude Ruffier, appeared thereafter; even then he did so purely because of a complex succession arrangement put together with crown approval by his uncle, the ageing bishop of Uzès; this occurred in the later 1650s, a decade in which five members of mendicant orders were nominated, the highest number for any decade since the 1590s. The heyday of the old orders had obviously passed, while even if the presence of the mendicants was not necessarily sustained after 1661, their contribution and the variety of the orders from which they were drawn, showed that they managed to remain closer than the monastics to the religious dynamism of the age.

---

43   ASV, N Fr 89, fo 408, Condé to pope, 19 July 1651; *ibid*, fo 109, Louis XIV to Innocent X, 1 Nov 1652; *ibid*, fo 111, same to same, 18 June 1653.
44   BN, MS Fr 20661, fos 426–8, Louis XIV to pope, the Jesuit general, and Cardinal de Vallançay in Rome, 14–17 June 1653. Ventadour was released from his Jesuit vows in April 1654, took the habit at Cluny a month later, and was professed as a monk there in July 1654.
45   Grillon, *Papiers de Richelieu*, iv. 508, Bérulle to Richelieu, 3 Aug 1629. Achille de Harlay-Sancy claimed that Bérulle had ordered him to drop his personal refusal to accept episcopal office in the late 1620s: BAV, Barb lat 7960, fo 4, Harlay to Cardinal Francesco Barberini, 5 Sept 1631.
46   BN, MS Fr 15611, fo 6v, Henri Arnauld to président Barillon, 9 Jan 1641.
47   E Riboulet, *Etude historique sur Msgr Guillaume Le Boux évêque de Périgueux et prédicateur ordinaire de Louis XIV* (Paris 1875), 5.

IV

However, it is no less apparent that when compared to the Spanish kingdoms, the Austrian lands, and perhaps elsewhere in Catholic Europe, the French episcopate contained a much lower proportion of members drawn from the religious orders.[48] It is time therefore to turn our attention to the majority of those bishops who were members of the secular clergy, and whose pre-episcopal careers were not dictated to them by the superiors of religious orders. As on other questions treated in this study, information of pre-episcopal activities improves in quantity, if not necessarily in quality, from the 1610s onwards. As mentioned earlier, one reason for this improvement is that the papal enquiry into newly chosen bishops included a specific question asking if they had held an office which had entailed the cure of souls or the 'government' of a church. As far as can be established, the manner in which the question was formulated did not imply that either of these activities was to be more highly regarded than the others, but the witnesses who were invited to comment on them and on the manner in which the new bishop had discharged his responsibilities, took widely varying views of what they held to be the most appropriate preparation for the episcopate.[49] The often flattering nature of their responses may be treated with some scepticism, but on questions of fact and detail they are often unrivalled.

It would be difficult to think of any period in the history of the church when the cure of souls in the conventional sense of directing a parish was regarded as a prime qualification for episcopal office. The more aristocratic the origins of bishops, the less likely service of a parish would have appealed to them. But in periods when their social background was more heterogeneous, the record might be expected to be different. Comparison across the centuries, however, is hampered by the fact that being *curé* of a parish did not always possess the same meaning. It was not until well into the seventeenth century that it could be assumed that the titular *curé* of a parish was *actually* serving in the parish rather than, as had been common in previous centuries, treating it as just a benefice to be collected like other benefices, and then traded up when better opportunities came along. Nicolas Briroy of Coutances was *curé* of his native parish from the age of sixteen onwards, but it is uncertain whether he ever served in it as an ordained priest before migrating to the cathedral chapter of Coutances. Likewise, the first Bertier bishop of Rieux,

---

48 In the Spanish kingdoms, the proportion of regulars in the episcopate in the seventeenth century varied from one-quarter to one-third, as emerges from the data in Maximiliano Barrio Gozalo's five-part study, 'Perfil socio-económico de una élite de poder, 1600–1840', *Anthologica Annua*, 28–34 (1981–7).

49 The Latin text of Urban VIII's questionnaire, article 11, refers to the 'regimen alterius ecclesiae', and the word *ecclesia* has sometimes been translated as meaning diocese (e.g. Jadin, 24), but Blet, citing a late seventeenth-century manual of curial practice, merely says 'l'administration de quelque Eglise' ('Le Concordat de Bologne et la réforme tridentine', *Gregorianum*, 45 (1964), 277).

Jean, had held several parishes in or near Toulouse, but what we know of his career makes it likely he regarded them as no more than benefices.

Nevertheless, Briroy and Bertier figure among the twenty-two bishops in our period known to have been *curés* of a parish. They were assuredly not the only ones who did not serve in them, and there were possibly five more titular *curés* who fit alongside them. But as the twenty-two bishops in question are reasonably evenly distributed across the years under study here, the likelihood is that a rising proportion of them actually *did* serve in one or more parish for a time. Two of them have no other known activity to their credit, but one may judge how much they had in common by their episcopal fortunes. François Hyver was Richelieu's predecessor as bishop of Luçon, and it was as the docile *curé* of the Richelieu family parish that he was chosen to act as their caretaker bishop. Pierre Donnaud was a *curé* in his native diocese of Mirepoix in Languedoc, but he did have the advantage of having his uncle as bishop before him. In contrast, six of these bishops had held Parisian parishes which, being reserved for graduates of the Paris theology faculty, were not without prestige, and all six held royal almonerships or other positions in addition to their parishes. It is no accident that four out of the seven bishops who, as far as can be established, still held a parish at the time of nomination should have been drawn from the Parisian élite of the parish clergy.

One striking feature of the seventeenth-century French church should be briefly noted in this context, namely the development of informal kinds of 'cure of souls' capable of attracting ecclesiastics who were not otherwise interested in becoming parish priests or in the 'government of a church'. They began to appear most strongly from the 1630s onwards, and included the priestly communities of Saint-Lazare and Saint-Sulpice, as well as the older one at Saint-Nicolas-du-Chardonnet all of which, before giving rise to seminaries for the reform of the clergy, acted as centres for a partly parish-based apostolate; priests affiliated to them also participated in the preaching missions organised by Vincent de Paul and Jean-Jacques Olier in dioceses as diverse as Chartres and Clermont. At least twelve bishops nominated in the 1640s and 1650s obtained their initiation into preaching and pastoral administration through these communities, which involved preaching, confessing and charitable work in a number of dioceses. Some of these men – Pavillon, Caulet, Vialart, Perrochel and Salignac – went on to become respected figures in the episcopate during Louis XIV's personal rule. As these communities expanded and became more institutionalised, so their role in the careers of future bishops shifted in emphasis, with activities of the kind just mentioned taking second place to what might be termed pre-sacerdotal formation. The Cardinal de Retz was not the only future bishop to have frequented the *conférences de mardi* organised by de Paul at Saint-Lazare for the instruction of the clergy, attendance at which Retz's uncle had made obligatory for the future priests of his diocese; as early as 1637, Vincent de Paul could already claim that four recently nominated bishops had attended Saint-

Lazare.⁵⁰ It was Saint-Sulpice which would in due course emerge as not just the most famous of French seminaries, but also as a seminary which future bishops were well advised to attend if they seriously wished to be considered for the episcopate. Such a development was still somewhat remote in the age of Richelieu and Mazarin.

V

In discussing these innovations and the bishops associated with them, we have moved into a clerical world which, for all its pastoral activism, was increasingly remote from that of France's parishes and those who held them. By contrast, one of the most obvious potential reservoirs of future bishops were the chapters, cathedral and collegiate, which dotted the ecclesiastical landscape of France. In 'la France des six cents chapitres', they were, in the words of their most recent historian the 'classe intermédiaire du premier ordre de l'Etat'.⁵¹ The cathedral chapters might progressively have lost the power to elect bishops freely well before the Concordat of Bologna, but that did little to reduce the attractiveness of a canonicate to ecclesiastics whose ambitions were for something more than a parish or some minor benefice. The *douceur de vivre* associated with this specimen of the corporate clergy was legendary, the duties attached to the tenure of a canonicate anything but onerous. It would be surprising if these attractions did not tempt at least some future bishops, not least because holding such a position might also enable an individual to play a role, formally or informally, in the affairs of the dioceses to which the chapters belonged.⁵² Moreover, if canons were sufficiently influential to secure election to meetings of provincial or local estates, or to a provincial or even general assembly of the clergy, then they might be able to break through into a wider world of ecclesiastical patronage which could eventually bring a bishopric as its reward. In practice, this kind of opportunity seems to have been limited increasingly to canons who were dignitaries of the chapter, or who held offices such as those of vicar-general or *official* in the service of a reigning bishop. But as well as acting as rungs on a patronage ladder which could lead to the episcopate itself, these offices also provided a minimum of experience of diocesan affairs and administration generally, since the chapters still retained a rightful role in the running of a diocese. A canon who became a vicar-general, *official*, *promoteur* or the like, was in effect one of the right-hand

50 Vincent de Paul, *Correspondance, Entretiens, Documents*, ed Pierre Coste, 14 vols (Paris 1922–5), i. 373–4, letter to Jean de Fonteneil, 8 Jan 1637.
51 Philippe Loupès, *Chapitres et chanoines de Guyenne aux xvii⁵ et xviii⁵ siècles* (Paris 1985), 41ff. There is a useful map locating, though not identifying, the chapters at pp 48–9.
52 Few studies of cathedral and other chapters have dealt in any detail with the early modern period, with most concentrating on the medieval centuries. A valuable recent exception is Loupès, *Chapitres et chanoines de Guyenne*, which does not confine its comments to south-western France.

men of the bishop who chose him; depending on the extent to which the bishop was absent or was not inclined to take an active role in diocesan government, such officials could find themselves shouldering a large part of the diocesan administrative burden; it was these same canons who were often elected vicars general by the chapter to govern the diocese during episcopal vacancies. On the other hand, if canons were content to remain as dignitaries of their chapter – provost, dean, archdeacon, cantor, *théologal* or sacristan, to name but the most common – that experience would not be negligible should they become bishops, especially in enabling them to deal with the perennial tension in relations between bishops and their cathedral chapters. Finally, even a simple canon who did little more than reside in his cathedral town could observe at close hand the challenges of governing a diocese, and would in any case play a part in managing the affairs, especially financial, of often wealthy and powerful chapters.[53] Proud of their traditions and jealous of their autonomy, the cathedral chapters regarded themselves as the bishops' natural auxiliaries and councillors, rather as the parlements did with respect to the crown.

Forming the aristocracy of the clergy, the chapters were a world replete with hierarchy and distinctions. In approaching the subject of bishops whose careers had taken them along this particular path, it is best to begin with the widest common denominator, the members of cathedral chapters, and then gradually focus on those of them who had progressed beyond a simple canon's stall to higher office and responsibility.

It appears that at least 106 future bishops were at one time or another – though not necessarily at the moment of their nomination – canons of a cathedral chapter. This represents just 30 per cent of the episcopate, and while it was a proportion which did not oscillate wildly during the period as a whole, one development may be noted, since it is closely related to others which arise elsewhere in this study. The lowest proportion of all is to be found for Henri IV's reign, when just under 26 per cent of bishops were cathedral canons; that proportion rose to nearly one-third under Louis XIII, before falling back again during the Mazarin ministry to a proportion slightly higher (by one point) than for Henri IV's reign. The bulge recorded for Louis XIII's reign actually came largely in the 1610s, and to a lesser degree in the 1620s, when young and well connected ecclesiastics were appointed bishops, especially coadjutors, in considerable numbers.

In addition to these cathedral canons, we should note the presence among the episcopate of a much smaller group, that of former canons of collegiate churches. They number only fourteen in all, and only one of them appears not to have held an office or dignity within his chapter. For the most part, these

---

53 See Loupès, *Chapitres et chanoines de Guyenne*, part ii. For a spirited evocation of the assiduity of the chapters in managing their affairs, see also Emmanuel Le Roy Ladurie, *Les Paysans du Languedoc*, 2 vols (Paris 1966), which is based to a large extent on the archives of chapters like Béziers and Montpellier.

chapters were less attractive or distinguished than those of the cathedrals, but two well known exceptions to the rule should be mentioned here — Saint-Martin of Tours and the Sainte Chapelle of Paris. It would be misleading to regard them as more aristocratic than other chapters, but entry was reserved to those with good background and, perhaps more importantly, good connections. Between them they provided six of the fourteen bishops holding canonicates in non-cathedral chapters, and while that hardly qualifies them as seminaries for bishops, it reveals the possibilities open to the best connected of their members.

Pluralism was not unknown in cathedral, and doubtless other, chapters, but it was not as rife as might be imagined, and the French chapters seem to have been significantly different from those of the highly aristocratic *Reichskirche* in this regard. Only eleven of the bishops are recorded as having held two cathedral canonicates, but because the precise chronology of their careers remains obscure, it is not clear whether more than four or five well placed – or fortunate – individuals held these canonicates concurrently. At any rate, a bishop like Charles de Balsac of Noyon, who was an archdeacon of Tours and dean of Rouen before his family's close connections to Henri IV gained him the see of Noyon in the late 1590s, was rather an exception. More common was the pattern represented by Nicolas Bourgoing of Coutances or Fulcran Barrez of Agde, men whose successive activities took them from one diocese to another, but without enabling them to hold more than one canonicate at a time. The last bishop of this type was Bernard Despruets, canon of Saintes and later *théologal* of his native Lescar, who was nominated to Saint-Papoul in 1636. Finally, only five instances have been found of bishops holding canonicates in a cathedral and in another collegiate church, too few for the question of simultaneous or successive tenure to be of much moment.

What *is* of some moment, however, is the fact that nearly two out of every three (70 out of 106) of the cathedral canons who became bishops were officers or dignitaries of their chapter. The numerical strength of individual French chapters could vary enormously, thereby making access to their principal positions more or less easy, with a canon's social origins and connections as well as the identity of the patron in whose gift they were, also playing a prominent part in the process of internal advancement. In the larger chapters, accession to such a dignity was a first critical step beyond the ranks of the ordinary canons, but it should not be thought that within these highly introverted clerical corporations, the hierarchy of dignities was one of merit; young and well connected individuals, often mere tonsured clerics still at college or university, were just as likely to begin their careers as archdeacons or cantors of a cathedral as among the ranks of the ordinary canons. The factors which enabled this to happen were also those which would later bring the same individuals into the wider world of church politics and patronage.

As for the remaining thirty-six 'mere' canons who never occupied the stalls reserved for the chapter's office-holders, it could hardly be argued that they were somehow plucked from utter anonymity on being appointed bishops. All but ten of them were either canons in their native diocese, related to the reigning bishop, or became bishop of the diocese in due course; in a number of cases, they combined all three. It should not be imagined that the ten odd-men-out themselves lacked for compensating advantages of one kind or another, and some of these advantages – such as being a minister like Guillaume du Vair or brother of a royal favourite like Henri de Baradat – were quite unmatched. For those without such advantages, a measure of geographical mobility was common, as exemplified in the career of a man like Jean de Salette. He faithfully served his fellow convert from Protestantism, Cardinal du Perron, in his dioceses of Evreux and Sens, where he was successively a canon and vicar-general, and the cardinal's patronage was probably crucial in enabling him to return at last as bishop to his native see of Lescar in 1609.

This kind of geographical mobility raises other questions about the role of the chapters, cathedral or collegiate, as 'providers' of bishops. Did membership of a chapter alone constitute realistic grounds for aspiring to episcopal office, or were other advantages needed? How far was a peripatetic career like that of Salette, with his dependence on a powerful church patron, typical of the canons of the time who later became bishops? As hinted in the previous paragraph, the most useful way of approaching the problem is to ask three related questions: how many were canons of their native dioceses, how many were related to the reigning bishop, and how many went on to govern the diocese in question? In response to the first of these questions, it appears that fifty-five, or slightly more than half of the 106 bishops (51.8 per cent), were canons of cathedral chapters in their native dioceses. A cursory chronological survey makes it clear that there were no major shifts in this crude one-in-two ratio between the age of Henri IV and the ministry of Mazarin. Seventeen of the fifty-five canons also went on to become bishops of their native dioceses, with nine of them succeeding members of their own family as bishops. Not all canons were equal, of course, and all but two of the seventeen were office-holders within their chapters; as for the two exceptions, they merely happened to be nephews of the reigning bishops!

Of the fifty-one canons who were *not* natives of the dioceses in whose cathedral they served, fourteen had a connection which, at the very least, came a close second – namely that the reigning bishop there was a member of their own family. This applies primarily to bishops appointed before about 1630, with only a few cases of the connection evident thereafter. Nothing resembling a single pattern can be found for the remaining thirty-seven canons, but in many cases the link between an outsider and a canon's stall in a particular cathedral was a bishop, as we saw in the case of du Perron and Salette. Sébastien Bouthillier had no links whatever with the chapter of Luçon until his boyhood friend and patron, Richelieu, used his right to appoint cathedral canons there in Bouthillier's favour. Where bishops enjoyed extensive presentation rights to canonicates in their cathedrals, the opportunities for outsider clerics were always likely to be greater, especially if the bishops themselves were outsiders. Moreover, what we saw of family ties or activities in a previous chapter might also explain why a future bishop belonged to a particular chapter. Jean de Barrault's family seat was in the Bordeaux diocese, but his father's office of *sénéchal* of neighbouring Bazas doubtless facilitated his son's entry into the chapter there before going on to become its bishop in 1611. From a tender age, Camille de Neufville was a canon-count of the socially exclusive chapter of Lyon, where his Paris-born father had recently become governor; by the time he became archbishop forty years later, Neufville himself had become governor of the city and neighbouring provinces. Successive Villars archbishops of Vienne were Lyonnais by birth, but the two dioceses were contiguous, so it was only to be expected that there would be canons and dignitaries from the Villars family in the Vienne chapter once the first Villars archbishop had been installed there under Henri III. Claude Gelas was a Lyonnais who moved further afield in search of preferment, becoming bishop of Agen in 1609: but here, too, the connection was his Villars uncle, Nicolas, who was bishop of Agen before him, and who enabled him to enter the chapter there before securing his episcopal succession.

Claude Gelas was not merely a canon and archdeacon of Agen before succeeding as bishop there, he was also vicar-general to his uncle. This in turn brings into focus a different subgroup, one that is important for other reasons – namely those canons who had stepped beyond even the highest positions in their chapters and who formally served in the administration of a diocese as a vicar-general, *official* or some other senior post. It is, of course, true that neither cathedral dignitaries nor episcopal officials had necessarily to be canons of the diocese's cathedral, but as far as can be established, this was generally the case for the bishops under discussion here.[54] Among those who held administrative posts under a reigning bishop, only four appear not to have been cathedral canons, and three of them were from religious orders which precluded such membership;[55] in two further cases, it has been impossible to discover if they were cathedral canons or not.[56] But even if they had been, that would not seriously alter the fact that only thirty-one future bishops had acted as vicar-general, *official* or *promoteur* to a reigning bishop – twenty-eight of them as vicars-general, three as an *official*, while five had held both posts.

By the eighteenth century future bishops could expect to serve a term of variable length in diocesan administration, usually as a vicar-general, before

---

54 Loupès, *Chapitres et chanoines de Guyenne* 72–3.
55 These were: Vervins, a Dominican, Gault, an Oratorian, and Ruffier, a Cistercian. The fourth was Etienne Puget, who was suffragan bishop of Metz for many years before his nomination to Marseille in 1643.
56 They were Péréfixe of Rodez and Grasse de Cabris of Grasse.

standing a realistic chance of episcopal promotion, and this pattern may have begun to take root under Louis XIV. For the period under study here, clear signs of such a development are extremely hard to find; if anything, the record is one which seems to point in the opposite direction! Thirteen, or not far short of half of the vicars general in question, became bishops under Henri IV, often in circumstances in which administrative experience was anything but the principal consideration. Only one vicar-general, Le Prestre of Quimper, and one *official*, Grasse de Cabris of Grasse, became bishops during the first fourteen years of Louis XIII's reign, a period which, as we saw, witnessed an influx of men who held canonicates and offices in cathedral chapters – a discrepancy which was hardly accidental. From the mid-1620s onwards, vicars general appeared again at desultory intervals among the newly appointed bishops, with the late 1630s and early 1640s witnessing something like a comeback on their part. But this was not sustained, and for the eighteen years of Mazarin's ministry, there were long periods during which no vicar-general or *official* figured among those joining the episcopate. With just six former vicars-general among the eighty-nine bishops seated after May 1643, there is little evidence of a trend taking shape that would become the normal pattern for future bishops in subsequent generations. Moreover, an analysis of the thirty-one individuals in question shows that they acceded to the offices of vicar-general or *official* in ways that differed hardly at all from the way in which canons entered cathedral chapters; they served primarily in their native dioceses and frequently because the ruling bishops were from their own families.

Yet with a total of 126 future bishops who had been canons of cathedral or other chapters, or episcopal officials, their contribution to the episcopate was anything but negligible, standing as it did at just over 35 per cent of its total strength for the period. But the point made for the chapters of Guyenne, namely that a canonicate was something of a 'narrow gate' when it came to obtaining the mitre is one that can be applied to France as a whole.[57] In the French church, where the Spanish practice of submitting the names of deserving ecclesiastics from vacant dioceses for selection as the new bishop never took root, despite occasional suggestions to that effect, local eminence as a cathedral canon, dignitary or vicar-general was not a sure passport to episcopal office.[58] It is worth noting that only thirty-nine of the 106 cathedral canons went on to become bishops of the diocese where they had previously been canons. Moreover, an unknown number of nephews of reigning bishops, endowed with all the prebends and administrative offices they could wish for, were overlooked when vacancies arose, however hard they might try either to create or to prolong a quasi-dynastic episcopal presence; reigning bishops regularly failed in their efforts to obtain their nephews as coadjutors, the

---

57 Loupès, *Chapitres et chanoines*, 260.
58 The clear majority of Spanish bishops was drawn from the ranks of the cathedral chapters. See the figures in Barrio Gozalo, 'Perfil de una élite de poder' (n 49, above).

surest method of keeping a diocese in family hands. Holding capitular prebends or diocesan office was a valuable, but not a sufficient, stepping-stone to the episcopate, and those who owed them to their families or their patrons usually attempted to transcend their limitations by seeking office outside of the dioceses to which they found themselves attached.

VI

Among the wider horizons of the clerical 'aristocracy', the royal court enjoyed pride of place. With the formal right to nominate bishops belonging to the king, it is no surprise that clerics in search of preferment, episcopal or otherwise, should turn their attention to the court. The most obvious way in which to do this was to acquire an office in one of the various households which formed the nucleus of the French court. The size and variety of the royal ecclesiastical establishments varied over time, though like the court generally, depressingly little is known about their organization or development.[59] Insofar as we can judge, Henri IV left the reconstitution of his own ecclesiastical household to successive grand almoners, Renaud de Beaune and Cardinal du Perron, but no notable change in its basic structures appears to have been made by them. Its principal dignitaries (grand almoner, first almoner, and master of the royal chapel) were invariably bishops, with a cardinal as grand almoner of France from du Perron onwards; a hierarchy like this not merely facilitated contacts between aspiring clergy and those bishops who were sufficiently favoured to hold major offices in the king's chapel, but also the constitution of specifically ecclesiastical clientage groups at court. There were considerable differences between the actual and the theoretical size of the royal ecclesiastical household, differences which reflect those of the court generally. A small core of serving almoners (*aumôniers ordinaires*) were in regular attendance for a given period of service (*par quartier*). There were just eight of them at any time for most of Henri IV's reign, rising very slowly to fifteen by the end of Louis XIII's reign;[60] in 1638, for example, only eight out of thirteen appear to have been paid for actual service.[61] The list of official court preachers was shorter still, oscillating between four in 1604 and fourteen in 1643.[62] By contrast, the number of unpaid almoners, who included several bishops, was consistently far higher, rising, for example, from

---

59 Some general observations about the size and organisation of the court are to be found in Jean-François Solnon, *La Cour de France* (Paris 1987), esp ch 2. See also Jacqueline Boucher, 'L'Evolution de la maison du roi: Des derniers Valois aux premiers Bourbons', *XVII Siècle*, no 136 (1982), 359–79.
60 BN, MS Fr 7854, fos 183–207, 'Estat des officiers de la maison de Henri IV 1590–1610', at fos 183–7v; Eugène Griselle, ed, *Etat de la maison de Louis XIII*, 1.
61 Griselle, *Etat de la maison de Louis XIII*, 138
62 BN, MS Fr 7854, fo 187r; Griselle, *Etat de la maison de Louis XIII*, 8.

thirty-one in the early 1590s to 197 by 1599; it stood at 240 by the beginning of Louis XIII's reign, falling back to 188 by 1621.

Moreover, the king's own household was only one of several at court, even if it was the largest and most attractive. Both Marie de' Medici and Anne of Austria, but especially the former, maintained chapels and a clerical household of a similar kind to their royal husbands, while Gaston d'Orléans and Philippe d'Orléans, brother of Louis XIV, did likewise, albeit on a much reduced scale. These households represented so many opportunities for leading members of the royal family, and their favourites, to employ and promote ecclesiastics in search of a foothold at court.

In the event, a total of eighty future bishops, or between one-fifth and one-quarter of the episcopate, held one of these court offices between 1589 and 1661, with the almoners and masters of the king's own chapel claiming the lion's share with sixty-nine of the total number. This may appear to be a rather small contribution, but the limited size of the ecclesiastical households needs to be kept in mind. As far as the king's own household was concerned, it was the almoners, masters of the chapel, and preachers who alone stood a serious chance of obtaining episcopal office. If the surviving evidence can be trusted, it seems that the unpaid, honorary almoners of Henri IV's reign were more successful than the serving almoners when it came to obtaining episcopal office. Under his son, however, that pattern seems to have been gradually reversed until the unpaid almoners (who in any case included numerous reigning bishops), not to mention the chaplains, henceforth stood no real chance of promotion. Only four of the successful almoners were members of religious orders, and all four were made bishops under Henri IV. Thereafter, almoners who became bishops were drawn entirely from the secular clergy, and the regulars tended to be restricted to positions as court preachers.

Approximately three out of every four of the court almoners and preachers who became bishops served Henri IV and his royal successors, while the remainder served in a variety of other royal households. Among the latter, the largest contingent served Marie de' Medici during the thirty years between her arrival in France and her exile in 1631. With most of them being appointed during the late 1620s, it seems likely that had it not been for her disgrace in 1630–1, her household would have continued to act as a conduit towards the episcopate. It is worth noting that several members of her household nominated in the late 1620s were preachers rather than almoners, itself a sign that the *dévots* around her were concerned to promote ecclesiastics with at least one obvious episcopal talent. Of course, several of these bishops were less clients of the queen mother than of Richelieu, Bérulle or others in Marie's entourage.

In contrast, during the entire period of Louis XIII's reign, neither Gaston d'Orléans nor Anne of Austria could expect to promote a comparable number of their ecclesiastical clients to episcopal office; their households were kept under constant surveillance, and many of their members were clients of Richelieu and other ministers rather than of Gaston or Anne. The Bouthillier brothers, Sébastien and Victor, held almonerships in the households of Anne of Austria and Gaston, but their elevation to the episcopate, in 1621 and 1626 respectively, owed nothing to the patronage of either one of them. It was only after Louis XIII's death that Gaston, by then *lieutenant général du royaume* during Louis XIV's minority, could obtain some success, but even then it was limited to two members of his household, Mathieu Bourlon and Louis Barbier de la Rivière, and it only occurred during or after the Fronde. Considering the difficulties she experienced with both Louis XIII and Richelieu in the 1630s, it is surprising to see three members of Anne of Austria's household – Etienne de Villazel, Charles-François de Raconis, and Henri de Maupas – becoming bishops in 1631, 1636 and 1640 respectively. But each of these men had sufficiently wide connections and experience not to be wholly dependent on Anne's fortunes, even if Maupas's nomination seems to have come as a surprise to at least one observer.[63] As regent after May 1643, Anne's fortunes could hardly have been different, but her ecclesiastical household remained small – in stark contrast to that of Marie de' Medici as queen mother – and only one of its members, Jacques de Montrouge, entered the episcopate thereafter. It was to the household of the young Louis XIV that clerics in search of bishoprics tended to gravitate, which of course enabled Mazarin, *surintendant* of the king's household as well as principal minister, to play a considerable role as a patron to them.

The ultimate ambitions of the royal almoners were no secret to contemporaries. When a former almoner (who had also grown up with Louis XIII), Bishop Litolfi of Bazas, opposed ministerial financial demands in the 1641 Assembly of Clergy, the king was particularly irate, which led the ever observant Henri Arnauld to comment that 'cella ne servira pas aux Aumosniers qui prétendent à l'épiscopat'.[64] Bishops who proved obstructive in 1641, or at other times, were hardly unheard of, but in this case, Louis XIII probably felt all the angrier because of Litolfi's past personal service to him. Indeed, it was the serving almoners who could legitimately claim that they had obtained episcopal office on the basis of merit, since for the most part their social status was such (most were from recently ennobled or commoner families) as to preclude rapid advancement. For their part, Louis XIII, Marie de' Medici and Anne of Austria went to considerable lengths to publicise their personal patronage of these men when raising them to the episcopate.[65] Of Louis XIII's eight serving almoners in 1638, three became bishops under his successor. Louis XIII himself had apparently promised to make one of them, Eustache le Clerc de Lesseville, a bishop, but died before he could keep his

---

63 BN, MS Fr 15611, fo 250v, Henri Arnauld to president Barillon, 7 Sept 1641.
64 *Ibid*, fo 62, letter to president Barillon, 20 Mar 1641.
65 Several letters to this effect written to Urban VIII and the Barberini cardinals can be found scattered througout BAV, Barb lat 7938–46.

word.⁶⁶ Anne of Austria and her entourage attended the consecration of another, Jacques de Bernage, dean of the royal almoners, as bishop of Grasse in January 1654.⁶⁷

By comparison with the almoners, the royal preachers appear as the poor relations when it comes to episcopal patronage. The fact that only fifteen official court preachers – some of them also royal almoners – were rewarded with the mitre would seem to suggest as much, and that the subject therefore calls for little further comment. Yet this would be a clear case of statistics telling only part of the story, since here was an activity which could never fully be accounted for by the numbers of those honoured with a court office. A brief analysis will help to show how significant preaching was in shaping the character of the French episcopate. The Catholic Reformation, taking its cue from the Council of Trent, strove hard to persuade Europe's bishops that preaching was their principal duty, and in the wake of Trent leading figures in Italy like Borromeo and Paleotti, attempted to implement this programme, while admitting their personal difficulties in preaching, given their utter lack of preparation for the task.⁶⁸ Although the subject has not been much discussed in French historiography, there is little evidence of comparable apprehension or reluctance to preach on the part of France's bishops. Perhaps the experiences of the wars of religion, especially the crisis of the Catholic League, and later the controversies with Protestant pastors, compelled the middling and upper ranks of the French clergy to engage in oratorical activities, sacred and profane, to a far greater degree than their Spanish or Italian counterparts ever needed to do. From the opening of the seventeenth century onwards, there was also the example of mentor-figures like François de Sales, Cardinal du Perron and other episcopal orators, such that young bishops like Richelieu or Jean-Pierre Camus had no hesitation about preaching, at court or elsewhere, whatever the actual quality of their preaching.⁶⁹ A younger generation of bishops like Camus, Godeau and Lingendes, carried on that tradition, paving the way for great preaching

---

66 ASV, PC 57, fo 104, evidence of Henri de Maupas, bishop of Le Puy, on behalf of Lesseville, 1658. Evidently, the king's death dashed Lesseville's hopes, and he subsequently left royal service for an office in the parlement of Paris. He was only nominated to Coutances in 1658, when the reigning bishop, Claude Auvry, one of Mazarin's confidants, was anxious to resign it on favourable financial terms.
67 BN, MS lat 17025 (vol ii), fo 121.
68 For a brief introduction, with bibliography, see John W O'Malley, 'Saint Charles Borromeo and the *Praecipuum Episcoporum Munus*: His Place in the History of Preaching', in John M Headley and John M Tomaro, eds, *San Carlo Borromeo. Catholic Reform and Ecclesiastical Politics in the Second Half of the Sixteenth Century* (Washington DC 1988), 139–57. For the wider question of the revival of eloquence and its rules, see Marc Fumaroli, *L'Age de l'éloquence. Rhétorique et 'res litteraria' de la Renaissance au seuil de l'époque classique* (Geneva 1980).
69 For example, de Sales's letter of 1604 to André Frémiot, recently installed as archbishop of Bourges, has often been regarded as virtually a treatise on how to preach: *Oeuvres complètes de Saint François de Sales* (Annecy ed), 27 vols (Annecy 1892–1964), xii. 301. He had written in a similar vein in the previous year to Antoine Revol of Dol, *ibid*, 89.

bishops like Bossuet and Massillon. An impressive proportion of the surviving funeral sermons for both Henri IV and Louis XIII were delivered by bishops or by men who would become bishops in subsequent years.[70] Bishops also preached regularly at masses held during the assemblies of clergy and other such gatherings. In early 1646, for example, four bishops, past and present, preached the traditional Lenten sermons in distinguished Parisian churches.[71] Striking confirmation of this characteristic of the French episcopate is to be found in, of all places, the instructions to the new papal nuncio in 1624:

> as for religion, many ecclesiastics, *and bishops in particular*, flourish in the kingdom of France, to whom God has given a superior talent as preachers, and He has willed that they deploy it to the greatest effect near to areas infected with heresy by giving them the priestly and apostolic charge of these churches.[72]

Few were better placed than Urban VIII (himself a former nuncio to France) and his officials to express a comparative judgement of this kind on the French episcopate, even if the exaggerations of the text are patent enough. The attraction of sermons given by well-known preachers grew further in the following decades, making the most successful preachers and their career prospects a subject of widespread speculation. Richelieu himself is reported as commenting on an Advent sermon in late 1639 which had attacked the incompetence of the archbishop of Paris, saying that the preacher 'spoke provocatively either in order to obtain a bishopric or to be put in the Bastille, but that he would obtain neither of them'.[73]

As already noted, the number of preachers officially attached to royal households who became bishops in our period was a rather modest fifteen. No fewer than six of them were members of religious orders, reflecting an older tradition which saw preaching as an activity more fitting for the regular than for the secular clergy.[74] Of course, the number of official court preachers was always smaller than that of almoners, serving and unpaid, so that the success

---

70 See Jacques Hennequin, *Henri IV dans ses oraisons funèbres, ou la naissance d'une légende* (Paris 1977).
71 ASV, N Fr 93, fo 73, *avvisi* of 23 Feb 1646. The bishops were Raconis of Lavaur, Grillié of Uzès, Camus the former bishop of Belley, and the coadjutor of Montauban, Pierre de Bertier.
72 *Recueil des instructions générales aux nonces ordinaires de France de 1624 à 1634*, ed Auguste Leman (Lille 1920), 24, instructions for Bernadino Spada, nuncio to France 1624–7. The italics are mine.
73 BN, MS Fr 15610, p 356, Henri Arnauld to president Barillon, 18 Dec 1639: '(il) parloit hardiment pour avoir un Evesché ou pour estre mis dans la Bastille, mais qu'il n'auroit ny l'un ny l'autre'. The preacher, named Hersant, may have had more reason to fear the Bastille than hope for a bishopric, but Richelieu's indulgence towards him can readily be understood, since he delivered a rebuke to Archbishop Gondi only a few weeks later: *ibid*, 389, Arnauld to Barillon, 8 Jan 1640.
74 See Larissa J Taylor, *Soldiers of Christ. Preaching in Late Medieval and Reformation France* (Oxford 1992).

rate of preachers in becoming bishops may not actually be significantly lower. This is all the more noteworthy since arguably the major obstacle faced by the court preachers in becoming bishops was their often undistinguished social origins, and indeed only about three of the fifteen could lay claim to any kind of noble status. This latter detail may also help to place their success in some wider perspective. Their oratorical ability may have helped obtain dioceses for them, but it was not quite enough to obtain major sees. Offsetting this to some extent was the fact that five of them benefited from also being royal almoners, an unusual combination which became far less common after Henri IV's reign, but which at the turn of the century was a sign of royal favour. The last of the almoner-cum-preacher bishops to be nominated was Jean de Lingendes, whose sermons brought him to the attention of Richelieu who helped elevate him to the episcopate. Indeed, during the 1630s the cardinal was instrumental in reviving, albeit briefly, a tradition that seemed to have been dying out since the episcopal appointment of the last such preacher, Claude de Rueil, in 1621. No fewer than six court preachers, of whom Lingendes was the last, were nominated bishops between 1630 and 1639.[75] He might not have had any successors during the Mazarin ministry had it not been for the promotion of the Franciscans Faure and Ithier towards the end of the Fronde, a promotion which owed as much to their political services as to their sermons.[76]

The term 'apostolic charge' used by the papacy in its instructions to the nuncio in 1624 seems to indicate Rome believed that the French crown consciously gave dioceses with a strong Protestant presence to men who would preach there rather than simply administer them. As a generalisation, this does not withstand scrutiny, since it makes untenable assumptions about the crown's freedom of action – though it would be worth discovering how far bishops not known as preachers before their promotion actually felt the need to develop such skills after taking over such dioceses. As already observed, noted preachers were just as likely to receive small, out-of-the way, or modestly endowed dioceses, and at least one of them protested bitterly at the meagre reward for his services, represented by an upland diocese in Provence.[77] Yet there are indications that at least some dioceses were actually treated as special cases requiring particular types of bishop. Two (out of three) of Henri IV's nominations to Montpellier were of experienced and highly respected preachers – the Benedictine Jean Garnier and Pierre Fenouillet, the disciple of François de Sales. When Fenouillet's succession was eventually settled in the mid-1650s, it was reported that Montpellier was given to François Bosquet, bishop of Lodève, not so much for his preaching

---

75 Lingendes was one of several bishops whose provisions were delayed by disputes between France and the papacy, and he was not confirmed until 1642.
76 AAE, France 891, fo 183, Mazarin to Ithier, 31 Aug 1653.
77 AAE, France 886, fo 311, Charles Paulin, S J, to Mazarin, 24 Dec 1652, referring to François Faure, briefly bishop of Glandèves.

skills, but for his great learning which it was hoped would counter-balance the activities of the Protestant academy there.[78] After the Languedoc revolt of 1632, two of the province's most Protestant-dominated dioceses, Uzès and Nîmes, were given to Nicolas Grillié, bishop of Bazas, and Anthime-Denis Cohon, both former court preachers. Jean Bertaut, the poet and royal almoner, was not known as a preacher before his nomination in 1606 to the diocese of Séez which boasted a large Protestant population, and that may have soon led Henri IV to promise the diocese to the experienced Portuguese preacher, Jacopo Suarez, in the event, no doubt, of Bertaut's death or resignation. The king's promise to Suarez was duly honoured by Marie de' Medici in 1611, but by then he was so old and infirm that almost immediately a much younger man, Jacques Camus de Pontcarré, was nominated as his coadjutor – a reminder that preaching alone could not solve all problems caused by an assertive Protestant minority.[79]

It would be absurd to suggest that the titular court preachers were victims of their own success, since their numbers were far too limited for that. But there is evidence to suggest that by the middle decades of the century those with their eye on episcopal office, royal almoners included, had come to realise that the ability to preach successfully, especially in Parisian churches, was an accomplishment which, if not absolutely indispensable, was at least a serious advantage in the competition for the mitre. Increasingly, witnesses testifying on behalf of incoming bishops singled out their preaching, especially in response to questions about their experience, or lack of it, regarding the cure of souls; no doubt that evidence was also inflated, but there seems little reason to deny its factual basis, and the trend which it seems to point to. Moreover, once this pattern began to set, it tended to become self-reinforcing. Quite how aspiring bishops learned to preach remains something of a mystery. While homiletics was never part of the curriculum of the theology faculties, it may be that with an increasing number of theology graduates among the episcopate, the often elaborate public disputations and defences of theses helped to develop skills which could be applied to the art of preaching. Here, too, the models they looked to may not necessarily have been bishops. It is rarely pointed out that influential professors like André du Val and Abra de Raconis (*prédicateur ordinaire* to Anne of Austria before becoming bishop of Lavaur in 1636), were themselves highly active preachers.[80] It is thus perhaps ironic that, despite the self-help methods they may have had to employ, the bishops of seventeenth-century France may be thought of as better preachers than theologians.

78 ASV, N Fr 109, fo 288, *avvisi* of 16 July 1655.
79 BAV, Barb lat 7961, fo 92, Suarez to Cardinal Maffeo Barberini, 25 Oct 1611; *ibid*, fo 93, same to same, 3 May 1613; ASV, PC 13, fo 5, royal letter of nomination for Camus specifically mentioning Suarez's infirmities, 6 June 1612.
80 For André du Val's extensive preaching activities, see de Sales, *Oeuvres*, xii, 188, n 1.

If preachers, who were hardly typical representatives of either the clerical courtier or the episcopal hopeful, were capable of attracting royal patronage, it is only to be expected that men with other qualities would prove just as successful – even if they were not formally attached to the court by holding office there. Indeed, the number of future bishops enjoying formal ties with the court in the widest sense was in some respects remarkably limited. Far more future bishops reached their appointed station through connections of a more indirect kind to the court and the ministry. One obvious route was service in the houses of the *grands* in a variety of roles – as preceptors, as confessors or almoners, or even as favourites. In some cases, as we have already seen with bishops like Bertaut or du Perron, this was a temporary stepping-stone to court office itself. Roland Hébert and Pierre de Hardivilliers, successive archbishops of Bourges, were confessors to the prince of Condé. He was primarily responsible for their promotion as he sought to have compliant archbishops in a province of which he was master. Before setting foot in the royal household itself, Jean de Lingendes served as tutor to Henri IV's bastard son, the comte de Moret, and it seems likely that other bishops of similar social background may have performed similar services. We have already noted the role of Louis Barbier as Gaston's favourite for many years until his promotion to Langres in 1655. Mazarin's willingness to settle accounts in this way with men like Barbier was no less evident in the elevation of Conty's favourite, Daniel de Cosnac, to Valence less than a year earlier; as Conti's *premier gentilhomme*, Cosnac played a major part in negotiating his master's marriage to one of Mazarin's nieces.

In the light of this discussion, it may come as a surprise that in only eight cases can it be said with any confidence that it was the service of the *grands* which led directly to episcopal preferment. In others, such as those of du Perron, Bertaut or Lingendes just cited, the connection to the *grands* was indirect, an important stepping-stone, but not the only one, towards the final prize. The principal reason for this low figure is that the notion of service is elusive, and that it can easily shift into subtly different degrees of clientage. In certain situations clientage could give rise to a greater degree of dependence than relations of service. Jean Martin, bishop of Périgueux, was an experienced vicar-general of the diocese who had been secretary in the ecclesiastical chamber of the 1588 Estates General, but it was the patronage of the powerful Bourdeille family which enabled him to become bishop of Périgueux in 1601 on terms so abject as to make him seem little more than a family chaplain. Claude de Rébé owed his elevation to the coadjutorship of Narbonne in 1622 to his service to the Guise family, and it was evidently their intention that he should act to preserve the late Cardinal de Joyeuse's influence in that diocese on their behalf. Within a year or two of succeeding as full archbishop, their relations had broken down irretrievably, and Rébé's dependence evaporated as he came to rely on protection from Richelieu. Sometimes, frequently recycled stories of service and dependence seem to rest on singularly slight foundations. It seems, for example, that Charles de Montchal was never preceptor to the young Cardinal La Valette, and therefore not a household 'dependent', any more than Philippe Cospeau was of the cardinal's father, Epernon, who had him made bishop of Aire in 1606.[81] On the other hand, as Montchal was briefly principal of the College of Autun in the University of Paris while La Valette was a student, some less precise link, not definable as a master-servant tie, seems quite probable, and might explain La Valette's decision in 1627 to select Montchal as his successor in the archbishopric of Toulouse.

Household service to ecclesiastical *grands*, especially cardinals, was no less perennial an attraction to ambitious clerics. Approximately fifteen bishops owed their careers and, in most cases, their mitre to the patronage which flowed from such service, stretching from Arnaud d'Ossat, who had served as secretary to Paul de Foix and Cardinal Joyeuse, to Gilbert de Clérambault, who had served Richelieu, but especially Mazarin before his promotion to Poitiers in 1658. Here, too, degrees of actual service or dependency varied, and the language used by contemporaries to describe both is full of potentially misleading traps. Paul-Antoine de Fay-Peyraud accompanied Cardinal de Joyeuse to Rome and remained with him there, but this hardly made him a Joyeuse client: his Montmorency ancestry would itself have sufficed to secure him the see of Uzès on his return to France.[82] In 1603, Ossat reported that he had just obtained papal provisions to Alet for Pierre Polverel, 'un serviteur de M le cardinal de Joyeuse', but the nature of that service remains unclear, as Polverel was also the nephew of the reigning bishop of Carcassonne, who did have close ties to Joyeuse.[83] The fact that nine out of the fifteen bishops under consideration had been attached to the service of Richelieu and Mazarin points to both the possibilities and limitations of this pattern of accession to the episcopate. On the one hand, it clearly underlines their willingness to reward some of their most active servants. On the other hand, as cardinals who were also ministers closely involved with the nomination of bishops, they had the opportunity to reward far more individuals than 'ordinary' cardinals could ever aspire to; their dual positions make them highly untypical of ecclesiastical *grands* generally. Yet they had to be careful to avoid being seen to raise 'mere' servants to the episcopate. The matter was a sensitive one, and the idea that servants, even of cardinals, might become bishops for no other reason than the will of their masters was repugnant to contemporaries. The accusations made against Richelieu by his bitterest enemies to the effect that he was intent on debasing the episcopate by filling it with dependants and men of

---

81 Leonce Couture, 'La Vérité sur les débuts de Cospéan évêque d'Aire', *Revue de Gascogne*, 41 (1900), 519, for a refutation the legend which was first propagated by Amelot de la Houssaye, *Mémoires historiques, politiques, critiques et littéraires* (Amsterdam 1725), ii. 165.
82 ASV, PC 13, fos 195–210, evidence *de vita et moribus*, 20 Nov 1612.
83 'Lettres inédites du cardinal d'Ossat', ed P Tamizey de Larroque, *Revue de Gascogne*, 13 (1874), 289–90, Ossat to Jacques de Harlay, 24 Feb 1603.

inferior birth, were testimony enough to the strength of opinion on the subject.[84] In fact, both Richelieu and Mazarin largely confined themselves to promoting those of their servants who had carried out a wide range of administrative and confidential duties, with their respective *maîtres de chambre* being the most successful. The privilege of cardinals to make their own arrangements for a successor should they wish to resign their diocese was one that the crown respected throughout the period, and no doubt this was an additional reason for seeking their patronage; at least a half-dozen cardinals under Henri IV and Louis XIII handpicked their own successors without any obvious external pressure, but it is noteworthy that in no case was their diocese conferred on a member of their household.

VII

Because the function of a bishop was ultimately to govern a diocese and because dioceses might also be crucial to the government of particular provinces, the extent to which political activity generally, whether ecclesiastical or not, could assist those anxious for advancement should not be underestimated. Inevitably it is far easier to trace these elements in a bishop's curriculum vitae when they took on an institutional form than when they were episodic, almost 'freelance' activities. But it would be unwise to imagine that the former weighed more heavily in the scales when it came to filling vacant dioceses since, as suggested earlier, specific services rendered to the crown might outweigh even the most commendable record of sustained service.

In attempting to propose a typology of the political activities of future bishops, we do not need to return to those bishops who had originally followed secular careers, but simply to recall that most of them had been magistrates, with a minority following military careers; on these grounds, their claim to episcopal office was one which could not but appeal to royal ministers and the king's entourage. By contrast, ecclesiastics in what might be called secular offices were few and far between, especially towards the upper ranges of the pyramid of political power. For that reason, it comes as an even greater surprise that two archbishops, Camille de Neufville of Lyon and Anne de Ventadour of Bourges, were both provincial governors at the time of their promotion to the episcopate! The practice was not unknown in the previous century with figures like Cardinal de Tournon occupying such

---

84 The *locus classicus* of this accusation against Richelieu is the mémoires of Charles de Montchal, *Mémoires de Mr de Montchal archevêque de Toulouse contentant des particularités de la vie et du ministère du cardinal de Richelieu*, 2 vols (Rotterdam 1718). Years later, he was also accused of nominating only those who shared the theological views of the Jesuits, which concurred with his own: see Pierre Blet, 'Louis XIV et les papes aux prises avec le jansénisme', *Archivum Historiae Pontificiae*, 31 (1993), 114.

positions, but there was a significant difference in that even then it had been limited to men who were *already* senior churchmen. But Neufville's and Ventadour's nominations came in 1649 and 1653 respectively, critical dates for the crown, already embroiled in the Fronde and looking to win or keep powerful families or individuals on its side.

By contrast, diplomacy in all its forms was historically an activity in which members of the clergy were extensively involved, and both the French crown and the papacy were accustomed to rewarding them with bishoprics, not to mention red hats, for their efforts; as often as not, it was a matter of raising their status sufficiently so that they would be treated properly when despatched to conduct negotiations on the crown's behalf. By comparison with the sixteenth century, the number of future bishops who made their reputation in this way under Henri IV and his successors was limited, and the tendency was to reserve diplomatic missions for ecclesiastics who were already bishops or cardinals. And it was in Rome that they made or confirmed their reputations, not on missions to Europe's secular princes. Only Cardinal d'Ossat might be ranked with the most distinguished, and in life as in death his reputation was probably all the greater because of the modesty of his social origins. Beginning as an embassy secretary in Rome, standing in as a *chargé d'affaires* in moments of upheaval such as the League, he went on to win admiration for his skill in defending Henri IV in the face of a medley of difficulties in a hostile curia. The career of Denis Simon de Marquemont, which partly overlaps with Ossat's, illustrates the possibilities which Rome might still offer ambitious French clerics. He was a leading curial magistrate (an Auditor of the Rota) for many years, then an occasional *chargé d'affaires* during ambassadorial absences, with the long deferred red hat only coming at the very end of an essentially Roman career, one that was interrupted only by brief periods of residence in his diocese of Lyon. But despite the opportunity to attract court patronage through service, official or unofficial, in Rome, these men had no real successors, with the possible exception of Henri Arnauld, even though a number of future bishops resided for several years in Rome; the services rendered and connections established there were doubtless valuable to them on returning to France, but it was not diplomatic service *per se* which brought them the mitre in the end. Louis XIV's ecclesiastical diplomats, personified by Cardinals d'Estrées and Janson, were established bishops well before they were trusted with diplomatic missions.

It was, therefore, political activity *within* France which promised the most attractive rewards. Summarising the record of politically active future bishops is no simple matter. That men like Richelieu and Mazarin used their household members for political and administrative tasks is well known, especially from the time of the siege of La Rochelle onwards. At one time in the mid-1640s, at least three bishops (one serving, two to be appointed later) were engaged in administering French-occupied Catalonia – Michele Mazarin, Hyacinthe Serroni and Pierre de Marca. For the same reason, royal almoners were also likely to be employed on particular missions, though few specific traces of them have survived. In 1643, however, François Bosquet was denied the see of Pamiers because Anne of Austria insisted on giving it to one of her almoners, Jacques de Montrouge, who, it was impressed on Bosquet, had risked his life in her service.[85]

Fortunately for men like Bosquet, political activity was not confined to the court. A variety of political forums survived or were even gathering strength, in which individual members of the clergy could advertise their talents and seek patrons and protectors. These different bodies, and clerical involvement in them, should be seen as overlapping in certain respects rather than being somehow separate. As many of them have attracted relatively little scrutiny as far as the clergy's presence there is concerned, only a brief look at each of them will be possible here. Provinces with their own estates certainly offered some such openings, especially where the clergy played a leading role in their affairs; yet these openings in turn were probably limited by the dominance of the episcopate within the clerical estate, a situation which, of course, suited the crown very well. Individual instances of what they might lead to may be given here. Emery Marc de la Ferté, a canon of Rouen and a royal almoner, was one of the deputies who presented the *cahiers* of the Norman estates at court in 1630, and subsequently appears to have conducted unspecified political assignments for Richelieu.[86] Estates like those of Brittany and Béarn seem to have offered slightly more scope for second-rank clergy and in some instances, perhaps not entirely without discreet prompting, they publicly supported the claims of individual clerics to episcopal office. The Breton Estates, which in 1647 had demanded that the province's bishoprics be reserved for Bretons, formally petitioned the queen mother in 1649 on behalf of François de Visdelou for the coadjutorship of Quimper.[87] Had the Estates General not vanished after 1614 (and, to a lesser extent, the Assemblies of Notables after 1627), they, too, would in all probability have provided a platform for rising or well connected clerics to make their names. Admittedly, this is purely hypothetical, but it would seem to be the logical inference to draw from the fact that while only four of Henri IV's future bishops appear to have attended the Estates General of 1576 or 1588, twice that number of bishops emerged from the ranks of the second-order ecclesiastical deputies to the 1614 Estates General.

However, if there was one estate in seventeenth-century France which did

---

85 BN, MS Fr 15720, fo 331v, Charles de Montchal, archbishop of Toulouse, to François Bosquet, 21 July 1643.
86 ASV, PC 37, fo 314, evidence of Pancrace Bétille, doctor of the Sorbonne, Dec 1637; Henri de Frondeville, *Les Présidents du parlement de Normandie* (Rouen 1953), no 56, p 409.
87 ASV, PC 48, fo 796, petition from 'les gens des trois estatz du pays et duché de Bretagne', 25 June 1649. The petition refers to article 1 of their *cahier* of 1647, and the response of the royal council of 16 Feb 1649. They added that the reigning bishop had long wanted Visdelou in this role 'sans aulcune consideration de parenté ny alliance, mais seullement pour ses qualitez'.

not lack opportunities to meet publicly and discuss their affairs, it was the clergy. In addition to the gatherings just evoked, the affairs of the *Clergé de France*, with the assemblies, general and provincial, that they spawned, provided regular openings of a kind not otherwise available for second-order clergy. These assemblies, as is well known, came into existence after 1560 for financial reasons, and were the price which the crown had to pay in return for continuing financial assistance from the French church. The 'great' assemblies were held once every ten years, with lesser 'accounting' assemblies meeting at intervals between them; but these latter assemblies, although smaller in numbers, could also find themselves called upon to provide additional funds for the crown or to discuss thorny questions affecting church-state relations. Gradually, the assemblies worked out elaborate procedures for electing deputies, voting, and rotating certain key offices among the 'provinces'. For example, no second-order ecclesiastic could be elected a deputy by a province in which he was not a benefice-holder, which at times led to unedifying scrambles to bend the rules in order to meet the minimum conditions required; the rules of course favoured those clerics who held several benefices in more than one diocese or province. Furthermore, despite the rules for elections, it was often alleged that the bishops pulled all the strings, ignoring conventions and ensuring the success of their own candidates.[88] The accusation was made in particular by Richelieu, who was anything but inactive himself when it came to urging the election of particular bishops to assemblies, and so it should therefore not be taken as objective fact. To the extent that episcopal control was a reality, it is not difficult to see how it might work in favour of younger clerics from their own families, their vicars-general, or others enjoying their favour – and thereby reinforcing the patterns of patronage observed earlier in this chapter. Certainly disputed elections were invariably the first item of business during the ensuing general assemblies, proof of how keen the competition for deputyships was. The 1655–6 Assembly, to give but a single example, had to adjudicate between the claims of Dominique de Ligny and Bernard de Sariac, both of whom would become bishops within a few years![89]

A total of fifty-two future bishops served as deputies to one or more assemblies of clergy between 1579 and 1655–7. That figure may be an understatement, especially for the early period, though there was a tendency for the size of assemblies to expand over the years. The total number may not seem particularly high. What is of particular interest, however, is the long-term trend revealed by these figures. Under Henri IV, incoming bishops who

---

88 BN, MS Fr 15720, fos 111–12, 'Mémoire de l'ordre qu'il seroit à propos de tenir pour nommer les députez de l'assemblée' (1645), which details the criticisms made of the disorders and factions, attributed mainly to the bishops, and calling for the strict observance of the rules voted in 1615.

89 *Collection des procès-verbaux des assemblées générales du clergé de France,* ed A Duranthon, 9 vols (Paris 1767–8), iv. 13.

had been deputies to assemblies of clergy were thinly spread through the list of new bishops, numbering no more than twelve in all. It is only in the years following the consecutive meetings of the Estates General and a 'great' Assembly of Clergy in 1614–15 that something like a surge of nominations of former deputies to the assemblies is distinctly visible, though only one bishop emerged from among the clerics attending the 1617 Assembly of Notables. From the mid-1620s to the late 1640s, there is no obvious sign of episcopal patronage being showered upon those attending assemblies of clergy. Richelieu kept a vigilant eye on their doings, clashing notoriously with that of 1641. The surviving evidence suggests that his primary concern was to control the assemblies by securing the election of reliable *serving* bishops as deputies, and especially the election of compliant *agents-généraux*.[90] The experiences of the Fronde, the emergence of the Jansenist question, and Mazarin's dispute with the exiled Retz over the government of the diocese of Paris, just to mention the most serious problems, all led Richelieu's successor to adopt a far more calculated use of episcopal patronage in his dealings with the assemblies. He would leave abbeys and bishoprics vacant while they were in session with a view to inducing the deputies to adopt a line favourable to his demands or policies.[91] Seventeen, or virtually one-third of the total number of deputies to become bishops between 1589 and 1661, were nominated during the final decade of the Mazarin ministry, especially in the aftermath of the marathon Assembly of 1655–7; the duration of this particular assembly ensured that the longer it lasted, the more attractive benefices – dioceses and abbeys – became available for well-measured distribution.[92] Such tactics did not die with Mazarin, and were if anything further refined during Louis XIV's rule. The Assembly of 1682, best known for adopting the celebrated Gallican articles, may not be typical, but no fewer than thirteen of its second-order deputies became bishops, most of them relatively quickly, in subsequent years.[93]

Mazarin shared at least one other conviction with Richelieu in this domain – namely that it was crucial to secure the election of the right men as *agents-généraux*, as it was they who administered the clergy's business in-between assemblies and generally played a major role in church-state relations at a

90 For one instance his attempts to ensure the election of well-disposed bishops in 1641 and his answers to anticipated objections that some of them had been deputies to the 1635 Assembly, see Avenel, *Lettres*, vi. 741–3, letter to Condé 23 Dec 1640; 749, to Chavigny, 18 Jan 1641; 784, *avis* to Louis XIII about deputies to assembly, late Apr/early May 1641.
91 This was first remarked upon during the 1645 Assembly: 'La distribution des bénéfices vacants qui sont quatorze Abbayes, 2 évêchés et archeveschés ne se faira pas à ce qu'on croy pendant ladite assemblée, c'est un boucquet qu'on leur veult faire sentir': AAE, France 852, fo 18, Jacques Gaudin to Abel Servien, 8 July 1645. For Mazarin's own thoughts on how best to use the vacant sees of Bazas and Tréguier, see Blet, *Clergé de France et monarchie*, ii. 8.
92 ASV, N Fr 110a, fo 287–8, *avvisi* of 11 May 1657. Reigning bishops could be rewarded with gifts of vacant abbeys, or transferred to more attractive sees.
93 This figure is derived from the 'liste des députés de l'assemblée de 1682', printed and annotated in Pierre Blet, *Les Assemblée du Clergé et Louis XIV de 1670 à 1693* (Rome 1972), 603–10.

routine bureaucratic level. This would be ground enough for thinking that it was the *agents-généraux* who, of all the French clergy, stood the best chance of becoming bishops. But to take that view would be to adopt the perspectives of the generation of the 1630s onwards. In fact, their chances depended very closely on the ebb and flow of relations generally between the crown and the successive assemblies. The *agents* had to tread a hazardous path between the assemblies which elected and supervised them, on the one hand, and the crown and its ministers, with whom they dealt regularly and who could dangle enticing promises before them, on the other; to lean too much in one or other direction would jeopardise their chances at a time when relations between the assemblies and the crown were still apt to lead to conflicts which neither side could prevent or control. The assemblies resented Richelieu's tactics over the election of *agents* in the 1630s and in 1641, and were sufficiently independent in spirit to break the career of at least one of them before the cardinal had had the opportunity to reward him with a mitre. As in most things, the hand of Mazarin is much less visible, but the successes speak for themselves – four *agents-généraux* and three other officials of the assemblies being among those elevated to the episcopate during his ministry.

It would be possible and perhaps illuminating, too, to extend this study of pre-episcopal careers yet further. But the accumulation of perspectives on pre-episcopal activities would not of itself unlock the secret of success in obtaining a vacant diocese. It would, in any case, be focused less on careers or activities of the kind just seen, and more on the elusive, if essential, quest for patronage. It would, of course, be quixotic to suggest that career, experience, and patronage could ever be clearly separated in any age, and this chapter has repeatedly afforded evidence to the contrary. It would make even less sense in an age when a pre-episcopal career that had become standard by the eighteenth century had not yet become the norm, and when the road towards the episcopate was characterised by a diversity which this chapter will have made abundantly clear.

Further, if not quite final, evidence of this diversity is surely to be found in the one thing that most bishops of this period have in common, namely the tenure of benefices *in commendam*. This form of benefice-holding had expanded rapidly under François I and his successors, and was still in progress in the early seventeenth-century. At least 155, or 44 per cent, of the bishops nominated between 1589 and 1661 already held at least one abbey or priory *in commendam*. In the case of some bishops, as already noted, there is no other pre-episcopal activity that can be credited to them. If there was an ecclesiastical spoils system during the *ancien régime*, this was it, and France's bishops were among its principal beneficiaries. The higher their social status, and the closer they positioned themselves to the sources of crown patronage, the better endowed they were likely to be with such benefices, and often from an early age. The competition for episcopal office would probably have differed in important respects had this outlet not been so readily available. The learned but shrewd Peiresc, himself an abbot *in commendam*, was assuredly not alone in thinking – and recommending others to do likewise – that for all the prestige and honour it might confer, a bishopric was more likely to bring toil and trouble than an abbey *in commendam*.[94]

Meanwhile, for those who went on to become bishops, the tenure of one or more benefices *in commendam* was less a sign of activity (since only a minority resided in, or took the trouble to administer them personally) than of success in attracting church patronage from the crown, a success which, given favourable conditions, might be repeated several times before, and indeed after, their accession to the episcopate. For those in search of episcopal rank, benefices like these were extremely useful bargaining counters which, depending on the circumstances, could mean the difference between the success and failure of one's hopes. Nothing would be gained by rehearsing the criticisms made of the *commende* and the bishops who benefited so much from it, but one of its most important effects on the episcopate has rarely attracted any notice. No doubt that effect was entirely unintended, but the manner in which these benefices were so commonly awarded, resigned and exchanged, probably contributed more than anything else to accustoming the French upper clergy to the geographical dispersion of their interests. By the time they were in a position to aim for episcopal office, they were no longer imprisoned in a 'territorial' attitude to the diocesan map of France.

---

94 *Lettres de Peiresc*, ed P Tamizey de Larroque, 8 vols (Paris 1888–98), vii. 579–82, letter to Cardinal Bentivoglio, 19 Apr 1622.

CHAPTER 8

Bishops and Dioceses: Patterns of Episcopal Tenure 1589–1661

THE FIRST, INDISPENSABLE requirement before an individual could become a bishop, was, as we noted in an earlier chapter, a vacant diocese. But the connection between bishops and dioceses was not as simple or accidental as that observation, taken in isolation, might suggest. The present chapter will attempt to show, among other things, just how complex the connection could be, since, over the centuries, it had given rise to elaborate legal and theological developments. The growth of what might be called a theology of episcopal office was a prolonged process which began in the early church, and which was still not completed by the seventeenth century. As recently as the Council of Trent, the apparently anodine proposal that bishops were obliged to reside in their dioceses because they held them directly of God, triggered off a row which nearly crippled the Council, raising as it did the insoluble question of the relation of episcopal and papal authority, and of local churches to the universal church. In the end, the impasse was only broken by shelving the discussion.

Not all propositions concerning episcopal office were quite so explosive, while some, inevitably, tended to be little more than a set of pious aspirations. Others had come to form a body of what might be called working principles which, although they might be frequently infringed, were nevertheless regarded as deserving respect, even to the extent of requiring special dispensations when not observed. One such principle, which applied not just to bishops but to the clergy in general, required that they be born of properly married Catholic parents, and indeed the papal enquiry into new bishops included a question specifically to that effect. The point is not a minor one, since it was marriage which formed the subject of one of the most widely used metaphors in relation to bishops and dioceses, and which is of particular interest in the present context. The marriage in question was that of the bishop to his diocese, his *ecclesia*. First expounded in the fourth century, the metaphor aimed to present the bond between a bishop and his diocese as being as indissoluble as the union of husbands and wives. It followed naturally that bishops could not be removed involuntarily from their sees, unless truly exceptional circumstances like heresy or treason were present; their security of tenure was a necessary consequence of their mystical marriage. But the real intention behind this development appears, in the conditions of the early church, to have been to inhibit both the poaching of bishops by one church from another, and the movement of ambitious bishops from poorer to richer or more prestigious dioceses. Theological positions like this duly found their way into classic canon law which, if it did not in the event categorically outlaw the movement of bishops between dioceses, at least attempted to discourage it by making it very difficult in practice; as we saw, it suspected resignations and exchanges of dioceses as likely to involve arrangements entailing a degree of simony. Gallican tradition, with its own strong emphasis upon episcopal dignity and rights, also strongly underlined the autonomy and stability of the episcopate. Reform-minded writers in the *bonus pastor* tradition reworked these ideas in the fifteenth and sixteenth centuries, and were closely followed by hagiographers and preachers who extolled the bishop who remained faithful to his diocese.

Paradoxically, one possible reason why they did so was that by then theory and practice had come to diverge. The early church's strenuous attempts to prohibit inter-diocesan movement by individual bishops as part of a personal *cursus honorum* were gradually abandoned during the Middle Ages, a change facilitated by the appearance of formal papal sanction for such movement; disapproval of ambition remained as rhetorically powerful as ever, of course, but the kings and popes who played increasingly important roles in the choice of bishops all wanted the freedom to exercise their patronage of individual bishops with fewer restraints. No doubt, the 'marriage' between bishops and their dioceses was more visible when they were still elected by the cathedral chapters which in so many respects 'represented' the *ecclesia* in question. But papal provisions and royal nominations combined gradually to dilute this sense of union, not least when 'outsiders', French or non-French, were the beneficiaries. As royal nominations became increasingly common, the papacy seemed at times to revert to a more judgemental stance on this question. In the course of the negotiations for the Concordat of Bologna, and also on numerous later occasions, it felt the need to point out that while the king of France might be moved by the desire to give 'good' (i.e. well endowed or high status) dioceses to individual bishops, out of a wish to reward them personally, the pope's responsibility was the rather different one of ensuring that dioceses were endowed with good bishops.[1]

It is not necessary to assume that this latter sentiment was widely or deeply held, in Rome or even among the French episcopate itself, in order to

---

1 Jules Thomas, *Le Concordat de 1516. Ses origines, son histoire au xvie siècle*, 3 vols (Paris 1910), ii. 65–6. The French clergy held the same view, as was made clear to Henri III by the Bishop of Saint-Brieuc in the 1579–80 Assembly of Clergy: 'Sire, l'on ne doit pourvoir aux personnes par Eglises, mais l'on doit pourvoir aux Eglises par personnes'. Quoted in Pierre Blet, 'Le Concordat de Bologne et la réforme tridentine', *Gregorianum*, 45 (1964), 255.

recognise that dioceses were themselves actors in the making of the episcopate. It is fair to say that in the minds of contemporaries, they tended to be passive, if rather unpredictable actors, falling vacant at times or in ways that were often unforeseeable, and thus complicating the plans of those in search of a mitre. Nor was it only the king of France who thought in terms of dioceses which might be more or less attractive to episcopal contenders. There were, throughout our period, repeated instances of individuals being nominated to a vacant bishopric, only to procrastinate before seeking their papal provisions in the hope that a more attractive diocese would become available in the meantime.

There is also some direct evidence of contemporaries' own thinking, much of it negative, on the subject. As we saw, this sometimes surfaced as a consequence of their keen interest in the financial value of bishoprics. Richelieu's famous indictment of his own diocese of Luçon as 'le plus vilain évêché de France, le plus crotté et le plus désagréable', was not based on financial considerations, but it may stand as a classic expression of this outlook, and he was not alone in being so scathing towards his ecclesiastical 'bride'.[2] When the young Henri de Béthune was nominated to Bayonne in 1626, having just missed out on the archbishopric of Lyon, his father objected that his son could not possibly be expected to accept Bayonne. It was too remote and the language spoken there was unintelligible; it was, quite simply, beyond the pale.[3] At the opposite end of the spectrum, we find Hugues de Lionne warmly recommending Bayeux to his reluctant father in 1659: 'Bayeux is such a prosperous place and life is so pleasant there, that a pigeon only costs a shilling'.[4]

But it is only rarely that we are vouchsafed statements of the attitudes of individual bishops, and it would be unrealistic to attempt a systematic analysis of their intentions in accepting a particular diocese or in seeking a transfer to another on the basis of a haphazard collection of *obiter dicta*. Yet that difficulty does not dispose of the need to consider the making of the episcopate from the point of view of the dioceses rather than simply of their bishops and their careers. What it means is that that the discussion has to focus mainly on 'objective' patterns of episcopal tenure and movement, and not on the explicit intentions that lie behind them.

In attempting to study the episcopate from this dual perspective, several closely connected questions arise. At the most basic level, one may ask to what extent was the French episcopate a stable one, corresponding (or not) to the

---

2 *Lettres, instructions diplomatiques et papiers d'état de Richelieu*, ed D L M Avenel, 8 vols (Paris 1853–76), i. 24, letter to Mme de Bourges [Apr 1609].
3 BN, MS Fr 3678, fos 108v-9r, Philippe de Béthune, ambassador in Rome, to Raymond Phélypeaux, secretary of state, 4 Nov 1626.
4 'Lettres inédites de Hugues de Lionne', ed Ulysse Chevallier, *Bulletin de la Société d'Archéologie et de Statistique de la Drôme*, 11 (1877), 14, letter of 7 Feb 1659: 'Bayeux est un pays si gras et où il fait si bon vivre, qu'un pigeon n'y vaut qu'un sol'.

ideals which churchmen themselves professed to believe. If it exhibits a higher degree of stability than other episcopates of the time, how is this peculiarity to be explained and what is its significance? If, on the other hand, there was a measure of mobility, what was its basis? Did it constitute a mechanism of reward or promotion of which both bishops and the crown could take advantage? Was there a hierarchy of first-, second- and third-rank sees of the kind that has been detected in contemporary Castile, a hierarchy which was known to contemporaries, and which helped to 'structure' the episcopate in ways which did not necessarily correspond to its formal hierarchy? Linked to these questions, at least in part, is the issue of the extent to which bishoprics remained in the hands of particular families over a number of generations, and which therefore removed them from the purview of those in search of mobility, geographical or hierarchical. And even if most dioceses were not the preserve of particular families, it would still be illuminating to know how extensive was the pool of families from which the episcopate of this period was drawn.

Straightforward as it may seem, finding answers to these questions is not without its share of supposition and approximation. In fact, the issues that they raise potentially touch on virtually every important aspect of the French episcopate's history, but the purpose of the present chapter is the relatively modest one of providing a bridge between the material and perspectives sketched in the previous chapters and the history of episcopal patronage in those which are to follow.

I

With 351 bishops filling 113 dioceses during this period, the average diocese was host to fractionally more than three bishops (3.1 in fact!). By any standards, this would seem a particularly low turnover for a period spanning seventy-two years, since, looking at the figures from a diocesan viewpoint, it suggests an average episcopal tenure of approximately twenty-four years. As we shall see, the actual length of the average episcopal career for the bishops appointed in this period is itself remarkably close to that figure, although the method of calculating it is necessarily rather different. For the present, however, such a figure is of interest in that it draws attention to the limitations of royal patronage, suggesting not merely how prolonged a process the changeover from one episcopal generation to another might be, but also that the very notion of clearly defined episcopal generations may itself be difficult to sustain.

Since the actual duration of careers was a crucial element in determining the stability of the episcopate, and therefore in conditioning access to its ranks, it is essential to look first at the key factors helping to determine it. Only in the light of such an analysis can the broad patterns of the relations between bishops and dioceses be adequately investigated. Clearly, the underlying common determinant of episcopal tenure was, for want of a better term, a demographic one. Assuming that bishops normally enjoyed perfect security of tenure, the duration of the average episcopal reign largely depended on the age at which individuals became bishops and the age at which they either died or retired. Here, too, successive accounts of the *ancien régime* episcopate have created an enduring image of men being raised to high office while still remarkably young – and thus unready and inexperienced. It should be said that such images sometimes derive directly from contemporary denunciations of individual instances of this kind of premature promotion, but they have not led to wider interest in the subject. In particular, the obvious implication of such an image has rarely been followed up – namely that the turnover of bishops must have been exceedingly slow since episcopal careers would normally have have been extremely long! Some careers indeed were, but it would be a mistake to assume that seventeenth-century bishops were at all times immune to disease, discomfort, and sudden death, however much we might be inclined to think that their social condition insulated them from such unforeseen hazards.

But demography might not be the sole determinant of episcopal tenure. Old age and family interests, not always working hand-in-hand, might persuade bishops to retire outright or to take as a coadjutor a younger man who was guaranteed the succession on the bishop's death or, more rarely, on his subsequent resignation. Resignation was the ultimate negation of the mystical marriage between bishops and their dioceses, and even when the reason was old age, it was something which, in keeping with church tradition, neither the papacy nor bishops themselves regarded as a normal course of action. It may also be added here that retirement or resignation was technically a *cessio regiminis*, the termination of the rule of a diocese, and did not entail the loss of the episcopal 'character' which, like priestly orders, could not be lost. Retired bishops, mostly cardinals who were no longer willing or able to retain a diocese, often continued to play an important part in the affairs of the French church, but one need only mention men like André Frémiot of Bourges or Jean-Pierre Camus of Belley to realise that less elevated figures could do likewise. It is thus necessary to determine how far it was death rather than resignation which determined the length of episcopal tenure.

It is at this point that the fragility of the data available for our purposes becomes most apparent. Fortunately, the problem does not concern episcopal careers as such, since the records of the papal confirmation of bishops, as well as the dates of retirement or death, are usually perfectly accurate. However, the same cannot be said for the dates of either their birth or nomination to their dioceses, both of which are essential for a comprehensive study of the episcopate. For the most part, the problem is less acute for dates of nomination, especially for the period from around 1610 onwards. Dates of birth are a different matter, and the fact that men achieved distinction in later life by being raised to the episcopate did not always lead to the kind of detailed biographical curiosity which historians would most welcome. It should also be said that most of the information we possess for the age of incoming bishops derives from the enquiries conducted by the papacy after their nomination. The stipulations of the Council of Trent to the effect that copies of certificates of baptism (as well as evidence of clerical orders or university degrees taken by incoming bishops) should be submitted to the enquiry, were rarely observed in France. It was therefore left to the enquiry's witnesses to determine the age of the bishops in question, and some witnesses were clearly guessing what that might be, as they themselves regularly admitted, on the basis of their physical appearance![5] Underage nominees were particularly unlikely to provide too many opportunities to discover their true age, while one or two were known to have gone to some lengths actually to conceal it from Rome.[6] Thus, what we have in a large number of cases is the age – and hence the year of birth – which Rome finally adopted as the most credible. It is with these essential caveats in mind that calculations of the age at which men became bishops in this period will be attempted.

The patterns which emerge from this analysis are of interest in several respects. Omitting those twenty-four bishops for whom no information at all is available, the overall average age at which bishops were nominated between 1589 and 1661 was $37\frac{1}{2}$ years. However, with the average time-lag between nomination and papal confirmation being sixteen and a half months, the age at which they received their provisions was just a fraction short of thirty-nine (38.9 in fact). For all its fragile basis, it is a figure which certainly dispels the legend of an underaged episcopate. Bearing in mind not just the patterns of life-expectancy in the seventeenth century, but the age at which bishops' contemporaries frequently assumed major responsibilities, the conclusion that the average bishop entered the episcopate at a relatively advanced stage in his career seems inescapable.

But an average based on 327 bishops and spanning seven decades is bound to conceal at least some variations, if not outright surprises. Closer analysis is clearly desirable (Table 8.1).

---

5   Witnesses repeatedly formed their impression of a bishop's age 'ex vultu eius', i.e. on the basis of his facial features. However, not all were reduced to such guesswork. Frequently, witnesses included parish priests who had checked their parish registers, former fellow-students or long-standing friends of the bishops, all of whom had a good idea of their age.
6   This is famously the case with the young Richelieu, though Rome clearly did not regard the deception as seriously as did some of Richelieu's later detractors: see Joseph Bergin, *The Rise of Richelieu* (New Haven and London 1991), 70. In the late 1610s, Paul V was assured that Louis de La Baume of Viviers was three years older than he actually was; it was only twenty years later that the deception was discovered, and in 1639 Urban VIII granted him a dispensation and obliged him to spend 1,000 écus in good works of the pope's designation; he also felt it necessary retrospectively to validate all La Baume's episcopal acts in the intervening period, which he regarded as invalid because of his initial offence: *Hierarchia Catholica*, iv. 284, 'Pompeiopolitan', n 2; *DHGE*, xviii, cols 537–8.

Table 8.1 Average age of incoming bishops

Decade	a	b	c
1589–1600	40.0	2.2	42.2
1601–10	34.1	1.4	35.5
1611–20	31.2	1.4	32.6
1621–30	37.8	1.1	38.9
1631–40	39.8	1.4	41.2
1641–50	39.0	1.1	40.1
1651–61	40.8	1.0	41.8
Totals	37.5	1.37	38.9

Table: a = age at nomination; b = time-lag for papal confirmation; c = age at papal confirmation

As this decade-by-decade breakdown of the average age at which bishops received their nomination and papal provisions shows, there was no consistency or linearity to the process. Later chapters will offer more detailed explanation of why this was so. For the present, a few brief comparisons will suffice. It may come as a surprise that some of the highest averages for a single decade come not at the end of the period but at the very beginning. There are two explanations: the first is that an inordinate number of those nominated bishops in the 1590s, during the most disruptive phase of the wars, had to wait much longer than most of either their predecessors or successors before obtaining their papal provisions. Delays of anything from three to six years were not unusual, and they clearly helped to raise the average age of incoming bishops far more than was normally the case. Incidentally, as the table also shows, the delay between nomination and confirmation steadily declined thereafter, although a spate of underage nominations in the 1610s and political difficulties with Rome during the mid- and late 1630s either slowed or temporarily reversed the downward trend. However, delay in obtaining provisions was only a secondary factor in determining the age profile of bishops. In the case of Henri IV's first cohort of bishops, the underlying reason for the high average age is that an unusual number of those appointed were elderly commoners or members of religious orders. In normal circumstances, they could not realistically have expected episcopal office, but in the particular circumstances of the 1590s and early 1600s, they appealed not so much to the crown as to patrons and families seeking to keep particular dioceses under their control who were willing to promote men already well into middle age. By the final decade of Henri IV's reign, the average age of new bishops had dropped considerably, which can be explained at least in part by the return of particular noble families to the episcopate. This in turn led to a rising number of young, underage nominations. The further drop registered in the 1610s, while less sharp in relative terms, had the effect of producing the youngest crop of bishops during the entire period. It is attributable to an acceleration of trends already present in the later part of Henri IV's reign; but the main reason was the large contingent of coadjutor-bishops appointed then, not out of any sudden need for their services, but out of a concerted push by reigning bishops and well-placed families to ensure episcopal office for nephews in the case of the former or younger sons in the case of the latter. The pendulum swung firmly in the opposite direction during the 1620s and, although a number of underage nominations were made then, the decade set a trend which was to be confirmed, steadily rather than spectacularly, over the following generation. The most 'representative' decade for the period as a whole as far as the age at nomination was concerned was the 1640s, while it was not until the 1650s that the average for nominations set in the 1590s was overtaken, albeit by the narrowest of margins.

This analysis needs to be taken a step further, since the figures for the average age of incoming bishops emerging from even a decade-by-decade breakdown of the data might prove to be no more than mathematical abstractions. The distribution of bishops into age groups conveys a more precise impression of the real age of incoming bishops over time (Tables 8.2, 8.3).

Of the next two tables, it is the second (Table 8.3) which, by organising the data in ten-year groups, proves the more useful, since it enables comparisons to be made with the overall averages already discussed. One further column ('j') of figures has been added to each table in order to take account of the one age-statistic that contemporaries would have been clearly conscious of – namely the requirement that episcopal nominees should have reached the age of twenty-six. At least forty-five royal nominees, or one in about eight bishops, failed to meet that condition, some admittedly by only a few months. The proportion of underaged bishops may not seem particularly high, but when we remember that elsewhere in Europe incoming bishops had to be in their thirtieth year, it is clear that the French church had, since the Concordat of Bologna, enjoyed especially favoured treatment. By the European yardstick, nearly eighty, or over one-fifth of French bishops, would have been underage at the moment of their nomination. As Table 8.3 shows, the vast majority of these underaged bishops were nominated during the 1600s and the 1610s, virtually disappeared during the 1630s and 1640s, only to creep

Table 8.2 Episcopal age-groups by reign

Reign	a	b	c	d	e	f	g	h	j
Henri IV	108	12	7	26	27	22	10	4	19
Louis XIII	154	11	8	48	46	24	13	4	22
Early Louis XIV	89	1	0	13	35	28	10	2	4
Totals	351	24	15	87	108	74	33	10	45

Table 8.3 Episcopal age-groups by decade

Decade	a	b	c	d	e	f	g	h	j
1589–1600	57	7	3	10	16	10	7	4	8
1601–10	54	5	4	17	13	12	3	0	11
1611–20	52	4	6	25	8	5	3	1	15
1621–30	57	6	2	14	20	9	4	2	6
1631–40	39	1	0	8	15	8	6	1	1
1641–50	41	1	0	6	17	13	4	0	1
1651–61	51	0	0	7	19	17	6	2	3
Totals	351	24	15	87	108	74	33	10	45

a = total nominations; b = age unknown; c = 11–20; d = 21–30; e = 31–40; f = 41–50; g = 51–60; h = 61–70; j = under 26 years old

back in again during the 1650s. The identity of the handful – five in all – for whom exceptions were made from the 1630s onwards is itself not without interest. Two of them were the Fouquet brothers, François and Louis, who benefited successively from the goodwill of Richelieu and Mazarin; a further two, both nominated in the early 1650s, were the future Cardinals Forbin-Janson and Estrées, while the only underage nominee of the 1640s, Louis de Gondrin, was pushed forward in the early days of the regency as coadjutor to his uncle, Archbishop Bellegarde of Sens. All five cases make it clear that only favour and protection at the highest level could ensure premature promotions to the episcopate after the 1620s, but even then the numbers involved were so few that ambitions to join the episcopate at an early age were becoming increasingly unrealistic.

Returning to the remainder of the data, especially in Table 8.3, a number of patterns suggest themselves. The first is that *very* young nominees, i.e. under the age of twenty, were more numerous than is generally realised – and they do *not* include Henri IV's bastard son, Bishop Henri de Bourbon-Verneuil of Metz, who is so often taken to be typical of early modern child-bishops.[7] It should also be noted that all of these adolescent bishops were nominated between the 1590s and the 1620s. The papacy's usual response to the nomination of such young men was to require them to wait several years before granting provisions, so the fact that even three of them were confirmed while still under twenty years of age is unusual in itself. The papacy was usually more unyielding than that, but in the early decades of our period it was hardly in a position to insist on the application of strict Tridentine standards to the French church: to have done so would have meant that

---

7   Bourbon-Verneuil's see of Metz, it will be recalled, was not part of the French church until the reign of Louis XIV.

particular episcopal vacancies would have lasted even longer. This is evident in the papacy's response to French nominees who were over twenty years old when nominated. Clement VIII and his successors might protest at infringements of the terms of the concordat, but exceptions could be, and frequently were, made for candidates who had reached their early to mid-twenties, and dispensations were issued which allowed them to be consecrated while still under the minimum age. Thus, no fewer than thirty-two of the forty-five underage nominees received their provisions while still under the age of twenty-six; some, like Richelieu, were no more than twenty or twenty-one when confirmed, but most tended to be twenty-four or twenty-five years old.

The evolution of the contingent of bishops nominated between the ages of twenty-one and thirty is consistent with what we have already seen in this chapter, and which would lead us to expect them to be at their most numerous during the 1610s and 1620s. In fact, it is apparent from Table 8.3 that the sudden jump observable for the 1610s, when over half of all bishops nominated were under thirty years of age, was unmistakably taking shape during the last decade of Henri IV's reign, when the king was looking favourably on the episcopal ambitions of several noble and ministerial families. By the 1630s, however, this age-group had fallen back to the point where it contributed just one in five incoming bishops, and it would fall again in the following two decades, contributing only one in eight bishops by the 1650s. It is indicative of the changes in the character of episcopal nominations that by the latter decade, the number of bishops in their twenties at their nomination should be overtaken for the first time since the 1590s by that of bishops who were in their fifties or even sixties.

So much for the groups at either extremity of the age spectrum. What of the majority of the episcopate? The question can be answered in a number of ways. With the average age of new bishops standing at 38.9 years, we may begin by noting that for the period as a whole, 210 out of 351 bishops (just around 60 per cent) were aged forty or under at the time of their nomination. As might be expected, this proportion, too, was anything but stable: it stood at its highest during the 1610s, when three out of every four bishops belonged to this category, but thereafter it slipped steadily, until by the 1650s, it was matched almost exactly by that of bishops in their forties or over when nominated to their first diocese. Such a gradual convergence towards the average age at nomination for the period as a whole would lead us to expect that the bulk of the episcopate consisted of men who were in their thirties and forties at the time of nomination. The distribution of this age-group over time is also significant. Under Henri IV, it accounted for around 45 per cent of bishops, falling to a mere 25 per cent during the 1610s. However, it exceeded the 50 per cent mark for the first time in the 1620s, and rose steadily thereafter, reaching a temporary peak of 73 per cent in the 1640s, before falling slightly to 70 per cent in the last decade of the Mazarin ministry.

Variations on such a scale in the age at which men became bishops in this period suggest that explanations need to be sought in the realms of crown patronage and the pressures to which it was subject. Yet, despite the fluctuations that we have just observed, it is equally clear that the episcopate was becoming more homogeneous, at least in the sense that it was chosen increasingly from men in their thirties and forties. As with other features of the episcopate at this time, this process had its *temps forts* and *temps faibles*. It was during the 1630s that underaged bishops became virtually a thing of the past, with exceptions (none involving any nominee who was not in his early twenties at least) henceforth being made only for a handful of *amis du pouvoir*, while it was arguably during the 1640s that the biggest effort was made to recruit a mature episcopate. And, as we shall see later, these and other developments are a fairly faithful reflection of the evolution of royal episcopal patronage during the same period.

II

In sharp contrast to what we have just seen, the figures for the duration of episcopal careers appear to be far more constant. It will be evident from Table 8.4 that, on a decade-by-decade basis, the trend moves within a range of just over five years, which is approximately half of the range for the nomination ages. By this calculation, the average episcopal career for the bishops of the period as a whole was 23.7 years.

But, as we saw with the age at which men became bishops, there is no inevitable or marked trend towards longer episcopal tenure. The low average for those nominated in the 1590s, as indeed of the 1630s, is a corollary of their high average age at the time of appointment, and which in both cases entailed a greater than average number of episcopal tenures of less than ten years. In contrast, it is only to be expected that the large numbers of young bishops nominated in the 1610s and 1620s would enjoy longer careers than their immediate predecessors and successors, but even here the increase clearly did not correspond to the age differential at the outset of their careers. In relative terms, it was the bishops appointed in the 1640s and the 1650s who did best of all; despite the fact that the average age at nomination had been rising steadily since the 1620s, they still managed to enjoy careers that were lengthening past the twenty-five year mark for the first time. It is here that the data for the average age of bishops at death contained in Table 8.4 are of crucial importance. In particular they point to the demographic reasons why the young bishops of the 1600s and 1610s did not enjoy longer careers than their older successors, and why the latter did rather better. It would be idle to speculate about the variations in life expectancy for such a small group of geographically dispersed men as France's bishops, but after the *malheurs du temps* – epidemics, *mortalités*, and numerous forms of unrest – of the period

Table 8.4 *Career duration averages and their determinants*

Decade	Age at Provs	Career length	Age at Death
1589–1600	42.2	20.1	62.3
1600–10	35.5	24.7	60.2
1611–20	32.6	24.4	57.0
1621–30	38.9	24.3	63.2
1631–40	41.2	22.9	64.1
1641–50	40.1	24.0	64.1
1651–61	41.8	25.6	67.4
Average	38.9	23.7	62.6

stretching from the wars of religion to the Fronde, it seems reasonable to suppose that, for the bishops and the social élites generally, the conditions of life improved markedly in Louis XIV's France.

If the trend in the durations of bishops' careers is less fluctuating than that of their age at nomination, it is because demographic factors were its principal determinants. Therein lies the importance of the fact that episcopal resignations were relatively limited in number. Fifteen of the bishops in office on Henri IV's accession resigned in later years, all but two of them during Henri's reign itself. In contrast, thirty-six episcopal careers, involving just over one in every ten of the bishops appointed between 1589 and 1661, ended in this fashion, though it is also clear that a number of planned resignations were overtaken by the death of the bishops in question. No doubt the reasons why a bishop might decide to resign could vary considerably, but not enough information is available to classify the cases which we are dealing with here. However, a few observations on the resignations which did occur may help provide a wider perspective than a purely demographic one on the manner in which bishops' careers might end.

Firstly, of the thirty-six resignations which did take effect, four were forced upon the bishops in question. Unlike the sixteenth century, none was in any way connected to theological unorthodoxy or ecclesiastical irregularity; all four were occasioned by political activity, and specifically rebellion against the crown – Delbène of Albi and Saint-Bonnet of Nîmes for their part in the Languedoc revolt of 1632; Henri de Guise of Reims for his participation in the Bouillon-Soissons revolt of 1640–1; and lastly, the most celebrated of all, the resignation of the exiled Frondeur and archbishop of Paris, the Cardinal de Retz, in 1661. On the other hand, the deposition of René de Rieux of Saint-Pol-de-Léon in 1635 for complicity in Marie de' Medici's flight into exile, was set aside ten years later, and he died in office. In addition, it seems highly likely that a few other resignations were engineered by the 'masters' of the dioceses in question – as, for example, those of François Hyver of Luçon (around 1605) and André Frémiot of Bourges (1621), which were brought about by the Richelieu family and the prince of Condé respectively. Only one bishop resigned voluntarily in order to embark on a secular career: the unconsecrated Louis de Valois left the see of Agde in 1622 in order to become comte d'Alais and head of his house. The similarly unconsecrated Henri de Guise would undoubtedly have done the same and resigned from Reims in 1641 in order to become duc de Guise, but he was deposed before he could achieve his objective of ensuring Reims would remain in reliable hands – precisely what Louis XIII and Richelieu were most anxious to avoid.

As for the remaining resignations, which show no signs of *force majeure* at work, it would be tempting to consider them as acts of retirement. In the absence of direct evidence that would throw light on individual decisions, such an argument would have to be based on considerations of age. Here, however, the factual evidence is far from being what one might expect. Three bishops resigned while still in their twenties, four while in their thirties, which suggests either unsuitability for, or premature disenchantment with, episcopal office. On the other hand, it is likely that those resigning between the ages of forty and eighty were, in differing degrees, thinking mainly of retirement, although the fact that the largest single contingent among them, numbering eight in all, were only in their forties would tend to weaken the force of such an argument. No less significant is the fact that not one of the thirty-three genuinely aged bishops – crudely defined as those who were eighty or over at the time of death – retired. It is perhaps here that we can best see the weight of tradition, which disapproved in principle of episcopal resignations.[8] The Bishop of Sarlat resigned to a designated successor in 1623, but when he went to Rome to explain his decision to the pope, the latter refused to accept his reasons and ordered him back to his diocese, which he governed until his death in 1639.[9] But it was not principle alone which prevented bishops from leaving office. Resignations, especially when delayed too long, became objects of suspicion, particularly if there was any hint that an elderly bishop had been taken advantage of by family members, servants, or clerics with episcopal ambitions. We have already seen the problems which the paralysed bishop of Conserans, Bruno Ruade, created in the early 1640s when he attempted to resign his see to two contenders. Here as elsewhere, the suspicion was that his servants held him in thrall and had been bribed to extract a favourable decision from him. Other cases could be cited, not all relating to elderly bishops. Early in 1604, the mental health of Archbishop Albert de Bellièvre of Lyon, son of the chancellor of France but still in his

---

8 For a discussion of this question in a general European context for the eighteenth century, see Owen Chadwick, *The Popes and the European Revolution* (Oxford 1981), 184–5.

9 *Mémoires du clergé, ou recueil des actes, titres et mémoires concernant les affaires du clergé de France*, 15 vols (Paris 1771), xi, cols 659–61; *Chronique de Jean Tarde*, ed Gaston de Gérard (Paris 1887), 338–40. The bishop's would-be successor engaged in litigation in France to oblige him to honour his resignation, but after five years of effort he abandoned his case.

early thirties, collapsed, but it was strongly objected in Rome that he could not legally resign Lyon to a successor if he was not of sound mind; given the identity of the *dramatis personae*, it is hardly surprising that this argument was discreetly set aside in an effort to avoid embarrassment.[10] But for the great majority of Bellièvre's and Ruade's episcopal colleagues, their careers ended with their deaths, the very unpredictability of which directly affected the calculations of those in search of episcopal office and the crown's own ability to engineer, if we may paraphrase Richelieu on this subject, an episcopate 'à son souhait'.[11]

III

It might also be imagined that one reason why aged bishops did not need to retire was because there was a convenient alternative – that of taking on coadjutors who could be relied on to perform most of the essential functions of a diocesan. It is certainly the case that at least some of the bishops with coadjutors did retire in all but name well before death.[12] But others, possibly because they had not been especially willing to accept they needed a coadjutor in the first place, did not see why they should take a back seat, even when the coadjutor in question was a nephew or relative, and continued to hold all effective power in their diocese until their death. However, the fact remains that almost three-quarters of the aged bishops mentioned above were unwilling either to resign or to take on a coadjutor. In such circumstances, it is not to be wondered that rumours of the death or the terminal illness of elderly bishops circulated so often and so quickly throughout this period, precipitating lobbying and petitions by both powerful families and ambitious clerics with an interest in the succession.

Yet the fact that aged bishops did not always co-opt coadjutors who would duly succeed them does not close the file on the question of the presence of coadjutors among the episcopate. While not unknown, coadjutorships were even more uncommon in the sixteenth century than were suffragan bishops; in an age when both the crown and the papacy still tolerated a high turnover rate of dioceses through resignations, transfers and exchanges, coadjutorships probably did not appear especially useful to those involved. It was not in response to developments in France, let alone to problems arising from them, that the Council of Trent decreed that coadjutorships were only justified by

---

10   See below p 396.
11   Richelieu, *Testament politique*, ed Françoise Hildesheimer (Paris 1995), 89.
12   AD Nièvre, 3E1, vol 697, 24 Aug 1640, Bishop Eustache du Lis, on account of his great age, confers the temporal administration of Nevers on his nephew and coadjutor, Laurent de Chéry. Léger de Plas, bishop of Lectoure (1599–1635) took a coadjutor in 1609, and then retired to his native village for the last fifteen years of his life: Antoine Degert, 'Les Dernières années de Léger de Plas', *Revue de Gascogne*, n.s. 12 (1912), 27–37 .

their 'necessity and evident utility'. The subsequent reduction in practices such as episcopal pluralism, the holding of dioceses 'in administration', and the right of regress, gradually ensured that dioceses were less freely available than before. Coadjutorships only tended to be attractive in a context in which the underlying connection between bishops and their dioceses had become more stable. It is also possible that this attractiveness owed something to the fact that sixteenth-century France had also experienced a powerful reinforcement in patrimonial attitudes to the possession of secular office, especially through the mechanism of the *survivance*, and that this was in some way bound to affect attitudes towards church office.

At any rate, some fifty-four of the 351 bishops nominated between 1589 and 1661 began their careers as coadjutors. As with resignations, the number would have been higher had not arrangements for coadjutorial appointments been superseded by the death of the reigning bishops. Particular attention will be paid in later chapters to changes in coadjutorial nominations, on account of what they reveal of the attitudes of bishops, families, and the crown itself in relation to episcopal office. It will suffice to comment here on a few general features of this practice.

At the outset of Henri IV's reign, there were no coadjutors among the episcopate, and for much of his reign, Henri IV would not make nominations of this kind. But from the early 1600s onwards, this began to change; by the time of his death in May 1610, he had agreed to ten coadjutorships in all, and was engaged in initiating moves for at least two others. The overall total, representing less than 10 per cent of the 108 nominations in all made by Henri IV, may seem modest enough, but it should be noted that most of those which did take effect dated from the last three years of his reign. In this regard, the record of Louis XIII's reign offers both contrast and continuity. No fewer than thirty-five (or over 20 per cent) of the 154 bishops nominated under him began their careers as coadjutors – probably the highest proportion of the entire *ancien régime*. In fact, two-thirds of these coadjutors were nominated in less than a single decade, the 1610s, and to that extent they may be seen as accelerating a development dating from the final years of Henri IV's reign. As might be expected, the inflation of coadjutorships elicited a strong reaction from the papacy and reformist elements in the French church, as a result of which the number of coadjutorships dropped substantially, especially from the 1630s onwards. The four decades from the 1620s onwards produced fewer coadjutors than the 1610s alone – twenty-one against twenty-three.

These statistics are indicative of a significant change in attitudes towards the transmission of episcopal office. The large numbers of coadjutors appointed in the 1610s were not really intended to assist the genuinely old members of the existing episcopate, but to fulfil family ambitions. A substantial number of them were underage, and had to wait several years before obtaining their provisions; they were also the least likely to proceed quickly to consecration, without which a coadjutor was wholly incapable of assisting a reigning bishop. Although similar family ambitions are evident in the nomination of coadjutors in the 1640s and 1650s, they were by now older at the time of nomination; underage candidates were the exception, and indeed their average age was no longer markedly out of line with that of other episcopal nominees. Since the 1630s, all incoming coadjutors were at least subdeacons, and most of them were priests, and not mere clerics or even students still at the threshold of their careers. For these reasons, the whole process of becoming a consecrated coadjutor-bishop was considerably speedier than a generation earlier. Changes are also visible in the way in which coadjutorial nominations were handled, especially in Rome. During the 1610s, depositions made to the papal enquiries into newly nominated coadjutors to the effect that a reigning bishop was advancing in years or in some way incapacitated, constituted the only real evidence of whether there was a genuine need for a coadjutor. Over a generation later, such laisser-faire seemed out of season. In 1653, it was the dean and chapter of Vienne who formally vouched for the illness and incapacity of their archbishop, Pierre de Villars.[13] In 1657, Nicolas Grillié of Uzès, aged sixty-six and suffering from failing eyesight and a speech defect (a serious blow to a highly regarded preacher like him), also sought a coadjutor. In order to ensure a favourable outcome, he submitted a certificate from two doctors of the Paris medical faculty, the text of which was duly authenticated for transmission to Rome by the vicar-general of Paris.[14] A year later, Dominique Séguier, bishop of Meaux and brother of the chancellor of France, wished to take his nephew as coadjutor, but the Roman consistorial congregation charged with preparing episcopal confirmations was not satisfied with the dossier it received.[15] It commissioned a separate enquiry into the Meaux succession, and although a medical certificate from a Paris doctor was produced, the congregation (which had also examined the Grillié case with considerable care)[16] insisted on establishing the 'utility' of giving the ageing Séguier a coadjutor.[17] Taken together, these developments ensured that coadjutor bishops would be as indistinguishable from reigning bishops as the difference between them in

---

13   ASV, PC 53, fo 245, certificate of 1 July 1653. Villars himself wrote to Innocent X to explain his decision: ASV, Lettere de Vescovi 25, fo 387, 30 June 1653.
14   ASV, PC 56, fo 379, certificate of 8 June 1657, itemising Grillié's ailments, and to which Grillié himself referred in general terms in his act of resignation: fo 375, 11 May 1657.
15   *Ibid*, fos 28–44, enquiry conducted by papal nuncio, 17 Jan 1658.
16   *Ibid*, fo 372, for the consistorial congregation's discussion and recommendations, 15 Dec 1657. Yet his coadjutor, Jacques de Grignan, bishop of Saint-Paul-Trois-Châteaux, was not approved until Sept 1658.
17   ASV, Processus Datariae 37, 7 Dec 1658, unfoliated dossier inserted after fo 157. This contains the medical certificate, dated 19 Jan 1658, but it is not clear if it had been submitted with the original text of the enquiry. Séguier was thought to be nearly seventy years old, but was in fact sixty-five in 1658, a discrepancy which could easily have been designed to strengthen the argument for a coadjutor.

status would allow. That they should have virtually disappeared during Louis XIV's personal rule comes as no great surprise.

IV

Thus far the discussion of episcopal careers has been conducted in something of a void, as if questions of age, career duration, and so on were of interest purely in their own right. However, their real significance will only emerge if they are related to the dioceses which received them and experienced their rule, however long or short their tenure might be. It was noted earlier in this chapter that the average diocese was host to three incumbents between Henri IV's accession and the death of Mazarin. As a first step in linking bishops to dioceses, we may turn to the map of France's dioceses in order to determine which of them most fully corresponded to, or diverged from, this average. Before doing so, it should also be pointed out that to say there were 351 bishops nominated between 1589 and early 1661 is not the same as saying that between them France's dioceses experienced 351 episcopal reigns in same period. That figure needs to be substantially augmented in two ways. Firstly, we should add the 98 bishops who were still in office at the time of Henri IV's formal accession in 1589. Admittedly, some of them had only a nominal hold on their dioceses or did not survive for very long into his reign, but others continued in office until the 1610s and 1620s, with one of them (Péricard of Avranches) enduring until 1639. But as every episcopal generation comprised a greater or lesser number of bishops from previous ones, there is nothing unusual about the numbers just cited.

More pertinent for our present purposes is the need to take account of the number of bishops who moved from one diocese to another during the same period; they, too, include some bishops who were already in office before Henri IV's reign. We should even include among them the one bishop, Charles Miron of Angers who, having first resigned his diocese in 1616, returned to it six years later when his successor died, before spending the last two years of his life as archbishop of Lyon. Altogether this exercise in aggregation (pre-Henri IV bishops plus transfers of all kinds) produces a much larger corpus, one with a total of 515 episcopal reigns (including coadjutors and unconsecrated but ruling bishops) in our period. From a purely arithmetical angle, this means that the average diocese was host to 4.5 rather than 3.1 bishops between 1589 and 1661.

An initial impression of the actual variations in the tenure of dioceses can be gleaned from the accompanying table and maps.

The first of the two columns of figures (Table 8.5) includes *all* bishops actually holding dioceses between 1589 and 1661, regardless of when they took up office. It will be evident from the table that the purely arithmetical

Table 8.5 *Numbers of bishops per diocese 1589–1661*

No of bishops	All bishops	Bishops nominated post 1589
1	0	1 (0.8)
2	4 (3.5)	23 (20.3)
3	20 (17.6)	33 (29.2)
4	33 (29.2)	31 (27.4)
5	34 (30)	19 (16.8)
6	19 (16.8)	6 (5.3)
7	3 (2.6)	0 (0)

Figures in brackets represent percentages. Because the episcopate was numerically relatively complete in 1589, the figures for three bishops in column one should be compared with those for two bishops in column two, those for four in column one with those for three in column two, and so on.

average of 4.5 bishops per diocese calculated above is not without foundation, since 67 out of the 113 dioceses had either four or five bishops during this period. In turn, this substantial, well-balanced cluster of averages (34 and 33 respectively) fits well into a wider pattern which shows, as a glance at the rest of the table reveals, that the 'spread' of episcopal reigns on either side of the cluster was itself remarkably symmetrical. Only four dioceses had as few as two bishops in all, a quite remarkable achievement made somewhat easier in three cases by the fact that they were vacant for several years at the beginning of Henri IV's reign. At the opposite end of the spectrum, only three dioceses, Lyon and the contiguous Provençal dioceses of Aix and Riez, were occupied by as many as seven bishops in the same period (see Map 5).

If we turn our attention to the second column of figures which deals solely with patterns of tenure among the bishops nominated between Henri IV's accession and Mazarin's death, it will be evident that there was relatively little overall change, except at the margins where a variation of a few figures either way can appear seriously to alter the percentages showing in the first column. But such variations are insignificant if compared with the sixty-four dioceses which had either three or four bishops, a figure which corresponds closely to the sixty-seven with four or five in the previous column. The only diocese to stand entirely alone here is that of Viviers, to which only one bishop was appointed in our period! Indeed, it was governed by just two bishops between 1573 and 1690, itself a quite extraordinary record. The second of them, Louis de la Baume de Suze, was the son of a noble family which had long controlled the diocese. Nominated as coadjutor in 1613, when he was aged only eleven, he obtained his provisions in 1617 by concealing his real age, but then proceeded to rule Viviers alone from 1621 to 1690; at his death,

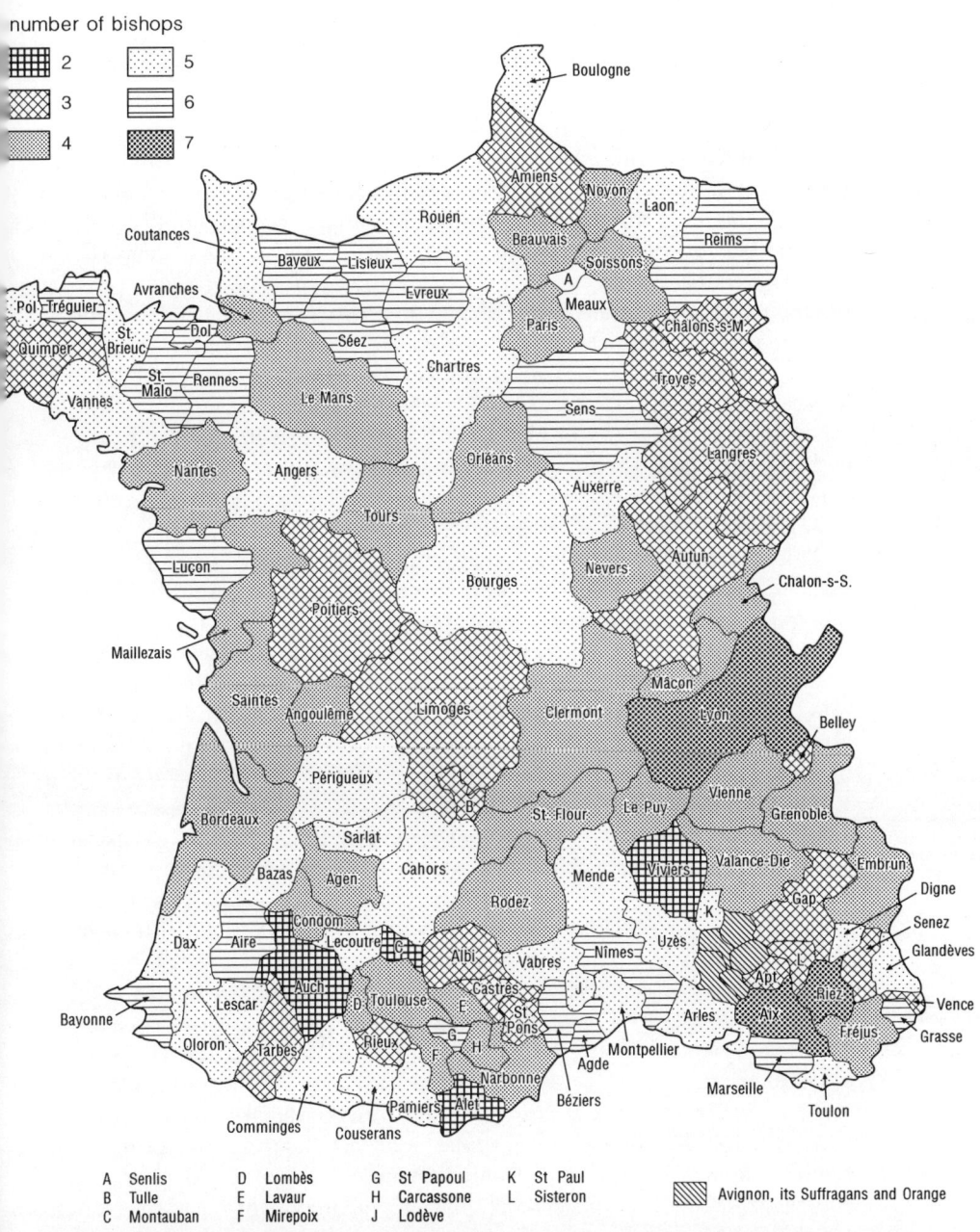

5 *All bishops per diocese, 1589–1661*

he was thought to be the longest-serving bishop in Christendom![18] At the other end of the spectrum, six dioceses — widely scattered and on the periphery of the kingdom without necessarily being insignificant for all that — were host to no fewer than six new bishops between 1589 and 1661 (see Map 6).

This brief sketch of the broad patterns of episcopal tenure can be complemented by considering the factors which, in addition to the demographic ones, ensured that dioceses would have either more or fewer bishops than the average. Foremost among them is the question of episcopal mobility, which can first be studied in relation to dioceses rather than to the bishops themselves. Overall, it emerges that less than 40 per cent of dioceses attracted a reigning bishop from elsewhere during this period, and that of the thirty-eight which did, only eleven managed to do so more than once. Indeed, by this reckoning, France's most desirable dioceses were Sens and Lisieux, attracting three apiece (see Map 7). To this statistic may be added the somewhat unusual cases of the six dioceses which were subject to direct exchanges between three pairs of ruling bishops, although these 'permutations' say far less about the relative attractiveness of the dioceses themselves than about the motives of the individual bishops who effected them.

This leaves a total of no fewer than seventy-five dioceses which at no time managed to tempt a ruling bishop to migrate there. Yet it would be inaccurate to regard these dioceses as somehow 'equal' for all that. It is possible to make an initial distinction between them by recording which dioceses saw their own bishops move elsewhere and how often this occurred, bearing in mind, of course, that the effect of every move was to increase the number of bishops governing the dioceses in question. A total of twenty-eight dioceses belong in this category. A majority of them (sixteen) only lost one bishop in this way, while ten lost two, and a mere two lost three. By this reckoning, the least popular dioceses in France were Bayonne and Aire, both in the extreme south-west, but a glance at the map shows that virtually all of these twenty-eight dioceses were geographically peripheral, and evidently the fact that some of them were relatively wealthy could not dissuade their bishops from seeking to move elsewhere (see Map 8).

Dioceses attracting and dioceses losing bishops are not totally unconnected, however, since a total of seven (Rennes, Evreux, Chartres, Nantes, Maillezais, Bayonne and Agde) experienced both types of movement. The only diocese to emerge from a comparison with a net gain was Evreux, which lost one but attracted two bishops; all of the others either managed a zero-sum parity or, like Maillezais and Bayonne, were net 'losers'. If we bring these figures together, it appears that only fifty-nine (52.2 per cent) dioceses had experience of any kind of episcopal movement, inward or outward. No less worth noting is how limited was the movement which did occur: of the fifty-

---

18 *Hierarchia Catholica*, iv. 284, 'Pompeiopolitan', n 2.

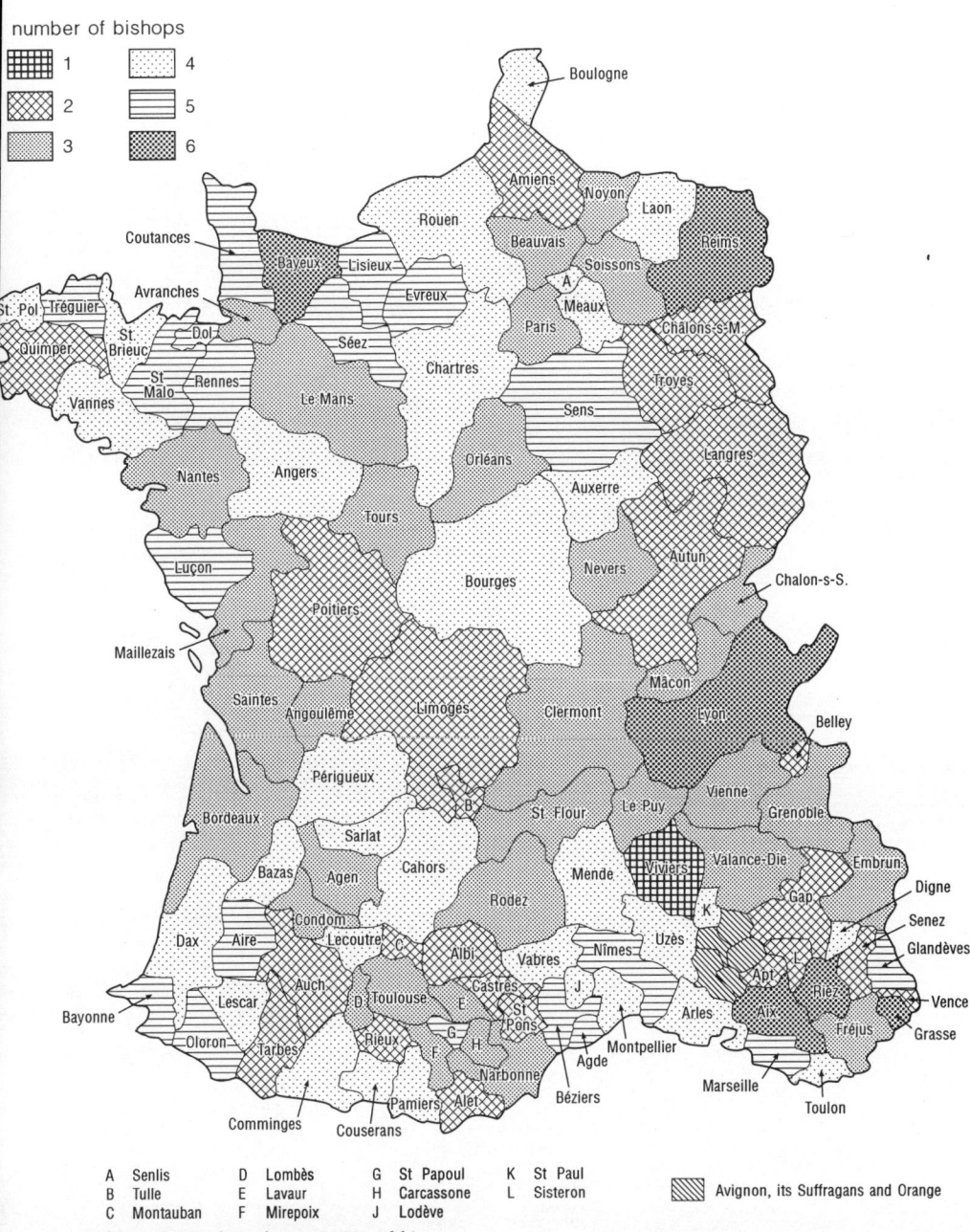

6 Bishops nominated per diocese, 1589–1661

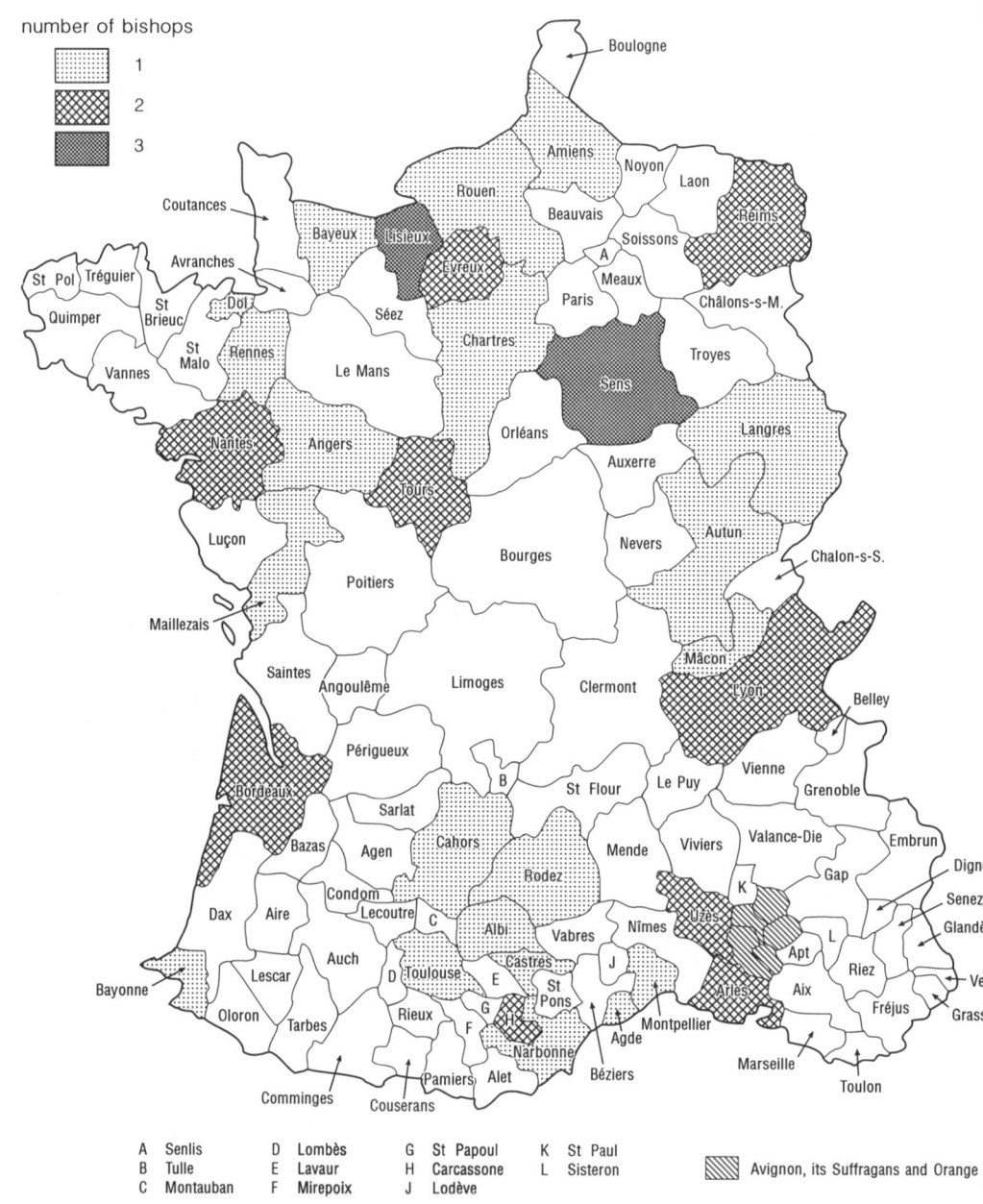

7 *Dioceses attracting reigning bishops*

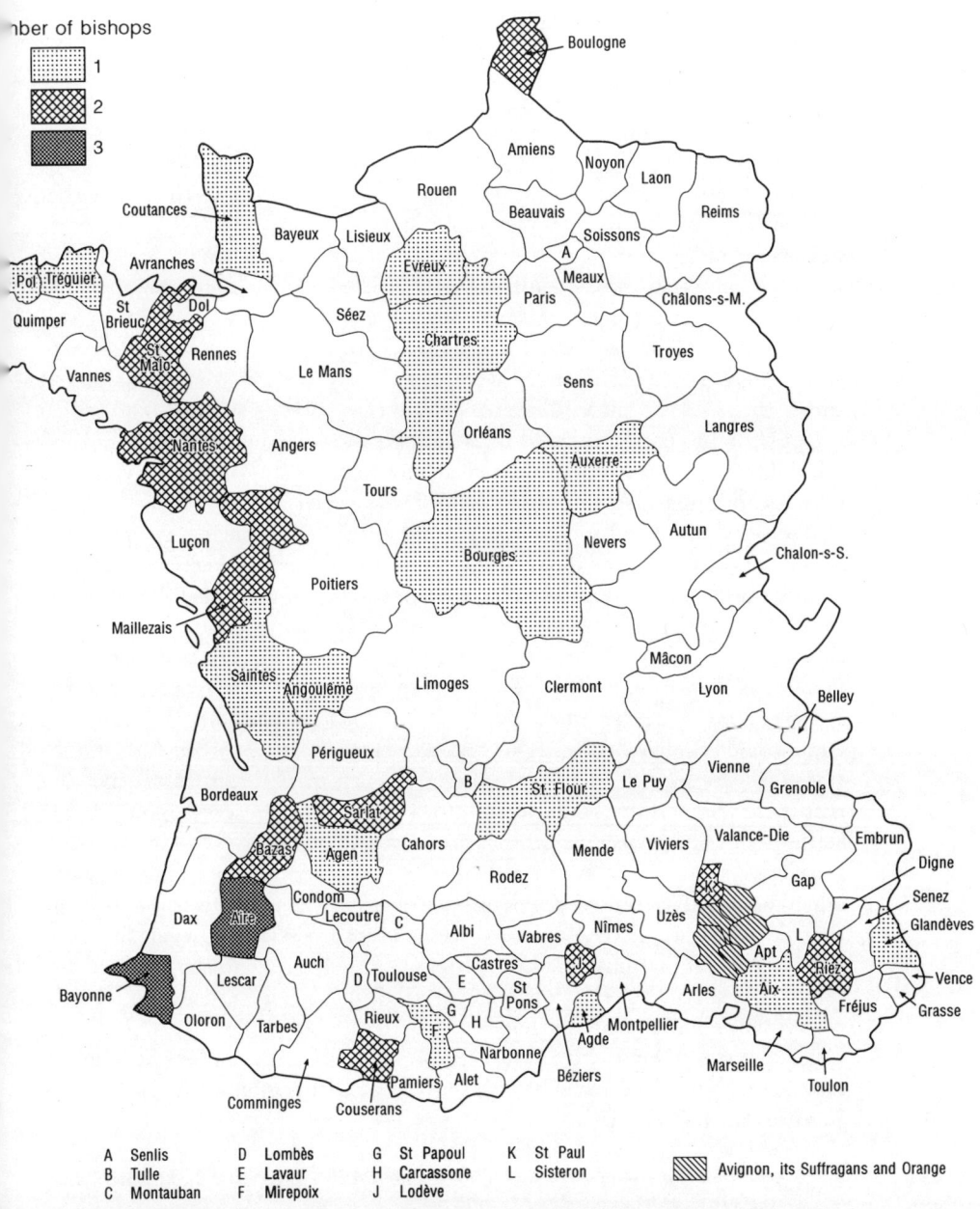

8 *Dioceses losing bishops*

nine dioceses in question, thirty-seven experienced only one transfer, inward or outward, while four dioceses shared the record for the highest totals for arriving or departing bishops – a mere three!

No less pertinent are the conclusions to be drawn from a further brief comparison of the two sets of dioceses. Both included sees which would be regarded as being of the first rank by any standards. Reims, Rouen and Lyon all attracted reigning bishops, but in this period Auch and Paris still remained beyond the grasp of ruling bishops, as indeed did all but one of the remaining five northern sees which had a peerage attached to it. Another comparison, based mainly on geographical location and revenues, of the more run-of-the-mill sees in both groups, leads to a similar conclusion, namely that while contemporaries were fully aware of differences in status, wealth, and other amenities from one diocese to another, there was not, at least during this period, anything resembling the tier-like structure of the Castilian episcopate, where particular dioceses were consciously treated as stepping-stones along the road to more desirable bishoprics. While successful Castilian bishops might commonly hold between two and four dioceses before achieving their ultimate ambitions, it is clear that the French bishop who managed to extricate himself from his first diocese was exceptional.[19]

If a formal ladder of success had existed within the French episcopate, one would expect to find the fifteen (fourteen until 1622 when Paris was elevated to this status) archbishoprics to have played a regular and pivotal part in the transfers. A total of forty-one archiepiscopal nominations were made during this period, a figure which is roughly in line with the rate of nominations to France's bishoprics as a whole. Twelve of these nominations favoured reigning bishops, and a further three were of archbishops (Beaune, Joyeuse, and Alphonse de Richelieu) clearly in search of better pastures.[20] But these fifteen transfers were scattered randomly throughout the period as a whole, showing that there was as yet no intention on the crown's part to reserve archiepiscopal status to existing bishops whose capacity and reliability had been found satisfactory and, therefore, that there was no perception that archiepiscopal office necessarily required previous episcopal experience. It was only during the 1620s that a different approach seemed a real possibility, when six out of the fifteen nominations (coadjutorships included) to archbishoprics were of reigning bishops, but this was not sustained in subsequent decades. Overall, the evidence points to archbishoprics being treated no differently to other sees – they were as likely to be given to young ecclesiastics, members of religious orders, or even to men who were heavily dependent on powerful nobles like Joyeuse, Crillon, or Condé.

19   See the tables for episcopal mobility in the mainly Castilian dioceses studied by Maximilano Barrio Gozalo, 'Perfil de una élite de poder', *Anthologica Annua*, 30–1 (1983–4), 241; 32 (1985), 56; 33 (1986), 217; 34 (1987), 80; 38 (1991), 61.
20   In the case of Joyeuse, it will be recalled, this was less true, since he kept his previous archbishopric of Toulouse.

There were several possible reasons why archbishoprics were treated in this way. Their geographical location or their limited financial endowment reduced the attractiveness of some of them such as Bourges or Embrun, while it was widely held that the parlements of Aix and Toulouse quite deliberately made life impossible for their archbishops. Equally importantly, a number of archbishoprics were successfully cornered for two or more generations by particular families – Paris by the Gondis, Vienne by the Villars, Reims by the Guise, Rouen by the Harlay – something which they also had in common with several 'ordinary' dioceses. Consequently, the temptation to 'reserve' them in advance of a vacancy through coadjutorships was naturally pursued by these families, but also by other ecclesiastics and their patrons. It is significant in this regard that thirteen of the forty-one archiepiscopal nominations were of a coadjutorial type, and that nine of them were in favour of individuals aiming to succeed a family member in the see or, as with the Guises at Reims, to recover a see traditionally held by family members. The most unusual coadjutor-archbishops were surely Victor Bouthillier and François Fouquet, both of whom abandoned their previous bishoprics in order to secure archiepiscopal status at some indeterminate future date.

To understand the episcopal transfers which did occur in this period, we must also look at other factors, focusing on the behaviour of bishops rather than on any inbuilt traditions of tenure or mobility. Between 1589 and 1661 an overall total of fifty-two transfers of bishops occurred. As on so many other issues, the statistic is not a clear-cut one, for reasons which derive from the unexpected variety which characterises the movement of bishops and which sheds some unusual light on contemporary practices. Firstly, it is slightly inflated by the fact that six of these moves were occasioned, as we have seen, by three direct exchanges of dioceses between reigning bishops. Secondly, the period also witnessed a number of 'paper' transfers which never actually took effect, and which have been discounted. For example, Christophe de Lestang, bishop of Lodève, obtained the see of Alet in 1594, but he was either unable or unwilling to set foot there, and in the end he gave up Lodève, which he still nominally held, in return for Carcassonne in 1603; it is the latter exchange which should be regarded as a genuine one, not the former. Thirdly, although not included in the figure because it is of a slightly different order, we may also note here three cases of retired bishops making a comeback to their original dioceses. Only one of the three, that of Charles Miron to Angers in 1621, was a clear case of a bishop arguing that he was entitled to recover his diocese by the ancient right of regress, now that his direct successor was dead.[21] The other two cases witnessed bishops returning from contrasting forms of involuntary 'retirement' – René de Rieux had been stripped of Saint-Pol-de-Léon in 1635, while Denis Cohon had abandoned Nîmes in 1644 (and

---

21 The right of regress had in theory been suppressed by the Council of Trent, and was followed by the Ordonnances de Blois: François Pérard-Castel, *Traité sommaire de l'usage et pratique de la Cour de Rome*, 2nd ed (Paris 1717), 373–4.

then Dol in 1648) because of his unpopularity and isolation. On the other hand, a bishop like Jean de Lingendes, who resigned Sarlat in 1647 and then accepted the nomination to Mâcon in late 1650, properly belongs in the category of mobile bishops, although his transfer was punctuated by a period of 'retirement'. Moreover, an unquantifiable number of bishops had a claim, if not actual papal provisions, to a particular diocese, which they subsequently proceeded to exchange for another, more attractive diocese, but it would be a mistake to regard them as genuine transfers. Once papal provisions had been obtained and paid for, there was an obvious financial deterrent to rapid movement to another diocese, one which could only be overcome if bishops enjoyed powerful patronage and could look forward to holding a much wealthier see. Frequently undocumented, this kind of bargaining forms the wider setting in which the exchanging of dioceses took place; it cannot count for our purposes as entailing formal transfers from one diocese to another, but it should not be ignored altogether, if only because it was often the reason for otherwise unexplained delays in filling vacant dioceses. Henri de Béthune's father might have protested fiercely in 1626 against the offer of Bayonne to his son, but he was not foolish enough to reject it out of hand; instead, his son formally accepted the nomination, and held onto it, apparently without attempting to obtain his provisions, until 1629 when the opportunity arose to trade in his title in exchange for Maillezais, a less remote and far better endowed diocese.

Looking at these figures in personal rather than diocesan terms, it emerges that the period under study here saw fifty bishops in all abandon their first diocese.[22] Eight of these men had become bishops under Henri III or Charles IX. The remaining forty-two represent just over one-eighth of the bishops nominated between 1589 and 1661, though it should be noted that a further eighteen of them, all nominated during the Mazarin ministry, were to change diocese during Louis XIV's personal rule. Philippe Cospeau and François Fouquet were the only ones who had the distinction of moving twice during this period, though a further six of Mazarin's appointees eventually caught up with them during the personal rule. Yet no matter how we combine these figures and the percentages that they represent, the overall conclusion will be the same – that there was a remarkably low level of movement within the episcopate.

A closer analysis of the chronology and nature of the transfers may offer some initial indications of why this was so. It might be thought that under Henri IV, when civil war had given rise to serious divisions within many dioceses between bishops and local authorities, especially in cathedral towns, that there would have been fairly extensive transfers or exchanges of this kind.

22 This figure excludes three bishops who were brought into a French diocese from one not part of the French church as understood at the time. They were Horatio Montano who came to Arles from Penna in Italy in 1598, and Jean-Vincent de Tulles and Hyacinthe Serroni, both of whom were originally bishops of Orange.

In fact, the total for his reign was a modest one of eleven in all. Of these, only three transfers (those of Cardinal Givry from Lisieux, Lestang from Lodève and Bourgneuf from Saint-Malo) were a direct result of a desire to leave dioceses which bishops no longer controlled or where they no longer felt welcome. Five transfers involved the crown extending its patronage to reward political support or services in the last phase of the wars from the likes of Charles de Bourbon-Navarre, Jacques du Perron, Renaud de Beaune, Philippe du Bec and Arnaud d'Ossat. The last transfer under Henri IV was in fact an exchange between two bishops, and it neatly combined two elements that we have just seen: La Rochefoucauld of Clermont, a former *ligueur* now returned to favour and elevated to the rank of cardinal, moved to Senlis and nearer the court, while Antoine Rose, bishop of Senlis and successor to the notorious *ligueur* Guillaume Rose, sought refuge from incident and harassment in the cardinal's distant see of Clermont. Finally, the transfer of Cardinal Joyeuse from Toulouse to Rouen in 1604 bears a superficial resemblance to those of Beaune, du Perron, or Ossat, but it was more complex than any of them and was in several respects *sui generis*. Joyeuse was the last remaining male member of his house and the inheritor of its political influence; with his brother-in-law, Montpensier, ensconced as governor of Normandy, tenure of Rouen, rich and far closer to court than Toulouse, was an alluring prospect. Nor was Joyeuse required to give up his previous see of Toulouse in order to claim Rouen; like French cardinals of earlier generations, he was an unrepentant pluralist.

Thus the transfers effected under Henri IV were limited and, with three exceptions, essentially promotions effected with crown sponsorship of prominent churchmen. This impression is confirmed by looking at the figures from a different angle: only eight of Henri IV's own 108 appointees changed their diocese – three during his reign, and all but one of the remaining five under Louis XIII.[23] The king's own ability or willingness to use this type of royal patronage to reshape the episcopate thus did not go very far. Around 1600, he seemed fully determined to transfer or force the resignation of Bishop Corneilhan of Rodez, given the enduring hostility between him and the municipal authorities, but Corneilhan stood his ground and Henri soon abandoned his plans.[24]

The proportion of transfers during Louis XIII's reign was not markedly higher, but that it formed part of a rising curve is clear when it is placed alongside the evidence from the years of Mazarin's ministry. By now normal

---

23 The exception was Charles de Noailles who retained his first diocese of Saint-Flour until 1646 when he moved to Rodez, only to die in 1648.

24 *Recueil de lettres missives de Henri IV*, ed X Berger de Xivrey and J Guadet, 9 vols (Paris 1843–76), ix, 228, Henri IV to Montmorency, undated: 'J'ay ceu tant de partycularytés de ce quy est antre les habytans de ma vylle de Rodès et de l'evesque, que ie ne panse pas quyls ce puyssent jamès rejoyndre. C'est pourquoy je continue an ceste resolusyson que l'evesque commue son diocèse . . . vous pryant, mon compère, y dysposer l'evesque et luy fere comprendre que c'est mon yntansyon.'

episcopal tenure had been restored to dioceses which had often been vacant or held in varying degrees of irregularity under Henri III or even Henri IV, an improvement which should have made transfers of a more 'ordinary', careerist kind objectively easier to envisage. At any rate, between 1610 and 1643, there were eighteen transfers which involved just seventeen bishops, an average of approximately one for every two, rather than for every three, years as under Henri IV. The Mazarin ministry witnessed twenty-three transfers involving twenty-two bishops, an average in excess of one per year. Moreover, a comparison of the record of the bishops actually appointed during each reign gives a sharper sense of increasing mobility. Where only eight of the bishops nominated by Henri IV moved to another diocese, twenty-seven of those appointed under Louis XIII did so, a figure matched exactly by those promoted by Mazarin even though three-quarters of these latter had to wait until after the cardinal's death before taking up their new diocese.

To the extent that no bishop could be compelled, even by the crown, to accept a lesser diocese than the one he already held, it seems platitudinous to describe all transfers as in some way promotions. Yet some subtle differences can be gleaned from the surviving evidence. In some respects, bishops engaged in exchanges probably represent the optimum vantage-point for the purpose of weighing up losses and gains, but there were simply too few of them to allow any wide-ranging conclusions. Two of the three cases of this type involved one party (Antoine Rose of Senlis, Denis Cohon of Nîmes) who was anxious to abandon his existing diocese, and who may be taken to have done less well than their partner in the exchange.[25] Yet even in these cases, each party obviously expected some kind of gain, however asymmetrical or dissimilar it might be. François de Donadieu, who exchanged his see of Auxerre with Gilles de Souvré for that of Comminges in 1624–5, was apparently under no pressure to move, and the initial prospect was a highly attractive one – that of returning to his native region, where his brother was bishop of Saint-Papoul, while Comminges itself was much wealthier than Auxerre. Although he soon regretted his decision, it was too late to withdraw and he was outmanoeuvred by Souvré in the negotiations which followed.[26] For his part, Souvré, as befitted the son of one of Henri IV's closest compan-

---

25 Rose of Senlis had succeeded his uncle in a small, easily governed diocese close to Paris, whereas his new diocese of Clermont was enormous and difficult to manage. Cohon, originally from Le Mans, admittedly moved closer to his geographical origins by leaving Nîmes for Dol, but Hector Douvrier was a Toulousain for whom Nîmes, despite its turbulent Protestant population, represented a real coup.

26 Donadieu resigned his claim to Comminges to his nephew, Barthélemy de Griet de Donadieu, even before his papal provisions arrived, but then went on effectively to administer Comminges on his nephew's behalf! See E Molinier, *La Vie de Messire Barthélemy de Donadieu de Griet, evesque de Comenge* (Paris 1639), 144–78; Abbé Lebeuf, *Mémoires concernant l'histoire civile et ecclésiastique d'Auxerre et de son ancien diocèse*, 4 vols (Paris 1848–55), ii. 214–16. Documents relating to this affair are in AN, MC, VI, 431, 10 Mar, 8 Apr 1625; vol 432, 28 Sept 1625; vol 433, 15 Apr 1626.

ions, was also extremely well endowed with valuable abbeys, and so he could easily afford to accept a less wealthy see, not least because of its unquantifiable advantages: Auxerre was much less peripheral than Pyrenean Comminges, and it offered attractive opportunities for political activity in a *pays d'états* like Burgundy.

But for the great majority of 'simple' transfers, the advantages which bishops might have envisaged cannot be approached in this way. Perhaps the nearest in kind to those just observed were those of the ten or so bishops who changed diocese in this period primarily because the conflicts they encountered within their first dioceses impelled them to look elsewhere. Five cases of this occurred at the end of the religious wars, and entailed either political animosity (Nantes, Saint-Malo and Senlis) or a hostile occupation of the episcopal temporalities (Lodève and Lisieux). But such problems did not disappear entirely in subsequent decades, as we saw in the case of Cohon at Nîmes, even if they lacked the specific characteristics of the conflicts of the League. As late as the 1650s, embattled bishops like Dony of Riez and La Vallette of Mirepoix, both obtained transfers to other dioceses; in both cases, it was claimed that their zeal as reformers had stirred up local animosity, but it seems likely that there were political reasons for Dony's transfer.[27] However, if every bishop who faced such local hostility had succeeded in transferring to another diocese, total episcopal mobility in seventeenth-century France would have been several times greater. Most bishops faced with such problems had to live with them; it was only a well connected minority which could escape them by changing their diocese.[28]

In one sense, this is underlined by the fact that the great majority of those who did obtain a transfer had to wait many years for the opportunity to do so; nothing distinguishes the French episcopate more sharply from its Castilian counterpart than the slow, often *ad hoc* nature of episcopal transfers. The record for brevity of tenure was held by Alphonse de Richelieu who spent only two years at Aix before his brother secured the primatial see of Lyon for him. Nicolas Grillié and Gaspar de Daillon had served only marginally longer terms at Bazas and Agen when the 1632 revolt in Languedoc precipitated their transfer to Uzès and Albi respectively, where political and ecclesiastical control needed to be restored. The same considerations brought a rapid change of diocese after the Fronde for Mazarin allies like Pierre de Marca (from Conserans to Toulouse after four years) and François Faure (from Glandèves to Amiens after two years). But for the majority, not excluding

---

27 BAV, Barb lat 7961, fo 59, Dony to Cardinal Francesco Barberini, 8 June 1652.
28 Samuel Martineau of Bazas left his diocese during the Fronde because of the hostility of the duc d'Epernon, and later suffered from that of the parlement of Bordeaux. But it was in vain that he asked Mazarin in 1659 to transfer him to the Breton see of Dol: René Toujas, 'Les Démêlés de Samuel Martineau évêque de Bazas (1646–1667) avec le parlement de Bordeaux', *Actes du 104ᵉ Congrès National des Sociétés Savantes: Section d'histoire moderne et contemporaine*, ii (Paris 1981), 51–62.

those who enjoyed political support at court or in the ministry, the wait could be a long one; only about one-third of the bishops who changed diocese managed to do so less than ten years after entering the episcopate. Even the two dioceses which had the highest number (three) of bishops transferring elsewhere, Bayonne and Aire, still managed to retain them for an average of eleven and fifteen years respectively.

However, none of this should disguise the fact that the majority of transfers can unambiguously be described as promotions. We have already noted the twelve nominations which had the effect of raising reigning bishops to the rank of archbishop. Nor should we overlook the three existing archbishops who also moved, with two of them trading less prominent for better placed archbishoprics. More unexpected is the behaviour of the five reigning bishops (Cardinal Givry, Victor Bouthillier, Nicolas Sévin, François Fouquet, and Jacques de Grignan) who left their original dioceses in order to serve for an indeterminate period as coadjutor to an elderly bishop! But in each case, the paradox is only superficial, the logic of the choice the same – *reculer pour mieux sauter*. They gave up an insignificant, troublesome, or peripheral diocese in the knowledge that after a period of reduced activity, a far more attractive future beckoned. As for the remaining transfers, they exhibit few distinguishing features, and generally entailed not one but a varying combination of concerns, ranging from geographical advantage to the attractions of a richer or more prestigious see.

V

Lengthening careers (the rising age of accession to office notwithstanding) and a correspondingly slow turnover of episcopal generations: these were two of the major reasons for the limited nature of episcopal mobility and for the peculiar shapes it took during this period. There was another which is perhaps less decisive, but which is of particular interest for reasons which extend far beyond its impact on episcopal mobility. This is the persistence of particular family interests within the upper reaches of the French church. The phenomenon has already been alluded to in a number of specific contexts, but it requires more systematic consideration, not least from the perspective of continuity and discontinuity in the tenure of dioceses over succeeding generations. To what extent were certain dioceses the preserve of particular families? How many families, broadly speaking, could normally expect to contribute to the episcopate? To put it at its most provocative – was there, in this period, an ecclesiastical version of 'la France des deux cent familles'? The answers that follow here will be limited to suggesting general patterns, since later chapters will devote attention to many of the precise circumstances of the changes that did occur.

Changes over time mean that no single approach or set of figures can fully convey the extent of the quasi-dynastic connections within the episcopate. Many of them emerge at a given moment, only to disappear again after a relatively short period of time. Sometimes these lines are discontinuous, temporarily broken by the conditions of the wars of religion, the vagaries of royal goodwill, or the difficulties experienced by the families themselves in sustaining them. These discontinuous forms of family presence in the episcopate pose further problems, as they do not fit into conventional categories; above all, in the absence of satisfactory family histories, they are the most difficult to explain convincingly.

With these caveats in mind, the most useful starting point for discussion would seem to entail a rapid tour of France's dioceses in search of those which experienced what might be called quasi-dynastic successions. These latter are taken here to mean the unbroken tenure of a bishopric by at least two members of the same family which, given the celibate character of the episcopate, should include members from both paternal and maternal lines. To prevent the analysis from remaining a static one, it is perhaps best to begin with those two-generational episcopal tenures which straddled the late Valois-early Bourbon divide, and in which a bishop appointed under Charles IX or Henri III was succeeded by a family member under Henri IV or, more rarely, Louis XIII. At least thirty, or just over a quarter of all dioceses, fall into this category. This may not seem a particularly large proportion, but like every snap-shot statistic, it does not tell the full story. Firstly, at least five more successions of this kind had been arranged at various times during the reigns of Henri IV or Louis XIII, and would have taken effect had four coadjutor-bishops not died before their 'predecessors', and had the fifth not been obliged by intense local hostility to move to a different diocese. Secondly, the figure obviously cannot take account of the extent to which a proportion of the bishops seated under Henri III and Henri IV were caretakers installed by families which were temporarily unable to provide a bishop of their own, but who were sufficiently powerful – and determined – to impose a bishop of their own choice and on their terms. It is probable that up to fifteen bishops of the late sixteenth and early seventeenth century can be regarded as fitting this description. No doubt, the intention of such families was to recover the dioceses in question by installing one of their members as bishop in the next generation. This did indeed happen in several cases, but in others the longevity and, albeit less frequently, the resourcefulness of the incumbent bishops, as well as the changing climate of politics and royal patronage, frustrated their ambitions.

A comparison between this situation and that which obtained at the end of Mazarin's régime, offers a simple yardstick by which to measure the staying-power of these episcopal 'dynasties'. Of the original thirty, only four were now left – the Bonsis at Béziers, the Gondis at Paris, the Villars at Vienne, the Salignac at Sarlat. In fact, only the first three of them had survived intact throughout the entire period, but by 1661 the Gondis were on the point of losing Paris for good because of the politics of the Cardinal de Retz; as for the last of the four, that of Sarlat, there had been a twenty-year interruption of Salignac tenure there between 1639 and 1659, when the isthmus was finally repaired with the nomination of François de Salignac, uncle of Fénélon. The collapse in the number of episcopal dynasties based in the same diocese could hardly be more spectacular, but its interpretation is anything but straightforward.

Further scrutiny of the four episcopal dynasties just cited may open up some lines of explanation. It is particularly interesting that the three families who were successful in keeping an uninterrupted grip on the same diocese were, despite their ambition and titles, not long-standing members of a putative provincial aristocracy determined to preserve its local power at all costs. The Gondi family had been Lyon-based bankers and financiers until the mid-sixteenth century when Pierre became bishop of Langres, and only later did they acquire both high noble titles and the see of Paris. The Villars, also of Lyon bourgeois stock, moved more slowly in the same social and ecclesiastical direction. Geographical factors were also less than crucial in their success in retaining their dioceses. The Bonsi family even remained resident in Florence, while the Gondi presence in Paris, as that of the Villars in Vienne, was more a consequence than a cause of their tenure of the bishopric in question. The same point is emphasised by the fact that the Villars also held the distant see of Agen between 1587 and 1630. These three families all managed to retain their dioceses by preserving and, in some cases, improving their social positions, but above all by taking full advantage of their political connections at court. Indeed, of the four families, it was the Salignac, who *were* of genuine old stock and firmly rooted in the Sarladais, who had the greatest difficulty in keeping their grip on a local see, even though the condition of Sarlat did not render it particularly attractive to outsiders.[29]

A closer look at the thirty episcopal dynasties present in the late sixteenth and early seventeenth century shows only about one-third of them consisted of bishops drawn from families with roots in or near to the diocese in question. Most of these dioceses were to be found in southern France, especially in the Dauphiné-Provence and Languedoc-Guyenne regions, where dioceses were more numerous anyway, but where local noble power also tended to be historically more firmly rooted. Furthermore, only nine out of the thirty dynasties were drawn from old noble families and, as might be expected, it was they which furnished most of the dynasties with local connections to particular dioceses. In sum, episcopal succession spread over two or more generations was the preserve of neither local nor old noble families. It seems that once they had gained a foothold in a particular diocese, regardless of its location, bishops and their relatives tended to direct their immediate efforts towards retaining what they already had for the next

---

29 See below, pp 491–2.

generation rather than placing all their hopes in a transfer to other, more desirable or more advantageously located dioceses.

However, the gradual disappearance of all but a handful of the episcopal dynasties present at the beginning of this period is, not surprisingly, far from being the full story. Within the chronological boundaries of this study, new names and families also made their appearance. Nor was the phenomenon dying out with the passage of time, since some of these uncle-nephew successions were only beginning to appear during the 1640s and 1650s. The scale of this continuing pattern can be gauged in a number of ways. Firstly, no fewer than fourteen of the new dynasties which took shape from Henri IV's reign onwards were still in place at the end of the Mazarin ministry. Three or four of them involved more than two generations of bishops from the same family, among them the Bertier bishops of Rieux, who were set to remain in the episcopate through the entire personal rule of Louis XIV. Secondly, a total of twenty-one new two-generational successions also developed at different times during this period, only to die out before the beginning of the personal rule. There are certain common features, as well as some overlap, between the two sets of dynasties. In both categories, there were a number of instances in which family tenure was not wholly continuous, but in all these cases, their comeback was probably helped in no small measure by local family connections. For example, the Béarnais Bertrand Deschaux was bishop of Bayonne from 1598 to 1617, when he became archbishop of Tours, but his decision to leave Bayonne was probably facilitated by the appalling treatment he received at the hands of the dominant local aristocrat, the violent Antoine de Grammont.[30] Yet he obtained some posthumous satisfaction in 1643 when his nephew, Jean d'Olce, bishop of distant Boulogne, was able to return as bishop to Bayonne, where he reigned in relative peace for almost forty years. During our period also, six dioceses shared the unusual record of having been host to two entirely unrelated sets of family dynasties, each of which held episcopal office there for two generations.[31]

The division of the spoils between families of *épée* and *robe* background among these episcopal groups is also of interest. Among the 'new' dynasties still in place in 1661, the honours were evenly divided; by contrast, among those which had disappeared, dynasties of robe and bourgeois origins had outnumbered the *épée* by three to one. As we saw in an earlier chapter, the social character of the episcopate was at its most diverse between the 1590s and the 1640s, enabling men of robe and lower social backgrounds not just to enter its ranks, but even to ensure family tenure into the next generation. The problem, as always, was how to sustain that kind of success, and it is noteworthy that the dynasties of such origins which were still in place around

---

30 P Tamizey de Larroque, 'Bertrand d'Eschaux évêque de Bayonne', *Revue de Gascogne*, 20 (1897), 297–310.
31 Agde, Meaux, Rouen, Sens, Senlis, Saint-Paul-Trois-Châteaux.

1660 were drawn primarily from the *grande robe* (royal council, parlements, etc) which enjoyed precisely the kind of rank and influence with enabled them to compete effectively with men of old noble or *épée* background.

The degree of success in prolonging family tenure of a particular diocese was also variable. Eighteen of the thirty dynastic successions under discussion were confined to just two generations of bishops, a statistic which clearly indicates the difficulty of keeping a sustained grip on a diocese. The record, both for the duration of tenure and the number of family members involved, belongs unquestionably to the Bonsi family, six of whom held Béziers without interruption between 1576 and 1672, with the last of them, Cardinal Pierre, moving on to hold the archbishoprics of Toulouse (1672–4) and Narbonne (1674–1703). Only two families, the Gondis and the Villars, managed four unbroken reigns, with a further nine families registering three. Here, too, the honours for durability were not manifestly reserved for bishops of high or ancient social status, but were spread relatively widely across *épée* and *robe* groups. Moreover, it would be wrong to underestimate the nature of such successes by imagining that they were a matter of families keeping their patronage connections well-oiled. If evidence from the *Reichskirche* is any guide, it is clear that sustaining episcopal ambitions over several generations could exact a high price, and even lead to the extinction of the families in question.[32]

But the full extent of the presence of particular names and families in the episcopate will not be revealed by the scrutiny of succession lists on a purely diocese-by-diocese basis. Mobility, even of the limited kind that we have already seen, ambition, rising families, and crown patronage all combined to ensure a wider distribution of bishops from particular families within the episcopate. By way of example, we may consider the case of not one, but two, of the dynasties holding the same diocese, Saint-Paul-Trois-Châteaux on the western edge of the Dauphiné, for two or more generations, because it neatly demonstrates the opportunities available to families that were in a position to exploit them. Members of the Adhémar de Monteil de Grignan family do not figure as bishops of Saint-Paul either at the very beginning or the very end of the period considered here, which might suggest that they differed little from most other families with transient episcopal ambitions. Saint-Paul-Trois-Châteaux was close to the family's principal lands at Grignan, near Valence. Between 1585 and 1630, the diocese was successively held by Antoine Gaume and his nephew Antoine de Cros. But this particular case of dynastic continuity is deceptive on all counts, since the bishops in question were both natives of Grignan itself, and dependents of the Grignan family. Apparently Bishop

---

32   Rudolf Reinhardt, 'Kontinuität und Diskontinuität. Zum Problem der Koadjutorie mit dem Recht der Nachfolge in der neuzeitlichen Reichskirche', in *Der dynastische Fürstenstaat*, ed J Kunisch (Berlin 1982), 145.

de Cros was, as one source innocently says, 'esteemed and presented' to the king by the comte de Grignan himself.³³ By 1630, when de Cros died, the young François de Grignan had established himself as a serious candidate for the succession. He had studied at the College of Clermont, taking his doctorate in theology around 1628. Moreover, he was also close to the *dévot* networks of court and capital, particularly to the duc de Ventadour, who confided in him his wish to found what would soon become the *Compagnie du Saint-Sacrement* and which Grignan was to join from its inception.³⁴ What his family pedigree might not have sufficed to secure on its own at this juncture, was put beyond doubt by the powerful but discreet support that he enjoyed from the Jesuits and the *dévots*, and he duly obtained the nomination to Saint-Paul in early 1630. In April 1643, still *bien en cour* and by now a well regarded bishop, he obtained the *brevet* as coadjutor to Archbishop Barrault of Arles, but Barrault's death three months later ensured that Grignan succeeded directly to the full title to Arles.³⁵ Moreover, his credit was strong enough to transfer his former see of Saint-Paul to his younger brother, Jacques, whose pre-episcopal career strongly resembled his own. In 1657, after over a decade at Saint-Paul, Jacques de Grignan also looked around for something better and found it in the form of another coadjutorship, that of Uzès. One reason he was able to make the move to Uzès was that, for a second time in a generation, the see of Saint-Paul could be utilised to satisfy the exigencies of the bishop of Uzès for one of his nephews.³⁶ The Grignan had been powerful enough to use Saint-Paul as a springboard to far better positions within the French church, and continued to turn out bishops under Louis XIV. After holding Saint-Paul for nearly thirty years, they provided two successive archbishops of Arles.

It would be absurd to claim that a case-history as uncommon as this might apply to more than a minority of the episcopate; it merely serves to show what families and individuals were likely to do where circumstances permitted. For that reason, the presentation of family interests under the heading of success or failure in retaining a particular diocese over several generations, can only be part of the story. The work of a generation of historians of early modern France would suggest that the family alliances, which the different strata of society cultivated so assiduously, were also likely to be put to purposeful use

---

33 L-A Boyer de Sainte-Marthe, *Histoire de l'église cathédrale de Saint-Paul-Trois-Châteaux avec une chronologie de tous les évêques qui l'ont gouverné* (Avignon 1710), 244. Antoine Gaume, his uncle, was almost certainly the comte de Grignan's candidate for the see in 1585: *ibid*, 242.
34 *Annales de la Compagnie du Saint-Sacrement*, ed H Beauchet-Filleau (Paris 1900), 10–11, 14.
35 *Gallia Chr Nov: Saint-Paul-Trois-Châteaux*, cols 593–4, quoting from an unpublished *mémoire* of the comtesse de Grignan. Grignan's initial nomination as coadjutor lapsed when Barrault died, and his letters of nomination to Arles were not issued until 31 Mar 1644, which may suggest some kind of struggle over the see during the early months of the regency.
36 *Ibid*, col. 604; ASV, PC 56, fos 371–94, which contains some of the relevant contracts agreed between Grignan, Bishop Grillié and his nephew, Claude Ruffier.

throughout the church, especially by those who were not tied to particular local horizons. Thus some attempt to analyse the presence and density of family links within the episcopate *as a whole* is called for.

The task may seem to require no more than the tabulation of a series of figures based on the family histories of the bishops in question. Unfortunately, this is not so, since it is only when the focus shifts away from direct successions that we are confronted with the most obvious consequences of a celibate episcopate. With the rare exceptions of widowers entering the episcopate and being followed by their sons, successions themselves were never of a father-son type. Uncle-nephew ties are the best known, partly because they are the easiest to trace, even when they occurred in the maternal rather than paternal line of the families in question. But nepotism (used purely descriptively here) is only one feature of the inevitably indirect, collateral ties that linked different generations of ecclesiastics, whether they became bishops or not. An exhaustive analysis of all the possible family ties between the bishops of our period would require a 'total' genealogical history of a kind which simply does not exist. Even in the case of well-known families, the extent of blood ties and their import for the families in question can easily escape discovery. For example, Pierre de Broc served as Richelieu's *maître de chambre* before becoming bishop of Auxerre in 1637. He seems to have come to the cardinal's attention sometime after 1624, when his eldest brother Jacques married Marguerite de Bourdeille who, in her marriage contract, made a point (as well she might in 1624!) of describing Richelieu as her *allié*.[37] This 'alliance', which apparently existed only *via* previous ties to the Brézé family, hardly makes the former bishop of Luçon a cousin of the bishop of Auxerre, but it shows how widely conceived family ties were held to be by contemporaries, especially if political power gave them a compelling incentive to do so. How many such connections there may have been between bishops is quite impossible to gauge without exhaustive genealogical research, so the figures which follow can therefore be safely regarded as minima.

Paradoxically, it may be easier to delimit the maximum extent of these family relations by looking first at bishops located at the opposite end of the spectrum, i.e. those who, as far as can be discovered, were totally *unrelated* to any previous, contemporary, or later bishop, in either their own or any other diocese. As Tables 8.6 and 8.7 show, the label 'unrelated' appears to apply to 131 of the 351 bishops nominated between 1589 and 1661 (37.3 per cent of the total). A broad subdivision of the figures for the reigns of Henri IV and Louis XIII, as well as for the ministry of Mazarin, suggests that this was not a wholly random feature of the French episcopate, since the overall proportion of 'loner' bishops remained rather static between the 1590s and early 1640s, and then moved rapidly upwards until these bishops accounted for fractionally under half of the bishops nominated during the Mazarin years as a whole.

---

37   Ambroise Ledru, *Histoire de la maison de Broc*, 2 vols (Mamers 1898), ii. 562–3.

Table 8.6   Unrelated bishops by reign

Reign	Total	Unrelated	Percentage
Henri IV	108	36	33.3
Louis XIII	154	51	33.1
Mazarin	89	44	49.4
Totals	351	131	37.3

Table 8.7   Unrelated bishops by decade

Decade	Total	Unrelated	Percentage
1589–1600	57	20	35.08
1601–10	54	16	29.62
1611–20	52	11	21.15
1621–30	57	23	40.35
1631–40	39	16	41.02
1641–50	42	22	52.38
1651–61	51	23	45.09

A decade-by-decade analysis, which can be regarded as free of inbuilt assumptions about how or why change occurred, shows that the trend was much less simple than that just suggested. The figures point to developments which will be examined at greater length, if not from the same perspective, in subsequent chapters. Firstly, the relatively high percentage of unrelated bishops recorded for the 1590s is due to the nomination of a large number of non-noble bishops from dependent backgrounds, while in the second part of Henri IV's reign better connected bishops began to make their appearance again. But it was during the 1610s that the proportion of bishops without family connections reached its nadir for the entire period – scarcely more than one in five; this is a development consistent with what we have seen previously in relation to bishops who were underage or not in full orders being promoted at this juncture. At any rate, judging by the figures, the subsequent reaction was a strong one, and although the detailed picture for the 1620s is not a consistent one, there is no doubt that the proportion of unrelated bishops began to climb quite sharply and then level out during the 1630s. It rose again significantly during the 1640s to exceed the 50 per cent mark for the first time, only to drop again during the last decade of Mazarin's ministry owing to the rising number of bishops related to predecessors or to fellow bishops in other dioceses.

Despite the fact that, in numerical terms at least, these figures deal with a minority of bishops and from what might be termed a 'negative' angle, they clearly hint at important variations within the episcopate and in the directions taken by crown patronage. To get beyond this point, we need to consider what was happening to the remaining bishops – over 60 per cent – who in one way or another were related to others on the bench. The simplest presentation of the available evidence is that given in Table 8.8. It should be noted at the outset that the total number of bishops to be considered under the different headings amounts to 220, though that figure will not appear anywhere in the table itself. But it is not so much the total figures for any one category that are of particular interest as the shifts experienced by each one in relation to the others.

The total number of bishops related to an immediate predecessor or a successor was 123, or just 35 per cent of the episcopate, and 55 per cent of the 220 inter-related bishops under consideration here. The first three columns in Table 8.8 represent an attempt to differentiate the available data on the bishops who were party to these quasi-dynastic successions. The overall decline in the practice is evident from a comparison of the first two columns, albeit with the spectacular exception of the figures for the 1610s as far as bishops related to predecessors are concerned. The decline in the number of bishops related to their immediate successors, in contrast, shows a far greater degree of regularity. The third set of figures, dealing with bishops related to both their predecessor and successor, inevitably reflects the vagaries of the preceding two columns, but the total, a modest eighteen, reinforces the point made earlier about how difficult it was to hold the same diocese for more than one or two generations.[38] At any rate, the overall decline in diocese-based dynasties from the 1620s and especially the 1630s onwards, is clearly confirmed by the figures from the first three columns. It is especially visible from a comparison of the second and third columns, which show that virtually none of the new bishops of the 1640s and 1650s were to have a relative as their immediate successor.

This trend naturally raises the question as to whether the French episcopate was becoming progressively more atomised as the century wore on. The answer would only be affirmative if it was held that territorial, diocesan successions were crucial to the argument. But the evidence presented hitherto, and not merely in this chapter, should suffice to challenge that assumption, and demonstrate that, given a chance, bishops and their families were attracted by the prospect of obtaining better dioceses which might be remote from their family's geographical centre of gravity – rather like those ambitious provincial office-holders who were tempted by places closer to the top of the pyramid of royal service.

Consequently, any attempt to understand the presence of family networks

---

38 Six of these three-generational dynasties begin with a bishop seated before Henri IV's reign.

Table 8.8   Related bishops

Decade	1	2	3	4	5	6
1589–1600	15	20	6	8	4	8
1601–10	16	11	3	17	11	12
1611–20	25	13	7	23	5	6
1621–30	11	8	2	16	3	8
1631–40	3	5	0	15	8	4
1641–50	6	1	0	10	7	2
1651–61	7	1	0	12	11	9
Totals	83	59	18	101	49	49

Column 1 = bishops related to predecessors; column 2 = related to successors; column 3 = related to both predecessor and successor; column 4 = related to other contemporary bishops; column 5 = related to bishops of a previous generation; column 6 = related to bishops of a later generation

in the episcopate needs to look beyond diocese-based dynasties. This is the purpose of the final three columns of Table 8.8, which list the numbers of bishops who were related to earlier, contemporary, or later bishops who were *not* holders of the same diocese as they themselves. No doubt the figures are probably too low under the headings of both earlier and later bishops, since full information would require more extensive research on the pre-Henri IV and the post-1661 bishops. Nevertheless, excluding from both groups the dynasties of bishops that we have already discussed, it appears that forty-nine bishops were from families which in previous generations had produced one or more bishops, a figure that is matched exactly by those families which would later – down to the end of Louis XIV's reign at least – produce bishops. This kind of intermittent presence in the episcopate may seem less impressive than the continuous dynastic kind, but in many cases it was spread over a long time-scale, and to that extent it represents a different form of staying power on the part of the families concerned. And of course, some of them, like the Colbert, Maupeou and Nesmond, all of whom first entered the episcopate under Mazarin, were only in the early stages of distinguished careers in both church and state.

But perhaps the most interesting result concerns the number of bishops related to *contemporaries* among the episcopate. Of the 100 individuals who fit into this bracket, sixty-three were cousins of one kind or another, but it is likely that exhaustive family histories would augment that figure. During this period, twenty-two brothers in all held dioceses simultaneously; four more, for example the Richelieu brothers, did not quite manage to do so, but it would be absurd to regard them as anything other than contemporaries.[39] In fact, when account is taken of dioceses passing directly from one brother to another, the overall total for brothers in the episcopate was forty-five. Uncles and nephews reigning simultaneously – something which should not be confused with coadjutorial arrangements – were clearly the exception rather than the rule, with fewer than ten being appointed in this period. The most unusual case of all was that of the two brothers-in-law, Artus de Lionne and François Servien, scattered to opposite ends of the kingdom in their dioceses of Gap and Bayeux respectively. When Lionne's son offered to obtain Servien's diocese of Bayeux as a kind of retirement present for his father in 1659, he demurred, not because his origins or career to date made such a move unthinkable, but because his advanced age – he was born in 1583! – made it impractical.[40]

Taken together, the evidence of the extent to which the episcopate was criss-crossed by family ties of different types is thus multifold. The 351 bishops nominated between 1589 and 1661 were drawn from about 240 different families. Some of these ties were particularly dense, as when they took the form of the dynastic tenure of particular dioceses or the simultaneous presence of brothers or nephews in the episcopate generally; others were more episodic, with certain families disappearing only to reappear again a generation or more later and, usually, in more distinguished dioceses. Despite this, it would be mistaken to regard access to the episcopate in this period as restricted to a narrow circle of families and individuals. As we saw, pressure in that direction could be intense at different times, notably during the wars of religion and again during the 1610s, but by the 1620s and especially the 1630s, it became clear that neither these nor other efforts to perpetuate family control of particular bishoprics would succeed. There were growing countervailing pressures whose objective was to ensure that incoming bishops conformed to the changing image of the episcopate which, in their different ways, the crown and the church looked for in those joining its ranks. For example, the decision to break the long Salignac tenure of Sarlat in 1639, despite the availability of a family candidate who was not without serious credentials and who would later hold Sarlat, was part of such a reaction. This is not to claim that episcopal patronage was increasingly subordinated to a clear, dominant 'ideal' of a Tridentine kind: that would simply ignore a great deal about the actual workings of both the monarchy and the church. What is does imply, however, is that the making of the episcopate cannot be understood without an extended analysis of the manner in which the royal prerogative of choosing bishops was exercised throughout the years under study here.

39 Cardinal Richelieu resigned Luçon in 1623, while his brother succeeded to Aix in 1626. The remaining brothers were Cardinal La Valette, who resigned Toulouse in 1627, and his half-brother, Louis de la Valette-Nogaret, bishop of Mirepoix from 1629 onwards.
40 He had apparently turned down the neighbouring archdiocese of Embrun in 1648 when he was already sixty-seven years old.

III
THE CROWN AND THE EPISCOPATE

CHAPTER 9

The Episcopate and the Wars of Religion

THE ATTEMPT AT a structural presentation of some of the most prominent features of the French episcopate has made it possible to identify some important changes occurring in its ranks over approximately three-quarters of a century. But on its own, this presentation could not embrace all of the factors capable of explaining why things developed as they did, or which of those factors played a decisive part in changing the face of the episcopate. For that reason, it is essential to complement what has been done so far with a 'political' analysis, the focus of which is the process (to be regarded as the sum of all those influences and actions) by which individuals became bishops in the French church during the same period. The analysis can be labelled 'political' in that its ultimate focus is firstly on the manner in which decisions to name bishops were made by the crown; secondly, on the individuals and groups involved in that process; and thirdly, on the extent to which the changing balance of relationships between the *dramatis personae* affected the character of the episcopate which resulted from them. It should be added that the term 'political' employed here has a purely descriptive connotation, and refers simply to the process of selecting bishops itself; beyond that, it is not intended to convey value judgements, even implicitly, or to suggest that episcopal nominations were 'merely' political.

The following chapters are a study in the exercise of one form of royal power, but since ecclesiastical issues were not neatly fenced-off from other political considerations, the analysis will have to take some account of political developments within the French monarchy generally. As noted earlier, the power to choose bishops belonged *pleno jure* to François I and his successors, and it was all the more important for being a formal rather than an informal prerogative (as had been the case before the Concordat of Bologna), one which in ensuing generations individuals and groups eyeing their chances of episcopal office had to adapt to, and work with. For that reason, the main focus in the following chapters is quite properly the crown in the widest sense, that is, the king, his ministers and favourites, the royal family, and the world of the court. It would, of course, be naïve to imagine that a Henri IV, a Louis

XIII, or even a Louis XIV made their episcopal decisions spontaneously or unprompted. In times of political weakness, the part played by the crown in selecting bishops might be minimal, little more than a formality, but, because all decisions had to be made in the king's name, the difference between the king as a necessary political fiction and an active political reality is not always easy to establish. Expressions like 'the king' or 'Henri IV' always contain an element of both, and in the pages that follow they are employed as a convenient short-hand for that wider political world in which decisions were taken, and as a consequence of which some men became bishops and others did not.

By comparison, the papacy's role in the making of the episcopate was a secondary one. Apart from the confirmation of individual royal nominations, it had come to consist in policing royal nominations and protecting some lesser residual rights of its own. It responded primarily to French decisions and initiatives, but had relatively few opportunities to contribute its own. The French monarchy may not always have been willing or able to appoint bishops who were to Rome's liking, but it did make quite sure that, with a few rare exceptions, the papacy would never be in a position to appoint directly men of its own choosing. Admittedly, the papacy could and sometimes did refuse to endorse royal choices, but even then it was the crown which enjoyed the right of selecting a suitable replacement. If a second nominee were unacceptable in Rome, the pope might then, and only then, appoint his own choice of bishop. This never happened under Henri IV or his successors, and possibly at no time after the 1516 Concordat.[1] However, to describe the papacy's role as secondary is not to say it was insignificant in the evolution of the episcopate; deprived of the power to make bishops directly, it could resort to discreet but effective diplomatic pressure, as well as to encouraging reform-minded or pro-papal groups in the French church to help it achieve its objectives.

It is a truism to say that no social or professional group can be fully understood in isolation, as if it were the product of spontaneous generation; all such groups fit into some kind of continuum involving both predecessors and successors. This is especially true for the French bishops we are considering here, if only because the episcopate was among the most ancient institutions of both church and society. Its sheer antiquity, of course, offers some guarantee that it would normally be characterised by solid continuity rather than by constant change, thus making the historian's task of fitting a given generation of bishops into a historical context that much the easier. In the present case, however, tracing the main contours of the French episcopate before Henri IV's reign is rendered anything but straightforward by the

1   Frederic J Baumgartner, *Change and Continuity in the French Episcopate: The Bishops and the Wars of Religion 1547–1610* (Durham, North Carolina, 1986), 12, shows that this was certainly the case during the sixteenth century.

successive impact of the Concordat of Bologna, the Protestant Reformation, and the wars of religion.

I

The subject of the sixteenth-century French episcopate is hardly a new one, and no useful purpose would be served by systematically considering every feature of its historiography here; at the risk of partiality, the following pages focus largely on a series of related developments concerning the manner in which bishops were made by the successors of Francis I, developments which have a direct bearing on the episcopate of Henri IV and Louis XIII. For a number of reasons, the reputation of sixteenth-century bishops, both with contemporaries and later historians, has, on the whole, been a rather negative one. The first of these, frequently repeated in accounts of the impact of the Reformation, is the allegedly disastrous effects of the Concordat of Bologna which opened the floodgates of royal episcopal patronage, and enabled François I and his successors to nominate to French bishoprics a variety of royal servants, courtiers, Italian cardinals and others, many of whom were simple clerics who fell well short of the minimum age for bishops; large numbers of such nominations were, it is held, made with little or no regard for diocesan needs, let alone for the conditions governing such appointments which François I himself had had written into the clauses of the concordat. Worse still, these bishops seemed to trade in bishoprics and other benefices as if they were dealing in commodities, holding several at once, or acquiring them only to dispose of them almost immediately while reserving most of the revenues for themselves.

Clearly, it would be mistaken to judge the calibre of any episcopal generation merely in the light of the manner in which it acquired office in the first place. Recent historiography has also shown that there was vitality as well as variety in the ranks of the episcopate under Francis I and Henri II. That is not, however, the point at issue here. For all its exaggerations, the older view of an episcopate characterised by high rates of turnover, has a solid basis in fact; it is the one which is immediately suggested by even a cursory comparison of the succession lists for France's dioceses in the sixteenth century with those of the seventeenth and eighteenth. Much of the criticism of church abuses, both within Catholicism and in the new Protestant churches, focused on the virtual secularisation of episcopal office. And while recent research has pointed to the continuing vitality of the late medieval, Gersonian tradition of reform, and revealed the efforts of highly active bishops in sixteenth-century France, it still seems to be the case that had success depended primarily upon its bishops, French Catholicism would have found the struggle against Calvinism in particular a highly unequal one.²

The Reformation and the wars of religion, it need hardly be said, had a highly disruptive effect upon the French episcopate, one from which it would take many years to recover. Not only did the period witness the Calvinist assault on both the idea and the reality of episcopal power, but the wars also altered relations between the crown and those social groups which normally aspired to episcopal office, and thus provided the essential backdrop to much of what was to happen during the reigns of Henri IV and Louis XIII.

The response of the episcopate in general to the challenge of Calvinism was, by and large, slow, un-coordinated, and defensive. Few bishops seemed to have grasped what it was that was driving large numbers of people first into dissidence and then into open assault upon the old church, and most relied upon the machinery of repression to repel this newest challenge to their authority. It has even been suggested that with high-born aristocratic bishops rallying to its side, Calvinism might have won wider support had its Genevan leaders not been so hostile to the principle of an episcopal church.³ That hostility did not prevent a small number – about twelve in all – of those French bishops who sympathised with the Reformation from embracing Calvinism during the 1550s and 1560s. Most of them quit the mitre and married, but some attempted to retain office. The papacy condemned seven bishops on heresy charges in 1566, but the judgements were never actually enforced, partly on the grounds that they infringed the Gallican liberties of the French church, partly because enforcement at this point would have constituted additional provocation to the Calvinist churches. The most distinguished episcopal convert was Admiral Coligny's brother, Cardinal Odet de Châtillon, bishop of Beauvais who, although married and no longer a bishop, declared his intention at the end of the third war of religion (1570) to recover his benefices, claiming that the terms of the treaty of Saint-Germain restoring the Huguenots to their offices and dignities should apply to episcopal as much as to secular office.⁴ The best known of these bishops, however, is Antonio Caracciolo of Troyes, who tried to persuade the Genevan authorities that he could both remain a bishop and serve the local Calvinist church as its pastor!⁵ Gabriel de Clermont, bishop of Gap, also obtained letters-patent in 1570 restoring him to the see he had held for forty years, but in this case 'restoration' was tempered by a crucial condition – that he would

---

2 For some of these correctives, see Nicole Lemaître, *Le Rouergue flamboyant: le clergé et les fidèles du diocèse de Rodez 1417–1563* (Paris, 1988); Jacques Le Goff and René Rémond, eds, *Histoire de la France religieuse*, ii (Paris, 1988), part ii, chs 1–2; Charles Piétri et al, *Histoire du christianisme*, viii. *Le Temps des confessions*, ed Marc Venard (Paris 1992), esp part iii, ch 1.
3 Baumgartner, *Change and Continuity*, 141.
4 *Ibid*, 129–31.
5 *Ibid*, 133–4.

promptly resign Gap, having no doubt negotiated favourable terms for himself, to a 'personnage catholique'. This he duly did. Meanwhile another claimant to the see of Gap had obtained provisions from the papal curia, on the grounds, as Clermont's letters-patent rather testily put it, that Gap was somehow vacant 'pour le seul faict de la religion'.[6]

The interesting point about these examples is that there was indeed pressure to allow bishoprics to remain in the hands of bishops who had adopted the Protestant faith, and that the crown, and to a lesser extent, the papacy were slow to acknowledge the reality of episcopal sympathy towards the new faith, let alone the actual defections that ensued. Though a number of bishops would continue to be suspect during the 1570s and 1580s without anything having been proven against them, it had at least become clear that men openly professing Calvinism would no longer be tolerated in the ranks of the episcopate, as in the case of Clermont of Gap. Despite earlier prevarication, it was by now firmly established that episcopal office was *not* like other offices, and that it could indeed be vacated 'pour le seul faict de la religion'. Firm action against individual bishops was, as already suggested, partly limited by the fact that direct papal intervention was unpopular in France, with even heresy trials being regarded as an infringement of Gallican liberties; inaction was also partly due to sheer inertia, but also to a reluctance to exacerbate the political tensions of these years by exemplary punishment of bishops who strayed from the narrow path of Catholic orthodoxy. However, from this time onwards, papal nuncios in France had standing instructions to ascertain as much as possible about candidates for episcopal office. These instructions were not systematic in character. They did not deal with the general suitability of candidates, but reflected, among other things, Rome's abiding fear that heretics might slip into high church office, a fear that was not to disappear for several years.

Thus, whatever might happen in dioceses as far apart as Beauvais, Troyes or Gap, French bishoprics were not about to go the way of a considerable number of German dioceses during the Reformation, when they were either abolished by the territorial princes or experienced a variety of experiments in alternating Catholic and Protestant 'administration'. Unlike the Empire, French bishoprics had ceased to be dominated by powerful and self-willed cathedral chapters monopolised by sons of the aristocracy; despite their different problems, the crown, the papacy and the French episcopate itself all reacted strongly enough to ensure the survival of the latter. Of course, this was not enough to prevent certain bishoprics, and in particular episcopal lands and

---

6   *Gallia Chr Nov*, Gap, Instrumenta, no 77, cols 334–6. Interestingly, however, the contract also stipulated that should the new bishop himself wish to resign Gap, he would require Clermont's prior agreement. Rome refused to accept that the incoming bishop, Paparin, could obtain Gap on the grounds that Clermont had resigned it to him, but insisted that his accession be on the grounds that Clermont had been removed for heresy. The distinction is an important one.

rights, from being actually occupied by Huguenots. In numerous dioceses, iconoclastic 'furies', erupting mostly in the 1560s, wrought considerable damage on cathedrals and bishops' residences, damage which was often not made good until the mid-seventeenth century, if not later.[7] On the other hand, some dioceses, such as Embrun, Cahors or Mende, did not suffer in this way until the later 1570s. Where it occurred, the occupation of lands and temporalities, often by Huguenot nobles, rendered a certain number of dioceses effectively inaccessible to the bishops holding title to them. This was especially true in Béarn, Gascony, parts of Languedoc, Provence and Dauphiné, and would only cease for the latter provinces during Henri IV's reign. As the wars of religion further sapped royal power, a comparable occupation of temporalities by powerful Catholic nobles such as Montmorency-Damville, Joyeuse, and others also gathered pace. Finally, the crown-sponsored 'alienations' of ecclesiastical lands also played a part in weakening the position of bishops within dioceses and provinces.

II

But not everything should be attributed to the wars, the aristocracy or the Huguenots, even if between them, they undoubtedly contributed to the remarkable turnover rates for bishops which, under Charles IX and to a lesser extent under Henri III, were the highest recorded for the entire *ancien régime*. An exhaustive scrutiny of episcopal nominations for these years would no doubt show that other, more conventional features of ecclesiastical politics were also at work. Pluralism, simony, and a high level of horse-trading in benefices among prelates and great families also reached a peak in the second half of the century, a process which did little to stabilise the episcopate in what were already difficult times. It may be too easy to exaggerate how rife such practices were or how disastrous their impact was, and to fall into the trap of taking the polemical views of sixteenth-century critics and reformers as factually unassailable. Absentee bishops, for example, were not necessarily the indifferent careerists that they have often been portrayed as being. Many, if not most, of them ensured that through vicars-general and, occasionally, suffragan bishops, their dioceses were adequately administered. Yet, even making such allowances, it seems clear that such measures could not really make up for the lack of a resident, even moderately energetic bishop who

---

7   The classic, and to date the most detailed study is Victor Carrière, 'Les Epreuves de l'église de France au xvie siècle', in his *Introduction aux études d'histoire ecclésiastique locale*, iii (Paris 1936). A more recent study, with particular emphasis on religious symbolism, has been attempted by Olivier Christin, *Une Révolution symbolique. L'Iconoclasme huguenot et la reconstruction catholique* (Paris 1991).

alone would have possessed the necessary power and prestige to initiate action beyond the timid routines of diocesan administration.[8]

Sixteenth-century France witnessed the heyday of episcopal pluralism, though it certainly was not something it invented. Not surprisingly, it was practised almost exclusively by high noble families enjoying extensive royal patronage, such as the Amboises, the Guises, the Châtillons and the Bourbons, and by powerful individual figures like Cardinals Tournon and Joyeuse. It provides the most visible evidence of the extent to which François I and Henri II, in particular, used their powers under the concordat for the purposes of political and financial reward. The record shows that the beneficiaries must have viewed their dioceses with considerable detachment, and, in many cases, as purely temporary acquisitions. Many dioceses which were snapped up by pluralists were not (and perhaps were not intended to be) held for very long, but were either passed on to ecclesiastical clients or exchanged for more desirable sees; in either case such transfers usually involved the retention of a pension, which of course may have been the real object of the exercise. The assaults of the Calvinist Reformation and the debates of the Council of Trent did much to curtail episcopal pluralism, and by the reign of Henri III it was becoming rarer. Yet legislation rarely made things disappear in early modern France, and Bourbon family prelates, for example, did not see why such self-denial should apply to them. The king's own contribution, though limited, is not without interest. In 1581, the eighteen-year-old François de Joyeuse, younger brother of the king's favourite, became archbishop of Narbonne; seven years later he obtained the archbishopric of Toulouse. Despite this, he did not give up Narbonne until 1600, and even then he retained all but a small fraction of its revenues. Henri IV not merely confirmed his control of both Toulouse and Narbonne, but in 1604 allowed him to add the archdiocese of Rouen to his collection, without in any way diminishing his rights over the two southern sees. Joyeuse was, of course, by then a cardinal, the Protector of France in the Roman curia, and above all heir to his family's immense power and patronage in southern France - and by that token, a worthy successor to the great churchmen of the age of Francis I and Henry II. Yet there is no doubt whatever that Joyeuse was an energetic bishop and an able administrator who made notable attempts to reform his various dioceses along Tridentine lines. He was a Renaissance-style prelate who played a leading role in the affairs of an episcopate that was in transition, and his would be the last case of an episcopal pluralist in seventeenth-century France.[9]

Partly intertwined with episcopal pluralism was the phenomenon of the

---

8   See the remarks by Marc Venard in *Le Temps des confessions* (*Histoire du christianisme*, viii), 426–7 (see above n 2).
9   No full modern study of Joyeuse exists, but some elements of his career can be gleaned from Pierre de Vaissière, *Messieurs de Joyeuse (1560–1615)* (Paris 1926).

granting of a substantial number of French dioceses to Italian prelates by François I and his successors. Not every Italian becoming a bishop in sixteenth-century France belonged to this category, since some were members of religious orders or natives of Savoy or Piedmont who had settled in France long before they became bishops. The royal largesse referred to here was largely a consequence of France's struggle with the Habsburgs for control of Italy, and the involvement of numerous Italian families on the French side, several of whom moved to France after the collapse of French power in Italy in the late 1550s. Some of the beneficiaries had settled in France as a result of royal or princely marriages during the century, notably those of Catherine de' Medici to Henri II, or of Anna d'Este to the duc de Guise. All were court-based families with direct access to the highest levels of royal power.[10] Overlapping with these developments was the concern of the crown to sustain and provide pensions for a pro-French party in the Roman curia, and a corresponding readiness to use French dioceses for that purpose. Some of these developments have all the signs of age-old, Roman curial benefice-hunting about them, especially as it tended to be prime sees like Auch, Aix, Albi and other rich southern dioceses which were handed around by ecclesiastics with names like Farnese, Medici, Strozzi, Ridolfi, and Este. Under Henri IV this trend declined, and though Henri was prepared to indulge in limited gifts of this kind, he gradually came to prefer monetary pensions.[11] Because of his own origins and political aspirations, Mazarin would later engage in limited efforts to revive the earlier tradition and to place fellow Italians in the episcopate.

III

The survival of the episcopate after 1560 was one thing, and the preceding discussion has not attempted to offer a full explanation of it. The kind of bishop who took up office during the same period is of no less interest for our present purposes. It is time to look more closely at the overall composition of the episcopate itself, and to identify some of its principal features in the years preceding Henri IV's succession. Perhaps the most convenient point of departure for such an analysis would be to examine the condition of the episcopate as it was in August 1589, on the eve of the new king's nominal accession to the throne. But as this might in turn yield an excessively static portrait of the bishops who happened to be in office in 1589, both the timescale of the discussion and the questions to be raised in the following pages may be expanded by drawing directly upon one of the most blistering attacks on the

---

10 Baumgartner, *Change and Continuity*, 112–13, for some comments on papal attempts to eradicate pluralism.
11 Bernard Barbiche, 'L'Influence française à la cour pontificale sous Henri IV', *Mélanges d'Histoire et d'Archéologie de l'Ecole Française de Rome*, 77 (1965), 277–99.

state of France's bishoprics – that prepared for a confrontation with Henri III by the 1579 Assembly of Clergy. The Assemblies of Clergy would later play their own particular part in the making of the episcopate, but were still in the early stages of development during this reign, and were certainly not dominated by hotheads. Yet the 1579 Assembly drew up an unprecedented document to accompany its critique of the king's behaviour towards France's bishoprics.[12] Nothing like it, as far as is known, was ever to surface again during the *ancien régime*. Eschewing for the most part criticism of individuals, it itemised the names of all French dioceses it regarded as either nominally vacant (but actually in lay hands thanks to the granting of *économats*), or else held by straw men (*confidentiaires*) who allowed laymen to draw episcopal revenues and exercise the bulk of episcopal patronage in the dioceses. Its originators confessed their ignorance about the state of certain ecclesiastical provinces, and were only concerned with certain types of abuses. Of course, bodies like a General Assembly traditionally painted matters in sombre colours, and historians using such criticisms may all too easily replicate what may be an unrepresentative and excessively negative portrait of France's upper clergy. Yet contemporaries were agreed that the episcopate under Henri III was in a state of crisis, and no account of the workings of episcopal patronage can exclude this sentiment from its purview.

What patterns emerge from a consideration of the bare facts about France's bishops and dioceses on the eve of the change of the ruling dynasty? In view of the criticisms of Henri III made at the time, it may come as something of a surprise that there were 98 bishops 'en exercise' for 110 dioceses (excluding the two Béarn sees) in mid-1589. This figure is considerably more than might be expected from earlier accounts, although it should be said immediately that clear and simple categories like 'occupied' or 'vacant' bishoprics do not always adequately reflect sixteenth-century realities. In a few cases – fewer, in any case, than might be imagined from reading complaints from Rome – it may be doubted whether certain royal nominees ever sought, let alone obtained papal provisions, while their extended possession of a diocese would nevertheless seem to have given them some form of recognised tenure, and that their tenure excluded any notion among their contemporaries that the dioceses in question had somehow been left vacant. The fact that several bishops were not consecrated also renders their episcopal 'identity' even more nebulous. Narbonne, for instance, continued to be in the hands of Cardinal Joyeuse who was promoted to Toulouse in 1588, while Bayeux was held 'en administration' rather than 'en titre' by Cardinal de Bourbon after 1586. But as far as one can judge, only ten dioceses were indisputably vacant at Henri IV's accession.

Equally unexpected is the fact that most of these diocese had not been

12 L Serbat, *Les Assemblées du clergé de France* (Paris 1906) remains the standard study, and can be complemented by the financially oriented analysis of Claude Michaud, *L'Eglise et l'argent sous l'ancien régime. Les Receveurs généraux du clergé de France aux xvie-xviie siècles* (Paris 1991).

vacant for a significant length of time. Only Auch and Vabres in southern France were without a bishop since 1585; most of the remainder had only fallen vacant in 1588 or early 1589, and even had nominations to all of them been promptly made by Henri III, 'normal' delays in obtaining provisions in Rome could easily account for continuing vacancies up to the time of his assassination in August 1589. It will been seen later that, as far as vacant dioceses are concerned, the most serious problems were still to come in the first decade of Henri IV's reign.

Thus, whatever failures could be imputed to Henri III, it would seem that leaving dioceses vacant for extended periods was not one of them, at least in the later years of his reign. But of itself, this reveals relatively little about the king's exercise of episcopal patronage. It has been claimed that Henri III had only limited opportunities to rebuild the episcopate, since he only made about half the number of nominations that had occurred during the reign of his brother Charles IX, which was of virtually identical length.[13] But if that comparison suggests anything, it is that the 1560s and early 1570s were a particularly unattractive time to be a bishop, and that the high number of appointments made at the time is indicative of a rapid turnover of bishops and, consequently, of an unstable, rather than a new or different, episcopate. Not surprisingly, it was during the explosive first years of his reign that Henri III had the most difficulty in nominating bishops.

If we return to the figures quoted above, it emerges that of the ninety-eight bishops seated in 1589, five were survivors from the age of Henri II, three from the short reign of François II, and thirty-six from that of Charles IX, while Henri III himself had placed no fewer than fifty-four of them. In fact, it seems that he made about seventy-seven nominations in all (judging simply by the number of those who received papal confirmation), if we take into account transfers from one diocese to another and the appointment of those bishops who had either died or retired before mid-1589. The annual average of nominations (again including transfers and the like) for his reign as a whole was thus nearly five, with the inevitable dips and peaks from year to year mainly as a result of episcopal mortality and retirements. Of particular interest here, however, is the fact that by far the largest contingent was nominated and received papal confirmation in just two years, in 1587 and 1588, when no fewer than eighteen were installed. There were no papal provisions granted at all in 1589, but this should not be taken to mean that Henri III had somehow failed to make nominations to vacant sees – there is direct evidence to the contrary for at least Vienne (a coadjutorial nomination), Grasse and Coutances. It was simply that as a monarch who had been excommunicated for the Guise murders, he could no longer expect his candidates to be confirmed in Rome. With his own assassination following in

---

13 Michel Péronnet, 'Les Nominations épiscopales sous Henri III' in *Henri III et son temps*, ed Robert Sauzet (Paris 1992), 288.

August 1589, the same logic applied even more implacably in the case of his still Huguenot successor. As suggested earlier, it was after, rather than during, the reign of Henri III that vacant dioceses began to accumulate in large numbers. Moreover, if we look at the ten dioceses which the 1579 Assembly specifically named as vacant and in the hands of administrators, it emerges that only two, Alet and Lectoure in Languedoc and Gascony respectively, still remained vacant a decade later, though the second of these dioceses had been in the *de facto* possession of an illegitimate and still unconsecrated half-brother of Henri IV, Charles de Bourbon, since about 1573. All the other dioceses cited as vacant in 1579 were filled between 1580 and 1584. Alet and Lectoure excepted, the ten dioceses that were vacant in 1589 were not the same as those vacant ten years previously.

Thus far the evidence suggests that Henri III's legacy should not be seen in terms of a depleted episcopate, but rather of an inexperienced one, at least in the sense that many of its members were quite new to office in 1589. Although Henri III was neither criticised nor complimented on this particular point, the implications of this pattern for the episcopate's behaviour during the last phase of the religious wars hardly need emphasising, and will be considered later.

IV

The major weaknesses of the episcopate as it took shape under Henri III lay elsewhere, and contemporaries were not sparing in their criticism of them, whether in verse, pamphlets, formal remonstrances, or private correspondence. The most solemn attack was the one we have already noted, that made by the Assembly of Clergy of 1579, the essentials of which were often repeated by other critics and historians of Henri III. According to this view, the king either left dioceses vacant for long periods and appointed *économes* to manage them in the interests of powerful laymen, or else he abdicated his personal prerogative to nominate bishops by allowing others to choose *their* candidates for him to rubber-stamp; in both cases, it was argued, laymen, usually powerful nobles, enjoyed both the revenues and the patronage of the sees concerned.[14] As the correspondence of its nuncios abundantly shows, the contemporary papacy shared the views of the assembled representatives of the French church.[15] Could it be that the price paid for a relatively complete episcopate in 1589 was one which comprised rather too many bishops who were under the thumb of lay patrons?

14 *Mémoires du clergé, ou recueil des actes, titres et mémoires concernant les affaires du clergé de France* xiv (Paris 1771), 1090, for the article of the 1579 *cahier* to this effect. See Pierre Blet, 'Le Concordat de Bologne et la réforme tridentine', *Gregorianum*, 45 (1964), 254–5.
15 *ANG*, ii. 136, general instructions to new nuncio, Girolamo Ragazzoni, Sept 1583. Similar opinions are to be found throughout the *ANG* volumes (vii and viii) covering the years 1578 to 1583.

This, it need hardly be said, is a particularly difficult question to answer satisfactorily. The parties to the arrangements which were so widely criticised rarely left behind a written record of malpractice, especially when it came to confidentiary arrangements. Only a careful scrutiny of contemporary comment can bring us closer to the inner workings of episcopal patronage under Henri III.

Of the twenty-three bishoprics highlighted by the 1579 Assembly, twelve were vacant and in the hands of *économes* acting on behalf of various members of the aristocracy and upper clergy. In the assembly's view, most of these vacancies had lasted much too long to be attributable to simple delays in the granting of provisions in Rome. Clearly it suited the beneficiaries that the crown was willing to allow *économats* either to be renewed at regular intervals, or to run indefinitely with its tacit approval. In the case of the dioceses controlled by Montmorency-Damville through *économats*, his own officials later admitted that it would be highly embarrassing if it were revealed in the courts that episcopal temporalities had been leased out alongside his other estates.[16] For its part, the papacy suspected that this situation was also due to the fact that the clerics actually nominated to the vacant sees were in no hurry to seek papal confirmation, because they were either ignorant, undeserving, or heretics. Henri III's first reaction to the protests over the *économats* in the late 1570s was to blame them on past difficulties, and he did at least proceed to fill most of the vacant sees, so that a decade later, the problem could seem much less serious. As we have seen, few of the ten dioceses vacant in 1589 could be regarded as deliberately rather than temporarily so.

Pinning down the presence of confidentiary bishops is far more problematic for several reasons, some of which extend well beyond the ecclesiastical sphere. Even the 1579 Assembly could only point unequivocally to three dioceses – Luçon, Viviers, and Albi – as being held *en confidence*, and it had to rely on hearsay evidence in the case of several others. Yet an attempt should be made to explore the question, apart from the obvious consideration of its impact on both the autonomy and calibre of the episcopate. First, the practice would not disappear with Henri III, but would continue in various guises under Henri IV; secondly, the papacy, and in particular Pope Sixtus V (1585–90), regarded it as one of the major afflictions of the French church; and lastly, it was one of the principal complaints made by the 1579 Assembly, a body dominated by bishops and therefore not naturally prone to disparaging either throne or altar. But whereas the reformer or critic could denounce confidentiary bishops as examples of the moral corruption which drew divine wrath down on to France and its people, historians need to approach them from a different angle. They can be seen as one of the possible consequences

---

16 Arch Chantilly, L/xxvi, fo 28, Claude Convers to Montmorency, 3 Sept 1597: 'si à tout propos l'on faict voyr publicquement en justice l'estat de voz affaires et les particularités quy doivent estre maniées plus discrettement et mesmes pour raison du bien ecclésiastique qui est comprins en voz fermes'.

of the way in which royal ecclesiastical patronage evolved during the sixteenth century and of the pressures to which it was subject. This in turn raises a series of questions about contemporary practices where patronage, in both the broad and the narrow senses suggested in an earlier chapter, is concerned. Without some prior consideration of these issues, it is impossible to make much sense of the confidentiary nominations which did occur.

At the most basic level, it is essential to acknowledge that the conferral of episcopal office was an act of patronage – or, as contemporaries called it, of 'liberality' or of 'grace'. As is well known, the later medieval monarchy often expected to appoint to offices on the recommendation of influential figures both at court and in the provinces. It saw nothing wrong in principle with soliciting them for the names of clients whom they wished to see promoted, as a result of which office became a form of royal maintenance for clients of great nobles. The systematic selling of royal office would alter that in due course, even though it was far from removing the need for patronage when seeking office.[17] Patronage was so taken for granted that it elicited surprisingly little direct comment, whether it be in royal service or in the church. In the case of the church, however, the gradual shift from elected to nominated bishops was bound to produce innovations in existing language and practice. Although the Concordat of Bologna formally acknowledged the king of France's personal right to nominate bishops, it provided no infallible guide as to how this right was actually exercised. Of itself, it produced no revolution in the habits of the monarchy in the dispensing of church patronage, nor did it suppress at a stroke a whole range of long-established customs, fully embedded in canon law, such as that of resigning bishoprics (or other benefices) to named successors, or of regaining possession of benefices should successors die or wish to part with them. The Council of Trent, as we have noted, took a strong line in its attempts to outlaw some of these practices, such as that of 'reserving' benefices in advance of their becoming vacant (*expectatives*, as they were called), but though some of its decrees might find their way into royal ordinances, they were never adopted as a whole by the French monarchy.[18] In practice, therefore, the royal prerogative to choose bishops was conditioned by a broad web of attitudes and behaviour which were highly resistant to change, not least because some were of the crown's own creation.

It is all too easy to argue from assumptions based on the later history of French royal absolutism that earlier monarchs were always directly responsible for choosing bishops, and that they wished to be. This was not so. Among the customs of the monarchy just referred to was that of setting aside apanages for the younger sons of French kings or jointure lands for dowager

---

17 Christopher Stocker, 'Office as Maintenance in Renaissance France', *Canadian Journal of History*, 6 (1971), 21–44.

18 Jean Bernhard, Charles Lefebvre, Francis Rapp, *L'Epoque de la Réforme et du concile de Trente* (*Histoire du droit et des institutions de l'église en Occident*, xiv) (Paris 1989), 376ff.

queens who normally only took possession of them after their royal husbands' death. Apanages and dower lands usually included one or more royal duchy or county, and specifically included all the elements of royal domain within their boundaries. The grant of royal domain was the crucial factor here, since it brought with it the right to present to offices and benefices within the area defined in the relevant apanage. Several such grants were made by the crown in the sixteenth and early seventeenth centuries, and while explicit mention was not normally made of presentations to vacant bishoprics, it was generally assumed that these were included in them. Such an assumption was certainly made when Henri III's younger brother, François, added the duchies of Anjou, Touraine and Berry to his apanage of Alençon in 1576.[19] That the assumption was shared by Henri III himself is made perfectly clear in his letter to Gregory XIII in 1577 asking him to confirm Anjou's chancellor, Renaud de Beaune, then bishop of Mende, as archbishop of Bourges 'in order to satisfy the requests made to me by my brother ... and because Beaune is the principal advisor to my brother, who is duke and lord of the said province of Berry'.[20] No less interesting is the fact that Henri IV's first wife, Marguerite de Valois, sister of Henri III, received from Charles IX as part of her dowry several royal counties, particularly in southern France, and also the power to exercise her patronage rights there *during* rather than after her marriage, making her privileges the nearest to a female version of the apanage. Among those to which she could present her candidates for royal approval were the southern dioceses of Agen, Cahors, Condom, and Rieux near Toulouse. The political upheaval that followed the ill-fated marriage and her subsequent estrangement from Henri IV did not reduce her resolve to protect her prerogatives, and it was at her insistence that Henri IV renewed them, explicitly mentioning church benefices, in October 1594.[21] Thereafter, it was not for want of trying that Marguerite did not manage to reward more than one or two of her servants with episcopal office.[22] In more conventional fashion, Mary Stuart received the county of Touraine and the duchy of Poitou as her dower lands, Catherine de' Medici the counties of Clermont and the Auvergne, while Henri IV's second wife, Marie de' Medici, received the royal domain of Brittany as well as that of the Auvergne, with similar rights to present to church benefices great and

---

19 Mack P Holt, *The Duke of Anjou and the Politique Struggle during the Wars of Religion* (Cambridge 1986), 16, quoting Etienne Pasquier's comment upon the *apanagiste*'s rights concerning benefices. Professor Holt kindly confirmed to me that Pasquier's view was shared by Anjou and Henri III as well.
20 *Lettres de Henri III*, ed Michel François, iii (Paris 1972), 416–17, letter of 27 Oct 1577: 'pour satisfaire aux postullations qui m'ont esté faictes par mondict frère ... comme estant (Beaune) la première personne auprès de mondict frère, duc et seigneur dudict pays de Berry'.
21 AD Haute-Garonne, B 1909, fos 274–5, letters-patent of 2 Oct 1594.
22 *Ibid*, 6 J 61, nos 13, 17, for her efforts to get Agen and Condom for Jean de Bertier, 1596 and later (n.d.).

small.[23] By the time of Gaston d'Orléans and Anne of Austria, however, the crown's attitude to such grants had begun to change significantly.

It would be excessive to claim that the door to broader surrenderings of royal powers to nominate bishops was inevitably opened by the granting of apanages and dower rights. The latter were few in number and were highly formalised, while the candidates for bishoprics presented by their holders were ultimately subject to royal approval before submission to Rome. Nor were such grants in some way predestined to lead to abuses in episcopal nominations. The state of France's bishoprics as depicted by both the 1579 Assembly and the papacy might well have been reached by other routes. Yet these privileged grants were an important element in the fragmentation of the royal prerogative, not least when those of Alençon, Marguerite de Valois, and Catherine de' Medici existed simultaneously thoughout most of Henri III's reign. In fact, among the most protracted and widely reported attempts to install a confidentiary bishop was that made by none other than Alençon who held the presentation rights to the attractive Norman diocese of Lisieux; from the available evidence, it is clear that Catherine de' Medici fully supported her youngest son's action there. When Lisieux fell vacant in 1578, Alençon turned it over to one of his clients, Marshal Fervacques, governor of Lisieux, who nominated one Jean de Bonnechose, a man whose merits were so debatable that an exasperated Gregory XIII insisted on an episcopal commission to examine him.[24] But rather than risk such an eventuality, Fervacques proposed instead Jean de Vassé who was confirmed by Rome in late 1579.[25] However, when he died in 1583, Alençon again allowed Fervacques to choose a candidate for his approval, although in the event Rome refused him its approval for reasons similar to those in the Bonnechose case, and the episode was only closed with Alençon's death in 1584.[26] In this instance, the power to pick a bishop had in effect been delegated not once, but twice.

With cases like this, the idea that French kings should also informally 'delegate' their powers to choose bishops to other individuals was unlikely to shock their sixteenth-century contemporaries. The crucial question then was not so much who would become bishop of a given diocese, but how far the real beneficiaries of royal largesse were free to extract concessions from bishops who owed their episcopal promotion to their patronage. In an age when, for

---

23   Mark Greengrass, 'Mary, Dowager Queen of France', in Michael Lynch, ed, *Mary Stewart, Queen in Three Kingdoms* (Oxford 1989), 172–3.
24   *ANG*, viii. 423, Como to Dandino, 15 June 1579; p 438, same to same, 3 July 1579; p 461, Dandino to Como, 2 Aug 1579.
25   *Lettres de Henri III*, iv. nos 3264–5, 3342, letters to Rome, Feb-Apr 1579 strongly supporting Bonnechose's nomination and reputation; no 3502, nominating Vassé to Pope, 17 Sept 1579, Bonnechose having withdrawn. *ANG*, viii. 216, 327, 356–7, 369, 374, 378–80, 407, 423, 438, 461, correspondence of nuncio and papal secretary of state, 1578–9, over the Lisieux affair.
26   *ANG*, ii. 209–10, 228, 256, 269–70, nuncio's correspondence over Lisieux vacancy, 12 Mar, 16 Apr, 21 May and 25 June 1584.

example, a number of bishops were nominated at an early age, it was clearly difficult to justify a royal grant either in terms of their personal services or qualities, but the services of someone else – a parent, a relative, or a patron – might be adduced in their place, and so vicariously fulfil the conditions for a justifiable nomination. But the form of words used in making nominations did not necessarily mean that the incoming bishop was intended to be no more than a caretaker for the rest of his career: all depended on the identity of the incoming bishop. In reply to Roman criticism of the abuse of *économats*, both Catherine de' Medici and Henri III protested that they could not but reward the services of families and individuals to the crown.[27]

While we should, perhaps, not attach too much importance to linguistic conventions or chancery formulae, the fact that the patronage relations involved in many episcopal nominations came to be so openly affirmed under the successors of François I is no accident. The manner in which practices whereby individuals were explicitly nominated to church benefices on behalf (*en faveur de*) of someone else began to proliferate under Charles IX and continued under Henri III – when this kind of expression regularly found its way into the actual texts of *brevets* or letters of nomination – led to rising unease among critics and reformers. The purpose of such language was not simply to impress or to flatter: it was nothing less than to indicate that the real beneficiary of the king's grace was the patron cited by name and in whose 'favour' the grant was therefore being made. It was this shift which made the appearance of the caretaker bishop possible.

It remains unclear whether the later medieval church ever adopted a clear view of the admissibility of such public expressions of patronage and dependence where appointments to major benefices were concerned, and that in turn may explain its slowness to respond to what was occurring in sixteenth-century French. The Roman curia had its own complex language and practice of patronage, which it was in no hurry to dismantle, but in late sixteenth-century France its nuncios were on the alert over what they regarded as improper episcopal nominations in which patrons seemed intent on confiscating most of the rights of their episcopal clients. That they were vigilant is evident, as we saw, in Rome's intense suspicion of Alençon's nominees for Lisieux in both 1579 and 1583, but also in several other cases. At one point, a despondent nuncio confessed that it was simply not possible for him to collect information on all of those nominated to bishoprics.[28] By the seventeenth century, as we shall see, such expressions of outright dependency among bishops would become widely unacceptable.[29]

---

27 *ANG*, viii. 550, Dandino to Como, 4 Dec 1579.
28 *Ibid*, 192, Dandino to Como, 21 July 1578.
29 For example, three Paris theologians led by André du Val argued very strongly in 1622 that using phrases like 'en considération des services' or 'sur le recommendation' of the duc de Guise in seeking papal provisions for his son to a number of abbeys was unacceptable and smacked of simony: BN, MS Fr 15518, fo 81.

V

It is commonly held that with the political disorders of the 1560s and 1570s, Catherine de' Medici and Charles IX went beyond the earlier practice, and explicitly permitted certain individuals, essentially courtiers, to present to them for nomination to the pope their choice of bishop for a vacant diocese. This is not to say that older instances cannot be found. In 1572, Charles IX acknowledged that the former Cardinal de Châtillon had actually received Beauvais and several abbeys under Henri II as a special favour to Constable Montmorency, and that it was, therefore, to the latter that they had really been given; Châtillon could be said to hold them 'directly' of Montmorency, and only 'indirectly' of the crown.[30] The difference between this and traditional practice may not seem considerable, especially as Montmorency had been acting on behalf of a member of his own family. Yet after 1560 instances of such concessions reflected the increasing political difficulties facing the crown, and its need either to reward supporters or to acquire the support of powerful individuals deemed necessary to maintaining its political position. Moreover, unlike the Beauvais case, they hardly ever involved members of the same family.

If the crown's political weakness was one opportunity which noble families might use to gain — or at times regain — a hold on local bishoprics, a new incentive also emerged after 1560 with the enforced sale of church properties in order to pay royal debts and finance annuities owed to purchasers of *rentes*. Between 1563 and 1587 several such sales occurred throughout France, and though it is clear that older accounts of the spoliation of the church were exaggerated, it remains true that valuable items of episcopal property were coveted by noble families who in some cases persuaded weak or absentee bishops to sell certain estates at almost bargain prices. Sometimes the process was little short of usurpation.[31] Whatever the methods used by those concerned, the fact is that their acquisitions needed protecting should bishops attempt to reclaim them. Only detailed local research could prove how widely this happened and which dioceses were most affected by it, but in sees as widely separated as Montpellier, Coutances, and Saint-Pol-de-Léon, it is clear that noble purchasers of episcopal estates subsequently paid uncommonly close attention to the choice of bishops.

The foregoing discussion should make it easier to see why contemporary references to confidentiary arrangements almost invariably begin by saying that the king turned over a blank *brevet de nomination* to the person he wished to reward. It was then up to the recipient to find an ecclesiastic willing to become a bishop on terms which usually required him to forego most of the revenues, as well as the right to nominate to certain benefices and offices in the

---

30 BM Toulouse, MS 612, fo 336, *brevet* of 4 Jan 1572. I wish to thank Dr Joan Davies for this reference.
31 See Michaud, *L'Eglise et l'argent sous l'ancien régime*, esp part i, chs 3,5

diocese concerned, and even to vacate the bishopric if summoned to do so. In the case of Beauvais in 1572, the *brevet* of Charles IX shows far more clearly than any other text of its kind how completely the crown could divest itself of its powers: the king, who had recently granted Beauvais to the Cardinal de Bourbon, issued a separate *brevet* which stipulated that should Bourbon die in office, Constable Montmorency's son, Marshal Damville, was free to dispose of the bishopric and the accompanying abbeys,

> using the names of whomsoever he judges fit for the purpose. His Majesty wishes it to be known that in this matter, all letters and dispensations from the curia and elsewhere shall be issued at the request of the said marshal, without there being any need for further orders from His Majesty, apart from that given in the present brevet.[32]

Montmorency could not have wished for a freer hand, though he never, in fact, nominated a client to Beauvais. He later used Charles IX's grant to strike a bargain with Bourbon over the see of Carcassonne which, as governor of Languedoc, was of no less interest to him.[33]

The case of Coutances in lower Normandy is also of interest because it fell vacant only late in Henri III's reign, and it helps to illustrate the changes in relations between the crown and the aristocracy. The elderly and indolent Artus de Cossé died in October 1587, having been no match for the formidable Marshal Matignon, royal lieutenant-general in Normandy and the most powerful nobleman in the Cotentin. Moreover, Matignon had recently managed to gain possession of the major episcopal barony of Saint-Lô and other lands, and he was anxious to preserve them for the future; having a bishop in Coutances *à sa dévotion* was perhaps the most effective means to such an end.[34] In December 1587, Henri III obligingly nominated Matignon's son, Lancelot, to Coutances, but Lancelot died in early 1588 while on his way to Rome to obtain papal confirmation. Like many noble families during the

---

32 BM Toulouse, MS 612, fo 336, *brevet* of 4 Jan 1572: 'pour les mettre au nom de telz personnaiges capables qu'il advisera; veut et entend Sadite Majesté qu'audit cas toutes lettres et dispenses en soient expédiées à la requeste dudit sieur Mareschal tant en cour de Rome que ailleurs, sans en attendre autre plus exprès commandement de Sadite Majesté que ce qu'elle en a délivré par ce present brevet.'

33 *Ibid*, fo 334, *quittance* of 30 Dec 1578. It emerges from this that Montmorency gave up his claims on Beauvais and his pensions off Bourbon's benefices, and in return Bourbon undertook to secure the resignation of the incumbent bishop of Carcassonne, Annibale Rucellaï. Montmorency had obtained a *brevet* from Henri III in July 1578 allowing him to fill Carcassonne with a nominee of his choice once Rucellaï's resignation was handed over to him. In fact, Rucellaï refused to resign or exchange benefices with Bourbon, and Montmorency simply usurped the episcopal lands and prerogatives in Carcassone for nearly fifteen years.

34 Archives du diocèse de Coutances, unnumbered file on the episcopal temporalities, 1497–1693, accounts for 1586. René Toustain de Billy, *Histoire ecclésiastique du diocèse de Coutances*, ed A Héron (Rouen 1886), iii. 186. Billy, who clearly had access to archives that have since vanished, wrote his well-documented history around 1708–9 after years of research conducted while a *curé* in Coutances diocese.

religious wars, Matignon did not have a second son groomed for a career in the church. The seventeenth-century historian of Coutances wrote that Henri III then sent Matignon a blank *brevet de nomination* to Coutances, enabling him to find his own successor to Cossé. We do not know what sort of understanding, verbal or written, was struck between Matignon and the bishop he chose, the elderly Nicolas Briroy, for many years canon and vicar-general of Coutances. But there can have been little doubt in anyone's mind as to what was intended, and the underlying relationship is made perfectly clear in the *brevet* of October 1588 which ratified Briroy's nomination to Coutances:

> Today, the 29 October 1588, the king being at Blois and wishing to gratify Monsieur the maréchal de Matignon in accordance with the gift he made to him for one of his children on 21 December 1587 of the see of Coutances vacant since the death of Messire Artus de Cossé: His Majesty confirms this gift and again wishes and is pleased that, in consideration of the said maréchal and in place of his son, Messire Nicolas de Briroy (...) be appointed to the said vacant diocese.[35]

As elsewhere, the Coutances evidence deals merely with the circumstances of Briroy's nomination, but is silent about the conditions of his tenure. These were not the king's concern, but the language of the concession to Matignon should leave no doubt about the freedom he was given to deal with Briroy.

Most of the bishops promoted as a result of *brevets* of this kind tended to be members of religious orders or commoners drawn from the ranks of local cathedral chapters or of diocesan administrators; once promoted to the episcopate, it was held that neither kind of bishop would possess the social standing or relations to resist their creators. This certainly seems to have been the view of Cardinal Como, Gregory XIII's secretary of state, who concluded in 1583 that the royal nominee to Bayeux, who was suspected by the nuncio of being a caretaker, was 'a noble, and therefore above suspicion of being a *confidentiaire*'.[36] But the case of Nicolas Briroy, son of a Cotentin noble family, shows that such assumptions could be mistaken. It is, however, revealing that at least a quarter of Henri III's bishops cannot be classified in social terms, which in the circumstances of the reign can be regarded as constituting at least indirect evidence that they were men heavily dependent on noble patronage.

Of course, the actual arrangements made between patrons and clients tended to remain private, signed under privy seal or filed away among notaries' minutes, no mention of them ever surfacing in official documents or royal letters. But rumours and allegations, once they had leaked out, could never be wholly suppressed let alone disproved. Because of the ambiguities of

---

35 Toustain de Billy, *Histoire ecclésiastique de Coutances*, iii. 187, for the text of the *brevet*.
36 *ANG*, vii. 553, Como to Castelli, 23 May 1583.

the language and the veil drawn across such practices by those concerned, it remains difficult to identify the extent to which Henri III – and Henri IV after him – allowed arrangements of this kind to flourish. Arrangements which were in part clandestine and which were adapted to different circumstances were in any case unlikely to follow a single model.

This is why the efforts of the 1579 Assembly to uncover them as part of an attempt to reform the higher clergy serves as a useful starting point. The assembly clearly regarded cases of simony and *confidences* as so rampant that three-quarters of all French benefices were affected by the disease, and it resolved to ask the king to refuse entry to the episcopate and other benefices to individuals tainted by them, as well as to require incoming bishops to swear on taking possession of their sees that they had not indulged in simony or confidentiary practices in order to become bishops.[37] The deputies were particularly incensed that confidentiary arrangements were considered valid by the king's council when litigation arose; the situation was so bad in their view that it strengthened their long-standing demand for a return to episcopal elections. In a conference with members of the king's council, the assembly's representatives claimed, with masterly understatement if not deliberate irony, that since Charles IX's reign the king's goodwill – which it was not politic to question in any circumstances – had not been strong enough to withstand either the *malheurs du temps* or, more specifically, the importunity of benefice-hunters. When the members of the council proved understandably reluctant to make any concession on the principle of royal nominations, the abbot of Cîteaux did not hesitate to defend episcopal elections in terms of royal self-interest, painting a bleak picture of what had been, and would continue to happen, if nothing were done:

> the king was in the process of gradually losing control of the nominations, since most of the benefices were in the hands of the leading noble families, who regarded them as hereditary; as a result of which, when they fell vacant the king could not refuse to give them to these families. It was thus easy to see that in a short time the king would no longer be able freely to confer a prelacy. But if elections were restored for a time, the benefices would little by little escape from these families, and would once again become freely disposable.[38]

As we saw, of the twenty-three sees highlighted by the 1579 Assembly, eight were thought to be held under confidentiary arrangements which merit

---

37 *Collection des procès-verbaux des assemblées générales du clergé de France*, ed A Duranthon, 9 vols (Paris 1767–78), i. 133–5.
38 *Ibid*, i. 127–8: 'peu à peu il (the king) s'en alloit perdant les nominations, étant la plupart des bénéfices entre les mains des plus grandes Maisons de France, lesquelles les tenoient comme héréditaires; de sorte que venant à vacquer, le Roi ne pouvoit les leur refuser, dont il étoit aisé à voir que d'ici à quelque temps le Roi n'auroit moyen de donner aucune Prélature; mais qu'étant les Elections remises pour un temps, les Bénéfices sortiroient peu à peu de telles mains, et viendroient en pleine disposition.'

brief examination.³⁹ The assembly was, as we saw, categorical about only three of them. It regarded Viviers as being held *en confidence* and was convinced that the comte de Suze pocketed its revenues. In fact, Jean de l'Hôtel had only been bishop since 1575, but in December 1583, he meekly signed an act resigning Viviers to Suze's son, a move which would constitute *prima facie* evidence of the truth of the assembly's charge. However, Suze's son declined the succession and later married, while l'Hôtel reigned for over forty years until he was required to accept a son from the next generation of the La Baume de Suze family as his coadjutor and successor during the 1610s.⁴⁰ Luçon was another diocese which the assembly found to be in the hands of a confidentiary bishop, even though it failed to identify the beneficiary of the arrangement. Because of Luçon's later history, it is tempting to guess that it was Cardinal Richelieu's father who was master of the diocese, but this seems doubtful in 1579. More likely it was Joyeuse, since the bishop, René de la Salla, was a known Joyeuse relative and client, as was his original intended successor, Antoine de la Bruyère.⁴¹ It was not until La Bruyères apparently declined Luçon that Henri III permitted François de Richelieu, himself connected to the Joyeuses, to pick the successor of his choice and thus to place his own uncle, Jacques du Plessis, in the episcopate while ensuring that Jacques would not interfere in the running of the diocese. What is noteworthy about the Luçon case, apart from the identity of those involved, is how it passed without interruption from one confidentiary settlement to another, a move that would be repeated during the 1590s.⁴² It is hardly surprising, therefore, that the next generation of Richelieus – and of other families involved in similar arrangements – should regard presenting their candidate to Luçon as virtually an acquired right and would not hesitate to press for it to be honoured by the crown.

The 1579 Assembly also stated that Albi, possibly the richest diocese in France at the time, had a bishop who surrendered all its revenues to 'Monsieur de Strozze', namely Filippo Strozzi, colonel-general of the French infantry and a favourite of Catherine de' Medici. The wealth of Albi meant it had always attracted highly connected cardinals, both French and Italian, and the crown was prepared to use it to build and maintain a French party in the Roman curia. In 1579 it was nominally held by Giuliano de' Medici who was also archbishop of Aix – though quite what arrangement he had made over Albi with Strozzi, to whom he was related, remains a mystery!

If the 1579 Assembly could only be categorical about these three

39 The assembly's list and comments are printed in Serbat, *Les Assemblées du clergé de France*, appendix xvii, pp 383–4.
40 Augustin Roche, 'Chronologie des évêques de Viviers', *Revue du Vivarais* (1931), 274–5, with text of resignation, 30 Dec 1583.
41 *ANG*, ii. 269, Nuncio Ragazzoni to Como, 25 June 1584. Better known as the abbé de Villeloin, la Bruyères's name figured in the 1596 settlement in Languedoc between Henri IV, Montmorency and Joyeuse.
42 See Joseph Bergin, *The Rise of Richelieu* (New Haven and London, 1991), 47–8.

bishoprics, it nevertheless went on to cite others which appeared to be no less subject to confidentiary arrangements. It could do no more than assert that Nîmes 'was endowed with a bishop who, it is said, is no more than a pensioner of Monsieur de Joyeuse who collects its revenues'. It turns out that Nîmes did indeed have a bishop since 1573, the Dominican Raymond Cavelesi. He had in fact undertaken, in a private contract, to resign Nîmes whenever and to whomever he might be called upon by Joyeuse to do so, and to turn over to Joyeuse his temporalities and rights to appoint to offices and benefices.[43] The pliant and powerless Cavelesi would be used later by Cardinal Joyeuse in his attempts to retain control of Narbonne after acquiring the see of Toulouse in 1588. Montpellier's bishop, Antoine Subject, was also rumoured to be the caretaker, not of a powerful nobleman, but of a secretary of state, Simon Fizes, who had bought church property in the diocese – the barony of Sauve from which he took his title – and who was also governor of Montpellier in the early 1570s.[44]

The 1579 Assembly also found evidence of two confidentiary bishops in Brittany but it regarded the dioceses of Languedoc and Gascony as by far the worst off, with at least half of their dioceses being either vacant or held irregularly. The situation of Languedoc, it claimed, was so bad that not a single bishop had performed the Easter rites there in 1579, 'since there is virtually nobody in these dioceses apart from *économes*'.[45] The assembly also confessed that it had no evidence at all for the fifteen Provençal dioceses where strong noble and protestant interests were keen to control episcopal appointments.

How far did the assembly's criticisms elicit the same positive response from Henri III as its strictures over vacant bishoprics? How different was the condition of the episcopate a decade later? On a conservative estimate, it would seem that there may have been as many as sixteen cases of *confidences* by 1589: that is, twice the number detected by the assembly ten years earlier. This was partly because some of the dioceses reported vacant and administered by *économes* in 1579 – such as Agde, Tarbes, Condom – were subsequently filled by confidentiary bishops, while other sees not mentioned at all in 1579 were granted *en confidence* in later years – among them Pamiers, Castres, and Saint-Pons. In 1578 the nuncio, Dandino, reported that Montmorency-Damville had given Agde to his treasurer Jean Martin, whom Dandino suspected of being a Huguenot, though the nomination was never confirmed; three years later, Bernard du Puy became bishop of Agde, and it was no secret that he was completely in Montmorency's

---

43 L Ménard, *Histoire civile ecclésiastique et littéraire de la ville de Nîmes* (Nîmes 1873), v. 79–80. Cavelesi was only entitled to an annual pension of 1,200 *livres*.
44 On Fizes, see Hélène Michaud, *La Grande chancellerie et les écritures royales au xvie siècle* (Paris 1967), 153, n 1; E Le Roy Ladurie, *Les Paysans du Languedoc* 2 vols (Paris 1966), i. 366–7, for his purchase of episcopal barony of Sauve in 1563.
45 *Procès-verbaux*, i. 123: 'n'y ayant dans tous les Evêchés quasi que des Econornes'.

pocket.⁴⁶ The same nuncio was convinced, rightly it seems, that the new bishop of Pamiers was a caretaker for a Gascon military noble, Esparbès de Lussan.⁴⁷ The new bishop nominated to Bayeux in 1583 was widely regarded as a caretaker of the princess of Conty, but he died in 1586 and after that the see remained vacant for a decade and a half.⁴⁸ The decline that we noted earlier in the number of vacant dioceses may, therefore, have been achieved only through a rise in the number of *confidences* or analogous arrangements.

Contemporaries seem to have regarded both *économats* and *confidences* as equally unacceptable abuses. Yet from an historian's point of view, this equation is not entirely satisfactory. The paradox of confidentiary arrangements is that the bishops in question were very often experienced local churchmen and administrators who were familiar with local conditions and often proved to be conscientious and active bishops. The opprobrium attached to them was based on other considerations. The corruption, if one may use the term, which their appointments entailed was institutional rather than personal. The papacy and French critics alike feared that if it were allowed to take root, the *confidence* would rob the episcopate of its distinctiveness by secularising most of its temporalities and powers of patronage and jurisdiction; bishops would then be little more than chaplains to the powerful noble families who engineered their elevation. First in 1564, but especially in 1569, with the aptly named bull, *Intolerabilis*, Rome attempted to define as well as to condemn for the first time this unfamiliar form of simony, and at least one French provincial council, that of Bourges in 1584, adopted the papal condemnation.⁴⁹ In the context of the wars of religion, with their often vicious local antagonisms, the fear of a permanently debilitated episcopate was an understandable one.

The emergence of confidentiary bishops from roughly the 1560s onwards can easily lead to the assumption that the French episcopate was increasingly a victim of the cupidity of the lay aristocracy. But *confidences* and analogous arrangements would not have been possible without clerical collusion, as was repeatedly observed at the time. If this is obvious enough where those individuals seeking to become bishops were concerned, it is less often realised how far powerful members of the clergy were themselves exploiting fellow clerics. It is a one sided view that the clergy, especially the upper clergy, were limited to roles in which they were subservient clients and their patrons were always laymen; such a view, when applied to situations like that of the wars of religion, can lead to a repetition of the old *clericis laicos* dirge of Boniface

---

46 ANG, viii. 228, Dandino to Como, 16 Sept 1578.
47 *Ibid*, 615, 620, 625, Dandino to Como, 1, 13 and 22 Mar 1580. It may be noted that the first two of these letters were sent in code, suggesting that the material was sensitive enough not to take the risk of its being intercepted.
48 ANG, vii. 540–1, Castelli to Como, 2 May 1583; p 553, Como to Castelli, 23 May 1583.
49 P-T Durand de Maillane, *Dictionnaire de droit canonique et de pratique bénéficiale* (Paris 1771), i. 366–9.

VIII and his disciples. In general, historians have not paid much attention to the potential for powerful patronage connections to develop within the ranks of the clergy, connections which could involve domination as much as assistance. Practices such as pluralism, the 'reservation' of revenues, the right to recover benefices one had held in the past should a successor die or wish to resign them – all of these conferred considerable freedom of initiative on sixteenth-century bishops, and on none more so than its leading figures. Cardinals, in particular, were expected to promote their clients into the episcopal order, and their freedom to resign and transfer dioceses with relatively little interference was crucial to their ability to do so. When the 1579 Assembly drew up its list of irregularly held bishoprics, it revealed that one-third of the vacant sees administered by *économes* were in fact controlled by leading ecclesiastics. The papacy was not well pleased to see the Cardinal d'Este, who dominated Narbonne by this means, placed at the head of the list which, for good measure, also included the Cardinal de Birague, Charles de Bourbon and Renaud de Beaune.[50]

For his part, Henri III showed few signs of wishing to curtail this particular manifestation of ecclesiastical liberty. Renaud de Beaune seems to have had an entirely free hand to settle the succession at Mende when he was given Bourges by the king's brother in 1577 and, as befitted the son of François I's leading financier, he sought to drive as hard a bargain as he could manage. If it took him four years to get papal confirmation as archbishop of Bourges, it was because he did his best to hold on to Mende in one way or another.[51] Arguably, the duc d'Alençon, Beaune's patron, played a greater role in the succession at Mende than did Henri III himself, although Mende was certainly not in his gift.[52] After one or more possible settlements failed to take shape, it was, finally, Beaune's own vicar-general in Mende, Adam de Heurtelou, who succeeded him.[53] He agreed to surrender an abbey and pay a hefty pension to Beaune, signing a contract the terms of which could hardly have been more explicit, namely that the nomination 'of the person of the said Heurtelou to the said bishopric was made by His Majesty on behalf, and on the supplication and petition of, the said sieur de Bourges'.[54]

50 *ANG*, viii. 456, Dandino to Como, 21 July 1579.
51 AD Lozère, G 60, Jean de la Marthonie to a Captain Lambert at Mende, 28 Feb 1584, with a detailed offer to Beaune of 10,000 *livres* per annum in a pension from Mende and other benefices, in return for letting him have Mende.
52 *Ibid*, G 57, letter to Beaune, n.d., asking him to postpone his resignation of Mende for a few months so that he could find a way of satisfying Monsieur de la Fin, his *chambellan*.
53 *Ibid*, G 60, undated letter (ca 1585) to a Roman cardinal whose name is given here as Reballer.
54 AN, MC, LXXVIII, 135, agreement of 31 May 1586: '... qui avoyt esté faicte audit evesché de la personne dudit de Heurtelou par Sa Majesté à la faveur, prière et requeste dudit sieur de Bourges'. In an earlier agreement of the previous year, it had been agreed that the cost of the papal bulls would be paid by de Beaune, which gave him a financial hold on Heurtelou, who was also required to pay an annual pension of 5,000 *livres* from the revenues of Mende (LXXVIII, 133, 15 Oct 1585). I wish to thank Olivier Poncet for bringing these notarial documents to my attention.

Henri III, clearly, could be quite accommodating towards arrangements suggested by certain bishops themselves. In 1582, he gave the see of Castres to his wife's brother, the Cardinal de Vaudémont, but when he quickly decided to part with it, Henri gave him a free hand to find a candidate, who would have to agree to pay Vaudémont a substantial pension.[55] The king's generosity to the Joyeuse family is also well known and, as we have just seen, it extended to their ecclesiastical clients and interests; nor did it cease when Henri's favourite was killed at Coutras in 1587, since his younger brother, Cardinal François de Joyeuse, received Toulouse in addition to Narbonne in 1588.

VI

It may be objected at this point that the developments we have been discussing appear to have affected only a minority of dioceses under Charles IX and Henri III. In fact, the real purpose of this discussion has been to use a particular set of problems in order to understand the world of royal patronage which made them possible in the first place. But above all, it can now be suggested that an episcopate which took shape in such a context was not ideally placed to confront a challenge at least as acute as that represented by the rapid emergence of Protestantism in the 1550s and 1560s – that of the Catholic League and the Bourbon succession. As we saw, well over half of the bishops of 1589 gained office under Henri III, and a high proportion of these only did so during the 1580s. No fewer than twenty newcomers had been appointed since 1585 when the Catholic League was reborn and the politico-religious climate began to deteriorate sharply. These were hardly propitious conditions for new bishops to take up office in dioceses which were soon to differ sharply in their reaction to the events of 1588–9. It may also be suggested that a certain lack of experience of the realities of episcopal office accounted in part at least for the hesitancy of many, especially recently appointed bishops when faced with the decision of how to react to Henri IV's accession. In fact, the positions taken by the bishops during the decade after 1584 have yet to be fully elucidated, and it may well be impossible to discover much about some of them, because of absenteeism, timidity, or uncongenial local conditions. As far as their adherence to the Catholic League is concerned, it is essential to appreciate that their support was never constant and that circumstances, both national and local, were crucial in bringing new episcopal recruits to its ranks. Moreover, once they had joined the League, their attachment was no more unbreakable than that of other adherents, either clerical or lay; some bishops are known to have become disenchanted by it at diocesan level rather than by its response to broader national developments; in some

---

55 ANG, ii. 257–8, Ragazzoni to Como, 28 May 1584. See also *Mémoires de Jacques Gaches*, ed Charles Pradel (Paris 1879), 291.

cases, the behaviour of local *ligueurs* may have made individual bishops revert towards neutrality and gradual recognition of Henri IV.[56]

At any rate, Henri III's ecclesiastical policies had no more endeared him to the French church and its leaders than his other policies had won him the support he desperately sought to achieve. His nominations to bishoprics and other major benefices, together with the successive sales of church property and an apparent reluctance to make war on the Huguenots, were the main reasons for this lack of popularity, which is evident in the criticisms voiced inside and outside of the assemblies of clergy. The continuing calls for a return to episcopal elections may have been a matter of tactics for the bishops attending the assemblies, but even if they were intended to pressurise the king into making acceptable episcopal appointments, at the very least they were a public expression of dissatisfaction with his performance.[57] He could not, therefore, count on many churchmen defending his government after the death of his only surviving brother Anjou-Alençon in mid-1584 and the resurgence of the Catholic League which followed. Those who did so, like Renaud de Beaune or Claude d'Angennes of Le Mans, were seen as defending royal inactivity over heresy or even as advocating a measure of religious toleration. On the other hand, high-ranking figures like Cardinals Guise and Bourbon or Pierre d'Epinac, archbishop of Lyon, were associated from an early date with the League and its determination to prevent Henri IV from succeeding to the throne. Despite such examples, the great majority of the bishops behaved with considerable caution after 1584: for them the succession crisis could remain just a worrying possibility for as long as Henri III was still alive, while Sixtus V's excommunication and banning of Henri of Navarre from the succession in 1585 made it conveniently unnecessary for them to take a potentially problematic personal stance on such questions. These factors are reflected in the figures available for episcopal support for the League in these years: from approximately eleven around 1585, the total rose to twenty-four by the critical year of 1589 – in other words, to about a quarter of the episcopate then in office.[58]

Unity of episcopal response was not forthcoming even in the wake of the Guise murders of December 1588 and Henri III's own assassination the following August. Seventeen of the twenty-six bishops present at the Estates General of 1588 were or would later become *ligueurs*, but it should not be forgotten that a substantial minority was, even after the Guise murders, prepared to face attack for being royalists or, worse still,

---

56 Christopher Stocker, 'Orléans and the Catholic League' *Proceedings of the Western Society for French History*, 16 (1989), 12–21.
57 *ANG*, ii. 482, Nuncio Ragazzoni to Cardinal Rusticucci, 25 Nov 1585; Serbat, *Les Assemblées du clergé*, 282ff.
58 Baumgartner, *Change and Continuity*, 158–60. This figure is higher than the same author's total of eight given in an earlier study: 'Crisis in the French Episcopacy: The Bishops and the Succession of Henry IV', *Archiv für Reformationsgeschichte*, 70 (1979), 282.

politiques.⁵⁹ It was, however, the murder of Henri III himself rather than that of the Guises, and thus Henri IV's accession *de jure*, which pushed some former royalists into the League, and obliged the large body of episcopal *attentistes* to commit themselves. After 1589–90, the number of neutral bishops shrunk to about ten or twelve in all. Such adherence was no doubt facilitated by the fact that, despite Henri IV's declaration of Saint-Cloud (August 1589) to maintain the Catholic church and to seek religious instruction, only part of the great nobility declared their support for him in 1589–90; the new pope, Gregory XIV, proved an intransigent opponent of the king, renewing the 1585 excommunication, and even sending papal troops to France to support the League. It would take the cautious Clement VIII (1592–1605) some time to abandon such rigid positions and to envisage accepting Henri IV as France's rightful king.⁶⁰ Some bishops subsequently assumed a leading role in local Leagues, often alongside lay members of their own families, while others were nudged into joining because pro-League pressure was so strong in their dioceses or episcopal towns. Even Cardinal Joyeuse, who had been prepared to go to Rome to defend Henri III over the Guise murders, returned to Toulouse after the king's death and threw himself into the League's cause in upper Languedoc. The high-water mark of episcopal support for the League thus came between 1589 and 1591, when just over half of the reigning bishops came out on the side of the League, while thirty-six have been described as *politiques*, leaving a small group (some of whom had fled their dioceses altogether) without any label at all.⁶¹ Not even the Italian bishops who owed so much to royal patronage remained immune to such temptation, and men like Alexander Canigiani of Aix, Antonio Cuppis of Sisteron, Horatio Birgue of Lavaur, and Luca Alemanni of Mâcon were among the most zealous *ligueurs* of the entire episcopate.⁶²

The geographical scatter of League bishops is also interesting to note, though again rigid patterns and conclusions should be eschewed. Burgundy, Champagne and Picardy were traditional centres of Guise influence, and most of the bishops there followed the League; Normandy was another, and three of its bishops were determined supporters of the League. Brittany and Provence were, as observed earlier, the two provinces which were least integrated, both politically and ecclesiastically, into the French monarchy, and the League may have seemed to some of their bishops an opportunity for greater autonomy. The remainder of the episcopal *ligueurs* were largely concentrated in the great dioceses of the centre and south-west, with Bordeaux and especially Toulouse as the main poles of attraction. Joyeuse power in upper

---

59 Baumgartner, *Change and Continuity*, 162.
60 Michael Wolfe, *The Conversion of Henri IV. Politics, Power and Religious Belief in Early Modern France* (Cambridge, Mass. 1993), 56–8.
61 Baumgartner, *Change and Continuity*, 166ff.
62 Jean-François Dubost, 'Les Italiens en France au xvie et xviie siècle' (Thesis, Université de Paris-I, 1992), 606–9.

Languedoc had developed in opposition to that of the Montmorency governors of the province, whose power was greater in eastern Languedoc and in the more northerly, upland dioceses of Mende, Le Puy and Viviers. Montmorency patronage and power ensured that bishops here would be a combination of royalists and *politiques*, while those of upper Languedoc and its Pyrenean extension proved to be mostly *ligueurs*. It may also be suggested that in provinces whose Estates met more frequently and undertook far more activities during the League years, it was inherently more difficult for bishops, who were often entitled to preside over the Estates in question and to organise tax-assessment and collection within their respective dioceses, to avoid committing themselves to one cause or another.[63]

There is, however, one important respect in which this geographical pattern is misleading. The personal preferences of bishops, whether royalist or *ligueur*, are no indication of the affiliations of their dioceses, or more specifically of their cathedral cities. Two more *ligueur* cities than Paris and Nantes would be hard to imagine, but towns like Saint-Malo, Auxerre and Beauvais were scarcely less so, and all made their bishops extremely uncomfortable, especially when they were known previously to have been supporters of Henri III's policies. Philippe du Bec of Nantes was subject to persecution and vituperation from the *ligueur* parlement based in Nantes itself, which may have been both cause and effect of his open royalism and early support for Henri IV. Cardinal Gondi of Paris subscribed to the League for a time, but like Jacques Amyot of Auxerre, he found that even so his motives were open to intense suspicion from *ligueurs*. But while Amyot died without accepting Henri IV in 1593, Gondi had abandoned both Paris and the League in 1591. The *ligueurs* of Beauvais arrested and ransomed their royalist bishop Nicolas Fumée, treating him so roughly that he soon died.

The numerous clashes that followed the events of 1588–9 in many dioceses had as much to do with local issues as with wider national divisions. Old conflicts often took on a new lease of life in this period. Rivalries between towns over the location of royal courts, for example, could determine a decision for or against the League, but the result might be that an episcopal town closed its gates to its *ligueur* bishop, as happened in Clermont in 1589.[64] At virtually the same time, the city of Châlons-sur-Marne snapped up the chance to shake off Guise control and refused entry to its *ligueur* bishop, Cosme Clausse. Other examples of such desires to reassert urban self-rule could be cited, and in some cases they found episcopal authority and jurisdiction blocking their path.[65] One of the worst examples of such a clash occurred

---

63 J Russell Major, *Representative Government in Early Modern France* (New Haven and London 1980), ch 8. Between 1585 and 1596, the rival Estates in Languedoc met a total of thirty-seven times (p 228).

64 See Joseph Bergin, *Cardinal de La Rochefoucauld: Leadership and Reform in the French Church* (New Haven and London, 1987), 21–2.

65 See Baumgartner, *Change and Continuity*, ch 9, for more detail and statistics of episcopal political affiliations in these years.

in Rodez in June 1589 when the bishop's palace was broken into, its furniture smashed, the building burned down, and the bishop himself imprisoned. The incident originated in fear of the bishop's designs to extend his jurisdiction over the city, and to use military means in the form of a citadel adjoining his palace to do so. Leaguer and royalist parties crystallised around this dispute, one of the most enduring and venomous of the time.[66] The radical *ligueur consuls* of Marseille heaped vituperation upon their royalist bishop, François Ragueneau, who had fled to Italy, even petitioning the pope as late as 1595 for his removal.[67]

Elsewhere, internal conflicts took some time to appear. The League's oath of union was taken in Le Puy, as in many other towns, at Easter 1589, in response to overtures from a delegation from Toulouse which included the bishop of Castres. But later, despite the continuing leadership of the Toulouse league, cracks began to appear in the union, followed by a massacre of royalists in 1593 and an insurrection in 1594. The elderly bishop Antoine de Senneterre had quit Le Puy well before that, and died in November 1592.[68] At Orléans, Jean de Laubespine had also fervently embraced the holy union in early 1589 and become deeply involved in its activities, but within two years he was clearly disenchanted, complaining about unruly preachers and his own humiliation by insolent local League leaders.[69]

Defections like those of Senneterre or Jean de Laubespine were the outcome of local conflicts, and did not always have a wider, national impact. But even though they did not lead to declarations of support for Henri IV, such defections made the labours of those bishops who backed the new king, either in 1589 or later, that much the less Sisyphean. There can be no question of rewriting the history of Henri IV's long-drawn out conversion to Catholicism here, but at crucial stages along the way episcopal support played a major part in it. Initially, in August 1589, only about seven bishops accepted the Bourbon succession, with two cardinals, Lenoncourt and Vendôme, following suit a few months later. But when, in February 1590, the latter invited Leaguer bishops to a meeting at Tours to prepare for Henri IV's religious instruction, they achieved nothing whatever beyond some angry responses from committed *ligueurs* like Bishop Hennequin of Rennes.[70] A year and a half later in July and September 1591, new meetings organised at Mantes and Chartres by royalist clergy were also comprehensively ignored by *ligueurs*, and attracted fewer than ten bishops in all. Only one bishop, Escars of Langres,

---

66 AD Averyon, G 497, attempted settlement of dispute before notary, 1 Sept 1589. This conflict would drag on for several decades, with Richelieu himself being called upon to settle it as late as 1629!
67 ASV, N Fr 43, fos 4–6, Consuls to Clement VIII, n.d.; to 126, same to same, 26 Apr 1595, fos 138–9, same to same, 1 July 1595.
68 Bernard Rivet, *Une Ville au xvie siècle: Le Puy-en-Velay* (Le Puy 1988). Rivet claims the bishop left in 1593, which is clearly impossible.
69 Wolfe, *Conversion of Henri IV*, 77; Stocker, 'Orléans and the Catholic League', 12–21.
70 Wolfe, *Conversion of Henri IV*, 77–8. This book is by far the best study available of the royal conversion.

publicly recognised Henri IV as a result of these two assemblies. Yet the committed support of men like Claude d'Angennes of Le Mans and Renaud de Beaune of Bourges, both close advisers to the king, as well as of others like Philippe du Bec of Nantes or Nicolas de Thou of Chartres was important, as they denied the League the prize of an episcopate united against Henri IV; in addition, they worked on public opinion, sharpening Gallican sensitivity to papal interference in France's affairs and preparing the ground for the king's final conversion. Thirteen bishops attended the League's own Estates General of January 1593, which may not seem much of a triumph, but the uncertainty of travel and safety was such that *any* assembly of this kind was a minor miracle. By then, however, the political winds were blowing more strongly in Henri IV's favour, with the result that the Estates failed to elect a Catholic monarch as had been intended, and eventually agreed to discuss the conditions for Navarre's conversion. Yet when the king's formal instruction leading to his conversion commenced in July 1593, it only attracted royalist ecclesiastics and a single former Leaguer bishop, Givry d'Escars.[71] Thereafter, episcopal acceptance of Henri IV nationally was to be no more rapid than that of other groups, and it would take his formal absolution by Clement VIII in September 1595 to bring round the remaining defenders of the Leaguer cause.

---

71   BN, MS Fr 3430, fos 28–40, *procès-verbal* of royal absolution and conversion, July 1593.

CHAPTER 10

Henri IV and the Stabilisation of the Episcopate

THE CRISIS OF the Bourbon succession was not the only one facing France's bishops after Henri III's death. For all its seriousness, the dynastic issue was resolved without lasting damage to them collectively. The threat of a schismatic 'national' church under episcopal leadership which Rome had feared around 1591–3 never materialised because there was at this point no strong, legitimate monarch to take the initiative and command episcopal adherence; left to themselves, the higher clergy were unlikely to find the cohesiveness or singlemindedness required in order to create the kind of national patriarchate which Rome periodically warned against. And whatever doubts they may have entertained about the manner and the motives of the royal conversion of 1593, most of the bishops who had not already done so proved willing to recognise Henri IV and did so in the year or two which followed. The formal papal absolution of September 1595 left the dwindling band of Ultras with little reason to fight on, with the exception of those in unsubdued provinces like Brittany. When it came, the edict of Nantes did, of course, revive their suspicions of Henri IV, but episcopal criticism was muted and contrasts sharply with the reaction to events a decade previously. Nor, for all the bitterness that had characterised numerous confrontations between *ligueurs* and royalists, does it seem that the experiences of the League left lasting divisions within the episcopate. Individual prelates like Renaud de Beaune might remain objects of suspicion because of their role as advisers to Henri IV in the years before his conversion, but open ideological rifts were not an immediate legacy of the League. Admittedly, both Gallican and Ultramontane attitudes hardened in the generation after the end of the wars, but they were also fuelled by a number of other causes, and they did not lead to an episcopate bedevilled with factional disputes.

The second crisis of the episcopate during the final phase of the League proved less easy to resolve because it was of a different order, and concerned the condition of the episcopate itself. As we saw, whatever the quality of his nominees, Henri III had not, in his last years at least, left French dioceses without bishops. He had probably made nominations to most of the ten sees vacant at the time of his death, but not surprisingly Rome was in no mood to confirm the decisions of an excommunicated king, and the best that his nominees could hope for was to be adopted in due course by Henri IV or by the League. In either case, the prospects of rapid promotion to episcopal rank cannot have seemed especially bright. At the outset of his reign, therefore, Henri IV was faced with an episcopate which was relatively 'full' and, apart from a few of its members, was in no hurry to rally to his side as the rightful claimant to the throne. It would thus be mistaken to take as fact the comments of later observers that a substantial proportion of France's bishoprics were simply left vacant during the League. It was not until the mid-1590s that it was possible to make such a claim, and even then the figures given for vacant dioceses could vary widely. In November 1596, the recently arrived papal legate, Cardinal Medici, calculated that 'up to forty or so' sees were vacant.[1] As one of his principal objectives was the restoration of the episcopate, we may assume he did not quote such a figure lightly, yet uncertainty remains as to the basis of his statements. He did not provide his own list of vacant sees, and his conception of an episcopal vacancy may differ from that of a modern historian, so it is imperative to look at the question not merely of the number of vacancies, but of the context in which they had arisen in the first place.

I

The first assumption that should be discarded is that if there were so many empty bishoprics by 1596, it was because nominations had not been made to them since 1589. If anything, the exact opposite was true, with multiple nominations to particular dioceses emanating from the rival claimants to the royal prerogative. A brief analysis of the ensuing confusion is essential for an understanding of the problems of reconstruction to be discussed later. To begin with, it seems unlikely that the League's short-lived 'king', Charles X, made or even confirmed any episcopal nominations before his death in May 1590, since he was the prisoner of Henri IV![2] On the other hand, there is little doubt that the duc de Mayenne, as the League's *lieutenant-général du royaume*, fully intended to nominate to vacant sees. His dependence on papal or local support in France did not make him sympathetic to ideas of direct papal nomination or of a return to elections by cathedral chapters; until such time as France had a legitimate Catholic monarch, he regarded it as his duty to

---

1 ASV, Fondo Borghese I, 646, fo 71, letter to Cardinal Pietro Aldobrandini, papal secretary of state, 24 Nov 1596. Medici's exact expression was 'sin a quaranta in circa'.
2 It has been claimed that he nominated a new bishop of Fréjus, but as the reigning bishop only died in late 1591, long after Bourbon had died, this is clearly impossible. See H Espitalier, 'Les Evêques de Fréjus du xiiie à la fin du xviiie siècle', *Bulletin de la Société d'Etudes Scientifiques et Archéologiques de la ville de Draguignan*, 22 (1898–9), 4, for this assertion.

preserve the crown's rights. Irritated perhaps by the activities of the papal legate Caetani who disposed of abbeys and other benefices, but not as far as is known, of bishoprics,[3] Mayenne bluntly instructed his agent in Rome in early 1591 that unless papal provisions were granted 'on my nomination and recommendation' he would not recognise them or allow their holders to draw the revenues of their benefices.[4] He received an assurance to that effect from Gregory XIV, but it is not clear that the papacy really wished to allow him the free hand he demanded.[5] At least Mayenne did not suffer from poor channels of communication to Rome: apart from the services of his agent there, Jacques de Diou, he could fall back upon the papal envoys in France, as well as men like Cardinals Joyeuse and Pellevé, both present in Rome at different times after 1589.

On only one occasion did Mayenne give any clue to his intentions on these questions. Writing to the *prévôt des marchands* of Paris in December 1590, he urged him to assure the preachers of the capital that, as far as promotions to ecclesiastical 'dignities' were concerned, Mayenne would prefer them to all other candidates; this was a time, he added, in which 'it was more necessary than ever to maintain the people in their present state of devotion'.[6] Although it is impossible to determine quite how many *brevets de nomination* Mayenne may have granted, the preachers do not appear to have done especially well, doubtless because Mayenne's relations with the radicals of the League soured so badly after 1590. It may be doubted if Mayenne really intended to populate the episcopate with hell-raising preachers, but it comes as a considerable surprise to learn that the notorious *ligueur* Jean Boucher could claim from his exile in Brussels in September 1594 that he had been nominated by Mayenne to the prominent see of Beauvais.[7] Boucher's cause was truly hopeless by then, and his nomination was all the stranger since, within days of Bishop Nicolas Fumée's death in March 1593, Mayenne had given Beauvais to Pierre d'Epinac, archbishop of Lyon and ecclesiastical leader of the League since 1588. At that point in the League's fortunes, Epinac may well have wished to exchange Lyon, which had forsaken the League's cause, for the more secure and fervently *ligueur* town of Beauvais. It appears that it was only after he had

---

3 See Anne-Cécile Tizon-Germe, 'Juridiction spirituelle et action pastorale des légats et nonces en France pendant la ligue 1589–1594', *Archivum Historiae Pontificae*, 30 (1992), 186.
4 *Correspondance de Mayenne*, ed E Henry and C Loriquet (*Travaux de l'Académie Impériale de Reims*, vols 29, 33, 35, Reims 1860–63), iii. 33–4, to Jacques de Diou, 11 May 1591; *ibid*, 66–7, to same, 22 May; *ibid*, 76, to the pope, 22 May. Tizon-Germe, 'Juridiction spirituelle et action pastorale', 187, surmised that Filippo Sega, legate after Apr 1592, had orders to respect Mayenne's claims.
5 *Correspondance de Mayenne*, i. 410–11, Mayenne to Jacques de Diou, agent in Rome, 23 Jan 1591; *ibid*, iii. 76, to the pope, 22 May 1591. The papal concession was also reported by an English source in Rome: *Lists and Analyses of State Papers, Foreign, 1590–91*, ed R B Wernham (London 1969), 405, Apr 1591.
6 *Correspondance de Mayenne*, i. 330, letter of 22 Dec 1590.
7 AN, L 728, Beauvais, dossier no 3. This is the enquiry *de vita et moribus* for Boucher's promotion to Beauvais, and the witnesses on his behalf were all fellow *ligueur* exiles.

recognised Henri IV the following year, in May 1594, that he renounced his claim to Beauvais, thus making way for Boucher's nomination.[8]

Of Mayenne's other nominees, only those of Reims, Noyon, Conserans, Montauban, and Glandèves were successful in obtaining papal provisions. Curiously, it was in northern France, where Guise patronage had historically been strongest, that Mayenne had least success in filling vacant dioceses. After the murder of Cardinal Guise, Reims passed directly to Cardinal Pellevé of Sens, a long-standing Guise client, but Mayenne proved unable to repeat this success in 1594 on Pellevé's own death. He appears to have nominated the *ligueur* bishop of Rennes, Aymar Hennequin, who promptly took the oath of fidelity before the parlement of Paris.[9] But Henri IV no less promptly appointed to Reims one of his most devoted episcopal supporters, Philippe du Bec of Nantes, and although du Bec had to wait four years for Rome's approval, no rival apart from the ephemeral Hennequin emerged to challenge his claim. Moreover, Pellevé's own original see of Sens was also a long-standing Guise diocese, and when he was finally compelled by Rome to resign it after moving to Reims, Mayenne nominated his own uncle, Claude de Guise, abbot of Cluny, as Pellevé's successor.[10] But he failed here, too, and it was Henri IV's own champion, Renaud de Beaune, who secured both the title to and, after many years of waiting, possession of Sens.[11] In addition to Beauvais and Sens, Mayenne designated candidates to Evreux, Troyes and Noyon in 1593, with largely similar outcomes. Nominated by early 1593, Jean Munier, Mayenne's choice for Noyon, died within months of his confirmation by Rome in February 1594 and without taking possession of his diocese.[12] Mayenne was unable to impose his choice of successor. When the neutral bishop of Troyes died in September 1593, Mayenne took an even bigger risk by nominating François Péricard, bishop of Avranches since 1588, as his successor. Although Péricard, from a family of noted Guise servants originally from Troyes itself, took up residence there, he did not hold out

---

8 AN, MC, VIII 408, 20 Mar 1593, *régale* settlement between Epinac and canons of Sainte Chapelle. Fumée had died on 2 March, so Mayenne had clearly not delayed in finding a successor. The League's Estates General was sitting at this time.

9 Père Anselme de Sainte-Marie, *Histoire généalogique et chronologique de la maison royale de France et des grands officiers de la Couronne*, 9 vols (Paris 1726–30), ii. 76, quoting from the registers of the parlement, 2 Apr 1594. Hennequin's oath was made on account of the peerage attached to Reims.

10 ASV, Fondo Borghese I, 636, fo 150, duc de Guise to pope, 15 Oct 1593. Pellevé himself was clearly reluctant to leave Sens, and appealed several times for extensions of the six-month deadline set by Rome: ASV, Fondo Borghese I 462-8, fos 45, 62, 88, letters to Cardinal Aldobrandini, 4 Mar, 8 Apr and 16 Sept 1593 respectively.

11 AN, V^5 1227, fo 268, letters-patent of 22 Jan 1598 recalling that Beaune had been nominated in 1594 'à l'instant' of Pellevé's death.

12 ASV, Fondo Borghese I, 462-8, fo 62, Pellevé to Cardinal Aldobrandini, 8 Apr 1593, describing Munier as a 'doctor of theology and a good preacher, but more virtuous than rich'. AN, MC, VIII 408, 1 Sept 1593, *régale* settlement between Munier and the Sainte Chapelle. Bishop Genevois's death is given here as 'vers la feste Saint Rémy' of 1592, and not Oct 1593, as stated in *Hierarchia Catholica* and other sources.

there for very long.¹³ Unlike the others, however, Péricard did at least have a diocese to return to, and he was to remain at Avranches for over half a century. Mayenne's choice of a bishop for Evreux, Godefroy de Billy, also had to make way for Henri IV's candidate, the future Cardinal du Perron, but he was not definitively relegated to the ranks of the forgotten losers: after a suitable wait, Henri IV gave him the see of Laon in 1601.¹⁴ Finally, Anne de Murviel, a relative of Mayenne's second wife, became bishop of Montauban in 1600, having originally been nominated by Mayenne around 1594–5. His ultimate success, however, was due to the fact that Henri IV proved willing to adopt him as his own candidate after Mayenne had recognised him as lawful king in December 1595.¹⁵

From the evidence available, it is clear that Mayenne's ability to exercise the crown's prerogatives in the ecclesiastical sphere was qualified. Indeed, it may be wondered how much of a voice he had in promoting the successful candidates to Conserans in the Pyrenees, whose bishop resigned the see to his nephew, or to Glandèves in eastern Provence which was then in Savoyard hands. In both cases, it seems highly likely that his approval was sought as a kind of insurance, enabling those in question to seek papal confirmation and to defend their title in case of a backlash later. In any case, by the time Mayenne was making the nominations discussed above, circumstances were beginning to change adversely for him. The new pope, Clement VIII, elected in January 1592, was far more cautious in his dealings with the League than his predecessor; although in no hurry to accept Henri IV's title, he was increasingly reluctant to confirm episcopal nominations which might needlessly antagonise him. If Mayenne failed in subsequent negotiations towards a settlement with Henri IV which would include presentation rights to the bishoprics in his Burgundian governorship, it was not merely because the king was hostile to such deals, but also in part because of Mayenne's limited success during previous years.

Mayenne was not the only one anxious to establish his formal right to have a say in making episcopal appointments during these years. The case of Brittany is also of particular interest in this regard. Like Provence, it was not subject to the 1516 Concordat, and French kings only nominated its bishops by virtue of special indults granted *ad hominem* by Rome to individual French monarchs. Henri III's indult lapsed with his death, and Rome was extremely slow to grant one to Henri IV, even after his absolution in 1595. Meanwhile, Mayenne's cousin, Mercoeur, *ligueur* governor of Brittany and would-be champion of its privileges, claimed the right to choose the province's bishops,

13   ASV, Fondo Borghese I, 636, fo 147, duc de Guise to Cardinal Aldobrandini, 29 Sept 1593. AN, MC, VIII 408, 25 Nov 1593, *régale* settlement between Péricard and Sainte Chapelle.
14   AN, MC, VIII 408, 10 Apr 1593, *régale* settlement between Billy and Sainte Chapelle.
15   Camille Daux, *Histoire de l'église de Montauban*, 2 vols (Montauban 1882–6), ii. 3, who claims he received papal confirmation 'sur la proposition de Mayenne' and with royal approval.

and in 1594 he even thanked the pope for accepting his case.[16] But despite this, he enjoyed relatively few opportunities to exercise such rights. In 1590, he merely supported Georges d'Aradon's election by the canons of Vannes cathedral and wrote to Rome in his support. Nor does he appear to have tried to fill the see of Dol whose bishop died the following year. When Vannes became vacant for a second time in early 1596, the chapter again elected a bishop and Mercoeur recommended him to the pope,[17] but circumstances had changed considerably since 1590: Clement VIII was now keen to prove, less to Mercoeur than to Henri IV, that since no indult had been granted since 1589, his rights as pope to nominate Brittany's bishops came first, and he proceded, in 1596, to name his own choice of successor to Vannes.[18] But neither Mercoeur's candidate nor even Clement VIII's was successful, and it was Henri IV who would later capture Vannes for a nominee of his own. It is not known if Mercoeur tried to make nominations to Saint-Brieuc or Rennes when they, too, fell vacant in 1595–6; at any rate, despite the fact that the governor defied Henri IV until early 1598, it was the royal nominees to both sees who were confirmed in due course.[19]

It is apparent from other evidence also that the papacy wished to retain a free hand in French ecclesiastical affairs, however much it might have to please Mayenne or Mercoeur. For example, it was the papacy that was mainly responsible for the uncle-to-nephew succession at Conserans in 1592 and, as we saw in the case of Brittany, it was also keen to demonstrate that, in the two provinces which were not covered by the terms of the concordat of Bologna, it had recovered its liberty of action since Henri III's excommunication. It was for this reason that Rome confirmed the only overt episcopal election of these years, that of the *ligueur* Georges d'Aradon at Vannes. The same considerations governed its direct appointment of the famous Hebrew scholar, Gilbert Génébrard, to be archbishop of Aix in May 1591, and of his friend Gérard Bellenger to Fréjus in December 1592.[20] Guillaume le Blanc had originally been nominated to Vence by Henri III in 1588, but by the time he obtained papal confirmation in 1592, it was with a view to uniting Vence and Grasse as a single diocese, an idea which both the papacy and Savoy promoted.[21] It was Rome, too, which appointed the vice-legate of Avignon, Grimaldi, to be administrator rather than bishop of Toulon between 1589 and his death in

16 ASV, Fondo Borghese I, 636, fo 210, letter to Clement VIII, 8 Oct 1594.
17 *Lettres du cardinal d'Ossat*, ed Amelot de la Houssaye, 5 vols (Amsterdam 1718), ii. 76–8, Ossat to Villeroy, 10 Mar 1596.
18 *Ibid*, ii. 40–3, 267–8, Ossat to Villeroy, 22 Feb and 19 Oct 1596 respectively. Ossat himself did everything he could in the curia to prevent any *démarches* from being made on behalf of the elected candidate, Jean Juhel, who had been one of Sega's most active clerical servants during his 1592–4 legation.
19 The king's choice for Rennes was Ossat himself, who would become a cardinal a few years later.
20 *Gallia Chr Nov*, i. cols 129–31, 401–2.
21 G Doublet, 'Guillaume le Blanc évêque de Grasse et de Vence à la fin du xvie siècle', *Annales du Midi*, 13 (1901) 176–89, 346–65.

1592.²² Moreover, the papacy was also willing to take advantage of France's disorders to strike out beyond Provence and Brittany: it directly appointed the Scots *ligueur* and exiled bishop of Rosse, John Lesley, to Coutances, also in December 1592.²³

But the contrasting fortunes of these men illustrate the political changes occurring around them and the limits to independent papal action. Aradon was not challenged at Vannes, although he spent much of the time in Paris; protected by the virtual autonomy enjoyed by Brittany during the League, he died in 1596, still refusing to recognise Henri IV.²⁴ But Génébrard, Bellenger and Lesley all finished up as exiles from their dioceses. Génébrard had at least actually governed Aix for a time before taking refuge in the *ligueur* stronghold of Marseille, which probably sealed his fate, but neither Bellenger nor Lesley were ever bishops of their respective sees on anything but paper.²⁵

The papacy's position during these years can also be gauged from the activities of its envoys in France. Between 1589 and 1594, it was represented not by nuncios, but mainly by legates wielding considerably wider powers of jurisdiction in both spiritual and temporal matters. This shift reflected papal determination not to allow the disputed royal succession to paralyse the church or its own jurisdiction. The successive legates Caetani and Sega both strongly supported the Catholic League, and in addition to granting faculties to absolve from heresy in several dioceses, they used their powers to intervene in dioceses held by openly royalist bishops. In 1590, the *ligueur* parlement sitting at Nantes actually deprived Philippe du Bec of the administration of Nantes diocese, and a vicar-general was appointed by the cathedral chapter. But in 1593, Sega insisted on replacing him with a vicar-general of his own, who remained in post for the next five years. The legate acted similarly in the diocese of Angers, though with less success, and he also issued powers to Bishop Péricard of Avranches enabling him to govern Troyes, to which Mayenne had just nominated him. Such intervention in the French church, particularly in defiance of incumbent bishops, was as unprecedented as it was short-lived, and it was hardly surprising that the legates' decisions were quashed outright by the Paris parlement after the League's collapse.²⁶

Finally, the legates tried to broker two major episcopal successions which reflect familiar and continuing problems of family power and ecclesiastical patronage. When Caetani arrived in France in late 1589, the widow of the duc de Guise was pressing hard to ensure the late cardinal's benefices went to her

---

22 *Gallia Chr Nov*, v. cols 639–40.
23 *Hierarchia Catholica*, iv. 161; Bernard Jacqueline, 'L'Evêché de Coutances au temps de la ligue: John Lesley évêque de Coutances 1592–1597', *Revue du Départment de la Manche*, 10 (1968), 95–101.
24 Tizon-Germe, 'Juridiction spirituelle et action pastorale', 190.
25 *Gallia Chr Nov*, i. cols 131–2, 402; Espitalier, 'Evêques de Fréjus', 4–5.
26 Tizon-Germe, 'Juridiction spirituelle et action pastorale', 200, 213–18.

eight-year-old son. Caetani had difficulty persuading her that the see of Reims should not be included, so it was agreed in the end that the trustworthy Pellevé of Sens should have it, but pay a pension to young Guise. A few years later, with the ageing Pellevé in Rome and Guise's son still too young to take office, Sega, having succeeded Caetani as legate, tried to ensure that Reims would continue to have a true Catholic (i.e. a pro-League) archbishop by pressing for the promotion of another *ligueur* and Guise client, Bishop La Rochefoucauld of Clermont, with La Rochefoucauld's own brother stepping into his shoes at Clermont.[27] Neither objective was within Sega's grasp, however.

The Guises also had a close interest in the fortunes of Auch, reputed to be France's richest bishopric. It was vacant since the death in 1586 of Cardinal d'Este, brother of the duchesse de Nemours, the first wife of duc François de Guise. Henri III had nominated Nemours' second son, the marquis de Saint-Sorlin, to Auch, but he was only seventeen years old in 1590, and went on to follow a military career, eventually succeeding his elder brother as duc de Nemours. In 1590, Caetani agreed to support Nemours' choice of a stop-gap archbishop, a Paris preacher called Cristin, though nothing came of this.[28] Four years later, Sega tried again, but this time he supported a candidate agreed by the Auch chapter who also happened to be Mayenne's secretary! But here, also, too much time had been lost, and Clement VIII may have been relieved not to have had to approve as archbishop of Auch a man whose status seemed little better than that of a Nemours *confidentiaire*.[29]

II

Whereas a Mayenne or a Mercoeur was never more than a faction leader who was bound to promote his own supporters, Henri IV was a faction leader who was determined to gain recognition as France's rightful king. Like them, he was anxious to protect and exercise his royal rights, but for the Most Christian King to be an excommunicate and a heretic in the eyes of the majority of his subjects was a serious handicap for several years. Ecclesiastical matters might appear secondary compared to the task of conquering a kingdom, but neither could they be neglected; even had he wished to, Henri IV could not avoid making decisions in matters of church patronage from the earliest days of his reign. An apposite illustration of this is provided by unfinished episcopal business from his predecessor's reign. After Henri III's death, some at least of those designated by him to bishoprics feared for the value of their nominations, and sought new titles from Henri IV. We know that the king

27 ASV, N Fr 32, fo 88, Sega to Rome, 13 Feb 1591.
28 Tizon-Germe, 'Juridiction spirituelle et action pastorale', 220.
29 ASV, N Fr 36, fo 410, Sega to Cardinal Aldobrandini, 19 Apr 1594. I would like to acknowledge here the assistance I received on these questions from Mme Tizon-Germe.

confirmed the existing nominee to Grasse in December 1589,[30] Nicolas Briroy to Coutances in May 1590,[31] and René de Daillon, one of his leading clerical advisers, to Bayeux, probably around the same time.[32] The poet-bishop of Châlon-sur-Sâone, Pontus de Thyard, had also obtained Henri III's permission, only days before the king's death, to resign his see to his nephew, Cyrus, and Henri IV duly confirmed the grant in March 1592, 'in consideration of the services of the sieur de Bissy, governor of Verdun in Burgundy', brother of Cyrus.[33] In September 1590, he reassured Orazio Rucellaï, an active Italian financier, that the benefices held in France by his absentee brother, Annibale Rucellaï, bishop of Carcassonne, would be at his disposal should Annibale die, 'so that you can nominate any capable person you wish to them'.[34] It is not possible to say if Henri IV was approached by other Henri III nominees, some of whom may have been reluctant to have dealings with a Huguenot monarch, but the possibility cannot be ruled out. There is some slight evidence, in fact, that in uncertain times ecclesiastical hopefuls were not beyond hedging their bets by seeking more than one nomination: in October 1590, Marguerite de Valois proposed Jean de Bertier for an abbey in her gift to *both* Henri IV and Mayenne in the hope that they would put his name forward for confirmation by Rome.[35]

In such cases, however, Henri IV was largely reacting to events triggered by the initiative of the parties concerned; as the language they employed itself strongly suggests, the royal responses can be seen largely as a matter of obliging allies or winning the support of others whose interests could be tied thereafter to Henri IV's own. Direct royal nominations to sees which were either vacant in 1589 or became so later, were a very different proposition, and require patient reconstruction and interpretation.

For obvious reasons, Henri IV was in no position for several years to follow the normal practice of despatching bishops' letters of nomination to Rome for its approval. Indeed, since the Guise murders, relations between the French

---

30   Grasse had been given in May 1589 by Henri III to Georges de Poisseux, brother of one of his *gentilshommes de la chambre*, the sieur de Passage, in recognition of his services: AD Alpes-Maritimes, G 11, *brevet* of 27 May 1589 and marginal note of confirmation by Henri IV on 30 Dec 1589. Unfortunately, Poisseux was reputed to be a Huguenot!
31   René Toustain de Billy, *Histoire ecclésiastique du diocèse de Coutances*, ed A Héron, 3 vols (Rouen 1874–86), ii. 190–2.
32   AN, MC, VIII 409, 14 Sept 1594, *régale* settlement for Bayeux between Daillon and Sainte Chapelle. Daillon claimed that Henri III had nominated him in February 1589, but gave no date for Henri IV's confirmation.
33   AD Saône-et-Loire, F 565, royal *brevets* of 27 July 1589 and 20 Mar 1592.
34   *Recueil de lettres missives de Henri IV*, ed X Berger de Xivry and J Guadet, 9 vols (Paris 1843–76), iii. 213–14, letter of 10 July 1590: 'pour y nommer telles personnes capables que vous y désirés'. 'Capable' here refers to persons in the clerical state, not those of any particular ability or experience.
35   AD Haute-Garonne, 6 J 61, no 15, *brevet* of 1 Oct 1590. The *brevet* also claims that Mayenne had confirmed Marguerite's presentation rights as stipulated in her dowry settlement of 1572.

church and the curia were thrown into confusion, not least where the provision of consistorial benefices was concerned. It was this growing confusion which eventually led the *grand conseil* to issue a decree in September 1590 designed to arrest the process by which benefices were falling into the hands of lay *économes* who were illegally administering them, both spiritually and temporally (*au spirituel comme au temporel*). By separating the two spheres of administration, the council hoped to ensure that only qualified clergy could conduct spiritual affairs and fill vacant benefices generally, and thus to prevent the administrators of episcopal temporalities from straying beyond their powers. The council specifically ordered royal judges to recognise only those claims to possession of benefices made by those appointed by fellow ecclesiastics.[36] This decree, in fact, went on to become the legal foundation of a system which endured for several years. Its effect was to institute a system of *économats spirituels* which would be more bitterly criticised in later years than even the lay *économes*, on the grounds that the spiritual *économes* were often no more than intruders or caretakers for noble families, and did not even have to obtain an episcopal nomination in order to fulfil their functions. Moreover, under these rules, those holding episcopal nominations could also apply to the *grand conseil* for a decree granting them lawful possession of their bishoprics or other benefices. These measures were rounded off in late 1590 by a formal ban on seeking papal provisions which remained in force until January 1596; it applied to bishoprics as much as it did to minor benefices. While the ban remained in force, benefice-holders great and small were subject to the *grand conseil*'s ruling. It is, therefore, a misapprehension simply to say that Rome refused recognition to the king's nominees during this period as there are few signs that any of them sought papal confirmation in the first place. By the same token, not having to consider Roman reactions may actually have led the king to make more rather than fewer episcopal nominations, and to have acquiesced in the extension of the *économats*, lay and spiritual. With the exception of Mayenne and the League, the French church was, in its legal structures at least, virtually a 'national' church between 1590 and 1596, and it is hardly surprising that talk of a French patriarchate in 1591 should have caused such anxiety and offence in Rome.[37]

In such circumstances, following the details of Henri IV's episcopal appointments before and even after 1595, and piecing together something like a coherent account of his actions, is extremely difficult, not least because the surviving evidence is itself patchy. Yet it is quite clear that he made far more actual nominations to bishoprics than the record of subsequent papal confirmations would indicate: some of his first nominees to vacant sees

36 AN, V⁵ 153, decree of 5 Sept 1590.
37 See Frederic J Baumgartner, 'Renaud de Beaune, Politique Prelate', *Sixteenth-Century Journal*, 9 (1978), 99–109. Beaune was suspected of wanting to become patriarch of a French national church in 1591 and later, hence the papacy's hostility to him in later years, especially over his transfer from Bourges to Sens.

subsequently withdrew, some resigned to other parties in return for pensions, while others still were obliged to abandon their ambitions because they stood little or no chance of gaining effective possession of their designated see. A roll-call, admittedly partial, of those who failed to become bishops at this time, includes a son of the duc de Bouillon, Alexandre de La Marck, and the future Marshal de l'Hôpital (both nominated to Meaux), Ennemond Revol (Dol), Louis Séguier dean of Notre Dame of Paris (Laon), the future marquis de Coeuvres (Noyon), René Benoist, the so-called *pape des Halles* (Troyes), and the poet Philippe Desportes (Rouen). Brief as it is, this list seems more impressive than that of those who eventually became bishops, while the identity of some of the individuals concerned suggests that the focus of particular family ambitions for their sons were changing as rapidly as the political context in which 'paper' nominations to vacant dioceses were made.

In such circumstances, the last thing we should expect was that Henri IV was in a position to act consistently during the early part of his reign where vacant bishoprics were concerned. He faced years of grinding military and political exertion as he tried to gain general recognition as king and to pacify the realm. The geography of his progress is mirrored in the episcopal nominations he made, yet it is quite apparent, particularly from what we have seen of the fate of some of Mayenne's nominations, that Henri was also anxious not to be confined to making them solely in provinces which he actually controlled. Above all, he was ready to regard bishoprics and church benefices generally as a natural part of any political package, and it is not surprising that a king who, as he himself confessed, negotiated and purchased the obedience of his subjects rather than conquered his realm, should have made concessions to the noble families who had their eyes closely fixed on local bishoprics.

As far as we know, Henri IV failed to make an attempt to dispose in one way or another of only about twelve of the thirty-six dioceses that were either already vacant in 1589 or that became so up to the end of 1595. We may divide his choices into three broad categories – individual nominations, *économats*, and outright gifts to non-clerical figures – though the second category may also be a disguise for the third. Some of the king's actual nominations appear so peculiar in retrospect, that it may well be asked if they were ever intended as genuine episcopal nominations at all. In 1590, for example, he apparently 'gave' Auch to Charles de Gontaut, second son of his comrade-in-arms, Biron, when Henri III had earlier given it to the Nemours family.[38] Having obliged Marshal Matignon in 1589 by confirming his candidate for Coutances, Henri also nominated Matignon's own son, the comte de Torigny, to the see of Montauban.[39] The nomination of Ennemond Revol to the Breton see of Dol in 1592 was a direct reward to his father, Louis, one

---

38 F Caneto, 'Souvenirs relatifs au siège d'Auch', *Revue de Gascogne*, 15 (1874), 346.
39 Daux, *Histoire de l'église de Montauban*, i. 105.

of the king's key Catholic advisors in the years before his conversion, but Revol, a councillor in the *grand conseil*, never showed any inclination to become a bishop.[40] After the death of the *ligueur* bishop of Meaux, Louis de Brézé in 1590, Henri gave it to no less a figure than the duc de Bouillon for his son, Alexandre, then a student. The Brézé and La Marck-Bouillon families were, of course, related by marriage, yet it is surprising to learn that the arch Protestant Bouillon should seem as willing for his son to become bishop of Meaux as he was to have him educated at a Jesuit college![41] The future Marshal d'Estrées was nominated to Noyon, probably about the same time (late 1594 or early 1595), but he soon discovered a more suitable vocation.[42] Virtually all of these individuals were young, and possibly not even tonsured clerics, so their nominations were no more than poorly disguised gifts of the vacant dioceses to their families. On the other hand, the diocese of Luçon was given to François Hyver, parish priest to the Richelieu family, when their episcopal uncle, Jacques, died in 1592. Hyver was at least in orders, and thus in theory a suitable choice, but there was never any question that his was anything other than a 'confidentiary' nomination.

In a limited number of cases, however, Henri IV showed his willingness and ability to gratify individual clerics rather than their fathers, brothers or other relatives. It need hardly be pointed out how much such personal recompense was necessary if Henri was to extend the ecclesiastical support he already enjoyed and attract clerical allies in the future. The nominations of René de Daillon du Lude to Bayeux and of Jacques du Perron to Evreux in 1591 were well deserved rewards for their counsel and fidelity to the royal cause. René Benoist was another cleric closely involved in the events leading to Henri's conversion, and his reward was the post of royal confessor and the gift of the see of Troyes in 1593. The translations, decided in 1594 but not completed for several years, of du Bec from Nantes to Reims and of Beaune from Bourges to Sens, were even more telling demonstrations of royal gratitude. But the scope for royal munificence was limited and, these few cases apart, it could not be said that the new king was able to do much to reward ecclesiastical supporters who were *not* already bishops; it was only later in his reign that non-episcopal followers, Benoist apart, would enter the episcopal ranks. It was not merely the king's lay followers who could complain that Henri was too busy trying to rally former enemies to satisfy their demands to reward his own friends and supporters.[43] Like Mazarin just after the Fronde,

---

40 Michael Wolfe, *The Conversion of Henri IV. Politics, Power and Religious Belief in Early Modern France* (Harvard 1993), 109, 111, 118, 121–2.

41 AN, MC, VIII 409, 15 Dec 1594 *régale* settlement between Bouillon and Sainte Chapelle. Unfortunately, the act gives no idea of when young La Marck was nominated to Meaux.

42 *Ibid*, 411, 25 Aug 1595, *régale* settlement of 25 Aug 1595.

43 See Richard Bonney, *Political Change in France under Richelieu and Mazarin 1624–1661* (Oxford 1978), 85, quoting the English ambassador, George Carew, to this effect.

Henri found that there were so many accumulated debts which had to be paid that there was little room for pure royal grace.

During these years the king also disposed of vacant dioceses, and especially their revenues, through *lettres d'économat* which were not always accompanied by an episcopal nomination. Toulon, vacant since 1592, was one such case, Lectoure in 1595 was another.[44] The *économe* appointed for Bordeaux in late 1591 was still there in 1598, though Jean le Breton asserted that he had been nominated archbishop at virtually the same time.[45] Some of the ten or more sees for which we have no evidence at all may also have attracted similar royal grants. The king's first nominee to Uzès, Jean Rousse, was a canon of Uzès, and in order to protect its rights and revenues, as well as to ensure religious services, the king also appointed him as both spiritual and temporal *économe* in April 1595.[46] But this was unusual, and some of the surviving royal patents simply assert that the king had made an episcopal nomination, without, however, revealing the candidate's identity.[47]

In addition to these *économats*, with their strong suggestion of unnamed lay beneficiaries, Henri IV continued the practice of his predecessors of simply granting bishoprics to named individuals with power to select their own candidates. For example, Aix-en-Provence, vacant in 1591, was 'granted' to Hurault de Maisse, ambassador at Constantinople, to dispose of in favour of a candidate of his choice.[48] Gilles de Souvré, another close ally, was given Tours, another archiepiscopal see, on condition that Philippe du Bec become archbishop, and 'on condition of reaching an agreement with you for an honest and reasonable recompense'.[49] Nothing came of this particular grant because Tours was not vacant, but the royal intention could hardly have been more clearly spelled out. Epernon was given a free hand with the diocese of Aire when Bishop Foix-Candale, to whom he was related by marriage, died in 1594.[50] As late as 1597, Henri de Noailles received the privilege of

---

44 *Gallia Chr Nov*, v. cols 640–1, text of *économat* for Toulon, 20 Mar 1593; AN V⁵ 1227, fo 137, *économat* of Lectoure 1 Mar 1595.
45 AN, V⁵ 1227, fos 144–5, letters-patent evoking the lawsuits of Fayet, *économe* of Bordeaux, 7 Apr 1595; fos 261–2, new evocation for Fayet, 21 Apr 1598. The reason given for the first evocation was that many of the archiepiscopal lands and revenues were actually in the hands of magistrates from the Bordeaux parlement! AD Gironde, G 254, for Le Breton's claim that he had been 'pourvu' (presumably on application to the *grand conseil*) as archbishop on 1 Jan 1592, but had not been able to take up residence.
46 AN, V⁵ 1227, fo 153, *économat* of Uzès, 11 Apr 1595, registered by the *grand conseil* on 14 July.
47 AN, V⁵ 1227, fo 66, *économat* for Auxerre, 1 Mar 1593; fo 67, *économat* for Beauvais, 15 July 1593.
48 ASV, Misc Arm I, 28, fos 447–8, Italian copy of Hurault's letter to the canons of Aix, 4 Jan 1594, explaining the king's original grant of 22 Nov 1591.
49 *Lettres missives de Henri IV*, iv. 73, letter to Souvré, 24 Dec 1593: 'avec honneste et raisonable récompense dont ledict sieur de Nantes (du Bec) conviendra avec vous'. The king here reminded Souvré of this earlier gift, but with no indication of when it had originally been made.
50 Arch Chantilly, L/xxvi, fo 17, *brevet* to Epernon for this purpose, 28 Feb 1594. Foix-Candale having died only three weeks earlier, Epernon had clearly lost no time in pressing his demands.

nominating his candidates to both Dax (held previously by two of his uncles) and Saint-Flour, where his lands and clientage were strongest.[51] The king's generosity could extend even to dioceses that were not actually vacant: in 1594 the vicomte de Bourdeille was allowed to nominate his choice for Périgueux, a privilege he did not exercise until 1599.[52] But the individual who benefited most from this form of generosity was another military commander, Crillon – 'brave Crillon' as the king called him. In October 1591, as we saw, he obtained the southern diocese of Saint-Papoul, while that of Fréjus followed soon afterwards.[53] At some subsequent date, he also acquired some claim on the revenues of Toulon, possibly through the appointment of an *économe* in March 1593.[54] Crillon's appetite was obviously sizeable, considering that he had already been granted the revenues of the archbishopric of Arles by Henri III.[55]

Nor, as suggested earlier, did Henri IV confine his decisions over what to do with vacant dioceses to the provinces which he effectively controlled; however little chance his candidates may initially have had of entering their dioceses, he did not wish to give Mayenne and the League a free hand in the areas they held. The nominations of Daillon and du Perron to sees in Normandy, a largely pro-League province, are cases in point. Equally clear is the intention behind the nomination of his own half-brother, Charles de Bourbon, to Reims in 1591, even though his prospects of success there were virtually non-existent. At that point Henri IV's authority in northern France was slight, yet, despite his failure to take major cities like Paris or Rouen in 1590–2, his control of other areas grew steadily, and included episcopal towns like Lisieux, Evreux and Chartres. As we saw earlier, Mayenne obtained papal provisions to Noyon for Jean Munier only because he retook the town from royalist forces in April 1593, but when Munier died in July 1594, it was too late to repeat that success.[56] One by one, Henri IV nominated to the vacant sees of northern France, culminating in those of Reims, Sens, and Rouen in 1594, and in so doing he showed that he had undermined independent Guise ecclesiastical patronage in its heartlands well before Mayenne submitted to him.

The royal progress was opposed by numerous *ligueur* bishops throughout France, more publicly and provocatively by some than by others. Several of these were subject to reprisals of one kind or another, usually the seizure of their temporalities. Bishop Jean de Laubespine of Orléans endured such treatment, but in May 1593 the *conseil privé* ordered that restitution be made

51 BN, MS lat 17021, fo 17, 10 Aug 1597.
52 *Lettres missives de Henri IV*, iv. 1036, letter of 10 Nov 1594.
53 AD Haute-Garonne, B 1972, fo 114, *brevet* of 18 Oct 1591 (Saint-Papoul); *Gallia Chr Nov*, i. cols 258–9 of *instrumenta* (Fréjus).
54 *Gallia Chr Nov*, v. cols 640–1, for text of *économat*, 20 Mar 1593.
55 *Gallia Chr Nov* (Arles), col. 935, contract of Nov 1595 with incoming archbishop, recalling Henri III's grant.
56 ASV, Fondo Borghese I, 462–8, fo 62, Pellevé to Aldobrandini, 8 Apr 1593.

to him on the advice of the 'commissioners in attendance on the king with responsibility for the property of those in rebellion'.[57] The bishop of Limoges faced similar reprisals, and his revenues were given by Henri IV to the Protestant duc de la Force, while the parlement of Paris ordered the arrest of his brother, the bishop of Amiens.[58] However, it seems that most of the troubles encountered by bishops, royalist or *ligueur*, during these years were not the result of direct royal persecution, but overwhelmingly of local conflicts. Some exiled *ligueur* bishops gathered in Paris or other known *ligueur* towns like Toulouse or Marseille, while others made their way to Rome. Exiled royalist bishops moved to Tours, the seat of a royalist rump parlement, and later joined the king's entourage itself in Chartres, Saint-Denis, and Paris. In early 1591, it was reported that of Brittany's nine bishops, five were *ligueurs* and four were royalists. More significantly, six of them had quit their dioceses, while one, the bishop of Saint-Malo, was under house arrest in the town.[59] Even though hardly any bishops were direct victims of the violence of these years, there was a large body of displaced bishops by the time peace was restored, and several of them were slow to return to their dioceses, either because of continuing local feuds or because of the extent of their own partisan commitment, especially *ligueur*, during the final conflict.

If Henri IV made any distinctions among the pro-League bishops, it was possibly between those who had been appointed under his predecessors, and those promoted since Henri III's death. The former were generally treated more leniently. Of course, some of them, like the hard-line Italian bishop of Mâcon, Alemanni, simply refused to recognise the new king; he preferred to return to Italy and begin a new episcopal career there.[60] Bishop Givry of Lisieux, an active *ligueur* who was made a cardinal against the king's wishes in 1596, was given no help whatever to reclaim his diocese, still effectively in marshal Fervacques's hands, and he had little option but to resign it on the best conditions he could negotiate.[61] But this was exceptional. After all, Guillaume Rose, the most radical bishop among the Paris Sixteen, eventually returned from exile to his diocese of Senlis, while the scarcely less pugnacious bishop of Comminges, Urbain de Saint-Gelais who led the Toulouse league

---

57 *Inventaire des arrêts du conseil privé, règnes de Henri III et de Henri IV*, ed François Dumont, 5 vols (Paris 1969–78), i. no 1836, decree of 3 May 1593: 'commissaires ordonnés par le roi près sa personne sur le fait des biens des rebelles'. The decree also suggests that Laubespine was no longer regarded as a supporter of the League.
58 AD Gironde, 1 B 16, fos 145v-6v, registration of letters-patent of 17 July 1594 ordering the restitution of Limoges revenues to the bishop; BN, MS Fr 18328, fos 125–6, decree of 9 July 1594, ordering arrest of La Marthonie of Amiens.
59 *Lists and Analyses of State Papers, Foreign, 1590–91*, ed R B Wernham (London 1989), 310–11, Feb 1591.
60 *Lettres d'Ossat*, ii. 291–2, Ossat to Villeroy, 19 Nov 1596. Alemanni was later to enjoy considerable favour under Clement VIII and Paul V.
61 AN, MC, VIII 415, 30 Aug 1597, *régale* settlement for Lisieux following Givry's resignation. See H de Formeville, *Histoire de l'ancien évêché-comté de Lisieux*, 2 vols (Lisieux 1873), i. p. ccxlii.

for much of the early 1590s, returned to his Pyrenean seat where he remained unmolested for nearly twenty years.[62]

In contrast, Henri IV seems to have felt no particular obligation towards those bishops who were nominated during the League by Mayenne or others, and he did little to save them subsequently. In some instances, of course, he had made his own nominations to the dioceses in question, but it was only with the collapse of the League that his men were in a position to capitalise on the king's grace. Génébrard of Aix was possibly the most famous victim of the change. His *ligueur* activities in radical Marseille left him unprotected, but it was in fact the former *ligueur* parlement of Aix, seeking to demonstrate its new loyalist credentials, which pursued him with considerable vindictiveness. In doing so, it was being pushed hard by the royal intendant sent to Provence, who was none other than Paul Hurault, nephew of Ambassador Hurault de Maisse to whom Henri IV had given Aix in 1591. Initially, Hurault, a convert from Protestantism, presented himself as the temporal *econome* of Aix, but he soon let it be known that he was also the royal nominee to the archiepiscopal title itself. Hurault's alliance with the Aix parlement left Génébrard helpless, and the latter's pleas to Henri IV remained unanswered. He ended his days in exile in Avignon and Burgundy.[63] A similar fate befell his fellow-papal nominee at Fréjus, Gérard Bellenger, who died without ever taking possession of his diocese. Guillaume le Blanc of Vence also became bishop of Grasse in 1592, but subsequently failed to hold his see in the face of opposition from Henri IV's own nominee.[64] Finally, Clement Isnard of Glandèves, another Mayennist-papal bishop who was a subject of the duke of Savoy, found himself in serious difficulties after the League, when he was faced with a crown-appointed *econome* and the seizure of his temporalities.[65] In all of these cases, the parlement of Aix was in the vanguard of the attack, despite the fact that Bellenger was a former councillor there.

With the exception of Isnard, who survived thanks to strong papal intervention, what all these men lacked was protection in high places which might have negated local attacks on them. As the exception which proves the rule, we can point to the experience of Jérôme de Lingua, whose uncle had resigned the see of Conserans to him in Rome under papal auspices in 1593. When Lingua arrived in Paris for the Assembly of Clergy in 1595, he was faced with a stern letter from the king to the assembly ordering it to deny him entrance on suspicion that he was either a *confidentiaire* or that he illicitly paid a pension to a layman. This royal pre-occupation with canonical niceties must have

---

62 Jean Lestrade, 'Un curieux groupe d'évêques de Comminges: Urbain de Saint-Gelais 1570–1613', *Revue de Comminges*, 23 (1908), 254–66; 24 (1909), 28–41, 97–112.
63 *Gallia Chr Nov*, i. cols 129–33. ASV, N Fr 43, fo 232, Génébrard to pope, 20 Apr 1595.
64 Le Blanc's numerous letters to Rome, sometimes signed 'l'infelicissimo vescovo di Grassa', are in ASV, N Fr 42, fos 449, 529–31, 539, 545, 550, 551–2, 560–1, 580–1 (1598–9).
65 ASV, Fondo Borghese I, 80, fo 91, Cardinal Aldobrandini to Cardinal Medici, papal legate in France, 17 May 1597, asking him to defend Isnard's rights.

intrigued some delegates, but it was not long before the assembly received a second letter from the king, saying that he had changed his mind over Lingua, as a result of the good offices of his *grand écuyer*, Roger de Bellegarde, and that he had retroactively granted Lingua his *brevet de nomination* to Conserans! Questioned by Cardinal Gondi, the president of an assembly that was seriously agitated about *confidences* and pensions, Lingua denied the allegations against him and claimed that it was only when he returned from Rome to France that his troubles really began, with his opponents alleging that he did not have the king's nomination. As a result, he thought it best to approach Henri IV for assistance in keeping his diocese; the king consented, but required him to pay a pension to 'an unnamed ecclesiastic', a condition which Lingua accepted, as he put it, *ad redimendam vexationem*.[66] What actually happened seems to have been the reverse of what was said, at least by Henri IV: Lingua got his provisions in 1593 without having to pay a pension to anyone save his retiring uncle, and he was not a *confidentiaire*. As for the 'vexation' to which he alluded, it probably came from Bellegarde himself: the 1595–6 manoeuvre enabled Bellegarde to reassert long-standing family patronage over Conserans, and it was to Bellegarde's brother that Lingua had to pay the newly established pension, a move which made him look more like a *confidentiaire* than he had hitherto.[67]

The Conserans affair also has the merit of suggesting that the king's handling of episcopal disputes during these years was often pragmatic to the point of taking the line of least resistance. This, in turn, reflects his general handling of the nobles and towns who, having fought against him since 1589, were beginning to move towards him by 1593–4. It also reflects in particular his desire to avoid general settlements with Leaguer leaders who, by obtaining numerous favours for their clients or dependents, would find their patronage bases considerably enhanced for the future.[68] The price he paid was arguably to give individual, second-rank leaders more than they might have obtained under general settlements. Sully, for example, was sent to negotiate with Villars-Brancas, the *ligueur* governor of Rouen, when he offered to treat with Henri IV in 1594. Among his many demands, Villars included most of the late Cardinal de Bourbon-Vendôme's benefices, and specifically the archdiocese of Rouen, which he wanted for his secretary, Philippe Desportes. Henri IV was willing to accept a poet as archbishop – France, after all, had its share of them from Pontus de Thyard to Jean Bertaut – but when Desportes declined the honour, the king unexpectedly recovered some freedom of manoeuvre and exploited it by quickly nominating his own half-brother,

---

66   *Collection des procès-verbaux des assemblées générales du clergé de France,* ed A Duranthon, 9 vols (Paris 1767–8), i. 525–6, 3 Feb 1596, for the assembly's handling of the case, and the text of the second royal letter of 29 Jan.
67   ASV, PC 13, fos 245–70, for evidence that the pension, of 5,000 *livres*, was payable to César-Auguste de Bellegarde. He may have been a tonsured cleric in 1596, but he married later.
68   Wolfe, *Conversion of Henri IV*, 180–1.

Charles de Bourbon, to Rouen.[69] When Vitry, the League's governor of Meaux, turned over the city to the king in early 1594, he was liberally rewarded, and the bishopric was subsequently earmarked for his young son. Even Constable Montmorency, when he asked if he could have Meaux for his brother-in-law, was told that it was not available and that the king could not let Vitry down, 'seeing how useful a servant he is'.[70] For all his pedigree, the young duc de Guise was too insignificant a political figure to extract major concessions in his 'abolition' of October 1594, though he did get a promise that his younger brother would become archbishop of Reims 'when he comes of age' – a distant prospect that can hardly have troubled the king at that point.[71] As we saw, Mayenne and Mercoeur's settlements both excluded presentation rights to bishoprics, but the king's flexibility was demonstrated at Montauban, where he did not press a candidate of his own, but instead transferred his support to Mayenne's existing nominee, Anne de Murviel. The Nemours family was treated in a similar fashion with the king finally accepting their claim to the see of Auch, the actual nomination being postponed until 1597.

However, it was not always possible to avoid general settlements. From an ecclesiastical point of view, the two most unsettled provinces were Provence and Languedoc. The price of pacification in Provence was, however, the removal of the much disliked governor, Epernon, so the king was fortunate to be spared from having to make concessions to a powerful, entrenched figure there. The new governor, the inexperienced duc de Guise, was new to Provence and would take a considerable time to establish a power-base there. In Provence, it was the lesser, but well-connected local nobles who continued to dominate the ranks of the episcopate.

Languedoc, the condition of whose bishoprics had so exercised the Assembly at Melun in 1579, was a different matter. While still very extensive, the power of the long-standing Montmorency governors was challenged, especially during the League, by the Joyeuse and their allies; this rivalry had always involved competition for and control of bishoprics, not least because the young Cardinal de Joyeuse was himself a formidable ecclesiastical empire-builder. During the 1580s and early 1590s, the main disputes had been over the sees of Nîmes, Uzès, Carcassonne, Alet, Lodève, and Albi. Carcassonne, Lodève and Albi were 'occupied', militarily as well as administratively, by the opposing camps, their bishops having either quit (Rucellaï of Carcassonne) or not been able to enter them at all (Delbène of Albi). The price of pacifying Languedoc was the recognition of Joyeuse influence alongside that of the governor, Montmorency-Damville, now Constable of France and an absentee who mainly resided at court.

---

69 *Lettres missives de Henri IV*, iv. 205–6, king to Sully, Aug 1594.
70 *Ibid*, iv. 809, letter to Montmorency, 10 July 1597: 'm'étant si utile serviteur qu'il est'.
71 BN, MS Fr 23039, fos 103–5, 22 Oct 1594: 'lors qu'il sera en aage'. See also *Lists and Analysis of State Papers, Foreign, 1593–4*, ed R B Wernham (London 1989), 347.

The overall settlement, finalised at Folembray in January 1596, envisaged two *lieutenances-générales* for the province, one for Joyeuse based on Toulouse and covering twelve dioceses in all, including Alet, Lodève, Albi and Carcassonne in western Languedoc, and one for Montmorency's son-in-law, Ventadour, in the eastern and northern areas. Both parties could therefore look forward to consolidating their political control and advancing their clients in a province which accounted for one-fifth of all France's bishoprics. Other ecclesiastical demands, not confined to either bishoprics or to Languedoc, also loomed large in the secret additional articles for Joyeuse in the Folembray settlement. This was partly because the new *lieutenances-générales* did not correspond perfectly to the existing spheres of influence of either Joyeuse or Montmorency, and neither was immediately prepared to give up what he had already, or might still acquire, in return for what might prove to be mere paper concessions. It should be added, of course, that these rivalries also gave Henri IV some room for manoeuvre, and allowed him both then and later to reject certain demands. Cardinal Joyeuse, who still held the archiepiscopal sees of Toulouse and Narbonne, was confirmed as Protector of France in the Roman curia, a post which demonstrated his political importance beyond Languedoc. The king also agreed that his client Christophe de Lestang, the combative bishop of Lodève, would move to Alet and resign Lodève to 'a capable person'. Joyeuse asked that the king confirm Mayenne's earlier nomination of Antoine de Bruyères to an unnamed bishopric, and also that the Gascon see of Aire, vacant since 1594, be given to another client, Pierre Polverel; but Henri IV rejected both suits on the grounds that he had already disposed of the dioceses to his own servants, and could not go back on his word to them. And when Joyeuse asked for approval of the choice of the governors and consuls of Le Puy for their next bishop (Alexandre de la Rochefoucauld, though he was not mentioned by name), the reply was a pointed refusal – 'the king will make sure that a suitable person is chosen' – the language of which served notice of the king's wish, if nothing more, to make his own choices.[72]

III

During the years from 1589 to 1595, Henri IV was operating in a largely 'national church' context, facing a divided French church and a papacy publicly committed to the League. But his piecemeal pacification of the

---

72 Claude Devic and Joseph Vaisette, *Histoire générale du Languedoc*, ed E Roschach, 16 vols (Toulouse 1872–1904), xii (2), cols 1533–64: 'le roy sçaura faire bonne election pour ladite charge'. See Mark Greengrass, 'Aristocracy and Episcopacy at the end of the Wars of Religion in France: the Duke of Montmorency and the Bishoprics of Languedoc', in *L'Institution et les pouvoirs dans les églises de l'antiquité à nos jours. (Miscellanea Historiae Ecclesiasticae*, viii) (Brussels and Louvain 1987), 356–63.

realm, his conversion and, more importantly, his reconciliation with Rome through the absolution of September 1595, were bound to change this. In addition to the adoption of the decrees of Trent in France, one of the principal conditions of the absolution was a strict observance of the Concordat of Bologna. As both king and pope realised, the resumption of normal relations with Rome had some way to go in practice, but the fact that du Perron, nominated to Evreux by Henri IV in 1591, should have been the first of his nominees to receive papal confirmation only weeks after the king's absolution, was in itself highly symbolic. Arnaud d'Ossat, who had served as secretary to du Perron as well as Joyeuse, immediately realised its significance, which he summed up with his celebrated conciseness to Villeroy: 'with this the king has begun to enjoy the right to nominate, and the pope to fill consistorial benefices that are vacant in France'.[73]

Pressure on the king also grew within France once normal church-state relations resumed. As might be expected, the General Assembly of Clergy, which began in Paris in December 1595, revived the criticisms aired by its predecessors; it drew an extremely lurid picture of the moral condition of the French church, but did not confine itself to the familiar, moralising jeremiads. The clergy's anger was directed especially against the 'monstrous spiritual *économats*' issued in recent years by the *grand conseil* and other secular magistrates which, by subverting ecclesiastical jurisdiction, had left forty dioceses vacant. In his formal speech presenting the assembly's remonstrances, the bishop of Le Mans, Claude d'Angennes, repeated these points, attacking in particular the return in all but name to a system of lay investiture at every level of the church, and demanding the adoption of Trent and the restoration of episcopal elections. Never, he said, had the French church been in a position where six to seven archdioceses were vacant, along with thirty or forty others sees; furthermore, Angennes asserted, if one were to look more closely at the remainder 'one would find several *confidentiaires* or caretakers, or men who obtained these offices by illicit means which are condemned by the holy canons'.[74] Angennes had firmly supported Henri IV from the beginning of his reign, so the thrust of his complaints was all the more difficult to ignore.

When confronted on these questions, Henri IV's response was to postpone the resolution of past problems until a projected Assembly of Notables could meet; for the future, he agreed to revoke all the spiritual *économats* granted to those nominated to bishoprics – which meant that vacant dioceses should be administered, as in the past, by officials (*vicaires capitulaires*) chosen by cathe-

---

73 *Lettres d'Ossat*, i. Letter to Villeroy, 18 Dec 1595.
74 Pierre Victor Palma-Cayet, *Chronologie novénaire* (*Choix de chroniques et mémoires sur l'histoire de France*), 2 vols (Paris 1836), ii. 80–3, for an abridgement of Angennes's address at Folembray in Jan 1596: 'il s'en trouveroit aucuns confidentiaires et gardiens, ou parvenus à ceste dignité par voies illicites et reprouvées par les saints decrets'. See Louis Serbat, *Les Assemblées du clergé de France: origines, organisation, développement 1561–1615* (Paris 1906), 311–12.

dral chapters, until such time as royal nominees were confirmed as rightful bishops. Like Henri III before him, the king was asked to publish papal condemnations of 'simonies et confidences', but on this point he was equally evasive, declaring that he would have to 'give it particular consideration'.[75] Finally, he agreed to lift the ban on seeking provisions in Rome; his decree to that effect of 30 December 1595 was quickly registered by the *grand conseil* and the parlement of Paris and within months Ossat was reporting that royal letters of nomination for new bishops had begun arriving in Rome.[76] Joyeuse's confirmation as Protector of France also followed in January 1596, signalling the king's intention of sending him back to Rome 'in order to retain the goodwill of the pope and to restore the reputation of my affairs there'. Before doing so, however, Henri recognised the need to adress the especially thorny question of 'how we are to proceed in respect of those benefices which became vacant after my break with the Holy See, and to which both the pope and myself have made appointments'. On Joyeuse's recommendation, he convened an informal council consisting of Joyeuse, Gondi, the Chancellor Cheverny, and Bellièvre to deal with the disputed nominations but, unfortunately for us, he also insisted that their deliberations be kept secret for fear of intrigues in Rome to undermine their recommendations.[77] Cardinal Gondi, who reported regularly to Rome during these months on both the Assembly of Clergy and the consultations in the king's entourage, struck a consistently pessimistic note. They had made little progress over the existing *économats spirituels*, he insisted, because all the ministers would say was that a line should be drawn under past mistakes, and that the papacy should simply forgive and forget them; such ministerial timidity, Gondi concluded, derived largely from their fear of the *grandi del regno* who were involved in the most serious abuses.[78]

While the king's handling of the episcopate for much of the 1590s suggests a man who had more serious matters to worry about, the papacy for its part was genuinely anxious to effect a reconstruction and, once it had recognised Henri IV, it took most of the significant initiatives. His absolution being a conditional one, the formal confirmation of his acceptance of its terms provided a useful opportunity effectively to reopen relations by sending a new legate, also with extensive powers, to the French court. Cardinal Alessandro

---

75 *Procès-verbaux*, i. 152–7, *pièces justificatives* for the 1595–6 Assembly. The king's words were reported as 'adviser particulièrement'.
76 AN V⁵ 1227, fos 161–2, decree of 30 Dec 1595, registered by *grand conseil*, 9 Jan 1596; Palma-Cayet, *Chronologie novénaire*, ii. 44; *Lettres d'Ossat*, ii. 162, Ossat to king, 16 July 1596.
77 *Lettres inédites du roi Henri IV au chancelier de Bellièvre du 8 février 1581 au 23 septembre 1601*, ed E Halphen (Paris 1872), 201–2, letter to Bellièvre, 15 Mar 1596: 'pour conserver la bonne volonté du pape et y remettre mes affaires en réputation'; and to determine 'quel chemin nous tiendrons pour la provision des bénéfices vacquans depuis ma division avec le Saint Siège ausquels le pape a pourveu de son costé comme j'ay fait du mien'.
78 ASV, Fondo Borghese I, 462–8, fos 242–3, to Aldobrandini, 2 Apr 1596; *ibid*, fos 246–7, to same, 20 Apr 1596; *ibid*, fos 252–4, to same 6 May.

de' Medici was given a wide-ranging commission in early May 1596, one in which ecclesiastical considerations loomed much larger than the normal diplomatic questions.[79] Medici was to press the king to help exiled bishops return to their dioceses and temporalities, and to protect those who had been confirmed by the papacy during the years of the League. He was not formally empowered personally to settle conflicts involving the upper clergy because theirs were 'consistorial' benefices, and therefore reserved for pope and curia. But there is no doubt that he was expected to negotiate with those holding nominations to, or claims on, episcopal office and other major benefices, in order to persuade them to seek provisions in Rome, and to press laymen to surrender their hold on major benefices. Indeed, an agent was sent ahead of Medici to court, and one of his tasks was to compile a list of dioceses and other major benefices, and to enquire into how and by whom they were held, with a view to reporting to the legate on his arrival.[80]

Medici, like the Roman curia generally, had formed the bleakest picture of conditions in France, and its church in particular. Based on decades of reports from nuncios and other observers, that picture had probably been given additional sharpness in recent years by the French bishops who were in exile in Rome, and by pathetic appeals for help from the likes of Génébrard of Aix or Le Blanc of Vence.[81] Yet the legate's views had already begun to mellow by the time he reached Lyon and had encountered or heard about the Dauphiné bishops, as well as Archbishops Villars of Vienne and Epinac of Lyon. It comes as a surprise to note that his first impressions of former *ligueur* bishops were, if anything, more negative than of the others. The more he saw for himself and met French clerics, the less despondent he became about the state of the church and the episcopate; soon he was warning Rome that its assumptions about the French church as a nest of irredeemable heretics needed serious modification.[82] Even a former bogeyman like Angennes, whom Rome had wished to put on trial in 1591, now seemed a devout ecclesiastic anxious to assist in the work of reconstruction.[83] The dozen or so royal nominees who presented themselves to Medici in the months after he reached Paris appeared to him worthy, qualified men, but he quickly realised that the real problems would be with those less willing to show their faces. A sense of the initial

---

79 Klaus Jaitner, ed, *Die Hauptinstruktionen Clemens' VIII für die Nuntien und Legaten an die europäischen Fürstenhöfen 1592–1605*, 2 vols (Tübingen 1984), ii. 450–69, instructions of 10 May 1596. Medici became Pope Leo XI for a few weeks in Apr 1605.
80 ASV, Fondo Borghese III, 73, fos 370–1, Antonio Grimani, bishop of Torcella, to Cardinal Aldobrandini, 13 July 1596.
81 *Lettres d'Ossat*, i. 445–6, Ossat to Villeroy 23 June 1595, reporting news reaching Rome that Henri IV had been granting *économats spirituels*, and that Génébrard had sent a copy of the one issued for his see of Aix. The *brevet d'économat* dated 19 Nov 1594, and Hurault's letter to the canons of Aix, are in ASV, Misc Arm I, 28, fos 447–8, 451.
82 ASV, Fondo Borghese I, 646, fos 11–12v, Medici to Cardinal Aldobrandini, 25 June 1596.
83 ASV, Fondo Borghese III, 73, fos 370–1, Bishop of Torcello to Aldobrandini, 13 July 1596.

uncertainty, as well as of the work done by Medici, is conveyed by the fact that on arriving in Paris, he thought about forty dioceses were vacant, but that a few months later he revised the total to 'thirty-three or possibly more'.[84] The king himself evidently welcomed Medici's mediation, aware that his own previous decisions had created awkward problems which he could not readily resolve without either breaking promises or offending Rome; as a result, he appeared more than willing to let Medici search for compromise solutions over disputed bishops or dioceses, such as Lisieux, Aix, or Glandèves.[85] At no other time during the entire period under study did a papal representative play such a key part in the making – or perhaps remaking – of the French episcopate, and he did so with royal blessing.

Once installed in Paris, Medici began, in his own words, to work on the consciences of the leading figures among those holding benefices without proper title or provisions; he set about finding *tempéraments* and arrangements for disputed sees and, on Rome's advice, he promised to treat them case by case and, equally revealingly, in accordance with the 'quality of the families and persons concerned'.[86] Finding solutions, however, depended on the ability to reconcile highly divergent interests. One of the most difficult cases was that of Cardinal Givry who had been forced out of his see of Lisieux during the wars, but who was determined to fight for his reinstatement. In 1596 he finally abandoned his efforts and reluctantly accepted instead a pension and two abbeys, followed somewhat later by the coadjutorship of Langres. Medici welcomed such commonsense, even though it involved ignoring canonical propriety, and he was clearly irritated by the refusal of others, such as the papally appointed Leaguer archbishop of Aix, Génébrard, to behave equally reasonably.[87] In general, he showed considerably less sympathy than did Rome itself for ex-Leaguer bishops like Givry who were unable to negotiate their own way back to their dioceses, and he pressed them not to prolong old confrontations unnecessarily.[88]

Medici was even more convinced that nothing would be achieved by imposing the strict letter of canon law on those involved in *confidences* and *économats*, since these had long been regarded as perfectly acceptable and normal. He therefore proposed that, in return for surrendering direct lay control of major benefices, they be given pensions off the revenues. In private, he expressed reservations about this idea, but he admitted that the *grands* and

---

84 ASV, Fondo Borghese I, 646, fo 71, Medici to Aldobrandini, 24 Nov 1596; *ibid*, fo 121, same to same 26 Jan 1597.
85 *Ibid*, fo 215–16, Medici to Aldobrandini, 21 June 1597.
86 ASV, Fondo Borghese I, 80, fo 58, Aldobrandini to Medici, 18 Mar 1597; Fondo Borghese I, 646, fo 179, Medici to same, 23 Apr 1597.
87 ASV, Fondo Borghese I, 646, fo 72, same to same 24 Nov 1596; *ibid*, fo 100, same to same 28 Dec 1596.
88 ASV, Fondo Borghese I, 80, fos 49v–50, Aldobrandini to Medici, 18 Nov 1596; *ibid*, fo 75, same to same, 18 Mar 1597, for expressions of papal support for these bishops.

others involved were of considerable help to him as legate in other ways.[89] This approach was first tried - or at least became public knowledge – in respect of Auch, which had been in dispute since 1586 before Henri IV finally accepted the Nemours claim in 1593. Although the intended beneficiary, the marquis de Saint-Sorlin, became duc de Nemours in 1595, neither he nor his mother, Anna d'Este, were willing to relinquish Auch, and they continued to administer it through spiritual and lay *économes*.[90] Cardinal Medici remonstrated with the duchess about the bad example a leading Catholic family like hers was setting. Six months or more later, a deal was struck whereby Léonard Destrappes, a Nemours client who was then a councillor in the Paris parlement, would become archbishop, while the duc de Nemours would collect an enormous pension of 8,000 *écus* off Auch, with the unusual proviso that he could retain it even were he to marry. Similar deals had either already been agreed by Henry IV or were still being discussed in 1596-7: at Beauvais, for example, the new bishop, René Potier, agreed to pay a pension of 2,000 *écus* to marshal Schomberg's son, although he was a military man.[91] However, Medici's initiative over Auch angered several bishops, doubtless because it seemed that the papacy itself was a party to what they regarded as a major scandal. A meeting of bishops was held in Paris at Cardinal Gondi's residence, where they expressed their alarm at the granting of pensions to married laymen: this was, they claimed, unheard of and against all the provisions of canon law; it would give royal and papal sanction to the strong-arm tactics being employed by powerful families. The discussions seem to have been heated, with Medici and his advisers having to rebut the claim that such pensions were tantamount to a secularisation of ecclesiastical property. Medici himself argued strongly that it was a matter of choosing the lesser of two evils in order to free major church offices from secular control: that, after all, was what really mattered, and pensions could be regarded as mere 'profane matters' which the pope would take care to circumscribe.[92] Medici, who complained that these unhelpful 'impertinences' would make a difficult task even more so, stuck to his chosen course, asserting that he was not making or applying general principles, but merely 'particular graces'.[93] The bishops' protest was ignored; Rome had little sympathy for them, and new pensions would continue to be demanded from incoming bishops.[94] Some of the heaviest pensions ever granted during the sixteenth or seventeenth centuries were conceded under Henry IV, and some of the bishops who were required

89 ASV, Fondo Borghese I, 646, fo 121, letter of 26 Jan 1597.
90 See above, p 372.
91 ASV, Fondo Borghese I, 646, fo 226, Medici to Aldobrandini, 13 July 1597.
92 ASV, Fondo Borghese III, 73, fos 455–6, Alessandro Giusti to Aldobrandini, 9 May 1597, for a detailed report of this case written on Medici's instructions.
93 ASV, Fondo Borghese I, 646, fos 226–7, Medici to same, 13 July 1597, for a long report on these discussions.
94 ASV, Fondo Borghese I, 80, fo 72, Aldobrandini to Medici, 25 Aug 1597, for the papacy's rejection of the bishops' views.

to pay them do not appear very different from some of the *confidentiaires* we have already seen.

However difficult it may be to measure Medici's influence, there is no doubt that his legation coincided with, and stimulated, some significant developments. Of the thirty-six dioceses vacant at one time or another up to the end of 1595, only ten or possibly eleven appear not to have attracted a nominee, while a further six had been filled without reference to Henri IV; the remaining twenty all had 'évêques nommés' by 1596 when Medici arrived, even though several of these men would disappear from sight during the following years, abandoning their efforts to become bishops for one reason or another. Thereafter, the simple factual record of Henrician nominees applying to Rome for papal provisions, and securing them, during the final years of the century is eloquent enough – one in 1595, two in 1596, seven in 1597, eight in 1598, eighteen in 1599, seven in 1600 and 1601, and nine in 1602. These figures show that dioceses were being filled quite rapidly around the turn of the century, thereby restoring the episcopate to something near full strength at a time when the religious energies unloosed during the wars, and especially by the League, were being directed increasingly towards the material and spiritual reconstruction of the church. In fact, most episcopal nominees were relieved that the ban on papal provisions had been lifted: after the conflicting nominations of recent years, they did not need to be reminded of the value of the provisions in establishing themselves as the rightful bishops of their dioceses. Some, of course, took longer than others to react, as is evident from the embarrassed letter written to Clement VIII by no less a figure than the newly created Cardinal Sourdis in 1599. He apologised profusely for the bad example which he, a cardinal, had given the French church by effectively occupying the archbishopric of Bordeaux without proper title for several years.[95]

Neither the changes of the mid-1590s nor Medici's diplomacy were enough to bring about a revolution within the French episcopate. Many familiar problems remained. Commenting on Cardinal Givry's reluctant resignation of Lisieux in 1597, Henri IV wrote that Givry had been wise to abandon a diocese where he was openly challenged, as the king put it in a telling phrase, 'by people, who having force on their side, took full advantage of it'. He added that the pope should not believe that 'things had yet been restored in France to such a state that justice and my authority are respected everywhere'.[96] The wars of religion might seem a thing of the past, but the political edifice presided over by the king remained brittle, the struggle for stability never quite finished. Yet it would be quite wrong to assume that

---

95 ASV, Fondo Borghese I, 462–8, fo 369, letter to Clement VIII, 15 May 1599.
96 BN, MS Dupuy 212, fo 84, letter to duc de Luxembourg-Piney, ambassador in Rome, 11 Aug 1597: 'par personnes qui ayant la force en la main, s'en faisoient croire... les choses soient encores remises en ce Royaume en estat tel que la justice et mon auctorité soient partout respectées'.

only a monarch with the kind of authority enjoyed by Louis XIV could ever impose his own policies and men. Like his predecessors, Henri IV had absorbed the lessons of ruling by manoeuvering and dividing those competing for power in both the state and the church. The old saw that 'the king can do anything he wishes, but not everything he wishes' seems particularly applicable to Henri IV. His success in pacifying the realm may have left him indebted to many people, but it also gave him some considerable advantages.

IV

The evolution of the episcopate during the remainder of Henri IV's reign reflects this reality in several ways. It should be reiterated, however, that a satisfactory analysis, and especially any attempt at a statistical presentation, is hampered by a serious lack of information about many of the new bishops, some of whom rank among the most obscure of the two following centuries. Indeed, the same obscurity surrounds many of the nominations themselves, particularly their timing. As a result, assumptions have to be made in many cases, based as far as possible on contextual evidence, but there is a danger that they may well distort the overall pattern which emerges. For example, it makes quite a difference if it is assumed that dioceses were simply left without nominated bishops for many years, or if nominees chosen relatively rapidly themselves proved slow to seek papal approval and consecration. Bearing in mind these problems, it is best to begin with an analysis of some general features of the Henrician episcopate, and only then turn to a closer study of their significance.

Despite the impressive numbers obtaining papal provisions after 1596, many French sees remained without bishops for many years. The average length of episcopal vacancies in excess of one year (which could be regarded as sufficient for a newly nominated bishop to obtain his papal provisions) during Henri's reign as a whole was higher than at any time during the period covered in this book. This is partly explicable by the conditions obtaining between 1589 and 1596. For those vacancies continuing or arising after 1598, delays in obtaining papal provisions fell sharply. In general, it was with dioceses already vacant for several years that Henri IV continued to have the greatest difficulties after his conversion and reconciliation with Rome. Of the 108 bishops (who do not include the seven incumbents moved to new sees after 1589) effectively installed during Henri's entire reign, only twenty-six had been clearly nominated before the end of 1596 when Franco-papal relations returned to a normal state, and nearly half of the latter were chosen in 1596 alone. No fewer than forty-one nominations were made between 1597 and 1601, easily the highest concentration for the whole period covered in this study. Thereafter, the turnover settled down to between a maximum of eight and a minimum of four nominations a year, but tailed off substantially during the last years of the reign. Apart from coadjutorships, only seven nominations were made by Henri IV after 1606, with just two in 1609, and one in early 1610.

These figures can be viewed in other ways, too. Not all of the nominations made during the king's reign were of the same type or arose in the same way. In all, eighty-two vacancies arose from the death of reigning bishops, and as such they constituted the nearest thing to an open competition for the choice of a successor. A further twenty-three dioceses changed hands as a result of resignations of one of two types – nineteen resignations in favour of a named successor, and four so-called 'simple' resignations made 'into the king's hand'. The total number of successions arising out of resignations would have been higher were it not for the fact that the death of some incumbent bishops occurred while resignation settlements were awaiting confirmation in Rome; death automatically cancelled such arrangements and reopened the succession, but in practice it does seem that the crown usually allowed the successor originally designated to succeed.[97] Cardinal d'Ossat was still bishop of Bayeux when he died in April 1604, but the transmission by resignation of his diocese to a member of the Angennes family, which he had negotiated in the previous year, went ahead anyway, despite the fact that the original successor, Jean d'Angennes, ran away to fight in the Netherlands![98] Lastly, the number of coadjutorial nominations made by Henri IV – which were, in effect, deferred resignations – was a rather modest ten, most of them arising in the king's latter years.

It is pure coincidence that the number of episcopal nominations of all types – 115 – made during Henri IV's reign tallies closely with the number of bishoprics in the entire French church (Lescar, Oloron and Belley included, since the king appointed to all three of them). As we have just seen, eighty-two dioceses became vacant through death, but since some dioceses experienced this fate more than once during the king's reign, the total number of sees affected in this way amounted to just seventy in all. In fact, twenty-two dioceses, or just over a fifth of the total, escaped nomination altogether between 1589 and 1610, though this proportion diminishes when we realise that in nominating coadjutors, the king was effectively making firm episcopal choices for the future. It is thus fair to say that while Henri IV may not have nominated to all of France's dioceses, his reign nevertheless saw a very substantial turnover in the episcopate. How did the king use this

97 In certain instances, royal letters of nomination explicitly ordered the quest for papal provisions to continue without interruption even if the reigning bishop died before the process was complete: see *Gallia Chr Nov*, i. cols 285 and *instrumenta*, col 184, for such instructions concerning the succession at Apt in 1606.
98 BN, MS Fr 17363, fos 82v-3v, *brevet* of 7 Oct 1603. The *brevet* cited Ossat's and the house of Angennes's services as the basis of the resignation, and permitted Ossat to retain a pension and to fill benefices within the diocese. A particularly interesting point is that the *brevet* left a blank for the Christian name of Ossat's intended successor.

opportunity? How far can he be said to have either pursued or achieved a given policy? And who were the principal beneficiaries of the changes in the episcopal ranks?

Before attempting to answer these questions, it should be noted that some of the categories habitually employed to classify individuals or families in this period need to be treated with some caution. As we have seen, labels such as *ligueurs*, royalists, or even *politiques*, are problematic because so many individuals, both lay and clerical, hesitated to take sides in the politico-religious conflicts at all; some initally embraced the League, only to shuffle later on towards neutrality or support of the royal cause, while yet others manoeuvred from one side to another in an effort to survive or simply to pursue their immediate self-interest. The bishop of Rodez was an ardent *ligueur* until the local insurrection of June 1589, after which he found himself on the receiving end of some rough treatment from the inhabitants and the *ligueur* parlement of Toulouse. Nor were family affiliations consistent across generations or between different branches of the same family. When this could be the experience of families and individuals like royal ministers of the past, present and future such as Villeroy, Bellièvre and Jeannin, it is hardly surprising to find considerable variation in the behaviour of less powerful groups. Finally, in the case of incoming bishops who were either not French at all, or who owed everything to lay patronage, it is pointless to categorise them in relation to the religious conflicts; as far as the second group are concerned, if labels have to be apportioned at all, it should be to their patrons rather than to the bishops themselves.

With these caveats in mind, we can divide Henri IV's bishops into a number of broad categories. The largest consists of those who, whether personally or through their families, can be identified as royalists during the later years of the wars and who continued in royal service in some demonstrable way thereafter. But such a loose category is itself in need of subdivision, if we are to attempt a more nuanced analysis of episcopal fortunes. It was noted earlier that in the years before his conversion and absolution, Henri IV had only managed to nominate a handful of clerics who had served him directly in one way or another. This situation would change thereafter, though not spectacularly, with the re-appearance of a normal royal court and its ecclesiastical household. A total of fourteen known members of that household would be nominated bishops by Henri IV.[99] But since many household offices were unpaid sinecures, and these, too, would grow in number as the reign progressed, the nature and extent of personal service to the king by court-based, incoming bishops still remains difficult to establish. It seems that only about fifteen of the 108 incoming bishops can be regarded as having served him directly, and that their promotion can be attributed, at

---

99 BN, MS Fr 7854, fos 183–207, *Estat des officiers* of king's household 1590–1610. This list may not be complete, and some of its entries are manifestly inaccurate.

least in part, to personal merit. Two of them, Bertrand Deschaux of Bayonne and Jean-Pierre d'Abbadie of Lescar, had earlier personal and family connections to the king in Béarn. The Gascon Arnaud d'Ossat had already shown his diplomatic skills in Rome by the time he received the see of Rennes in 1596, and the red hat would follow four years later. Gaspar Dinet was another who had served the king in Italy while holding high office in the order of Minims, and for this he received first a post of *prédicateur du roi* and then the see of Mâcon in 1599. Paul Hurault, Génébrard's persecutor and successor at Aix, may have originally been 'presented' to the king by his uncle, Hurault de Maisse, but when he arrived in Provence it was on an official mission of pacification as a *maître des requêtes*, and this probably enabled him to stake his claim effectively to the archbishopric.[100]

These examples apart, there are few signs to suggest that the king was in a special hurry to reward personal service, and some of his clerical supporters had to wait several years before claiming theirs. Claude de Morenne had been one of the few Parisian *curés* to defy the League and openly support the royalist cause, and yet it seems unlikely that he would have become a bishop had he not been in a position to succeed his elderly uncle Claude du Molinet at Séez in Normandy in 1600. Adrien d'Amboise, the royalist grand master of the College of Navarre and *curé* of Saint-André-des-Arts, obtained the remote Breton see of Tréguier in 1604. But another royalist Parisian *curé*, Chavagnac, received nothing at all, possibly because of his opposition to the edict of Nantes. René Benoist, *curé* and royal confessor, was exceptional in being given a diocese – that of Troyes – as early as 1593, but he never secured papal approval. Jean de Salette, a Béarnais and a convert like the king, who assisted du Perron at the Fontainebleau debate in 1600, succeeded Abbadie at Lescar in 1608. Apparently, Henri wished to nominate the Jesuit Pierre Coton, later to become his confessor, to Arles in 1603, but he refused the honour in accordance with his Society's constitutions.[101] Even had this not been the case, refusal on the grounds of political prudence would have been in order for the recently recalled Jesuits whose enemies were still powerful. Finally, the concept of royal service can arguably be extended to the king's two consorts, especially where the evidence is of direct personal service to them. Marguerite de Valois obtained the coadjutorship of Rieux for Jean de Bertier in 1600, though by then Bertier was *agent-général* of the clergy and well regarded by the king, who even wrote to the old bishop of Rieux to congratulate him on his choice of successor.[102] Marguerite was also at least partly instrumental in ensuring that Condom went to the nephew of the incumbent bishop, who was

100 AD Bouches-du-Rhône, B 3339, fo 92, for Hurault's letters as royal commissioner, 23 Sept 1595.
101 *Gallia Chr Nov*, Arles, cols 942–3.
102 AD Haute-Garonne, 6 J 61, no 11, letter of 22 Dec 1601, 'pour la bonne volonté que je porte audit Bertier fondée sur ses mérites, les sermons qu'il m'a faictz, et l'espérance que J'ay qu'il remplira bien dignement ceste place'.

one of her almoners.[103] Service to Henri's new queen, Marie de' Medici, brought similar rewards for her confessor, the Italian Franciscan, Jacopo Turicella, appointed to Marseille in 1604, and also her first almoner, the poet Jean Bertaut, successor to Morenne at Séez in 1606.

But this is only part of the story: personal services or loyalty were not a *sine qua non* for such preferment. Incumbent royalist bishops also exploited their own personal support of Henri IV to promote the younger generation from their own families. This is particularly evident in the case of leading royalist prelates. Cardinal Gondi, a key figure in the royal entourage during the mid-1590s despite his earlier equivocation, transmitted Paris to his young nephew Henri in 1596, while another Italian, Thomas de Bonsi, did the same at Béziers, also in 1596. Philippe du Bec obtained Nantes for his nephew, Jean, when moving from Nantes to Reims, but it remains unclear whether the nomination of André Frémiot to Bourges was in any sense a gift to Renaud de Beaune as he departed to Sens rather than a reward to Frémiot and his family for their loyalty.[104] Claude de Morenne's accession to Séez was at least as much in recognition of his uncle's unwavering royalism as of his own. Less highly placed figures could achieve similar ends. One of the king's longest serving almoners, Etienne Bologne, seems to have been perfectly content to remain in the royal chapel, yet he was clearly instrumental in obtaining the see of Digne in Upper Provence for his brother, Antoine. But perhaps the most intriguing succession in this regard is that of Charles de Saint-Sixte at neighbouring Riez: his uncle, Bishop Eleazar de Rastelles had been a dedicated *ligueur*, while Saint-Sixte himself had been strongly royalist in the Estates of Provence during the League. His succession in 1598 to Riez, in which long-standing Gondi patronage of Saint-Sixte was probably crucial, had the double effect of satisfying family aspirations while rewarding personal rather than family fidelity in the new bishop.[105] Finally, incumbent royalist bishops were also attracted by coadjutorships – especially later in the reign, when the bishops of Rodez, Mende, and Albi all secured successors from their own families. In all, two-thirds of the eighteen direct family successions which took place under Henri IV were to the benefit of those with known royalist affiliations during the last phase of the civil war.

As so often in this period, it is especially difficult to identify the public activities or partisan affiliations of second-order clergy *before* their elevation to

103 Adrien Clergeac, *Chronologie des archevêques, évêques et abbés de l'ancienne province ecclésiastique d'Auch et des diocèses de Condom et de Lombez* (Paris 1912), 158; Ludovic Mazeret, *Chroniques de l'église de Condom* (Condom 1927), 277, 295. Condom was also a Monluc fief, so Marguerite's influence there in 1603 may not have been quite so dominant.

104 It is not known when Frémiot first received his nomination to Bourges, which complicates the problem of establishing a connection with Beaune's move to Sens, but it was reported to Rome from Marseille in 1595 that such a nomination had been made: ASV, N Fr 43, fo 138, consuls of Marseille to Clement VIII, 1 July 1595.

105 *Lettres d'Ossat*, iii. 282, to Villeroy, 19 Feb 1599. J A Pithon-Curt, *Histoire de la noblesse du comtat Venaissin*, 4 vols (Paris, 1743–50), iii. 337.

the episcopate. But with considerable numbers of them attaining office at an early age under Henri IV, it is fair to assume that it was the services and influence of their families which were crucial to their success. This in turn introduces a world which, needless to say, embraces far more than those present at court and with access to the king, but the latter were certainly best placed to obtain what they sought. Favourites, both male and female, ministers, and other *commensales* had always been able to promote their own family members, and to act as patrons and brokers for others without a foothold at court. But as myths abound as to Henri IV's behaviour generally when it came to royal patronage, some scepticism about them seems imperative here. First of all, Henri IV was much less generous than Henri III towards friends and favourites. Admittedly, the young comte de la Chapelle, who would become known as Cardinal Sourdis, owed his spectacular advancement to both his cousin Gabrielle d'Estrées, mistress of Henri IV, and to his mother, Isabelle Babou, whose family was celebrated for its amorous favours to many French monarchs. Likewise, Charles de Balsac owed his diocese-cum-peerage of Noyon to his family, who included Henriette d'Entragues, another royal mistress. But these seem to be the only two instances of their kind. The king's nomination of his own son by the marquise de Verneuil to the see of Metz, often quoted as an example of royal insouciance towards episcopal office, actually reflects the need to ensure that that politically and strategically important city was in reliable hands. Arguably the king proved more generous to the families of less elevated personal servants. Two brothers of his personal physician, André du Laurens, became archbishops of Embrun and Arles in 1601 and 1605 respectively, while Adrien d'Amboise, brother of another physician, obtained the Breton see of Tréguier in 1604. It is worth noting that in the case of Honoré du Laurens, the royal nomination was made 'in consideration of the services I daily receive from du Laurens, my personal doctor', despite the fact that Honoré was himself *avocat-général* at the Aix parlement, and therefore hardly an insignificant figure.[106] Late in his reign, Henri made strenuous efforts to ensure the coadjutorship of Langres for the young son of one of his favourite companions, the financier Sébastien Zamet.

Ministerial and aristocratic political influence understandably weighed more heavily in royal calculations than personal preferences. French monarchs had always made a point of promoting members of ministerial families, not merely to satisfy ambition and reward service, but also to extend royal control of certain areas or dioceses. Possibly because of the mixed confessional make-up of his entourage, Henri IV rewarded fewer such individuals or families than other kings before and after him. In the first decade of his reign, in particular, Henri IV appointed bishops from these milieux to several dioceses

---

106 Balthazar Clapiers-Coulonges, *Chronologie des officiers de cours souveraines*, ed marquis de Boisgelin (Aix 1909–12), 161–2: 'en considération des services que du Laurens, mon médécin ordinaire, me rend journellement'.

(and especially archbishoprics like Arles, Aix, Lyon, Embrun, Sens, Tours) which had previously had *ligueur* holders, and which it was important to put into reliable hands. Other nominations were more conventional. Chancellor Cheverny's young son, Philippe Hurault, obtained Chartres in 1598 in succession to his great-uncle Nicolas de Thou, and as an explicit reward for the chancellor's merits and services to the crown.[107] But the most substantial ministerial success was that of Cheverny's successor, Bellièvre, whose son Albert succeeded the *ligueur* Epinac at Lyon in 1599 and who, when he lost his mental balance in 1604, was succeeded by his brother Claude. Lyon, with its turbulent record during the League, was too important to treat lightly, and with a Bellièvre (from an old Lyon family) as archbishop, an astute blend of native and ministerial power could be regarded as capable of healing past divisions and enhancing royal control.[108] The king's leading minister, the Protestant Sully had no one from his own family to promote, but this did not prevent him from making it clear that he wanted a voice, as governor of Poitou, in selecting the next bishop of Poitiers.[109]

Sub-ministerial families, as well as those of leading magistrates, also attracted a considerable share of episcopal nominations. If names like Laubespine, Revol, Potier, La Guesle, Frémiot, du Sault, Camus, La Croix de Chevrières, and du Vair figure among the king's choices, it is because they stemmed from such high-profile backgrounds, with several of them drawn from the senior ranks of provincial parlements. Indeed, this list alone is enough to suggest how the close interweaving of high robe families, both ministerial and *parlementaire*, enabled the better placed among them to secure episcopal office for sons of related families. Louis Revol had briefly been secretary of state to Henri III and Henri IV (1588–94), and it was to his son, Ennemond, that Henri IV first gave the see of Dol in 1592; when he finally abandoned his claim to it ten years later, it was his cousin, Antoine, who was nominated in his place.[110] The Laubespines had produced secretaries of state and ambassadors as well as bishops since the days of Henri II; they would have to wait until 1630 for further ministerial preferment, but in the meantime they could count on the patronage of no less a ministerial figure than Villeroy, husband of Madeleine de Laubespine. As we saw earlier, some of those initially nominated to dioceses but who subsequently failed to proceed further, were also drawn from exactly the same social and professional back-

---

107 AN, MC, VIII 417, *régale* settlement for Chartres 'donné en faveur de haut et puissant seigneur Philippe Hurault chancelier de France', 5 Dec 1598.
108 Bonney, *Political Change in France under Richelieu and Mazarin*, 12–13, 142, shows that Lyon was one of the first places to have regular intendants under Henri IV and Louis XIII - evidence of how important it was in the eyes of the royal council.
109 See Joseph Bergin, *The Rise of Richelieu* (New Haven and London 1991), 75, for the relevant references.
110 Trani, Camille, 'Les Conseillers du grand conseil au xvie siècle (1547–1610)', *Paris et l'Ile-de-France: Mémoires*, 42 (1991), 202. Trani mistakenly regards Antoine as Ennemond's nephew.

grounds. Achille de Harlay de Sancy, the son of a recent convert from Protestantism who was nominated to Lavaur while still a student in 1604, was the only one of them who eventually became a bishop, but that was not until over a quarter of a century later, and after he had been successively an ambassador to Constantinople and a priest of the Oratory![111]

For a king who began his reign with as many financial debts as Henri IV, it is remarkable how few sons of financial office-holders figure among his bishops. Apart from the case of Zamet, which did not yield actual results until 1612, one can point to only two bishops clearly drawn from such a background – Claude Dormy of Boulogne and Jacques Martin of Vannes. Of course, other bishops were drawn from families that had once been directly involved in financial affairs or that had strong ties to financial milieux – Jean-Pierre Camus of Belley and Henri de Gondi are but two examples of the former, Godefroy de Billy of Laon a case of the latter.[112]

In all, thirty-eight (35.2 per cent) out of the 108 bishops taking office between 1589 and 1610 were drawn from *robe* families of one kind or another, stretching all the way from the son of an Avignon municipal office-holder to those of successive chancellors of France. This figure tallies almost perfectly with the number of bishops drawn from older noble families, but it would be misleading to conclude from these figures that the spoils were divided evenly between the two sides. The influence of the older nobility can only be measured fully by taking into account the number of commoner bishops who owed their elevation to them, irrespective of whether or not they are to be regarded as *confidentiaires*.

If we discount the two *ligueur* bishops of Vannes and Glandèves installed in the early 1590s, it appears that about half of the bishops of older noble origins were drawn from families who had supported the king's cause at some time before his conversion; of the remaining half, at least six were *ligueurs*, while the political stance of the others has not been identified. As noted earlier, the timing of and the motives for partisan allegiance among older noble families varied considerably, making accurate listing hazardous. At any rate, it does seem that the proportion of sons of royalist nobles becoming bishops under Henri IV who owed their advancement to their families' services rather than their own is considerably higher than for other groups. This is underscored by two separate but convergent facts: firstly, the higher than usual number of them who were clearly underaged when nominated to their dioceses; secondly, the equally high proportion who were nominated to dioceses presently or previously held by members of their families. It was thus entirely logical in the circumstances for the surviving *brevets* or letters of nomination to be silent about the new bishops themselves (except for the rather formulaic expression of royal hopes for their future actions) but quite

111 AN, V^6 1178, fos 41, 199, decrees of *grand conseil*, 12 Oct and 1 Dec 1603, referring to Achille de Harlay as 'nommé par le Roy à l'évesché de Lavaur'.
112 For Billy, see Daniel Vidal, *Critique de la raison mystique* (Grenoble 1990), 248–9.

explicit about the 'merits and services' to the crown of one or more members of their families.

The future Cardinal Richelieu is as good an example of this pattern as any. He was no more than seventeen when he received his *brevet*, the text of which has never been found, but it would almost certainly have referred to the services of his late father who was First Captain of the royal bodyguard when he died over twelve years earlier. Richelieu was, moreover, designated to a diocese which his great uncle had held between 1585 and 1592, when a confidentiary nomination was made by Henri IV. Similar promotions were obtained by scions of better known families with names like Angennes, Salignac, Guise, Noailles, Corneilhan, and Gelas de Léberon. Cyrus de Thyard succeeded his uncle at Chalon-sur-Saône not because of what either of them had accomplished, but because Cyrus's elder brother was one of the few royalist town governors in Mayenne's province of Burgundy. The two Donadieu brothers, both confusingly called François, who became bishop of Auxerre in 1599 and of Saint-Papoul in 1607, owed their elevation to the favour enjoyed by another brother, the royalist governor of Angers.

Numerous other examples of the king's willingness to recognise his debts to the nobility and their expectations of high church office could be cited, but without altering the general picture. What does need to be stressed, however, is that the crown retained a degree of freedom in the choice of diocese for these new bishops. The examples of Auxerre and Chalon show that Henri IV was perfectly capable of nominating outsiders as bishops in a particular province when it suited his purpose: in these two cases, his purpose was almost certainly that of undermining any claim Mayenne might have had to promote candidates of his own there. Most of his nominations to Breton dioceses followed a similar pattern, especially in the early years of the reign, when his nominees were not merely royalists but also non-Bretons. He appears to have been much less concerned about Provence whose bishoprics continued to be dominated by local noble families. The exception in this region was the archbishopric of Embrun, which the Protestant Lesdiguières was anxious to control through a client, but the king made it clear he was unwilling to oblige him.[113] Such disparities in the king's behaviour may in turn derive from differences in attitude and expectation within the nobility itself. Given the sterling support Henri IV had had from the Angennes family, it might be thought that they might have pressed to retain Le Mans when Bishop Claude died in 1601, but Henri offered it instead to the former *ligueur* and provincial governor, the Marshal de Lavardin, for his son. But, as we saw, the next generation of the Angennes family was amply rewarded with the diocese of

---

113 BAV, Barb lat 5287, fo 15, Cardinal Aldobrandini to Cardinal Medici, legate, 15 Oct 1596. In 1600, when the archbishop, Lesdiguières's enemy, died, Henri IV allowed Créqui, the latter's son-in-law, to collect its revenues for several months (BN, MS Fr 4222, fo 450, *brevet* of 20 July 1600 'le Roy estant à Lyon'), but then nominated Honoré du Laurens, who had no connection to either man, as archbishop.

Bayeux after Ossat's death in 1604. Such geographical displacement, however, probably worried a family of the standing of the Angennes, with their wide horizons and past history, far less than it would, say, the Salignac with respect to Sarlat, the Corneilhan to Rodez, the Isnard to Glandèves, or the Iharse to Tarbes.

It is hardly surprising, given the methods adopted by Henri IV to win acceptance as rightful ruler, that former *ligueurs*, whether bishops or not, were still able to attract a measure of episcopal patronage once the succession crisis had ended. Incumbent bishops fared better in this regard than second-order clerics, almost certainly because of the king's desire to win over influential figures in the episcopate. We have seen Cardinal Givry's failure to retain Lisieux, but as a cardinal whose services in Rome and elsewhere the crown could not afford to forgo, Givry could not be banished into limbo. So Henri IV enabled him to become coadjutor to his uncle, the bishop of Langres, in 1603. Five years later, he moved him to the opulent see of Metz, but then angered him enormously by insisting that he resign the Langres coadjutorship which the king wanted for the twenty-year-old Sébastien Zamet.[114] Guillaume Rose, the League's bishop in armour, was succeeded at Senlis by his nephew Antoine, but this may well have been a reward for the latter's service to the king.[115] François de la Rochefoucauld of Clermont finally became a cardinal in 1607, and exchanged his see for that of Senlis in early 1610 with Antoine Rose, who was unable to escape from harrassment by the Paris parlement at Senlis.[116] The Villars family's League past did not damage the prospects, ecclesiastical or otherwise, of its numerous and ambitious progeny, who would flourish hugely in succeeding generations. Pierre II de Villars, the former *ligueur* archbishop of Vienne was even a candidate for a red hat; he managed to get his nephew Jérôme as his coadjutor in 1598, while his other episcopal nephew Nicolas, bishop of Agen, had in all probability completed arrangements for a coadjutorial succession for his own brother, Pierre III, before his sudden death in December 1608. Subsequently, Pierre III preferred to wait his turn in order to succeed Jérôme at Vienne, and in the meantime he ceded his claims to Agen to his cousin, Claude Gelas, son of a committed *ligueur* consul of Lyon, who became bishop there in 1609. Such complex manoeuvres are unthinkable without the virtual certainty of personal royal benevolence.[117]

---

114   BN, MS Fr 18003, fo 164, Denis Simon de Marquemont to king, Rome 8 July 1608; MS Fr 3540, fo 10, king to ambassador, 6 Aug 1608; MS Fr 18003, fo 243, Brèves to Villeroy, 2 Sept 1608; MS Fr 3790, fo 23, king to Brèves, 17 Mar 1610.

115   BN, PO 2546, dossier 56929 (Rose), fo 44, for a reference to a mission to Rome in 1602. This document, which enumerates the family's services to the crown and ignores everything else about them, needs to be treated with caution, though its factual content may well be accurate enough.

116   See Joseph Bergin, *Cardinal de La Rochefoucauld. Leadership and Reform in the French Church* (New Haven and London 1987), 36–7.

117   There is, unfortunately, no adequate study of this leading family of Lyon merchant origins which would produce peers and marshals of France under Louis XIV.

These exceptions apart, *ligueur* clerics needed either powerful patrons or family members – and ideally, both – in order to acquire bishoprics. The case of Anne de Murviel of Montauban is already familiar: he owed his career to Mayenne, who was both his relative and patron, as nothing at all is known about Murviel's own pre-episcopal affiliations or activities. François Rouxel de Médavy of Lisieux, Jean-Richard de Genoulhac of Tulle, and Guillaume Péricard of Evreux were all sons of prominent figures in the League whose local power networks were not destroyed by its defeat. It is less clear how or why Godefroy de Billy, Mayenne's nominee to Evreux in 1593, succeeded to Laon in 1601, or the Poitevin Melchior Marconnay became bishop of Saint-Brieuc the following year.[118] In these cases, and perhaps in others, it is likely that earlier family ties to the court were revived and strengthened under Henri IV, enabling them to tap into the fund of church patronage.[119]

V

It was, as might be expected, in Languedoc that some of the most prolonged difficulties with regard to bishoprics arose during Henri IV's reign. As remarked earlier, the Folembray settlement of 1596 had attempted to define separate Montmorency-Ventadour and Joyeuse spheres of influence, but each side had continuing aspirations to dominate dioceses outside their respective domains. This was of more than academic interest, since several dioceses were vacant in the area and had been at the centre of bitter conflicts for some years. Although litigation and rivalry were protracted, peaceful solutions to these disputes were probably rendered more possible by the fact that, after the return of the Marshal Joyeuse to his Capuchin's cell in 1599, the head of the Joyeuse affinity was his brother the cardinal: his frequent absences from Languedoc and his office of Protector of France in Rome required him to act as more than simply the manager of a particular set of interests.[120]

Few Languedoc sees could hope to escape competition when they fell vacant. Of course, each case has its own individual complications, but the

---

118 *Arrêts du conseil privé (Henri IV)*, ed Dumont, no 1998, decree of 23 Apr 1596 against Marconnay which refers to his 'rebellion'.

119 Billy was related to the Brichantau family, and was succeeded by two brothers from that family at Laon. His promotion to Laon may have been a royal gift to Antoine de Brichantau, a strong supporter of Henri IV since 1589. See Manfred Orléa, *La Noblesse aux états-généraux de 1576 et 1588* (Paris 1980), 138–41.

120 For example, Montmorency's daughter wrote to her father in 1597 asking him to write to Joyeuse to ensure that their candidate for Uzès would be supported in Rome; she added that Epernon had previously written to Joyeuse to that effect: Arch Chantilly, L/xxxii, fo 106, letter of 12 Mar 1597.

overall picture which can be pieced together may illuminate the general problems facing both the crown and the episcopate under Henri IV.[121] Joyeuse's efforts at Folembray to secure Le Puy for a *ligueur* in 1596 were too obvious to be disinterested, but in the event Ventadour's influence in the Velay proved the stronger. Henri IV was thus able to ignore the *ligueur* Alexandre de la Rochefoucauld in favour of Jacques de Serres, a cousin of the more famous Huguenots Jean and Olivier de Serres.[122] Prolonged disputes also centered on the sees of Nîmes and Uzès, still prominent centres of Huguenot power, both of which fell vacant in 1594–5. Nîmes had been in the hands of a Joyeuse confidentiary bishop, the Dominican Cavalesi, since 1573, and his attempts to resign it in 1588, presumably under Joyeuse auspices, to another Dominican, Louis Vervins, had come to nothing despite Henri III's consent at the time.[123] When Cavalesi died in August 1594, Joyeuse and his supporters in Nîmes did everything they could to press Vervins's case, while Montmorency promptly obtained a royal nomination for Pierre de Valernod, 'who has always belonged to my house' as the Constable later said of him.[124] The rival candidates lobbied hard, and instigated local enquiries to discredit each other in the eyes of the legate Medici, who personally approved of Valernod, and Rome.[125] But continuing Joyeuse obstruction ensured that it was only in early 1598 that he finally got his provisions.[126] The neighbouring see of Uzès was by now more securely under Montmorency control, so much so that the Constable's daughter could request the see for the Carmelite Louis Vigne in 1597, on the clear understanding, as she asserted years later, that he would hold it until such time as her own son came of age.[127]

Problems also arose in upper and Mediterranean Languedoc. The Joyeuse had occupied several dioceses, such as Albi, during the League, seizing revenues and imposing taxes, and were reluctant to relinquish control. However, there was an incumbent bishop of Albi, the royalist Alphonse Delbène,

---

121 It is likely that some of the bargaining over church patronage in Languedoc was channelled through successive papal vice-legates in Avignon rather than through papal nuncios in Paris, and that systematic research in the surviving papers of the legation would yield some interesting discoveries.
122 Devic and Vaisette, *Histoire générale du Languedoc*, xiibis, document no 446, article 90 of Folembray settlement.
123 ASV, N Fr 43, fo 117, Canons of Nîmes to Clement VIII, 14 Sept 1594, recalling Henri III's nomination, which they dated to 24 Nov 1588.
124 ASV, Fondo Borghese I, 636, fo 285, Montmorency to Aldobrandini 31 Aug 1596: 'qui a tousjours esté de ma maison'.
125 ASV, Fondo Borghese I, 646, fo 90, Medici to Aldobrandini, 20 Dec 1596.
126 For Valernod's career as a resident bishop, see Robert Sauzet, *Contre-réforme et réforme catholique en bas-Languedoc. Le Diocèse de Nîmes au xviie siècle* (Louvain and Paris 1979), 52ff.
127 Arch Chantilly, L/xxxii, fo 106, Marie de Montmorency to Constable, 12 Mar 1597. She was an illegitimate daughter, and was married to Jean de Fay-Peyraud, *sénéchal* of Beaucaire. In 1612, Louis XIII repeated this argument when requesting the coadjutorship of Uzès for her son, Paul-Antoine: BN, MS Fr 3792, fo 59, letter to Ambassador Brèves in Rome, 20 July 1612.

who had been appointed as long ago as 1588; it was with the greatest difficulty that he finally entered his diocese for the very first time in 1598![128] But it is the career of Christophe de Lestang, a leading Joyeuse client, which best illustrates the experiences of the province's episcopate, and the difficulties of a settlement. Lestang had been bishop of Lodève since 1580, but the diocese was occupied *manu militari* by Montmorency, and as a riposte Henri III allowed Lestang to take control of Carcassonne in 1585. But Montmorency also had a strong personal claim to dispose of Carcassonne, one which went back to the late 1570s, and Lestang was only able to remain there for four years. It was for that reason that he looked for another diocese, and in 1594 he obtained papal provisions to Alet, which had long been vacant.[129] Joyeuse's intentions were revealed in the Folembray settlement, which stipulated that Lestang would surrender Alet to Joyeuse in exchange for an abbey, and that Joyeuse would present his candidate for the see; Lestang would also resign his other diocese of Lodève 'to a capable person', also presumably of Joyeuse's choosing.

But nothing so straightforward came of Joyeuse's efforts at consolidating his domination of regional episcopal patronage, especially as Lodève was no longer dominated by Joyeuse or Lestang, but by Ventadour. Instead, it was Carcassonne which eventually provided the key to a settlement, though not until 1602. Montmorency remained as determined as ever to assert his rights to dispose of the diocese, but the absentee Annibale Rucellaï, who had technically resigned it in 1579 and returned to Rome, still claimed to be the rightful bishop, and had the full support of his patron, Clement VIII. Montmorency's repeated efforts in the late 1590s to get the crown to declare the see vacant and to present his own candidate, came to nothing in the face of such tenacious opposition.[130] In addition, as we saw, in 1590 Henri IV himself had promised to dispose of Carcassonne in favour of someone to be nominated by Rucellaï's brother, but it may be doubted how firmly wedded he remained to that promise a decade later. At any rate, Bishop Rucellaï's death in 1601 paved the way for a settlement of a kind which had been suggested to Montmorency several years earlier and which involved all three dioceses in dispute during the previous twenty years.[131] Lestang duly surrendered his theoretical title to Alet in return for Carcassonne. Montmorency also gave up his claims to Carcassonne, but not before exacting a hefty pension for

---

128   See Delbène's own account of his experiences during the decade following his confirmation: ASV, N Fr 42, fos 338–9, 15 July 1599, letter to Clement VIII. Other letters and appeals against Joyeuse occupation in *ibid*, fos 342, 355.

129   Greengrass, 'Aristocracy and Episcopacy', 360–2.

130   *Arrêts du conseil privé*, ed Dumont, i. 48, decree of 14 Nov 1597, requiring Rucellaï to resign Carcassonne to Jean-Anthoine de Thézan within three months.

131   Arch Chantilly, L/xxiv, fo 209–212, Claude Convers to Montmorency, 25 Oct 1595; L/xxvi, fo 126v, same to same (1596?), reporting discussions with the Constable's advisors on this question.

one of his almoners as his price.¹³² Alet now went to Pierre Polverel, whom Joyeuse had long wished to make a bishop and, after his sudden death, to his brother, Etienne. Finally, Lestang resigned his original see of Lodève to a candidate designated by Ventadour, the obscure Augustinian Gérard de Robin, but this transfer only took effect from January 1605.¹³³

Now the chronology of these moves coincides too closely with those of Cardinal Joyeuse himself to be a simple accident. In 1600, he finally disposed of his first archdiocese, Narbonne, to Louis Vervins, his candidate for bishop of Nîmes after Cavalesi's death in 1594. His choice of Vervins for Narbonne drew criticism from some quarters, possibly from Montmorency, leading Henri IV to revoke his initial letters of nomination in early 1598, and to write somewhat enigmatically to Rome, 'I do not wish this Dominican to take up this diocese for several important reasons connected to my service'.¹³⁴ However, Joyeuse evidently changed the king's mind and Vervins's nomination went ahead two years later. For all practical purposes, he was Joyeuse's caretaker, since all the revenues save a small annual pension still belonged to the cardinal. Far more surprising, however, was Joyeuse's own move from Toulouse to Rouen in 1604, though he continued to hold Toulouse for almost another decade and attempted to keep a close eye on the province. At first glance, it might seem as if Joyeuse, having now 'placed' his Languedoc clients and seen relations with Montmorency improve considerably, was intent on further extending his ecclesiastical influence. It is more likely that he had reached something of an impasse. The house of Joyeuse, of which he was now the head, faced extinction with him. Meanwhile Montmorency-Ventadour power was recovering strongly in Languedoc, as was evident from the amalgamation in 1599 of the two *lieutenances-générales* (created in 1596) in Ventadour's hands. On the other hand, Normandy was far from being *terra incognita* for the Cardinal. Both directly and through related families, the Joyeuse had long had interests of various kinds in the province, and the cardinal's brother, Anne, had been its governor in the 1580s. Villars-Brancas, the governor of Rouen who had negotiated his terms with Henri IV in 1594, was also a cousin of the cardinal. In 1604, when the latter finally replaced Henri IV's half-brother, Charles de Bourbon-Navarre, at Rouen, the duc de Montpensier, husband of Joyeuse's niece, was provincial governor, making such a move all the more attractive.

Despite these advantages, Joyeuse did not manage to build up an episcopal

---

132 Arch Chantilly, L/lxiii, fo 8, concordat of 25 Apr 1602 superseding an earlier agreement of 31 Jan 1601. The pension off Carcassonne was set at 5,000 *écus*, and was to be paid at Chantilly.
133 Ernest Martin, *Histoire de la ville de Lodève*, 2 vols (Montpellier 1900), ii. 372.
134 BN, MS Dupuy 212, fo 195r, Piney, ambassador in Rome, to king, 7 Mar 1598, returning the letters of nomination; *ibid*, fo 215v, king to Piney, 21 Apr 1598: 'je ne veulx pas que ce jacobin (Vervins) entre en ceste église pour plusieurs raisons qui importent à mon service'.

clientèle in northern France comparable to that of Languedoc. Years later, in a kind of *apologia pro vita sua*, the cardinal confessed that his duties as Protector of France and as head of his house, had led him to hope that he might achieve more in Rouen than elsewhere, 'even by relying on the authority and goodness of the late Monsieur de Montpensier', only to conclude that that, too, had been a mistake.[135] Henri IV clearly valued his political and diplomatic skills, and was prepared to satisfy him personally, but he would also seem to have set limits to his wider ambitions. Even in Languedoc itself, the king managed to avoid a complete carve-up of its bishoprics among clients of Montmorency and Joyeuse. A small number of bishops were protected by powerful men like Epernon and Crillon, while royalist bishops like Delbène of Albi were restored to their sees and developed their links with Montmorency. Even Montmorency's client bishop of Nîmes, Valernod, was effectively protected against his patron when the Constable turned against him and demanded his resignation in 1609.[136] Henri IV had no fewer than three opportunities to nominate bishops of Montpellier between 1596 and 1607, and on each occasion he chose his own men – first a royalist councillor in the Toulouse parlement, Guitard Ratte (1596), and then two preachers in his own service, Jean Garnier (1602) and the famous Pierre Fenouillet (1607). When Ratte was on his deathbed in 1602, Ventadour hastily wrote to Montmorency to press the king to honour his promise to grant the next vacant bishopric in Languedoc to him for his son, adding that he would present someone else until such time as his son came of age.[137] As a leading Huguenot centre, it was possible to insist that Montpellier needed an active proseltysing bishop, and not a caretaker of the kind Ventadour had in mind. But the most ironic twist was still to come, for when Bishop Garnier himself died in 1607, it was Sully who was instrumental in securing Montpellier for Pierre Fenouillet, a disciple of François de Sales and a highly regarded preacher.[138]

In the light of these and other cases mentioned above, it comes as no surprise to learn that Henri IV was willing to continue some of his predecessors' other practices regarding episcopal preferment. One reason for some of the extended vacancies, especially well into his reign, was the royal readiness to use French bishoprics in an effort to rebuild French influence in Rome.

---

135   BN, MS Fr 18006, fos 577–9, Joyeuse to Villeroy, 13 Nov 1611: 'mesmes par le moyen de l'auctorité et bonté de feu Monsieur de Montpensier'. Henriette-Catherine de Joyeuse was to become duchesse de Guise in 1611 after her first husband's death.
136   Arch Chantilly L/xcvii, fo 144, Jean-Baptiste Fortune to Montmorency, 26 May 1609; AD Gard, G 69, declaration by Jean de Fay-Peyraud in favour of Valernod. See Sauzet, *Contreréforme*, 114.
137   BN, MS Fr 3589, fo 77, letter of 6 July 1602. According to Ventadour, the doctors had given up all hope of Garnier recovering, and he died the following day.
138   BN, MS lat 17027, fo 155, quoting Sully's memoires to that effect. Independent evidence of this – essential where Sully's assertions are concerned – in MS Fr 18003, fo 275, Brèves to Villeroy, 13 Sept 1608.

While this had been common practice under his predecessors, and Italian incumbents of French bishoprics were numerous, especially but not exclusively in southern France, by Henry IV's time this practice began to diminish sharply. In 1600, when Ossat moved from Rennes to Bayeux, the Breton see was given to Seraphim Olivier-Razali, a curial official of Franco-Italian origin, but after two years of inaction he declined it for himself and negotiated for it to be transferred to François Larchiver, then rector of Saint-Louis-des-Français in Rome.[139] The following year Carcassonne, which had been held by the absentee Annibale Rucellaï for many years, attracted strong interest from a fellow Italian but, as we saw, the Joyeuse-Montmorency rivalry over the see ensured that it would be unavailable for disposal in this way.[140] In 1603, Henri IV was informed of Italian interest in Arles and Marseilles, but only *after* he had made firm nominations to both sees. The king regretted this and promised to reserve benefices in future for curia-based candidates; he even promised to accept fewer resignations in future, since they diminished the pool of disposable ecclesiastical patronage.[141] In 1604 Angoulême was offered to the Italian Dominican Serafino Banqui, but two years later he surrendered his title to Antoine de la Rochefoucauld.[142] The younger Cardinal d'Este was especially courted by the French crown during these years, and when rumours of the death of the bishop of Comminges circulated in 1602, it was suggested that his well-endowed diocese would help to persuade Este to support French interests in Rome. Although Comminges proved not to be vacant, a decision was apparently taken to 'reserve' it for Este.[143]

It was, therefore, not for lack of effort or interest that Henri IV failed to imitate his predecessors' generosity towards Italian, and especially Roman based ecclesiastics.[144] Ultimately, however, it was the disruption and damage

---

139 AAE, CP Rome 18, fo 217, Henri IV to Ambassador Sillery, 18 Apr 1600, nominating Olivier, called Serafin here. See also *Lettres d'Ossat*, iii. 541–2, letter to king, 9 May 1600, undertaking to resign Rennes to him.
140 *Lettres d'Ossat*, iv. 304–5, letter to Villeroy, 13 Mar 1601, for the terms offered by Ludovico Anguissola, a papal official.
141 *Lettres inédites de Henri IV à M de Béthune ambassadeur de France à Rome (8 avril au 29 décembre 1603)*, ed E Halphen (Paris 1897), 132–3, letter of 3 Dec 1603.
142 *Lettres missives de Henri IV*, vii. 78–9, letter to grand duchess of Tuscany, 18 Jan 1607, on La Rochefoucauld's journey to Florence to negotiate with Banqui. Earlier references to this exchange and the litigation arising out of it can be found in *Inventaire des arrêts du conseil privé*, ed Dumont, ii. fasc 3, p 49, decree of 17 Feb 1606; AN, MC LIV, 466, contract of 29 Mar 1606. Apparently, Henri IV offered Angoulême to Banqui because he had once warned him of an attempt on his life.
143 BN, MS Fr 3487, fo 70, Villeroy to Béthune, 21 Sept 1602; MS Fr 3496, fo 60, Béthune to Villeroy, 27 Jan 1603. Béthune concluded that even with Comminges, Este would be hard to secure, a familiar experience with high-born Italian prelates. See *Lettres missives de Henri IV*, ix. 303–4, undated letter to Gilles de Souvré: 'et pour l'evesché de Commenges, sy elle eut vacqué je l'eusse donné à quelque Cardynal à Rome pour y fere mes aferes'.
144 BN, MS Fr 18005, fo 140v, Brèves, ambassador in Rome, to Villeroy, 2 Apr 1610: 'J'ay faict scavoir à M le Card de Mantoue (Este) la bonne intention de Sa Mté en son endroit sur l'advis de la mort de l'Evesque de Comminge. La nonce en advisera Sa Sté.'

caused by the wars which ensured that Roman or Italian prelates increasingly preferred rewards of a safer and more secure kind – pensions off bishoprics and abbeys rather than the benefices themselves, with all their attendant problems of possession, management, and litigation. Thus the Italian bishops actually nominated by Henri IV were for the most part long settled in France, not high-ranking prelates from the curia in search of sinecures; the latter he satisfied, at least partly, through pensions payable not by the treasury, but by bishoprics like Auch and Angoulême.[145]

VI

For its part, the papacy was not tempted to lapse into complacency about the French episcopate once Cardinal Medici returned from his legation in September 1598. However, its role thereafter cannot be characterised in simple terms, and has to be approached from a number of directions. It should not be thought of as purely a matter of applying a Tridentine view of what the episcopate should be.

For one thing, the papacy played its own part in keeping a considerable number of dioceses vacant for many years. There were different reasons for this. For one thing, its suspicion and indeed resentment of some of the king's men was slow to recede. Both du Bec and Daillon had to wait until 1598 for their provisions, Beaune until 1602, while Benoist was humiliatingly forced to abandon his claims to Troyes after eleven fruitless years of royal pressure on Clement VIII.[146] Resentment was strongest against Beaune because of his alleged ambition to become head of a French national church and his unauthorised absolution of Henri IV in 1593, and Clement VIII regularly responded to French pressure to confirm his transfer to Sens by claiming that Beaune would simply not win a vote by the cardinals in consistory.[147] In Benoist's case, the king's exasperation was so great that in 1603 he momentarily threatened to revert to the pre-1596 system under which the *grand conseil* could authorise those nominated to bishoprics to take possession and administer them.[148] It was Benoist's earlier translation of the Bible which

---

145 See Bernard Barbiche, 'L'Influence française à la cour pontificale sous Henri IV', *Mélanges d'Histoire et d'Archéologie de l'Ecole Française de Rome*, 77 (1965), 277–99, for Henri's attempts to rebuild a French party in Rome after the League, when Spanish influence had been preponderant.
146 The Benoist claim, first to Angers and then to Troyes occurs repeatedly in papal and royal diplomatic papers down to 1604, when Benoist himself finally abandoned his claims. See E Pasquier, *Un curé de Paris pendant les guerres de religion. René Benoist, le pape des Halles 1521–1608* (Angers 1913).
147 ASV, Fondo Borghese I, 80, fo 97, Aldobrandini to Medici, 16 Sept 1596; fo 112v, same to same 7 June 1597; *Lettres d'Ossat*, iii. 309, Ossat to Villeroy, 25 May 1599.
148 *Lettres inédites de Henri IV à M de Béthune (1603)*, ed E Halphen (Paris 1897), 46, letter of 4 June 1603.

proved the ultimate stumbling block, and the papacy persisted in regarding it, if not actually as heretical, then at least as sufficient evidence of Benoist's doubtful orthodoxy for him to be unacceptable as a bishop; no amount of explanation or defence of Benoist could break down Roman resistance.[149] Other Henrician nominees were quizzed on similar grounds, especially if they had been subject to any kind of censure by the Paris faculty of theology under Henri III or the League. The Benedictine preacher Jean Garnier was initially welcomed in Rome as an excellent choice for Montpellier in 1602, and was warmly recommended to the pope by Henri IV as one of his *prédicateurs ordinaires*.[150] But when it was learned that one of his books had been criticised by the faculty during the wars, it needed all the support he enjoyed at court to persuade Clement VIII, who particularly wanted an energetic bishop for a Protestant stronghold like Montpellier, to approve him.[151] It seems, therefore, that Rome was more sensitive on matters of orthodoxy than on the personal qualities of episcopal nominees during these years, and that that sensitivity could extend to individuals who were in any way tainted with Huguenot associations. Paul Hurault had to wait until 1599 for his bulls to Aix, not just because he was party to the campaign against Génébrard, but even more so because of his Protestant birth. In September 1597, Medici had received a coded instruction to warn the king against nominating sons of heretics like Hurault 'who are abhorred by the canons, as you know, unless they are eminent men of reliable doctrine'.[152] The same warning was repeated in the instructions to subsequent nuncios.

Elsewhere, delays in filling sees were due to the papacy taking a strictly legalistic line by flatly refusing to grant provisions to royal nominees to dioceses which had been given Mayennist or papal bishops during the League, regardless of whether these bishops had ever taken possession of their sees. So Coutances, Aix, Fréjus all had to wait until these nominal bishops died before successors were confirmed by Rome. In addition, Clement VIII felt strongly that his predecessors had not defended papal nomination rights vigorously enough, and he attempted to exercise them when he felt entitled to do so.[153] In 1601 and 1603, the bishops of Carcassonne and Alet respectively died in

---

149 ASV, Fondo Borghese I, 462–8, fos 318–21, for Gondi's extensive efforts to defend and excuse Benoist, 15 May 1597.
150 Formal letter of nomination, 26 Sept 1602, in Bernard Barbiche ed, 'Lettres originales de Henri IV à Clement VIII', in *Miscellanea in onore di Monsignore Martino Giusti* (Vatican City 1978), i. 64–5.
151 *ANG*, iv. 344, Aldobrandini to Del Buffalo, papal nuncio, 10 Sept 1602, for Pope's recommendation; *ibid*, 374, 386–7, 390–1, 411, for subsequent exchanges between Rome and Del Buffalo over Garnier, 4 Nov, 2 Dec, 16 Dec 1602, and 13 Jan 1603 respectively; BN, MS Fr 3496, fos 41, 45v, 51v, Béthune to Villeroy, 10 Sept, 21 Oct, and 2 Dec 1602 respectively.
152 ASV, Fondo Borghese I, 80, fo 119, letter of 9 Sept. The Italian refers to 'uomini eminenti et securi'.
153 *Lettres d'Ossat*, iv. 305, letter to Villeroy, 13 Mar 1601.

curia, and the pope's reaction was to insist that in such circumstances, the right to choose a successor was his.¹⁵⁴ But in each case, he soon realised he could not turn the clock back or overcome resistance from France, and after some delay he accepted the king's nominations instead.

The papacy's slowness was also partly based on its long-standing mistrust of the processes by which French bishops were chosen, and the real identity of the individuals nominated. This suspicion can be exaggerated, since Rome was no less anxious than the crown to see a restored, active episcopate in France, and that as quickly as possible.¹⁵⁵ Clement VIII proved far more generous than his successors towards newly-appointed French bishops by granting them a record number of total or partial reductions of annates in response to pleas founded on the damage done to revenues during the wars; in many cases, as Ossat regularly noted in his reports to the court, he even took it upon himself to sign the reduction papers *motu proprio* after consistories had met and approved royal nominees - never a popular move in the college of cardinals who drew part of their income from such sources of income.¹⁵⁶

At the same time, there was more to the curia's role in shaping the episcopate than *ad hoc* responses to developments in France. Its approach can also be followed through the activities of its nuncios. Their status, both personal and diplomatic, might be less impressive than that of a legate, and French nuncios, unlike their counterparts in Spain, possessed no powers of jurisdiction. But as defenders of the Gallican liberties were wont to object, this did not keep them out of matters episcopal. After virtually a decade of interruption, a new line of resident nuncios began in early 1599 with the arrival of Gasparo Silingardi, whose principal task was to obtain the adoption of the decrees of Trent promised by Henri IV as part of his absolution. The virtually identical instructions given to successive nuncios in 1599, 1601, and 1604 all placed vigilance over episcopal nominations close to the top of each nuncio's hierarchy of responsibilities, arguing that a reformed episcopate was an essential part of a restored and pacified kingdom. Singled out for special attention on each occasion were the *billets, brevets* and *lettres d'économat* which still enabled abuses to endure and kept benefices vacant. Rome's repeated insistence on the proper observance of the concordat was largely intended to eliminate them altogether. Heretics and the sons of heretics were also unacceptable to Rome as candidates for bishoprics, the latter because 'born of infected roots, their fruits were suspect'.¹⁵⁷ In general, whenever vacancies

---

154 *Lettres inédites de Henri IV à Béthune (1603)*, 102, letter of 21 Sept 1603.
155 Jaitner, *Hauptinstruktionen Clemens' VIII*, i. 584, n 4, for reference to papal brief to all French bishops urging visitations, synods and seminaries.
156 *Lettres d'Ossat*, ii-v, *passim*, for frequent references to this question in Ossat's reports on papal consistories.
157 Jaitner, *Hauptinstruktionen Clemens' VIII*, ii. 583.

arose, the nuncio was to keep his eyes open and find out who was being put forward for episcopal nomination; should undesirable names appear, he was to take pre-emptive action, warning the king of the dangers, one of which was that the pope might be compelled to reject the king's choices.[158] If the repetition of these views in successive instructions tends to suggest that there was something formulaic about them, nothing could be more instructive than a comparison with the instructions given in 1604 to the new nuncio to Madrid: there the papacy's complaint was that the Lerma régime under Philip III had descended from the virtual perfection which obtained under Philip II when it came to the care that was exercised over the choice of bishops, and that patronage concerns now loomed much larger than had been the case or than was desirable.[159]

The language of the French nuncios' instructions might seem designed to produce confrontation, but this would be to miss the point. In fact, the papacy usually had relatively little stomach for fights over episcopal nominations, and it placed considerable faith in the ability of its nuncios to head off disputes by prompt diplomacy; the latter could be held to have failed when unsuitable nominations were actually made and rejection by Rome was rendered more awkward because of the loss of face to both king and candidate that it would entail. It is, therefore, hardly surprising to find more frequent and sustained reference to the problems of the episcopate in the correspondence of both the papal nuncios – and indeed of the French ambassadors in Rome – during the decades stretching from the mid-1590s to the 1610s than at any other time during the seventeenth century. It seems highly unlikely that nuncios were ever able to obtain nominations for individual clerics they knew and approved of. But in some cases, they were able to dissipate suspicion or mistrust in Rome of certain royal choices. It would not be excessive to claim that one of the reasons why Jean Garnier finally got his provisions to Montpellier in late 1602 was because Del Buffalo did *not* act upon his instructions to raise the pope's objections with Henri IV, but instead put together a dossier of evidence on Garnier which convinced Clement VIII that he deserved his provisions.[160]

From the papacy's point of view, the principal problems fell into two categories. The first involved the crown more directly than the second. The nomination of underaged bishops in the late 1590s and early 1600s exasperated Clement VIII, who threatened to refuse the necessary dispensations and reminded the king of his promises to curtail the

---

158 *Ibid*, ii. 577–96 (1599), 662–88 (1601), 725–49 (1604). Only the correspondence of Del Buffalo, nuncio from 1601 to 1604 has been published in full: *ANG*, vol iv.

159 *Ibid*, ii. 777–8, instruction for Tommaso Lapi, Dec 1604.

160 *ANG*, iv. 374, 386–7, 390–1, 411, for Del Buffalo's correspondence with Aldobrandini over Garnier, 4 Nov, 2 Dec, 16 Dec 1602, and 13 Jan 1603 respectively.

practice.¹⁶¹ The suggestion, for example, that the experienced Philippe du Bec might not become archbishop of Reims unless he agreed to take a young Guise as his coadjutor from the outset was met with a categorical refusal.¹⁶² The second category of problems had less to do with the crown than with the intense pressures from nobles, and concerned *confidences*, suspicions of malpractice surrounding resignations, and the unwillingness of laymen to surrender control of major benefices, bishoprics not excluded.¹⁶³ The Cardinal-legate, Medici, had suspected that such practices were widespread, but what surprised him most was the extent to which they were regarded as normal by those involved; in his view, the position would only be improved by a sustained assault on the consciences of all those engaged in them, both laypeople and ecclesiastics.¹⁶⁴

It should cause no surprise that an examination of the extent to which such problems continued under Henri IV faces the same difficulties as we encountered under Henri III. Distinguishing a case of outright *confidence* from arrangements which enabled powerful figures to retain most of a bishopric's revenues in the form of pensions or patronage rights, remains problematic, but at least first-hand evidence for several of them is more abundant than for the previous reign. The fact that early in his reign Henri IV, like his predecessor, 'gave' a considerable number of dioceses to nobles, with or without accompanying *lettres d'économat*, and that many of these dioceses remained vacant for several years, was always likely to give rise to episcopal nominations at a later date which carried the marks of these experiences. To some extent, this can in turn be connected to a development noted, and diversely interpreted, by previous historians of the subject – namely, the presence of an unusually high number of commoners among the bishops nominated by Henri IV. But the connection is one that needs to be demonstrated case by case rather than assumed. While the nomination of a commoner bishop may

---

161 *Lettres d'Ossat*, v. 185, Ossat to Villeroy, 2 Dec 1602. In fairness to Henri IV, he did attempt to refuse bishoprics to underage sons of his closest friends, which was perhaps the most difficult decision, though his reasons were not always consistent: see *Lettres missives de Henri IV*, ix. 303–4, undated letter to Gilles de Souvré: 'Souvenés vous de ce que vous m'avés ouy dire que ie suis résolu doresnavant de ne donner plus les éveschés que à personnes qui les puissent desservyr et non les fere desservyr par autruy, et que faysant bien estudyer et nourryr celluy de voz enfans que vous avés destyné pour estre d'eglyse an bon ecclésyastyque, que vous aymant comme ie fay, il ne ne manquera d'estre pourveu de dygnyté an l'église, et pour l'évesché de Commenges sy elle eut vacqué je l'eusse donné à quelque Cardinal à Rome pour y fere mes aféres.'
162 *Lettres d'Ossat*, ii. 443–5, Ossat to Villeroy, 22 Mar 1597; BN, MS Dupuy 212, fo 80v, Luxembourg-Piney, ambassador in Rome, to Henri IV, 26 Aug 1597, for Guise lobbying in Rome for the Reims coadjutorship.
163 For example, see the papers and reports arising from a suspected simoniacal resignation of Apt in Provence by its bishop in 1606: BN, MS Fr 18001, fo 11, Halincourt, ambassador, to Villeroy, 25 Jan 1606; ASV, Fondo Borghese II, 248, fos 73, 274, 531, Barberini to Borghese, 22 Feb, 27 June and 27 Dec 1606; *Gallia Chr Nov*, i. cols 285–6.
164 ASV, Fondo Borghese I, 646, fos 37–8, Medici to Cardinal Aldobrandini, 11 Oct 1596; fo 121, same to same, 21 Jan 1597.

alert us to possible anomalies, we have already seen a sufficient number of these bishops not to infer that they should be regarded *ipso facto* as caretakers; figures as eminent as du Perron, Ossat, Garnier, Fenouillet and Philippe Cospeau provide weighty evidence to the contrary. It is not the social origins of bishops alone, but the circumstances of their dioceses and of their nomination which enable one to test the validity of the charges laid against several of Henri IV's bishops.

While making these allowances, it still appears that up to half of Henri IV's commoner bishops were bound, either formally or informally, to powerful aristocrats or local noble families; the idea that the king possessed either the desire or the freedom of action required in order to promote social harmony and national reconciliation by choosing bishops from all social classes seems to fly in the face of political and social realities after a generation of civil and military turbulence.[165] In the early 1580s, the papal secretary of state ventured to say that a candidate for the see of Lisieux could not be a caretaker because he was of noble birth. Such a view would be inaccurate for Henri IV's reign, when a number of bishops of sword or robe origin were party to confidentiary arrangements or something quite close to them. Nicolas Briroy of Coutances was from a noble family of the Cotentin, but owed his mitre entirely to Marshal Matignon. Jean Martin, as we have seen, was from a Limousin office-holding family, but as bishop of Périgueux he was wholly at the mercy of the Bourdeille clan. Henri de Noailles's choice for bishop of Saint-Flour, Raymond Rouchon, was no more than a domestic, and his masters treated them as such. The Richelieu family never allowed François Hyver to become the consecrated bishop of Luçon, which made it all the easier to cast him aside when the future Cardinal received the royal nomination in 1602.

About half of these 'dependent' Henrician bishops can fairly be regarded as *confidentiaires*, but it is the status of the other half which is the more difficult to convey. The duc d'Epernon took all the credit for promoting the celebrated Sorbonnist, Philippe Cospeau, to the episcopate, paying for his papal provisions, his *équipage*, and even a carriage to get him to his Gascon diocese of Aire, but only after claiming for himself a substantial pension off the diocese, which he had in any event kept vacant for the previous twelve years.[166] As we saw, Cardinal Joyeuse was even more tightfisted in his treatment of Louis Vervins, his personal choice of successor as archbishop of Narbonne, leaving him just a modest pension for his needs. The fact that a number of these new bishops were, like Vervins, members of religious orders, in addition to being commoners, was not wholly accidental, since they could more readily be held to be capable of living off limited incomes than sons of the nobility. And there

---

165 J Michael Hayden, 'The Social Origins of the French Episcopacy at the Beginning of the Seventeenth Century', *French Historical Studies* 10 (1977), 27–38; Péronnet, *Les Evêques de l'ancienne France*, i. 496ff.
166 BN, MS lat 17021, fo 81 'extraict de la vie de Mre Philippe Cospeau'.

is a major paradox in this particular development.¹⁶⁷ It is that many of these bishops, especially when they were both commoners and regulars who were well into middle age, were often experienced administrators and preachers, possessing more pastoral abilities than their noble counterparts. Several went on to become highly active reforming bishops, but it may be asked how much even those intent on religious revival actually achieved, given their limited control over the dioceses which they held.

In the context of episcopal patronage, however, a major key to understanding the condition of these bishops lies in the pensions which they were required to pay to those – or their nominees – who obtained their bishoprics for them. Henri IV ratified some of the most extravagant demands for pensions off bishoprics of the entire *ancien régime*. Even if incoming bishops made no other promises or concessions to the pensioner that would have placed them among the ranks of confidentiary bishops, the fact remains that the size – at least in relation to episcopal revenues – of some of these pensions could not but exacerbate the bishops' dependence. The real test would come when bishops either would not or could not pay the pensions in full or in good time, and when litigation, accompanied by the seizure of their temporalities, duly followed. It is quite clear from two lawsuits in 1602–4 that the *conseil privé*'s jurisprudence envisaged the enforced resignation of the offending bishops as a logical and acceptable outcome in such instances. To that extent, it implied that episcopal tenure was conditional, not absolute, as canon law required it should be. When French bishops had complained under Henri III that the council enforced confidentiary arrangements in disputes between bishops and patrons, it was probably this kind of attitude that they had in mind. Moreover, the identity of the parties to the cases in 1602–4 is also revealing of developments under Henri IV. The first concerns a diocese we have already seen more than once, Auch, and its archbishop since 1599, Léonard Destrappes, who owed a huge pension of 8,000 *écus* to the duc de Nemours. It is hard to know whether Destrappes was just stalling, or whether he experienced genuine difficulty in finding such a substantial sum of money, but he had been summoned several times by Nemours to pay up before the 1603 court action.¹⁶⁸ A rather pathetic appeal by him to Chancellor Bellièvre in December 1603 shows him freely acknowledging himself as a humble client of the Nemours family, but complaining bitterly about the harsh treatment he was receiving from the duc's mother.¹⁶⁹ At any rate, in January 1604, the *conseil privé* summoned him to appear before it at the duc's request. To ensure the pension was paid, it wished the leases of Auch's temporalities to be made before magistrates; and it concluded pointedly by saying that if Destrappes found the pension too high, he could resign Auch to a person who would be selected by Nemours.¹⁷⁰ The threat against Destrappes was not

---

167 Hayden, 'Social Origins of the French Episcopacy', 37–8.
168 AN, V⁶ 1178, fo 42, decree of 28 Oct 1603.
169 BN, MS Fr 15897, fo 96, letter of 27 Dec 1603.
170 AN, V⁶ 7, no 263, decree of 7 Jan 1604.

implemented, however, and a few years later, the Nemours pension was reduced by a third and transferred to the crown for patronage uses in the Roman curia.[171]

The other lawsuit of 1602–3 is more startling still, in that it pitted Archbishop Philippe du Bec of Reims against his nephew, Jean, bishop of Saint-Malo. The latter owed his uncle a pension of 2,000 *écus* off Saint-Malo and an abbey he held since 1599, a pension which was either the archbishop's reward for having promoted his nephew, or perhaps an indemnity for the loss of revenue in transferring from Nantes to Reims. At any rate, in two successive decrees, the council ordered Jean du Bec to pay up or else resign his see (and the abbey) in favour of successors chosen by his uncle.[172]

Relations between patrons and their episcopal dependents did not always go to the brink in this way. Yet these cases show the range of possibilities inherent in certain episcopal successions which, like that involving the du Bec, could set cleric against cleric, and even one member of a family against another. The generalisation of pensions off bishoprics under Henri IV went much further than it did under his successors, and accounts in part for the continuing fragility of the episcopate. An unusual feature of these developments was the extent to which another member of a bishop's family was allowed to claim a legally enforceable pension off a diocese. It had always been widely accepted that family *pietas* would ensure that reigning bishops would use their incomes to educate, marry and generally assist members of their family, but the obligation was a moral, customary one. When, however, a father or elder brother insisted that a formal pension for them, or another cleric of the family, be contained in a bishop's nomination and papal provisions, it is clear that something had changed. The bishops who protested in Paris in 1596 against the Nemours pension off Auch were in no doubt about the dangers, and condemned the secularisation of church revenues. The Nemours pension was the largest of all, but it was not isolated. For a time the *grand prieur* de France, and later Cardinal Joyeuse, held one for 20,000 *livres* off Albi, the Monluc family one for 10,000 *livres* off Condom, the Lansac family 10,000 *livres* off Comminges, and Henry IV's own *brave* Crillon 4,000 off Fréjus and 5,000 off Arles.[173] But it is just as legitimate to regard these specially earmarked pensions as part of an attempt to retain control over the temporal administration of dioceses, in the hope that it would enable those involved to strongly influence any subsequent episcopal nomination. It was for

---

171 AN, MC, VIII, 564, for a series of agreements between Sully, Sillery Jeannin (on behalf of the king) and Nemours and his creditors, 4 Oct, 24 and 26 Nov 1604.

172 AN, V^6 1175, fo 368, 2 Apr 1602; V^6 1177, fo 249, 10 Mar 1603. The second decree simply says that du Bec should resign to someone to be presented to him, and does not specify if he was to be chosen by the archbishop.

173 ASV, Acta Miscellanea 53, fo 272; ASV, N Fr 42, fos 338–9, Bishop Delbène to Clement VIII, 7 July 1599 (Albi); L Mazéret, *Chroniques de l'Eglise de Condom*, p 295; AN, V^6 1180, fo 454 (Comminges); ASV, Fondo Borghese, I, 636C, fo 32, Henry IV to Paul V, 28 Apr 1608 (Fréjus); *Gallia Chr Nov* (Arles), 942.

this reason that papal provisions in this period commonly specified that the various pensions owed by a new bishop should only be paid on condition that a fixed sum, usually rather modest in size compared to the pensions, remain at the bishop's disposal. And, as we saw in a previous chapter, Paul V was even willing to grant pensions off benefices to laymen provided the benefices themselves were returned to at least nominal ecclesiastical control.[174]

The papacy was not alone in trying to restore what it considered to be right order in the French church. The successive assemblies of clergy, as we saw, regularly adopted a critical stance over benefices, and bishoprics in particular. At the end of each assembly, the clergy presented their remonstrances, which might form the basis of a royal edict issued in the following months or years, the terms of which, if not necessarily immediately enforceable, at least helped to keep the spotlight on, for example, abuses relating to the acquisition and transmission of benefices.[175] Under Henri IV, the assemblies of 1595, 1598 and 1605 all reiterated earlier demands for the return to episcopal elections, though after seeing the determination of both Mayenne and the king to defend the Concordat of Bologna, it may be wondered how seriously they pursued the return to elections. But the assembled clergy also fretted about existing royal practice. In 1598, the archbishop of Tours made the closing address to the king, and criticised his ecclesiastical appointments, underlining the need to end the scandals of entrusting major offices to men who merely held them on behalf of others, even of women and military men. As in 1596, Henry replied by referring to the difficulties he had until recently had with his realm, and rejected any responsibility by claiming that these scandals pre-dated his reign.[176] In December 1605, the archbishop of Vienne made substantially the same charge and the same recommendation. This time, the king was more assertive, putting the clergy on the defensive. Referring to the abuses cited by the clergy, he answered,

> in the matter of simony and confidences, begin by healing yourselves and by stimulating others to follow your good example. As for the elections, you see for yourselves how I make them. I take pride in the fact that those whom I have elevated are very different from those of the past. What you have said to me redoubles my determination to do better in future.[177]

174 See ch 4, 149.
175 See the 'édit rendu sur les remontrances du clergé assemblé à Paris, qui statue sur la repression du crime de simonie, sur les appels comme d'abus, la tenue des conciles etc, sept 1610', in *Recueil général des anciennes lois françaises*, ed F A Isambert et al, 29 vols (Paris 1821–33), xvi. 9–14.
176 *Lettres missives de Henri IV*, v. 33, king's reply, 28 Sept 1598.
177 *Ibid,* vi. 565, 'réponse du roy Henri IV à M. Pierre de Villars': 'pour ce qui est des simonies et confidences, commencés à vous guérir vous-mesmes et exciter les autres par vos bons exemples à bien faire. Quant aux élections, vous voyés comme j'y procède. Je suis glorieux de voir ceux que j'ay establis estre bien differens de ceux du passé; le récit que vous avés faict me redouble le courage de mieux faire à l'advenir.'

There is no record of anyone present trying to contradict the king on either occasion, and it is fair to say that the king's own verdict on his policy towards the episcopate has been widely accepted by historians. In 1598 he distanced himself from the practices of past years and reigns; by 1605, he was effectively asserting that he had reshaped the French episcopate. Possibly for diplomatic reasons at least, the clergy in 1605 agreed with him: they did compliment him upon the good choices he had made of bishops but, equally, that did not prevent them from repeating the complaints of 1595 and 1598, as they would do again in 1614–15. It should also be clear that neither the habitual reserve nor the guarded language of papal diplomacy could hide the fact that Rome consistently worried throughout Henri's reign about his decisions, and about the poor quality of royal nominations to the French episcopate taken as a whole.

In view of these enduring problems, it would be somewhat naïve to talk in terms of a far-reaching reconstruction of the episcopate under Henry IV. The crisis of the episcopate which had begun in the 1560s and reached its paroxysm during the last phase of the religious wars, could only be overcome by means of a restoration of political stability, and by a return to normal relations with Rome. Thereafter, the long-term recovery of the episcopate would be closely dependent upon the recovery of church lands and an enhancement of bishops' control over their clergy, a task that was still not completed, to the bishops' satisfaction at least, until the late seventeenth-century. In this wider perspective, the changes occurring during Henri IV's reign were, as we have seen, rather too limited in scope to be safely regarded as decisive, but they were not negligible for all that. By restoring peace, and by containing Catholic nobles and *ligueurs* as much as the Huguenots, his reign contributed above all to the stabilisation of the French episcopate. Modest though this may sound, such stabilisation was important. Henri's power to achieve more than that was decidedly limited, and he acknowledged this by compromising with local families and demands. To argue that the crown possessed a general policy when it came to choosing bishops would be flying in the face of the facts. However, fears about how far this pragmatism would take Henri IV rendered both the French clergy and the papacy less than ecstatic eulogists of his handling of episcopal patronage. It is surely significant that one of the earliest recommendations from Paul V to Henri's widow after his assassination was a firm exhortation to her to attempt to present better candidates for the mitre than her late husband had done.[178]

---

178 ASV, Fondo Borghese I, 907, fos 175–8, Borghese to Ubaldini, 30 May 1610.

CHAPTER 11

Consolidation and Contradiction

THE CHAOTIC BEGINNINGS and abrupt end of the reign of Henri IV have meant that historians have always experienced difficulty in evaluating its achievements and, in particular, in placing them in any long-term perspective. It is a problem which confronts the historian of the church as much as it does the historian of foreign, financial or domestic affairs, though it does so in a different way. It is all the more paradoxical, therefore, that when one begins to consider the decades which followed Henri's assassination, his shadow and that of his reign often seem to loom large in the background, and almost imperceptibly become a yardstick by which to measure the events and achievements of the first two decades of his successor's reign. In this way the thing to be measured itself becomes the ruler, and the resulting ambivalence is no doubt one of the reasons why interpretations of the reigns of the first two Bourbons have differed so much.

Moreover, a long-entrenched periodisation for the reign of Louis XIII has proved exceptionally resilient to serious challenge. The Regent Marie de' Medici, who acted as official caretaker for Louis XIII until October 1614 and then unofficially until the coup d'état of April 1617, has rarely had a good press, either as a political figure in her own right or as mentor to her son. The opening years of Louis XIII's personal rule have fared little better, dominated as they were by the royal favourite, the duc de Luynes, until his death in late 1621, and by a series of unstable, short-lived ministries during the following years. Historians almost palpably sigh with relief when the masterly hand of Richelieu can be seen moving, from April 1624 onwards, to take hold of the plough – or, as he himself might have said, with his fondness for naval metaphors, the ship of state. Like a piece of classical theatre, the next eighteen years would possess a unity of purpose and action, and witness profound changes; they would see an intelligent and highly strung, but imperious and detested cardinal, emerge more clearly than even Louis XIII as the authentic, albeit uncrowned, successor to Henri IV.

The problem with this schema lies not just with the broad brush-strokes, however flamboyant or subdued their presentation may be, but with the fine detail as well. The extended regency of Marie de' Medici is a case in point. When not portrayed as politically inept or unable to concentrate for long on matters of state, she is often represented as rather too inclined to accommodate papal and Spanish interests. Surrounding herself with fellow-Italians and ecclesiastics, she has often been portrayed as governing France in almost conscious defiance of the healthy Gallican maxims of her husband and his predecessors. This view of the regency culminates in the often repeated canard that even the papal nuncio, Roberto Ubaldini, was invited to attend council meetings during his extended period of service in France (1607–16). Thus France exchanged a monarch who could rarely be found closeted with any ecclesiastic apart from his confessor – and even then the occasion was newsworthy – for a regent who lost little time in allowing the levers of power to fall into the hands of those who were increasingly identified as *dévots*. Subsequently, Louis XIII and his first favourite, Luynes, enabled the *dévots* to consolidate their position, responding positively to their demands for strong action against the Huguenots and for a Catholic foreign policy. It would take the emergence of Richelieu for the *dévot* legacy first to be challenged and then abandoned, both in the realm of policy and of personnel, with the dispersal of the *dévot* party grouped around the queen mother after the political crisis of 1630; under his direction, a more authoritarian monarchy, committed to openly secular goals both at home and abroad, was able to develop in a relatively short time, and would be fostered by Mazarin and Louis XIV.

While individual parts of this interpretation will doubtless survive, much of it remains open to serious question. One reason is that it has always focused heavily on the individual dramatis personae – kings, regents or ministers – and their personal preferences, whether explicitly stated or observable in their behaviour, without sufficient consideration of the context in which they operated. For the most part, the freedom of action implicit in such interpretations seems excessive when confronted with contemporary realities; this is as true of Marie de' Medici and her friends – Italian, ecclesiastical or otherwise – as it is of Richelieu, with his constant need to retain royal trust and to construct enduring political alliances that would help to fortify him against sudden eviction from office.

The evolution of the French episcopate in the two decades following Henri IV's death is just one of several ways in which the received wisdom can be tested and amended. It is not being suggested here that either 1610 or 1630 represent major, but hitherto unrecognised, turning points, and ample evidence of significant continuities on both sides of these terminal dates will appear in due course. Nevertheless, the chronological scope of the present chapter has not been settled upon at random: it is intended to suggest that as far as ecclesiastical patronage and policy are concerned, there are powerful grounds for attempting to revise the generally accepted sequence of developments, and to offer alternative explanations of the underlying causes of that sequence. Briefly, it will be argued that the readiness of the regency and its successor régime to make extensive concessions to reigning bishops and their families had very little to do with the alleged presence of *dévots* in the counsels of the government. On the contrary, it was this readiness, the roots of which require examination, which triggered an increasingly vigorous response from reformers and *dévots* alike during the late 1610s and early 1620s. This reaction did not carry everything before it, and it only gained ground slowly in the face of entrenched interests and traditional uses of church patronage. In this perspective, the arrival of Richelieu in office in 1624 was not in itself of particular significance, and the following years witnessed an unstable mixture of old and new uses of episcopal patronage. What disappeared after 1630 was a particular manifestation of *dévot* activity; what survived was much less visible or political in the narrow sense, but it was sufficiently strong to thrive under both Richelieu and the early years of Mazarin. Meanwhile, the episcopate of the 1610s and 1620s, taken as a whole, still had more in common with that of Henri IV than it did with that of the middle decades of the century. The pages that follow represent an attempt to understand the gradual emergence of a more self-confident episcopate while not ignoring the contradictions and ambiguities which also characterised it.

I

It is considerably easier for the historian to plot the course of episcopal patronage in the 1610s and 1620s than for the reign of Henri IV, when a simple lack of information about vacant dioceses makes even basic general statements about the episcopate subject to endless qualification. The gradual elimination of such irregularities such as rival nominations, *économats*, etc coupled with the survival, from the early 1610s onwards, of more satisfactory records of episcopal appointments, is the underlying reason for the difference – though the significance of the change should not be exaggerated. A brief survey of trends in nominations during the 1610s and 1620s will not be without its surprises.

In the two decades after Henri IV's death, a total of 112 new men entered the ranks of the episcopate, which translates into a somewhat higher year-on-year average than for the whole of the period studied in this book. This is mainly accounted for by a steady stream of retirements, but also by higher than usual rates of episcopal mortality, especially during the 1620s; in 1621 alone, twelve bishops died or retired, in 1625 eleven, in 1628 eight. In fact, the difference between the two decades is striking, with the overall number of careers ending through death or retirement being over twice as many in the 1620s as it had been in the 1610s. Thirty-six deaths or retirements affecting thirty-seven dioceses are recorded for the years 1610 to 1619, but seventy-one for the period 1620 to 1630 inclusive. Three of these in all (one from the 1610s, two from the 1620s) may be discounted for our purposes, since they involved the deaths of coadjutor bishops, which did not create vacancies that automatically required new appointments to be made.

Nothing could be more natural than to infer from these figures that few episcopal nominations were made in the 1610s and that a correspondingly large number occurred thereafter, but it is one of the most intriguing paradoxes of the period that this is not so. Allowing for the uncertain dating of several royal nominations, it emerges that forty-nine were made between mid-1610 and 1619, and sixty-two during the following eleven years. These figures do, of course, show that more nominations *were* made in the 1620s, but they only take on their true significance when seen in the light of the figures for deaths and retirements given above − forty-nine nominations against thirty-six deaths and retirements in the 1610s, but only sixty-two against sixty-nine in the 1620s. At first sight, it seems that during the 1610s, more bishops were created than there were places for, while there seems to have been a puzzling failure during the 1620s to keep the ranks of the episcopate filled. Neither impression actually fits the facts.

The underlying reason for this state of affairs was the inordinately large number of coadjutor-bishops nominated during the two decades. Of the 112 incoming bishops, no fewer than thirty-four were coadjutors. Such a proportion, accounting for 30 per cent of nominations, is without equal for any other period of the *ancien régime*; it also accounts for 55 per cent of all coadjutors nominated between 1589 and 1661! But these nominations were not evenly spread across the two decades: only eight were made during the 1620s, with all of the remaining twenty-six occurring between 1610 and 1618. The scale of the phenomenon becomes clearer still when it is realised that a comfortable majority (55 per cent) of *all* episcopal nominations made between 1610 and 1618 was of coadjutors.

Moreover, these figures represent only those coadjutorships which actually took effect. Close analysis of all the appointments of these years suggests that, were it not for premature death of reigning bishops, who include men like Cardinals du Perron and Sourdis, and the slowness of the beneficiaries of royal largesse to seek papal provisions, the total number of coadjutorial or analogous nominations would have been higher than the thirty-four recorded.

In his later years, as we saw, Henri IV had agreed to a number of coadjutorial successions, but what had been a mere trickle between 1607 and 1610 became a virtual flood thereafter. As early as 1608, Henri IV had tried to obtain the coadjutorship of Langres for Sébastien Zamet, but Cardinal Givry, who was already coadjutor there, managed to keep him at bay by promising to resign and then obtaining successive postponements. There was the additional problem in that Zamet was underage. It was decided after Henri's death, that an intermediate solution should be negotiated on his behalf – that the pope should grant him the right of 'access' to Langres, which would effectively reserve the bishopric for him.¹ At Sully's insistence, Henri IV, had already paved the way for just such a succession arrangement at Poitiers, in 1607, when Henri de Chasteignier de la Rocheposay, a man with excellent personal and family connections in Rome, was confirmed as future bishop of Poitiers without actually becoming coadjutor at all.² There were, therefore, recent precedents to point to when a similar demand was made in 1612 for the underaged Gilles de Souvré, son of the young king's governor, in respect of the diocese of Comminges.³ In early 1614, the crown simultaneously issued *brevets de réserve* in respect of Auch to Cardinal Gonzaga and an unnamed son of the duc de Nevers, a decision which can probably be explained in connection with the aristocratic revolt of 1614 in which Nevers was a major participant.⁴ Meanwhile Zamet and Souvré duly became bishops of Langres and Comminges in 1615 and 1617 respectively, but only after their predecessors had died. Nothing in the official record would lead one to suspect that theirs were always intended to be variations of coadjutorial successions, let alone that they had been in the making for several years. As far as can be determined, there were seven cases in which the original intention was to arrange a coadjutorial succession between 1610 and 1630, but in which intentions were overtaken by events, and the death of reigning bishops made coadjutorships redundant. All but two of these arose during the 1610s. In retrospect, the most interesting development, though a limited one, is the willingness to continue, or perhaps to revive, the practice of formally 'reserving' – with *brevets* to prove it - particular sees for high-born clerics, a practice outlawed by Trent and repeatedly decried in the age of Charles IX and Henri III. To those who observed royal episcopal patronage closely, such moves would have been an unmistakable sign of generosity in responding to particular family interests.

Never far removed from coadjutorial arrangements was the practice of bishops retiring outright by resigning their dioceses to named successors. For the most part, it is safe to assume that in these cases the initiative came from the bishops themselves rather than from the crown, but much depended upon their age and state of health. Elderly or infirm bishops could expect to be courted by ambitious younger clerics or, more usually perhaps, by their families, with a view to a coadjutorship or a resignation *in favorem* with

1 BN, MS Fr 3790, fo 23, king to Brèves, ambassador in Rome, 17 Mar 1610, recalling his original intention for Langres.
2 BN, MS lat 18384, p. 194–5, *brevet* of 30 Sept 1607; BN, MS Fr 3540, fo 23, Henri IV to Brèves, 13 Oct 1608. In fact, the proper forms were probably not observed. There was no formal act of resignation by Bishop Saint-Belin, which meant that Rome failed to grant the coadjutorship the king appears to have wanted for La Rocheposay.
3 BN, MS Fr 3792, fo 81, Louis XIII to Brèves, 30 Sept 1612.
4 *Inventaire des titres de la maison de Nevers de l'abbé de Marolles*, ed J Soultrait (Nevers 1873), cols 527, 609. Neither of these reserves ever took force, and in 1622, the son of a former keeper of the seals, Dominique de Vic, was nominated coadjutor to Auch.

immediate effect. But in view of what we have seen of the position of the many dependent bishops installed under Henri III and Henri IV, it would be unwise to assume that a large measure of free co-option was involved in all resignations. Fifteen instances of episcopal resignations occurred between 1610 and 1630, but this time the majority is clustered in the 1620s. Five of them were the consequence of bishops being transferred or promoted from one see to another rather than the results of retirement; the outgoing incumbent probably enjoyed some freedom to select a successor with whom he could negotiate satisfactory terms, since pensions for departing bishops were often involved in such transfers. A further six resignations involved cardinals retiring from episcopal duties, and it was accepted that they, at least, had an entirely free hand in choosing their successor. If the last Guise cardinal failed in his attempts to resign Reims in the late 1610s, it was because his deeply suspicious brother, the duc de Guise, strongly disputed his right to dispose freely of the see, and the cardinal was in any case usually out of political favour.[5] Cardinal Sourdis had made arrangements to take his brother as coadjutor at Bordeaux in late 1627, but died in February 1628 before this had been confirmed in Rome.[6] The best known of these resignations was Richelieu's transfer of Luçon in 1623 to Emery de Bragelongne, the son of a Parisian office-holding family related to Richelieu's clients, the Bouthillier. The interest of this particular resignation, however, lies primarily in the person of the resigning bishop, not in the diocese or the successor.

Of much greater interest, especially in the light of what we have seen in previous chapters, was the resignation ten years earlier by Cardinal Joyeuse of his two archdioceses of Toulouse and Rouen, each a major prize in its own right. These resignations, too, were years in the making, and may have first been mooted as early as 1609 or early 1610.[7] Joyeuse was an able administrator who was closely in tune with contemporary ideas about church reform, especially concerning the formation of the lower clergy, but in practice he spent much of his time at court or in Rome, where his office of Protector of France made him a major figure. It may well be that Henri IV was as happy to see him absent from Languedoc as Constable Montmorency. The problem for Joyeuse was less a matter of finding a successor than of timing. It was only in 1611 that he finally recognised that he was unlikely ever to become a resident bishop again, and that his hopes in moving to Rouen in 1604 of being able to spend more of his time in a diocese that was not far from court had, by his own admission, come to

---

5 See Joseph Bergin, 'The Decline and Fall of the House of Guise as an Ecclesiastical Dynasty', *Historical Journal*, 25 (1982), 793–5.
6 *Lettres de Peiresc*, ed Philippe Tamizey de Larroque, 8 vols (Paris 1888–98), vii. Peiresc to M d'Andraut, 26 Feb. 1628; ASV, PC 26, fo 406, Louis XIII to Urban VIII, 11 Feb 1628.
7 BN, MS 500 Colbert 353, p 366, Marie de' Medici to Brèves, 12 Nov 1612 claiming that Joyeuse had resigned Toulouse three years previously to La Valette.

nothing.⁸ Joyeuse's choices as successor in Toulouse and Rouen could scarcely have been more different, and they encapsulate the contrasting faces of his career. For Toulouse, which he decided to part with first, he picked Louis de la Valette, the eighteen-year-old son of Henri III's other favourite, Epernon. Still nominally a university student, La Valette would go on to become a cardinal and a leading military commander for Louis XIII without ever bothering to have himself consecrated archbishop of Toulouse, which he, too, would resign in 1627. For Rouen, Joyeuse chose François de Harlay, son of a great Parisian office-holding family who would be the first of a long line of bishops of that name, and a man whose origins, tastes, and learning made him the very antithesis of La Valette. To the very end, Joyeuse, who was the last episcopal pluralist in French history, represented the Renaissance prince-prelate but also the newer breed of churchman who was willing to regard high episcopal office as a pastoral duty as well as a perquisite to be distributed to those enjoying a distinguished pedigree and favour.

As for the remaining four of the fifteen resignations, too little is known about them to suggest any overall pattern. But it seems fair to guess that the resignation of André Frémiot of Bourges in 1621 was, if not forced upon him, then at least made with some reluctance: he was to remain highly active in church affairs for the next twenty years, having ceded Bourges to the confessor of the prince of Condé, governor of Berry and a man with little time for people who did not owe their station to him.⁹

By comparison with the plethora of coadjutorships, actual or intended, and the outright resignations, the number of dioceses which became available as a result of death and without pre-arranged successions, was small by comparison with either earlier or later decades. For the 1610s the total was a modest twenty-one, for the 1620s a somewhat more respectable thirty. These figures suggest something of the constraints and the opportunities with which both candidates for mitres and the crown itself were confronted.

Before turning to examine the reasons for these features of the post-Henrician episcopate, it is worth pausing to look at some related developments. Round figures of the kind that have just been presented invariably do not tell the whole story, and usually raise as many questions as they answer in the history of sixteenth- or seventeenth-century France; it is therefore worth looking at the statistically marginal cases if we wish to shed a more searching light on the subject.

Episcopal patronage was never confined in any generation to the making of new bishops, and opportunities for new men to enter the episcopate were often provided by the movements of incumbent bishops. Thus to the figure of 112 new bishops should be added a far smaller, but not insignificant, figure

8 BN, MS Fr 18006, fos 577–9, Joyeuse to Villeroy, 13 Nov 1611. See above, pp 403–4.
9 *Lettres de Peiresc*, vii. 572, Peiresc to Cardinal Bentivoglio, 14 Dec 1622: 'Il (=Condé) se plaict maintenant à Bourges plus que jamais depuis qu'il y a mis un nouvel archevesque à sa dévotion comme vous aurez sceu.'

for other exercises in episcopal patronage. Between 1610 and 1630, thirteen reigning bishops were transferred from their first diocese to another, with only one of those transfers being a simple swap of dioceses between two bishops. Only four out of the thirteen bishops involved had taken up office before Henri IV's death, while several of the others were relatively new to the episcopate when they made their move. As far as this generation of bishops was concerned, the longer one had been in office, the less likely one was to be moved or promoted; episcopal mobility had clearly slowed considerably since the previous century, even for the leading members of the episcopate. The most interesting exception here is that of Charles Miron, who had been bishop of Angers since 1588. A staunch royalist during the League, he emerged in the 1610s and 1620s as a vociferous defender of episcopal authority and an Ultramontane who was much appreciated in Rome – a most unusual trajectory, given the tendency of defenders of episcopal rights to be Gallicans and opponents of papal claims. Miron resigned Angers outright in 1616, but when his successor died in 1621, he exercised the option of recovering it – he was one of the very last French bishops to use the right of regress which had been common enough until the previous century, but which had been condemned by Trent.[10] Five years later, as we saw, it was Miron whom the pope, with royal agreement, designated archbishop of Lyon, an appointment which led the parlementaire cleric and scholar, Peiresc, to comment: 'there is considerable apprehension about him in Lyon, and it is a great reproach to those who should have known him (better) that they allowed him to recover Angers and, above all, installed him in Lyon'.[11] As an important archiepiscopal see, Lyon was clearly coveted, and to be transferred there was also to be promoted, as was demonstrated when Alphonse de Richelieu, already archbishop of Aix-en-Provence, quickly moved to Lyon on Miron's death in 1628. The days when archiepiscopal status was reserved for men who were already bishops were still some way off, but it is clear that no reigning bishop in these decades could hope to move up to archiepiscopal rank unless he was in some way – whether personally or through family connections – in high favour at court, as is clear from the promotions of Bertrand Deschaux (Bayonne to Tours 1617), Octave de Bellegarde (Comminges to Sens, 1622), Miron and Alphonse de Richelieu (Lyon), Henri de Sourdis (Maillezais to Bordeaux, 1628), and Victor Bouthillier (Boulogne to the coadjutorship of Tours, 1630).

10 The last, in the period under study here at least, was Henri de Sponde of Pamiers, who resumed his office for a few months in 1643 after the death of his nephew and successor, Jean. The practice was condemned at Trent because it diminished a new bishop's absolute tenure of his office by allowing his predecessor to retain a residual right in it.
11 *Lettres de Peiresc*, i. 94, letter to Pierre Dupuy, 22 Nov 1626: 'on l'appréhende grandement à Lyon, et c'est un grand reproche à ceux qui le pouvoient cognoistre de l'avoir laissé rentrer dans Angers et encores plus de l'avoir logé à Lyon'. A former secretary to Guillaume du Vair, Peiresc was a friend and correspondent of numerous bishops, and closely interested in ecclesiastical politics, especially in Provence. See above, p. 51.

The remaining five episcopal transfers, while not involving hierarchical mobility in the strict sense, can be regarded as promotions nonetheless, as all but one brought the beneficiaries from peripheral to more geographically 'central' dioceses, which also happened to be better endowed and generally more significant (e.g. Bayonne to Angers, Tréguier to Rennes, Riez to Lisieux). And it can fairly be assumed that Balthasar de Budos, nephew of Constable Montmorency, regarded his move from being just the coadjutor of Castres to bishop of the 'patrimonial' see of Agde in 1626, as promotion, though he did not enjoy the rewards for long. In the case of the one exchange of dioceses, that of Comminges and Auxerre in 1624–5, the beneficiary clearly was Gilles de Souvré, the reigning bishop of Comminges, although the official grounds for the exchange was François de Donadieu of Auxerre's alleged desire to move closer to his place of birth. Indeed, it was the mixture of chagrin and remorse he felt over being bamboozled by Souvré that almost immediately prompted Donadieu to resign Comminges to his nephew.[12]

Mention should also be made at this point of those who proved less fortunate than these happy few. Nicolas Coëffetau, the respected Dominican preacher who had served as suffragan bishop of Metz, was nominated to Marseille in 1621, but died within a short while of being confirmed by Rome and before taking possession of his see.[13] At Coutances, an identical fate befell the otherwise obscure Guillaume le Blanc, who died in his home-town of Agen, unconsecrated and without ever setting foot in Coutances.[14] In addition, some of the coadjutors appointed during the 1610s failed to succeed to their designated see, though most of them did play active, if subordinate, roles during their coadjutorship; some even attended assemblies of the clergy and played a part in the affairs of the French church generally. Perhaps the most luckless of them were François and Henri de Boivin, successive coadjutors to their uncle, François Péricard, at Avranches since 1611. Nothing is known about François Boivin, who was perhaps never consecrated; his place was taken in 1616 by Henri, who in turn died after twenty-two years service in February 1639, to be followed into the grave by his nonagenarian uncle a mere nine months later![15] Pierre de Donnaud similarly served his eponymous uncle at Mirepoix from 1610 until his death in 1621. In both cases, the loss was all the greater since each of the dioceses then slipped out of family control.

12   Abbé Lebeuf, *Mémoires concernant l'histoire civile et ecclésiastique d'Auxerre et de son ancien diocèse*, (Paris 1848–55), ii. 214–15. E Molinier, *La Vie de Messire Barthélemy de Donadieu de Griet evesque de Comenge* (Paris 1639), 160–1. Numerous notarial deeds concerning this complex exchange can be found in AN, MC, VI, 431, 10 Mar, 8, 15 and 28 Apr 1625; VI, 432, 28 Sept 1625.
13   *Gallia Chr Nov*, ii. 610–12.
14   René Toustain de Billy, *Histoire ecclésiastique du diocèse de Coutances*, ed A Heron, 3 vols (Rouen 1874–6), ii. 221–2.
15   François Boivin is known only from the record in Eubel, *Hierarchia Catholica*, iv. 328, 'Tarsen'. For this reason, he does not figure among the bishops included in the corpus of this book.

Others fared rather better in warding off such disaster, but not without difficulty. It was in 1621 that the Bonsi family came closest to losing Béziers which it held without interruption from 1576 to 1669. Cardinal Jean de Bonsi retired for all practical purposes to Rome in 1616, content to leave his see of Béziers in the hands of his young nephew and coadjutor, Dominique. The latter's death in April 1621 sent his uncle into a panic, as there was no obvious successor and the cardinal's own health was also declining fast. In fact, he died three months later, but by then he had done just enough to ensure that another nephew previously designated for a secular career, Thomas, would take his place;[16] even then, his plans were nearly wrecked when Thomas had to be prevented from running away to a monastery or joining the Jesuits rather than accept the unexpected responsibility now thrust upon him. In the event, Béziers remained safely in Bonsi hands for almost fifty more years.[17] Louis de Bologne became coadjutor to his brother at Digne in 1613, but he was paralysed by a stroke before his consecration. This made consecration impossible (paralysis was a canonical impediment), but he did at least survive to govern Digne for over a decade after his brother's death, solving the problem of how to administer the diocese *in spiritualibus* by obtaining a nephew, Raphaël de Bologne, friend and protector of Gassendi in later years, as his coadjutor between 1617 and 1628.[18]

Finally, we noted in the previous chapter that under Henri IV several individuals were offered bishoprics only to decline them, though it is impossible to say whether they did so from personal unwillingness or because of the difficult post-war conditions in the dioceses. Interestingly, far fewer such cases have been found for the years covered in this chapter, though more would appear again in mid-century. Less well known – and less easy to understand – are the few coadjutor bishops who, duly nominated and confirmed by Rome, never took the one step that was indispensable for a coadjutor seriously intent on an episcopal career – that of having themselves consecrated. Whether some, lined up too early in their careers for episcopal office, suffered from the same jitters as Thomas de Bonsi, is hard to determine. Dreux Hennequin, whose family boasted several bishops, was an unconsecrated coadjutor of Soissons from 1612 onwards, but when his uncle died in 1619, he quickly renounced his claim and carried on with his career as a councillor in the Paris parlement.[19] Pierre Dinet was nominated coadjutor of Mâcon in 1615, confirmed in 1616, but he, too, was unconsecrated when

---

16 BN, MS Clairambault 377, fo 713, Cardinal Bonsi to Phélypeaux de Pontchartrain, 30 May 1621. See above, pp 250–1.
17 There is a voluminous correspondence about the Béziers succession in BN, MS Fr 18015–16, all the more so as Cardinal Bonsi lived in Rome, and it was hoped that the pope would be able to dispose of some or all of his benefices.
18 Gassendi was a canon and dean of Digne cathedral.
19 BN, MS Fr 3791, fo 3, letter to Rome, 14 Jan 1611 about his nomination; BN, MS Fr 17364, p 155, Louis XIII to Paul V, n.d. (but 1619), asking him to confirm Charles de Hacqueville to Soissons in place of Hennequin.

he died in early 1618.[20] As we saw in an earlier chapter, Jacques Ribier abandoned his title to Grasse in 1636 to enable Godeau to hold it simultaneously with Vence. By contrast, others still, like Pierre Habert, the *maître des requêtes* nominated coadjutor of Cahors in 1622, only had themselves consecrated when their predecessor died, and this may also suggest some reservations about an episcopal career on their part.[21] The coadjutor of Grenoble, Alphonse de la Croix, went a step further: still only just past thirty years of age, he actually succeeded his father in May 1619, having been consecrated coadjutor in 1614, but within less than a year he had resigned his diocese, and lived in retirement until 1637.[22] All of these coadjutors, apart from Habert, were designated to follow close family members into the episcopate, but when the crucial moment came, they opted for another, perhaps quieter life. Such hesitations or rejections, coming after rather than before formal confirmation, distinguishes them from those who preferred to renounce an initial nomination, and raises intriguing questions of motivation and, for want of a better term, vocation. None of them, unfortunately, gave any explanation of their reasons. Where Thomas de Bonsi's reaction was precipitate but short-lived, the coadjutors of the 1610s and early 1620s often had plenty of time to consider their position, and the extremely relaxed circumstances of most of their nominations meant they were under little immediate pressure to commit themselves to a full episcopal career.

II

These developments within the episcopate were, it need hardly be said, connected to the wider ecclesiastical and political context which appeared after the assassination of Henri IV. The regent could hardly imagine, however many ministers and policies of her late husband she wished to retain, that the political landscape would remain unaltered. While leading members of the aristocracy tried to tunnel their way into positions of power by threats of revolt, court favourites, notably the Italian Concini and his wife, were effectively achieving the same ends more discreetly from the early days of the regency onwards. It is well known that Marie de' Medici, counselled by the experienced but fearful Villeroy, was prepared to make extensive concessions of cash, governorships and other perquisites to the aristocracy in order to keep the peace during her son's minority.[23] In advocating such a general loosening of the patronage strings, Villeroy did not make any mention of whether – or

---

20 ASV, PC 13, fos 821–43, enquiry *de vita et moribus*, 20 Mar 1615; *Gallia*, iv. col 1102.
21 For Habert, *DHGE*, xxii, col 1392. See above, p 247.
22 ASV, PC 13, fos 285–308, enquiry *de vita et moribus*, 8 June 1612.
23 See Salvo Mastellone, *La Reggenza di Maria de' Medici* (Florence 1962), esp ch 3; Richard Bonney, *The King's Debts. Politics and Finance in France 1589–1661* (Oxford 1981), 73–6.

how far – church patronage should be included, but neither he nor his contemporaries can have expected it to be unavailable for such purposes.[24] However, in the absence of any general statement, even of a retrospective kind, of the regency's intentions with regard to episcopal patronage, we have to discern the latter by a close analysis of its record as well as of the criticisms of it made by other interested parties.

If we look at the first two years of the regency (May 1610–May 1612), we find that royal episcopal nominations, which numbered fourteen in all, show early signs – which may admittedly be more telling in retrospect – of what was to come. The first four nominations were of men *intended* as coadjutors.[25] At the same time, Agde, Poitiers, and Toulouse went to candidates already singled out in the later years of Henri IV, while Saint-Pol-de-Léon in Brittany was effectively reserved for René de Rieux, son of the most powerful nobleman in the area and a *fidèle* of Marie de' Medici. Only Séez, Embrun, Périgueux and Lyon went to ecclesiastics with no known family claim to them. In the case of Séez, where the candidate was the elderly Portuguese Franciscan, Suarez, a coadjutor was nominated to succeed him only months after Rome had confirmed Suarez.[26] As for Lyon, the Bellièvre family was so weakened after the death of its second archbishop in April 1612, that it could no longer furnish a serious candidate to a diocese which was no stranger to episcopal dynasties. Quite what happened is unclear, but the crown's first choice was, it seems, Guillaume Fouquet de la Varenne (later bishop of Angers 1617–21), son of one of Henri IV's personal favourites, but he refused the honour for reasons that remain unknown.[27] Years later, Cardinal Jean de Bonsi reminded the secretary of state, Puysieux, that he, too, had obtained a promise of Lyon at this juncture, but that he had waived it in order to oblige the court.[28] The eventual successor to Bellièvre was Denis Simon, a Parisian serving as a highly placed curial official in Rome and better known by the family's *nom de terre* of Marquemont. The hand of Villeroy is unmistakable in this important placement, all the more so as his own son, who as French ambassador in Rome (1606–9) had worked closely with Marquemont, had

---

24 See Mastellone, *Reggenza*, 229–34, for the text of the 'Advis de Monsieur de Villeroy donné à la Reyne en 1611', but which makes no mention of ecclesiastical patronage.
25 They include Dreux Hennequin, nominated coadjutor of Soissons in Jan 1611, but who failed to have himself consecrated and later resigned his title to Soissons.
26 Saurez received his provisions in Jan 1612, and Jacques Camus was nominated coadjutor in June 1612 on the grounds that Suarez was by now 'valétudinaire et quasy du tout interdit de pouvoir doresnavant s'acquitter de sa charge'. No explanation was given for his sudden incapacity to fulfil his duties. ASV, PC 13, fo 5, letter of nomination for Camus as coadjutor, 6 June 1612.
27 BN, MS Fr 18007, fo 198v, Brèves to Villeroy, 25 May 1612; *ibid*, fo 259, same to same, 20 July 1612: 'au reffus de Mons de Chésy . . .'. It was reported that he would have needed a dispensation, as he was under the canonical age, but that was hardly a major obstacle, especially as he was about twenty-five years old in 1612.
28 BN, MS Fr 18013, fo 91, Bonsi to Puysieux, 16 Mar 1619.

only been installed a few months previously as governor of the Lyonnais.[29] Marquemont was a long-standing correspondent and client of Villeroy, who valued him highly.[30] This evidence of ministerial patronage is also borne out by the nomination of Guillaume d'Hugues to the archbishopric of Embrun a few months before Marquemont: for two years, the French ambassador in Rome had been bombarding Villeroy and Puysieux with glowing accounts of his ability and the usefulness to France's interests of his extensive connections as Minister-General of the Franciscans.[31] Both the Lyon and Embrun appointments were ministerial initiatives, facilitated by the absence (in Lyon) and the disregarding (in Embrun) of strong claims by members of the families of the previous incumbents.

It was, however, from mid-1612 onwards that the flood of coadjutorships discussed above really began, and for the next five years two-thirds of all episcopal nominations were of this variety. These nominations were not all identical. The first category, which accounts for nearly two-thirds of the coadjutors named during the remainder of the 1610s, involved an unparalleled exercise in crown-approved episcopal nepotism. The speed with which reigning bishops, their families, and patrons reacted to the changed circumstances is not in doubt, even though a familiar lack of information about patronage connections also causes difficulties when it comes to interpreting success and failure. At any rate, most of the beneficiaries were sons of noble families, old and new. But the crown seems to have been particularly forthcoming towards bishops who sought to secure their sees for their nephews, doubtless on the grounds that satisfying their ambitions would give them a strong incentive to continue serving its interests in the provinces. Of course, such royal goodwill could offend other noble families equally keen to gain possession of particular dioceses. The example of Pierre de Fleyres, bishop of Saint-Pons in Languedoc, is particularly enlightening in this regard. Before his elevation in 1587, Saint-Pons had been held by a member of the Castelnau de Clermont family, and Henri III seems to have allowed Clermont to present Fleyres formally to him as his personal choice as successor. Nearly thirty years

---

29   Robert R Harding, *Anatomy of a Power Elite. The Provincial Governors of Early Modern France* (New Haven and London 1978), 225. At the same time, Villeroy's young grandson, Camille de Neufville, was already being provided with church benefices in Lyon at this juncture, especially the abbey of Aisnay and a canon's stall in the noble chapter of Saint-Jean (MS Fr 18007, fo 349v, Brèves to Puysieux, 13 Oct 1610; J Beyssac, *Les Chanoines de Lyon* (Lyon 1914), 195. The ambition to succeed where the Bellièvres, despite their Lyon family roots and connections, had failed is clear, and it would be fulfilled. Camille de Neufville was both governor and archbishop of Lyon for forty years under Louis XIV.

30   Cécile Pozzo di Borgo, 'Denis Simon de Marquemont, archévêque de Lyon et cardinal (1572–1626): La Carrière d'un prélat diplomate au Saint-Siège au début du xviie siècle', *Archivum Historiae Pontificiae*, 15 (1977), 265–94, for an account of his career.

31   BN, MS Fr 18005, fo 131, 140, Brèves to Henri IV and Villeroy respectively, 2 Apr 1610; MS Fr 18006, fo 285, same to Villeroy, 9 July 1611; *ibid*, fo 499, same to Puysieux, 28 Sept 1611; MS Fr 18007, fo 88, same to regent, 1 Mar 1612; *ibid*, fo 94, Hugues to regent, 2 Mar 1612, thanking her for the gift of Embrun.

later, in 1616, the Clermont family, like several others who did not have young promotable ecclesiastics among their ranks a generation earlier, wished to recover the diocese by means of a coadjutorship. But Bishop Fleyres was now evidently unwilling to oblige his former patrons, and an enraged Monsieur de Clermont, who could still not bring himself to refer to Fleyres as anything other than a 'vilain' and 'that son of a judge in one of my estates', wrote indignantly in protest to Louis XIII to remind him of his predecessor's concession and to demand the *survivance* of Saint-Pons for his son.[32] His plea, however, was ignored, perhaps because it was unsupported, and a few years later Fleyres himself obtained his nephew as his coadjutor. By the 1610s the Fleyres were no longer the 'vilains' of Clermont's imagination, not least because in the intervening generation they had succeeded in establishing themselves as a well connected office-holding family with bases in Rodez, Toulouse and Montpellier. Jean Martin, the *confidentiaire* bishop of Périgueux, does not appear to have tried to imitate Fleyres before his death in 1612, possibly because his reign was shorter and he had been too heavily dependent on his Bourdeille patrons, but neither did the Bourdeille family recover it either before or after his death; the new bishop apparently persuaded Louis XIII some years later to revoke his predecessors' concessions to them.[33]

Bishops who, like Martin, were not from established noble or office-holding backgrounds, or who did not personally enjoy some unusual connection at court, fared much less well in extending family tenure of their sees. A second, albeit smaller, category of coadjutor appearing in these years is that of sons of older noble families who, like Clermont, were anxious to stake their claim to dioceses currently held by some of the commoner bishops installed under Henri III or Henri IV. The La Baume de Suze family reclaimed Viviers in this fashion, having held it in the previous generation, while Montmorency's daughter obtained the coadjutorship of Uzès for her son in 1612, after it was pointed out to the king that it had been 'reserved' to that end by Henri IV as long ago as 1591.[34] It may also be assumed that Balthasar de Budos, the Constable's nephew, was originally appointed coadjutor of Castres in 1614 in order to restore Montmorency family control of a diocese held since 1583 by a Joyeuse client.

Finally, it should be noted that the crown was not wholly reduced to rewarding noble families or existing bishops. Five of the incoming coadjutors

32 BN, MS Clairambault 368, fo 424, letter to king, n.d. (1616): 'un fils d'un juge d'une de mes terres'.
33 See above, p 80.
34 BN, MS Fr 3792, fo 59, Louis XIII to Brèves, 20 July 1612: 'sachant que le feu Roy dez l'année 1591 (que l'évesché d'Uzès avoit vacqué par la mort de feu Mre Robert de Girard) auroit désiré que l'ung des enfans du sr Perault sénéschal et gouverneur de Beaucaire et Nismes en feust pourveu s'il en eust alors quelqu'un de capable, J'ay daultant plus agréable, maintenant que je suis informé du soing qu'a eu ledit sr de Perault depuis ce temps de faire instruire ès saintes lettres et nourrir en la piété et dévotion Mre Paul Antoine de Fay son filz.'

nominated during the 1610s were sons of financiers or well-placed office-holders.

The remaining non-coadjutorial nominations made between 1612 and the late 1610s are no less interesting, and serve to reinforce the arguments just presented. When dioceses fell vacant through death, it was the aristocracy who proved best placed by far to take advantage of the opportunities, a fact which was to remain largely unchanged throughout the following decade. From what we saw about the diocese of Conserans in the previous chapter, it would be a surprise to see anyone but a Bellegarde, or a client of theirs, succeed as bishop when Jérôme de Lingua died in 1612, while the see of Autun was 'reserved' for the son of the marquis de Ragny who was not only governor of the Nivernais, but whose eldest son was married to a Gondi. Joachim d'Estaing succeeded Antoine Rose at Clermont because, in addition to powerful family connections in the region, he was the nephew of Cardinal La Rochefoucauld, a former bishop of Clermont who was also close to Marie de' Medici to whom the right to present bishops of Clermont belonged as part of her jointure. Clearly, success was all the more likely if one enjoyed good *entrées* at court. This last factor accounts for the persistence of ministerial and high robe patronage generally, however advantaged the aristocracy and old nobility might be. It enabled Guillaume du Vair, keeper of the seals, to obtain the see of Lisieux for himself in August 1617, just as it had previously enabled his nephew Guillaume Aleaume to become bishop of Riez in 1614 and Louis Duchaine coadjutor of Senez in 1617; both dioceses were situated in Provence, where du Vair had long served as first president of the parlement at Aix[35]. Likewise, the Potier family's secretaryship of state and personal service of Marie de' Medici helped ensure their continued tenure of Beauvais after René Potier's unexpected death in October 1616.

It is, however, far less easy to determine who played the main part in the distribution of episcopal office during these years. The political instability of the period makes it intrinsically hard to think in terms of a crown picking and choosing with sovereign control from the scrum of contenders for the mitre. Yet it is only natural that there should be some suspicion that the Concinis were discreetly pulling the patronage strings offstage, given the attention they paid to such questions. But with positive evidence in such short supply, the temptation to fantasise about the extent of their influence should be resisted. As we saw, the episcopal promotions between 1610 and 1612 were sufficiently varied to leave ample freedom to figures as diverse as Cardinal Joyeuse and Villeroy to play the leading roles. Thereafter, the flood of coadjutorships was such as to render implausible any suggestion that one particular individual was in control. It may, therefore, be suggested – as it was at the trial of Léonora, Concini's wife, in 1617 – that they extracted kickbacks

---

35 Duchaine was son of the second president of the parlement who had been a staunch royalist like du Vair during the religious wars.

from those seeking preferment at court, ministers not excluded, rather than promoted to the episcopate men of their own choosing.³⁶ The Florentine ambassador reported in late 1616 that it had cost the Potier a large bribe of 22,000 *livres* to Léonora in order to ensure that Beauvais remained in family hands.³⁷ By the time the Concinis raised their own sights high enough to obtain the archbishopric of Tours for Léonora's brother, Sébastien, the tide was about to turn savagely against them. Sébastien duly obtained his papal provisions in December 1616, but before he could have himself consecrated or installed in Tours, the Concinis were executed and Sébastien himself, though unharmed, immediately realised that Tours would never be his and resigned his title outright. The new régime of the young Louis XIII and his mentor-favourite Luynes was not committed to serious changes in the way in which bishoprics were filled, and young coadjutors in particular continued to be nominated in succeeding years. However, by 1617–19, other voices were beginning to be raised, demanding improvements in the calibre of the episcopate, voices which were the culmination of several years of protest and debate.

III

It was in Rome that the first rumblings of dissent and criticism were heard. Moreover, they are sufficiently different in origin and scope from the familiar discontents of the curia with the exercise of episcopal patronage in France as to repay close analysis. Mention was made in the previous chapter of a papal plea of May 1610 to Marie de' Medici urging her to nominate worthy candidates to the episcopate. In fact, the nuncio had been instructed to impress the importance of just this on the regent only weeks after Henri IV's death.³⁸ The timing of the more formal reminder of 1611 is not easy to explain, but it may well have been sparked initially by the impact of allegations made directly to Paul V by a French cleric, Olivier du Bois, about the general laxity of procedures in France for establishing the credentials of newly nominated bishops, as well as the untrustworthiness of the evidence about them enclosed in the enquiries *de vita et moribus*. He was also critical of the papacy for being insufficiently tough with French candidates and for granting provisions too readily.³⁹ The pope's response was to commission an enquiry from Joyeuse.⁴⁰ The findings of this enquiry have never come to light, but it led to the brief of August 1611 and an accompanying instruction to Ubaldini, the nuncio, to discuss with the regent the pope's concern at the unsatisfactory state of the French church and the need for greater respect for episcopal

---

36 Fernand Hayem, *Le Maréchal d'Ancre et Léonora Galigaï* (Paris 1910), 217ff.
37 I owe this information to Jean-François Dubost to whom I extend my thanks.
38 ASV, Fondo Borghese I, 907, fos 175–8, Borghese to Ubaldini, 30 May 1610.
39 ASV, Lettere de Vescovi 19, fo 69, du Bois to Paul V, 9 Oct 1610.
40 BL, Add MS 8721, fos 419–21, Borghese to Ubaldini, 5 July 1611.

office.⁴¹ It was Villeroy who fielded Ubaldini's questions and, like his late master Henri IV, he argued that unfavourable circumstances were at the root of the problem.⁴² It should be noted, in addition, that the early 1610s were years of bitter debate in France over the question of regicide, papal powers, and royal sovereignty, a debate into which the papacy was drawn, sometimes by the incaution of its defenders. Ubaldini did not flinch from controversy, but if there is scant evidence that he advised the regent on matters of policy, he had already, it seems, been playing a more active role than his predecessors in personally conducting the enquiries *de vita et moribus* for newly nominated bishops.⁴³ He also remonstrated with the regent when particularly unacceptable nominations to bishoprics, like that of the young sons of the duc de Ventadour and the comte d'Auvergne in 1612, were being mooted.⁴⁴ In this way, the curia was probably better informed than hitherto about the crown's choices, and therefore in a position to challenge individual promotions as well as criticise the general manner in which bishops were selected in France.

In the short term, there was not much by way of a positive response from within the French church itself to Paul V's plea of 1611. But the papacy was not inhibited by this lack of co-operation, and it was in August 1613 that the French ambassador first began reporting its objections to the coadjutorships that were becoming increasingly numerous.⁴⁵ There was, after all, nothing new about Rome's unhappiness with the condition of the French episcopate, so it was arguably another, far more prosaic feature of French episcopal politics that exasperated the curia more persistently and tangibly for much of the 1610s: the fact that letters of nomination of new bishops (coadjutors included) seemed to be followed almost without exception with pressing requests for the total or partial reduction in the sums payable for the much disliked annates. Where Clement VIII had been willing to make frequent financial concessions to French bishops in order to ensure vacant sees were filled quickly, his successor Paul V was beginning by 1607–8 to complain about French demands, countering them with claims about the poverty of the papacy itself.⁴⁶ In the 1610s, the bitterness would be even greater, with

---

41 L von Pastor, *History of the Popes*, 40 vols (London 1894–1953), xxvi. 464–6, for the text of the brief.
42 *Ibid*, 55.
43 It may be an accident that the texts of these enquiries for French prelates only survive in the Vatican archives from about 1611 onwards. But this seems unlikely, not least because the first volume in which they appear (PC 13) contains exclusively French material covering the years 1611 to 1615, which makes it unique among the volumes I have seen for the years up to 1661. This in itself suggests some practical response in the curia to perceived problems in France.
44 ASV, Fondo Borghese I, 907, fo 595, Borghese to Ubaldini, 6 June 1612.
45 BN, MS Fr 18008, fo 445v, Brèves to Villeroy, 13 Aug 1613.
46 BN, MS Fr 18003, fo 392v-4, Brèves to Puysieux 24 Dec 1608, for an early instance of papal reluctance, even though the case involved the duc de Nevers and the comte d'Auvergne; MS Fr 18008, fo 388v-9, Brèves to Marie de' Medici, 8 July 1613, summing up developments since he had become ambassador in 1609, and suggesting some agreement with the curia over a revision.

complaints that the French were ungrateful when concessions were made, and seemed to regard them as something they had a right to expect.[47] Indeed, for a time after 1610 it seems that the crown and its agents in Rome believed that the long-sought-for reduction in the assessed value of French benefices for the payment of annates could be achieved, thus satisfying an oft-voiced grievance against the curia.[48] But on this point the papacy, fearing similar demands from elsewhere, absolutely refused to budge; almost anything seemed preferable to such a major change, and even the granting of individual reductions could always be represented as acts of grace or favour to the beneficiaries.[49] The rejection of continuing French demands for a general revision of the ratebooks meant that the stream of requests for favourable treatment continued to grow.[50]

One possibly surprising outcome was that Rome's existing doubts about the manner in which episcopal nominations were handled in France were reinforced in the process. Given the reluctance of cardinals and curial officials to make financial concessions which affected them directly, it did not take long for complaints also to arise in Rome about abuses in the use of royal letters of recommendation or support for demands for the reduction in the annates payable by incoming bishops.[51] It was objected as late as 1617 that royal letters of recommendation inspired by secretaries of state were too numerous to be regarded as genuine expressions of royal favour, and therefore only aroused suspicion; if it was to mean anything, royal favour needed to avoid being indiscriminate and should be self-evidently 'de propre mouvement'.[52] The suspicion was that the secretaries of state were abusing their position and collecting 'gratifications' from those seeking such recommendations, just as the ambassador and the bankers and their agents in Rome were suspected of either selling their influence or pocketing the difference between what was paid by those seeking provisions and what should have been payable.[53]

Contrary to what might be expected, curial self-interest was, therefore, one

47 ASV, Fondo Borghese I, 907, fo 437v, Borghese to Ubaldini, 8 Nov 1611, refuting French arguments as inflated and untenable. The annates payable in respect of coadjutorships were also lower than in the case of a normal vacancy caused by death.
48 BN, MS Fr 18006, fo 631, undated letter on presentation of memoir concerning reduction of annates (1611). MS Fr 18010, fo 387, Tresnel to Puysieux, 2 Feb 1616.
49 ASV, Fondo Borghese I, 907, fo 437, Borghese to Ubaldini, 8 Nov 1611, claiming that even Cardinal Joyeuse agreed that there was no real foundation to the French arguments.
50 French demands were not dropped overnight, and in 1619 the new ambassador was instructed to press them again: BN, MS Fr 17364, p 93, instructions to Annibal d'Estrées, marquis de Coeuvres.
51 As early as 1608, the French ambassador reported that these requests were 'une viande que Sa Saincteté gouste mal volontiers': BN, MS Fr 18803, fo 348v, Brèves to Puysieux, 30 Nov 1608.
52 BN, MS Fr 18003, fo 393-4, Brèves to Puysieux 24 Dec 1608, for Paul V's own claim that royal instructions were 'solicited' and thus not genuine; MS Fr 18011, fo 291, Marquemont, archbishop of Lyon, to Louis XIII, 3 Nov 1617.
53 BN, MS Fr 18009, fo 227v, Tresnel, ambassador, to Puysieux, 10 July 1614, for accusations against bankers; fos 318, 341, same to same, 9 Nov and 8 Dec 1614 respectively, for Tresnel's attempts to regulate their behaviour.

root of the demand for improvements in the episcopate, and it helped to focus attention on what was seen as the misuse of royal patronage. In such circumstances, it is easier to understand Roman irritation with the nomination of coadjutors, some of whom were so underaged as to make a mockery of the term coadjutor, or with demands that future bishops like Zamet or Souvré be granted special rights of 'access' to dioceses because of their age – and, of course, to have them all cost free.[54] Moreover, the papacy did not confine itself to verbal remonstrances. A brief look at the record shows that there were often considerable time-lags, sometimes lasting several years, between the initial nomination of these bishops and the grant of papal provisions. This was caused in some cases by a lack of haste on the part of the nominees themselves, but there is also clear evidence that Paul V deliberately refused to be rushed into granting provisions, especially to coadjutors. He openly responded to requests from the French ambassadors for provisions by saying there would be time to consider them case-by-case later, especially where nominees were too young. Zamet and Souvré each waited several years before receiving formal confirmation, despite strong pressure from powerful patrons or, as in Souvré's case, spending considerable time in Rome himself.[55] Cardinal Bonsi was informed in August 1613 that the Béziers coadjutorship would not be dealt with until the cardinal himself came to Rome to put the case for his underaged nephew; the nuncio could in the meantime conduct the enquiry *de vita et moribus*, but for the rest there was no rush, given Dominique Bonsi's age.[56] Originally nominated, it seems, as early as 1612, he was not confirmed as coadjutor of Béziers until August 1615.[57] In most of these cases, however, it seems as if the pope was merely intent on delaying rather than refusing outright the confirmation of candidates. But firm rejections were not ruled out, even if in practice they were probably rare. When Ambassador Tresnel presented a coadjutor for Noyon in 1616, the pope was ready for him: the coadjutor nominated was disreputable in both his private behaviour and his views, even though his brother was a president in the Paris parlement whom it might be dangerous to alienate.[58] Paul V ignored this last consideration, and said he knew that Noyon had no need of a coadjutor, as its bishop was still young enough to perform his duties there; the ambassador was firmly invited not to raise the idea again, and nothing more was heard of it.[59]

54 ASV, Fondo Borghese I, 896, fo 182, Borghese to Ubaldini, 31 Aug 1613, for objections to coadjutorships.
55 BN, MS Fr 18010, fo 437, Tresnel to Puysieux, 8 May 1616, reporting that Souvré had sent to France to seek his father's permission to stay on a few more months in Rome. His provisions were dated Feb 1617.
56 ASV, Fondo Borghese I, 896, fos 182, 186, 200, Borghese to Ubaldini, 31 Aug, 1 Sept, and 10 Oct 1613 respectively.
57 ASV, PC 13, fos 411–48. The enquiry was not completed until 18 Jan 1614, but Bonsi's profession of faith was dated 1 Aug 1612!
58 BN, MS Italien 1269, fos 249–52, Ubaldini to Borghese, 27 Sept 1615.
59 AAE, CP Rome 23, fo 404, Tresnel to Marie de' Medici, 31 Dec 1616.

It will be apparent from this discussion that the deliberations of the Estates General and Assembly of Clergy of 1614–15 did little to persuade the papacy that things were about to improve in France. Indeed it was in 1617, with the demand for coadjutorships showing no signs of abating, that Paul V openly declared to Archbishop Marquemont that 'the very frequency of these coadjutorships is making benefices hereditary, thereby depriving virtue of hope of reward, and it also means that the coadjutors themselves do not feel indebted to Your Majesty in the way they should'.[60] Such language must have strongly reminded the king's ministers of the arguments made in France against the sale and especially the hereditary tenure of office with the introduction of the *droit annuel* in 1604.

IV

In the short term, the papacy's criticisms evinced little response in France, as a beleaguered regency and post-regency government sought by all available means to win or maintain support. More to the point, France's bishops seemed more anxious to join the scramble to take advantage of the crown's liberality than to criticise it or the forms it took. Yet when they came together in the regular assemblies of clergy, they could not avoid addressing general issues. By the end of Henri IV's reign, attitudes had begun to shift slightly away from the earlier insistence on the restoration of episcopal elections, though such a restoration was still invariably included in their remonstrances to the crown. In 1605, Jérôme de Villars of Vienne had, as we saw, called for their restoration, but he also added that if this was not forthcoming, then at least good nominations should be made. Three years later, we find André Frémiot of Bourges thanking Henri IV for his wise use of his right to nominate bishops, and conceding that the loss of the right to elect bishops had not been so disastrous after all. At the end of the 1610 Assembly, the new regent was addressed by the bishop of Avranches; he, too, asked for elections to be restored, but then urged her to ensure that when dioceses became vacant they be filled after taking the advice of well intentioned people, though what precisely he meant by that he did not say. The debates of the Estates General of 1614–15 and the regular Assembly of Clergy which followed it were of greater importance, both because of the extremely large number of ecclesiastical deputies participating in them, and the seriousness of the main issues facing them (the reception of the decrees of Trent, reform in both church and state, the issue of royal sovereignty and papal powers, etc). The shift in official attitudes occurring during the Estates is highly significant, however

60 BN, MS Fr 18011, fo 291, Marquemont to king, 3 Nov 1617: 'ces Coadjutoreries si fréquentes rendent les bénéfices héréditaires, ostant l'espérance à la vertu, et font que les Coadjuteurs ne ressentent pas tant l'obligation qu'ilz doibvent avoir à Vostre Majesté.'

inevitable it may seem in retrospect. After some preliminary debate, the clergy decided that they would simply demand the restoration of episcopal elections. Yet, by the time the finishing touches had been put to their *cahier de doléances*, it was the minority view evident in that earlier debate which had come to prevail: for the first time, there was no mention at all of elections, and their concern was how best to ensure that the royal privilege of nominating bishops was exercised as it ought to be. So long as the assembled clergy had been content to repeat their demand for elections as the cure for all evils – rather like the abolition of the sale of offices in relation to reforming the administration of justice and finance – little was, or indeed could be, done to concentrate attention on how to ensure better candidates were promoted. In 1614–15, the clergy proposed that a commission of six ecclesiastical and two lay members of the royal council be delegated to examine the credentials of those whom the king wished to nominate to the episcopate and to invalidate nominations made before such scrutiny was conducted. The commission could instigate enquiries about candidates at diocesan level and collate information about candidates collected there.[61]

Such a proposal, which contained in embryonic form the idea of a *conseil de conscience*, was both too new and too ambitious to be acceptable to the ministers of Marie de' Medici who undertook to examine the demands made by the individual Estates. It was always likely to incur the suspicion of being an attempt to appropriate part of the king's prerogative, and to deny him a free hand in dispensing his fund of patronage. Yet, unlike other proposals raised in 1614 which the royal council hoped to bury quietly by procrastination or inaction, it did not vanish into oblivion. Neither the post-Estates régime that was increasingly dominated by Concini nor, after his elimination in April 1617, that of Luynes, was sufficiently free of trouble to undertake reforms in church or state. But, as already noted, the political upheavals of these years did gradually begin to offer greater opportunities to leading figures among the clergy to press for improvements in the provision of bishops. Because of the highly impersonal language in which the debates of the ecclesiastical assembly were recorded, it is extremely difficult to identify by name the deputies who took the lead in pressing for the reform of episcopal nominations in 1614. But in the subsequent years, leading churchmen such as Henri de Gondi, first Cardinal de Retz and nominal president of the council from 1618 until 1622, and Cardinal La Rochefoucauld, who succeeded both du Perron as Grand Almoner of France in September 1618 and Retz as council president in 1622, were clearly associated with demands for improvement. So, too, were less elevated churchmen, such as Bishop Miron of Angers and Lestang of Carcassonne. They could count on support from Rome and its new

---

61 See Pierre Blet, 'Le Concordat de Bologne et la réforme tridentine', *Gregorianum* 45 (1964), 262–4, for a characteristically clear summary of changing clerical objectives.

nuncio, the celebrated Guido di Bentivoglio, as well as from Louis XIII's new Jesuit confessor, the enterprising Jean Arnoux.[62] Something of the growing ecclesiastical influence is evident in the fact that no fewer than six senior churchmen, Retz and La Rochefoucauld among them, were included among the new *chevaliers* of the élite royal order of the *Saint Esprit* in late 1619.[63]

Equally significant for the experiences of subsequent decades is the fact that just as senior ecclesiastics were finding political roles to play, Louis XIII's own real political apprenticeship was beginning. His promise to the nuncio, made shortly after Concini's murder, to choose more suitable bishops may have a distinctly formulaic ring to it, but in the following years he would respond positively to both complaints and recommendations put to him personally by the nuncio, his confessor, and churchmen like La Rochefoucauld.[64] On one such occasion, he frankly revealed the dilemma of every king who was a dispenser of patronage by pleading that if only the pope took a strong line in refusing dispensations and concessions to those seeking benefices, it would be considerably easier for him to keep to his promises to improve nominations.[65] The reply from Rome was a perfect complement to the king's plea: if the pope made such concessions, it was because he was usually pushed into making them, on account of the force of pressure on him from France, and to which the king was himself often a party.[66] At any rate, Louis XIII's conscientious attitude towards church affairs thereafter has its roots in these and other exchanges during the early years of his personal rule, and should not be regarded merely as a product of the years of supposed *dévot* political dominance during the 1620s.

The first signs of this change of attitude are evident in the discussions at the Assembly of Notables held in Rouen in late 1617, and in particular in the resolve to pursue ideas left unanswered since being first aired at the Estates three years previously, notably that of a *conseil de conscience*. Specific complaints were made at Rouen against the abuse of coadjutorial nominations which were being forced upon bishops who had no need of them; for a while, it was even thought that the crown was willing to respond to them by revoking all coadjutorships. Having criticised them longer than anyone else, Rome now found that particular cure excessive, as it seemed to revoke coadjutorships that

---

62 See Joseph Bergin, *Cardinal de La Rochefoucauld. Leadership and Reform in the French Church* (New Haven and London 1987), 128–9.
63 Père Anselme de Sainte-Marie, *Histoire généalogique et chronologique de la maison royale de France et des grands officiers de la Couronne*, 9 vols (Paris 1726–30), ix. 132–55.
64 *La Nunziatura de Francia de Giudi di Bentivoglio*, ed Luigi di Steffani, 4 vols (Florence 1863–70), i. 507–8, Bentivoglio to Borghese, 22 Sept 1617, for the nuncio's first discussions with the king and Arnoux; *ibid*, ii. 538–9, same to same, 15 Aug 1618, reporting on further discussions, especially about coadjutorships.
65 *Ibid*, iii. 501, Bentivoglio to Borghese, 11 Sept 1619.
66 Archivio di Stato, Ferrara, Fondo Bentivoglio 18–13, no 236, Borghese's reply, 7 Oct 1619.

had already been settled.⁶⁷ An extensive reform edict was drafted after the assembly had finished and was published in mid-1618. It was somewhat limited in scope, but it did propose that provincial assemblies should draw up for submission to the king a list of suitable episcopal candidates, and promised to put an end to coadjutorships and 'reservations' of dioceses.⁶⁸ In separate attempts to regulate the activities of the secretaries of state in mid-1617, similar injunctions were issued against the 'reservation' of bishoprics and the practice of giving them 'in favour of' anyone other than the episcopal nominee himself.⁶⁹

Few of these ideas had much effect in the short term. Provincial councils were so rare as to be non-existent by the early seventeenth century, and neither the council nor the parlements was anxious to see any change in this. The reform edict of 1618 was never registered by the parlement, let alone enforced, while Rome felt compelled to send the nuncio a specially compiled list of recent coadjutorships and other graces bestowed on French clerics in order to underline the urgency of action rather than words.⁷⁰ Yet for all that, the discussions of 1617–18 did herald a different climate with regard to church patronage. Even though there were fresh cases of episcopal nepotism, the number of coadjutors being nominated began to drop sharply by 1618, and would never again reach the levels of the preceding years. Indeed, rumours even reached Rome in mid-1618 that the crown had already published, or was about to publish an edict banning coadjutorships outright. This had the curious effect that the French coadjutorial nominees who happened to be there at the time took fright and promptly stopped haggling over annates; as Archbishop Marquemont reported from Rome, some of them would have paid over twice what they had to rather than wait to discover that their nominations had been revoked *en bloc* by the crown.⁷¹

A particularly revealing sequel to these developments is provided by the deliberations chaired by La Rochefoucauld and involving Retz, Arnoux, and Bishop Lestang of Carcassonne in September 1619, at a time when the reform of the religious orders was also being discussed. After a review of episcopal problems, they concluded that Pierre Valernod of Nîmes was now too old to perform his functions effectively, and recommended that he be given three

---

67 Steffani, *Nunziatura di Bentivoglio*, ii. 214–15, 303, Borghese to Bentivoglio, 16 Jan and 18 Mar 1618 respectively. Rome's fear was that the revocation would be indiscriminate, and might include coadjutors who were already confirmed and consecrated, something it could not accept: see *ibid*, ii. 339, Bentivoglio to Borghese 25 Apr 1618.
68 *Ibid*, ii. 129.
69 See Orest Ranum, *Richelieu and the Councillors of Louis XIII* (Oxford 1963), 185–9, *règlement* of 21 June 1617, arts. 1, 3.
70 AS, Ferrara, Fondo Bentivoglio 18–12, no 198, and accompanying letter (no 197) of 8 July 1618.
71 BN, MS Fr 18012, fo 284r, letter to Louis XIII, 18 June 1618. In the same letter, Marquemont listed in detail the French bishops who had recently obtained financial concessions from the curia, and did so in response to letters from France accusing Cardinal Bonsi of not defending French interests there robustly enough.

months to choose a coadjutor capable of discharging episcopal office. The bishop of Viviers, they concluded, was equally incapable of action, but since the young Louis de la Baume seemed likely to get approval to be his coadjutor, the only immediate solution seemed to lie in the appointment of a suffragan bishop who could stand in for him until he was old enough to be consecrated. Finally, Retz undertook to try to persuade the nonagenarian Bishop Briroy of Coutances to choose a coadjutor.[72] The implication of the discussions was evident: despite all the appointments made during the 1610s, particularly of coadjutors, the real pastoral needs of some dioceses had been ignored in the scramble for office. Unfortunately, it is impossible to say whether other such conferences were held during these years, as no allusion to them has been found, but the possibility that less formal discussions of episcopal affairs took place should not be ruled out. The problem, as always, was also one of action, and it should be noted that the 1619 proposals were not especially successful. Admittedly, the bishop of Coutances died in March 1620, but La Rochefoucauld would lament in 1621 what he called the 'scandalous nomination' of his successor.[73] Valernod announced in early 1623 that he had decided to take a coadjutor in 1619, but did not offer any explanation for his lack of haste in following up his decision.[74] The young coadjutor of Viviers, who had in fact already been confirmed by Rome, succeeded as bishop there in 1621 but was not consecrated until 1628; there is no sign that a suffragan was ever brought in during the lengthy interval.[75]

However limited their ability to achieve results, it is beyond doubt that the reformers brought pressure to bear and that this began to make itself felt in the late 1610s. The pro-Jesuit La Rochefoucauld certainly showed a sustained interest in promoting a wide range of reforms; his position as grand almoner and, after 1622, his place in the king's council enabled him to become, albeit on a limited scale, a one-man *conseil de conscience* for several years thereafter. Moreover, the cause of reform could only be strengthened by the return to court of Marie de' Medici and her followers, after the revolt of 1620. Their political influence grew steadily in subsequent years, but their contribution to reform is a complex question, with historiographical clichés often blurring the overall picture. They are often collectively portrayed, quite wrongly, as being somehow co-extensive with the *dévot* phenomenon as a whole, largely

---

72 Paris, Bibliothèque Sainte-Geneviève, MS 3238, fos 343–4, record of discussions ordered by the king, 1 Sept 1619.
73 Rome, Corsini Library, MS 713, fo 240, La Rochefoucauld to Arnoux, n.d., referring to this case, 'je vois déjà en l'exemple marqué en vostre lettre de la nomination dernière pour l'éveché de Coustance, qu'au lieu d'en réparer la faute pour l'avenir, on s'en veut ayder pour appuy d'autres plus grandes'. The new bishop was Guillaume le Blanc, canon of Agen, but he died before taking up office, and was briefly followed by Nicolas Bourgoing (1623–5).
74 Robert Sauzet, *Contre-réforme et réforme catholique en bas-Languedoc. Le Diocèse de Nîmes au xviie siècle* (Louvain-Paris, 1979), 201.
75 *DHGE* xviii. cols 537–8; Sauzet, *Réforme catholique et contre-réforme*, 344.

because the leading figures among them - who included the likes of Richelieu, Bérulle and Marillac - all shared a strong personal interest in church reform. But it is essential to realise that Marie's followers were extremely diverse in background and interests, and that those who dominated the so-called *parti des dévots* associated with her were those members of the established court and provincial nobility, like Epernon, Guise, and Retz, whose families' extensive ecclesiastical interests, built up over several generations in several cases, were not necessarily compatible with those of church reform as a whole; while they might patronise particular religious orders and causes, their behaviour over the years, some of which will be noted later in this chapter, bears its own distinctive witness to the contradictions within the *dévot* movement. Furthermore, neither the Luynes régime nor its short-lived ministerial successors were powerful or determined enough to forgo the use of church patronage for political purposes, and Cardinal La Rochefoucauld, for one, recognised in 1622 that interfering with the bargaining power of noble families over church office could be highly dangerous and might well lead straight to disgrace.[76] The best that could be hoped for was a challenge to the most indefensible transgressions, and thereby to chip away at traditions they could no longer accept.

Indeed, a perfect example of what could be done and how limited the scope for change still was, is provided by the succession at Reims in 1621, when the last Guise cardinal died.[77] As in 1588, the next generation of family ecclesiastics was represented by an underage boy (a seven-year-old to be precise), who was already provided for with part of his great-uncle Joyeuse's magnificent collection of abbeys; as in 1588, the idea that Reims might escape from family control after nearly a century of virtually uninterrupted tenure, was not readily entertained by the Guises. But what is especially interesting is that in 1621, the attack upon 'hereditary' tenure and underaged promotions was led by La Rochefoucauld and Arnoux, the king's Jesuit confessor, both men with long-standing ties to the Guise family. Louis XIII was initially perfectly willing to give the Guises what they wanted, and even the nuncio's initial reaction was to say that in view of the Guises' historic services to the church and to Catholicism, he would do nothing to prejudice their chances of success.[78] But the king soon proved susceptible to the reformers' arguments about what was at stake in this case, and asked to be advised 'for the relief of his conscience' ('pour la décharge de sa conscience') by two successive commissions of theologians. There followed a nine-month deadlock in which the two sides besieged the king and his entourage, but, in the end, the Guises had to surrender Reims and the abbot-generalship of the abbey and order of Cluny. Towards the end, La Rochefoucauld was excluded from the affair because of his strong anti-Guise stance, but not before he had persuaded the

76   Rome, Corsini Library, MS 713, fo 238, La Rochefoucauld to Arnoux, n.d.
77   See Bergin, 'The Decline and Fall of the Guise as an Ecclesiastical Dynasty' 795-6.
78   BAV, Barb lat 8054, fo 35, Ottavio Corsini to Cardinal Ludoviso, 12 July 1621.

king that this was a matter of conscience and that the Guises would have to make concessions over Reims and Cluny. There were by now three candidates for Reims – Georges Péricard, the bishop of Avranches, who was a Guise client; André du Val, a professor of theology at the Sorbonne thought to be virtually deaf; and, lastly, an English Benedictine, William Gifford, who was already a suffragan bishop in Reims.[79] The short-list was hardly outstanding, and contained no one of genuine personal or social distinction. Significantly, all three candidates were elderly, and therefore unlikely to hold the see for very long, which is what led La Rochefoucauld to say that the Guises were proposing something akin to a *confidence*, with a view to 'hereditary succession'.[80] It was Gifford who was finally chosen, but the duc de Guise and his forceful Joyeuse wife could take some comfort from the outcome: Gifford was not only elderly, he was an exile with few powerful patrons, he was poor, and he was unlikely to cut an impressive figure as archbishop of Reims given that he was to be denied the well-endowed abbey of Saint-Rémy which was normally 'united' to the archbishopric.[81] Meanwhile, young Henri de Guise's claims to succeed Gifford could only become stronger as time passed. And, indeed, within four years the duc de Guise, emboldened by his step-daughter's marriage to Gaston d'Orléans in 1626, was making plans to ensure that Gifford would consent to 'choose' his son as his coadjutor.[82] A formal petition was put to Urban VIII to the effect that only Guise power could protect Reims from the depredations of the duc de Bouillon and other Huguenots in Sedan, and the pope's advisers recommended that Henri de Guise be granted 'access' (a variation on the 'reservations' we have already seen) to Reims when he reached the proper age.[83] This is almost certainly the reason why, on Gifford's death in April 1629, Henri de Guise, still only fourteen years old, succeeded him without opposition or discussion, since the papacy's response had probably pre-empted a repetition of what had happened in 1621–2.

Obviously, few episcopal successions could rival the *éclat* of that of Reims, and there would be no point building a general argument upon such a case. Gifford's tenure was too short to produce enduring results within a much neglected diocese, and Henri de Guise – who, like his late uncle, was more

---

79 BAV, Barb lat 8055, fos 61–2, Corsini to Ludoviso 9 Feb 1622; *ibid*, fo 78, to same, 23 Feb 1622.
80 In his letter to Arnoux already cited: Rome, Corsini Library, MS 713, fo 242r.
81 AAE, CP Rome 23, fo 102, Chancellor Sillery to commandeur de Sillery, ambassador in Rome, 6 Oct 1622, on Gifford's inability to pay the 12,000 *livres* for his provisions; BN, MS Fr 17588, fo 212–13, memorandum on union of Reims and Saint-Rémy.
82 Bibliothèque Sainte-Geneviève, MS 3249, fo 287, Jean Frizon, SJ, to La Rochefoucauld, 11 Apr 1626, reporting that Gifford had taken steps to resign Reims in favour of Henri de Guise; BL, Add MS 8730, fo 310, *avvisi* of 20 Oct 1626 explicitly connecting the duc's plans and the Orléans marriage.
83 ASV, Acta Camerarii 16, fos 190v-1r, consistory of 14 June 1627, acting on a report requested from the consistorial congregation.

than 'un peu subject aux femmes'[84] – showed virtually no interest in its affairs during his twelve-year tenure which finished with his being stripped of it for rebellion in 1641. Consequently, the leadership which archbishops of Reims, and earlier Guise incumbents in particular, had exercised for so long within the French church was seriously eclipsed after 1588; thereafter Guise tenure of the see was merely accompanied by mediocrity, and the standing of Reims would only recover with the long tenure of the masterful Charles-Maurice Le Tellier under Louis XIV.

The interest of the contrasting Reims successions of 1622 and 1629 lies in the way they illustrate the obstacles encountered by those hoping to bend the crown's use of its church patronage towards even moderately reformist standards. A victory like that of 1622 might impress contemporaries, but it did not of itself set the kind of precedent that La Rochefoucauld had hoped it would. Each case of this kind had to be fought on its merits, because much more was involved than just 'reform' versus 'inertia', and reformers knew they could not simply count on past gains to win future arguments. Nor, it should be added, was there anything intrinsically anti-aristocratic about attempts to change episcopal nominations. But what the reformers did increasingly attack was the assumption, which had long been common to both the crown and the aristocracy in particular – though it was also made by ministers and other close servants of the monarchy – that the merits and services of the parents and families of episcopal nominees were a sufficient warrant or qualification for high office for their sons. All through the previous century, as we saw, *brevets* and letters of nomination to Rome had repeated the same basic formulae, occasionally adding that such offspring inspired high hopes for future service and distinction in their calling. The letters of Henri IV, Marie de' Medici and Louis XIII continued to make liberal use of such considerations. By the early 1620s, opposition to such language and its implications was growing among the king's ecclesiastical entourage. This opposition emerges most clearly in the Reims succession of 1621 when it was suggested that Gifford might officially be described as receiving Reims 'in consideration of the services of the duc de Guise', a phrase that was so objectionable to La Rochefoucauld and those close to him as to smack of simony.[85] This attack on the conventional language of patronage was also slow to bear fruit, though a change of tone and emphasis is perceptible in letters and *brevets* of the 1620s and 1630s, when the claims or services of the candidates themselves became increasingly prominent.

---

84 This was the view of Cardinal Louis de Guise expressed in Rome in 1609 and relayed by the ambassador: BN, MS Fr 18004, fo 45, Brèves to Villeroy, 18 Feb 1609.

85 BN, MS Fr 15518, fo 81, *avis* of Duval, Isambert and another doctor of the faculty. They suggested any other wording than that originally suggested, even that of 'on the recommendation of the duc de Guise'.

V

Needless to say, it was easier to change formulae than the realities which they might either conceal or reveal. In looking for the ingredient which enabled reform to extend beyond the realm of linguistic cosmetics, it is tempting to point to the arrival of Richelieu in office in 1624. In some respects – though not always in the ways or for the reasons that might be expected – there is much truth in the familiar view that his extended period of ministerial tenure allowed reformers to experience more than occasional success and, indeed, enabled their concerns to become part of official policy. But the extent of change, and the question of Richelieu's own part in it, is something which can only be established if the evidence is evaluated in the traditional perspective of royal episcopal patronage.

The attempt to assess the record of Richelieu's early years in office needs to begin by returning to the figures for episcopal promotions presented earlier in this chapter, and to the contrasts noted there between the 1610s and the 1620s. The principal effect of the large number of coadjutors appointed during the 1610s was, as we saw, to ensure that vacancies did not arise when incumbent bishops died in the 1620s and later; this is especially striking in both the early and the later 1620s. And although new coadjutorships arose much less than previously, those that did were not fundamentally different from the coadjutorships of earlier years, except perhaps that they were less the monopoly of the families of reigning bishops. The coadjutorships of Auch and Narbonne were probably the most prized among them. The first went to Dominique de Vic, first nominated in early 1622, and whose father Méric had died in office as keeper of the seals just after Luynes in late 1621. His son's elevation was a recognition of the keeper's long service and his brother's favour, but it meet opposition and it needed reconfirmation by Louis XIII in May 1624.[86] The grounds for opposition to him remain unknown, but they may have been based on de Vic's unsuitability, since on the day after he had completed the enquiry *de vita et moribus*, the nuncio reported to Rome that de Vic had and still kept a mistress.[87] No such suspicion surrounded the coadjutor nominated to Narbonne in 1622 with full Guise support, and Claude de Rebé's thirty-year episcopal career in Languedoc would be a distinguished one. Overall, however, with the Gondis retaining Paris (1622), the Guises recovering Reims (1629), and Cardinal Sourdis completing arrangements before his death for his brother's accession to Bordeaux (1627–8), the opportunity to make high-ranking episcopal nominations were extremely limited after the early part of the decade.

---

86 BAV, Barb lat 7940, fo 42, Louis XIII to Cardinal Barberini, 7 May 1624; BN, MS Fr 3666, fo 36, Raymond Phélypeaux d'Herbault, secretary of state, to Béthune, ambassador in Rome, 7 May.

87 BAV, Barb lat 8057, fo 238, Corsini to Ludoviso, 4 July 1622.

But coadjutorships are not the only measure of continuity and change. The continuing power of noble and aristocratic patronage was evident in other ways, too. The most obvious form of it is represented by the recovery of dioceses previously held by families or dependants, of which the Reims successions of 1621 and 1629 are but one instance. It was also in 1621, during the siege of Montauban, that Condé insisted on having his personal confessor, Roland Hébert, as archbishop at Bourges, the capital of the prince's governorship of Berry. Condé had already secularised – 'pillaged' would be more accurate, as was widely said at the time – a number of church properties there, and needed an archbishop who would not challenge him. As even a cursory reading of Louis XIII's letter nominating Hébert to Bourges shows, this was a case of *confidence* in all but name:

> It is our pleasure that our dear cousin, the prince of Condé, should recompense the (outgoing) archbishop of Bourges in order to confer it on Messire Roland Hébert, grand penitentiary of Notre Dame of Paris. Since Hébert owes his elevation to this dignity to our said Cousin and has no personal means with which to pay for the bulls of the said archbishopric, we beseech Your Holiness to despatch them to him *gratis*.[88]

A few years later, the Matignon family finally produced a bishop of their own line after a generation of 'confidentiary' dependants at Coutances. First nominated in 1625, the twenty-year-old Léonor de Matignon was not consecrated until 1633. In 1628, Epernon finally moved his illegitimate son, Louis de la Valette, into the coadjutorship of Mirepoix, a see held since the late 1580s by his client Pierre de Donnaud. Old noble families like Forbin, Grasse, and Villeneuve also began to appear, or in some cases reappear, among the episcopate of Provence during these years.

As in the past, royal favourites continued to expect and get episcopal office for close relatives. Surprisingly for such an adept dispenser of patronage, Luynes was in some ways the exception, possibly because his family, for whom he secured three duchies in four years, had virtually no ecclesiastical representatives. But his successors did. Roger de Bellegarde's brief period of favour in the early 1620s enabled his nephew, Octave, bishop of Comminges, to move to Sens, while Bellegarde also ensured, according to his own later claim, that Comminges was given to a rather inoffensive Carthusian monk, Bruno

---

[88] BAV, Barb lat 7940, fo 122, Louis XIII to Gregory XV, 22 Sept 1621. 'Nous avons eu bien agréable que nostre trèscher Cousin le prince de Condé récompensant l'archevesché de Bourges pour le mettre entre les mains de Messire Roland Hébert grand pénitencier de l'église Notre Dame de Paris . . . Or comme il est tiré à ceste dignité par nostredit Cousin et qu'il n'a aucunes commoditez pour satisfere aux bulles dudit archevesché, nous supplions Vostre Saineteté . . . de les luy vouloir faire depescher gratis.' The phrase 'récompensant l'archevesché de Bourges' refers to the terms agreed by Condé for the resignation of the previous archbishop, André Frémiot; the king's letter goes on to refer to the exchange of benefices which that entailed.

Ruade.[89] Another favourite, the future Marshal Toiras, enabled his brother to become coadjutor of Nîmes in 1623, and his uncle, Louis Claret, bishop of Saint-Papoul in 1626.[90] Finally, François de Baradat obtained Noyon (and the attached peerage) for his brother, Henri, during his relatively brief period of favour in the mid-1620s. Moreover, the Baradat promotion provides a fascinating coda to one prominent element of episcopal patronage which we have already noticed in several contexts. Twenty-five years later, during the Fronde, Bishop Baradat negotiated terms with Barbier de la Rivière, Gaston d'Orléans's favourite who would later become bishop of Langres, for his retirement from Noyon which, because of war damage, he claimed no longer enabled him to 'uphold the dignity of being a peer of France' which was attached to it. But his brother, Louis XIII's former favourite, reacted energetically and promptly lodged a strong protest with Gaston, 'claiming that since the late king had gratified him with this benefice in reward for his services, his brother should keep it in their family so long as there were members capable of holding it, and asking that the king in his goodness should keep it for him'.[91] A more concise or perfect expression of aristocratic attitudes to church dignities would be hard to find, and it was probably one of the last of its kind to be made so publicly, in respect of bishoprics at least. In 1651, it appeared old-fashioned and inconvenient, but as an expression of attitudes still current in the 1620s, it was unerring.

It is perhaps in Languedoc that, for all its untypical characteristics, we can best measure the changes of these decades. Cardinal Joyeuse's outright resignation of Toulouse in 1611–12 was itself a recognition that as the sole surviving – and celibate – male of the family, he could only hope to perpetuate its influence by indirect means; the choice of Epernon's son as his successor may well have been inspired by the hope that the duke, who already had at least two episcopal clients in the south-west, might step into his shoes in the region. But although the new archbishop of Toulouse became a cardinal in 1621, and played a considerable political part in the conflicts of the late 1610s and early 1620s, he never became a successor figure to Joyeuse in Languedoc, partly because he was neither ordained nor consecrated. By the time he resigned from Toulouse in 1627, his father was governor of neighbouring Guyenne, yet, despite the promotion of his illegitimate son to Mirepoix in 1629, Epernon's patronage in Languedoc remained marginal. Moreover, his influence in Guyenne itself was limited by the presence of a counterweight

---

89 AAE, France 834, fo 59, Bellegarde to Chavigny 11 Sept 1639.
90 *Les Papiers de Richelieu* (*Politique intérieure: Correspondance et papiers d'état*), ed Pierre Grillon, 6 vols (Paris 1975 – in progress), iii. 52–3, 'mémoire concernant M. de Toiras', 6 Feb 1628.
91 BN, MS Fr 25025, fo 420, nouvelles de la Fronde, 14 May 1651: 'soutenir la dignité de pair de France . . . disant que le feu Roy l'ayant gratiffié de ce bénéfice pour recompense de ses services, son frère le devoit laisser dans la maison tandis qu'il y auroit des personnes capables de le tenir, et que le Roy auroit la bonté de le luy conserver.' Bishop Baradat did not go through with his retirement, but other objections and objectors were instrumental in defeating his efforts.

with powerful support at court, Sourdis, in the see of Bordeaux. The other heirs to Joyeuse's capital of influence were the Guises, thanks to Henriette-Catherine de Joyeuse's marriage to the duc de Guise in 1611. Despite their inheritance, there is little to suggest that they attempted to build any kind of distinct Guise clientèle among the bishops of Languedoc. Even the accession of Claude de Rebé to the Narbonne coadjutorship appears to have been a piece of opportunism made possible by the large pension that the archbishop had formerly paid to his patron, Joyeuse.[92] It is arguably better to see the Guises' role in a more limited and entirely different perspective - not that of creating an episcopal clientèle in Languedoc, but rather of enabling erstwhile Joyeuse protégés there to enjoy continuing protection and, in some cases, even to secure coadjutorships for their younger relatives. Christophe de Lestang of Carcassonne, who had always been the most prominent among them, found a senior position in the royal chapel after the end of the wars, and was well respected at Louis XIII's court. He was not the only Joyeuse client to take advantage of the opportunities to take on a nephew, Vital de Lestang, as his coadjutor (1613). So, too, did Bernard Daffis at Lombez (1614) and Jean de Fossé at Castres (1626).

If the Joyeuse clientèle fragmented relatively quickly, that of Montmorency and Ventadour only seemed to gain in solidity. The established political position of neither family was seriously challenged, either provincially or nationally, before the late 1620s, while the passage of time and the extensive activities of the provincial Estates acted to strengthen existing ties or create them where they had not been especially strong. If, as we saw, the bishop of Saint-Pons was able to defy his former patron, Clermont, over his succession in 1616, it was partly due to ties formed with Montmorency, whose revolt the bishop would join in 1632. Elsewhere, Montmorency and Ventadour experienced little difficulty with their episcopal clients at Béziers, Le Puy, and Viviers. A mysterious attempt in 1609 to discredit Valernod of Nîmes came to nothing, though his choice of coadjutor in 1622 fell on Claude de Saint-Bonnet-de-Toiras, another Montmorency client, while Uzès had a Montmorency family coadjutor nominated as early as 1611.

But it was the treatment of the core dioceses of Agde and Lodève which is the most revealing of the persistence of patterns inherited from the previous century. The long serving confidentiary bishop of Agde, Bernard du Puy, died in 1611, but in 1607 Henri IV had already agreed that Montmorency's twelve-year-old grandson, Louis de Valois, should become his coadjutor.[93] This was clearly a method of reserving the bishopric, one which du Puy's

---

92   AAE, France 1632, fos 177–9, for evidence of Guise attempts to force Rebé in 1643 to pay a pension off Narbonne to which Vervins had consented after Joyeuse's death but only on condition that he would not actually be required to do so! Copies of notarised agreements to this effect from 1615–16 between Vervins and Mme de Guise at fos 178–9.
93   Recueil de lettres missives de Henri IV, ed X. Berger de Xivrey and J Guadet, 9 vols (Paris 1843–76), vii. 422–3, king to Paul V, n.d. (1607).

subsequent death did not disturb, and which, resembling other nominations made during the 1610s, kept Agde at least formally vacant until Valois was confirmed by Rome in May 1618. But as we saw, he was never consecrated, and he resigned it outright sometime in 1622. It was not until 1626 that the former Constable's nephew, Balthasar de Budos, who had been coadjutor of Castres for nearly a decade, was finally nominated to succeed to Agde. He reigned for less than two years, and when he died in 1629, the see went to a dependent bishop from the neighbouring diocese of Béziers who was not even a blood relative, Fulcran de Barrez.

The fate of Lodève was analogous, but in some respects more symptomatic of future developments. After the confidentiary bishop Robin died in 1611, it had as its 'bishops' between 1611 and 1626 a succession of Ventadour's own sons – though 'succession' is scarcely an apt term to use, as it is virtually impossible to establish anything like a clearly defined sequence.[94] The real point, however, is that all three were minors under the tutorship of their father or eldest brother, and none of them may even have obtained a formal royal nomination until the early 1620s, when François de Ventadour sojourned in Rome, whence he returned in 1624 with his provisions as Bishop of Lodève.[95] But almost immediately he joined his former 'episcopal' brother, Charles, in preferring a military career, and drowned off La Rochelle in August 1625. This, according to the next bishop, was a turning point: even before young Ventadour's death, Louis XIII had bluntly told the duke and his wife that he would no longer tolerate such behaviour, and asked them to arrange for a proper succession. The new bishop was Jean Plantavit, a converted Huguenot minister from Nîmes and a scholar.[96] Crucially, however, what Plantavit, the source of this information, did *not* reveal was why Louis XIII suddenly lost patience with the Ventadours' treatment of Lodève. In the absence of any other evidence, it may be suggested that La Rochefoucauld or someone close to him took a hand in working on the king's conscience, as Plantavit had for several years been in La Rochefoucauld's service. By the time Plantavit himself, who was lucky to escape being implicated in Montmorency's 1632 revolt, came to casting around for a successor in the mid-1640s, he fixed his choice on a scholar-cleric from a different background, François Bosquet. As for the Ventadours, despite remaining loyal during the 1632 revolt, their influence within Languedoc went into decline but, having escaped the fate of their Montmorency relatives, they showed considerable resilience. Indeed, the ecclesiastical members made a somewhat spectacular breakthrough during and after the Fronde, when first Anne, once

---

94 Ernest Martin, *Histoire de la ville de Lodève*, 2 vols (Montpellier 1900), ii. 373–4.
95 The source for this is Jean Plantavit, *Chronologia praesulum Lodovensium* (np. 1634), 403–4, but no trace of François de Ventadour's provisions is to be found in Eubel, *Hierarchia Catholica*, iv. p 72, 'Agathen'.
96 Plantavit, *Chronologia praesulum Lodovensium*, 404–5; Martin, *Histoire de la ville de Lodève*, 374.

'bishop' of Lodève, became archbishop of Bourges in 1651, and his youngest brother, Louis-Hercule, became bishop of Mirepoix in 1655.

No single province can be held to be representative of France as a whole, and Languedoc less than most. Its experience of episcopal patronage in the 1610s and 1620s was one of limited change. There was certainly no assault on existing patterns of provision from above. Indeed, even when Louis XIII finally lost patience with the Ventadours over Lodève, he proved to be generosity itself, giving them six months in which to come up with a man of their choice and an arrangement that would suit them. The principal change, as we saw, was the disappearance of Joyeuse influence and the fact that it was not replaced by anything comparable, despite an Epernon presence among Languedoc's bishops. Further change would greatly depend on how far surviving patronage networks endured, reformed or disappeared in years to come.

VI

It is in the context of such developments that the role of the Richelieu ministry should be evaluated. As a chapter in the wider history of royal patronage and policy towards the church, the long ministry of Richelieu obviously deserves close attention. It is also fortunate that, for perhaps the first time in the monarchy's history, ministerial and other papers are sufficiently numerous and interesting for a study of ecclesiastical patronage at the highest level to be illuminating. Of course, these papers are much less complete than might be wished, a fact which all too often leaves the historian guessing about ministerial influence over numerous royal decisions. Yet the subject is worth pursuing for other reasons. For the first time in the period covered by this study, it is possible to examine in some depth the fundamental question of the advice given to the king in ecclesiastical affairs, an incidental bonus of which is that we can also approach from an unusual angle the perennial question of Richelieu's relations with Louis XIII and the extent of ministerial powers to fashion decisions of which the king could be expected to approve. Finally, there is the often ignored fact that Richelieu the cardinal-minister remained as committed as he had been throughout his own episcopal career to improving the condition of the French church. How far did he attempt to use his ministerial influence to pursue such objectives through episcopal patronage and how successful was he? How far was he – or indeed anyone in his position – free to ignore the pressures and interests of families and social groups clamouring for episcopal preferment? Not all of these questions can be answered with equal assurance, though an attempt which pays close attention to the successive phases of Richelieu's contribution to changing the episcopate is the one most likely to yield satisfactory conclusions.

Of course, much of the discussion of the record of Richelieu's ministry has been traditionally pre-empted by the opinions expressed in the pages of the Cardinal's *Testament Politique*. Whatever its value as an expression of Richelieu's thinking, it is worth remembering that the *Testament Politique* contains a series of assertions and comparisons which, rather like Henri IV's replies to the clergy's complaints a generation before, have had a lasting impact on the historiography of his age in general, and also on particular issues within it. As befitted a work purporting to emanate from a prince of the church, its discussion of French society begins with a chapter on the church and the problem of how it might be reformed. Although less well known than other parts of that controversial document, one of the chapter's better known passages offered a combination of reminiscence and advice to the king on ecclesiastical appointments:

> When I recall how, in my youth, I saw nobles and other lay persons holding, by means of *confidences*, not merely the majority of priories and abbeys, but also parish cures and bishoprics . . . I confess that it is no small consolation to see that these disorders have been so totally eliminated during your reign. In order to continue and increase this blessing, Your Majesty needs only, in my opinion, to take particular care to fill bishoprics with men of merit and exemplary life.[97]

As has happened with other issues, Richelieu's direct comparison of the experiences of his youth and of subsequent improvements seemed to speak with genuine authority, and has readily been repeated by biographers and by historians of the French church. Yet this consensus rests on remarkably slight foundations, since surprisingly little research has been done on the contributions of Richelieu and Louis XIII to church reform at the point where they could exercise greatest influence – namely, in the selection and nomination of bishops.[98] If for no other reason, the claim made in the *Testament Politique* requires balancing with some attempt to describe and define the roles of both king and cardinal in achieving the results which the *Testament Politique* so clearly enunciated.

One claim that, surprisingly perhaps, was *not* made in the *Testament Politique* was that on returning to office in 1624 Richelieu had recommended specific ecclesiastical objectives to Louis XIII. But if he did not have anything

---

97 Richelieu, *Testament Politique*, ed Françoise Hildesheimer (Paris 1995), 87–8: 'Quand je me souviens que j'ai veu, dans ma jeunesse, des gentilshommes et autres personnes laïques posséder par confidence, non seulement la pluspart des prieurés et abbayes, mais aussi des cures et des évêchés . . . J'avoue que je ne reçois pas peu de consolation de voir que ces désordres ayent esté si absolument bannis sous votre régne . . . Pour continuer et augmenter cette bénédiction, V(otre) M(ajesté) n'a autre chose à faire, à mon avis, que d'avoir un soin particulier de remplir les évêcezs de personnages de mérite et de vie exemplaire.'

98 Much of what follows is closely based on my essay, 'Richelieu and his bishops? Ministerial Power and Ecclesiastical Patronage under Louis XIII', in Joseph Bergin and Laurence Brockliss, eds, *Richelieu and his Age* (Oxford 1992), 175–202.

resembling a 'policy', he did, at least, have considerable personal experience of episcopal patronage. The manner of his own promotion to Luçon in the early 1600s was typical of many under Henri IV – protracted, uncertain, litigious, and more an *affaire de famille* than a personal odyssey. Moreover, the terms under which he resigned it to a hand-picked successor in 1623 provide additional evidence of how enduring such 'proprietary' views of the tenure of a particular diocese could be. In his early career, he had sought at least once to exchange Luçon for another diocese, that of Poitiers, but he had been frustrated in his attempts, probably by no less a figure than Sully; this, as we have also seen, was a not uncommon experience for French bishops.[99]

But it is also essential to realise that Richelieu's pre-ministerial experience of episcopal patronage went considerably further than that of the general run of bishops. Mainly as a result of the fact that he became Marie de' Medici's principal adviser in 1619, he took a direct hand in the exercise of episcopal patronage which arose from the grant of apanages and jointure rights to members of the royal family, which we saw in an earlier chapter. In Marie de' Medici's case, the actual exercise of presentation rights to the seven Breton and the two Auvergne bishoprics of Clermont and Saint-Flour only commenced after Henri IV's death in 1610. But as she was regent during several years of her widowhood, disentangling her different roles remains virtually impossible. There is, however, little to suggest that she was particularly successful in promoting individuals enjoying her favour to the episcopate during these years.[100]

The situation changed abruptly after Marie's disgrace and internal exile in 1617. As already noted, how, or indeed whether, she should be permitted to exercise these rights at all was one of many bones of contention between her and the court from 1617 to 1620. Three months after her fall, one of her entourage reported to Richelieu that the bishop of Rennes was rumoured dead and that, on hearing of it, 'members of the council pointed out to the king that he should not allow her the power to confer benefices and offices in the present situation, as it would enable her to oblige too many people'.[101] In June 1619, when talks for a settlement with her were in full swing, she attempted to nominate her candidate to Rennes – which was now, in fact, vacant – and insisted on regarding a positive response as a test of the court's

99 See Joseph Bergin, *The Rise of Richelieu* (New Haven and London 1991), 58–63, 70–3, 75.
100 For example, she turned down Cardinal Sourdis's request for Sarlat, rumoured to be vacant in 1612, saying that she had previously promised it to the son of Florent d'Argouges, her personal treasurer. But young d'Argouges did not get Sarlat or any other bishopric either in later years. BN, MS Fr 6379, fo 84, Marie to Sourdis, 27 Oct 1612.
101 AAE, 771, fo 157v, abbé Tantucci to Richelieu, 13 July 1617: 'ceulx du conseil ont remonstré au Roy qu'il ne doibt pas permettre que la Reyne aye le pouvoir de conférer les bénéfices et donner les offices en l'estat que nous sommes, car la Reyne auroit le moyen d'obliger trop de gens'.

good faith.¹⁰² But despite confirmation of her jointure rights a few months later in September 1619, suspicion of her remained strong.¹⁰³ The revolt of 1620 ensured a continuing unwillingness to satisfy her: Rennes, not surprisingly, was filled without reference to her in 1619. However, the settlement which followed the 1620 revolt did take effect, enabling Marie to exercise her presentation rights again during the 1620s. In addition, she was governor of Anjou after 1619, with the result that when Charles Miron of Angers became archbishop of Lyon in 1626, the dominant voice in the choice of a successor to Miron at Angers appears to have been hers – or at least that of her entourage.¹⁰⁴

Now all of this afforded opportunities to a man like Richelieu, whose influence in the queen mother's affairs grew steadily during the early 1620s. Protecting his patron's privileges demanded considerable alertness, as he was reminded from Rome by his friend Sébastien Bouthillier.¹⁰⁵ Louis XIII and his ministers were probably reluctant to allow Marie's influence in Brittany, for example, to grow unchecked. Nantes, being one of the most important Breton sees, needed to be in the hands of a reliable bishop. Yet Marie and Richelieu may not have been the prime movers in the transfer of Philippe Cospeau, one of the cardinal's earliest mentors, from Aire to Nantes in 1621.¹⁰⁶ Instead, they had to settle for an agreement whereby the diocese of Aire went to Richelieu's close friend, Sébastien Bouthillier, whom he would almost certainly have preferred to see in Brittany.¹⁰⁷ Further opportunities for episcopal patronage in Brittany would only come later in the 1620s.

What is already obvious, however, is that Richelieu, even had he not become a royal minister, would have continued to be far more closely associated with bishop-making on the queen mother's behalf throughout the 1620s than virtually any of his fellow ecclesiastics. If this suggests that Richelieu's

102 BN, MS Fr 15699, fos 413v-4r, Marie de' Medici to Cardinal La Rochefoucauld, 23 June 1619, insisting on presenting the bishop of Marseille to the see of Rennes – 'c'est une affaire où il n'y a nulle difficulté'. La Rochefoucauld was one of those negotiating with the queen mother.
103 AAE, France 772, fo 132, *brevet* of 24 Sept 1619 confirming her rights.
104 ASV, N Fr 66, fo 163, Bernadino Spada, papal nuncio in France, to Cardinal Antonio Barberini the elder, 24 Oct 1626; fos 275–6, same to Cardinal Francesco Barberini, 4 Dec 1626; fos 279–83, same to same, 20 Dec 1626.
105 AAE, CP Rome 23, fos 36–7, Sébastien Bouthillier to Claude Bouthillier, Rome, 1 June 1621, urging vigilance lest benefices be filled without the queen mother's knowledge, and asking for a full list of benefices at her disposal to be sent to Rome. He added that three Breton abbeys had recently been filled without her knowledge.
106 Emile Jacques, *Philippe Cospeau. Un ami-ennemi de Richelieu* (Paris 1989), 83–4, who shows that there were several candidates in addition to Cospeau and Bouthillier, and that Marie's initial choice, Philippe Thibault, actually declined the offer.
107 At some later date, Richelieu obtained Bouthillier's presentation to Saint-Malo, but news of the reigning bishop's death proved to be false: AAE, CP Rome 23, fos 51–4, Sébastien Bouthillier to Claude Bouthillier, no date, thanking Richelieu for his favour.

experience and concerns were, as befitted a key figure in the queen mother's entourage, focused purely on the political mechanics of episcopal nominations, we should not forget that he had long been associated with the reformist movement, and belonged to circles which were increasingly active in seeking to improve episcopal nominations.

There can be little doubt, therefore, that as he returned to office in 1624, Richelieu saw himself as playing a part in the crown's episcopal patronage – a part which his cardinal's rank seemed to make all the more natural. Quite how much influence he expected to wield is much harder to determine. Despite the king's long-standing dislike or fear of him, there were some grounds for Richelieu's expectations. We have already seen something of Louis XIII's political apprenticeship and his evident willingness to listen to criticism and advice on ecclesiastical affairs. But in the uncertain political climate of the early 1620s, it still remained unclear how far the king was capable of matching his good intentions with traditional pressures from courtiers, patrons, families, and individual clerics. Indeed, it may well be that Louis XIII himself did not quite know how far he would actively seek counsel concerning episcopal nominations from any one minister, let alone allow himself to be guided by it, even if that minister were at the same time a leading figure in the French church.

Contrary to expectations, surprisingly little is known about Richelieu's initial actions or attitudes as minister in or after 1624. These have to be pieced together from a variety of sources, and not merely from some of the well-known and endlessly-quoted disquisitions on reforming the realm which were drafted during the first two years of his ministry. A rather general note from late 1624 on the presentation of requests to Louis XIII may provide some indication of his early thinking:

> the Cardinal will observe the following procedure where requests to be made of the king are concerned: he will inform the king of them, and will personally deal with those which the king refuses to grant. As for those which the king does wish to grant, he will pretend not to want to raise them, but will advise the parties themselves to make their petitions directly to the king, so that the grace comes purely from him and that they may be obliged to him alone.[108]

But even such an apparently self-effacing code of behaviour only made sense if, as Cardinal Bérulle recognised a few years later, Richelieu already had

---

108 Grillon, *Papiers de Richelieu*, i. 105: 'le Cardinal gardera cet ordre en toutes les demandes qu'on voudra faire au Roy: (savoir) qu'il en advertira Sa Majesté, et se chargera en sa personne du reffus de celles que Sa Majesté ne pourra accorder. Et pour celles qu'elle [Louis XIII] voudra donner, il fera semblant de n'en vouloir parler; cependant il conseillera les parties de faire leurs demandes eux-mesmes au Roy, afin que la grace vienne purement de luy et qu'ils ayent obligation à luy seul'. This document is not dated, but is related to proceedings against La Vieuville in late 1624.

a general licence to present all kinds of petitions directly to the king.[109] How far Richelieu gave his personal support to the notion of a council for ecclesiastical affairs as outlined in the so-called *règlement général* of 1625 we can also only guess, but it is clear that he made no attempt to implement it subsequently.[110] It is generally believed that this proposal (and the others on church reform) was drafted by Charles Miron, who had taken part in both the Estates General of 1614 and the Assembly of Notables of 1617, and was therefore more identified than Richelieu with their work, and with that of the 1617 assembly in particular. Clearly, like other reform ideas aired at these earlier meetings, that of a *conseil de conscience* was far from dead nearly a decade later. If such a *conseil* was not to see the light of day for many years, it was partly because there were, and continued to be, differing views as to how – and indeed, by whom – it should be implemented.

By contrast, Richelieu's reaction to the disgrace of Gaspar Seguéran, the king's confessor, in late 1625, is far more revealing. Seguéran was dismissed shortly after having been sharply attacked by Richelieu's old friend, Bishop Laubespine of Orléans, for, among other things, his presumption concerning the distribution of major church benefices.[111] Seguéran's less combative successor, Jean Suffren, was long known to Richelieu as Marie de' Medici's confessor, and the cardinal's warning to him on his appointment could hardly have been more explicit: 'Put aside any ambition to dispose of bishoprics and abbeys, as these are things which should depend directly on the king, like all other graces' – though Richelieu did concede that Suffren could warn the king directly if a matter of conscience arose concerning such appointments.[112] This warning notwithstanding, it is perfectly clear that Richelieu was generally prepared to employ the confessor in the circumstances which he had indicated.[113] What that could entail in concrete terms is illustrated by a case which arose two years after Suffren became royal confessor, a case which sharply delineates the roles of each participant. In late 1627, the cardinal wanted to promote the well-recommended Jean Daffis to the episcopate, but he was only twenty-four years old.[114] It was to Suffren that the task of discussing the merits of his case with Louis XIII fell. He reported to Richelieu

109 *Ibid*, iii. 241, Bérulle to Richelieu [28 Apr 1628].
110 *Ibid*, i. 248–69, 'règlement pour toutes les affaires du royaume' [1625], at p 249. See the discussion by Robin Briggs, 'Richelieu and Reform', in Bergin and Brockliss, eds, *Richelieu and his Age*, esp 79–81.
111 E Griselle, *Louis XIII et Richelieu* (Paris 1911), 21–2, quoting the diary of Robert Arnauld d'Andilly.
112 Grillon, *Papiers de Richelieu*, i. 239, undated letter but probably late 1625: 'N'ayez point l'ambition de disposer des éveschez et des abbayes, estant chose qui doit dépendre immediatement du roy, ainsy que toutes autres graces'.
113 *Ibid*, iii. 374–5, Suffren to Richelieu, 10 July 1628. Here Suffren merely makes a general allusion, but its meaning is obvious enough: 'Je traite amplement avec Sa Majesté de ce que nous avions arresté pour le bien de l'Eglise, et [il] me semble tout à fait résolu à suivre vostre advis, auquel vous sçavez comme promptement je m'y suis porté'.
114 ASV, PC 25, fo 318, letter of nomination, 31 Dec 1627.

that the king's scruples would be eased if the pope could first be persuaded to grant Daffis a dispensation – an interesting reversal, not so much of roles, as of the normal sequence of an episcopal nomination. The confessor concluded with a general statement of his position since 1625, professing that he had been only too happy to behave in accordance with Richelieu's guidance: 'My fear of being dragged into matters concerning benefices, as my predecessors were, is the reason for my reserve. I have maintained this reserve for the past two years and it suits me well. I was confirmed in it by what it graciously pleased you to communicate to me in writing when I took up my post.'[115] Suffren continued in the same vein until he abandoned Louis XIII and Richelieu and chose to go into exile with Marie de' Medici in 1631.

If it is characteristic of Richelieu's political style to seize such an opportunity to neutralise a royal confessor, it would be hasty to see it as heralding an immediate move on his part to monopolise advice to the king on how episcopal patronage might be distributed. Indeed, there is ample evidence that Richelieu was extremely cautious over bishoprics during his early years as a minister. Successive royal favourites such as Baradat and Toiras secured bishoprics for members of their families between 1625 and 1627, and there are no signs that Richelieu tried to come between the king and his favourites at the time, however much he might comment upon their behaviour once they had fallen.[116] Indeed, the same could be said in respect of several episcopal promotions between 1625 and 1629, mostly of young and inexperienced scions or, failing that, clerical dependants, of powerful noble houses like the Guise, Epernon, Souvré, Matignon, or Montmorency.

Richelieu's caution in such instances suggests the actions of a man who knew when to leave well alone. But it was not just the power of royal favourites or great noble families, many of them close allies of his patron, Marie de' Medici, which could inhibit him. A number of sources show that he also experienced difficulty, even failure, early in his ministry in obtaining bishoprics for a small group of individuals, at least one of whom was a close personal associate; this might be less significant were it not for the fact that, here, most of the opposition came from fellow churchmen rather than from courtiers. In 1626, Mathieu de Morgues was formally nominated, only to be prevented from becoming bishop of Toulon by Cardinal La Rochefoucauld and, to a lesser extent, the papal nuncio, both of whom regarded him as being

115 Bibliothèque de l'Institut, MS Godefroy 15, fo 394: 'La crainte que j'ay qu'on ne m'embarque en ces matières béneficiales comme mes prédécesseurs s'y estoient laissés porter me fait d'estre réservé. J'ay vescu depuis deux ans avec ceste reserve et m'en suis fort bien trouvé, à quoy encore m'a confirmé ce que de vostre grace il vous pleust me faire entendre par escrit au commencement de ceste charge.' The letter is undated, but was probably written around the time of Jean Daffis's nomination to Lombez on New Year's Eve, 1627.
116 See Grillon, *Papiers de Richelieu*, iii. 52–3, 'mémoire concernant M de Toiras', 6 Feb 1628, in which Richelieu criticises Toiras, noting that his brother and uncle both received bishoprics during his term of favour.

too outspokenly Gallican.[117] In the end, de Morgues had to abandon his efforts, blaming Richelieu's lack of support for his public humiliation, and thereby opening a wound which would eventually make de Morgues the most deadly of the Cardinal's pamphleteering enemies.[118] La Rochefoucauld also held up the appointment of Henri de Sponde to Pamiers, and Richelieu had to use the good offices of the papal nuncio to talk La Rochefoucauld out of his opposition to Sponde.[119] La Rochefoucauld successfully frustrated the young Henri de Béthune's designs on Lyon in 1626, when Richelieu seemed to support him.[120] Richelieu may well have been on the way to becoming a dominant figure in the council, but there were others in it, or close to it, who still possessed the ability to frustrate him. In no sense had the responsibility for episcopal and church reform generally been delegated irrevocably to him, and it was clear enough to well-placed contemporaries that if there was a guardian of the king's conscience over episcopal patronage during these years, it was La Rochefoucauld, not Richelieu.

This evidence of limited success in influencing episcopal nominations – both in preventing certain nominations and in promoting others – fits well with the overall record of appointments during Richelieu's first years in office. That record strongly suggests that Richelieu experienced much less difficulty in promoting the claims of candidates who were *dévots* or members of the queen mother's wider circle than he did with those who were personal clients. It also suggests, though perhaps more tentatively, that a policy of close collaboration with the queen mother and her entourage did much to ease the advancement of those candidates who did enjoy close personal association with Richelieu. At any rate, it would be misguided to assume that Richelieu, even after his ministerial elevation, effortlessly dominated the queen mother's entourage. The *dévot* circles in which he moved were not highly regimented, and did not look exclusively to Richelieu for advancement.

For example, one might have expected Richelieu to have been most effective in placing allies in bishoprics in the gift of the queen mother. In fact, less than half a dozen opportunities to fill dioceses in this manner arose between 1620 and 1631. In 1621, as we saw, Philippe Cospeau, obtained the important see of Nantes; ten years later, Achille de Harlay, one of the authors of Richelieu's *Mémoires*, received that of Saint-Malo, but the original nominee had been Michel de Marillac's son, who died before

117 BN, MS Fr 23200, fos 3v-4r, Morgues to Richelieu, 16 June 1626, thanking him for nomination to Toulon.
118 ASV, N Fr 65, fo 213v, Spada to Barberini, 22 June 1626; BN, MS Fr 3671, fo 32, Louis XIII to Ambassador Béthune, 6 May 1627, expressing unwillingness to accept papal objections to Morgues's promotion; *Lettres de Peiresc*, i. 795, Pierre Dupuy to Peiresc, 28 Dec 1626; *ibid*, 312, Peiresc to Dupuy, 1 Aug 1627..
119 BL, Add MS 8730, fo 138, 19 Dec 1625; fo 157, 16 Jan 1626. Spada agreed to talk to La Rochefoucauld as if he had not been prompted by Richelieu at all.
120 Bergin, *La Rochefoucauld*, 133–4.

receiving his provisions.¹²¹ None of the other nominees was particularly identified as a Richelieu man, and in the competition for vacant bishoprics it is clear that Marillac, Bérulle, and others felt free to press the claims of their own candidates, protégés, or family members. Bérulle actively sought the see of Dol in Brittany for the abbé de Saint-Cyran in 1629, though it was not Richelieu, but the queen mother's chief physician, Vautier, who appears to have frustrated him by engineering an appointment of his own 'candidate'.¹²² The same applies to nominations to bishoprics elsewhere in France. It may come as a surprise that Bérulle, so universally regarded as the champion of a reformed clergy, was much stronger than Richelieu in his support for Camille de Neufville-Villeroy for the Lyon succession in 1626, even though he was barely twenty years old and a simple cleric.¹²³

Nevertheless, it is equally plain that Richelieu did register several striking personal successes as a patron of episcopal hopefuls during these early years and, what is arguably more important, that he did so not merely in Brittany. Firstly, in addition to well-known *dévots* like Miron promoted to Lyon, Charles de Montchal to Toulouse, Jean Jaubert de Barrault from Bazas to Arles, there were other figures like Clement Bonsi of Béziers, Louis Dony d'Attichy of Riez, and Nicolas Grillié of Bazas – all of whom were strongly supported by the queen mother and others of her circle, Richelieu himself included. Alongside them we can list Richelieu's own brother, Alphonse, archbishop of Aix and then Lyon; Victor Bouthillier, successively bishop of Boulogne and coadjutor-archbishop of Tours; Henri de Sourdis elevated, in the face of some strongly worded *dévot* criticism, from Maillezais to the archbishopric of Bordeaux; Jean Daffis appointed bishop of Lombez, Harlay de Sancy of Saint-Malo as we saw, and Sylvestre de Marsillac of Mende.¹²⁴

---

121 Grillon, *Papiers de Richelieu,* iv. 101–2, Richelieu to Denis Bouthillier de Rancé, ca. 15 Feb 1629, 'Quant à Saint-Malo, puisque M de Marillac le demande, je crois que la reine mère luy doit accorder'. Further letters exchanged between Richelieu, Marillac, Bouthillier and the queen mother offer interesting insights into Marillac's anxiety each time Saint-Malo was rumoured vacant: *ibid,* 535, 539–40, 587–8, 681–2, Aug-Nov 1629. Harlay, a former Oratorian, was a contemporary of the cardinal's at university, and had been nominated by Henry IV to the diocese of Lavaur in his youth.

122 Jean Orcibal, *Jean Duvergier de Hauranne, abbé de Saint-Cyran et son temps* (Louvain 1947), 284.

123 Bérulle initially suggested Henri de Béthune, then aged twenty, for the coadjutorship of Lyon in 1624, so that Marquemont could remain in Rome in royal service: *Correspondance de Pierre de Bérulle,* ed Jean Dagens, 3 vols (Louvain 1937–9), ii. 527, Bérulle to Villauxclercs, secretary of state, 6 Nov 1624. Archbishop Marquemont resigned Lyon in favour of Neufville just before his death in Sept 1626, and the king initially seemed willing to nominate him (BAV, Barb lat 8059, fo 236, 245, Spada to Cardinal Barberini, 4 Aug and 30 Sept 1626 respectively). Marquemont's death reopened the question of succession. For Bérulle's support, see *Correspondance,* iii. 280, Bérulle to Claude Bertin, 28 Sept 1627; *ibid,* 346, to Richelieu, 3 Dec 1627.

124 Richelieu's association with Sourdis was greatly strengthened during the siege of La Rochelle, when Sourdis proved his organisational abilities. Marsillac was a maître de chambre in Richelieu's own household. See Maximin Deloche, *La Maison du cardinal de Richelieu* (Paris 1912), 75–7.

These successes, especially those of men closely associated with the Cardinal, did not escape contemporary notice. Richelieu's own surviving correspondence would lead us to believe that it was in 1628 that he began to receive letters and petitions explicitly requesting his favour or intervention over appointments to vacant dioceses – but it is difficult to imagine that it did not happen earlier than that. Marie de' Medici, Gaston d'Orléans, Marillac, Bérulle and others were among those regularly soliciting his intercession with the king; but while Marie and Gaston would feel free to approach Louis XIII directly – and pointed that out in their letters to Richelieu – it is less clear that men like Marillac or Bérulle enjoyed direct access to the king on such matters.[125] This resort to Richelieu as intermediary could perhaps be seen as a fortuitous consequence of his accompanying Louis XIII on the military campaigns of the late 1620s, and of the petitioners' temporary absence from the royal entourage, but there is good reason to think that it amounted to far more than that by this juncture. Richelieu's first direct, written request to Louis XIII to appoint a particular individual (Raymond de Montaigne) to a given diocese (Condom) also dates from February 1628.[126] Unfortunately, the text of the king's reply – if indeed there was one at all, since the 'vacancy' proved to be yet another false alarm – has not survived, but a few months later, it was Louis XIII's own turn to write to Richelieu on hearing that the archbishop of Paris was dead. If Paris was now vacant, the king wrote tantalisingly, 'you know who is to have it'.[127] But in fact Paris was not vacant either and, unfortunately for historians, neither Louis XIII nor Richelieu would ever have the opportunity of revealing the name of their choice as the next archbishop of Paris.[128] Hypothetical though both of these choices were, they do at least show clearly that by 1628 consultations and exchanges between king and minister over episcopal patronage were routinely taking place, and that in at least some cases, provisional decisions were being made in advance of actual vacancies. In this sphere at least, something like an *entente cordiale* between king and minister was already beginning to take shape, one which, as we shall see, would mature further in the following decade or so.

VII

Confirmation that the overall quality of episcopal nominations had been improving during these years came from a possibly surprising source – the

125 For examples of this, see Grillon, *Papiers de Richelieu*, iii. 419–20, Marie de' Medici to Richelieu, 8 Aug 1628; *ibid*, 538, Gaston to Richelieu, 21 Oct 1628.
126 *Ibid*, 66, *précis* of letter of 13 Feb. He had been informed, wrongly as it transpired, that the bishop of Condom was dead. Montaigne had formerly been president of the *présidial* court at Saintes.
127 *Ibid*, 507, letter of 27 Sept 1628: 'vous sçavez bien pour qui c'est'.
128 It can hardly have been a member of the Gondi family, since the future Cardinal de Retz was only sixteen at the time.

papacy itself. For decades, Rome had worried mainly about abuses, whether they took the form of 'confidences et simonies' or the proliferation of coadjutorships. The instructions given in early 1621 to the new nuncio, Ottavio Corsini, fully reflected Rome's traditional anxieties over the granting of bishoprics in France, anxieties which had not been laid to rest by the pattern of nominations during the 1610s.[129] Yet three years later, in 1624, Roman attitudes had begun to shift, if we are to judge by the terms of the instructions given to Corsini's successor, Bernadino Spada. It was admitted that the granting of benefices to lay persons was still a scandal, but the king was steadily working to remedy it. However, there was no suggestion that bishoprics were affected by these abuses, which mainly involved abbeys and priories held *in commendam*, and France's bishops were even complimented for their unusual talent in preaching. In 1627, the incoming nuncio, Guidi di Bagno, was instructed to pay close attention to episcopal nominations, but not in the same way that his predecessors had. The focus had again shifted: with recent Gallican alarms (occasioned by the Santarelli dispute of 1626) uppermost in its mind, the curia was now concerned with ensuring that the doctrine of incoming bishops was as sound as their behaviour was exemplary; Spada's achievement in helping to prevent Gallicans from being nominated bishops was expressly cited as the example Bagno should follow.[130] It is unnecessary to argue from this change of language and focus that some kind of revolution in episcopal patronage had occurred during the early to mid-1620s. Rome's changing perception was based in part on the knowledge of the growing seriousness with which episcopal patronage was being handled in France, but it probably also had something to do with the change of pontificate in 1623, and the election of the former nuncio to France, Maffeo Barberini, as Urban VIII. His information and knowledge of the French church meant that he could bypass the stereotypes which commonly found their way into curial attitudes to particular churches, and thus redirect Rome's approach to episcopal nominations.

But general instructions to nuncios may only be a partial guide to Roman attitudes at this time. As we saw in an earlier chapter, what is equally illuminating, though largely unremarked upon, is the papacy's demands on incoming bishops from roughly the second half of the 1620s onwards that they devote specific sums per annum from their revenues, over and above what they were obliged to spend by existing law, on rebuilding cathedrals and episcopal residences or on refurnishing cathedrals where that was needed but had not been done. Rome also demanded that they found seminaries, *monts-de-piétés*, and an office of penitentiary in their diocesan administrations. Some of these demands were also included in the general instructions to incoming nuncios but they were increasingly imposed on individual bishops when

---

129 ASV, N Fr 57, fos 14–16, instructions dated 4 Apr 1621.
130 *Recueil des instructions générales aux nonces ordinaires de France de 1624 à 1634*, ed A Leman (Lille 1920), 24–5 (Spada), 97 (Bagno).

receiving their provisions – in other words, the papacy was not relying solely upon the activity of nuncios, but was trying to bind bishops in conscience at the outset of their careers to carry through the particular requirements it was placing upon them.[131]

In the short term, the papacy may have had no more success in these than in its other demands but, taken as a whole, this change in Rome's approach presupposes an episcopate which was, at the very least, no longer regarded in the same way as it had been in the previous generation or more. It is hardly a coincidence that the instructions given to Giorgio Bolognetti and Ranuccio Scotti, appointed nuncios to France in 1634 and 1639 respectively, were for the first time in generations entirely silent about the choice of bishops.[132] Moreover, when Scotti came to draft the *relazione finale* of his turbulent nunciature in early 1641, he mentioned episcopal nominations only in connection with the problems he had encountered over the conduct of the enquiries *de vita et moribus* into the royal nominees, and these problems were jurisdictional rather than substantive in nature.[133]

---

131 The chronology and the range of these demands can be followed in *Hierarchia Catholica*, iv, whose entries for incoming French bishops are in turn based on the consistorial archives in ASV.
132 *Recueil des instructions générales*, 169–203 (Bolognetti); *ANG*, v (*Correspondance du nonce en France, Ranuccio Scotti, 1639–1641*, ed Pierre Blet) (Rome 1965), 91–9.
133 *ANG*, v. 584.

CHAPTER 12

A Turning Point?

IT WAS SUGGESTED in the previous chapter that the arrival of Richelieu in high office in the mid-1620s did not of itself suffice to effect a clear transformation, let alone an immediate one, either in the character of the episcopate or in the mechanisms by which bishops were chosen. The Cardinal's occasional declarations of intent directed towards royal confessors and others do not warrant the sweeping conclusions which have often been drawn by historians of his second ministry. In reality, his contribution to episcopal patronage has to be placed in a wider continuum, and not seen merely in terms of personal preferences about the kind of men he wished to see become bishops. The progressive strengthening of his political position entered a new phase in the aftermath of the Day of the Dupes, and gave him and his ministry the kind of political leeway without which no amount of good intentions would have yielded results.

It is equally essential to bear in mind that the activities of the *dévots* who were concerned with the reform of the episcopate, beginning with the process of bishops' selection, pre-dated Richelieu's ministerial accession, and that they continued to enjoy independent freedom of action during his early years in office. The political crisis of 1630 which saw the defeat of the challenge to Richelieu by Marie de' Medici and her *dévot* supporters, whose political influence was consequently eliminated, has too readily been seen as a complete defeat for the *dévots*. This is a mistaken notion, because it takes too seriously the notion of a unified party gathered around the queen mother in opposition to the chief minister. Had there been a party of that kind, Richelieu and the policies with which he was associated by 1630 would have faced a much more serious and prolonged challenge than they did. In fact, Richelieu's dispute with the *dévots* took place within rather narrowly defined boundaries – foreign policy and internal reforms – and was not a generalised conflict, as is clear from the large number of them who rallied to him during and after the *grand orage* of 1630. What they, and a younger generation of *dévots*, were to discover was that both king and chief minister supported a wide range of religious and moral objectives that coincided with theirs. The new *Compagnie du Saint-*

Sacrement, founded after some false starts only months before the Day of the Dupes, acted for over a generation as a powerful focus for such aspirations, and there is no doubt that Louis and Richelieu were amply informed of its activities, through the royal confessor and other sources. Among the *dévots'* primary objectives was the reform of the clergy, and though this has usually been seen in terms of the lower clergy, there is no question about the keenness of their concern to see the exclusion from the episcopate of individuals they considered unworthy of office. The extent to which Richelieu drew upon them for both episcopal candidates and advice on nominations will appear later in this chapter. Almost immediately after the death of Richelieu and Louis XIII, a regency government effectively directed by a foreign cardinal consented to the establishment of a specially devised *conseil de conscience*, whose primary task it was to advise on the nomination of bishops. This, clearly, was an attempt to institutionalise the aspirations of the *dévots* and to ensure that the gains made during the previous reign could be preserved in the new political circumstances of Anne of Austria's regency.

I

Before attempting to discuss the record of the Richelieu years from the later 1620s to the end of Louis XIII's reign, a rapid survey of the essential facts of episcopal patronage will provide a framework by which to judge the wider significance of these years for the episcopate. After a relatively high number of nominations – seventeen in all – between 1628 and 1630 inclusively, vacant bishoprics became far less common. Between 1631 and the king's death in May 1643, a total of forty-two new bishops, who included a small number of coadjutors, joined their colleagues on the bench. This modest figure compares with 154 for the reign of Louis XIII as a whole, seventy-five for the period of Richelieu's term in office after 1624 and eighty-nine for Mazarin's ministry, of which twenty-five were made before the onset of the Fronde. Apart from suggesting in crude quantitative terms that the Richelieu ministry may not have had exceptional opportunities to reshape the episcopate, these figures may not seem especially revealing. Their significance becomes much clearer when they are translated into annual averages for nominations. For the period from 1610 to 1661 as a whole, there was an average of 4.75 nominations a year, a figure which is roughly similar to those for the reign of Louis XIII (4.6) and Mazarin's ministry (4.9). But as soon as we subdivide these wider time-spans, interesting variations begin to emerge. In particular, the average falls to barely more than four nominations (4.05) per year for Richelieu's ministry as a whole. But it is for the years from 1631 to the death of Louis XIII that we can really see the delayed effect of the nomination of a large number of young coadjutor-bishops during the 1610s; fewer dioceses fell vacant through the death or retirement of ageing bishops, especially from the early 1630s onwards, just at the time that the Richelieu régime was becoming more dominant. As a consequence, the average fell to 3.5 nominations per year for the period 1631 to 1643, the lowest for the entire period covered in this book. Indeed, the openings available to Louis XIII and Richelieu would have been fewer still were it not for the deposition of a number of bishops implicated in rebellion during the 1630s. By comparison, Mazarin was more fortunate throughout the duration of his ministry as a whole, and especially during the first five years, when no fewer than twenty-five new bishops were nominated. Moreover, episcopal nominations were not evenly spaced out, with fat years and lean years alternating according to the vagaries of mortality, depositions, resignations, and to other factors. The bulk of them were clearly concentrated in the years 1631, 1635–7 and 1640. In between we find some particularly lean years, with 1632, 1638 and 1641 witnessing only two, and 1642 only one nomination. Needless to say, the patience of seekers after episcopal office was severely tested as a consequence of declining opportunities. No wonder, therefore, that Peiresc could write in 1636 to a Roman correspondent in search of a bishopric that 'one really does need a lot of good fortune to get hold of one of these prelacies'.[1]

But, as we have seen before, changes in the episcopate were not just a matter of injecting new blood into an ageing body. The movements of reigning bishops, especially where they involve demonstrable promotion, are no less significant a part of the history of the episcopate. For several reasons, the seven episcopal transfers occurring during the period from 1631 to 1643 are of particular interest.

Three of these transfers were directly connected to some of the most unusual and controversial of all episcopal nominations of the *ancien régime*. They occurred during the 1630s, with the deposition of bishops compromised by flight abroad with Marie de' Medici or by implication in the 1632 revolt in Languedoc; a few years later, the last Guise archbishop of Reims was also deposed for similar reasons. The numbers involved may have been small, but the consequences were not.

René de Rieux, bishop of Saint-Pol-de-Léon in northern Brittany, was the first of these offenders. From an ancient Breton noble family particularly close to Marie de' Medici, he was accused of lending his carriage to her for her escape to Flanders in 1631 and then of compounding this 'crime' by paying her an unauthorised visit in exile. But although his other benefices were confiscated in 1631,[2] no action against his tenure of Saint-Pol-de-Léon was taken until 1634, and he was only finally deposed in May

---

[1] *Lettres de Peiresc*, ed Philippe Tamizey de Larroque, 8 vols (Paris 1888–98), iv. 162, to Jean-Jacques Bouchard, 1 Aug 1636.
[2] *Les Papiers de Richelieu (Politique intérieure: Correspondance et papiers d'état)*, ed Pierre Grillon, 6 vols (Paris 1975 – in progress), vi. 594, Louis Testu, *chevalier du guet*, to Richelieu, 19 Sept 1631.

1635.³ Meanwhile, four bishops, all closely connected to Montmorency, the provincial governor of Languedoc, had been implicated in the revolt there in 1632. The political embarrassment caused by their activities must have been considerable. Neither the participation of bishops in the wars of religion, nor the rebellion and flight into exile of the Cardinal de Retz after the Fronde, gave rise to the kind of response which was to follow. Whether the crown would have proceeded unilaterally against the bishops, as it had during earlier centuries, is a moot point, but it was probably thanks to Richelieu that no such 'secular' action occurred. The price extracted, however, was a papally appointed commission of four French bishops entrusted with full powers to try and judge their offending colleagues. The desired outcome was guaranteed by the nature of the commission's membership – Barrault of Arles, Séguier of Auxerre, Victor Bouthillier, and Noailles of Saint-Flour were all either allies of Richelieu or personally close to him.⁴ But the process took time as Rome was extremely reluctant to endorse any trial of bishops, and when judgement day arrived, retribution was tempered by a measure of leniency. Bishop Toiras of Nîmes escaped a trial because his brother, the extremely able Marshal Toiras, was still in sufficient favour; but that was not enough to save him completely, and he was obliged to resign his see, after which he quietly returned to his pre-episcopal status as a canon of Montpellier cathedral.⁵ Alphonse Delbène of Albi was the only Languedoc bishop to be formally deposed because of his complicity in the revolt; indeed, some believed that it was he who had pushed Montmorency into rebelling in the first place. Whatever hope there might have been of leniency towards him was probably dashed by his decision to leave France for exile in Italy. His diocese, one of France's richest, was given to the lordly Gaspard de Daillon du Lude, who had been bishop of Agen since 1631 and a cousin of Languedoc's new governor Schomberg. Bishop Fay-Peyraud of Uzès, a cousin of Montmorency, was probably only spared the dishonour of a similar fate by his death in 1633. Another recently-appointed bishop, Nicolas Grillié of Bazas, was promptly moved into Uzès as his successor. Like Fay-Peyraud, Pierre de Fleyres, bishop of Saint-Pons, died in Paris during his trial, but his coadjutor-nephew was not troubled by the commission, and went on to govern the diocese for nearly twenty years. Finally, Bishop Plantavit of Lodève, also closely identified with Montmorency, was brought to trial, but the charges were not quite strong enough to convict him of *lèse-majesté*. As the presiding judge, Barrault

3   Alain de Solminihac, *Lettres et documents*, ed Eugène Sol (Cahors 1930), 126, Archbishop Barrault of Arles to Alain de Solminihac, 17 July 1634. At that juncture, Barrault thought they would have finished with Rieux by late October, but the final sentence was not given until late May 1635!
4   Achille de Harlay, bishop of Saint-Malo, was originally designated one of the judges, but when he declined the responsibility, he was replaced by Séguier.
5   Robert Sauzet, *Contre-réforme et réforme catholique en bas-Languedoc. Le Diocèse de Nîmes au xviie siècle* (Louvain-Paris 1979), 213–14.

ambiguously reported to a close episcopal confidant, 'we sent him back to his diocese for him to perform his duties there. We acquitted him on the basis of a royal declaration, and we concluded that he had acted in accordance with the declaration in Languedoc.'[6]

Despite the obvious concern to observe legal formalities, the depositions of Rieux and Delbène proved to be hotly contested. It took two years to find someone willing to accept Rieux's see of Saint-Pol. The ambitious Robert Cupif did so in 1637, but he would have ample time to rue his recklessness in later years. Rieux himself never accepted his deposition and, after sustained protests, he triumphantly witnessed its reversal during the Assembly of Clergy of 1645, where other bishops who had fallen foul of Richelieu were also publicly rehabilitated. But Rieux was the only one actually to regain possession of his diocese.[7] Delbène and his supporters also worked strenuously for his rehabilitation during the 1640s, but with less success: although personally vindicated, he failed to recover Albi.[8] These depositions and the clamour of their victims for rehabilitation during the regency added a sour note to relations between the Mazarin régime and the French clergy, especially during the General Assemblies of 1645 and 1650.

The 'deposition' of Henri de Guise, archbishop of Reims, was far more *sui generis*, and to that extent consistent with Guise's entire ecclesiastical career. His relations with Louis XIII and especially with Richelieu were as difficult as might be expected from a prominently placed member of the younger generation of this marked family.[9] Deposition when it came was largely automatic. Not only did he join the duc de Bouillon at Sedan in revolt in 1639–40 but, after the deaths of his elder brother and father, he became duc de Guise; for a man who was neither ordained nor consecrated, a secular career was now unavoidable.[10] It will come as no surprise that little was left to chance about his succession: despite Guise's attempts to resign his benefices to individuals of his own choosing, Léonor d'Etampes of Chartres, a faithful

---

6 Solminihac, *Lettres et documents*, 126, Barrault to Solminihac of Cahors, 17 July 1634: 'nous l'avons renvoyé dans son diocèse pour y faire les fonctions de sa charge et (nous) l'avons deschargé purement, en conséquence d'une declaration du Roy, au désir de laquelle nous avons trouvé qu'il avoit satisfait dans le Languedoc.'
7 See P Peyron, 'L'Evêché de Léon de 1613 à 1651', *Bulletin d'Histoire et d'Archéologie du Diocèse de Quimper* 15 (1915), 266–7, 294–304, 334–6, 356. There is also a concise account of the conflict in Pierre Blet, *Le Clergé de France et la monarchie. Etude sur les assemblées du clergé de 1615 à 1666*, 2 vols (Rome 1959), ii. 20–3.
8 Blet, *Clergé de France et la monarchie*, ii. 56–8.
9 BAV, Barb lat 8021, fos 76–7, duchess of Guise to Cardinal Barberini, 26 Feb 1639, pleading for a new dispensation for her son to take taking clerical orders as Louis XIII and Richelieu had commanded him to do. The duchess feared her wayward son would act rashly if not given time to think fully about such a serious step, not least because he seemed far more anxious to marry the duke of Mantua's daughter with whom he was passionately in love. She appealed to papal goodwill by saying, 'c'est une oeuvre de charité d'avoir compassion des affligés'!
10 The papal records use the term 'privatio' to describe the termination of Guise's tenure: Eubel, *Hierarchia Catholica*, iv. 295, art 'Rhemensis'.

client of Richelieu, had been lined up to succeed him at Reims long before Guise was formally condemned for treason in September 1641.[11]

In the cases of Albi, Uzès and Reims, the transfer of trustworthy ruling bishops was an obvious way of regaining control of dioceses which might otherwise remain difficult to control. If this solution was not adopted in the case of Saint-Pol-de-Léon, it was doubtless because no reigning bishop was willing to take such a risk immediately after Rieux's deposition. The remaining episcopal transfers of these years – four in all – were more conventional in nature, and all involved bishops who were closely connected to the Richelieu ministry generally, or indeed to the cardinal personally.

The great majority of the episcopal nominations made during these years were occasioned by the death of the reigning bishop creating a vacancy. In such cases, the royal decision was, in theory at least, relatively straightforward. Most of the coadjutors appointed in the 1610s had by now succeeded as ruling bishops, and would not be replaced by a new generation of bishops until the 1640s or 1650s. A limited number of coadjutorships were arranged during the 1630s, but in a context which was rather different from that of either the 1610s or indeed the early years of the regency of Anne of Austria, when altered political conditions enabled several aristocratic families to obtain concessions reminiscent of the 1610s. The number of vacancies arising from resignations by incumbent bishops, a move usually preceded by complex negotiations over the succession, also fell sharply after 1630. Apart from the hapless bishop of Nîmes, forced to resign in 1633, only one other bishop, Richelieu's own successor at Luçon, Emery de Bragelongne, retired outright. He was persuaded to facilitate the cardinal's attempts to become abbot-general of the Cistercian order by offering the bishopric to Pierre Nivelle, abbot of Cîteaux since 1625. Thus, although the opportunities for nominating bishops were admittedly fewer in the last decade or so of Louis XIII's reign than they had been previously, it can be suggested that a far higher proportion of the opportunities which did arise were more 'open'.

It may be appropriate, especially as a preface to developments to be considered later in this chapter, to conclude this brief *tour d'horizon* of nominations by noting that, as in the past, an unknown number of episcopal nominees resigned or returned their nominations either voluntarily or as a result of difficulties encountered in obtaining the necessary papal provisions.[12] In contrast to the reign of Henri IV, when it was problems within individual dioceses – lay control of temporalities, a hostile Huguenot presence, the

---

11 Henri Arnauld's frequent accounts of Guise affairs between 1639 and 1641 are in BN, MS Fr 15610, pp 59, 68, 72–3, 78–9, 125, 198–9, 221, 292–3, 305, 398–9, 458, 645, 836, 898–9; MS Fr 15611, fos 22, 75, 326.
12 In the case of the see of Saint-Pol-de-Léon in Brittany, whose bishop had, as we have seen, recently been deposed, several candidates were nominated but then declined to proceed further, before a sufficiently determined candidate was eventually found. See Peyron, 'L'Evêché de Léon de 1613 à 1651', 266–7.

condition of cathedrals or episcopal residences, and so on – which were instrumental in deterring certain candidates from pressing their claims to the mitre, some at least of those who refused episcopal status in the age of Richelieu and Mazarin were probably moved by reasons of a quite different order. Given the changing religious climate of these years, defections and failures of this kind are of more than passing interest. Those who declined episcopal honours did so after a good deal of hesitation and soul-searching – though, here, the historian has to be wary of hagiographical motifs, such as the 'sense of personal unworthiness', which dominate contemporary accounts.

Whether the abbé de Saint-Cyran was ever formally offered the see of Bayonne (his native diocese) by Richelieu in order to entrap or stifle him in high office, has never been clearly established, but he was widely believed to have received and refused such an offer. That in turn has given rise to much discussion of an alleged aversion on the part of extreme *dévots* for high office, in the church as much as in the state.[13] It was, apparently, only after Bérulle's successor as superior-general of the Oratory, Charles de Condren, had died, that it was learned that he had refused the see of Reims, presumably in 1640 when Henri de Guise was in revolt against the crown. Henri Arnauld, the future bishop of Angers, commented on this item of news without any cynical intent: 'this will make a good subject for the funeral oration which the Bishop of Saint-Brieuc will deliver'.[14] There is little doubt, too, that Jean-Jacques Olier, the *curé* of Saint-Sulpice and founder of the famous seminary, could himself have become a bishop had he really wished to, as he was offered Châlons-sur-Marne in 1640 and Comminges in 1644.[15] Omer Talon's brother, Charles-François, *curé* of Saint-Gervais in Paris, was another who should have had no difficulty in donning the mitre, given his brother's reputation and his own high personal standing as one of the *agents-généraux* of the French clergy after 1635. Indeed, in 1635 he was given the Breton see of Saint-Pol-de-Léon, after the deposition of René de Rieux.[16] But, after initially accepting the nomination, Talon realised that this gift could be a poisoned chalice and, even as Rome was dragging its feet about confirming him, he returned his *brevet* and appears not to have sought another diocese

---

13 Jean Orcibal, *Jean Duvergier de Hauranne, abbé de Saint-Cyran et son temps* (Louvain 1947), 515–16. From the evidence here, it seems that Cardinal La Valette was used as an intermediary to sound out Saint-Cyran, but that he made no actual offer to him of Bayonne. On this aversion, which also affected royal office-holding, see the arguments of Lucien Goldman, *The Hidden God* (London 1964).

14 BN, MS Fr 15611, fo 6v, Arnauld to président Barillon, 9 Jan 1641: 'voilà un bel endroit de son oraison funèbre que Monsieur de Saint-Brieuc fera.' Monsieur de Saint-Brieuc was Etienne Villazel, a highly regarded preaching bishop.

15 Gilbert Cherest, *L'Evêque de la paix. Félix Vialart de Herse, évêque et comte de Châlons-sur-Marne, pair de France* (Châlons-sur-Marne 1976), 6, 11–12 (Châlons); AAE, France 849, fo 116, Gaudin to Servien, 12 Mar 1644 (Comminges)

16 BN, MS Fr 23200, fos 1–2, Charles Talon to Michel Le Masle, Richelieu's secretary, 2 Sept 1635

thereafter.[17] Alain de Solminihac declined the see of Lavaur in April 1636, but accepted that of Cahors (which had just been turned down by Jacques Camus, bishop of Séez!) two months later, after Richelieu had written to say that the king rejected his reasons for refusing the honour and, more to the point, had satisfactorily assured Solminihac that the episcopate would not prevent him from continuing his efforts to reform the canons-regular in the south-west.[18] Finally, edifying anecdotes have long been current about the behaviour of newly nominated bishops, like Etienne Pavillon or Jean-Baptiste Gault, who apparently panicked on being chosen and had to be ordered by their directors of conscience to accept God's will.[19] As far as can be established, reservations about one's personal fitness for the episcopate rather than – as alleged for Saint-Cyran - about episcopal office itself, first became a notable feature of French religious experience during the rise of *dévot* influence. In cases like those of Condren, Olier and even Solminihac, it would also seem that the obligations and objectives they had previously set themselves remained paramount, and doubts about how, if at all, they could still be pursued if they became bishops, persuaded them to decline episcopal honours. Refusals and hesitations of this kind, to the extent that they have not been exaggerated for hagiographical purposes, were relatively new, and would be difficult to find in the age of Henri III or Henri IV; they are also expressive of some of the most original features of the Catholic reform as it developed under Louis XIV. With a figure like Richelieu playing a central role in the distribution of episcopal patronage, such attitudes were likely to inform as well as to complicate the search for new bishops.

II

The gradual expansion of Richelieu's episcopal patronage, and of the king's readiness to seek his advice, already well in evidence by the late 1620s, continued after the political crisis of 1630. Both aspects can be examined from a number of angles, none of which may be conclusive on its own, but together they provide converging evidence of the extent of his effectiveness. Continuity and expansion are clearly visible in the fate of the queen mother's ecclesiastical patronage, with which Richelieu had been involved for so long. After her flight abroad in July 1631, her presentation rights in Brittany and

---

17 Peyron, 'L'Evêché de Léon de 1613 à 1651', 266.
18 Solminihac, *Lettres et documents*, 133–8, for the extensive correspondence concerning this affair. See Eugène Sol, *Le Vénérable Alain de Solminihac, abbé de Chancelade et évêque de Cahors* (Cahors 1928), 80, quoting Richelieu's letter of 27 Apr informing Solminihac of the king's response, though of course this response was at least partly inspired by Richelieu himself.
19 Pavillon's director of conscience was none other than Condren, who ordered him to accept the see of Alet.

the Auvergne obviously lapsed. In the event, neither Clermont nor Saint-Flour fell vacant until well into Louis XIV's minority, but Brittany was a different matter, with all but one diocese being vacated through death between 1629 and 1642. After Louis XIII's death, Anne of Austria exercised jointure rights in Brittany and the Auvergne similar to those of Marie de' Medici, but there is no evidence of how – or indeed whether – she was entitled to present to vacant dioceses there.[20] In any event, a major blow had already been struck against the tradition of formally alienating episcopal patronage to members of the royal family when, in 1626, Gaston d'Orléans received his apanage of Chartres, Blois and Orléans on his first marriage. After extensive scrutiny of previous arrangements, he was permitted to appoint to all offices and benefices within his apanage, with the significant exception of its bishoprics, which were explicitly excluded from the settlement.[21] This decision, taken before Gaston's political leanings had become apparent, shows that considerations of how episcopal patronage should properly be handled had been taken into account. This, of course, did not prevent Gaston from insisting later that he had at least an interest in who was appointed to the two dioceses in question, nor from pushing for bishops who were at least *personae gratae* to him. But Gaston's political adventures led him regularly into exile and disgrace, which made it all the easier to ignore his arguments.

From the 1630s onwards, therefore, the crown was far less restricted than in the past by formal concessions of patronage rights. Richelieu, who had previously benefited from such concessions, now made the most of their removal. Moreover, he became governor of Brittany in 1631, and this ensured that he inherited Marie's influence in filling its bishoprics. Direct evidence of his exercise of episcopal patronage in Brittany is surprisingly scant, despite his power and the many sources of advice he had there. Achille de Harlay, as befitted a bishop who owed his elevation to Saint-Malo in 1631 to the cardinal, was one of the most important channels of advice and information about Bretons in search of a mitre. The record, in any case, speaks for itself. It began, as we saw, with the negotiation in late 1630 of Victor Bouthillier's strategically important move from the bishopric of Boulogne to the coadjutorship of Tours – an unusual, but not unique, move for a reigning bishop to make. Although not in Brittany itself, Tours was the metropolitan see for all the Breton dioceses, and persuading both Louis XIII and Bertrand Deschaux, the reigning archbishop and an old mentor of Richelieu, to agree to this particular succession arrangement was a considerable success for the

---

20   Ruth Kleinman, *Anne of Austria, Queen of France* (Columbus, Ohio, 1985), 174, provides details of revenue-yielding jointure, but says nothing of patronage rights.
21   Bibliothèque de l'Arsénal, MS 4207, fos 1–7, terms of Gaston's apanage, July 1626, with additions (fo 8), 31 July 1626; BN, MS Fr 3668, fo 128, memorandum on terms of apanage, filed with Philippe de Béthune's papers for 1626.

cardinal.²² During the next decade, the key Breton bishoprics – Saint-Malo, Nantes, Rennes and Saint-Brieuc – all went to men who were unmistakably clients of Richelieu. Lesser and more remote dioceses, like Tréguier or Quimper, went to men known to him at least by repute, thanks to members of his entourage, and who thus had his full approval and support.

Among the Breton bishops in office around 1630, only René de Rieux caused problems by siding with the queen mother during the political crisis of 1630–1. The matter of his succession provides some evidence of Richelieu's ecclesiastical patronage at work. As we saw, Omer Talon's brother was initially nominated to succeed him, but he quit – in the face, it seems, of Rome's reluctance to grant his provisions. Richelieu then appears to have had some difficulty finding a replacement. He relied upon his entourage to find a candidate willing to take on an evidently recalcitrant diocese and a well-regarded old noble family; a number of Breton ecclesiastics, one of whom would become bishop of Quimper a few years later, were put forward. One of these potential bishops apparently said he would prefer to die on learning that he was being offered Saint-Pol!²³ The eventual bishop, Robert Cupif, was a Parisian of Angevin origin, but above all he was cousin to François Fouquet, one of the cardinal's closest advisers with family connections in Brittany; Cupif was also reported upon favourably by Bishop Harlay.²⁴ Cupif was typical of Richelieu's Breton bishops in one important respect: all but one of them, the bishop of Quimper, were outsiders, even in dioceses which were thought to need Breton-speaking bishops.

However, it would be a mistake to imagine that either before or after 1630 Richelieu or the *dévots* were confined to Marie de' Medici's former spheres of influence when it came to bishoprics. There is no obvious geographical limitation to the episcopal appointments of Richelieu clients during the 1630s. These embraced dioceses as far apart as Arles, Marseille and Grasse in Provence; Bazas, Dax and Bayonne in Guyenne and Gascony; Auxerre, Chartres, and Lisieux in northern France, in addition to those of Brittany. In this context, and in view of what we know of Languedoc's history of episcopal patronage, the cardinal's handling of episcopal successions there should prove illuminating. The 1632 revolt was so ill-considered that it was poorly supported, and even some close relatives and friends of Montmorency, both lay and clerical, who might have been expected to join him, refrained from doing

---

22   See Michel de Marillac's view of Tours, expressed when the archbishop was rumoured to be dying in 1628: 'C'est une pièce digne d'un grand et sage prélat, ayant ces trois grandes provinces et toutte la Bretagne': Grillon, *Papiers de Richelieu*, iii. 483, letter to Richelieu [ca 12 Sept 1628].

23   AAE, France 1505, fo 386, Harlay to Richelieu, 1 Feb 1637. The future bishop of Quimper was René du Louet, then a senior member of the chapter of Saint-Pol, and who, according to Harlay, was 'fort mal avec Monsieur l'ancien évesque', whom he had served in senior positions.

24   AAE, France 1504, fo 166, Harlay to Richelieu, 24 July 1637; *ibid*, fo 177, same to same, 9 Mar 1637.

so: the bishop of Montmorency's quasi-patrimonial see of Agde did not participate and escaped all blame. Traditional Montmorency or Marie de' Medici clients, like the Bonsi bishops of Béziers, did likewise. Joyeuse's successors in Narbonne and Toulouse, both outsiders of recent elevation, also remained aloof. Claude de Rebé of Narbonne was, as we saw, originally a Guise client who might well have become personally disaffected by his erstwhile patrons' disgrace and exile in 1631, but their periodic demands for payment of a hefty pension off Narbonne, had already driven Rebé to seek the protection of Richelieu and the royal council.[25] The presence of a royal or court-oriented episcopal clientèle makes it easier to understand why only four of the province's twenty-two bishops were implicated in the revolt.[26]

The débâcle, however, opened up the province to further external penetration, and its new governor, Schomberg, took a close interest in subsequent years in episcopal patronage; he began by having the rebel bishop of Albi replaced by his own first cousin, the incumbent bishop of Agen.[27] Only two other dioceses were similarly affected – Nîmes and Uzès – both of which were confided to reliable and energetic outsiders, each of whom was connected to Richelieu for several years via *dévot* networks.[28] For the remainder of Richelieu's ministry, relatively few dioceses fell vacant in Languedoc as elsewhere, but the policy of nominating outsider bishops not beholden to local patronage was strongly sustained; it could be said to have culminated in the transfer, only weeks after Louis XIII's death, of François Fouquet from Bayonne to Agde. Whatever the province's subsequent troubles, the episcopate would not be party to them, and the piecemeal remaking of the Languedoc episcopate was well expressed in its energetic response to the Spanish invasion of 1637, when most of the bishops played no small role in organising military counter-measures.

Despite revolt and its governor Guise's flight into Italian exile in 1631, Provence and its bishops posed fewer difficulties for the Richelieu régime. It may be argued that timing played a part in this initially, since the two key archdioceses there, Aix and Arles, were awarded to dependable outsiders, the Norman Louis Bretel and the long-standing bishop of Bazas, Jaubert de Barrault, in 1630 and 1631 respectively. Later in the decade, sees like Grasse,

25 Grillon, *Papiers de Richelieu*, vi. 608, Rebé to Richelieu, 30 Sept 1631 referring to his difficulties with the Guises. AAE, France 1632, fos 177–9, for a dossier of papers concerning this quarrel, 1616–43.
26 See the general discussion in William Beik, *Absolutism and Society in Seventeenth-Century France* (Cambridge 1984), esp 235–7.
27 Evidence for this under Richelieu has not been found, but it seems reasonable to assume it did not emerge *ex nihilo* under Mazarin, as documented in AAE, France 1634, fos 163–4, 188–9, letters to Mazarin, 22 Sept and 31 Dec 1645 respectively, about the see of Lodève.
28 Sauzet, *Contre-réforme et reforme catholique en Bas-Languedoc*, for a brief study of Anthime-Denis Cohon, the incoming bishop of Nîmes. Nothing substantial has ever been written about the new bishop of Uzès, Nicolas Grillié, a long-standing friend of Bérulle.

Toulon, and Marseille were treated in similar fashion, with all three being given to northerners. Only one native Provençal, Scipion de Villeneuve, bishop of Grasse (1632–6), briefly joined the ranks of the province's episcopate between 1630 and 1643, a statistic which contrasts sharply with the predominance of native Provençaux among the bishops in previous decades.

It would, of course, be wrong to claim that the experience of these three provinces was somehow representative of the French episcopate as a whole after 1630. With their traditions of provincial autonomy, there was every reason to pay special attention to them; more to the point, all were *pays d'états* in which the bishops played a major political and administrative role, especially at a time when the crown was seeking to raise more and more revenue to sustain its escalating financial commitments. But the evidence from these years, including the pre-Fronde regency, shows that in other provinces incoming bishops were just as likely to be outsiders with strong connections to the court, the ministry and *dévot* circles. This seems to be the case particularly in the dioceses of Guyenne, Gascony and the Pyrenean regions which had also tended to be occupied by sons of local noble families. The arrival of a Litolfi at Bazas, a Fouquet in Bayonne, and a Lingendes at Sarlat are the most striking examples of such a pattern.

Another measure of Richelieu's influence can be gauged from an examination of the speed or slowness with which episcopal vacancies were filled. In an age when rumour was rife, news of episcopal vacancies might take some time to confirm, depending on where the diocese was, or whether the court was itself on the move. Allowing for this, it is remarkable how quickly decisions to appoint known Richelieu clients were made, though there are some interesting exceptions. Alphonse de Richelieu's nominations to Aix and to Lyon came within three days and five days respectively after the previous archbishops' deaths.[29] Henri de Sourdis was appointed to Bordeaux on the very day his brother died. In the first of these cases, the presumption must be that the decision to promote Alphonse was made in advance of the vacancy arising.[30] In the second, it emerges that Henri de Sourdis had been proposed months earlier as coadjutor to his brother, so that the decision over the Bordeaux succession had also been taken in advance of the actual vacancy.[31] Most of the other nominations came between a week and a month of a predecessor's death, but with most of them clustering at the shorter end of that spectrum. Admittedly, Abra de Raconis got Lavaur three months after it fell vacant, but this delay seems due to his reluctance to accept it because of

---

29 Grillon, *Papiers de Richelieu*, iii. 427, Louis XIII to Richelieu, 11 Aug 1628: 'l'on me vient de dire que l'archevesque de Lion est mort. Je vous ay voulu escrire ce mot pour vous dire que, en ce cas, je le désire donner à Mr l'archevesque d'Aix, vostre frère.'
30 Charles Miron, his predecessor at Lyon, was ill for some time before his death early Aug 1628.
31 BAV, Barb lat 7941, fo 127, Louis XIII to Cardinal Barberini, 10 Dec 1627, informing him of nomination as coadjutor and seeking papal provisions.

its remoteness. Grasse in Provence was vacant for six weeks before Antoine Godeau was finally nominated, but this was largely because Richelieu had attempted to find a native Provençal for that poorly endowed see. The frequently prolonged vacancies of French bishoprics during the 1630s and early 1640s were not due to royal negligence, not even in cases such as those we have just seen in which royal decisions were not especially rapid; the delays were, in fact, the direct consequence of disputes with the papacy which, for reasons that had nothing to do with candidates' suitability, took several years to ratify numerous royal nominations in 1635, 1637–8 and 1641. Known clients of Richelieu fared no better than other episcopal nominees while these logjams endured.[32]

No less pointed evidence of Richelieu's influence is provided by the fact that of the six bishops transferred or promoted during the last decade of his ministry, five were known clients of his. As we have seen, he had succeeded in demonstrating in the late 1620s that he could achieve this kind of promotion for his clients by securing Lyon for his own brother, Bordeaux for Henri de Sourdis, followed by the coadjutorship of Tours for Victor Bouthillier in 1630. During the remainder of his ministry, he engineered six further episcopal transfers. Two of them were to archbishoprics and, though separated from each other by a decade, they both arose from Richelieu's quarrels with the Guise family who had long been powerful allies of Marie de' Medici. Promoting the bishop of Bazas, Jaubert de Barrault, to the see of Arles in late 1630 was designed to place a well-known client in a key Provençal diocese, given that the archbishop was called upon to play a major part in the Estates of the province; Barrault could be relied upon to keep the duc de Guise, governor of Provence, and his clients under observation. In the event, Guise's self-imposed exile in Italy ensured there would be no such conflict. In 1641, Richelieu made sure that an even closer client, Bishop Etampes of Chartres, broke the Guise grip on Reims when the last Guise archbishop, now duc de Guise, was forced to resign his rights there. In between these dates, Languedoc required close attention after the 1632 revolt, and the task of regaining mastery of two of the dioceses most directly involved in the revolt – Albi and Uzès – was entrusted to reliable men, the existing bishops of Bazas and Agen. The links between Richelieu and the two remaining bishops to be promoted during the 1630s, Philippe Cospeau and Dominique Séguier, are too well known to require further elaboration. Clearly, by this time only bishops closely identified with the cardinal could aspire to promotion.

---

32 See Blet, *Le Clergé de France et la monarchie*, i. part ii, chs 5–7, for the best study. Delays were most obvious in 1635 and again in 1637–8, and were occasioned by disputes about the role of Antonio Barberini as protector of France, which included presenting French bishops in consistory, as well as over who should conduct the enquiries *de vita et moribus* in France. See the memorandum on this point for Marshal d'Estrées, French ambassador to Rome in AAE, CP Rome 63, fos 137r–9v, 20 Apr 1638.

We can also form some idea of the *modus operandi* of the Richelieu régime where bishoprics were concerned by observing other, not dissimilar permutations of dioceses. One instance of episcopal musical-chairs involving well-scattered dioceses – Boulogne, Bayonne and neighbouring Aire-sur-l'Adour – provides a particularly telling illustration of this. As we saw, Sébastien Bouthillier, the first of all Richelieu's friends to become a bishop, got the see of Aire in 1621 when Philippe Cospeau vacated it to move to Nantes, but Bouthillier died suddenly in January 1625. Soon afterwards, his brother Victor, was nominated to succeed him at Aire, but he evidently did not relish moving to such a remote diocese, and so resigned his title to Gilles Boutault, whose exact connection to the Richelieu-Bouthillier circle at that point remains obscure. A year later, however, in 1626, Victor Bouthillier became bishop of Boulogne which he in turn resigned in 1632 to Jean d'Olce after becoming coadjutor-archbishop of Tours. The key to this particular transaction lies in the identity of the *other* parties: Bertrand Deschaux of Tours was a former bishop of Bayonne, and Jean d'Olce, a native of that diocese, was also his nephew. Deschaux accepted Bouthillier as his coadjutor at Tours in return for transmitting Boulogne to Dolce. Meanwhile, in 1629, in an unrelated development, Richelieu secured the vacant see of Bayonne, which had remained without a proper incumbent since 1626, for Raymond de Montaigne. When Montaigne himself died in 1637, Bayonne went to the eldest son of the cardinal's councillor, François Fouquet. Six years later, only months after Richelieu's death, Fouquet moved from Bayonne to Agde. This time, Bayonne did not long remain vacant, and it fell to Bishop d'Olce of Boulogne, who was only too pleased to return from Boulogne to his native Bayonne, which he then governed for almost forty years. All along the way, these carefully managed exchanges were facilitated by the survival of the practice, much disliked by certain reformers, of resigning benefices in favour of named individuals. Resignations, of course, required formal royal approval before they could begin to take effect, but with the main beneficiaries in these instances being close allies of Richelieu, the task of obtaining such approval was not a daunting one.

In these examples of coordinated episcopal movements, which may appear peculiar because they are so extended in both time and space, the impression is of a clientèle's growing confidence in its power to achieve its ambitions; it is also one in which certain bishoprics appear to become the virtual *chasses gardées* of a limited number of ministerial families. It is, however, more than just an impression, as is clear from the record of episcopal nominations from 1631 to Louis XIII's death. Of the forty-two new bishops made during these years, at least half were of men who were close enough to Richelieu, either through family connections, personal service, or other associations, to be regarded as owing their preferment to his personal influence. A closer look at them will reveal some of the main features of the cardinal's network of *créatures*.

The extended Richelieu family had always been rather fragile, its fund of ecclesiastics distinctly limited. The cardinal's elder brother, Alphonse, was temperamentally more suited to being a Carthusian than an archbishop, though he gamely supported his ministerial brother by accepting Aix and Lyon in quick succession. But his independence and moodiness reduced his further usefulness to Richelieu. More distant relatives, especially on the female side of the family, also benefited from his influence. Daniel de la Mothe-Houdancourt, briefly bishop of Mende (1624–8), was an early example of this, though household service to Marie de' Medici in the early 1620s was just as useful in his advancement; his younger brother, Henri, obtained Rennes in 1640 soon after graduating from the Sorbonne, and ended his career as archbishop of Auch. Gabriel Beauvau of Nantes (1635–67) could also claim a blood relationship to Richelieu, but actual personal service to the cardinal was probably more decisive in his elevation. He was one of a handful of future bishops who were members of Richelieu's personal ecclesiastical household, which was not especially numerous. It was Richelieu's successive *maîtres de chambre*, dignitaries with important administrative functions, who fared best, reflecting the cardinal's respect for those who could govern as well as preach or pray. Beauvau's predecessor in this office, Sylvestre de Marsillac, followed La Mothe-Houdancourt as bishop of Mende 1628, while Beauvau's successor, Pierre de Broc occupied the see of Auxerre vacated in 1637 by Dominique Séguier when he moved to the more convenient see of Meaux. The last Richelieu household member to get a bishopric, in late 1641, was the cardinal's confessor, Jacques Lescot, though his predecessor, Pierre Desclaux, had helped to obtain the see of Dax for his brother in 1638.

The remaining episcopal clients were drawn from the cardinal's wider circle. The most prominent among these were members or relatives of ministerial families, actual or future, who owed their political fortunes to Richelieu – for example, the Bouthillier, the Séguier, and the Fouquet. Mention has already been made of several bishops drawn from these families, but it should not be thought that ministerial influence was confined to those bearing the family name. During his first tenure of ministerial office (1631–6), Abel Servien obtained the see of Gap for his brother-in-law, Artus de Lionne, father of Louis XIV's first foreign secretary.[33] Denis de la Barde, bishop of Saint-Brieuc in 1641, was a nephew of Claude Bouthillier, while Félix and Charles Vialart, bishops of Châlons-sur-Marne and Avranches respectively, were cousins of Chancellor Séguier. The only ministers not to place a relative in the episcopate were Bullion and Sublet des Noyers, though in the case of the latter it was not for want of effort.[34] Episcopal preferment was not confined to ministerial clients of Richelieu. Sons of second-rank, but well-placed royal officials were also favoured. François Malier du Houssay, son of an *intendant des*

33 AAE, CP Rome 81, fo 573, undated letter from Abel Servien to Richelieu, about the difficulties encountered over the coadjutorship.
34 BN, MS Fr 15610, p 168, Arnauld to Barillon, 4 Sept 1639.

finances, became coadjutor of Troyes in 1634, while his elder brother, Claude, after a career as a *maître des requêtes*, ambassador, and *conseiller d'état*, went on to become bishop of Tarbes under Mazarin. The celebrated Etienne Pavillon of Alet was not just a *dévot*, but also the son of a prominent financier, while Jacques Danès de Marly, nominated to Toulon in 1638, was a former *maître des requêtes* and intendant-designate in Languedoc.

Beyond these groups gathered round the ministry and the council, we encounter a necessarily more nebulous circle consisting of the many religious figures whom Richelieu knew personally or who were strongly recommended to him by others – Godeau, the poet and founding member of the Académie Française; the Gault brothers, members of the Oratory and very active in Sourdis's diocese of Bordeaux; well-known preachers like Noël Deslandes or Jean de Lingendes, whose papal provisions Richelieu insisted on paying himself. Richelieu's status as a cardinal, and his continuing interest in ecclesiastical affairs of all kinds, from the teaching of theology in universities to the reform of the religious orders and secular clergy alike, made him into a sort of magnet capable of attracting clerical clients from an extremely wide range of backgrounds and spheres of activity.

This change in the contours of the episcopate was closely connected to another equally significant development – the temporary decline in the presence of the aristocracy and *noblesse d'épée* among the episcopate. The principal losers in the power struggles around 1630 were not so much the *dévots* as the aristocracy. Scarcely one-third of all bishops nominated between the 1630s and early 1640s can be regarded as stemming from the older nobility, and with the exception of Daillon du Lude or Maupas du Tour, none of them was the bearer of an especially distinguished name; all of the others were of middling families of provincial nobility. Moreover, if Léonor d'Etampes de Valençay was elevated to the see of Reims in 1641, it was not because his genealogy was somehow on a par with the status of the archbishopric, but rather because he was a well-known Richelieu factotum: in the event, neither his record nor his new rank would save him from being disgraced by his master in 1642. Of course, their lack of success did not render the aristocracy indifferent to the fate of bishoprics during these years. The fact that he was in provincial exile for his earlier support of Marie de' Medici did not deter Roger de Bellegarde from approaching Richelieu in 1639 to recommend one of his nephews as successor to the ageing bishop of Conserans, since the Bellegarde family had dominated the diocese since Henri III's time.[35] When Orléans was rumoured vacant in April 1641, Condé's son, the comte de Béthune-Charost, and the Ventadour family all interceded with Richelieu for their own candidate.[36] No decision needed to be made, as Orléans proved not

---

35 AAE, France 834, fo 59, Bellegarde to Chavigny, 11 Sept 1639.
36 BN, MS Fr 15611, fos 90, 96, 103, letters from Henri Arnauld to Barillon, 24 Apr, 5 May and 12 May 1641; AAE, France 840, fo 55, Béthune to Richelieu, 26 May 1641.

to be vacant, but the aristocracy, with the Ventadour especially prominent among them, were to begin their episcopal comeback under Mazarin. Their eclipse under Richelieu was short-lived, but the fact that it happened at all may come as a surprise in view of the fact that the cardinal's supposed preference for nobles among the episcopate – their birth naturally endowing them with the habit of authority so necessary in a bishop – has long been accepted on the basis of the extended discussion of the subject in the *Testament politique*. To the extent that this discussion represents Richelieu's thinking on the subject, it seems remarkably ambivalent in retrospect, with each statement hedged around with so many reservations as to blunt its persuasiveness. If these qualifications are taken into account, it will be less surprising to learn that the actual rather than the theoretical exercise of episcopal patronage for much of his time as a minister did not prove advantageous to the established aristocratic families.

III

With so many converging, if often indirect, indices of Richelieu's success in peopling the episcopal bench, the question of his relations with Louis XIII over the exercise of that very personal royal prerogative of nominating bishops needs to be addressed. Understandably, the cardinal's success in obtaining benefices for protegés and clerical acquaintances encouraged, both at the time and subsequently, the tendency to think that Louis XIII simply ratified the cardinal's choices. But it would be a mistake to perpetuate a view which is partly based on throwaway comments of members of Richelieu's entourage itself. We need not take at its face value the statement of Effiat, the *surintendant des finances* who, in passing on information to the cardinal in early 1629 about the reputedly vacant bishopric of Lodève, wrote that he did so 'so that you may dispose of it as you please'.[37] Instead, the practice of consultation and even prior agreement between king and minister already noted for the end of the 1620s was extended and became routine in subsequent years. Indeed, it is precisely because Louis XIII found it so normal to seek the cardinal's opinions over major church appointments, that there is much less direct evidence of exchanges of opinion between them during the 1630s. For much the same reason, Richelieu was under less pressure than ever to consider a formal *conseil de conscience*, and the appointment of his brother as grand almoner of France in 1632 ensured that he would not need to fear competition from another leading ecclesiastic. Clearly Louis XIII, who had consulted the previous grand almoner, Cardinal La Rochefoucauld, as late as 1630, was now willing to allow Richelieu to add to his existing role the one previously filled

---

37 Grillon, *Papiers de Richelieu*, iv. 106–7, letter of 15 Feb 1629: 'affin que vous en disposiès comme il vous plaira'

by La Rochefoucauld of ensuring that episcopal appointments were of an acceptable standard.[38]

But while enjoying considerable liberty to advise and guide the king, Richelieu was careful not to overreach himself, and he appreciated the political dangers that doing so entailed. For example, in August 1630, he replied to Louis XIII that he had no one to recommend for the see of Orléans, but advised him in a general way to take his time before deciding whom to nominate.[39] In the event, Louis did precisely the opposite, and filled the position as fast as possible in order to prevent his brother, Gaston, from staking a claim to it for one of his clients. Gaston did indeed protest during the following months at the lack of respect shown for his interests on this occasion. In August 1630, as the major crisis of his ministry was brewing, Richelieu could certainly not afford to antagonise Gaston, whose interest in the see of Orléans he presumably realised; in the circumstances, leaving the decision to Louis XIII made eminent political sense, while also making it more difficult for Gaston to blame the cardinal for the outcome.[40]

Problems of this kind seem to have been less frequent in the 1630s, with fewer sons of well-placed nobles or clients of the *grands* finding a place among the episcopate. Yet there was no observable change in Richelieu's behaviour towards Louis XIII. Hearing the diocese of Tréguier was vacant in 1635, he wrote to Bouthillier:

> If the king considers père Deslandes – whom he had destined for Périgueux but which is not actually vacant – for Téguier, then I believe he (Deslandes) will perform well there. However, if his Majesty has someone else in mind, I submit to this, knowing full well that His Majesty's prudence is such that he will not make a bad decision.[41]

In recommending candidates for benefices to the king, Richelieu frequently covered himself by letting them understand that he could not vouch for the king, who might already have given his word to someone else. That

---

38 Joseph Bergin, *Cardinal de La Rochefoucauld. Leadership and Reform in the French Church* (New Haven and London 1987), 135.
39 Grillon, *Papiers de Richelieu*, v. 490–1, Richelieu to Bouthillier, 8 Aug 1630.
40 *Ibid*, v. 578–9, Claude de Bullion to Richelieu, 30 Sept 1630; *ibid*, 622–3, Louis XIII to Richelieu, 28 Oct 1630; *ibid*, 628–9, Suffren to Richelieu, 1 Nov 1630. As we have seen, Gaston did not enjoy presentation rights to dioceses within his apanage of Orléans, Chartres, and Blois, but felt strongly that he had a rightful interest in the choice of bishops there. In 1641, when Lescot, Richelieu's confessor was appointed to Chartres, Gaston again tried to prevent him from accepting it: see Pierre Blet, 'Vincent de Paul et l'épiscopat français', in *Vincent de Paul. Actes du colloque international d'études vincentiennes* (Rome, 1983), 88–9.
41 *Lettres, instructions diplomatiques et papiers d'état de Richelieu*, ed D L M Avenel, 8 vols (Paris 1853–76), v. 246, letter of 20 Sept 1635: 'Sy le roy considère le père Deslandes, qu'il avoit destiné pour Périgueux, qui n'est pas vacant, pour Tréguier, je croy qu'il s'en acquittera bien. Sy cependant Sa Majesté a quelque autre pensée je m'y sousmets, sçachant bien que la prudence de S.M est telle qu'Elle ne sçauroit faire un mauvais choix.'

may appear, and doubtless occasionally actually was, a convenient pretext, but we would be well advised to view it in the context of a sharp reminder which Richelieu issued to Bouthillier's son, Chavigny, in 1638: 'when I propose something to the king, it is not a demand, but a simple proposition'.[42] This outburst suggests either that Chavigny had been too forward with Louis, or perhaps that the king had been irritated by a suggestion from Richelieu himself. At any rate, just four days later, Richelieu wrote to the king, possibly on this same issue but almost certainly in response to a direct request from Louis: 'His Majesty could do no better in my opinion than to gratify the Bishop of Lavaur with the diocese of Lisieux, should it fall vacant'.[43] Two days after that again, he was able to write thanking Louis XIII for agreeing to transfer the bishop of Lavaur to Evreux. In the meantime, however, another candidate had emerged for Evreux, the abbot of Saint-Denis of Reims, and Louis evidently sought the cardinal's comments on him, too. Richelieu's answer read as follows:

> As for the abbot of Saint-Denis's claim, I have nothing to say other than that I think that the king should persevere in the resolution he took not to rush into filling bishoprics, so as to have the necessary time to enquire into the life and behaviour of candidates. I know of nothing that might be said against M de Saint-Denis.[44]

Exchanges like this were probably usual enough, but are only occasionally documented; when looked at closely, they can be highly illuminating. The somewhat cryptic passage just quoted proves to be unexpectedly instructive on several counts. Firstly, it recalls earlier resolutions about the need for considered appointments, resolutions which may not always have been implemented, but which were evidently not being ignored for all that. It then goes on to argue that this kind of approach would give the crown the time necessary to conduct its own enquiry into the 'life and morals' of candidates. As far as can be determined, this was something which it never managed to do in any formal sense, however many enquiries or verbal reports may have been made on individuals seeking bishoprics. That there was still room for improvement here is dramatically illustrated by the fact that in

---

42 *Ibid*, vi. 113, letter of 25 Aug 1638: 'quand je propose une chose au roy, ce n'est pas une demande, mais une simple proposition'.
43 *Ibid*, 118, letter to Louis XIII, 29 Aug 1638: 'Sa Majesté ne scauroit mieux faire, à mon avis, que de gratiffier M de Lavaur de l'évesché d'Evreux, s'il vient à vacquer.'
44 *Ibid*, 132–3, letter to Chavigny 31 Aug 1638: 'Quant à la prétention du sr de Saint Denis, je n'ay rien autre chose à dire sinon que je croy que le roy doit persister à la resolution qu'il a prise de ne se haster pas de donner les éveschez, afin d'avoir le temps de faire une bonne perquisition de vita et moribus. Je ne sçay rien à dire contre M de Saint Denis.' In the event no nomination to Evreux was made at this time, since news of the incumbent bishop's death was false.

late 1638 the abbé de Loyac was nominated to Toulon, only for Louis XIII to ask him to return his *brevet* when it was discovered his eyesight was too poor![45] It was left to the papal nuncio to conduct written enquiries using witnesses, but the difference – and it was a major one – between the two enquiries was that the nuncio only conducted his *after* someone had been selected for promotion. Finally, Richelieu's advice to Louis ends with a distinctly cautious last sentence, in which he only confirms that he is unaware of any reason why the abbot of Saint-Denis might not be considered for Evreux. How much Richelieu had been able to learn about him at this point is impossible to guess, but at least it did not damage his chances of promotion. In the event, the abbot in question, Henri de Maupas du Tour, who was then in Anne of Austria's service, became bishop of Le Puy a few years later.

This standing responsibility to inform the king and protect his conscience, which Louis XIII expected Richelieu to exercise, is also implicit in a number of other remarks scattered through the cardinal's correspondence. When, in 1631, the princess of Condé asked Richelieu to intervene with Louis XIII in order to get the see of Auxerre for the prince of Conty, then a mere two years old, the answer was reasoned and polite but firm: the idea of such a promotion, he concluded, was 'a proposition which, as you well know, the king cannot grant'.[46] Likewise a candidate for suffragan-bishop of Metz in 1634 was peremptorily turned down with the words, 'on no account could I ever propose to make a bishop of him, given the kind of man he is'.[47]

This *entente cordiale* between king and minister over appointments, and Richelieu's lack of interest in a formal mechanism or *conseil de conscience* did not entirely preclude the development of certain working arrangements concerning the distribution of episcopal patronage. Richelieu was certainly aware of the need to avoid snap nominations and the dangers they entailed, an awareness expressed most clearly in 1630 when he wrote that bishops 'should be selected not by accident, but through properly considered election'; this in turn was something which could only be achieved 'by keeping in mind from

45 *Ibid*, 228, Richelieu to Chavigny, 1 Nov 1638; *Lettres de Jean Chapelain*, ed Philippe Tamizey de Larroque, 2 vols (Paris 1880–3), i. 307–8, Chapelain to Antoine Godeau, 28 Oct 1638, who refers to his 'fort mauvaise veue'. It was around this time that the case of Joachim d'Estaing, the virtually blind bishop of Clermont, was brought to the crown's attention, which would help to account for the king's reaction in Loyac's case.
46 Grillon, *Papiers de Richelieu*, vi. 594–5, letter of 21 Sept 1631: 'une proposition que, vous sçavez bien, le roi ne peut effectuer.' It should be added that within days, Dominique Séguier, brother of Pierre, keeper of the seals, was appointed to Auxerre.
47 Avenel, *Lettres de Richelieu*, iv. 711, letter to Cardinal La Valette, 20 Apr 1635: 'je ne voudrois pour rien du monde proposer de le faire evesque, estant tel qu'il est'. As the bishop of Metz was the unconsecrated Henri de Bourbon-Verneuil, Louis XIII's illegitimate brother, the diocese was effectively administered by his suffragan.

this point onward the names of those whom they (kings) wish to gratify in a year or so from now'.[48] Eight years later, as we have just seen, he wrote to the king recommending that he persevere in his resolution not to nominate bishops hastily, so as to have sufficient time to conduct a proper enquiry into candidates life and morals.[49] Unfortunately nothing further is known about the nature or date of the king's resolution, or what, if any, arrangements were made for its implementation. Although the evidence is slight, Richelieu also seems to have developed some awareness that not all French bishoprics, especially those in distant provinces, were equally attractive to potential, even worthy, candidates, an awareness which probably derived from a combination of personal experience and from his extensive travels around France in the late 1620s and 1630s. Writing to the incoming bishop of Saint-Papoul in March 1636, Richelieu promised him that 'the manner in which he exercises his office will provide His Majesty with the opportunity to seek out other persons of good repute in the depths of the provinces'.[50] A month later, when the bishop of Grasse in Provence died, Richelieu could think of no one to recommend to the king, but he wrote to Louis that Sublet des Noyers, the secretary of state, would attempt to find out who the worthy clerics in Provence were, as a small diocese like Grasse was unlikely to attract outsiders.[51] But Sublet's researches 'dans le fonds des provinces' evidently proved unsuccessful, and Richelieu's own scepticism was confounded when Antoine Godeau, a northerner and a distinguished founding member of the Académie Française, accepted the royal nomination; he went on to confound both friends and contemporaries by remaining faithful to his tiny upland diocese for the next thirty years or more.

Despite these difficulties, it may be argued that something like a pool of potential candidates did emerge over the years, at least to the extent that their names were mentioned more than once when vacancies arose; it would probably be an error to think that there was some kind of ranking of candidates involved here, if only because some of them were made to wait several years before they became bishops. But although the evidence is anything but comprehensive, what there is has the additional advantage of affording a further insight into the nature of the exchanges between the king and his minister. It is especially ironic that, as we have already seen more than once already, much of this evidence only exists because of the repeated reports reaching the king and his ministers, as well as candidates for the mitre, their

---

48 Grillon, *Papiers de Richelieu*, v. 490–1, letter to Bouthillier, 8 Aug 1630: 'doivent estre pris non par hasard, mais par grande eslection ... (il faut avoir) dès cette heure en l'esprit ceux qu'ils voudroient y pourvoir dans un ou deux ans'.
49 Avenel, *Lettres de Richelieu*, vi. 132–3, Richelieu to Chavigny, 31 Aug 1638.
50 *Ibid*, v. 992, letter to Bernard Despruetz [late Mar/early Apr 1636, and not Oct, as Avenel suggested, Despruets having been nominated by Louis XIII on 30 Mar]: 'la façon dont il s'acquittera de sa charge donnera lieu à Sa Majeste de rechercher dans le fonds des provinces d'autres personnes de bonne reputation'.
51 *Ibid*, v. 468, Richelieu to king, 19 May 1636.

patrons, and their families, that such and such a bishop had either died, was in imminent danger of death, or was thought to be beyond all hope of recovery. If the frequency of such rumours is evidence of anything, it is probably of contemporary perceptions about the need to move quickly if a bishop were indeed dead, and indeed of how difficult it was to sustain any resolve on the part of the crown to avoid precipitate nominations. It is not inconceivable that some of these rumours were deliberately started with a view to discovering who could expect to receive royal favour. At any rate, such news would lead king and minister to exchange views and names, as in the case of Paris in early 1628, even if they knew that they should await confirmation of the rumours of death; meanwhile, patrons could be expected to begin pressing the claims of candidates of their own. In at least some instances, an actual decision to nominate was made, clearly with some speed, and even a *brevet de nomination* given to the successful candidate; in 1628, for example, Louis XIII actually wrote to offer the archbishopric of Tours, then rumoured vacant, to no less a figure than Cardinal Bérulle.[52] When here as elsewhere, the news proved to be false, the process obviously had to stop, but not before it had produced some acknowledgement that a particular individual had been deemed worthy to join the episcopal bench. This did not necessarily imply any express right to succeed if, or when, the diocese in question became vacant, or indeed to become a bishop at all, but such a candidate's claims would manifestly be even harder to resist in future. We noted above how Richelieu reminded Louis XIII in 1635 that the Dominican Noël Deslandes had previously been recommended for Périgueux when it was thought to be vacant, and suggested that the king could now offer him Tréguier instead. In the event, Tréguier was vacant, and Deslandes was formally nominated a mere two two days later.[53] The official *Gazette* reported that the nomination was a reward for Deslandes's long years of activity and preaching, and that it had been made 'on the request of His Eminence'.[54] There is considerably more evidence of this practice of 'reserving', not so much dioceses (as frequently happened under Henri III and Henri IV), but individuals for promotion, both before and after 1635. Raymond de Montaigne did not get Condom, as Richelieu had requested in 1628 when it was mistakenly thought to be vacant, but he duly obtained Bayonne the following year. When Henri de Sourdis was moved to Bordeaux in 1628, the queen mother promptly asked that his former see of Maillezais go to her almoner, Nicolas Grillié, who, as she reminded Richelieu, had earlier been promised Vence when it, too, was rumoured to be vacant.[55] The following year she renewed her appeal for Grillié when it seemed Maillezais would be

---

52 *Correspondance de Pierre de Bérulle*, ed Jean Dagens, 3 vols (Louvain 1937–9), iii. 428, 21 Oct 1628.
53 Avenel, *Lettres de Richelieu*, v. 245–6, letter of 20 Sept 1635.
54 BN, MS lat 17029, fo 90, 6 Oct 1635.
55 Grillon, *Papiers de Richelieu*, iii. 397–8, letter to Richelieu, 25 July 1628.

moved to La Rochelle and, later in 1629, Grillié's name was also suggested for the see of Dol in Brittany.[56] His patience was finally rewarded when he got Bazas in 1630, only to be promoted to the troubled diocese of Uzès a few years later. Achille Harlay de Sancy was first recommended for the southern diocese of Vabres, when it was rumoured vacant in April 1631, and duly got Saint-Malo a few months later when Marillac's son died before receiving his papal provisions.[57] A similar impression of certain individuals being designated for preferment emerges no less clearly from Louis XIII's admittedly isolated request to the pope in early 1631 to confer a titular bishopric *in partibus infidelium* on Dominique Séguier, brother of the future chancellor, 'as he waits to be appointed to a bishopric in our kingdom'.[58] It is hardly surprising that by September 1631 it was Séguier, and not the infant prince de Conty, who should be nominated to the first desirable see to become available, that of Auxerre. Towards the end of the decade, in November 1639, Henri Arnauld reported the common view that Bishop Etampes of Chartres had already been selected to become archbishop of Reims once Henri de Lorraine-Guise had finally been ejected or obliged to resign, though it took a further two years for the transfer to be confirmed.[59] Henri Maupas du Tour, abbot of Saint-Denis of Reims, was a contender not merely for Evreux in 1638, as we saw, but also for Avranches in 1640, before he finally got Le Puy in 1641.[60]

This pattern, in which the names of particular individuals regularly appeared when dioceses became available, amounted to far more than just the sum of the inevitable court gossip, even if it does not necessarily mean some sort of list or order of preference of the kind suggested in 1614 and 1617 was being kept. In 1637, Jean Chapelain, the academician, penned a shrewd summary of what was now happening in the course of commenting on Henri Arnauld's problems over the see of Toul in Lorraine to which he had been elected: 'even if he does not become bishop there, he will still have been judged worthy of being one, and if he is not to be bishop of Toul, he will not fail to become one somewhere else'.[61] For someone so clearly identified as an *episcopabile*, Arnauld had to wait rather a long time — eleven years to be precise — but it was no secret by the early days of the regency that not only would

---

56 *Ibid*, iv. 61–2, Marie de' Medici to Richelieu, 29 Jan 1629; *ibid*, 556, Bouthillier to Richelieu, 19 Aug 1629.
57 *Ibid*, vi. 225, Châteauneuf to Richelieu, [11 Apr 1631].
58 BAV, Barb lat 7942, fo 22, letter to Urban VIII, 14 Feb 1631: 'en attendant qu'il soit nommé à quelque évêché en nostre Royaume'. By Sept, Séguier had in fact been nominated to the see of Auxerre, although that of Saint-Brieuc had fallen vacant a few months earlier than Auxerre.
59 BN, MS Fr 15610, p 305, letter to Barillon, 27 Nov 1639.
60 Avenel, *Lettres de Richelieu*, vi. 132–3, Richelieu to Chavigny, 31 Aug 1638; BN, MS Fr 15610, p 412, Arnauld to Barillon, 15 Jan 1640; MS Fr 15611, fo 250v, same to same, 7 Sept 1641.
61 *Lettres de Chapelain*, i. 196, letter to Godeau, bishop of Grasse, 28 Jan 1638: 'quant il ne seroit pas évesque, on ne laissera pas de l'en juger digne, et s'il ne l'est pas à Toul, il ne se peut manquer de l'estre ailleurs'.

Arnauld become a bishop but, more unusually by then, that he had also been promised the see of Angers when it became available.[62]

IV

The principal effect of this outline of the relations between king and minister, as well as of the methods they adopted in choosing bishops, is to focus renewed attention not just on Richelieu, but on the milieu in which he moved. It was from this milieu that both bishops themselves and also pressure and advice about matters episcopal arose. It would be jejune to imagine that the results which he, the king and reformers of the episcopate aimed for, could have been achieved by a single, all-knowing individual.

To begin with, it should be borne in mind that the cardinal's entourage were not merely beneficiaries of episcopal patronage; the very success they enjoyed in this respect inevitably meant that they in turn also tended to become a secondary source of such patronage and support. They were all the more likely to be utilised as an avenue to Richelieu and the king by those seeking bishoprics and other benefices at a time when episcopal vacancies were fewer in number. Begging letters and letters of thanks to secretaries and close associates of Richelieu testify to this, though it should be said that the cardinal had no desire to encourage independent activity on the part of those he employed in his personal service.[63] For the same reason, it remains difficult to follow, let alone accurately assess, the activities of his entourage as a broker of church patronage, since he rarely evinced any willingness to have subordinates make up his mind for him. In 1629, for example, Claude Bouthillier reported to Richelieu on a wide-ranging discussion between himself, Bérulle, Marillac, and the cardinal's own niece as to which of several candidates was best suited to fill one of the Breton dioceses then thought to be vacant. Bouthillier evidently received a firm and prompt rebuke from Richelieu for his pains, for he assured him virtually by return of post that he had not opened his mouth, nor would he, on such a subject; he concluded by affirming that he had no wishes other than those of Richelieu himself in these matters.[64] Ten years later, Henri Arnauld reported that Sublet des Noyers was busy attempting to obtain a bishopric for the abbé de Champigny but, despite his high favour with the cardinal, he had no success whatsoever.[65] Much more discreet was the duchesse d'Aiguillon, the cardinal's niece, whose personal

---

62 AAE, France 848, fos 2–3, 4 Jan 1643, Brézé, Richelieu's brother-in-law and governor of Angers, to Mazarin, reporting news of the existing bishop's death, and asking that Arnauld be his successor.
63 Letters to Charpentier, Richelieu's principal secretary who corresponded with a wide range of bishops and other figures, are to be found in BN, MS Baluze 333.
64 Grillon, *Papiers de Richelieu*, iv. 556, Bouthillier to Richelieu, 19 Aug 1629; *ibid*, 570–1, same to same, 31 Aug 1629.
65 BN, MS Fr 15610, p 168, Henri Arnauld to president Barillon, 4 Sept 1639.

involvement with the world of *dévot* reforms and reformers generally made her a natural channel for those intent on pressing their names and advice on Richelieu, but her discretion makes it impossible to show whether she was instrumental in securing episcopal office for particular individuals.

Looking beyond the inner circle of Richelieu's entourage, there is good reason to believe that ecclesiastics, some of them bishops, played a role in influencing the selection of bishops during the cardinal's ministry. The first, and most valuable of these, was probably Bérulle, although by the time of his death in 1629 he and Richelieu had fallen out. However, his role as an influential counsellor of Marie de' Medici and his long years of intensive activity as superior of the reforming Oratory, ensured that he had an unrivalled knowledge of French ecclesiastics, both Parisian and provincial. Bérulle did not always back winners, as we saw in the previous chapter when he actively sought episcopal office for Henri de Béthune and Camille de Neufville-Villeroy. But it is not unrealistic to suggest that he helped to shape Richelieu's own approach to episcopal patronage. Discussing the need to send a bishop to serve Henrietta Maria in England, he recommended that Richelieu leave incumbent bishops to serve in their dioceses, and 'in that case, you might consider Grillié, Saint-Cyran and others who are under consideration for episcopal office'.[66] Both Grillié and Saint-Cyran were widely known to be close friends and disciples of Bérulle. When the question of what to do with La Rochelle during the siege first arose, Bérulle was equally quick to reveal his candidate, Bernard Despruets, for the new bishopric. A canon of Saintes who hailed originally from Béarn, Bérulle regarded Despruets' skill as a preacher and controversialist as what was most needed in La Rochelle. But he also had a very different reason for proposing Despruets: 'it would be a great example if the king were to take from the cathedral in order to make him a bishop of that diocese a canon who has no idea of becoming a bishop, and whom nobody is considering for such an office'.[67] Despruets was one of several Bérulle disciples to become a bishop, though in his case not until 1636. There is no evidence as to how Richelieu reacted to Bérulle's suggestion that bishops should be selected from among men who were not known to be candidates for high office, but it may not have been entirely forgotten. It is worth noting that towards the end of the cardinal's ministry, this was precisely the impression that certain gifts of bishoprics and other benefices left on a diligent observer like Henri Arnauld.[68]

Philippe Cospeau was another source of advice and a patron of future

---

66 *Correspondance de Bérulle*, iii. 397, letter to Richelieu, 25 July 1628: 'En ce cas, vous pouvez considérer Grillet, Saint-Cyran et autres qui sont exposés à cette dignité'.
67 *Ibid*, iii. 346–7, letter to Richelieu, 3 Dec 1627: 'qu'il serait de grand example que le Roi tirât du même chapitre un chanoine qui n'y pense point, et à qui personne ne pense pour le faire évêque de la même église'.
68 BN, MS Fr 15610, p 28, letter to Barillon, 23 Mar 1639; MS Fr 15611, fo 326v, to same, 27 Nov 1641.

bishops. He was both a close episcopal supporter of Bérulle and a former mentor to Richelieu, but, if only because of the company he kept, which included Epernon, the Vendômes, and Anne of Austria, Cospeau remained sufficiently independent of the cardinal not to be regarded as just another client among many. His episcopal experience of three dioceses in three different provinces inspired considerable respect on Richelieu's part.[69] At least two bishops, Nicolas Grillié and Etienne Villazel, also disciples of Bérulle, explicitly recognised that they owed their formation and pre-episcopal careers to Cospeau, and it was almost certainly through Cospeau and Bérulle that both entered the queen mother's service as preachers, and then went on to become bishops in the early 1630s. Harlay of Saint-Malo, despite his reputation as a Richelieu client, was another bishop to acknowledge Cospeau as his model. When these men became bishops, the *Gazette* contained a fulsome, and most unusual, eulogy, not so much of them as of Cospeau: 'Not even Plato ever had as many pupils as this good prelate ... and it is true that the exercises which they performed before the king since they left his school served them no less well than those which they first took with him.'[70] Cospeau also knew, and gave evidence on behalf of, too many other incoming bishops before the papal nuncios for their recourse to him to have been a simple coincidence. He may have been appointed to the *conseil de conscience* in 1643 because of his personal links with Anne of Austria, but it was also in recognition of the discreet role he had played earlier in discerning and nurturing episcopal potential.

No evidence of episcopal influence in the choice of bishops comparable to that of Cospeau has come to light, probably because it did not exist. Indeed, it is not altogether clear whether Cospeau's influence with Richelieu and Louis XIII survived past the mid-1630s, but his example shows how valuable a reigning bishop could be as an intermediary in the making of bishops. It is also evident from one or two nominations of the 1630s that candidates used the good offices of Henri de Sourdis of Bordeaux, but that was probably more because of his known service to Richelieu than of his reputation as a role-model for would-be bishops.

At any rate, it should be clear by now that for a cardinal who saw himself as a champion of church reform until the end of his life, episcopal patronage could not be reduced to an elaborate exercise in political fixing. Richelieu's increasingly dominant ministerial position during the 1630s and the king's growing reliance on him for guidance on episcopal patronage reduced the need to satisfy powerful noble families, and allowed him to turn for information and advice to a wide spectrum of those second-generation *dévots* whose reformist activities he supported; several of them were drawn from the second-order clergy and some of them, as we saw, refused to accept bishoprics

---

69 See the judgement of Richelieu's attitude to Cospeau in Retz, *Oeuvres*, ed Marie-Thérèse Hipp and Michel Pernot (Paris 1984), 160.
70 BN, MS lat 17027, fo 39, 5 Sept 1631.

for themselves while being anything but indifferent about the condition of the episcopate. The historiography of this relationship has, to say the least, been somewhat peculiar. Generations of biographers of figures like Père Joseph, Vincent de Paul or Charles de Condren have readily claimed that they had sufficient influence with Richelieu, or were well-enough regarded by him, to present to him the names of deserving candidates. But as independent evidence of this influence has been hard to come by, the biographers' assertions have been either ignored or dismissed as starry-eyed hagiography. Assessing the record can be all the more difficult if the objective is to isolate the individual influence which determined a particular bishop's promotion; to try to do so is probably futile since everything we know about both French society and patronage shows that multiple influences and support were the best guarantee of success. For instance, the nomination of the Gault brothers to Marseille in 1639 and 1641 could simply be attributed to Condren's influence, as they were members of the Oratory of which he was superior-general at the time. But they had both spent many years working under Sourdis's direction in a variety of capacities in Bordeaux, and one of them, Jean-Baptiste, had also been Sébastien Zamet's grand vicar at Langres. Likewise, when Vincent de Paul, then general of the Congregation of the Mission, wrote to one of his subordinates in early 1637 stating that three ecclesiastics who had attended his *conférences des mardi* at Saint-Lazare – Godeau, Fouquet and Pavillon – had become bishops and another had recently been nominated for a coadjutorship, he was obviously claiming at least some of the credit for the outcome.[71] The academician Godeau and François Fouquet could clearly be said to have had other influential mentors, not excluding the cardinal himself!

At any rate, it is clear that throughout the 1630s reformers, whether they were bishops or not, were in regular and intensive contact, not just with each other, but with courtiers and ministers, aristocrats and highly placed royal officials. Condren almost certainly did play a key role in ensuring that Hugues Labatut would become bishop of Comminges in 1637, since the old bishop had, before his death, entrusted to Condren the business of negotiating with the court.[72] The evidence for Vincent de Paul's involvement in episcopal politics is more elusive, but he certainly had considerable dealings with Richelieu in the late 1630s, some of them involving a foundation in the new town of Richelieu. It was hardly a matter of chance that when the archbishop of Paris insisted from 1638 onwards that all future priests follow a brief retreat at Saint-Lazare under de Paul's direction prior to taking orders,

71 Vincent de Paul, *Correspondance, Entretiens, Documents*, ed Pierre Coste, 14 vols (Paris 1922–5), *Corespondance*, i. 373–4, letter to Jean de Fonteneil, 8 Jan 1637.
72 Jean Contrasty, *Histoire des évêques de Comminges* (Toulouse 1940), 339–40 for the text of Condren's letter to Richelieu with a view to settling the Comminges succession by resignation, and pointing out that the bishop, Donadieu de Griet, who was also a disciple of Condren, was now 'aux extremitez'.

considerable numbers of theology faculty graduates with both career prospects and ambition began attending.[73] His *conférences des mardi* also continued as before and, along with the rural missions organised by de Paul, continued to attract participants like Félix Vialart, Etienne Caulet or François Perrochel who would become bishops from 1640 onwards. This development did not go unnoticed. Paul de Gondi, surely the most celebrated of all coadjutor-bishops, judged it wise to make a good impression at the *conférences* if he was to achieve his ambition of succeeding his uncle as archbishop of Paris, not least because his family had been in considerable disgrace since 1630. The Gondis may have had to wait until Richelieu was dead before there was any point in attempting to ensure the Paris succession, but young Gondi had long since made the impression that he had intended.[74]

V

In addition to these developments, we may point to a number of others which will serve to conclude this attempt to understand the changing character of the episcopate during the Richelieu ministry. Not all are directly related to episcopal patronage in the strict sense, yet they provide an important sense of the wider context in which the latter was exercised.

Apart from the changes in the social origins of the episcopate already noted for the 1630s, the evidence presented in an earlier chapter showed that the episcopate of these years was increasingly a well-educated body. Bishops without university degrees disappeared altogether by 1635 at the latest, having been in a distinct minority since the later 1620s. Moreover, an increasing number of these bishops were either doctors or licentiates in theology or law, and not mere baccalaureates (like Richelieu himself); both the doctorate and the licentiate, especially in theology, required serious, sustained study; and even some of those bishops taking law degrees are, as we saw, known to have devoted at least a few years to studying theology. In the emergence of an episcopate that was increasingly university educated and theologically literate, we may see one tangible result of Richelieu's attempts to reform the Theology Faculty of the University of Paris, and make it an unofficial seminary for future higher clergy.[75]

The evidence of enduring *dévot* influence in Richelieu's entourage may also help to explain some other novel aspects of his interest in the behaviour of France's bishops at different times during the 1630s, and his sense of

---

73 De Paul, *Correspondance*, i. 525, letter to Antoine Lucas, 13 Dec 1638.
74 Retz, *Oeuvres*, 172. Gondi had already impressed leading *dévots* like de Paul and Cospeau, with whom he appears to have been on particularly good terms. For Henri Arnauld's positive view of Retz, see BN, MS Fr 15611, fos 593–5, Arnauld to Barillon, 24 Dec 1642.
75 See L W B Brockliss, 'Richelieu, Education and the State', in Joseph Bergin and Laurence Brockliss, eds, *Richelieu and his Age* (Oxford 1992), 252ff.

responsibility for that behaviour. Two cases have emerged from the late 1630s of bishops newly arrived in their dioceses writing detailed reports on their state to Richelieu at his explicit request, but it is not known if they were isolated episodes or part of a more systematic interest on his part.[76]

Furthermore, it would be difficult to think of any other period in the sixteenth or seventeenth centuries when bishops were subject to so much admonition for their shortcomings from a royal minister. The bishops of Nîmes and Reims, and perhaps a few others, were lectured over their undignified private lives, while Harlay of Rouen was rounded upon for his wayward opinions which landed him in trouble, not least in Rome.[77] On hearing that the archbishop of Paris had been attacked publicly by a preacher for his behaviour, Richelieu reportedly reacted by saying the preacher was in search of either a mitre or a spell in the Bastille! Yet within two weeks Richelieu himself rebuked Gondi to his face for his negligence.[78] More telling, perhaps, is the fact that bishops who had once been close to him or worked under his direction, were disgraced over the years, especially in the late 1630s and 1640s. Bishop Marsillac of Mende was the first of those to feel the minister's disfavour and battled against local detractors to regain favour.[79] Archbishops Sourdis and Etampes, both far more senior figures and Richelieu clients, also endured disgrace, though in neither case was it on religious grounds.

Richelieu's concern was such that in 1638 he even requested Urban VIII to authorise a commission of French bishops directed against 'ill-living bishops through the threat of investigation into their lives'.[80] Nothing ever came, or was indeed ever likely to come, of this proposal, which bears the imprint of Richelieu's liking for special commissions, though it would have been worth knowing how he himself actually conceived of it. In any case, Rome, which had only reluctantly agreed to the commission to judge the Languedoc bishops in the early 1630s, was not anxious to repeat the experience, especially as the bishops who were now being targeted by Richelieu were not explicitly mentioned in his proposal; the idea of a tribunal enjoying sweeping licence to supervise France's bishops was as unacceptable to Rome as it would

---

76 AAE, France 836, fos 12–13, Hugues Labatut on diocese of Comminges, 6 Aug 1640; *ibid*, 838, fos 138–9, Godeau on Grasse, 12 Apr 1641.
77 Avenel, *Lettres de Richelieu*, iv. 510–11, [late 1633] (Harlay of Rouen); *ibid*, v. 960 [1636] (Cohon of Nîmes); *ibid*, vi. 378–9, 8 June 1639 (Guise of Reims). Cohon's private life was widely held to be disreputable, and he was apparently threatened with a trial: see Sauzet, *Contreréforme et réforme catholique*, 226–7.
78 BN, MS Fr 15610, pp 389–90, Arnauld to Barillon, 8 Jan 1640.
79 AAE, France 1632, fos 15–16, Marsillac to Richelieu, 18–7–1639; *ibid*, 835, fo 297, same to same, 22 July 1648; *ibid*, 838, fo 13 and 273, same to same, 13 Jan and 19 June 1641; *ibid*, 836, fos 72–3, Arpenon, a Marsillac adversary, to Richelieu, 8 Sept 1640, keeping up the attack on Marcillac.
80 Avenel, *Lettres de Richelieu*, vi. 228–9, memorandum for Chavigny, 1 Nov 1638: 'evesques mal vivans par l'appréhension de la recherche de leur vie'.

have been to the French church itself.[81] Yet there is evidence that a limited and possibly exploratory attempt was actually made in 1639 to deal with some delinquent bishops, without waiting for papal approval. Henri de Sourdis of Bordeaux, not the perfect model of a resident bishop but an effective administrator who enjoyed Richelieu's confidence, was commissioned to investigate the state of the dioceses of Sarlat and Périgueux. By his own account, he put together a damning dossier against the respective bishops, but Bishop Salignac of Sarlat died before any action could be taken against him. Sourdis strongly recommended that Richelieu ensure the appointment of a successor who would be a man of action as well as a preacher, since no one else could revive a diocese that was so 'perdu au spirituel'. But Richelieu only registered half of this message, and secured the nomination of Jean de Lingendes, a distinguished preacher. Neither he nor the cardinal may have properly realised the kind of task that awaited him, but by the time his provisions arrived in 1642, Lingendes was already searching for an escape in a preceptorship to Louis XIV. The essential accuracy of Sourdis's diagnosis of the state of Sarlat and the kind of bishop it needed, was confirmed by the vigilant *dévot* bishop of Cahors, Alain de Solminihac, in 1643.[82] As for neighbouring Périgueux, Sourdis merely informed Richelieu that 'the file for proceedings . . . is ready to be despatched to Your Eminence whenever you should desire it', leaving the initiative entirely to him.[83] But not knowing exactly what Sourdis had been asked to do, nor what his 'proceedings' amounted to, it is hard to conjecture how it might have been acted upon, though the intention may simply have been to compel the bishop of Périgueux to accept a young and active coadjutor who could initiate the work of religious restoration. At any rate, there is no sign that any action was subsequently taken against Bishop de la Béraudière whose collected sermons, published in 1635 with the appropriate title of *Otium Episcopale*, could scarcely have impressed an advocate of active resident bishops like Sourdis.

In fact, the history of coadjutorships during the 1630s is of particular interest, since it offers an unusual measure of both the ambition and the limits of royal power with regard to bishoprics. This is so despite the fact that their numbers dropped to just four, all of whom were nominated in 1633–4. The total would be higher, though only slightly, if we add two cases, that of Artus de Lionne of Gap and Félix Vialart of Châlons, both of whom were initially

---

81 *ANG*, v. 220, Barberini to Scotti, nuncio, 23 Dec 1639; *ibid*, 242, Scotti to Barberini, 20 Jan 1640.
82 Solminihac, *Lettres et documents*, 290, Solminihac to Vincent de Paul, 3 May 1643. Though nominated in June 1639, Lingendes's bulls were only delivered in July 1642.
83 AN, Marine B/4, vol 1, fos 281v-2r, Sourdis to Richelieu, 28 Apr: 'la procédure . . . est en estat d'estre envoiée à Vostre Eminence lors qu'elle le souhaitera'. This is a copy, and it seems misdated, as the bishop of Sarlat died on 2 May 1639, not on 20 Apr as Sourdis's letter would lead one to believe.

nominated as coadjutors to bishops who died before their intended coadjutors had been confirmed in Rome.[84]

But striking as it is, it is not the scaling down of the number of coadjutorships which is the only interesting feature of this change; it is the shift in intention and initiative which demands attention. Though two of the four were nephews of existing bishops, their nominations came much closer than those of the past to respecting the canonical principles governing their elevation – the capacity to relieve the burden on elderly or infirm bishops. Eustache de Chéry was of the nephew-bishops nominated in 1633, but by 1640, his uncle was one ready to turn over to him total responsibility for his diocese, which Chéry had probably administered *de facto* in previous years.[85] Until his premature death, Jean de Sponde also appears to have governed Pamiers for his ageing uncle, Henri. The remaining coadjutors, both actual and intended, were experienced men intended to offer positive assistance to ageing bishops, not relatives of incumbent bishops anxious to defend a quasi-patrimonial claim to a bishopric.

Their appointments, contrasting as they did with common practice, raise the crucial question of who took the initiative in seeking a coadjutorship – the reigning bishop, the coadjutor in search of promotion, or the crown itself. The bishop of Troyes agreed to take on François Malier, son of an *intendant des finances*, as coadjutor in 1634, but over a year later the matter had still not been resolved in Rome, which objected to the nomination, possibly because the reigning bishop regretted his decision. But royal determination to proceed is clearly evident in the terms of a stern letter to Rome from Louis XIII, who wrote that 'I would be failing in my duty to God if my subjects in this diocese did not have someone capable of performing the functions of a bishop there'.[86] The case of the slightly earlier coadjutorship of Montauban is far better documented, if only because it was such a prolonged struggle. After the city's fall in 1629, the task of re-catholicising it and the diocese seemed especially pressing, but its bishop, Anne de Murviel, Mayenne's client from the 1590s who had been bishop there for thirty years, seemed to lack the energy for a Catholic reconquest of Montauban similar to that being attempted in the other former Protestant strongholds of Nîmes or La Rochelle. Within a short while a campaign to persuade him to take a coadjutor was launched, orchestrated by successive first presidents of the Toulouse parlement, Gilles le Masuyer and Jean de

---

84 AAE, CP Rome 81, fo 573, Servien to Richelieu, undated letter explaining history of attempts to obtain coadjutorship of Gap for Lionne; for Vialart, BN, MS Fr 15610, p 865, Arnauld to Barillon, 25 Nov 1640, Vialart nominated coadjutor; *ibid*, p. 903, Arnauld to Barillon, 16 Dec 1640: 'voillà M l'abbé Vialart en possession bien plustost qu'il ne pensoit'.

85 AD Nièvre, 3E1, vol 697, act of 24 Aug 1640. The bishop refers only to the temporalities of Nevers here, which can be seen as implicitly recognising that his nephew already exercised the spiritual government of the diocese.

86 BN, MS lat 17029, fos 123, 127, royal letters to Noailles, ambassador in Rome, 29 May 1634 and 11 Oct 1635.

Bertier.⁸⁷ It took five years of sustained pressure on Murviel, during which he received some stinging rebukes from Richelieu himself, before he finally consented to accept Pierre de Bertier in 1634.⁸⁸ In one such exchange, Richelieu expressed his astonishment that Murviel 'was refusing the good which the king wishes to do you'.⁸⁹ Bertier, a doctor of the Sorbonne and a promising preacher, certainly had the qualities needed, and could readily find episcopal models to follow in his own family; but the family's standing as prominent Richelieu clients and *dévots*, as well as its connections within the diocese of Montauban were surely not without a bearing on the outcome.⁹⁰

A few years later again, in early 1638, Vincent de Paul reported that one of those attending his *conférences*, a Monsieur Barreau, had been nominated coadjutor to Sarlat, but 'without the consent of the bishop', Louis de Salignac.⁹¹ This admission is crucial, for Barreau never followed in Malier or Bertier's footsteps; in this case, the imposition of coadjutors from above had probably gone a step too far. Murviel's protracted resistance shows how difficult it was to impose them on reluctant bishops, regardless of the objective needs of a diocese; only a combined 'local' and 'central' campaign could expect to achieve success. But even where coadjutors were imposed on reluctant bishops, results could fall far short of expectations: until his death in 1652, Murviel largely prevented Bertier from taking a major part in the administration of his diocese, and the marginalised coadjutor was left to concentrate on enhancing his name as a preacher of talent.⁹² The Salignac family had held Sarlat for far longer than Murviel had Montauban, and were

---

87 It seems likely that Murviel's family had earlier received some kind of undertaking that his nephew would succeed to Montauban, which would have certainly fortified his opposition to Bertier; when it finally came, the bishop's acceptance of Bertier had to be approved before a notary by his nephew, who thereby renounced his claims of the see: ASV, PC 34, fos 404–32, Bertier's enquiry *de vita et moribus*, at fos 405–6.
88 Grillon, *Papiers de Richelieu*, iv. 682, Le Masuyer to Richelieu 23 Nov 1629; *ibid*, v. 623–4, same to same, 28 Oct 1630; *ibid*, 729–30, Richelieu to Murviel [1630?]; *ibid*, vi. 48–9, Murviel to Richelieu, 20 Jan 1631.
89 Avenel, *Lettres de Richelieu*, iv. 540–1, Richelieu to Murviel [Feb.] 1634.
90 ASV, PC 34, fos 405, 411–12. Both Murviel's acceptance of Bertier and the king's letter of nomination make explicit mention of the Huguenot problem as the basis for the coadjutorship. Murviel even referred to fact that Bertier had 'plusieurs parents dans le parlement de Toulouse par l'auctorité desquelz les droictz des ecclésiastiques pourront estre conservez'. For the Bertier family and Richelieu, see Beik, *Absolutism and Society*, and Beik, 'The Parlement of Toulouse and the Fronde' in Mack P Holt, ed, *Society and Institutions in Early Modern France* (Athens, Georgia and London 1991), 133.
91 De Paul, *Correspondance*, i. 525, de Paul to Antoine Lucas, 13 Dec 1638: 'mais sans le consentement de l'évêque'.
92 AAE, CP Rome 81, fos 115–16, Bertier to Mazarin, 10 Mar 1643, relating his travails since 1634 and Murviel's obstructionism, which he feared would be all the easier henceforth, given that Richelieu was now dead. Bertier wrote years later to Mazarin with the same complaint: 'je ne suis pas seulement sans employ dans mon ministère et sans revenu suffisant à ma condition, mais encore persécuté sans cesse et cru coupable sans raison': quoted in de Paul, *Correspondance*, ii. 504–5, n 4.

evidently not prepared to relinquish it without a fight. Indeed, as already suggested, it may well be that Sourdis's commission from Richelieu to investigate the dioceses of Sarlat and Périgueux in 1639 was designed to break the bishops' resistance to crown-sponsored coadjutors. Even under the leadership of a determined and well-advised cardinal-minister, the ability of the crown to refashion the episcopate was constrained by episcopal autonomy. Adopting what might be termed an active policy of sponsoring coadjutors unrelated to reigning bishops also required more persistence than might have been imagined. As early as 1630, for example, Michel de Marillac urged Richelieu to obtain a coadjutor for Gap whose bishop he described as a disgrace, but the bishop's agreement to a nominee acceptable to the crown, Artus de Lionne, did not materialise until 1634.[93] The disgrace of Lionne's brother-in-law, Servien, as a minister in 1636, stalled the procedure, emboldening opponents to think the pressure would now vanish. The bishop of Gap died before Lionne could become his coadjutor![94] This method of choosing bishops obviously ran the risk of causing more friction than benefit, either to dioceses or the crown.

Yet the fact that such aspirations could be pursued at all cannot be dismissed as quixotic merely because results were so limited. They were part of a change in attitudes and standards which was noted by certain contemporary observers, a change which might have been less noticeable had vacant bishoprics been more plentiful during these years. Mention was made earlier of Peiresc's remark that one needed much good fortune in order to obtain a bishopric, and his comment may be seen as expressing the difficulty of a provincial faced with the growing inaccessibility of episcopal patronage in an age when the few openings that did arise were channelled towards northerners and ministerial clients generally. In his correspondence with the exiled parlementaire, president Barillon, Henri Arnauld, who was no provincial but a native Parisian and an attentive observer of court politics between 1639 and 1643, regularly reported on the competition for vacant bishoprics. He remarked more than once on the surprise caused by several of the outcomes, ranging from the nomination of Eustache Gault to Marseille in March 1639 to that of Jacques Lescot to Chartres in late 1641.[95] But the peculiar mix of new and old attitudes when it came to disposing of bishoprics was probably best expressed in August 1639 by Jean Chapelain. As secretary to the Académie Française, he gravitated in the circles around Richelieu. Replying to a French correspondent in Rome who had confided to him his ambitions to

---

93 Grillon, *Papiers de Richelieu*, v. 392, Marillac to Richelieu, 13 July 1630; ASV, PC 37, fo 899, royal letter of nomination of Lionne to Gap, 24 May 1637, referring to earlier nomination of 25 Aug 1634.
94 AAE, CP Rome 81, fo 573, Servien to Richelieu, '1637'.
95 BN, MS Fr 15610, p 28, letter to Barillon, 23 Mar 1639 (Gault); MS Fr 15611, fo 326v, to same, 27 Nov 1641: 'ce qui vous surprendrez . . . est que M Lescot aura très asseurément l'évesché de Chartres'.

obtain a French bishopric through the intervention of his Roman patrons, Chapelain disabused his friend with some pithy, even irreverent advice:

> in order to become a bishop in France, one needs to be resident in France itself, be a great preacher and a royal almoner, or if not, then to be in favour with the powers that be, or else be a saint. But even when there are individuals who fulfil some of those conditions, they are still left to vegetate as they witness their disciples overtake them.[96]

Comments of this kind could not have been made of episcopal patronage in previous decades. They were only made possible by the changed political circumstances of the 1630s and early 1640s, when reformist pressures could effectively be brought to bear on the crown, thanks in part to a ministry which was more unified and tightly controlled than in the past. If Richelieu achieved results, it was because being both cardinal and leading minister he was uniquely placed to do so. Equally crucial to the whole process was the willingness, even alacrity, of a conscientious Louis XIII to accept Richelieu as both purveyor of advice, patron of would-be bishops, and guardian of his conscience. There is no serious sign that Louis ever chafed at this particular element of his relationship with Richelieu, despite an occasional sarcastic comment which reminded contemporaries of the underlying tension is his relationship with the cardinal. Nor is there any evidence that Louis was tempted to emulate his father by openly boasting that he had transformed the episcopate. Yet the gradual emergence of an unmistakable readiness to treat royal episcopal patronage as something which required information, reflection, and even a measure of foresight and anticipation took place in the context of institutional inertia. At least part of this was a matter of personal influence and political circumstances. It remained to be seen how much of it could be sustained in the changed political conditions following the deaths of king and minister.

---

96   BN, MS Naf 1886, fo 179–84, Chapelain to Jean-Jacques Bouchard, 23 August 1639: 'pour estre évesque en France, il faut estre en France et grand prédicateur et aumosnier du roy ou favory des puissances ou béat, et avec tout cela il y en a qui ont partie de ces conditions qui s'y morfondent et qui voyent passer leurs escoliers avant eux.' I would like to thank Christian Jouhaud for bringing this text to my attention.

CHAPTER 13

The Mazarin Years

IN THE BROAD sweep of French history the ministry of Mazarin seems to parallel that of Richelieu with uncanny exactitude – one cardinal succeeded by another whom he had groomed as his successor, who pursued similar policies at home and abroad, and whose ministry, to cap it all, also lasted eighteen years. But such a parallel, which only becomes persuasive from the perspective of the very last years of Mazarin's ministry when a number of objectives common to both ministers had finally been achieved, disguises a multitude of dissimilarities along the way. There is no need to retrace them in detail here, beyond pointing to the long minority of Louis XIV and the political upheavals collectively known as the Frondes which came so close to altering the whole direction of France's political development. The evolution of the episcopate during these years, it will be argued here, is more revealing of the discontinuities between the two ministries than of their enduring common threads. As political circumstances changed, so the responses to them altered the 'parallelogram of forces' which between them determined who succeeded and who failed in obtaining episcopal office during these years.

During the regency following Louis XIII's death (1643–51), it was inevitable that ecclesiastical patronage could not be managed in the same way that Richelieu, with steady royal backing, had done for so long. The dying king's willingness to allow figures like Gaston d'Orléans and Condé a formal role in the regency was the beginning, not the end, of change. If past regencies were any yardstick, the *grands* would expect to be listened to and their interests satisfied, in the church as elsewhere. This particular regency, however, differed from past precedents in that the continuation of a major war on several fronts kept many nobles busy for years and, for a time at least, presented the ministry with a less impossible task than might have been expected, bearing in mind the numbers of nobles who emerged from prison or exile with grievances against Richelieu and the late king. But a crisis in relations between the crown and the nobility was not to be avoided: it was only deferred for several years.

There was, however, one immediate change for which there was no precedent, and which could not be ignored by any of those, from ministers to episcopal hopefuls, interested in the fate of France's bishoprics. The establishment of a *conseil de conscience* in June 1643 constituted a striking response to altered circumstances. It was an unmistakable attempt by the reformers and *dévots* to retain and consolidate the influence which, however informally, they had acquired by the later years of Louis XIII's reign. The obvious justification for something more formal at this juncture was that the king was a minor, and that the task of minding his conscience should be exercised collectively. And with a long royal minority in the offing, and hence the prospect of political uncertainty or even unrest, such a body appeared the best hope of ensuring that the standards which had gradually become accepted in previous years, would continue to be upheld.

Mazarin, for obvious reasons, began his ministerial career with a rather limited ecclesiastical clientèle. But this former client of the Barberinis had had ample opportunity to observe the ways of the French monarchy, and was no beginner in the arts of governing through diplomacy and finesse rather than by fiat. His well-documented unwillingness to take full priestly orders and commit himself irrevocably to an ecclesiastical career was no doubt the main reason why he never took the opportunity of joining the ranks of the French episcopate itself, as he might have been expected to do;[1] and when he did actually obtain a bishopric, after the Fronde, it was with geopolitical concerns in mind, both personal and political, since he kept the French-controlled but imperial see of Metz from 1653 to 1658.[2] Meanwhile, as his ministerial position strengthened, his capacity to attract both a lay and clerical clientèle grew. But there was nothing automatic about this on the part of groups or individuals who judged patrons by deeds rather than by words. Mazarin, for reasons of both personal temperament and political circumstance, was prone to make promises which he then found hard to fulfil. Apart from extending his embryonic clientèle, his approach appears to have been to exploit his position as minister-cum-favourite in order to attach to himself and his interests as many as possible of those needing his patronage. There is more than a grain of truth in Retz's bold assertion that the imperious Richelieu was succeeded by a cardinal who apologised for the fact that his rank did not allow him to act as the humble servant of those who approached him to the degree that he would have wished.[3]

1 See Madeleine Laurain-Portemer, *Etudes Mazarines* (Paris 1981), 'Le statut de Mazarin dans l'église', 19–153.
2 See Joseph Bergin, 'Mazarin and his Benefices', *French History* 1 (1987), 7.
3 Cardinal de Retz, *Oeuvres*, ed Marie-Thérèse Hipp and Michel Pernot (Paris 1984), 178: 'L'on voyait sur les degrés du trône, d'où l'apre et redoubtable Richelieu avait foudroyé plutôt que gouverné les humains, un successeur doux, bénin, qui ne voulait rien, qui était au désespoir que sa dignité de cardinal ne lui permettait pas de s'humilier autant qu'il l'eût souhaité devant tout le monde.'

I

As in previous chapters, it will be useful to review the broad trends of episcopal patronage before attempting to examine in detail the challenges and responses of the Mazarin years. Indeed, the factual record of nominations between 1643 and early 1661 contains some valuable pointers to issues to be discussed later. A total of eighty-nine new bishops were installed during Mazarin's ministry, fourteen more than for for the correspondingly long ministry of Richelieu. Most of these nominations arose before and during the Fronde, with just thirty-one nominations being made between 1654 and 1661. But that is only part of the overall picture. Levels of episcopal mobility also continued to rise, and are reflected in the twenty-six transfers or exchanges involving reigning bishops between 1643 and 1661; they sometimes – particularly after the Fronde – gave rise to quite complex and protracted exchanges of dioceses and other benefices. One consequence of this was a considerable number of prolonged vacancies, as candidates either jostled for the nomination or used their nomination to one diocese as a bargaining chip with which to secure a more desirable one.

Coadjutors also made something of a comeback, especially in the early years, and again in the early and mid-1650s, but, though some of these cases are of particular interest, the scale of the phenomenon was much reduced by comparison with the 1610s and 1620s. On the other hand, even the record of the 1610s might have been completely outstripped and *every* French diocese (and abbeys and priories, too) might conceivably have had a coadjutor had a highly bizarre scheme hatched in late 1647 borne fruit. Facing the stark prospect of an empty treasury and in search of financial expedients of the kind that would spark the Fronde a few months later, Mazarin and his finance minister d'Hémery proposed that the king should forego all his church patronage rights for two years, during which time the current holders of benefices in his gift might choose their own successors freely in return for paying one year of their revenues into the treasury over a period of two years. A later version of the same proposal included a threat that those unwilling to nominate their own coadjutors would forfeit their right, and the king would act in their place.[4] The idea probably came from Hémery but Mazarin took it seriously enough to ask the ambassador in Rome in December 1647 to pursue it with papal officials.[5] Even without the political crisis that had begun in 1648, there is little doubt that the suggestion, which presumably had not received much, if indeed any, discussion at court, would have foundered in the face of Roman resistance. Its revival in November 1649, when Hémery was

4 BN, MS Fr 25025, fo 129, *nouvelles de Paris*, 12 Nov 1649.
5 *Lettres du cardinal Mazarin pendant son ministère*, ed A Chéruel and G d'Avenel, 9 vols (Paris 1872–1906), ii. 585–6, letter to Fontenay-Mareuil, ambassador, late Dec 1647. Here Mazarin outlines the workings and advantages, even to the curia, of the scheme.

recalled from disgrace, was even more ephemeral, and seems to have been regarded as just a desperate move by a bankrupt government.[6] For the most part, however, the Mazarin régime kept well clear of such novel ways of doing things; indeed the longer it endured, the more the often complex horse-trading over vacant dioceses tended to resemble that of an earlier age.

The early years of the regency were, in any case, to be unusually busy ones for all those concerned with episcopal office. No fewer than twenty-five of the eighty-nine new bishops seated between 1643 and 1661 had been nominated by the end of 1647, while a number of other promotions were already well in train.[7] The appearance of so many opportunities to create new bishops was, as always, partly a matter of luck. Episcopal mortality rates did indeed favour the new régime from the outset: for example, six bishops died in 1643, five in 1645, and no fewer than ten in 1646. But there was more to what was happening than simply the filling of dead men's shoes.

As already noted, these were years of considerable mobility within the episcopate, far more than had been the case in recent times, as if bishops themselves were taking advantage of the changed political environment to further their ambitions or to extricate themselves from unpleasant situations. No fewer than nine reigning bishops changed bishopric before the Fronde. The triangular move in mid-1643 of François Fouquet from Bayonne to Agde and of Jean d'Olce from Boulogne to Bayonne was completed with the elevation of one of Vincent de Paul's closest allies, François Perrochel, to Boulogne; here was an exchange which the *dévots* could only support, but it was probably facilitated by the fact that neither Bayonne nor Boulogne figured among France's most desirable dioceses. The case of the much promised and often postponed bishopric for La Rochelle was also reopened in 1643, but it was not finally established until 1648; even then it only became practically possible after Henri de Béthune of Maillezais had succeeded Sourdis at Bordeaux in 1646. The one straight episcopal 'permutation' of these years, that between bishops Cohon of Nîmes and Douvrier of Dol in 1644, was an early reminder of unhealed wounds since Richelieu's time. Cohon's position at Nîmes as successor to Saint-Bonnet (forced to resign in 1633) rapidly deteriorated after Richelieu's death, and his own pugnacity and lifestyle did nothing to improve matters there. His choice of an exchange partner is not without interest either, as Cohon, originally from Angers, moved northwards to the small Breton diocese of Dol, hoping for 'some peace after the storm which battered me', Hector Douvrier, a Toulousain and

---

6 BN, MS Fr 25025, fo 129, *nouvelles de Paris*, 12 Nov 1649.
7 For example, Jean d'Estrades had been nominated to Périgueux in 1646, but preferred to bide his time until a more attractive diocese came along: Condom was much richer and less neglected, and was given to him in 1648, which meant in effect that Périgueux remained vacant for well over two years.

former member of Marie de' Medici's household, returned with evident eagerness to Nîmes and his native province.[8]

Moreover, Bishops Delbène of Albi and Rieux of Saint-Pol-de-Léon were rehabilitated by the 1645 Assembly of Clergy and the manner of their original condemnation was denounced in a posthumous attack on Richelieu's political methods.[9] In theory this outcome was without prejudice to any reigning bishop, but while Delbène had no success in reclaiming Albi, Rieux, benefiting no doubt from his family's entrenched local position, effectively undermined the authority of Robert Cupif at Saint-Pol, and left him with little option but to resign and move to Dol in 1648.[10] This move was in turn facilitated by Cohon's brief but unhappy experience at Dol, which he abandoned to Cupif in 1648.[11]

Not all changes were dictated by considerations of this kind. Some involved individuals or families who would later figure prominently in the episcopate of Louis XIV; by the same token, they suggest that established and older noble families were also well placed to take advantage of the new régime's need to consolidate its position by cultivating them. The elevation in 1643 of François d'Adhémar de Grignan from Saint-Paul-Trois-Châteaux to Arles and his younger brother's immediate accession to Saint-Paul, long a quasi-patrimonial bishopric under Grignan control, was the first of them.[12] Henri de Béthune's translation from Maillezais to Bordeaux, Léonor de Matignon's move from Coutances to the wealthy Lisieux, or that of Charles de Noailles from Saint-Flour to Rodez are other instances of a similar pattern.

Above all, one can point to the three important coadjutorships – important as much for the individuals as for the dioceses involved – put in place shortly after Louis XIII's death and highly reminiscent of an earlier age. Easily the most celebrated was that of Paris and Paul de Gondi – 'Monsieur le coadjuteur' to his contemporaries during the Fronde. Despite his low opinion of Gondi's uncle, the archbishop of Paris, Richelieu had nevertheless flatly rejected all suggestions of a coadjutorship for the nephew; the family was under a political cloud during the 1630s and Paul de Gondi himself became personally suspect to Richelieu for his associations and ideas by 1639.[13] The

8   AAE, CP Rome 83, fo 441, Cohon to Brienne (?), 6 June 1644. See Robert Sauzet, *Contre-réforme et réforme catholique en bas-Languedoc. Le Diocèse de Nîmes au xviie siècle* (Louvain-Paris 1979), 226–7, 244–6.
9   Pierre Blet, *Le Clergé de France et la monarchie. Etude sur les assemblées du clergé de 1615 à 1666*, 2 vols (Rome 1959), ii. 20–34.
10 BN, MS Fr 17362, fos 170–3, three letters from Cupif to Séguier, 1646–7 describing Rieux's activities and requesting the chancellor's protection.
11 Sauzet, *Contre-réforme*, 229.
12 In fact, Grignan was initially granted the coadjutorship of Arles by Louis XIII, but the archbishop, Barrault, died before it could take effect. See Retz's reference to this case below, n 20.
13 Derek Watts, *Cardinal de Retz: The Ambiguities of a Seventeenth-Century Mind* (Oxford 1980), 279.

Gondis could only take heart from the Cardinal's death, as is clear from the fact that within days of the event, the idea of a coadjutorship for Paris was revived.[14] With a Sorbonne doctorate in theology and so many family members who were widely admired models of *dévot* behaviour, there was then little reason to imagine Paul de Gondi becoming anything other than an ideal bishop, though his official nomination was delayed until a month after Louis XIII's death.[15] A few months later still, the coadjutorship of Sens was also settled in favour of Louis de Gondrin, nephew of Octave de Bellegarde, another leading figure in the episcopate. Henri Arnauld had reported in late 1639 that such an idea had been mooted, though Arnauld thought Archbishop Bellegarde would not consent to it.[16] But more to the point, Bellegarde family credit was particularly weak in 1639, and even had the archbishop not had his own reasons for opposing such a deal, concessions might not have been forthcoming.[17] By late 1643, however, things looked rather different: young Gondrin, who had been active in the Olier circle at Saint-Sulpice, was by now a far stronger candidate and, though there were some reservations about his possible leanings towards Jansenist ideas, they were soon swept aside.[18] The third of these early coadjutorships came only months later, in early 1644, and saw the Villeroy family, destined for higher status and enduring favour from Mazarin and Louis XIV, establish a first toehold in the episcopate, when Ferdinand de Neufville became coadjutor to his uncle, the unwell and often absent Harlay de Sancy, at Saint-Malo.[19]

This sequence of coadjutorships entailing traditional uncle-to-nephew successions and benefiting high-ranking court-based families (allowing for the rapid rise of the Villeroy) was one sign that episcopal nominations might well follow a different pattern than in recent years. In his memoirs, Retz later attributed the delay in approving his coadjutorship after Richelieu's death to the opposition of Sublet des Noyers, but he also noted that Louis XIII had

14　BN, MS Fr 15611, pp 593–5, Arnauld to Barillon, 24 Dec 1642: 'une chose qui est secrette et dont j'ay beaucoup de joye est que Mons de Paris veut faire pour Mons l'abbé de Rets tout ce qui pourra despendre de luy. J'espère que nous le verrons coadjuteur et bientost.'
15　BN, MS Fr 15610, pp 244–5, Henri Arnauld to Barillon, 6 Nov 1639: 'M l'abbé de Retz prescha à Pontoise le jour de la Toussaint admirablement bien'. As is well known, in his own *Mémoires* written decades later, Retz cynically interpreted his own motives in attending de Paul's *conférences de mardi* and behaving like a model ecclesiastic.
16　*Ibid*, letter of 6 Nov 1639. The proposal was apparently made as part of negotiations to enable Louis XIII's ill-fated favourite, Cinq-Mars, to acquire the duc de Bellegarde's office of *premier écuyer* to the king.
17　Louis-Henri de Gondrin, son of Marshal Bellegarde's sister, Paule, and future archbishop of Sens, was only nineteen years of age at the time, and there would almost certainly have been stiff opposition to any such premature promotion.
18　Pierre Blet, 'Vincent de Paul et l'épiscopat de France', in *Actes du colloque international d'études vincentiennes* (Rome, 1982), 89.
19　ASV, PC 45, fo 57, royal letter of nomination as coadjutor, 15 Apr 1644.

been so criticised for consenting to the coadjutorship of Arles for Bishop Grignan of Saint-Paul, that he had promised not to grant any others.[20] If true, this would indicate the extent to which opposition to such nominations had taken root in the final years of his reign. It also suggests how, in the aftermath of the deaths of Richelieu and Louis XIII, both participants and observers might be uncertain as to how things would develop. The prospects of those candidates who could have counted on Richelieu's favour were understandably in some doubt. Henri Arnauld reported in late December 1642 that Richelieu had designated the Carmelite friar, Léon de Saint-Jean, for Conserans if its bishop were to resign or die, but within a few weeks of the cardinal's death the coadjutorship was awarded to Pierre de Marca, who was closely connected to Chancellor Séguier. In the same letter Arnauld wrote that Narbonne was also rumoured vacant, and that the bishop of Rennes (La Mothe-Houdancourt, Richelieu's cousin) would get Narbonne, while Rennes itself would fall to Hardouin de Péréfixe, the cardinal's last *maître de chambre*. Such talk left Arnauld to conclude that major changes did not seem in store as yet: 'you can see from this what the position of the relatives and servants of the late Cardinal is'.[21] With the cardinal dead and Mazarin's future far from certain, former ministerial clients of Richelieu's like Séguier, Chavigny, and Sublet des Noyers briefly emerged as would-be patrons of future bishops, but in the event they enjoyed very limited success. For example, in March 1643 Sublet, who was now thought to dominate the king's confessor, wanted the vacant see of Agde for the abbé de Champigny against the claims of Anne de Ventadour whose Montmorency relatives had long dominated the see, but Sublet's disgrace soon terminated his activities. As Arnauld put it, 'there is intrigue in the matter', and not for the only time it was a *tertius gaudens*, François Fouquet, a Richelieu client who was already bishop of Bayonne, who emerged the victor in mid-1643.[22] Chavigny, who had so long acted as a vital intermediary between Richelieu and those in search of patronage, was another loser in the political struggle with Mazarin, but as he remained a minister without portfolio he retained some influence, and petitions for bishoprics from several *grands* continued to be directed to him.[23]

20 Retz, *Oeuvres*, 170: 'Comme le roi avait pris des engagements assez publics de n'en point admettre, depuis celle qu'il avait accordée à Monsieur d'Arles, l'on balançait . . .'.
21 BN, MS Fr 15611, fo 598, letter of 31 Dec 1642: 'par là, vous voyès en quelle posture sont les parents et les serviteurs du défunt'.
22 *Ibid*, fo 659, letter of 8 Apr 1643; fo 664, 15 Apr; *ibid*, fo 667, 19 Apr, when he reported Agde had not been granted, adding 'il y a intrigue dans cette affaire. On doute que Mons l'abbé de Mesmac (Anne de Ventadour) puisse l'avoir.'
23 See Longueville's request for Aix for the late archbishop's relative, the dean of Rouen cathedral (AAE France 848, fo 100, letter of 16 Nov 1643, reminding him of a previous petition) and Epernon's request for the see of Vabres for a cousin (*ibid*, fos 196–8, 24 Nov 1644). Neither obtained satisfaction, suggesting that Chavigny's powers as a patron had seriously declined.

II

By late 1643, Mazarin had survived the first challenge to his ambitions as Richelieu's successor from the *cabale des importants*, and the *conseil de conscience* had been formally constituted. Conflicts between him and the *dévots* would arise over the years to come, and it is these rather than the record of their cooperation which have tended to attract attention. As far as the choice of bishops was concerned, the 'conflict' version of events is not without its elements of truth, but it would be a mistake to conceive the history of episcopal patronage during the minority of Louis XIV purely in these terms. Only a more detached review of the evidence as a whole can hope to reach conclusions which do justice to the complexity of motives and pressures of those involved.

Judging by the identity of the bishops nominated before the Fronde, the evidence points to a relative equilibrium of influence and success on the part of the ministry, the nobility and the *dévots* respectively, though these categories should not be viewed too rigidly, let alone as mutually exclusive. The number of French clerics in Mazarin's personal entourage was small to begin with, so it would be wrong to expect to see him repeat what Richelieu himself had been able to do only during the 1630s. But his first obvious success, in early 1644, was at least identical to one of Richelieu's earliest moves – the nomination of his own brother, the Dominican Michele, to the see of Aix, in spite of strong support by the governor Alais and the duc de Longueville for alternative candidates. However, the episcopal career of Michele Mazarin, who like Alphonse de Richelieu also became a cardinal, was to prove extremely short; he spent most of his few remaining years with the French administration of occupation in Catalonia and died in Rome in 1648. Not only was there no other family member available to take his place, but his death in Rome led to a prolonged tussle with the papacy over who had the right to nominate his successor at Aix. Meanwhile, Mazarin waited until 1646 before placing two non-family protégés, Claude Auvry and Jean-Vincent de Tulles (the latter already bishop of Orange), in the sees of Avranches and Lavaur respectively. This enabled another Italian dependant, the Dominican Serroni, to obtain Orange, where he faithfully served the cardinal until he was rewarded with the see of Mende only weeks before Mazarin's death in early 1661.[24] In addition, Mazarin's ministerial position meant that he was extremely well placed to act as a patron to bishops in trouble such as Cupif and Cohon, or to problematic candidates like Marca and Bosquet, who would later figure among his most prominent allies in the episcopate. The same kind of patronage was naturally extended to servants of Anne of Austria

---

24 Serroni may in fact initially have been a friend of Mazarin's brother, Michele, a fellow Dominican: *Mémoires de Philippe Gourreau de la Proustière*, ed Béatrix de Buffevent (Paris 1990), 159.

like Jacques de Montrouge who was initially preferred to Bosquet for Pamiers because, it was said, he had risked his life in the regent's service. Whatever the veracity of that assertion, it was Mazarin's protection which enabled Montrouge to hold on to Pamiers until he could exchange it for Saint-Flour which he found more attractive. Men like these would form the nucleus of the Mazarinist party among the episcopate during the Fronde.

Meanwhile, as we have seen, the claims of noble patrons and their clients had become more pressing after Louis XIII's death, partly in reaction to the lean years that had preceded. They had, as we saw, never accepted that their influence should be so reduced. Gaston d'Orléans may not have enjoyed formal presentation rights in his apanage, but he was as anxious as ever to demonstrate that his interests in episcopal nominations there deserved consideration. Chartres fell vacant in 1641 with Bishop Etampes's translation to Reims, and Gaston pressed hard for it to be given to his favourite, the abbé de la Rivière. But he was again ignored and it went instead to Richelieu's confessor, Jacques Lescot, whose Roman provisions did not arrive until a few months after Louis XIII's death. Gaston was still not resigned to the outcome, and was by then arguably better placed to make his voice heard. For his part, Mazarin, still in a weak political position and anxious not to alienate the king's uncle, sought to defuse the conflict by pressing Lescot not to have himself consecrated to Chartres, but to wait until some other diocese became available to which he could be transferred without undue fuss.[25] Interestingly, it was not Mazarin, but Lescot, who frustrated Gaston by ignoring the minister's advice and having himself consecrated. As it was, Gaston had to wait until 1646 for his first success, when Orléans itself was given to Alphonse Delbène, the nephew of the bishop of Albi deposed for his part in Gaston's 1632 revolt. In the absence of direct evidence, it may be assumed that Mazarin behaved rather as Richelieu had done in the early years of his ministry and did not oppose the Gondi, Gondrin and Neufville coadjutorships which were authorised in the following months; they, too, were part of a process of stabilising the régime by satisfying the ambitions of the families in question.

Moreover, in the coming years, the regency also demonstrated a noticeable readiness to promote sons of nobles actively serving in the royal armies or in provincial military posts. For example, among the new bishops nominated before the Fronde, one-quarter were sons or brothers of present or future *maréchaux de France*.[26] Apart from their own pedigree, such candidates could obviously count on some influential supporters. In 1643, Louis de Bassompierre, the illegitimate son of Marshal Bassompierre and Henriette d'Entragues, was put forward by Alais, governor of Provence, for the archbishopric of Aix, and Alais underlined how important the see was to the

25 Blet, 'Vincent de Paul et l'épiscopat de France', 88.
26 Neufville, Choiseul, Aumont, Bassompierre, Gassion, and Estrades.

good government of the province.²⁷ But the new régime was not exactly rushing to reward Richelieu's former victims either, and the abbot Bassompierre had to wait until November 1646 before obtaining the much less grand see of Saintes, having briefly accepted that of Oloron in Béarn. Another Richelieu victim, Epernon, was even less successful, and his pleas of loss and spoliation failed in 1644 to keep the see of Vabres in family hands.²⁸ The duc de la Rochefoucauld was no less anxious to promote his son Louis – younger brother of the Frondeur – to the episcopate from the early days of the regency. Mazarin supported his efforts to gain the wealthy diocese of Comminges in early 1644, but nothing came of their plans.²⁹ Six months later, Chavigny was informed that the duc had given up his designs on Angoulême, where the main family estates were situated, though, as Angoulême was not actually vacant at this time, it may be that he had been angling for a coadjutorship there.³⁰ His persistence finally paid off in 1646 when Louis was nominated to the small Gascon diocese of Lectoure. Louis's own personal inclinations may have had relatively little to do with his elevation, as it does not appear that he set foot in Lectoure between his confirmation in 1649 and his premature death in 1654.³¹

The suggestion that family services rather than personal merits were being rewarded in at least some of these cases is hard to avoid.³² In 1647 the semi-official *Gazette* announced that Pierre Gassion was given Lescar in Béarn and a promise of other benefices in open recognition of the services of his brother, Jean, the late Marshal Gassion.³³ It announced the nomination of Anne de Ventadour to Bourges in 1649 in similarly glowing terms – it was a case of 'His Majesty's wishing to reward the great services which members of the house of Ventadour have rendered to the state'; the candidate's own piety and doctrine were also mentioned, but later.³⁴ Mazarin pressed the ambassador in

---

27 BN, MS Baluze 175, fo 3, Alais to Mazarin, 27 Oct 1643. '[Il] tient la première place dans nos estats et nos assemblées, et peut beaucoup servir ou nuire aux affaires du Roy'.
28 AAE, France 848, fos 196–8, letter to Mazarin, 24 Nov 1644. The late bishop of Vabres and his predecessor were cousins of Epernon from the Cornusson branch of the La Valette family. In 1645, Epernon was pushing the claims of Jean de la Valette-Cornusson, brother of the late bishop, but his candidature was probably opposed by Vincent de Paul in the *conseil de conscience*: Vincent de Paul, *Correspondance, Entretiens, Documents*, ed Pierre Coste, 14 vols (Paris 1922–5), ii. 504, de Paul to Charles Montchal of Toulouse, 24 Feb 1645.
29 AAE, France 849, fo 116, *nouvelles de Paris*, 12 Mar 1644.
30 AAE, France 850, fo 129, La Rochefoucauld-Liancourt to Chavigny, Oct 1644. The duc's reasons were not explained, but Chavigny's assistance in the future was requested.
31 ASV, N Fr 89, fo 37, Louis XIV to Innocent X, 7 Feb 1647, extolling the services and merits of the house of La Rochefoucauld, in addition to the candidate's own worth.
32 See the duc de la Rochefoucauld's letter of thanks to Chavigny for the gift of Lectoure to his son 'le petit abbé': AAE France 1632, fo 300, letter of 3 May 1646.
33 BN, MS lat 17027, fo 242, 26 Oct 1647. The new bishop was himself a canon of Lescar, and a former military man; two other brothers were in royal service, one as an intendant, the other as a *maréchal des camps et armées du roi*.
34 BN, MS lat 17024, fo 160, 20 Nov 1649: 'Sa Majesté voulans reconnoistre les grands services que ceux de la maison de Ventadour ont rendus à l'Estat'.

Rome to overcome papal delays in confirming Jean d'Estrades for the see of Condom, reminding him in the strongest terms how much the new bishop's brother, another military commander and diplomat, meant to him.[35] It was, however, the nomination in 1647 of Edouard Molé, son of the first president of the parlement of Paris, which elicited the most unqualified statement to this effect from Mazarin himself, one which he repeated several times.[36] The fact that he felt it necessary to ask Vincent de Paul to take the candidate in hand and offer him instruction in the duties of a bishop was a tacit admission that the younger Molé's personal claims to preferment were distinctly limited.[37] Both Molé and La Rochefoucauld died young, while Estrades quit Condom after just ten years, and lived on until 1684.

The evidence from these years suggests that Mazarin's capacity to steer clients, dependants, and men like Edouard Molé into episcopal office grew gradually, and only became sustained from about 1645–6 onwards; but even then, he was far from having things entirely his own way. For example, Mazarin appreciated, like Richelieu before him, that the Assemblies of Clergy needed to be humoured. The Assembly of 1645, the first of the regency, was firmly bent on restoring the dignity of those bishops who had fallen foul of Richelieu, either through deposition during in the 1630s or through expulsion from the tempestuous Assembly at Mantes in 1641. It was in 1645 that commentators noted, for the first time it seems, that major benefices were being deliberately kept vacant while the assembly was in session, as an inducement to its members to conduct themselves as the crown desired.[38] But Mazarin had little control over the assembly's mood. As far as bishoprics were concerned, there is no clear evidence that this well-leaked policy worked, or that the vacant bishoprics in question were given as a reward to loyal deputies. Even so, it was a tactic that Mazarin would use again in later years, and not always with more success.

Meanwhile, during the pre-Fronde years, in addition to rewarding earlier services and existing clients and satisfying at least a cross-section of powerful interests, the cardinal also had to take account of the *dévots* both as candidates for episcopal office and, as happened in the case of men like Vincent de Paul, as patrons and scrutineers of those who were candidates themselves. It would be easy to give the impression that the two sides were locked into irreconcilable positions, since the surviving evidence is often the product of the conflicts which did arise. Equally it would be misleading to imply that the *dévots* themselves were somehow afflicted with an anti-noble animus. The fact

---

35 BN, MS Baluze 331, fo 46, letter to Fontenay-Mareuil, 7 Jan 1648.
36 *Lettres de Mazarin*, ii. 899, Mazarin to Molé and Hémery 21 May 1647; *ibid*, 924, to Molé, 18 July, underlining the gift of Bayeux as a recognition of the first president's services at a time when the parlement's cooperation was essential for the crown.
37 De Paul, *Correspondance*, ii. 563–4, Mazarin to de Paul, Feb 1646.
38 AAE, France 852, fo 18, Jacques Gaudin to Abel Servien, 8 July 1645. Gaudin regularly informed Servien, then French negotiator at Munster, of events in France.

is that some of the sons of court or military nobles who obtained dioceses during these (and subsequent) years had, like Choiseul, Gondi, Grignan and others, pursued extended university studies, and some had even taken the doctorate in theology; still others had frequented de Paul's *conférences* or Olier's parish and seminary at Saint-Sulpice, or even been involved in the activities of the *Compagnie du Saint-Sacrement*. As was the case with many of those made bishops under Richelieu, their personal affiliations were multiple and overlapping. The abbé Bassompierre was well regarded by both Mazarin and Vincent de Paul; the same appears to have been true of Gilbert de Choiseul, bishop of Comminges, whose family had stood firmly by Gaston d'Orléans throughout the crises of the 1630s; Henri Arnauld also won the cardinal's unstinting praise for his 'probity and ability' during a mission to Rome before his nomination to Angers. The *dévots*' quarrel was not with the nobility, great or small, but with the types of candidate and the methods of episcopal nomination to which the regency régime seemed in some instances rather too willing to resort.

In any event, there is no doubt that *dévots* continued to enter the episcopate in significant numbers during the regency, especially in the early years when the new régime was still finding its feet. The variety of their backgrounds, attainments and activities was considerable, following no single pattern. Perrochel of Boulogne and Caulet of Alet were both close friends and collaborators of de Paul, as were later choices like Sévin of Sarlat and Brandon of Périgueux, both nominated with a view to bringing order and reform to long-neglected dioceses. As we saw previously, exchanges of bishoprics also involved existing as well as incoming *dévot* bishops. Some of the latter, such as Brandon, had already been proposed for bishoprics under Richelieu.[39] The Grignan brothers, like the Gault brothers before them, were deeply involved with the *Compagnie du Saint-Sacrement*: when François de Grignan, the elder of the two, moved from Saint-Paul-Trois-Châteaux to Arles on Archbishop Barrault's death in 1643, it was a case of one founding member of the *Compagnie* taking the place of another.

III

The continuing success of the *dévots* in gaining episcopal office after 1643 cannot be fully understood without reference to the activities of the body usually known as the *conseil de conscience*. The publicity which in previous decades had accompanied proposals for some sort of *conseil de conscience* contrasts sharply with the discretion with which such a body was inaugurated within weeks of Louis XIII's death, in late May or early June 1643. Scarcely anyone at the time commented in any detail on the innovation – not even the

---

[39] De Paul, *Correspondance*, ii. 389.

papal nuncio, who might be thought to have had a special interest in informing Rome of what was afoot.⁴⁰ But rather than regretting such silence, we should perhaps see it as evidence of the changes which had gradually occurred in the previous decades, changes which made the move towards a council, especially during a regency government, seem a natural step to take and not an outright innovation likely to elicit extended comment from contemporaries. Yet its immediate origins should not be neglected for all that. Only a month before his death, Louis XIII, evidently missing Richelieu's advice and reflecting on how to fill the gap left by his disappearance, asked Vincent de Paul to send him a list of those he felt worthy of episcopal office – and that at a time when no more than two dioceses were actually vacant! It may also be, as de Paul says somewhat cryptically in his account of the king's request, that there had even been some discussion of a special 'seminary' under his direction for those who were candidates for episcopal office – an altogether more far-reaching idea.⁴¹ Years later, Jacques Dinet, Louis XIII's last confessor, wrote that it was through him that the king had approached not just de Paul, but also the Jesuits and others, asking them for a list of candidates who would be ranked 'in order of their ability and merits'.⁴² If accurate, this statement would credit Louis XIII with the paternity of the *feuille des bénéfices* administered by the royal confessor which only came into being many years later under Louis XIV. At any rate, there can be no mistaking the continuity linking these final efforts of Louis XIII and the beginnings of the *conseil de conscience*. Before its first formal meeting, which was apparently held on 4 June 1643,⁴³ the regent had 'had a list of deserving persons in the kingdom drawn up in order to fill the bishoprics which would become vacant'; to help her implement her plans, 'she chose a number of bishops to deal with the matter'.⁴⁴ At that first meeting, two episcopal nominations were discussed and one was decided upon in principle; the merits of François Bosquet, then serving as *intendant* in Languedoc, were also discussed and his name was put second on the list of *episcopabili*, though interestingly his claim to the see of Pamiers was not raised by his patron in attendance at the meeting, Archbishop Montchal of Toulouse, for fear of damaging his

---

40 See Blet, 'Vincent de Paul et l'épiscopat de France', 87–90. A letter from the bishop of Cahors, Solminihac, some weeks earlier makes it clear that de Paul did not lack for advice about episcopal affairs: de Paul, *Correspondance*, ii. 389, letter of 3 May 1643.
41 De Paul, *Correspondance*, ii. 387–8, letter to Bernard Codoing, in Rome, 17 Apr 1643.
42 'Derniers moments de Louis XIII racontés par le père Dinet son confesseur', *Le Cabinet Historique* 12 (1886), 232–3: 'une liste où ils seroyent rangés selon l'ordre de leur suffisance et de leur mérite'. This account was edited and published as the *Idée d'une belle mort ou d'une mort chrétienne dans le récit de la fin heureuse de Louis XIII* (Paris 1656).
43 BN, MS Fr 15720, fos 329–30, memorandum on affair of Pamiers succession, 1643.
44 *Ibid*, fo 332v, the precentor of Narbonne cathedral to François Bosquet, 5 June 1643: '(elle a) fait faire une liste de personnes bien méritantes du royaume pour remplir les Eveschés qui viendront à vacquer, et à cet effect elle a nommé certains evesques qui en prendront le soin'.

chances.⁴⁵ Unfortunately for historians, the subsequent reporting of the *conseil*'s deliberations never again matched that of its inaugural session.

Nevertheless, the early membership of the *conseil* provides some valuable pointers to its nature and activities. The presence of the regent, Mazarin and Chancellor Séguier was wholly in keeping with normal conciliar practice, and also a reminder that its principal business was to advise on how to dispense royal patronage. The hierarchical structures of church and state were acknowledged by the inclusion of two bishops and, like a number of other decisions in the early days of the regency, the individuals rewarded with places in the *conseil* were men who were personally close to Anne of Austria herself. The more important of the two bishops on the *conseil* was Bishop Potier of Beauvais, Anne's long-serving grand almoner (since 1624) whom, so it was briefly thought in 1643, she wished to make a cardinal and the ministerial successor to Richelieu. Another of Anne's favourite bishops, Philippe Cospeau, who had moved from Nantes to Lisieux in 1635, was also chosen to serve, but he had only a few years to live. More surprising in the longer perspective of the crown's traditions but in itself a striking testimony to recent developments, was the presence of two second-order clerics in the new body, Vincent de Paul and Jacques Charton, the *grand pénitencier* of Notre-Dame and director of the Parisian seminary known as the 'Trente-Trois'. Indeed, there may well have been some plan for a larger membership than this, possibly with representatives from more far-flung provinces. Certainly Montchal of Toulouse, who was at court in May-June 1643, was assured that he had been chosen to sit on the *conseil*; he did in fact, as we saw, attend its first session, about which he is the only known source of information.⁴⁶

Whatever the original plans for the *conseil*'s membership, they were probably affected by the political tussles which soon followed Louis XIII's death. Mazarin's emergence as the effective chief minister during mid- to late 1643, after he had swept aside the challenge of the *cabale des importants*, was a severe blow to Bishop Potier's ambitions for a red hat and the position of chief minister in particular. The wings of the new *conseil* were almost certainly clipped in the process, and Mazarin subsequently enjoyed more freedom of action with respect to ecclesiastical patronage than Potier, de Paul, and others would have wished. Indeed, Anne of Austria eventually ordered Potier back to his diocese, and he may have played no further part in the affairs of the

---

45 *Ibid*, fos 329–30, memorandum on Bosquet-Pamiers case. Bosquet's claim to succeed to Pamiers was based on Henri de Sponde's resignation in his favour. The other case discussed was probably that of François Perrochel, whose formal letters of nomination to Boulogne were signed only a few days later, on 9 June. Etienne Puget was also nominated to Marseille at this time.

46 *Ibid*, fo 332v, the precentor of Narbonne to François Bosquet, 5 June 1643; *ibid*, fo 331, Montchal to Bosquet, 22 June 1643.

conseil.⁴⁷ Cospeau was treated in the same way, and does not appear to have been replaced when he died in 1646. As de Paul implied in June 1648, this left the *conseil* without any episcopal membership at all for a time.⁴⁸ Bishop Cohon may have been brought into it at some time during the Fronde, but was excluded from it when his patron, Mazarin, went into exile in early 1651.⁴⁹ In the reorganisation which followed, there was still only one place for a bishop, Péréfixe of Rodez, Louis XIV's preceptor, while Charton and de Paul were joined by the young Louis XIV's first confessor, the Jesuit Charles Paulin.⁵⁰

The history of the *conseil* has often been summarised in terms of the relationship, not to say antagonism, between its two leading figures. The tendency to do so has been powerfully reinforced by the fact that it is their papers which have survived down to our time; even now, only the most fleeting glimpse of the activities of its other members is possible. Mazarin was, of course, a member of the *conseil* from the outset, but it is not usually realised that in the declaration of 20 April 1643 which constituted Louis XIII's political testament, Mazarin, as a member of the planned regency council, was explicitly entrusted with particular responsibility for ecclesiastical patronage, and that Anne of Austria was required to seek his advice when making church appointments.⁵¹ Even though the restrictions placed on Anne's powers of regent in the king's will were lifted after his death, the role intended for Mazarin in church affairs was not one of them.⁵² Thus, irrespective of the role envisaged for the new *conseil*, Mazarin – provided, of course, he could stay in power – had a prior and highly unusual personal claim to a powerful voice in ecclesiastical affairs, based on a solemn royal declaration, and he was unlikely to overlook it. This of itself would justify his readiness to act independently of the *conseil* and in concert with a willing regent over ecclesiastical matters. For that same reason papal nuncios normally raised Roman concerns over episcopal nominations directly with Mazarin and Anne of Austria rather than with members of the *conseil*.⁵³ It was also to the chief minister's advantage that the *conseil* was not empowered actually to initiate royal nominations. That privilege formally belonged to the regent who, once she had provisionally selected a candidate for a bishopric, put his name before

---

47   Ruth Kleinman, *Anne of Austria, Queen of France* (Columbus, Ohio 1985), 141, 145, 168–9.
48   De Paul, *Correspondance*, iii. 319, letter to Joseph Dehorgny, 25 June 1648.
49   BN, MS Fr 25025, fo 390v, *nouvelles de Paris*, 17 Mar 1651.
50   Antoine Dubuisson-Aubenay, *Journal des guerres civiles, 1648–1652*, ed Gustave Saige, 2 vols (Paris 1883–5), ii. 26, 1 Mar 1651. BN, MS Baluze 327, fo 1, François II de Harlay to François I de Harlay, archbishop of Rouen, 1 Mar 1651, who makes no mention of Péréfixe however.
51   Kleinman, *Anne of Austria*, 137–8.
52   A Lloyd Moote, *The Revolt of the Judges: The Parlement of Paris and the Fronde 1643–1652* (Princeton 1971), 64–6, makes no mention of the actual contents of the will in his analysis of its emasculation by the parlement of Paris.
53   Blet, 'Vincent de Paul et l'épiscopat de France', 88–9.

the *conseil* for investigation and report; it was only after it had made a positive recommendation (which also required Mazarin's personal signature) that a definite nomination could be made.[54] With such liberty of action, it is not hard to see why Mazarin would later evince irritation at what he saw as the *conseil*'s attempts to exceed its brief.

The best known, though not the most powerful, member of the new *conseil* was, of course, Vincent de Paul, whose long career was so intimately tied to an impressive range of reform activities within the French church. After Louis XIII's death, it was arguably his new position as director of conscience to Anne of Austria rather than his 'official' place in the *conseil* which accounted for his influence. In any case, it is inconceivable that he could have retained his place on the *conseil* for nearly ten years without enduring support inside as well as outside that body, even when its membership was reduced in numbers. Rumours of his impending disgrace were common almost from the beginning of the *conseil*'s existence. The most widely known instances date from early 1644 when Mazarin was reported to be furious with him because he disagreed with de Paul over who should be the new bishop of Comminges.[55] De Paul also appears to have angered Anne of Austria by saying that she could not nominate Louis Barbier, Gaston's favourite, as coadjutor of Narbonne until he became a priest and improved his morals.[56] But it is easy to take such incidents out of context and leave them incomplete. It is rarely pointed out that only a few weeks after the first of them, Anne of Austria decided to defer nominating a bishop for Comminges for a month. A shrewd but anonymous commentator wrote of this standoff: 'père Vincent is not so powerless as to be unable to prevent the gift of Comminges to Monsieur de la Rochefoucauld's son at Cardinal Mazarin's request, asking instead for it to be given to Monsieur Olier, curé of Saint-Sulpice'.[57] This particular deadlock was only resolved by giving Comminges to a third party, Gilbert de Choiseul, while Louis Barbier had to wait a further eleven years before obtaining a bishopric. Neither Anne nor Mazarin's anger arising from differences of opinion over episcopal candidates was sufficient to remove de Paul from the *conseil*; it was only as late as 1652 that he was finally ousted, but even then it was for having too openly demanded that Mazarin abandon ministerial office for good during the Fronde, a very different matter. De Paul has variously been described as president of the *conseil*, which is quite implausible, or as its secretary, which is far less so but not actually the case. Such a role was filled by one of the secretaries of state, if not by Anne of Austria's own *secrétaire des commandements*, who after 1646 was none other than Hugues de Lionne. This made the

---

54 François Pérard-Castel, *Traité sommaire de l'usage et pratique de la Cour de Rome*, 2nd ed (Paris 1717), 388.
55 AAE, France 849, fo 75, 20 Feb 1644.
56 Olivier Lefebvre d'Ormesson, *Journal*, ed Adolphe Cheruel, 2 vols (Paris 1860–1), i. 153, 17 Mar 1644.
57 AAE, France 849, fo 165, 12 Mar 1644.

secretary's role one of key intermediary between Anne, Mazarin and the *conseil*.[58]

As his regrettably incomplete correspondence shows, de Paul was a major conduit for reformist-*dévot* pressure and advice about episcopal nominations, and he actively invited information and advice on such matters from his correspondents when he felt it was needed.[59] Unfortunately, his ability actually to put the names of individual candidates before the regent and chief minister is much less easy to determine. If, however, we can judge by his own papers as well as by incidental statements from Mazarin in particular, it seems that, in institutional terms at least, he was the *conseil*'s *promoteur* and *rapporteur*, entrusted mainly with the thankless role of devil's advocate when it came to assessing the merits of candidates for high church office. In that sense, he was – and was expected to be – the conscience of the *conseil de conscience*.[60]

The subsequent history of the *conseil* faithfully reflects the ambiguities which surrounded its birth. There was no formal announcement of its inception, let alone any published declaration outlining its responsibilities. Even its title was somewhat elusive; it referred to itself officially as the *congrégation des affaires ecclésiastiques*, a wording which may indicate its anomalous and less than full conciliar status; on occasion, de Paul called it simply the *conseil des choses ecclésiastiques*.[61] Mazarin was just as imprecise, once loosely referring to it as 'those entrusted with directing the queen's conscience'.[62] At any rate, it is clear from subsequent years that it did not concern itself merely with royal church patronage, but with a wide range of ecclesiastical affairs, such as disputes between religious orders, the establishment of seminaries, and so on. That it met regularly during the early years of its existence at least, and occasionally more than once weekly, is also beyond doubt, though Mazarin's

---

58 Dubuisson-Aubenay, *Journal des guerres civiles*, ii. 26, 86, shows that during the Fronde there was bad blood between Lionne and the secretaries of state over Lionne's role in reporting the *conseil*'s decisions to the regent. On one occasion, Brienne refused to accept Lionne's role, and insisted on circumventing him and the *conseil* in handling church patronage with the regent. See also BN, MS Baluze 327, fos 1–2, François II de Harlay to his uncle, the archbishop of Rouen, 1 Mar 1651, on the role of the different secretaries 'pour depescher les expéditions après les résolutions prises'. At this juncture, the younger Harlay was at court attempting to become coadjutor to his uncle, hence his attention to such details.

59 See de Paul, *Correspondance*, ii. 504, de Paul to Charles Montchal of Toulouse, 24 Feb 1645, asking Montchal to enquire about Jean de la Valette-Cornusson, who was anxious to succeed his brother as bishop of Vabres. His claims were suspect to de Paul who was not even sure if he was in priestly orders.

60 Dubuisson-Aubenay, *Journal des guerres civiles*, ii. 72, is the only source to use the term *promoteur*, but it is in many ways the most accurate analogy, since ecclesiastical tribunals in France all had an official known as a *promoteur* whose duty it was to handle the cases coming before them.

61 De Paul, *Correspondance*, ii. 527, letter to Brienne, secretary of state, 2 June 1645.

62 *Lettres de Mazarin*, ii. 855, letter to comte d'Alais, 7 Feb 1648 (wrongly dated to 1647): 'ceux qui ont la direction de la conscience de la Reyne'.

private *carnets* show him trying to prevent this.⁶³ But how precisely it conducted its business is much less apparent. Its surviving papers are perfect models of discretion, conveying no hint whatever of how it made its decisions. They invariably take the form of recommendations to the regent that she might nominate a particular individual to a diocese or some other benefice. Like decrees of the royal council generally, they merely register decisions actually made, revealing nothing of the discussions which preceded them, let alone those proposals that were rejected or deferred. In fact, most of the extant decisions concern abbeys and other lesser benefices in the crown's gift; not until April 1645 is there any mention in its records of a recommendation for a bishopric, that of Isaac Habert for Vabres, and even then the proposition is laconic in the extreme.⁶⁴ Yet it had been directly concerned with episcopal patronage from the very outset, and at least a dozen episcopal nominations must have passed through it before Habert was proposed to the regent!

More regrettably still, it is impossible to determine whether the initial resolve to list deserving candidates in order of merit was upheld in practice during subsequent years. If the experience of François Bosquet noted earlier is anything to go by, it was not, since it was not until early 1648 that he got approval to become coadjutor of Lodève. Even though the Bosquet case was unusual in certain respects, and thus not a safe basis for generalisation, it seems highly improbable, especially in the circumstances of a royal minority, that either Anne of Austria or Mazarin would have wished to have their hands tied by a tightly defined order of precedence when bishoprics became available. This hypothesis would seem to be borne out by evidence from later years suggesting that candidates were only formally presented for the *conseil*'s approval once they were reasonably sure of obtaining it.⁶⁵ The tussles or disagreements over which individual to propose for a vacant see were normally resolved informally, and the assembled *conseil*'s task was probably for the most part a rubber-stamping one. But open disputes in sessions of the *conseil* did occur, in the early years at least, and when they did they were necessarily harder to resolve, involving as they could a loss of face for one or more of those concerned. But once again, the evidence which exists does not always clearly distinguish disagreements over episcopal nominations which took place informally from those which either erupted, or were continued, during the *conseil*'s sessions. Bosquet, for example, was formally proposed by Mazarin himself for approval as coadjutor of Lodève during a formal session in December 1647, but de Paul objected that there were dubious clauses in

63 Georges Minois, *Le Confesseur du roi: Les directeurs de conscience sous la monarchie française* (Paris 1988), 395, quoting from Mazarin's private *carnets*.
64 AAE, France 851, fos 120–1, *congrégation* of 3 Apr 1645. The *résultats* of the *conseil* for these years are filed chronologically alongside other state papers in these volumes.
65 AAE, France 875, fo 266, *nouvelles de Paris*, [1651?].

Bishop Plantavit's resignation, which held up his nomination for several months while the claims against him were investigated.[66] The comte d'Alais, governor of Provence, strongly supported Nicolas de Valavoire for the Provençal see of Sisteron in 1648. Mazarin, while conceding that Valavoire was under-age and still lacked some of 'the preparations required by those in charge of the queen's conscience', promised to do everything he could for him.[67] But the opposition was evidently too stiff: Valavoire did not get Sisteron, and had to wait a further four years before the neighbouring see of Riez came his way.

IV

Clearly Vincent de Paul and the circles in which he moved had formed definite ideas on who would make good bishops. They were also concerned in varying degrees with what might be called the 'ideological' leanings of candidates, a problem which would loom increasingly larger, in the 1650s and later as Jansenism became a major issue. In the meantime, strong Gallican views among prospective bishops also aroused their suspicions, and Rome, as Pierre de Marca discovered, proved less willing to overlook such sentiments than reports of behaviour unbecoming in future bishops.[68] Their demand for active and resident pastoral bishops was not new in itself, but proven personal experience mattered far more than expectations of good performance, whatever their basis might be; they were decidedly reluctant to put their faith in candidates whose claims were based mainly on prior family service, even in the episcopate. It is not hard to see how all of this could lead to friction with the regent, Mazarin and wider circles at court and beyond. At times, the gap between the sides could be a wide one, as when the outspoken bishop of Cahors wrote to de Paul in 1648 lamenting the state of the neighbouring diocese of Rodez and expressing incomprehension over a proposed successor there to Charles de Noailles: 'I cannot believe that because of considerations of state, the Queen could possibly nominate to this diocese a person who does not have the required qualities for its reform; it would pain me greatly if that

---

66 BN, MS Fr 15720, fo 341, 'justification du sieur Bosquet'; *ibid,* fo 339, for an undated draft of a resolution by the *conseil de conscience* accepting Plantavit's resignation in favour of Bosquet: this was presumably the outcome of the session of 24 Dec 1647 anticipated by Mazarin. The accusation was that Bosquet had only obtained Plantavit's resignation by promising to buy his library, a chapel and a house belonging to him in Lodève, and that such a promise constituted a form of simony.

67 *Lettres de Mazarin,* ii. 885, letter to comte d'Alais, 7 Feb 1648 (wrongly dated 1647, since the bishop of Glandèves only died in Jan 1648).

68 Blet, 'Vincent de Paul et l'épiscopat de France', 89, for opposition to episcopal office for Robert Constantin, a Sorbonne theology graduate who fell into the category of those who were suspect 'sur l'intégrité de la doctrine'.

were to happen'.⁶⁹ However, the evidence of conflicting priorities over episcopal choices is usually much less explicit than this, and has often to be gleaned, sometimes by reading between the lines, from a variety of sources. At the same time, it would be simplistic to assume that Mazarin, whatever the accusations made against him, was wholly 'political' in his views on episcopal office. He may have resented the constraints which a body like the *conseil de conscience* represented, but if there were fewer outright collisions between the two sides than might be imagined, it was probably because Mazarin was prepared to accept the standards which the *conseil* was attempting to apply. He may not have pressed too strongly the claims of Louis de Guise or Nicolas de Valavoire for this reason. Writing to the comte de Parabère in 1648 to explain why he did not even ask for, let alone obtain, the see of Tarbes for his son, Mazarin cited the 'lack of the required age and priestly orders, which constitute insuperable obstacles to his receiving the rank of bishop at this point'.⁷⁰

A particularly vivid impression of what making bishops in these years could entail is provided by the correspondence between de Paul and his longstanding friend and advisor, Alain de Solminihac, the energetic bishop of Cahors. How distinctive this correspondence may have been is difficult to say, but it is the only one of its kind to have survived for the entire period covered by this book. Of course, it offers only a partial view of the workings of episcopal patronage, but it is all the more invaluable in that it gives particular weight to Solminihac's own ideas and outbursts; de Paul, by contrast, appears as a discreet, self-effacing recipient of warnings and recommendations, though the exchanges between the two must have been less one-sided in reality. The perspective they offer is, therefore, that of a forceful *dévot* bishop from the provinces who had long known de Paul, Olier, and many other reforming figures within the clergy; over the years he evidently enjoyed ready access to Richelieu, as well as to Anne of Austria. Moreover, Cahors was an ideal vantage point for south-west France in general, since it was contiguous with more dioceses than any other in the entire realm – ten in all. But Solminihac's concerns were not limited to minding his neighbours' business, and he occasionally looked further afield. He was one of those, for example, who denounced the 'atheism' of Philibert de Lavardin, nominated to Le Mans in 1648.⁷¹ Mostly, though, he deplored the inadequacies of his own episcopal neighbours, and the dreadful state of their dioceses which, as he repeatedly insisted, made his own task in Cahors even harder. His intention, clearly, was to use de Paul to spark a sense of urgency in the capital about the need to ensure that a generation of ageing, no longer active bishops was succeeded by

---

69 Alain de Solminihac, *Lettres et documents*, ed Eugène Sol (Cahors 1930), 370, Apr 1648.
70 *Lettres de Mazarin*, iii. 1068, letter of 24 Oct 1648: 'le deffaut de l'aage et de l'ordre de prêtrise, (qui) se trouvent des obstacles invincibles pour recevoir présentement le caractère d'évesque'.
71 De Paul, *Correspondance*, iii. 351, letter to de Paul, 28 July 1648.

one consisting of what he repeatedly called 'apostolic men' filled with higher ideals of what a bishop should be and do.

For years under Louis XIII and Richelieu, Solminihac had bemoaned the 'desolation' of the dioceses of Périgueux and Sarlat. He had high hopes that Jean de Lingendes, nominated in 1639 but not consecrated until December 1642, would become an effective bishop of Sarlat, and wished to draw him into his own vision of episcopal action. He was therefore dismayed when, by mid-1643, Lingendes seemed intent on returning to Paris as a tutor to Louis XIV.[72] Sarlat remained vacant in all but name until Lingendes finally resigned in 1646, the same year as the bishop of Périgueux finally died. The Sarlat succession proved a great success from both Solminihac's and de Paul's point of view, since the new bishop, Nicolas Sévin, was their candidate. But Périgueux was a different matter, since its fate was tied to that of Condom, another of Cahors' neighbours. It was first given, in mid-1646, to Jean d'Estrades whose career was largely in his brother's hands, and who in any event was on the lookout for a 'better' diocese. Condom duly came his way over a year later, but it was not the prolonged vacancy which this entailed that troubled Solminihac most. Rather it was the prospect of the deceased bishop of Condom's unqualified nephew laying claim to Périgueux as his 'reward' for facilitating Estrades's succession at Condom. For his part, de Paul vigorously resisted the nephew's ambition, and Solminihac thundered in one of his letters to him: 'I cannot imagine how it is possible to think of giving dioceses to such persons'.[73] Solminihac may not have been aware that there was another candidate for Condom, Louis de Guise, illegitimate son of the last Guise cardinal. For a time at least, Guise had Mazarin's support, but he was opposed by de Paul. Mazarin tried to force de Paul to concede that his opposition to Guise boiled down to an unspecified question of fact, and insisted that he, Mazarin, knew for certain that the alleged fact was untrue. He therefore asked de Paul to conduct an enquiry and report to the *conseil*, since the issue was important to him.[74] But the report was probably a negative one, since Guise dropped out of the running, and Mazarin was happy to support Jean d'Estrades for Condom instead. The irony is that, over ten years later, long after de Paul had left the *conseil de conscience* which no longer enjoyed much independence, Estrades, still relatively young but in all probability a reluctant bishop from the outset, quit the episcopate outright by resigning Condom to his former rival, Guise. Yet Solminihac's exertions over Périgueux were far from being in vain. After the prolonged delay he could finally write in mid-1648 to congratulate de Paul warmly on having secured the nomination of Philibert de Brandon, widower of Chancellor Séguier's niece and the very model of what Solminihac meant by 'an apostolic man'.[75]

72 *Ibid*, ii. 389, letter to de Paul, 3 May 1643.
73 *Ibid*, 256, letter of 4 Dec 1647.
74 *Ibid*, 248, Mazarin to de Paul, 10 Oct 1647.
75 *Ibid*, 344, letter of ?? July 1648.

Solminihac's correspondence with de Paul also shows that he fretted over three dioceses on his eastern periphery – Rodez, Saint-Flour and Tulle. Saint-Flour only became vacant when its long-serving bishop, Charles de Noailles, moved to Rodez in 1646. It was first given to Claude Auvry, Mazarin's client, and then, when he declined the offer, to Jacques de Montrouge, who had been designated for Pamiers three years previously but who did not really want it. Both Anne and Mazarin were determined to reward him for services rendered, and Saint-Flour suited him better than Pamiers. By 1650 Solminihac, however, was denouncing him to de Paul: 'his spiritual exercises consist entirely in hunting, and with a musket on his shoulder'. Only then does the bishop recall, virtually *en passant*, that de Paul had opposed Montrouge's episcopal ambitions at the outset and regret that his views had not prevailed at the time.[76]

For his part, Charles de Noailles only survived his transfer to Rodez by two years, dying in March 1648. Very quickly, Solminihac approached Anne of Austria with a gloomy account of the state of Rodez diocese, and protested to de Paul about a nomination he had heard of and which seemed to be founded on 'considerations of state'.[77] Who the candidate in question was remains unknown, but it was almost certainly not the ultimate winner, Hardouin de Péréfixe, preceptor to Louis XIV and future archbishop of Paris. Originally a Richelieu client, he had recently been a vicar-general of Rodez itself: his nomination was one about which Solminihac could feel well pleased.

As for Tulle, the reigning bishop had been installed as long ago as 1599. A reported attack of apoplexy in 1650 prompted Solminihac to begin attempts to influence the choice of an eventual successor. As on previous occasions, he asked de Paul to pave the way by presenting the regent with an account of the poor state of the diocese. His own choice of candidate was François de la Mothe-Salignac, dean of Carennac in Solminihac's diocese, and he urged de Paul to support him by adding that he personally regarded him as the fittest man in Guyenne to govern Tulle.[78] But Tulle would not fall vacant for nearly three more years, and it would be given to one of Mazarin's most loyal servants. The dean of Carennac would have to wait much longer for his reward, but when it came it cannot have displeased either him, Solminihac or de Paul: in 1658 he was finally nominated to Sarlat, which Bishop Sévin had left to become coadjutor to Solminihac at Cahors. Salignac's elevation ended the twenty-year gap in his family's tenure of Sarlat which began in 1568 and ended with his own death in 1688.

---

76 *Ibid*, iv. 25, 25 May 1650: 'enfin tous ses exercises sont la chasse, in brevibus, un fusil sur le col'.
77 *Ibid*, iii. 293–4, letter to de Paul, Apr 1648. The approach to Anne of Austria was made via Louis XIV's governess, Marie-Cathérine de la Rochefoucauld, marquise de Senecy, was a committed *dévote* with extensive family connections in the region.
78 *Ibid*, iv. 24–5, letter to de Paul, 25 May 1650. On La Motte-Salignac, uncle of Fénelon, see *Correspondance de Fénelon*, ed Jean Orcibal, vol i: *L'Abbé de Fénelon, sa famille, ses débuts* (Paris 1972), ch 3.

Casting his eye somewhat further afield in 1651, Solminihac also raised the question of Montchal's succession at Toulouse, again asking de Paul to advise the regent that the diocese was in a worse state than was generally believed and, more worryingly, that Jansenism had take root there. As far as he was concerned, there was no prelate in the region, or indeed elsewhere, who was right for such a post, especially as the parlement of Toulouse was a perpetual thorn in the archbishop's side.[79] Although Solminihac had no successor to suggest for Montchal, it may well be that some of his reflections were, however faintly, heard and digested at court, for the new archbishop, Pierre de Marca, bishop of Conserans, was himself a former president of a parlement and a determined anti-Jansenist.

However, it is perhaps appropriate that Solminihac's long correspondence with de Paul over episcopal questions should tail off over the question of his own succession at Cahors. It is also remarkably rare, considering how frequent they were in the period, to have any record of a bishop's own reaction to rumours of his death. At Christmas 1650, Solminihac nearly died from blood entering his lungs. The news instantly triggered the despatch of special messengers to court in order to canvass the vacant see.[80] Epernon's brother, the bishop of Mirepoix, was one of the candidates. Another was Cyrus de Villers, a royal almoner close to Anne of Austria and a future bishop of Périgueux, but there were probably others.[81] These developments made Solminihac, whose health was otherwise very robust, write to de Paul for him to remind the regent of her promise to him as long ago as 1646 to nominate an 'apostolic man' as his successor in case of death.[82] Quite what kind of solution he had in mind he did not say, for he later claimed that he was neither old nor incapacitated enough to require a coadjutor; he may have left it to de Paul to unravel his precise intentions. At any rate, Anne of Austria replied by giving him permission to select a coadjutor of his choice.[83] By July 1651 he had made up his mind in a manner which, though unusual, was not without precedent. He was by then so impressed with Sévin of Sarlat that he could think of no one more suited to the task of perpetuating his own vision of episcopal action into the next generation.[84] As we saw, it was not until 1657 that Sévin was finally confirmed as his coadjutor – a striking

---

79 De Paul, *Correspondance*, iv. 244–5, to de Paul, 29 Aug 1651. He even reminded de Paul of his prediction in 1645 that whoever became archbishop of Bordeaux would be unhappy there, and claimed that Henri de Béthune sorely regretted his promotion from Maillezais.
80 AAE, France 874, fo 11, Léon de Saint-Jean, Carmelite, to Mazarin, 19 Jan 1651: 'La mort de M l'Evesque de Cahors est certaine, le bénéfice estant de 40,000 livres il est aisé d'en tirer l'establissement de vostre serviteur'. Père Léon protested that he did not actually want Cahors, only a pension from its revenues.
81 Solminihac, *Lettres et documents*, 460, Jacques Vitet to Solminihac, Paris 1 July 1651.
82 De Paul, *Correspondance*, iv. 145–7, to de Paul, 25 Jan 1651.
83 *Ibid*, 154, de Paul to Solminihac, 18 Feb 1651.
84 *Ibid*, 219–20, to de Paul, 2 July 1651; *ibid*, 634–5, to Anne of Austria, same date.

reminder of the continuing complexity of episcopal politics in post-Fronde France.[85]

V

It was inevitable that the Fronde, even when it did not involve actual civil war, would bring new pressures to bear on the workings of episcopal patronage. Hitherto the spoils had been fairly evenly divided between the various parties concerned, possibly because a higher than usual number of bishoprics had been available for distribution since 1643. This indeed would continue to be the case into 1648, and again from 1651 to 1653. 1649 and 1650 were lean years, though only relatively so. Indeed, when Colbert and Le Tellier were attempting in late 1650 to obtain an abbey from Mazarin for one of Le Tellier's sons, then a student, it was the scarcity of vacant abbeys rather than of bishoprics that they remarked upon, and that dictated the tactics which they decided to employ.[86]

Moreover, delays of one kind or another in filling vacant bishoprics during these years prevented any sudden drying up of episcopal patronage. Indeed, as the Fronde developed, it served to widen the circle of those competing for major church offices and hoping that the régime's weakness would enhance their chances of success. In mid-1651, at the height of the military conflict, the bishop of Poitiers died, and one source claimed that there were at least ten candidates to succeed him.[87] Such a proliferation may not be quite typical in every case, but one inevitable result of it was that candidates would have to have recourse to as many intermediaries and patrons as possible if they were to be successful. As the political pendulum swung back and forth during the Fronde, figures like Gaston d'Orléans and Condé attracted the attention of candidates who were not otherwise attached to them. As one candidate remarked in 1651, 'one needs to be on good terms with everyone'.[88] In such circumstances it is not hard to see why nominations might not be made for several weeks or even months. At times Anne and Mazarin were compelled to

---

85 *Ibid*, 490–1, 2 Oct 1652; *ibid*, 496–8, 17 Oct 1652; *ibid*, 517–18, 31 Oct 1652; *ibid*, v. 169–71, 26 July 1654. See also Orcibal, *Correspondance de Fénélon*, i. 47.
86 BN, MS Fr 4209, fos 57–8, Colbert to Le Tellier, 16 Sept 1650. Their plan was to obtain the promotion to the episcopate of a cleric already holding an abbey which in acknowledgement of their good offices he would agree to dispose of in Le Tellier's son's favour. But Mazarin was extremely wary, and did not believe Le Tellier had had so little reward for his services to date: See their correspondence in *ibid*, fo 101, Colbert to Le Tellier, 3 Oct 1650; fo 129, to same, 12 Oct 1650; fos 135v-6, to same 17 Oct 1650; fos 161–5, to same, 24 Oct 1650. Le Tellier did, however, succeed in obtaining one of the deceased bishop of Saint-Pol-de-Léon's abbeys some months later: BN, MS Fr 25025, fo 394, *nouvelles de Paris*, 24 Mar 1651.
87 BN, MS Fr 25025, fo 460, *nouvelles de Paris*, 18 Aug 1651.
88 BN, MS Baluze 327, fo 1v, François II de Harlay to Archbishop Harlay, 1 Mar 1651: 'il fault estre bien partout'.

announce that a nomination would not be made until the court had returned from a provincial expedition to Paris, which was simply another way of admitting that there was a deadlock. In the case of Poitiers, the competition was largely terminated when Anne announced it was to be given to no less a figure than Cardinal Antonio Barberini, whose status was enough to silence the remaining candidates.

At any rate, there seems to be little doubt that the political crisis which opened in 1648 made Mazarin more conscious of the need for episcopal support and of its value. This had consequences for the choice of new bishops as well as for promotions and transfers of existing ones. Dony d'Attichy of Riez, disgraced in 1647 for alleged opposition to royal demands in Provence, was 'restored' to his diocese in November 1648.[89] The siege of Paris in early 1649 began the process whereby bishops were drawn into political activity in a manner unprecedented since the League. A large number of them were present in the city itself, and from an early date during the siege moves were made to assemble them in order to mediate between the crown and the parlement.[90] Mazarin for his part tried to rally episcopal support with letters to individual bishops applauding their loyalty.[91] Others, such as Bishop Matignon of Lisieux, were potentially dangerous enemies, and in early 1649 the cardinal entreated him not to be drawn into revolt, despite his close family connections with the duc de Longueville, the Frondeur governor of Normandy.[92] Later, when Mazarin was under attack from the parlement, the Assembly of Clergy of 1650–1 could not but line up behind him in defence of a general principle – that cardinals were entitled to hold office – however much ecclesiastics like Retz or La Rivière might themselves wish to grab Mazarin's place in the ministry.[93]

From the outset of the Fronde, Mazarin had also been able to count on a small band of devoted episcopal supporters like Cupif and Cohon, both of whom had quit their dioceses, as well as Tulles of Lavaur, Auvry of Coutances and Boutault of Aire; pigeonholed as 'Mazarins', they were often unpopular, and two of them, Cohon and Boutault, were actually arrested in Paris during the blockade of the city in January 1649 on suspicion of passing information

---

89 AD Saône-et-Loire, G 465, *lettre de cachet* of 19 Oct 1647 denouncing him for his role in factional activity in the Estates, followed by letters from Hémery and Brienne and a second *lettre de cachet* exculpating him, 24 Dec 1647. See also *Lettres de Mazarin*, iii. 1073, letter of 28 Nov 1648, declaring his restoration. Evidently, the dispute had taken more than a few months to settle.
90 Dubuisson-Aubenay, *Journal des guerres civiles*, i. 107, 9 Jan 1649. The diarist claims there were up to three dozen bishops in Paris at the time.
91 See *Lettres de Mazarin*, iii. 1087, 1093, 1095, 1108, for letters to the bishops of Lavaur, Comminges, Sens, Saint-Pol-de-Léon and Bazas. No doubt other unpublished letters in the same vein could be found.
92 *Ibid*, 1080, letter to Matignon, 10 Jan 1649.
93 Although naturalised as a Frenchman in 1639, Mazarin's enemies treated him as an Italian adventurer like Concini, and the parlement renewed a decree against foreigners' holding office in France.

to the court.⁹⁴ This group would grow in numbers as the Fronde progressed. Bishops who previously had no particular ties to Mazarin now looked to him for protection against local enemies.⁹⁵ Tulles, Cupif, Boutault, and Péréfixe of Rodez all declined to attend a memorial service organised by the Assembly of Clergy in December 1650 for the dowager princess of Condé as they were 'too close to the cardinal to participate in an event which the court is not happy with'.⁹⁶

At the same time, Mazarin also had a number of second-order clerics active in his service, some of whom were engaged at various times in composing *Mazarinades* in his defence; they were frequently lampooned by name in the *Mazarinades* put out by the cardinal's adversaries.⁹⁷ Episcopal office would be the reward claimed by a number of them in the aftermath of the Fronde. Meanwhile, provincial Frondes also saw unpopular bishops, like Marsillac of Mende, Daillon of Albi, or Dony of Riez, having to face local hostility.⁹⁸ In Dony's case, the outcome was a growing desire to find a diocese somewhere else, and while he would undoubtedly have preferred Aix-en-Provence (where he might have turned the tables on his enemies in the province), he was finally happy enough to settle for Autun in Burgundy in 1652.⁹⁹ In Languedoc, it was the behaviour of the parlement of Toulouse and its high-handed treatment of the province's bishops, many of whom it threatened to arrest, which led to furious protest by the Assembly of Clergy meeting in Paris in 1651.¹⁰⁰ Even though there were no religious issues *per se* at stake during the Fronde, a cross-section of France's bishops found themselves drawn into the conflicts it spawned throughout the country.

VI

Turning to the evidence of episcopal nominations during the Fronde, it is apparent that Mazarin was more anxious than ever to maintain and even extend the control of patronage which he had been slowly building up in previous years. Throughout 1648, which witnessed the nomination of no

---

94 Dubuisson-Aubenay, *Journal des guerres civiles*, i. 162, 177; BN, MS Fr 25025, fo 19, *nouvelles de Paris*, 22 Jan 1649: Cohon was locked up in a house belonging to the Oratory.
95 *Lettres de Mazarin*, iv. 730, letter to Bishop Doni, 12 June 1651. Archbishop Béthune of Bordeaux and Bishop Martineau of Bazas both experienced problems with the parlement of Bordeaux, and turned to the court for protection.
96 BN, MS Fr 25025, fo 332, *nouvelles de Paris*, 16 Dec 1650: 'qui sont trop amis de M le cardinal pour se trouver en une action dont la cour n'est pas satisfaitte'.
97 See Hubert Carrier, *Les Mazarinades*, 2 vols (Geneva 1989–91), i. 191, n 617; ii. 31–2.
98 Beik, *Absolutism and Society*, 195. In both Mende and Albi trouble had begun before 1648, and in Albi the deposed Bishop Delbène continued to have much local support.
99 On his desire for Aix, see ASV, N Fr. 89, fos 240–1, Anne Doni, bishop's sister, to Innocent X, 29 Oct 1648; *Lettres de Mazarin*, iii. 1131, Mazarin to Doni, 20 July 1649.
100 Beik, *Absolutism and Society*, 211–12; Beik, 'The Parlement of Toulouse and the Fronde', 139–40.

fewer than eight new bishops, it was men who were either personally or through their families close to the court and the ministry who took the lion's share. They included figures as diverse as Bosquet of Lodève and Brandon of Périgueux, both of whom had long been candidates for the mitre, in addition to Beaumanoir of Le Mans whom, it will be recalled, Solminihac denounced as an atheist. Georges Aubusson de la Feuillade, brother of Marshal d'Aubeterre, might have become bishop of Gap rather than archbishop of Embrun (both in the Dauphiné) had not Lionne's father, bishop of Gap, refused the gift of Embrun obtained for him by his son.[101] The fate of the see of Aix-en-Provence should not have caused problems either, since both Mazarin and the pope wanted the same successor, Cardinal Grimaldi, a former nuncio to France and a friend to Mazarin; instead Innocent X's insistence on exercising the right to make the nomination himself (Michele Mazarin had died in Rome) led to a seven-year deadlock! Further evidence of ministerial confidence can be seen in the nomination of Péréfixe to Rodez or of Claude Malier du Houssay, a former ambassador to Venice, to Tarbes. The following two years, 1649 and 1650, witnessed only eight nominations between them, but although the profile of the new bishops is at first sight not markedly different, the political crisis was beginning to have an effect, politicising the process to a greater degree than had obtained hitherto. Furthermore, the reduced fund of vacant dioceses sharpened the competition for episcopal office, leading contemporary observers to comment more regularly on such questions.

The arrest of the princes in January 1650 and the year-long civil war which ensued proved the first real challenge to the ministry's control of episcopal patronage — and Mazarin's in particular. Significantly, the cardinal proved unable to manage the Assembly of Clergy of 1650–1, something which its defence of cardinals' rights to hold political office in France could not quite obscure; in his dealings with a particularly truculent assembly, he was even forced on the defensive by the Delbène bishops still looking for their uncle's restoration to Albi.[102] The policy of keeping abbeys and dioceses vacant while the assembly was sitting also proved unfruitful, since it refused the crown a much needed *don gratuit*, and in any case it was still in session when Mazarin went into exile in March 1651.[103]

The most widely remarked conflicts over vacant bishoprics arose in late 1650 when the dioceses of Mâcon, Clermont and Séez fell vacant within weeks of each other. All three illustrate the changing realities of episcopal patronage

101 ASV, PC 49, fo 8, evidence of Jacques Danès, bishop of Fréjus, 7 Apr 1649.
102 See Blet, *Clergé de France et la monarchie*, ii. chs 2–3, for a full account of the 1650–1 Assembly. BN, MS Fr 25025, fo 327, *nouvelles de Paris*, 2 Dec 1650.
103 BN, MS Fr 25025, fo 325v, *nouvelles de Paris*, 25 Nov 1650. The identity of the author of these reports has not been established, but it is evident that he was extremely close to, and well informed about, the ecclesiastical milieux of the time; the reports are a uniquely valuable source for the ecclesiastical politics of the Fronde years, far superior to the reports of the papal nuncio or other observers.

as the Fronde deepened. That of Séez took the longest to fill, nearly five months, because the three leading candidates enjoyed considerable support from different quarters.[104] Moreover, Séez was also in Longueville's governorship of Normandy, which made finding a bishop for it at this time a particularly delicate matter. The Franciscan, François Faure was an active Mazarin client with known episcopal ambitions; the abbé Camus de Pontcarré was a nephew of the previous bishop and enjoyed Gaston d'Orléans's support;[105] finally, there was François Rouxel de Médavy, brother of the powerful comte de Grancey who would become a *maréchal de France* in early 1651. The longer the vacancy lasted and the more the political situation worsened, the more Médavy's claim strengthened; when Séez was finally awarded to him in April 1651, Gaston's protests were of no avail.[106] It may also be noted that at around the same time Robert Cupif's former see of Saint-Pol-de-Léon in Brittany was given to Marshal Boisdauphin's brother in preference to a court candidate who was close to Anne and Mazarin.[107]

The Clermont and Mâcon successions were less protracted but were no less indicative of the crown's growing difficulties. Mazarin had previously promised Clermont to Jean de Lingendes, the former bishop of Sarlat who was close to both Anne of Austria and Gaston d'Orléans, and the promise was no secret. But the Bishop of Clermont, who had been blind since the 1630s and had for years resisted all pressure to take a coadjutor, finally yielded to family pressure in his last months and agreed to co-opt his brother Louis d'Estaing as his coadjutor. Likewise, the bishop of Mâcon had attempted during his last months to resign his see to Louis de Chandenier, a close associate of Vincent de Paul who evidently pressed Mazarin to honour the arrangement.[108] There were other candidates, for Mâcon in particular, among them Gaston d'Orléans's former favourite Louis Barbier, who had by now become a Condé supporter! In the case of Clermont, Louis d'Estaing could count on the support of Gaston, as well as on his own family's powerful relatives.[109] After initially declaring that decisions would be postponed until the court could return from the military campaign in the south-west, the crown's hand was soon forced by the scarcely veiled threats of the vicomte d'Estaing to ignite conflict in the Auvergne where the family's lands were

104 *Ibid.*
105 *Ibid*, fo 343, *nouvelles de Paris*, 30 Dec 1650.
106 *Ibid*, fo 409v, *nouvelles de Paris*, 14 Apr 1651.
107 *Ibid*, fo 394r, *nouvelles de Paris*, 24 Mar 1651; fo 405r, 4 Apr 1651. The other candidate is given here as the abbé de Jacinthe (*sic*): in fact he was Cyrus de Villers-la-Faye, abbé de Jassin.
108 *Lettres de Mazarin*, iv. 635, Mazarin to de Paul, 29 Sept, announcing that a decision about Mâcon was being postponed until the court returned from Bordeaux. De Paul's original letter has not been found.
109 BN, MS Fr 4208, fo 117, Colbert to Le Tellier, 8 Oct 1650; fo 129, same to same, 12 Oct. Colbert had hoped to obtain Mâcon for Barbier with a view to extracting an abbey from him in return for Le Tellier's son. Mazarin later promised to do just that next time a bishopric fell vacant. Le Tellier finally got an abbey formerly held by René de Rieux of Saint-Pol-de-Léon in Mar 1651: BN, MS Fr 25025, fo 394v, 24 Mar 1651.

located.¹¹⁰ Mazarin moved smartly to placate him, deciding that the old bishop's resignation (which had no force after his death) should be allowed to stand after all. The same logic was not applied to Mâcon: the old bishop's resignation to Chandenier was ignored and the see was given to Lingendes.¹¹¹

In these three instances, only one 'natural' court candidate proved successful. Meanwhile, existing bishops and well-placed families were beginning to awaken to the opportunity of taking advantage of the crown's difficulties. Beginning in May 1650, when Choart de Buzenval obtained his *brevet de nomination* to Beauvais, where his uncle Augustin Potier only had weeks to live, coadjutorships began to reappear, and they would remain a prominent feature of the next few years. Indeed, half of all the nominations between 1650 and 1653 were either coadjutorships or the result of resignations of one form or another. The full extent of this activity is disguised by the formal record since, as is indicated by the Beauvais and Clermont cases, plans for co-opting coadjutors were overtaken by the death of the bishops involved.

With Mazarin's ministerial authority weakening, one might have expected political rivals such as Gaston d'Orléans or Condé to take advantage of his difficulties. Condé's younger brother, Conty, was for a time during 1648 an official French candidate for a cardinal's hat, which might have enabled him to challenge Mazarin directly for ministerial office.¹¹² But it was only in late 1649, when Mazarin was briefly eclipsed by Condé himself, that the latter registered his one undoubted success - the nomination of his cousin Anne de Ventadour to the archbishopric of Bourges in November 1649. But his mprisonment in January 1650 and then civil war eliminated any further influence on royal patronage. That Condé was aiming to achieve more than merely preserve Bourges as the *chasse gardée* that it had been since the early 1620s is evident from a move in mid-1651, during Mazarin's first exile, to obtain 'quelque évesché' for Ventadour's younger brother.¹¹³ But since Louis-Hercule de Ventadour was at that moment a Jesuit, and neither the papacy nor the Society was prepared to permit him to move straight into a bishopric, another rapid promotion was impossible; by the time the younger Ventadour was eventually nominated to Mirepoix, it was Condé, not Mazarin, who was the exile.

Gaston d'Orléans, for his part, was in many ways far better placed than Condé to act as a major patron, as is evident enough from the number of

110 ASV, N Fr 101, fo 365v-6, *avvisi di Parigi*, 15 Oct 1650, 'obbligata al Conte Destain, acciò non armare in Overnia, dovè è molto potente'. As another commentator put it in retrospect, Louis d'Estaing obtained Clermont 'plus de force que de gré': BN, MS Fr 25025, fo 452, 4 Aug 1651.
111 Dubuisson-Aubenay, *Journal des guerres civiles*, i. 339, 14 Nov 1650; 'Correspondance inédite du maréchal de Gramont et de Hugues de Lionne (Sept-Dec 1650)', ed H Courteault, *Annuaire de la Société de l'Histoire de France* (1925), 267, Lionne to Gramont, 14 Oct 1650.
112 ASV, N Fr 89, fo 45, Louis XIV to pope, 7 Nov 1648.
113 *Ibid*, fo 408, letter to pope, 19 July 1651.

candidates for mitres who sought and obtained his support during the Fronde. He had registered one or two successes before the Fronde, but not perhaps the one that mattered most to him. His desire to advance his favourite and leading councillor, Louis Barbier de la Rivière, had been no secret since 1643, but early attempts to obtain Agde or the coadjutorship of Narbonne had failed.[114] As for their experiences during the Fronde, the problem seems to have been one of tailoring ambition to reality, since each time Barbier's chances improved, he and Gaston seemed to raise the stakes. By mid-1649, Barbier was even a candidate for a red hat, and it was widely believed that he, too, wished to supplant Mazarin.[115] In his ambition to succeed, Barbier abandoned Gaston and rallied to Condé in late 1649, but his timing could hardly have been worse. While invariably a candidate in subsequent years for sees like Reims and Noyon, both of which had peerages attached to them, he was made to wait until 1655 before his hour came.[116] Where Gaston is known to have supported other candidates for episcopal office during the Fronde, it appears that he was capable of delaying or postponing decisions, but not of imposing his own choices.[117]

If there were losers at all during these years, they were the *dévots*, despite the elevation of men like Brandon and Henri Arnauld; and it may be wondered if Arnauld would have obtained Angers with so little difficulty in early 1649 had it not been so solemnly promised to him during previous years.[118] The abbé Chandenier's claim to Mâcon got short shrift over a year later and was more typical of *dévot* fortunes. Solminihac's worries in late 1650 and early 1651 about the fate of Cahors should he die before ensuring an acceptable successor was co-opted, should be seen in this context.[119] Moreover, it is extremely difficult to imagine the *conseil de conscience* continuing to function normally in the midst of blockades of Paris, court peregrinations throughout the country, Mazarin's exiles, and several abrupt changes within the ministry. Its members were doubtless widely separated for extended periods of time, which may explain why mentions of it are extremely rare. But it was reshuffled in March 1651, just as Mazarin began his first exile; the royal confessor

---

114 Lefebvre d'Ormesson, *Journal*, 153, 17 Mar 1644.
115 ASV, N Fr 89, fos 40, 66, Anne of Austria to Innocent X, 9 June 1648 and 9 Apr 1649 respectively; *ibid,* fos 42, Louis XIV to pope, 4 June 1648; *ibid,* fo 67, Condé to pope, 10 Apr 1649; *ibid,* fo 82, Anne of Austria to pope, 8 Oct 1649; *ibid,* fo 93 Louis XIV to pope, 26 Jan 1650.
116 BN, MS Fr 25025, fo 115, 22 Oct 1649 (Reims); *ibid,* fo 420, 15 May 1651 (Noyon). AAE, 893bis, fo 157, unsigned minute of a settlement in favour of La Rivière, 16 July 1654.
117 BN, MS Fr 25025, fos 428v-2r, 16 May 1651, for the see of Alet, wrongly rumoured vacant. The nomination to Mâcon was delayed by Gaston, who also supported the abbé de Pontcarré for Séez when his uncle, Bishop Jacques Camus de Pontcarré, died in 1650, but without success: *ibid,* fo 343, 30 Dec 1650.
118 *Lettres de Mazarin*, iii. 1087, letter to anonymous correspondent, 4 Feb 1649. Arnauld's *brevet de nomination* was issued on the same day as his predecessor died – such alacrity was rare.
119 See above p 516.

and Bishop Péréfixe of Rodez joined it under the presidency of Châteauneuf, the new but short-lived keeper of the seals, while Cohon, one of Mazarin's most loyal episcopal clients, was excluded.[120] The timing alone suggests that this move was a conscious attempt to ensure that episcopal patronage was restored to its normal framework, and above all to remove it from Mazarin's control. Earliest reports indicated that it was conducting its business as usual, despite the continuing differences between Hugues de Lionne and the secretaries of state over the reporting of its resolutions to the regent.[121] However, an early discordant note was struck by Louis XIV himself in June 1651 when, having asked for a benefice for the poet Benserade, Anne of Austria answered that she would first have to refer the case to de Paul; to which the young king retorted 'that he did not care what père Vincent thought'.[122]

By then, however, it had become evident that Mazarin was determined even in exile to control decision-making as much as possible, in the ecclesiastical as much as in the political sphere generally. Quite how the *conseil* itself reacted to this remains a mystery. But within days of its reconstitution in late February 1651, one careful observer, François de Harlay, wrote presciently: 'some people believe that the cardinal still has a major role, though others will become involved in its business. It will not be a bad idea to be on good terms with everyone'.[123] These suspicions were rapidly confirmed, and the archbishop of Reims was told that if he wished to resign two of his abbeys he should first seek Mazarin's permission, which was duly given. Harlay commented that 'this shows which approach one needs to take'.[124] Harlay himself was far from being a disinterested observer at this juncture, since he was using his deputyship to the Assembly of Clergy to canvass for the coadjutorship of Rouen, where his uncle had been archbishop since the mid-1610s. His own experiences, as he conveyed them to his uncle, shed some valuable light on how a candidate in his position could manoeuvre in such uncertain conditions. For obvious reasons, he carefully noted the changes to the *conseil de conscience* in March 1651 and Mazarin's string-pulling from his exile.[125] He approached the *conseil* not through de Paul, but through Charton whom he and his uncle were determined to flatter and win over to their cause. But though favourable to their case, Charton declined to declare himself openly as

---

120 BN, MS Fr 25025, fo 390v, 17 Mar 1651; BN, MS Baluze 327, fo 1v, François II de Harlay to Archbishop Harlay, 1 Mar 1651. Harlay makes no mention of either Péréfixe or Cohon, perhaps because the changes were not complete by the date of his report.

121 *Ibid*, fo 390v, 17 Mar 1651: 'le conseil de conscience se tient à présent tous les lundy'; Dubuisson-Aubenay, *Journal des guerres civiles*, ii. 26, 'toutes les affaires de bénéfices s'y expédient aisément'. In July 1651, it was meeting under the presidency of Chancellor Séguier: *ibid*, 86.

122 AAE, France 875, fo 190, 14 June 1651: 'qu'il n'avait que faire du père Vincent'.

123 BN, MS Baluze 327, fo 1v, letter to Archbishop Harlay, 1 Mar 1651.

124 *Ibid*, fo 12, letter to Archbishop Harlay, 12 Mar 1651: 'cela fait voir le chemin qu'il fault tenir'.

125 *Ibid*, fos 1–2, letter of 1 Mar 1651.

their advocate, alleging difficulties arising from his opposition to another coadjutorship then under discussion.[126] When Harlay finally set about presenting his petition for the coadjutorship to Anne of Austria in late March 1651, he made sure that the bishop of Lavaur, one of Mazarin's most trusted servants, was on hand to press the regent on his behalf.[127] He had also taken care to lobby the Assembly of Clergy for its support, should it be necessary to play such a card. Anne of Austria gave her consent, and Harlay jubilantly reported the news to his uncle.[128] Their correspondence thereafter is lost, but it was not until late May that the case was formally approved by the *conseil de conscience* and Harlay, who would be one of the dominant churchmen of Louis XIV's personal rule, finally got his *brevet de nomination*.[129] The time-lag suggests that he may have cried victory too soon, and that it may have been necessary after all to bring pressure on the crown from the Assembly of Clergy to overcome whatever opposition there may have been in the *conseil* and elsewhere. But the Harlay de Champvallon family were loyal Mazarinists, and the exiled cardinal claimed the credit for the successful outcome, which in his opinion also proved how devoted he was to them.[130]

As is well known, resentment against Mazarin's continuing domination of government from Germany grew in the months following his exile. The six episcopal nominations made during the first half of 1651 did nothing to allay it, quite the contrary, since they largely benefited either men close to him, bishops seeking to co-opt successors, or nobles with whom Mazarin was anxious to strike bargains. However, the nomination of François Servien to Fréjus, which was briefly rumoured vacant in mid-July 1651 helped, albeit in a minor way, to bring matters to a head.[131] Certainly it contributed to the growing antagonism, not just against Mazarin, but against Servien's brother, Abel, and the other Mazarinist ministers (Le Tellier and Lionne) who had remained in post during the cardinal's exile. They were regarded as keeping the regent in thrall to Mazarin, and their removal from court followed a few days after Servien's nomination.[132]

By that date, mid-1651, the united opposition to Mazarin was on the verge of collapse, and Condé soon re-ignited the civil war that was to last with little

---

126 *Ibid*, fos 25–6, letter of 23 Mar 1651. The coadjutorship to which Charton was opposed was that of Soissons, but it would be pushed through in August 1651 in favour of Mathieu Bourlon. Charton had been on the *conseil de conscience* since 1643.
127 *Ibid*, fo 33, letter of 29 Mar 1651.
128 *Ibid*, fo 35, letter of 31 Mar 1651.
129 Dubuisson-Aubenay, *Journal des guerres civiles*, ii. 72–3. The author, well informed, writes that the *conseil* approved Harlay's coadjutorship on 23 May, and de Paul reported to Anne of Austria three days later; she then ordered the *brevet* to be drawn up by the secretary of state. See also AAE, France 875, fo 148, Gabriel Naudé to Mazarin, 3 June 1651.
130 *Lettres de Mazarin*, iv. 733, letter to marquis de Champvallon, 26 June 1651.
131 AAE, France 875, fo 239v, Bluet to Zongo Ondedei, 17 July (?) 1651; BN, MS Fr 25025, fos 444–5, *nouvelles de Paris*, 21 July 1651; *ibid*, fo 449v, 28 July.
132 Dubuisson-Aubenay, *Journal des guerres civiles*, ii. 91, 19 July.

interruption until Louis XIV entered Paris in October 1652. Moreover, with just one exception, episcopal nominations ceased altogether for virtually a year, until May 1652. This was mainly because opportunities to make them were extremely limited, something which could hardly have been anticipated. But it also seems as if the inaction was deliberate. When Montchal of Toulouse died in August 1651, Anne of Austria announced that she would not fill the vacant see – or any other post – until after the Estates General had met, 'in order to have the means of keeping people in line'.[133] But with Conty and Ventadour of Bourges as candidates for Toulouse, the stakes were much higher than usual, and procrastination was clearly in order, even without an Estates General. For his part, Mazarin was anxious to avoid appearing to make decisions, but it is also probable that he was not averse to obliging the numerous candidates in search of a falling supply of bishoprics to have recourse to him and in that sense to tie their own futures to his. Though not an archiepiscopal see like Toulouse, Poitiers, which fell vacant in July 1651, was a key see in western France, and it was also well endowed; as we saw earlier, it immediately attracted up to ten candidates who included two cardinals – Antonio Barberini and the former nuncio, Grimaldi – and a reigning bishop in search of a more placid flock.[134] Mazarin was informed about the various candidates, and was strenuously lobbied by his own client Louis Guron de Rechignevoisin, who had set his heart on succeeding La Rocheposay in his native Poitiers.[135] Mazarin's own preference, clearly expressed in his secret correspondence with the regent was, however, for Barberini, with Guron in third place behind the abbé Parabère. Were it to come to a competition between the latter two candidates, Mazarin wanted Parabère rather than Guron, 'having some reservations about the latter in the present circumstances, since he is an open Mazarinist'.[136] While Mazarin's awarness of his and his followers' predicament could hardly have been more acute, it should be noted that although Barberini was thought to be *persona grata* to both Condé and Gaston d'Orléans, there was no rush to confirm his nomination to Poitiers, which occurred nearly a year later in August 1652. But it is also revealing for the future course of episcopal patronage that at least three of the candidates for Poitiers would also become bishops within less than two years.[137]

133 BN, MS Fr 25025, fo 469, *nouvelles de Paris*, 1 Sept 1651: 'afin d'avoir de quoy mesnager les esprits'.
134 *Ibid*, fo 460, *nouvelles de Paris*, 18 Aug 1651. The bishop was Dony of Riez who had burned his bridges in his old diocese.
135 AAE, France 876, fo 222, 5 Aug 1651; *ibid*, fos 257–8, same to same, 12 Aug. Both Guron and Parabère were sons of established noble families from Poitou.
136 *Lettres du cardinal Mazarin à la reine, la princesse palatine etc*, ed M Ravenel (Paris 1836), 226–7, letter of 16 Aug 1651: 'ayant quelque scrupule du dernier dans la conjoncture présente, car il est Mazarin déclaré'.
137 Apart from Guron, they were Cyrus de Villers-la-Faye, and Michel Tubeuf.

VII

By the time Antonio Barberini was formally nominated to Poitiers in mid-1652, the end of the Fronde was imminent, although Mazarin's second exile would extend into early 1653. It has been argued that the Fronde did not really end at this juncture, but that it managed to rumble on in coming years, at the very least as an abiding preoccupation in the minds of the king and his subjects.[138] Despite the undeniable impact of war, tax revolts, and noble disaffection in certain provinces, it may be doubted whether this thesis is generally valid; what can be said is that the crown's continuing problems made it aware how fragile victory over rebellion was, and how much needed to be done to mend its fences with the social and professional élites who had played the major part in the Fronde.[139] As far as the present study is concerned, what is of interest is that thorny religious and ecclesiastical issues only came to the forefront just as the embers of political rebellion began to cool during the 1650s. The row over Cardinal de Retz's imprisonment, exile, and right to govern the diocese of Paris in defiance of the crown on the one hand, and the condemnation of the five propositions attributed to Jansen on the other, dominated the religious setting of the later years of the Mazarin régime. Perhaps the longest and most tense General Assembly of the entire century met between October 1655 and March 1657 and wrestled with the financial, political and theological issues they raised, coming to conclusions that were not always to the liking of the crown or the papacy. Such considerations played their part in the evolution of the post-Fronde episcopate, alongside others which had already begun to appear before and during the Fronde. However, certain features of Mazarin's political style also came to the fore during these years, some of which make the exercise of episcopal patronage after the Fronde oddly reminiscent of an earlier age.

As noted earlier, the number of bishops nominated after the Fronde was lower overall than the average for the first decade of the regency. This was partly because coadjutorships and resignations before and during the Fronde had, as in previous decades, the effect of reducing the number of vacancies arising at a later juncture. But the effects of this reduction were not uniformly spread across the 1650s, and a brief look at the timing of post-Fronde nominations will suggest something of the style and methods employed by the Mazarin régime. For example, there were no fewer than ten episcopal deaths in 1652, but only two the following year. But as we have just seen, no episcopal nominations were made at all between mid-1651 and May 1652, with the result that there was a considerable volume of patronage still

---

138 Richard M Golden, *The Godly Rebellion: Parisian Curés and the Religious Fronde 1652–1662* (Chapel Hill, NC, 1981).
139 See Beik, *Absolutism and Society*, esp ch 13.

accumulating just as the Fronde was dying out – enough indeed for reports to circulate by May 1653 that over 400,000 *livres* worth of benefices of all kinds were available for distribution.[140] A similar situation arose just a few years later, and it was no less deliberately contrived. Only one nomination was made between October 1655 and March 1657 – that of Louis Fouquet, brother of the *surintendant des finances*, to Agde – and the reason was that the General Assembly of the Clergy was in session between those dates. When it finally ended its marathon deliberations in March 1657, the distribution of bishoprics and abbeys which followed was widely, almost officially, reported. The assembly did not fall in with Mazarin's plans in all respects, and successfully defended episcopal autonomy by thwarting his efforts to deprive the exiled Retz of his rights to govern the diocese of Paris by means of his vicars-general. Mazarin nevertheless used the patronage at his disposal to reward those deputies who had served the crown well, and did so with considerable publicity. It was not just a matter of rewarding second-order deputies with the mitre; contemporary sources could only point to three immediate cases of that, though a further five fellow-deputies would become bishops within two to three years.[141] Existing bishops benefited, too: some obtained abbeys *in commendam*, two moved to another diocese, and three uncle-to-nephew coadjutorships were arranged.[142] Archbishop Rebé of Narbonne was one of those whose efforts to secure his nephew as his successor did not succeed; but just as the assembly opened, he agreed to take François Fouquet as his coadjutor, while Fouquet 'bought out' Rebé's nephew's interest in Narbonne with a promise to provide him with benefices worth an impressive 50,000 *livres* a year in revenue.[143]

As even those who failed to obtain their primary goals managed to do business, it is clear that the assembly served as a stage for a considerable amount of bargaining, and its inordinate length ensured that the results could all take final shape within a very short while of its termination. It was the first time that Mazarin had managed to use this carrot - benefices in return for cooperation - with any real success, and for that reason it can be viewed as a sign of his increased control of ecclesiastical patronage. The fact that there were no nominations at all between October 1659 and the weeks immediately before Mazarin's death in early March 1661, suggests he was preparing to repeat the exercise during the 'small' Assembly of Clergy which began in June 1660. This time, however, sensing that he might not live long enough to do so, Mazarin completed a clutch of no fewer than five nominations in the four weeks before his death, four of them in a single week! On this occasion, it was not members of an assembly in session who were rewarded, but mostly

---

140 ASV, N Fr 107, fo 158, *avvisi* of 9 May 1653.
141 ASV, N Fr 110a, fos 287v-8, *avvisi* of 11 May 1657.
142 *Ibid*, fo 316, *avvisi* of 25 May 1657.
143 ASV, N Fr 109, fo 528, *avvisi* of 2 Nov 1655. Rebé was himself to be a president of the assembly.

Mazarin's own clients, one of whom was, fittingly, a brother of Colbert. The result of this final spate of delayed nominations was that there was not a single vacant bishopric to which Louis XIV could make a nomination on the cardinal's death.[144]

The impression that Mazarin enjoyed a freer hand than hitherto in the selection of bishops is also reinforced by the fate of the *conseil de conscience*. As we saw, its reorganisation in 1651, when it was successively headed by Châteauneuf and Chancellor Séguier, was itself a feature of Mazarin's removal from office and no doubt gave it a partisan character. De Paul's removal in mid-1652 for his anti-Mazarin stance could not but damage its standing. Thereafter, its history becomes shadowy in the extreme. Mazarin probably judged it better to retain it in a truncated form than to abolish it outright. Its other members seem to have been Pierre de Marca of Toulouse, Péréfixe of Rodez, and the royal confessor of the day, which probably meant that its actual business consisted of exchanges between the chief minister and the confessor. Until his death in 1653, Louis XIV's confessor, Charles Paulin corresponded actively with Mazarin, whether in exile or not, over episcopal nominations and was capable of expressing his views quite bluntly: for example, when Camille de Neufville was being considered for Lyon in 1653, he argued that he 'is really not suitable for Lyon. His establishment there would be contrary to both christian and secular policy'.[145] But if the outcome of this particular contest is anything to judge by – Neufville obtained Lyon and he would rule there for forty years – Paulin's influence was decidedly limited during his few years in the *conseil*. His successor, François Annat, outlived Mazarin. He was the first to administer the *feuille des bénéfices*, but while Mazarin lived, his influence, the struggle against the Jansenists apart, also seems to have been fairly negligible.

VIII

Mazarin's own position in the French church also changed appreciably during the final period of his ministry. The fact that he held the see of Metz as an unconsecrated bishop for six years probably mattered less in this regard than the huge accumulation of abbeys which he held *in commendam*. These were scattered throughout France, one predictable consequence of which was the extension of an ecclesiastical clientèle which had grown steadily since the early 1640s. The bishops of the dioceses in question found themselves

---

144 One possible exception to this is the diocese of Rieux, vacant since Jean-Louis de Bertier's death in 1657. Apparently, his nephew André was then nominated, but as he did not obtain his provisions until 1662, he may not have fully accepted the original nomination during Mazarin's lifetime.

145 AAE, France 892, fo 224, to Mazarin, n.d. [Apr 1653?]: '(il) n'a aucune qualité pour Lion. La politique chrestienne et mondaine sont contraires à son establissement.'

involved to some extent in dealing with the cardinal's interests.[146] By the mid-1650s, he was ready to establish a special council to deal with his ecclesiastical interests, and no fewer than five reigning bishops were proposed as possible presidents of this body.[147]

But, as recent research suggests, it is essential not to misinterpret the nature or the context of Mazarin's freedom of action during these years. His position at the end of the Fronde was similar in certain respects to that of Henri IV sixty years previously: victory did not constitute a *tabula rasa* with respect to friend and foe, or the immediate past. There were numerous debts to be discharged, some of them for loyalty and services rendered, others in respect of promises of one kind or another made to win the loyalty of former enemies or neutrals; as so often, such obligations were in competition with each other. Moreover, putting the régime together again required more than just setting straight the record of past services or promises. Unlike Henri IV, the post-Fronde régime still had a hugely expensive war to fight, which in turn meant that the continually evolving mix of social and political forces in these years made it impossible simply to look backwards.

For one thing, there was a need to rebuild royal authority in the provinces, especially in those which had been most affected by the Fronde. Languedoc, which had remained quiescent since the 1632 revolt, experienced internal upheaval during the Fronde, not least because of acute rivalry between the different holders of power and authority there. Its bishops had protested against persecution by the parlement of Toulouse and looked to the crown for protection.[148] The evidence suggests that a careful choice of new bishops was one way of rebuilding royal influence in the province's affairs once the Fronde had ended. Sixteen episcopal nominations were made there, beginning with that of Pierre de Marca to Toulouse in 1652, and two features of the sequence are of particular note. Firstly, exactly half of the nominations consisted in fact of the transfer of existing bishops whose past record proved where their loyalties lay. Of the remainder, four were outsiders, and four were natives of the province (if we count a Bonsi as a Languedocian by adoption); the latter were carefully selected and, as sons of families with long records of royal service, could be relied upon to uphold the crown's authority. One particular nomination best conveys the changed climate of these years – that of Denis Cohon to a second term at Nîmes in 1655. He had, it will be recalled, quit Nîmes in the face of local hostility in 1644, when the crown did little to

---

146 BN, MS Baluze 176, fo 341v, Colbert to Mazarin, 9 Sept 1657: 'Je supplie V. E. de signer les lettres cy jointes à Mrs les évesques dans les diocèses desquels V. E. a des abbayes et bénéfices affin qu'ils fassent faire la taxe du don fait au roy par le clergé avec justice et égalité.'

147 *Lettres, instructions et mémoires de, Jean-Baptiste Colbert*, ed Pierre Clément, 10 vols (Paris 1861–82), i. 268–9, Colbert to Mazarin, 21 Oct 1656 (?). This bishops were Godeau of Vence, Péréfixe of Rodez, Neufville of Saint-Malo, Auvry of Coutances and Séguier of Meaux.

148 See Beik, 'The Parlement of Toulouse and the Fronde', esp 139–40.

dissuade him from moving to Dol in Brittany. Resigning Dol in 1648, he had spent the entire Fronde in Mazarin's household service, but in 1655 Mazarin was prepared to allow him to return to Nîmes after his successor's death. This time he could count on far greater support in his renewed battles with an assortment of local adversaries.[149]

Provence also experienced considerable turbulence during the Fronde, with Marseille even holding out against royal authority until 1659. Similar care was taken with the nomination of bishops there, though the long vacancy of Aix (from 1648 to 1655) cannot have helped the crown's cause. Seven episcopal nominations occurred in the decade after 1651, but because of the province's small and relatively poorly endowed bishoprics, transferring bishops there from other dioceses, especially from the outside, was not practicable. Among the new bishops, most were outsiders obtaining their first promotion. The two native bishops, Nicolas Valavoire of Riez and Toussaint de Forbin-Janson, coadjutor of Digne and a future cardinal, were both from families closely identified with the Mazarin ministry.

Normandy was the third province to have been heavily involved in the Fronde, thanks mainly to its governor Longueville, brother-in-law of Condé, and one of the princes imprisoned by Mazarin in 1650. Its geographical position and its fiscal contributions gave it inordinate importance, though the scope for episcopal patronage there was limited by the fact that it only included seven bishoprics in all. With no fewer than three well-known 'Mazarins' among its bishops (Auvry of Coutances, Boutault of Evreux, and from 1651 onwards, Boylesve of Avranches), the bishop whose loyalties caused serious concern to Mazarin was Longueville's cousin, Matignon of Lisieux (previously of Coutances, where his family had long been the dominant power). All of the remaining dioceses were secured for clients or loyalists, beginning with Gilles de Boutault's transfer from Aire in Gascony to Evreux in 1649, and consolidated by the Harlay and Servien successions in Rouen and Bayeux respectively.

The steady return of older noble families to the ranks of the episcopate which we observed during the 1640s continued thereafter, not least during the Fronde which saw the elevation of names like Aubusson, Ventadour, Estaing, Rouxel de Médavy, and Laval de Boisdauphin among others. Perhaps most striking of all was the acceptance of the young duc d'Aumale, Henri de Savoie-Nemours, as the new archbishop of Reims in early 1651 – despite the fact that his brother commanded a Frondeur army![150] But as in the case of his father, the duc de Nemours who was given Auch in the 1590s, the sudden death of an elder brother meant that dynastic politics (he, too, became duc de Nemours) and marriage (to Longueville's daughter) supervened. When he

149 Sauzet, *Contre-réforme*, 216, 311, 379ff.
150 BN, MS Fr 25025, fos 314, *nouvelles de Paris*, 23 Oct 1650; *ibid*, fo 323, 18 Nov 1650; *ibid*, fo 413, 21 Apr 1651; Dubuisson-Aubenay, *Journal des guerres civiles*, ii. 52, 8 Apr 1651.

finally resigned Reims without ever being confirmed by Rome in 1657, his successor was Antonio Barberini, who in turn abandoned his claim to Poitiers to Mazarin's serving *maître de chambre*, Louis de Clérambault, brother of marshal Clérambault. The Fronde had taught Mazarin the importance of cultivating the *grands*, through marriage alliances where possible.[151] Daniel de Cosnac's reward for facilitating his master Conty's marriage with one of the cardinal's nieces was the see of Valence in 1655, the same year as that in which Gaston's former favourite, Barbier, finally obtained Langres. César d'Estrées, a future cardinal, was given Laon in early 1653 as part of an arrangement for the governorship of La Fère which Mazarin was extremely anxious to acquire.[152] The new Bishop of Oloron in 1652 almost certainly owed his mitre to the influence of his cousin, the future marshal d'Albret.[153] The fate of Lyon is perhaps the most eloquent of all in this context. When Alphonse de Richelieu died in March 1653, his cousin Marshal La Meilleraye made a powerful appeal for it to remain in the Richelieu family, an appeal based on past services and family sentiment; he argued that the hopes of the Richelieu family, which at that juncture had neither males nor offices, but only 'filles maryées', lay with Bishop La Mothe-Houdancourt of Rennes, whose elevation to Lyon would greatly reinforce its position.[154] But although Mazarin would later entrust the La Meilleraye family with no less a responsibility than that of perpetuating his own title and lineage, in 1653 he measured things differently. After some delay, Lyon was given to Camille de Neufville, whose claim to it, as we saw, was regarded as completely unsustainable by the royal confessor, Paulin.[155] But like Ventadour of Bourges before him, Neufville was a *grand* in his own right: as acting governor of the Lyonnais, he had kept it loyal during the Fronde. Political calculation and family pressure, rather than personal inclination on Neufville's part secured

---

151   See R J Bonney, 'Mazarin and the Great Nobility during the Fronde', *English Historical Review* 96 (1981), 818–33. R Oresko, 'The Marriage of the Nieces of Cardinal Mazarin', in Rainer Babel, ed, *Frankreich im Europäischen Staatensystem der frühen Neuzeit* (Sigmaringen 1995), 109–51.

152   BN, MS Fr 25026, fo 244, *nouvelles de Paris*, 29 July 1653. Strangely, Mazarin tried to pull out of this agreement and to prevent d'Estrées from becoming bishop of Laon, but he was either unsuccessful or changed his mind: AAE, France 896, fos 13–14, letter to Marshal d'Estrées, 2 Mar 1655, apologising for his decision to oppose César's nomination and and offering to accept any other candidate of the marshal's choice! César d'Estrées finally received his papal provisions in Aug 1655.

153   V Dubarat, *Notices historiques sur les évêques de l'ancien diocèse d'Oloron* (Pau 1888), 43. The grant of a pension of 3,000 *livres* to François d'Amanieu d'Albret seems to put the question beyond reasonable doubt.

154   AAE, France 892, fo 218, M de la Guelfe (?) to Mazarin on La Meilleraye's behalf, n.d. (end Mar 1653); *ibid,* fo 228–9, La Meilleraye to Mazarin, 4 Apr 1653.

155   *Ibid*, fo 223–4, to Mazarin, Apr 1653. Neufville was apparently reluctant to become an archbishop, since it would require taking priestly orders and episcopal consecration. Although forty-six years old in 1653, he was still apparently merely a tonsured cleric.

an archiepiscopal succession, the rationale of which evidently escaped Louis XIV's confessor.[156]

The Lyon case, coming as it did in 1653, illustrates one of the problems confronting the Mazarin régime at the end of the Fronde. With the demand for ecclesiastical patronage outstripping supply, it was a question of rewarding one ally in the place of another, and in other circumstances, Henri de La Mothe-Houdancourt might well have been preferred to Neufville. Shortly afterwards, Mazarin had to refuse the count Francesco Bonsi's petition for a Languedoc bishopric (his family still held Béziers), alleging the number and the 'qualities' – an ambiguous term which could just as easily mean 'claims' as 'fitness' – of the existing candidates for the dioceses vacant there.[157] Yet the cardinal did succeed in rewarding quite a number of his clerical clients during and especially at the end of the Fronde. Sitting client-bishops benefited by his willingness to transfer them to a new diocese, and indeed practically all of the transfers between 1648 and about 1655 were of clients in search of better fortune. Equally, known 'Mazarins' like Guron, Faure, Ithier, and Valavoire all received episcopal office in the bumper years 1652–3 when vacancies were especially numerous; other associates with personal-service ties like Zongo Ondedei, a fellow-Italian, and Gilbert de Clérambault, followed in later years.

Yet for the reasons just alluded to, Mazarin's methods of rewarding support did not always attract unadulterated gratitude. It was La Rochefoucauld, one of the losers in the Fronde, who subsequently reflected that 'ingratitude is the normal form taken by acknowledgement'. Some of Mazarin's new bishops of 1651–3 would probably have accepted such a verdict on their master's behaviour, and it says something of the peculiar climate of these years that some of the most scathing criticism of him came from his own ecclesiastical clients and supporters, bishops included. Having, as they saw it, run serious risks to themselves and their prospects on Mazarin's behalf during the civil war, their expectations of reward once it had ended were commensurably high, and possibly unrealistic. Mazarin disappointed a number of them, not so much by refusing them rewards altogether, as by the kind of rewards he was ready to offer them.

Clearly, not all of them appreciated the problems that even a victorious Mazarin still faced, or the promises he had made to others in order to win

---

156 BN, MS Fr 20663, p 429, Louis XIV to Cardinal Pamphili, 8 Aug 1653. This letter commending Neufville to the cardinal-nephew can be read as a classic statement of the case Paulin could not see or accept: 'les grands et signalez services que ceux de la maison de Villeroy ont de tout temps rendus à cet estat joinct à ceux que m'a rendus mon cousin le duc de Villeroy pendant le gouvernement qu'il a eu de ma personne, mesme ceux qui m'ont esté rendus par le sieur abbé Dayné (sic) son frère, mon lieutenant général en mes provinces de Lionnois, Forestz et Beaujolois, me convient de prendre en affection ce qui regarde leurs interestz.'

157 *Lettres de Mazarin*, v. 710, letter of 2 May 1653.

them round. Both Dony of Riez and Tulles of Lavaur tried hard to obtain Aix-en-Provence, but Mazarin declined to support them, having firmly committed himself to Cardinal Grimaldi in the conflict with his enemy, Innocent X, over who had the right to nominate to Aix after Michele Mazarin's death.[158] Mazarin's oldest French client, Claude Auvry, bishop of Coutances since 1646, was desperate to leave it within a few years, and in 1652 he declared he did not really mind whether Mazarin gave him Amiens or Montpellier, though ideally he would prefer Amiens; somewhat later, he set his eyes on Langres with its peerage and seat in the Paris parlement.[159] Nothing came of any of these efforts, and he was left to resign Coutances outright, rather than as part of the expected transfer to a more desirable see, in 1658.[160] Cupif, the unhappy bishop of Saint-Pol-de-Léon moved to Dol in 1648, was another client desperately in search of evidence of Mazarin's favour, the lack of which reduced him to asking the cardinal for bread and water and a straw mattress in the Paris Châtelet so as not to be 'odious to the public'.[161] His subsequent relations with Mazarin may have been less acerbic, but shortly before his death in 1659, he accepted the bishopric of Killala in the west of Ireland – possibly the most bizarre move made in the whole period by a French bishop, and one which suggests that Cupif had abandoned hope of ever exchanging Dol for another French diocese.[162] Archbishop Harlay of Rouen wrote a blisteringly caustic memorandum in 1653, presumably for submission to Mazarin, when he discovered that Mazarin preferred Rebé of Narbonne for a seat in council, despite announcing that he would reward him for his fidelity during the Fronde.[163] The Franciscan François Faure was extremely displeased with his reward in 1651, the obscure Provençal see of Glandèves, having set his sights on Montpellier.[164] His attitude elicited a withering put-down from the royal confessor: 'A poor Cordelier is unhappy with becoming a bishop and having 12,000 *livres* a year. He believes he secured the return of

---

158 AAE, France 874, fo 65, Tulles to Mazarin, 13 Feb 1651; *Lettres de Mazarin*, iv. 751, to Tulles, 5 Sept 1651; *ibid*, v. 714–15, to Cardinal Orsini, 13 June 1653. For Doni's statement of his claim, AAE, France 886, fo 358, undated memorandum wrongly attributed to Pierre de Marca. Doni eventually received Autun and, apart from the drop in revenues that he had to accept, was happy enough with the outcome.
159 AAE, France 891, fo 340, Auvry to Mazarin, 24 Nov 1653, when Bishop Zamet was rumoured dead.
160 Joseph Toussaint, *Claude Auvry évêque de Coutances et trésorier à Paris de la Sainte-Chapelle* (Avranches 1981), 134. Auvry's case was not helped by his furious rows with his metropolitan, Harlay of Rouen, in 1655 and with the canons of the Sainte Chapelle, and he seems to have become a rather solitary figure.
161 BN, MS Baluze 175, fo 60–1, letter to Mazarin, n.d.: 'odieux au public'.
162 *Dictionnaire historique, géographique, et biographique du Maine-et-Loire*, ed Célestin Port, 3 vols (Paris and Angers 1874–8), i. 871.
163 BN, MS Baluze 327, fos 34–5, no date, but pre Mar 1653.
164 AAE, France 885, fos 284–5, 27 Oct 1652, anonymous petition to Mazarin for Montpellier, in which the author refers to his existing diocese as so remote as to offer him no chance to 'servir le publicq'. The reference to a remote diocese (such as Glandèves was) suggests this may well have been Faure's petition.

Paris to obedience to the king – may God help him!'[165] In this case, at least, Mazarin's opinion of Faure was evidently somewhat higher than Paulin's, for he transferred him to Amiens in 1653. Glandèves then went to his fellow 'pauvre Cordelier', Dominique Ithier, who was thereby rewarded for his imprisonment and trial by the Ormée in Bordeaux for his efforts to open the city gates to Mazarinist forces. Louis de Guron, who openly claimed the credit for the pacification of Poitou, had in fact played a considerable role in the restoration of royal authority in the west and Bordeaux. But, as we saw, he failed to obtain Poitiers to which he felt entitled as a result, and had to settle for the tiny and comparatively insignificant see of Tulle instead. It was not the choice of diocese which chagrined him most, however, but the fact that *after* accepting it he had to give his consent to a pension of 3,000 *livres*, one-third of its modest revenues, to persons whom Mazarin had not yet named; and even though he had been told that he would not have to pay it and that he would be given a better see in due course, he could not restrain himself from writing to the cardinal to complain bitterly of his treatment of him, which he regarded as a public humiliation. 'I am driven to believe', he wrote, 'that you have no respect for me and that I shall never do other than waste my time in the service of your interests', after which he went on to enumerate the benefits reaped by numerous other clients of Mazarin 'who are not of the same calibre or consideration as I am'; he finished by saying that 'the thanks which I owe to your Eminence are not of the order which I would have wished them to be, or which I hoped to offer you'.[166]

On this kind of evidence, personal services by clerics lacking wider social or political support were insufficient to win them dioceses commensurate with their loyalty to Mazarin. Even the cardinal's Italian confidant, Ondedei, came to suspect that the gift of the see of Fréjus in 1655 was designed not so much to bring him closer to his native country, but to keep him far away from court. If Gilbert de Clérambault did better than the others by obtaining Poitiers in 1657, it was not merely because of his services as Mazarin's *maître de chambre*, but also because of his social distinction and family services in other capacities, particularly military.

By comparison, however, the more time passed, the better the political and financial milieux that regrouped around the ministry after the Fronde fared. Gabriel de Boylesve, brother of the great financier and tax-farmer, Claude de Boylesve, bargained his way into Avranches in 1651, but miscalculated in his attempts to bargain his way out of it and into Saint-Malo several years

---

165 AAE, 886, fo 311, Charles Paulin to Mazarin, 24 Dec 1652: 'Un pauvre cordelier n'est pas content d'estre evesque avec 12,000 livres de rente. Il croit estre la cause de la reduction de Paris à l'obéissance du roy. Dieu le sauve s'il luy plaist.'

166 BN, MS Baluze 252, fos 163–4, Guron to Mazarin, 23 Nov 1652: 'Je dois croire que vous n'avés nulle estime de ma personne et que ie n'ai jamais que perdre mon temps en m'attachant à vos intérests . . . (des hommes) qui ne sont pas de ma volée et de ma considération . . . les remerciemens dont ie suis obligé à Vostre Eminence ne sont pas tels que ie les eusse souhaitté et que i'esperois vous randre.'

later.[167] As we saw, Abel Servien's brother, François, was given Fréjus when it was rumoured vacant in mid-1651, and it seems thereafter as if he was promised the first vacant diocese that would suit him. As we have seen, he accepted Carcassonne in 1652, but only provisionally, and finally switched, after a two-year hiatus, to the more congenial see of Bayeux. The family of Nicolas Fouquet, Servien's fellow *surintendant des finances*, also did particularly well when it again put its collective mind to matters episcopal a few years later. The eldest son, François, had held the well-endowed see of Agde in Languedoc since 1643, and Fouquet loyalty during the Fronde naturally emboldened the family to aim higher still. The coadjutorship to the ageing Claude de Rebé of Narbonne was extremely attractive on several counts and had long been sought after, as it combined prestige, considerable revenue, and a major political role in Languedoc; at the end of the Fronde Rebé was denied the coadjutorship for his nephew, despite his long-standing loyalism in a turbulent province.[168] How much the Fouquet brothers had to do with the intrigues to frustrate Rebé it is impossible to say, but in October 1655, the *brevet* of the coadjutorship was granted to François Fouquet, whose younger brother, Louis, was obligingly given Agde in his place[169]. One of the most interesting elements of this settlement was the provision, once François succeeded Rebé as archbishop, for a pension of 25,000 *livres* off Narbonne payable to yet another brother, the abbot Basile Fouquet, chief of Mazarin's secret police. Such a huge pension recalls that imposed on Auch in the 1590s; it also suggests that it was the redoubtable Basile Fouquet, rather than his more famous brother, who was the real fixer in this *affaire de famille*. It is equally likely that Fouquet influence helped their cousin Jean de Maupeou to obtain Chalon-sur-Saône in 1658, though 'Messieurs de Maupeou' had long since been in search of a bishopric for him.[170] Chancellor Séguier's political fortunes may have been in steady decline since the end of the Fronde, but not to the extent that a family with such vast connections was unable to pursue its other ambitions. Dominique Séguier co-opted his nephew, Dominique de Ligny, as his coadjutor at Meaux in 1658, while a few years later, Jacques Séguier, another cousin, was nominated to Lombez. Alongside bishops from Paris-based financial families like Tubeuf and Colbert, but also lesser known names like Le Clerc de Lesseville and Bourlon, we find others from provincial backgrounds like Pingré from Amiens and Thoreau from Poitiers. All of these

---

167 AAE, France 1507, fo 116, Mazarin to Boyslève, 14 Oct 1659, implying that Boyslève had failed to keep his promises to François de Villemontée who had been nominated to Saint-Malo and who was apparently willing to exchange it for Avranches and 12,000 *livres'* worth of benefices.

168 ASV, N Fr 107, fo 362v, *avvisi*, 3 Oct 1653. At this juncture, the rumour was that Cardinal d'Este was anxious to obtain the coadjutorship.

169 AAE, France 894, Nicolas Fouquet to Mazarin, 8 Nov 1655, asking for Mazarin's approval of the agreement between his brother and Rebé.

170 AAE, France 886, fo 226, Charles Paulin to Mazarin, 17 Dec 1652, when they hoped to obtain Amiens for him.

names point to the closeness of the links between ministerial and financial interests, and the two were rarely closer than during and following the Fronde.[171]

This particular combination of noble, ministerial and financial families in the post-Fronde episcopate can also be explained by looking at the methods adopted by Mazarin now that he had a freer hand than before to dispose of church patronage. Essentially, these weighted the odds heavily in favour of candidates whose status and connections had already enabled them to accumulate benefices *in commendam*. It was in 1651 that one of the cardinal's tactics, which he would employ with increasing frequency when bishoprics were being filled, was first specifically identifed by an attentive, but unknown observer, as 'son micque mac ordinaire'. In this particular instance, it consisted in obliging Louis d'Estaing to surrender his abbey of Bellaigue in return for the nomination to Clermont, a bargain which enabled Mazarin to dispose of Bellaigue to a son of the comte de Matha. Estaing protested before a notary against the extortion involved in this transaction, and provoked the regent's anger by making his protest public during the cardinal's exile.[172] Exchanges of benefices were not at all uncommon before the 1650s, and often occurred when bishops were retiring outright or transferring from one diocese to another; as we have already seen, there is abundant evidence that they were capable of driving hard bargains, especially where there were marked differences in revenue between the old diocese and the new. But this was some way from the situation which increasingly obtained in the 1650s, when most candidates for episcopal office had to be ready to surrender abbeys or similar benefices as part of the nomination process. A determination to exploit church patronage to the full is perfectly evident here, and Mazarin may well have been willing to employ such methods because of the scarcity of other forms of patronage as rewards for those to whom he was indebted. Equally, he may have been influenced by the practices of the papacy, which he knew at first hand, in considering certain offices or sinecures as *vacabili*: that is, to be vacated once their incumbents were elevated to higher office. As we saw, Le Tellier and Colbert attempted to get hold of an abbey for Le Tellier in just this way in 1650, and Mazarin did not disown the principle of what they wished to do. Probably the most spectacular instance of this arose in relation to Carcassonne and Bayeux between 1652 and 1654 when, as we saw, a succession of candidates bid against each other for Carcassonne, offering to surrender benefices and pay annual pensions valued at only slightly less than the revenues of Carcassonne itself. Whether the candidates were simply incited to improve their offers in competition with each other, or whether there was a target figure set from the beginning and which approximated to

---

171 See Julian Dent, *Crisis in France. Crown, Financiers and Society in Seventeenth-Century France* (Newton Abbot 1973); Daniel Dessert, *Argent, pouvoir et société au grand siècle* (Paris 1984).
172 BN, MS Fr 25025, fo 452, *nouvelles de Paris*, 4 Aug 1651.

the annual income of Carcassonne, it is impossible to say. When Barbier de la Rivière obtained the bishopric of Langres he had so long sought in 1655, it was reported that he had had to surrender benefices of virtually the same annual value as Langres, despite the damage it was reported to have suffered from military operations.[173]

It did not take very long for this kind of message to be heard and understood, so that in some cases that we know of, the surrender of benefices was offered rather than demanded. Camille de Neufville's offer to cede his abbey of Lagny and to pay a pension of 6,000 *livres* no doubt enhanced his claim to Lyon in 1653, while Jacques de Grignan simultaneously offered to do likewise with an abbey of his if he could obtain the bishopric of Saint-Pons.[174] The bishop of Chalon-sur-Saône offered an abbey with an income of 12,000 *livres* if Mazarin would transfer him to Chartres after Jacques Lescot's death in 1656.[175] Later that year, Hugues de Lionne claimed to have a fully-prepared plan for the exchange of benefices in order to obtain the succession to his elderly father at Gap for a nephew, Charles de Lionne; two years later, Lionne was ready to employ similar methods in an attempt to keep Bayeux in family hands by persuading his own father to move there.[176] It would seem as if the unusually long vacancies which affected several dioceses after the Fronde were the product of an environment in which complex exchanges of dioceses and other benefices or pensions were being negotiated by several parties at once. This is not to say that rapid, straightforward nominations were no longer being made, but rather that the rising number of extended vacancies – some in excess of a year or two – suggest a measure of self-confidence on the part of both patrons and candidates sufficient for them to engage in a relatively untroubled fashion in extended bargaining over episcopal office.

The other feature of Mazarin's 'micque mac ordinaire' consisted in the proliferation of pensions payable by newly appointed bishops from the revenues of their dioceses, incidental examples of which have just been seen. The days when Louis XIII had vowed to eliminate pensions altogether were long since forgotten, and Mazarin may not have been aware of the late king's intentions at any point. At any rate the number and the scale of pensions which began to be imposed on bishoprics from 1652 onwards is too striking to have been a mere accident, and must be viewed as part of Mazarin's struggle to find additional sources of financial patronage in the church. For

173 ASV, N Fr 109, fo 61, *avvisi*, 26 Feb 1655. One abbey, Saint-Pierre-de-la-Vallée, was said to be worth 18,000 *livres* a year. ASV, PC 52, fo 652–3, for evidence that its revenues had fallen from 40,000 to about 10,000 *livres*, 2 Mar 1655.
174 BN, MS Fr 25026, fo 224v, *nouvelles de Paris*, 23 May 1653.
175 BN, MS Baluze 176, fo 259, Colbert to Mazarin, 23 Aug 1656.
176 'Lettres inédites de Hugues de Lionne', ed Ulysse Chevallier, *Bulletin de la Société d'Archéologie et de Statistique de la Drôme*, 11 (1877), 298, letter to Humbert de Lionne, 18 Dec 1656. To facilitate the plan, Lionne expected his father to resign Gap. For Bayeux, where Lionne's uncle, François Servien, had just died, see *ibid*, 12 (1878), 11–14, letter to Artus de Lionne, bishop of Gap, 7 Feb 1659.

example, François Faure escaped without a pension when nominated to Glandèves in 1651, but his successor at Glandèves, Ithier, was not so fortunate just two years later, losing nearly half his modest income in the process. Only a small number of incoming bishops avoided having to pay pensions, either because their dioceses were too poorly endowed or too damaged by war. No more than five in all escaped because they were personally close to Mazarin, but it is worth noting that this only happened in the later 1650s. Previous to that, even close servants like Cohon, Clérambault and Guron had to consent to pensions, sometimes substantial, if they wanted a bishopric.

What is striking about many of these pensions – if we exclude cases where bishops resigned and retained a pension for their remaining years – is how numerous rather than how valuable they were individually. This was no consolation to those, like Guron, Marca or Serroni, who felt they deserved to be treated better by their patron. Guron's bitter resentment we have already seen, but it was Marca who harassed Mazarin most systematically after being obliged to pay five separate pensioners a total of 12,000 *livres* a year from the see of Toulouse. Marca eschewed Guron's biting remarks, and instead made endless business-like proposals to Mazarin as to how his lot could be alleviated, and was not above suggesting how some or all of his pensions might even be offloaded onto the dioceses of newly-nominated colleagues![177]

Nor can the *affairisme* which seems typical of so many of Mazarin's dealings over France's bishoprics after the Fronde be completely divorced from his own personal affairs. There is no proof that the cardinal personally extorted pensions from incoming bishops, as has been alleged on more than one occasion, though the obscurity of many of the pensioners throughout the 1650s inevitably raises the question of whether or not they were acting in their own name or simply as straw-men for others. However, it is significant that Colbert, who was in charge of Mazarin's personal finances from the early 1650s onwards, should figure so prominently in his dealings over church benefices; it was a position which enabled the Colbert clan to begin establishing a position in the upper reaches of the church, one that was crowned by the very last of Mazarin's episcopal nominations, that of Nicolas Colbert to Luçon. Many of the abbeys *in commendam* which Mazarin was himself busily accumulating throughout the 1650s were liable for the payment of pensions. A constant refrain in his correspondence with Colbert was the need to get rid of either the benefices or the pensions, and the audacity and cynicism of some of the solutions advocated by Colbert was, like those of Marca, only possible

---

177 BN, MS Fr 6892, fo 397–8, Marca to Le Tellier, 14 Oct 1654, suggesting that if Castres fell vacant, 9,000 of the 12,000 *livres* owed in pensions by Marca off Toulouse could be transferred to it. For extensive quotations from similar letters from Marca to Mazarin, in 1654 and 1656 respectively, see P Jansen, *Le Cardinal Mazarin et le mouvement janséniste français* (Paris 1967), 44, n 49.

because they knew that Mazarin himself was perfectly willing to consider them.[178]

VII

It is hardly surprising that the uneven pattern of episcopal patronage should reflect the wider political fortunes of the Mazarin régime. Ultimately, it was these, rather than the personal attitudes of Mazarin or of others involved in appointing bishops, which account for the discontinuities which we have seen in this chapter. If the régime of Louis XIII and Richelieu emerged from the political crisis of 1630 with a greater freedom of movement, the same does not appear to be true of the Mazarin régime after the upheaval of the Fronde, which required much careful bridge-building with a wide range of social and other interest groups. Mazarin's own role appears with far less clarity than that of his predecessor, partly because he did not have to deal with an exacting adult monarch like Louis XIII, and partly because his personal political style and his shifting ministerial power deterred him from acting as openly as Richelieu had done.

The discontinuities just mentioned were further highlighted by the institutional novelty that was the *conseil de conscience*, the very existence of which was bound to polarise approaches to the making of bishops. But its work, and its success, too, probably depended more on the fortunes of its principal members than on its institutional status. Much less is heard of its activities after the Fronde, yet it would be a mistake to regard the whole experiment as a failure brought on by massive political pressures. On the contrary, it proved to be an essential stage in the crown's internalisation of the central demands of the reformers for an adult, well-educated and reasonably experienced episcopate which was prepared to take the government of their dioceses seriously.

The contribution of the *conseil* was unlikely to be forgotten if only because the emergence of Jansenism added a new twist to the making of the episcopate. Although evidence as to how candidates for the mitre with known Jansenist leanings were dealt with during these years is virtually non-existent, it is probable that the Jansenist issue only seriously entered the crown's calculations from the mid-1650s onwards, with the formal condemnation of the five propositions by Innocent X, who showed a close interest in the opinions of the French episcopate at the time of the publication of the bull *Cum Occasione*.[179] It is clear that ever since his part in the interrogation of

---

178 See Joseph Bergin, 'Mazarin and his Benefices', *French History*, 1 (1987), 3–26; G Charvin, 'Colbert intendant des abbayes de Mazarin', *Revue Mabillon*, 36 (1946), 15–47, 87–119, who quotes extensively from the correspondence between Mazarin and Colbert, parts of which remain unpublished.
179 ASV, N Fr 107, fos 399, 405–10, Nuncio Bagno to secretary of state, 31 Oct 1653, in response to papal desire to know who were those who might spread Jansenist ideas.

Saint-Cyran in 1638, Vincent de Paul had championed strict theological orthodoxy, parting company with some of his early associates when they seemed to lean too much towards suspect ideas. As we saw, bishops like Solminihac of Cahors, de Paul's most assiduous episcopal correspondent, were already sufficiently concerned about the spread of Jansenist ideas in particular dioceses to warn of the need to appoint bishops of proven orthodoxy.[180] Nevertheless, the crown's capacity to identify and exclude Jansenists from the episcopate was not infallible, despite the presence of a powerful and vigilant anti-Jansenist like Pierre de Marca in the *conseil de conscience* in the 1650s, and it would remain so under Louis XIV. Arguably, it was the high-minded, ascetic clerics whom the *dévots* were so anxious to see enter the episcopate who were the most likely to adopt positions that were either openly Jansenist or close to them. Moreover, as often as not, this move towards Jansenist convictions would occur *after*, rather than before, their episcopal elevation. Few would have foreseen in the 1640s or 1650s that bishops like Gondrin of Sens, Pavillon of Alet, Choart of Beauvais, or Louis Fouquet of Agde would be widely identified with Jansenism in subsequent decades.

It is not being suggested that the emergence of *dévot* demands and of doctrinal problems such as Jansenism fundamentally altered the crown's approach to episcopal nominations. There was no radical overhaul of the workings of royal ecclesiastical patronage which continued to ensure that status, service and family activities remained crucial to those in search of high office. In the final analysis, it is clear that the making of the episcopate was itself – like the collective biography of the men studied in these pages – a process that was subject to continual evolution.

---

180 See above, p 516.

Conclusions and Comparisons

WITH THE *commerce des bénéfices* in such robust health in the dying years of the Mazarin régime, it is tempting to think that the wheel had merely come full circle to rest at a point not that far from where it had been under Henri III and the early years of Henri IV. But it would be highly misleading to conclude on such a disabused note since, as far as the make-up of the episcopate itself was concerned, the similarities over three-quarters of a century were in several important respects more formal and apparent than real. Even when developments occurred in the 1640s or 1650s which resemble those of half a century earlier, closer inspection shows that there were subtle, but important differences. Ministerial and courtly nepotism, to take just one example, remained as real as ever, but it was by now absolutely out of the question for bishoprics to be granted to fathers for their underaged sons or to powerful nobles for as yet unnamed caretakers. At twenty-five, Louis Fouquet was easily the youngest bishop nominated to office after the Fronde, but the unease which his appointment caused is evident from the apologetic memorandum prepared for despatch to Rome, and which listed nominations of bishops of a similar age since that of Charles Miron as long ago as 1588.[1] Otherwise, sons or brothers of Mazarin's clients were invariably men of often considerable experience rather than mere *fils de famille*. Gabriel de Boylesve was not merely the brother of the great financier, Claude, but also his associate and a man of experience in his mid-fifties.[2] Michel Tubeuf, brother of the influential *intendant des finances*, Jacques, was a former *agent-général* of the clergy also in his early fifties, as was François Servien, brother of Abel. None of these men entered the episcopate with anything like the facility of the son of a minister like Philippe Hurault de Cheverny or of a great financier like Sébastien Zamet – both of whom were assured of episcopal nominations while still in their teens – half a century earlier. Even a man like Nicolas Colbert

---

1 ASV, N Fr 110a, fo 36, undated memorandum, probably from early 1657. It was also pointed out that Fouquet had been a *conseiller* in the Paris parlement for five years, and thus had professional experience: *ibid*, fo 94, nuncio to papal secretary of state, 20 Feb 1657.
2 Daniel Dessert, *Argent, pouvoir et société au grand siècle* (Paris 1984), 548.

was in his early thirties when nominated to Luçon in early 1661, having been royal librarian since 1656. Sons of leading noble families like Forbin-Janson, Estrées, or Clermont-Tonnerre might be rather younger on entering the episcopate, but they were in fact in a minority even for their social group. Moreover, it is hard to imagine Catherine or even Marie de' Medici admitting – as Anne of Austria did in 1657 in respect of Mazarin's client, Ondedei – that she could not in conscience regard a particular nominee as fit to govern a diocese, an indiscretion which, as we saw, seriously delayed the grant of Ondedei's provisions while Rome tried to establish what Anne had really meant![3]

Of course, the use of the term 'experience' itself begs a number of questions. To some extent, it relates to the age of incoming bishops rather than to specific expertise. As we saw in an earlier chapter, the pre-episcopal careers of French bishops in this period varied enormously – the more aristocratic the incoming bishop, the less likely he was to have done much more than accumulate benefices *in commendam*; commoners, on the other hand, were those most likely to have preached widely and to have held positions within a diocesan administration. From the evidence available, it does not seem that contemporaries demanded a particular kind of prior experience in new bishops. Instead they looked for *hommes de mérite* who would discipline and reform their clergy, conduct visitations, defend their jurisdiction and temporalities, as well as preach.

Other apparent similarities turn out to mean different things when viewed in their proper context rather than set against each other in isolation. As we have seen, a high proportion of new bishops during the 1590s and 1630s were commoners by birth, but there the similarity ends: a considerable, if elusive number of those of the 1590s were dependents of powerful noble families, if not outright *confidentiaires*. Those of the 1630s, on the other hand, were appointed during the dominant years of the Richelieu ministry, when the influence of the nobility over ecclesiastical patronage was at its lowest point, and the new bishops owed far less to noble patronage, and considerably more to their own abilities and ecclesiastical affiliations.

Likewise, the return in force of sons of the old nobility in the 1640s and 1650s was not simply a resumption of earlier patterns. One important difference was that by then even the families of the *grands*, old and new, had largely come to accept the demands of reformers of the episcopate. Their offspring were, among other things, now prepared to endure the *épreuves* of university study, even to the extent of taking the licentiate or doctorate in theology, something which would have been virtually unthinkable a generation or so previously. They were also prepared to accept direction from the likes of Vincent de Paul at Saint-Lazare and, somewhat later, from Olier and the emerging seminary at Saint-Sulpice.

3 See above, p 17.

This was an important development for the future: the nobility's willingness to accept that episcopal office was only available for men in middle age (by seventeenth-century standards at least), and that it required serious academic preparation and other pre-episcopal activities, meant that its sons would again enjoy the advantages which, all other things being equal, they held over all other groups competing for the rank of bishop. Even the obligation of theological studies which had previously been so repugnant, could become an additional advantage to noble families, given their length and cost. When the *Gazette* announced that the 'theses' of, say, an abbé La Rochefoucauld or a Harlay de Beaumont had been attended by leading figures from the court and the judiciary and were a splendid success, it is difficult not to conclude that a subtle but effective mechanism for the promotion of young 'men of distinction', in whom birth was both confirmed and enhanced by merit, was at work. The fact that the sons of the nobility increasingly needed more than their pedigree or their families' *états de service* to the crown by way of entitlement to a mitre makes it clear that the requirements and improvements which had been painfully but cumulatively built into episcopal patronage from the 1610s onwards remained in place, regardless of whether there was a fully fledged *conseil de conscience* to enforce them.

I

The *conseil de conscience* itself was not, as we saw, merely a bureaucratic arrangement for the processing of the crown's ecclesiastical patronage, since those who promoted the idea from the outset were unmistakably church reformers, and not bureaucrats. When it finally came into being, it was as a result of their determination to preserve what had so far been achieved and ensure that it would not be undone in the unpredictable circumstances of the regency of Anne of Austria. But it is also essential to see the *conseil* and the results it helped to achieve as arising from wider developments within the French church. It has been argued that jurisdictional themes were more important than theological ones in the thinking of the Council of Trent and the post-Tridentine church generally as far as the episcopate was concerned. Within the Italian peninsula itself, this jurisdictional turn was due mainly to the centralising pressures exerted by the Roman curia in the interests of papal primacy, but also by the problems experienced by local episcopates in defending their perceived rights. In the literature devoted to episcopal office there, the emphasis was firmly on the concept of *buon governo*, which stressed practical skills, prudence, and the avoidance of excessive enthusiasm, even in defence of episcopal rights. The French church was in less danger than most from papal efforts at centralisation, though its bishops were no strangers to conflicts with the secular royal courts over jurisdiction, conflicts in which they regularly strove to obtain ministerial and conciliar support. Jurisdictional and 'governmental' issues could, therefore, never be regarded as trivial, but there is also little doubt that the seventeenth-century French episcopate inherited and developed further the Gallican traditions in relation to the dignity and importance of episcopal office. From François de Sales and Bérulle onwards, the dignity of episcopal office was enhanced by emphasising the idea that priests were set apart from the rest of the church by their participation in the priesthood of Christ, an idea which was such a defining feature of French thinking in the seventeenth century; bishops were, logically, the most complete expression of that priesthood, as only they could confer priestly orders. This was a major reason why episcopal consecration loomed so large in both the theory and practice of episcopacy in seventeenth-century France, since it symbolised the unique character of episcopal status. The contrast between the Spanish and French episcopates here may also indicate underlying differences in status. For example, one papal nuncio in late sixteenth-century Spain experienced difficulty in persuading Spanish bishops to abandon the tradition of private consecrations in favour of a public ceremony. Moreover, the energetic responses which were forthcoming every time the French religious orders attempted, however indirectly, to devalue episcopacy during the different phases of the seculars-regulars controversy shows just how firmly such views had struck root – as is clear again from the public expression of thanks by the 1635 Assembly of Clergy to the abbé of Saint-Cyran for his defence of episcopal office against the attacks of the regulars.[4] Such controversies were often about jurisdiction, but to a surprising extent they also focused sharply on both pastoral and doctrinal aspects of episcopacy. Interestingly, it was only later in the century, in the age of the reforming, philojansenist pope, Innocent XI, that Roman and Italian church circles would begin to absorb French thinking and to approach episcopal questions from a more theological and less purely practical or governmental point of view.[5]

Some of this thinking was, in turn, inspired by historical models. The search for an episcopate which would recreate as far as possible that of the early church – in line with reformist thinking since Erasmus and the humanists – was common to both Catholic and Protestant churches (where the latter retained the office of bishop). But, as has been shown for Jacobean England, where the attractions of an apostolic episcopate based on Saint Paul and early church sources were considerable, real-life bishops found the ideal hopelessly remote in practice.[6] They might have been shorn of much of their wealth under Henry VIII and his successors, but they retained considerable estates,

---

[4] Officially the assembly merely thanked an author known to them only as Petrus Aurelius, the nom-de-plume used by Saint-Cryan for his works, especially the *Vindiciae Censurae Facultatis Theologiae in Spongiam*, published in 1632. See Jean Orcibal, *Jean Duvergier de Hauranne, abbé de Saint-Cyran et son temps* (Louvain 1947), 334ff.

[5] Mario Rosa, 'L'Immagine del vescovo nel Seicento', *Richerche di Storia Sociale e Religiosa*, 46 (1994), 51–2, 58–9.

[6] Kenneth Fincham, *Prelate as Pastor. The Episcopate of James I* (Oxford 1990), esp chs 1 and 8(1).

not to mention social and political obligations which, in a country with a far less developed network of royal officials, made them much more important government agents than the majority of French bishops could ever be.[7] The latter may not have gone back quite as far as their English counterparts in the search for role models, but at the 1625 Assembly of Clergy, Bishop Etampes of Chartres boldly made the claim that 'through their learning, our prelates, or at least the majority of them, are reviving the memory of Irenaeus, Aymeric, Sidonius, Yves, Fulbert and other famous men who were our predecessors'.[8]

The question of a learned episcopate was, as Etampes's claim suggests, closely associated in contemporary thinking with that of an apostolic one, since both were part of the humanist-reformist tradition. It is here, perhaps, that the limitations of a theologically led ideal of episcopacy are most apparent. Contemporary comment of the kind to be found in Richelieu's *Testament Politique*, for example, was generally unfavourable to book-learning in bishops, unless it was a complement to the basic abilities required to govern a diocese effectively. Charles d'Abra de Raconis was a Paris philosophy professor before becoming bishop of Lavaur, but his colleague, the bishop of Valence, deplored his lack of savoir-faire in his diocese.[9] Louis XIII's remark about Raconis's university colleague, Jacques Lescot of Chartres, as a fine pedant of a bishop, also reflects this general reluctance to consider men of academic learning as natural candidates for the mitre.[10] And in practice, only a handful of university professors entered the ranks of the episcopate. Mendicants might not be regarded as more naturally fit to govern dioceses, but their preaching skills frequently gave them an advantage over academics aspiring to similar status. These reservations about the appropriateness of academic learning in bishops did not, however, preclude the emergence of an episcopate that was increasingly theologically literate, as its involvement in the Jansenist and other controversies demonstrated, nor was that theological competence confined to those who had formally taken theology degrees. From Jean-Pierre Camus to Bossuet and Fénélon, the episcopate produced able writers in several genres, although no theological or philosophical thinker of real distinction. Instead considerable numbers of bishops engaged in theological controversy with Huguenots, a more practically oriented form of intellectual activity. Even more of them proved to be antiquarians, collectors of books and manuscripts, and patrons of scholars, activities which brought them into regular

7   Felicity Heal, *Of Prelates and Princes. A Study of the Economic and Social Position of the Tudor Episcopate* (Cambridge 1980), esp ch 10. See also Heal, *Hospitality in Early Modern England* (Oxford 1990).
8   Quoted in Pierre Blet, 'L'Idée de l'épiscopat chez les évêques français du xviie siècle', in *L'Institution de les pouvoirs dans les églises de l'antiquité à nos jours*, ed Bernard Vogler (Louvain 1987), 311.
9   BN, MS Baluze 333, fo 114, letter to Charpentier, Richelieu's secretary, 11 Sept 1641.
10 BN MS Fr 15611, fo 382v, Henri Arnauld to president Barillon, 3 Feb 1642. Lescot was also Richelieu's confessor.

intercourse with men of similar interests, both inside and outside France.[11] Overall, the impression is one of an episcopate whose educational and intellectual attainments were spread widely rather than deeply.

II

The peculiar position of the French episcopate was only partly the result of its own internal make-up or self-image, and needs to viewed in a set of wider contexts, both French and European. It would be difficult to find a Catholic church in early modern Europe whose affairs were dominated as much by its bishops as was that of France. There are several reasons for this. For one thing, the great monastic orders no longer produced outstanding religious figures whose personal standing could enhance the power and prestige of the orders in question. The contrast here with parts of the Empire, the Habsburg hereditary lands included, where abbots of the 'princely' monasteries could wield considerable influence, and frequently went on to take episcopal office, is (for all the peculiarities of the *Reichskirche*) particularly striking.[12] In France, the almost systematic expansion, especially in the sixteenth century, of the commendatory system of benefice-holding virtually 'decapitated' the monastic orders, including even the most prestigious like Cluny and to a lesser extent Cîteaux. Individuals from the monastic orders might become bishops in seventeenth-century France, but as we saw they were never numerous, and their presence declined steadily by mid-century. Few of the old orders were more than partially revitalised through reform, and what little reform there was tended to generate minority congregations within the orders in question.

Nor did the mendicant orders succeed in acquiring, let alone preserving, the kind of influence in the French church which the Dominicans, Franciscans or Jesuits enjoyed in the Iberian and Italian churches generally. The absence of an Inquisition may be one reason for this contrast, since it provided an important vehicle for mendicant influence, especially in Spain, where many of its officials went on to become bishops. In France the office of royal confessor was held by a Jesuit, whose Society's constitutions forbade its members from accepting episcopal office! In Spain, for instance, Franciscans and Dominicans could enjoy more influence than any bishop, partly because of the Inquisition and the confessorship, but partly also because of the monarchy's regular recourse to *juntas* of theologians when making political decisions. It is

---

11 These activities can best be approached through the published correspondence of *savants* like the brothers Dupuy, Peiresc and Chapelain, but much of it remains unpublished. Chancellor Séguier, himself a keen collector of books and manuscripts, was in regular correspondence with several bishops on such subjects.
12 See Rudolf Reinhardt, 'Die hochadeligen Dynastien in der Reichskirche des 17. und 18. Jahrhunderts', *Römische Quartalschrift*, 83 (1988), 224.

difficult to judge if there was less tolerance in France than elsewhere in Europe of mendicants entering the episcopate (an aversion which seems to have affected the monastic orders rather less), but without the obvious advantages that they enjoyed in the Spanish kingdoms, their claims on episcopal office were considerably more difficult to establish; in proportional terms, regulars entering the seventeenth-century Castilian episcopate outnumbered their French counterparts by as many as between two or three to one, and their numbers were still rising in the second half of the century when, as we saw, they were fading strongly in France. One feature that French and Castilian mendicant bishops shared, however, was that they usually acceded to office at a more advanced age than other bishops, and that in turn partly explains why the average age of incoming bishops was consistently higher south of the Pyrenees throughout the seventeenth century. Moreover, mendicants in France were commonly given relatively insignificant or otherwise unattractive dioceses, and no doubt because of their orders' practice of religious poverty, individually or corporately, they were widely held to be the obvious choices to fill poorly endowed sees. A systematic study of contemporary views would almost certainly suggest that they were not generally regarded as suitable for episcopal office. Similar views also circulated in Italy and curial circles, one of whose spokesmen wrote in the mid-seventeenth century, 'a bishop is a man of government, and regulars do not know how to govern'.[13]

Finally, the cathedral chapters of France failed to preserve the considerable power and prestige which they had possessed for much of the central and later Middle Ages. Their loss of the right to elect bishops and the fact that, with exceptions such as the chapter of Lyon, they did not turn themselves into proud aristocratic corporations of the kind that was common in the Empire and the eastern marches of France, but were accessible to sons of royal officials and urban patricians, meant that their ambitions were blunted and their horizons were increasingly local. They could, of course, still be formidable opponents locally, as many a bishop learned to his cost down to the Revolution, but this could not hide the fact that both locally and nationally, they carried less and less weight in church affairs as the *ancien régime* progressed, while episcopal powers grew correspondingly.[14] Such trends might have been offset had the number of French bishops who were members of cathedral chapters been higher than the figure of around 30 per cent. As it was, a proportion of the canons in question probably treated their positions as attractive sinecures which did not bind them tightly to the chapters in question and to their interests. Here, too, the contrast with Castile is striking. Despite a similarly centralised form of royal episcopal patronage, approximately two out of every three bishops throughout the early modern period were drawn from the chapters, a fact which suggests at the very least that their

---

13 Quoted in Rosa, 'L'Immagine del vescovo nel Seicento', 55.
14 See Loupès, *Chapitres et chanoines de Guyenne*, part 1, chs 1–2, part IV, chs 1–2.

members clearly corresponded more than any other group to the working ideal of the episcopate held by the monarchy there.

Not only could the monastic, mendicant and corporate clergy not compete with the episcopate in the affairs of the French church, but the episcopate was also among the major beneficiaries of the crown's dispensation of the many abbeys and priories tenable *in commendam*, especially once the grip the great nobility had on many of the most valuable of them under Henri III and Henri IV had been brought to an end. This, it may be argued, offered the bishops (as well as other clerics not necessarily interested in episcopal office) yet another opportunity to dominate the old orders. Elsewhere in Catholic Europe, such opportunities were, it seems, severely limited, thus denying individual bishops a potentially attractive mechanism for substantial ecclesiastical empire-building. In Spain, for example, the absence of well-endowed benefices without cure of souls deprived the crown of an obvious way of rewarding its clerical servants, with the effect that promotion to episcopal office was actively sought by such men with relatively little resistance from the crown.[15]

It should be noted here that another obvious consequence of the *commende* was that individual bishops – usually the highborn and well connected – drew considerable financial benefit from it. The more benefices they accumulated in this way, whether before or during the episcopate, the greater their personal as distinct from their episcopal revenues, which in turn created a hierarchy of personal episcopal wealth which could be seriously at variance with the institutional hierarchy that we saw in an early chapter. This is not the full picture, however, since the *commende*, in turn, almost certainly affected individual attitudes to episcopal office, though this is a subject still to be explored. A wealthy *abbé de cour* might, in particular circumstances, be much less worried about accepting a poorly endowed bishopric than would a cleric with limited means; another might decide that, compared to a lucrative *in commendam* sinecure, episcopal office was altogether more trouble than it was worth, and there is no shortage of evidence to show that otherwise worldly or ambitious clerics would hesitate on such purely pragmatic grounds before becoming candidates for the mitre.[16] On the other hand, there are few signs that French bishops, unlike their Venetian counterparts (mostly in Venice's overseas territories) abandoned their dioceses because of chronic under-endowment. Candidates are known to have hesitated occasionally before accepting a diocese because of lack of means with which to pay the cost of annates and provisions – but that was a different matter.[17] Moreover, incom-

---

15 See A D Wright, 'Church and State in Post-Tridentine Spain', in *Catholic Times and Tastes. Essays in Honour of Michael E Williams*, ed Margaret A Rees (Leeds 1987), 319.
16 See *Lettres de Peiresc*, ed Philippe Tamizey de Larroque, 8 vols (Paris 1888–98), iv. 60, letter to Jean-Jacques Bouchard, Aix 6 June 1636.
17 See BAV, Barb lat 7960, fo 54, Philippe Cospeau to Cardinal Barberini, 8 Jan 1631, referring to Nicolas Grillié's nomination to Bazas, Cospeau wrote that 'sa pauvreté est si extreme qu'il court fortune d'y estre nommé sans fruit' – unless his provisions were issued *gratis*.

ing French bishops did not normally face the prospect, as did their Roman counterparts, of having to surrender their benefices on their elevation to the episcopate. As we saw, benefices might have to be traded in order to acquire episcopal office, but this was never based on the principle that benefices, unlike offices, were of their nature *vacabili*. Nor did French bishops really have to face the kind of prolonged fiscal extortion which in seventeenth-century Castile appears to have had the effect of deterring some individuals from accepting episcopal office and reigning bishops from accepting promotions to more distinguished and better endowed sees. It could not be said of the French episcopate, as it has of their Castilian counterpart, that 'the fiscal capacity of the Spanish church was always a prime motivator of the Crown's preferment policy',[18] even at the relatively *ad hoc* level of maximising the financial benefits to be derived from pensions payable by bishops to third parties. And in death, the personal estates of French bishops were not threatened by either papal or royal claims to impose the so-called 'right of spoil' (*ius spolii*) which so envenomed relations between bishops, crown, and papacy in Spain, Naples and elsewhere.

III

The French church, like others in Catholic Europe, was 'governed by the twin principles of authority and hierarchy', though from a distance it might seem that a 'lack of clear jurisdictional lines, maldistribution of ecclesiastical wealth, and uneven territorial boundaries created an institution without strong cohesion'. If this judgement, made by a recent historian of the *ancien régime* Spanish church, does not quite fit that of France, it was in part because it could not be said that it 'lacked an institutional means of developing an independent stance against either king or pope', or that 'without a collective means of expression, the church accepted the direction marked for it by the Bourbon monarchy'.[19] One important reason for this is that just when the ecclesiastical 'congregations' of the Castile-León church were entering a period of decline, the French Assemblies of Clergy were still growing in vitality. This is no place to attempt a summary of their history, but merely to comment on their importance for the episcopate, actual and potential. It is probably fair to say that by deterring the French monarchy from imitating its Castilian counterpart, and specifically from imposing heavy financial burdens on their sees, the assemblies played no small part in ensuring the bishoprics remained highly attractive to French ecclesiastics. Not only were the assemblies dominated by bishops, but they also gradually became an important

---

18 Helen E Rawlings, 'The Secularisation of Castilian Episcopal Office under the Habsburgs, c. 1516–1700', *Journal of Ecclesiastical History*, 38 (1987), 69.
19 William J Callahan, *Church, Society and Politics in Spain 1750–1974* (Cambridge, Mass. 1984), 7–8.

stepping-stone towards episcopal office itself. As we saw, the Mazarin ministry in particular made a point of keeping vacant sees unfilled during assemblies in order to persuade second-rank deputies to support royal policies or demands, while reigning bishops could look forward to the grant of benefices *in commendam* if they also conformed. From at least the mid or late 1620s, the Richelieu ministry went to great trouble, not always successfully it should be realised, to ensure the election of well-disposed deputies, episcopal and non-episcopal, to the assemblies. The fact that no fewer than five *agents généraux* obtained bishoprics after the Fronde reinforces this point, since their office gave them unrivalled experience of the affairs of the French church and made them the normal intermediaries between the crown, the council, the financiers, and the French church generally. Their success underlined not merely the extent to which the upper clergy, at the centre of which stood the reigning bishops, had come to play a major role in defining and determining the shape of the episcopate, but also revealed the ecclesiastical character of episcopal patronage.

IV

None of this should be construed as making family connections and secular patronage of all kinds irrelevant in the making of the French episcopate: there is, quite simply, far too much evidence to the contrary. As already noted, factors such as the *commende*, the assemblies of clergy, and the relatively limited financial burdens imposed by the crown, ensured that the seventeenth-century French church experienced no serious difficulties in attracting the able as well as the ambitious to the episcopate. Admittedly there were individual refusals at various times, and although the reasons for declining a nomination changed over time, these refusals should not be interpreted as a *general* reflection on the desirability (or lack of it) of French dioceses. In any case, whatever negative effects they might have had were more than offset by the renewed presence of churchmen, epitomised by Richelieu and Mazarin, in leading ministerial positions. Ambitious ecclesiastics needed few stronger incentives than that to compete for episcopal office.

The enduring attractiveness of the episcopate only served to make connections and patronage networks all the more vital to individual success. But, as the preceding pages have shown, the interpretation of these networks and their influence is far from straightforward. For one thing, our information about them and how they functioned in more than a limited number of cases is quite thin and frequently indirect. Both the geography of the French church and the variety of its 113 dioceses suggest that talk of highly centralised mechanisms of control through an over-arching patronage system is illusory, even though the emergence of a generation of cardinal ministers did help to focus ecclesiastical networks in ways that might otherwise not have happened.

The elusiveness of patronage ties should also be seen as a consequence of at least two underlying features of the French church. The first is that there was nothing like a single dominant springboard to a career in the episcopate, although with the benefit of hindsight it can be said that this was beginning to change in a limited way by the middle of the seventeenth century. The second element, which emphasises both the diffuseness and the pervasiveness of patronage ties, is that most French bishops were part of a much wider world of royal ecclesiastical patronage for many years before obtaining a place in the episcopate. Here too, the well born and well connected had inherent advantages over other social groups, which enabled them to acquire benefices *in commendam* often from an early age, or to hold office in the ecclesiastical households of the royal family. By the same token, both features underline the extent to which future bishops were embedded in circles based on family ties, but also on more unpredictable ties of friendship, service, dependency, etc, and which were at least in part ecclesiastical rather than secular in nature. Ultimately, it was probably these well oiled ecclesiastical networks which enabled the episcopate to recover relatively quickly from the upheavals of the wars of religion and the attempts of the nobility to gain lasting control of diocesan sees. The process was supported by the crown, which appreciated the broader political value of an episcopate which was not reduced to the role of chaplains to the nobility.

V

Of course, the role of the crown gave formal shape to the whole process of making bishops, obliging all of those with an interest in vacant bishoprics to turn towards it. But what is clear, if perhaps also surprising, is the prolonged absence of any *esprit de système* in the making of nominations. Certainly, there was very limited reglementation compared to that which existed in the Castilian church of Philip II and his successors. The limited extent of bureaucratic provision for the handling of episcopal patronage is all the more surprising given the sheer size of the French church and the diversity of its dioceses. At no particular point do we encounter any attempt openly to define criteria for the screening or selection of candidates. It is curious, for example, that the *conseil de conscience*, especially in its very early years, appears never to have made pronouncements of the kind made a half-century previously by Philip II.[20] It is no less unexpected to find that on occasion men like Bérulle

---

20 Maximiliano Barrio Gozalo, 'Perfil socio-económico de una élite de poder: los obispos de Castilla la Vieja 1600–1840, *Anthologica Annua*, 28–9 (1981–2), 75–6, quoting the terms of the *Instrucción que debe observar la Cámara en las consultas para la provisión de prelacías* of Jan 1588.

or Vincent de Paul, known for their championship of a reformed episcopate, actively supported young and inexperienced candidates for office such as Henri de Béthune, the young Retz, Paul de Gondi, Henri de Guise, or Louis Fouquet. In addition, knowledge of personal moral failings, especially of Guise or Gondi, weighed less than the conviction that individuals like them might still serve a positive purpose thanks to the ultra-*dévot* entourage in which they and their families moved. Examples of this kind of thinking may not be abundant but they do indicate an awareness of the need to balance the merits of deserving but relatively isolated individuals against wider considerations of what would make a bishop, for all his personal defects, effective in a given diocese.

Consequently, it is fair to say that competition for episcopal office remained highly 'open', and not confined to a narrow range of candidates who met a clearly acknowledged set of requirements. By the same token, the crown's ability, let alone determination, to keep the distribution of episcopal office separate from other forms of royal largesse was highly variable. Moreover, on the evidence presented here, it does not appear that the French crown had a distinctive 'agenda' or policy of its own when nominating bishops. It was not, for example, under the same intense pressure to reward with bishoprics its servants, secular as well as clerical, as was the case in Venice or Spain, where the promotion of such individuals ensured not merely that the average age of incoming bishops was considerably higher than in France, but that many of them had not taken any orders.[21] Nor, for all the talk of Gallican sensitivities, did the crown ever go the lengths which Venice could in attempting to ensure that only men known to be closely in tune (*confidenza*, as it was called) with the Republic's Erastian preferences and unsympathetic to either papal or ecclesiastical concerns, were promoted, especially to the principal sees of the Terraferma.[22] Indeed, as we saw, episcopal candidates with known Gallican views commonly faced a difficult problem in obtaining papal confirmation.

The same point is underlined by the changing social profile of the episcopate between 1589 and 1661. The episcopates of France, Castile, the Austrian hereditary lands, and even the Spanish Netherlands in the seventeenth century were not wholly dissimilar in that all four experienced a considerable degree of social diversity. In the circumstances, it seems clear that the 'external' royal nomination of bishops was always more likely to produce a socially heterogeneous episcopate than 'internal' election by cathedral chapters.[23] Ideally, this contention needs to be proved in a comparative context, but there are relatively few possibilities for a comparison on this point by the seventeenth century. However, in the Empire, but also in a quasi-independent bishopric like Liège

---

21   *Ibid*, 80–3; Rawlings, 'Secularization of Episcopal Office', 71–3; Menniti Ippolito, *Politica e carriere ecclesiastiche*, 47.
22   Ippolito, *Politica e carriere ecclesiastiche*, esp ch 3.
23   See Johann Rainer, 'Die Politik der Bischofsernennung in Österreich 1648–1803', *Römische Quartalschrift*, 85 (1990), 231.

where bishops were still elected by cathedral chapters, bishops were almost always canons of the chapters in question, but above all sons of great aristocratic or ruling families.[24] It was rare for the chapters to look for candidates from a different background from their own, and their corporate traditions gave them a singlemindedness and continuity of purpose which even monarchies like that of France or Castile could rarely achieve.[25] The paradox is that an elective system was just as capable as any other of producing episcopal dynasties, with or without resort to coadjutorial arrangements, and that despite its ostensibly anti-dynastic principles.[26]

It is also clear that the period covered by this book played a crucial part in giving France a stable, long-serving episcopate. As we have seen, the average age of incoming bishops – which consistently exceeded forty from the 1630s onwards – was higher than is often imagined, even though it was still at least ten years lower than in contemporary England and Castile whose incoming bishops could justifiably be described, particularly in terms of contemporary life-expectancy, as elderly.[27] Seventeenth-century Castilian bishops might live a few years longer than their French counterparts, but the average episcopal career there did not exceed approximately fourteen years, compared to nearly twenty-four for their French counterparts. But arguably this was not the crucial factor differentiating the two episcopates. It is clear that the overall rates of episcopal transfers in seventeenth-century Spain and Italy were much higher than in France. Several Italian commentators during the pontificates of Paul V and Urban VIII complained of what they termed the scandal of frequent transfers, though figures that would reveal the actual extent of the phenomenon are still lacking.[28] For their part, Clement VIII and his successors protested, especially to Philip II and Charles II on this same point, while Philip IV's confessor's hostility to the practice was publicly known and doubtless influenced the king's instructions of 1656 which attempted to limit the frequency of transfers.[29] But none of this seems to have had much effect,

24 Stefan Kremer, *Herkunft und Werdegang geistlicher Führungsschichten in den Reichsbistümern zwischen Westfälischen Frieden und Säkularisation* (Freiburg-im-Breisgau 1992) *passim*; Alfred Minke, 'Die "belgische" Episkopat nach 1648 – ein Vergleich', *Römische Quartalschrift* 83 (1988), 364–78.

25 See Günter Christ, 'Selbstverständnis und Rolle der Domkapitel in der geistlichen Territorien des alten deutschen Reiches in der Frühneuzeit', *Zeitschrift für Historische Forschung*, 16 (1989), 257–328.

26 See Rudolf Reinhardt, 'Kontinuität und Diskontinuität. Zum Problem der Koadjutorie mit dem Recht der Nachfolge in der neuzeitlichen Germania Sacra', in J Kunisch, ed, *Der dynastische Fürstenstaat. Zur Bedeutung von Sukzessionsordnungen für die Entstehung des frühmodernen Staates* (Berlin 1982), 114–55.

27 Barrio Gozalo, 'Perfil socio-económico de una élite', *Anthologica Annua*, 38 (1991), 58, for a description of Spanish bishops as 'venerables ancianos'; D R Hirschberg, 'Episcopal incomes and expenses, 1660–c. 1760', in Rosemary O'Day and Felicity Heal, eds, *Princes and Paupers in the English Church 1500–1800* (Leicester 1981), 223, who calcuates that the average age of English bishops for the period 1660–1760 was 55, and 52 for the years 1688 to 1760.

28 Rosa, 'Immagine del vescovo nel Seicento', 56–8.

29 Barrio Gozalo, 'Perfil socio-económico de una élite', *Anthologica Annua*, 38 (1991), 61–2.

and transfer rates remained consistently high. The main consequence was that for the century as a whole the average duration of episcopal tenure per diocese was only slightly more than seven years, about half of the total average length of episcopal careers generally.

Viewed in this perspective, the French episcopate can be shown to have achieved a high level of stability in a relatively short period after the upheavals of the sixteenth century. With episcopal transfers the exception rather than the rule, the average duration of episcopal careers – which was 23.7 years for the years 1589 to 1661 – was not significantly higher than the average for the tenure of individual dioceses.

The advantages of diocesan tenure which averaged in the region of twenty years hardly need emphasising. Apart from giving French bishops both the time and the continuity to impose their brand of Catholic reform, it served to streamline diocesan administrative practices and defend episcopal rights and jurisdiction, as well as to improve the management of, and the revenues from, episcopal temporalities. Even more so, it ensured that each generation of bishops had a genuine opportunity to maintain and build their connections to local élites, and to play a significant part in provincial affairs generally. Of course, this stability and longevity had its negative side, too, since all too often it meant that little could be done with elderly or infirm bishops whose inactivity could be prolonged and damaging to their dioceses; it was almost certainly a factor accounting for the uneven geographical development of reform in the seventeenth-century French church.

The wider implications of all this for church-state relations generally await further exploration. Certainly, it can be suggested that the stability just described was an additional factor in sustaining French episcopal autonomy in relation to the monarchy. By comparison, the Spanish crown seems to have been dealing with an altogether more dependent, pliant episcopate, and the frequency with which it moved bishops around from one diocese to another was probably both cause and effect of that particular relationship. Over the longer term, it may also help to explain the limited extent of Spanish episcopal authority within dioceses as well as the limited results of efforts to carry through the objectives of Tridentine reform there. Of course, it would be easy to imagine that the French monarchy was envious of its Castilian counterpart's control of the episcopate, but it does seem that the temptation to treat the map of France's dioceses as a chessboard was never particularly strong. If anything, the monarchy seems to have appreciated the benefits of a stable episcopate, with transfers under Louis XIV being limited mainly to the filling of archiepiscopal sees. It is probably no accident that the high transfer rates typical of the Spanish church only finally plummeted when the Bourbons succeeded the Habsburgs there.[30] Former royal servants regularly entered the French episcopate, but their numbers were relatively limited, and

---

30   *Ibid*, 62–3.

their earlier secular careers did not automatically guarantee them a major role in church-state politics, let alone the best dioceses; even former provincial intendants, who were used to being moved from province to province, usually found that on becoming bishops their days as peripatetic royal commissioners were over and that they would be wedded to a single diocese for the rest of their career.

VI

It would be easy to dismiss the changes which occurred within the French episcopate in this period as minor adjustments which were not immune to reversal were circumstances, political and otherwise, to alter. But this would be to underestimate the nature of the challenge and of the efforts made in response to it. If we are to avoid unrealistic conclusions about its evolution over time, it is essential to view the episcopate not merely in the broad perspective of other European churches, but also in relation to particular social developments within France. It is all too easily forgotten that French bishops belonged to a society in which offices of all kinds had increasingly become both venal and hereditary, and that this process was driven by powerful social pressures at every level. Church offices and benefices were subject to those same pressures, and historians have shown how families and social groups were able to establish an impressive grip on a whole range of benefices, ranging from parishes and chaplaincies to canonicates in chapters and places in monasteries with a *numerus clausus*.[31] Indeed, many of the formal ethical and legal mechanisms, notably those of resignation and reversion, which subsequently enabled offices to be kept from one generation to the next, were originally developed by the late medieval church, in which they continued to be widely practised during the early modern centuries. Subsequent moves towards the full venality (under François I and his successors) and heredity of royal office (under Henri IV) had profound social and cultural repercussions, and it would be naïve to imagine that they did not affect attitudes to church offices and benefices. Court offices, governorships, military officerships and so on, which were in the king's direct gift, were subject to intense competition. For obvious reasons, they were 'political' and favour-driven, so that the forms of venality which applied to them were more 'customary' and uncodified than those which applied (especially after the *droit annuel* was introduced in 1604) to the mass of legal and financial offices throughout the realm. Bishoprics and benefices tenable *in commendam* were similarly in the king's gift, and it is clear that for much of the sixteenth century large numbers of them were distributed liberally in order to satisfy a

---

31 See Louis Châtellier, 'Société et bénéfices ecclésiastiques, 1670–1730: le cas alsacien', *Revue Historique*, 224 (1970), 75–98; Loupès, *Chapitres et chanoines de Guyenne*, 231ff.

wide range of court and provincial noble families, who equally naturally expected such largesse to come their way. It is possible to see the subsequent appearance of a practice such as the *confidence* between Charles IX and Henri IV or the pressure for coadjutorships during the 1610s as expressions of the social pressure to bring bishoprics closer to the forms taken by royal 'liberality' with regard to other venal offices.

Consequently, any effort to prevent episcopal office from moving in the direction of contemporary *vénalité* had to impress on the crown (broadly conceived) the reasons why bishoprics should be treated differently from other offices, and in doing so to follow the terms of the Concordat of Bologna or the Council of Trent rather than the political arithmetic of the day. Clearly, the views of kings and their advisers, as well as of the wider circles of influential courtiers and patrons, as to how best to employ episcopal patronage varied, but it is clear that as the seventeenth century progressed a consensus slowly emerged. It was one in which the average bishop was at least in his mid-thirties, had taken a university degree, was in orders, and increasingly had engaged in one or more ecclesiastical activities; and if he was also more than likely to be drawn from the nobility, old and new, he was nevertheless expected to conform in large measure to the expectations just described.

But this was only part of the picture. The clergy who competed for episcopal office were themselves usually drawn from families who held office of one kind or another, and who would naturally tend to see offices as venal and hereditary. This trait would in turn have been exacerbated by the *commerce des bénéfices* in which the great majority of future bishops indulged, sometimes personally, sometimes through their families, and often from an early age. Court almonerships were effectively bought and sold, while benefices tenable *in commendam* were sinecures divorced from any pastoral or residential duties and were subject to intense competition and frequent horse-trading. If persuading the crown to treat episcopal office differently from the other forms of patronage at its disposal was no small task, it was surely no less difficult to educate ecclesiastics long accustomed to the *commerce des bénéfices* to view bishoprics as radically different. Ultimately, it may be impossible to judge how decisively attitudes among those involved in the making of the episcopate in any generation were transformed, but on the evidence that we have seen in these pages, the years from Henri IV to the death of Mazarin represent a crucial stage in the emergence of an episcopate which by the later seventeenth century had in many ways become a model for much of Catholic Europe.

Biographical Dictionary

ADDITIONAL ABBREVIATIONS

This list of abbreviations should be completed by that on p xi.

abp	archbishop
AC	Assembly of Clergy
av-gen	*avocat-général*
B/b	Born
bacc	baccalaureat
bp	bishop
coadj	coadjutor
coll	college
cons	consecrated/consecration
cons	*conseiller*
cons-cl	*conseiller-clerc*
D/d	Died
doct	doctor(ate)
EG	Estates General
gov	governor
in c	*in commendam*
in utr	*in utroque iure*
lic	licentiate
lt-gen	*lieutenant général*
MR	*maîtres des requêtes*
ND	Notre-Dame
nom	nominated, nomination
OSA	Order of St Augustine
OSB	Order of St Benedict (Benedictines)
O Cist	Order of Cîteaux (Cistercians)
OFM	Order of Friars Minor (Franciscans)
OP	Order of Preachers (Dominicans)
O Prem	Order of Premonstratensians
parlt	parlement
pres	president
proc-gen	*procureur-général*
provs	papal provisions
resign	resigned
sgr	seigneur
SJ	Society of Jesus (Jesuits)
SR	*Secrétaire du Roi*
St	Saint
uncons	unconsecrated
univ	university
vg	vicar-general
(Bourges)	refers to diocese in which benefices were located

BIOGRAPHICAL DICTIONARY

THE BIOGRAPHICAL SKETCHES which follow are not intended to embrace the entire careers of the individuals concerned – that would easily fill an entire volume. Their purpose is more practical. Written in close connection to the main text, they are designed to provide some idea of the broad social and family background as well as the pre-episcopal careers of the 351 bishops who form the corpus of this book. A brief explanation of the dictionary's format will be of help.

Without attempting to devise a rigid framework which would apply equally in each case, but which might impose a pre-conceived unity on those who became bishops in this period, it seemed important to cover certain common features. Each notice begins with the bishop's name, the dates of his episcopal career and the diocese(s) he held and, if he was a member of a religious order, the name of the order in question. Wherever possible, consideration has then been given to the family circumstances of each bishop, in the hope of elucidating the kind of advantages – social, ecclesiastical or otherwise – which might have helped individuals on the road to the episcopate. As for the bishops themselves, comment has focused primarily on their education, their benefices, their offices and activities, and the orders they had taken before the episcopate. Beyond this, comment and information varies, covering issues such as patronage connections, the circumstances of individual nominations, and so on. Each notice concludes with the factual details of episcopal nomination, papal approval, consecration, transfers, death, etc.

For reasons of space, considerable numbers of abbreviations have been used References have frequently been given in highly condensed form, and only those not cited in the bibliography are given in full.

Where there are several bishops from the same family, sketches have followed chronological rather than alphabetical order. I have also, where possible, tried to indicate which sources apply to a given bishop from the same family; rigid separation is impossible, and a fair amount of overlap in the sources cited is inevitable.

Any attempt at an alphabetical dictionary like this has to confront the problem of family names. With so many bishops known by *noms de terre* rather than by patronymics, the only rule which appears not to generate unnecessary confusion or absurdity is that of common usage. On occasion, however, I have italicised the patronymics of bishops better known by other names. I have as far as possible provided cross-references where more than one name has been used for individuals.

Abbadie, Jean-Pierre d'. Lescar 1599–1609. Profile of this Béarnais family only becomes clear with bp's father, who held succession of important legal-admin offices in the service of king of Navarre from 1529 until his death, ca 1567. Ennobled by office, his social origins are evident from marriage to daughter of merchant of Oloron and status as late as 1547 as a *bourgeois* of Osse.

B. ca 1529 Maslacq. 5th son of Bertrand and Jeanne de Florence. No information on education, but held doct in law, and may have studied with brothers Jean, Pierre, and Gassiot in Paris, Toulouse etc. Successively MR and *cons* (in 1573) of Navarre. Like father, he managed to remain Catholic while in royal service – possibly less difficult under Henri IV than under Jeanne d'Albret. Marriage in 1581 to Bernardine de Luger, dame de St-Castin, greatly consolidated Abbadie position among leading robe families of Béarn. Sister Isabelle was grandmother of Pierre de Marca, abp of Toulouse and Paris. A widower after 1588, Abbadie was leading figure among Béarn Catholics in 1590s, joining several deputations to king and court in 1594 and 1598. Elevation to episcopate by Henri IV, who liked him, was logical step after king's promise in 1595 to restore Catholicism in Béarn.

No date for nom, but probably 1598. Provs 4–6–1599. Cons date unknown. D. 8–5–1609.

Sources: AD Pyr-Atlantiques, E 1996. Dufau de Maluquer, 'La Maison d'Abbadie de Maslacq', *Mémoires de la Société Royale du Canada*, 2nd ser (Ottawa 1895), 73–113. Denis Labau, *Lescar, histoire d'une cité épiscopale* (Pau 1975), vol ii. Pierre de Marca, *Histoire de Béarn*, ed V Dubarat, 2 vols (Pau 1894–1912). *DBF*, i. cols 44–51.

Abra. *See* **Raconis**

Adhémar. *See* **Grignan**

Aleaume, Guillaume. Riez 1614–22, Lisieux 1622–34. Family originated in Brie region, where they held lands and bp's grandfather, Nicolas, was *procureur* in *élection* of Rozay-en-Brie. Nicolas (?-1622), father of bp, settled in Paris, becoming *cons* in *grand conseil* (1579) and parlt (1582). Marriage to sister of Guillaume du Vair, future keeper of the seals, was crucial to his and son's career. On close terms, Du Vair and Aleaume both suffered for their royalism during League, but were to benefit subsequently. Despite these advantages, neither family managed to progress much further, since Guillaume du Vair never married, while his brother Pierre was bp of Vence in eastern Provence.

B. Paris 1585. Son of Nicolas and Antoinette du Vair. Studied humanities and philosophy at coll of Calvi, Univ of Paris, and law at Orléans, becoming doct in utr, ca 1613. Original career choice was *cons* in Paris parlt, where he was 'received', 18–7–1613. Only months later, uncle, G du Vair, first pres of Aix parlt, helped to obtain Provençal see of Riez for him. Then just a simple cleric, he quickly took minor orders (19–9–1614) and subdiaconate (20–9–1614) as 'bishop-elect of Riez'. Not long resident in Riez, he moved to Lisieux in 1618 to assist aged bp du Vair, whom he formally succeeded after his death.

Nom to Riez 19–4–1614. Provs 18–5–1615. Cons 15–11–1615. Transferred to Lisieux 14–3–1622. D. 29–8–1634.

Sources: ASV, PC 13, fos 486–517; PC 34, fos 1–22. AN, Z^{1}o, 241. BL, Add MS 21434, fo 14. Trani, 'Conseillers du grand conseil', 97. *DBF*, i.1370–1.

Amboise, Adrien. Tréguier 1604–16. One version of family's origins traces them to a bastard son of Chaumont d'Amboise, admiral of France under Louis XII, but this perhaps was used to disguise more humble origins when bp's father, Jean, sought naturalisation in 1566. B. in Douai, Jean (?-1584) moved to Paris where he was surgeon and *valet de chambre* to Charles IX and Henri III. A man of considerable learning. During bp's generation family achieved its greatest distinction: his brother Jacques held more socially and professionally respectable position of *médécin ordinaire* to Henri IV in 1594, when he also became rector of Univ of Paris, which he had led into recognising Henri IV. Eldest brother, François, did better still, moving into law, and becoming *avocat du roi* at the *cour du trésor*, av-gen at *grand conseil*, and after period of exile during League, MR in 1596. He had obtained letters of ennoblement in 1589.

B. Paris 1551. 2nd son of Jean and Marie Fromager. Educated (like brothers) at king's expense at coll of Navarre, where brother François was teaching. Adrien served as rector of univ in 1579, and took lic in theology, 1582, but possibly not doct. Early career was academic, but also wrote poetry and at least one play, *Holopherne tragédie sainte* (pub 1580). During League, his royalism, shared with his brothers, meant he kept relatively quiet in Paris, but city's submission in 1594 enabled them all to reap rewards. Rapidly appointed a *prédicateur* and royal almoner in 1594, he was *curé* of St-André-des-Arts in 1595, the same year Henri IV made him grand master of coll of Navarre as part of an effort to master and reform univ.

Nom 1603. Provs 2–8–1604. Cons 1604. D. 29–7–1616.

Sources: Dante Ughetti, *François d'Amboise (1550–1619)* (Rome 1974) (with numerous documents). Saulnier, *Parlement de Bretagne*, i. 26–8. Trani, 'Conseillers du grand conseil', 98–9; Tallemant, *Historiettes*, ii. 282, 1142–3. *DBF*, ii. 480–1.

Angennes, Jacques. Bayeux 1606–47. One of early modern France's most prominent noble families, the Angennes achieved real distinction under François I and successors. Bp's grandmother embraced Protestantism, and some family members were Protestant until early 17th C. Bp's father's generation prospered to extraordinary degree, rising to top ranks at court, in military and diplomatic activities, and in the church, thanks especially to favour of Henri III. Having voted for execution of Guises in 1588, Louis and and brother, Nicolas, quickly rallied to Henri IV in 1589. Equally strong ecclesiastical presence is evident under Charles IX and Henri III in careers of Cardinal de Rambouillet and his brother Claude, successively bp of Noyon and Le Mans. Like his brothers, Claude rallied early to Henri IV, and was one of his key clerical advisors during 1590s.

B. ca 1582. Son of Louis, marquis de Maintenon, and Françoise d'O, sister of Henri III's *surintendant des finances*. Originally destined for military career, early education was probably minimal and *chevaleresque*. Nom to Bayeux only when elder brother, Jean, declined and fled abroad to seek military adventure. Consequently, only became cleric in Jan 1605 (i.e. *after* his nom) and was still in minor orders when confirmed by Rome, which also accepted he had by now acquired doct in canon law, possibly in Rome itself.

No date for nom (Bayeux vacant since Ossat's death in May 1604). Provs 5–5–1606. Cons in Rome 27–8–1606. D. 16–5–1647.

Sources: AN, Z¹o, 241; MC, XXIX, 112, 25–7–1604 (*régale* settlement). ASV, Acta Camerarii 14, fo 37. Anselme, ii. 421–33. M Orléa, *La Noblesse aux états généraux de 1576 et de 1588* (Paris 1980) 131–7. Vidal, *Critique*, 270–1. Wolfe, *Conversion of Henri IV*, 74. *DBF*, ii. 1095–6.

Anglure. *See* **Bourlemont**

Aradon, Georges d'. Vannes 1590–6. The only bp successfully elected in this period, Aradon owed his advancement to a combination of political circumstances and local family power. Of middling noble rank by 15th C, family members regularly appeared in Breton military affairs (*montres, réformations*) between 1443 and 1536, but in early 17th C their lands (most of them in Vannes diocese itself) and title passed to house of Lannion.

B. Quimperley near Pontivy 29–9–1564. Son of René and Claude de Guého. Nothing known of education, though probably had lic in utr – suggestion he was doct of theology can be safely discounted. *Cons* in Rennes parlt Dec 1586, he and brothers organised and dominated Catholic League in native Vannetais, and also helped establish its parlt at Nantes, 1590. Abbot in c of La Meilleraie, O Cist (Nantes) and deacon at time of election, but quickly ordained priest. Cons in Paris where he was active deputy to League's EG of 1593. Took possession of Vannes in 1594, and remained an intransigent supporter of Mercoeour and League. D. without submitting to Henri IV.

Vannes vacant since 1588, the cathedral chapter chose Aradon as successor, 'a la sollicitation du duc' (Mercoeur), 13–2–1590. Provs 10–3–1593. Cons 1593. D. 31–6–1596.

Sources: AD Morbihan, 55 G 2. Saulnier, *Parlement de Bretagne*, i. 35–36; ii, 869. Gallet, *Seigneurie bretonne*, 137,159, 288, 418. *DBF*, iii. 196–7.

Arbaut de Bargemon, Antoine. Sisteron 1648–66. Family first appears with a notary at Aups in 1410. Gradual process of social advancement in course of 16th C through office-holding, though some branches were fined for usurpation of noble status in 17th-C *recherches*, possibly for attempting to graft themselves onto older provençal noble family of same name. In 16th C, there were several generations of officiers in *chambre des comptes* at Aix, which brought ennoblement, and bishop's family descended from them. By contrast, bp's mother's family, the Rochas d'Aiglun, had been noble for generations. In ecclesiastical sphere, family first gained a place in Aix cathedral chapter in 1549 and as this was sustained in later generations, chapter was natural starting point for future bp of Sisteron.

B. 11–11–1602 Aix. Son of Jean-Baptiste, sgr de Podenière and Bargemon, and Anne de Rochas d'Aiglun. Nothing known of early education, but credited with lic in theology (probably from Aix). Canon of Aix from 1619, his family was sufficiently well placed to enable him to rise further than predecessors in local church hierarchy, culminating in provostship of cathedral (1637) and key diocesan posts of vg and *official* for 5–6 years before episcopal nom. This suggests he had trust and patronage of Michele Mazarin, absentee abp of Aix, which contributed to his final promotion. In 1648, several witnesses testified to his independent wealth and means. Subdeacon (1625), deacon (1627), and ordained priest in 1638.

Nom 8–7–1648. Provs 28–9–1648. Cons 7–2–1649. D. 26–5–1666.

Sources: ASV, PC 50, fos 568–90. BN, Doss bleus 615 (doss Arbaud). Blanc, *Origines des familles provençales*, 32–5. Clapiers-Coulonges, *Chronologie des officiers*, 79, 88. Dolan, *Entre Tours et clochers*, 343–4. *DBF*, iii. 253–4.

Arnauld, Henri. Angers 1649–92. Arnauld and family appear so archetypically Parisian and *dévot* that even the broad outlines of their history contain surprises. Moved to Paris during 16th C from Herment in Auvergne, where they had served the Bourbon family whose disgrace in 1523 they (like other notable 'Parisian' families) survived. Including a considerable number of Protestants for several generations, bp's father and grandfather only reverted to Catholicism soon after 1572 massacres. Like fellow Auvergnat, Jean du Vair, Antoine I served as proc-gen to Catherine de' Medici (who protected him during the massacre of 1572), while his two marriages allied him to office-holding and financial families, du Bourg and Forget de Fresnes. Ennobled in 1577. Bp's father's marriage – to daughter of fellow barrister of comparable provincial origins – was relatively modest in social terms, but more spectacular professionally, given influence and connections of father-in-law, Simon Marion, who ended career as av-gen in Paris parlt. Bp Henri was one of 20 children, many of whom, both male and female, entered the church. While he and youngest brother, Antoine, are the best remembered of the sons, Arnauld political activities were far more prominent in 1610s and 1620s, when their eldest brother Robert was *intendant des finances*; his (and family's) ministerial ambitions were shattered by Richelieu, though Louis XIV made amends later.

B. 30–10–1597 Paris. 2nd son of Antoine II and Catherine Marion. Little known of education, except took lic in canon law at Orléans. Although tonsured in 1615, he practised law until 1619, when father's death freed him to enter church. Took orders in Rome, Sept 1624, where he had settled in 1621, acting as secretary to Cardinal Bentivoglio, former papal nuncio to France. But Brûlart patronage, which had helped him and family, collapsed after 1624. Abbot in c of St-Nicholas-d'Angers 1623, royal almoner 1624, archdeacon (1633) and dean (1636) of Toul, he was nom bp by Louis XIII in Sept 1637, but despite enjoying its revenues until 1641, his promotion failed in face of determined papal opposition. Unofficial French emissary in Rome 1645–8, mainly in order to reconcile Innocent X and Barberinis. Long regarded as natural 'episcopabile', slowness with which became bp probably derives from being virtually promised Angers succession several years before see became vacant.

Nom 30–1–1649 (the day after his predecessor's death). Provs 4–4–1650. Cons 29–6–1650. D. 8–6–1692.

Sources: ASV, PC 48, fos 118–29. Bonnot, *Hérétique ou saint?* Vidal, *Critique*, 90–2. *DBF*, iii. 868–73. *DGS*, 108–9, 110–11.

Attichy. *See* **Dony**.

Aubusson de la Feuillade, Georges. Embrun 1649–69, Metz 1669–79. Old noble family originally from Marche town of same name, though its claim to 9th C origins may be doubted! La Feuillade branch of this prolific clan dates from early 15th C. Thereafter, marriages with famous families like Rochechouart, La Trémouille, Pot de Rhodes, as well as military and court offices ensured they remained among leading families of military nobility. Ecclesiastical careers, male and female, were also frequent throughout 15th and 16th C but, with the exception of Cardinal Pierre who as grand master of knights of St John defended Rhodes against the Turks, were of secondary importance compared to other activities. In early 17th C, service to Marie de' Medici and especially Gaston d'Orléans predominated. Abp's father was killed by royal forces during Gaston and Montmorency's revolt of 1632, and his estate confiscated. Despite this, abp's brother remained faithful to Gaston, and family recovered from their disgrace after Richelieu's death, aided no doubt by the death of 3 of bp's brothers in royal service in 1630s and 1640s, while another brother, François III, would achieve eminence as Marshal La Feuillade and close friend of Louis XIV.

B. 1606 Vouet (Limoges). Son of François, comte de la Feuillade and *premier chambellan* of Gaston d'Orléans, and Isabelle Brachet. Early education was partly at SJ coll in Reims. Apparently attempted to join SJ, only changing his mind shortly before taking the habit. Studied theology at Sorbonne (with Choiseul bp of Comminges), taking 1st place in lic, 1642, followed by doct and election as *socius* of Sorbonne. Deputy to AC of 1645, where he served as *promoteur*, an important post for aspiring ecclesiastics. Priest and abbot in c of Solignac, OSB (Limoges) before episcopate. Initially nom to Gap when Artus de Lionne was given Embrun, but they negotiated an exchange of their respective claims after Lionne declined Embrun.

Nom to Embrun 13–11–1648. Provs 21–6–1649. Cons 12–9–1649. Transfer to Metz 1669. D. 12–5–1679.

Sources: ASV, PC 49, fos 1–23; PC 46, fo 346; PC, 49, fo 367v. BN, MS lat 9153, fo 93. Anselme, v. 318–50. Beauchet-Filleau, *Dict du Poitou*, i. 159–60. *DGS*, 816–17.

Aumont, Roger d'. Avranches 1645–51 (resign).   Although grandson of a marshal of France and brother of another, the career of the bp of Avranches is as obscure as his origins in great nobility were illustrious. Through marriage, Aumont were closely allied to an astonishing range of great families, whether of the aristocracy or the *robe ministérielle*. A few family members adopted Protestantism for a time, but in subsequent generations, associations were of *dévot*, even Jansenist nature. Their status and influence seem to have sufficed to propel Roger into episcopate.

B. ca 1610 (by his own account). Son of Jacques, *prévôt* of Paris and Ile-de-France, and Cathérine-Charlotte de Villequier, widow of François d'O. Destined early for church career, but nothing known of education, and probably took no degree. Royal almoner by 1625 (a sinecure, given his age). Well-endowed with benefices via family influence, he was abbot in c of St-Pierre-d'-Uzerche, OSB (Limoges), Beaulieu, Bouzelles and Longvilliers, O Cist (Boulogne) well before becoming bp (all of which he retained thereafter). Apparently difficult and violent in character, but not an inactive bishop, whose reasons for resigning are unknown, but may relate to ill-health or troubles of Fronde.

Nom 3–11–1644. Provs 20–3–1645. Cons 14–5–1645. Resign 5–1–1651. D. 25–3–1653.

Sources: Anselme, iv. 865–79. BN, MS lat 17022, fo 66. AN, Y 138, fo 57, 9–6–1599 (c.m. of parents); MC, XXIV, 310, 30–3–1623; XXIV, 314, 6–1–1625; LIII, 9, 25–3–1653 (testament). *DBF*, iv. 626–42.

Auvry, Claude. Coutances 1646–58 (resign).   Parisian family of relatively modest origins and circumstances. Bp's father was a master stocking-maker around the time of his marriage. Bp's brother and sisters all married in same social milieu, so there are few signs of social or professional mobility. Claude, one of the alleged models for Boileau's *Lutrin*, manufactured his own career far from his native milieu, initially in Rome and, after his return, in the Mazarin circle.

B. Paris 1606. Son of Claude and Catherine des Jobars. Early studies in Paris under Abraham Bazire, but moved to Rome, where he completed philosophy and took doct in theology, dedicating theses to Urban VIII! Barberini patronage enabled him to obtain subordinate, but valuable, post of clerk of the consistory in 1632 and 1635. The same patronage also brought him benefices, inc that of archdeacon of Toul, and priory of Chastenoy, both in Lorraine. Probably encountered Mazarin, the decisive influence on his subsequent career, through Barberinis. Accompanied Mazarin to Paris, 1639, becoming his *maître de chambre*, a position of trust (in which his successor was Gilbert de Clérambault, bp of Poitiers). Priest since 1641, originally nom to St-Flour, but quickly switched to Coutances when Léonor de Matignon was transferred to Lisieux in 1646. A staunch Mazarinist during Fronde which he spent in Paris, he was also anti-Jansenist. Treasurer of Ste Chapelle, 1653, he clashed with other bishops, including his abp, Harlay of Rouen. This led to his resignation in 1658. Not averse to a hard bargain, he vacated Coutances on condition his successor, Leclerc de Lesseville, paid him pension of 12,000 *livres* a year.

Resign of Coutances by Matignon 29–7–1646. Nom 18–8–1646. Provs 3–12–1646. Cons 15–2–1647. Resign Sept 1658. D. 9–7–1687.

Sources: ASV, PC 46, fos 308–21. BN, MS lat 17025 (1), fos 159–60. AN, Y 140, fo 6. Cauchie, *Documents pour servir à l'histoire littéraire du xviie siècle*, 77–82. Carrier, *Les Mazarinades*. *DBF*, iv. 777–9. Golden, *Godly Rebellion*, 51.

Balsac, Charles de. Noyon 1597–1625. Family derived its patronymic from town of same name near Brioude, in the Auvergne, where its origins go back to 14th C. It produced several branches, of which the Entragues was the most famous, thanks to Henri IV's mistress, Henriette. Prior to that, a series of distinguished marriages had consolidated their position among France's leading noble families. Guise protégés in 1550s and 1560s, some of them moved towards royalist stance under Henri III, with others, like Charles, governor of Orléans and father of Henri IV's mistress, playing his own game in 1580s and 1590s. There was also a family ecclesiastical tradition, which produced a bp of Valence and an abbot of Vézélay in late 15th C, but it seems probable that bp of Noyon owed his elevation primarily to personal and political connections of his elders at court rather than to any personal achievements.

B. date unknown. Son of Thomas, sgr de Montaigu, and Anne Gaillard, illegitimate sister of Francis I. Nothing known of education, but Rome accepted he had lic in canon law. Tonsured in 1579, apparently joined Carthusians when young – but presumably left before taking vows. Subsequently archdeacon in Rouen cathedral, and dean of Tours. Obtained Noyon (vacant since July 1594) in 1596 because willing to bargain and exchange benefices with d'Estrées and others, who controlled Noyon. He initially took possession of it under *grand conseil* rules, 29–12–1596.

No date for nom. Provs 15–9–1597. Cons 8–2–1598. D. 29–11–1625.

Sources: Anselme, ii. 435–41. *DBF*, iv. 1519–23.

Baradat, Henri de. Noyon 1626–60. 'De souche récente et de noblesse discutable', Baradat family originated near Condom in Armagnac, and only emerged from relative obscurity in mid-16th C, when bp's grandfather served in regiment of Navarre. His eldest son Guillaume (father of bp) followed his example, serving Catherine de' Medici and, from 1590 onwards, Henri IV, who made him captain of Monceaux, and captain of a company of infantry in 1596. He also acquired lands east of Paris. Eldest of his 5 sons, François, was briefly Louis XIII's favourite, becoming *premier écuyer* (April 1625) and lt-gen of Champagne (June 1626), before being disgraced in Dec 1626. His favour lasted just long enough to secure peerage-see of Noyon for Henri, and during Fronde he managed to persuade Henri to remain as bp of Noyon in the hope of securing it for younger member of family.

B. 1598. Son of Guillaume, sgr de Darmery, and Suzanne de Romain. Educated by SJ at Reims and La Flèche, he later took doct in canon law, Paris. Canon of ND de Paris 1613, he also obtained in c priory of Les Essarts, provostship of Favières, and abbey of Clermont, O Cist (thanks to his uncles Joachim Baradat and Léon Lescot).

Nom 7–12–1625. Provs 30–3–1626. Cons 2–8–1626. D. 20–8–1660.

Sources: ASV, PC 22, fos 524–39. Anselme, ii. 442–5. Grillon, *Papiers de Richelieu*, i. 197. *DBF*, v. 153–8.

Barberini, Antonio. Reims 1657/67–71. The highpoint of 'Cardinal Antoine's' career had long since passed before his elevation to Reims. This was no more than an epilogue to his period as papal nephew under Urban VIII, when his behaviour, political activities, and personal enrichment made him powerful enemies. Not least of these was Urban VIII's successor, Innocent X, whose plans for retribution obliged Antonio (and more briefly, his brother Francesco) to find refuge in France under Mazarin's protection, their erstwhile client and foe of Innocent.

B. Rome 4–8–1607. Youngest son of Carlo and Constanza Magalotti. Cardinal in 1627, fled to France in 1644, and as former Cardinal Protector of France in Rome, remained identified with French interests thereafter. Nom to Poitiers in August 1652, but both Innocent X and Alexander VII refused to confirm appointment. Even when Mazarin, who made him grand almoner of France, had him nom to Reims, he had to wait 10 years for provs, on account of continuing disputes over his Roman interests. But by 1667, when provs were finally granted, he was permanently resident in Italy, and quickly selected Charles-Maurice Le Tellier as coadj.

Nom (in place of Henri de Savoie-Nemours) 1657. Provs 18–7–1667. D. 3–8–1671.

Sources: AN, MC, LIII, 10, 11–12–1652 (nom to Poitiers). *DBI*, vi. 164–7. *DGS*, 158–9.

Barbier de la Rivière, Louis. Langres 1655–70. Another case of a self-made man making a career for himself within clerical and court circles, since depiction of parents as 'nobles et honorables' reveals rather than disguises his modest social background – about which he was highly sensitive, not least because critics during Fronde exaggerated it.

B. 1593 Montfort-l'Amaury. Son of Antoine, *dit* la Rivière, and Cécile Lemaire. Tonsured 29–3–1603, so evidently destined early for church career. Nothing known of studies, but seems to have had doct in utr. Having taught philosophy at coll du Plessis, his career took decisive turn when he was brought into Gaston d'Orléans's household, initially as tutor and then as almoner, by Pierre Habert, Gaston's first almoner (later bp of Cahors). By 1640s, when officially first almoner (prestigious sinecure since he was a mere cleric and not ordained priest until 1655!) to Gaston's wife, both fortune and ambitions escalated. Gaston's influence brought both benefices (inc several wealthy abbeys) and entry into royal orders of chivalry. From at least 1644, he also sought episcopal office and even the red hat which, during Fronde, was seen (and not merely by Barbier or Gaston) as a means of supplanting Mazarin as chief minister. Bitter rival of Retz and Mazarin, his political adventures during Fronde finally lost him Gaston's confidence, and see of Langres was distinctly a consolation prize. His testament shows how hugely successful (with legacies in excess of 600,000 *livres*) his financial operations were.

Nom 25–2–1655. Provs 15–11–1655. Cons 2–1–1656. D. 30–1–1670.

Sources: ASV, PC 52, fos 642–57. AN, Z¹a 515 (Gaston d'Orléans household); MC, CV, 834 (testament); CV, 835, 27–3–1670 (*inventaire après décès*). *DBF*, v. 343–4. Anselme, ii. 237.

Bargemon. *See* **Arbaut.**

Barrault, Jean *Jaubert* **de.** Bazas 1611–31, Arles 1631–43. The Jaubert de Barrault family originated in Limousin where they can be traced back to late 14th C. Subsequently, service under Charles VIII in Italy extracted them from their purely provincial setting. Bp's father began as page at court of Charles IX, and served Henri III and Henri IV in a variety of increasingly prominent roles – *sénéchal* and gov of Bazadais, 1582, vice-admiral of Guyenne, 1585, *cons d'état*, 1600, ambassador to Spain, 1602, to Savoy, 1611. He was also close to Bérulle, whom he helped in bringing reformed Carmelites from Spain to France. His eldest son Henri succeeded as gov of Bazadais and was also ambassador to Spain, 1629–35, where he clashed violently with Olivares. Bp's father's office as gov of Bazadais enabled him to obtain see from Henri IV for son at very early age, and to keep it vacant until old enough to obtain papal approval. Well educated, he proved to be an active and cultivated bishop who was close to centre of *dévot* movement (a virtual founder-member of *Compagnie du St Sacrement*) and to SJ. Political reliability bought him promotion to Arles in 1631, and selection as French candidate for the red hat between 1631 and 1634.

B. ca 1583. Son of Emery, and Guyonne de la Motte. Early education at Bordeaux, where he took lic in utr, Jan 1598. Also studied at La Flèche, ca 1606–9 (with other future bps, Plantavit and Dominique Bonzi), completing theology studies in Rome. Tonsured on 9–6–1591, was subdeacon by the time he obtained his provs. Abbot in c of Solognac (Limoges), 1600, and prior in c of St-Aubin (Bazas), he was also archdeacon of Bazas before 1611. D. before concluding negotiations to obtain François de Grignan, bp of St-Paul-Trois-Châteaux, as coadj of Arles.

Nom to Bazas Feb. 1605. Provs 25–5–1611. Cons 7–8–1611 in Rome. Nom to Arles 20–7–1630. Provs 12–5–1631. D. 30–8–1643.

Sources: ASV, Acta Misc 98, fo 858. AD Gironde, G 798, fos 188v-9r (degrees). BAV, Barb lat 7942, fos 33, 87 (red hat candidature). *Lettres inédites de Henri IV à M de Béthune (1604)*, 14–15. Delpech, 'Lettres de JJ de Barrault', 303–21, 416–29, 453–9. Clergeac, *Chronologie*, 91. *DBF*, xviii, cols 508–10.

Barrez, Fulcran de. Agde 1629–43. Family migrated at an unspecified date from the Vivarais to Pouzolles, near Clermont-de-Lodève, where father was a simple *bourgeois*. Bp's brother was barrister in *sénéchaussée* court of Béziers, while his nephew described himself as an *écuyer* and *viguier* of Pouzolles, though it is clear their status was that of small-town *notables*.

B. 1574 Pouzolles. Son of Jean and Anne de Crussy. Educated at Univ of Toulouse ca 1598–1600, where took doct in utr. Subdeacon of Agde ca 1599, he probably took priestly orders soon afterwards. Despite modest origins, he fitted remarkably quickly, and well, into ecclesiastical milieux of both Béziers and Agde, and it was no doubt his long years of service as right-hand man to the often absent bps of Béziers that brought him wider attention, not least because Bonsis were close to Montmorencys. Canon of St-Aphrodisie of Béziers, he was vg and *official* of Cardinal Bonsi at Béziers 1605–21, and during episcopal vacancies. Deputy to EG, 1614, canon and sacristan of Agde chapter before 1619, although he apparently refused offer of see of Agde from Louis de Valois when he resigned it in 1622. In the end his nom to Agde was largely due to Montmorency influence and control there, but he was not compromised by revolt of 1632.

Nom 1–7–1629. Provs 19–11–1629. Cons 2–2–1631. D. March 1643.

Sources: ASV, PC 24, fo 472; PC 26, fos 235–45. AN, G^8 87. AD Hérault, G 3, pp 136, 145–6. *DBF*, v. 587–8.

Bassompierre, Louis de. Saintes 1646–76. Few court nobles of Louis XIII's reign had such a brilliant and dramatic career as bp's father. Descended from a Lorraine noble family from Haroué, south of Nancy, where it can be traced to 13th C, and whose traditions were of service to both duke and Emperor, it was bp's father who disrupted such patterns by attaching himself to Henri IV. Thereafter his rise was meteoric – colonel general of Swiss 1614, *chevalier des ordres* 1619, marshal of France 1622, close confidant of Louis in the early 1620s, ambassador to Spain 1621, Switzerland 1625, England 1626 – only for his career to be broken in 1631 by Richelieu. After 12 years in Bastille he returned to court, but died in the same year his son became bp. A bibliophile and military intellectual with wide interests and curiosity, and a good library.

B. 17–8–1610. Illegitimate son of François (never married) and Marie-Charlotte de Balsac d'Entragues. Initially reared by uncle, Charles de Balsac, bp of Noyon, spent 10 years at coll of Navarre under its grand master, Pereyret. Appears to have followed virtually all of theology course at Sorbonne (with P de Bertier), but took lic in canon law, Paris, instead. Uncle obtained him as coadj in c for his abbeys of St-Georges-de-Boscherville, OSB (Rouen) and Chézy, OSB (Soissons). Priest for some years before nom, devout and retiring, esteemed by Vincent de Paul and Olier, but also by Mazarin, who originally designated him for Oloron diocese. Mazarinist during Fronde, not easy in a region where Condé and Dognon were powerful adversaries.

Bp Raoul (transferring to Maillezais-La Rochelle) resign Saintes to Bassompierre, 20–11–1646. Royal nom 26–11–1646. Provs 7–12–1648. Cons 17–1–1649. D. 1–7–1676.

Sources: ASV, PC 50, fos 946–76. BN, MS Fr 33047, p 495 (naturalisation of relatives of bp's father, Dec 1620); MS lat 9958, fo 59. J-P Labatut, *Noblesse, pouvoir et société en France au xviie siècle* (Limoges 1987), 81–3. Bondois, *Le Maréchal de Bassompierre*. Dangibeaud, 'Louis de Bassompierre évêque de Saintes', 75–98, 170–89. Tallemant, *Historiettes*, i. 594–604. *DGS*, 168. *DBF*, v. 765–6.

Beaumanoir de Lavardin, Charles de. Le Mans 1610–37. Ancient noble family of Breton origins had settled in Maine by 16th C. Both father and grandfather of first bp were Protestants, with father converting to Catholicism after 1572 massacres (in which grandfather died). Like many other nobles, he shuffled in subsequent decades between service to Navarre, Henri III (serving under Joyeuse) and, later still, Catholic League. *Chevalier of St Esprit* and marshal of France in 1595 (as reward for accepting Henri IV as king), he obtained governorship of Maine few years later. Bp Charles's nom to Le Mans in 1601 was extension of this search for strong local power, as he was no more than 15 at time, and had to wait 9 years for provs. Bp's eldest brother, Henri (father of 2nd bp), further consolidated family's position by marriage.

B. 1586. Son of Jean (1551–1614), and Catherine de Longueval, 2nd of three wives. Educated mostly at Univ of Paris, where enrolled in arts faculty 1594–1601, and studied along with Bp Etampes of Chartres under Cospeau. Rome accepted he had doct in utr. Deacon by the time Rome granted provs in 1610.

Nom 1601. Provs 18–8–1610. Cons Nov 1610. D. 17–11–1637.

Beaumanoir de Lavardin, Philibert-Emmanuel de. Le Mans 1649–71. B. 1617. Son of Henri and Marguerite de la Baume de Suze; nephew of Charles (above). Studied humanities and philosophy at La Flèche, followed by theology at Univ of Paris, but took doct in canon law. Office and honours came his way in 1640s – royal almoner, deputy for Tours at AC of 1645, when also ordained priest. Abbot in c of St-Leger, OSB (Saintes) and ND de Beaulieu, OSA (Le Mans). Preached in Paris, and possibly before court. Having failed in ambition to succeed uncle at Le Mans in 1637 (aged 20!), he set about preparing himself systematically for episcopal office. Despite attending de Paul's St-Lazare conferences (like Retz), he was denounced as atheist and his nom to Le Mans was held up for several months.

Nom 13–11–1648. Provs 1–3–1649. Cons 25–4–1649. D. 27–7–1671.

Sources: Anselme, vii. 379–90; *DGS*, 838 (family). BN, MS lat 9957, fo 45; MS Fr 5755, fo 79v. ASV, PC 34, fos 497–9 (Charles); PC 48, fos 641–63. Solminihac, *Lettres et Documents*, 378. Tallemant, *Historiettes*, ii. 297–8, 1151 (Philibert).

Beaumont. *See* Péréfixe

Beauvau de Rivarennes, Gabriel de. Nantes 1636–67 (resign). Family history and lineage are less than perfectly clear, but it seems fair to regard their 17th-C descendants (by then split into several branches) as faithfully prolonging traditions of the *noblesse militaire*. Marriages were in same social milieu, and one in particular, although somewhat brief, was probably decisive for bp's career – that of Jean, sgr du Rivau, to Richelieu's eldest sister, Françoise, ca 1597. Bp's father fought with/for Henri IV in last phase of wars, while brother, Louis, died at siege of Turin in 1641.

B. date unknown. 2nd son of Louis, sgr de Rivarenne, and Charlotte Brillouet. Student at Univ of Paris ca 1623–5, but no evidence of degree. Spent most of pre-episcopal career in Richelieu's service, chiefly as *maître de chambre* in wide variety of capacities (esp military organisation and logistics) for several years. Lt-gen in April 1636, then *cons d'état*, he continued to serve in military capacity after episcopal nom, until Fuentarrabia debâcle (1638) brought about loss of favour. Priest by time of nom, dean of Nîmes chapter, also held abbeys of Turpenay, OSB (Tours) and Ivry, OSB (Evreux) in c. Episcopal career ended ingloriously, and forced to resign under family pressure.

Nom 4–3–1635 (after transfer of Cospeau to Lisieux). Provs 18–2–1636. Cons 27–4–1636. Resign 1667. D. 9–1–1668.

Sources: BN, P Or 254, doss Beauvau; MS lat 9958, fo 83; MS. lat 17027, fo 188. BAV, Barb lat 7942, fo 147. Beauchet-Filleau, *Dict du Poitou* i. 393. Deloche, *La Maison du cardinal de Richelieu*, 77. *DBF*, v. 1204–5.

Bec. *See* **Du Bec**

Belleau, Jean de. Meaux 1624–37. Bp owed his elevation less to influence (far from negligible) of his own direct family – which was of Norman *noblesse militaire* background, with worthy *états de service* for 16th C – than to the fact he was nephew of Jean de Vieuxpont, bp of Meaux 1602–23.

B. Courson (Lisieux) 1590. Son of Geoffroy and Charlotte de Vieuxpont, sister of bp of Meaux. Before attending school, he lived with uncle at Meaux, who entrusted him to care of canon of Meaux who was episcopal secretary, Jean Madoulet. Humanities and philosophy followed in SJ colls at Caen and Rouen. Despite 3 years of theology in Paris under André du Val and Isambert, he took lic in canon law. Canon of Meaux for many years, also priest by time of nom.

Nom 17–8–1623. Provs 15–7–1624. Cons 1624. D. 16–8–1637.

Sources: ASV, PC 18, fos 303–28. BN, P Or 273, doss 5958.

Bellegarde, Octave de *St Lary* de. Comminges 1612–22, Sens 1622–46. An interesting and unusual case of only son entering church. St Lary family originated from place of same name near St-Gaudens in SW France, where it can be traced to Raymond who also acquired (by marriage in 1498) the *seigneurie* of Bellegarde in Burgundy, though this did not drastically alter family focus or interests. That was occasioned by service in Italian wars, during which Raymond's sons, Pierre (?–1571) and Roger served under the marshal Thermes. Pierre married Thermes's niece, and Roger, a future marshal of France (and grandfather of bp), married Thermes's own widow. It also helped, *in fine*, that their sister, Jeanne, was mother of Henri III's favourite, the duc d'Epernon! Thermes-Bellegarde legacy was preserved into next generation, in the person of 3rd brother, Jean's son, Roger II, *grand écuyer de France*, and favourite of Marie de' Medici and Louis XIII until his disgrace in 1631.

B. Feb 1587 Saintes. Posthumous son of César, gov of Saintonge, and Jeanne de Lyon, daughter of first prest of *cour des monnaies*. Grew up mostly in care of maternal grandfather, beginning humanities and philosophy in Toulouse, and completing studies in Paris, with lic in canon law, but no real evidence that he was also lic in theology. Priest by time of nom, also had some experience as preacher. As well endowed with benefices as social standing might suggest – abbot in c of St-Germain-d'Auxerre (1607), La Bénisson-Dieu *alias* Nizors, O Cist (Comminges) in 1609, and dom of Aubrac (Rodez) before nom to Comminges. Transfer to Sens thanks to his cousin, Roger II, the *grand écuyer*. His refusal to accept archiepiscopal status for Paris (at expense of Sens) did not prevent him from playing major role in affairs of French church for several decades.

Nom Dec 1611 or Jan 1612. Provs 2–12–1613. Cons 25–5–1614. *Brevet de nom* to Sens 14–11–1621. Provs 18–12–1623 (delayed by problems arising from establishment of archbishopric of Paris). D. 26–7–1646, having obtained nephew, Louis de Gondrin, as coadj.

Sources: ASV, PC 13, fos 245–70; PC 18, fo 160. AD Yonne, G 2. Anselme, iv. 295–309. Clergeac, *Chronologie*, 62, 67. *DBF*, v. 1331–2.

Bellièvre, Albert de. Lyon 1599–1604 (resign). This old Lyon bourgeois family, originally from Bresse area, can be traced back to Hugonin, a notary there in 1433. Owed much of its early advancement to successive generations' activities in ecclesiastical affairs of Lyon and its abps, a connection which they subsequently cultivated. There was, not surprisingly, a strong presence of younger sons since 15th C in Lyon chapters of St-Jean and St-Paul, though apparently none rose to office or much influence outside of their chapters. Bellièvres also displayed cultural and antiquarian interests, culminating in those of Claude, the chancellor's father, and obviously transmitted to the abps' generation. Status as urban notables was taken big step further by Claude (1487–1577), who served as proc-gen and briefly as first pres of Grenoble parlt (1541–4). It was his son, Pomponne, future chancellor of France and father of the abps, who really reaped the rewards, marrying daughter of a pres in Grenoble parlt, but then moving to Paris, advancing rapidly thanks to patronage of Catherine de' Medici, which led, after a multitude of offices and activities, to his appointment as chancellor in 1599, at virtually the same time as see of Lyon fell vacant with death of Pierre d'Epinac.

B. ca 1570 Lyon. Eldest son of Pomponne, chancellor of France, and Marie Prunier (m. 1569). Nothing known of early education, but enrolled in Paris arts faculty in 1594. Subsequently took doct in utr. Abbot in c of Jouy-en-Brie, O Cist (Sens) 1594, St-Cybard, OSB (Angoulême) by 1596, attended Fontainebleau colloquy of 1600. Learned and pious, but never in good health, was obliged to resign Lyon because of mental breakdown, ceding his place to brother, Claude.

Nom 25-1-1599. Provs 29-3-1599. Cons 6-6-1599. Resign 1604. D. 1621.

Bellièvre, Claude de. Lyon 1604–12. B. 1576. Younger brother of Albert (above). Tonsured Dec 1586, designated early for church career. No information about education, but apparently took lic in utr, which enabled him to become *cons-cl* in Paris parlt. Only when brother was obliged to resign as abp in 1604 did he hurriedly take full orders, being ordained priest a week before episcopal cons.

Nom mid-1604. Provs 1-10-1604. Cons 12-12-1604. D. 26-4-1612.

Sources: AD Rhône, Fonds Frecon, Doss rouges, vol 2. Claude de Bellièvre, *Souvenirs de voyage en Italie et en Orient, notes historiques, pièces et vers*, ed C Perrat (Geneva 1956), pp ii-xiii. AN, MC, LXXVIII, 191, 4-12-1607 *inventaire après décès* of Chancellor Bellièvre. BI, MS 1354, fo 11. *DBF*, v. 1359-62 (family-general). AN, Z^{1}o 240. BN, MS lat 9956, fo 113, Oct 1594; MS Fr 15897, fos 30, 32. *DBF*, v.1359-60 (Albert). AN, Z^{1}o 240-1 (Claude).

Bentivoglio, Guido. Riez 1622–5 (resign). The celebrated cardinal's brief presence among the French episcopate is probably the least of his achievements, coming only after he had left France and the most interesting parts of his career had ended. B. 4-10-1577 into former ruling dynasty of Ferrara, he was papal nuncio in Flanders 1609–16, and France 1616–21, returning to Rome in 1621 as cardinal with prospect of becoming Cardinal Protector of France there, thanks to support of Puysieux, French secretary of state, who was also responsible for securing see of Riez for him in a manner reminiscent of an earlier age.

Brevet de nom to Riez 22-5-1622. Provs 11-7-1622. Resign 16-10-1625. D. 7-9-1644.

Sources: ASV, Fondo Pio 88 (Puysieux-Bentivoglio correspondence). BN, MS Fr 17364, p 533. *DBI*, viii. 634-8.

Bernage, Louis. Grasse 1653–75. Family was settled in Paris by later 16th C, but otherwise origins unknown. First 2 Parisian generations were lawyers. Grandfather of bp, Louis, sgr de Dixmont, was a barrister in parlt, as were 2 sons, Pierre (bp's father) and

Jehan; another, Gilles, took a wholly different road, becoming one of the *cent gentilshommes du roi*. The youngest, Jacques, was canon of ND de Paris and royal almoner, a crucial factor in bp's early career. Family marriage connections in each generation were in remarkably similar socio-professional milieux (Dennet, Le Picart, Le Gras). Family's professional and social status was substantially advanced in bp's own generation, when they became an office-holding family which would produce a provincial intendant in Louis de Bernage at Limoges, 1697.

B. Paris, ca 1605. Son of Pierre, barrister at *grand conseil* and *conseil privé*, and Louise le Picart. Early education probably in Univ of Paris colls, where he may also have studied law, but apparently took doct in utr at Orléans. Succeeded uncle, Jacques Bernage, as royal almoner in 1628, became a 'serving' almoner in personal attendance on Louis XIII in 1638, when was also ordained priest. By 1653 he was *doyen* of royal almoners.

Antoine Godeau, preferring to keep his other diocese of Vence, resign Grasse to Bernage 22–2–1653. *Brevet de nom* for Bernage, 23–2–1653. Nom to pope 24–2–1653. Provs 23–11–1653. Cons 25–1–1654. D. 6–5–1675.

Sources: ASV, PC 52, fos 226–40. AD Alpes-Maritimes, G 11. BN, MS Fr 32989, fos 280v-1r. BN, P Or 300, dossiers 6580–1. AN, MC, XXIV, 325, 4–1–1629, 4–4–1629; XXIV, 313, 6–9–1624; XXIX 143, 12/23–4–1624. *Hommages à la chambre de France (xive-xvie siècles)* ed Mirot and Babelon, iii. nos 1947–8. Griselle, *Etat de la maison de Louis XIII*, no 38, 4868; Doublet, 'Les visites pastorales de Louis de Bernage', 297–316, 534–59. *DBF*, vi. 36–7.

Bertaut, Jean. Séez 1607–11. B. 1555 into Norman family of college teachers and clerics. Father, François, was a master at Dubois college, Caen. Early education under father, who taught him Greek and Hebrew. Univ law studies followed, possibly in Paris, and took lic in canon law. Norman origins were probably useful in securing him tutorship in powerful Matignon family, through whom he was introduced to Charles IX, and for whose bastard son, the duc d'Auvergne, he acted as tutor. He frequented court circle around Henri III, where his poetry was appreciated, becoming *secretaire de cabinet* and *lecteur ordinaire* to king. Played small part at conferences at Suresnes in 1593, by which time patronage of fellow Norman, the future cardinal du Perron, had become vital to him. His writings as poet of peace and restoration were not unimportant to his career at this point. He obtained abbey of Aunay in c from Henri IV, who made him first almoner to Marie de' Medici (a sinecure, as priestly orders were not required). But priest by time of nom. Françoise Bertaut, dame de Motteville, daughter of Pierre Bertaut and lady in waiting to Anne of Austria, was his niece.

Nom 4–6–1606. Provs 5–3–1607. Cons 11–11–1607. D. 8–6–1611.

Sources: Grente, *Jean Bertaut*. *DBF*, vi. 175–6. *DGS*, 191–2, 1066.

Bertier, Jean de. Rieux 1602–20. One of the most prolific of robe families where bishops are concerned, the Bertier remained firmly anchored in Toulousain society, resisting attractions of a move to Paris on more than one occasion. Their itinerary is the classic one of so many robe families – emerging in later 15th C from trade, they entered municipal office, then chancery office in Toulouse parlt, before moving in force into councillorships in parlt by second half of 16th C. Thanks also to development of several solid branches (notably those of Montrabé and St-Geniès), they became the leading parlementaire family of early 17th-C Toulouse, with marriage connections to most of the dominant consular and parlementaire families. They could boast 7 councillors for the period between 1568 and 1723, when they were present without interruption in parlt, while no fewer than 9 members of the extended Bertier family were present in the same court around 1650. Louis (d. 1560), father of first bp, seems to have been one of few members to serve outside Toulouse itself (as SR). His son, Philippe (d. 1611), pres in Toulouse parlt, was father of Jean II, first pres of parlt, and Jean-Louis bp of Rieux. Earlier generations had regularly produced ecclesiastics, but until 5th known generation, that of 1st bp of Rieux, they held mainly minor benefices, parishes included.

B. ca 1556. Son of Louis, sgr de Montrabé, and Marguerite de Tappie de Roques Montels, daughter of a *marchand bourgeois* of Agen. Probably educated in Toulouse, held doct in utr. Canon of Rieux while student, canon and archdeacon of Tarbes in 1578, of Toulouse by 1583, where also archdeacon in 1590. Nominal *curé* of St-Martial (Toulouse), Massac and Paynan (Lectoure), but probably without serving in any of them. An extremely active figure before episcopate, he did not rely soley on other family members for career. Almoner to Marguerite de Valois (1584), he (and other family members) played major role in running her affairs, part of her dower lands being located around Toulouse, and played part in negotiating her divorce from Henri IV. Deputy to ACs of 1585 and 1595, he served as *agent-général* of clergy for over decade after 1595. Remained active in these roles for years, and only began to reside in Rieux after Marguerite's death in 1615. By then nephew was already installed as his coadj. It was through Marguerite's patronage, which inc presentation rights to Rieux itself, that he entered episcopate.

Nom coadj of Rieux 7–7–1601. Provs 25–2–1602. Cons 6–4–1603. Succeeds 31–8–1602. D. 15–7–1620.

Bertier, Jean-Luis de. Rieux coadj 1616/20–62. Baptised in Toulouse 28–10–1579. Son of Philippe, sgr de Montrabé, pres in parlt, and Catherine de Paulo, sister of second pres of parlt (m. 1569). Educated at Toulouse, studying along with Bps Iharse of Tarbes and Corneilhan of Rodez and taking doct in utr. Canon and grand archdeacon of Toulouse, *cons* in diocesan *chambre des décimes*, and metropolitan judge for ecclesiastical province of Toulouse. Priest for few years before nom. Attended ACs of 1612 and 1615 as deputy for Toulouse province. His coadj-succession to Rieux was first mooted in 1608, owing to uncle's involvement in affairs of Marguerite de Valois and French clergy. In turn, sought in 1657 to take nephew, André-François, as coadj, but without evident effect before death.

Procuration from uncle to take him as coadj 12–4–1611. Nom to Rome 9–11–1610. Provs 19–9–1616. Cons 25–6–1617. Succeeded 1620. D. 8–6–1662.

Bertier, Pierre de. Montauban coadj 1636/51–74. B. 13–1–1606. Son of Jean, sgr de Geniès, pres in parlt and Eléonor de Desplats de Gragniague. Early education at SJ coll of Tournon (with Jacques de Grignan), philosophy at coll of Harcourt, Paris (with H de Béthune), probably under Jacques Lescot (future bp of Chartres), ca 1626–7. Doctorate in theology at Sorbonne, taking 1st place in lic, 1632. Canon and archdeacon of Toulouse, abbot in c of Restauré, O Prem (Soissons) before 1630, preached in Paris, esp at St-Germain-l'Auxerrois, Senlis etc. Ordained priest in 1632. Nom as coadj of Montauban was culmination of years of pressure on Bp Murviel of Montauban by senior parlementaires from Toulouse, led by Bertier family members, and ministers.

Nom as coadj. 9–1–1634. Provs 7–4–1636. Cons 31–8–1636. Succeeded Sept 1652. D. 28–6–1674.

Sources: AD H-G, 6 J series, Bertier family archives. Vindry, *Parlementaires* (Toulouse), 165. Michaud, *Grande Chancellerie*; Michaud, *Les Formulaires de la grande chancellerie*, 106–10. Villain, *France moderne*, iii. 39. Navelle, *Familles toulousaines*, ii. 142–56. *DBF*, vi. 229–333 (family-general). AD H-G, 6 J 61 (personal papers); 6J 44, no 62 (testament). AN, V⁶ 1180, fo 656v (Jean). ASV, PC 13, fos 676–94. AD H-G, 6J 46, no 54 (Jean Louis). ASV, PC 34, fos 404–32; PC 28, fo 896v. BN, MS lat 15400, p 159 (Pierre).

Béthune, Henri de. Maillezais 1629–46, Bordeaux 1645–80. Scion of one of the most durable and prolific of all French aristocratic families, rarely far removed from the leading roles in court, politics, or military and diplomatic activity, and related by marriage to impressive range of similar families. Otiose to recount their *états de service*. Bp's father was younger brother of Sully, but a Catholic who served two terms as French ambassador in Rome (1601–5, 1624–30), where he was resident when son born and when he was first chosen to be bp of Bayonne. Disappointed with such meagre reward for his own services, and feeling his untried son deserved something better (e.g. Angers, Limoges, Lyon!) he did little to press for provs to Bayonne, and plumped instead for Maillezais when Henri de Sourdis succeeded to Bordeaux in 1628. Subsequently tried to obtain a better see for his son, and lived long enough to see him elevated to Bordeaux in 1646.

B. 7–9–1604 Rome. Son of Philippe, ambassador to papacy, and Catherine Le Bouthillier de Senlis, 1st wife. Humanities and philosophy at coll of Harcourt, Paris (with Pierre de Bertier), but also at coll of Clermont ca 1621–2 (with Ferdinand de Neufville), and privately in Rome during father's second embassy, but did not take degree (for which papacy granted dispensation on episcopal confirmation, 1629). First almoner (a sinecure) to Nicolas duc d'Orléans, 1610. Abbot in c of Le Jard (Luçon), les Alleuz, OSB (Poitiers) and Cadouin, O Cist (Sarlat) before nom to Maillezais. Exchanged Cadouin with Sourdis when he accepted Maillezais in place of Bayonne. None of this prevented Béthune from being exemplary bishop in troubled period and region(s).

Nom to Bayonne 1–10–1626 (no provs). Nom to Maillezais 22–3–1629. Provs 19–11–1929. Cons 6–1–1630. *Brevet de nom* to Bordeaux 21–11–1646. D. 11–5–1680.

Sources: ASV, PC 48, fos 402–33. BN, MS Fr 3678, fos 108v-9, 113v-14. AAE, CP Rome 40, fos 46–8. AD Gironde, G 257 (Maillezais, 1629); G 260 (Bayonne 1627, Bordeaux 1646). *Archives Hist de la Gironde*, xiv, 67–8; xxiii, 523–4. *Corr de Bérulle*, iii. 249, 280, 346. Isabelle Aristide, *La Fortune de Sully* (Paris n.d.). Peyrous, *La Réforme catholique à Bordeaux*, ii. 714–25. *DBF*, vi. 349–50.

Billy, Godefroy de, OSB. Laon 1601–12. From old noble family of Soissonnais traceable to 12th C (Anselme), and characterised by solid marriage alliances (e.g. Vieuxpont, Orgemont, Brichantau) and military service, as well as a more discreet ecclesiastical presence in 15th and early 16th C. Connections to Guises arose mainly from Brichantau marriage, and many family members were active militarily during wars of religion. This did not prevent individual members adopting Protestantism and supporting prince of Condé during wars. Two of Bp Godefroy's brothers were ecclesiastics: Jacques 1535–81, OSB was a distinguished scholar, friend of Génébrard, and author of works of piety, while Jean was influential Carthusian mystic.

B. ca 1536. 4th son of Louis, sgr de Billy-sur-Ourcq and gov of Guise, and Marie de Brichantau. Nothing known of education. Professed monk of St-Denis-en-France, where he later became prior and vg from 1575 for abbot in c, Cardinal Louis de Guise. Also succeeded maternal uncle, Crespin de Brichantau, as abbot in c of St-Vincent-de-Laon, OSB, and St-Jean-d'Amiens, O Prem. Translator of Vives and various works of spirituality. Deputy to EGs of 1576, 1588, 1593, and known for strong *ligueur* sympathies. Participated in Suresnes conference for Henri IV's conversion with Epinac of Lyon and Péricard of Avranches on behalf of 1593 *ligueur* EG. Nom by Mayenne to Evreux, but failed to obtain provs in face of competition from Henri IV's nominee, du Perron. Nor was he first choice for Laon in 1598: Louis Séguier, canon of ND de Paris, was original royal choice, but he dropped out in 1599 or 1600.

No date for nom to Laon (vacant since Aug 1598) but 1600 at latest. Provs 19–2–1601. Cons 6–5–1601. Took nephew, Brichantau, as coadj 1608. D. 28–3–1612.

Sources: AN, MC, VIII, 408, 10–4–1593 (Evreux, 1593); VIII, 418, 16–1–1599; VIII, 422, 21–2–1601 (Laon *régale*, 1598, 1601). ASV, PC 7, fos 429–30 (search for a suffragan bp of Laon, 1606). Anselme, ii. 116–29. Vidal, *Critique*, 248–9. *DBF*, vi. 484.

Boisdauphin. *See* **Laval**

Boivin de Pericard, Henri. Avranches coadj 1616–39 (non successit). One of several coadjs who failed to outlive incumbent of see, Henri Boivin (or Boyvin) was from family whose origins lie in merchant bourgeoisie of 15th C Rouen and which in generation of bp's father made striking transition from commercial activities to office-holding – 2 brothers were *cons* in Rouen parlt, while another was SR and treasurer to Estates of Normandy in 1577; similar career patterns are visible in next generation. Bp's father's marriage to Anne Péricard, daughter of Jean, proc-gen in Rouen parlt, was another crucial step in their advancement and brought them into the Guise clientèle in Normandy, in which the Péricards were a major force.

B. ca 1585 Rouen. Son of Roman Boivin, sgr de Vauroy and *cons* in Rouen parlt, and Anne Péricard. Early schooling probably in Rouen, but after 1605 studied theology in Paris under André du Val and others, taking bacc in theology there. Elected *socius* of Sorbonne, taught philosophy for a time. Priest before 1615, he also preached in some Parisian churches. Dean of Rouen cathedral before 1615, a post he retained after becoming coadj. Although he did not live to govern Avranches, was an active coadj, who also helped administer Reims for Henri de Guise-Lorraine, 1633–9.

Procuration from uncle, François Péricard, to take Boivin as coadj 8–8–1615. Nom 16–2–1616. Provs 3–8–1616. Cons 28–5–1617. D. 12–2–1639.

Sources: ASV, PC 13, fos 785–92. Frondeville, *Conseillers*, 492–8.

Bologne, Antoine de, Minim. Digne 1602–15. Original family name of these three bps was Capizuchi, originally from Bologna – hence perhaps name (Bologne) normally used by them. But their claims to eminent medieval Roman lineage were bogus, for although episcopal office helped them move upwards socially, the elder branch was condemned in the 1667 *recherches de noblesse* for usurpation of noble status; they were recognised as noble in 1690s by intendant Lebret, to whom large dossier of forgeries was presented! In fact, they moved to France during early 16th C, settling as *bourgeois* in Barcelonette, then at Digne and Salon, where grandfather of first 2 bps, Claude, was still living in 1539. Patronage of Catherine de' Medici may initially have enabled them to find place at court, where they became a virtual dynasty of royal chaplains and 'serving' almoners under Henri IV and Louis XIII, which entailed regular personal attendance on kings; another brother, Julien, was a *gentilhomme de la chambre du roi* under Henri IV. Bps initially owed their elevation to their brother Etienne, royal almoner, who had assisted Henri III at his death and enjoyed the favour of Henri IV. He obtained see of Digne from Bp Coquelet by offering him abbey of Livry which he held in c.

B. Barcelonette, date unknown. Son of Rodolphe and Delphine de Francon (m. 1539). Brother of Etienne (above). Joined order of Minims at relatively young age, most of his education was within order, hence probably took no degree. Appears to have been prior of Minims at Mâcon before episcopate.

Nom to Digne on resign of Bp Coquelet (probably Jan 1602, but possibly earlier). Provs 27–3–1602. Cons 9–6–1602. Took brother Louis as coadj 1613–15. D. 24–9–1615.

Bologne, Louis de. Digne coadj 1613/15–28. Brother of Antoine (above). Date and place of b. unknown. Chaplain in ordinary to dauphin until 1609, almoner thereafter, he was apparently Louis XIII's religious tutor. Prior in c of Val des Ecoliers (Paris), in succession to brother Etienne, and which he retained while coadj. Took possession of Digne by proxy 2–1–1616 and governed it until death. But by 1616 was physically incapacitated and could not be cons. Hence decision to take nephew, Raphaël, as coadj in 1617.

Nom coadj 31–5–1612. Provs 17–6–1613. Succeeded to Digne 24–9–1615. D. 1–2–1628.

Bologne, Raphaël. Digne coadj 1617/28–57. Nephew of Antoine and Louis above. B. April 1590 at Mondovi, son of Jean and Jeanne de Trièves. Initially destined for military career, early education was probably minimal. Only when paralysed uncle, Louis, needed coadj did he change course, studying at both Paris and Pont-à-Mousson and obtaining lic in canon law. Subdeacon when confirmed coadj by Rome.

No date for nom as coadj. Provs 17–4–1617. Cons date unknown. Took future Cardinal de Forbin-Janson as coadj in 1655. D. Oct 1657.

Sources: Blanc, *Origines des familles provençales*, 124–5. Dumont, *Arrêts du conseil privé (Henri IV)*, no 5656. Griselle, *Etat de la maison de Louis XIII*, nos 345–8. Oroux, *Histoire ecclésiastique*, ii. 291–2. *Gallia*, iii. cos 1134–5. *DBF*, vi. 885 (family-general). AN, MC, XII 34, 11 Feb 1602 (Antoine). ASV, PC 13, fo 273; *Lettres de la main de Louis XIII*, ed Griselle, i. 308–9. AD Alpes de Haute-Provence, 1G 4 (Louis). BN, MS lat 9958, fo 158v; MS Fr 20661, fo 169 (Raphaël).

Bonsi, Jean de. Béziers 1596–1621. Assuredly one of the most enduring episcopal 'dynasties' of early modern France. Holding Béziers between 1576 and 1669, and finishing with Cardinal Pierre, successively abp of Toulouse and Narbonne until 1703. They bettered the record of their Florentine counterparts, the Gondi bps of Paris – all the more remarkable in that the Bonsis remained resident in Florence, forming an integral part of senatorial aristocracy, with only individual members becoming naturalised Frenchmen when their careers so required. First formal relations with France arose through Antonio Bonsi, bp of Terracina, who was extraordinary nuncio sent by Clement VII Medici in 1532 to negotiate marriage of Catherine de' Medici and future Henri II. Thomas, first bp of Béziers, came to France as administrator of Béziers for his uncle, Cardinal Lorenzo Strozzi, bp of Béziers, in 1550 and his successor Giuliano de' Medici. When Medici transferred to Aix in 1571, and his designated successor withdrew, Thomas was nom bp in 1575. By now Bonsis were well placed to benefit from Medici patronage and French royal largesse towards Italian (esp Florentine) families like them, although they were a notch lower at this juncture than Strozzis, Ridolfis and others who could aspire to major French sees and red hats. Thereafter, each generation of Bonsi bps was educated and carefully groomed for their careers in Florence, and sent to France at appropriate moment, though Clement and Pierre were largely educated in French SJ schools. Thomas II was the only one of them not originally designated for church, but the almost simultaneous deaths of Cardinal Jean and Dominique his coadj at Béziers, in 1621, produced a succession crisis which compelled him to take up church career in order to keep Béziers in family hands. In Languedoc, successive bps enjoyed close ties to Montmorency governors.

B. Florence 1560. Son of Domenico, senator of Florence and minister of Grand Duke of Tuscany, and Costanza Vettori; nephew of Thomas I, bp of Béziers 1576–96. Educated, in accordance with family tradition, at Padua, where he took doct in utr. Early career was as well respected lawyer in Rome and Florence. Apparently offered see of Florence, but preferred to succeed uncle at Béziers. In minor orders when confirmed by Rome. Benefices and offices (esp in service of Marie de' Medici) followed rather than preceded episcopal office, culminating in red hat.

Nom 1596. Provs 11–2–1598. Cons 30–9–1598 in Rome. Cardinal in 1611. D. in Rome 4–7–1621.

Bonsi, Dominique. Béziers coadj 1615–21. B. Florence, 1591. Eldest son of Pietro, senator of Florence, and Lucrezia de Manelli. Began education in Florence, continued at Béziers ca 1607, followed by 3 years at La Flèche (in company of Barrault of Bazas), and ending in Paris, where completed philosophy and 3 parts of theology course, but coadjutorship of Béziers beckoned well before he could take degree. Still mere cleric when nom, he was first almoner (a sinecure) to Marie de' Medici and prior in c of Solesmes, OSB (Le Mans) by 1612. Chronology of coadjutorship confusing: probably first moved in mid-1612, when took required profession of faith, though enquiry *de vita et moribus* was not done until Jan 1614. Papal disapproval of underaged bps was also responsible for delay in granting provs. By then, uncle had retired to Rome, and he administered Béziers with full powers until premature death in 1621, pre-deceasing uncle by a few weeks.

No date for nom as coadj. Provs 31–8–1615. Cons 31–1–1616. D. 30–4–1621.

Bonsi, Thomas II de. Béziers 1622–8. B. 1601. Brother of Dominique and Clement. Initially educated at Béziers under uncle Jean's supervision, spent some time at La Flèche. Naturalised in March 1609, page at court as comte de Vaillan, 1615, destined for secular career until sudden death of Dominique in 1621 required change of family strategy and (despite his personal reluctance) an episcopal career.

Nom July 1621. Provs 10–1–1622. Cons 13–4–1626 in Rome (delayed because of age). D. 7–8–1628.

Bonsi, Clement de. Beziers 1629–59. B. 1598 Florence. Brother of Dominique and Thomas II. Educated at Pisa, where took doct in utr. Canon of St Peter's Rome in early 1621, priest in 1626. Passed over by Cardinal Jean for Béziers succession in 1621, but succeeded in 1628 with Richelieu's support. Despite traditional family relations with Montmorency, he remained loyal during 1632 revolt.

Nom after Aug 1628. Provs 17–11–1629. Cons date unknown. D. 6–10–1659.

Bonsi, Pierre de. Béziers 1660–9, Toulouse 1669–73, Narbonne 1673–1703.
B. Florence 15–4–1631. Son of Francesco and Christina Riario. Sent to France in 1641, studied humanities and philosophy in SJ coll at Béziers. Then studied theology in Paris in mid-1650s, but took doct in canon law, Toulouse, instead. Abbot in c of St-Sauveur, OSB (Lodève) in succession to uncle, Clement, in 1654. Deputy to AC of 1655 for Narbonne province. Ordained priest in Paris, Pentecost 1659, only months before episcopal nom.
   Nom to Béziers 11–10–1659. Provs 7–6–1660. Cons 12–12–1660. Abp of Toulouse 1669, Narbonne 1673, cardinal 1672. D. 11–7–1703.

Sources: ASV, PC 13, fos 411–48; PC 53, fos 656–68; PC 58, fos 514–28; Processus Datariae 8, fos 222–31. BN, MS Fr 33047, pp 485, 501 (naturalisations, 1601, 1602, 1637); MS lat 9957, fo 162v. Griselle, *Etat de la maison de Louis XIII*, nos 2112, 2417, 2420, 2440. *DBI*, xii. 375–6, 381–2, 388–95, 397–8. Dubost, 'Les Italiens en France au xvie et xviie siècles'. *DBF*, vi. 1061–3. *DHGE*, ix. 1141–3. *Gallia*, vi. 370–5. Beik, *Absolutism and Society in 17th Century France*.

Bosquet, François. Lodève 1648–57, Montpellier 1656–76. Perhaps one of the most self-made men among French bps, though better known as provincial intendant than as bp. Family long established in Narbonne, where several generations practised as notaries (inc that of his father). That and evidence of municipal office-holding made them a family of urban *notables*. On mother's side, bp's social connections may have been slightly better. His two sisters married in financial circles, one husband being a receiver of taxes in Narbonne, the other of *gabelles* at Marseille.
   B. 28–5–1605. Son of Durand, notary at Narbonne, and Jeanne le Noir. Early education at SJ coll of Béziers, followed by law studies in Toulouse, leading to doct in utr, ca 1622. Scholar and editor of texts from early in his career, he formed wide range of relationships and friendships (inc future bps like Montchal, Plantavit, Marca) in Languedoc and Paris during 1620s and 1630s, which enabled him to obtain pension payable by abp of Auch as early as 1624. These ties, and others to political/ministerial figures like Séguier, were crucial to subsequent career – classic case of workings of patronage and friendship, allied to being in right place at right time. Judge and *lieutenant criminel* of Narbonne, he helped keep it loyal during 1632 revolt, after which political favour and commissions followed, thanks mainly to Séguier and Pierre de Marca. Proc-gen in Rouen parlt during Séguier mission in Normandy 1639–40, *cons d'état*, 1639. One of few non-MR and provincial officials to become intendant (Montauban *généralité* 1641–2, Languedoc 1642–6). Unmarried and ordained priest in 1646, his ambition to enter episcopate was no secret from at least early 1640s, when he failed to secure either Pamiers or Conserans. Long negotiations, giving rise to suspicions of simony, preceded his accession to Lodève.
   Nom to Lodève April 1648 (following resign of see by Plantavit). Provs 28–9–1648. Cons 20–12–1648. Moved to Montpellier, Jan 1656 (but did not resign Lodève until May 1657). D. 24–6–1676.

Sources: ASV, PC 49, fos 528–44; Acta Misc 97, fo 28. Henry, *François Bosquet*. Martin, *Histoire de la ville de Lodève*, ii. 375 (important corrections to Henry's account). M Foisil, *La Révolte des Nu-pieds* (Paris 1970), 323. *DBF*, vi. 1136–8.

Boucicault Etienne *le Meingre* **de, OFM. Grasse 1604–24.** The le Meingre adopted Boucicault as their name in the hope of grafting themselves onto an old noble family identified with a marshal of France under Charles VI. On this basis, they fraudulently obtained confirmation of their noble status in 1597, but eldest branch was condemned for usurpation in 1667. In fact, le Meingres can only be traced to bp's great-grandfather, Pierre Gros *dit* Boucicault, a fisherman at Stes-Maries-de-la Mer in late 15th C, and his son, Jacques, also a fisherman. Bp was one of 3 sons of Etienne, a peasant from near Arles, and it was brothers Claude and Trophime (same Christian name as marshal Boucicault!) who obtained recognition as nobles in 1597. Ten years later, Trophime was describing himself as 'écuyer de la ville d'Arles, consr et mre d'hostel de la maison de la royne Marguerite'.

B. Arles ca 1567. Son of Etienne le Maingre and Madeleine d'Urbane (m. 1565). Nothing known of education, but may have been partly in schools of Capuchin order which he joined in 1582, but switched to Observant branch of Franciscans in 1597. Accession to Grasse, typical of many promotions under Henri IV, only possible by negotiating with Georges de Poisseux (who had received royal nom years previously thanks to his brother's influence with Henri III and Henri IV, but had failed to obtain papal approval). Le Meingre's provs were then delayed because Rome regarded Guillaume le Blanc (d. 1601) as rightful bp of Grasse since the early 1590s.

Nom 8–4–1598. Provs 24–3–1604. Cons 30–5–1604. D. 17–4–1624.

Sources: Blanc, *Origines des familles provençales*, 129–31. AD Bouches-du-Rhône, B 3339, fos 752–60, *lettres de noblesse* (24–9–1597). AN, MC, XXIX 160, 31–3–1608. *DBF*, vi.1243. *Gallia*, iii. cols 1177–80.

Bourbon-Navarre, Charles de. Rouen 1597–1604 (resign). Of the 3 Bourbon ecclesiastics with identical names in late 16th C, he is the least known. Half-brother of Henri IV, he was illegitimate son of Antoine de Bourbon, king of Navarre, and Louise de la Béraudière, aunt of François, future bp of Périgueux. Status and career before nom to Rouen are particularly hard to follow. At best he held see of Lectoure in Gascony for many years 'in administration' rather than as titular bp, and he did not attempt to play church or political role like his two namesakes, Cardinal Bourbon ('Charles X') and Cardinal Vendôme. Henri IV attempted to place him in Reims in 1591, but was unable to dislodge the Guises. Not first choice for Rouen in 1594, and only nom when Philippe Desportes, the poet, refused it. It seems fair to date his episcopal career from accession to Rouen, rather than from any one of earlier 'associations' with a particular diocese. Short episcopate ending in resignation, it seems even a major archdiocese held few attractions for him.

Nom 13–11–1594. Provs 26–3–1597. Resign 1604 to Cardinal Joyeuse. D. 15–6–1610.

Sources: Clergeac, *Chronologie*, 49. AD Marne, G 51, fo 226 ('nom' to Reims 1591). *DBF*, vi. 1395.

Bourgoing, Nicolas. Coutances 1623–25. Another bp of highly obscure social and family background. Although Parisians, they were apparently unrelated to better known Bourgoing family of office-holders or Edme Bourgoing, the prior of Jacobins executed in 1590s.

B. Paris ca 1568. Identity of parents unknown. Probably educated in Univ of Paris, and took doct in theology at coll of Navarre. Well-known preacher, whose anti-*ligueur* stance seems to have attracted attention of Henri IV, who secured him seat as canon at St-Malo, ca 1599 (where also canon-*théologal* for time). Thereafter, career was split entirely between

St-Malo and Coutances, owing less to patronage of Henri IV or Louis XIII than to local bps and esp powerful Matignon family, who appointed him *curé* of St-Lô, and then to canon's stall in Coutances cathedral chapter, where he held variety of major positions (*théologal* from 1609, *official* in 1620). Elected deputy to Norman Estates (1612, 1614) and AC of 1619, he was only nom bp of Coutances after two previous attempts to find successor to Bp Briroy (d. 1620) had come to nothing. Obviously highly experienced, he was too elderly in 1623 to be anything other than a Matignon family caretaker.

Brevet de nom 4–4–1622. Provs 10–5–1623. Cons 9–7–1623. D. 19–4–1625.

Sources: Coutances, Archives de l'Evêché, M 41. ASV, Misc Arm XII 144, fo 259. Toustain de Billy, *Histoire ecclésiastique du diocèse de Coutances*, ed Héron, iii. 223–5. Guilloton de Courson, *Pouillé de l'archévêché de Rennes*, i. 641. *DHGE*, x. 228–9. *DBF*, vi. 1502–3.

Bourlemont, Charles-François *Anglure* de. Aire 1650–9, Castres 1659–64, Toulouse 1664–9. Despite myths of crusader origins/exploits (esp by regular use of name Saladin!), this was genuine old noble family traceable to 14th C, whose offices and alliances were considerable. Their 'frontier' geographical roots ensured their services were as much to dukes of Burgundy and Lorraine as to kings of France. While bp's father was close to duke of Lorraine, there was a discernible shift of attention towards French interests in careers of several members of bp's generation.

B. 8–5–1605 Bourlemont. Son of Claude and Angélique d'Adjacet de Aquaviva (of Roman origin with connections to Barberini and other families); godson of Duke Charles III of Lorraine. Early education (to philosophy at least) at Pont-à-Mousson, followed by doct in utr, but univ unknown. Given his mother's family's relations with Urban VIII, Roman career was obvious one for Charles, who may have completed his education there before embarking under Barberini patronage on curial career, which enabled him to become *primicier* of Metz cathedral in 1630 and Urban VIII's preferred candidate for see of Toul in 1630s, an ambition frustrated by Louis XIII and Richelieu. Louis, Charles-François's younger and more famous brother, also began career in Rome where he was an auditor of the Rota and French *chargé d'affaires* before becoming bp of Fréjus and later abp of Bordeaux under Louis XIV. Charles may also have followed Mazarin (another Barberini client) into service of French crown, becoming royal almoner ca 1639. Priest for several years, abbot in c of ND de la Crete, O Cist (Langres), St-Pierre-des-Monts, OSA (Metz) and Ste-Trinté-de-Beauchamp, OSA (Toul) before episcopate.

Nom to Aire 20–4–1649. Provs 10–1–1650. Cons 25–3–1650. Transferred to Castres 17–2–1659, to Toulouse 15–9–1664. D. 29–11–1669.

Sources: ASV, PC 48, fos 1–16; PC 57, fos 205–17. Poull, *Le Château et les seigneurs de Bourlement*. Lacger, *Etats administratifs*, 332–3. Bourquin, *Noblesse seconde et pouvoir en Champagne*, 38ff. *L'Intendance de Champagne à la fin du xviie siècle*, 260–1, 271.

Bourlon, Mathieu. Soissons coadj 1651/56–85. Solidly established and well-connected Parisian bourgeois and office-holding family of second rather than first rank, and enjoying considerable wealth. Transition from *grand commerce* to offices occurred during 16th C, with bp's own father serving as *auditeur* (later *maître*) in *chambre des comptes*, and marrying daughter of a pres in the same court, in 1612. Their marriages accurately reflect this shift, with a noticeable cluster of financial office-holders by early 17th C, but improving steadily thereafter to include even *noblesse d'épée* unions. Three of bp's brothers became *cons* in parlts or *grand conseil*. Through related families such as Netz, Le Gras, Hac and Lallemant, they formed part of Parisian *dévot* circles.

B. Paris (St-Eustache parish), ca 1613. Son of Mathieu and Chrétienne Bailly. Entire education probably Parisian, culminating in 1st place in 1640 lic in theology, quickly followed by doct. Abbot in c of Chartreuve, O Prem (Soissons) by 1640, also active as preacher. Participated in efforts to relieve distress during Fronde, esp in Picardy and Soissonnais, in association with uncle, Bp Le Gras of Soissons. Enjoying considerable patrimonial wealth, he was originally nom to Lavaur in 1644, but abandoned it because retiring bp wished to retain most of revenues. The services of Le Gras relatives to Anne of Austria over many years were another factor in his career, and were cited explicitly in his letter of nom to Soissons.

Procuration from Bp Le Gras to take Bourlon as coadj 22–8–1651. Nom to pope 28–8–1651. Provs 16–12–1652. Cons 2–2–1653. Succeeded Le Gras in 1656. D. 26–10–1685.

Sources: ASV, PC 51, fos 817–41. AN, Y 138, fo 297, c.m. of bp's uncle Nicolas Bourlon and Marie Lalemant 24–4–1579; MC, XXIX, 127, c.m. of bishop's parents, 6–5–1612. BN, P Or 471, doss 10490; Doss bleus 125. BN, MS lat 15440, p 169; MS Fr 15720, fo 342–3 (Lavaur, 1644); MS Fr 8327 (family epitaph, St-Eustache). Poutet, 'Docteurs de Sorbonne', 240. Tessereau, *Chancellerie*, 288, 329, 465. *DBF*, vi. 1518.

Boutault, Gilles de. Aire 1627–49, Evreux 1649–61. Family originated in Poitiers, but moved to Tours, where its members appear as undistinguished merchants before and during bp's lifetime.

B. 1594 Tours. Son of Charles and Marie Viart. Educated initially in SJ coll at Poitiers, then at coll of Navarre, ca 1606. Credited with doct in theology from Paris, but claim may have been inflated. In fact, owed advancement essentially to patronage of highly connected Souvré family, and of Gilles, bp of Comminges and Auxerre in particular, in whose household he boarded while studying in Paris, before accompanying him to Italy (possibly as tutor-preceptor as well as travelling companion) in 1616. Subsequently served Souvré as vg in Comminges. By time he obtained Aire (for which he was third rather than first choice) in 1626, he was priest and royal almoner, a well-known preacher, and well endowed with offices and benefices: abbot in c of St-Rémy of Sens (which he surrendered in order to obtain nomin to Aire), canon and archdeacon of Tours as well as protonotary apostolic. As bp of Aire, he energetically served Richelieu as military organiser in SW during Spanish campaigns there. Strongly Mazarinist during Fronde, for which his transfer to Evreux was evidently a reward.

Nom to Aire 19–4–1626. Provs 27–1–1627. Cons 14–3–1627. Nom to Evreux 17–4–1649. Provs 15–11–1649. D. 11–3–1661.

Sources: ASV, PC 24, fos 653–702; PC 49, fos 24–37. BN, P Or 476, doss 10664. Beauchet-Filleau, *Dict du Poitou*, i. 705. *DHGE*, x. 266. Griselle, *Etat de la maison de Louis XIII*, nos 32, 1625. Clergeac, *Chronologie*, 76. *DBF*, vii. 38.

Bouthillier, Sébastien. Aire 1621–5. This ministerial family's roots lay in Angoulême where its earliest known generations exercised municipal and then royal office in early 16th C (e.g. Sébastien, grandfather of bps, began as barrister at local *sénéchaussée*, but by end of career was royal judge and *sénéchal* of la Rochefoucauld). Having tried military career, his best known son Denis also turned to law and migrated with brother and fellow barrister, Jean, to Paris where he married daughter of a Dijon lawyer. A highly successful legal career followed, esp at *grand conseil*, where he specialised in church affairs (esp benefices) and his opinions were widely sought, though he never moved beyond position of barrister. If his actual connection to Richelieu's barrister-grandfather, La Porte, remains to be elucidated, there can be no doubt that he and family's later association with the cardinal was decisive in their rapid rise to ministerial office. It also enabled families related to Bouthilliers via marriages of two of Denis's offspring (Bragelongne and La Barde) to enter episcopate in 1620s and 1630s.

B. ca 1580. Son of Denis and Claudine Macheco. No information on education, but took lic in utr. Inseparable companion of Richelieu, became canon and dean of Luçon during his episcopate, and in late 1610s, first almoner to Marie de' Medici. Priest for some time before episcopate, he was on diplomatic mission to Rome when nom to Aire, vacated by Philippe Cospeau. Richelieu and Marie de' Medici subsequently tried to obtain a northern (preferably Breton) see for him, but career was cut short by early death.

Nom 1621. Provs 13–10–1621. Cons 24–10–1621 in Rome. D. 17–1–1625.

Bouthillier, Victor. Boulogne 1627–30, Tours coadj 1631/41–70. B. 1597. Younger brother of Sébastien. Studied humanities and philosophy in Univ of Paris, where Bp Etampes may have taught him briefly, and theology in both Paris and Louvain, but does not seem to have taken degree. Tonsured on 22–3–1608, joined Bérulle's Oratory ca 1614–15, already priest. Left Oratory in 1621 to take brother Sébastien's place as canon of ND de Paris. First almoner to Gaston d'Orléans, Oct 1626. Nom to Aire after brother's death, he preferred Boulogne. Abbot in c of St-Rémy of Sens, OSB, in 1626, which he obtained from Boutault in return for surrender of claim to Aire!

Nom to Boulogne 26–12–1626. Provs 29–11–1627. Cons 9–4–1628. Nom coadj of Tours 12–11–1630. Provs 1–11–1631. Succeeded to Tours 1641. D. 12–9–1670.

Sources: Louis Le Clert, *Notice généalogique sur les Bouthillier de Chavigny* (Troyes 1907). *Inventaire-sommaire des archives communales de la ville d'Angoulême* (Angoulême 1889); *Inventaire-Sommaire des archives de la Charente, E series* 4 vols (Angoulême 1880–1906). AN, Y 123, fos 297–9, c.m. of Jean Bouthillier 2–10–1581; LXXXVI 314, 8–2–1630, *inventaire après décès* of Denis Bouthillier. Ranum, *Richelieu and the Councillors of Louis XIII* (family-general). *Corr de Bérulle*, ii. 186. BAV, Barb lat 7939, fo 74. BN, MS Fr 3668, fo 19 (Aire, 1625) (Sébastien). AN, Z^{1}o 241 (tonsure); MC, LXXXVI 459, 15–10–1670, *inventaire après décès*. Batterel, *Mémoires domestiques de l'Oratoire*, i. 384–401 (Victor).

Boylesve, Gabriel de. Avranches 1651–67. Ennoblement of Marin Boylesve, lt-gen. of Angers *présidial* in 1587, provoked a bitter controversy at time over family's history and claims to lineage, and led one later historian to uncover 10 generations before that of bp of Avranches! But while there may be scraps of evidence for service to dukes of Anjou and Orléans in 15th C, most of family's numerous offices in 16th C were municipal, in law and finance, which put them on margins of notability and nobility, and their connections were to families of similar background in Angers – including Grimaudet family with its relations to Cupifs and Fouquets. Bp's father was the first to transcend these local horizons, becoming *cons* at Rennes parlt in 1593, and his long career there enabled succeeding generations to follow in his footsteps (11 Rennes *cons* in all!). While bp was an active partner in financial activities of his brothers, Charles and Claude, it was the latter, secretary to Fouquet after 1642, who was instrumental in their spectacular rise to wealth, office and preferment – all of which were left in ruins by *chambre de justice* after 1661.

B. 1–3–1595 Angers. Son of Charles, sr de Malnoë and *cons* at Rennes parlt, and Marie de Nicolas, 1st wife. Education was mainly, perhaps wholly, at Angers, finishing with doct in utr. Tonsured in 1612, ordained priest in 1623, early career was modest enough, though an uncle was canon of Angers and chancellor of the univ in early 1610s. Served as almoner to Bp Charles Miron of Angers (to whom his father was previously connected), was also schoolmaster at St-Maurice, Angers, becoming chancellor of Angers Univ in 1629. Also *cons* at Angers *présidial*, he moved first to Rennes, finally to Paris parlt by 1640s, when he also became canon of ND de Paris and royal almoner. While based in Rennes he had held parish of Alloire (Vannes) and attended the Breton Estates. Before nom to Avranches, he was abbot in c of St-Aubin-aux-Bois, O Cist (St-Brieuc), ND de Berdoues, O Cist (Auch), St-Georges-sur-Loire, OSA (Angers). He surrendered latter benefice to Roger d'Aumont in order to secure Aumont's resignation of Avranches to himself.

Nom 5–1–1651. Provs 28–10–1651. Cons 10–12–1651. D. 3–12–1667.

Sources: ASV, PC 51, fos 1–16; BN, MS lat 18345, fo 214 (ennoblement 1587). Trani, 'Conseillers du grand conseil', 119; Saulnier, *Parlement de Bretagne*, i. 152. Dessert, *Argent pouvoir et société*, 548; Anselme, ii. 116–29. Farcy, *Histoire généalogique de la maison de Boylesve*. Godet de Soudé, *Dict des anoblissements*, 9. *DBF*, vi. 826.

Bragelongne, Emery de. Luçon 1623–35 (resign). Family apparently originated from near Sens, where Thomas de Bragelongne was a tax-receiver in late 15th C, but by 1540s at the latest they were already prominent Parisians, with impressive marriage connections, and holding array of municipal, royal and other offices. Wealthy and prolific, their matrimonial ties were to families just below very top rank of Paris office-holders (Bouthillier, Abra de Raconis, Chesnard, Le Nain). Pierre, great-grandfather of bp, was a *procureur* at Châtelet in 1536, while his son Thomas was *prévôt des marchands* by 1558. It was generation of his offspring which began to make serious advances into offices, both parlementaire and financial. Bp's father and brother (Claude) were both pres in Paris parlt, while another brother, Pierre, was comptroller general of Marie de' Medici's household until 1621. Marriage alliances of female members were just as important in each generation – e.g. bp's sister Anne married Jean le Nain, while Marie married Claude Bouthillier (1606), which explains their subsequent ties with Marie de' Medici and Richelieu.

B. Paris ca 1580. Son of Martin, pres in Paris parlt, *prévôt des marchands* (1602), and Cathérine d'Abra de Raconis (relative of future bp of Lavaur). Probably educated in Paris, he apparently took doct in canon law. Ordained priest 20–12–1614. Almoner to Marguerite de Valois in 1612. Dean of St-Martin-de-Tours and abbot in c of Vaast, OSA (Le Mans) by the time of nom, which he owed entirely to Richelieu, outgoing bp of Luçon. His career there ended in 1635 when Richelieu persuaded him to make room for Pierre Nivelle.

Richelieu resign Luçon to Bragelongne 19–5–1623. Nom 31–5–1623. Provs 29–4–1624. Cons 4–6–1624. Resign Oct 1635. D. 1669.

Sources: ASV, PC 18, fos 94–106. AN, MC, XIX 243 (c.m. of bp's parents, 20–3–1569); MC, CV, 355, 20–8–1615 (*inventaire après décès* of bp's mother); MC, XIV, 10, 3–1–1612. BN, P Or 490, Bragelongne doss. BI, MS 1354, fo 21. *DBF*, vii. 136. *DHGE*, x. 372.

Brandon, Philibert de. Perigueux 1648–52. Originally from Issoire in Auvergne, members of Brandon family dispersed in several directions in 16th C, but without wholly abandoning their Auvergnat roots. Bp's great grandfather, Pons, was *cons* in both Paris (1532) and Rennes parlts, his grandfather, Antoine, became MR in 1580, while father, also Antoine, began his career as pres and *trésorier de France* at Moulins, but later moved to Paris where he became *maître aux Comptes* and married into influential and well established family of Parisian officeholders. Bp's own marriage and that of his sister (to Lemaître de Bellejamme, the future intendant of Picardy) were intended to consolidate their social and professional rise into high Parisian robe.

B. Moulins ca 1597. Son of Antoine and Charlotte Gayant, daughter of Thomas, pres in *Enquêtes*, Paris parlt. Nothing known about education, but apparently took doct in utr. Following in footsteps of paternal and maternal relatives, he began career as *cons* in Paris parlt (received 18–2–1622). In 1630 married Marie-Charlotte de Ligny, niece of future chancellor, Pierre Séguier. Marriage was brief, but brought Brandon valuable patronage and relations. A true *dévot*, he was an early (1631) and active lay member of *Compagnie du St Sacrement*, and was close to reformed religious orders like Carmelites of Pontoise, where only daughter became nun. After wife's death, he took priestly orders (before 1637) on advice of Bérulle's successor, Condren (as did his brother, Balthazar, who joined Vincent de Paul's new congregation). Then studied theology informally with Oratorian, Denis Amelotte, and threw himself into the missionary, charitable, and other activities of Vincent de Paul, Olier and others over several years. Episcopate was too short and the SW too turbulent for him to realise *dévot* hopes of restoring his diocese. By time of death he was massively in debt.

No date for nom to Périgueux, but probably March-June 1648. Provs 28–9–1648. Cons 22–11–1648. D. 13–7–1652.

Sources: ASV, PC 37, fo 160; PC 50, fos 137–48. BN, P Or 492, doss 11078. BL, Add MS 21434, fo 23 (*cons* in parlt, 1622). AN, MC, CX, 124, *inventaire après décès* of bp, 27–7–1652. Etchéchoury, *Maîtres des requêtes*, 210–11. *Lettres et mémoires adressés au chancelier Séguier* ed Mousnier, i. 152; ii. 1189. Séguier, *Lettres a son frère*, ed Hours, 60. Michaud, *Grande Chancellerie* 74, n 5. Pierre de Bessort, *Livre-journal 1609–1652*, ed P Tamizey de Larroque (Paris 1893), 63–4, 105, 121.

Breslay, René. Troyes 1605–41. Family had long lived in Angers and its environs, holding various offices since mid-15th C, when their ancestor Jean Breslay was successively *sénéchal* of Chenillé (1436), *bailli* of Sablé (1456), and finally *juge ordinaire* of Angers. Enduring or spectacular mobility did not ensue, and family long remained involved with municipal magistracies and law practice in local courts, esp at *présidial*. Their alliances were with families of same type. Nor did occasional external success (e.g. a councillorship in Rennes parlt or a presidency in *grand conseil*) transform their fortunes.

B. Angers May 1557. Son of Etienne and Françoise de Hériz. Education did not include taking degree (surprising for someone of his social background), which led to accusations of ignorance when nom to Troyes. *Curé* of Bazouges-sur-Loire (where he probably did not serve), canon of St-Pierre *collégiale* in Angers, 1574, his career was facilitated principally by his able brother, Pierre, who died in 1583, leaving René to succeed him as canon and *chantre* of Angers cathedral, where he later became grand archdeacon (1599). By then fellow Angevin, René Benoist, confessor to Henri IV, had received him in Paris, obtaining a royal almonership for him (1596), confiding various tasks to him and, finally, when his own prolonged efforts (1593–1604) to obtain papal confirmation as bp of Troyes proved fruitless, resigned his title to Breslay. Through similar patronage he held two abbeys in c before episcopate.

Nom probably early 1604. Provs 18–7–1605. Cons 25–9–1605. D. 2–11–1641, having taken François Malier du Houssay as coadj in mid-1630s.

Sources: BN, P Or 500, dossier 11331. Launay, *Les Avocats d'Angers de 1250 à 1789*, 5, 28, 84. Launay, *Recherches sur les familles des maires d'Angers*, iii. 87–108. Saulnier, *Parlement de Bretagne*, ii. 170–1. Port, *Dict du Maine-et-Loire*, i. 511–12. Prévost, *Diocèse de Troyes*, ii. 419–82. *ANG*, iv. 552, 656, 677, 689, 710. *DBF*, vii. 219–20.

Bretel, Louis de. Aix 1631–44. Having been peasants in the *pays* de Caux and merchants in Le Havre, the Bretel settled into legal practice and councillorships in Rouen parlt during 16th C. A rapid rise to eminence followed during generation of abp's grandfather, Raoul (1527–98), sgr de Grémonville, *cons* (1570), then pres *à mortier* (1585) in parlt. Also a *cons d'état*, he was ennobled in 1588. His only son, abp's father, consolidated these advances, succeeding father as pres in parlt (1597). His marriage to Françoise le Roux d'Infréville (1574) brought family into wider circles, some of them Parisian (e.g. Potier de Blancmesnil), while members of abp's generation (11 children in all) would serve, among others, Marie de' Medici and Richelieu. Their marriage connections to senior parlementaire families of Rouen like Groulart and Maignart also ensured they were close to *dévot* circles in Normandy and beyond.

B. Rouen 9–4–1584. Son of Louis and Françoise le Roux. Studied humanities and philosophy in Rouen and Paris, followed theology course in Paris, before taking doct in utr at Orléans. Canon of Rouen by time ordained priest in Paris 18–4–1609. Entered Rouen parlt as *cons-cl* around same time. Canon and dean of Lisieux for nearly 15 years, he became dean of Rouen in 1620s. Deputy to AC of 1625 for Rouen province, where was also abbot in c of Aulnay-sur-Odon, O Cist (Bayeux) and St-Victor-de-Calais, OSB (Boulogne) for many years.

Nom 13–2–1630. Provs 4–10–1631. Cons 11–1–1632. D. 27–3–1644.

Sources: ASV, PC 13, fos 366–8; PC 28, fos 1–32. AN, Z^{1}o 241 (ordination); G^8 87 (AC elections). BN, MS Fr 32989, fo 199. Frondeville, *Présidents*, 266–72. Griselle, *Etat de la maison de Louis XIII*, no. 2566. Trani, 'Conseillers du grand conseil', 120–1. Grillon, *Papiers de Richelieu*, vi. 596. Dewald, *Formation of a Provincial Nobility*, 95, 89, 285–6.

Brichantau, Benjamin de, OSA. Laon coadj 1608/12–19. A military noble family from Chartres region traceable to 14th C, but not always particularly active or holding important court or military posts thereafter, despite prestigious marriage alliances – Chabot, Lenoncourt, Hôpital de Vitry, Billy, Bauffremont, La Rochefoucauld. But generations of bps' grandfather and father were highly active during wars of religion, with father Antoine changing sides on more than one occasion as he searched for patronage and advantage – moving from Antoine de Bourbon to Guises, then to Anjou-Henri III, to Guises again, and finally back to Henri III in late 1580s. After some hesitation, he recognised Henri IV in 1590, refusing Mayenne's offers of governorship of Normandy. Henri IV refused to confirm his appointment by Henri III in 1589 as admiral of France, but made him a *chevalier of St Esprit*. Ecclesiastical activities and connections were already visible, esp since bps' grandfather had married a niece of Cardinal de Lenoncourt, and his brother Crespin was abbot of St-Vincent de Laon and briefly bishop of Senlis in 1559–60.

In following generation, it was patronage of Cardinal La Rochefoucauld and then closeness of Nicolas de Brichantau to Louis XIII, that facilitated elevation of Benjamin and Philibert to Laon.

B. 10–9–1585 Paris. Son of Antoine, marquis de Nangis, and Antoinette de la Rochefoucauld, sister of François, Cardinal La Rochefoucauld. Nothing known of education, but probably took doct in canon law in Paris. Tonsured with his brothers in June 1599, became canon-regular in Parisian abbey of Ste-Geneviève 14–04–1601, taking vows in 1602, and becoming coadj-abbot in 1607. Also held abbey of Barbeaux, O Cist (Sens) in c before episcopate.

Nom coadj to cousin G de Billy, ca 1607. Provs 23–6–1608. Cons 13–5–1610. Succeeded Billy 1612. D. 13–7–1619.

Brichantau, Philibert de. Laon 1621–52. B. 25–7–1588 in Paris. Younger brother of Benjamin (above). Nothing known of education, does not appear to have taken degree. Tonsured in 1599, and may have joined the knights of Malta and accompanied Champlain to Canada. Succeded cousin Bp Billy of Laon as abbot in c of St-Vincent-de-Laon in 1612, but was still simple cleric at time of nom as bp. The premature death of brother Benjamin in 1619 precipitated an unexpected career change, and it was through Cardinal La Rochefoucauld that Brichantau family tenure of Laon was prolonged for another generation.

Nom July 1619. Provs 19–4–1621. Cons 1621. D. 21–11–1652.

Sources: Anselme, vii. 887–9. Orléa, *Noblesse aux états-généraux de 1576 et 1588*, 138–41. AN, Z^1o 241 (ordinations). *DBF*, v. 1191–2; vii. 282. *DHGE*, x. 672–3. Hayden, *France and the Estates General of 1614*, 236.

Briroy, Nicolas. Coutances 1597–1620. Cotentin middling noble family which died out by mid-17th C when its titles and lands passed by marriage into Harcourt family.

B. Fierville 1526. Son of Guillaume, sgr de Fierville, and Gillette de Thienville. Nothing known of studies but apparently took lic in utr. Nominally *curé* of Fierville from 1541 onwards. Later canon (1570) and archdeacon (1574) of Coutances, he owed his pre-episcopal career largely to Artus de Cossé, an inactive and often non-resident bishop of Coutances (1560–87), for whom he virtually ran diocese for many years, acting as vg after 1575. Deputy to EG of Blois 1576, AC of 1579–80, and Rouen provincial council of 1581. This gave him experience which marshal Matignon, the real master of Coutances diocese, looked for in successor to Cossé, although the elderly Briroy was not his first choice candidate. Henri III explicitly nom Briroy as favour to Matignon, an arrangement which Henri IV confirmed. Briroy attempted to take Charles Prévost, vg of Sens, as coadj in 1610, but despite his great age, this move failed.

Nom Oct 1588, renewed by Henri IV 16–5–1590. Provs delayed until 15–9–1597, since papacy confirmed John Lesley (d. 1597) as bp during League. Cons 7–12–1597. D. 22–3–1620.

Sources: Coutances, Archives de l'Evêché, M 41. BN, P Or 522, doss 11,171; Doss bleus 137, doss 3381. AN, MC, VIII, 409, 27–8–1594 (*régale* for Coutances). Toustain de Billy, *Histoire ecclésiastique de Coutances*, ii. 187, 190–2; iii. 138–53. Guy Chamillart, *Recherche de la noblesse faite en 1666 en la généralité de Caen* (Paris-Caen 1887), 146, 314. Berthelot du Chesnay, *Les Missions de Saint Jean Eudes*, 337.

Broc, Pierre de. Auxerre 1637–71. This old noble family originated in the parish of same name near Angers. Military and political service of various kinds was a regular feature of its history in later Middle Ages. In mid-16th C, eldest branch survived thanks to a younger son, Mathurin (grandfather of bp) who served under Daillon du Lude, and whose marriage to Louise de Lavardin in 1566 confirmed family's existing affiliations and standing. Their son François married Françoise de Montmorency-Fosseux without his parents' consent, for which he was disinherited, so that lands and title went to bp's uncle, Sébastien. Ecclesiastics were not esp prominent before bp's generation, but a Pierre de Broc played an important part in AC of 1585. A series of indirect ties (via marriage) to Richelieu and his extended family brought several members of de Broc family into cardinal's service by late 1620s and early 1630s.

B. 25–2–1602 Courtalain. 3rd son of François and Françoise de Montmorency-Fosseux. Studied humanities and philosophy at La Flèche and Orléans, followed by several years of theology under Nicolas Isambert in Paris, where he took doct in canon law. By 1624, when eldest brother married Marguerite de Bourdeille in a high-society wedding at Louvre, bp and family had moved into Marie de' Medici-Richelieu-Effiat circles. Royal almoner before 1624 and best known as abbé de St-Mars, Pierre was well endowed with other benefices (inc ND de Broc and ND de Fontenelles) before episcopate, thanks no doubt to patronage of Richelieu, whose service he entered by 1630 at the latest and whose *maître de chambre* he was for several years. Priest since 1629, Richelieu also imposed him as an additional *agent-général du clergé* on reluctant AC of 1635 ('la souveraine faveur a fait apaiser force criards, lesquels auraient été bien fondés').

Nom (following Dominique Séguier's transfer to Meaux) 7–9–1637. Provs 19–12–1639. Cons 4–3–1640. D. 7–7–1671.

Sources: ASV, PC 37, fos 88–112; Griselle, *Etat de la maison de Louis XIII*, no 2364. Ledru, *Histoire de la maison de Broc* (vol ii includes family docs). *ANG*, ii. 115 (1585 AC). Blet, *Clergé de France et monarchie*, i. 402. Deloche, *Maison de Richelieu*, 80–3. Tallemant, *Historiettes*, ii. 615–16, 1397–8. *DBF*, vii. 378–81. *DHGE*, x. 789–80.

Budos, Balthasar. Castres coadj 1616–26, Agde 1627–9. This well established Languedocian family of *noblesse seconde* served Joyeuse family in 1570s-80s, but owed most significant advancement to Constable Montmorency-Damville, with whom it subsequently formed extremely close ties, not least because bp's own sister, Louise, was Montmorency's 2nd wife, while his 3rd wife, Laurence de Clermont-Montoison, was relative of bp's mother! Given nature of Montmorency power in their Languedoc governorship, not surprising that Budos family held important political and military posts there – e.g. bp's brother was lt-gen in Gevaudan and Cévennes, and vice-admiral of France. Bp's own career fits well into Montmorency efforts to maintain a strong presence in Languedoc episcopate.

B. 1594 Portes. Son of Jacques, sgr de Portes, and Catherine de Clermont-Montoison. First educated by SJ at Rouen, then at La Flèche. After few years of theology in Paris under du Val and Isambert, took doct in canon law there. Subdeacon in 1614, when Jean de Fossé of Castres agreed, no doubt in response to Montmorency promptings, to take him as coadj. Subsequent move to Agde, before he could succeed Fossé as bp of Castres, was also occasioned by internal Montmorency family politics, after Louis-Emmanuel de Valois (son of Charlotte de Montmorency and future comte d'Alais) resigned see of Agde in early 1620s.

Procuration from bp of Castres for coadj 5–6–1614. Nom 5–10–1614. Provs 3–10–1616. Cons 15–8–1617. Nom to Agde (vacant since 1622) 26–6–1626. Provs 30–8–1627. D. 24–6–1629.

Sources: ASV, PC 13, fos 653–74; PC 24, fos 463–701. AD Tarn G, 1265, pp 44–7. Anselme, ix. 154–5. Vindry, *Etat Major*, 257. *DHGE* x. 1050–1. *DBF*, vii. 614. Berthelot du Chesnay, *Les Missions de Saint Jean Eudes*, 329–30.

Cabris. *See* **Grasse**

Camelin, Barthélemy. Fréjus 1599–1637. Condemned for usurping noble status in 1668 and 1697, Camelin family invented legend of Italian origins, complete with references to service of kings in distant past. In fact, they can only be traced as far as grandfather of Bp Barthélemy: Jacques Camelin was a small merchant at Fréjus, as were sons Thomas and Jacques II. Bps were drawn from a second branch founded by Jacques II, whose elder son, Charles I, was *écuyer* of Fréjus, while *his* son, Bernard, also *écuyer* of Fréjus, abandoned claim to noble status 1667, as did his brother, Charles II. Rather than family rank and influence 'making' bps, this was a case of episcopal office helping to 'make' a family.

B. Fréjus 1562. Son of Jacques II, merchant of Fréjus, and Claire Villy. Appears to have studied theology, but probably took law degree. Canon of Fréjus in 1577, ordained priest some years later, and archdeacon of Fréjus in 1596. Ambitious, turbulent, authoritarian, he was unscrupulous in dealings with Fréjus chapter and those around him. Nom to Fréjus after Henri IV had evicted *ligueur* appointee Gérard Bellenger, Camelin's theoretical predecessor, and given see to Planchier, lieutenant of Crillon, who allegedly arranged Camelin's succession in return for pension to one of Crillon's relatives, Louis de Bertons. Camelin's nom to Fréjus was distinctly unwelcome in Fréjus and Rome, and it was only after Bellenger's death that papacy granted Camelin's provs.

Brevet de nom 1–8–1594 (registered by Aix parlt 24–3–1597). Provs 1–9–1599. Cons 5–1–1600. Took nephew, Pierre, as coadj 1621. D. 15–6–1637.

Camelin, Pierre. Fréjus coadj 1621/37–54. B. Fréjus 22–11–1579. Son of Georges and Jeanne Gaybier. Destined for church from early age, studied at Avignon, where took degree in utr. Tonsured 7–4–1593, ordained subdeacon (1600), deacon (1602) and priest (Dec 1605) by episcopal uncle, who also resigned office of archdeacon of Fréjus to him, and secured him other benefices in later years (e.g. priory of Revest, 1613). Career was shaped entirely by uncle, who, even after taking him as coadj, allowed him scarcely any say in running of diocese. Shortly before death, he failed in attempt to obtain Jean de Grasse, briefly an uncons bp of Grasse 1625–8, as coadj.

Nom coadj 31–12–1620. Provs 20–6–1621. Cons 5–12–1621. Succeeded 1637. D. 4–12–1654.

Sources: BN, P Or 578, doss 13371. AN, V[6] 1181, fos 197v, 140. AD Bouches-du-Rhône, B 3339, fo 408. Blanc, *Origines des familles provençales*, 145–7. H Espitalier, 'Les Evêques de Fréjus du xiiie à la fin du xviiie siècle', *Bulletin de la Société d'Etudes Scientifiques et Archéologiques de la ville de Draguignan*, 22 (1898–9), 3–331. *Gallia Chr Nov*, i. cols 405–6. Borricand, *Nobiliaire de Provence*, i. 281, iii. 1393–4.

Camus de Pontcarré, Jacques. Séez coadj 1613/14–50. Originally from Auxonne (not Auxerre), family held municipal office there in 15th and early 16th C. Jean Camus, baron de Bagnols, was the first to settle in Lyon, where he was a *marchand-épicier* in 1519; by 1540s, he had become one of Lyon's richest merchants, which led to municipal office-holding and ennoblement. Expanding rather than abandoning this mainly Lyonnais base, his 3 eldest sons (Antoine, Jean, and Claude) rose no less rapidly to become major financial figures by mid-century, not least as *receveurs généraux du clergé* in 1560s. They also developed extensive family ties in financial and office-holding milieux through numerous marriages of male and female members in Lyon and Paris. Jean Camus, sgr de St-Bonnet, grandfather of Jean-Pierre (below) was successively notary to Paris parlt, secretary to *conseil des parties* under Charles IX, and *intendant des finances* under Charles IX and Henri III. His youngest brother, Geoffroy, sgr de Pontcarré (father of Jacques, below), was successively notary (1566) and *cons* (1568) in parlt, MR (1573), and *cons d'état* (1585).

B. 1584 Bordeaux. Eldest son of Geoffroy and Jeanne Sanguin de Livry, from one of Paris's most distinguished office-holding dynasties. Godmother was wife of marshal Matignon, lt-gen of Guyenne. Studied at Univ of Paris (with Guy Champion, bp of Tréguier), and took lic in utr. Resident in St-Merry parish from ca 1605, became canon of ND de Paris early 1614. Also held priory of Orhères in c by then. Subdeacon when nom coadj, ordained deacon and priest in Aug 1614. Refused offer of Cahors in 1636.

Procuration from bp of Séez to take Camus as coadj 17–3–1612. Nom 6–6–1612. Provs 17–1–1613. Cons 31–8–1614. Succeeded 30–5–1614. D. 4–11–1650.

Camus, Jean-Pierre. Belley 1609–29 (resign). B. Paris 3–11–1584, baptised at St-Jean-de-Grève 5–11–1585. Son of Jean, sgr de St Bonnet, gov of Etampes, and Marie des Contes. One of 20 children, cousin of Jacques, above, nephew of future marshal Marillac. Began studies in Paris arts faculty in 1594, where probably took lic in canon law. Seems to have practised as barrister for 4 years, before turning to church career. According to one tradition, he nearly entered Carthusians, but changed mind and took major orders, May 1607. One of most prominent episcopal preachers and writers of age, he proved even more active once he had resigned from Belley. Given abbey of Aulnay, O Cist (Bayeux) as pension on resignation, he served as vg to Harlay of Rouen, before retiring to *hôpital des Incurables* in Paris. Nom bp of Arras in 1650, but d. before provs could be granted.

No date for nom to Belley, but possibly 1608 (predecessor d. in 1604). Provs 25–5–1609. Cons 30–8–1609. Resign 1629. D. 26–4–1652.

Sources: Bluche, *Origins des magistrats*, 116–17. Michaud, *Grande Chancellerie*, 167, n 4. Michaud, *L'Eglise et l'argent*, 149–53 (essential). Frondeville, *Présidents*, 103–6. Etchéchoury, *Maîtres des Requêtes*, 213 (family-general). ASV, PC 13, fos 1–21. AN, Z^{1}o 241. *Humanisme et politique. Lettres romaines de Christophe Dupuy à ses frères 1636–45*, ed P J and K P Wolfe (Tübingen 1988), 12 (Jacques). BN, MS Fr 32588, p 125; MS lat 9956, fo 100. AN, Z^{1}o 241. *DBF*, vii. 1013–14. *DGS*, 262. Tallemant, *Historiettes*, i. 840; ii. 66–70 (Jean-Pierre).

Caset de Vautorte, Louis. Lectoure 1655–71, Vannes 1671–87. Family possibly originated in Vautorte in Maine, where they were active as merchants, notaries and legal practitioners in late 15th and early 16th C, by which time some of them had settled in Laval. *Seigneurie* of Vautorte, held by several families in previous centuries, was only bought in 1575 by Jean Caset, bp's grandfather. Eldest of his 2 sons, Jean II, was *cons* at Rennes parlt in 1586, and married twice, but it was Louis (1588–1651, father of bp), only son of his 2nd marriage to Jeanne Bignon, who inherited Vautorte and was successively *juge ordinaire* of Le Mans, *cons* at Rennes parlt, and later pres in *Enquêtes* chamber from 1624. In turn, it was his eldest son, François (brother of bp), who did most to advance family's fortunes. Av-gen at *grand conseil*, intendant in Limoges, Provence, etc and with French army in Germany, he conducted several diplomatic missions in Italy and Germany in 1640s and 1650s, having married (1634) Marie Marcel, daughter of prominent, well connected Parisian robe family.

B. 1617 Laval. Son of Louis and Renée Fréart (relative of Fréart de Chantelou family). Nothing known of early education, but studied theology at Sorbonne for a time. Described in letter of nom as doct of theology, in reality he held lic in utr. Successively *curé* of Vautorte and Charné-Ernée, but unclear if actually served in them. Archdeacon of Laval in Le Mans cathedral for some years before nom. Apparently preached in several Parisian churches and possibly at court. Tonsured in April 1627, priest for ca 10 years before nom.

Nom to Lectoure 17–2–1655. Provs 14–5–1655. Cons 21–9–1655. Transferred to Vannes 1671. D. 13–12–1687.

Sources: ASV, PC 52, fos 597–611. AN, MC, LI 491, 30–1–1634 (c.m. of François Caset, bp's elder brother). Pointeau, 'Notice sur les seigneurs de Vautorte'. *Lettres et mémoires adressés au chancelier Séguier*, ed Mousnier, i. 155–61. Angot, *Dict de la Mayenne*, i, 479–80; iv. 161–2.

Caulet, Etienne. Pamiers 1645–80. Originally from Cadars, Caulets settled in Rodez where they rose to wealth and municipal prominence during first half of 16th C. While Bernard (d. 1531), bp's great-grandfather, was a shopkeeper, his son Hugues held municipal office, was *receveur des deniers* for *comté* of Rodez, and later became sgr de Cadars. His younger brother Guillaume moved to Toulouse, and family's centre of gravity quickly shifted there. *Cons* in parlt in 1545, his religious leanings attracted suspicion during the religious disturbances of 1562–3. Hugues's son, Jean-Georges, father of bp, began as a *cons-secrétaire de la chambre du roi*, before becoming pres of *trésoriers de France* at Toulouse, 1586. By later 16th and early 17th C, the Caulet family was extremely well connected in both parlt, finance, *eaux et forêts* and office-holding circles of Toulouse and Languedoc generally, and at highest levels, esp via marriage of daughters (notably to Melet, Duranti, Reich de Pennautier families). This socio-professional integration was rapid, sidestepping *capitoulat* or other habitual preliminaries in Toulouse. Although less distinguished, their church connections were numerous and influential enough. Bp's uncles, Pierre Caulet and Bonaventure de la Font, were abbots of Volusien de Foix before him, and closely connected to powerful *dévot* networks of Toulouse.

B. 19–5–1610 Toulouse. 2nd son of Georges, pres of *trésoriers de France*, and Marguerite de Garaud, daughter of a pres in parlt. Initially educated by private tutor, attended SJ coll at Toulouse, continuing at La Flèche, and ending in Paris (coll de Laon) with doct in canon law. Abbot in c of St-Volusien-de-Foix, in 1627, thanks to uncle and mentor, Bonventure de la Font. Apparently tempted by secular career, but came under influence of Condren, superior of Oratory, and entered St-Magloire seminary. Ordained priest ca 1636, established close ties with Olier, Vincent de Paul and other clerical reformers, and was involved in establishing seminaries of St-Lazare, and later St-Sulpice. Also participated in rural missions and other initiatives in late 1630s and early 1640s. His long episcopate was famous for its reforming austerity, during which he adopted Jansenist principles and proved a determined opponent of crown in *régale* dispute.

Resign by Jacques de Montrouge of claim to Pamiers to Caulet 10–6–1644. Nom 14–6–1644. Provs 16–1–1645. Cons 5–3–1645. D. 7–8–1680.

Biographical Dictionary 593

Sources: ASV, PC 44, fos 135–53. J-M Vidal, *François-Etienne de Caulet évêque de Pamiers 1610–1680* (Paris 1939); Vindry, *Parlementaires* (Toulouse), 217, 253. Villain, *France Moderne*, iii (1), 800–2. Navelle, *Familles toulousaines*, iii. 113–20. Barrau, *Dict du Rouergue*, iv. 181–4.

Caylar. *See* St-Bonnet

Cazet. *See* Caset

Champion, Guy. Tréguier 1619–35. Originally probably Breton rather than Norman, family were part of bourgeoisie of late-medieval Rennes, where from 1450s onwards they held variety of municipal offices. Also served dukes of Brittany, especially in financial capacities. Further social and professional advancement followed, and brought membership of order of St Michel to several members of family under Charles IX and his successors. It was for bp's eldest brother, René, that family lands were 'erected' into barony of Cicé, the *nom de terre* by which they were subsequently best known. Guy, bp of Tréguier, was first of several bps from this family, whose most illustrious member, Abp Champion de Cicé of Bordeaux, briefly served as keeper of the seals on eve of French Revolution.

B. ca 1583. Son of François, *chevalier de St-Michel* and royalist during League, and Françoise de la Chapelle. Educated largely in Univ of Paris, where studied with Jacques Camus, and probably took doct in canon law. Along with Camus, became *cons* in Paris parlt, suggesting he may initially have embarked on secular career. Only tonsured as cleric in Jan 1603, and ordained deacon in May 1611. By then abbot in c of St-Etienne of Fontenay, OSB (Bayeux). Also canon of ND de Paris, probably through patronage of Henri de Gondi, bp of Paris, to whom Champion was *familiaris*.

Nom 6–5–1619 (following the transfer to Rennes of brother-in-law, Pierre Cornulier, who resigned the see to Champion). Provs 2–10–1619. Cons in 1620. D. 14–9–1635.

Sources: ASV, PC 16, fos 267–87; PC 16, fos 291–308. AN, Z^{1}o 241 (ordination). Saulnier, 'L'Enfeu des Champion à Saint-Sauveur de Rennes 1519–1792', 169–95; Saulnier, *Parlement de Rennes*, i. 213–14. Kerhervé, *L'Etat breton aux xive et xve siècles*, 320–1, 869, 924, 942.

Chasteignier de la Rocheposay, Henri-Louis. Poitiers 1612–51. A well known noble family from Poitou in the service of the kings of France since Charles VIII, if not earlier. Successive members played active roles at court and in military engagements during wars of religion. Bp's father, a close companion of Henri III, supported Henri IV, who amply rewarded him and his children. Family's confessional allegiances were divided, but strong evidence of humanistic eirenicism is evident in their patronage of scholars like Scaliger. If anything, nobility of bp's mother's family, which was from Berry, was more impressive, and its Protestant affiliations more numerous. Bp's own acute sense of family's status later led him to employ André Duchesne to write its history and genealogy.

B. Tivoli 6–9–1577. Son of Louis (?-1595), sgr d'Abain, ambassador to Rome, gov of Haute and Basse Marche, and Claude du Puy. Reared by mother, who turned Protestant after her husband's death. Tutored initially by Tilenus and famous Scaliger, whom he accompanied to Leyden, 1591. But soon parted company with these Protestant mentors, deciding to follow church career after father's death and mother's conversion. Settled in Rome, where he took minor clerical orders, 2–6–1596. As later career shows, his learning was considerable, but hardly reflected in bacc in canon law attributed to him in 1607.

Although royal almoner to Henri IV in July 1601, he continued to reside in Rome where he moved in papal circles, and became a papal chamberlain. Through curial and French court connections, obtained several benefices in c – Nanteuil, OSB (Poitiers), St-Cyprien of Poitiers, OSB, La Couture, OSA (Luçon), Stafarda, O Cist (Turin, Piedmont). Henri IV granted him *brevet* promising him succession to Poitiers, 30–9–1607, but it was not followed up nor did it lead to coadjutorship for him before death of St-Belin, his predecessor. But Marie de' Medici honoured the king's promise. Combative and learned, *grand sgr* and political figure, he famously opposed, *les armes à la main,* prince of Condé in 1614.

Nom 1611. Provs 19–3–1612. Cons on 13–5–1612. D. 30–7–1651.

Sources: AD Vienne, H1, vol 2; BN, MS lat 18384 (copies of family papers). *Lettres missives de Henri IV*, iv. 201. Formon, 'Henri-Louis de la Rocheposay évêque de Poitiers (1612–1651)', 165–231. *DBF*, viii. 730–3.

Chery, Eustache de. Nevers coadj 1633/43–69. Family took its name from fief of Chéry in Bourbonnais, which they no longer owned after 1493. Traceable to Nicolas de Chéry, siegneur of Moulin-Porcher around 1350, they settled in Nivernais in 16th C, intermarrying with local middling *noblesse*, culminating in 1588 in 3rd marriage of Nicolas to Marguerite du Lis, daughter of Pierre and Eliane de St-Phalle, and sister of Bp Eustache du Lis. Other marriage connections, albeit indirect, were established between the two families during same century. Such connections were doubtless facilitated by father of Bp Eustache, Nicolas, serving in military 'compagnie' of Michel du Lis, who had himself served marshal Bourdillon and the duke of Nevers.

B. 23–11–1592. Son of Nicolas and Marguerite du Lis, sister of bp of Nevers. Scarcely anything known of education, but was enrolled in Paris arts faculty in 1621, though may not have taken degree. Uncle's patronage provided him with benefices and major offices in Nevers. *Curé* of Poiseux, Nevers, for a time, he was successively canon, treasurer (1618) and grand archdeacon in cathedral, and *official* (1628) of Nevers diocese. Almoner to Marie de' Medici in 1627, having attended 1625 AC along with uncle.

No date for nom as coadj, but possibly early 1633. Provs 26–9–1633. Cons in 1634. Succeeded uncle 1643 (but had administered diocese since 1640). Took nephew, Laurent de Chéry, as coadj 1659, but outlived him. D. 10–11–1669.

Chery, Laurent de. Nevers coadj 1659–61 (non successit). B. 26–3–1620 Moussy. 2nd son of François, sgr de Montgason, and Jeanne d'Armes. Studied humanities with SJ, followed by some theology at SJ coll in Bourges, having dedicated his (philosophy?) theses there to Marie Gonzaga, Queen of Poland and member of ducal family of Nevers. Subsequently took lic in canon law, Bourges, ca 1647. Thanks to episcopal uncle, he became both canon and grand archdeacon of Nevers, and then vg ca. 1653, having been ordained priest ca. 1651.

Procuration from uncle to take him as coadj 7–5–1657. Nom 31–5–1657. Provs 13–1–1659. Cons 27–4–1659. D. before succeeding to Nevers 31–1–1661.

Sources: AD Nièvre, 2F 29–30, 354, 416, 436; BN, P Or 736, doss 16827. A de Villenant, *Nobiliaire de Nivernois*, ii (Nevers 1900), 506–11. *Inventaire des titres de Nevers*, ed Soultrait, cols 137, 384–5, 681, 694–5 (family-general). AD Nièvre, 3E 1, 697, 24–8–1640; 1G 3. AC Nevers, BB 22, fos 108–9 (Eustache de Chéry). ASV, PC 56, fos 166–83 (Laurent de Chéry).

Chevrières. *See* **La Croix**

Choart de Buzenval, Nicolas. Beauvais 1650–79. Originally from Brie, family settled in Paris by mid-15th C. Jean was a *procureur* at Châtelet (d. 1445), while his son, Jean II, was *lieut-civil* of *prévôté* of Paris and important municipal figure under Louis XI. Subsequent generations remained within this world of judicial and financial officeholding, without making spectacular advances, but family connections were solid and extensive (e.g. Refuge, Allegrain). A change in profile is evident with Eustache, grandfather of bp of Beauvais, who carried out diplomatic missions under Henri IV, and his only son, Theodore (1577–1616), who followed a military career. Latter's marriage to Madeleine Potier de Blancmesnil in 1608 strengthened existing connections, although individual members continued to hold middling offices in *chambre des comptes* and elsewhere in 17th C.

B. 25–7–1611 Paris. Son of Théodore, sgr de Buzenval, and Madeleine Potier, sister of René and Augustin, successive bps of Beauvais. Educated at coll of Navarre, took doct in canon law in Paris. Briefly *cons* at Rennes parlt (1630–1), he accompanied duc de Créqui on embassy to Rome 1633–4, and became *cons* in *grand conseil* on return, later an MR and *cons d'état*. Only turned towards ecclesiastical career in 1643, when political eclipse of uncle, Bp Potier of Beauvais, blighted his political prospects. Entered Oratorian seminary of St-Magloire, taking priestly orders at some point before episcopal nom. A pro-Jansenist reformer who lived austerely, refusing early condemnations of Jansenism and imposing rigorist pastoral practices on his diocese.

Nom 11–5–1650. Provs 3–10–1650. Cons 8–1–1651. D. 21–7–1679.

Sources: ASV, PC 48, fos 283–302. AN, MC, LXXXVIII, 1312, Dossier of Choart family marriage contracts; MC, LXXXVI 184, 20–4–1608 (c.m. of bp's parents). Anselme, ii. 305–7. Bluche, *Origine des magistrats*, 132–3. Vindry, *Ambassadeurs*, 50. *DBF*, viii. 1175–9. *DGS*, 324.

Choiseul, Gilbert de. Comminges 1646–70, Tournai 1670–89. Although family lineage extended back for several centuries, its greatest achievements, socially and politically, were still to come in 18th C. Originally from southern Champagne, it developed numerous branches over centuries: that of du Plessis-Praslin commencing in later 16th C with Ferry, bp's father. By then, their extensive marriage alliances included several important noble families, especially among *noblesse militaire* whose activities resembled their own. Bp's own brother, Ferry II, temporarily threatened their position by joining Gaston d'Orléans' revolt 1632. Fidelity to Gaston survived unshaken through remainder of Louis XIII's reign, and he served as captain of his guards. During regency, he returned to royal service, became *maréchal de camp*, but supported Condé during Fronde, for which he again lost his regiment and offices. Meanwhile, his better known brother, César, became marshal of France (1645), minister of state (1652), and *duc et pair* (1665).

B. 1613 Paris. Son of Ferry, comte du Plessis-Praslin and Madeleine de Barthélemy (daughter of Guillaume, *cons* in *grand conseil*, and Marie Hennequin). Early education apparently in SJ coll at Reims, continuing in Paris, where took MA in 1637. Also studied theology there (in company of Abp La Feuillade of Embrun), obtaining lic in 1642, followed by doct and election as *socius* of Sorbonne. Ordained priest in 1641, having already accumulated several benefices in c – Boulencourt OSA, Basse-Fontaine, O Prem, Chantemerle, OSA, and St-Martin, OSA (all in Troyes diocese). Retained all but

Chantemerle on nom to Comminges. Rigorist rather than Jansenist, he was one of the doctors who refused to sign censure of Antoine Arnauld in 1655. Also strongly Gallican, he worked closely with Bossuet in 1682 Assembly which produced the 'four articles'.

Brevet de nom to Comminges 23–5–1644. Formal nom 30–5–1644. Provs 6–2–1646. Cons 8–4–1646. Transferred to Tournai 1670. D. 31–12–1689.

Sources: ASV, PC 46, fos 334–62. BN, MS lat 17025, fo 107; MS lat 16573; MS lat 9153, fo 83; MS lat 15440, p 173. Poutet, 'Docteurs de Sorbonne', 244. Clergeac, *Chronologie*, 56; Anselme, iv. 817–64 (extensive genealogy); Bourquin, *Noblesse seconde en Champagne*. R Butler, *Choiseul: Father and Son* (Oxford 1980). *DGS*, 324, 510. *DBF*, viii. 1204–5.

Claret, Louis de. St-Papoul 1626–36. Family's *nom de terre* was St-Félix but should not be confused with that of another Toulouse parlementaire family, the St-Félix. Clarets seem to have originated in or near Montpellier, where retained connections despite moving into Toulouse legal and office-holding circles during 16th C. Bp's mother was from much older noble family from same region, the Pelets de Vérune, some members of which were well entrenched in Montpellier chapter. Clarets own social success is evident from marriage of bp's sister to Aymar de Caylar de St-Bonnet, father of Claude de St-Bonnet, bp of Nîmes (1621–33) and Marshal Toiras, while his niece, Louise de Claret, married Bernard Reich de Pennautier, father of the celebrated financier, in 1621.

B. Toulouse at unknown date. 3rd son of Jean, sgr de St-Félix, and Philippe de Pelet de Vérune. Early studies probably in SJ coll, Toulouse, after which took law degree, also probably in Toulouse. Evidently destined for church career, he became canon of Toulouse and later succeeded a relative, Pons de Claret, as canon and provost of Montpellier cathedral. Also entered Toulouse parlt as *cons-cl* in 1600, serving until 1626. Also vg of Toulouse under its uncons archbp, Cardinal La Valette, during 1610s. Activities and influence ensured he served on several commissions in Languedoc and on delegations to court under Henri IV and Louis XIII. Also deputy to several ACs (1605, 1610, 1619). For all his experience, his elevation to St-Papoul was facilitated by the favour at court of Toiras relatives in mid-1620s.

Nom 5–5–1626. Provs 2–12–1626. Cons in 1627. D. 2–3–1636.

Sources: ASV, PC 24, fos 632–49; BN, Doss bleus 560, doss 14766. AD Haute-Garonne, B 419, fos 61, 471; B 439, fo 87. AD Hérault, G 1483. Anselme, vii. 789. Michaud, *L'Eglise et l'argent*, 319. Vindry, *Parlementaires* (Toulouse), 264. *DBF*, viii. 1359. J Segondy, 'La Famille languedocienne du maréchal de Toiras', *XXXIX Congrès de la Fédération Hist. du Languedoc Méditerrannéen et du Roussillon* (Montpellier 1976), 199–232.

Clausse, Henri. Châlons-sur-Marne coadj 1608/24–40. Family owed rapid rise to prominence, as indeed its ecclesiastical position, to Cosme, son of a modest *correcteur* in *chambre des comptes*, who entered service of future Henri II as secretary in 1540. In 1547, the new king made him *secretaire des finances*, and in due course he became one of the 4 secretaries of state. Like his colleagues, he and his family married within same circle of influential royal servants. Cosme's own marriage to Marie de Bourges eventually brought see of Châlons into family's grasp, since her brother, Jérôme, bp of Châlons (1556–71), resigned it to Nicolas Clausse, first of 3 members of family to hold it, in 1571. Thereafter, family's activities declined, but its influence, which enabled it to retain the see (and peerage) of Châlons, was preserved mainly via related families such as Neufville-Villeroy. Henri, last of the 3 Clausse bps of Châlons, remains the least known.

B. ca 1586. Son of Henri, successively *cons d'état, grand maître des Eaux et Forêts de France*, ambassador to Swiss in 1580s, and Denise de Neufville, daughter of Villeroy, the secretary of state. Nothing known of education, nor whether he took degree. Cleric at time of nom, he took minor and major orders between May and Dec 1611, and became priest in early 1612. Also held priory of St-Lau (Rouen) in c before episcopate. He administered see of Reims for several years under papal commission during episcopate of underage Henri de Guise. Had initiated steps to take Félix Vialart as coadj shortly before death.

No date for nom as coadj to uncle, Cosme. Provs 28–4–1608. Not cons until 16–8–1615. Succeeded uncle in 1624. D. 13–11–1640.

Sources: AN, Z^1o 241 (clerical orders). BN, MS lat 18290, fo 153v. Anselme, viii. 944–7. Michaud, *Grande Chancellerie*, 119, 132. Sutherland, *French Secretaries of State*. AD Marne, G 25, p 550; G 386 (*inventaire après décès*, 1640). *DBF*, viii. 1396–7.

Clérambault, Gilbert de. Poitiers 1658–80. Family lineage was ancient rather than distinguished, with some members tried for serious crimes by *grands jours* of Poitiers in 1567. Also related to Richelieu family from late 15th C. Only acquired *seigneurie* of Palluau, in Luçon diocese, by which they would generally be known thereafter, in early 17th C. Jacques, bp's father, was well rewarded for his energy in opposing Soubise revolt in Poitou, 1625, but family's true flowering was due largely to bp's younger brother, Philippe (1620–65), who served very effectively against Condé during Fronde in Berry and elsewhere, for which he was made a marshal of France in 1653, and gov of Berry in 1655.

B. 1611. Son of Jacques, baron of Palluau, and Louise Rigaud de Millepieds. Little known of education, but probably did not include univ attendance, since he only took doct in canon law in Paris a few weeks *after* his nom to Poitiers! Ordained priest at virtually same time (Oct 1657). He may have been member of Richelieu's entourage, but service to Mazarin as *maître de chambre* (a major household office) from 1646 onwards constituted his principal claim to episcopal preferment.

Nom 1–9–1657 (on resign of Antonio Barberini, who had failed to obtain papal provs). Provs 1–4–1658. Cons 21–7–1658. D. 3–1–1680.

Sources: ASV, PC 55, fos 395–411. Anselme, vii. 582–5. *DBF*, viii. 1460–2.

Clermont-Tonnerre, François de. Noyon 1661–1702. This powerful and well-connected family originated in the Dauphiné, and served the crown in military campaigns and in provincial posts, especially during 16th C. At same time, its interests shifted partly to Burgundy, where bp of Noyon's grandfather inherited Tonnerre title and married Catherine-Marie d'Escoubleau, sister of the 2 Sourdis brothers, archbps of Bordeaux. At least 2 other family members were bps during 16th C. These traditions of service were continued by succeeding generations, not least by bp's father, who became lt-gen of Bourbonnais in 1661.

B. Paris 1629. 3rd son of François and Marie Vignier de St-Liébault (widow of Urbain de Créqui). Early studies at coll of Clermont, Paris, followed by philosophy and theology at Univ, culminating in lic in theology in 1660, and doct in Feb 1661. Preached in several Parisian churches, ordained priest about 4 months before nom. Abbot in c of St-Martin, OSB (Langres).

Nom 27–2–1661. Provs 8–8–1661. Cons 2–10–1661. D. 15–2–1701.

Sources: ASV, PC 59, fos 342–58. BN, MS lat 16573, Nov 1660. Anselme, viii. 907–39. *DBF*, viii. 1514–18. Poutet, 'Docteurs de Sorbonne', 274. *Intendance de Champagne à la fin du xvii siècle*, 246–7.

Cohon, Anthime-Denis. Nîmes 1633–44, Dol 1644–8, Nîmes 1657–70. The humble origins of this masterly figure were widely commented on during his lifetime. From Craon near Le Mans, Cohon family members can be traced back to 1450s. Scattering later to neighbouring provinces, some 18th-C descendants resident in Angers were still trying to claim noble status on rather dubious grounds. Bp's father was a candle merchant who may have supported Catholic League, as bp's godfather clearly did. But it was his uncle, Jean, who was the decisive figure in Denis's career. Canon and archdeacon of Le Mans before becoming canon of Chartres, and holder of several other benefices, he educated his nephew, transferred his benefices to him, and did everything to advance the career of a young man with considerable natural energy and ambition.

B. 4–9–1595 Craon. Son of François, candle merchant, and Renée Hallay. Education probably began at Le Mans under uncle's direction. Completed humanities and studied law at Angers, where he probably took doct in utr. May have studied theology for a time in Paris, ca 1617, but took no degree there. Tonsured in 1610, ordained priest in 1619. By then, canon of Le Mans (and later grand archdeacon), he had begun to shine as preacher, esp in Paris, which brought him post of royal *prédicateur* in 1621. Subsequently made strong impression on Richelieu and his entourage, who were instrumental in his elevation to episcopate. Thanks initially to uncle, acquired several benefices in c before episcopate, with more to follow (and to exchange) later. His unpopularity forced him to leave Nîmes in 1644 for Dol, where his position also became rapidly untenable. By 1648, had quit Dol to live in Paris where he openly supported Mazarin during Fronde, for which cardinal gave him Nîmes for second time in 1655.

Nom to Nîmes 19–11–1633 (after the forced resign of bp Caylar de St Bonnet). Provs 24–7–1634. Cons 29–11–1634. Nom to Dol 19–2–1644. Provs 19–11–1644. Resign Dol 24–11–1648. 2nd nom to Nîmes 23–7–1655. Provs 27–8–1657. D. 7–11–1670.

Sources: ASV, PC 45, fos 284–300; PC 48, fos 659–60; PC 55, fos 252–67. Angot, *Dict de la Mayenne*, i. 688. Sauzet, *Contre-réforme et réforme catholique*, 217–44. Duine, *Un politique et un orateur au xviie siècle*. Duine, 'Cohon évêque de Nîmes et de Dol, précepteur des neveux de Mazarin, prédicateur du roi', *Bulletin de la Commission Historique et Archéologique de la Mayenne*, 23 (1907) 407–28, 24 (1908). *DBF*, ix.138–40.

Colbert, Nicolas. Luçon 1661–71, Auxerre 1671–6. Few families in French history can have projected such an idealised vision of their origins and advancement in the service of the crown as the Colberts. Municipal office in Reims, international trade, banking activities in Paris and Lyon, financial office-holding of various kinds characterised a family with branches based in Reims, Troyes and Paris, and leaves little of myth of Louis XIV's minister as self-made man intact. Colbert's own father was a financier of second rank whose business acumen was not infallible. Marriage alliances to families from same milieu provided them with solid foundations, while early patronage of Michel le Tellier was crucial to Jean-Baptiste, bp's brother and future minister, as it enabled him to enter Mazarin's personal service during Fronde. Mazarin's inability – or unwillingness – to distinguish between his private affairs and those of crown, allowed Colbert to extend his connections as well as to place a large number of brothers and cousins in coveted positions. Nom of Nicolas to Luçon was one of Mazarin's last decisions, just a month before his death, and was all the more welcome in that the Colberts had for years been pestering the ageing bp of Luçon to take Nicolas as his coadj.

B. 1628 Reims. Son of Nicolas, *sieur* de Vendières, and Marie Pussort. Early studies in Jesuit coll at Reims, followed by theology in Paris, where he took 2nd place in lic in 1658, and doct in 1659. Elected *socius* of Sorbonne, having been *prieur* there while student. Canon of Mâcon as early as 1651, fraternal favour with Mazarin obtained him post of royal librarian in 1656 and, more conventionally, a collection of benefices in c (ND du Landais, O Cist (Béziers), St-Sauveur-des-Vertus, OSB (Châlons-sur-Marne), St-Vincent-sous-Vergy, and St-Denis of Nogent-le-Rotrou, OSB (Chartres)). Also also *prévôt* of Rugny. Ordained priest in 1657.

Nom to Luçon 8–2–1661. Provs 30–5–1661. Cons 24–7–1661. Transferred to Auxerre 1671. D. 5–9–1676.

Sources: ASV, PC 51, fos 947–58; PC 59, fos 179–90. AD Saône-et-Loire, 2G 21. BN, MS lat 15440, p 202. Poutet, 'Docteurs de Sorbonne', 266. J-L Bourgeon, *Les Colbert avant Colbert* (Paris 1973).

Corneilhan, Bernardin *Vernède* de. **Rodez coadj 1605/14–45.** Patronymic Vernède. Family originated from Corneilhan in Armagnac, to west of Auch. Of long if relatively undistinguished lineage, they owed their ultimate fortune to admittedly short-lived marriage in 1515 of Jean to Jeanne Marguerite d'Armagnac, sister of Cardinal Georges d'Armagnac, a powerful ecclesiastical and political figure in Languedoc, successively bp of Rodez and abp of Toulouse. Not only did the family then settle in Rouergue, but it was also through the cardinal that Jacques, the first Corneilhan bp, acquired sees of Vabres (1548) and Rodez (1561), both previously held by Armagnac himself. Jacques was succeeded in 1580 by his nephew François, whose tribulations arising out of conflicts of Catholic League in Rodez were legendary, and which carried over into his successor's reign.

B. 1579. Son of Antoine and Jeanne de Lau. Little known about education, but studied at Toulouse with Jean-Louis Bertier, future bp of Rieux, and took lic in theology there. Canon of Rodez and archdeacon of Conques, ordained priest in April 1604. Prior in c of St-Mont, O Cluny (Auch) before episcopate.

No date for nom as coadj to uncle. Provs 3–8–1605. Cons 1–1–1606. Succeeded uncle in 1614. D. 8–9–1645.

Sources: AD Aveyron, G 201, fo 69 (1604). BN, MS Lat 17028, fos 117–27 (3 episcopal testaments); MS Fr 20477, fo 365. Barrau, *Dict du Rouergue*, iii. 133–43. Anselme, vii. 270–1. Navelle, *Familles toulousaines*, iii. 229. Dubédat, *Histoire du parlement de Toulouse*, i. 531–2. *DBF*, ix. 672–3.

Cornulier, Pierre. Tréguier 1617–19, Rennes 1619–39. The royal historiographer, du Haillan, traced this family to ancient house of Cornillé, but there are few signs of them anywhere before 16th C. Bp's father, Pierre, owed his fortune and advancement to Jean de Brosse, duc d'Etampes and gov of Brittany under Francis I, serving both him and his successor as secretary, before becoming *trésorier général* of Breton finances in 1570. Mayor of Nantes for a time, he also served Mercoeur when he became gov in 1588. After Cornulier's death, Mercoeur protected his offspring, and bp's eldest brother, Claude, succeeded father as *trésorier* in 1588, serving as royal commissioner at Breton estates of 1590 and 1593, only to turn against League and Mercoeur soon afterwards.

B. 1575 Nantes. Son of Pierre, and Claude de Comaille, daughter of Toussaint, *intendant des affaires* of Admiral Annebault. Nothing known about education, but held lic in utr by 1593. Seems to have been ordained priest few years later. *Cons-cl* in Rennes parlt in 1597, an office he held until 1616. Offices and attractive benefices also came his way: dean of Nantes after 1593, abbot in c of Ste-Croix-de-Guingamp, OSA (Tréguier) in 1598, St-Méen, OSB (St-Malo) in 1601, and ND de Blanche Couronne, OSB (Nantes) in 1612. Attendance at 1614 EG showed he had become a prominent figure in Breton clergy.

Nom to Tréguier 1616. Provs 3–4–1617. Cons date unknown. Resign Tréguier to brother-in-law, Guy Champion, when nom to Rennes on 7–5–1619. Provs 29–7–1619. D. 21–7–1639.

Sources: ASV, PC 16, fos 291–308. BN, P Or 862, doss 19,322. Saulnier, 'L'Enfeu des Champion à Saint-Sauveur de Rennes 1519–1792', 169–95; Saulnier, *Parlement de Bretagne*, i. 262–71. *Supplement à la généalogie de la maison de Cornulier imprimée en 1847* (Nantes 1860), 114–17. *DBF*, ix. cols 710–12.

Cornusson. *See* **La Valette de Cornusson**

Cosnac, Daniel de. Valence 1655–87, Aix 1687–1708. From established old noble family of the Limousin. B. June 1626, 3rd son of François, marquis de Dugnac, and Eléonor de Talleyrand de Chalais. Educated mainly at coll of Navarre, where he apparently studied theology for up to 3 years under Denis Guyart, who later claimed that he had defended his theses and taken bacc in theology. He was tonsured at early age, but if destined for clerical career by his family, it did not prevent him from throwing himself into politics during Fronde, when he was *premier gentilhomme* to Conti and one of his principal advisers. Having helped negotiate his patron's marriage to Mazarin's niece, he persuaded him to obtain see of Valence for him from the cardinal. Ordained priest in mid-1654, possibly just after his nom. His episcopal career was no less political than the circumstances of his entry to upper clergy.

Nom to Valence 24–6–1654. Provs 21–4–1655. Cons 24–10–1655. Abp of Aix 1687. D. 18–1–1708.

Sources: ASV, PC 53, fos 1243–59. Daniel de Cosnac, *Mémoires*, ed J de Cosnac, 2 vols (Paris 1852). *DBF*, ix. cols 748–50.

Cospeau, Philippe. Aire 1606–21, Nantes 1621–36, Lisieux 1636–46. The only French bp of this period from the Spanish Netherlands, Cospeau originated in the *bonne bourgeoisie* of Mons, where his family were established and frequently held municipal office since early 15th C. Bp's father was accused of association with the rule of the Calvinists during their brief domination of Mons in 1572, and was forced to flee, but returned later after being pardoned.

Baptised 15–2–1571 at Mons. 3rd son of Louis, medical doctor, and Michelle Mainsent. Took humanities at coll of Houdain, Mons, and continued studies in Louvain arts faculty from 1588 onwards, where his masters included celebrated Lipsius and Jesuit Lessius. He probably began theology studies in Louvain but, apparently reluctant to pursue them there, moved to Paris, around 1598. Lic in theology at Sorbonne in 1604, but never took final *épreuves* for doct. Naturalised in Nov 1601, by which time he had become priest. Taught philosophy in Univ of Paris and was respected preacher, activities which attracted the patronage of Angennes-Rambouillet family and duc d'Epernon. A canon of St-Germain, Mons by 1588, he resigned in 1598, but was made a canon of Cambrai in 1605. One of the most admired figures of French episcopate, he drew over a generation of ecclesiastics and future bps to him. Member of first *conseil de conscience* in 1643.

No date for nom to Aire (but ca early 1606). Provs 4–12–1606. Cons 18–2–1607. Transferred to Nantes 1621, to Lisieux 1635–6. D. 8–5–1646.

Sources: ASV, PC 34, fos 494–514 (Nantes 1635). BN, MS lat 15440, p 129. Emile Jacques, *Philippe Cospeau: Un ami-ennemi de Richelieu 1571–1646* (Paris 1989).

Cous, Antoine de. Condom coadj 1604/17–47 (resign). B. 2–1–1573 at Treignac in the upper Limousin, Antoine was the son of Philippe and of Marie du Chemin, sister of Jean du Chemin bp of Condom since 1581 in succession to Jean de Monluc, whom he had served in several senior positions. All the signs are that the 1581 succession was dictated by the Monluc family, and both du Chemin and Cous would pay heavy pensions off Condom, a wealthy diocese, to members of Monluc family. Relatively little known about family background, but likely that his episcopal uncle was key to career. It appears he studied in Bordeaux, where his uncle, a strong *ligueur*, was often to be found, and that he took at least the lic in utr there. A canon of Condom at 15, he later became archdeacon and vg to uncle around 1598, having been ordained priest in 1595. Travelled to Rome to obtain provs as coadj, and became client of Cardinal du Perron there.

No date for nom as coadj. Provs 15–3–1604. Cons 28–3–1604 in Rome. Succeeded uncle 1616. Resign Condom to Jean d'Estrades in 1647. D. 15–2–1648.

Sources: ASV, Acta Misc. 97, fo 108. *Gallia*, ii. 970–1. Clergeac, *Chronologie*, 158. Mazéret, *Chroniques de l'église de Condom*, 251–319.

Cros, Antoine de. St-Paul-Trois-Châteaux 1599–1630. Cros became bp for reasons very similar to those of Antoine de Cous. Modest, obscure family from village of Grignan who, like their relatives the Gaumes, were dependents of the Adhémar de Grignan family who secured St-Paul for both these bps. Thanks to bp's patronage, some of his siblings settled at St-Paul, with one or two clerics among them entering his personal service. Little is known of them after 1630 when Grignan family took direct control of St-Paul.

B. Richerenches 1565. Son of Etienne and Anne Gaume, sister of Antoine Gaume, bp of St-Paul (1585–98). Nothing known of education, but was regarded as holding doct in utr. May not have been intially destined for ecclesiastical career at all, as not even a cleric when nom: it is possible his uncle died prematurely, and he was, unexpectedly perhaps, put forward by the comte de Grignan as successor.

No date for nom. Provs 19–7–1599. Cons 19–7–1599. D. 24–2–1630.

Sources: *Hierarchia Catholica*, iv. 344, 'Tricastrin', n 3. *Gallia*, i. 732. *Gallia Chr Nov*, iv. cols 562–82. *DBF*, ix. 1278. Villain, *France moderne*, ii. 316. Boyer de Sainte Marthe, *Histoire de l'église cathédrale de Saint-Paul-Trois-Châteaux*, 244–55.

Crusy. *See* **Marsillac**

Cupif, Robert. St-Pol-de-Léon 1640–8, Dol 1648–59. This Scottish family settled in Anjou in 1440–50s and subsequently developed several branches, some of whom were active in legal profession, the *échevinage* of Angers (4 mayors), and variety of local financial and *présidial* offices during 16th and early 17th C. But it was non-Angers based branches (inc that of bp of St-Pol) which proved the more vigourous and adventurous. *Surintendant* Fouquet's grandmother was a Cupif, while bp's sister, Marie, married Christophe Fouquet de Chalain, pres *à mortier* in Rennes parlt. Bp's father began as barrister before entering Paris parlt. Bp was nearly upstaged by a cousin, François, doct of Sorbonne, who converted to Protestantism in 1636 and ended career as pastor in the Dutch republic.

B. Paris, ca 1600. Son of Elie, originally from Angers, and Marie Grimaudet, daughter of an *élu* from Angers. Studied humanities and philosophy in Univ of Paris, and law at Angers, where he took lic in utr, ca 1622. Ordained priest some years later, ca 1627. Brother-in-law, Fouquet de Chalain, probably instrumental in facilitating his pre-episcopal career in Brittany. Initially prior of Folgoat, became canon and archdeacon of Quimper, ca. 1626, and vg and *official* there for over 10 years. Not original choice of successor to deposed René de Rieux, but recommended to Richelieu by Harlay de Sancy, bp of St-Malo and, in all likelihood, by Fouquet relatives.

Nom to St-Pol-de-Léon 26–3–1637. Provs 16–1–1640. Cons 25–3–1640. Unable to control Léon after Richelieu's death and Rieux's rehabilitation in 1645. Transferred to Dol in 1648. Provs 13–11–1652. D. 21–9–1659.

Sources: ASV, PC 38, fos 414–30. AAE, France 1504, fo 166. BN, MS Baluze 175, fos 58–65. AD Côtes d'Armor, 5G 562. AD Ile-et-Vilaine, 5 Fa 27 (docs on Dol transfer 1648). Port, *Dict du Maine-et-Loire*, i. 869–71. De Launay, *Recherches sur les familles des maires d'Angers*, ii. 27–60. D Dessert, *Fouquet* (Paris 1987). DHGE, xiii. 1112–13.

Dabbadie. *See* **Abbadie**

Daffis, Jean. Lombez coadj 1594/7–1614. As befitted one of the most notable parlementaire dynasties of southern France, members of Daffis (de Affis, d'Affis) family moved in and out of the most senior offices in Bordeaux and Toulouse parlts for over a century, though origins and effective family seat were Toulousain. Despite claims to medieval noble title, they only emerged from merchant class of Toulouse to hold municipal office from 1442 onwards. Law practice (initially as professors at univ) followed for nearly 3 generations before they somewhat slowly moved into office in parlt with Jean I (*cons* in 1536, first pres in 1563), father of first Daffis bp. Thereafter their parlementaire record was impressive. Jean's son, Guillaume, first pres in Bordeaux. Later generations also served in both parlts – e.g. Jean II, father of last Daffis bishop of Lombez, was first pres in parlt of Navarre, where he contributed to restoration of Catholicism, before temporarily filling same position in Bordeaux (1628–31). Daffis family was strongly anti-Huguenot, championed militant Catholicism of Toulouse, and acted as protectors of SJ, as well as other Counter-Reformation orders (Capuchins, Récollets). Family's episcopal record was scarcely less continuous and remarkable, although confined to second-ranking diocese, and resembles that of another rising Toulouse parlementaire family, the Bertier.

B. ca 1554 Bordeaux. Son of Jean, first pres of Toulouse parlt, and Catherine Tournoer. Nothing known of education, but held doct in utr. Canon of Toulouse and provost of St-Sernin church, served as vg to often absent Cardinal Joyeuse after he became abp in 1588. Papal nuncio, Ragazzoni, thought Henri III wanted to make him abp of Toulouse in

1584, but he was suspected of keeping a mistress. Ardent member of Toulouse Catholic League, but circumstances of his nom to Lombez remain obscure.

No date for nom as coadj. Provs 19–1–1594. Cons date unknown. Succeeded 1597. D. 1–2–1614.

Daffis, Bernard. Lombez 1614–27. Baptised 7–6–1586 in Bordeaux. 2nd son of Guillaume, first pres of Bordeaux parlt, and Lucrèce des Places. Educated by SJ in Toulouse, where he also began univ studies, completing them in Bordeaux (where Bp Maytie of Oloron was fellow student) and taking doct in utr. Protonotary apostolic and royal almoner, also well endowed with benefices before episcopate: abbot in c of La Case-Dieu, O Prem (Auch), in 1610, St-Martin-de-Brenne (Luçon), and 2 other priories. Tonsured in 1595, ordained subdeacon in Dec 1605, and priest between 1611 and 1614. Appears to have contracted some form of marriage which he travelled to Rome to have annulled in 1607.

Brevet de nom 30–1–1614 (2 days before uncle-predecessor's death, so may initially have been designated as coadj). Provs 17–3–1614. Cons 1–6–1614. D. 20–12–1627.

Daffis, Jean. Lombez 1628–57. B. 1604 Bordeaux. Son of Jean II, then second pres in Bordeaux parlt, and Catherine Loupès. Educated initially at La Flèche and Paris until ca 1620, then at Bordeaux, where obtained docts in canon law and theology – unique combination for bp of his generation. Tonsured in 1617, deacon by time of nom, ordained priest day before his cons! Already had some experience as preacher, thanks to goodwill of Cardinal Sourdis of Bordeaux. Underage when nom which caused some discussion and embarrassment in king's entourage.

Nom 31–12–1627. Provs 21–8–1628. Cons 12–11–1628. D. 16–11–1657.

Sources: Vindry, *Parlementaires* (Bordeaux), 39; *ibid* (Toulouse), 141–2, 238. *DBF*, ix. 1472–3. Navelle, *Familles toulousaines*, iv. 2–11 (family-general). ASV, Misc Arm XII, 216, fo 323. *ANG*, ii (Nunciature of G. Ragazzoni), 255, 272. Dubédat, *Parlement de Toulouse*, i. 488. Vindry *Parlementaires* (Toulouse), 276 (Jean). ASV, PC 13, fos 311–43; Acta Camerarii 14, fo 265. AM Toulouse, GG 193. Clergeac, *Chronologie*, 164. L Bertrand, 'Bernard d'Affis, évêque de Lombez', *Revue de Gascogne*, n.s., 5 (1905), 515–16 (Bernard). ASV, PC 25, fos 317–63. AD Gironde, G 803, fo 387. BI, MS Godefroy 15, fo 394 (Jean).

Daillon du Lude, René. Bayeux 1598–1600. This old family emerged into limelight under Charles VII and Louis XI, and from then its leading members held high court office, numerous military commands, and provincial governorships. Jean II, father of René, was typical in this regard, active in the Italian campaigns and in quelling disorders in France (e.g. Guyenne), as was René's brother, Guy, gov of Poitou from 1560 onwards. Bp Gaspard's father was *sénéchal* of Anjou, lt-gen of Auvergne, and gov of Gaston d'Orléans 1608. Extensive marriage alliances (e.g. Motier de la Fayette, Schomberg, Illiers, Batarnay, Laval) faithfully reflect their activity and status.

B. 1526. Younger son of Jean II, comte du Lude after 1545, and Anne de Batarnay. Little known about early career. Received see of Luçon in 1553 in succession to an uncle, but unclear if, uncons, he ever effectively took possession of it, and in any case, he exchanged it for ND des Chastelliers, O Cist (Saintes). Subsequently, all but abandoned any pretence of being cleric, taking up arms in defence of Catholicism in Poitou during religious wars and becoming gov of Niort. A commander of Henri III's new military *Ordre du St Esprit* from its inception. Rallying to Henri IV in 1589, he became a leading ecclesiastical advisor in following years. Apparently, marshal Matignon, his brother-in-law, obtained see of Bordeaux for him after death of Abp Prévost in 1591, but he declined it. See of Bayeux seems to have been held 'en administration' by Cardinal Bourbon after 1586, but Henri III may initially have nom Daillon to it in early 1589, a gift renewed by Henri IV.

No date for nom. Provs 11–2–1598. Cons date unknown. D. 8–3–1600.

Daillon, Gaspar de. Agen 1631–4, Albi 1634–76. B. 1602 Paris. Son of François comte du Lude, and Françoise de Schomberg, sister of marshal Henri de Schomberg. Educated mostly at La Flèche, where Bp Barrault of Bazas tonsured him ca 1614. Took doct in canon law in Rome, where he resided for many years before entering episcopate. Deputy to 1625 AC for Bordeaux province. Also 'inherited' abbey of Chasteliers from previous family incumbents. Transfer from Agen to Albi arose out out 1632 revolt in Languedoc, and installation of his cousin Hallwin-Schomberg as new provincial gov. A difficult, authoritarian bp, he provoked frequent friction in his diocese.

Nom to Agen 5–1–1631. Provs 12–5–1631. Cons 24–8–1631. Nom to Albi Oct 1634. Provs 28–1–1636. D. 25–7–1676.

Sources: ASV, PC 34, fos 382–402. Anselme, viii. 188–92. Vindry, *Etat major*, 66, 185–6, 188. *Chronique d'Etienne de Cruseau*, i. 50–1. *DBF*, ix. 1499–1504.

Danès de Marly, Jacques. Toulon 1640–58 (resign). Originally relatively modest, but numerous family of merchants present in Paris from 15th C, where they were strongly represented in drapery, haberdashery, and related trades during early to mid-16th C, and whose marriage alliances were in same social milieu. Subsequently, its various branches were not notably successful in improving their fortunes, marriages with families like Hennequin and Séguier notwithstanding, so that 2 best known members were bps – Pierre, distinguished humanist bp of Lavaur (1497–1577) and Jacques (below). In second half of 16th and early 17th C, various family members held royal offices, esp as SRs or in *chambre des comptes*. Bp's father was Huguenot during early 1560s at least, but reverted to Catholicism before his marriage, gave up business, and entered world of office-holding via a post of *notaire-secretaire du roi* in 1568.

B. Paris 1600. Son of Jacques, sgr de Marly, successively pres in *chambre des comptes*, MR, *cons d'état*, and Anne Hennequin. Probably educated in Univ of Paris, e.g. studied philosophy coll of Calvi under Jacques Lescot (later bp of Chartres). Lic in civil law at Orléans in 1622. Pres in *chambre des comptes*, *cons* in *grand conseil*, MR, *cons d'état*. Married Madeleine de Thou, daughter of Jacques, the historian. Both his wife and only son pre-deceased him, leading him to abandon his commission as a provincial intendant and take orders, priesthood included, which he did in Jan 1639, only months after episcopal nom.

Nom 30–10–1638. Provs 9–1–1640. Cons 6–5–1640. Resign to Pierre Pingré, June 1658. D. 5–6–1662.

Sources: ASV, PC 38, fos 698–716. BN, MS Fr 32989, fo 248. AN, MC, LXXVIII, 130 (c.m. of bp's parents, 14–9–1584). Tessereau, *Chancellerie*, 135. Michaud, *Grande Chancellerie*, 172. Vidal, *Critique*, 218, 306. *Gallia Chr Nov*, v. 659–62. D Richet, *De la Réforme à la révolution* (Paris 1992). *DBF*, x. 90–1.

Davy. *See* **Du Perron**.

Delauro, Thomas. Vabres 1594–9. Family was long resident near, and in, Rodez, where they were among leading tax-payers and *notables* by early to mid-16th C. They also included several generations of notaries, which enabled Hugues, bp's father, to serve as secretary and notary to episcopal admin of Rodez from 1530s to 1570s. Patronage of Cardinal d'Armagnac and his successors, Jacques and François Corneilhan, was evidently considerable in family's ascent into governing élite of Rodez. Bp's brother Antoine succeeded their father as notary and secretary to *évêché*, but also became *greffier* of Estates of Haut-Rouergue. Delauro family members supported Bp Corneilhan in crisis of 1589 and later in Rodez. They continued to prosper in subsequent generations, providing numerous canons and number of judges and magistrates of Rodez. Despite this, they were in no position to retain see of Vabres after 1599 in face of much more powerful La Valette-Cornusson interest, though Georges Delauro, *cons* at Rodez présidial and canon-cantor of Rodez cathedral, held pension off Vabres under bp Thomas's successor.

B. Rodez, probably early 1530s. Son of Hugues and Rose Boniol. Nothing known of education, but was bacc in canon law by 1555, and doctor in utr by 1569. Canon of Rodez in 1555, in succession to Jacques de Corneilhan, bp of Vabres, and cantor there in 1569. A priest by 1550, he later served Corneilhan as vg of Rodez. Also held priory of St-Amand in c before episcopate. Deputy to AC of 1579–80, in place of bp of Rodez.

No date for nom to Vabres (vacant since 1585), but possibly during 1589 and with Mayenne's support. Provs 1–6–1594. Cons date unknown. D. 29–9–1599.

Sources: AD Aveyron, E 1782 (testament of Antoine, 1603), G 191, pp 101–2; G 195, fos 133–4; 15J, vols 1–2, 13; AC Rodez, CC 75, 148, 158; Duranthon, *Collection des procès-verbaux des assemblées du clergé de France*, i. 117.

Delbène, Alphonse II. Albi coadj 1608–34. One of the most prominent Florentine financial and merchant families to attach themselves to French interests, via world of Lyon banking, since early 16th C, when forced out of Florentine politics by their anti-Medici republican positions. Naturalised in 1533, their financial services to monarchy were extremely important, especially under Henri II, whom Albisse Delbène served in several capacities, not least as *surintendant des finances*. They also brought wider social and political opportunites, which included 2 initial episcopal promotions – in 1561 to Nîmes, in 1588 to Albi, one of France's richest dioceses and held by Italian families like Medici, Strozzi or Ridolfi since 1560s. Meanwhile, abandoned their financial roles for those of courtiers and landed proprietors, with male and female members serving in households of Henri IV and Louis XIII, but also of Marie de' Medici and Gaston d'Orléans. Endogamy within fellow Italian families also gave way to alliances with French upper nobility. Royal goodwill flowed from such activities, but their position was severely shaken by Languedoc revolt of 1632 in which Alphonse II, bp of Albi, played prominent role. Yet damage limited, as crown appeared unwilling to disgrace family as a whole, which would help explain appointment of Barthélemy as bp of Agen in 1636 and that of Alphonse III to Orléans in 1646, though by then Gaston d'Orléans's patronage paid clear dividends.

B. 1580. 3rd son of Julien and Catherine Tornabuoni. No information on education, but appears to have taken doct in utr. Canon in 1598 and first archdeacon of Albi in 1602, thanks to his uncle and predecessor; abbot in c of St-Pierre-d'Hautvilliers, OSB (Reims) by similar means. Before 1632 revolt, had been important political figure in Languedoc:

gov of Albi, *lieutenant du roi* in Albigeois, *cons* in Toulouse parlt and *chambre des comptes* of Montpellier.

Nom coadj 22–9–1607. Provs 4–2–1608. Cons 1608. Succeeded Feb 1608. Deposed for rebellion 19–7–1634, exiled in Florence. Rehabilitated in 1645, but failed to regain Albi. D. 5–1–1651.

Delbène, Barthélemy. Agen 1636–56. B. 1606. 4th son of Pierre and Anne Delbène (cousins). Early education at La Flèche (along with Denis de La Barde), philosophy in Paris, it seems, ending with lic in canon law, Paris. He may also have studied theology for 2 years in company of future Bp Grangier of Tréguier at Sorbonne, ca 1626–7. Abbot in c of St-Pierre-d'Hautvillers, OSB (Reims). Resided in Rome for several years in entourage of Cardinal Barberini. Simple cleric at time of nom. The most curious element in his episcopal career is how soon it followed disgrace and deposition of uncle, bp of Albi. It may have been calculated to appease Rome and Delbène's Barberini patrons.

Nom 1–3–1635. Provs 9–6–1636. Cons 2–11–1636. D. 20–5–1656.

Delbène, Alphonse III. Orléans 1647–65. B. 1600 in Sens dioc. Elder brother of Barthélemy above. Educated partly in Paris, partly in Toulouse, where took doct in canon law. Held abbey of Mezières, O Cist (Chalon-sur-Saône) in c from 1609 onwards, following death of Alphonse I of Albi, and was also provost of St-Selve (Albi). Also seems to have served as vg of bp of Rieux for his lands located in Auch diocese. Ordained priest Mar 1646 in obvious expectation, given his age, of episcopal nom.

Nom 4–5–1646. Provs 21–1–1647. Cons 27–5–1647. D. 20–5–1665.

Sources: Vidal, *L'Ancien diocèse d'Albi*, 12–42. Lacger, *Etats administratifs*, 311–12. Compayré, *Etudes historiques et documents inédits sur l'Albigeois*, 103–11. Dubost, 'Les Italiens en France aux xvie et xviie siècles', 269–70, 300–1, 447, 623–4, 629–32. *DBF*, x. 762–3 (family-general). ASV, PC 34, fos 467–87 (Alphonse III); PC 46, fos 85–103 (Barthélemy).

Deschaux, Bertrand. Bayonne 1599–1617, Tours 1617–41. The Deschaux were an ancient noble family from Béarn-Navarre, allied to the Albrets, but despite remaining Catholic were reconciled with Albrets during the 1570s. Such Béarnais connections were no disadvantage in 1590s, when their kinsman became Henri IV. Yet although a bp in his native region and enjoying obvious royal goodwill, Bertrand experienced considerable harrassment from Antoine de Grammont gov of Bayonne, and willingly moved to Tours in 1617.

B. 1556 Baigorry (Béarn). Son of Antoine, vicomte de Baigorry, and Catherine de St Esteben. Nothing known about education, possibly because originally destined for secular, military career. Circumstances in which he turned towards church are obscure, as are those of his initial nom by Henri IV to Bayonne. Nominally an almoner to Henri IV before episcopate, he was not even a tonsured cleric until June 1598.

Nom to Bayonne 1595, renewed in face of papal non-approval 22–9–1597. Provs 17–3–1599. Cons in 1599. Nom to Tours 11–5–1617. Provs 26–6–1617. Took Victor Bouthillier as coadj in 1630. D. 21–5–1641.

Sources: BN, Doss bleus 249, doss 6462. AN, Z^{1}o 240 (tonsure). Anselme, iv. 133. *Lettres missives de Henri IV*, i. 850; iv. 1066. Orcibal, *Saint-Cyran*, 102–3. *DBF*, xii. 1109–10. Tamizey de Larroque, 'Bertrand d'Eschaus', *Revue de Gascogne*, 5 (1864), 596–616; 20 (1879), 297–310, 403–11.

Desclaux, Jacques. Dax 1639–58. Relatively obscure family from Mugron in the Landes, which only began to emerge as office-holders in generation *after* that of bp: by later 17th C, they held parlementaire office and produced a bp of Lescar (1681–1716). Virtually nothing known about earlier generations. Richelieu connection was clearly decisive in ecclesiastical sphere, and it may well have helped to propel younger generations into a new social and professional world.

B. 1593. Son of Armand and Françoise de Cabannes. Educated by SJ at Agen and esp Toulouse, where he took bacc in theology. Briefly principal of coll at Aire under Cospeau, and successively *chapelain* of Buglose, *curé* of Ste-Croix, Meilhan, and Ygos (1631) before episcopate. Although Cospeau may have influenced his early career, it was the favour enjoyed by his brother Dominique (d. 1638), Richelieu's confessor, which was almost certainly key to his episcopal advancement.

Nom 21–11–1638. Provs 11–4–1639. Cons 2–6–1639. D. 4–4–1658.

Sources: ASV, PC 37, fos 114–26. Clergeac, *Chronologie*, 37, n 3 (ref to papal dispensation *super defectus gradus doctoratus*). JP Labatut, *Noblesse, pouvoir et société en France au xviie siècle*, 174. Deloche, *Maison de Richelieu*, 90. Degert, *Histoire des évêques de Dax*, 323. *Gallia*, i. 1059–60. *DBF* x. 1290.

Deslandes, Noel, OP. Treguier 1636–45. Celebrated in his own time for his rise from obscurity, Deslandes was, by own later account, born ca 1573 at St-Cyr-du-Gault, in Tours diocese, son of Michel and N . . . Thibaut, both long dead before he became widely known and said to be of extremely modest origins. Entering Dominican convent at Blois at an early age, he studied in the order, completing his humanities at Bourges, and taking lic and doct in theology in Paris, 1608. A priest from 1608, he established a reputation as preacher, with long experience in various towns and dioceses, and worked at request of bps like Sourdis of Bordeaux and Etampes of Chartres. He was also prior of Jacobin convent, rue St-Jacques, and provincial of Dominicans, 1626–8. His reputation ensured he was long regarded as candidate for mitre, but his long wait (proposed for Nantes in 1621, and 62 years old at nom) and his diocese (Tréguier in northern Brittany) suggest the reward was both slow and less than readily granted.

Nom 22–9–1635. Provs 28–1–1636. Cons in 1636. D. 19–8–1645.

Sources: ASV, PC 34, fos 515–36; fo 456v. BN, MS lat 15440, p 135. Touron, *Hommes illustres de l'ordre de St Dominique*, v. 268–78. J Hennequin, *Henri IV dans ses oraisons funèbres* (Paris 1977), 267. *DBF*, x. 1417 (erroneous on several counts).

Despruets, Bernard. St-Papoul 1636–55. Despruets (or Despruetz) family were notaries from Garos in Béarn (Lescar diocese). Bp may also have been related to Jean Despruetz (1521–96), energetic abbot-general of Prémontré, but nature of connection is unclear. During 16th C, several members were *curés* or minor local church dignitaries. The same pattern, but on a higher and more successful level, is evident in next century. While Bernard's elder brother was still a notary, his other 4 brothers were cathedral canons, 2 in Saintes, 2 in Lescar.

B. 1583. Son of Jean, notary at Garos, and N . . . Little known of education, but partly in Toulouse, where a canon of Lescar tutored him for time and where he obtained a doct in theology. *Curé* of Orthez in Béarn, ca 1614, centre of activity soon moved to Saintes, where he became cathedral canon and was involved in disputations with local Protestant pastors in 1618. Although background to this move is obscure, it helped him establish close ties with Bérulle, esp in connection with local Carmelite convent which he tried to reform/govern on Bérulle's behalf. One of the doctors who approved Bérulle's *Grandeurs de Jesus* in 1623, and regarded by Bérulle as a worthy candidate for episcopal office in later years. Probably priest from early 1610s, he subsequently became canon and *théologal* of Lescar, probably in late 1620s.

Nom 30–3–1636. Provs 1–9–1636. Cons 9–11–1636. D. 20–7–1655.

Sources: ASV, PC 30, fos 158–79. AD Pyrénées-Atlantiques, *Inv sommaire* E series, vols 1273–1316 (numerous family references). Pierre de Marca, *Histoire de Béarn*, i. cxxxix. *Corr de Bérulle*, iii. 346. *DBF*, xi.42.

Destrappes, Léonard de. Auch 1599–1629. The Destrappes (only spelling used by family members) was a Nevers family that only emerges from anonymity with Jean, notary at Nevers, ca 1512. Two generations later, abp's father was apothecary, and though related to other familes of urban *notables* (not least to most famous of Nevers notarial families, the Marions) there was little to suggest any rapid social or professional mobility. Abp's own brother was an *élu* at Nevers by 1591, while a nephew would follow him into Paris parlt a generation later.

Baptised at St-Angle church, Nevers, 3–10–1558. Son of Jean, *marchand-apothicaire* and *controleur des deniers communs* of Nevers, and 1st wife, Jeanne Olivier. No information on education, but law degree can be assumed as *cons* in Paris parlt by early 1595. No evidence to suggest any early decision to direct him into the church, and it may be simply that he left Nevers to seek his fortune in Paris, as had Simon Marion, the notary's son whose success there may have inspired a wish to emulate him. Marion's patronage may also have enabled him to enter parlt, and above all the service of Nemours family, which had held title to Auch since 1586 and was directly responsible for his change of career in 1597. Only in anticipation of episcopal office that he took all minor and major (priesthood included) orders in Feb-May 1597. There is, consequently, no truth in view that he was ever Capuchin!

Nom April 1597. Provs 3–11–1599. Cons Jan 1600. Took Dominique de Vic as coadj 1622. D. 29–10–1629.

Sources: AD Nièvre, 3 E 1, vols 367, 369–71. BN, P Or 2875, doss 63786. AN, Z^1o 240 (for orders taken, 1597); MC, XXXVI 75, 20–2–1595. *Gallia*, i. 1005.

Diharse. *See* **Iharse**

Dinet, Gaspard, Minim. Mâcon 1600–19. Originally from Forez, it seems, family had settled in Moulins by early 16th C, where legal practice led to office-holding, financial and judicial, esp in admin of duchy of Bourbonnais, which was frequently held by members of royal family (e.g. as jointure). Such activities may well have opened doors to wider opportunities: Jacques II, Bp Gaspard's brother, was MR in service of Henri III's widow, Louise de Lorraine.

B. 6–1–1569 Moulins. Son of Jacques I, treasurer-chancellor of principality of Bourbonnais, and Philippine Euvraud. Probably educated in schools of order of Minims, whose convent at Vincennes he entered and where he took the habit in 1586. Apparently later sent to study theology in Rome. Tonsured in 1582, priest in 1591. His pre-episcopal career was partly Roman: held major offices within order, as secretary general and visitor of Minims in Spain and Italy, later as provincial of French Minims. *Prédicateur du roi* ca 1595, he apparently refused the superior-generalship of his order in 1597. Well regarded in Henri IV's entourage, his promotion meant Mâcon exchanged a fugitive Italian *ligueur* for a royalist Frenchman returning from Italy.

No date for nom, but probably in 1598. Provs 2–8–1599. Cons 6–1–1600. D. 30–11–1619.

Dinet, Louis. Mâcon 1619–50. B. 1592. Son of Jacques II brother of Bp Gaspard and *avocat au conseil*, and Jeanne Bardon. He was not originally designated as uncle's successor at Mâcon, but Pierre Dinet, who obtained his provs as coadj in 1617, d. suddenly and uncons in Jan 1618. Louis was apparently pressed to take over as successor-designate at relatively short notice. Quickly became canon of Mâcon and bacc in canon law, which suggests extremely limited studies. Deacon at time of confirmation as bp, he also held abbey of St-Sulpice-de-Bugey, O Cist (Belley) in c before episcopate. Brother of Jacques Dinet, SJ, future confessor to Louis XIII.

No date for nom (but it may have originally been as coadj to Bp Gaspard, who died in Nov 1619). Provs 28–9–1620. Cons 25–4–1621. D. 3–10–1650.

Sources: AD Allier, 5J, 2184. ASV, PC 13, fos 821–43 (on Pierre, original coadj-designate 1617). Thuillier, *Diarium Minimorum*, ii. 263–5 (Gaspar). *Gallia*, iv. 1102. *DBF*, xi. 374–6.

Dolce. *See* **Olce.**

Donadieu, François. Auxerre 1598–1623, Comminges 1625 (resign). These 3 bps were from a noble family from Mirepoix in western Languedoc, whose filiation only becomes clear in early 16th C. The wars of religion brought them out of provincial anonymity for a time at least, thanks essentially to activities of Pierre, sgr de Puchairie, elder brother of first 2 bps, both confusingly named François. After initially serving in Admiral Joyeuse's household and as nominal captain in navy, he supported Henri IV against League, becoming gov of Angers, lt-gen (1593) and *sénéchal* of Anjou (1596). Unmarried, he appears to have done most to advance careers of his ecclesiastical brothers, and it was his nephew, Barthélemy de Griet (below) who was originally designated as his heir and successor.

B. ca 1560. Son of Jean, sgr de Puchairie, and Madeleine d'Hautpoul. Nothing known of education, but papacy accepted he held doct in theology from the Sapienza, Rome. Not the original candidate for Auxerre, he was only a cleric when confirmed by Rome, to which he had travelled in order to obtain his provs (which enabled him to obtain his theology degree). Obtained abbey of Bellebranche, O Cist (Le Mans) in c in 1599.

Brevet de nom to Auxerre 6–1–1599. Provs 4–6–1599. Cons 1–7–1599 in Rome. Resign to transfer to Comminges in 1623, but despite grant of provs by Rome, never served as bp there, and resigned title to nephew Barthélemy (below). D. 5–1–1640.

Donadieu, Francois, OSB. St-Papoul 1608–26. B. 1563. Younger brother of François (above). Nothing known about education, but Rome accepted he held bacc in theology and doct in canon law. Entered Benedictine order at unknown date, and was successively prior of Montolieu (where vg of Cardinal Guise, the abbot in c), and in 1588 'regular' abbot of St-Hilaire-de-Carcassonne. He seems to have rejected see of Auxerre soon after Jacques Amyot's death, possibly because unwilling to meet brother Pierre's financial demands!

Nom 28–2–1607. Provs 3–3–1608. Cons June 1608. D. 6–4–1626.

Donadieu, Barthélemy de *Griet* **de. Comminges 1625–37.** B. 24–8–1592 Montesquieu-Volvestre. Son of Ferréol de Griet, sgr de Villepinte, and Jeanne de Donadieu, sister of Donadieu bps of Auxerre and St-Papoul. Hagiographical tradition that grew up around him after death makes it difficult to unravel his career. Early education seems to have been in Toulouse, though in view of early career, he may well not have completed humanities and philosophy studies at this time. Uncles pressed him into military career, and obliged him, in 1617, to take Donadieu name and arms as heir of Pierre, sgr de Puchairie. Gov of Domfront in Normandy, fought against Huguenots of the Midi in 1620–1 (along with Hugues de Labatut, later bp of Comminges). Through Charles de Condren, Bérulle's successor as superior of the Oratory, he abandoned his military career, entered St-Magloire seminary in Paris, and proceeded to take orders in early 1625. He may also have resumed/completed education at this time, obtaining doct in canon law. Elevation to episcopate result of uncle's decision not to implement his transfer to Comminges in 1624. But ironically, then allowed uncle virtually to administer Comminges in his name!

Nom 23–4–1625. Provs 6–10–1625. Cons 8–12–1625. D. 12–11–1637.

Sources: BN, P Or 1011, doss 23,053; Cab d'Hozier 121, doss 3161. Lebeuf, *Mémoires concernant l'histoire civile et ecclésiastique d'Auxerre*, ii. 197–216. *DBF*, xi. 503–4 (family-general). AN, V⁵ 1228, fo 102; MC, VI, 431–3 (notarial records of Auxerre-Comminges exchange, 1623–5) (François, bp of Auxerre). ASV, PC 21, fos 365–84. AD Haute-Garonne, B 1912, fo 48. Molinier, *La Vie de Messire Barthélemy*. Contrasty, *Histoire des évêques de Comminges* (Barthélemy).

Donnaud, Pierre. Mirepoix coadj 1610–21 (non successit). Nephew of an Epernon protégé, Pierre de Donnaud, bp of Mirepoix (1587–1630), who is said to have declined archiepiscopal see of Vienne and, later, Bordeaux and Toulouse.

B. 1578. Son of Dominique, a merchant at St-Ybars, and Jeanne de Salinier, 1st wife, both of whom died when Pierre was young. Brought up by uncle, bp of Mirepoix, who supervised his early education; completed his studies at Univ of Toulouse and, later, Paris, where he studied theology and took doct. Ordained deacon and priest in Paris, 1603, by which date he held *curé* of Puyvert (Mirepoix).

No date for nom as coadj. Provs 8–11–1610. Cons in Rome 21–11–1610. D. 14–7–1621, predeceasing uncle.

Sources: ASV, Acta Misc 98, fo 150; Acta Camerarii 14, fo 163. Villain, *France moderne*, iii (2), 1562–4. *DBF*, xi.528–9

Dony d'Attichy, Louis. Minim. Riez 1629–52, Autun 1652–64. The Doni (or Dony in its French form) were an old Florentine merchant family, one of whose branches settled in Avignon in earlier centuries. However, Octavien, father of bp, came directly from Florence. Starting as a secretary to Catherine de' Medici, he soon became involved in financial affairs, and gradually rose to become Catherine's *intendant des finances* and later Marie de' Medici's *surintendant des finances* (1610–14), which made him virtually a ministerial figure for a time. Marriage in 1588 to Valence de Marillac, sister of Michel, future keeper of the seals, sealed his entry into world of *grande robe*, and also ensured that next generation would move in *dévot* political circles.

B. Paris, St-Jean-de-Grève parish, 10–1–1598. Son of Octavien and Valence de Marillac; godson of duc d'Epernon. Studied humanities and philosophy at La Flèche (and possibly at SJ coll in Bourges), and later at coll of Navarre. By 1614, he had taken habit of the Minims, perhaps owing to influence of Olivier Chaillou, Minim confessor of Marillac-Attichy family. Another brother, Achille, became well known SJ. Completed studies in Minim order, and hence took no univ degree. But learned Hebrew and Greek, and wrote the history of his order while still in early 20s. Tonsured in 1609, deacon in March 1620, priest in Feb 1622. Resident in Rome, ca 1624, he held various posts of authority within his order (corrector of Paris house, provincial of Bordeaux in 1628). Driven out of Riez during Fronde owing to local animosities as much as his reforming activities, and though he initially wanted the vacant see of Aix, he finally settled for Autun.

Nom to Riez (where he succeeded fellow Minim, La Fare) 5–10–1628. Provs 8–10–1629. Cons 7–4–1630. Nom to Autun 2–5–1652. Provs 23–9–1652. D. 1–7–1664.

Sources: BN, Cab d'Hozier 121, doss 3164; MS Fr 33047, p 475 (naturalisation of father, 1575); MS Fr 32588, p 180 (baptism). ASV, PC 26, fos 202–30; N Fr 89, fos 240–1. BAV, Barb lat 7961, fo 59. AD Saône-et-Loire, G 464. Thuillier, *Diarium Minimorum*, ii. 2–6. *Gallia*, i. 413–14. Vidal, *Critique*, 101–8. Pillorget, *Mouvements insurrectionnels en Provence*, 623, 648, 691. Dubost, 'Les Italiens en France aux xvie et xviie siècles', 234, 334–5, 433, 681.

Dormy, Claude, OSB. Boulogne 1600–26. Nephew of Claude-André, 1st bp of Boulogne in 1567, whose family roots lay in the Charollais and the barony of Vinzelles, acquired in 15th C. Bp's father was apparently the first to move to Paris, where he ended as a pres in *Enquêtes* chamber of parlt. Bp's brothers moved in political and financial circles, one serving as a *trésorier général* de France, another as *intendant* to duc de Nemours.

B. 1563 in Mâcon diocese. Son of François, and Claude de Sève 1546, daughter of Bénigne, first pres in *chambre des comptes*, Dijon. Nothing known about education, but Rome accepted he had doct in canon law (probably from Paris). Destined for clerical career, he was ecclesiastical deputy to 1588 EG. By the time he was ordained deacon in March 1596, he was prior of St-Martin-des-Champs (Paris) and vg of the order of Cluny – which makes it clear he was also a professed Benedictine monk. In the years before nom as bp, he forged useful patronage links with Constable Montmorency.

Brevet de nom 18–2–1599. Provs 26–6–1600. Cons 13–8–1600. D. 30–11–1626.

Sources: BN, Cab d'Hozier 121, doss 3178; Carrés d'Hozier 229; MS Naf. 11863, fo 31. Michaud, *Grande Chancellerie*, 153, 162. AN, Y 117, fos 195–8; Z^{1}o 240 (ordination); MC, VIII 419, 9–9–1599 (*régale* settlement for Boulogne). Archives du château de Chantilly, L/xxxv, fos 120, 127; xlviii, fo 20. Chesnaye-Desbois, *Dict de noblesse*, vi. 955–8.

Dossat. *See* Ossat

Douvrier, Hector. Dol 1630–44, Nîmes 1644–55. Douvrier (or Ouvrier) family originated in the Auvergne, where main branch remained, at Aurillac. Rigal, son of Guillaume and Jeanne de Monteils, settled in Toulouse where he was barrister in 1510, but *capitoul* by early 1540s. Office in parlt beckoned in next 2 generations, with bp's father and uncle both becoming *cons* there in 1570–80s. Marriages with better positioned families (e.g. Nupces, Melet, Potier) also followed, and consolidated family's professional and social gains.

B. Toulouse ca 1588. Son of Renaud (or Rigal), and Béatrice Potier de la Terrasse, daughter of Etienne, MR. Little known about early education, but took doct in canon law in Paris, and doct in civil law in Toulouse. *Cons* in Toulouse parlt, as was brother Jean (later a pres in *Enquêtes*). Tonsured in 1601, ordained priest on 29-3-1625 in Paris, where he had by then settled. Almoner to Marie de' Medici in 1624, also obtained priories of St-Pierre-de-Montaud and Montesquieu (both in Rieux diocese) and abbey of St-Memmie, OSA (Châlons-sur-Marne) in c in 1630. One of several candidates for Dol succession, membership of Marie de' Medici's household was a major advantage as she enjoyed presentation rights to the see.

Brevet de nom to Dol 1-9-1629. Formal nom 6-9-1629. Provs 10-6-1630. Cons 2-8-1630. Exchanged Dol with Cohon for Nîmes in 1644. D. 20-6-1655.

Sources: ASV, PC 27, fos 306–41; PC, 45, fos 284–300. Sauzet, *Contre-réforme*, 244–6. Vindry, *Parlementaires* (Toulouse), 207, 240, 273. AN, Z^{1}o 241 (ordination). Griselle, *Etat de la maison du roi Louis XIII*, no 2434. AN, MC, XCV, 63, 14-4-1632. Orcibal, *Saint-Cyran*, 284, n 1. Villain, *France moderne*, iii (1), 433–8. Navelle, *Familles toulousaines*, viii. 144–6.

Du Bec, Jean. St-Malo 1598–1610. Nephew of Philippe du Bec, bp of Nantes and abp of Reims (d. 1605). As name suggests, family originated near Bec abbey in Normandy, where it was settled for several generations. Bp's father, Charles, embraced Calvinism after 1562, and was active in military campaigns until mid-1570s, when he may have reverted to Catholicism and royal service.

B. 1540. 2nd son of Charles, vice-admiral of France, and Madeleine de Beauvillier de St-Aignan. Brought up Protestant, travelled extensively throughout Europe, and on return home converted to Catholicism, in Feb 1572. Engaged in military campaigns versus Huguenots. Embraced ecclesiastical state around 1577, becoming abbot in c of Mortemer, O Cist (Rouen) in 1578, but failed to secure the deanship of Nantes, 1579. Uncle unsuccessfully attempted to resign see of Nantes to him in 1582. Henri IV also offered Nantes to him in 1594 after nom uncle to Reims, but years of *ligueur* hostility to uncle rather than to himself made prospect of governing Nantes unpalatable, so he readily exchanged title for St-Malo, whose bp, René de Bourgneuf, was anxious to move to Nantes.

Nom 30-10-1596. Provs 14-9-1598. Cons 14-3-1599. D. 20-1-1610.

Sources: BN, MS Baluze 59, fos 159–60. AD Ile-et-Vilaine, G 54 (abjuration, testament, etc). *DBF*, xi. 884–6.

Duchaine, Louis. Senez coadj 1618/23–71. Well-known Aix family ennobled in 16th C via offices in parlt, where bp's grandfather, Guillaume (d. 1578) and father, Louis, both served as *cons*. Father played a major, albeit inevitably shifting, role during League in Provence, rallying early to Henri IV while opposing Epernon's government of Provence. His royalism brought its rewards, as second pres in Aix parlt (his fellow royalist Guillaume du Vair being first pres), and ensured that he remained an important provincial figure under Henri IV. This in turn enabled bp's own brother to succeed to father's office in 1613.

B. 7-7-1589 Aix. 3rd son of Louis and Anne de Bausset, daughter of prominent royalist figure in Provence. Nothing known of education, save he had doct in law. Canon of St-Sauveur of Aix, deputy to ACs of 1612 and 1615. Deacon at time of confirmation as coadj. Administered neighbouring see of Riez for the non-resident Cardinal Bentivoglio 1622-5.

Nom coadj to Jacques Martin 31-8-1617. Provs 2-4-1618. Cons 17-6-1618. Succeeded to Sisteron Feb 1623. D. 11-3-1671.

Sources: Vindry, *Parlementaires* (Aix), 24, 33. Clapiers-Coulonges, *Chronologie des officiers*, 15-17, 20, 54, 68, 75, 79, 88. AD Bouches-du-Rhone, BB 3345, fo 277 (nom). Borricand, *Nobiliaire de Provence*, i. 313. *Encylopédie départementale des Bouches-du-Rhône*, ed Paul Masson (Paris 1913-33), iv (2). 170. *DBF*, xi. 1161-3.

Du Haut. *See* **Salies**

Du Laurens, Honoré. Embrun 1601-12. Rise to prominence of this family was meteoric, and was partly work of bp and brothers, as they were originally a peasant family from near Chambéry. Father, Louis Laurens (b. 1511) studied in Turin and Paris, where he turned to medicine. Settling in Tarascon as a doctor, he married Louise Castellane, daughter of Honoré, a *médecin ordinaire* of the king. Eldest son, André, took full advantage of this connection, becoming Marie de' Medici's and Henri IV's *médecin ordinaire*, and a fount of favour for his brothers Honoré and Gaspard. His son, Richard, went on to serve as *médecin ordinaire* to Louis XIII. Another of André's brothers, Antoine, was an *avocat au conseil*, while Jean was major figure in Capucin order in Marseille and Provence, and is said to have rejected episcopal office. Their Castellane relatives are not to be confused with well-known Provençal noble family, the Castellanes, nor should rendering of the name as *du* Laurens mislead in way it was obviously intended!

B. 7-3-1554 Tarascon. Son of Louis and Louise Castellane. Nothing known of early studies, though his Castellane uncle persuaded him to study medicine for time. Switched to law, which he studied at Turin and Avignon, where he probably took law degree. On completion of studies, he practised as barrister at Aix parlt, married Anne d'Ulmo, whose father he duly succeeded as av-gen there in 1581. Leading figure among Aix *ligueurs*, he acted as their envoy to pope in 1591, and attended EG of 1588 and 1593. Is said to have attracted Henri IV's attention during and after Suresnes conference which paved way for royal conversion, but death of his wife (1591) gradually led him to retire and take clerical orders. Influence of his brother, the king's physician, was (as *brevet de nom* makes clear) decisive in obtaining see of Embrun for him in face of competition from family of outgoing archbp; he achieved the same result a few years later for his other brother, Gaspard, in respect of Arles.

No date for nom, but probably 27-7-1600. Provs 24-1-1601. Cons 24-2-1601 in Rome. D. Jan 1612.

Du Laurens, Gaspard, OSB. Arles 1605-30. B. 14-9-1567 Arles. Youngest brother of Honoré (above). Little known of education, except studied law at Orléans and Aix, and took doct in utr, possibly at Avignon. Abbot of St-Pierre-de-Vienne, OSB (Vienne) in 1597, he also entered the Benedictine order and took monastic vows. Ordained priest well before his nom, which he owed to brother, André. Failed more than once to secure nephew, Antoine, doct of Sorbonne, as coadj and successor.

Nom Dec 1603. Provs 27–6–1605. Cons 10–8–1605. D. 12–7–1630.

Sources: Ch de Ribbe, *Une famille au xvie siècle* (Paris 1867). Borricand, *Nobiliaire de Provence*, ii. 718–20; *Encyclopédie départementale des Bouches-du-Rhône*, ed Paul Masson (Paris 1913–33) iv (2), 293. Griselle, *Etat de la maison de Louis XIII*, no 2985. Clapiers-Coulonges, *Chronologie des officiers*, 161–2, Vindry, *Parlementaires* (Aix), 51–2. *Gallia Chr Nov* (Embrun), 943. *DBF*, xii. 67–71 (family-general). ASV, Acta Misc 97, fo 84. *Gallia Chr Nov* (Arles), 942–56. *DBF*, xii. 68 (Gaspard). BN, MS Fr 4222, fos 450v-2r (*brevet*). ASV, Misc Arm XII, 144, fo 468. *DBF*, xii. 69–70 (Honoré).

Du Lis, Eustache 1606–43. Family claimed they could be traced back to 14th C, but only in early 16th does their profile emerge with any clarity. By mid-century, bp's father, Pierre, and uncle, Michel, were both in service of Marshal Bourdillon, who introduced them to entourage of duke of Nevers and wife. These connections were decisive, leading them to participate in military campaigns during 1550s and 1560s, but also to obtain positions in royal households. Bp's father d. relatively young, having married 3 times. In following generation, Marguerite du Lis, bp's sister, married Nicholas de Chéry, whose son, Eustache, succeeded his uncle as bp of Nevers in 1640s (see Chéry).

B. 1561. 2nd son of Pierre and Elie de Saint-Phalle (m. in 1558), his 3rd wife. Nothing known of education, and may originally have been destined for military career. If true, this did not last long for, by 1588, when he was clerical deputy to EG, he was also canon and treasurer of Nevers cathedral. Rome accepted in 1606 he was a lic in utr. Prior in c of St-Gildard in 1589, he served as vg of Bp Sorbin of Nevers for 12 years, and was almoner in Henri IV's household by 1602.

No date for nom, but probably very soon after Arnaud Sorbin's death on 1–3–1606. Provs 17–7–1606. Cons 19–11–1606. Took nephew Eustache de Chéry as coadj 1633, turning over full control of diocesan admin to him in 1640. D. 17–6–1643.

Sources: ASV, Acta Misc 98, fo 275. AD Nièvre, 2F, 30, 416. Villenant, *Nobiliaire de Nivernois*, ii. 506–11, 608–16. *DBF*, xii. 91.

Du Louet, René. Quimper 1641–68. Various members of Louet family (without the *particule*) were in the service of dukes of Brittany in 14th and esp 15th C, but their subsequent history and connection to bp are uncertain. By mid-16th C at least, they were well entrenched among Breton nobility, esp in Quimper area itself, with successive family members becoming *chevaliers* of royal order of St Michel.

B. 1584. Son of Jean, sgr de Coatjunval, and Marie de Brezal. Educated in part at coll of Nantes, he took lic in utr, possibly at Angers. Canon of St-Pol-de-Léon by 1606, and cantor (the first 'dignity' of the chapter) 2 years later, he was ordained priest in 1610. Also served Bps Neufville and Rieux as *promoteur*. Following Rieux's deposition (1635) he administered diocese as vg and *official* elected by chapter until Robert Cupif became bp in 1640. Also Cupif's vg when nom to Quimper. Harlay of St-Malo had recommended him for St-Pol in 1637, but he may have wished to avoid such a troublesome succession. By then, he had strong reputation as preacher in both French and Breton, which made him serious candidate for a Breton-speaking see like Quimper. In close contact with Père Joseph, he was instrumental in founding convent of Calvairian nuns in Quimper in 1634.

Nom 23–12–1640. Provs 1–12–1642. Cons 1–1–1643. Took François de Visdelou as coadj in 1651 and then, after he moved to St-Pol (1662), François de Coëtlogon in 1666. D. 11–2–1668.

Sources: ASV, PC 40, fos 289–302. AAE France 1505, fo 386. Kerhervé, *Etat breton aux xive et xve siècles*, 317, 714, 827, 921, 928. *La Bretagne en 1665 d'après Colbert de Croissy*, ed Kerhervé, 193. Carné, *Chevaliers bretons* (1884), 234–6. Fagniez, *Le Père Joseph et Richelieu*, i. 118. *DBF*, xii. 86.

Du Lude. *See* **Daillon**

Du Perron, Jacques *Davy* de. **Evreux 1595–1606, Sens 1606–18.** The celebrity of Cardinal du Perron belies his modest origins. Father, Julien Davy, was native of either St-Lô or St-Sauveur-Lendelin in the Cotentin, and seems to have been of respectable but undistinguished bourgeois stock. A medical doctor by profession, he embraced Calvinism and fled to Switzerland, settling in Bern, whence he subsequently returned to serve as pastor and preacher in Dieppe and perhaps later in Vire, apparently dying in Paris in 1583. Early biography of his most famous son is understandably obscure because of his parents' movements and precarious existence once they had embraced Calvinism.

B. 25–11–1556 probably in Bern. Son of Julien and Ursule le Cointe, daughter of gentry family from Cotentin. Childhood was spent in Switzerland where his education began, though it was probably completed in France. His prodigious memory and precocity led him, like his fellow Norman, Jean Bertaut, into entourage of another powerful Norman, marshal Matignon, whose patronage enabled him to enter academic and court circles around Henri III, who made him a *lecteur royal* and appreciated his rhetorical and poetic abilities. Become Catholic by 1578 at the latest. Briefly supported Cardinal Bourbon's claim to throne (as 'Charles X') in 1589, but soon rallied to Henri IV whose cause he served industriously in subsequent years (esp in preparing his conversion) and to whom he became first almoner in early 1590s. Patronage of Gabrielle d'Estrées also vital during these years, and she is said to have obtained Evreux for him, though he was not even cleric when nom. Rewards for his service and skills were considerable – cardinal in 1604, grand almoner of France 1606, and abp of Sens 1606. His learning and oratorical abilities made him a magnetic figure in early 17th-C church, and attracted aspiring clergy, some of them future bps, even though his wider influence on royal church patronage remains difficult to establish.

Date of nom to Evreux unclear, but probably 1591. Provs 11–12–1595. Cons 27–12–1595 in Rome. Transferred to Sens 1606. D. 5–9–1618.

Du Perron, Jean *Davy*. **Sens coadj 1617/1618–21.** B. ca 1565 Vire (?). Brother of Jacques (above). Nothing known about education (though Rome accepted he had lic in utr), early career, or when he converted to Catholicism. Subsequent activities remain just as obscure, and he evidently lived largely in the shadow of brother, the cardinal. A mere cleric at time of promotion to Sens, it seems likely that his brother, during the last year of his life, pushed him into the limelight, obtaining abbeys of St-Taurin, OSB (Evreux) and ND de Lyre, OSB (Evreux) in c for him in 1617, and arranging the coadjutorship of Sens.

Nom as coadj of Sens 10–10–1617. Provs 18–12–1617. Cons 22–7–1618. Succeeded 5–9–1618. D. 24–10–1621.

Du Perron, Jacques II *le Noël*. **Angoulême 1636–46, Evreux 1648–9.** B. St-Lô ca 1590. Son of Robert le Noël, sgr de Grancy, and Marie du Perron, cousin of Jacques and Jean du Perron (above). Little known of him or family's activities – apart from those of episcopal uncles. A student in Paris arts faculty in 1614–15, it is not clear that he took degree. Uncles' patronage was crucial to early career, lasting just long enough for him to gain a foothold in court and church circles. Abbot in c of St-Taurin and Lyre in succession to Jean, his uncle (1622) and a priest before 1628, he became grand almoner to Henriette Marie, queen of England (1630), whom he served for several years in England.

Nom to Angoulême in 1635. Provs 28–1–1636, Cons 14–6–1637. Nom to Evreux 30–8–1646. Provs 24–8–1648. D. 14–2–1649.

Sources: *DHGE*, xiv. 1130–6. *DBF*, x. 397–8; xii. 339–41. Pierre Féret, *Le Cardinal du Perron. Orateur, controversiste, écrivain* (Paris 1879). AN, MC VIII, 409, 14–9–1594 (*régale*, Evreux). BN, MS Fr 18011, fo 304 (Jean). ASV, PC 49, fos 41–61. BN, MS lat 9957, fo 167v (Jacques Le Noël).

Du Sault, Jean-Jacques de. Dax 1598–1623. This Bordeaux parlementaire family orginated in Saintonge, and settled in Bordeaux on establishment of parlt in 1472, of which Pierre I was first *greffier*. Bps were descended from junior branch of family which developed from mid-16th C. Having briefly held office in Paris (*grand conseil*) and though also holding a variety of posts in chancery and elsewhere, du Sault family became identified thereafter with post of av-gen in Bordeaux parlt, which they held for over a century after 1568. Well calculated marriages, in Bordeaux and elsewhere, ensured they formed part of small parlementaire élite of Bordeaux through the following century. These alliances also enabled family members to becomes canons and dignitaries within chapters of Bordeaux and Dax.

B. 1570. Son of Charles, av-gen, and Anne Godin, grand-daughter of chancellor under Francis I. Educated by SJ in Bordeaux, he took doct in law, probably also in Bordeaux. Ordained in his early 20s, canon of Bordeaux cathedral chapter, and dean of prestigious chapter of St-Seurin, as well as first almoner to Marguerite de Valois – all of which demonstrate the extent of family relationships. But he owed his nom to Dax to Henri de Noailles, comte d'Ayen, whose uncles had held see for many years, and to whom Henri IV granted the right of presenting his candidate for succession in 1597. Nature and origin of his (or his family's) links with Noailles remain obscure.

Nom 1597. Provs 25–5–1598. Cons 1599. Took his nephew Philibert as coadj 1617. D. 23–5–1623.

Du Sault, Philibert. Dax coadj 1618/1623–38. B. 25–3–1598 Bordeaux. Son of Charles II sgr de l'Espine, av-gen, and Marguerite de Cruseau, daughter of a pres in parlt of Bordeaux. Nothing known of educational background, though Rome accepted he held lic in utr. Subdeacon, canon of Dax, and holder of minor priory in Dax diocese at time of his nom – and had obviously been groomed for episcopal succession there. He was dean of St-Seurin of Bordeaux while coadj in Dax.

No date for nom as coadj. Provs 23–7–1618. Not cons until 14–5–1623. Succeeds 25–5–1623. D. 2–11–1638.

Sources: ASV, Misc Arm XII, 144, fo 117. AD Gironde, G 805, fo 364; *Inventaire-sommaire*, B series (family office-holding). Vindry, *Parlementaires* (Bordeaux), 125–6 and xxvii-viii (*état-civil* notes). Bourousse and O'Gilvy, *Nobiliaire de Guyenne* i. 176; ii. 221–32. Degert, *Histoire des évêques de Dax*, 300ff. *DBF*, xii. 843–7.

Du Serre, Charles-Salomon, Gap 1600–37. Like so many episcopal (and non-episcopal) families, the du Serre claimed 13th-14th C origins, but little is known of them before early-mid 16th C, when 3 different branches began to emerge in Upper Provence/ Dauphiné region. Bp's father, Antoine, who founded the Thèze branch, served under Admiral Annebault and at siege of Metz, in 1552. 3 of his 5 sons were killed in military encounters during wars of religion, leaving only bp and his brother Daniel, both of whom were also active militarily in the wars. Charles-Salomon may even have served under Huguenot chief Lesdiguières, since some family members were Protestant. His mother, who was Huguenot, may have been connected to Lesdiguières by earlier family marriage, although there is also firm evidence of Guise (via Mayenne) patronage.

B. 1572. Son of Antoine, sgr de Thèze, and Marguerite Bonne d'Auriac. Nothing known of education, which apparently included serving as page in household of dukes of Guise and Mayenne and which, if true, would have meant early conversion to Catholicism. Not in orders when nom to Gap. It was almost certainly the marriage, in 1594, of his sister, Suzanne, to Claude de Paparin, nephew of the elderly Pierre Paparin, bp of Gap, which was decisive in change of direction and willingness to embrace an ecclesiastical career. Must have been initially nom as Paparin's coadj of Gap, since provs issued only 4 weeks after predecessor's death on 1–8–1600. Agreed to take Artus de Lionne as coadj in 1634, but d. before Lionne was confirmed by Rome.

No date for nom but probably early 1600. Provs 30–8–1600. Cons 28–5–1601. D. 16–5–1637.

Sources: Blanc, *Origines des familles provençales*, 415. AD Hautes-Alpes, *Répertoire de la série G*, ed P Guillaume (Gap, 1897), iii. pp xvii-xviii, 361–4. *Gallia Chr Nov* (Gap), 519–211.

Du Tour. *See* **Maupas**

Du Vair, Pierre. Vence 1602–38. The philosopher-minister and his brother were 1st-generation Parisians, whose origins were in the Auvergne, where grandfather, Jean, was simple *bourgeois* of Tournemire. His son, also Jean, moved to Paris, where he served as barrister in Paris parlt, but also, and crucially, as proc-gen to Catherine de' Medici and duc d'Anjou, future Henri III. Became MR in 1573 as reward for his services, and took orders after his wife's death. Dean of St-Marcel-lès-Paris in 1585, he set an example which both of his sons were to follow *ab initio*. His daughter Antoinette married Nicolas Aleaume, father of Guillaume, bp of Riez and Lisieux.

B. 1561 Paris. Son of Jean and Barbe François; younger brother of Guillaume below. Little known of education, but studied theology and usually referred to as doct of Sorbonne. Prior in c of Brienne and Monfaucon, he almost certainly owed episcopal elevation to influence of brother, a trusted royal servant in Provence, after his arrival in 1596. Pierre obtained nephew Jacques Ribier as coadj in 1636, but after du Vair's death he renounced succession rights in favour of Antoine Godeau, bp of neighbouring Grasse.

Nom 17–5–1601. Provs 15–4–1602. No date for his cons. D. 28–6–1638.

Du Vair, Guillaume. Lisieux 1617–21. B. 7–3–1556 Paris. Elder son of Jean and Barbe François. Received humanistic education in France and Italy, took law degree and practised as lawyer before becoming *cons* in Paris parlt (1584). Tonsured cleric from early age, he never married. Emerged from political conflicts of League (during which he composed his best known works e.g. *De la constance*) with reputation for independence, rectitude, and philosophical high-mindedness, which saw him become an MR (1594), *cons* d'état (1596), and first pres of Aix parlt from 1599 until 1616, when he was briefly keeper of the seals. Gift of see of Lisieux was regarded as a means of softening his subsequent fall from political favour. Episcopal office had been on his mind much earlier in his career, though he may have vacillated when he had to decide. Having asked in vain for sees of Riez (1597) and Arles (1603), he proved unenthusiastic when actually offered Marseille (also in 1603).

Nom 11–8–1617. Provs 26–10–1617. Cons 1618. D. 3–8–1621.

Sources: R Raudouant, *Guillaume du Vair, l'homme et l'orateur* (Paris 1907). Etchéchoury, *Maîtres des Requêtes*, 222; Trani, 'Conseillers du grand conseil', 97. AD Bouches-du-Rhône, B 3339, fo 361; B 3340, fo 275. *Gallia Chr Nov*, ii. 602. E Roux, *Auvergnats en Provence*, 125, 163–4. Jarno, 'Du Vair évêque de Marseille?', 195–7. *DBF*, xii. 950–2.

Du Vergier, Claude. Lavaur 1606–36. One of the more obscure of Henri IV's bps, du Vergier's progress is particularly difficult to chart. Family had lived in Dun-sur-Auron in Berry, where they held municipal, seigneurial and prevotal offices from mid-15th C. Later, some members moved to Bourges, where bp's father, Claude, practised law and was *procureur du roi* at the *présidial* court by 1566. It seems that his eldest son, Louis, was a secretary to duc d'Alençon (Berry was part of his apanage) and to Admiral Joyeuse, which, if true, would plausibly account for attraction of Toulouse for his other son, Claude, future bp. Other members of family followed him to Languedoc, where brother Jérôme became a *trésorier de France* in the Toulouse *généralité*, while his son, Jérôme II, administered temporalities of Lavaur diocese for his uncle.

B. ca 1566 Bourges. Son of Claude and Marie Gassot. Neither nature nor place of studies is known, but he may have taken doct in utr in native Bourges. Early career was, it seems, that of barrister in Paris parlt, to which he may have been drawn by presence of relative, Jules Gassot, secretary in Henri III's service. In 1592, obtained an office of *cons-cl* in Toulouse parlt, but not being in orders, his reception was opposed in parlt and delayed until May 1595. He was still a mere cleric on being nom to Lavaur in 1605.

Nom 21–8–1605. Provs 24–4–1606. Cons 16–7–1606. D. 25–3–1636.

Sources: ASV, Acta Misc 98, fo 871. Vindry, *Parlementaires* (Toulouse), 248. *Inventaire-Sommaire des archives communales, Dun-sur-Auron* (Bourges 1938). AD Cher, 2 F 251; Haute-Garonne, B 1972, fo 105, B 215, fo 385, B 248, fo 87. A Vidal, 'Du Vergier, évêque de Lavaur et les siens', *Revue Historique du Tarn* 17 (1900), 73–86. Lacger, *Etats administratifs*, 347. *DBF*, xii. 1026.

Elbène. *See* **Delbène**

Eschaux. *See* **Deschaux**

Esclaux. *See* **Desclaux**

Escoubleau. *See* **Sourdis**

Esdresses, Jean d'. Lectoure coadj 1609/35–46. Son of relatively little known noble family from the Limousin, he owed his elevation to his elderly uncle, Léger de Plas, bp of Lectoure since 1599.

B. 30–7–1582. Son of Gaspard, marquis d'Esdresses, and Isabeau de Plas, sister of bp de Plas. Nothing known of education, but Rome accepted he was *magister* (presumably lic) in theology. Pre-episcopal career equally obscure, but was probably in uncle's entourage at Lectoure. Subdeacon at time of confirmation by Rome. Although did not succeed his uncle fully until 1635, he governed Lectoure from 1620 onwards, when de Plas effectively retired elsewhere. Enjoys distinction of probably being only bp of this period whose personal austerities were publicly cited in *Gazette de France* after his death ('une chaisne de fer garnie de pointes et... plusieurs disciplines, haires et cilices').

Nom as coadj Dec 1608. Provs 3–8–1609. Cons 4–10–1609. Succeeded 24–3–1635. D. 12–4–1646.

Sources: BN, MS lat 17026, fo 51. Clergeac, *Chronologie*, 49. S d'Estresse de Lanzac, 'Essai de bibliographie de Jean d'Estresses, évêque de Lectoure', *Bulletin de la Société des Etudes du Lot*, 60 (1939), 130–5. M Bordes, *Histoire de Lectoure* (Toulouse 1975).

Esparbès de Lussan, Joseph. Pamiers 1605–25. An old noble family from near Fezensaguet in Gascony, spawning numerous branches in 16th C, and which could boast good marriage connections, both in old nobility and emerging robe (e.g. Lauzières-Thémines, St-Félix). Military careers were the most common, partly through the order of Malta, with individual members serving different causes or *chefs* during wars of religion (Navarre, Mercoeur, Henri III), and with its most distinguished branch, that of Aubeterre, producing a marshal of France under Louis XIII. Bp's father (who founded the Brazais branch) seems to have been a classic 'cadet de Gascogne': acquiring lands through marriage into northern noble family, he was highly active under Henri III, esp in Normandy, as *mestre de camp* in Picardy regiment, and as gov of Rouen. Henri IV made him gov of Nantes in 1598.

B. ca 1580. 2nd of two sons of Joseph, sgr de Couarde-sur-Mer, and Jeanne du Bois-Rouvray, dame de Brazais (in Burgundy). Little known of early education, but studied philosophy and theology at Univ of Paris, and Rome accepted that held lic in theology. In minor orders (acolyte) at time of nom. There is no truth in story that Henri III nom Esparbès to Pamiers in 1579 when he was a boy, and that Gregory XIII refused him – he was not born until 1580! But his predecessor, Bp Barrau, whose brother was married to an Esparbès, had been nom either through Esparbès family pressure or in order to ensure their loyalty. Joseph's succession to Pamiers in 1605 was thus not unpredictable.

Nom mid-1605 (Bp Barrau d. 5–6–1605). Provs 19–12–1605. Cons Feb 1608. D. 5–12–1625.

Sources: ASV, Misc Arm XII, 144, fo 100; PC 18, fo 44. BN, Doss bleus 255, doss 6511. Anselme, vii. 448–62. Villain, *France moderne*, iii (2), 1250–60. J-M Vidal, *Schisme et hérésie au diocèse de Pamiers* (Castillon 1931), 256–7, 278–9. *DBF*, xii. 1496–1501. *DGS*, 133–4.

Espinay de St-Luc, Arthur d'. Marseille 1619–21. Few French clerics could feel as entitled to episcopal preferment as the son of this old Breton noble family whose ties among upper nobility were truly phenomenal, and whose activities (military, diplomatic, courtly, political) were impressive in both range and numbers.

B. ca 1589. Son of François, sgr de St-Luc, grand master of royal artillery, and Jeanne de Cossé-Brissac. Nothing known of education, but he appears to have taken doct in utr.

Deputy to AC of 1615 for province of Tours. Abbot in c of Breton abbeys of Redon, OSB (Vannes) and St-Pierre-de-Rillé, OSA (Rennes). Subdeacon at time of nom.

No date for nom. Provs 28–1–1619. Not cons by time of death 14–8–1621 (although he had taken possession of see).

Sources: *Gallia Chr Nov*, ii. 609–10. *DBF*, xiii. 13–14.

Estaing, Joachim d'. Clermont 1615–50. Estaing family originated in the Rouergue, where they were powerfully ensconced, politically and ecclesiastically, by early 15th C. Made partial move into Auvergne as barons of Murol, in 16th. François d'Estaing, bp of Rodez in early 16th C, was famous as an early reformer. Subsequently, Estaings maintained their provincial eminence, with bps' father's marriage being crucial to their ecclesiastical ambitions in next generation.

B. 1589. Son of Jean and Gilberte de la Rochefoucauld, sister of Cardinal La Rochefoucauld. Early education in SJ coll at Lyon, completed philosophy at Univ of Paris, where he also followed part of theology course. Rome accepted that he had doct in canon law, probably from Paris. Tonsured at Rodez in March 1607, canon-count of Lyon cathedral, in 1608. Prior in c of Charlebois (Clermont) and St Fleuret d'Estaing (Rodez), was subdeacon at time of nom. Though he succeeded Antoine Rose at Clermont, his uncle, Cardinal La Rochefoucauld (bp of Clermont until 1610) was instrumental in securing diocese for him from Marie de' Medici, who enjoyed presentation rights there. Increasingly blind after 1630 and only administered diocese with help of successive suffragan bps.

Nom 2–8–1614. Provs 12–1–1615. Cons 31–5–1615. D. 11–9–1650.

Estaing, Louis d'. Clermont 1651–64. B. 1601 at Estaing. Younger brother of Joachim (above). Apparently studied in SJ coll in Lyon, ca 1617–18, and coll of Clermont (Paris), ca 1622–4, though took lic in theology at Cahors. Tonsured in June 1612, subdeacon in 1619, ordained priest ca 1635. Canon-count of Lyon, possibly in succession to brother, in 1615, later held post of almoner to Anne of Austria. Abbot in c of Belleaigue before episcopate. Little sign of any personal activities or interests during pre-episcopal period. For years, brother Joachim had refused to accept need for coadj at Clermont, despite his obvious incapacity, and rejected family pressure. Shortly before death, he signed papers to obtain coadjutorship for Louis, but that might well have achieved nothing had not the circumstances of Fronde obliged Mazarin to satisfy Estaing family ambitions.

Nom 6–2–1651. Provs 9–6–1651. Cons 25–8–1651. D. 15–3–1664.

Sources: AD Aveyron, G 201. P Charbonnier, *Une autre France*, 2 vols (Clermont-Ferrand 1984). Lemaître, *Le Rouergue flamboyant*. Welter, *Réforme ecclésiastique dans le diocèse de Clermont*. Beyssac, *Chanoines de l'église de Lyon*, 193, 196. *DBF*, xiii.63–4 (family-general). ASV, PC 13, fos 399–408. AAE, France 772, fo 271v (Joachim). ASV, PC, 48, fos 680–717; PC 48, fos 701–17. BN, MS Fr 25025, fo 309 (Louis).

Estrades. Jean d'. Condom. 1648–58 (resign). Despite claims to medieval origins and chivalric status, Estrades family appears gradually to have emerged from bourgeoisie of Agen in 15th and early 16th C, when members still held municipal and royal office, esp as lieutenants and judges in local courts, as late as 1550s. Thereafter, military activities altered their fortunes and prospects, with bp's father rallying early to Henri IV, whose court he later frequented, also serving as governor to his illegitimate sons, the comte de

Moret, and later the ducs de Beaufort and Vendôme. An uncle of the bp, also called Jean, was a well known Jesuit preacher and controversialist. But it was bp's brother, Geoffroy, who capitalised most fully on these connections, beginning career as a page to Louis XIII, and after faithful service to him and Mazarin in military and esp diplomatic capacities, became marshal of France. He also seems to have taken it upon himself to promote Jean to episcopate.

B. ca 1608 Agen. 2nd son of François and Suzanne de Secondat de Montesquieu (m. 1604). Studied humanities and philosophy with SJ at Agen, and some theology at Sorbonne, but took doct in canon law, probably from Paris. A priest since 1638, prior in c of Tomboeuf and Lusignan, OSB (Agen) and St-Jean de la Vannaudière, OSA (Limoges). Originally designated for Périgueux in 1646, his brother's favour secured more desirable see of Condom, which ageing Bp Cous was persuaded to resign outright to him.

Nom to Condom 7–7–1647. Provs 10–2–1648. Cons 19–4–1648. Resign 1658, exchanging Condom for abbey of Chaalis with Charles-Louis de Guise. D. 12–6–1684.

Sources: ASV, PC 46, fos 264–81. BN, P Or 1059, doss 24,906; Doss bleus 257, doss 6581; MS Baluze 331, fo 46. Anselme, vii. 599–602. *DGS*, 554. *DBF*, xiii.132–8. Tallemant, *Historiettes*, ii. 663–6.

Estrées, César. Laon 1655–81 (resign). Little would be gained by itemising the activities, 'alliances' and status of a family whose members would continue to add distinction to the Estrées name under Louis XIV and after. Their connection to Henri IV via his mistress, Gabrielle d'Estrées, was extremely important in consolidating their influence, and while still young the cardinal's father was briefly nom bp of Noyon in 1595 by Henri IV. On mother's side, César was a first cousin of Henri de Béthune, abp of Bordeaux, but that did not exhaust range of Estrées relatives in French upper clergy.

B. 5–2–1628. 3rd son of François-Annibal, marquis de Coeuvres, Marshal d'Estrées, and his 1st wife, Marie de Béthune-Charost, daughter of Philippe de Béthune, his fellow ambassador in Rome. Nothing known of early education, but studied theology at coll of Navarre as pupil of Jean de Launoy, taking lic in theology in 1650 and becoming a *socius* of Sorbonne. Abbot in c of ND de Longpont, O Cist (Soissons) and Doudeauville, OSA (Boulogne), and cleric at time of nom, he was ordained deacon in Nov-Dec 1653. For some reason, Mazarin appears to have wished to revoke his nom *in extremis* while his provs were being sought in Rome, but he either failed to do so or changed his mind.

Nom 26–2–1653. Provs 30–8–1655. Cons 26–9–1655. Cardinal 1672. Resign Laon 1681. D. 18–12–1714.

Sources: ASV, PC 52, fos 561–77. BN, Doss bleus 257, doss 6584; MS lat 15440, p 190. Vindry, *Etat-major*, 205. *DBF*, xiii. 141–54. *DGS*, 555–6. *DHGE*, xv, 1087–8.

Etampes de Valençay, Leonor d'. Chartres 1621–41, Reims 1642–51. Valençays were a cadet branch of a family which originated in Berry and initially rose to prominence in ducal service there during 15th C, when 3 members also became bishops. In subsequent generations, marriages to sword and high robe families enabled them to serve successive kings as govs, household officers, and military figures, with ensuing prominence culminating in elevation of bp's brother, Jacques, to status of marshal of France (1651) and of another, Achille, to cardinal (via order of Malta rather than normal church career).

B. 6–2–1589. Son of Jean, sgr de Valençay, and Sarah d'Applaincourt. Educated mostly at Univ of Paris, from humanities through philosophy (at Harcourt) to theology (at Navarre), where pupil of Cospeau, among others. Lic in theology in 1612, elected *socius* of Sorbonne, and taught philosophy for a time at univ. Deputy for Anjou clergy at EG of 1614. Abbot in c of St-Pierre-de-Bourgueil, OSA (Chartres), La Couture and La Cour-Dieu, O Cist (Orléans). Nom to Chartres was due partly to Hurault family connections (which made him relative of his predecessor, Philippe Hurault), partly to marriage of his sister, Charlotte, to Puysieux, secretary of state, in 1615. A fellow student of Richelieu, much of episcopal career was spent in service to cardinal, for which see of Reims in 1642 was ultimate reward. Notoriously acquisitive and spendthrift, he d. all but bankrupt and had to be buried at expense of AC of 1650. In Sept 1650, he agreed to take Henri de Savoie-Nemours as coadj; nom in Nov 1650, but never received his provs and resigned claim to Reims to Antonio Barberini in 1657.

Nom to Chartres June 1620. Provs 17–8–1620. Cons 13–12–1620. Nom to Reims 16–11–1640. Provs 10–11–1642. D. 8–4–1651.

Sources: ASV, PC 40, fos 629–52. AN, MC, XXIV, 302, 11–1–1615 (c.m. Puysieux-Charlotte d'Etampes). BN, MS lat 15440, p 140; MS Fr 4222, fos 464–5 (Reims, 1650). Anselme, vi. 526, 542–3. Vindry, *Etat-major*, 409. *DBF*, xiii. 164–76. Tallemant, *Historiettes*, i. 422–32. R Sauzet, *Les Visites pastorales dans le diocèse de Chartres pendant la première moitiè du xvii*^{e} *siècle* (Rome 1975).

Faure, François, OFM. Glandèves 1651–3, Amiens 1654–87. Relatively little known about bp's background, not least because family name was such a common one, though their origins appear to lie in the Angoumois. Some evidence of military tradition in the form of an uncle who was a captain in Henri III's guards, while bp's father was gov of Mirebeau in Poitou – so possibly some connection to Richelieu, who owned extensive lands there.

B. 9–11–1612 Ste-Quiterie. Son of Jean and Gabrielle Martin, 'parents nobles mais pauvres'. Early studies with SJ and Dominicans (whom he joined briefly before switching to OFM at Angoulême) he continued in Paris, where Bp Guron of Tulle knew him as a theology student. Took 8th place in theology lic of 1644, followed by doct. Taught philosophy in Angoulême, Le Mans and Paris houses of OFM. Professed as OFM when 16 years old, he was later provincial superior of Tours. Ordained priest in mid-1630s he was extremely active as preacher from ca 1630. Like several contemporary bps, he owed career to activities within order and to abilities as preacher. First patrons were comte de Brassac and wife, whose father, Montausier, he converted; they seem to have introduced him to entourage of Anne of Austria, who made him one of her *prédicateurs ordinaires*, ca 1640. Obtained similar post in Louis XIV's service in 1649. Some sources credit him with converting future James II and Christina of Sweden! During Fronde, he played active role as mediator, and also as one of Mazarin's pamphleteers. Discontented with meagre episcopal reward first offered by Mazarin, he quickly exchanged Glandèves for Amiens.

Nom to Glandèves 6–3–1651. Provs 9–6–1651. Cons 3–9–1651. Nom to Amiens 28–3–1653. Provs 23–3–1654. D. 11–5–1687.

Sources: ASV, PC 49, fos 158–72. BAV, Barb lat 7959, fo 1. BN, Doss bleus 262, doss 6752. BN, MS lat 15440, p 176. Oroux, *Histoire ecclésiastique*, ii. 476–7. F Pouy, 'Histoire de François Faure, 77e évêque d'Amiens 1612–87', in *Mémoires de la Société des Antiquaires* *de Picardie* 25 (Amiens, 1876), 137–286. 'Poutet, Docteurs de Sorbonne', 246. *DBF*, xiii. 740–2.

Fay-Peyraud, Paul-Antoine. Uzès 1613–33. This old Vivarais noble family can be traced to mid-14th C, though its genealogy remains rather confused. Beaucaire seems to have been their real power base, where successive generations held office of *sénéchal*. Combination of judicious marriages to families with episcopal and church connections (St-Gélais, La Baume de Suze) allied to military activity during Italian (and later religious) wars helped them to prosper in eastern Languedoc. Bp's grandfather was one of several members (who also inc Jean de St-Gélais, bp of Uzès!) to become Protestants, but he reverted to Catholicism more quickly than the others. Entry into Montmorency-Damville's service during crisis of 1575 was also decisive in promoting their interests in next 2 generations, creating a link that was sealed by bp's father's marriage in 1590 to Marie de Montmorency, Constable's illegitimate daughter.

B. ca 1583. Son of Jean, sgr de Vezonobre, *sénéchal* of Beaucaire and later Nîmes, gov of Haute Bresse, and Marie de Montmorency (her 2nd marriage). Destined by parents for episcopal career, he studied almost wholly in Jesuit coll at Avignon, where took lic (and perhaps the doct) in theology, in 1612. Despite Montmorency ties, also served in household of Cardinal Joyeuse in Rome and elsewhere. Cleric at time of nom, he held no benefices, but had been handsomely endowed by father. Uzès had been virtually reserved for him since at least 1597, when Henri IV allowed his parents to find caretaker (the Carmelite friar, Louis de Vigne) until such time as son came of age. Implicated in Montmorency's revolt of 1632, he d. during his trial for rebellion.

Procuration from Bp Vigne to take Fay as coadj 7–7–1612. No date for nom, but probably soon after Vigne's procuration. Provs 21–10–1613. Cons 1614. D. 4–4–1633.

Sources: ASV, PC 13, fos 191–219. Arch. de Chantilly, L/xlv, fo 185. Nicod, 'La Maison de Fay-Peyraud', 145–58, 203–12, 281–96, 315–38, 379–89. Gigord, *Noblesse de la sénéchaussée de Villeneuve-de-Berg*. Villain, *France moderne*, ii. 377–8. *DBF*, xiii. 883–5.

Fenouillet, Pierre. Montpellier 1608–52. Family was long settled in Annecy, where they figured among the bourgeois *notables*, despite a Jean Fenouillet having been secretary to Philibert II of Savoy ca 1498. During 16th C, they were notaries, schoolmasters etc, marrying into merchant and 'town-hall' families at best, as is evident in the generation of bp's father.

B. ca 1573 Annecy. Son of Antoine, master at Annecy coll, and Jeanne de Verney, daughter of local merchant. After father's early death, he was reared by uncle, Claude, a notary. Began education at Annecy coll under father's direction, later studied at SJ coll of Tournon. Continued with theology studies, leading to doct in the subject, probably at Louvain. First patron and career-model was François de Sales, bp of Annecy-Geneva, who helped him become canon of Annecy in 1604 and *curé* of Arenthon. Previously he had been *théologal* and *grand maître des escolles* of Gap cathedral (1600). Ordained priest in late 1602, he later moved to Paris, where his preaching in city churches and court, as well as other activities, attracted patronage of duc de Nemours and, crucially, of Sully, who was instrumental in securing see of Montpellier for him.

No date for nom (but post 15–9–1607, death of bp Jean Garnier). Provs 10–9–1608. Cons 23–11–1608. D. 24–11–1652.

Sources: AD Haute-Savoie, E 399, 439–41, 459. *Repertoire de la série G des AD Hautes-Alpes*, iv (Gap 1901), xxxiv-v. BN, MS Fr 33047, p 547 (naturalisation, March 1608). *DBF*, xiii. 996.

Fleyres, Jean-Jacques de. St-Pons coadj 1622/33–52. Nephew and successor of Pierre de Fleyres, bp of St-Pons 1587–1633, his family was originally from Albigeois, but settled at Espalion in Rouergue by early 16th C. They practised law, moving gradually upwards through both municipal office and seigneurial/royal judgeships to position of syndic of Estates of Rouergue by 1617 for bp's father. In this, as in a subsequent generation, marriages in legal and robe circles brought them close to Toulouse financial and parlementaire families such as Caminade (1589), Caulet (1645), etc. His uncle Pierre originally obtained St-Pons in 1587 through patronage of Clermont de Calvimont family, whom his father and brother both served as judges, only for the Fleyres to assert their independence in the next generation, and to retain see against Calvimont protests. Bp Pierre's involvement in 1632 revolt in Languedoc came close to disaster, but the case against him was dropped and nephew succeeded without difficulty.

B. ca 1590 Espalion. Son of Jacques, sgr de Combres and baron of Bozoul, syndic of Rouergue Estates (1617), and Antoinette Gaubert de Caminade, sister of a pres in Toulouse parlt. No details on education, but took doct in utr, probably in Toulouse. A cleric, he obtained in c priories of St-Crespin-en-Vabrais, St-Salvy-de-Carcabes and St-Maurice, ca 1609. His coadjutorial nom was probably a protracted affair, given the angry objections of Fleyres' erstwhile Calvimont patrons.

No date for nom. Provs 5–12–1622. Cons 1623. Succeeds to St-Pons 1633. D. 1652.

Sources: ASV, PC 21, fo 663v. BN, P Or 1167, doss 26,560; Carrés d'Hozier 259, Fleyres doss; MS Clairambault 368, fo 424. AD Aveyron, E 1433, 1786. Navelle, *Familles toulousaines*, iii. 8. Barrau, *Dict du Rouergue*, iii. 275–7. Villain, *France Moderne* iii (2), 1559–61. *DBF*, xiv. 66.

Forbin de Soliès, Auguste. Toulon 1627–38. Probably the most celebrated family of early modern Provence, the Forbins originated in Langres, but settled in Marseille where they were involved in trade and mercantile activities in 14th and 15th C. Spawned numerous branches which in following centuries intermarried with virtually every noble family (old and new) of any distinction in Provence, while never quite abandoning earlier links in Marseille and its leading families. Military and esp naval activities were developed partly through the order of Malta, which attracted so many recruits from Provençal nobility. Forbin vitality is evident in fact that Bp Auguste was son of the *eighth* branch of the family. Bp's father was (like members of his mother's family) active as a *Carciste* during Catholic League in Provence.

B. ca 1570. Son of Palamède, sgr de Soliès and gov of Toulon, and Jeanne de Vins, daughter of Gaspard, *cons* at Aix parlt. Nothing known of education, but Rome accepted he held doct in theology. Tonsured in Paris in 1598, which suggests (he was 28 at the time) he was not initially destined for church career at all. Provost of Pignans, OSA (Fréjus), no trace of his activities before episcopate. Original choice of bp for Toulon in 1626 was Mathieu de Morgues, and Forbin was only chosen after Morgues encountered too much resistance, esp in Rome.

Nom 30–6–1627. Provs 21–1–1628. Cons 9–4–1628. D. 5–4–1638.

Forbin-Janson, Toussaint de. Digne coadj 1655/7–68, Marseille 1668–79, Beauvais 1679–1713. B. 30–12–1629 (though one source claims 1626). Son of Gaspard, marquis de Janson, and Claire de Libertat. Educated mainly in Paris, studying humanities, philosophy and theology, although he took theology doct in Valence. Ordained priest in June 1653, he held abbey of Janson and priory of Villeneuve (Sisteron) in c. At time of nom as coadj, his considerable private means were noted in papal enquiry, no doubt to strengthen case for having coadj in such a poorly endowed diocese. He went on to be one of the major ecclesiastical diplomats of Louis XIV's reign.

Brevet de nom June 1653. Provs 5–7–1655. Cons 14–5–1656. Transferred to Marseille 1668, to Beauvais, 1679. Cardinal 1690. D. 24–3–1713.

Sources: Blanc, *Origines des familles provençales*, 243–8. Maurel, 'Structures familiales et solidarités lignagères à Marseille au xve siècle', 675–81. *DBF*, xiv. 396–418 (family-general). ASV, PC 25, fos 292–314. AN, Z^{1}o 240 (Auguste). ASV, PC 53, fos 209–26. BN, MS Fr 20661, fo 169 (Digne coadj, 1653) (Toussaint).

Fossé, Jean II de. Castres coadj 1627/32–54. Relatively little known about this bp's background, but the most important fact is he succeeded an uncle and namesake at Castres. However, family was well established in Toulouse, where they served as notaries for much of 16th C, activities which probably enabled bp's father to become a *banquier expéditionnaire* specialising in transactions involving church benefice, and to serve successive abps of Toulouse, Cardinals Armagnac and Joyeuse, both major benefice-holders throughout southern France. Certain family members were also enthusiastic *ligueurs* in Toulouse. Parlementaire office also beckoned by early 17th C, thanks largely, it seems, to families to which they were related by marriage (Mérigot, Mansencal, Maynial), and Mérigots' ecclesiastical activities also appear to have been useful to them. Patronage of Henri III's brother-in-law, Cardinal de Vaudémont, ennabled Jean I de Fossé to receive see of Castres in 1583: Vaudémont was permitted to dispose of the gift of Castres as he wished, and Fossé connections to Joyeuse probably enabled Jean I to avail of the opportunity.

Jean II (so called here purely to distinguish him from uncle) b. Toulouse ca 1574. Son of Jean and Cardone Portal. Probably educated in Toulouse where he also obtained doct in law. *Cons-cl* at Toulouse parlt, 1607, but not 'received' until possibly 1620. Successively canon, grand archdeacon, and provost of Castres during uncle's episcopate. Like uncle a generation earlier, was not initial choice of successor for Castres: his opportunity only arose when Balthasar de Budos, coadj since 1616, moved to take up see of Agde in 1626–7.

No date for nom as coadj (but soon after nom of Budos to Agde in June 1626). Provs 27–1–1627. Cons 12–3–1628. Succeeded 1632. D. Sept 1654.

Sources: AN, V^6 10 no 90, *arrêt* of *conseil privé*, 19–6–1606; V^6 12, no 161, *arrêt*, 19–11–1607. AD Haute-Garonne, B 1913, fo 219; B 213 fos 95–6, 5–7–1603. Arch Mun, Toulouse, GG 193, 26–8–1574. Lacger, *Etats administratifs*, 332. Dubédat, *Parlement de Toulouse*, 619, 625. Navelle, *Familles toulousaines*, vii. 156. *DBF*, xiv. 564.

Fouquet de la Varenne, Guillaume. Angers 1616–21. Family, originally from La Flèche, north of Angers, has no proven connection to better known Fouquet family, also natives of Angers. Their social origins, by same token, were much more modest than their later status would readily suffer, hence *flou* which surrounds their early history and activities. Both bp's father and grandfather began in service (allegedly as *écuyers de cuisine* but probably as something less elevated!) to Henri IV's sister, Catherine, through whom Guillaume, bp's father, entered king's service, becoming his close companion and receiving impressive tokens of royal favour in following years. Gov of La Flèche and Angers (1604), *contrôleur-général des postes*, he was ennobled by Henri IV in 1598. Persuaded king to install the new SJ coll at La Flèche, his home town. Marie de' Medici made him lt-gen of Anjou in 1610. That his son should become bp of Angers seems entirely consistent with father's career.

B. 1586. Eldest son of Guillaume, and Catherine Foussart, his 1st wife, also a native of La Flèche. Nothing known of education, but apparently held lic in utr. Cons at Paris parlt in 1605, MR in 1609. Holder of several abbeys in c from early age (St-Nicolas-d'Angers, St-Lomer-de-Blois, Moutier St-Jean, Ainay in Lyon), thanks to paternal favour. Refused see of Lyon after death of Albert de Bellièvre in 1612, possibly because not yet really intent on church career. Canon and provost of St-Martin-de-Tours, he traded these offices for provostship of Angers chapter a few years before his episcopal nom. Subdeacon at time of confirmation by Rome. Decision to accept see of Angers in 1616 on retirement of Charles Miron was probably less difficult than that of Lyon in 1612. After his early death in 1621, Miron reclaimed possession of Angers.

Resign by Miron of Angers to Fouquet 1–2–1616. Nom to pope 4–2–1616. Provs 13–6–1616. Cons 1616. D. 9–1–1621.

Sources: ASV, PC 13, fos 758–78. BL, Add MS 21434, fo 7 (*cons* in parlt). BN, MS Fr 32785. Port, *Dict du Maine-et-Loire*, ii. 195. DBF, xiv. 722–4.

Fouquet, Francois. Bayonne 1639–43, Agde 1643–56, Narbonne coadj 1656/9–73. The fate of this family's most famous member has tended to eclipse its broader history and associations, from its Angevin origins through its *années de faste* (thanks to prolonged patronage of Richelieu and Mazarin) to collective disgrace visited by new régime of Louis XIV after 1661. From political and religious point of view, their closeness to Parisian *dévot* circles, lay and clerical, on both sides of the family, is of particular importance and, for all the differences of emphasis, rivals that of families like the Arnaulds in its intensity and effects.

B. 26–7–1611. Eldest son of François, MR and advisor to Richelieu, and Marie de Maupeou. Studied humanities, philosophy and some theology in SJ coll of Clermont, but took lic in canon law. Destined for lay career, began career as *cons* at Paris parlt, in 1633, but abandoned it by 1635, when he prepared to take orders, becoming treasurer of chapter of St-Martin-de-Tours. After 1661, exiled from Narbonne to Alençon for several years.

Nom to Bayonne 2–5–1637. Provs 28–2–1639. Cons 15–5–1639. Nom to Agde 23–6–1643, Provs 16–11–1643. Nom coadj of Narbonne 9–1–1656. Provs 16–10–1656. Succeeded Cl de Rebé in 1659. D. 19–10–1673.

Fouquet, Louis. Agde 1657–1702. B. 4–2–1633. Youngest brother of François (above). Studied humanities and philosophy at coll of Clermont, and took doct in utr at Orléans. Initially (like François) *cons* in Paris parlt (Aug 1653). Unofficial French envoy to Rome 1655–6, when brother moved from Agde to coadjutorship of Narbonne, and see of Agde was offered to him. Cleric at moment of nom. Received abbey of Ham, OSA (Noyon) in c in 1659 'pour luy donner moien de plus en plus soustenir sa dignité dans l'église'. He later moved close to Jansenist positions as bp, and was a founder of the *Nouvelles Ecclésiastiques*. Exiled (like his brother) from his diocese in 1661, he only returned to Agde in 1691.

Nom 31–10–1656. Provs 28–5–1657. Cons 2–3–1659. D. 4–2–1702.

Sources: D Dessert, *Fouquet* (Paris 1987) (family). ASV, PC, 37, fos 151–68. BL, Add MS 21434, fo 36 (François). ASV, PC 54, fos 62–86; PC 57, fo 753. BL, Add MS 21434, fo 62. Azéma, U*n prélat janséniste. Louis Fouquet, évêque et comte d'Agde* (Louis).

Frémiot, André. Bourges 1603–21 (resign). The abp is probably best known as, firstly, the brother of Jeanne de Rabutin-Chantal, disciple of François de Sales and foundress of the Visitation order of nuns, and, secondly, as great-uncle of Mme de Sévigné. The Frémiots (or Frémyots) were originally a Burgundian family of notaries and officials in provincial *chambre des comptes* who moved into Dijon parlt from mid-16th C onwards. A pres *à mortier* in parlt in 1581, bp's father and family were leading royalists in a province dominated by Mayenne and Catholic League, but could do little for Henri IV's cause there until Burgundy returned to allegiance.

B. 26–8–1573. Son of Celse-Bénigne, sgr des Buttes, and Marguerite de Berbisey. Began education under Claude Robert (first author of *Gallia Christiana*), then studied abroad during League wars, taking doct in law at Padua. Like father, he benefited from restoration of royal authority in Burgundy. Abbot in c of St-Etienne of Dijon, OSA, in 1595, *cons* at Dijon parlt, in 1597. Nom to Bourges depended on transfer/promotion of Abp Beaune to Sens which, first decided in 1595–6, was not agreed by Rome until 1602. If not actually nom to Bourges in 1595–6, virtually certain it was effectively reserved for him at that point. After highly active episcopate, he resigned and retired to Paris in 1621, probably under pressure from Condé, new gov of Berry.

No date for nom. Provs 16–6–1603. Cons 7–12–1603. Resign to Roland Hébert, 1621. D. 13–5–1641.

Sources: BN, Naf 11865 (*Nobiliaire du xvie siècle*). ASV, N Fr 43, fo 138 (rumours of nom to Bourges, 1595). Vindry, *Parlementaires* (Dijon), 143, 162, 177. Vidal, *Critique*, 97ff. *DBF*, xiv. 1188–91.

Garnier (or Granier), Jean, OSB. Montpellier 1602–7. Virtually nothing is known about his personal or family background. B. ca 1554 at Bourguignons, near Bar-sur-Aube. He was almost certainly the Jean Garnier who was ordained deacon in Paris in 1572. Entered OSB abbey of Montieramey (Troyes) at early age, and studied in Univ of Paris, taking doct in theology at Sorbonne. *Curé* of St-Albin in Châlons-sur-Marne from 1594 onwards, but widely known as preacher 'aus mylleures vylles de mon Royaume' (Henri IV in his letter nom him to Montpellier), for which he was made *prédicateur ordinaire* and almoner to Henri IV, ca 1594. Episcopal promotion may owe something to the fact that he assisted Biron before execution in July 1602.

Nom 26–9–1602. Provs 11–12–1602. Cons 1603. D. 15–9–1607.

Sources: ASV, Misc Arm XII, 145, fo 266. AN, Z^{1}o 239 (ordination). AD Marne, G 22, fo 15; G 52, fo 172. *Studi in onore di Martino Giusti* (Vatican 1978), pp 64–5. *Journal de Pierre de l'Estoile 1601–1610*, 76. *DBF*, xv. 499.

Gassion, Pierre. Lescar 1648–52. This Béarnais family had a solid record of service to the rulers of Navarre, and have been described as 'an excellent example of the middle-managers of the principality', though their genealogical pretensions were mocked by Tallement des Réaux and others in bp's own lifetime. Most of its members appear to have become Protestant in mid-16th C, with several active as lawyers and members of *conseil souverain* of Navarre – e.g. bp's grandfather, Arnaud, and father, Jacques, who was an MR under Henri IV, *pres à mortier* in *conseil souverain* (1583), and *cons d'état* (1598). But episcopal office was much more than a reward for ancestral fidelity/service, since bp's own generation distinguished itself, switching successfully into military roles. One brother, Jean, became a highly regarded marshal of France (1643), another was a *maréchal des camps* in the army, though the eldest stuck to tradition, and served as pres *à mortier* at Pau parlt from 1628, and as intendant of Navarre 1640–8.

B. 4–4–1616. Youngest son of Jacques and Marie d'Esclaux. Born Protestant, like his brothers, but abjured ca 1632–2, as did father. Nothing known of early education in Protestant schools, but it may have been limited, since his early career was military. After conversion, studied theology at Sorbonne, taking 8th place in 1646 lic. Canon of Lescar and abbot in c of St-Vincent-du-Lucq, OSB (Oloron), ordained priest in 1646, he also preached in Paris before episcopate.

Nom 20–7–1647. Provs 13–1–1648. Cons 7–3–1648. D. 23–4–1652.

Sources: ASV, PC 47, fos 28–41. BN, MS lat 15440, p 176. Anselme, vii. 536–9. Dufau de Maluquer, *Armorial de Béarn*, i. 103. Chesnaye-Desbois, *Dict de noblesse*, ix. 19–24. Tallemant, *Historiettes*, ii. 78–87. M Greengrass, 'The Calvinist Experiment in Béarn', in A Pettegree, G Lewis, A Duke, eds, *Calvinism in Europe 1540–1620* (Cambridge 1994), 125. *DBF*, xv. 626–9. *DGS*, 645.

Gault, Jean-Baptiste, Oratorian. Marseille 1642–May 1643. Despite celebrity of bp and elder brother, Eustache, whose careers were inseparable, little is known of their background, but family seems to have been one of bourgeois *notables* in militantly Catholic city of Tours, where bp's father 'passa par toutes les charges qui peuvent donner du lustre à un bourgeois de sa ville' (Batterel). The brothers were the only children of their parents' marriage.

B. 29–12–1595. Son of Jacques and Marguerite Poitevin. Studied humanities in SJ coll at Lyon (from 1607), rhetoric and philosophy at La Flèche, followed by theology for 3 years at Sorbonne and in Rome for a year, but took no degree in it. Appears to have taken lic in canon law at Bordeaux, presumably in order to hold office in episcopal administration there. Joined Bérulle's Oratory with Eustache in 1618 and played an active part in its expansion, helping to found the Madrid house, and later serving as superior of several French houses (Dijon, Le Mans and Montauban). He and brother organised missions, preached extensively in provincial cities, and taught theology and philosophy in Oratorian houses. VG of Bp Zamet of Langres for a time, Jean-Baptiste and Eustache contributed actively to Henri de Sourdis's efforts to reform Bordeaux diocese. Jean-Baptiste became curé of Cussac and Ste-Eulalie in 1634, master of ceremonies and secretary to Sourdis, while his brother directed diocesan seminary for several years. Eustache was nom to Marseille in 1639, but d. suddenly in March 1640, only weeks after Rome had granted his provs but before he could be cons or take possession of his see. Jean-Baptiste's succession was consistent on all counts.

Nom 10–5–1640. Provs 14–7–1642. Cons 5–10–1642. D. 23–5–1643 'en odeur de sainteté' during plague.

Sources: ASV, PC 40, fos 511–33. Valois, *Inventaire des arrêts*, no 179, 9–2–1593. AAE, France 835, fos 85–6. *Corr de Bérulle, passim*. Batterel, *Mémoires domestiques de l'Oratoire*, i.

103–47. Peyrous, *Réforme catholique à Bordeaux*, i. 228. Dessert, *Argent, pouvoir et société au grand siècle*, 543. DBF, xv. 758–9.

Gelas, Claude. Agen 1609–30. No relation to the Gelas de Leberon, bps of Valence, this bp was a son of a Lyon merchant family of Italian (or Piedmontese) origins, originally called Gella, and settled in Lyon since early 16th C, where it figured prominently among merchant and muncipal élite. *Echevins* of Lyon by 1550s, involved in *grand parti* with Henri II, they married into families of similar standing, in particular the prolific Villars clan. Bp's father was an *échevin* during Catholic League, and a deputy (along with Guillaume Villars) to *ligueur* EG of 1593! He was forced out of office in 1594 because he refused to accept the defeat of League, but Villars patronage was probably decisive in following generation.

B. 1564. Son of Guillaume and Jeanne de Villars, sister of Nicolas, bp of Agen. No information on education, but early career presupposed a law degree. Cons at Paris parlt, 21-1-1597. Subsequently treasurer of Ste Chapelle of both Paris and Vincennes. Canon and grand archdeacon of Agen before 1602, also served as vg to uncle, Nicolas Villars. Attended AC of 1602 as deputy for Bordeaux province. Cousin Pierre de Villars, abp of Vienne (1626–53), was originally designated to succeed to Agen, but when he preferred the coadjutorship of Vienne, Gelas was nom in his place.

No date for nom, but probably mid-Dec 1608. Provs 29–4–1609. Cons 25–10–1609. D. 26–12–1630.

Sources: AN, Y 5268; G^{8*} 87 (AC, 1602). AD Rhône, Fonds Frecon, *Dossiers rouges*, 6 (*familles consulaires*). AC Lyon, BB 129, 131. Anselme, v. 104. DBF, xv. 955.

Gelas de Leberon, Pierre-André. Valence 1598–1622. These 2 bps were sons of a noble family from Condomois-Armagnac region, where it was settled since at least later 15th C. Military roles predominated during following century, not least because of their kinship relations to better known families of the region – e.g. Monluc, Pardailhan. It was as successor to a deposed relative, Jean de Monluc, that bp's uncle, Charles, became bp of Valence in 1574, and no doubt such influential connections helped them retain see into following generations.

B. date unknown, but possibly late 1560s. Son of Antoine, sgr de Leberon, and Marguerite de Gessac. Nothing known of education (though Rome accepted he had doct in utr) or of pre-episcopal career, but evidently groomed to succeed uncle, who resigned Valence (and other benefices later) outright to him in late 1590s.

No date for nom. Provs 17–8–1598. Cons date unknown. D. 15–9–1622.

Gelas de Leberon, Charles-Jacques. Valence 1622–54. B. ca 1592. Son of Lysander, *maréchal de camp*, and Ambroise de Voisins. No information on education, but Rome accepted he had doct in canon law. Abbot in c of Bonnecombe, O Cist (Rodez) and Flaran, O Cist (Auch), he was a simple cleric at time of nom. Resided in Paris from 1646 onwards.

No date for nom (but probably soon after uncle's death). Provs 22–5–1623. Cons 2–2–1624. D. 5–6–1654.

Sources: ASV, Acta Misc 98, fo 880; Misc Arm XII, 146, fos 177, 197. BN, Doss bleus 308, doss Gelas. Bibl. Mazarine, MS 3246 (family documents). Chesnaye-Desbois, *Dict de la noblesse*, ix. 114–16. DBF, xv. 956.

Génébrard, Gilbert, OSB. Aix 1591–7.   Son of Auvergnat family settled in Riom by early 16th C, but otherwise too modest to have left many traces.

B. 1537 Riom. Son of Pierre, notary and *procureur* at Riom *présidial* court, and Anne de Richevoye. Joined first Franciscans and then Benedictines at early age. Education probably began in Benedictine abbey-schools (Mozac and St-Alyre in Clermont), whence he went on to study in Paris, becoming doct of theology (1563). The institutional and personal patronage of fellow Auvergnat, Guillaume Duprat (bp of Clermont but also abbot in c of St-Alyre), was vital to early career in Paris, but his own intellectual distinction (esp as Hebraist) duly brought him celebrity and a professorship at *Collège Royal*. Pierre Danès offered to resign his see of Lavaur to him in 1576, but move was blocked by Blois EG, which wished to see episcopal elections restored. He threw himself into League in Paris (where preached notorious *sermon du Béarnais* in Feb 1593) but esp in Marseille, and episcopal promotion followed from this *engagement*. But his effective tenure of Aix was brief, and the parlt there joined in persecuting him after it had itself returned to royalist allegiance. He offered full submission to Henri IV in Dec 1595, after his papal absolution, but the political circumstances of his appointment made him highly vulnerable and the process of ostracisation, orchestrated partly by successor, Paul Hurault, had gone too far by then.

Appointed to Aix by papal *motu proprio* 10–5–1591 (predecessor d. in Rome). Cons 10–5–1592 in *ligueur* Paris. D. 16–2–1597 'in exile', at Semur.

Sources: ASV, N Fr 43, fo 232. *Gallia Chr Nov*, i. 129–33. Roux, *Auvergnats en Provence*, 31–72. *DBF*, xv. 1003–4.

Genoulhac, Louis de Gourdon de. Tulle 1599–1653.   This old family of well-connected Limousin military nobles stretched back to 14th C, with the famous Galiot de Genoulhac holding offices of *grand écuyer de France* and *grand maître de l'artillerie* under Francis I. Ecclesiastical record less remarkable, but it was particularly pertinent to bp's career, as 2 of his uncles preceded him at Tulle between 1560 and 1586.

Louis (erroneously named Jean-Richard in some sources) b. ca 1574. Son of Louis, gov of Bordeaux, and Anne de Montberon, his 1st wife. No information on education, but Rome accepted he had doct in canon law. Tonsured in 1588 at Bordeaux, subdeacon by time of confirmation by Rome. After death of uncle, Flotard, bp of Tulle, in 1586, see passed to Antoine de la Tour, an ageing vg and family client who resigned to Jean de Visandon in 1594. Unclear if Visandon ever really obtained papal provs, and his claim to succession was not recognised by Tulle chapter after La Tour d. in Sept 1595. Tulle thus remained vacant until Genoulhac family obtained royal nom for the underage Louis.

No date for nom. Provs 8–11–1599. Cons 1–5–1600. D. 13–1–1653.

Sources: ASV, Misc Arm XII, 216, fo 163. AD Gironde, G 794, fo 378, (tonsure). Anselme, viii. 162–7. Vindry, *Etat-major*, 197–8. Clement-Simon, *Tulle et le bas-Limousin pendant les guerres de religion*, 109, 157–8. *Lettres d'Ossat*, iii. 428.

Gifford, William, OSB. Reims 1622–9   The only Englishman of his generation in French episcopate. B. April 1554. 2nd son of John (from old Hampshire gentry family) and Elizabeth Throckmorton. Entered Lincoln coll, Oxford, in 1569, but as a Catholic he soon left for Louvain, where he was pupil of Bellarmine in 1573–7. Further studies in Paris, Rome, and Pont-à-Mousson, where took doct in theology, in 1584. Ordained priest in 1582, taught in several colls before serving as Cardinal Allen's secretary in Rome until latter's death in 1594, when returned to Spanish Netherlands and became dean of St-Pierre chapter in Lille (1595). A long-standing Guise pensioner, active in English recusant circles, he supported obedience by Catholics to Elizabeth and James I, opposing the more extreme voices among his fellow exiles. His stance made him attractive to the English government, and in 1606 he was suddenly expelled by Archduke Albert on secret allegations of spying for London on exiled recusants. Settling in France, he entered OSB and was professed in July 1609 as Gabriel de Ste-Marie, and did much thereafter to help expand English Benedictine congregation in France. Also dean of St-Malo chapter 1611–18, was naturalised in Feb 1617, when Cardinal Guise of Reims (who was not in orders) took him as suffragan bp. Administered Reims in following years, distinguishing himself as preacher. Despite vast experience, he was too old by 1622 to achieve much in badly neglected diocese.

Original nom as suffragan of Reims, ca July 1616. Provs 22–10–1617. Cons 23–9–1618. Nom abp of Reims, March 1622. Provs 5–12–1622. D. 11–4–1629.

Sources: *DBF*, xv. 1496. *DHGE*, xx. 1281–3. *DNB*, vii. 1185–7. BN, MS Fr 33047, p 491 (naturalisation). BN, MS Italien 1269, fo 388 (suffragan 1616). AAE, CP Rome 23, fo 102. Bergin, *Cardinal La Rochefoucauld*, 130–2. L Hicks, 'The Exile of Dr William Gifford from Lille in 1606', *Recusant History*, 7 (1964), 214–38. John Bossy, *The English Catholic Community* (London 1975), 28, 33. Yves Chaussy, *Les Bénédictins anglais refugiés en France au xviie siècle (1611–1669)* (Paris 1967). A Lottin, *Lille citadelle de la contre-réforme?* (Westhoek 1984), 339, n 13.

Glandevès de Cuges, Toussaint de. Sisteron 1606–48. One of the oldest and most prolific of Provençal noble families which spawned numerous branches (at least 8 by mid-17th C) through generations of intermarriage with virtually all leading noble families of province (Grimaldi, Villeneuve, and esp Forbin). Declared noble to 14th degree in 1669 *recherches*. Military activities seemed to dominate in most generations, sliding into adventurism during wars of religion, though individual family members were also tempted by office in Aix parlt in same period.

B. ca 1585. Son of Antoine, sgr de Cuges, and Diane de Forbin-Janson. Nothing known of education, but Rome accepted he had doct in utr. An underage cleric at time of nom, he succeeded the former *ligueur*, Antonio Cuppis, who resigned Sisteron in circumstances which raised suspicions in Rome of duress and produced much litigation in Paris. Peiresc later praised him as excellent preacher.

Nom 1605. Provs 16–1–1606. Cons July 1606. D. 17–1–1648.

Sources: ASV, Misc Arm XII, 145, fo 511. Blanc, *Origines des familles provençales*, 285–91. Clapiers-Coulonges, *Chronologie*, 47, 75. Vindry, *Parlementaires* (Aix), 43–4. *DBF*, xvi. 342–6. *Correspondants de Peiresc*, ed P Tamizey de Larroque, x. 13–15. Borricand, *Nobiliaire de Provence*, i. 571–5. Dumont, *Arrêts du conseil privé* (Henri IV), ii. 176, 295, 424, 439, 577 (disputes with predecessor).

Godeau, Antoine. Grasse 1636–53, Vence 1639–72. The Godeau family in general and bp's father in particular were as obscure as he was himself celebrated in his lifetime, but key influences on his early career were those exerted by wide kinship network on *mother*'s side (Targer, Grangier, Conrart, Goulas etc). Targer family, some of whom had either been or still were Protestants, were wealthy Parisian merchants and esp finance officials by Godeau's generation.

B. and baptised at Dreux 24–9–1605. Son of Antoine, lieutenant in *eaux et forêts* admin at Dreux, and Jeanne Targer. Studied humanities and philosophy at coll of Navarre, followed by law in Paris and Orléans, where took lic in utr, in 1625. An only son, initially destined for secular career, he enrolled as barrister at Paris parlt in Jan 1626, but soon abandoned the bar for poetry, attracted by literary 'academy' around Valentin Conrart (his first cousin) and Chapelain. Also frequented Rambouillet salon for several years and, having attracted Richelieu's attention, became a founding member of Académie Française. His turn towards church career surprised contemporaries, but was genuine and definitive: episcopal career combined active diocesan administration with extensive preaching and literary activity. Ordained priest 12–5–1636, no more than a month before nom to Grasse. Held no benefices before 1636, but was known to enjoy considerable private wealth. In 1639, also appointed to neighbouring (and equally miniscule) see of Vence but the union, which Rome approved in 1644, was unpopular in each diocese, and after Fronde (during which his political activities alienated him from Mazarin's supporters) Godeau was forced to make a choice of diocese, but opted to retain Vence at expense of Grasse, his original diocese.

Nom 21–6–1636. Provs 22–9–1636. Cons 14–12–1636. D. 17–4–1672.

Sources: ASV, PC 34, fos 361–79. BN, P Or 2797, Targer doss. AN, MC, XXVI, 61, 13–8–1636 (*partage* Marie Targer). Doublet, *Godeau évêque de Grasse et de Vence*. DGS, 662. DBF, xv. 425–7.

Gondi, Henri. Paris 1597–22. With 4 successive bps (and abps) of Paris (1568–1661), Gondis must rank as one of the most successful of many Italian banking families who settled in France, initially in Lyon, and later in Paris where favour of their fellow Florentine, Catherine de' Medici, rapidly enabled them to reap political, military and ecclesiastical dividends from their financial talents. Surviving periods of unpopularity as foreigners and favourites during reigns of Charles IX and Henri III, by early 17th C they were fully part of the great nobility, to whom they were now connected by numerous marriages, and also benefited from second round of Florentine patronage through Marie de' Medici. By now their political and military activities were being complemented by increasing affinities to *dévots*, at court and elsewhere, exemplified by activities of parents of last Gondi abp of Paris. Latter's political activities during Fronde have inevitably overshadowed much of their previous history and activities, though it is less often noted that Retz's rebellion came at a time when Gondi family as such was *en voie d'extinction*.

B. 1572. Son of Albert, marshal of France, and Claude-Catherine de Clermont (widow of baron de Retz). No information on education, but took lic in utr. He was abbot in c of Buzay when he took minor orders in Sept 1597. Ordained deacon and priest in Dec 1597. Became first Cardinal de Retz in 1618

Nom 2–11–1596 (on resign of Cardinal Pierre de Gondi). Provs 16–6–1597. Cons 1–3–1598. D. 12–8–1622.

Gondi, Jean-François de. Paris 1622–54. B. 1584 Paris. Younger brother of Henri (above). Studied at coll of Tournon (ca 1605) along with Claude de Rebé, abp of Narbonne, but not known if he took degree. Canon and dean of ND de Paris, he was also master of music in Louis XIII's chapel until 1631. Took nephew as coadj in 1643.

No date for nom (but shortly after brother's death in Aug 1622). Provs 14–11–1622. Cons 19–2–1623. D. 21–3–1654, having taken nephew as coadj in 1643.

Biographical Dictionary

Gondi, Jean-François-Paul. Paris coadj 1643/54–61 (resign). B. 20–9–1613. 3rd son of Philippe-Emmanuel, comte de Joigny, *général des galères* and later priest of the Oratory, and Marguerite de Silly de Rochepot. Educated at coll of Clermont from 1625 onwards, then studied theology in Paris, taking 1st place in 1638 lic, ahead of La Mothe-Houdancourt, future bp of Rennes and Richelieu's protégé – a piece of defiance which prevented him from taking doct until 1643! Also appears to have studied canon law, but took no degree. Tonsured in June 1623, canon of ND de Paris in 1627, ordained subdeacon 3 months before nom, while remaining orders quickly followed his famous (by his own account) retreat at St-Lazare under Vincent de Paul, a former family chaplain. Family's evident ambition for him to succeed his uncle was blocked while Richelieu lived, but they persuaded Louis XIII and later Anne of Austria to agree to coadjutorship for him. After 1646, uncle virtually turned over admin of diocese to him. As full abp, he never set foot in Paris, having been arrested in Dec 1652 before escaping to exile in Rome in mid 1654.

Brevet de nom as coadj 12–6–1643. Provs 5–10–1643. Cons 31–1–1644. Cardinal Feb 1652. Resign 5–6–1662. D. 24–8–1679.

Sources: Retz, *Ouevres* [Pléaiade ed.]. Dubost, 'Les Italiens en France au xvie et xviie siècle' (*passim*). S Bertière, *La Vie du cardinal de Retz* (Paris 1990). D Julia and M-M Compère, *Les Collèges français xvie-xviiie siècles*, i (Paris 1984), 700. AN, Z^{1}o 241 (ordinations). ASV, PC 43, fos 185–211 (papal enquiry, 1643). DHGE, xxii. 575–83.

Gondrin, Louis-Henri de Pardailhan, de. Sens coadj 1645–74. The Pardailhans, sgrs de Gondrin, were an old noble family from the Armagnac, whose activities were overwhelmingly military and whose kinship ties were essentially to similarly active families from the same region. Abp's father's marriage to Paule de Bellegarde, sister of duc de Bellegarde and cousin of abp Octave de Bellegarde, was obviously crucial to Sens succession. Paule de Bellegarde's extraordinary energy and ability were no less vital, given her husband's death in 1624; the Bellegarde connection was further reinforced in 1638 by abp's brother's marriage to his first cousin, Anne-Marie de Bellegarde. As abp of Sens, Gondrin became embroiled in Jansenist controversies, and his independence was feared even by Louis XIV whose mistress, Mme de Montespan, was Gondrin's niece.

B. 1620 Gondrin. 7th son of Antoine-Arnaud, sgr de Gondrin and Montespan, and Paule de Bellegarde. After early studies in Toulouse and La Flèche, undertook theology at Sorbonne for 3–4 years but, not unusually, took lic in canon law, in Paris. Prior in c of St-Orens (Auch), obtained an age dispensation to be ordained priest in late 1643. Also active in Olier's parish of St-Sulpice before nom.

Procuration from uncle, Bellegarde, to take him as coadj 15–10–1643. Nom to pope 4–11–1643. Provs 6–2–1645 (delayed because he was underage). D. 19–9–1674.

Sources: ASV, PC 44, fos 621–52; Secr dei Brevi 924, fo 926 (age dispensation, Aug 1643). BAV, Barb lat 7944, fos 60–1 (Bellegarde-Gondrin marriage dispensation, 1638). Vindry, *Etat-major*, 9–10, 384. Monluc, *Commentaires*, 482ff. J Lestrade, 'Acte de décès de Paule de Bellegarde, dame de Gondin', *Revue de Gascogne* 14 (1914), 354–5. DHGE, xxi. 586–90. DBF, xvi. 572–3.

Gourdon. *See* **Genoulhac**

Grangier, Balthasar. Tréguier 1646–79. Family's early history little known, but no doubt that they were well settled in Paris by the early 16th C, where increasingly their relations were to financial circles, esp those involving military-financial liaisons with the Swiss. Having served both Henri III and Catherine de' Medici, bp's grandfather was successively treasurer (1569–73) and ambassador (1577–94) to Swiss leagues; his career owed much to patronage of Chancellor Bellièvre, himself a former ambassador to the Grisons. Bp's own father entered Paris parlt in 1598. On mother's side, bp was related to another prominent Parisian family of merchants and office-holders which was related to, *inter alios*, the Choart family.

B. Paris ca 1606. Son of Timoléon, sgr de Liverdis, and Anne du Refuge. Little known of education except that took lic in canon law (probably in Paris) and spent over 2 years studying theology under Jacques Lescot, ca 1626–7 (in company of Barthélemy d'Elbène, bp of Agen). Royal almoner (for brief period?) in mid-1620s, was also prior in c of St-Martin-de-Selle (Périgueux) and abbot of St-Barthélemy of Noyon, OSA. Subdeacon before 1635, ordained priest, ca 1639–40. Dean of Lisieux, in 1639, thanks to patronage of Cospeau, who thought highly of him and probably helped bring him to attention of ministerial and *dévot* circles.

Nom 22–2–1646. Provs 16–7–1646. Cons 18–11–1646. D. 2–2–1679.

Sources: ASV, PC 34, fo 480–1; PC 47, fos 432–50. Vindry, *Ambassadeurs* (Paris 1903), 45. Blanchart, *Catalogue des conseillers*, 111. Vidal, *Critique*, 214–15. *DBF* xvi. 1023. *La Bretagne en 1665 d'après Colbert de Croissy*, ed Kerhervé, 133.

Grasse de Cabris, Jean de. Grasse 1625–9 (resign). Obscure and short-lived figure of episcopate descended from one of Provence's most ancient and prolific noble families, which produced at least 7 bps between the 11th and 18th C. Family's centre of gravity was in diocese of Grasse itself, where the Cabris branch had existed for generations. Alliances with best Provençal families ensured family members occupied numerous offices locally.

B. 1600. Son of César, sgr de Cabris, and Marthe de Barrause. Studied humanities at Avignon and philosophy in Paris (along with B Corneilhan, bp of Rodez), taking doct in canon law there, having followed theology course for several years under André du Val and others. Normally resident in Paris, tonsured in March 1612, he was subdeacon in 1625 when nom to Grasse. His attendance at AC of 1628 led to dispute as to whether uncons bishops could rightfully be deputies. Despite taking possession of Grasse, he declined to have himself cons and resigned it in 1629 to Jean Guerin, exchanging Grasse for Guerin's priory of l'Enfourchure. Thereafter he remained in Provence where he was active as *vicaire apostolique* of Antibes, and might well have become bp of Agen or coadj of Fréjus in 1653, but Bp Camelin of Fréjus's plans were thwarted at court. Grasse's ambivalence towards episcopal office, while not unusual, remains difficult to understand, particularly in someone of his social and geographical origins.

Nom 20–4–1624. Provs 15–9–1625. Resigned without being cons, ca 1629. D. in 1691

Sources: ASV, PC 21, fos 624–39. BN, P Or 1399, doss 31,492. Borricand, *Nobiliaire de Provence*, i. 586–91. Doublet, *Godeau évêque de Grasse et de Vence*, i. 65, 69, 71–2. Espitalier, 'Evêques de Fréjus', 54. *DBF*, xvi. 1067.

Griet. *See* **Donadieu de Griet**

Grignan, François de Castellane d'Adhémar de. St-Paul-Trois-Chateaux 1630–44, Arles 1645–89. Best known *via* Mme de Sévigné (whose daughter was comtesse de

Grignan and thus niece by marriage of the bps), Adhémars were one of the genuinely old noble families of the Valentinois, although Grignan bps were descended from Castellane family which inherited Grignan title in mid-16th C. Thereafter, Grignan fortunes prospered again, esp under Louis XIV, when Mme de Sévigné's son-in-law was lt-gen and virtual gov of Provence, and where his episcopal uncles (esp François) played considerable supporting rôles, as key members of Provençal governing élite. Domination of small see of St-Paul via dependent bishops (esp 1585–1630) was also an important asset, but it is clear that their enormously influential *dévot* connections would have helped secure episcopal preferment for their members.

B. 27–8–1603 at Grignan, near Valence. Son of Louis-François, comte de Grignan, and Jeanne d'Ancezune de Corderousse, daughter of Louis, sgr de St-Romain. Studied humanities at SJ colls of Avignon and Carpentras, followed by philosophy and theology at coll of Clermont, Paris. Unable to graduate at Paris, took doct in theology in Valence. Abbot in c of Aiguebelle, O Cist (St-Paul-Trois-Châteaux), ordained priest shortly after nom to St-Paul. Deputy to AC of 1628 for Arles province. A founder member of *Compagnie du St Sacrement*, he was highly regarded by SJ. Abp Barrault of Arles, who cons him, had made necessary arrangements to take him as coadj just before death in 1643.

Nom to St-Paul 12–3–1630. Provs 16–12–1630. Cons 14–9–1631. Nom coadj of Arles, 5–5–1643, nom renewed for full title 31–3–1644. Provs 16–1–1645. D. 9–3–1689.

Grignan, Jacques de Castellane d'Adhémar de. St-Paul-Trois-Chateaux 1645–57, Uzès coadj 1657/60–74. B. 1615. Younger brother of François. Educated initially at SJ coll of Tournon (along with Jean-Vincent de Tulle and Pierre de Bertier), followed by 4 years of theology at Sorbonne, where he apparently defended theses, but did not take degree. Ordained priest in 1640. Deputy to AC of 1641 where he was elected an *agent-général du clergé*, a coveted post which frequently led to episcopal office.

Nom to St-Paul (vacated by brother François) 18–4–1644. Provs 20–3–1645. Cons 14–5–1645. Nom coadj of Uzès 22–5–1657. Provs 30–9–1658. Succeeded to Uzès, Feb 1660. D. 13–9–1674.

Sources: AD, Bouches-du-Rhône, B. 3339, fo 58, c.m. of parents (4–6–1595). *Gallia Chr Nov*, (St Paul), 595–7. Anselme, ix. 85–6. Borricand, *Nobiliaire de Provence*, i. 15–17, 297–9, 601–3. Kettering, *Patrons, Brokers and Clients*, 104–11. R Duchêne, 'Argent et famille au xviie siècle: Mme de Sévigné et les Grignan', *Provence Historique*, 15 (1965), 205–28, 16 (1966), 3–41, 587–620. DGS, 680. DHGE, i. 557–8, xxii. 215–16. DBF, xvi. 1216–17 (family-general). ASV, PC 28, fos 855–83; PC 44, fos 154–71; 45, fo 58. BN, MS lat 17021, fo 178 (Arles 1643). Retz, *Oeuvres*, 170 (François). ASV, PC 45, fos 752–77; PC 56, fos 371–94 (Jacques).

Grillié, Nicolas. Bazas 1631–3, Uzès 1633–60. Career of this widely admired bp (name also spelled Grillet) was a classic case of ecclesiastical mobility, owing little to prior family connections. Family (which should not be confused with others of same name in Mâconnais and Provence) was a rather modest one from Braye-sur-Seine, near Provins, where father was probably an *élu* (*iudex taillarum* in Roman sources) of whom nothing else is known. A number of family members figured among local clergy in generation before bp, making modest ecclesiastical prospects realistic.

B. Braye-s-Seine, ca 1593. Son of Jean and Louise Truffe. Education probably began at Provins, where Jean Grillié was dean of ND du Val, and continued in Paris where resided in Cistercian coll of St-Bernard (which had strong Provins connection). Encounter with Cospeau in early 1610s (by Cospeau's own account) was turning-point, and Grillié soon joined him in Aire diocese (serving him for 3 years) and Toulouse, where he took doct in theology, ca 1615. Ordained priest, ca 1618. Under Cospeau's auspices, he developed reputation as preacher, not least in Paris, and through him became *prédicateur ordinaire* to Marie de' Medici and Louis XIII. Influence and patronage of Bérulle, who also held high opinion of his talents, was perhaps more important to later career, and persuaded Marie de' Medici to demand episcopal promotion for him several times in late 1620s. Dean of ND du Val, Provins, in 1629, he held no other benefices before episcopate. Took Jacques de Grignan bp of St-Paul-Trois-Châteaux as coadj at Uzès in 1657 (with his own nephew, Claude Ruffier, obtaining Grignan's see of St-Paul-Trois-Châteaux).

Nom to Bazas 30–12–1630. Provs 24–3–1631. Cons in mid-1631. Transferred to Uzès 1633. D. 12–2–1660.

Sources: ASV, PC 24, fo 698; PC 28, fos 777–806, 907–34. BAV, Barb lat 7960, fo 54. AN G^8 87. AD Yonne, G 198 (ND de Provins). *Corr de Bérulle*, ii. 33, 42, 140; iii. 497. *DBF*, xvi. 1229–30.

Grimaldi, Jerome de. Aix 1655–85. Former nuncio to France (1641–4) and a cardinal before his nom to Aix, Jérôme Grimaldi-Cavalleroni was as well suited as any Italian curial figure to hold episcopal office in France. Moving from their Genoese seat, one branch of Grimaldi family had struck down roots in Provence as early as 14th C. Nor were they strangers to episcopal office, before or after this period (e.g. they provided bps of Rodez, Besançon and Noyon in 18th C). A Barberini protégé, Jérôme was vice-legate in the papal states in 1626, and a gov of Rome in 1628. Mazarin connection facilitated by their common Barberini clientship, which would explain both men's difficult relations with Innocent X after 1644. His nom to succeed Michele Mazarin at Aix was a sign of consistency on Cardinal Mazarin's part, but led to 7 years vacancy at Aix, since Innocent X insisted on right to nom its abp, as Mazarin's brother had died in curia. Grimaldi went on to become much respected and resident abp, the antithesis of the curial benefice-hunter.

Nom 20–9–1648. Provs 30–8–1655. D. 4–11–1685.

Sources: *DBF*, xvi. 1237–7. *DHGE*, xxii. 245–9. Kettering, *Judicial Politics and Urban Revolt*, 307–9.

Guerin, Jean de. Grasse 1630–2. One of the most obscure and short-lived bishops of the period.

B. in Clermont diocese, date unknown. Identity of parents also unknown. Not certain if he or family were actually Auvergnats, and it is possible he was related to Aix parlementaire family of same name which, if true, might mean he was distantly related to his predecessor at Grasse. Nothing known of studies or early career, except that he was prior in c of L'Enfourchure, O Grandmont (Sens) and almoner to Louis XIII by 1616. Circumstances in which he obtained Grasse are a mystery, but nom followed resignation of uncons Jean de Grasse.

Nom 1629. Provs 4–3–1630. Cons 1–8–1630. D. 7–4–1632.

Sources: AN, MC, LXXXIII, 289, 30–12–1616. *Gallia*, iii. 1180. Grillon, *Papiers de Richelieu*, v. 525. *DBF*, xvi. 1490–1.

Guise. *See* **Lorraine**

Guron de Rechignevoisin, Louis. Tulle 1653–71, Comminges 1677–93. By the terms of bp's parents' marriage contract, the Gurons were required to adopt the Rechignevoisin name. Bp's family belonged to middling nobility of Poitou, where they fought on Catholic side during wars of religion. Having supported and served Henri IV, bp's father became a busy client of Richelieu from mid-1620s in western France, and in general enjoyed a considerable military and diplomatic career. Bp himself fully maintained this tradition of ministerial service/devotion.

B. Nov-Dec 1617 at Guron. Son of Jean, *introducteur des ambassadeurs* under Louis XIII, and Marie de Rechignevoisin, his 2nd wife and cousin. Studied humanities at SJ coll of Poitiers, moved to coll of Harcourt (Paris) for philosophy, followed by theology at Sorbonne. Took 4th place in theology lic of 1644, followed by doct and election as *socius* of Sorbonne. Ordained priest ca 1644, abbot in c of Moreaux (Poitiers) before episcopate. But service to Mazarin (following that of father to Richelieu) was key to career. Particularly active during Fronde, when served as *commissaire* in Poitou, Saintonge, Angoumois, and Béarn, and contributed to restoration of royal control in Bordeaux, shortly before nom as bp.

Nom to Tulle 2–8–1652. Provs 26–5–1653. Cons 2–11–1653. Transferred to Comminges 1677. D. 20–5–1693.

Sources: ASV, PC, 53, fos 1209–30. BN, MS Baluze 252, fos 156–93; MS lat 15440, p 176. Vindry, *Etat-major*, 83. Grillon, *Papiers de Richelieu*, i. 407. *DBF*, xvii. 363–4.

Habert, Isaac. Vabres 1645–68. Family originally from Issoudun, where grandfather Pierre b. Along with brother François (a court poet under Henri II), Pierre moved to Paris and began as a *maître-écrivain*, and indeed a writer – a vocation pursued by later generations. By 1560s he was also 'suivant les finances', becoming SR by 1587 and 'bailli du Louvre et de l'artillerie de France et garde des sceaux d'icelle' by 1596. Bp's father followed same path, trying his hand at poetry during 1580s, perhaps because his father was in circle of Henri III.

B. Paris 1600. Son of Isaac, SR, sgr des Ternes, and Catherine Poncet. Educated in Univ of Paris, took 2nd place in 1626 lic in theology, followed by the doct, having been prior of Sorbonne in 1624. Ordained priest, ca 1626, canon and *théologal* of ND de Paris by 1631. Much involved in univ politics and ecclesiastical controversies of 1620s and 1630s, he gained greatest notoriety in 1642 when, at Richelieu's instigation, he openly preached against Jansen's work at ND.

Approved for Vabres by *conseil de conscience* 3–4–1645. Nom 3–4–1645. Provs 18–9–1645. Cons 17–12–1645. D. 15–9–1668.

Sources: ASV, PC, 28, fo 819; PC 45, fos 819–34. AAE 851, fos 120–1. *DBF*, xvii. 452–3. Tessereau, *Chancellerie*, 226.

Habert de Montmort, Pierre. Cahors coadj 1622/27–36. Unrelated to Isaac (above), bp was from an Artois family which moved to Paris during early 16th C, where grandfather, Philippe, ended his career as a clerk of *greffe criminelle* of parlt. Bp's father (Louis 1530–1622) did most to establish family's fortunes, holding a series of important financial offices during a very long career, and laying basis of next generation's financial activities and wealth, which also enabled them to become important figures in Parisian intellectual life.

B. Paris, date unknown. Son of Louis and Marie Rubentel. Nothing known of education, but law degree may be assumed. Cons at Paris parlt in 1599, MR in 1611. Well endowed with benefices, abbot in c of ND de Coulombs (Chartres), La Roche (Chartres-which he obtained via Rubentel family), ND de Bouhours, O Cist (Laon), prior of St-Arnoul-de-Crépy, O Cluny (Senlis). Although often a deputy to ACs from 1605 onwards, reluctant to take orders, despite being pressed to do so by father (esp in his will, 1621). Having served Cardinal de Guise and other *grands*, was first almoner (an attractive sinecure) to Gaston d'Orléans before nom to Cahors.

Nom Nov 1621. Provs 2–5–1622. Cons 2–5–1627. Succeeds 29–3–1627. D. 27–2–1636.

Sources: BN, MS Fr 32785, p 447; MS Fr 3540, fo 72. AN, MC, LXXXVIII, 46, 19–2–1614 (Guise service). Luc Boisnard, *Les Phélypeaux* (Paris 1986), 62. Cauchie, *Documents pour servir à l'histoire littéraire du xviie siècle*, 86–9. Y Labbé, 'Une famille de noblesse de robe: Les Habert de Montmort, seigneurs du Mesnil-Saint-Denis 1543–1720', *Paris et Ile-de-France* 39 (1988), 7–119. *Lettres et mémoires au chancelier Séguier*, ii. 1202–3. *DHGE*, xxii. 1392. *DBF*, xvii. 452, 456–60.

Hacqueville, Charles de. Soissons 1620–53. Like the Haberts de Montmort, the Hacquevilles originated in Artois, and settled in Paris, where by mid-16th C they had entered the major courts (*grand conseil, conseil privé*, parlt), and in the process intermarried with some of best known robe families, in particular the Hennequins, whose family network was impressively wide, and who may have impelled bp's father into following several Hennequin members into Parisian League, in which they played such a prominent part. But Hacqueville service to Guise family would also have pushed them in same direction. Bp's father became (apparently reluctantly) a *ligueur* pres in parlt in 1591, but was forced back into *grand conseil* after League's defeat in 1594. In next generations, their *ligueur* commitment found itself transmuted into *dévot* activities and affiliations.

B. 1572 Hacqueville. Son of André and Anne Hennequin, daughter of Dreux, pres in *chambre des comptes*. Early studies in SJ coll in Paris, after which studied some theology, but took lic in canon law, probably in Paris. Close to SJ, whose houses he frequented over many years. A priest, also preached, esp in St-Nicholas-du-Chardonnet, Paris. Archdeacon of Vexin in Rouen diocese, whose parishes he visited and which he helped to administer for Cardinal Joyeuse, the frequently absent abp. Obtained see of Soissons when cousin, Dreux Hennequin, uncons coadj there since 1612, declined the succession after death of Bp Jérôme Hennequin in March 1619.

Nom 22–4–1619. Provs 12–8–1619. Cons 1619 in Rome by Paul V. D. 27–2–1623.

Sources: ASV, PC 16, fos 186–200. BN, MS Fr 32989, fo 23v. Etchéchoury, *Maîtres des requêtes*, 227. Trani, 'Conseillers du grand conseil', 151–2. Descimon, *Qui étaient les Seize?*, 157–8. A Lapeyre and R Scheurer, *Les Notaires et sécretaires du roi sous les règnes de Louis XI, Chartes VIII et Louis XII*, 2 vols (Paris 1978), ii. 159. Chesnaye-Desbois, *Dict de noblesse*, x. 189–91. *DBF*, xvii. 477–8.

Hardivilliers, Pierre. Bourges 1642–9. Relatively little is known of abp's family, except they were apparently of Picard origin and his parents settled in Paris before or relatively soon after his birth. Their circumstances seem to have been relatively modest, with family ties to merchants and a Paris notary. Some of them left Paris for Berry during Pierre's episcopate, doubtless in hope of improving their fortunes.

B. ca 1579 (but possibly 1581 by his own, much later account). Son of Pierre and Barbara Joly. Studied humanities and philosophy at Univ of Paris, and was resident MA at coll of Boncourt in 1610. Also studied theology there (along with Charles de Condren), took 1st place in theology lic (1616), and doct soon afterwards. Rector of the univ in 1611–12 session, opposed SJ efforts to reopen coll of Clermont, the univ's main potential competitor. By 1614, when ordained deacon, held two modest benefices. Went on to serve as *curé* of Parisian parish of St-Laurent for about 10 years, moving to St-Benoît after ca 1628, where he established reformed community of priests, activities which naturally brought him into contact with follow reformers of secular clergy – Bérulle, Olier and others. Member of *Compagnie du St Sacrement* from at least 1633 onwards.

Nom 31-3-1639. Provs 10-11-1642. Cons 8-2-1643. D. 9-10-1649.

Sources: ASV, PC 40, fos 140–56; PC 47, fo 241. AN, Z^1o 241 (ordination). Argenson, *Annales de la Compagnie du Saint-Sacrement*, ed Beauchet-Filleau, 42. Jean Jenny, 'Un archévêque réformateur, Pierre de Hardivilliers', *Bulletin de la Société d'Emulation du Bourbonnais*, 55 (1971), 597–610. *DHGE*, xxiii. 349. *DBF*, xvii. 638–9.

Harlay de Champvallon, François de. Rouen coadj 1613–51 (resign). The history of this celebrated and prolific clan seems so inextricably intertwined with that of the Paris parlt in 16th and 17th Cs that its broader history has not been attempted, so its numerous and important non-robe activities, insofar as they are taken into account at all, appear as deviations from the norm rather than as normal advances upon robe office-holding, however distinguished. In fact, from mid-16th C onwards, when different branches of the family began to form, they were attracted to courtly, military and diplomatic roles, and it is noteworthy that none of the 3 bps of this period was drawn from the parlementaire branch. Father of first abp of Rouen, best remembered for his liaison with Marguerite de Valois, was one of the first to follow a military career, while his cousin, Nicolas, sgr de Sancy, embraced Protestantism and was a close ally of Henri IV during final phase of the religious wars. His conversion to Catholicism became celebrated for attack on him and motives by Agrippa d'Aubigné.

B. 1586. Son of Jacques, sgr de Champvallon, and Catherine de Lamarck. Educated almost entirely, it seems, at Univ of Paris, he took 1st place in theology lic, 1610, became doct soon afterwards, and was elected *socius* of Sorbonne. Tonsured in March 1603, deacon in 1609, ordained priest in 1611. Abbot in c of St-Victor, OSA (Paris) before 1607, he had some experience as a preacher, but in later years was known for considerable, if somewhat undirected, learning.

Procuration from Cardinal Joyeuse to take Harlay as coadj 4-6-1613. Nom 16-6-1613. Provs 9-9-1613. Cons 2-3-1614. Succeeds Aug 1615. Resign to nephew, François II, 9-5-1651. D. 22-3-1653.

Harlay de Champvallon, François II. Rouen 1651–71, Paris 1671–95. B. 14-8-1625. 2nd son of Achille, marquis de Brevel and Champvallon, and Odette de Vaudetar, his 1st wife. Like uncle probably studied mainly at Univ of Paris, where took MA in 1643–4, and studied theology at Sorbonne, taking lic in 1644. Canon of Rouen, ordained priest in late 1649–early 1650. Abbot in c of Jumièges in succession to uncle in 1645, deputy to, and *promoteur* at, AC of 1650, which proved ideal opportunity to extract coadjutorship for him from crown during Mazarin's first exile. As abp of Paris under Louis XIV, gained deserved reputation for political and administrative ability and for his notorious private life.

Procuration from uncle for coadj 9-5-1651. Nom 23-5-1651. Provs 28-10-1651. Cons 28-12-1651. Transferred to Paris 1671. D. 6-8-1695.

Harlay de Sancy, Achille de, Oratorian. St-Malo 1631-46. B. 1581. 3rd son of Nicolas, sgr de Sancy, successively MR, ambassador, *surintentant des bâtiments*, gov of Chalon-sur-Saône, and Marie Moreau du Tremblay. Early education obscure, but studied philosophy under Cospeau at coll of Lisieux, ca 1599, followed by doct in law and, over 20 years later (after return to clerical career), bacc in theology. Expert in Hebrew and other languages. Nom to Lavaur ca 1603, just after completing studies, but turned it down to assume elder brother's title and follow military career. Subsequently ambassador to Constantinople, where he learned Hebrew and other languages, but was involved in unsavoury activities. Returned to France in 1618, entered the Oratory in 1619, was ordained priest in 1620. Thereafter, he preached, personally financed new Oratorian foundations, accompanied Bérulle and Henriette Maria to England in 1625-6, and conducted other diplomatic missions. A senior figure in Oratory, he was potential successor to Bérulle as superior-general, an (unrealised) ambition which his patron, Richelieu, seems to have held for him. Known to desire episcopal status, he was made several offers in 1620s, but none came to anything. Only received St-Malo after death of Marillac's son, the original nominee, in 1631.

Nom 15-8-1631. Provs 10-11-1631. Cons Jan 1632. Took nephew F de Neufville-Villeroy as coadj 1645. D. 20-10-1646.

Harlay de Césy, Roger. Lodève 1657-9. B. 1616. Eldest son of Philippe, sgr de Césy and long-serving ambassador in Constantinople (1619-39), and Anne de Béthune. Nothing known of early education, but may have studied theology in Paris, even though took doct in theology at Bourges in 1656 (years after completing his studies, and probably in anticipation of episcopal promotion). Ordained priest ca 1647, he was credited with converting a number of Armenians to Catholicism. Abbot in c of St-Pierre of Auxerre, OSA, and ND de Chaalis, O Cist (Senlis), he was deputy to AC of 1655.

Nom 3-6-1657. Provs 24-9-1657. Cons 2-6-1658. D. 14-3-1659.

Sources: Etchéchoury, *Maîtres des Requêtes*, 227-8. *DBF*, xvii, 658-9, 662-6. *DHGE*, xxiii 378-80 (family-general). ASV, PC 13, fos 89-111. BN, MS lat 15440, p 135. BN, 500 Colbert 353, p 406. *Revue de Gascogne*, 13, pp 289-90. Tallemant, *Historiettes*, ii. 39-42 (François I). ASV, PC 53, fos 530-61. AAE 851, fo 152, 8-5-1645, *conseil de conscience*. *DGS*, 709-10 (François II). ASV, PC 28, fos 937-59. AN V^6 1222, 10-10-1603 (Lavaur, 1603). Batterel *Mémoires domestiques de l'Oratoire*, i. 178-212. Charles E Williams, *French Oratorians and Absolutism 1611-1641* (New York 1989), 245 (Achille). ASV, PC 54, fos 880-94. Martin, *Histoire de Lodève*, ii. 376 (Roger).

Hébert, Roland. Bourges 1622-38. At the time of his birth, abp's family was resident in Beaumont-sur-Oise, north of Paris, where father was a modest merchant. His parents (and probably other family members) subsequently moved to Paris, but their social and economic success there was limited enough, judging both by offices they held and their marriages. Several family members were clearly active in Catholic League.

B. ca 1564. Son of Raoul and Catherine le Ret. Probably educated at Univ of Paris schools, where also studied theology, taking bacc in 1593 and lic in 1598, which opened up prospect of ecclesiastical advancement within Paris. *Curé* of St-Côme parish by 1604, later obtained the more prominent post of *pénitencier* of ND. Deputy to EG of 1614 for

Paris clergy. His service as confessor to Condé during incarceration in Bastille (1616–19) was turning point in his career, as it was Condé, appointed gov of Berry in 1621, who opened the way for Hébert's episcopal promotion by negotiating resignation of his predecessor, André Frémiot.

No date for nom, but probably Sept 1621. Provs 14–3–1622. Cons 16–5–1622. D. 21–6–1638.

Sources: ASV, PC 17, fo 206. AN, MC, LXXXV, 61, 7–12–1561; MC, XXIII, 223, 15–7–1604 (marriages). BN, MS Fr 17364, pp 476–7 (nom to Bourges). Descimon, *Qui étaient les Seize?*, 154–6; Hayden, *Estates-General*, 236. *DBF*, xvii. 811.

Houdancourt. *See* **La Mothe-Houdancourt**

Houssay. *See* **Malier**

Hugues, Guillaume d', OFM. Embrun 1612–48. There is no truth in the legend of Languedoc family of ancient noble stock. Originally from Poujol near Aniane, where abp's father was a mere *bourgeois*. Family members followed abp to Provence, where they entered nobility via fief-holding, and later persuaded intendant to accept their noble status on the basis of proofs dating from 1090! In fact, abp was probably key to their upward movement: several family members were canons and dignitaries of Embrun during his episcopate, while the next generation moved towards military careers and intermarriage with local nobility.

B. 1564 Poujol-sur-Orb. Son of Michel, sgr de Vilaret, and Delphine du Pré. First schooling apparently in SJ coll at Rodez. But as he entered Franciscan/Cordeliers house in Avignon at early age, completed education in Franciscan *studia*. Of considerable ability, he was successively guardian of Avignon and other southern French Cordelier houses, becoming Minister-General of order in 1601. Also had good reputation as preacher. His unofficial diplomatic activities in Rome were valued by Henri IV and Marie de' Medici, their ministers and ambassadors, and ultimately played no small part in promotion to Embrun, which the crown was anxious to prevent from falling into hands of dependent of Huguenot gov of Dauphiné, Lesdiguières, who made no secret of ambition to play the local bishop-maker.

Nom 18–1–1612. Provs 3–9–1612. Cons 16–9–1612 in Rome. D. 27–10–1648.

Sources: AD Alpes de Haute-Provence, E 1550 (family papers). Chesnaye-Desbois, *Dict de Noblesse*, x. 851–3 (myth of ancient nobility). Blanc, *Origines des familles provençales*, 317. *Gallia*, iii. cols 1096–7. *DBF*, xvv. 1484, 1486–7 *DHGE*, xxv. 1994–5.

Hurault de Cheverny, Philippe. Chartres 1608–21. Celebrity of Hurault family was more short-lived than that of the Harlays, but few could rival their record during 16th C, when they produced 2 chancellors of France. In previous centuries, their activities had been similar to those of many Loire-valley families serving the crown, moving in due course to Paris and esp to offices in the chancery of parlt. Typical examples of the *grande robe* which was developing under Francis I and successors, the Huraults owed their ascension in part to their early financial activities (esp under Francis I), in part to marriages with other financial and robe families (Beaune, Poncher, L'Hôpital, de Thou etc). By later 16th C, offices in parlt or as MR (no fewer than 9 during the century) had become more common. Diplomatic and other political activities flowed naturally from such a broad social and professional base. At least one branch, the Belesbat, from which the abps of Aix were descended, became Protestant for a time. In some ways, episcopal office was a coda to the most distinguished chapter of their history, though bps had figured among earlier generations.

B. 19-9-1579. 3rd son of Philippe, chancellor of France, and Anne de Thou, sister of Jacques-Auguste de Thou. Nothing known of education, he apparently held lic in utr. Held no fewer than 5 abbeys (inc St-Pierre-en-Vallée and Pontlevoy) in c before episcopate. When uncle, Nicolas de Thou, bp of Chartres died in 1598, he was promised the succession 'donné en faveur de haut et puissant sgr Philippe Hurault, chancelier de France' though, because of age, the search for papal confirmation was deferred for several years.

Nom, Nov 1598. Provs 7-1-1608. Cons 1608. D. 27-5-1621.

Hurault de l'Hospital, Paul. Aix-en-Provence 1599-1624. B. date unknown. Son of Robert, sgr de Belesbat, chancellor to Marguerite de France, duchess of Savoy, and Madeleine de l'Hôpital, daughter of Chancellor of France. Nothing known of education, but early career presupposes law degree. Born Protestant, Paul began as cons in parlt of Paris, becoming MR later. Having converted to Catholicism, was tonsured on 21-9-1593, ordained deacon and priest in June 1597 as *electus Aquensis*. Sent to Provence in 1594 as royal commissioner after submission to Henri IV, he duly obtained royal nom to Aix (via uncle Hurault de Maisse, to whom Henri IV had granted privilege of presentation) and played important part in hounding *ligueur* abp, Génébrard, out of Provence. Rome would not grant him provs until after Génébrard's death.

Nom Nov 1595. Provs 10-3-1599. Cons 12-3-1599 in Rome. D. 8-9-1624.

Hurault de l'Hospital, Guy. Aix-en-Provence coadj 1618/24-25. B. date unknown. Son of Michel, chancellor of Navarre, sgr de Fay, and Olympe du Faur de Pibrac; nephew of Paul (above). No information on education, but took doct in utr. Tonsured on 23-3-1608, ordained subdeacon and deacon in Feb 1615.

Brevet de nom as coadj 11-12-1617. Provs 2-4-1618. Cons 1619 in Paris. Succeeded to Aix Sept 1624. D. 3-12-1625.

Sources: Michaud, *Grande Chancellerie*, 401-2. Etchéchoury, *Maîtres des requêtes*, 231-8. R Descimon, *L'Hospital. Discours pour la majorité de Charles IX* (Paris 1993). Tallemant, *Historiettes*, 388-90. *DGS*, 320. *DBF*, xviii. 57-62, 67-71. *DHGE*, xviii. 412-15 (family-general). AN, MC, VIII, 417, 5-12-1598 (Chartres *régale*). ASV, Fondo Borghese III, 73, fo 480 (Philippe). AN, Z^{1}o 240 (ordination). *Gallia Chr Nov*, i. 129-35. ASV, Sec dei Brevi 270, fo 173 (Paul). AN, Z^{1}o 241 (ordination). *Gallia Chr Nov*, i. 136-7 (and *instrumenta*, 110). BAV, Barb lat 7940, fo 92 (Guy).

Hyver, François. Luçon 1599-ca 1605 (resign). The fact that Hyver was Richelieu's predecessor as bp of Luçon has only helped to keep him in almost total obscurity. Nothing is known of his background, or family circumstances

B. date unknown, but Rome accepted he was 44 in late 1590s and held lic in canon law. *Curé* of St-Jean-de-Braye by 1590s, when Richelieu family, patrons of parish, presented him to Henri IV as its candidate for successor to Jacques de Richelieu (d. 1592) at Luçon. He was intended purely as caretaker until Richelieu family had son capable of entering episcopate.

No date for initial nom to Luçon, but possibly 1592-3 (Jacques de Richelieu had allegedly resigned to him shortly before death). Provs 17-3-1599. Not cons, resign title to future Cardinal Richelieu, ca 1602, but probably continued in post until 1605. D. date unknown.

Sources: ASV, Misc Arm XII, 145, fo 114. AN V^5 1227, fo 120. *Mémoires du clergé ou recueil des actes*, xi. 430–4.

Iharse, Sauvat II d'. Tarbes 1602–48. With a name spelled as diversely as Diharce and Deherse, identifying the background of these bps is tricky. What is known is that they were a noble family from Bigorre, but who numbered at least a few modest legal practitioners in the bp's own generation. More crucially, they were clients of the Grammont clan who dominated Tarbes during most of 16th C and who regarded it as virtually a family heirloom. Bp Sauvat I of Tarbes (1580–1601) was clearly a Grammont *confidentiaire*, and it is unthinkable that his nephew succeeded him without Grammont patronage. Subsequently, his own character and his lengthy reign enabled him to acquire a measure of independence of his patrons.

B. ca 1576 (by his own later account). Son of Pierre, sgr de Chémia, and N . . . Little known of education, except studied in Toulouse for a time along with Jean-Louis de Bertier, bp of Rieux. Abbot in c of Arthous, O Prem (Dax) and in minor orders at time of nom.

Nom ca July 1601. Provs 3–6–1602. Cons 24–6–1602 in Rome. D. 7–10–1648.

Sources: ASV, PC 13, fo 681v-2r. Clergeac, *Chronologie*, 103. Soulet, *Traditions et réformes religieuses*, 51. *Lettres de Henri III*, iii. 444. G Balencie, 'Chronologie des évêques de Tarbes', *Revue de Gascogne*, n.s., 5 (1905), 75–9. *DBF*, xviii. 137–8.

Isnard, Clément. Glandeves 1593–1604 (resign). These 2 bps were among the most obscure of the entire period. Sons of a Nice patrician family unrelated, apparently, to Provençal families with a similar name.

B. ca 1560 Nice. Identity of parents unknown, as is virtually his whole pre-episcopal career. Owed his episcopal promotion entirely to political conditions in eastern Provence in early 1590s, when Savoyard influence was dominant. Glandèves was vacant for some years, and Isnard owed position to duke of Savoy (of whom he was a subject), albeit on Mayenne's formal nom. These circumstances endangered his tenure of Glandèves after reassertion of royal authority in 1595–6, and royal *économe* was appointed on grounds that Isnard's title was void. Only strong Roman intervention protected him against Génébrard-style reprisals, but not before he was obliged to surrender a substantial slice of diocesan revenues to one of Henri IV's grantees. His resignation to nephew may have been designed to draw a line under earlier problems.

No date for nom. Provs 18–8–1593. Cons 19–12–1593 at Nice. Resign 1604. D. 11–5–1612.

Isnard, Octave. Glandeves 1605–25. B. ca 1575 Nice. Identity of parents unknown. No information on studies, but Rome accepted he held doct in utr. Subdeacon when uncle resigned to him in 1604.

Sources: AD Bouches-du-Rhône, B 3337, fo 161. ASV, Fondo Borghese I, 80, fo 91; III, 86b, fo 30. *DBF*, xviii. 217.

Ithier, Dominique, OFM. Glandèves 1654–72. Though Ithier was a relatively common Bordeaux family name, bp's background is fairly obscure, no doubt because it was modest enough. Father was *procureur* in local lawcourt, and hence not even on lowest rung of office-holding ladder. Mother's family background is no less obscure.

B. 1607 Bordeaux. Son of Geoffroy and Jeanne de Lamothe. Entered Franciscans very young, and took doct in theology within the order. Priest from 1635, served as superior of Cordelier houses in Toulouse, Bordeaux and elsewhere, and was later provincial superior of Aquitaine. A 'definitor' of his order, he also went on missions to Spain on behalf of Franciscan Minister-General. Active and reputable preacher in many parts of France, was appointed *prédicateur du roi*, probably in mid-1640s. His involvement with cousin Pierre (a merchant) and other Cordeliers in Bordeaux Fronde as a Mazarinist (for which he was imprisoned by Ormée rebels) brought him notoriety, and led Mazarin to reward him with modest see of Glandèves when fellow-Cordelier Faure abandoned it for Amiens in 1653.

Resign of Glandèves by Faure to Ithier 29–3–1653. Nom 11–10–1653. Provs 13–4–1654. Cons 21–6–1654 D. 12–9–1672.

Sources: ASV, PC 52, fos 192–210. AD Gironde, G 754, no 69. AAE, France 891, fo 183. Sal A Westrich, *The Ormée of Bordeaux* (Baltimore 1972), 87–92. DBF, xviii, 231–2.

Jaubert. *See* **Barrault**

La Barde, Denis. St-Brieuc 1642–75. Although Parisian, the family background is relatively obscure, though they may have come from Marche in central France. Probably merchants during 16th C, they moved into law practice, but remained undistinguished until generation of bp's father, whose marriage to Bonne Bouthillier in 1596 was decisive, bringing them in next generation into service of Marie de' Medici and Richelieu, with bp's brother, Jean, acting as queen mother's secretary before being sent as ambassador to the Swiss (he was also ennobled in 1640).

B. in Paris parish of St Cosme et St Damien, 1600. Son of Jean, barrister in Paris parlt, and Bonne Bouthillier, sister of Claude Bouthillier, later *surintendant des finances*. Educated in part at La Flèche (along with B Delbène, bp of Agen), returned to Paris for theology, where he took 1st place in 1630 lic, and doct shortly afterwards. Canon of ND de Paris and prior in c of St-Voulges at La Ferté-Millon, OSA (Soissons), ordained priest ca 1630, he served as director of *dévot* congregation for *propagation de la foi* during 1630s. Went to Rome on diplomatic mission in 1633. Ministerial favour secured him coveted post of *agent-général du clergé* at AC of 1641, which was increasingly regarded as a stepping-stone to episcopal office, even for those with lesser connections than La Barde.

Nom 10–6–1641. Provs 26–5–1642. Cons 6–7–1642. D. 22–5–1675.

Sources: ASV, PC 34, fos 467–87; PC 40, fos 159–74. AN, MC, CV 580, 21–1–1627 (*inventaire après décès* of Bonne Bouthillier). Batterel, *Mémoires domestiques de l'Oratoire*, ii. 154–7. Poutet, 'Docteurs de Sorbonne', 234. BN, MS lat 15440, p 157. Godet de Soudé, *Dict des anoblissements*, 6. Chesnaye-Desbois, *Dict de noblesse*, ii. 319.

Labatut, Hugues. Comminges 1640–4. Very little is known of the origins of this bp who was native of Rieux diocese.

B. 1582. Son of Guillaume and Soubirane de Du de la Vézolle. Early education apparently in SJ coll at Béziers, but career until mid-1620s was military: he participated (along with his predecessor, Bp Griet) in Huguenot wars of early 1620s. It was probably only after he turned to church that he resumed studies, taking doct in canon law in Paris, in Feb 1626. Ordained priest around same time, became canon and archdeacon of Comminges, where he served as *official* and vg of Donadieu de Griet, his predecessor, who decided to take him as coadj-successor, but d. before arrangements could be completed. However, thanks to intervention of Condren with Richelieu, Griet's plans were realised. During prolonged interregnum at Comminges (1637–40), Labatut governed diocese as chapter's vg.

Nom 30–11–1637. Provs 3–12–1640. Cons 27–1–1641. D. 10–2–1644.

Sources: ASV, PC 21, fo 381; PC 38, fos 232–64. BN, MS lat 17025, fo 106. AAE, France 836, fos 12–13. Clergeac, *Chronologie*, 56. Contrasty, *Histoire des évêques de Comminges*, 339–40.

La Baume de la Suze, Louis-François. Viviers coadj 1618/21–90. One of the most powerful of old noble families from the Dauphiné and Vivarais, a position reinforced over generations by intermarriage with the Alleman, Tournon, Lévis de Ventadour, and other families, but whose horizons and kinship networks were far from provincial. Members in successive generations held important political posts, esp governorships. Bp's grandfather was gov of Provence (1578–9) and *chevalier du St-Esprit* (1581).

B. ca 1602 Suze-la-Rousse. Son of Rostaing, comte de la Suze, and Catherine de Grolée de Meuillon, his 2nd wife. Nothing known of education, which cannot have been far advanced by time nom coadj of Viviers; no evidence he took degree. Predecessor, Jean de l'Hôtel, owed elevation entirely to La Baume family, who regarded him as caretaker until a family member could recover Viviers. Having misled pope about his real age in 1617, the young coadj's misdemeanour was discovered in 1639 and his episcopal acts had to be revalidated by Rome, which also inflicted a penance upon him! When he d. in 1690 he was reputedly the oldest bp in Christendom.

Nom coadj ca 1613. Provs 13–11–1617. Cons 17–12–1628. Succeeded 6–4–1621. D. 5–9–1690.

Sources: BN, MS Fr 33047, p 465 (naturalisations, 1543). Anselme, ix. 71–2. Vindry, *Etat-major*, 43. *DHGE*, xviii. 537–8. Sauzet, *Contre-réforme*, 344.

La Beraudière, François. Perigueux 1614–46. B. in Poitiers diocese, ca 1556 to established and well-connected Poitevin noble family. Son of René and 2nd wife Catherine Herbert, dame de Sigon. Half-sister, Louise, was mistress of Antoine de Bourbon and mother of Charles de Bourbon-Navarre, abp of Rouen 1597–1604. Nothing known about education, but was lic in utr. Entered Paris parlt as *cons* in 1587, and married Elisabeth de Dormans, daughter of Charles, sgr de Bièvre, a *maître des comptes*. Widowed during 1590s, he may have retained office in parlt for some years after entering church. Abbot in c of Noaillé, OSB (Poitiers) in 1597, dean of Poitiers cathedral (1598), but also resided in St-Séverin parish, Paris, preaching and debating with Huguenots. Delivered funeral sermon for Henri IV in Poitiers cathedral, 1610. Ordained deacon on 29–3–1603, he was priest for several years before nom.

Nom probably late Jan-Feb 1612. Provs 17–2–1614. Cons 13–7–1614. D. 14–5–1646.

Sources: Beauchet-Filleau, *Dict du Poitou*, i.450–1. AD Vienne, *Inventaire de la série G*, i. p ix. Anselme, i. 144, iv, 42, 428. Vindry, *Etat-major*, 395. Blanchart, *Catalogue des conseillers*, 103.

La Croix de Chevrières, Jean de. Grenoble. 1607–19. One of Grenoble's most prominent parlementaire families by early 17th C, their origins were in Romans, where they continued to own lands in 17th C, but original patronymic was Guerre. Jean Guerre, first bp's grandfather, was a merchant who adopted name La Croix by marriage. An advantageous marriage also enabled Bp Jean's father, Félix, to enter world of officeholding in Grenoble parlt by 1540s. A *cons* and av-gen there, he was also an MR, *intendant de justice* and finally *cons d'état*. D. 1583 leaving successive generations well placed to pursue their ambitions.

B. 1555, Jean was one of 4 sons of Félix and Guyonne Portier. Took doct in utr. *Cons* and av-gen at Grenoble parlt in succession to father, later MR, *intendant des finances* for Mayenne's army in Dauphiné, he served Henri IV as ambassador to duke of Savoy *inter alia*, becoming pres *à mortier* in 1603–4. Married Barbe d'Arsac 1577, by whom he had 8 children before she d. in 1594. Nom to Grenoble somewhat mysterious, as Henri IV hurriedly revoked (citing reasons of state in doing so) nom of intended bp, Charles Mansel.

No date for nom, but 1607. Provs 4–7–1607. Cons 9–12–1607 at Grenoble. Took son as coadj in 1614. D. 10–5–1619.

La Croix de Chevrières, Alphonse de. Grenoble coadj 1614/19–20 (resign). B. Grenoble 1588. Son of Jean (above) and Barbe d'Arsac. Took his humanities and philosophy in SJ coll at Tournon, followed by doct in utr at Valence. Briefly practised as barrister at Grenoble parlt, presumably with a view to succeeding father, but soon abandoned law, again perhaps to follow in father's clerical footsteps. In the 2 years before episcopal nom, he studied theology (but also some Greek and Hebrew) in Jesuit coll at Lyon, and was reported to have preached and held disputations with Protestant ministers. Still a mere cleric when nom in 1612.

Procuration from father to take him as coadj 19–5–1612. Nom probably May-June 1612. Provs 3–3–1614. Cons 9–11–1614. Succeeds on father's death, 10–5–1619, but resign 1620. D. 1637.

Sources: Vindry, *Parlementaires* (Grenoble), 83, 87–8. Maurice Virieux, 'Le Parlement de Grenoble au xviie siècle' (*Thèse de doctorat d'état*, Université de Paris-IV 1986, pp 167–9) (family-general). ASV, Fondo Borghese II, 249, fos 120–1, 150–1. BN, MS Fr 18002, fo 161. *Lettres missives de Henri IV*, vii. 259–60, 308–9 (Jean). ASV, PC 13, fos 285–308 (Alphonse).

La Fare. *See* **Lopis**

La Faye. *See* **Villers-la-Faye**

La Fayette, François Motier de. Limoges 1627–76. Boasting a marshal of France by mid-15th C, the Motier de la Fayette family, whose lands were mainly in Auvergne-Bourbonnais, was long associated with Bourbons, both during Hundred Years' War and later. Kinship ties were extensive and impressive (Maubac, Silly, La Marthonie, Daillon du Lude, de la Tour, Montmorin). By bp's generation, court office appears more prominent than traditional military activities – Louis XIII's infatuation with bp's niece, Louise de la Fayette, represents a vignette of this.

B. 1590. 3rd son of Claude and Marie d'Alègre, daughter of old noble family. Virtually no information on education (though possibly studied at SJ coll of Riom) or whether took degree. Tonsured in 1603, abbot in c of ND de Dalon, O Cist (Limoges), canon-count of Lyon in 1610, and first almoner to Anne of Austria from 1617 onwards, to whom aunt, Mme de Sénécy, was first lady-in-waiting. Apparently nom to Tréguier in 1619, but evidently reluctant to accept such a minor see, and settled for pension off its revenues instead.

Nom 4–4–1627. Provs 29–11–1627. Cons 19–3–1628. D. 3–5–1676.

Sources: ASV, PC 16, fo 269. AN, Z^{1}o 241 (ordination). Anselme, iii. 821; iv. 334; vi. 714; vii. 56–67. Broutin, *Réforme pastorale au xviie siècle*, i. 258–9. Aulagne, *La Réforme catholique du xviie siècle dans le diocèse de Limoges*, 125–31.

La Ferté, Emery *Marc* de. Le Mans 1639–48. Family was almost certainly of Rouen bourgeois origins, despite their claims to old noble origins. Bp's grandfather, Pierre, was *premier huissier* of parlt of Rouen, and a district militia captain during Catholic League, while bp's father began as an *élu* at Neuchâtel, and went on to become *cons* in *cour des aides* in Rouen (1586). This steady progress was maintained in following generation, when bp's brother, Scipion, was MR and provincial intendant, while his other siblings also fared well, marrying into Rouen office-holding families (Faucon, Jubert, Becdelièvre) at *comptes*, *aides* and parlt, not to mention financial circles.

B. 16–1–1608. Son of Louis and Anne Baudouyn, daughter of former *cons* at *grand conseil* and lt-gen of Evreux. Little known of education, but studied partly in Paris, where was MA in 1625–6, and took bacc in theology, ca 1630. Ordained priest, ca 1633, canon of Rouen cathedral and, possibly, royal almoner. Deputy to 1630 Estates of Normandy, he performed political services there for Richelieu and accompanied Alphonse de Richelieu during mission to Rome 1635. Nom to Le Mans in preference to Philibert de Beaumanoir who eventually succeeded him.

Nom 30–11–1637. Provs 28–22–1639. Cons 1–5–1639. D. 30–4–1648.

Sources: ASV, PC 37, fos 302–27. *Lettres de Peiresc*, iv. 134–5. Frondeville, *Présidents*, 408–11. Tallemant, *Historiettes*, ii. 647–8. *Lettres et mémoires au chancelier Séguier*, ii. 1218–19.

La Feuillade. *See* **Aubusson**

La Guesle, François. Tours 1597–1614. One of several Auvergnat families to settle in Paris during 16th C and to rise rapidly in office-holding hierarchy there, for which they had been prepared (like so many others) by prior service to ducs de Bourbon. They first appeared in Paris parlt with bp's father, Jean, sgr de la Chaux, who was *cons* and proc-gen, 1571–83, and pres *à mortier* 1583–4. Bp's brother, Jacques, distinguished himself as proc-gen of parlt during League, and his services to Henri IV's cause may well have been instrumental in obtaining episcopal office for François.

B. 1562. Son of Jean and Marie Poiret de Laureau. Nothing known of education, but he held doct in utr. Abbot in c of Vauluisant, O Cist (Sens) in 1580, and Cerisiers, OSB (Bayeux) before 1590. *Cons* in Paris parlt (in 1587) and canon of ND de Paris before ordination as priest in June 1588.

Nom Jan-Feb 1596. Provs 7–2–1597, Cons 1597. D. 30–10–1614.

Sources: BN, MS Fr 33047, p 469 (naturalisation, 1546). AN, Z^{1}o 240 (ordination); MC, VIII, 411, 27–3–1596 (Tours *régale*); P 725(ii), 28–4–1597, *serment de fidelité* as abp of

Tours. Vindry, *Parlementaires* (Dijon), 141–2. Blanchart, *Catalogue des conseillers*, 104. *Lettres de Henri III*, iv. 341–2.

La Madeleine de Ragny, Claude de. Autun 1620–52. This family of old nobles from Charollais region settled in Nivernais during 16th C, although its earlier genealogy seems highly imaginative! Through marriage in 1522 bp's grandfather Girard, *bailli* of Auxois, acquired Ragny title and other lands, but family's later fortunes owed a great deal (as did those of du Lis and Chéry families) to his wife's 2nd husband, marshal Bourdillon, who acted as key mentor to bp's father at court, utilising links to Guises and other great families. Marriage of François, bp's father, also enhanced family's standing and connections, while his loyalty to Henri III and Henri IV brought him governorship of Nivernais and promotion as *chevalier du St-Esprit*. In bp's generation, his brother Léonor's marriage to Hippolyte de Gondi cemented previous court connections.

B. 1591. Son of François, marquis de Ragny, and Catherine de Marcilly (daughter of Philibert, governor of Orléanais and Berry). Nothing known of education, but Rome accepted he had lic in canon law and was subdeacon at time of nom. Abbot in c of Cervon (Autun) before episcopate. Family's provincial power and court connections, allied with political circumstances of Marie de' Medici's regency, greatly facilitated the nom of an underaged son to Autun, even though, not unusually in these years, provs were not sought for several years.

No date for nom, but probably early 1613 (predecessor, Pierre Saulnier, d. in late Dec 1612). Provs 18 May 1620. Cons 21–9–1621. D. 21–4–1652.

Sources: Anselme, ix. 113–14, 146–7. Tallemant, *Historiettes* ii. 1163. H de Jouvencel, 'François de la Magdelaine de Ragny gouverneur du Nivernais 1543–1626 et sa famille' *Bulletin de la Soc Nivernaise des Lettres, Sciences et Arts*, 31 (1943) 131–56. AN, MC, VI, 309, 15–6–1624 (Autun *régale* settlement).

La Marthonie, Raymond *Mondot* **de. Limoges coadj 1615/18–27.** Originally a Périgord family of office-holders in Bordeaux parlt, the La Marthonies first achieved distinction at beginning of 16th C, when Pierre, whose mother was a Pompadour, was successively first pres of Bordeaux parlt 1499–1515, and then of Paris 1515–16, while his younger brother, Gaston, became bp of Dax 1523–44. Pompadour influence and episcopal traditions were instrumental in creating an enduring family tradition (as salient as their parlementaire attachments) which duly saw two of Raymond's uncles enter episcopate in late 16th C.

B. ca 1581. Son of Gaston and Françoise de la Bastide. Studied at SJ coll of Périgueux for ca 8 years, then moved to Paris to follow law course, but appears to have taken doct in canon law in Toulouse. Canon and provost of Amiens cathedral, where uncle, Geoffroy, was bp, he was also active in Périgueux diocese (where family seat was located) since elected as clerical deputy to EG of 1614. Prior in c of St-Jean-de-Celle, and a deacon when nom coadj.

Procuration from uncle, Henri, to obtain him as coadj 12–2–1615. Nom 4–2–1615. Provs 20–7–1615. Cons 20–9–1615. Succeeded to Limoges 7–10–1618. D. 11–1–1627.

Sources: ASV, PC 13, fos 606–25. BN, Carrés d'Hozier 418, fo 113 (c.m. of bp's parents, 1573). Vindry, *Parlementaires* (Bordeaux), 37, 59, 112. Aulagne, *Réforme catholique dans le diocèse de Limoges*, 11–15, 67–74.

La Mothe-Fénélon. *See* **Salignac**

La Motte-Houdancourt, Daniel. Mende 1624–8. Relatively little is known about this family (whose Houdancourt lands in the Beauvaisis were acquired by marriage) before early 16th C. It was the 3rd marriage of bps' father which was to bring them out of obscurity, as it created a link to the La Porte and (indirectly) Richelieu family which they cultivated to enormous effect in following generation.

B. 1595. Son of Philippe and Louise Charles, daughter of Antoine Charles, sgr du Plessis-Piquet. Educated in SJ colls of Pont-à-Mousson and Tournon, where he studied humanities and theology. Subsequently took lic in utr and theology from Angers (unusual, but Rome accepted it was true). Had some experiece of preaching in Angers and Paris. Grand archdeacon of Angers, he became first almoner to Marie de' Medici in 1621. Abbot in c of Souillac, OSB (Cahors), but was still simple cleric at time of nom.

Nom 18–11–1623. Provs 7–10–1624. Cons 2–11–1625. D. 5–3–1628.

La Motte-Houdancourt, Henri. Rennes 1640–64, Auch 1664–84. B. 1612. Younger brother of Daniel above. Little information on education, but was Paris MA in 1630–1. Studied theology at Sorbonne, where took lic and doct in 1638. Abbot in c of Souillac (Cahors) in succession to brother. Subdeacon at time of nom, which he owed entirely to Richelieu's patronage.

Nom to Rennes 31–7–1639. Provs 17–12–1640. Cons 1–1–1642. Transferred to Auch 1664. D. 1684.

Sources: Anselme, vii. 530–3. ASV, PC 18, fos 179–200 (Daniel); PC 38, fos 598–636 (Henri). Griselle, *Etat de la maison de Louis XIII*, no 2432. Poutet, 'Docteurs de Sorbonne', 239.

La Porte. *See* **Le Porc**

Larchiver, François. Rennes 1602–19. B. Plouézoch, northern Brittany, ca 1565. Son of modest family and unknown parents. Pre-episcopal career also obscure. A priest with doct in canon law, he spent many years in Rome, where was successively rector of St-Yves-des-Bretons (1598) and St-Louis-des-Français (1600). Accession to Rennes was fruit of unusual circumstances and his presence in Rome. Henri IV initially nom Séraphim Olivier-Razali, an influential French curial official and cardinal in 1604, as Cardinal d'Ossat's successor at Rennes, but he was reluctant to keep the see and, with royal approval, negotiated a settlement with Larchiver who consented to pay Olivier-Razali a pension in return.

Nom, 11–3–1602. Provs 17–6–1602. Cons 24–6–1602 in Rome. D. 22–2–1619.

Sources: ASV, Misc Arm XII, 145, fo 416. AN, MC, VIII, 584, 7–9–1613 (Rennes *régale*). *Lettres d'Ossat*, iii. 541–2. Taillandier, *Histoire ecclésiastique et civile de la Bretagne*, iii, Catalogue des évêques et abbés, xi-xii.

La Rivière. *See* **Barbier**

La Rochefoucauld, Antoine. Angoulême 1608–34. It would be superfluous to elaborate on the pedigree of bps drawn from this ancient and prolific noble family which had scattered widely throughout France, though it may be said that the activities of some of its myriad branches remain difficult to plot – true for the father of bp of Angoulême. Family's ecclesiastical connections were a prominent feature of its history, past and to come.

B. 1574 Paris. 4th son of Antoine, sgr de Chaumont, and Cécile de Montmirail. Nothing known of education, but apparently took lic in canon law. Subdeacon at time of nom, which itself followed grant by Henri IV in 1604 of Angoulême first to Marie de' Medici's confessor, Turicella and then to a Florentine Dominican, Serafino Banqui, both of whom declined it. Banqui apparently took his time in doing so, and then negotiated settlement (not dissimilar to that of Larchiver for Rennes a few years earlier) which generated much litigation with La Rochefoucauld.

No date for nom, but probably early 1606. Provs 13–8–1607. Cons 5–6–1608. D. 24–12–1634.

La Rochefoucauld, Louis de. Lectoure 1649–54. B. 23–12–1615 Poitiers. Son of François, first duc de La Rochefoucauld, and Gabrielle du Plessis de Liancourt; brother of the Frondeur. Studied humanities and philosophy with SJ, esp at coll of Clermont (along with Jacques de Grignan), where also studied some theology, under mentorship of Cardinal La Rochefoucauld; though he may also have done so briefly at Toulouse, he took lic in canon law. Well endowed with benefices in c, he held La Réau, Celle-sur-Belle, OSA (Poitiers), St-Jean-d'Angély, OSB (Saintes) and the priory of Lanville, OSA (Angoulême) at time of nom. Ordained priest in 1644. Father's episcopal ambitions for son were no secret, and Lectoure was only one of several dioceses considered before 1646. His personal inclinations remain in doubt, and he died without ever setting foot in Lectoure.

Brevet de nom 10–3–1646. Nom 2–5–1646. Provs 11–10–1649. Cons 8–12–1649. D. Dec 1654.

Sources: Labatut, *Les Ducs et pairs au xviie siècle* (family-general). AN, MC, LIV, 466, 29–3–1606. *Gallia Chr Nov*, ii. 602–3. *Lettres Missives de Henri IV*, vii. 78–9 (Antoine). ASV, PC 49, fos 354–76. AAE, France 849, fo 116; 850, fo 129. BN, MS lat 17026, fo 51. Clergeac, *Chronologie*, 49 (Louis).

La Rocheposay. *See* **Chasteignier**

Laubespine, Gabriel de. Orléans 1604–30. Family, originating in the Beauce and prominent merchant and municipal *notables* of Orléans by mid-15th C, won real distinction and power within a very short span of time in mid-16th C, thanks to a clutch of able secretaries of state, bishops, and diplomats, whose activities enabled them to marry into families like themselves (Bochetel, Villeroy), but also into *épée* families such as the la Châtre and Clutin.

B. 26–1–1579. Son of Guillaume, baron de Châteauneuf, and Marie de la Châtre; brother of future *garde des sceaux* (1630–3, 1651). Educated in Paris, where took bacc in theology, in 1604, and elected *socius* of Sorbonne. Learned, he was respected by contemporaries as authority on Fathers of Church. Subdeacon at time of nom to Orléans, where predecessor was brother Jean (d. 1596), but it was another brother, Guillaume, who was initially nom to succeed him. Gabriel did not replace him as royal nominee until 1600 at the earliest.

No date for nom. Provs 15–3–1604. Cons in Rome 28–3–1604. D. 15–8–1630.

Sources: BI, MS 1354, nos 12, 69. AN, MC, VIII 412, 15–6–1596. Anselme, vi. 558–64. Etchéchoury, *Maîtres des requêtes*, 241–4. Trani, 'Conseillers du grand conseil' 167.

Laurens. *See* Du Laurens

Lauro. *See* Delauro

Laval de Boisdauphin, Henri. St-Pol-de-Léon 1651–61, La Rochelle 1661–93. An old noble family of considerable distinction, the Laval were long related to the Montmorencys and others of similar status. Bp's brother was a key Mazarin military ally in the later Fronde, which won him a marshal's baton and helped secure St-Pol-de-Léon for Henri. Bp's mother was a patron of Port-Royal, and her religious austerity left its mark on her episcopal son.

B. 2–3–1620. Son of Philippe-Emmanuel and Marie de Souvré, famous as marquise de Sablé. Nothing known of early studies, but Bp Marmiesse of Conserans claimed he had followed theology course at Sorbonne for 3 years and was about to defend theses for lic, but distracted by other activities! Distraction did not prevent him from taking doct in utr. Abbot in c of ND de Pierreneuf, dean of St-Martin-de-Tours, ordained priest ca 1645. Deputy to 1650 AC for Tours province.

Nom to St-Pol-de-Léon 30–3–1651. Provs 19–6–1651. Cons 27–8–1651. Transferred to La Rochelle, Nov 1661. D. 22–11–1693.

Sources: ASV, PC 49, fos 451–66. Pérouas, *Le Diocèse de la Rochelle*, 230–1. Séguier, *Lettres à son frère*, ed Hours, 73, n 5.

La Valette de Cornusson, François I. Vabres 1600–22. Both bps in this period are among the most obscure members of episcopate, but family's episcopal ambitions for them were nurtured by tenure of Vabres between 1561 and 1585 by an uncle of Bp François I. Natives of the Rouergue, they were militarily active in the region and around Toulouse, and produced a famous Grand Master of Malta in mid-16th C. Distantly related to La Valette-Epernon family, their other kinship connections were far from negligible. Father of first bp was decorated by Henri III with Order of St Esprit in 1583, while Henri IV also valued his support and confirmed him as *sénéchal* of Toulouse after religious wars.

B. Cornusson 1565. Son of Jean, *sénéchal* of Toulouse, and Gabrielle de Murat. All that is known of pre-episcopal biography is that he became abbot in c of Moissac, OSB (Cahors) in 1597.

No date for nom, but probably mid-1600. Provs 15–12–1600. Cons Jan 1601. Took nephew as coadj 1618. D. 2–8–1622.

La Valette de Cornusson, François II de. Vabres coadj 1618/22–44. B. 1590. Son of Jean II, *sénéchal* of Toulouse, and Ursule de Loubans de Verdales, 2nd wife; nephew of François I (above). Nothing known of education or degrees taken. A simple cleric at time of nom, and obviously groomed for just one role, that of succeeding uncle at Vabres.

No date for nom as coadj. Provs 8–1–1618. Cons 4–3–1618 in Rome. Succeeded uncle 2–8–1622. D. 20–11–1644.

Sources: Anselme, ix. 81. *Lettres missives de Henri IV*, iv. 235–6. Barrau, *Dict du Rouergue*, ii. 365–404. Chesnaye-Desbois, *Dict de noblesse*, xix. 424–9 (family-general). *Gallia*, i 171–2. Vidal, *Diocèse d'Albi*, 21–2 (François I).

La Valette, Louis de Nogaret de. Toulouse 1613–26 (resign). Career of duc d'Epernon, most famous of all 'cadets de Gascogne' and father of the 2 bps, is too well known to need recapitulation. The favour he enjoyed at hands of Henri III was carefully translated into enduring social and political capital by this shrewd and dominant figure whose patronage networks were extensive and well managed by a master politician.

B. 1593 Angoulême. 3rd son of Epernon and Marguerite de Foix-Candale, sister of François bp of Aire (d. 1594). Educated mostly at SJ coll of La Flèche and Univ of Paris, where he completed philosophy course. A simple cleric, he was first almoner (a sinecure) to Louis XIII before episcopate. Magnificently endowed, as might be expected, with opulent benefices – ND de Berdous, O Cist (Auch), Gimont and Grandselve (all 1600), with several more to follow at various dates. Father originally planned to keep Aire vacant until he came of age, but abandoned idea ca 1605, enabling Cospeau, who remained attached to Epernon family thereafter, to succeed in 1606. Six years later, Cardinal Joyeuse offered him a far more desirable see, Toulouse, but his personal inclinations remained to the end military rather than ecclesiastical.

No date for nom (but profession of faith dated 31–1–1612). Provs 26–8–1613. Never cons. Cardinal 1621. Resign to Charles de Montchal, 1626. D. 1639.

La Valette, Louis de Nogaret. Mirepoix coadj 1629/30–56, Carcassonne 1656–79. B. ca 1598. Illegitimate son of duc d'Epernon, mother unknown. A student taking philosophy course at SJ coll in Bordeaux when tonsured and took minor orders in 1618. Ordained priest in July 1628, abbot in c of Ile-de-Medoc, OSA (Bordeaux) in 1627. Unlike his half-brother, he proved to be active, resident bp, whose transfer to Carcassonne was occasioned by clashes with Huguenots and other opponents.

No date for nom as coadj, but during 1628. Provs 28–5–1629. Cons 22–12–1629. Succeeded to Mirepoix 1630. Transferred to Carcassonne 1656. D. 10–9–1679.

Sources: *DGS*, 540–1. ASV, PC 13, fos 33–50 (Cardinal). ASV, PC 51, fos 884–95. A de Lantenay, 'A propos du second mariage du duc d'Epernon', *Revue de Gascogne*, 26 (1887), 509–10, 27 (1888), 83–4 (Louis, bp of Mirepoix).

Lavardin. *See* **Beaumanoir**

La Vieuville, Charles-François Coskaer. Rennes 1660–76. Family is probably best known for having produced the minister (and father of the bp) whose disgrace was engineered by Richelieu in 1624. Natives of Artois, they had settled in Champagne by 16th C, where they joined ranks of local *noblesse seconde*, active mainly in military roles. Partly because of earlier Nevers family patronage, they remained consistently loyal to crown during religious wars, when Guise and League offered powerful counter-attractions. Bp's grandfather was rewarded for his loyalty, becoming *grand fauconnier* and gov of Mezières, Reims, etc and lt-gen of Champagne under Henri IV, and taking Catherine d'O (sister of Henri III's *surintendant des finances*) as 2nd wife. Bp's father combined both of these examples in more audacious way. Marrying the daughter of a professional financier, he became (a short-lived) *surintendant des finances* in 1623 and (after long disgrace of the Richelieu years) again during Fronde, while also being made a *duc et pair* along the way.

B. Paris, ca 1625. Son of Charles and Marie Bouhier de Beaumarchais. Nothing known of education, but had lic in canon law, which may have been taken around time of episcopal nom. Early career was a military one: he served in the Dutch Republic, and was known simply as comte de la Vieuville. Change of career remains mysterious, but probably occurred soon after father's death (1653). Ordained priest ca 1654–5 in Limoges, where he held abbey of St-Martial in c.

Bp Lamothe-Houdancourt of Rennes resign to La Vieuville 1–8–1659. Nom 30–8–1659. Provs 16–2–1660. Cons 4–4–1660. D. 29–1–1676.

Sources: ASV, PC 58, 267–80, fos 828–43. AN, MC, CXII, 372, 15–2–1676 (*inventaire après décès* of bp). Anselme, viii. 758–61. Bourquin, *Noblesse seconde et pouvoir en Champagne*, esp 105–6.

Leberon. *See* **Gelas**

Le Bouthillier. *See* **Bouthillier**

Le Boux, Guillaume, Oratorian. Dax 1659–66, Périgueux 1666–93. This bp, known simply as Boux before the episcopate, was famous for his modest social origins, as his father was variously described as a boatman, a *petit marchand* or a notary.

B. St-Maurice-de-Souzai, near Saumur 30–6–1621. Son of Pierre Boux and Barbe Lecourt. Apparently began career as domestic servant in Oratorian house at Blois before being formally accepted into congregation (June 1638). Educated in its colls, but took no degree until episcopal nom, and then it was perfunctory lic in canon law, probably from Paris law faculty. Taught in various Oratorian colls (Troyes, Riom, Vendôme), but real reputation was as preacher, as befitted a disciple of Sénault, fellow Oratorian. He preached widely throughout France, even defending court versus Retz in his preaching. This no doubt attracted attention, enabling him to preach repeatedly in Paris and at court in 1654–7. Priest from ca 1645, *curé* of Epernay for 3 years, he may also briefly have held a parish near Saumur.

Nom to Dax 2–10–1658. Provs 26–5–1659. Cons 4–4–1660. Transferred to Périgueux 1666. D. 4–8–1693.

Sources: ASV, PC 57, fo 424–38. Batterel, *Mémoires domestiques de l'Oratoire*, ii. 580–98. Riboulet, *Etude historique sur Guillaume le Boux*. Degert, *Histoire des évêques de Dax*, 357.

Le Clerc, Rene, Minim. Glandeves 1627–51. The fact that this bp was born in Beauvais (where his family also owned *seigneurie* of Blicourt) has hindered attempts to identify him and his family. In reality, they were Parisians. Bp's father briefly held office in Beauvais during League, but otherwise he and family's activities were essentially focused on Paris, where they were undistinguished *bourgeois* in Henri III's reign, although connected to police officials of the Châtelet through bp's mother, sister of *commissaire* Louchart, one of the more unsavoury leaders of Parisian *Seize*. Bp's elder brother, Thomas, held several financial offices (*commissaire des guerres, receveur des tailles* at Beauvais) and by time he married in 1607, was an SR and principal clerk to Puysieux, the secretary of state, a quite remarkable transformation.

B. ca 1590 Beauvais. Son of Thomas, *commissaire des guerres*, and Marguerite Louchart. Entered order of Minims at Tours, and was professed there, in 1610. Educated in order's schools, he consequently took no degree. Active preacher in Paris and elsewhere, he became first superior of Minim house at Beauvais (financed partly by his brother), in 1617, and later at Vincennes. Provincial superior in Burgundy at time of nom to Glandèves, which was initially given to Augustin de Thou, who declined it and ceded claim to Le Clerc.

Nom 19-6-1626. Provs 7-9-1626. Cons 14-2-1627. D. 9-2-1651.

Sources: ASV, PC 22, fos 190-204. AN, MC, IX, 231, 22-4-1577, 9-5-1577; CIX, 58, 9-9-1599; XII, 38, 31-8-1607; XVI, 217, Sept 1624 (family docs). Thuillier, *Diarium minimorum*, 67-8.

Le Clerc de Lesseville, Eustache. Coutances 1659-65. One of several Parisian families of the same name, the Leclerc de Lesseville family was native of Melun, where Nicolas, bp's grandfather, was originally a mere merchant-tanner. But in a short space of time (1576-90) he made his fortune in Parisian financial milieux, becoming SR and sgr de Lesseville. Thereafter descendants were mostly office-holders (esp in *chambre des comptes*) and intermarried with established finance and robe families such as the Camus de Jambeville, Le Boulanger, Le Gras and Fortia, though a few members broke with tradition in later generations and followed military careers.

B. 1614 Paris. Son of Nicolas, *maître* (later *doyen*) of *chambre des comptes*, and Catherine Le Boullenger, daughter of parlementaire family. Educated probably wholly at Univ of Paris, MA in 1629-30. Took 5th place in 1636 lic (followed by doct) there (having studied with abp Aubusson of Embrun), and elected *socius* of Sorbonne. Also served term as rector of univ, and was later *curé* of parish of St-Gervais and St-Protais. Abbot in c of St-Crespin-de-Soissons, OSA, canon of ND de Paris, he was also a serving almoner to Louis XIII, who apparently promised to make him a bp, but d. before fulfilling that promise. Having then taken lic in utr, he became *cons-cl* in Paris parlt (July 1645) possibly because episcopal ambitions seemed unrealisable, though attendance at 1650 AC suggests he had not given up hope.

Resign by Claude Auvry of Coutances (reserving a pension of 12,000 *livres*) to Leclerc 23-7-1658. Nom 13-9-1658. Provs 13-1-1659. Cons 23-3-1659. D. 8-12-1665.

Sources: ASV, PC 57, fos 93-114. BN, MS lat 15440, p 164; MS Fr 32989, fo 259; P Or 1399, doss Le Gras. BL, Add MS 21434, fo 52. P Coquelle, 'Six testaments de bourgeois de Meulan, de 1498 à 1589', *Mémoires de la Société Historique et Archéologique de l'arrondissement de Pontoise et du Vexin*, 40 (1930), 73-80. Bluche, *Origines des magistrats*, 249-50.

Lefebvre de Caumartin, François. Amiens coadj 1617-52. Amiens was a suitable episcopal seat for Lefebvre de Caumartin, since family originated in Ponthieu, where they became sgrs of Caumartin in early 16th C, and where bp's grandfather was *général des finances* for Picardy in mid-century. By then ties to Paris and robe office-holding there were strengthening, as career of bp's father makes clear. *Cons* in parlt (1579), MR (1585), pres in *grand conseil* (1587), intendant in Poitou (1588), Picardy (1590), *cons d'état* (1594), intermediary between Henri IV and Marguerite de Valois, ambassador to Swiss 1605, he was classic example of experienced royal servant rewarded in his last year with keepership of seals. Marriage in 1582 to Marie Miron, daughter of Robert, intendant and *contrôleur général des finances*, enhanced family's prior financial foundations, and also brought him close to circles around Henri III. Bp's elder brother, initially destined for church career, switched to robe office-holding, and was briefly provincial intendant and ambassador to Venice (1624).

B. 1592 Amiens. Son of Louis and Marie Miron, sister of Charles, bp of Angers. Nothing known of education or if he held degree. Abbot in c of St-Quentin-en-l'Isle, OSB (Noyon), and subdeacon at time of nom, which he owed to paternal favour.

No date for nom, but 1613. Provs 4–12–1617. Cons 13–5–1618. Succeeded 17–12–1617. D. 27–11–1652.

Sources: BN, MS Fr 32989, fo 28v. Anselme, vi. 543–6. Mousnier, *Lettres et mémoires au chancelier Séguier*, ii. 1211–12. Etchéchoury, *Maîtres des requêtes*, 247. Trani, 'Conseillers du grand conseil', 169–70.

Le Gouverneur, Guillaume. St-Malo 1610–30. Bp's entire career was spent in his native city, where family can be traced to late 15th C. Two generations later, in mid-16th C, they were still solidly bourgeois, despite acquisition of lands and seigneurial title. Bp's father was a younger son. Family continued to be prominent in St-Malo during and after bp's tenure. Early career was facilitated by patronage of a well-placed ecclesiastical uncle.

B. St-Malo 12–7–1573. Son of Jean, sgr de St-Etienne, and Guillemette Crosnier, his 3rd wife (m. in 1569). Nothing known of education, but held lic in canon law. Ordained priest at unknown date, he succeeded an uncle (who had also been vg to 3 bps of St-Malo) as dean of cathedral chapter in 1592, and became rector of parish of Paramé in 1598. Deputy to AC of 1602 and 1608. Price of nom to St-Malo was a heavy pension to relative of his predecessor. J du Bec.

Nom 29–1–1610. Provs 30–8–1610. Cons 20–2–1611. D. 25–6–1630.

Sources: ASV, Acta Misc 98, fo 146. AN G^8 87. BN, MS Fr 3790, fo 17. P Paris-Jallobert, *Anciens registres paroissiaux de Bretagne (St Malo)* (Rennes 1900) ii. 125–7; iv. 28. *Lettres missives de Henri IV*, vii. 853. Guilloton de Courson, *Pouillé historique de l'archévêché de Rennes*, i. 601, 657.

Le Gras, Simon. Soissons 1624–56. Until mid-16th C, the Le Gras family was based in Troyes, where they were related to important *notable* families. By time bp's father married in 1579, a partial move to Paris was underway, and he himself was barrister in parlt. But his main activities were in financial sphere, as receiver of the church tax, the *décimes*, in Sens diocese (1583) and, more importantly, as *trésorier de France* in Paris by 1590s. Further advances followed in bp's own generation, mainly via brother, Nicolas, who initially succeeded father as *trésorier de France* in Paris, while also becoming *secrétaire des commandements* (a key post) to Anne of Austria (1624–46). Another brother, Louis, was a monk of St-Denis.

B. Paris 1–6–1589. Son of Simon and Louise Danois. Early studies in SJ colls at Verdun and Bourges, where he learned Greek and Hebrew, followed by theology at Sorbonne during early 1610s, and leading to lic in 1616. Tonsured in Paris March 1603, ordained deacon and priest in March 1614. Prior in c of St-Pierre-de-Courtenay, O Cluny (Sens), he was coadj to uncle Claude le Gras in abbey of St-Corneille-en-Champagne (Soissons). Close to SJ, he preached in Parisian churches, and was serving almoner to Louis XIII at time of nom.

Nom 7–5–1623. Provs 16–10–1624. Cons 17–11–1624. Took Mathieu Bourlon as coadj 1652. D. 28–10–1656.

Sources: ASV, PC 18, fos 65–92. AN, Y 121 fo 181 (c.m. of bp's parents); Y 124 fo 524, (1583); Z^{1}o 241 (ordinations). Charmeil, *Les Trésoriers de France*, 247, 218.

Le Meingre. *See* **Boucicault**

Le Noël. *See* **Du Perron**

Le Porc de la Porte, André. St-Brieuc 1618–31. An old noble family which included a *connétable* of Nantes in 15th C, the Le Porc de la Porte experienced considerable internal conflicts during wars of religion, when bp's father turned Protestant and became a close dependent of his famous maternal uncle, François de La Noue. Died a Protestant in 1613, but his wife (who was lady-in-waiting to Catherine de' Medici, was later remarried to, firstly, Claude de la Trémouille, baron de Noirmoutier, and, secondly, Claude Gouffier, duc de Roannez) probably reared their children as Catholics from birth. They held some lands in St-Brieuc diocese, but it is more likely bp's mother's subsequent marriages to high-ranking nobles helped André to become bp in 1618.

B. 1593. Son of René, sgr de Vézins in Anjou, and Anne de Maillé de la Tour-Landry (daughter of François, comte de Châteauroux, and Diane de Rohan). Nothing known of education or whether he took degree, though as bp had reputation as patron of learning and music, and of reformed religious orders. A simple cleric at time of nom.

Nom 1618. Provs 3–9–1618. Cons 1620. D. 22–6–1631.

Sources: ASV, Acta Misc 97, fo 280. Anselme, iv. 176, vii. 503. Port, *Dict du Maine-et-Loire*, ii. 502–3.

Le Prestre, Guillaume. Quimper 1614–40. Le Prestre belonged to Breton *chevaleresque* family which was long and solidly entrenched in Quimper region. Grandfather had been *échanson* to Mary Stuart in 1560, and *maître d'hôtel* to Catherine de' Medici, as well as gov of several Breton towns (inc Concarneau). Bp's father continued these traditions. Gov of Concarneau, lt-gen of Quimper diocese, *chevalier of St-Michel*, he led the *ban* and *arrière ban* under Mercoeur in 1585. He supported League as gov of Concarneau, but recognised Henri IV *moyennant finance* in 1594. Family domination of Quimper made Guillaume a strong candidate when diocese became vacant in 1614, but internal family politics required he pay a considerable pension to one of his brothers.

B. 1587. Son of Louis, sgr de Lézonnet and gov of Concarneau, and Claude Bizieu, his 2nd wife (m. in 1577). Nothing known of education, but unlikely he took degree. Ordained priest in 1614 and dean of Guémenée *collégiale*, he served as vg to predecessor at Quimper. Also assisted Bp Martin of Vannes as *promoteur* during his diocesan visitation of 1611.

Brevet de nom 15–3–1614. Royal nom to pope 6–5–1614. Provs 17–11–1614. Cons 1615. D. 8–11–1640.

Sources: ASV, PC 13, fos 347–62. Anselme, vii. 717–30. *Lists and Analysis of State Papers, Foreign*, ed R B Wernham, ii (1590–1), 310. Bluche, *Les Magistrats du parlement de Paris*, 47. Carné, *Chevaliers bretons*, 316–18.

Lescot, Jacques. Chartres 1643–56. Career of this bp is in marked contrast to his modest origins in merchant bourgeoisie of St-Quentin in Picardy. Even names of parents are unknown, but father (1609–19) and brother were both *échevins* in their native town.

B. St-Quentin 1–8–1593. Little known of early education, but studied philosophy and theology in Paris, where he took 2nd place in 1622 lic (followed by doct) in theology.

Initially a highly regarded professor of philosophy, he succeeded Philippe de Gamaches as professor of theology in 1625. Also participated in missions organised in his future diocese of Chartres. A priest since 1622, canon and *théologal* of Amiens (his native diocese), as well as abbot in c of Toussaints de l'Isle, OSA (Châlons-sur-Marne) and La Chapelle-aux-Planches before episcopate. Almost inevitably, he attracted attention of Richelieu, *proviseur* of Sorbonne, at whose invitation he played a part in affair of Gaston d'Orléans's marriage (1635) and campaign against St-Cyran (1638). Confessor to the cardinal in late 1630s, he was the last member of his household raised to the episcopate.

Nom to Chartres (which Léonor d'Etampes vacated for Reims) 13–12–1641. Provs 22–7–1643. Cons 8–11–1643. D. 22–8–1656.

Sources: ASV, PC 40, fo 150; PC 42, fos 285–308. BN, MS lat 15440, p 147. BAV, Barb lat 7944, fo 155 (abbey of La Chapelle). AN, MC, C, 244, 22–8 and 16–9–1656 (Lescot's testament and *inventaire après décès*); Robert Sauzet, *Les Visites pastorales dans le diocèse de Chartres pendant la première moitie du xviie siècle* (Rome 1975), 32.

Lestang, Vital de. Carcassonne coadj 1615/21–52. Original family name of Vital was Guilhon, and claims to noble status going back to 15th C and manufactured by his more famous uncle and predecessor, Christophe in 1618, were spurious. Natives of Brive in Limousin, they were bourgeois married to fellow bourgeois families from both Brive and Tulle. No traces survive until Bp Vital's grandfather, Etienne Guilhon *dit* de Lestang, who was barrister at Bordeaux parlt in 1530s-40s, lt-gen at Brive 1559, deputy at EG 1560, and pres of restored Brive *présidial* in 1576. His son, Antoine (uncle of bp) inherited presidency from father, but emerged as leading Catholic figure in region during later wars of religion, serving Mayenne and the Guise party while his younger but more able brother, Christophe, bp of Lodève, supported Joyeuse interests in Languedoc, having originally been protégé of Bp Duprat of Clermont and, later, of René de Birague, chancellor of France. Joyeuse protection and Henri IV's policy of reconciliation in Languedoc enabled both brothers to retain offices and influence in subsequent years, although Christophe was eventually obliged to move to see of Carcassonne in the face of Montmorency-inspired difficulties in Lodève. Their sister Antoinette married Guillaume Polverel and their sons became bps of Alet.

B. Malzieu near Mende 23–4–1588. Son of Léonard, who settled in Gévaudan, and Anne Descorières(?). Early education apparently in SJ coll of Toulouse, where he completed humanities and philosophy. Later moved to Paris, residing in SJ house while studying theology under du Val and others, taking bacc in theology, ca 1612. Ordained subdeacon in Paris, Feb 1612 and priest in Dec 1612, he appears to have preached in one or more churches there. Uncle Christophe's court office in royal chapel and wider political/ecclesiastical activities were crucial in securing mitre for him. Prolonged process by which he became coadj is revealing example of episcopal patronage during regency of Marie de' Medici.

Procuration from uncle to take him as coadj 30–7–1611. Nom 5–10–1613. Provs 9–2–1615. Cons 24–2–1615 in Rome. D. 28–9–1652.

Sources: ASV, PC 13, fos 536–51. AN, Z^{1}o 241 (orders). G Clement-Simon. 'Célébrités de la ville de Brive: les de Lestang, les Meynard de Lestang, les Polverel', *Bulletin de la Société Scientifique, Historique et Archélogique de la Corrèze*, 14 (1892) 533–611. *Cartulaire et archives des communes de l'ancien diocèse de Carcassonne*, ed A Mahul, v (Paris 1867), 496–8 (testament of Bp Christophe de Lestang).

Lévis de Ventadour. *See* **Ventadour**

L'Hospital. *See* **Hurault**

Ligny, Dominique de. Meaux coadj 1659–81. Relatively little known of family before generation of grandfather, Jean, an extremely active financier during 1580s and 1590s whose career was crowned by his tenure as *trésorier de l'Epargne* (1601–17), an office he transmitted to his son Etienne. Etienne's brother, Jean (father of bp) was *cons* in Paris parlt at time of his marriage to Charlotte Séguier in 1609, and went on to become MR. Thereafter, as bp's own career demonstrates, the Séguier (but also the Vialart and Castille) connection was to serve them extremely well.

B. Paris, where baptised 26-1-1619. Son of Jean, sgr de Rentilly, and Charlotte Séguier, sister of chancellor. Educated mostly at Univ of Paris, where took MA, ca 1638, but does not appear to have taken degree then. Early career was secular one, and was known as the sieur de Marsilly. For several years he was a *grand maître des eaux et forêts*, but remained unmarried. Probably his uncle, Bp Séguier of Meaux, persuaded him to change to an ecclesiastical career. Ordained deacon in 1654–5, he only took lic in canon law in 1657, after his nom to coadjutorship. Abbot in c of St-Jean of Amiens, O Prem, dean of Meaux in 1657, he attended AC of 1655–7.

Procuration from Bp Séguier to take Ligny as coadj 2–5–1657. Nom 11–1–1658. Provs 13–1–1659. Cons 9–3–1659. Succeeded 12–3–1659 (on uncle's outright resignation). D. 27–4–1681.

Sources: ASV, PC 56, fos 28–44; Processus Datariae 37, fo 157. BN, MS Fr 32588, p 288. AN, MC, LIV, 472, 3–2–1609 (c.m. of parents). Tessereau, *Chancellerie*, 252. Richet, *De la Réforme à la Révolution*, 265. O Poncet, 'Une utilisation nouvelle de la rente constituée au xvie siècle: les membres du conseil au secours des finances de Henri III', *Bibliothèque de l'Ecole des Chartes*, 151 (1993), 345–6.

Lingendes, Jean de. Sarlat 1642–7, Mâcon 1651–65. This family from Moulins emerged from shadows in early 16th C, after Jean and son Antoine had practised as notaries at Chaveroche during mid to late 15th C. Antoine's son Jean, was lt-gen of duchy of Bourbonnais from 1540s onwards, while his sons Pierre (*trésorier de France* at Moulins, 1591), Antoine (*receveur* of *aides* and *tailles* in the Bourbonnais, 1587), and Michel (father of bp) moved into local financial and judicial offices, with *présidial* court at Moulins attracting their attention, mainly as stepping-stone, from mid-century onwards. Service to successive members of royal family who held royal domain of Bourbonnais was no less important in providing ties to a wider world, and bp's generation was identified mainly with Gaston d'Orléans and Anne of Austria. She rewarded them by confirming their alleged noble status in 1646, when they argued that they were of ancient noble extraction but had 'derogated' in earlier generations. Bp's uncle, Jean, was reputable poet, and another, Claude, a Jesuit preacher of considerable ability.

B. 1595. Son of Michel, a younger son and *marchand-bourgeois* of Moulins, and Marguerite Belein. Studied humanities, philosophy, and theology in SJ coll at Bourges, he took doct of theology there, ca 1624. Closeness to SJ (he was member of Jesuit sodality as student and later) had family origins. His earliest position was apparently as tutor to comte de Moret, bastard son of Henri IV, but later served Gaston d'Orléans (briefly) and Anne of Austria, though the timescale of these activities is obscure. He was priest from ca 1626. In demand as preacher, he was royal almoner and *prédicateur ordinaire* to Louis XIII by 1626. Richelieu was among those who admired his preaching, and was instrumental in obtaining Sarlat for him, even making a point of paying for his papal provs, as he held no benefices before episcopate. Experience at Sarlat, a much neglected diocese, was brief and unhappy, and he virtually left it within a year. But episcopal ambitions survived beyond his formal resignation several years later. Mazarin promised him Clermont until events of Fronde made that impossible and he was persuaded to take Mâcon instead.

Nom to Sarlat 22–6–1639. Provs 14–7–1642. Cons 14–12–1642. Resign 27–9–1647. Nom to Mâcon 11–11–1650. Provs 13–2–1651. D. 2–5–1665.

Sources: ASV, PC 24, fo 701; PC 40, fos 689–709. BN, MS Fr 4139, fos 314–18 (confirmation of nobility 1646); P Or 1725, doss 40,022; Doss bleus 398, doss Lingendes. AAE, France 835, fos 131–2. AD Allier, 5J 3555. Griselle, *Etat de la maison de Louis XIII*, nos 3549, 3766, 4059, 4349 (Anne of Austria's service). Jean Valette, 'Jean de Lingendes, évêque de Sarlat' *Bulletin de la Société Historique et Archéologique du Périgord* 94 (1967) 210–32. C Grégoire, 'Le bureau des finances de Moulins (1587–1789)', *Bulletin de la Société d'Emulation du Bourbonnais*, 18 (1910).

Lingua, Jerome de, OFM. Conserans 1593–1612. Like his uncle and predecessor, François Bonard, Lingua was Piedmontese, but little more than that known of either his or uncle's background, which was probably as modest as notation in Roman sources – 'ex honesta familia' – suggests.

B. ca 1530–5 Mondovi. Son of Paulo and N... Bonardi, sister of Bp Conserans. Probably educated in Observant Franciscan order which he joined young, and Rome accepted that he held doct in theology, possibly from Turin (1556). He later settled in France, teaching in Paris Observant convent in 1580, and becoming canon and *théologal* of Couserans in uncle's service. Naturalised by Mayenne in 1592, he succeeded Bonard at height of League, when both men travelled to Rome and, with Mayenne's approval, obtained papal sanction for transfer of diocese, an action which nearly led to Lingua being forced out of office in 1595.

No date for Mayenne's nom. Provs 29–1–1593. Cons 14–2–1593 in Rome. D. 13–11–1612.

Sources: ASV, Acta Misc 95, fo 447. F J Samiac, 'Le Testament de Monseigneur Jérôme de Lingua évêque de Conserans' *Bulletin Historique des Anciens Diocèses de Pamiers, Mirepoix etc* 1 (1912), 86–92. C Douais, 'Documents pontificaux sur le siège de Conserans 1425–1619', *Revue de Gascogne*, 27 (1888), 439–62. *Procès-verbaux des assemblées du clergé*, i. 525–6.

Lionne, Artus de. Gap 1639–61 (resign). History of this family obscured by need to invent medieval noble origins in order to flatter Louis XIV's minister when he became chancellor of the royal orders. Originally from St-Quentin, they later settled at Romans, where a Jean Lionne was a notary in 1470s. In fact, a clear family profile only emerges with bp's father, Sébastien, who married a daughter of a pres in Grenoble parlt in 1574, which helped him move rapidly into financial offices in Dauphiné, serving as intendant of royal army there in 1589, and becoming first pres of *chambre des comptes* of Savoy-Piedmont at Lesdiguières suggestion. He was also ennobled by Henri III in 1580.

B. 1–9–1583 Grenoble. Son of Sébastien and Bonne de Portes. Studied humanities and philosophy at SJ coll of Tournon, and law at Valence, where he took doct in utr. After serving as barrister at Grenoble parlt, he became *cons* there (1605–13). Married Isabelle

Servien, sister of Abel, the future minister, and Hugues, minister under Louis XIV, was their only surviving son. After wife's death in 1612, he took orders (ordained priest in 1614 by own later account). Canon of Grenoble cathedral, he was extremely active in bringing Ursuline nuns to city, and in other religious causes. By late 1620s episcopal ambitions were no secret. Owed promotion to brother-in-law, Servien, but no less to son, Hugues, who by 1630s was Servien's principal *commis*. Even so, succession to Gap was difficult, protracted affair. Initially nom as coadj to incapacitated Bp du Serre, Lionne waited several years and by time Rome was ready to issue provs, du Serre was dead and new nom and negotiations had to follow. Refusing offers of Embrun (1648) and Bayeux (1659), he finally retired to Paris to live with son in 1661.

Brevet de nom as coadj of Gap 25–8–1634. 2nd nom, following Serre's death, 13–1–1636. Provs 11–4–1639. Cons 27–11–1639. Resign 19–4–1661. D. 18–5–1663.

Sources: ASV, PC PC 37, fos 899–925. BN, Doss bleus 398, doss 10736. Ulysse Chevallier, 'Notice historique sur la famille de Lionne', *Bulletin de la Société Départementale d'Archéologie et de Statistique de la Drôme*, 11 (1877), 51–73. Virieux, 'Parlement de Grenoble au xviie siècle', 215–17. Grillon, *Papiers de Richelieu*, iv. 197.

Lis. *See* **Du Lis**

Litolfi-Moroni, Henri. Bazas 1633–45. Family was of Mantuan extraction and several members served in French army during 16th C wars, as a result of which they settled in France and were naturalised at different times. Bp's father married a Norman heiress, while bp himself actually grew up in entourage of Louis XIII, to whom his father was first *maître d'hôtel* from 1602 onwards.

B. ca 1602. Son of Constantin, sgr de Gauville, and Nicole du Val. Early education at coll of La Marche, Paris (with abbé Marolles and others). Took doct in canon law at Paris, having studied theology, though not taking degree in it. Royal almonership (in 1623) was natural step for cleric of his background. Abbot in c of St-Nicolas-au-Bois, OSB (Laon) and priest at time of nom. Episcopal office obviously had significant effect on him, and he ended career virtually as *solitaire* at Port-Royal, the crown having blocked his attempts to resign Bazas to his Port-Royaliste seminary director.

Resign by Bp Grillié, transferring to Uzès, of Bazas to Litolfi, 5–6–1633. Nom pope 7–6–1633. Provs 28–11–1633. Cons 18–6–1634. D. 22–5–1645.

Sources: ASV, PC 32, fo 590–610. BN, MS Fr 33047, pp 485, 543 (naturalisations, 1570, 1600); MS Fr 4139, fo 163, 25–11–1637 (*confirmation* of noble status). AN, Y 141, fos 68v–70v, 15–3–1602 (c.m. of bp's parents). Griselle, *Etat de la maison de Louis XIII*, no 31. Dubost, 'Les Italiens en France au xvie et au xviie siècle'. Jean Mesnard, 'Un évêque de Bazas solitaire de Port-Royal: Henri Litolfi-Maroni', *Revue Historique de Bordeaux et du Dépt de la Gironde*, 10 (1961) 65–78.

Liverdis. *See* **Grangier**

Loménie, François de, O.P. Marseille 1624–39. Despite celebrity of this long-serving family of royal secretaries and secretaries of state, bp's own background is quite obscure. Originally from Limoges where most of family appears to have remained and held a variety of royal offices, Martial de Loménie (d. 1572) migrated to Paris in early to mid-16th C, where he eventually became *secrétaire des finances* by mid-1550s. His 2nd son

Antoine, first of family to hold Ville-aux-clercs title, went on to become a trusted secretary of state under Henri IV and Louis XIII, as was *his* son, Henri, first comte de Brienne, under Louis XIII. Members of bp's family from Limoges would migrate to Provence with him and claim noble status there by 18th C.

B. Limoges 1585. Son of Pierre, sgr de Faye and brother of Claude, sgr de Ville-aux-clercs, and Catherine Essenaud. Although father was Protestant, he was reared a Catholic by his mother. Nothing known of education, except that, having entered Dominicans, he studied in Paris convent, and took doct in theology at Paris, in 1622 (ranked 33rd). Despite membership of mendicant order, his uncle, Ville-aux-clercs, acted as willing patron with higher ambitions for him, establishing an early connection between him and Marseille in 1605 by obtaining pension off episcopal mense for him, despite Roman objections. Priest for several years before nom, he was also a *prédicateur ordinaire* to Louis XIII.

Procuration from Nicolas Coëffetau to take Loménie as coadj of Marseille 18–1–1623, but Coëffetau himself died before taking possession of Marseille (which he was apparently reluctant to accept!). Nom to Marseille 22–4–1623 (day after Coëffetau's death). Provs 13–5–1624. Cons 8–9–1624. D. 27–2–1639.

Sources: BN, MS Fr 33047, p 401; Doss bleus 400, Loménie doss; MS Fr 3488, fos 100–1, 106 (Marseille pension); MS lat 15440, p 147. *Lettres de Peiresc*, vii. 583, 962–5. *Gallia Chr Nov*, ii (Marseille) 611–12. Michaud, *Grande Chancellerie*, 95, 157, 121, 159. Tessereau, *Chancellerie*, 118, 148, 241. Blanc, *Origines des familles provençales*, 348.

Lopis de la Fare, François, Minim. Riez 1625–8. As name suggests, bp's family migrated from Spain to Avignon in mid-15th C, but myth of family connection to Fernán Lopez, constable of Castile, may be safely discounted! Thereafter several branches developed, with bp's grandfather settling at Carpentras and acquiring the la Fare title/lands through marriage there. Their assimilation into local nobility gathered pace in this and later generations, and is exemplified by bp's father's military activities in Montmorency's service towards the end of religious wars.

Baptised Hector 12–3–1584 at Carpentras. Son of Jérome, sgr de la Fare, and 2nd wife Isabelle de Guiramand. Joining Minims ca 1600, he took name François 'in religion', and studied within order's houses at Aix and Avignon, and in accordance with order's rules, took no degree. Unusually, he remained full member of order after becoming bp. Unclear if he also studied at Salamanca as one source suggests. Provincial superior in his order, and also well-known preacher, not least in Paris, where he preached Lenten sermons in 1622. Cardinal Bentivoglio, bp of Riez since 1622 but not particularly desirous of retaining it, selected him as successor, though how and why remains unknown.

Brevet de nom 28–4–1625. Provs 15–9–1625. Cons 26–10–1625. D. 28–9–1628.

Sources: ASV, PC 21, fos 323–36. *Gallia Chr Nov*, i. 638. *Lettres de Peiresc*, vii. 585; vi. 723. Pithon-Curt, *Noblesse du comtat Venaissin* ii. 199–224. Borricand, *Nobiliaire de Provence*, ii. 764–5.

Lorraine-Guise, Louis. Reims coadj 1602/5–21. The last 3 episcopal members of Guise clan were as undistinguished as their predecessors were able and influential, both ecclesiastically and politically. Only bp of Condom, no doubt because of his illegitimacy, felt obliged (like Epernon's illegitimate son at Mirepoix) to conform to standards of an increasingly exacting church and crown.

B. 1575. Son of Henri, duc de Guise, and Catherine de Clèves. Educated in Univ of Paris, but took no degree. Cleric to the end, he was neither ordained priest nor cons bp. His family failed in bid to obtain see of Reims for him in 1594, but although Henri IV refused it then, he agreed to a coadjutorial arrangement some years later. Louis probably secretly married Charlotte des Essarts, by whom he had 5 children (inc Charles-Louis below). Restless and rebellious during 1610s, he attempted to resign Reims in 1617, and was imprisoned in Bastille in 1620.

No date for his nom or (more surprisingly) for papal provs, but probably 1602. Succeeded Jan 1605. Unconsecrated. Cardinal in 1615. D. June 1621.

Lorraine-Guise, Henri. Reims 1629–41 (resign). B. 1614. Son of Charles, duc de Guise, and Henriette-Catherine de Joyeuse, niece of Cardinal de Joyeuse. A cleric for his entire episcopal 'career' and magnificently endowed with benefices in c, inc most of those belonging to his great-uncle, Joyeuse. Passed over for Reims in 1621–2 under *dévot* pressure, his succession there was carefully prepared in advance of ageing Abp Gifford's death, and was virtually foregone conclusion by 1629. As unfit for episcopal office as his uncle, he joined revolt against Louis XIII and Richelieu led by comte de Soissons, and was deposed as abp in 1641. But by then he had inherited father's title and cannot have regretted his change of status.

Lorraine-Guise, Louis de. Condom 1659–68. B. ca 1610. Son of Louis, cardinal de Guise (above) and Charlotte des Essarts (whom he later claimed were secretly married). Studied humanities at La Flèche, continued philosopy at coll of Harcourt, and took doct in canon law, Paris, ca 1653 (possibly in anticipation of episcopal preferment, given his age). Abbot in c of Chaalis, O Cist (Senlis) he was ordained priest ca 1651. Otherwise pre-episcopal career remains extremely obscure.

Procurations from Bp Estrades of Condom and Guise in order to exchange Condom for Guise's abbey of Chaalis 18/21–6-1658. Nom 30–6-1658. Provs 10–11–1659. Cons March 1660. D. 1–6-1668.

Sources: Bergin, 'The Decline and Fall of the House of Guise', 783–805 (with references). ASV, Acta Camerarii 16, fos 190v-91 (Henri); PC 57, fos 1052–68 (Charles-Louis). *DBF*, xxii. 1121–2.

Louet. *See* **Du Louet**

Malier du Houssay, Claude. Tarbes 1649–68 (resign). One of several Orléans families to enter episcopate in this period, the Maliers were merchants as well as muncipal and royal office-holders there for several generations after Jean, who was mayor in 1413. But by later 16th C, they were well established as a prominent financial office-holding family. Claude, grandfather of bps, was SR, while son, Claude, began as *trésorier de France* at Orléans but went on to become an *intendant des finances*. Successive marriages to Mélissant, Sublet and Bailleul families strengthened their ties to Parisian *grande robe* circles. In generation of bps, these activities were extended to include military and diplomatic positions.

B. Paris 1600. Son of Claude, *intendant des finances*, and Marie Mélissant. Studied humanities at coll de Navarre, took lic in canon law, Orléans, but he also appears to have studied some theology – possibly much later. Pre-episcopal career was secular, and built upon family's social and professional capital. *Cons* in Paris parlt, 19–7-1624, he was successively pres in the *requêtes du palais*, MR in 1631 (resign 1633), ambassador to Venice, and *cons d'état* on his return. Marriage to Marie de Bailleul, sister of Nicolas (intendant of Anne of Austria, pres in parlt and nominal *surintendant des finances* after 1643), also contributed to his advancement. After wife's death in July 1640, he became cleric.

Nom 28–10–1648. Provs 1–2–1649. Cons 25–4–1649. Resign to son Claude 1668. D. 21–9–1681.

Malier du Houssay, François. Troyes coadj 1636/41–78. B. 1603. Younger brother of Claude above. Educated almost wholly at Univ of Paris, where studied humanities, philosophy and theology, and took doct in canon law. Abbot in c of St-Pierre-de-Melun, OSB (Melun), he was priest at time of nom.

Nom coadj of Troyes 29–4–1634. Provs 7–4–1636. Cons 6–7–1636. D. 11–10–1678.

Sources: ASV, PC 50, fos 614–40. BL, Addit MS 21434, fo 26 (Claude). ASV, PC 34, fos 434–64 (François). BN, Doss bleus 421, doss 11242; AN, MC, 1, 34, 30–5–1600 (c.m. of bps' parents); CV, 424, 17–4–1642, *inventaire après décès* of Claude Malier (bps' father). AN, Y 130, fos 92–4. Tessereau, *Grande Chancellerie*, 155, 251, 278, 307. Mousnier, *Lettres et mémoires au chancelier Séguier*, ii. 1218.

Marc. *See* **La Ferté**

Marca, Pierre de. Conserans 1648–52, Toulouse 1654–62, Paris 1662. One of the most politically experienced bps of his generation, Marca faked an ancient lineage for family going back to 12th C, the better to disguise rather modest origins in Béarn village of Gan, near Pau. Though they can be traced back there to late 15th C, they only emerge from shadows with bp's grandfather, Jérôme, in mid-16th C, when he initially served as *avocat du roi* at the local court. Became an MR de Navarre, and a *cons* and pres in the *conseil souverain* of Navarre. His religious affiliations are also unclear, but he laid the foundations for subsequent generations. Bp's father seems to have started out as merchant, but by 1598 claimed to be a noble, by 1608 a sgr and deputy to Béarn Estates, securing a formal act of ennoblement in 1611. Family's marriages reflected their developing activities and ambitions, and brought them into kinship with Abbadie, Bordenave and other prominent Béarnais *robe* families.

B. 24–1–1594 Gan. Son of Jacques, *vice-sénéchal* of Gan, and Cathérine de Lartet. Early studies in SJ coll at Auch, followed by philosophy at Toulouse, where he also took the lic in utr. Subsequently enjoyed formidable reputation in history, law, theology etc., though Gallican opinions expressed in his political-ecclesiastical writings delayed episcopal promotion considerably. Although tonsured in 1608, early career was in royal office – *cons* (1615) and pres *à mortier* (1621) in parlt of Navarre, intendant in Béarn (1631–6) and later in French-occupied Catalonia, *cons d'état* in June 1639. Married Marguerite de Forgues, a widow, who d. in April 1631. Inactive for much of 1630s, he turned to scholarly pursuits, writing De *concordia sacerdotii et imperii*, published in 1641, and which embroiled him in controversy. Censured by Rome, he later retracted most of its Gallican theses. Having also served as one of Cinq-Mars's judges, his episcopal ambitions were unmistakable by early 1640s, but he had to struggle hard to secure nom (originally as coadj) to Conserans 1642–5, and then to face Roman disapproval of his Gallican writings. Only took orders once provs as bp had been granted by Rome. Subsequent episcopal career was closely tied to his moderation of previous Gallican views and increasingly invaluable services to Mazarin, who relied heavily on him (e.g. Jansenist crisis, Retz case etc). His ultimate reward, succession to Paris in 1662, was one he did not live to enjoy.

Nom to Conserans, Jan 1645 (originally mid-1643). Provs 13-1-1648. Cons 25-10-1648. Transferred to Toulouse 23-3-1654, to Paris 5-6-1662. D. 29-6-1662.

Sources: ASV, PC 46, fos 283-302. Marca, *Histoire de Béarn*, 2 vols. Gaquère, *Pierre de Marca*. DGS, 961-2.

Marconnai, Melchior. St-Brieuc 1602-18. In 19th C, this Poitevin noble family claimed to be descended from ancient Châtillon family from Champagne, but in fact their lineage was eminently respectable without such *extravagances*. Royal household service evident from at least the reign of Charles VII, while bp's own father, Pierre, was *premier maître d'hôtel* and *premier écuyer* to Catherine de' Medici, having previously served other members of royal family, and he was succeeded in these offices by eldest son, Charles. Female members also served in royal households, with bp's mother lady-in-waiting to Queen Elisabeth, wife of Charles IX. Altogether, patronage of Catherine de' Medici appears to have been enormously beneficial to them during religious wars, in which they participated, as they had in wars of Francis I and Henri II.

B. Poitou, date unknown. Son of Pierre, sgr de Froges, and Catherine de Soubsmoulins. Nothing known of education, or whether he took degree. Almoner to Catherine de' Medici, abbot in c of St-Pierre-de-Rillé, OSA (Rennes) in 1581 and Sept-Fons, O Cist (Autun) before episcopate. He was required to abandon latter abbey to one of Espinay family when promoted to St-Brieuc, suggesting Espinay influence may have played some part in his elevation, not least because of their Breton power and fact that St-Brieuc was vacant since Sept 1595! After 1589, he may have espoused the League's cause, and it appears chapter of Dol tried in vain to secure his promotion as bp of Dol in 1591 (a *conseil privé* decree of 1596 refers to his 'rebellion'). It is not certain that Marconnai was vg of Rennes before episcopate.

Nom Jan 1601. Provs 19-11-1601. Cons 3-2-1602. D. 7-3-1618.

Sources: AN, Y 130, fo 131-2 (c.m. of François, brother of bp, and Anne de Cluys, 1588); BN, P Or 1843, doss 42575. *Lettres de Catherine de Médicis*, x. 504-30 (householders), ix. 496 (legacy by Queen Mother of 10,000 *écus* to bp's father). Dumont, *Arrêts du conseil privé* (Henri IV), no 1998 (23-4-1596). Vindry, *Etat-major*, 36, 63-4. Beauchet-Filleau, *Dict du Poitou*, vi. 493, 503-4. AN, MC, XII, 33, 19-4-1601 (contract for papal provs).

Marmiesse, Bernard de. Conserans 1654-80. A Toulouse family of uncertain origin, the Marmiesses are difficult to trace beyond later 16th C, by which time they had begun gradual ascent from lesser law practice, via municipal office, to positions within local parlt. Pierre, bp's father, was a *capitoul* in 1614, and described as a *docteur et avocat* when he bought a town house in 1622. It was bp's own generation which made an important breakthrough (brother Jacques serving as *cons*, av-gen and pres *à mortier*), and which would enable them to remain in parlt into next century.

B. Toulouse 1620. Son of Pierre and Cecile de Lavit (?). Early education probably in Toulouse, but studied theology in Paris, where he took lic (ranked 22) in 1642, followed by the doct. Priest from ca 1644, also canon of Toulouse, for which province he was deputy to AC of 1645. Elected *agent général du clergé* in 1650 AC. Father's early ambitions for him to become bp of Conserans in 1642-3 failed, but major post of *agent général* made it hard to overlook him later. Ironically, his victorious rival of 1642–5, Marca, resigned Conserans to him on being transferred to Toulouse in 1652. Slowness in obtaining papal approval may relate to his activities as *agent général*.

Nom 6–6–1652. Provs 9–10–1654. Cons 12–11–1656. D. 22–1–1680.

Sources: ASV, PC 49, fos 458v-59; PC 51, fos 1392–1405. AN, V^6 1182, fo 126v (22–2–1606). BN, MS lat 15440, p 173. Jules Chalande, *Les Rues de Toulouse* (Toulouse 1919), ii. 316–17.

Marquemont, Denis *Simon* de. Lyon 1612–26. Marquemont, name by which cardinal was generally known, was no more than a *nom-de-terre* in the Vexin. Origins of Simon family are obscure, but they were resident in Paris, where they may once have been *marchands-épiciers* (as was one of cardinal's uncles) and where Simon was a common family name, from at least mid-16th C. Confusion arises also from the fact that the cardinal's grandfather and father were both called Denis, and held same offices in close succession. Grandfather (d. in 1577), was a *receveur des tailles* in Paris *élection*, while father, who succeeded him in this office, had become a secretary to Catherine de' Medici by 1583. This change of activity seems to have arisen via Laubespine patronage, which was probably a decisive element in Simon family fortunes. Cardinal's own godfathers were Edouard Molé and Guillaume de Laubespine-Châteauneuf, and his father succeeded François de Laubespine as an SR in 1585. Bp's early career in Rome was greatly facilitated by patronage of Villeroy and Puysieux, themselves related in variety of ways to the Laubespines.

Baptised at St-Eustache, Paris, 1–10–1572. Son of Denis and Marie Rouillard. Educated initially in Univ of Paris colls, he later studied law, in part (perhaps because of events of League years) at Angers, where he took doct in utr in Sept 1592. He taught law briefly in Paris after 1594, but having accompanied du Perron to Rome as secretary, he remained there, and by 1604 had become French Auditor of the Rota, a major church tribunal, a post which made him an unofficial French agent in curia, and regular correspondent of king and secretary of state. Tonsured in 1580, ordained priest in Dec 1603. Held priory of St-Germain-Buzelles, OSB in c before episcopate. Not first choice of abp of Lyon in 1612, he owed his elevation to Villeroy-Brûlart patronage.

Nom 1612. Provs 5–11–1612. Cons 11–11–1612 in Rome. Cardinal, Feb 1626. D. 16–9–126.

Sources: ASV, Rota Romana, *Processus in admissione auditorum*, vol 1, no 50. BN, MS Baluze MS 209, fo 142, deposition by E Molé for Marquemont; MS Fr 32588, pp 86, 94; MS Fr 18007, fo 262 (Lyon 1612). AN, Y 126, fo 153; Y 131, fo 7 (Laubespine relations). Tessereau, *Chancellerie*, 226. *Lettres de Catherine de Médicis*, x. 504–30 (household members). Pozzo di Borgo, 'Denis Simon de Marquemont,' 265–94.

Marsillac, Sylvestre de Crusy de. Mende 1628–60. Originating around Castelsarrasin area, Crusy family moved to the Rouergue in late 17th C. Clearly traceable only to Jacques de Crusy in early 16th C, it was through marriage of bp's father in 1565 that they acquired Marsillac lands/title. This marriage was broadly representative of their history, since it was via marriages rather than their own exploits that the family appears to have raised itself. Eldest males followed military careers, but were otherwise unremarkable. Bp's father and elder brother were both govs of Moissac and participated in wars versus Huguenots, while another served as captain in Louis XIII's guards.

B. 1581 Cahors. Son of Grimond, gov of Moissac and Françoise de Goué. Educated at Agen and Toulouse (probably in SJ colls), and took doct in canon law (not theology) from Cahors. A priest before 1618, and abbot in c of ND de Chastres, OSA (Saintes) and Marsillac before episcopate. Originally client of Cardinal Guise, and then of Richelieu, serving both men as protonotary, later becoming an almoner to Marie de' Medici. But as Richelieu's first *maître de chambre* he came to prominence, playing a leading role in organising military campaign against La Rochelle 1627–8 (like his predecessor at Mende, Lamothe-Houdancourt, who died during siege). Continued to serve Richelieu for over a decade after episcopal promotion, until he fell from favour in late 1630s and retired to diocese.

Nom 20–3–1628. Provs 31–7–1628. Cons 21–12–1628. D. 20–10–1660.

Sources: ASV, PC 25, fos 480–502. Acta Camerarii 15, fo 102. BAV, Barb lat 7939, fo 72; 7941, fo 65. Barrau, *Dict du Rouergue*, iv. 546–50. Deloche, *Maison de Richelieu*, 75–7. Grillon, *Papiers de Richelieu*, ii. 471.

Martin de Bellecize, Jacques. Vannes 1599–1622 (resign). The 3 bps of the name of Martin appointed under Henri IV were totally unrelated to each other, but this does not make discovering their identities any easier, and all 3 are among the more obscure episcopal figures of his reign. Bp of Vannes's family may have originated in the Limousin, but settled in Bordeaux where several members of father's generation held high-ranking provincial financial offices (inc 2 *receveurs-généraux* of taxes) and were also engaged in tax-farming activities. Bp's own generation began moving, not without initial difficulty, into office in parlt there, and one of his nephews, Jean Martin de Laubardemont, would achieve notoriety as an intendant under Richelieu and Mazarin.

B. Bordeaux, ca 1574 (but possibly 1577, as he himself claimed in 1611 to be 33 years old). Son of Jean, *trésorier de France*, and Antoinette du Faur. Education and pre-episcopal career are wholly unknown. In 1599 Rome accepted he had a doct in utr and was subdeacon. It is quite plausible that nom to Vannes, where he and his family had no known ties, was arranged by a sieur de Ste-Colombe, a captain in royal guards suspected by AC of 1579 of usurping the revenues of Vannes.

No date for nom. Provs 8–11–1599. Cons in Rome 8–11–1599. Resign Vannes in 1622 to S de Rosmadec in return for latter's abbey of Paimpont. D. 12–1–1624.

Sources: ASV, Misc Arm XII 146, fo 118; Acta Camerarii 13, fo 131; PC, fo 351. AN, MC, XXIX, 143, 11–1–1624 (bp's testament). BN, P Or 1871, doss Martin. AD Gironde, 3B, *insinuations* 1607, fo 174 (c.m. of Laubardemont's parents); C 3803, fo 92, C 3807, fos 98, 108. *Chronique d'Etienne Cruseau*, i. 53–4, 106–7, 143, 236. Jean de Métivier, *Chronique du parlement de Bordeaux*, i. 299, 526; ii. 37. Taillandier, *Histoire ecclésiastique et civile de la Bretagne*, iii (Catalogue des évêques et abbés de Bretagne, p xxxvii). Serbat, *Les Assemblées du clergé de France*, 384.

Martin, Jacques, OSB. Senez 1601–23. Family of this former Benedictine monk originated in hinterland of Marseille, but by grandfather's generation were Marseillais and *bourgeois honorables*. This and following generation held municipal office in Marseille and married into often older and better placed families (some of them of Italian extraction). Bp's own father was a municipal councillor and consul in late 1570s, and was beginning to adopt the trappings of nobility (*écuyer* etc) which, given ties to local noble families, was understandable. Connections to local ecclesiastical bodies, such as the abbey of St-Victor, were also well established before bp's generation. During upheavals of Marseille League, Martin family appears to have remained strongly royalist and anti-League.

B. ca 1547 in Marseille. 3rd son of François and Diane de Johanne, daughter of modest noble family. If he entered the abbey of St Victor at an early age, as seems likely, his education would have been mostly there, after which he took doct in canon law. Pre-episcopal career mostly within St-Victor, where he became 'sacristan' and vg to abbot in c. Also credited with attempting to reform St-Victor's dependent houses in neighbouring dioceses. Personal role during League unclear, but probably did not differ from other members of family.

Nom 14–4–1601. Provs 22–10–1601. Cons 3–3–1602. Took Louis Duchaine as coadj in 1617. D. 21–2–1623.

Sources: ASV; Misc Arm XII 145, fo 506. AD Alpes de Haute-Provence, 2 G 9. *Gallia*, ii. 891. Kaiser, *Marseille im Bürgerkrieg* (and unpublished research by same author).

Martin, Jean. Périgueux 1602–12. It seems, this family was from Limousin (where Martin was a common name). Some members moved to Périgueux where they held offices at *présidial* court in later 16th and early 17th C. Bp himself may have been part of this search for new opportunities.

B. ca 1560 in Limoges diocese. Mother was Catherine Penicailhe, but father's name unknown. Nothing known of education, but held a lic in utr. Canon of Périgueux from about 1580, he became precentor there, vg of bp Bourdeille in 1583, and deputy to EG of 1588, serving as a secretary of ecclesiastical chamber. Long service as *official* and vg to his predecessor, Bp Bourdeille, was crucial to his career. Accession to Périgueux (see above, pp 80–1) was entirely dependent on Bourdeille patronage, and made a *confidentiaire* of him.

Bourdeille resign Périgueux to Martin 15–11–1599. No date for nom. Provs 15–5–1600. Cons date unknown. D. 5–1–1612.

Sources: ASV, Misc Arm XII 145, fo 370. AN, MC, VIII, 561, 4–3–1603 (Périgueux *régale*). *Procès-Verbaux des Assemblées du Clergé*, i. 461. AD Gironde, G 793, fo 44 (vg of Périgueux, 12–4–1583). Dujarric-Descombes, 'Résignation de François de Bourdeille-Montancey, évêque de Périgueux', 394–402.

Martineau, Samuel. Bazas 1646–67. Several Martineau families were resident in Paris in late 16th and 17th C, but nature of ties (if any) between them are difficult to establish. In 1590s bp's father and uncle (Mathurin) were both in service of duc de Montpensier, his father as 'controleur général de sa maison et de ses finances', no small occupation and one which indicates financial background/activities, while another brother, Pierre, was a barrister in parlt. Bp's father was subsequently SR (d. 1626) and purchased barony of Thuré, by which family were later known for time.

B. Paris ca 1604. Son of Martin and Marie Redont, 1st wife. Little known of early education, but studied theology at Sorbonne, of which he was elected prior, under André du Val (whose anti-Richer views he shared and whose funeral oration he later delivered), taking 1st place in the lic (1628) followed by doct. Priest from ca 1631, highly active in Paris thereafter. Canon of ND de Paris, he administered the Hôtel-Dieu, which he helped to reform. Superior of Calvariennes (Père Joseph's congregation of nuns) and close friend of Carmel, esp of Pontoise, before episcopate. A mediator in 1649 troubles in SW, he was later openly Mazarinist, and joined court at Poitiers in 1651. His subsequent troubles with members of Bordeaux parlt were hardly surprising, and even led him to demand transfer to Dol 1659.

No date for nom. Provs 23–4–1646. Cons 17–6–1646. D. 24–5–1667.

Sources: ASV, PC 50, fos 818–27; N Fr 93, fo 80. BN, MS lat 15440, p 155; P Or 1875, doss 43152; Doss bleus 431, doss 11586. AN, Y 134, fos 170; Y 140, fo 488; Y 144, fos 417–18. Tessereau, *Chancellerie*, 253. Jeanne de Jésus Séguier, *Lettres*, 37–8, 65. Toujas, 'Les Démêles de Samuel Martineau, évêque de Bazas, avec le parlement de Bordeaux', 51–62.

Matignon, Leonor I Goyon de. Coutances 1632–46, Lisieux 1646–74 (resign). Originally from Brittany, this prolific family of military nobility, connected to the Rieux and du Guesclins (*connétables de France*) in 14th and 15th C, moved its centre of gravity to lower Normandy, where it owned extensive lands and was politically dominant by mid-16th C. Their greatest period of military and political distinction stretched from the wars of religion to those of Louis XIII, enhanced by their marriages to some of greatest noble families. Their domination of lower Normandy made them particularly interested in bishopric of Coutances.

B. 3–5–1604. Son of Charles, lt-gen in Normandy and marshal of France, and Eléonor d'Orléans-Longueville, sister of duc de Longueville. Educated mostly by SJ, member of one of their college sodalities of the Virgin, but did not attend univ or take degree. Cleric at nom, he had been destined for Coutances which had been held by series of caretakers, the last of whom died after brief episcopate in 1625. This explains not merely delay in formally nom the young Matignon, but also slowness with which his provs were sought in Rome.

Brevet de nom, ca July 1625. Formal nom 10–3–1627. Provs 29–3–1632. Cons 9–10–1633. Nom to Lisieux 22–7–1646. Provs 4–5–1648. Resign to nephew in 1674. D. 14–2–1680.

Sources: ASV, PC 31, fos 645–65. Archives de l'évêché de Coutances, M 41, p 530 (*brevet* presented to chapter, 16–7–1625). *Corr de Bérulle*, iii. 369–70. Anselme, v. 374–425. Vindry, *Etat-major*, 231–2. *DBF*, xvi. 869–70.

Maupas du Tour, Henri Cauchon de. Le Puy 1643–61, Evreux 1661–80. Old noble family from Champagne-Picardy, with a number of military commands and town governorships to their credit. Bp's grandfather, *grand fauconnier de France*, was well connected at court of Henri IV, while bp's father was successively gov and *surintendant de maison* to duke Charles III of Lorraine. But his ties to French court were no less strong, thanks to his marriage to Anne de Gondi, daughter of Marie de' Medici's *chevalier d'honneur*. Family's connections to La Vieuville, Richelieu's rival and predecessor, and to Guises and Joyeuses, did not harm them unduly, as bp's own elevation to episcopate from his post as grand almoner to Anne of Austria, clearly indicates.

B. 15–11–1604, and baptised 'pour les cérémonies' at court in March 1606, with Marie de' Medici as godmother, and Giovanni de' Medici as godfather. Son of Charles and Anne de Gondi. Studied philosophy and theology under SJ at Pont-à-Mousson, where he took his doct in theology, 1627. Abbot in c of St-Denis-de-Reims, OSA, which he helped reform. Royal almoner, and then grand almoner to Anne of Austria after 1634. Priest since 1629, he served as vg of Reims diocese under Henri de Guise. Very close to SJ and Parisian *dévot* networks generally, he was lifelong disciple of François de Sales, whose canonisation he worked tirelessly to bring about.

Brevet de nom and nom 30–8–1641. Provs 22–6–1643. Cons 4–10–1643. Nom to Evreux 1–7–1661. Provs 31–3–1664. D. 12–8–1680.

Sources: ASV, PC 42, fos 71–90. BN, MS lat 17678 (Maupas papers). Griselle, *Etat de la maison de Louis XIII*, no 3584. *DBF*, vii. 1438.

Maupeou, Jean. Chalon-sur-Saône 1659–77. Any family which produced not one but two chancellors of France was bound to be tempted to doctor its history, and the Maupeous were no exception. Originally from Poitiers, they suddenly emerged from obscurity with Vincent, a Parisian notary in mid-16th C who, perhaps because of his business clientèle, established extensive connections within a remarkably short period of time. Immediate descendants were able to capitalise on these (Miron, Laubespine, Verdun 'alliances', followed in early 17th C by Netz, Laisné, Fouquet, Villemontée, Feydeau and Quentin de Richebourg). Bp's grandfather, Pierre, founder of Monceau branch and son of the notary held (as did other brothers) financial offices, esp in *chambre des comptes*, and was also a 'secretary' in households of Henri III (1581) and his wife, and later served as household treasurer to Marshal Joyeuse. Bp's father (who founded the Bruyères branch) was successively *cons* (1602), av-gen (1604) and pres (1608) in *cour des aides*, and proc-gen of *chambre de justice* in 1624. By then the senior branch, which had been partly Protestant for some time, had reached the pinnacle of its influence, thanks to Gilles, the Protestant *contrôleur general des finances* and grandfather of *surintendant* Fouquet and his episcopal brothers. As their Protestant affiliations disappeared, so their *dévot* and religious ones became increasingly obvious, producing a large number of religious vocations, and in old age even bp's father engaged in religious controversies with Protestants and Jansenists alike.

B. Paris 20–9–1623. One of 17 children of René and Marguerite de Creil (daughter of Jean, a wealthy SR and financier). Nothing known of education, except he took doct in canon law, Paris, ca 1650. Priest ca 1651, he was dean of *collégiale* of St-Quentin-en-Vermandois, and succeeded Bp Grangier of Tréguier as royal almoner in 1646, thanks to Mazarin's protection.

Nom 30–7–1658. Provs 21–4–1659. Cons 9–5–1660. D. 2–5–1677.

Sources: ASV, PC 57, fos 394–407. BN, MS lat 18345, fo 208v (ennoblement of notary's sons, 1586). Maupeou, *Histoire des Maupeou*. Bluche, *Origine des magistrats*, 303. Dessert, *Foucquet*, 32–6.

Maytie de Mauleron, Arnauld de. Oloron 1597–1622. Scarcely anything known of social and family background of these 3 bps, whose diocese was occupied by Huguenots since time of Jeanne d'Albret. In 1595 Henri IV undertook to restore Catholicism there, but in face of local obstructionism nothing was achieved until after military campaign of 1620. Meanwhile, bps of Oloron and Lescar, who did not technically 'belong' to French church until 1620, were unable to reside in their dioceses and used successive ACs to press their case. Because church revenues were also in Huguenot hands for many years, bps also relied on tenure of local abbeys in c (e.g. St-Pé-de-Generez, OSB [Tarbes] and St-Vincent-du-Lucq [Oloron]) to supplement their meagre resources. All of which made Oloron (and Lescar) unattractive to outsiders for several generations, which facilitated the Maytie tenure of see for such a long (even if interrupted) period.

B. ca 1565 (by own later account), Arnauld I was son of Pierre and N. . . Studied law at Bordeaux with Bernard Daffis of Lombez, and took his lic in canon law there, late 1597. Ordained priest in Sept 1585. Prior of Ordiarp (1590), he became canon of Oloron in

1590s. Elected by chapter to govern vacant diocese in 1598. Rumours circulated later about how he obtained Lescar, and in particular that he signed an agreement with Charles de Luxe, gov of Soule, making him little more than a *confidentiaire*. This remains unproven, though Maytie's huge energy as bp would seem to make it unlikely. He co-operated actively with bps of Lescar to obtain restoration of Catholicism in Béarn.

No date for nom, but first mentioned in Jan 1597. Provs 21–5–1597. Cons date unknown. Took nephew as coadj. D. Sept-Oct 1622.

Maytie, Arnauld II de. Oloron coadj 1618/22–46. B. 1588 Mauléon. Parents' identity unknown. Took doct in canon law after completing his studies. Deacon at time of nom.

No date for nom as coadj to uncle. Provs 15–1–1618. Cons date unknown. Succeeded to Oloron Oct 1622. D. 20–6–1646.

Maytie, Arnauld-François. Oloron 1659–81. B. 1613. Son of N. . . Maytie, *lieutenant de robe longue* at Mauléon, and Madeleine d'Arbide. Educated in part at coll de Clermont (along with Montpezat de Carbon), but completed philosophy in Toulouse. Also studied theology there and took doct, though may also have taken law degree. Priest from ca 1648, he was canon of Oloron. Abbot in c of St-Pé (Tarbes) from 1635, he was, unusually, required to part with it on nom as bp.

Nom 11–4–1659. Provs 1–9–1659. Cons 11–4–1660. D. 2–7–1681.

Sources: Labau, *Lescar, histoire d'une cité épiscopale*, 57–9, 61–2. Abbé Menjoulet, *Chronique du diocèse et du pays d'Oloron*, ii. 159–276. Dubarat, *Notices historiques sur les évêques de l'ancien diocèse d'Oloron*, 40–4. Clergeac, *Chronologie*, 133 (family-general). ASV, PC 13, fo 322v. Fondo Borghese I, 646, fo 108. AD Gironde, 798, fo 12 (Arnaud I). ASV, PC 57, fos 735–50, 1250–1. BN, MS lat 17027, fo 244 (Arnaud-François).

Mazarin, Michele. Aix 1645–8. The much discussed and often misunderstood history of the Mazarin family is much less pertinent to French ecclesiastical career of Michele Mazarin than the ministerial patronage of his younger brother, who found his elder as difficult to manage as he did other members of his family.

B. 1607 Rome. Son of Pietro and Hortense Buffalini, 'jeune fille de sang bleu'. Educated first in Rome and then Bologna, where he took doct in theology. Entered Dominican order (1620), in which, thanks to Barberini patronage, he gradually rose to hold high office. Having served as provincial superior in Puglia and Rome, he became Master of Sacred Palace in 1643, but failed, because of Habsburg hostility, to become General of his order in 1642. Spent most of his time after 1644 in Catalonia, and only briefly resided in Aix before returning to Rome where he d., triggering long ensuing vacancy at Aix (see Grimaldi).

Nom Mar 1644. Provs 10–7–1645. Cons 23–7–1645 in Rome. Cardinal 1647. D. 1–9–1648.

Sources: ASV, Processus Datariae 24, fos 370–5. Touron, *Hommes illustres de l'ordre de Saint Dominique*, v. 278–84. *DGS*, 998–1002. G Dethan, *Mazarin, homme de paix à l'âge baroque* (Paris 1981). G Treasure, *Mazarin* (London 1995).

Médavy. See Rouxel de Médavy

Miossens, Jean de. Oloron 1652–8. Bp's real background obscured by his family's desire to identify with Albret family, sgrs de Miossens, an affiliation which could only add lustre to the name of Miossens, sgrs de Sanons! They are only clearly identifiable from mid-16th C, the generation of bp's grandparents (Bertrand and Jeanne de Lary), whose only son Henri-Bernard I (d. 1610) seems to have been a *gentilhomme de la chambre* to Henri IV. Catholic, he narrowly escaped execution in Pau during wars of religion. Marriage of bp's nephew to a daughter of Marshal d'Albret (1614–76) not only unleashed their genealogical imagination but, more importantly, made it possible for Jean to obtain Oloron at the end of Fronde, when the future marshal bargained with Mazarin for his loyalty.

B. 1607 (by own later account). Son of Henri-Bernard, baron de Sanons, and Françoise de Montesquieu, vicomtesse of Sardirac. Educated partly in Paris, where he took doct in canon law. Priest from ca 1640, *curé* of Turon for several years (credited with some Huguenot conversions), but also a canon of Lescar.

Nom 1–8–1652. Provs 13–11–1652. Cons 9–2–1653. D. 8–2–1658.

Sources: ASV, PC 53, fos 14–30, 1050. *Lettres missives de Henri IV*, ix. 177–8. Beaumont, *Pièces inédites tirées des archives de la maison de Miossens-Sansons*.

Molé, Edouard. Bayeux 1648–52. It would be difficult to find a family whose history is more closely identified with Paris and its parlt than that of bp of Bayeux. Yet Molé family originated in Troyes where they were prominent *bourgeois* from early 15th C. Only a century later, with the move of bp's great-grandfather, Nicolas, to Paris, did their parlementaire and *grande robe* identity begin to take shape, *via* marriage alliances with similar status families (Hennequin, Charmolue, La Grange Trianon). This social capital was built upon by bp's grandfather Edouard (*cons* in 1562, pres *à mortier*, 1602), and his son, the most celebrated of them all, Mathieu, father of the bp. *Cons* in 1606, pres in the *Enquêtes* 1610, proc-gen in 1614, first pres in 1641, twice keeper of the seals during Fronde, he was highly esteemed by Luynes and Richelieu alike, and acted with legendary firmness and courage at critical moments during Fronde, which his eldest son did not survive.

B. 1611. Eldest son Mathieu and Renée Nicolay. Studied humanities and philosophy at Univ of Paris colls, followed theology course to bacc level (but did not sit exam), he took doct in canon law, probably in Paris. Tonsured in Feb 1617, ordained priest ca 1644. Prior in c of Sermais, OSB (Châlons-sur-Marne) and St-Denis-en-Vaux, OSB (Poitiers), also canon of ND de Paris. Despite close ties to Olier (his second cousin) and other prominent *dévot* families, Molé was generally regarded as less than suitable candidate for episcopal office.

Nom 3–6–1647. Provs 23–11–1648. Cons 14–2–1649. D. 6–4–1652.

Sources: ASV, PC 48, fos 208–26. AN, Z^1o 241 (tonsure). BI, MS 1354, no 88. Anselme, vi. 570–6. Bluche, *Origines des magistrats*, 314–15.

Montaigne, Raymond de. Bayonne 1629–37. This nephew of Michel de Montaigne was descended from a converted Jewish family, the Eyquem, which migrated from Spain and settled into office in Bordeaux parlt during 16th C. Despite the essayist's own well known withdrawal from office in mid-career to live the life of a gentleman-scholar, his relatives continued to hold office there into 17th C.

B. 1580 Bordeaux. Son of Geoffroy, *cons* at Bordeaux parlt, and Perrine Guillot, from a Saintonge family. Studied humanities at coll de Guyenne, Bordeaux, and took doct in utr in Bordeaux while still 14 years old! Entire pre-episcopal career was that of secular magistrate. A *cons* at parlt (but 'en survivance' only) from 1593 onwards, he quickly turned elsewhere to make career, and served for many years at *sénéchaussée* court in Saintes, where, thanks to patronage of maternal uncle, Jacques Guillot, he became successively lt-gen and, after 1611, pres. Deputy for 3rd Estate at EG of 1614 (Michel Raoul, future bp of Saintes, was clergy's deputy). Married Marie de Maulevant, by whom he had 3 children, but she d. ca 1620, after which he took orders, becoming priest in 1622. Held abbey of Sablonceaux OSA (Saintes) in c before episcopate. A truculent, litigious character, he continued as pres of Saintes after ordination, and only the threat not to cons him in 1630 forced his hands on the eve of his cons. Richelieu had identified him as worthy of episcopal office over 18 months before his nom.

Nom 30–11–1629. Provs 4–3–1630. Cons 14–7–1630. D. 10–3–1637.

Sources: ASV, PC 27, fos 775–810. *Chronique d'Etienne Cruseau*, i. 120. Jean-Claude Dubé and Pierre Julien-Laferrière, *Les Bigot du xvie siècle à la Revolution* (Montreal 1988), 291–6. L Audiat, *Les Célébrités inconnus: un petit-neveu de Michel de Montaigne* (Vannes 1900). Dangibeaud, *Le Présidial de Saintes*.

Montano, Horace de. Arles 1598–1603. No obvious connection between Montano and see of Arles, except perhaps Arles was previously held by a fellow Italian, Silvio de Santacroce. B. 1540 at Rocca Gloriosa in Policastro diocese (Naples), Montano took lic in theology in Rome, where he was canon of St-Peter's before becoming bp of Penna and Atri in 1591. His succession to Arles was consequence of deal over revenues of Arles signed in 1595 between predecessor Santacroce and Louis Bertons de Crillon, to whom Henri III had granted revenues in 1586. Unclear how or why Montano became involved with either Crillon or Santacroce, but he was evidently willing to accept the Arles succession on terms suitable to the *brave* Crillon.

Nom, ca 1598. Provs 25–11–1598. D. 11–9–1603

Sources: AD Bouches-du-Rhône, B 3340, fo 165 (letters-patent enabling Montano to hold benefices in France, 29–5–1598). *Gallia Chr Nov*, iii. 928–41.

Montchal, Charles. Toulouse 1627–52. Frequently portrayed as an aggrieved aristocratic opponent of Richelieu, Montchal was in reality of relatively modest origins. As so often, an attempt was made at some point to graft family onto different Montchal family which had disappeared by 14th C. In fact, family profile only becomes clear from early 16th C, when Nicolas was an apothecary of Annonay. When his son, Mondon, also an apothecary, married Perette Broë in 1545, a real change in family fortunes began. While his brother François founded the Montpellier-Huguenot branch of financiers, and other members embraced Protestantism for a time, the rest of the family still remained within familiar local and social horizons (despite kinship ties to Serres and Villars families). The true source of their success was Perrette Broë's brother, Bon, a trusted servant of Cardinal de Tournon and Catherine de' Medici, diplomat, *cons* and pres in Paris parlt, but also an unmarried cleric who held benefices in c and who promoted his Montchal and Serres nephews in a way they could hardly have done themselves. His legacy was in every sense the basis of their advancement, although none of them held offices remotely resembling his. Abp's father was successively *contrôleur de l'artillerie* 1585, capt of royal château at Bourg-St Andéol, *contrôleur* of *grenier-à-sel* of Ste-Colombe, but used title of *écuyer* when he finally became *bailli* of Annonay, and thus deputy to Estates of Vivarais.

B. 1589 Annonay. Son of Antoine and Anne de Guillon. Studied mainly at Univ of Paris, where he was *boursier* and later principal of college of Autun (a family tradition), finishing with lic in canon law. Took minor and major orders in Dec 1614–April 1615, and became royal almoner at same time. Succeeded uncle Jean Montchal in 1612 as abbot in c of St-Amant-de-Boixe, OSB (Angoulême), of St-Sauveur-le-Vicomte, OSB (Coutances), but not as canon in Coutances cathedral, though canonicate in Ste Chapelle was ample compensation. The story that he was tutor to Cardinal La Valette in Paris in early 1610s, and that this explains his succession to Toulouse, appears unfounded, but other ties, established either then or later, cannot be ruled out.

No date for La Valette's resign or for Montchal's nom, but probably late 1626–early 1627. Provs 17-5-1627. Cons 9-1-1628. D. 22-8-1651.

Sources: ASV, PC 13, fos 720–1. BAV, Barb lat 3792, fo 117. AN, Z^1o 241 (orders). BN, P Or 2011, doss 46128; Doss bleus 458, doss 12326. Archives de l'évêché de Coutances, M 41, pp. 480–1, 327, 410. Tallemant, *Historiettes*, ii. 668–70. Villain, *France moderne* ii. 156–8, 225; Nicod, 'Généalogie de la famille de Montchal', 38–45, 72–5, 132–9, 193–6.

Montpezat de Carbon, Jean de. St-Papoul 1658–64, Bourges 1664–74, Sens 1674–85. One of the most aristocratic of Louis XIV's bishops, Montpezat was son of one of the innumerable branches of an old Agenais family which, through military activity and intermarriage, established themselves as a premier noble clan of Guyenne. Carbon was apparently a sobriquet given to one such branch in 16th C. Yet they were not to achieve major ecclesiastical office until generation of abp and brother, who became abp of Toulouse in 1676.

B. 1605, in Comminges diocese, where father held lands. Son of Jean-Antoine, *sénéchal* of Nébouzan, killed at siege of Montauban 1621, and Louise de St-Paul, dame de Vidaussan. Educated at coll of Clermont (along with Arnaud-François Maytie) ca 1629–30, he took doct in canon law, Paris. Deputy to ACs of 1650 and 1655, he served as secretary in latter, during which his nom to St-Papoul was negotiated. Priest from ca 1643, he was abbot in c of Mas d'Azil, OSB (Rieux).

Nom to St-Papoul 15-6-1657. Provs 3-6-1658. Cons 8-9-1658. Abp of Bourges 1664, Sens 1674. D. 5-11-1685.

Sources: ASV, PC 55, fos 376–92. AAE, France 898, fos 130–1. Blet, *Clergé de France et monarchie*, ii. 134. Monluc, *Commentaires*, 32. Bourousse and O'Gilvy, *Nobiliaire de Guienne*, iv. 269–348, esp 336ff. Navelle, *Familles toulousaines*, vii. 256–7.

Montrouge, Jacques de. St-Flour 1647–64. Parisian family of prosperous merchants, although difficult to trace further than bp's own father, whose 1st marriage to Claude Poullain in 1590 produced 5 children. 2nd marriage (in 1610) was to daughter of a Paris *élu* with rather better social and professional connections (several of them financial) than those of Montrouge family, though bp's father did later become an *échevin* of Paris.

B. Paris 1612. Son of Jacques and Geneviève de Secqueville, 2nd wife. Studied humanities and philosophy at coll of Navarre, taking 15th place in lic in theology, 1640. Canon and treasurer of St-Jacques-des-Pelérins for 14 years before episcopate. Almoner to Anne of Austria in 1634 and later one of her *prédicateurs*, it was his (unspecified) services to her which constituted his claim to episcopal office, and which gave him priority in 1643 over other contenders like François Bosquet.

Initially nom to Pamiers in 1643, but resign claim to Caulet on 10–6–1644. Nom to St-Flour 31–10–1646 (on transfer of Noailles to Rodez). Provs 8–4–1647. Cons 21–9–1647. D. 20–4–1664, having obtained and then declined Le Puy in 1661.

Sources: ASV, PC 44, fo 152; PC 45, fos 142v-44; PC 46, fos 428–49. AN, MC, CXII, 300, 3–2–1606, *inventaire après décès* of Claude Poullain; MC, XXXIV, 18, 18–3–1610 (c.m. of bp's parents). BN, MS lat 15440, p 170. Griselle, *Etat de la maison de Louis XIII*, nos 3589, 3626.

Morenne, Claude. Séez 1600–6. Family may have originated in Poitou, but their Parisian profile remains quite shadowy. Bp's father and brother (Gervais), were successively *cons* in the *chambre du trésor*, though Gervais later entered the parlt. Episcopal office came Claude's way thanks to patronage of royalist uncle and predecessor at Séez, Louis du Moulinet, who had himself succeeded a relative at Séez. One of the least understood of France's episcopal dynasties of this period, though the du Moulinet were related to several important robe families (Mangot, Luillier, Le Roy de la Poterie, Longueil).

B. Paris ca 1550. Names of parents unknown, as is his early career up to 1577, when he took doct in theology at Sorbonne, thanks to which he became *curé* of St-Merry. Uncle's patronage enabled him to become canon and provost of Séez cathedral, where he may also have held a parish briefly. Above all, he participated with 3 other Paris *curés* in the instruction and conversion of Henri IV in 1593, and temporarily lost his parish owing to his firm anti-League stance and defence of kings from attack by their subjects.

No date for resign of Séez by uncle. Nom 19–3–1599. Provs 23–10–1600. Cons 29–7–1601. D. 2–6–1606.

Sources: AN, MC, VIII 422, 10–3–1601 (Séez *régale*). BN, Doss bleus 476, du Moulinet doss. *Lettres missives de Henri IV*, v. 740 (19–3–1599). L Tabourier, 'Claude Privas de Morenne', *Bulletin de la Société Historique et Archéologique de l'Orne* 45 (1926), 335–49. Louis Hommey, *Histoire générale ecclésiastique et civile du diocèse de Séez*, iv (Alençon 1900), 67–158.

Murviel, Anne de. Montauban 1600–52. Family can be traced back to Antoine Murviel, sgr de Coujan near Béziers in 1425, but they only emerged from obscurity with marriage in 1509 (according to Père Anselme) of Jean, baron de Murviel, to Antoinette de Lettes de Montpezat, sister of Marshal de Lettes, gov of Languedoc. Nearly a century later, this connection proved crucial as far as obtaining the see of Montauban, held by a succession of Montpezat family members, was concerned. In 17th C, Murviel marriage ties were in both robe and *épée* circles, and included families of bps like the Bertier, Montchal, Percin de Montgaillard, etc. Succession to Montauban, vacant since death of the battling Bp Jacques des Prés in an ambush in 1589, was highly political. Both Mayenne and Henri IV had candidates for the see, which was also coveted by the marshal de Matignon for one of his sons, but it was because of a common Montpezat family connection (Mme de Mayenne's 1st husband had been a Montpezat!) that Murviel candidature triumphed, with Henri IV finally accepting Mayenne's suit and granting him a blank *brevet de nom*. Bp's brother had also sought Montmorency support to same end, using mother's family's connections, past and present, to impress the constable.

B. 1568 Murviel, near Béziers. Son of François and Françoise de Castelnau de Cuers. Nothing known of education or pre-episcopal career. The fact that he was not even cleric when nom to Montauban suggests something of nature and circumstances of his promotion.

No date for nom, but probably 1596. Provs 15–11–1600. Cons 15–8–1600. Took P de Bertier as coadj, 1636 D. 8–9–1652.

Sources: BN, Cab d'Hozier 252, doss 6685; Doss bleus 478, doss 12653; Arch de Chantilly, L/xxix, fo 10; L/xlv, fo 174. AD Hérault, 1 E 196, 910–14, 931 (misc family docs). La Roque, *Armorial de Languedoc* (Montpellier) i. 345. Anselme, vii. 189. Navelle, *Familles toulousaines*, vii. 286–7. Daux, *Histoire de l'église de Montauban*, ii. 3.

Nesmond, François de. Bayeux 1661–1715. Like the Bouthilliers, Nesmond family were natives of Angoulême, where they, too, were merchants who held municipal office in early to mid-16th C, but to whom the attractions of Bordeaux soon proved irresistible. Within two generations, they had achieved the highest office there, with bp's grandfather André, becoming first pres of parlt (1611–16). As he and his father before him had briefly been *cons* in *grand conseil* in Paris before moving to Bordeaux, his eldest son (and father of bp), François-Théodore's, decision to reverse the process and follow a Parisian career is not surprising. Initially a *cons* at Bordeaux, he became an MR in 1624, intendant in Condé's army 1628–9, and pres *à mortier* in Paris parlt in 1636. Entry to the higher reaches of parlt was facilitated by marriage to daughter of Chrétien de Lamoignon, whom he succeeded as pres *à mortier*. Also served as Condé's *intendant de maison* from at least 1631. Played an important role in parlt during Fronde, not least as a defender of the *grand* Condé's interests, an uncomfortable position which saw him become leader of a rump Frondeur parlt in 1652.

B. Paris 31–8–1629. Son of François-Théodore and Anne de Lamoignon. Early studies SJ, moving later to coll of Navarre, followed by theology under Gaston Chamillard at Sorbonne, where he took 5th place in 1652 lic, and doct soon after. Priest from ca 1654, active in priestly community of St-Nicholas-du-Chardonnet, and at St-Lazare under Vincent de Paul, he had some experience as preacher. Held abbey of St-Pierre-de-Chézy, OSB (Soissons) and the priory of La Voulte, O Cluny (St-Flour) in c before episcopate. Attended AC of 1655–7 as deputy for Bourges province.

Nom 27–2–1661. Provs 8–8–1661. Cons 19–3–1662. D. 16–5–1715.

Sources: ASV, PC 55, fo 638; PC 59, fos 318–41. Vindry, *Parlementaires* (Bordeaux), p 44. Trani, 'Conseillers au grand conseil', 194–5. *Inventaire-sommaire des archives de la Charente* [E series], 4 vols (Angoulême 1880–1906). AN, Y 165, fo 108v (c.m. of bp's parents, 10–9–1624). BN, MS lat 15440, p 195. Poutet, 'Docteurs de Sorbonne', 259.

Netz, Nicolas de. Orleans 1630–46. Family's history remains, despite its Parisian context and often impressive kinship ties, rather vague. Bp's father was the first figure to emerge distinctly, but his office of *cons* in *cour des aides* and a Maupeou marriage suggest a solid background and good connections. Bp's own generation sustained the advance, socially and professionally: brother, Pierre became a *maître d'hôtel ordinaire* to Louis XIII (1636) and married a Talon; another, Charles, was *cons* in the *cour des aides* before becoming MR, etc.

B. 18–2–1592 at Tours during League. Son of Nicolas and Marguerite Maupeou. No information on early education, but was Paris MA by 1612 and studied theology at Sorbonne (in late 1610s with Rebé of Narbonne), where he distinguished himself with 1st place in lic (1618) and doct. Tonsured in Dec 1605, ordained priest ca 1619, when he also became royal almoner and *curé* of St-Germain de l'Auxerrois, the parish of the Louvre! He held priories of Palaiseau (Paris) and Ste-Marie-Madeleine (Meaux) in c before promotion. Regarded as Richerist and Gallican because of his dislike of regulars and, possibly, his behaviour during Santarelli censure (1626–7), Rome was for time anxious to prevent him from becoming bp. But clearly well regarded by Louis XIII, Richelieu and queen mother. His hurried nom to Orléans in 1630 gave rise to friction with Gaston d'Orléans who resented not having voice in choice of bp there.

Nom 18–8–1630. Provs 27–1–1631. Cons 27–4–1631. D. 20–1–1646.

Sources: ASV, PC 24, fo 700; PC 28, fos 826–53. AN, Z^{1}o 241 (orders); MC, CIX 222, 30–12–1647 (*inventaire après décès* of Pierre de Netz, bp's brother). BN, MS lat 15440, p 143. Griselle, *Lettres de la main de Louis XIII*, i.100–1. Griselle *Etat de la maison de Louis XIII*, no 25.

Neufchezé, Jacques de. Chalon-sur-Saône 1624–58. Prolific Poitevin family of *noblesse seconde* rank was commonly known by title of barons des Francs (having long since lost its original title-lands of Neufchezé). Several members served in the Italian wars, and it was marriage of Léon, baron des Francs, to a sister of Marshal Saulx-Tavannes which enticed them to move in part to Burgundy. Bp's father was a *fidèle* of Henri III and Henri IV, whose successive marriages to Gabrielle de St-Gelais and Marguerite Frémiot brought his family closer than hitherto to ecclesiastical circles.

B. 25–10–1591 Poitou. Son of Jacques, baron of Bouzey in Burgundy, and Marguerite Frémiot, sister of André, future abp of Bourges. Education began in SJ coll at Dijon, followed by theology in SJ coll, Lyon. Rome accepted that held doct in theology on nom, but if true, it was probably from Bourges, since his studies and early career owed much to uncle, Frémiot, abp of Bourges. Chancellor of church and Univ of Bourges, where he also preached. Deputy to 1619 AC for Bourges province. Priest, he was abbot in c of Varenne, O Cist (Bourges), and also coadj of uncle's abbeys at time of nom.

Nom 7–1–1624. Provs 7–10–1624. Cons 29–12–1624. D. 1–5–1658.

Sources: ASV, PC 18, fos 162, 348–65. BN, Doss bleus 486, doss 12748. Vindry, *Etat-major*, 98, 357, 408.

Neufville-Villeroy, Camille de. Lyon 1654–93. The *états de service* of this celebrated ministerial and (later) military family scarcely need (and would defy) detailed recounting. Their political origins lie in small and closely knit circle of notaries and secretaries who served Louis XII and François I, a kind of conciliar oligarchy which was perfectly placed to benefit from subsequent expansion of government business. Bps' grandfather was classic example of the new secretary of state, and his extraordinarily long career firmly anchored Neufville-Villeroys in France's admin and political élite (Laubespine, Harlay, Brûlart de Sillery etc) while laying foundations for their wider social ambitions, finally realised in impressive style under Louis XIV, by the generation of the bps and the following one. The choice of Lyon as a provincial family power-base under Henri IV was not irrelevant to their ecclesiastical ambitions. Ironically, noble chapter of Lyon was unimpressed by future abp's lineage when he sought entry as canon there in 1611–12, since his 'nobility' was clearly inadequate by their standards, and powerful pressure had to be brought upon them to change their minds.

B. 22–8–1606 Rome (where father was ambassador). Son of Charles, marquis d'Halincourt and gov of Lyonnais, and 2nd wife, Jacqueline de Harlay, daughter of

Nicolas, sgr de Sancy. Nothing known of education, but some sources credit him with doct in theology. Tonsured in Lyon, Sept 1612, received as canon of St-Jean, Lyon, June 1613. Magnificently endowed with benefices from early age: abbot in c of St-Wandrille (1616), Ainay, Lyon (1617), St-Romain-de-Puy, (1617), Ile Barbe (1618), Lagny (1634), Noirlac (1636), Mauzac (1640) (which he exchanged for Montverdun in 1646). Lt-gen of Lyonnais, Forez and Beaujolais, 1646, a post previously held by father and elder brother, and which he exercised while abp. His personal ecclesiastical ambitions seem to have been uncertain for long time. Cardinal Marquemont tried to obtain the succession of Lyon for him in 1626, but d. before it could be arranged. Still probably too young for office, he was in no position to obtain Lyon in 1628 when Richelieu's brother moved there from Aix, and had to wait until his death in 1653, when Neufville's nom to Lyon was strongly opposed by the royal confessor, but by this juncture Mazarin's favour and Neufville's indispensability overrode all objections.

Nom 28-5-1653. Provs 12-1-1654. Cons 29-6-1654. D. 3-6-1693.

Neufville, Ferdinand de. St-Malo coadj 1644-57, Chartres 1657-90. B. 1608 Rome. Younger brother of Camille (above). Educated at coll of Clermont (fellow-student of Fr de Grignan and H de Béthune in 1621-2), followed by theology at Sorbonne for several years, but took doct in canon law instead. Abbot in c (after his brother) of St-Wandrille, OSB (Rouen). Deputy for Lyon province to 1635 AC. Ordained priest in July 1643 in preparation for episcopal office.

Procuration from uncle Harlay de Sancy to take him as coadj of St Malo, 27-6-1643. Nom 15-4-1644. Provs 13-6-1644. Cons 28-8-1644. Nom to Chartres 29-5-1657. Provs 24-9-1657. D. 8-1-1690.

Sources: Anselme iv. 639-44. Harsgor, *Un très petit nombre*, 251-2. Sutherland, *French Secretaries of State*. J Nouaillac, *Villeroy, secrétaire d'état et ministre* (Paris 1909). *DGS*, 1601-2. Beyssac, *Les Chanoines de l'église de Lyon*, 195. Tallemant, *Historiettes*, i. 218-20 (family-general). BAV, Barb lat 8059, fos 236, 245 (Lyon, 1626). BN, MS Fr 20663, fo 429. Colbert, *Lettres*, i. 495 (Camille). ASV, PC 45, fos 54-74; PC 48, fo 408; PC 54, fo 455 (Ferdinand).

Nivelle, Pierre, O Cist. Luçon 1636-60. The Nivelles were a solidly established Troyes family of paper merchants and printers, with business and kinship connections beyond Champagne. Bp's generation is 4th known to historians. Father's marriage in 1563 brought them into relations with the Hennequins, another prominent Troyes family which was by then also Parisian, and whose ties to merchant and office-holding families there were prodigious. Nivelles were themselves attracted to Paris, where Nicolas, a bookseller and printer was a member of Paris Sixteen, while a cousin from Troyes was household comptroller to duc de Guise. But it was bp's generation who first moved out of traditional local social and professional milieu, though modestly rather than spectacularly – one brother, Jean, was *lieutenant-particulier* in Troyes *élection*, another was *receveur du taillon*, while a 3rd was *cons* at Troyes *bailliage*.

B. 1593 Troyes. Son of Jean, *bourgeois* of Troyes, and Anne Morise (daughter of Jeanne Hennequin). Joined Cistericans, so probably studied in order's houses and then at coll des Bernardins, Paris, where he took doct in theology. Moved quickly upwards within Cistercian order: abbot of St-Sulpice, elected abbot-general in 1625, he became embroiled thereafter in conflicts generated by Cardinal La Rochefoucauld's efforts to reform his order. This ultimately led to episcopal promotion, since it was with a view to becoming abbot-general himself that Richelieu persuaded Nivelle to step down and accept his old diocese of Luçon, which Richelieu's direct successor, Emery de Bragelongne, obligingly vacated.

Resign of Luçon by Bragelongne to Nivelle, 30–10–1635. Nom 30–11–1635. Provs 22–9–1636. Cons 25–1–1637. D. 11–2–1660.

Sources: ASV, PC 35, fos 378–95; Kuno Böse, *Amt und soziale Stellung. Die Institution der élus in Frankreich im 16. und 17. Jarhhundert am Beispiel der Elektion Troyes* (Frankfurt 1986), ii. 231–2. P Zakar, *Histoire de la stricte observance de l'ordre cistercien jusqu'au généralat de Richelieu* (Rome 1966). Descimon, *Qui étaient les Seize?*, 196–7.

Noailles, Charles de. St-Flour 1609–47, Rodez 1647–8. One of oldest noble families of Limousin with military record stretching back to 12–13th C, but whose age of greatest achievement and prestige still lay in the future. By 15th C they were solidly entrenched among Auvergne-Limousin nobility (relatives included the Turenne and other families). Church ties were also strong by then. So successive generations during 16th C able to pursue their ambitions along several fronts, with both lay and clerical members gaining increasing distinction, as exemplified by political and diplomatic activities of François and Gilles, successive bps of Dax 1560–97. By 1590s, bp's father had established himself as dominant political figure in Upper Auvergne and his service to Henri IV was acknowledged not merely through personal political promotion, but also through the gift in 1597 of presentation rights to dioceses of Dax and St-Flour.

B. 27–7–1589. Son of Henri, comte d'Ayen, and Jeanne-Germaine d'Espagne de Panassac. Nothing known of education, but Rome accepted in 1609 he had doct in canon law, at which time he was still in minor orders. Abbot in c of ND de Valette, O Cist (Tulle) in 1603 and destined from outset for see of St-Flour. His predecessor, Rouchon, was an elderly caretaker (see above, pp 78–9 for circumstances of his promotion) who d. in 1602, after which, given Noailles's age, St-Flour was kept vacant for 7 years until he could obtain provs from Rome. Even then, cons was delayed for several more years. But he proved an active bp, and early member of *Compagnie du St Sacrement*.

No date for nom to St-Flour, but late 1602–early 1603. Provs 28–9–1609. Cons probably 1614. Transferred to Rodez 8–4–1647. D. 27–3–1648.

Sources: Kalas, 'Wealth, Place and Power in 16th century France'. *Annales de la Compagnie du Saint-Sacrement*, ed Beauchet-Filleau, 14. *DGS*, 1091–3.

Nogaret. *See* **La Valette**

Olce, Jean d'. Boulogne 1632–43, Bayonne 1643–81. The Olce (sometimes rendered as Dolce) family were relatively undistinguished nobles from Iholdy in Béarn, and bp owed his career almost wholly to family's connection to Bertrand Deschaux, bp of Bayonne and abp of Tours, who at each turn secured ecclesiastical advancement for his nephew.

B. 1605. Son of Pierre and Isabelle Deschaux, sister of Bertrand, abp of Tours. Studied humanities and philosophy at both Univ of Paris and with SJ (under whom also studied some theology), but took no degree. Canon of Tours thanks to his uncle, ordained priest in early 1632. Abbot in c of La Boissière, O Cist (Angers) before episcopate. His promotion to Boulogne was probably negotiated by uncle as *quid pro quo* for accepting

Victor Bouthillier as coadj in Tours, while his later transfer to Bayonne was facilitated by François Fouquet's wish to leave Bayonne for Agde in 1643.

Resign by V Bouthillier of Boulonge to d'Olce, 8–5–1632. Nom pope 16–8–1632. Provs 20–12–1632. Cons in 1633. Initially nom to Agde in 1643, but Fr Fouquet resign Bayonne to him 21–6–1643. Provs 31–8–1643. D. 8–2–1681.

Sources: ASV, PC 31, fos 705–23; PC 42, fos 156–77. *Armorial de Béarn*, ed Dufau de Maluquer, i. 205–6. *Gallia*, vi. 700. *DBF*, xi. 439.

Ondedei, Zongo. Fréjus 1658–74. B. May 1608 Pesaro, of parents unknown. Ondedei owed career (at least in France) entirely to Mazarin. After early studies, he took doct in utr at Bologna. Moved to Rome to pursue diplomatic/service career, and was successively auditor of papal nuncio to Spain, and of the Avignon vice-legate. But encounter with Mazarin, of roughly the same age and ambitions, was decisive. Mazarin took him under his wing, and he followed the cardinal to France in 1646, serving him in host of roles, and accumulating considerable wealth in the process. Later *cons d'état*, he was simple cleric at time of nom, with relatively little inclination towards episcopate, which may have been designed to ease him out of court (Colbert certainly wished him to stay away after Mazarin's death). The long delay between his nom and provs is due in part to complications arising out of Anne of Austria's incautious statement that she could not vouch for his suitability for episcopal office!

Nom 4–10–1655, Provs 8–7–1658. Cons 20–10–1658. D. 23–7–1674.

Sources: ASV, PC 54, fos 672–87. Espitalier, 'Evêques de Fréjus', 55–81.

Ossat, Arnaud d'. Rennes 1596–1600, Bayeux 1600–4. A virtual legend to contemporaries and subsequent generations, Ossat's diplomatic gifts, which were the basis of his reputation, also ensured he never set foot in either of his dioceses. He had virtually completed negotiations to resign Bayeux to Jean d'Angennes before death in 1604. His celebrity was all the greater for the obscurity of his origins.

B. 20–7–1537 Larroque (Auch diocese). Son of Bernard Deossat and N. . . Little known of early education, but by own account, he studied law at Bourges 1566–8, after which he headed for Paris to 'prendre la pratique de la cour de parlement et puis faire comme Dieu me conseillera'. Tonsured in Dec 1556, his early to middle career remains obscure, though he was tutor to sons of Marca family in late 1550s-early 1560s. By mid-1580s, he was in Rome, and served as secretary to Cardinal Joyeuse in Rome and Venice, ca 1589 and after. Returned to Rome with du Perron in 1594–5, and acted as virtual *chargé d'affaires* there until normal diplomatic relations were restored in late 1590s. His negotiating skills and defence of Henri IV's interests won him enormous respect and, crucially, patronage of royal ministers like Villeroy. Rennes was an early reward for his services, which were crowned by the red hat in 1599. Dean of St-Martin (Vabres), prior in c of Vesci OSB (Clermont) and abbot in c of Varenes, O Cist (Bourges) at time of nom.

Nom to Rennes 25–1–1596. Provs 9–9–1596. Cons 27–10–1596 in Rome. Moved to Bayeux 1600. D. 14–5–1604.

Sources: *Lettres d'Ossat*. A Degert, *Le Cardinal d'Ossat, évêque de Rennes et de Bayeux (1537–1604). Sa vie, ses négociations à Rome* (Paris 1894). P Tamizey de Larroque, 'Lettres inédites du cardinal d'Ossat', *Revue de Gascogne*, 13 (1872), 126–37, 187–90, 341–2.

Ouvrier. *See* **Douvrier**

Passelaigue, Jean de. Belley 1629–63. B. ca 1589 Sancoins. Son of Jean and Gilberte Coulombier, but origins are as obscure as those of Ossat. Educated partly by SJ at Clamecy and Nevers, but esp in Cluniac priory of La Charité which he entered as an *oblat*, ca 1596, and where he became professed monk ca 1605. He gradually came to hold prominent offices there and in order of Cluny – in 1613, he was vg of La Charité for Cardinal de Guise, and became claustral prior 2 years later, attempting to reform it and its dependent houses. Became full prior (*en titre*) of La Charité in 1625, but as the priory was so keenly coveted by members of powerful families over the years (Gonzaga, Guise, Richelieu), Passelaigue's tenure was blighted by conflict and litigation. His role as vg of order of Cluny under Richelieu's predecessor as abbot-general was also conflict-ridden, as it coincided with attempts at reform (and resistance to it from within). As with Pierre Nivelle at Cîteaux, Richelieu seems to have offered him episcopal office in order to lever him out of La Charité and Cluny's affairs, and Belley was conveniently available and not esp sought after.

Resign by Bp Camus of Belley to Passelaigue 17-1-1629. Nom 11-4-1629. Provs 19-11-1629. Cons. 24-3-1630. D. 12-8-1663.

Sources: ASV, PC 26, fos 496–517. *Histoire chronologique du prieuré de la Charité sur Loyre ordre de Cluny* (La Charité, 1991), 125–6. Paul Denis, *Richelieu et la réforme des monastères bénédictins* (Paris 1913). Maximim Deloche, *Un frère de Richelieu inconnu* (Paris 1923), 175–8.

Pause. *See* **Plantavit**

Pavillon, Nicolas, Congregation of the Mission. Alet 1639–77. A paragon of Jansenist austerity in his remote rural diocese, Pavillon's origins were Parisian (and before that Tourangeaux) and, in social and professional terms, almost wholly financial. Grandfather managed to be both barrister and poet, while father was mostly an official in *chambre des comptes*. Mother's family, La Bistrade, was much better connected, with relatives in *grand conseil* and *chambre des comptes*. When bp's sister married for 2nd time in 1647, virtually her entire entourage on both sides was made up of families long, and sometimes prominently, engaged in *les affaires du roi* (Quentin de Richebourg, Maupeou, Mithon).

B. Paris (parish of St-Sauveur) 17-11-1597. Son of Etienne and Catherine de la Bistrate. Early studies at coll of Navarre, after which he may have followed part of theology course, but he did not take degree on completion. His lic in canon law only taken in June 1637, just when he was nom to Alet and purely with view to episcopal promotion. Subdeacon in 1620, ordained priest of Congregation of Mission in 1627. Canon of Condom thanks to influence of Quentin de Richebourg, his financier-cousin. Best known before the episcopate as right-hand man of Vincent de Paul at St-Lazare, and de Paul could justifiably claim him for one of the 'évêques sortis de cette maison'. His preaching also attracted prominent attention in Paris, but succession to Alet in 1637 (coming during a period when vacant dioceses were scarce) was hotly contested. Pavillon's impeccable *dévot* credentials and his mentors' access to Richelieu may well have been decisive in his favour.

Nom 2-6-1637. Provs 16-5-1639. Cons 21-8-1639. D. 8-12-1677.

Sources: Dessert, *Argent, pouvoir et société*, 666. Déjean, *Prélat indépendent du xviie siècle*. Trani, 'Conseillers au grand conseil', 160–1.

Pelissier, Jean, OSB. Apt 1607–28. Originally, it seems, from Languedoc, Pélissier family consolidated its roots in Provence thanks to bp's father's marriage to a member of the Villeneuve-Trans clan, an old noble family whose network of relations and clients there was vast.

B. ca 1566. Son of Antoine, sgr de Simiane, and Jeanne de Trappard, daughter of Antoinette de Villeneuve-Trans. Nothing known of education, but it may have been mainly in Benedictine order, which he entered relatively young. Rome accepted he was doct of theology. A monk of St-André-de-Villeneuve-les-Avignon, later prior at Simiane, he apparently had some experience as preacher. The circumstances of his nom aroused intense suspicion in Rome, where the original intention of making him coadj to the elderly Italian bp, Periglio, led to allegations of simony and *confidence*, compounded by his agreement to pay a substantial pension to a nominee of the military commander Crillon, to whom Henri IV had given the diocese to dispose of. Periglio d. in the meantime, which dispensed Pélissier from a coadjutorial apprenticeship. He was succeeded at Apt by a Villeneuve-Trans relative.

No date for nom. Provs 28–5–1607. Cons details unknown. D. 28–9–1628.

Sources: ASV, Fondo Borghese II, 248, fo 531. *Gallia Chr Nov*, i. 285–6, (and *instrumenta*, 184). Terris, *Eveques d'Apt*, 112–13.

Péréfixe, Hardouin de Beaumont de. Rodez 1649–62, Paris 1662–71. From Poitevin noble family, bp's path to mitre was greatly facilitated by father's service as *maître d'hôtel* to Richelieu, and his own brief period as the cardinal's last *maître de chambre*, and his appointment, first moved by Richelieu in 1642 (and confirmed in 1644), as preceptor to Louis XIV, for whom he also wrote several historical works in that capacity.

B. 1606 Beaumont. Son of Jean, sgr de la Papinière, and Claude de Lestang. Educated by SJ at Poitiers, he studied theology at Sorbonne, where he took 3rd place in 1636 lic, followed by doct. Apart from his duties to the young Louis XIV, he was vg to his predecessor at Rodez, and helped to found seminary at Villefranche. A priest since early 1640s, abbot in c of Sablonceaux OSA (Saintes), and prior in c of St-Jarric before episcopate. It was as anti-Jansenist and authoritarian, but maladroit abp of Paris that he achieved contemporary notoriety.

Nom to Rodez 22–4–1648. Provs 1–2–1649. Cons 18–4–1649. Transferred to Paris 1662. D. 1–1–1671.

Sources: ASV, 47, fos 236–44; PC 50, fos 318–33. BN, MS lat 15440, p 164. Orest Ranum, *Artisans of Glory* (Chapel Hill, 1980), 327–8. G Lacour-Gayet, *L'Education politique de Louis XIV* (Paris 1923), 10–12. *DGS*, 1183–4.

Péricard, Guillaume, Evreux 1608–13. Best known for their association with the Guises during religious wars (esp during League), this Rouen-based family of parlementaires and clerics originated in Troyes where they were prominent merchants during 15th and 16th C, despite being ennobled by Charles VII in 1433! Bps were descended from a family member, Jean, who became proc-gen in Rouen parlt in 1558–70. By comparison with their Troyen antecedents, their Norman career was relatively shortlived, but did not lack for event or achievement. Only one of Jean's (above) sons,

Nicolas, had children, while his daughter Anne married Romain Boyvin, father of coadj-bp of Evreux (1616–39). No fewer than 3 of his sons became bps under Henri III (Georges and François, bps of Avranches in 1583 and 1588) and Henri IV (Guillaume, bp of Evreux, 1608). Nicolas became duc de Guise's secretary and a leading figure in Catholic League. From his marriage to Jeanne de Croismare, there were 2 sons and 2 daughters, of whom bishop of Evreux 1613–46, and Charles, father of bp of Angoulême (below). By that generation, male lines were dying out, possibly because of their remarkable success in producing bps and the number of sons entering the church or serving as *cons-cls* in parlt. Bishop of Angoulême proved to be the last surviving male.

B. 1548, Guillaume was son of Jean and Anne Martin, daughter of a *procureur* in Paris parlt. Destined for clerical career from early age, canon of Rouen, he served as vg of abp of Rouen. *Cons-cl* in Rouen parlt in 1571, he was militant *ligueur* in Rouen after 1588, but failed in attempt to become pres in parlt, 1592. Abbot in c of St-Taurin, OSB (Evreux). Deputy to ACs of 1600 and 1605 for Rouen province, he succeeded Cardinal du Perron in Evreux in 1608, 2 years after the cardinal's promotion to Sens. Du Perron, a fellow Norman, appears to have wished to retain Evreux and Sens, but negotiated Péricard's succession in return for his abbey of St-Taurin! Little is known of certain aspects of his career, least of all why, at the age of 60, he wished to enter episcopate, though it was almost certainly linked to ecclesiastical ambitions of the younger generation, hence the rapidity with which his nephew joined him as coadj.

No date for nom to Evreux. Provs 4–7–1608. Cons 1608. D. 26–11–1613.

Péricard, François. Evreux coadj 1611/13–46. B. 1587–8. Son of Nicolas and Jeanne de Croismare. Nothing known of education, but Rome accepted he had bacc in theology. In May 1610, he sought papal dispensation (because he was underage) in order to become canon and dean of Rouen. At that point he was subdeacon and protonotary apostolic, though by 1611 he was ordained deacon.

No date for nom as coadj. Provs 12–12–1611. Cons 16–12–1612. Succeeds Nov 1613. D. 21–7–1646.

Péricard, François. Angoulême 1647–89. B. 1619 Condé-sur-Hon. Son of Charles, baron des Botereaux, and Esther de Costentin. Educated initially under direction of uncle, bp of Evreux, he later studied in Paris, where he appears to have followed the theology course for 5 years, but chose to take lic in canon law instead. Priest from ca 1643, he helped to administer Evreux during uncle's last years. His nom to Angoulême was clear break with family tradition, but was occasioned by ambition of fellow Norman, Le Noël du Perron, to return to native Normandy.

Resign of Angoulême to Péricard by Le Noël du Perron 18–12–1646. Nom Dec 1646? (royal letter left undated!). Provs 18–2–1647. Cons 25–8–1647. D. 29–9–1689.

Sources: Kuno Böse, *Amt und soziale Stellung. Die Institution der élus in Frankreich im 16. und 17 Jht* (Frankfurt 1986) ii. 251–3. Frondeville, *Conseillers*, 501–2. Dewald, *Formation of a Provincial Nobility*, 90–2, 355 (family-general). ASV, Acta Misc 97, fo 599 (Georges, bp of Evreux); Acta Misc 97, fo 609. AN, MC, XII, 40, 14–5–1610 (François, bp of Evreux). ASV, PC 46, fos 404–26 (François, bp of Angoulême).

Perrochel, François. Boulogne 1645–75 (resign). Origins of this model *dévot* bp lay in Parisian *marchandise*. Grandfather, Valleran Perrochel, was one of its wealthiest *marchands-pelletiers*, offical *pelletier* to Henri III to whom he also lent money, while his grandmother, Marguerite Nicéron, was also from wealthy merchant background. Bp's father's generation improved on this capital, focusing their ambitions mainly in financial sphere. Uncle Valleran was a comptroller general of Marie de' Medici's household (1611–14) and *trésorier de France* at Tours, another uncle Guillaume was pres of the *trésoriers de France* at Amiens 1601–6, and later *maître des comptes* in Paris (1610–59), while his father was successively SR and *grand audiencier de France* (1598). Bp's brother, Charles, sgr de Grandchamp, appears to have been first family member to enter Paris parlt, in 1625. Their family relations (e.g. Niceron, Parfaict, Poussepin, Neufbourg, Buisson) were extensive, and included several ecclesiastics. Abbey of St-Crespin of Soissons, previously held by his Buisson relatives, was virtually family heirloom by time bp acquired it in 1637.

B. Paris 18–10–1602. Son of Charles and Marie Varlet. Nothing known of early education, but followed Paris theology course for ca 4 years, taking bacc, ca 1627–8. Abbot in c of St-Crespin, OSA (Soissons) in 1637, and canon of Arles for unknown period of time. A priest from ca 1633, participated in several missionary and preaching campaigns, e.g. in diocese of Bayonne under Fr Fouquet, and also in Auvergne. Particularly close to de Paul, Olier and other leading religious reformers.

Nom 9–6–1643. Provs 6–2–1645. Cons 11–6–1645. Resign 1675. D. 8–4–1682.

Sources: ASV, PC 44, fos 249–65. BN, P Or 2241, doss 50774; Cab d'Hozier 266, doss 7158; Carrés d'Hozier 490; Doss bleus 518, doss 13523; MS lat 17024, fos 90–1. AN, MC, XXVI, 61, 2–5–1636 (Arles canonicate). 'Testament de Msgr François Perrochel évêque de Boulogne 1643–77', *Mémoires de la Société Académique de Boulogne-sur-Mer*, 17 (1896).

Perron. *See* **Du Perron**

Pingré, Pierre. Toulon 1658–62. This wealthy and well connected financial family originated in Amiens, but by mid-17th C, it was equally at home in Paris, as its progress in less than a century suggests. Bp's grandfather, Antoine, was an *échevin* of Amiens in mid-16th C, while his younger brother became a *receveur-général des finances* for Picardy by late 1570s, and was ennobled by Henri IV in 1594 for services to royalist cause. Two generations later, marriage of bp's sister, Catherine, to Nicolas Sainctot in 1627 brought together an astonishing array of (mainly) financial families and social power on both sides (Hacqueville, Vertamont, Louvencourt, Camus, Bonnard, Fortia, Le Masuyer, Colbert, Danès, Sève, to name but a few). At mid-century, several Pingré family members still held important offices throughout Picardy. Their religious affiliations emerge less clearly, though a brother of bp Pierre was a Jesuit.

Baptised 18–2–1615 at St-Jean-de-Grève, Paris. Son of Henri, *trésorier de France* at Amiens, and Isabelle Raguenat. Little known of education, except he took lic in utr. at Orléans. Spent 20 years before episcopate as *cons* in the *cour des aides*. Reasons for change of career are (in contrast with those of his predecessor, Danès, at Toulon) unclear, but change seems to have come during Fronde. A priest from ca 1652, also canon of ND de Paris, royal almoner and protonotary apostolic at time of nom.

Contrat de permutation between Bp Danès of Toulon (who had signed Catherine Pingré's marriage contract in 1627 as an *ami*) and Pingré for see of Toulon and Pingré's priory of Sts-Pierre-et-Paul-de-Souvigny, O Cluny (Clermont), 28–7–1657. Nom 28–2–1658. Provs 17–6–1658. Cons 12–1–1659. D. 3–12–1662.

Sources: ASV, PC 55, fos 634–52. BN, MS Fr 32588, p 269 (baptism). AN, MC, CV, 269, 25–4–1627 (c.m. of Catherine Pingré). *Nouveaux hommages rendus à la Chambre de France xviie-xviiie siècles*, i (Paris 1988), nos 1686–7, 1701. Louvencourt, *Les Trésoriers de France de la généralité de Picardie ou d'Amiens*, 127–9. Pierre Deyon, *Amiens capitale provinciale au xviie siècle* (Paris 1967), 97–8, 259, 325–6, 554–5.

Plantavit, Jean. Lodève 1625–48 (resign). Few bps enjoyed *two* careers as different from each other as this Huguenot convert whose long public life has somewhat obscured his antecedents. His parents, both Protestants resident near Mende, were probably of middling noble rank, though the family's geographical origins may lie in or near Béziers.

B. 1576 Ste-Croix. Son of Christophe, sgr de Margon, and Isabelle Dassas. Early education was at Calvinist coll of Nîmes, after which he studied theology in Geneva, defending his theology theses in Montpellier, 1603. After brief period as schoolmaster in Nîmes coll, he was converted by Barthélemy Jacquinot SJ. Subsequently, he returned to studies, following philosophy and theology course at SJ colls of Rouen and later La Flèche, supported by funds from the French clergy. Embarked on 2-year grand tour of Germany and Italy, ending with doct in theology, Rome 1611, where he entered the circle of Cardinal La Rochefoucauld. On return to France, he engaged in debates with Huguenot pastors, became almoner to the future Queens of Spain and England, and also served as vg to La Rochefoucauld as grand almoner of France. Ordained priest in 1613–14, he obtained the abbey of Ruricourt, OSA (Beauvais) in c. He himself described how he became bp of Lodève, a see which had been in Ventadour hands and effectively vacant for over a decade: royal intervention forced Ventadours to allow proper episcopal nom to be made in 1625. Plantavit's closeness to Montmorency, gov of Languedoc, nearly cost him his diocese after 1632 revolt but the case against him was eventually dismissed. François Bosquet was not alone in coveting the ageing Plantavit's succession in the 1640s, but bp's terms for resignation nearly sunk Bosquet's chances of succeeding, such was *conseil de conscience*'s suspicion of anything smacking of simony.

Nom 29–3–1625. Provs 18–8–1625. Cons 19–10–1625. Resign to François Bosquet 1648. D. 28–5–1651.

Sources: PC 21, fos 339–63. BN, MS lat 18345, fos 187v, 192. (ennoblements, 1508–9). AD Hérault, IIE/40, vol 82 (testament and codicils of bp). Louise Guiraud, 'Qui a converti Jean de Plantavit de la Pause en 1604?' *Revue Historique du Diocèse de Montpellier* (1913) 145–55. Jean Plantavit, *Chronologia Praesulum Lodovensium* (1634), 402–4. Chesnaye-Desbois, *Dict de noblesse*, xv. 915–16. Henry, *François Bosquet*, 254–70. Luthard, 'Journal de Plantavit évêque de Lodève', 189–213, 323–44.

Plas, Leger de. Lectoure 1599–1635. From one of the many old noble families of the Limousin to produce bps in this period, Leger's uncle and great uncle had been bps of Bazas under Francis I, though there is no basis for view that as a young man he served the second of them in his diocese. For much of 16th C, family appears to have combined sword and robe (as well as ecclesiastical) activities quite happily, with members serving in Bordeaux parlt and *grand conseil* in Paris. Bp's father's marriage evidently reinforced their ties to Parisian robe and court circles, while marriage of bp's sister to Gaspard d'Esdresses, explains his subsequent choice of coadj and successor.

B. 1549 Curemonte. Son of Annat de Plas and Marie d'Etampes de Valençay. Sent early to school in Paris with brothers, where he did humanities and philosophy, after which he went to Toulouse ca 1565–6 to study law, but does not appear to have taken degree. Took orders when ca 30, but there is no proof he was ever an OSB monk. Prior in c of Layrac, O Cluny (Agen) when nom to Lectoure, which had been nominally vacant for many years, although Charles de Bourbon-Navarre held title to it until 1595 when he surrendered it and secular administrator was appointed to govern it. Background to Plas's nom remains unknown. Once he had secured coadj in 1620, he retired to native village.

No date for nom. Provs 19–7–1599. Cons 19–12–1599. Took Jean d'Esdresses as coadj 1609. D. 24–3–1635.

Sources: BN, P Or 2298, doss 51970; Doss bleus 526, doss 13,841. Clergeac, *Chronologie*, 49. Degert, 'Les Dernières années de Leger de Plas', Chesnaye-Desbois, *Dict de noblesse*, xv. 917–20 (confused).

Polverel, Etienne. Alet 1607–37. From a bourgeois family of Brive, this bp owed his advancement to his formidable uncle, Christophe de Lestang, bp of Lodève, Alet and Carcassonne, whose family were also natives of Brive.

B. ca 1570. Eldest son of Guillaume Polverel and Antoinette de Lestang, daughter of Etienne Guilhon-Lestang. Destined for military career, education was doubtless rudimentary. Along with brother, Pierre, he grew up under mentorship of Christophe de Lestang, and through him, the Polverels became clients of Joyeuse family, and of Cardinal Joyeuse in particular. An attempt to obtain the see of Aire for his brother Pierre in 1596 failed as Henri IV had already given it to Epernon. As part of subsequent Montmorency-Joyeuse-Lestang negotiations over disputed Languedoc dioceses, Pierre was nom to Alet, but d. in Rome in Aug 1603 having obtained his provs, though still uncons. A 4-year vacancy followed while Etienne was persuaded to abandon his military career and prepare himself for the episcopate, apparently taking a degree in utr and priestly orders before being given his provs by Rome. Lucky to escape conviction after 1632 revolt in Languedoc.

No date for nom to Alet, but possibly soon after brother Pierre's death (Aug 1603). Provs 30–7–1607. Cons date unknown. D. 25–4–1637.

Sources: ASV, Acta Camerarii 14, fo 71; Acta Misc 97, fo 608. Gustave Clement-Simon, 'Célébrités de la ville de Brive: Les Lestang, les Meynard de Lestang, les Polverel', 533–611.

Popian, Simon Etienne de. Cahors 1601–27. One of the most obscure of Henri IV's bps, as even exact name, not to mention family and background, are difficult to establish. Popian was a small town and *seigneurie* near Béziers which gave rise to family name, but by 16th C, it was in hands of Tuffet family, who called themselves Tuffet de Popian. No doubt that the bp was related to them, possibly through marriage in female line, and also that it was through members of that family that he made his early ecclesiastical career. His real name, therefore, may have been Tuffet de Popian, and his social status that of minor, landed nobility.

B. ca 1550. Identity of parents unknown. Nothing known of education, except that held doct in utr. Virtually all his pre-episcopal career was spent in cathedral chapter and episcopal admin of Béziers. Canon of Béziers since the 1570s, he succeeded uncle, François de Taraux de Tuffet, as precentor there in 1590. By then a long-serving *official* to Bp Thomas de Bonzi, whose patronage was no less important to his career. He was also prior in c of St-Vincent-de-Popian, OSB (Béziers) before episcopate. The circumstances of his accession to Cahors are also obscure, but common link may be marshal Thémines-Lauzières, a relative of previous bp of Cahors (Hébrard de St-Sulpice) who, in later years, appears to have been esp close to Popian. His patronage and regional power/ambitions would certainly have sufficed to win see for Popian, given circumstances of Henri IV's reign.

No date for nom to Cahors but 1601. Provs 10–9–1601. Cons 9–12–1601. Took Pierre Habert as coadj, 1622. D. 29–3–1627.

Sources: ASV, Misc Arm XII, 144, fo 337. AD Hérault, I E 1470–4 (Popian papers), G 363, 444. *Gallia*, i. 150.

Potier, René. Beauvais 1596–1616. The Potiers are classic example of how an old Parisian bourgeois family, which had engaged in fur trade, banking (as *changeurs*), and tax receiverships, moved steadily and inexorably over several generations into highest ranks of the robe, having been ennobled by office in 1528. Under Louis XI, Nicolas Potier (great-grandfather of bps) was *général des monnaies* and *prévôt des marchands*; by Louis XIII's reign, the family included 3 secretaries of state, as well as *cons* and pres in parlt. Bps' father, Nicolas (1540–1635), sgr de Blancmesnil and pres *à mortier* in Paris parlt, played a key role in this upward movement, thanks to his astonishingly long career, his marriage to heiress of a hugely influential parlementaire family, his strongly royalist stance during League, and his long services to Catherine and Marie de' Medici.

B. 1574. Son of Nicolas, pres *à mortier*, and Isabeau Baillet. Scarcely anything known of pre-episcopal career, or whether he had degree. His library, however, was one of a man of wide interests and learning. Canon of Chartres in 1594, he was probably mere cleric still engaged in studies when Beauvais succession arose that year. He quickly took minor orders in Sept 1594, and (with papal dispensation) major orders in early 1597, only days before cons. His predecessor at Beauvais, Nicolas Fumée was a royalist who d. as a result of mistreatment by the *ligueurs*, and for a time, Pierre d'Epinac of Lyon laid claim to the vacant see. But collapse of League ruined his chances, while Potier family royalism was about to be rewarded by Henri IV who, having gained control of Paris, was prepared to use episcopal patronage to tame the strongly *ligueur* town of Beauvais (bp was sgr of town).

No date for nom, but mid-1594. Provs 23–11–1596. Cons 24–2–1597. D. 4–10–1616.

Potier, Augustin. Beauvais 1617–50. B. date unknown. Younger brother of René above. Nothing known of education, but Rome accepted he had lic in utr. Episcopal accession was sudden, occasioned by death of brother, and it required use of his family's considerable influence (and a bribe to Concini's wife) to keep bishopric in their hands. Augustin was strongly anti-Gallican bp, close to Cardinal La Rochefoucauld. As grand almoner to Anne of Austria, he was briefly, in 1643, candidate for the red hat and rival to Mazarin for the place of principal minister (*cabale des importants*).

No date for nom but probably late 1616. Provs 21–8–1617. Cons 17–9–1617. D. 19–6–1650.

Sources: BI, MS 1354, no 94. AN, MC, LXXXVI, 84, 28–6–1573 (c.m. of bps' parents). E Barnavi and R Descimon, *Le Juge et la potence* (Paris 1985), 146–51. Bluche, *Origine des magistrats*, 357–8. Anselme, ii. 304–5. Etchéchoury, *Maîtres des requêtes*, 257–8. Trani, 'Conseillers du grand conseil', 103–5 (Baillet). AN, MC, VIII, 409, 27–7–1594 (Beauvais *régale*); LXXXVI, 215, 15–10–1616, *inventaire après décès*, René Potier. AD, Oise G 695 (testament and codicils of René Potier, 1616).

Puget, Etienne de. Marseille 1644–68. Later attempts to fabricate a suitable genealogy notwithstanding, bp of Marseille was quite unrelated to an ancient Provençal family (or the artists) of the same name. His family were natives of Toulouse, where several members were *capitouls* in late 15th and 16th C, but were of limited social distinction. Bp's own grandfather, Jean, was either stocking-merchant or apothecary from Toulouse, whose sons and grandsons 'made' the family name once they had moved into Parisian and court circles. Bp's father, also Etienne, was key figure in this process. Described in 1580 as simply 'suivant les finances', he became one of the 3 *trésoriers de l'Epargne* under Henri IV, and was prominent enough to enjoy royal protection against efforts of Sully and *chambre de justice* in 1607 to convict him! In the next generation, the most famous family member would be Puget de Montauron, the great financier, client of Richelieu, and patron of Corneille, while others would hold financial offices in family's birthplace, Toulouse.

B. ca 1588 Paris. Probably eldest son of Etienne, *trésorier de l'Epargne*, and Louise Prévost, 2nd wife (m. in 1587). Nothing known of education, but he appears to have taken lic in canon law. Early career was a secular one, but although he bought an office of SR, his activities remain highly obscure. Married Anne Hallé, daughter of a *maître des comptes*, but after her death in Sept 1613, he resigned his office, turned towards church career, and was ordained priest before 1623, when he became suffragan-bp of Metz (whose titular bp, Henri de Bourbon-Verneuil, Henri IV's son, was uncons). Also served as vg of Toul and Reims dioceses during late 1630s, and may have incurred Richelieu's ire in defending abp of Reims's rights. Nom to Marseille came just as *conseil de conscience* was being formed, and patronage of Augustin Potier of Beauvais may well have been a crucial advantage.

Nom to Dardania 'in partibus infidelium' 29–9–1623 (to succeed Coëffetau as suffragan of Metz). Provs 1623. Cons 1624. No date for nom to Marseille, but early June 1643. Provs 18–4–1644. D. 11–1–1668.

Sources: ASV, PC 18, fos 121–31; PC 45, fos 140–52. BN, MS Fr 32588, fo 208. Tessereau, *Chancellerie*, 35. Tallemant, *Historiettes*, ii. 530–42. F Bayard, *Le Monde des financiers au xviie siècle* (Paris 1988), 329–30. Navelle, *Familles toulousaines*, viii. 297–303. Blanc, *Origine des familles provençales*, 454–8.

Raconis, Claude-François d'Abra de. Lavaur 1639–46. Abra family hailed from Raconis in Piedmont, hence form of family name. They may have settled in France in the first half of 16th C through service in royal artillery, which led on to offices in financial admin, military and civilian. François (bp's grandfather) was naturalised in 1547, converted to Protestantism, lived at Sedan for a time, and engaged in diplomatic activities, it seems, for Huguenot cause. His 3 marriages laid the foundations of family's extensive connections in the world of finance, both Protestant and Catholic. His son, bp's father, was also raised a Protestant but converted to Catholicism as did his wife on her deathbed. By bp's generation, the Abra de Raconis were fully integrated into Parisian office-holding circles, and their Catholicism would be of the ardent *dévot* type.

B. ca 1595. Son of Olivier and Péronne de Flévin. Born Protestant but abjured early, apparently under influence of François de Sales. Educated virtually entirely in Univ of Paris, where studied theology under Nicolas Isambert, and took 2nd place (behind Netz of Orléans) in the lic exam, 1618, quickly followed by doct. Long-serving univ professor of philosophy, he published a general treatise on philosophy in 1617. Ordained priest ca 1616, *curé* of Courville (Chartres) for a while, but preaching was his real 'ministry', enabling him to become almoner and *prédicateur* to both Louis XIII and wife. Close to *dévot* networks, he was pillar of *Compagnie de la propagation de la foi* during 1630s, and strongly supported Richelieu against St-Cyran and his followers. Episcopal career blighted by poor health, but had little desire to live in distant Lavaur, which he attempted to resign to Mathieu Bourlon (later bp of Soissons) in 1644.

Nom 17–6–1636. Provs 10–1–1639. Cons 22–5–1639. D. 10–7–1646.

Sources: ASV, PC 37, fos 929–48. BN, MS Fr 33047, pp 467, 559 (naturalisations, 1509, 1547); MS lat 15440, p 143; Baluze 333, fo 114; MS Fr 15720, fo 342. AAE, France 835, fo 284–6. Tallemant, *Historiettes*, ii. 271. Vidal, *Critique*, 65–7.

Ragny. *See* **La Madeleine**

Raoul, Michel. Saintes 1617–30 (resign). Earliest known ancestor of these bps may have been a notary in Nantes diocese, ca 1426. Family moved to Anjou, and later held offices in Rennes parlt, though the outline of their activities in subsequent generations remains rather sketchy. Guillaume (father of Bp Jacques), was *procureur-syndic* of Breton Estates and pres in *chambre des comptes* at Nantes by 1598, while another brother was *cons* at Rennes parlt. By this juncture, their ties were essentially in municipal oligarchy of Nantes and parlt of Rennes, where they would be further strengthened during 17th C.

B. ca 1570 Angers. Son of Jean, sgr de la Guibourgière, and Marguerite Plainchesne. Educational history unknown, but held lic in utr. Dean of Saintes cathedral 1598, he was deputy to AC of 1605, where he was elected *agent-général du clergé*. Also deputy to 1614 EG. Probably priest long before nom. Arranged nephew's outright succession in 1630, and though he d. before it could take effect, crown allowed nom of Jacques to proceed.

Nom July 1617. Provs 18–12–1617. Cons 18–3–1618. D. 14–9–1630.

Raoul, Jacques. Saintes 1631–48, La Rochelle 1648–61. B. 1589 (by own later account) Nantes. Son of Guillaume, sgr de la Guibourgière, and Jeanne Simon. Studied mainly at La Flèche (along with René de Rieux, bp of St-Pol-de-Léon), and took lic in utr at Poitiers. *Cons* at Rennes parlt, 1616–21, *sénéchal* of city and county of Nantes, he served as mayor of Nantes, 1621–2. Also active in Estates of Brittany. M. Yvonne Charette, (daughter of a *cons* in Rennes parlt) in 1618, by whom he had 4 children. After her death, he took orders, being tonsured by Cospeau of Nantes, and assisted uncle at Saintes (possibly as vg). Active, vigilant bp in region with strong Protestant communities, and closely connected to Vincent de Paul and other reformers.

Resign by uncle, Michel, of Saintes to Jacques, 4–7–1630. Nom 23–1–1631. Provs 7–7–1631. Cons 11–1–1632. *Brevet de nom to Maillezais* 26–11–1646. First bp of La Rochelle 1648. D. 15–5–1661.

Sources: Saulnier *Parlement de Bretagne*, ii. 743–4. *Supplément à la généalogie de la maison de Cornulier imprimée en 1847* (Nantes 1860), 134. ASV, PC 28 fos 654v, 704–38. *Archives Historiques de la Gironde*, xxiii, 524. Pérouas, *Diocèse de la Rochelle*, 224 (Jacques).

Ratte, Guichard de. Montpellier 1597–1602. Family was from lower Languedoc, where earliest known members practised law, first in Gignac and then in Montpellier. Bp's father, Jean, *lic-ès-lois*, was *lieutenant* in the *viguerie* of Gignac before becoming *avocat du roi* at *présidial* of Montpellier from its foundation to 1565, when his son Etienne succeeded him. Etienne, who later held office in *chambre des comptes* there, adopted Protestantism during 1560s, but returned to Catholicism by early 1580s at the latest. Other family members, then and later, held similar offices, as did relatives such as Uzillis family.

B. 1552 Montpellier. Son of Jean and Marguerite de Cambous (m. in 1529). Early studies in Montpellier, followed by law, probably in Toulouse. Local family connections played important role from outset of career. Prior of Vailhauquès by 1574, canon of Montpellier in Sept 1575 (where Pierre and Etienne de Ratte preceded him), archdeacon by 1577, precentor by 1596. After taking minor orders and subdiaconate in 1579, he became key member of chapter, as well as vg of Bp Subject of Montpellier from 1584 onwards. Extensive activities on behalf of chapter and bishop throughout Languedoc, delegations to parlt of Toulouse and royal court, A *cons-cl* in Toulouse parlt by 1587, he established close links with Daffis and Duranti, and like them was persecuted for his royalism by Toulouse *ligueurs*. Bp Subject initiated moves to take him as coadj in the months before he died in Nov 1596.

Nom 15–6–1596. Provs 26–3–1597. Cons 29–6–1597. D. 7–7–1602.

Sources: ASV, Misc Arm XII, 145, fo 203. Vindry, *Parlementaires* (Toulouse), 252, 269. Guiraud, *La Réforme à Montpellier*, i. 469–75.

Raymond, Jean de. St-Papoul 1601–4. Raymond is one of the least known of Henri IV's bishops, despite almost certainly coming from a well-known Toulouse parlementaire family, with solid connections and ties. Family members had figured in parlt since 1550s, but Jean (*cons* 1556–88 and possibly father of bp) was given a hard time for alleged Protestant leanings in 1560s and early 1570s.

B. ca 1580. Identity of parents unknown. Education and early career equally obscure, but Rome accepted he held doct in canon law, Toulouse, and was priest by time of nom. As Henri IV had granted Crillon right to dispose of St-Papoul, it seems likely that Raymond owed elevation to whatever connections he may have had to Crillon or entourage.

No date for nom. Provs 28–5–1601. Cons 13–10–1602. D. 15–11–1604.

Sources: ASV, Misc Arm XII, 216, fo 244. AD Haute-Garonne, 6J 43 (c.m. of Isabeau de Bertier and Barthélemy de Raymond, 16–3–1603: bp as witness). Vindry, *Parlementaires* (Toulouse) nos 213–14.

Rebé, Claude de. Narbonne coadj 1622/8–59. This established noble family of Forez had, among other things, a record of placing younger sons in noble chapters like Lyon, and also enjoyed an *entrée* to cathedral chapter of Mâcon. But it was the Guise connection, which Abp Rebé himself may have established, which was decisive in taking them a step further up the church hierarchy.

Baptised 2–6–1587 at Amplepuis. Son of Claude, baron of Amplepuis, and Jeanne de Meysé. Studied humanities and philosophy in SJ colls of Lyon and Tournon (with J-Fr de Gondi and others), completing philosophy in Paris, where also studied law. Took doct in canon law at Valence, but subsequently studied theology at Sorbonne. With 2 of his brothers, became canon-count of Lyon cathedral (notorious for its rigour in establishing entrants' nobility) in 1601, *chantre* in 1621. Also provost of Mâcon in 1622. Tonsured May 1597, ordained deacon April 1620, he was priest by 1622. Attended AC of 1621 as deputy for Lyon province. Became tutor to young Henri de Guise in late 1610s, and was entrusted with administering his affairs (travelling to Rome for the purpose in 1622). As the Guise family, via the duchess (a Joyeuse by birth), had 'inherited' Cardinal de Joyeuse's interest in the tenure of Narbonne, their patronage of Rébé enabled him to slip into coadjutorship there at an opportune moment.

Nom to Narbonne coadjutorship 27–4–1622. Provs 8–8–1622. Cons 29–9–1622, Rome. Succeeded 1628. D. 17–3–1659, having taken F Fouquet of Agde as his coadj.

Sources: ASV, PC 17, fos 268–75. AN, Z^{1}o 241 (ordination). Beyssac, *Les Chanoines de Lyon*, 169, 190–1. Compère and Julia, *Les Collèges français*, i. 700.

Rechignevoisin. *See* **Guron**

Revol, Antoine de. Dol 1603–29. Revol's accession to episcopate was made possible by the one-generation 'miracle' which saw uncle, Louis, son of a notary from Dauphiné, become (after busy career in Provence, Dauphiné and Savoy) secretary of state in the last year of Henri III's reign, only for the favour which he subsequently found with Henri IV to be cut short by premature death in 1594. Before that, the see of Dol, which fell vacant in Sept 1591, had been given by Henri IV to his son, Ennemond, a *cons* in *grand conseil* who held it for a decade without seeking papal provs. Finally, preferring his secular career, he resigned it (on condition of substantial pension) to brother's son, Antoine, in 1603. Virtually nothing is known about other members of the Revol family, bp and parents included.

B. unknown date, but possibly ca 1573 (in 1548 according to some sources, though Rome accepted he was 30 in 1603!). Son of Antoine, archer in royal guard, and Benoite Chauvin. Views differ on early career: some claim he followed military career, others that he was canon of St-Ruf in Vienne. Became acquaintance and disciple of François de Sales, who evidently esteemed him, before 1602. Sales endeavoured to prepare him for episcopal office. It may be at this point that, still a simple cleric, he took his doct in utr and was ordained subdeacon.

Nom, probably late 1602. Provs 5–11–1603. Cons 4–11–1604. D. 6–8–1629.

Sources: ASV, Misc Arm XII, 144, fo 444; XII, 216, fo 378. AN, MC, XII, 35, 25–2–1603 (contract for papal provisions). François de Sales, *Oeuvres*, xii. 187–93. Sutherland, *French Secretaries of State in the Age of Catherine de' Medici*. G de Rivoire de la Batie, *Armorial du Dauphiné* (Lyon 1867), 599–601. Vindry, *Ambassadeurs*, 53. Wolfe, *Conversion of Henri IV*, 109–11. 118–22. Trani, 'Conseillers du grand conseil', 202.

Richelieu, Armand-Jean du Plessis de. Luçon 1606–23 (resign). The history of this genuine noble family of middling rank, with a record of court and military service, would be typical of that of so many nobles were it not for the unparalleled success of the cardinal in transforming their status and fortunes. Although the church served as his personal avenue to power, the Richelieus subsequently held virtually no ecclesiastical positions, let alone any of an episcopal character. The peculiar political circumstances of Henri III's reign were a crucial factor; and cardinal's father's loyalty was rewarded in part by king's *ad hoc* alienation of episcopal patronage, which enabled his uncle to become bp of Luçon in 1584, a 'gift' which Henri IV renewed for Alphonse and then Armand (in reality for their eldest brother) around 1600. Alphonse's later exit from the cloister was at behest of his brother, who needed every family ally he could place in high office.

B. Paris 5–9–1585. 3rd son of François and Suzanne de la Porte. Educated at coll of Navarre from 1594 onwards. An MA in 1605, he took bacc in theology in very short time, taking full advantage of prior episcopal nom. Sudeacon by 1606 when confirmed by Rome. If there is anything unusual about his episcopal career it is his resignation of Luçon so soon after becoming cardinal, as most cardinals would probably have aimed at getting a more desirable see, preferably an archbishopric.

First nom in late 1602. Provs 18–12–1606. Cons 17–4–1607 in Rome. Cardinal Sept 1622. Resign to Emery de Bragelongne May 1623. D. 5–12–1642.

Richelieu, Alphonse, Carthusian. Aix 1626–8, Lyon 1628–53. B. ca 1582. Older brother of Armand-Jean (above). Also educated at coll of Navarre 1594–1601 (along with Harlay de Sancy and Gabriel de Laubespine). Entered Carthusian order before he could take degree, but also to escape episcopate (at Luçon) in 1601–2, and was professed in 1602. A priest relatively soon afterwards, he went on to hold several offices in his order, and would undoubtedly have remained there had not brother insisted on his accepting episcopal office. But too independent and wayward to provide brother with political services he desired and needed.

Nom to Aix 6–12–1625. Provs 27–4–1626. Cons 21–6–1626. Nom to Lyon Sept 1628. Provs 27–11–1628. Cardinal Nov 1629. D. 23–3–1653.

Sources: ASV, PC 22, fos 169–89. M Deloche, *Un frère de Richelieu inconnu* (Paris 1935). Bergin, *Rise of Richelieu*.

Rieux de Sourdéac, René de. St-Pol-de-Leon 1619–35 (deposed), 1648–51. This Breton noble family, with origins in 11th C and boasting a constable of France in late 14th C, developed several closely knit branches and was related by marriage to a formidable array of great families, Breton and French. They held major political posts and military commands for generations thereafter. Strong supporters of Henri IV during League in Brittany, for which bp's father was well rewarded by Henri IV. Rieux-Sourdéac power was substantial in St-Pol-de-Léon region, obtaining important episcopal seigneurie of Ouessant from Bp Neufville in 1595. Like the Matignons at Coutances, this acquisition provided a powerful incentive to obtain St-Pol for one of theirs, and explains speed with which René was propelled into office. Rieux family's continuing favour and close ties to Marie de' Medici greatly facilitated such arrangements in early 1610s, but proved their Achilles heel when Marie fled France in 1631, and led to René being deposed as bp in 1635. Even then, their local power remained intact: his successor at Léon, Cupif, never enjoyed peaceful possession and was unable to control the diocese after Richelieu's death and René's rehabilitation by AC of 1645, which enabled him to return to his episcopal seat during his last years.

B. ca 1590–1. Son of René, sgr de Sourdéac, and Suzanne de St-Melaine-de-Boulenesque. Studied first in Univ of Paris colls (Grassins and Montaigu) in 1600–3, and later at La Flèche (with Jacques Raoul), ca 1605. In 1619 Rome accepted he was doct in canon law. Cleric by 1600 and subdeacon by 1619, he was abbot in c of ND du Rulecq (1600), and Daoulas, OSA (Quimper) in 1602 – with others to follow later. Nom (which may initially have been a simple 'réserve') came soon after Neufville's death in early 1613, but there was little urgency about seeking papal provs, given unchallenged family political (and admin) control of the diocese.

Nom 1613 (Neufville died 5–2). Provs 18–3–1619. Cons 1–11–1619. Deposed 31–5–1635. Rehabilitated 1645, formally restored 1648. D. 8–3–1651.

Sources: ASV, Acta Camerarii 15, fo 121v; Misc Arm XII, 145, fo 100; PC 28, fos 726–8. Vindry, *Etat-major*, 403–5. Gallet, *Seigneurie bretonne*, 126–34, 377–88. P Peyron, 'Eveché de Léon de 1613 à 1651', *Bulletin Diocésain d'Histoire et d'Archéologie du Diocèse de Quimper*, 15–16 (1915–16) (11–part study).

Robin, Gérard de, OSA. Lodève 1606–11. Obscurity of this bp due largely to his being chosen by duc de Ventadour to hold Lodève *en confidence* until one of his sons was old enough to accept succession (Robin was required to pay Ventadour's son a pension of 7,000 *livres* provided there remained 1,000 for himself!). Contrary to previous suggestions, he was not a native Languedocian.

B. in Geneva diocese, ca 1560. Son of Louis and Florette Tanay, both otherwise unknown and dead long before son's episcopal promotion. Nothing known of education, but entered Augustinian order of Hermits young, and doubtless frequented their schools. In 1605 was credited with doct in theology. Resident from 1598 onwards in his order's La Voulte convent of which he became prior in 1605. This brought him to attention of Ventadour, one of whose titles was baron of La Voulte! His episcopate was too short-lived to meet expectations of Ventadour, who was thereafter compelled to keep it vacant, under the nominal tenure of 3 different sons, until Plantavit's succession in 1625.

No date for nom, but ca 1604–5. Provs 3–4–1606. Cons in 1607. D. 15–1–1611.

Sources: EJ Hurault, 'Actes et lettres de Mgr L'Hostel évêque de Viviers', *Revue du Vivarais* (1931), 13–16 (text of Robin's episcopal enquiry *de vita et moribus*, 1605). Martin, *Histoire de Lodève*, ii. 372–4.

Rose, Antoine. Senlis 1602–10, Clermont 1610–14. This Champagne family settled in Chaumont-en-Bassigny (where earlier generations held a variety of middle-ranking offices, esp that of *prévôt*) and Provins, but notoriety stems wholly from career of bp's uncle and predecessor at Senlis, Guillaume, the radical Catholic League's own *évêque armé*. Latter's father, also Guillaume, was declared a noble and descendant of nobles in 1533, when in fact both he and his descendants were still struggling to reach lower levels of the hierarchy of ennobling offices! *Ligueur* bp's own promotion clearly did not eliminate strong rebellious streak, for which his less combative nephew would be made to pay at Senlis.

B. 1575. Son of Nicolas, sgr de Poirresons and *secrétaire de la chambre du roi*, and Catherine des Fours. Nothing known of education, but appears to have taken bacc in theology from Paris, and doct canon law (also Paris?). A priest, he was also royal almoner by 1601.

Nom to Senlis 1601 on uncle's resignation of title to him. Provs 12–11–1601. Cons in Rome 25–11–1601. Transferred to Clermont 1–3–1610. D. 31–1–1614.

Sources: ASV, Misc Arm XII, 145, fo 502. BN, P Or 2546, doss 56929; Doss bleus 581, doss 15282. Barnavi, *Le Parti de Dieu*, 83–4.

Rosmadec, Sebastien. Vannes 1622–46. An emblematic Breton noble family, comparable to Rieux and Rohan, with several generations of military commands and provincial lt-gens and govs, as well as numerous marriages to other well-known noble families, behind them. Prolific, they were scattered in different parts of Brittany, in whose Estates they also played a prominent role. Support for Henri IV during League yielded political and other dividends later.

B. 1585. Younger son of Jean and Marguerite Jégo, dame de Lesnevé. Nothing known of education, but apparently took lic in utr. Briefly monk of St-Germain-des-Prés, he returned to secular clerical state. Subdeacon when nom bp, he was abbot in c of Paimpont, OSA (St-Malo) in 1608. Elected deputy to 1614 EG by Breton Estates.

Nom as result of exchange with Bp Martin of Vannes of Rosmadec's abbey of Paimpont. Provs 14–11–1622. Cons 11–2–1624. D. 29–7–1646.

Rosmadec, Charles de. Vannes 1647–71, Tours 1671–1702. B. ca 1618. 3rd son of Mathurin, sgr de Jouan, and Jeanne de Trogoff de Fontenelles; cousin of Sébastien, predecessor at Vannes. Studied humanities and philosophy at coll of Navarre, followed by 4 years of theology at Sorbonne, but finishing with lic in canon law (Paris). Abbot in c of Le Tronchet, OSB (Dol) in 1640, ordained priest in 1646. By then he had political experience, having attended Breton Estates, but also some pastoral experience, having assisted Harlay de Sancy at St-Malo and cousin, the bp of Vannes, esp in conducting pastoral visitations. Arrangements for his succession to Vannes were in train before his predecessor's death.

Nom to Vannes 10–4–1647. Provs 1–7–1647. Cons 6–10–1647. Abp of Tours 1671. D. 10–3–1702.

Sources: ASV, Misc Arm XII, 146, fo 93 (Sébastien); PC 47, fos 542–72 (Charles). Carné, *Chevaliers bretons*, 366–77.

Rouchon, Raymond. St-Flour 1599–1602. From obscure commoner family of Cusance in Quercy, Rouchon owed episcopal elevation purely to patronage of Henri de Noailles, who needed a caretaker while his son, Charles, could come of age. Neither date of birth nor identity of family is known. That he was credited with a bacc in theology from Cahors suggests limited, and possibly, hasty studies. He served as priest in his native town before episcopate, the circumstances of which have been described above, p 79.

Nom 1597. Provs 10–3–1599. Cons 20–2–1600. Resign to Charles de Noailles, Nov 1601, but died before it could take effect, July 1602.

Sources: ASV, Misc Arm XII, 145, fo 494. BN, Doss bleus 383, doss 15343; P Or 2556, doss 57111. AD Lot, F 492, no 2. AN, P 563 (ii), no 2323 (*serment de fidélité* as bp).

Rousseau, Charles de. Mende coadj 1606/8–23. This bp was Angevin. Family's origins and professional status remain unknown, but almost certainly of middling bourgeois rank. In any case, Charles Rousseau owed entire career to episcopal uncle, the energetic and combative Adam de Heurtelou, who in turn owed his early career and episcopal promotion to Renaud de Beaune, his immediate predecessor as bp of Mende. During wars of late 1580s and 1590s, Heurtelou was client of Montmorency in Languedoc and committed supporter of Henri IV's right to the throne (while pressing him to convert). Consequently he was perfectly placed to secure Rousseau as his coadj and successor in 1606.

B. 1569 Mayet, near La Flèche. Son of Gilles Rousseau and Lucrèce de Heurtelou, sister of bp of Mende. Nothing known of education, but in 1589 he was bachelor in canon law;

when confirmed bp in 1606, Rome accepted he had doct in canon law. In fact, from early age uncle took charge of upbringing. Took orders (inc priesthood) in Mende in early 1589, where he was already canon and provost of cathedral. Prior in c of St-Pierre-d'Ispagnac, OSB (Mende), he was deputy to 1595 AC, and served as vg to uncle, for possibly as many as 15 years.

Nom coadj March 1606. Provs 4–12–1606. Cons in 1607. Succeeds uncle June 1608. D. 4–11–1623.

Sources: AD Lozère, G 2169, fos 1, 5v, 9, 29v, 41 (register of ordinations, 1589); G 38 (Mende chapter's records on Rousseau's succession as coadj). *Gallia*, i.107. Roucaute, *Le Pays de Gévaudan au temps de la ligue*, 184–9.

Rouxel de Médavy, François I. Lisieux 1599–1617. The Rouxel, originally from Brittany but settled in Normandy, may indeed have been a 'famille plus illustre qu'ancienne' (a description applicable to many noble families, those of 17th-C bps included), but held several military and political posts in Normandy during 16th and 17th Cs. The first of the 2 bps was brother of *ligueur* commander Pierre, baron de Médavy, gov of Verneuil and later lt-gen of Normandy, 'qui avoit été de toutes les rebellions' (Richelieu). François I was, more to the point, godson of Marshal Fervacques, who was instrumental in obtaining Lisieux for him at the end of the religious wars, when he (and Pierre above) struck hard bargains with Henri IV. Their continuing political importance and military services became fully apparent during Fronde when (in 1651) Mazarin was extremely anxious to bring 2nd bp's brother, long-serving military commander, comte de Grancey-Rouxel, to support him, a circumstance which enabled the latter to obtain a *bâton de maréchal* for himself and Lisieux for his brother.

B. unknown date. Son of Jacques, baron de Médavy, and Pierrette Fouques de Mannutot. Nothing known of education, or whether he took degree. Abbot in c of Cormeilles, OSB (Lisieux) and St-André, O Cist (Séez), and canon of ND de Paris on nom. Godfather Fervacques had effectively seized control of Lisieux in early 1580s, preventing its bps, who included Cardinal Givry, from governing it for many years. Fervacques refused godson entry to Lisieux, and only after the terrible marshal's death in 1612 did he first set foot in his cathedral!

Nom probably early-mid 1597. Provs 17–3–1599. No date for cons. D. 13–8–1617.

Rouxel de Médavy, François II. Séez 1651–71, Rouen 1671–91. B. 8–8–1604. Son of Pierre, comte de Médavy and Charlotte de Hautemer, comtesse de Grancey, daughter of Fervacques; nephew of François I (above). Nothing known of education, and did not, it seems, take degree. Spent long periods in Langres diocese, where he did some preaching. Ordained deacon in 1633, he was priest before his nom. Abbot in c of Cormeilles, OSB (Lisieux) after uncle's death, and St-André, O Cist (Séez) in 1630, and prior of Prigny, OSB (Sens) before episcopate. Served on a royal commission in 1639 concerning resistance of Rouen parlt to registration of fiscal edicts.

Nom 28–2–1651. Provs 25–9–1651. Cons 21–5–1652. Abp of Rouen, 1671. D. 29–1–1691.

Sources: *Lettres missives de Henri IV*, iv. 103–4. Vindry, *Etat-major*, 245. *DGS*, 675. O and P Ranum, eds, *The Century of Louis XIV* (London 1972), 43–4 (family). AN V^6 3, no 72, decree of *cons privé*, 10–10–1597. *Miscellanea in onore di Martino Giusti*, 45–6. Formeville,

Histoire de l'ancien évêché-comté de Lisieux, i. ccccxlii (François I). ASV, PC 50, fos 335–45. Louis Hommey, *Histoire générale, ecclésiastique et civile du diocèse de Séez*, 4 vols (Alenon 1898–1900), iv. 314–15. (François II)

Ruade, Bruno, Carthusian. Conserans 1623–45. Bp's background unclear, but family was almost certainly from Turenne area of Limousin, and of commoner status. 2 of its members, both called Gabriel, had moved to Paris by 1570s, and served in royal artillery. One of them (but which?) was father of bp.

Philibert (his baptismal name) b. Paris unknown date. Son of Gabriel and N... Nothing known of early education, but studied law in Paris, where he took lic in canon law (1607), followed in 1608 with doct in theology in Rome. At that point, entered papal college of notaries, declaring intention to serve pope. Also probably ordained priest there. But quickly changed his mind, returned to France, and joined Carthusians (the Paris convent of Vauvert) in 1610, and was professed under name of Bruno, by which he was known thereafter. Remained in Paris convent until nom. which arose with promotion of Octave de Bellegarde from Comminges to Sens. The choice of Ruade for successor was inspired by Bellegarde's cousin and companion of Louis XIII, the duc de Bellegarde. Towards end of life, Ruade was paralysed and incapacitated, giving rise to prolonged struggle for succession to Comminges described above, pp 84–6.

Brevet de nom 31-5-1622. Provs 7-6-1623. Cons 10-3-1624. D. 2-1-1645.

Sources: AD Haute-Garonne, E 292–95 (Bp Ruade's papers). AN, Y 120, fo 144, 11–12-1578. *Recueil de lettres de Révérendissime P Dom Bruno Ruade Chartreux Eveque de Couserans touchant sa promotion à sondit Evesché* (Paris 1623). BAV, Barb lat 7958, fo 12.

Rueil, Claude de. Bayonne 1621–8, Angers 1627–49. Frequently known by seigneurial name of Desmarests, Rueil family was well established as merchants and *bourgeois* in Paris well before early 16th C, when Jean de Rueil was *lieut-civil* of *prévôté* of Paris (1505). Later generations were associated with office-holding in *trésor* and *cour des monnaies*, where bp's own father became first pres by 1576. His marriage to Marie Boucherat, daughter of an av-gen in parlt, was of crucial importance thereafter, bringing them into much better placed circles, which included Beaulieu-Ruzé family, with a secretary of state and a bp of Angers among its members. This also made future bp a cousin of Marshal d'Effiat, *surintendant des finances* under Louis XIII who was instrumental in effecting his transfer from Bayonne to Angers.

B. 1581. Son of Jean, sgr des Marests, and Marie Boucherat, daughter of Edmond and Marie Ruzé. Father d. during bp's infancy and he was reared by uncle, Beaulieu-Ruzé, secretary of state. Nothing known of education, though took lic in utr at Angers, followed by theology studies in Paris. Family influence ensured he was well endowed with benefices/offices long before episcopate. Abbot in c of Hériveaux, OSA (Paris), canon of Chartres, canon and archdeacon of Tours since ca 1600, royal almoner to Henri IV and Louis XIII. His succession to Bayonne arose almost certainly out of his membership of Tours chapter, as Bertrand Deschaux, who became abp in 1617, retained his title to Bayonne for several years, which no doubt enabled Rueil to negotiate his way into the succession.

No date for nom to Bayonne (vacated by transfer of Bertrand Deschaux to Tours, 1617). Provs 15-11-1621. Cons 2-1-1622. Nom to Angers 19-2-1627. Provs 20-3-1628. D. 20-1-1649.

Sources: ASV, PC 50, fos 527–44. AN, MC, VIII, 9, 30–12–1505; XIX, 147, 8–4–1536; XCIX, 8, 6–1–1571; Y 93, fo 221; Y 96, f 415v. BN, MS Fr 32589, fo 113. *Corr de Berulle*, iii. 231. Trani, 'Conseillers du grand conseil', 116, 204.

Ruffier, Claude, O Cist. St-Paul-Trois-Chateaux 1658–74. Like his uncle and benefactor, Nicolas Grillié, bp of Bazas and Uzès, Ruffier was native of Provins/Braye-sur-Seine, and his origins were similarly modest. Grandfather's generation included an apothecary who was a local parish churchwarden in Provins. Father was a 'marchand' of Provins. Both Grillié and Ruffier families enjoyed close ties to local Cistercian priory at Braye, which seems to have been important for younger sons' clerical beginnings. In each generation, other family members followed bps to southern France to seek their fortunes, and some held office in Montpellier *chambre des comptes* under Louis XIV.

B. in Provins and baptised in St-Ayeul parish church 24–4–1609. One of several sons of Jean and Marie Grillié, sister of Nicolas, bp of Uzès. Attended Univ of Paris and, like uncle, resided in Cistercian coll des Bernardins. He had by then probably joined Cistercians, and was professed as monk of Charlieu, ca 1630. Completed studies by taking lic (ranked 10th) and doct in theology, 1638, and ordained priest shortly afterwards. Probably during early 1640s he gravitated towards Languedoc and uncle's service, acting initially as vg of abbot of Cîteaux in Languedoc and Provence, and then, for ca 15 years, as vg to uncle in Uzès diocese. Accession to episcopate also arranged by uncle, who in return for accepting Jacques de Grignan as his coadj at Uzès, opportunely obtained Grignan's own modest see of St-Paul-Trois-Châteaux for nephew.

Grignan resign St-Paul to Ruffier 11–5–1657. Nom 31–5–1657. Provs 8–7–1658. Cons 12–1–1659. D. 16–3–1674.

Sources: ASV, PC 55, fos 679–99; PC 59, fo 287. BN, P Or 2593, doss 57623. AD Seine-et-Marne, B 516, fo 16; B 615, E 1232, E 1618; 5 Mi 6296 (parish regs, St-Ayeul, Provins). *Gallia Chr Nov* (St-Paul), 610–17. BN, MS lat 15440, p 167. Poutet, 'Docteurs de Sorbonne', 239.

Saint-Bonnet de Toiras, Claude Caylar de. Nimes coadj 1621/25–33 (resign). The Caylar were a noble family from Languedoc, with medieval ancestry, though St-Bonnet title did not predominate until later 15th C. Bp's father and grandfather were both Huguenots, and active clients of Montmorency, gov of Languedoc. Bp's mother (daughter of Toulouse parlementaire family and sister of Louis de Claret, bp of St-Papoul 1626–36) apparently brought her children, who included future Marshal Toiras, back to Catholicism, though bp's father specifically disadvantaged Claude in his will because he had become an ecclesiastic!

B. date unknown. 4th son of Claude, sgr de Toiras and *sénéchal* of Montpellier, and Françoise de Claret. Nothing known of education, but Rome accepted he held doct in canon law. Canon and grand archdeacon of Montpellier, where family members on both sides had preceded him, he was abbot in c of St-Gilles, OSB (Nîmes) and Longvilliers (Boulogne). A priest, he attended AC of 1610 and was elected *agent-général du clergé* in 1619. Elderly and increasingly incapacitated predecessor, Valernod, took initial steps to co-opt him as coadj in 1619, but progress was very slow. Forced to resign for his part in 1632 revolt, his post-episcopal career was spent in Montpellier cathedral, where he resumed previous position of canon and provost.

No date for nom but probably 1621. Provs 25–10–1621. Cons 13–3–1622. Succeeded Nov 1625. Resign Feb 1633. D. 4–5–1642.

Sources: ASV, Misc Arm XII, 145, fo 273. *Gallia*, vi. 460–1. JB Segondy, 'La Famille languedocienne du maréchal de Toiras', *XX XIX Congrès de la Fédération Hist. du Languedoc Méditerrannéen et du Roussillon* (Montpellier 1976), 199–232. Sauzet, *Contre-réforme*, 201–15.

St-Sixte, Charles de. Riez 1599–1614. Originally from St-Sixte near Annecy (then in Savoy), family settled during 15th C in Avignon, where their activities were mostly mercantile and financial. By 3rd generation there, changes are evident: bp's father was *consul* of Avignon in 1563. He made a fortune out of confiscated Huguenot property, and served as financial adviser to cardinal of Armagnac, legate in Avignon. Also actively involved as military figure during wars in 1570s until his assassination in 1580. Wife was daughter of Cavaillon consular family.

B. 25–3–1557. Son of Pierre and Pernette de Rastelles, sister of bp of Riez. Partly educated in Paris, he took doct in civil law in Avignon in 1595. Prior of Pont St Esprit, he took royalist position (unlike his *ligueur* uncle, Bp Rastelle of Riez) in Provence during wars. Client of Gondi family, was protonotary apostolic and almoner to Henri IV before episcopate. May originally have been intended as coadj to uncle, but latter's death made it unnecessary. Poisoned by servant apparently suborned by someone with designs on Riez succession.

No date for nom. Provs 29–3–1599. Cons 3–10–1599. D. 13–4–1614.

Sources: ASV, Misc Arm XII, 145, fo 415. *Gallia Chr Nov*, i. 633–5. Teulé, *Chronologie des docteurs*, 44. Pithon-Curt, *Noblesse du Venaissin,* iii. 334–41. Labande, *Avignon au xve siècle*, 474. Hennequin, *Henri IV dans ses oraisons funèbres* (Paris 1977), 272.

St-Luc. *See* **Espinay**

Salette, Jean de. Lescar 1609–25 (resign). The 2 Salette bps descended from family whose early history is obscure, but which formed part of admin élite of Navarre by mid-16th C, when father of first bp was successively pres in *chambre des comptes* and in *conseil souverain* of Navarre. Like other families in similar position (e.g. Sponde), they became Protestants under Jeanne d'Albret, and remained so for some time thereafter. By generation of second bp, military careers were as prominent as *robe* professions; one brother was capt-gov of chateau of Oloron, while another was capt-gov of Pau, and was father of François-Charles, bp of Oloron 1682–1704.

B. 1564. Son of Jean and Astruge de Bussy – and half-brother of prominent Huguenot pastor, Arnaud de Salette. B. Protestant, educated 'aux eschollses' at expense of King of Navarre, he took doct in law in Toulouse, 1584. Date and circumstances of his conversion to Catholicism remain unclear, but by early 1590s was already canon of Lescar. Gravitated towards much better known convert, Cardinal du Perron, whom he (may have) assisted in conversion of Henri IV and, later, at Fontainebleau conference of 1600. A priest before then, he also became canon of Evreux under du Perron, and later accompanied him to Sens, where he served as vg. Du Perron's patronage was probably instrumental not merely in his becoming royal almoner, but above all in securing succession to Bp d'Abbadie at Lescar, since speed with which his provs were granted after d'Abbadie's death suggests a coadjutorial appointment was already in train.

No date for nom (d'Abbadie d. 8–5–1609). Provs 6–7–1609. No date for cons. Resign to nephew 3–8–1625. D. 1632.

Salette, Jean-Henri de. Lescar 1629–58. B. 1588. Son of Pierre, sgr de Montardon, and Suzanne de Zoller (daughter of capt of king's Swiss guard). Born Protestant, he abjured ca 1615, while studying in Paris. Had previously studied at Toulouse, where he returned to take his lic in utr. A priest from ca 1621, he was canon of Lescar and vg to uncle.

Resign of Lescar by uncle to Jean-Henri 12–7–1625. Nom 3–8–1625. Provs 12–2–1629. Cons 6–10–1630. D. 21–6–1658.

Sources: Haag, *France protestante*, ix. 113. P-V Palma-Cayet, *Chronologie novénaire*, ii. 44. *Armorial de Béarn*, ed Dufau de Maluquer, ii. 116–21. Labau, *Lescar, cité épiscopale*, 65–72. Clergeac, *Chronologie*, 142. AD Pyrénées-Atlantiques, E 2001, fo 191 (Jean's father's testament). ASV, PC 26, fos 550–72 (Jean-Henri).

Salies, Jean *du Haut* de. Lescar 1658–81. 'Natif de la maison noble Duhau de Berenx en Béarn' by his own account, but relatively little is known about him, though a brother of his was proc-gen at parlt of Pau.

B. ca 1594 Salies-de-Béarn. Identity of parents unknown, but both were Protestant. Converted to Catholicism at the 'age of reason', according to Pierre de Marca. Educated partly at Univ of Bordeaux where took bacc in theology, possibly ca 1620. Ordained priest some 10 years later. Dean of Bidache *collégiale* (1636) and abbot in c of Lahonce, O Prem (Bayonne), before episcopate. The deanship may have entitled him to preside over local Estates of Bidache and bring him to attention of higher political circles.

Nom 28–6–1658. Provs 30–9–1658. Cons 1–12–1658. D. 18–4–1681.

Sources: ASV, PC 56, fos 397–415. Labau, *Lescar, cité épiscopale*, 80–1. Clergeac, *Chronologie*, 142.

Salignac de la Mothe-Fénélon, Louis II de. Sarlat 1602–39. Abp Fénélon of Cambrai, the most illustrious member of this noble Périgord family, referred to the long line of provincial govs, royal *chambellans*, ambassadors, a *chevalier du St-Esprit*, and bps who had preceded him. Its past was more distinguished than its present by 17th C, when mounting financial problems limited their opportunities. Their tenure of Sarlat, which began in 1568, was rather undistinguished, esp under Louis II, but they were sufficiently resilient and involved in *dévot* religious causes to recover it after 20-year loss in 1659.

B. 1577. Son of Armand and Judith de Baynac. Nothing known of studies, or whether he took degree. Groomed to succeed uncle and namesake, who d. in Feb 1598. Although only 20 years old, Louis II (or rather his family) was in a position (Villeroy was close friend of new bp's uncle) to keep Sarlat vacant until late 1602 to enable him to be put forward for the succession. A negligent bp, he clashed with his metropolitan Cardinal Sourdis, and was not even represented at major provincial council of Bordeaux in 1624. Attempted to resign Sarlat in mid-1620s, but Urban VIII rejected his reasons. Henri de Sourdis later compiled damning report on the state of his diocese, which was probably instrumental in his nephew, François (below), being overlooked when successor was needed in 1639.

No date for nom. Provs 27–11–1602. Cons 26–1–1603. D. 22–5–1639.

Salignac de la Mothe-Fénélon, François II de. Sarlat 1659–88. B. 20–3–1607. Son of François and Marie de Bonnevel, heiress of Magnac. Early studies at SJ colls of Rouen and then Poitiers (along with Péréfixe), followed by doct in canon law from Paris, ca 1636–7. Tonsured in 1619, ordained subdeacon in 1631 and probably became priest soon afterwards. Dean of Carennac (Cahors), whose bp, Solminihac, regarded him highly, he became royal almoner in 1646. Pre-episcopal career was that of active *dévot* and reformer. An early member of *Compagnie du St-Sacrement,* he resided in St-Sulpice seminary/parish, engaged in missions and attempts to convert Protestants etc. Opportunity of becoming bp of Sarlat, denied him in 1639, arose in 1657, when Bp Sévin unexpectedly left to become coadj of Cahors and was refused permission to retain Sarlat.

Resign of Sarlat by Sevin to Salignac 23–6–1658. Nom to pope 31–10–1658. Provs 31–5–1659. Cons 25–5–1659. D. 1–5–1688.

Sources: *Correspondance de Fénélon,* i. Vindry, *Ambassadeurs,* 43. Peyrous, *Réforme catholique à Bordeaux,* i. 293–5 (family). ASV, PC 57, fos 338–54 (François).

Sanguin, Nicolas. Senlis 1623–51 (resign). Family, which may have originated in Troyes, was not alone in commissioning an impressive, but largely false, genealogy to embellish its history. In fact, they were one of most prolific and ubiquitous of Parisian marchant-cum-robe dynasties of late medieval and early modern period, comparable to the Hennequins or the Bragelongnes in sheer range of activities and 'alliances' (the latter include Le Camus, Marle, Louviers, Séguier, de Thou, du Mesnil, and many others!). One brother of Bp Nicolas, Christophe, sgr de Livry, was pres in Paris parlt (*Enquêtes*), *prévôt des marchands*, and husband of Elisabeth Séguier, while another, Christophe (father of Bp Denis) was principal *commis* of Puysieux, secretary of state. By then, tenure of court offices was also a feature of their history. Their ecclesiastical connections were equally wide, extending to religious orders and chapters of canons. Antoine Sanguin, bp of Orleans and Cardinal de Meudon (1493–1559), was by far the most distinguished of them.

B. 1580. Son of Jacques, sgr de Livry, and Marie du Mesnil. Studied humanities and philosophy at coll of Navarre (with Lefebvre de Lezeau), followed by lic in utr. Known as sgr de Tréon before episcopate, he became *cons-cl* in parlt on 20–7–1612. Ordained priest in April 1620, by which date also canon of Chartres. Handpicked for Senlis in 1622 by elderly Cardinal La Rochefoucauld who wished to resign it in order to concentrate on reforming the monastic orders.

Nom 10–3–1622. Provs 19–9–1623. Cons 12–2–1623. Resign to nephew Denis, 1651. D. 15–7–1652.

Sanguin, Denis. Senlis 1651–1702. B. 1621. Son of Christophe and Marion Dollé. Education supervised by uncle, Bp Nicolas, and completed by doct in canon law. Canon of Ste Chapelle ca 1637, he was also canon of Chartres and prior in c of Ste-Madeleine-de-Parthenay, OSA (Poitiers). Ordained priest ca 1646.

Resign of Senlis by uncle to Denis, 6–6–1651. Nom 20–6–1651. Provs 28–10–1651. Cons 14–1–1652. D. 13–3–1702.

Sources: BI, MS 1354, no 115. BN, P Or 2626–7, doss Sanguin. AN, MC, LIV, 493, 29–11–1619 (c.m. of parents of bp Denis). Anselme, viii. 263–6. Kuno Böse, *Amt und soziale Stellung. Die Institution der élus in Frankreich im 16. und 17. Jarhundert am Beispiel der Elektion Troyes* (Frankfurt 1986), ii. 293 (Troyes). AE Genty, *Livry* (Paris 1898)(family). ASV, PC 17, fos 202–24. AN, Z^{1}o 241 (ordination). BL, Addit MS 24134, fo 13 (Nicolas). ASV, PC 53, fos 775–805 (Denis).

Sariac, Bernard de. Aire 1659–72. Bp of Aire was born into junior branch, it seems, of long-established noble family which intermarried extensively with fellow Gascon nobility, e.g. the Montesquiou and Gondrin de Pardailhan families, whose horizons were probably broader and ecclesiastical interests considerable. Profile of bp's immediate family remains shadowy, though one brother served against Spaniards in 1630s and 1640s, becoming *maréchal des camps* in 1650. More to the point, one of bp's uncles, also Bernard, was abbot of Paimpont, OSA (St-Malo), first almoner to Gaston d'Orléans, and *agent général du clergé* in 1635, and his example and influence were probably decisive in enabling bp himself to enter service of Louis XIV's brother, Philippe d'Orléans.

B. Sariac, ca 1617. Son of Emery, sgr de Sariac and comte de la Barthe, and Marie de Parrou de Bucquet. Nothing known of education, but took doct in theology at Toulouse, 1645. Master of the chapel to Philippe d'Orléans, and abbot in c of Escale-Dieu, O Cist (Tarbes) and Lieu-Dieu, O Cist (Amiens) before episcopate. Ordained priest only weeks after his nom to Aire.

Resign of Aire by Bp Bourlement (transferring to Castres) to Sariac 20–6–1657. Nom 24–6–1657. Provs 10–3–1659. Cons 1–6–1659. D. 12–10–1672.

Sources: ASV, PC, 57, fos 268–84. BN, POr 2634, doss 58569; Cab d'Hozier 573; Doss bleus 599, doss Sariac. Chesnaye-Desbois, *Dict de noblesse*, xviii. 270–84 (confusing). Clergeac, *Chronologie*, 126, 77.

Sault. *See* **Du Sault**

Scarron, Pierre. Grenoble 1620–68. Bp's birthplace, Agen, should not mislead: he was unmistakably a member of this celebrated Lyonnais (and increasingly Parisian) family whose origins lie in Piedmontese town of Chieri (or Montaliers), whence Jacques Scarron migrated to Lyon where he was naturalised in Dec 1512. Descendants rose to prominence in commercial and esp financial affairs of Lyon and Dauphiné, before partly shifting focus to Paris in late 16th C. While bp's grandfather, Jean *l'ainé*, was a *marchand-épicier* and *consul* of Lyon 1546–9, his father was *cons* at Paris parlt 1568. But then and later, their massive involvement in royal finances at virtually every level (as well as equally valuable service to certain great noble families) was real source of their wealth, influence and connections, and made them so prominent in age of Richelieu and Mazarin.

B. 1584 Agen. Son of Jean Scarron and Marie Boyer. No information on education, but Rome accepted in 1620 he had doct in utr, which seems acceptable given his pre-episcopal career was essentially that of *cons* in parlt. A mere cleric when nom bp. Promotion beckoned unexpectedly when Alphonse de la Croix, coadj of Grenoble since 1614, decided within less than a year of succeeding father as bp, to resign see outright.

Nom June 1620. Provs 14–12–1620. Cons 7–3–1621. D. 6–2–1668.

Sources: BN, MS Fr 33047, pp 459, 473 (naturalisations 1512, 1560). BL, Addit MS 21434, fo 5. AD Rhône, Fonds Frécon, *dossiers rouges* 6 (Scarron).

Séguier, Dominique. Auxerre 1632–7, Meaux 1637–59 (resign). The collective biography of this emblematic family of Parisian *grande robe*, crowned by chancellorship of Pierre Séguier in 1635, is too well known to require exposition here. Yet it may be wondered why their prodigious family and professional ties did not lead them to hold high church office more frequently. Their church ties were indeed extensive, esp in ND de Paris. Louis Séguier refused diocese of Meaux in 1590s.

B. 2–8–1593 St-Denis. Son of Antoine, pres in Paris parlt, and Marie Trudert. Educated at SJ colls of Dijon and La Flèche (along with Bp Baradat of Noyon at La Flèche), with few years at coll of Lemoine, Paris, in between (1606–9). Took lic in utr at Orléans, ca 1612–13. *Cons-cl* in parlt of Paris, 1616, he was canon of ND de Paris, becoming dean there in 1623. Ordained subdeacon in May 1614, he became priest ca 1625. First almoner to Louis XIII in 1631, the year of episcopal promotion. Initially (and most unusually) the intention was to make him a bp without a French diocese, and to wait until suitable one became available. This arrangement (by which he would have become abp of Corinth *in partibus infidelium*) was soon overtaken by unexpected death of Gilles de Souvré, bp of Auxerre, in Sept 1632, though Séguier had briefly been nom to succeed Victor Bouthillier at Boulogne.

No date for nom to Corinth, but probably Feb 1631. Provs 10–11–1631. Nom to Auxerre 28–9–1631. Provs 7–6–1632. Cons 18–1–1632. Nom to Meaux 26–8–1637. Resign to nephew, Dominique de Ligny, March 1659. D. 16–5–1659.

Sources: Richet, *De la Réforme à la Révolution*, 155–306. BL, Addit MS 24134, fo 16. AN, Z^{1}o 241 (ordination). Griselle, *Etat de la maison de Louis XIII*, no 5. ASV, PC, 16, fo 275; PC 28, fos 808–20; PC 31, fos 634–42. Lebeuf, *Mémoires concernant l'histoire civile et ecclésiastique d'Auxerre*, iv. 229.

Serres, Jacques de, OSB. Le Puy 1597–1621. Known mainly thanks to its Huguenot members – Olivier, the champion of agriculture, and his brother Jean, the eirenicist pastor and royal historiographer under Henri IV – de Serres family was from Villeneuve de Berg in the Vivarais, but also settled at Annonay and Bourg-Saint-Andéol. Divergent religious affiliations date from 1550s. Active as local merchants and notaries at Villeneuve de Berg since 15th C, their real advancement began when father of Bp Jacques, Jean, notary at Villeneuve, married Barbe Broë from Tournon. Her brother, Bon Broë, made his career in service of Cardinal de Tournon and ended it as an unmarried pres in Paris parlt, having served Catherine de' Medici in several capacities. His protection and benefactions contributed decisively to advancing both the de Serres and their cousins, the Montchals. Locally, Broë alliance was also decisive, since Jean de Serres succeeded father-in-law, Jean Broë, as *greffier* of local Estates of Vivarais, a key position of political influence. Through Broë family, the de Serres were also related to the Villars. Family's advancement continued in generation of Charles, father of Bp Juste, as he became *juge royal* of the Vivarais at Annonay and was ennobled by letters in 1612, a status that was confirmed under Louis XIV.

B. ca 1550 Annonay. Son of Jean, *greffier* of Vivarais estates, and Barbe Broë. Nothing known of education, but appears to have taken lic in canon law. Through uncle, Bon Broë, became abbot in 1584 of Montebourg, OSB (Coutances), for which, unusually, he needed to become professed Benedictine monk. Ordained subdeacon in Paris, March 1585, he may have become priest shortly afterwards. Le Puy fell vacant in 1592, and *ligueurs* who dominated it until 1595 attempted to secure a favourable succession, as did Joyeuse in 1596. But power of duc de Ventadour in province was decisive and obtained de Serres's promotion (de Serres agreed to pay pension probably to a man of Ventadour's choice).

Nom probably Oct-Nov 1596. Provs 18–8–1597. Cons date and place unknown. Took nephew as coadj 1615–16. D. 28–1–1621.

Serres, Juste de, OSB. Le Puy coadj 1616/21–41. B. Annonay, 1592. Possibly eldest son of Charles, syndic of Estates of Vivarais, and Elisabeth du Fay-Gerlande (m. in 1591);

nephew of Jacques (above). Educated initially at SJ coll of Le Puy (along with cousin Montchal, future abp of Toulouse). Followed theology course in Paris under André du Val and Gamaches for 3 years to 1615, which probably led Rome to believe he held doct in theology, but in fact he probably obtained lic in canon law from Paris. Ordained subdeacon in 1615, around time of his coadj nom. Also co-opted by uncle as coadj-abbot of Montebourg in 1613, but Rome insisted that he, too, become professed Benedictine monk, which he did before 1616.

Procuration from uncle to obtain his nom as coadj 23–4–1615. Nom 13–7–1615. Provs 11–4–1616. Cons date and place unknown. Succeeded to Le Puy Jan 1621. D. 28–8–1641.

Sources: BN, P Or 2694, doss 59806; Doss bleus 612, doss 16,142; AD Ardèche, series C, *Inventaire-sommaire* (1877), for Vivarais Estates. Frondeville, *Conseillers*, 174. Gigord, *La Noblesse de Villeneuve de Berg*, 404–11. *Revue du Vivarais*, 36 (1929), 1–35. *DBF*, vii. 355–6 (family). ASV, Misc Arm XII, 144, fo 89. AN, Z^1o 240 (ordination). AN, MC, VIII, 415, 20–9–1597 (*régale* for Le Puy). *Gallia*, ii. 737–8. Valois, *Inventaire des arrêts, Henri IV*, no 3127 (Jacques). ASV, PC 13, fos 711–27; Acta Camerarii 14, fo 218v-19r; 15, fo 48 (Juste).

Serroni, Hyacinthe, OP. Orange 1647–61, Mende 1661–76, Albi 1676–87. B. Rome 30–8–1617, baptised Giacomo Felice. Names and circumstances of parents unknown. He apparently entered Dominican order in Fiesole in mid-teens, studied philosophy and theology at the Minerva, Rome, where he took the doct in theology, ca 1643. Taught these 2 disciplines there, where he was master of studies. Ordained priest in 1641. Through holding office in his order he encountered Michele Mazarin, a fellow Dominican and papal theologian, a relationship that was crucial for Serroni's subsequent career. He accompanied M. Mazarin to French-occupied Catalonia, and it was, naturally, through his brother's patronage that he was made bp of Orange, still notionally in direct papal gift, in 1647. Continued energetically to serve Cardinal Mazarin in various capacities in S France thereafter (e.g. as *intendant de la marine* in Toulon, 1654), and this service was rewarded with transfer to Mende in 1661 (one of Mazarin's last episcopal decisions). Went on to become first abp of Albi in 1676.

Provs for Orange 27–5–1647. Nom to Mende 28–2–1661. Provs 8–8–1661. Transferred to Albi 1676. D. 7–1–1687.

Sources: ASV, PC 46, fo 22–33; PC 59, fo 283–301. AD Lozère, G 45 (bp's testament). *Mémoires de Gourreau de la Proustière*, ed Buffevent, 159, 163. Touron, *Hommes illustres de l'ordre de Saint Dominique*, v. 600–13.

Servien, François. Bayeux 1654–9. This Dauphiné family rose socially and politically through membership of Grenoble parlt during 16th C. Bp's great-grandfather married daughter of a *cons* there in 1500. Bp's own father was one of 17 children, 2 of whom became important financial officials (as *receveurs-généraux*) in Tours and Rouen, valuable activities in family's later ascent to ministerial office, even though they continued to concentrate their activities in Dauphiné. Bp's father's own career and marriage of bp's sister to Artus de Lionne, *cons* at Grenoble before becoming bp of Gap and father of Louis XIV's minister, show this did them no harm.

B. Grenoble 1601. Son of Antoine, sgr de Biviers, *syndic-procureur-général* of Dauphiné Estates, *cons* in Grenoble parlt (1604), and Diane de Bailly; younger brother of Abel

Servien. Nothing known of education, but held doct in utr. Royal almoner and abbot in c of St-Maure and St-Jouin-de-Marnes, OSB (Poitiers). Ordained priest in Sept 1648. Apart from attendance at 1635 AC, little is known of pre-episcopal career: seems to have been borne along by his brother, Abel, and nephew, Hugues de Lionne. Originally nom to Carcassonne, he was slow to seek provs, and in the end he preferred more opulent diocese of Bayeux, previously held by member of Molé family which proved unable to find successor in its ranks (see above, pp 86–9).

Nom to Bayeux 23-5-1654 (having resigned claim to Carcassonne the same day). Provs 9-11-1654. Cons 10-1-1655. D. 2-2-1659.

Sources: ASV, PC 50, fo 152; PC 51, fos 511–24. BN, MS lat 17025, fo 46. Virieux, 'Parlement de Grenoble au xviie siècle', 272–4. Tallemant, *Historiettes*, ii. 192–4. Vidal, *Critique*, 273–5. *DGS*, 1442.

Sévin, Nicolas. Sarlat 1648–57, Cahors coadj 1657/59–78. Origins of this family, obscured by their later genealogical pretentions, lie in bourgeoisie of 15th C Orléans, whence some of them later scattered to Paris and Toulouse. By 17th C, there were several branches, though their social and professional success was somewhat uneven. Bp was descended from a notary at Orléans, whose grandson (and father of bp), Eléazar, was one of several family members to practice as barristers in Paris during 16th C. *Cons* in *prévôté* of Orléans (1586), he suffered for his royalism during League, which dominated Orléans for several years. Although his childen obtained *lettres de noblesse* in 1633, they were less dynamic and successful than other branches of the family (in both Paris and Toulouse), though it may be assumed they could count on their support and influence.

B. 1613. Son of Eléazar and Renée Vasse. Studied humanities and philosophy at coll of Clermont, followed by theology studies at Paris, though open to question if he really took doct (as nuncio accepted). Royal almoner and abbot in c of Wulmer, OSB (Boulogne) before episcopate. Ordained priest, ca 1640. Close ties to *dévot* figures, several of them belonging to wider Sévin family circle, but also to men like Bp Solminihac of Cahors, who were instrumental in obtaining episcopal office for him.

Resign of Sarlat by Bp Jean de Lingendes to Sévin 22-9-1647. Nom 30-9-1647. Provs 18-5-1648. Cons 26-7-1648. Transferred to Cahors as coadj 1657. Succeeded to Cahors 31-12-1659. D. 9-11-1678.

Sources: ASV, PC 50, fos 386–99. AAE 852, fo 66–7. BN, P Or 2700, doss 59945; Doss bleus 614, doss 16181. Vidal, *Critique*, 121–2, 225–9. Bluche *Origines des magistrats*, 389–90. Mme de Naurois-Sévin, *Généalogie de la famille Sévin* (Paris 1912).

Seytres, Gilles de. Toulon 1599–1626. Of Italian extraction (sometimes called Septres) this family first settled at Montélimar in early 15th C, and then in Avignon and the Comtat, where they engaged in mercantile activities and wide variety of municipal offices post-1450. Antoine de Seytres, *changeur* and *consul*, married his daughter to Gabriel de Tulle (ancestor of several bps of Orange from same socio-professional background). But it was intermarriage nearly a century later with Bertons family (also from northern Italy and also bourgeois and merchants by origin) which turned out to be the key to episcopal office.

B. Avignon, date unknown. Son of Louis, sgr de Caumont, and Marguerite de Bertons (m. in 1558), sister of Crillon, military commander and companion of Henri IV. Nothing known of education, but Rome accepted he held doct in utr. Subdeacon at nom, he appears to have had some physical disability, possibly a limp. His uncle Crillon, who had sharp eye for church patronage, probably played key role in his promotion.

No date for nom. Provs 19-7-1599. Cons details unknown. D. 2-5-1626.

Sources: ASV, Misc Arm XII, 216, no 32. *Gallia Chr Nov*, v. 641-50. Labande, *Avignon au xvie siècle*, esp 18, 24, 427, 549ff. Pithon-Curt, *Noblesse du Venaissin*, iii. 270-83 (misleading). P Hurtebise, 'La Famille de Tulle et le siège épiscopal d'Orange', *Archivum Historiae Pontificiae*, 25 (1897), 411-30. Blanc, *Origines des familles provençales*, 537.

Simon. *See* **Marquemont**

Solminihac, Alain, OSA canon-regular. Cahors 1636-59. The very model of pugnacious *dévot* bp, Solminihac was scion of junior branch of middling noble family originally from the Sarladais. But they and their activities remain rather obscure, if we except those of Pierre, sgr de Belet, *lic-ès-lois* and mayor of Périgueux in early 16th C! A similar lack of *éclat* is suggested by bp's father's marriage. They could, however, boast a number of ecclesiastics, and it was through them that the future bp obtained abbey of Chancelade — with which his name is as much associated as with the see of Cahors.

B. 25-11-1593. Son of Jean and Marguerite de Marquessac (daughter of *juge-mage* and lt-gen of *sénéchaussée* of Périgord). Nothing known for certain of early education. He took bacc in canon law at Cahors by 1614, and may later have taken some bacc exams in theology at Paris (but without taking degree). Initially abbot in c of Chancelade, OSA (Périgueux) in 1614 (in succession to uncle Arnaud de Solminihac), he subsequently became a professed canon-regular, and attempted to launch a reform of the order's houses in SW France in late 1620s and 1630s, which brought him into touch (as well as conflict) with Cardinal La Rochefoucauld, Vincent de Paul, and wider *dévot* networks of both Paris and provinces. He initially refused Lavaur in 1636, but accepted Cahors when Richelieu and Louis XIII insisted. As bp of Cahors, was assiduous correspondent of Vincent de Paul, constantly on look-out for suitable candidates for episcopal office in SW.

Brevet de nom 17-6-1636. Provs 22-9-1636. Cons 27-9-1637. Took Bp Sévin of Sarlat as coadj in 1657. D. 31-12-1659.

Sources: Sol, Le *Vénérable Alain de Solminihac*. Alain de Solminihac. *Lettres et Documents*. DGS, 1458.

Sourdis, François d' *Escoubleau* **de. Bordeaux 1599-1628 (also coadj of Maillezais 1605-15 but resign).** Old noble family from Thouars region of Poitou stretched back to 3th C. By 16th, it was the Alluye branch which became most prominent. Abps' grandfather and father were close companions of François I, Henri III and Henri IV, and remained firmly royalist during wars of religion. Their fidelity was powerfully reinforced by abps' maternal family, the prolific and influential Babou-Angennes-Rambouillet clan, whose role in French church affairs was considerable. Less distinguished but no less real, Sourdis church presence was represented by Jacques and Henri, bps of Maillezais (1543-61 and 1572-1615 resp). Numerous other marriages to court and high *robe* (e.g. Cheverny) families ensured they formed part of court élite and were well placed to benefit from royal bounty. Thanks to their cousin, Gabrielle d'Estrées, Henri IV's mistress, this was readily forthcoming, enabling François to become cardinal even before diocese had been found for him, an exceptional favour. Both Sourdis abps proved to be extraordinary figures, men of extreme contradictions: authoritarian, violent, temperamental, yet committed to good government and reform of their dioceses, even when, as in the case of Henri, they spent more time engaged in military and naval activities.

B. 25–10–1574. François was eldest son of François, marquis d'Alluye and gov of Chartres, and Isabeau Babou de la Bourdaisière. Educated at coll of Navarre, but initially destined for secular career, so may only have completed humanities course. As comte de la Chapelle, he embarked on military career, fighting at siege of Chartres in 1591, and was engaged to marry Catherine Hurault de Cheverny, the chancellor's daughter. But a séjour in Rome 1593–4 (where he encountered Federico Borromeo and Filippo Neri) changed his mind, and persuaded him to choose church career. Tonsured on return to France, was quickly nom for red hat by Henri IV. Only nom to Bordeaux in early 1598. In 1605, became coadj to uncle, bp of Maillezais, on understanding that he would vacate Bordeaux on succeeding to Maillezais. In the event, the opposite happened – he surrendered Maillezais to brother Henri, though only after a typically furious family row, and retained Bordeaux instead.

No date for nom to Bordeaux (but previous holder of *brevet de nom*, Jean Le Breton, resign his claim to Sourdis 8–2–1598). Provs 5–7–1599. Cons 21–12–1599. D. 8–2–1628.

Sourdis, Henri *d'Escoubleau* **de. Maillezais 1616–28, coadj Bordeaux 1627/28–45.** B. 20–2–1593, baptised at St-Germain-l'Auxerrois 15–10–1594. Henri IV was his godfather, Gabrielle d'Estrées his godmother. Younger brother of François above. Studied humanities and philosophy at coll of Navarre, followed by law studies, after which he took doct in utr. Tonsured in May 1605, was still simple cleric at time of nom. Initially intended only as coadj but quickly became full episcopal nom when uncle died in April 1615. Abbot in c of St-Jouin, OSB (Poitiers) before episcopate, his amassed a prize collection of wealthy benefices during his later years, whose value far exceeded that of his diocese(s). His episcopal career was colourful and turbulent.

Resign coadjutorial title to Maillezais by brother Cardinal de Sourdis to Henri 23–3–1615. Nom same date. Provs 18–5–1616. Cons 19–3–1623. Nom coadj of Bordeaux 10–12–1627; to full title 8–2–1628. Provs 16–7–1629. D. 18–6–1645.

Sources: Beauchet-Filleau, *Dict du Poitou*, ii. 285–90. Peyrous, *Réforme catholique à Bordeaux*, i (*passim*). *DGS*, 1462–3 (family). AD Gironde, G 254–5, 259 (Cardinal). ASV, PC 13, fos 802–16. BAV, Barb lat 7941, fos 127, 141. AN, Z^{1}o 241. *Lettres de Peiresc*, vii. 53–4 (Henri).

Souvré, Gilles. Comminges 1617–25, Auxerre 1626–31. This old noble family from the Perche rose rapidly to prominence owing to bp's father, who was close companion of both Henri III and Henri IV, under whom he reaped rewards (which included the marshal's baton) for his loyalty and military commitment. Henri IV made him gov of Touraine, and once 'gave' him the see of Tours when rumoured vacant in 1593, though Souvré had no son old enough (even by contemprary standards) for episcopate! Gov of Louis XIII as dauphin, he was no less well placed to benefit from ecclesiastical patronage 20 years later.

B. March 1596. Son of Gilles and Françoise de Bailleul. Studied mainly at coll of Navarre, where he followed both philosophy and theology course, but did not complete it or take degree. Pre-episcopal endowment with benefices was commensurate with father's favour: abbot in c of St-Florent-sur-Loire, OSB (Angers) and St-Calais, OSB (Le Mans), he was also treasurer of Ste Chapelle. Probably simple cleric at nom, which was a highly complex affair. Rome initially rejected coadjutorship of Comminges proposed for him in

1612 on age grounds, but under intense pressure from court (father's position as Louis XIII's gov was major consideration), Paul V accepted suggestion of granting him 'access' to see (inc keeping it vacant if necessary) in early 1613. Subsequently spent a period in Italy and Rome, which evidently enabled him to obtain full title to Comminges and be cons while several years underage.

Nom to Comminges ca Sept 1612. Provs for access, 31–1–1613. Cons 12–3–1617 at Ravenna. Nom to Auxerre (as result of exchange with Fr de Donadieu) 18–10–1623/22–10–1624. Provs 9–2–1626. D. 19–9–1631.

Sources: ASV, PC 21, fos 662–81; Secr dei Brevi 617, fo 104 ('access' to Comminges). BN, MS Fr 18007, fos 357v, 402, 410, 440v (Comminges succession, 1612). AD Haute-Garonne, 3G, vol 4. Clergeac, *Chronologie*, 55. *DGS*, 1466.

Sponde, Henri de. Pamiers 1626–43. Scholarly and literary exploits of members of this family have, if anything, helped to keep their early history obscure. Henri's father, Ennecot (French form of Iñigo), seems to have been either Basque or Spanish immigrant to Béarn. Converted to Protestantism, and served as secretary to Jeanne d'Albret, and Catherine and Henri de Navarre, becoming *cons* and MR of Navarre. Married twice: Huguenot poet Jean (1557–95) was son of 1st marriage, while Henri was one of 3 sons by 2nd wife.

B. 6–1–1568 Mauléon. Son of Ennecot and Sauvate de Hosta, a native of Pamplona. Godson of Henri de Navarre/Henri IV, he was reared Protestant, educated at king's expense at Orthez academy, and later (ca 1583–4) at Geneva. By 1591, having presumably converted to Catholicism, he was a law student at Bordeaux, but took lic in utr at Angers. Briefly practised law, but turned to the church and was tonsured in 1597. Accompanied Cardinal Sourdis to Rome ca 1600, and settled there. Ordained priest in March 1606. Nominally holding post of corrector in Penitentiary, he gained reputation as a scholar and historian who continued the Annales, the scholarly enterprise launched by Cardinal Baronius. Also rector of French church in Rome, St-Louis-des-Français, but resigned after clashing with Bérulle's Oratorians who took control there. Canon of St-Seurin of Bordeaux for many years before episcopate. His first attempt to resign Pamiers outright to his nephew (his coadj since 1634) was declared invalid by Rome, but second was accepted in 1641. Recovered title of bp for less than 2 months after his nephew predeceased him.

Nom 8–4–1626. Provs 20–7–1626. Cons 16–8–1626 in Rome. Took nephew as coadj 1634. D. 15–5–1643.

Sponde, Jean de. Pamiers coadj 1634/41–3. B. 1594 Mauléon. Son of Jean, poet and pres in La Rochelle *présidial* (i.e. half-brother of Henri, above), and Anne le Grand. Father converted to Catholicism in 1593, soon after his master, Henri IV. Nothing known of education or whether he had degree, but early career may have been secular, since not tonsured until April 1618. Pre-episcopal career generally remains obscure, until co-opted as coadj by uncle in 1633. Latter retired from Pamiers to Paris by late 1630s, hence desire to resign see outright to his nephew.

No date for nom. Provs 20–2–1634. Cons 2–7–1634 in Paris. Succeeds 1641. D. 31–3–1643.

Sources: Palma-Cayet, *Chronologie Novenaire*, ii. 44. Ruchon, *Essai sur la vie de Jean de Sponde*. *DGS*, 1468–9. E Droz, 'Les Années d'études de Jean et d'Henry de Sponde',

Bibliothèque d'Humanisme et de Renaissance 9 (1947), 141–50 (family). AD Gironde, G 798, fos 47–9. BL, Addit MS 8730, fos 138, 157. *Corr de Bérulle*, iii. 178; 'Lettres de Henri de Sponde', *Revue de Gascogne*,14 (1874), 547–52 (Henri). ASV, PC 22, fos 126–43. AAE, France 809, fo 140 (Jean).

Suarez, Jacopo, OFM. Séez 1612–14. The 'Cordelier portugais', as Pierre de l'Estoile and contemporaries called him, was born in Lisbon in Nov 1552. Nothing known of his family or early life, though as he joined Franciscans, was probably educated within the order. Accompanied Don Antonio, the Portuguese pretender, to France (arriving in 1579 by his own later account) and remained after his death in 1595. By then had acquired a reputation as popular preacher, preaching no fewer than 14 Advent or Lenten 'stations' in Paris, and some sermons were published. Successively *prédicateur ordinaire* to Marguerite de Valois and Henri IV, in whose memory he delivered an *oraison funèbre* in 1610. Also engaged in controversy with du Plessis-Mornay over Eucharist, though theological skills seem to have been somewhat limited. Henri IV apparently promised him a diocese, possibly even Séez itself, ca 1607, but did not live to keep his promise. By 1611, was hardly young or fit enough to govern a diocese, as decision to nom a coadj so quickly makes clear. Had to defend himself in Rome against rumours of being greedy and wealthy in 1611, and also suffered indignity of being expelled from Séez to Alençon by local Huguenots in 1613.

Nom after 8–6–1611 (death of Bp Bertaut). Provs 9–1–1612. Cons 4–3–1612. Agreed to take Jacques Camus as coadj, June 1612. D. 30–5–1614.

Sources: ASV, PC 13, fo 5 (Camus coadj). BAV, Barb lat 7961, fo 92–3 (2 *apologias*, 1611, 1613). Pierre de l'Estoile,*Journal 1601–1610*, 96–7. Hommey, *Histoire générale de Séez*, iv. 179–81.

Suze. *See* **La Baume de Suze**

Thoreau, Mathieu. Dol 1661–92. The Thoreau family held a succession of offices, municipal and royal, in their native Poitiers, where earliest known member, bp's grandfather, was a simple *procureur* (albeit possibly early in his career) at local *présidial* court, ca 1560. Bp was one of several sons of René, sgr de la Grimaudière, who was *trésorier général* at Poitiers from 1614 (and later pres of *trésoriers*), as well as mayor of Poitiers (an ennobling office) in 1621. Bp's own generation was esp energetic and, at least in the case of its clerics, less tied to its original milieu. Brother Gilles succeeded their father as *trésorier général* in Poitiers (1640–64), and another, René, was *cons* at Poitiers *présidial*, ca 1657. Another brother Philippe was chamberlain to Pope Alexander VII, and in 1656 obtained office of *chantre* in Dol cathedral thanks to his relations with Mazarin (though opposition prevented him from obtaining effective possession of it until 1661). Philippe paved the way for Mathieu's accession to Dol, since he was subsequently both vg of the diocese and gov of Dol itself (1663), and members of Thoreau family 'colonised' both church and secular posts there.

B. 14–4–1612 Poitiers. Son of René and N . . . Early studies at SJ coll of Poitiers (along with Bp Péréfixe), took doct in canon law, also at Poitiers. He held number of priories (Ste-Catherine-de-Laval, St-Jean-de-Montleveur and La Faye-Montjoult) in c before episcopate. Ordained priest ca 1645, became dean of Poitiers cathedral before attending AC of 1650. Elected *agent-général du clergé* by 1655 AC. Mazarin had already been alerted to his services and loyalism ('puissant en biens, vertu et parenté', as the royal confessor put it in 1652), and there was little doubt that Thoreau, partly through his brother, Philippe, enjoyed his goodwill as *agent-général*.

Nom 28–2–1661. Provs 8–8–1661. Cons 2.10–1661. D. 31–1–1692.

Sources: ASV, PC 59, fos 302–17; N Fr 110, fo 160. AAE, France 885, fo 33–4. Charmeil, *Trésoriers de France à l'époque de la Fronde*, 473. R Durand, 'Un chanoine de Dol au xviie siècle', *Annales de Bretagne*, 34 (1919–20) 486–91. A Bonvallet, *Le Bureau des finances de la généralité de Poitiers* (Poitiers 1883).

Thyard, Cyrus de. Chalon-sur-Saône 1594–1624. Ennobled in 1400, this Burgundian family had a long history of service to both the Burgundian dukes (inc Habsburgs) and, thereafter, the kings of France. Poet-bishop, Pontus de Thyard (uncle and predecessor of Cyrus) added intellectual lustre to their name during 16th C, while remainder of family continued their traditional military and political activities. One of relatively few noble families during later religious wars to defend royalist cause in Burgundy, dominated by Mayenne and Catholic League. Bp's parents both participated in this struggle, and his father was killed in action, which left Bp Pontus to bring up his nephews.

B. date unknown. Son of Claude, sgr de Bissy, and Guillemette de Montgomery, (m. in 1553). Nothing known of education, probably did not take degree. Ordained subdeacon in Sept 1586, was canon of Chalon cathedral by that date, and later grand archdeacon. Only days before his death, Henri III allowed Pontus to resign Chalon to Cyrus. Henri IV renewed the concession in March 1593, accepting ensuing resignation in May 1593 'in consideration of services of the sgr de Bissy gov of Verdun in Burgundy'. Loyalty clearly had its rewards.

Nom May 1593. Provs 24–1–1594. Cons in Rome, 20–2–1594. D. 3–1–1624.

Sources: AD Saône-et-Loire, F 561, 563, 565 (Thyard de Bissy papers). BN, MS lat 18345, fo 180v (ennoblement). AN, Z^{1}o 240 (ordination). Jeandet, *Pontus de Thyard*. Drouot, *Mayenne et la Bourgogne*. i. 63–4. *DGS*, 202.

Trappes. *See* **Destrappes**

Tubeuf, Michel. St-Pons 1654–64, Castres 1664–82. Forever associated with Mazarin, the Tubeufs were well-established Parisian, bourgeois family traceable back to late 15th C, with certain branches ennobled by offices during 16th C. But bp's grandfather never progressed beyond professor of barrister, while father began as barrister and later served as MR to Anne of Austria. Marriage to Marie Talon, sister of Omer, enhanced their kinship ties to robe families, but it was the wide-ranging activities of Jacques, Bp's brother, which did most to advance their fortunes, thanks to crown's financial needs and Mazarin's patronage.

B. Paris ca 1602. Son of Simon and Marie Talon; brother of Jacques, pres in *chambre des comptes* and *intendant des finances* (1643–50). Studied humanities at coll of Harcourt, and philosophy under Jacques Lescot (bp of Chartres) at Calvi, where he took MA, ca 1622. Followed theology course at Sorbonne, becoming bacc in theology ca 1628. Priest by 1630, he was royal almoner within a year. Abbot in c of St-Urbain, OSB (Châlons-s-Marne) and *prieur-curé* of St-Jean-de-Dammartin before episcopate. Personal and family connections began to bring some reward from early 1640s. Deputy to AC of 1641, elected *agent-général du clergé* in 1645, and served as secretary to 1650 AC. Brother's simultaneous rise to financial eminence in government circles rounded off these accomplishments, and made episcopal office increasingly certain, even if St-Pons was not necessarily the most desirable of dioceses.

Nom to St-Pons 20–6–1653. Provs 26–1–1654. Cons 12–4–1654. Nom to Castres 29–6–1664. Provs 6–10–1664. D. 16–4–1682.

Sources: ASV, PC 53, fos 393–411. AN, MC, XXXVI, 136, 6–5–1624 (*inventaire après décès* of bp's father); XVIII, 247, 4–4–1630; XXXIV, 332, 17–6–1631. Bluche, *Origines des magistrats*, 392, 403. Lacger, *Etats administratifs*, 333.

Tulles, Jean-Vincent. Orange coadj 1637/40–7, Lavaur 1647–68. Family, possibly of Italian origin, settled at Villefranche near Avignon by late 14th C, but contrary to later claims, only attained noble status by late 15th/early 16th C, when municipal office and fief-holding enabled them to merge into local nobility. Before that they were merchants and bourgeois intermarrying with similar families (inc Seytres family in 1480) of Avignon. They consolidated their previous advance during 16th C, when Antoine became first *consul* of Avignon in 1528 (a noble office), while other members held financial offices elsewhere in Provence; they also included professors and doctors in law at Univ of Avignon. Simultaneously moved into positions in the church, preparing the way for uninterrupted three-generation tenure of see of Orange between 1572 and 1646. Due largely to the bps the younger generations of family turned increasingly towards service of French interests.

B. Avignon ca 1611. Son of Pierre, sgr de la Nerte, and Lucrèce de Lascaris. Educated partly in Paris in early-mid 1630s (with Jacques de Grignan). Abbot in c of St-Eusèbe of Apt. Co-opted as coadj of Orange in 1637 by his uncle, Jean II de Tulle, whom he succeeded in 1640, having been consecrated on 13–4–1637 in Rome. His devotion to Mazarin while at Orange was considerable, and ensuing ministerial patronage duly enabled him, like his successor at Orange, Serroni, to move from Orange to a fully 'French' diocese.

Provs as coadj of Orange 16–3–1637. Succeeded 1640. Nom to Lavaur, 30–10–1646. Provs 27–5–1647. D. 3–12–1668.

Sources: ASV, PC 47, fos 529–36; PC 56, fo 391v-2; Processus Datariae 26, fos 191–5. Rolland, *Une Famille avignonnaise*. Hurtebise, 'La Famille de Tulle et le siège épiscopal d'Orange', 411–30. Pithon-Curt, *Noblesse du Venaissin*, iii. 448–55.

Turicella, Jacopo, OFM. Marseille 1605–18. B. in Tuscany ca 1560, very little is known about background or early career of this Franciscan friar who, having entered the order at early age and taken doct in theology, only arrived in France in mid-career with Marie de' Medici, to whom he was confessor and preacher. Previously held posts in his order in Tuscany, and preached in several major cities there. The tradition of Italian clerics acceding to southern French dioceses was not yet dead, and Turicella's promotion was not exceptional. Not first choice for Marseille, where his predecessor had been murdered by a servant (as would Turicella be himself). Only after Guillaume du Vair (then first pres of Aix parlt) refused it that Turicella, who had for some reason failed to secure claim on Angoulême (to which he was nom in Dec 1603) against fellow Florentine competitor, was nom. Private life as bp of Marseille, where he fathered a daughter whose mother demanded a dowry payable from bp's revenues, caused a scandal in Aix and Rome, which investigated and reprimanded him in virtual secrecy. He too was poisoned by one of his servants.

Nom to Marseille, early 1604. Provs 19–1–1605. Cons 20–3–1605. D. 19–1–1618.

Sources: *Gallia Chr Nov*, ii. 602–6. BN, MS Fr 33047, p 531 (naturalisation, 1603); MS Fr 3497, fo 99. BAV, Barb lat 7955, fo 47. Dubost, 'Les Italiens en France au xvie et au xviie siècle'.

Vair. *See* **Du Vair**

Valavoire, Nicolas de. Riez 1652–85. Valavoire was seigneurial name in bp's family since 13th C. Prominent in church, military affairs and order of Malta over several centuries, and thanks to marriages to families such as the Forbin (1538 and 1618), Villeneuve and others, they were firmly established among old and influential nobility of Provence. Bp's father and grandfather were both *viguiers* of Marseille (1603 and 1628 respectively). Father, marquis de Valavoire, was also a captain of one of comte d'Alais, gov of Provence's, companies of *gendarmes*, and later gov of Sisteron citadel. He and other family members supported Alais during Aix revolt of 1649. Such service brought them powerful provincial patronage, and with it the benevolent attention of Mazarin.

B. 1621. Son of Pierre, sgr de Vaux, and Gabrielle de Forbin-Soliès (m. 1618). After early studies, followed theology course leading to doct at Avignon. Priest in 1649, he spent 2 years before nom at St-Sulpice, where Olier, a witness in his inquiry *de vita et moribus* for Riez, directed him through the Spiritual Exercises, and where Valavoire preached and administered the sacraments. Prior of Vaux, he was deputy to 1645 AC for Aix province. With Alais's and Mazarin's support, was proposed for Sisteron in 1647, but refused on grounds of age by *conseil de conscience*. Mentioned in connection with see of Fréjus in 1651.

Resign by Dony d'Attichy (vacating Riez for Autun) of Riez to Valavoire 9–5–1652. *Brevet de nom* and royal nom 10–5–1652. Provs 14–10–1652. Cons 8–12–1652. D. 28–4–1685.

Sources: ASV, PC 53, fos 474–94. AAE, France 875, fo 239v. *Lettres de Mazarin*, ii. 855, 902. Blanc, *Origines des familles provençales*, 567–9. Kettering, *Patrons, Brokers and Clients*, 92–3.

Valernod, Pierre. Nîmes 1598–1625. Family were middle-ranking Dauphiné magistrates settled in area near St-Vallier. Their service to powerful Languedoc gov, Montmorency-Damville, enabled them to develop both wider ties and ambitions. Bp's brother, Jean, was secretary of Montmorency, as were his Maridat relatives, who together formed a tight admin oligarchy in the gov's service – from which they benefited in ecclesiastical as in secular sphere.

B. 25–5–1551 St-Vallier. Son of Jean and Françoise de Luc de Champfagot. Nothing known of education or whether he took degree. A priest, he was successively canon of Die (diocese of origin) and archdeacon of Carcassonne (Montmorency patronage?). Canon of Nîmes by 1583 where his maternal uncle, Bertrand de Luc, was vg and resigned precentorship of cathedral to him. See of Nîmes would almost certainly have escaped him, however, without continuing Montmorency support, as bp of Nîmes since 1573, Cavalesi, was a Joyeuse *confidentiaire*, and chapter of Nîmes wanted another Joyeuse client Louis de Vervins (later abp of Narbonne) as successor. Ensuing struggle for Nîmes was prolonged and unpleasant, hence 4–year vacancy. For some reason, Valernod later fell foul of Montmorency who was party to failed plan to unseat him ca 1608–9. By late 1610s,

largely incapacitated, he was persuaded to take Claude de Caylar de Saint-Bonnet as his coadj.
Brevet de nom 4–9–1594. Provs 7–1–1598. Cons 24–2–1598. D. 12–9–1625.

Sources: Arch de Chantilly, L/xxviii, fo 60; xxix, fos 12, 66; xxxi, fos 82, 105, 336; xxxviii, fo 337; xcvii, fo 144. AD Gard, G 69. Sauzet, *Contre-réforme*, 54–5; Villain, *France moderne* ii. 928.

Valois, Louis-Emmanuel de. Agde 1618–22 (resign). While a number of 17th-C bps left secular careers to become bps, the future comte d'Alais was one of only 2 who travelled in the opposite direction (Henri de Guise was the other). In both cases, a sudden shift in family imperatives dictated change of course, reversing what had once seemed an entirely appropriate church career. For Valois, grandson of Charles IX and mistress, Marie Touchet, and son of Charles de Valois, comte d'Auvergne, and Charlotte de Montmorency, a church career arose essentially from Montmorency family control of Agde (held by *confidentiaire* since the early 1580s) and the wish to preserve it as family heirloom. Valois, a younger son, was designated for this role. 'Princely' status ensured his road to episcopate would be unusual – like that of Henri IV's own son's accession to Metz. B. 1598, and brought up at Chantilly, plans were already afoot in 1608 to secure coadjutorship of Agde while old bp, Bernard du Puy, was still alive. A *brevet de nom* in his name was issued in mid-1611, after du Puy's death, but Roman dislike of underage episcopal noms stalled proceedings for several years. But there is little doubt that he took possession of, and governed, Agde between 1618 and 1622. Death of his elder brother in 1622 changed everything, and being unordained and uncons, he was free to choose secular career – in which, as the comte d'Alais, his principal role was that of gov of Provence (1636–53).

Nom initially mid-1611. Provs 14–5–1618. Never cons . Resign 1622. D. 13–11–1653.

Sources: ASV, Misc Arm XII 144, fo 22. Arch de Chantilly, L/xcii, fo 25; cvi, fo 238. AN, MC LIV, 477, 15–9–1611.

Ventadour, Anne de Lévis de. Bourges 1651–62. Powerfully entrenched in uplands of NE Languedoc (where barony of La Voulte constituted a strategic base and historic seat) as well as in the Limousin, this prolific family was long related by marriage to powerful local families (e.g. Tournon, La Baume de la Suze) whose political interests were far from merely local. These kinship ties were still being stengthened in 16th C, culminating in marriages with members of Montmorency family, which enabled first duc de Ventadour (father of the bps) to become right-hand man to his brother-in-law, Damville, gov of Languedoc, and (in 1596), lt-gen of Languedoc. Despite close political ties, Ventadours followed different path to Montmorencys in certain respects: the *dévot* affiliations of bp's eldest brother (founder of the *Compagnie du St-Sacrement*) were famous, while ecclesiastics had probably always been more numerous in their ranks than among Montmorency family. But bp's father's control of Lodève resembles Montmorency's behaviour over Agde.

B. ca 1605. Son of Anne, duc de Ventadour, and Marguerite de Montmorency, daughter of Constable Montmorency. Destined for church career, studied humanities at coll of Clermont (along with F de Neufville), and Univ of Paris. Later took theology at Sorbonne, but graduated as doct in utr at Orléans. Abbot in c of St-André-de-Meymac

(OSB, Limoges – title by which he was normally known before episcopate) and St-Martin-de-Ruricourt, OSA (Beauvais). Like parents, was active *dévot*, esp in *Congrégation pour la propagation de la foi*. A priest for many years, he was treasurer of Ste Chapelle. Became gov of Limousin (via brother's resignation) at same time as he acceded to primatial see of Bourges. According to Bp Plantavit, he had let Lodève 'slip through his fingers' in 1625, and family control of see thus ended.

Nom 11–11–1649. Provs 13–2–1651. Cons 30–4–1651. D. 17–3–1662.

Ventadour, Louis-Hercule de Lévis de, SJ/Cluny. Mirepoix 1655–79. B. 1613. Younger brother of Anne above. Educated virtually entirely at coll of Clermont (humanities, philosophy, theology), and thus took no degree. Joined SJ, becoming a professed member, and was ordained priest, 1639. Family pressure (inc that of cousin, Condé) during later Fronde led to his leaving SJ, but promptly received into Order of Cluny (May-July 1654). Sole object was to make him bp, since Rome would not consent to Jesuit becoming bp while still member of SJ.

Resign by Bp Nogaret of Mirepoix to Ventadour 6–5–1655. Nom 16–6–1655. Provs 25–10–1655. Cons 19–12–1655. D. 6–1–1679.

Sources: Anselme, iv. 1–44. Vindry, *Etat-major*, 272. Martin, *Histoire de Lodève*, ii. 373–4. Beyssac, *Chanoines de Lyon*, 194 (family). ASV, PC 48, fos 339–61 (Anne); PC 52, fos 966–93. BN, MS Fr 20661, fos 426–8 (Louis-Hercule).

Vernède. *See* **Corneilhan**

Vervins, Louis de, OP. Narbonne 1600–28. Few French abps were as modest in their origins as Vervins, whose family was from Baumes-de-Venise near Carpentras, where they were resident as commoners, and quite indigent ones, in 1550s. Abp was son of 'noble' Jean, *alias* Jean de Ronan, captain of Beaumes château, while his mother was from 'notable' Beaumes family of greater means and standing than the Vervins, but still quite modest. In fact, abp's father appears originally to have been domestic servant of baron de Baumes in 1550s! Widowed early, abp's mother probably placed him in the local Dominican house.

B. 4–8–1547. Eldest son of Jean and Madeleine de Buneis, his 2nd wife. Professed Dominican from Carpentras convent, he studied at Aix, where he took doct in theology. Extremely active within and without his order during later years of wars of religion. Served as vg of bp of Castres around 1578. Ten years later, he was Dominican prior in Carpentras, and in Avignon (1593). As *commissaire général* of his order, he was entrusted with reforming convents in province. Deputy to Inquisitor of Avignon (1588), he became Inquisitor (1590). Anti-Navarrist and active in Provençal politics in early 1590s. 'Nom' to Nîmes in 1588 with Joyeuse support, but defeated by Valernod and Montmorency. Joyeuse then handpicked him as successor at Narbonne, which he resigned outright to him while retaining all but fraction of revenues for own use.

No date for nom to Narbonne. Provs 17–7–1600. Cons 8–12–1600. Took Claude de Rébé as coadj 1622. D. 8–2–1628.

Sources: ASV, Misc Arm XII, 216, fo 367. Carpentras, Bibl Imguimbertine, MS 1362, fo 453–64 (enquiry *de vita et moribus* for Vervins, when nom to Nîmes). A Allègre, *Monographie de Baumes de Venise* (Carpentras 1888), ch 9.

Vialart, Charles, O Cist. Avranches 1640–4. Originally from Issoire in the Auvergne, where Michel was judge and *bailli* in 1507, this family only emerged from obscurity when Jean, Michel's grandson, migrated to Paris where, thanks to powerful patronage of Chancellor Duprat, who promoted so many of his fellow Auvergnats, he served as barrister in parlt, *lieut-civil* at the Châtelet, and later as a pres in Rouen parlt (1540–9). His 1st marriage, to Marie Séguier, may not have produced children, but it tied the Vialarts enduringly to the Séguiers (with whom they intermarried more than once in subsequent years). Grandson Félix (d. 1613, father of bp Charles) also served as barrister and MR in 1576, while his marriage to Jeanne Hennequin extended family's existing *robe* ties, and made them a leading Paris-based *robe* family, with impressive *robe* alliances, well into 17th C (Hennequin, Amelot, Ligny, Séguier, Danès, Olier). Partly because of such connections, they were close to the Guises during religious wars. *Grands catholiques*, they were *ligueurs* and *dévots* of first rank, esp parents of bp Charles, who enjoyed close ties with François de Sales.

B. 1592. Son of Félix, sgr de Herse, and Jeanne Hennequin, aunt of Jacques Danès, bp of Toulon. Little known of education, but took bacc in theology ca 1617 in Paris. Ordained priest ca 1618, he entered the reformed Cistercian congregation, the Feuillants, and as Charles de St-Paul became their 4th superior-general.

Nom 8–5–1640. Provs 26–5–1642. Cons 6–7–1642. D. 15–9–1644.

Vialart, Felix. Châlons-sur-Marne 1640–80. B. 3–9–1613. Son of Michel, MR and ambassador to Swiss, and Charlotte de Ligny; nephew of Charles (above) and 1st cousin of Dominique de Ligny (above). Studied humanities, philosophy and theology at coll of Navarre, took MA there in 1631, and 2nd place in lic in theology in 1638 (doct followed soon afterwards). Tonsured in 1623, ordained priest in Dec 1637 (not to be confused with namesake of previous generation who may have been a family role-model for the future bp). Abbot in c of Scarceaux, O Cist (Sens) before episcopate. Above all, disciple of Vincent de Paul, through whom also became close to Jean Eudes and Pavillon, future bp of Alet. Active both on missions and as confessor. Cousin Olier apparently refused see of Châlons and Vialart was put forward for coadjutorship, but since Bp Clausse, his predecessor, d. in late 1640, he immediately succeeded *pleno jure* there.

Nom 14–12–1640. Provs 26–5–1642. Cons 6–7–1642. D. 11–6–1680.

Sources: AN, MC, LXX, 56, *inventaire après décès* of Jean Vialart and 2nd wife Jeanne Poncet, 15–5–1578; MC, VIII, 110, 23–5–1581 (c.m. Vialart-Hennequin). Etchéchoury, *Maîtres des requêtes*, 268–9. Trani, 'Conseillers du grand conseil', 215–16; Frondeville, *Présidents*, 168–72. Richet, *De la Réforme à la Révolution* (for Séguier and robe ties) (family). ASV, PC 40, fos 1–27. AAE, France 835, fo 141–2. AN, MC, LXXIII, 358, 6–7–1640 (Charles). ASV, PC 40, fos 217–36. Z¹o 241 (ordination). BN, MS lat 15440, p 167. AD Marne, G 152. Chérest, *L'Evêque de la paix* (Félix).

Vic, Dominique de. Auch coadj 1625/29–61. From relatively obscure beginnings in Guyenne, where abp's grandparents still lived, this family rose meteorically in following generation. Abp's uncle, Sarred, was well-known captain in royal guards, but it was father's career which was decisive. Initially MR to duc d'Anjou and MR *de l'hôtel du roi* in 1582, his service of Henri IV, to whom he rallied early, saw him rise to prominence, with an impressive number of commissions/intendancies in different provinces, esp concerning edict of Nantes in 1598 and 1611. *Cons d'état* 1589, pres in *chambre des comptes*

(1590) and in Toulouse parlt (1597–8), he became ambassador to Swiss (1600–5) and *garde des sceaux* (1621). Little evidence of social integration into ministerial or parlementaire high-robe circles, perhaps because career was so individual and rapid, but sister's marriage to Chancellor Cheverny's secretary may have helped win him useful political patronage.

B. ca 1589. Son of Méric and Marie de Bourdineau. Studied at SJ coll of Ingoldstadt (during father's Swiss embassy), then at La Flèche, completing humanities and philosopy in Univ of Paris (with Esparbès de Lussan). Took bacc in theology at Sorbonne, Feb 1610. Abbot in c of Bec, OSB (Rouen), aged 7, was deacon at time of nom. His pre-episcopal career seems closely dependent on father's dictates: he became *cons* in Paris parlt in 1621 when he accompanied Louis XIII on military campaigns against Huguenots. Nom as coadj of Auch owed nearly everything to father's services to Louis XIII, but was opposed after his death. Rumours about de Vic's personal life delayed Rome's confirmation of his candidature.

Procuration from Destrappes, abp of Auch, to take de Vic as coadj, probably Nov-Dec 1622. No date for nom, but probably early 1623; renewed 7–5–1624. Provs 27–1–1625. Cons 25–5–1625. Succeeded to Auch 29–10–1629. D. 21–12–1661.

Sources: ASV, PC 18, fos 44–62. AN, Z^{1}o 241 (ordinations). BAV, Barb lat 8055, fo 238. BN, MS Fr 3666, fos 36–7; MS Fr 33047, p 471 (naturalisation of abp's uncle, François de Vic, 1565). Anselme, vi. 539–40. Etchéchoury, *Maîtres des requêtes*, 270–1. Vindry, *Ambassadeurs*, 50. Chesnaye-Desbois, *Dict de noblesse*, xix, 688–90.

Vieuxpont, Jean de. Meaux 1602–23. This Norman family of long-standing nobility, powerfully established in the Séez area, enjoyed impressive kinship network in province and beyond, one which included episcopal families of both sword and *robe* backgrounds, such as Billy and Belleau, not to mention Potier, Harcourt, Clérambault and Frémiot. Their continuous presence in royal *gendarmerie* throughout 16th C reflects family military traditions dating from Hundred Years' War.

B. 15–9–1559. Son of Guillaume and Madeleine Messay de Berthère. Nothing known of education, and probably did not have degree. Succeeded uncle Claude de Vieuxpont as abbot in c of St-Jean-de-Falaise, O Prem (Séez), which he retained until episcopate. He was also, probably thanks to an older family member, *grand chantre* of Séez cathedral chapter. Attended 1595 AC as deputy for Rouen province. Meaux succession was long and complex: vacant for virtually 10 years, during which several candidates came and went, but reasons for Vieuxpont's promotion remain obscure. Successor was nephew, Jean de Belleau, whom he groomed for mitre.

Nom 1601. Provs 22–4–1602. Cons 2–2–1603. D 16–8–1623.

Sources: BN, P Or 2991, doss 66478; Cab d'Hozier 333, doss 9364. AN, MC, LXXXVI 184, 22–4–1608 (Vieuxpont-Belleau); Y 142, fos 71v–5r (Vieuxpont-Potier marriage). Anselme, ii. 116–29. Vindry, *Etat-major*, 75, 85, 504. Chesnaye-Desbois, *Dict de noblesse*, xix 727–32. A Plaisse, *La Baronnie de Neubourg* (Paris 1961).

Vigne, Louis de, Carmelite. Uzès 1598–1620. B. 30–10–1558. Son of Jaume, a rope maker from Avignon, and N . . . Joined Carmelites of Avignon young, was no doubt educated by them, though may not have taken degree. Accession to Uzès engineered mainly by Marie de Montmorency, daughter of the Constable and mother of Paul-Antoine de Fay-Peyraud, whom she and her husband had, with royal approval, destined for the see.

Vigne was *confidentiaire*, whose task was to keep seat warm for Fay-Peyraud, which he duly did, and meekly agreed to co-opt him as coadj in 1613.

No date for nom. Provs 18–9–1598. Cons 13–12–1598. D 20–11–1620.

Sources: J Giraud, 'La Chronique de Jean de Rodolphe Roubert bourgeois d'Avignon 1582–1606', *Annales d'Avignon et du Comtat Venaissin*, 2 (1913) 217–42; Arch Chantilly L/ xlv, fo 185.

Villars, Jérome de. Vienne 1598–1626. Of the many old Lyon bourgeois families who rose into French nobility, few were as enduringly successful as the Villars, who can be traced to the city in early 14th C. Enriched by trading activities, they held consular office numerous times during the 2 centuries which it took them to emerge from ranks of Lyon patriciate. Along the way, they developed several branches, forming solid marriage alliances with equals among city's merchant and consular families (e.g. Bellièvre, Camus, Grolier, de Lange, Gelas), but also made number of 'external' marriages (Serres, Gayant), which led to limited amount of office-holding in Paris parlt. They were, like the Bellièvres, also well entrenched in Lyon church, esp its chapters. Only in 1586 that Condrieu branch, which produced the bps, was ennobled in person of Claude, captain and châtelain of Condrieu, brother of Pierre abp of Vienne. The most impressive phase in their social and political advancement was still to come, culminating in career of *maréchal-duc* de Villars, one of Louis XIV's and Louis XIV's longest-serving commanders. This chapter of their history clearly important to their episcopal record, which was as impressive as that of any French family of early modern period – 2 bps of Mirepoix (1561–79), 5 abps of Vienne in succession (1575–1693), and one bp of Agen (where he was succeeded by a nephew, Claude de Gelas) – and which, like those of the Montchal and Serres, was initially launched by Cardinal de Tournon.

B. 1547. Son of François and Françoise Gayant. Brother of Pierre II abp of Vienne (d. 1592). After studies (and, presumably, law degree) became *cons-cl* in Paris parlt 1594, and also canon and archdeacon of Vienne. He took major orders (priesthood included) in 1588, possibly in anticipation of episcopal promotion (given he was already 40). Also abbot in c of St-Pierre, O Cist (Bourges) before episcopate. His elevation to Vienne was obviously due to uncle's and family's standing, and he subsequently played prominent role in church affairs under Henri IV. Candidate for red hat in 1602, he lost out to Du Perron and La Rochefoucauld, and was later dropped.

No date for nom. Provs 8–4–1598. Cons 27–12–1598. Took nephew, Pierre III, as coadj 1612. D. 18–1–1626.

Villars, Pierre III de. Vienne coadj 1612/26–62. B. 1588. Son of Claude, sgr de Condrieu, and Charlotte Gayant. Studied humanities at Tournon, completed philosophy at Agen (also with SJ) where uncle, Nicolas, was bp. Took some theology at La Flèche, but finished with doct in utr, univ unknown. Canon and archdeacon of Agen thanks to uncle, but a simple cleric at time of nom. Originally intended as successor to Agen, and was nom coadj in 1608, but Paul V postponed confirmation because he was underage. In 1612 Villars family changed tactics: Pierre got coadjutorship of Vienne instead, with Agen now secured for cousin, Claude Gélas.

Procuration from uncle, Jérôme, for Pierre as coadj 30–8–1612. Nom 8–10–1612. Provs 1–7–1613. Cons 29–7–1615. Succeeded 18–1–1626. Took nephew Henri as coadj 1653. D. 25–5–1662.

Villars, Henri de. Vienne coadj 1653/62–93. B. 1621. Son of Claude, baron of Condrieu, and Charlotte de Calvisson. Studied humanities and philosophy with SJ at Vienne, followed by theology (3 years at Sorbonne) and law in Paris, finishing with bacc (Sept 1652) and doct (early 1653) in canon law. Ordained priest in June 1651, when he was also made vg of Vienne, where he was both canon and *capiscol* of cathedral chapter. Abbot in c of Ispagnac, attended 1650 AC as deputy for Vienne province, elected *agent-général du clergé*, and served as secretary of 1655 AC. With such *états de service*, his claim on episcopal office was virtually irresistible.

Nom as coadj of Vienne 28-2-1653. Provs 30-8-1653. Cons 1655. Succeeded uncle 1662. D. 27-12-1693.

Sources: AD Rhône, Fonds Frécon, *Familles consulaires*, Villars doss. BN, MS lat 18345, fo 208r (ennoblement). Labande, *Avignon au xve siècle*, 268. Anselme, v. 101ff. Pallasse, *La Sénéchaussée et siège présidial de Lyon*. Barnavi, *Parti de Dieu*, 99–100 (family). AN, Z^{1}o 240 (ordination) (Jérôme). ASV, PC 13, fos 228–43. BAV, Barb lat 7963, fos 44–5; 7985, fo 10. (Pierre III). ASV, PC 53, fos 232–57. AAE 891, fo 270, letter from Claude Auvry re coadjutorship (Henri 1653).

Villazel, Etienne de. St-Brieuc 1631–41. One of only 2 Toulousains to hold episcopal office in Brittany in this period, Villazel was son of little-known family from the city, where his father was barrister in parlt, and possibly later pres in *Eaux et Forêts* admin. Other family members (?) served as city councillors at different times between 1610s and 1660s, but they were condemned as *faux nobles* (on grounds of *dérogeance*) under Louis XIV. Bp's mother was apparently from an established Toulouse family, though the Campistron name was common enough there.

B. ca 1592 Toulouse. Son of Louis and Marguerite de Campistron. Probably educated in Toulouse, where he took doct in theology, ca 1618. He owed early career primarily to Cospeau, bp of Aire, who administered Toulouse diocese in mid-1610s for uncons Abp La Valette-Epernon. Subsequently, Villazel may have worked with Cospeau at Aire, and certainly served him as *auditeur* for nearly 10 years after transfer to Nantes in 1621. Also close to Bérulle who had high opinion of him. Able preacher, later praised for mastery of short sermon, he became *prédicateur ordinaire* to Louis XIII ca 1624, no doubt thanks to Bérulle's and Cospeau's influence. Also succeeded an uncle (?) as abbot in c of St-Sever, OSB (Coutances) in 1630. His episcopal promotion was copybook example of *dévot* influence at work.

Nom 20-8-1631. Provs 10-11-1631. Cons 1-2-1632. D. 1-6-1641.

Sources: ASV, PC 28, fos 647–76, 888–96; PC 34, fo 369v. Acta Camerarii 16, fo 374v. *Corr de Bérulle*, i. 293–4. J-B. Noulleau, 'Le Modèle d'un grand evesque', in his *Diverses oeuvres* (Paris 1665). Chalande, *Rues de Toulouse*, i. 473, ii. 213. Frêche, *Toulouse et la région Midi-pyrénéen*, 373.

Villemontée, François III de. St-Malo 1659–70. One of longest-serving of Richelieu and Mazarin's provincial intendants and only man to become bp while wife was still alive, Villemontée was of Auvergnat stock. Grandfather moved to Paris in mid-16th C and became *procureur du roi* at the Châtelet. Bp's father inherited this office, but later became pres in *cour des aides*, and married sister of an *intendant des finances*. This incorporation into world of Parisian office-holding, which bp took a stage further, was powerfully assisted by growing network of family ties there (e.g. Verdun, Vigny, Hotman, Fortia), while several of these related families themselves produced bps in this period – Netz, Maupeou. The Villemontée family was 'maintenue noble' in Champagne 1666, with assistance of bp's papers.

Baptised at St-Merry church, Paris, 8–11–1598. Son of François, sgr de Montgaillard, and 1st wife Jeanne de Verdun. Nothing known of education, but took lic in utr. Although tonsured in 1605, steered towards secular career. *Cons* in parlt (1620), MR (1626), became intendant in Poitou (1631), and *cons d'état* (1635). Séguier and esp Le Tellier patronage was crucial to career during these decades when he was a busy *commissaire départi* in the provinces. Married Philipppe de la Barre, daughter of a *contrôleur* of king's *écurie* and *payeur des rentes* of *hôtel de ville*, by whom he had 3 children. Marriage was well-known fiasco: separated in 1638, and agreed years later to live in perpetual chastity. This allowed Villemontée to take orders. Quickly ordained priest, he continued to serve as intendant, esp in Picardy, during 1650s. Rome was reluctant to confirm a married (albeit formally separated) bp, and Mazarin was in no hurry to press for his provs, needing his political services.

Nom 20–5–1657 (after transfer of Neufville to Chartres). Provs 4–11–1659. Cons 29–6–1660. D. 19–10–1670.

Sources: ASV, PC 57, fos 1006–26; AN, Z^{1}o 241, P 726, no 496 (iv). Mousnier, *Lettres et mémoires au chancelier Séguier*, ii. 1227. Tallemant, *Historiettes*, ii. 165–6. Saulnier, 'Un prélat au xviie siècle, François de Villemontée évêque de Saint-Malo, sa femme et ses enfants', *Bulletin et Mémoires de la Société Archéologique de l'Ile-et-Vilaine*, 32 (1903), 107–38.

Villeneuve des Arcs, Modeste de. OFM Récollet. Apt 1629–70. The common ancestor of the 2 Villeneuve bps was a genuinely old noble family, possibly of Aragonese origin, but already present in 13th C Provence. Spawned numerous branches, whose marriages over the centuries (continuing in 17th C) ensured they were related to virtually every prominent family in the province – e.g. Grasse-Cabris, Bouliers, Brancas, Forbin-Soliers. Their ecclesiastical presence in Provence was possibly less visible, but included earlier bps of Cavaillon, Fréjus, Vence and Riez, and in every generation second-ranking clerics seem to have been a feature. Geographical dispersion of family's various branches also greatly facilitated access to office, ecclesiastical and otherwise, throughout Provence. The barons des Arcs, one of the older branches, were powerfully entrenched in Grasse region, where their attempts to grab some of the temporalities of Vence (not a well-endowed diocese) during wars of religion caused furore. Bp's father (who was nephew and heir of Bp Bouliers of Fréjus, d. 1591) was unusual in turning attention beyond Provence, and seems to have resided primarily at court or in Paris, where he m. daughter of duc d'Hallwin in 1588. Well regarded by Henri IV, he became a *chevalier du St-Esprit* shortly before his death in 1613.

B. and baptised under name of Florimond at St-André-des-Arts, Paris, 12–10–1600. Son of Arnaud, baron (later marquis) des Arcs, and Elisabeth Hallwin de Piennes. Nothing known of education, but early entry into Franciscan order of Récollets at Avignon, where he took the name of Modeste, would explain his not taking a degree.

Nom 28–2–1629. Provs 20–8–1629. Cons 25–11–1629. D. 7–1–1670.

Villeneuve-Thorenc, Scipion de. Grasse 1632–6. Exact contemporary of his cousin, the bp of Apt. Baptised 2–1–1600. Son of Claude, gov of St-Paul-les-Vence, and Delphine de Villeneuve des Arcs (sister of bp of Apt). Studied humanities at Avignon, and later theology with SJ there, but perhaps also in Paris and Rome. Took doct of theology at Avignon 6–10–1621. Tonsured in 1612, he was subdeacon before 1622, and ordained priest in early March 1624. Canon of Vence under Pierre du Vair, he was prior of Thorenc, and attended 1628 AC as deputy for Embrun province. Regarded by Peiresc as man of great learning, he had preached in Vence, Grasse and Fréjus before the episcopate.

Nom 12–6–1632. Provs 20–12–1632. Cons 8–5–1633. D. 3–5–1636.

Sources: Blanc, *Origines des familles provençales*, 581–91. E Tisserand, *La Famille de Romée de Villeneuve dit le Grand* (Nice 1866). Labande, *Avignon au xve siècle*, 43, 525 (family). AN, Y 130, fos 88v-90v, (c.m. of bp's parents 21–2–1588); MC, LXXIII, 287, 1–8–1615, *inventaire après décès* of bp's father. *Lettres missives de Henri IV*, ix. 20. BN, MS Baluze 59, fo 330; MS Fr 32589, p 257 (baptism). *Gallia Chr Nov*, i. 286–7 (Modeste). ASV, PC 31, fos 601–24. *Lettres de Peiresc*, vii. 587, n 1 (Scipion).

Villeroy. *See* **Neufville**

Villers la Faye, Cyrus. Périgueux 1653–65. This old Burgundian family (often incorrectly given name of Villiers or Villars) first appears in later 14th C in service of dukes of Burgundy as *gruyers, châtelains* and *baillis*. This fidelity/service ensured steady social ascension in the following generations, though their horizons seem to have remained firmly provincial. During Catholic League, bp's grandfather's allegiance was to Mayenne, gov of Burgundy, and although he seems to have been a figure of secondary importance, his shift towards Henri IV in 1594 was a sign League's cause there was beginning to crumble. Bp's own father was youngest of 3 sons.

B. ca 1619–20. Son of Hercule, baron de Villeneuve, and Anne de Chastenay. Nothing known of education, but credited in 1652 with 2 docts, one in theology, one in canon law! Succeeded Abp Gondi of Paris as music master of king's chapel to Louis XIII in 1632 (which must have been a sinecure, given his age), and became royal almoner in 1643. Priest ca 1645. Moved in exalted *dévot* circles around Anne of Austria, whose confidence he appears to have enjoyed. Joined *Compagnie du St-Sacrement* in 1644, and became trusted director of sister *Congrégation pour la propagation de la foi* from 1646. Preached in several Parisian churches, and before court. Abbot in c of Caumont, O Prem (Reims) and Jassin (name by which he was usually known) before the episcopate. Loyalty during Fronde made him candidate for episcopal office, and he was mentioned in connection with both Cahors and St-Pol-de-Léon before Périgueux was vacated by death of another *dévot*, Bp Brandon. As bp, was devoted servant of Cardinal Antonio Barberini, whose French interests he seems to have looked after.

Nom 28–8–1652. Provs 21–7–1653. Cons 31–8–1653. D. 4–10–1665.

Sources: AD Côte d'Or, E 2126–45; 37 F 38–40, 60–2, 65 (family papers). Marie-Thérèse Caron, *La Noblesse dans le duché de Bourgogne 1315–1477* (Lille 1987), 147–53. Drouot, *Mayenne et la Bourgogne*, ii. 237, 234 n3, 314 n4, 320. Chesnaye-Desbois, *Dict de noblesse*, xix. 818–22. ASV, PC 53, fos 193–208. BAV, Barb lat 7961, fos 15–40. *Annales de la Compagnie du Saint-Sacrement*, 107. Griselle, *Etat de la maison de Louis XIII*, no 54. Oroux, *Histoire ecclésiastique*, ii. 400.

Visdelou, François de. Quimper coadj 1651–62, Léon 1662–8. Family figured prominently among nobility of St-Brieuc diocese during later Middle Ages, and were designated 'nobles d'ancienne extraction' in the 1669 investigations. Bp's father supported Henri IV during League, for which he was imprisoned and his property confiscated by Mercoeur. In bp's generation, familiar pattern of Breton nobles following both robe and sword careers was in evidence, with one of his brother's becoming successively *cons* and pres in Rennes parlt.

B. 1615 (by his own account). Son of Gilles, sgr de la Goublaye, and Françoise de Quellenec. Educated firstly at La Flèche, where may have started theology, continuing in Paris under François Hallier. But took lic in utr. Priest ca 1642, he held several parishes, but unclear whether having 'governed' them means he actually served as *curé*. More prestigious activities beckoned: canon and *chantre* of Quimper cathedral, and served as vg of diocese. He may also have preached in Paris before Anne of Austria. Deputy to Breton Estates, which seconded his episcopal ambitions by petitioning for nom as coadj in June 1649. Active coadj of Quimper for 10 years, he then negotiated transfer to St-Pol-de-Léon before actually succeeding to Quimper, but conditions of the transfer caused some criticism and delayed confirmation by Rome for several years.

Procuration from Bp du Louet for Visdelou as coadj 4–5–1650. Nom 18–5–1650. Provs 27–2–1651. Cons 7–5–1651. Nom to St-Pol-de-Léon 12–1–1662. Provs 7–7–1665. D. 18–5–1668.

Sources: ASV, PC 48, fos 781–96; PC 51, fo 5v. Saulnier, *Parlement de Bretagne*, ii. 857–8. Carné, *Chevaliers bretons*, 423–4.

Yver. *See* **Hyver**

Zamet, Sebastien. Langres 1614–55. Famous as Henri IV's companion and favourite financier, bp's father was an immigrant from Piedmont, where b. ca 1547. Once in France service to Catherine de' Medici proved key to later success. Having also served Henri III, he became an important financier to Catholic League 1589–92, before turning towards Henri IV (to whom he led a League delegation) in 1593. From then he totally supported king, which enabled him to develop his financial activities as a major royal creditor (involved in tax farming since early 1580s). He did not marry Madeleine Le Clerc du Tremblay, relative of the Père Joseph, until 1598, several years after their children, bp included, were born. Career originally intended for the future bp may not have been clerical one (he was 16 when tonsured), and it may well be that Henri IV himself determined it in his last years.

B. 1587. Son of Sebastien and Madeleine Le Clerc du Tremblay. Educated partly at Henri IV's new coll at La Flèche, followed by theology with Gamaches at Sorbonne, where he took bacc in theology 1608, but not full lic or doct, since not *in sacris*. Elected a *socius* of Sorbonne in 1609. Tonsured on 20–8–1603, he had succeeded a murdered uncle as abbot in c of Juilly, OSA (Meaux) in 1591, aged 4. By 1608, Henri IV was pressing Cardinal Givry to resign as coadj of Langres in order to promote young Zamet. Nothing finalised before king's death, but Marie de' Medici continued her husband's patronage.

Procuration from bp of Langres to take Zamet as coadj 21–10–1612. Nom on same date, renewed 10–11–1614 (Escars had since d., hence coadjutorship redundant). Provs 8–11–1614. Cons 18–6–1615. D. 2–2–1655.

Sources: ASV, PC 13, fos 368–94. AN, Z^{1}o 241 (tonsure). BN, MS lat 15440, p 139. *Lettres missives de Henri IV*, vii. 863. Prunel, *Sébastien Zamet, DGS*, 1628.

Individuals not Included in the Biographical Dictionary

Bellenger, Gérard: provs to Fréjus, Dec 1592, but never succeeded in entering diocese. D. 27-1-1597

Benoist, René: nom to Troyes by Henri IV in 1593, but never succeeded in obtaining provs; resigned his claim in 1604.

Coëffetau, Nicolas: nom to Marseille on 22-8-1621, but only 3 months before his death he was still describing himself as 'évêque nommé de Marseille'. His papal provs, dated Aug 1621, appear not to have been despatched ('expedited') from Rome, and he d. on 21 Apr 1623.

Dinet, Pierre: provs as coadj of Mâcon, Aug 1616, but he d., uncons it seems, in Jan 1618.

Dori-Galigaï, Simon: obtained provs to Tours 19 Dec 1616, but resigned it precipitately, without taking possession, in Apr 1617 after fall of Concini, his brother-in-law.

Gault, Eustache: papal provs to Marseille, 30 Jan 1640, but he d. of plague 13 Mar 1640.

Hennequin, Dreux: confirmed as coadj of Soissons, 30 Jan 1612. Resigned, uncons, in 1619, refusing succession to his uncle there.

Le Blanc, Guillaume: provs to Coutances 21 June 1621, but d. 4 months later in Agen, where he was a canon.

Lesley, John: provs to Coutances, Dec 1592, but unable to take possession; after collapse of the League, he was exiled to Brussels, where he d. in Dec. 1596.

Munier, Jean: nom to Noyon by Mayenne, mid-1593; papal provs 14 Feb 1594, but he d. 9 July 1594, not have taking possession of the see.

Polverel, Pierre: provs to Alet Feb 1603, but he d. 5 months later.

Ribier, Jacques: provs as coadj of Vence 23 June 1636, but never cons; resigned his claim on death of his uncle, Pierre du Vair, in June 1638.

Savoie-Nemours, Henri de: nom to Reims, initially as coadj to Léonor d'Etampes, 1650, then as his successor, 1651. But no evidence of papal provs or actual possession of Reims. Resigned after becoming duc de Nemours, ca 1657.

Touchard, Jean: nom to Meaux 1595 or early 1596; provs dated 28 July 1597. But he did not take possession of this hotly disputed see, and he d., uncons, date unknown.

BIBLIOGRAPHY

Manuscript sources

Paris

Archives des Affaires Etrangères (AAE)

Mémoires et Documents, France (France), 771–80, 830–52, 874–6, 885–98, 1504–7, 1632–4.
Correspondance Politique (CP), Rome, 12, 18–19, 23, 40, 63, 81, 83.

Archives Nationales (AN)

E 435.
G^8 87, G^{8*} 653.
L 728.
Marine B/4, vol 1
Minutier Central (MC), VI, 309, 431–3; VIII 408–23, 564; XII, 33–40; XXIV, 296; XXXIX, 143; LIV, 457, 465–6; LXXIII, 358; LXXVIII, 135, 207, 221; LXXXVI 184, 195, 215; LXXXVIII, 1312; XCI, 313, XCVI 48; CX, 124.[1]
P 725 vols i-ii, P 726, vols i-iii.
V^5 153, 1227–8.
V^6, 7, 12, 170, 263, 1175, 1171, 1177–80.
Z^1o 239–41.

Bibliothèque Nationale (BN)

Baluze 175–7, 252, 327, 331, 333.
Cabinet des titres; sub-series: Pièces originales, Dossiers bleus, Cabinet d'Hozier, Carrés d'Hozier.[2]
500 Colbert, 6, 98, 157, 180, 278, 353.
Clairambault 368, 377.
Dupuy 212.
Français (Fr) 3430, 3484, 3487–8, 3496–8, 3540–2, 3589, 3666–80, 3790–3, 4139, 4209, 4222, 4328, 6379, 6892, 7854, 10839, 15610–11, 15518, 15699, 15720, 15897, 17362–4, 17588, 18001–20, 18328, 20661–3, 20737–9, 23039, 23200, 25025–6, 32587–9, 32989, 33047.

[1] This list is incomplete, and does not account for random documents found in other *études* of the Minutier Central.
[2] I consulted dozens of volumes in each of these sub-series, and the relevant references, most of which refer to single families or individuals, can be found in the biographical dictionary.

Italien 1269.
Latin (lat), 9153–6, 9953–8, 15440, 16573, 17021–9, 18384.
Morel de Thoisy, 207, 229.
Nouvelles acquisitions françaises (Naf). 460, 188–56, 5116, 11854–6.

Bibliothèque de l'Arsénal, MS 4207.
Bibliothèque de l'Institut (BI), MS 1354. Collection Godefroy, MS 15, 269, 320.
Bibliothèque Mazarine, MS 3246.
Bibliothèque Sainte-Geneviève, MS 3238, 3249.

Provinces

Archives Départementales (AD)

Allier, 5J 2184, 3555.
Alpes de Haute-Provence, 2G 9, E 1550.
Alpes-Maritimes, G 11.
Aube, G 326–30, 462–3.
Averyon, G 79–80, 191, 195, 201, 497, 1023; 15J 1–2, 13.
Bouches-du-Rhône, B 3339; 5 G 611, 616, 683–6, 693.
Côtes d'Armor, 1 G 386–91, 403–10; 5 G 518–22, 562.
Côte d'Or, 37F 23, 34, 37–42, 60–5.
Gironde, 1 B 16. 3 B *insins*, 1607. C 3803, 3807. G 244–5, 249–57, 259–60, 754, 789–95, 796–8, 803, 805, 924.
Haute-Garonne, B 203, 1909, 1972. E 292–5. 1 G 280, 380–7, 391–6, 718, 726, 728. 6 J 43–4, 46, 61.
Haute-Loire, G 22–3, 106–10, 112–13, 775–7.
Haute-Savoie, E399, 459.
Hautes-Alpes, 1 E 1493.
Hérault, I E vols 96, 1470–4; II E 39, vol 1002, II E 40, vol 82; G 3, 363, 609.
Ile-et-Vilaine, G 54, 5 Fa 27.
Lot, B 1299, B 1334. F 492.
Lozère G 45, 57, 59–60, 651–2, 2169, 3031–4.
Marne, G 22, 51–2, 252–3, 306–45. 2 G 32–2, 161–2, 166.
Morbihan, 52 G 7.
Nièvre 1G 3, 18. 2F 29–30. 3E1, vols 369, 371, 697.
Oise G 618, 637, 695. H 7111, 7114.
Puy-de-Dôme 1 G 153, 175, 1772–5.
Pyrénées Atlantiques, E1284, 1309, 2J 195.
Rhône 1 G 290, 10 G 1458. Fonds Frécon, *dossiers rouges*, 2, 6.
Seine-et-Marne, B 516, 602. 6155 Mi 6200.
Saône-et-Loire, F 565, G 87, 431, G 465.
Tarn, G 264–5.
Tarn-et-Garonne, G 47.
Yonne G 2, 177, 452, 1630.

Carpentras, Musée Imguimbertine, MS 1362.
Chantilly, Archives du château: Series L, vols xxvi, xviii xxxxiii-ix, xxxi, xxxviii, xlv, lxiii, xcvii.
Coutances, Archives du diocèse de Coutances, M 41. Unnumbered file on the episcopal temporalities, 1497–1693.
Toulouse, Archives municipales, GG 193; Bibliothèque municipale, MS 612.

Rome

Archivio Segreto Vaticano (ASV)

Acta Camerarii 14–18, 53, 95–8.
Fondo Borghese, Series I, 80, 462–8, 636, 646, 896, 907. Series II, 248–50, 406, 474. Series III, 8a, 73, 86b, 127e.
Fondo Pio 88.
Lettere de Vescovi 19, 25.
Misc Arm, I, 28; XII, 144–6, 214–16; XLV, 2.
Nunziatura di Francia (N Fr), 32–6, 42–3, 65–7, 88–9, 93, 95, 97, 99, 101, 102, 104, 107–10a, 112–16, 119, 406.
Processus Consistoriales (PC), 7, 11, 13, 16–18, 21–2, 24–8, 30–4, 36–8, 40, 42–59.
Processus Datariae, 1, 3–4, 6–8, 11, 24, 26, 37.
Rota Romana, Processus in admissione Auditorum, vol 1.

Biblioteca Apostolica Vaticana (BAV)

Barberini latini (Barb lat), 5287, 7938–47, 7953, 7955–61, 7985, 8021, 8054–64, 8217–20, 8126–31, 8683–5, 9684.

Corsini Library, MS 713.

Others

Ferrara, Archivio di Stato, Fondo Bentivoglio 18, vols 12–13.
London, British Library, MS Add 8721, 8730, 21434 .

Primary Printed Sources

Acta Nuntiaturae Gallicae, eds Jean Lestocqouy, Pierre Blet *et alii* (Rome 1961 – in progress).
Archives Historiques de la Gironde, 58 vols (Bordeaux 1859–1932).
Cartulaire et archives des communes de l'ancien diocèse et de l'arrondissement administratif de Carcassonne, ed A Mahul (Paris 1867).
Chronique d'Etienne Cruseau, 2 vols (Bordeaux 1879–81).
Chronique de Jean Tarde, ed Gaston de Gérard (Paris 1887).
Collection des procès-verbaux des assemblées générales du clergé de France, ed A Duranthon, 9 vols (Paris 1767–8).
Correspondance de Pierre de Bérulle, ed Jean Dagens, 3 vols (Louvain 1937–9)
Correspondance de Fénélon, vol i: L'Abbé de Fénélon, sa famille, ses débuts, ed Jean Orcibal (Paris 1972).
Correspondance de Mayenne, ed E Henry and C Loriquet (*Travaux de l'Académie Impériale de Reims*, vols 29, 33, 35) (Reims 1860–3).
'Correspondance inédite du maréchal de Gramont et de Hugues de Lionne (Sept-Dec 1650)', ed Henri Courteault, *Annuaire de la Société de l'Histoire de France* (1925), 225–90.
Correspondants de Pieresc, ed P Tamizey de Larroque 10 fascicutes (Paris 1885).
De Paul, Vincent, *Correspondance, Entretiens, Documents*, ed Pierre Coste, 14 vols (Paris 1922–5).
'Documents pontificaux sur l'évêché de Conserans, 1425–1619', ed C Douais, *Revue de Gascogne*, 27 (1888), 349–57, 439–62.
Dubuisson-Aubenay, Antoine, *Journal des guerres civiles, 1648–1652*, ed Gustave Saige, 2 vols (Paris 1883–5).
Etat de la maison du roi Louis XIII, de celles de sa mère, Marie de Médicis; de ses soeurs Chrestienne, Elisabeth et Henriette de France; de son frère, Gaston d'Orléans; de sa femme, Anne d'Autriche; de ses

fils, le Dauphin (Louis XIV) et Philippe d'Orléans, comprenant les années 1601 à 1665, ed Eugène Griselle (Paris 1912).

Die Hauptinstruktionen Clemens' VIII für die Nuntien und Legaten an die europäischen Fürstenhofen 1592–1605, ed Klaus Jaitner, 2 vols (Tübingen 1984).

Humanisme et politique. Lettres romaines de Christophe Dupuy à ses frères 1636–45, ed P J and K P Wolfe (Tübingen 1988).

Isambert, François *et al*, *Recueil général des anciennes lois françaises*, 29 vols (Paris 1821–33).

Journal de Pierre de L'Estoile pour le règne de Henri IV, ed L-R Lefèvre, 2 vols (Paris 1948–58).

L'Intendance de Champagne à la fin du xviie siècle (Edition critique des mémoires 'pour l'instruction du duc de Bourgogne'), ed J P Brancourt (Paris 1983).

La Bretagne en 1665 d'après le rapport de Colbert de Croissy, ed Jean Kerhervé, François Roudaut and Jean Tanguy (Brest 1978).

La Noue, François de, *Discours politiques et militaires*, ed F E Sutcliffe (Geneva 1967).

Lefebvre d'Ormesson, Olivier, *Journal*, ed Adolphe Chéruel, 2 vols (Paris 1860–1).

Lettres de Catherine de Médici, ed H de la Ferrière and G Baguenault de la Puchesse, 11 vols (Paris 1880–1909).

Lettres de Henri III, ed Michel François, 4 vols (Paris 1972 – in progress).

Lettres de Henri IV concernant les relations du Saint-Siège et de la France, ed Bernard Barbiche (Vatican City 1968).

Lettres de Jean Chapelain, ed Philippe Tamizey de Larroque, 2 vols (Paris 1880–3).

Lettres de la main de Louis XIII, ed E Griselle, 2 vols (Paris 1914).

Lettres de Peiresc, ed Philippe Tamizey de Larroque, 8 vols (Paris 1888–98).

Lettres du cardinal d'Ossat, ed Amelot de la Houssaye, 5 vols (Amsterdam 1718).

Lettres du cardinal Mazarin à la reine, la princesse palatine etc, écrites pendant sa retraite hors de la France en 1651 et 1652, ed Jules Ravenel (Paris 1836).

Lettres du cardinal Mazarin pendant son ministère, ed A Chéruel and G d'Avenel, 9 vols (Paris 1872–1906).

Lettres et mémoires adressés au chancelier Séguier, ed Roland Mousnier, 2 vols (Paris 1964).

Lettres inédites de Henri IV à M de Béthune (1601–05), 8 vols, ed E Halphen (Paris 1889–1901).

Lettres inédites de Henri IV à M de Béthune ambassadeur de France à Rome (8 avril au 29 décembre 1603), ed E Halphen (Paris 1897).

Lettres inédites de Pierre de Marca au chancelier Séguier, ed. P Tamizey de Larroque (Paris 1881).

'Lettres inédites du cardinal d'Ossat', ed P Tamizey de Larroque, *Revue de Gascogne* 13 (1872), 126–37, 287–90, 340–2.

Lettres inédites du roi Henri IV au chancelier de Bellièvre du 8 février 1581 au 23 septembre 1601, ed E Halphen (Paris 1872).

'Lettres inédites de Hugues de Lionne', ed Ulysse Chevallier, *Bulletin de la Société d'Archéologie et de Statistique de la Drôme* 11 (1877), 272–306, 382–402; 12 (1878), 5–30, 105–38, 254–87, 313–44.

Lettres, instructions diplomatiques et papiers d'état de Richelieu, ed D L M Avenel, 8 vols (Paris 1853–76).

Lettres, instructions et mémoires de Jean-Baptiste, Colbert, ed Pierre Clément, 10 vols (Paris 1861–82).

'Lettres originales de Henri IV à Clement VIII', ed Bernard Barbiche, in *Miscellanea in onore di Monsignore Martino Giusti* (Vatican City 1978), i. 35–72.

Lists and Analyses of State Papers, Foreign, 1590–91, ed R B Wernham (London 1969).

Lists and Analysis of State Papers, Foreign, 1593–4, ed R B Wernham (London 1989).

Mémoires de Jacques Gaches, ed Charles Pradel (Paris 1879).

Mémoires de Philippe Gourreau de la Proustière, ed Béatrix de Buffevent (Paris 1990).

Mémoires des intendants pour le duc de Bourgogne: la généralité de Paris, ed A M de Boislisle (Paris 1881).

Mémoires du clergé, ou recueil des actes, titres et mémoires concernant les affaires du clergé de France, 15 vols (Paris, 1771).

Monluc, Blaise de, *Commentaires*, ed P Courteault (Paris 1964).
La Nunziatura de Francia de Giudi di Bentivoglio, ed Luigi di Steffani, 4 vols (Florence 1863–70).
Oeuvres complètes de Saint François de Sales (Annecy edition), 27 vols (Annecy 1892–1964).
Palma-Cayet, Pierre Victor, *Chronologie novénaire* (*Choix de chroniques et mémoires sur l'histoire de France*), 2 vols (Paris 1836).
Les Papiers de Richelieu (*Politique intérieure: Correspondance et papiers d'état*), ed Pierre Grillon, 6 vols (Paris 1975 - in progress).
Procès-verbaux des Etats-généraux de 1593, ed A Bernard (Paris 1842).
Recueil de lettres du Révérendissime Père Dom B Ruade Chartreux Evesque de Conserans touchant sa promotion à sondit Evesché (Paris 1623).
Recueil de lettres missives de Henri IV, ed X Berger de Xivrey and J Guadet, 9 vols (Paris 1843–76).
Recueil des instructions générales aux nonces ordinaires de France de 1624 à 1634, ed Auguste Leman, (Lille 1920).
Retz, François-Paul de Gondi, cardinal de, *Oeuvres*, ed Marie-Thérèse Hipp and Michel Pernot (Paris 1984).
Richelieu, Armand-Jean du Plessis de, *Testament Politique*, ed Françoise Hildesheimer (Paris 1995).
Séguier, Jeanne de Jésus, *Lettres à son frère chancelier de France (1643–1668)*, ed Bernard Hours (Lyon 1992).
Solminihac, Alain de, *Lettres et documents*, ed Eugène Sol (Cahors 1930).
Sully, Maximilien de Béthune, duc de, *Les Oeconomies royales*, ed D Buisseret and B Barbiche, 2 vols (Paris 1970–88)
Tallemant des Réaux, Gédéon, *Historiettes*, ed Antoine Adam, 2 vols (Paris 1960–1).

Reference Works, Dictionaries, etc

Anselme de Sainte-Marie, le Père, *Histoire généalogique et chronologique de la maison royale de France et des grands officiers de la Couronne*, 9 vols (Paris 1726–30).
Armorial de Béarn, ed A de Dufau de Maluquer, 2 vols (Pau 1893).
Barrau, Hippolyte de, *Documents historiques et généalogiques sur les familles et les hommes remarquables du Rouergue*, 4 vols (Rodez 1853–60).
Beauchet-Filleau, H, *Dictionnaire historique et généalogique des familles du Poitou*, 2nd ed, 3 vols (Poitiers 1891–1915).
Beaumont, Charles de, *Pièces inédites tirées des archives de la maison de Miossens-Sansons* (Pau 1885). [Originally published in *Bulletin de la Société des Sciences, Lettres et Arts de Pau*, 2 ser, 24 (1894–5)].
Blanc, François-Paul, *Les Origines des familles provençales maintenues dans le second ordre sous le règne de Louis XIV. Dictionnaire généalogique* (Thesis, Aix-en-Provence 1971).
Blanchart, François, *Les Eloges de tous les premiers présidents du parlement de Paris depuis qu'il a esté rendu sedentaire ensemble leurs généalogies, épitaphes armes et blazons en taille douce* (Paris, 1645).
Bluche, François, *L'Origine des magistrats du parlement de Paris au xviiie siècle. Dictionnaire généalogique* (Paris 1956).
Borricand, René de, *Nobiliaire de Provence*, 3 vols (Aix-en-Provence 1974–9).
Bourousse de Laffore, Jules, and O'Gilvy, Gabriel, *Nobiliaire de Guyenne et de Gascogne*, 4 vols (Bordeaux-Paris 1856–83).
Carné, Gaston de, *Les Chevaliers bretons de Saint-Michel* (Nantes 1884).
Clapiers-Coulonges, Balthazar, *Chronologie des officiers de cours souveraines*, ed marquis de Boisgelin (Aix 1909–12).
Clergeac, Adrien, *Chronologie des archevêques, évêques et abbés de l'ancienne province ecclésiastique d'Auch et des diocèses de Condom et de Lombez* (Paris 1912).
Dainville, François de, *Cartes anciennes de l'église de France* (Paris 1956).

Dictionnaire de biographie française, ed Roman d'Amat *et al*, (Paris, 1934 – in progress).
Dictionnaire de droit canonique, ed R Naz, 7 vols (Paris 1936–65).
Dictionnaire d'histoire et de géographie ecclésiastiques, ed A de Meyer *et al* (Paris, 1912 – in progress).
Dictionnaire de la noblesse, ed F Aubert de La Chesnaye-Desbois and Badier, 3rd ed, 19 vols (Paris 1866–76).
Dictionnaire du grand siècle, ed François Bluche (Paris 1992).
Dictionnaire historique, topographique et biographique de la Mayenne, ed A Angot and F Gaugain, 4 vols (Laval 1900–10).
Dictionnaire historique, géographique, et biographique du Maine-et-Loire, ed Célestin Port, 3 vols (Paris and Angers 1874–8).
Dizionario biografico degli Italiani (Rome 1960 – in progress).
Durand de Maillane, Pierre-Toussaint, *Dictionnaire de droit canonique et de pratique bénéficiale* (Lyon 1770).
Encylopédie départementale des Bouches-du-Rhône, vol 4, ii: *Dictionnaire biographique*, ed Raoul Busquet (Paris-Marseille 1931).
Farge, J K, *Biographical Register of Paris Doctors of Theology 1500–1536* (Toronto 1980).
Frondeville, Henri de, *Les Conseillers du parlement de Normandie au xvie siècle 1499–1594* (Rouen and Paris 1960).
————, *Les Conseillers du parlement de Normandie sous Henri IV et Louis XIII* (Rouen and Paris 1964).
————, *Les Présidents du parlement de Normandie 1494–1790* (Rouen 1953).
Gallia Christiana, ed Denis de Sainte-Marthe *et al*, 16 vols (Paris 1715–1865).
Gallia Christiana Novissima, ed Joseph Albanès, 7 vols (Valence 1899–1920).
Gams, P B, *Series Episcoporum Ecclesiae Catholicae* (Ratisbon 1873).
Gatz, Erwin, ed, *Die Bischöfe des Heiligen Römischen Reiches 1648 bis 1803. Ein biographisches Lexikon* (Berlin 1990).
Godet de Soudé, François de, *Dictionnaire des anoblissements. Extrait des registres de la Chambre des Comptes depuis 1345 jusqu'en 1660*, ed E de Barthélemy (Paris 1875).
Haag, Eugène and Emile, *La France protestante*, 10 vols (Paris 1846–59).
Hierarchia Catholica medii et recentioris aevi, ed Conrad Eubel *et al*, vols 3–5 (Munich 1923–52).
Hommages rendus à la chambre de France. Chambre des comptes de Paris. Série P (xive-xvie siècles), ed L Mirot and J-P Babelon, 3 vols (1932–85).
Inventaire des arrêts du conseil privé, règnes de Henri III et de Henri IV, ed François Dumont, 5 vols (Paris 1969–78).
Lacger, L de, *Etats administratifs des anciens diocèses d'Albi, de Castres et de Lavaur* (Albi and Paris 1921).
Lapeyre, André, and Scheurer, Rémy, *Les Notaires et secrétaires du roi sous les règnes de Louis XI, Charles VIII et Louis XII (1461–1515)* (Paris 1978).
Navelle, André, *Familles nobles et notables du midi toulousain au xve et au xvie siècles*, 11 vols (Fenouillet 1991–5).
Nouveaux hommages rendus à la chambre de France. Chambre des comptes de Paris. Série P (xviie-xviiie siècles), ed L Mirot and J-P Babelon, 2 vols (Paris 1988–9).
Rivoire de la Batie, G de, *Armorial de Dauphiné* (Lyon 1867).
Saulnier, Frédéric, *Le Parlement de Bretagne 1551–1790. Répertoire alphabétique et biographique de tous les membres de la cour*, 2 vols (Rennes 1909).
Tessereau, Abraham, *Histoire chronologique de la grande chancellerie de France*, 2 vols (Paris 1710).
Trani, Camille, 'Les Conseillers du grand conseil au xvie siècle (1547–1610)', *Paris et l'Ile-de-France: Mémoires*, 42 (1991), 61–218.
Valois, Noël, ed, *Inventaire des arrêts du conseil d'état (règne de Henri IV)*, 2 vols (Paris 1886–93).
Vidal, Jean-Marie, *Catalogues épiscopaux et listes de bénéfices des anciens diocèses ariégois* (Foix 1933).
Villain, Jean, *La France moderne*, 3 vols (St Etienne-Montpellier 1906–13).
Villenaut, A de, *Nobiliaire de Nivernois*, 2 vols (Nevers 1900).

Vindry, Fleury, *Les Ambassadeurs permanents français au xvie siècle* (Paris 1903).
——, *Dictionnaire de l'état-major français au xvie siècle. Vol 1: la gendarmerie* (Paris 1901).
——, *Les Parlementaires français au xvie siècle*, 2 vols (Paris 1909–12).

Secondary Studies

Alberigo, Giusseppe, 'Carlo Borromeo come modello di vescovo nella chiesa post-tridentina', *Rivista Storica Italiana* 79 (1967), 1031–52.
——, 'L'Episcopato nel cattolicesimo post-tridentino', *Cristianesimo nella Storia*, 6 (1985), 71–91.
Albert, M, *Histoire géographique, naturelle, ecclésiastique et civile du diocèse d'Embrun* (n.p. 1783).
Allègre, A, *Monographie de Baumes de Venise* (Carpentras 1888).
René de Voyer d'Argenson, *Annales de la Compagnie du Saint-Sacrement*, ed H Beauchet-Filleau (Paris 1900).
Aston, Nigel, *The End of an Elite. The French Bishops and the Coming of the Revolution 1786–90* (Oxford 1992).
Audollent, G, *La Création de l'archévêché de Paris* (Paris 1922).
Aulagne, J, *La Réforme catholique du xviie siècle dans le diocèse de Limoges* (Paris 1905)
Azéma, Xavier, *Un Prélat janéniste. Louis Foucquet évêque et comte d'Agde 1656–1702* (Paris 1963).
Barbiche, Bernard, 'L'Influence française à la cour pontificale sous Henri IV', *Mélanges d'Histoire et d'Archéologie de l'Ecole Française de Rome*, 77 (1965), 277–99.
Barnavi, Eli, *Le Parti de Dieu. Etude sociale et politique des chefs de la Ligue parisienne* (Louvain 1980).
Barrio Gozalo, Maximiliano, 'Perfil socio-económico de una élite de poder: les obispos de Castilla la Vieja, Leon, Galicia, etc, 1600–1840', *Anthologica Annua*, 28–9 (1981–2), 71–138; 30–1 (1983–4), 209–91; 32 (1985), 11–107; 33 (1986), 159–302; 34 (1987), 11–188; 38 (1991), 43–106.
Batterel, Louis, *Mémoires domestiques pour servir à l'histoire de l'Oratoire*, ed A-M-P Ingold, 5 vols (Paris 1902–4).
Baumgartner, Frederic J, 'The Case for Charles X', *Sixteenth-Century Journal*, 4 (1973), 87–98.
——, 'Crisis in the French Episcopacy: The Bishops and the Succession of Henry IV', *Archiv für Reformationsgeschichte*, 70 (1979), 279–301.
——, 'Renaud de Beaune, Politique Prelate', *Sixteenth-Century Journal*, 9 (1978), 99–109.
——, 'Humanism and Heterodoxy in the French Episcopacy under Francis I', *Proceedings of the Western Society for French History*, 8 (1980), 57–68.
——, *Change and Continuity in the French Episcopate: The Bishops and the Wars of Religion 1547–1610* (Durham, North Carolina 1986).
Beik, William, *Absolutism and Society in Seventeenth-Century France* (Cambridge 1984).
——, 'The Parlement of Toulouse and the Fronde' in Mack P Holt, ed, *Society and Institutions in Early Modern France* (Athens, Georgia and London 1991), 132–52.
Bell, David A, *Lawyers and Citizens. The Making of a Political Elite in Old Régime France* (New York and Oxford 1994).
Belleau-Dessalles, E, *Les Evêques italiens de l'ancien diocèse de Béziers (1547–1669)* (Toulouse and Paris 1901).
Bergin, Joseph, 'The Decline and Fall of the House of Guise as an Ecclesiastical Dynasty', *Historical Journal*, 25 (1982), 781–803.
——, 'The Guises and their Benefices 1588–1641', *English Historical Review*, 99 (1984), 34–58.
——, *Cardinal de La Rochefoucauld. Leadership and Reform in the French Church* (New Haven and London 1987).
——, *Cardinal Richelieu. Power and the Pursuit of Wealth* (New Haven and London 1985).
——, 'Mazarin and his Benefices', *French History*, 1 (1987), 1–26.

———, *The Rise of Richelieu* (New Haven and London 1991).

———, 'Richelieu and his bishops? Ministerial Power and Ecclesiastical Patronage under Louis XIII', in Joseph Bergin and Laurence Brockliss, eds, *Richelieu and his Age* (Oxford 1992), 175–202.

Bernhard, Jean, Lefebvre, Charles, Rapp, Francis, *L'Epoque de la Réforme et du concile de Trente* (Histoire du droit et des institutions de l'église en Occident, xiv) (Paris 1989).

Berthelot du Chesnay, Charles, *Les Missions de Saint Jean Eudes* (Paris 1967).

Bertrand, A L, *La Vie de Messire Henry de Béthune archevêque de Bordeaux 1604–1680*, 2 vols (Paris and Bordeaux 1902).

Beyssac, Jean, *Corévêques, suffragants et auxiliaires de Lyon* (Montbrison 1910).

———, *Les Chanoines de l'église de Lyon* (Lyon 1914).

Bien, David D, 'Manufacturing Nobles: The Chancelleries in France to 1789', *Journal of Modern History*, 61 (1989), 445–86.

Blet, Pierre, *Le Clergé de France et la monarchie. Etude sur les assemblées du clergé de 1615 à 1666*, 2 vols (Rome 1959).

———, *Les Assemblées du clergé et Louis XIV de 1670 à 1693* (Rome 1972).

———, 'Le Concordat de Bologne et la réforme tridentine', *Gregorianum* 45 (1964), 241–79.

———, 'Fidèle au pape, fidèle au roi', in Yves Durand, ed *Hommage à Roland Mousnier. Clientèles et fidélités dans l'Europe moderne* (Paris 1981), 315–32.

———, 'Vincent de Paul et l'épiscopat français', in *Vincent de Paul. Actes du colloque international d'études vincentiennes* (Rome 1983), 81–114.

———, 'L'Idée de l'épiscopat chez les évêques français du xviie siècle', in *L'Institution de les pouvoirs dans les églises de l'antiquité à nos jours*, ed Bernard Vogler (Louvain 1987), 311–23.

———, 'Louis XIV et les papes aux prises avec le jansénisme', *Archivum Historiae Pontificiae*, 31 (1993), 109–92; 32 (1994), 65–148.

———, *Le Clergé du grand siècle en ses assemblées 1615–1715* (Paris 1995).

Bluche, François, *Les Magistrats du parlement de Paris au xviiie siècle* (Paris 1960).

——— and Durye, Pierre, *L'Anoblissement par charges avant 1789* (Les Cahiers Nobles, vols 23–4, 1962).

Boase, Alan, *Vie de Jean de Sponde* (Geneva 1977).

Bondois, Paul M, *Le Maréchal de Bassompierre* (Paris 1925).

Bonnenfant, G, *Histoire générale du diocèse d'Evreux*, 2 vols (Paris 1933).

Bonney, Richard, *Political Change in France under Richelieu and Mazarin 1624–1661* (Oxford 1978).

———, *The King's Debts. Politics and Finance in France 1589–1661* (Oxford 1981).

———, 'Mazarin and the Great Nobility during the Fronde', *English Historical Review*, 96 (1981), 818–33.

Bonnot, Isabelle, *Hérétique ou saint? Henry Arnauld évêque janséniste d'Angers au xviie siècle* (Paris 1983).

Bossy, John, *The English Catholic Community 1570–1850* (London, 1975).

Boucher, Jacqueline, 'L'Evolution de la maison du roi: des derniers Valois aux premiers Bourbons', *XVII Siècle*, 136 (1982), 359–79.

Bourquin, Laurent, *Noblesse seconde et pouvoir en Champagne aux xvie et xviie siècles* (Paris 1994).

Boyer de Sainte-Marthe, L.-A., *Histoire de l'église cathédrale de Saint-Paul-Trois-Châteaux avec une chronologie de tous les évêques qui l'ont gouverné* (Avignon 1710).

Briggs, Robin 'Richelieu and Reform', in Joseph Bergin and Laurence Brockliss, eds, *Richelieu and his Age*, (Oxford 1992), 71–97

Brockliss, LWB, 'Patterns of Attendance at the University of Paris 1400–1800' *Historical Journal* 21 (1978), 503–44 [revised version in *Histoire sociale des populations étudiantes*, vol ii, ed Dominique Julia and Jacques Revel (Paris 1989), 487–526].

———, *French Higher Education in the Seventeenth and Eighteenth Centuries. A Cultural History* (Oxford 1987).

———, 'Richelieu, Education and the State', in Joseph Bergin and Laurence Brockliss, eds, *Richelieu and his Age* (Oxford 1992), 237–72
Broutin, Paul, *La Réforme pastorale en France au xviie siècle: Recherches sur la tradition pastorale après le Concile de Trente*, 2 vols (Tournai 1956).
Bush, M L, ed, *Social Classes and Social Orders in Europe since 1500* (London 1992).
Callahan, William J, *Church, Politics and Society in Spain, 1750–1874* (Cambridge, Mass 1984).
Caneto, F, 'Souvenirs relatifs au siège d'Auch', *Revue de Gascogne*, 15 (1874), 341–61.
Caron, Marie-Thérèse, *La Noblesse dans le duché de Bourgogne 1315–1477* (Lille 1987).
Carrier, Hubert, *Les Mazarinades*, 2 vols (Geneva 1989–91).
Carrière, Victor, 'Les Epreuves de l'église de France au xvie siècle', in Carrière, Victor *et al.*, *Introduction aux études d'histoire ecclésiastique locale*, 3 vols (Paris 1936).
Catta, E, 'Les Evêques de Nantes des débuts du xvie siècle au lendemain du concile de Trente (1500–1617)', *Revue d'Histoire de l'Eglise de France*, 51 (1965), 23–70.
Cauchie, Maurice, *Documents pour servir à l'histoire littéraire du xviie siècle* (Paris 1924).
Chadwick, Owen, *The Popes and the European Revolution* (Oxford 1981).
Chalande, Jules, *Histoire des rues de Toulouse* (Toulouse 1919).
Charmeil, Jean-Paul, *Les Trésoriers de France à l'époque de la Fronde* (Paris 1964).
Charvin, G, 'Colbert intendant des abbayes de Mazarin', *Revue Mabillon*, 36 (1946), 15–47, 87–119.
Châtellier, Louis, 'Société et bénéfices ecclésiastiques 1670–1730', *Revue Historique*, 224 (1970), 75–98.
Chaussinand-Nogaret, Guy, ed, *Histoire des élites en France, du xvie au xxe siècle* (Paris 1991).
Chaussy, Yves, *Les Bénédictins anglais réfugiés en France au xviie siècle (1611–1669)* (Paris 1967).
Cherest, Gilbert, *L'Evêque de la paix. Félix Vialart de Herse, évêque et comte de Châlons-sur-Marne, pair de France* (*Mémoires de la Société d'Agriculture, Commerce, Science et Arts de la Marne*, 1970–6).
Chevallier, Ulysse, 'Notice historique sur la famille de Lionne', *Bulletin de la Société d'Archéologie et de Statistique de la Drôme*, 11 (1877), 51–73, 172–202.
Christ, Günter, 'Selbstverständnis und Rolle der Domkapitel in der geistlichen Territorien des alten deutschen Reiches in der Frühneuzeit', *Zeitschrift für Historische Forschung*, 16 (1989), 257–328.
Christin, Olivier, *Une Révolution symbolique. L'Iconoclasme huguenot et la reconstruction catholique* (Paris 1991).
Clay, Christopher, '"The Greed of Whig Bishops": Church Landlords and their Lessees 1660–1760', *Past and Present*, 87 (1980), 138–57.
Clement-Simon, Gustave, *Tulle et le bas-Limousin pendant les guerres de religion* (Tulle 1887).
———, 'Célébrités de la ville de Brive: les Lestang, les Maynard de Lestang, les Polverel', *Bulletin de la Société Scientifique, Historique et Archéologique de la Corrèze*, 14 (1892), 533–611.
Clergeac, Adrien, *La Curie et les bénéfices consistoriaux. Etude sur les communs et menus services 1300–1600* (Paris 1911).
———, 'Le Temporel de l'archevêché d'Auch en 1617', *Revue de Gascogne*, n.s., 29–30 (1934–5), 86–8.
Cloulas, Ivan 'La Monarchie catholique et les revenus épiscopaux: les pensions sur les mitres de Castille pendant le règne de Philippe II', *Mélanges de la Casa de Velazquez*, 4 (1968), 107–42.
Compayré, Claude, *Etudes historiques et documents inédits sur l'Albigeois, le Castrais et l'ancien diocèse de Lavaur* (Albi 1841).
Compère, Marie-Madeleine and Julia, Dominique, *Les Collèges français, 16e-18e siècles*, 2 vols (Paris 1984–8).
Contrasty, Jean, *Histoire de la cité de Rieux-Volvestre et de ses évêques* (Toulouse 1936).
———, *Histoire des évêques de Comminges* (Toulouse 1940).
d'Avenel, Georges, *Richelieu et la monarchie absolue*, 3 vols (Paris 1884–90).
Dangibeaud, Charles, *Le Présidial de Saintes. Raimond de Montaigne, lieutenant-général et président 1568–1637* (Paris 1881).

———, 'Louis de Bassompierre, évêque de Saintes', *Bulletin de la Société des Archives Historique de la Saintonge et de l'Aunis*, 45 (1935), 75–98, 170–89.

Darricau, R, 'Comment les souverains pontifes et les rois de France concevaient la nomination aux bénéfices devenus vacants par la mort de leur titulaires en cour de Rome', in *Miscellanea in onore di Martino Giusti* (Vatican City 1978), i. 159–90.

———, 'Louis XIV et le Saint-Siège. Les indults de nomination aux bénéfices consistoriaux (1645–1670)', *Bulletin de Littérature Ecclésiastique*, 66 (1965), 17–34, 107–31.

———, 'La Posterità spirituale di San Carlo Borromeo in Francia nei secoli xvii-xix', *La Scuola Cattolica*, 112 (1984), 733–64.

Daux, Camille, *Histoire de l'église de Montauban*, 2 vols (Montauban 1882–6).

Degert Antoine, *Le Cardinal d'Ossat. Evêque de Rennes et de Bayeux 1537–1604. Sa vie, ses négociations à Rome* (Paris 1894).

———, *Histoire des évêques de Dax* (Paris 1903), 297–8.

———, 'Les Dernières années de Léger de Plas', *Revue de Gascogne*, n.s. 12 (1912), 27–37.

———, 'Saint Charles Borromée et le clergé français', *Bulletin de Littérature Ecclésiastique*, 4th ser, 4 (1912), 145–59, 193–213.

Déjean, E, *Un prélat indépendent du xviie siècle. Nicolas Pavillon évêque d'Alet* (Paris 1909).

Deloche, Maximin, *La Maison du cardinal de Richelieu* (Paris, 1912).

Delpech, G, 'Lettres de Jean Jaubert de Barrault', *Revue de Gascogne*, n.s. 14 (1914), 303–21, 416–29, 453–9.

Dent, Julian, *Crisis in Finance. Crown, Financiers and Society in Seventeenth-Century France* (Newton Abbot 1973).

'Derniers moments de Louis XIII racontés par le père Dinet son confesseur', *Le Cabinet Historique*, 12 (1886), 225–60.

Descimon, Robert, *Qui étaient les Seize? Mythes et réalités de la Ligue parisienne (1589–94)* (Paris 1983).

Dessert, Daniel, *Argent, pouvoir et société au grand siècle* (Paris 1984), 548.

———, *Fouquet* (Paris 1987).

Devic, Claude, and Vaisette, Joseph, *Histoire générale du Languedoc*, ed E Roschach, 16 vols (Toulouse 1872–1904).

Dewald, Jonathan, *The Formation of a Provincial Nobility. The Magistrates of the Parlement of Rouen 1499–1610* (Princeton 1980).

———, *Aristocratic Experience and the Origins of Modern Culture: France 1570–1715* (Berkeley and London 1993).

Dolan, Claire, *Entre Tours et clochers. Les gens d'église à Aix-en-Provence au xvie siècle.* (Sherbrooke, Québec 1981).

Doublet, G, 'Guillaume le Blanc évêque de Grasse et de Vence à la fin du xvie siècle', *Annales du Midi*, 13 (1901) 176–89, 346–65.

———, *Godeau évêque de Grasse et de Vence 1605–1672*, 2 vols (Paris 1911–13).

———, 'Les Visites pastorales de Louis de Bernage, successeur de Godeau à Grasse', *Revue d'Histoire de l'Eglise de France*, 3 (1912), 297–316, 534–59.

Doucet, Roger, *Etude sur le gouvernement de François I dans ses rapports avec le parlement de Paris*, 2 vols (Paris 1921–6).

———, *Les Institutions de la France au xvie siècle*, 2 vols (Paris 1948).

Drouot, Henri, *Mayenne et la Bourgogne. Etude sur la ligue en Bourgogne*, 2 vols (Paris 1937).

Dubarat, V, *Notices historiques sur les évêques de l'ancien diocèse d'Oloron* (Pau 1888).

———, *Etudes d'histoire locale et religieuse*, vol 1 (Pau 1889).

Dubédat, Jean-Baptiste, *Histoire du parlement de Toulouse*, 2 vols (Toulouse 1885).

Dubost, Jean-François, 'Les Italiens en France au xvie et xviie siècle', (Thesis, Université de Paris-I, 1992).

Dufau de Maluquer, A, 'La Maison d'Abbadie de Maslacq', *Mémoires de la Société Royale du Canada*, 2 sér (Ottawa 1895), 73–113.

Duine, F, *Un politique et un orateur du xviie siècle. Cohon évêque de Nîmes et de Dol. Essai de bio-bibliographie avec documents inédits* (Rennes 1902).

Dujarric-Descombes, A, 'Résignation de François de Bourdeille-Montancey, évêque de Périgueux (1599)', *Bulletin de la Société Historique et Archéologique du Périgord*, 15 (1888) 394–402.

Dupuy, Michel, *Bérulle et le sacerdoce* (Paris 1969).

Duval, Pierre, *Description de l'évêché d'Aire en Gascogne* (n.p. 1651).

Edelstein, Marilyn, 'The Social Origins of the Episcopacy in the Reign of Francis I', *French Historical Studies*, 8 (1974), 377–92.

———, 'Les Origines sociales de l'épiscopat sous Louis XII et François I', *Revue d'Histoire Moderne et Contemporaine*, 20 (1978), 239–47.

Erba, Achille, *La Chiesa sabauda tra Cinque e Seicento: Ortodossia tridentina, gallicanesimo savoiardo e assolutismo ducale (1580–1630)* (Rome 1979).

Espitalier, H, 'Les Evêques de Fréjus du xiiie à la fin du xviiie siècle', *Bulletin de la Société d'Etudes Scientifiques et Archéologiques de la ville de Draguignan*, 22 (1898–9), 3–331.

Etchéchoury, Maïté, *Les Maîtres des requêtes de l'hôtel sous les derniers Valois (1553–89)* (Geneva 1991).

Fagniez, Gustave, *Le Père Joseph et Richelieu*, 2 vols (Paris 1894).

Farcy, Paul de, *Histoire généalogique de la maison de Boylève* (Angers 1901).

Favier, René, *Les Villes du Dauphiné aux xviie et xviiie siècles* (Grenoble 1993).

Fincham, Kenneth, *Prelate as Pastor. The Episcopate of James I* (Oxford 1990).

Formeville, H de, *Histoire de l'ancien évêché-comté de Lisieux*, 2 vols (Lisieux 1873).

Formon, Marcelle, 'Henri-Louis Chasteigner de la Rocheposay, évêque de Poitiers (1612–51)', *Bulletin de la Société des Antiquaires de l'Ouest*, 4th ser, 3 (1955), 169–231.

Frêche, Georges, *Toulouse et le région Mid-Pyrénées au siècle des Lumières* (Paris 1974).

Gallet, Jean, *La Seigneurie bretonne (1480–1680). L'example Vannetais* (Paris 1983).

Gaquère, F, *Pierre de Marca, sa vie, ses oeuvres, son gallicanisme* (Paris 1932).

Gaudemet, Jean, *Eglise et société en Occident au moyen âge* (London 1984).

Gazzaniga, Jean-Louis, 'Les Evêques de Louis XI', in *Eglise et pouvoir politique. Journée internationale d'histoire du droit* (Angers 1987), 151–66.

Gemmiti, Dante, *Il Processo per la nomina dei vescovi. Richerche sull'elezione dei vescovi nel secolo xvii* (Naples 1989).

Gigord, Raymond de, *La Noblesse de la sénéchaussée de Villeneuve-de-Berg en 1789* (Lyon 1894).

Godeau, Antoine, *Eloges des évêques qui dans tous les siècles de l'Eglise ont fleury en doctrine et en sainteté* (Paris 1665).

Golden, Richard M, *The Godly Rebellion: Parisian Curés and the Religious Fronde 1652–1662* (Chapel Hill, NC 1981).

Goldman, Lucien, *The Hidden God* (London 1964).

Goulden, Cynthia A, 'Changes in the Episcopal Structure of the Church of France in the Seventeenth Century as an Aspect of Bourbon State-building', *Bulletin of the Institute of Historical Research*, 48 (1975), 214–29.

Greengrass, Mark, 'Aristocracy and Episcopacy at the end of the Wars of Religion: The Duke of Montmorency and the Bishoprics of Languedoc', in *L'Institution et les pouvoirs dans les églises de l'antiquité à nos jours. (Miscellanea Historiae Ecclesiasticae*, viii) (Brussels and Louvain 1987), 356–63.

———, 'Mary, Dowager Queen of France', in Michael Lynch, ed, *Mary Stewart, Queen in Three Kingdoms* (Oxford 1989), 171–94.

Grente, Georges, *Jean Bertaut, abbé d'Aunay, premier aumônier de la reine, évêque de Séez* (Paris 1903).

Griselle, E, *Louis XIII et Richelieu* (Paris 1911).

Guenée, Bernard, *Between Church and State* (Chicago 1991).

Guilloton de Corson, Amédée, *Pouillé historique de l'archevêché de Rennes*, 6 vols (Rennes 1880–6).

Guimart, Charles, *Histoire des évêques de Saint-Brieuc* (Saint-Brieuc 1852).
Guiraud, Louise, *La Réforme à Montpellier*, 2 vols (*Mémoires de la Société Archéologique de Montpellier*, 2 ser, vols 6–7) (Montpellier 1918).
Haigh, Christopher, *English Reformations* (Oxford 1993).
Harding, Robert R, *Anatomy of a Power Elite. The Provincial Governors of Early Modern France* (New Haven and London 1978).
Harsgor, Mikhaël, *Un très petit nombre. Des oligarchies dans l'histoire de l'Occident* (Paris 1994).
Hay, Denys, *Annalists and Historians: Western Historiography from the Seventh to the Eighteenth Century* (London 1977).
Hayden, J Michael, *France and the Estates General of 1614* (Cambridge 1973).
———, 'The Social Origins of the French Episcopacy at the Beginning of the Seventeenth Century', *French Historical Studies*, 10 (1977), 27–38.
Hayem, Fernand, *Le Maréchal d'Ancre et Léonora Galigaï* (Paris 1910).
Heal, Felicity, *Of Prelates and Princes. A Study of the Economic and Social Position of the Tudor Episcopate* (Cambridge 1980).
———, *Hospitality in Early Modern England* (Oxford 1990).
Henry, P-E, *François Bosquet. Intendant de Guyenne et de Languedoc. Evêque de Lodève et de Montpellier. Etude sur une administration civile et ecclésiastique au xviie siècle* (Paris 1889).
Hermann, Christian, *L'Eglise d'Espagne sous le patronage royal (1476–1834)* (Madrid 1988).
Hoffman, Philip T., *Church and Community in the Diocese of Lyon 1500–1789* (New Haven and London 1984).
Holt, Mack P, *The Duke of Anjou and the Politique Struggle during the Wars of Religion* (Cambridge 1986).
———, ed, *Society and Institutions in Early Modern France* (Athens, Georgia 1991).
Huppert, George, *Les Bourgeois gentilshommes. An Essay on the Definition of Elites in Renaissance France* (Chicago 1977).
Hurault, E J, ed, 'Lettres et actes inédits de Msgr de l'Hostel évêque de Viviers', *Revue du Vivarais*, 38 (1931), 1–16.
Hurtebise, Pierre, 'La Famille de Tulle et le siège épiscopal d'Orange', *Archivum Historiae Pontificiae*, 25 (1987), 411–30.
Idée d'une belle mort ou d'une mort chrétienne dans le récit de la fin heureuse de Louis XIII (Paris 1656).
Imbart de la Tour, Pierre, *Origines de la Réforme*, vol 2 (2nd ed, Paris 1946).
Ippolito, Antonio Menniti, *Politica e carriere ecclesiastiche nel secolo xvii. I Vescovi veneti fra Roma e Venezia* (Bologna 1993).
Jacqueline, Bernard, 'L'Evêché de Coutances au temps de la ligue: John Lesley évêque de Coutances 1592–1597', *Revue du Départment de la Manche*, 10 (1968), 95–101.
Jacques, Emile, *Philippe Cospeau, un ami-ennemi de Richelieu* (Paris 1989).
Jadin, Louis, 'Procès d'information pour la nomination des évêques et abbés des Pays-Bas, de Liège, et de Franche-Comté d'après les archives de la congrégation consistoriale', *Bulletin de l'Institut Historique Belge de Rome*, 6 (1928), 5–37.
Jansen, Paule, *Le Cardinal Mazarin et le mouvement janséniste français* (Paris 1967).
Jarno, E, 'Du Vair, évêque de Marseille?', *Revue d'Histoire Littéraire de la France*, 54 (1954), 195–7.
Jeandet, J-P Abel, *Pontus de Thyard seigneur de Boissy, depuis évêque de Châlon* (Paris 1860).
Jedin, Hubert, *L'Evêque dans la tradition pastorale du xvie siècle*, ed Paul Broutin (Brussels 1953).
Julia, Dominique, and Revel, Jacques, eds, *Histoire sociale des populations étudiantes*, vol ii (Paris 1989).
Just, Leo, 'Das Staatskirchentum der Herzöge von Lotharingen-Bar von 1445 bis 1633', *Archiv für Mittelrheinische Kirchengeschichte*, 5 (1953), 223–63.
Kagan, Richard L, *Students and Society in early Modern Spain* (Baltimore 1974).
Kaiser, Wolfgang, *Marseille im Bürgerkrieg. Sozialgefüge, Religionskonflikt und Faktionskämpfe von 1559–1596* (Göttingen 1991).

Kalas, Robert J, 'Wealth, Power and Place in Sixteenth-Century France: The Rise of the Selves and Noailles Families' (Unpublished Ph D thesis, New York University 1982).
Kamen, Henry, *The Phoenix and the Flame: Catalonia and the Counter-Reformation* (New Haven and London 1993).
Kerhervé, Jean, *L'Etat breton aux xive et xve siècles. Les ducs, l'argent, les hommes*, 2 vols (Paris 1987).
Kettering, Sharon, *Judicial Politics and Urban Revolt in Seventeenth-Century France. The Parlement of Aix 1629–1659* (Princeton 1978).
————, *Patrons Brokers and Clients in Seventeenth-Century France* (Oxford 1986).
————, 'Patronage and Politics during the Fronde', *French Historical Studies*, 14 (1986), 409–41.
————, 'Clientage during the French Wars of Religion', *Sixteenth-Century Journal*, 20 (1989), 221–39.
————, 'Patronage in Early Modern France', *French Historical Studies*, 17 (1992), 839–62.
Kishlansky, Mark A., *Parliamentary Selection: Social and Political Choice in Early Modern England* (Cambridge 1986).
Kleinman, Ruth, *Anne of Austria, Queen of France* (Columbus, Ohio 1985).
Knecht, R J, 'The Concordat of 1516: A Reassessment', in *Government in Reformation Europe*, ed H J Cohn (London 1971), 91–112.
————, *Renaissance Prince and Patron. The Reign of Francis I* (Cambridge 1994).
Kremer, Stefan, *Herkunft und Werdegang geistlicher Führungsschichten in den Reichsbistümern zwischen Westfälischen Frieden und Säkularisation* (Freiburg-im-Breisgau 1992).
Hommey, Louis, *Histoire générale, ecclésiastique et civile du diocèse de Séez*, 4 vols (Alençon 1896–1900).
Labande, L-H, *Avignon au xve siècle* (Avignon 1920).
Labatut, Jean-Pierre, *Les Ducs et pairs de France au xviie siècle* (Paris 1972).
Labau, Denis, *Lescar, histoire d'une cité épiscopale*, 2 vols (Pau 1975).
Labbé, Yvonne, 'Une Famille de noblesse de robe: les Habert de Montmort siegneurs du Mesnil-Saint-Denis 1543–1720', *Paris et Ile-de-France* (*Mémoires publiés par la Fédération des Sociétés Historiques et Archéologiques de Paris et de l'Ile-de-France*) 39 (1988), 7–119.
Lantenay, A de, *L'Oratoire à Bordeaux* (Bordeaux 1886).
Launay, Gontard de, *Les Avocats d'Angers de 1250 à 1789* (Angers 1888).
———— *Recherches généalogiques et historiques sur les familles des maires d'Angers*, 3 vols (Angers 1893–5).
Laurain-Portemer, Madeleine, *Etudes Mazarines* (Paris 1981).
Le Bras, Gabriel, *Etudes de sociologie religieuse*, 2 vols (Paris 1955–6).
————, *Introduction à l'histoire de la pratique religieuse*, 2 vols (Paris 1942).
Le Goff, Jacques, and Rémond, René, eds, *Histoire de la France religieuse*, vol 2 (Paris 1988).
Le Roy Ladurie, E, *Les Paysans de Languedoc*, 2 vols (The Hague 1966).
Lebeuf, Abbé, *Mémoires concernant l'histoire civile et ecclésiastique d'Auxerre et de son ancien diocèse* (new ed, Paris 1848–55).
Ledru, Ambroise, *Histoire de la maison de Broc*, 2 vols (Mamers 1898).
Lemaître, Nicole, *Le Rouergue flamboyant: le clergé et les fidèles du diocèse de Rodez 1417–1563* (Paris 1988).
Lemarchand, Guy, *La Fin du féodalisme dans le pays de Caux. Conjoncture économique et démographique, et structure sociale dans une région de grande culture, de la crise du xviie siècle à la stabilisation de la Révolution (1648–1795)* (Paris 1989).
Le Mené, J-M, *Histoire du diocese de Vannes*, 2 vols (Vannes 1878–9).
Lestocquoy, Jean, 'Les Evêques français au xvie siècle', *Revue d'Histoire de l'Eglise de France*, 45 (1959), 25–40.
Lestrade, Jean, 'Un curieux groupe d'évêques de Comminges: Urbain de Saint-Gelais 1570–1613', *Revue de Comminges*, 23 (1908), 254–66; 24 (1909), 28–41, 97–112.
Lloyd, Howell A., 'The Political Thought of Charles Loyseau', *European Studies Review* 11 (1981), 53–82.

Lormeau, E, *Des Menses épiscopales en France. Etude historique et juridique* (Alençon 1905).
Lottin, Alain, *Lille citadelle de la contre-réforme? (1598–1668)* (Westhoek 1984).
Loupès, Philippe, *Chapitres et chanoines de Guyenne aux xviie et xviiie siècles* (Paris 1985).
Louvencourt, A de, *Les Trésoriers de France de la généralité de Picardie ou d'Amiens* (Amiens 1896).
Luthard, M, 'Journal des actes de Jean Plantavit de la Pause évêque de Lodève (1626–1630)' *Annales du Midi*, (1913), 189–213, 323–44.
Major, J Russell, *Representative Government in Early Modern France* (New Haven and London 1980).
Marca, Pierre de, *Histoire de Béarn*, ed V Dubarat, 2 vols (Paris and Pau 1894–1912.).
Margadant, Ted W, *Urban Rivalries in the French Revolution* (Princeton 1992).
Martin, Ernest *Histoire de la ville de Lodève*, 2 vols (Montpellier 1900).
Martin, Georges, *Histoire et généalogie de la maison de Clermont-Tonnerre* (La Ricamarie 1986).
Mastellone, Salvo, *La Reggenza di Maria de' Medici* (Florence 1962).
Maupeou, Jacques de, *Histoire des Maupeou* (Fontenay-le-Comte 1959).
Maurel, Christian, 'Structures familiales et solidarités lignagères à Marseille au xve siècle', *Annales: Economies, Sociétés, Civilisations*, 41 (1986), 675–81.
Mazéret, Ludovic, *Chroniques de l'Eglise de Condom* (Condom 1927).
McClung Hallmann, Barbara, *Italian Cardinals, Reform and the Church as Property 1492–1563* (Los Angeles 1985)
McManners, John, 'Tithe in Eighteenth-Century France: a Focus for Rural Anticlericalism', in Derek Beales and Geoffrey Best, eds, *History, Society and the Churches* (Cambridge 1985), 147–68.
Ménard, Léon, *Histoire civile ecclésiastique et littéraire de la ville de Nîmes*, 6 vols (Nîmes 1754–5); new ed, 5 vols (Nîmes 1875).
Menjoulet, J-Maximien, *Chronique du diocèse et du pays d'Oloron*, vol 2 (Oloron, 1869).
Mesnard, Jean, 'Un évêque de Bazas solitaire de Port-Royal: Henri de Litolfi-Maroni', *Revue Historique de Bordeaux et du département de la Gironde* 10 (1961), 65–78.
Michaud, Claude, *L'Eglise et l'argent sous l'ancien régime. Les Receveurs généraux du clergé de France aux xvie-xviie siècles* (Paris 1991).
Michaud, Hélène, *La Grande chancellerie et les écritures royales au xvie siècle* (Paris 1967).
———, *Les Formulaires de la grande chancellerie 1500–1580* (Paris 1972).
Minois, Georges, *Le Confesseur du roi: Les directeurs de conscience sous la monarchie française* (Paris 1988).
Molinier, E, *La Vie de Messire Barthélemy de Donadieu de Griet, evesque de Comenge* (Paris 1639).
Moote, A Lloyd, *The Revolt of the Judges: The Parlement of Paris and the Fronde 1643–1652* (Princeton 1971).
Motley, Mark, *Becoming a French Aristocrat. The Education of the Court Nobility 1580–1715* (Princeton 1990).
Mousnier, Roland, *Les Règlements du conseil du roi sous Louis XIII* (Paris 1949).
———, *Institutions of France under the Absolute Monarchy*, 2 vols (Chicago 1979–84).
Murray, Alexander, *Reason and Society in the Middle Ages* (Oxford 1978).
Neuschel, Kristen B, *Word of Honour: Interpreting Noble Culture in Sixteenth-Century France* (Ithaca, N.Y. 1989).
Nicod, Emmanuel, 'La Maison de Fay-Peyraud', *Revue du Vivarais*, 11 (1903), 145–58, 203–12, 281–96, 315–38, 379–89.
———, 'Généalogie de la famille de Montchal', *Revue du Vivarais*, 30 (1929), 38–45, 72–5, 132–9, 193–6.
Orcibal, Jean, *Jean Duvergier de Hauranne, abbé de Saint-Cyran et son temps* (Louvain 1947).
Oresko, Robert, 'The Marriage of the Nieces of Cardinal Mazarin', in Rainer Babel, ed, *Frankreich im europäischen Staatensystem der frühen Neuzeit* (Sigmaringen 1995), 109–51.
Orléa, Manfred, *La Noblesse aux états-généraux de 1576 et de 1588* (Paris 1980).
Oroux, abbé, *Histoire ecclésiastique de la Cour*, 2 vols (Paris 1777).

Pallasse, Maurice, *La Sénéchaussée et siège présidial de Lyon pendant les guerres de religion* (Lyon 1943).
Pasquier, E, *Un curé de Paris pendant les guerres de religion. René Benoist, le pape des Halles 1521–1608* (Angers 1913).
Pastor, Ludwig von, *History of the Popes*, 40 vols (London 1894–1953).
Pérard-Castel, François, *Traité sommaire de l'usage et pratique de la Cour de Rome*, 2nd ed (Paris 1717).
Péronnet, Michel, *Les Evêques de l'ancienne France*, 2 vols (Lille 1978).
———, 'Quelques réflexions sur les critères d'analyse d'un groupe social: la noblesse dans une durée séculaire', in *L'Anoblissement en France xve-xviiie siècles. Théories et réalités* (Bordeaux n.d. [1985]), 148–9.
———, 'Les Nominations épiscopales sous Henri III' in *Henri III et son temps*, ed Robert Sauzet (Paris 1992), 283–92.
Pérouas, Louis, *Le Diocèse de la Rochelle 1648–1724: Sociologie et pastorale* (Paris 1964).
Perroy, Edouard, 'Social Mobility among the French *noblesse* in the later Middle Ages', *Past and Present*, 21 (1962), 25–38.
Peyron, P., 'L'Evêché de Léon de 1613 à 1651', *Bulletin d'Histoire et d'Archéologie du Diocèse de Quimper*, 15 (1915), 266–7, 294–304, 334–6, 356.
Peyrous, Bernard, *Le Réforme catholique à Bordeaux 1600–1719*, 2 vols (Bordeaux 1995).
Piétri, Charles, et al, *Histoire du christianisme*, vi, *Le Temps des confessions*, ed Marc Venard (Paris 1992).
Pillorget, René, *Les Mouvements insurrectionnels de Provence entre 1596 et 1715* (Paris 1975).
Pithon-Curt, J A, *Histoire de la noblesse du comtat Venaissin*, 4 vols (Paris 1743–50).
Plantavit, Jean, *Chronologia praesulum Lodovensium* (n.p. 1634).
Plongeron, Bernard, *La Vie quotidienne du clergé français au xviiiè siècle* (Paris 1974).
———, 'Charles Borromée, exemple et modèle: son influence en France (xvie-xixe siècles)', in *San Carlo Borromeo e il suo tempo* (Rome 1986), i. 493–525.
Pocquet du Haut-Jussé, 'Les Evêques de Bretagne dans la renaissance religieuse du xviie siècle', *Annales de Bretagne*, 54 (1947), 30–59.
Pointeau, Charles, *Notice sur les seigneurs de Vautorte* (Laval 1892).
Poulbrière, J-B, *Histoire du diocèse de Tulle* (Tulle 1885).
———, 'Une poignée de documents sur la Haute Auvergne', *Bulletin Historique et Scientifique de l'Auvergne*, 8 (1888), 67–100, 109–50, 167–217.
Poull, Georges, *Le Château et les seigneurs de Bourlemont, 1412–1964*, 2 vols (Corbeil 1962–4).
Poutet, Yves, 'Les Docteurs de Sorbonne et leurs options théologiques au xviie siècle', *Divus Thomas*, 81 (1978), 213–348.
Pouy, F, 'Histoire de François Faure, 77e évêque d'Amiens (1612–1687)', *Mémoires de la Société des Antiquaires de Picardie*, 3 ser, 5 (1876), 137–286.
Pozzo di Borgo, Cécile, 'Denis Simon de Marquemont, archevêque de Lyon et cardinal (1572–1626): La carrière d'un prélat diplomate au Saint-Siège au début du xviie siècle', *Archivum Historiae Pontificiae*, 15 (1977), 265–94.
Prévost, A E, *Histoire du diocèse de Troyes*, 3 vols (Troyes 1923–6).
Prunel, Louis N, *Sébastien Zamet. Evêque-duc de Langres, pair de France (1588–1655). Sa vie et ses oeuvres. Les origines du jansénisme* (Paris 1912).
Rainer, Johann, 'Die Politik der Bischofsernennung in Österreich 1648–1803', *Römische Quartalschrift*, 85 (1990), 225–35.
Ranum, Orest, *Richelieu and the Councillors of Louis XIII* (Oxford 1963).
Ravitch, Norman, *Sword and Mitre: Government and Episcopacy in France and England in the Age of Aristocracy* (The Hague 1966).
Rawlings, Helen E, 'The Secularisation of Castilian Episcopal Office under the Habsburgs, c. 1516–1700', *Journal of Ecclesiastical History*, 38 (1987), 53–79.
Reinhardt, Rudolf, 'Die hochadligen Dynastien in der Reichskirche des 17 und 18 Jahrhunderts', *Römische Quartalschrift*, 83 (1988), 213–55.

———, 'Kontinuität und Diskontinuität. Zum Problem der Koadjutorie mit dem Recht der Nachfolge in der neuzeitlichen Germania Sacra', in Johannes Kunisch, ed., *Der Dynastische Fürstenstaat. Zur Bedeutung von Sukzessionsordnungen für die Entstehung des frühmodernen Staates* (Berlin 1982), 114–55.

Ribbe, Charles de, *Une famille au xvie siècle d'après des documents originaux*, 3rd ed (Tours 1879).

Riboulet, E, *Etude historique sur Mgr Guillaume Le Boux, évêque de Périgueux et prédicateur ordinaire de Louis XIV* (Paris 1875).

Richet, D, *De la Réforme à la Révolution* (Paris 1992).

Rives, Jean, 'Les Refus de dîmes dans la ville d'Auch à la veille de la Révolution', *Actes du 96e Congrès National des Sociétés Savantes* (Toulouse 1971), ii. 237–57.

Rivet, Bernard, *Une Ville au xvie siècle: Le Puy-en-Velay* (Le Puy 1988).

Roche, Augustin, 'Chronologie des évêques de Viviers', *Revue du Vivarais*, (1931) 68–75, 127–34, 156–64, 228–37, 269–75.

Rolland, H, *Une famille avignonnaise. Les Tulle de Villefranche* (Paris 1909).

Rosa, Mario,'Diocesi e vescovi del Mezzogiorno durante il viceregno spagnolo: Capitanata, Terra di Bari e Terra d'Otranta dal 1545 al 1714', in *Studi in onore di Gabriele Pepe* (Naples 1970), 531–80.

———, 'Curia Romana e pensioni ecclesiastiche: fiscalità pontificia nel Mezzogiorno (secoli xvi-xviii)', *Quaderni Storici*, 42 (1979), 1015–55.

———, 'L'Immagine del vescovo nel Seicento', *Richerche di Storia Sociale e Religiosa*, 46 (1994), 49–59.

Rott, E, *Histoire de la représentation de la France auprès des cantons suisses, de leurs alliés et de leurs confédérés*, 10 vols (Paris 1900–35).

Roucaute, Jean, *Le Pays de Gévaudan au temps de la Ligue* (Paris 1900).

Roux, E, *Auvergnats en Provence* (Clermont-Ferrand 1967).

Ruchon, François, *Essai sur la vie de Jean de Sponde 1557–1595* (Geneva 1949).

Sahuc, Joseph, *Saint-Pons-de-Thomières, vol 1: les Archives, l'abbaye, l'évêché* (n.p. 1895).

Samiac, F J, 'Testament de Mgr Jérôme Lingua, évêque de Conserans (12–11–1612)', *Bulletin Historique des Diocèses de Pamiers, Conserans et Mirepoix*, 1(1912), 86–91.

Saulnier, Frédéric, 'L'Enfeu des Champion à Saint-Sauveur de Rennes (1519–1792). Notes et documents', *Bulletin et Mémoires de la Société d'Archéologie d'Ile-et-Vilaine*, 18 (1888), 169–95.

———, 'Un prélat au xviie siècle. François de Villemontée, évêque de Saint-Malo, sa femme et ses enfants', *Bulletin et Mémoires de la Société Archéologique de l'Ile-et-Vilaine*, 32 (1903), 107–38.

Sauzet, Robert, *Contre-réforme et réforme catholique en bas-Languedoc. Le Diocèse de Nîmes au xviie siècle* (Louvain and Paris 1979).

Schalk, Ellery, *From Valor to Pedigree. Ideas of Nobility in France in the Sixteenth and Seventeenth Centuries.* (Princeton 1986).

Schmidt, Peter, *Das Collegium Germanicum in Rome und die Germaniker* (Tübingen 1984).

Schmitt, Thérèse-Jean, *L'Organisation ecclésiastique et la pratique religieuse dans l'archidiaconé d'Autun de 1650 à 1750* (Autun 1957).

Schwinges, Richard C, *Deutsche Universitätsbücher im 14 und 15 Jahrhundert. Studien zur Sozialgeschichte des Alten Reiches* (Stuttgart 1986).

Serbat, Louis, *Les Assemblées du clergé de France: origines, organisation, développement 1561–1615* (Paris 1906).

Simard, Jean, *Une iconographie du clergé français au xviie siècle: les dévotions de l'école française et les sources de l'imagerie religieuse en France et au Québec* (Laval, Québec 1976).

Sol, Eugène, *L'Eglise de Cahors à l'époque moderne* (Cahors 1947).

———, *Le Vénérable Alain de Solminihac, abbé de Chancelade et évêque de Cahors* (Cahors 1928).

Solnon, Jean-François, *La Cour de France* (Paris 1987).

Soulet, Jean-François, *Traditions et réformes religieuses dans les Pyrénées centrales au xviie siècle* (Pau 1974).

Soultrait, J, ed, *Inventaire des titres de la maison de Nevers de l'abbé de Marolles* (Nevers 1873).
Stocker, Christopher, 'Office as Maintenance in Renaissance France', *Canadian Journal of History*, 6 (1971), 21–44.
——, 'Orléans and the Catholic League' *Proceedings of the Western Society for French History*, 16 (1989), 12–21.
Stone, Lawrence, 'The Educational Revolution in England 1560 to 1640', *Past and Present*, 28 (1964), 41–80.
——, ed, *The University in Society*, 2 vols (London 1974).
Strayer, Joseph R, *The Reign of Philip the Fair* (Princeton 1980).
Sutherland, N M, *The French Secretaries of State in the Age of Catherine de Medici* (London 1962).
Tackett, Timothy, *Religion, Revolution and Regional Culture in Eighteenth-Century France. The Ecclesiastical Oath of 1791* (Princeton 1986)
Taillandier, Charles, *Histoire ecclésiastique et civile de Bretagne*, 3 vols (Paris 1756).
Tamizey de Larroque, P, 'Bertrand d'Eschaux évêque de Bayonne', *Revue de Gascogne*, 20 (1879), 297–310.
Terris, Jules, *Les Evêques d'Apt, leurs blasons et leurs familles* (Avignon 1877).
Teulé, Alexandre-E. de, *Chronologie des docteurs en droit civil de l'université d'Avignon* (Paris 1887).
Thomas, Jules, *Le Concordat de 1516. Ses origines, son histoire au xvie siècle*, 3 vols (Paris 1910).
Thuillier, René, *Diarium patrum fratrum et suorum ordinis Minimorum provinciae Franciae sive Parisiensis qui religiose obierunt ab anno 1506 ad annum 1700* (Paris 1709).
Tizon-Germe, Anne-Cécile, 'Juridiction spirituelle et action pastorale des légats et nonces en France pendant la Ligue (1589–1594)', *Archivum Historiae Pontificiae,* 30 (1992), 159–230.
Toujas, René, 'Les Démêlés de Samuel Martineau évêque de Bazas (1646–1667) avec le parlement de Bordeaux', *Actes du 104e Congrès National des Sociétés Savantes: Section d'histoire moderne et contemporaine,* ii (Paris 1981), 51–62.
Touron, A, *Histoire des hommes illustres de l'ordre de Saint Dominique*, 6 vols (Paris 1743–9).
Toussaint, Joseph, *Claude Auvry évêque de Coutances et trésorier à Paris de la Sainte-Chapelle* (Avranches 1981).
Toustain de Billy, René, *Histoire ecclésiastique du diocèse de Coutances*, ed A Héron, 3 vols (Rouen 1874–86).
Tricoire, abbé, *Les Evêques d'Angoulême. Recherches historiques depuis les origines jusqu'à nos jours* (Angoulême 1912).
Ughetti, Dante, *François d'Amboise (1550–1619)* (Rome 1974)
Ultee, Maarten, *The Abbey of St Germain des Prés in the Seventeenth Century* (New Haven and London 1981).
Vaissière, Pierre de, *Messieurs de Joyeuse (1560–1615)* (Paris 1926).
Valette, Jean, 'Jean de Lingendes, évêque de Sarlat (14 sept 1642-27 sept 1647)', *Bulletin de la Société Historique et Archéologique du Périgord*, 94 (1967), 210–32, 95 (1968), 51–64.
——, 'Nicolas Sévin, évêque de Sarlat (2 avril 1648–sept 1657)', *Actes du 96e Congrès National des Sociétés Savantes: Section d'histoire moderne et contemporaine* (Paris 1971), 57–70.
——, 'François II de Salignac de la Mothe-Fénélon, évêque de Sarlat (15 avril 1659–11 mai 1688)', *Bulletin de la Société Historique et Archéologique du Périgord*, 99 (1972), 190–220.
Veillet, René, *Recherches sur la ville et sur l'église de Bayonne*, ed, V Dubarat and J-B Daranatz, vol 1 (Bayonne 1910).
Venard, Marc, *Réforme protestante, réforme catholique dans la province d'Avignon au xvie siècle* (Paris 1993).
Vidal, Auguste, 'Du Vergier évêque de Lavaur et les siens', *Reuve Historique du Tarn*, 17 (1900), 73–86.
——, *L'Ancien diocèse d'Albi d'après les registres des notaires* (Paris and Albi 1913).
Vidal, Daniel, *Critique de la raison mystique* (Grenoble 1990).
Vidal, Jean-Marie, *Histoire des évêques de Pamiers*, vol 3: *Schisme et hérésie au diocèse de Pamiers* (Castillon 1931); vol 4: *Henri de Sponde, recteur de Saint-Louis-des-Français, évêque de Pamiers*

(1568–1643) (Paris 1929); vol 5: *François-Etienne de Caulet, évêque de Pamiers (1610–1680)* (Paris 1939).

Virieux, Maurice de, 'Le Parlement de Grenoble au xvii⁣ᵉ siècle. Etude sociale' (*Thèse de doctorat d'Etat*, Université de Paris-IV 1986).

Watts, Derek, *Cardinal de Retz: The Ambiguities of a Seventeenth-Century Mind* (Oxford 1980).

Welter, Louise, *La Réforme ecclésiastique du diocèse de Clermont au xvii⁣ᵉ siècle* (Paris 1956).

Whitmore, PJS, *The Order of Minims in Seventeenth-Century France* (The Hague 1967).

Wolfe, Michael, *The Conversion of Henri IV. Politics, Power and Religious Belief in Early Modern France* (Harvard 1993).

Wright, A D, 'Church and State in Post-Tridentine Spain', in *Catholic Times and Tastes. Essays in Honour of Michael E Williams*, ed Margaret A Rees (Leeds 1987), 303–62.

Zeller, Gaston, *Les Institutions de la France au xvi⁣ᵉ siècle* (Paris 1948).

INDEX

The entries below do not include references to the Biographical Dictionary, which is itself in large part an index. But in order to facilitate locating the bishops of individual dioceses via the Dictionary the index entries for each diocese indicate the names of *all* the bishops for the period covered in this book, regardless of whether their names occur elsewhere in the index proper. The key references on individuals or subjects are printed in bold type.

Abbadie, Jean-Pierre d', bp of Lescar 393
Académie Française 4, 475, 480
Agde, bp of 260, 273, 305, 356, 470; see of 29, 100, 110, 149, 153, 161, 162, 177, 190, 312, 356, 424, 427, 446–7, 470, 497, 500, 523, 528, 536. *See* Barrez, du Puy, Fouquet, Valois
Agen 169, 195, 424; bp of 218, 221, 275, 470; see of 52, 110, 195, 321, 324, 348, 399, 472. *See* Daillon, Delbène, Gelas, Villars
agents-généraux du clergé 18, 86, 291, 393, 466, 290, 542; as candidates for episcopate 291, 551
Aiguillon, duchesse d' 483–4
Aire, bp of 97, 146, 155, 285; see of 312, 322, 377, 383, 411, 451, 473, 531. *See* Boutault, Bourlemont, Bouthillier, Cospeau, Foix-Candale, Sariac
Aix 175; abp of 83, 179, 355, 361, 370, 423, 456; parlement of 317, 395, 430; see of 29, 52, 110, 175, 266, 267, 310, 321, 342, 371, 377, 380, 387, 393, 396, 407, 470, 471, 474, 501, 502, 531, 519, 520, 534; Univ of 228, 229, 236, 238. *See* Canigiani, Grimaldi, Génébrard, Hurault, Mazarin
Alais. *See* Valois
Albi, bp 135, 304, 401, 470; see of 40, 41, 102, 103, 110, 113, 117, 171, 321, 342, 346, 355, 382, 383, 394, 401, 413, 464, 465, 472, 498, 520. *See* Daillon, Delbène
Albret, house of 175, 192, 195
Albret, Henri d'Amanieu, Marshal 532
Albret, Jeanne d' 39
Aleaume, Guillaume, bp of Riez, Lisieux 82–3, 430
Alemanni, Luca, bp of Mâcon 361, 379
Alençon, François de Valois, duc d' 78, 348, 349, 350, 358. *See* Anjou

Alès, see of 34
Alet, bp of 250, 260, 285, 407; see of 110, 117, 171, 317, 345, 382, 383, 402, 403. *See* Lestang, Pavillon, Polverel
Alexander VII, pope 52
Aliermont, comté of 98
Allen, William, Cardinal 257
Amboise, Adrien d', bp of Tréguier 393, 395
Amboise, family 341
Ambrose, Saint 208
Amiens 536; bp of 379; see of 110, 171, 321, 534, 535. *See* Faure, La Marthonie, Lefebvre de Caumartin
Amyot, Jacques, bp of Auxerre 150, 213, 362
Angennes, family 152, 391, 398–9
Angennes, Claude d', bp of Le Mans 360, 364, 384, 386, 398
Angennes, Jacques d', bp of Bayeux 250
Angennes, Jean d' 391
Angers 197, 221, 497; bp of 193, 195, 260, 309, 423, 427, 466; governor of 150, 398; see of 110, 115, 257, 317, 371, 423, 424, 451, 483, 505, 523; Univ of 226, 228, 234, 238. *See* Arnault, Fouquet, Miron, Rueil
Anglure de Bourlemont. *See* Bourlemont
Angoulême 197; bp of 155, 239; see of 110, 239, 405, 406, 503. *See* Du Perron, La Rochefoucauld, Péricard
Angoulême, Charles de Valois, duc d' 144–5
Angoumois 205
Anjou 40, 52, 451; duc d' 360; duchy of 348. *See* Alençon
Annat, François, Jesuit, royal confessor 529
annates 49, 67, 68, 69, 140, 92, 136, 408, 438, 549; demands for reduction of 432; source of anti-papal grievances 433; unpopularity of 65

740   Index

Anne of Austria 17, 53, 76, 77, 85, 95, 147, 196, 278, 279, 280, 283, 288, 349, 461, 465, 479, 485, 507, 508, 509, 511, 513, 515, 516, 521, 524, 525, 526, 543, 544; episcopal clients of 501; jointure rights of 468
Annecy 181
Annonay 207
anoblis 186
apanages 52, 53, 348, 349, 450, 468, 502
Apostolic Chamber 65
Apt, see of 30, 110, 447. See Pélissier, Villeneuve
Aquitaine 41
Aradon, Georges d', bp of Vannes 74, 370, 371
Archbishops: limited authority of 42
Arles, abp of 144, 206, 222, 327; see of 29, 38, 40, 110, 115, 117 146, 148, 154, 175, 378, 393, 395, 396, 405, 413, 456, 469, 470, 472, 498, 500, 505. See Barrault, du Laurens, Grignan, Montano, Santacroce
Armagnac 192
Arnauld, family 196, 257
Arnauld, Antoine 260
Arnauld, Henri, bp of Angers 37, 195, 257, 260, 261, 287, 466, 482–3, 484, 492, 499, 500, 505, 523
Arnoux, Jean, Jesuit, royal confessor 437, 438, 440
Arras, see of 36
Assemblies of Clergy 8, 18, 25–6, 28, 42, 76, 96, 109, 116, 123, 126, 136, 143–4, 151, 164, 213, 271, 279, 281, 288–90, 343, 345–6, 349, 354, 355, 356, 358, 380–1, 382, 384, 385, 424, 435, 464, 498, 504, 518, 519, 520, 524, 525, 527, 528, 545, 546; and episcopal elections 435–6; as springboard to episcopate 289–90, 550–1; attack *confidences* 354–6; criticise episcopal nominations 360, 383–5; demand restoration of episcopal elections 414; deputies to become bishops 289–90
Assembly of Notables 288, 290, 384–5, 437, 438, 453
Aubagne 98
Aubusson de la Feuillade, Georges, abp of Embrun 160, 520, 531
Auch 221; abp of 62, 149, 207, 372, 443, 474; chapter of 372; see of 103, 110, 113, 117, 146, 152, 316, 342, 344, 372, 375, 382, 388, 406, 412, 413, 420, 531, 536. See Destrappes, Este, Vic
Augustine, Saint 208
Augustinian Hermits 169
Aumont, César d' 130
Austrian lands 269; bishops in 553; monastic orders in 547
Autun, bp of 240; see of 73, 104, 110, 519; coll of (Univ of Paris) 285. See Dony, La Madeleine
Auvergne 79, 173, 190, 348, 450, 468, 521
Auvergne, Charles de Valois, comte d' 432. See also Angoulême

Auvry, Claude, bp of Coutances 93, 87, 94, 231, 501, 515, 518, 531, 534
Auxerre, bp of 157, 231, 328, 362, 398, 435; see of 110, 115, 117, 150–1, 171, 177, 191, 320, 321, 398, 424, 469, 479, 482. See Amyot, Broc, Donadieu, Séguier, Souvré
Auxonne 170
Avignon 5, 29, 38, 180–1, 182, 228, 237, 238, 241, 370, 380, 397; papacy at 31, 47, 48; Univ of 228, 229
Avranches, bp of 309, 371; see of 24, 30, 110, 368–9, 482, 501, 535. See Aumont, Boivin, Boylesve, Vialart
Aymeric 546

Babou, Isabelle 395
Bagno, Giovanni Guidi di, papal nuncio 458
bail général 125. See *fermes, fermiers-généraux*
Balsac, Charles de, bp of Noyon 218, 273, 395
Baluze, Etienne 5
Banqui, Serafino 405
banquier expéditionnaire 64, 66, 67, 69, 109
Baradat, François de 454, 445
Baradat, Henri de, bp of Noyon 55, 274, 445
Barberini, family 182
Barberini, Antonio, Cardinal, abp of Reims 22, 23, 125, 126, 179, 518, 526–7, 532
Barberini, Maffeo. See Urban VIII
Barbier de la Rivière, Louis, bp of Langres 55, 189, 218, 254, 279, 284, 445, 502, 509, 518, 521, 523, 532, 538
Barillon, Jean-Jacques, president 492
Barrault, family 275
Barrault, Jean-Jacques Jaubert de, bp of Bazas, Arles 220, 222, 231, 275, 327, 456, 463–4, 470, 472, 505
Barreau, Nicolas 491
Barrez, Fulcran de, bp of Agde 273, 447
Basle, council of 48, 65
Bassompierre, François de, Marshal 502
Bassompierre, Louis de, bp of Saintes 218, 502–3, 505
Bastille 281
Baumgartner, Frederic, historian 9, 186, 187, 188, 213
Bayeux, bp of 250, 391, 393; see of 87, 88, 93, 110, 116, 120, 152, 161, 162, 177, 260, 295, 332, 343, 353, 357, 373, 376, 399, 405, 531, 536, 537, 538. See Angennes, Daillon, Molé, Nesmond, Ossat, Servien
Bayonne, bp of 39, 93, 94, 110, 157, 158, 176, 223, 233, 249, 262, 325, 473; see of 295, 312, 318, 322, 325, 423, 424, 466, 469, 470, 471, 473, 481, 497. See Deschaux, Fouquet, Montaigne, Olce, Rueil
Bazas, bp of 222, 275, 279, 283, 470, 472; see of 110, 321, 456, 469, 471, 482. See Barrault, Grillié, Litolfi-Moroni, Martineau
Béarn 151, 175, 195, 249, 288, 340, 343, 393,

Index

484, 503; bishoprics in 39, 178; restoration of Catholicism in 39
Beaton, James, abp of Glasgow 74
Beaumanoir de Lavardin, family 151
Beaumanoir de Lavardin, Jean de, Marshal 398
Beaumanoir de Lavardin, Philibert-Emmanuel, bp of Le Mans 4, 513, 520
Beaune, Renaud de 152, 277, 316, 319, 348, 358, 360, 364, 365, 368, 376, 394, 406
Beauvais 168–9; bp of 59, 102, 250, 338, 362; see of 42, 110, 113, 120, 133–4, 160, 162, 339, 351, 352, 367, 368, 388, 430, 431, 522. *See* Choart, Fumée, Potier
Beauvau de Rivarennes, Gabriel de, bp of Nantes 474
Bec, abbey of 266
Bellaigue, abbey of 537
Belleau, Jean, bp of Meaux 41, 195, 218, 259
Bellegarde, family 499
Bellegarde, Octave de, bp of Comminges, abp of Sens 41, 84, 301, 423, 444, 430, 475, 499
Bellegarde, Roger de 41, 84, 381, 444, 475
Bellenger, Gérard 370, 371, 380
Belley, bp of 297; see of 37, 110, 115, 170, 391, 397. *See* Camus, Passelaigue
Bellièvre, family 170, 197, 427
Bellièvre Pomponne de, chancellor of France 170, 385, 392, 396, 412
Bellièvre, Albert de, abp of Lyon 260, 305–6, 396
Bellièvre, Claude de, abp of Lyon 260, 427
Benedictines 257, 266, 282, 407, 441
benefices 141, 160, 178, 179, 246, 269, 270, 347, 350, 360, 373, 375, 385, 406, 414, 433, 462, 464, 476, 477, 496, 503, 511. (*See in commendam*, Italians, pensions); consistorial 49, 374, 384; held by future bishops 218, 291–2, 543, 549–50, 551, 552; held by Italian prelates 373, 406; held by laymen 152–4, 247, 387, 410, 458; held *en confidence* 354; held *in commendam* 91, 94, 137, 264, 265, 266, 291, 547, 549, 551, 556, 557; included in apanages 348–9, 450, 468; nature of 90–1; presentation rights to 351–2; resignations of 473; trading in 337, 340, 537, 542, 557; use of by Mazarin 162, 290, 528, 537, 537–8, 539–40; use of during Assemblies of Clergy 290, 504, 528; used to bid for bishoprics 537; value of to episcopal candidates 224, 244, 245, 259, 292
Benoist, René 216 375, 376, 393, 406, 407
Benserade, Isaac 524
Bentivoglio, Guido di, papal nuncio, bp of Riez 82, 83, 179, 437
Bern 169
Bernage, Jacques de, bp of Grasse 76, 280
Berry 444; duchy of 348
Bertaut, Jean, bp of Séez 207, 217, 220, 262, 283, 284, 381, 394

Bertier, family 198–9, 325
Bertier, Jean de, bp of Rieux 149–50, 269–70, 373, 393
Bertier, Jean de, parlementaire 491
Bertier, Jean-Philippe de, abbé de 87–8
Bertier, Pierre de, bp of Montauban 24, 229, 243, 491
Bérulle, Pierre de, Cardinal 268, 440, 452, 466, 481, 483; disciples of 278, 484, 485; influence of 254, 457, 545; and episcopal nominations 456, 552–3
Béthune, Henri de, bp of Maillezais, Bordeaux 34, 64–5, 70, 93–4, 158, 169, 177, 230, 295, 318, 455, 484, 497, 498, 553
Béthune-Charost, Philippe de 475
Béziers, bp of 180, 182, 221, 250, 434, 470; see of 29, 110, 119, 175, 260, 323, 326, 394, 425, 446, 447, 533. *See* Bonsi
Billy, Godefroy de, bp of Laon 369, 397, 400
Birague, Cardinal 358
Birgue, Horatio, bp of Lavaur 361
Biron, Charles de Gontaut, duc de 375
Biron, Charles de Gontaut 375
bishops. *See* coadjutors, dioceses, episcopate, resignations; absenteeism among 89, 340–1; active in provincial estates 288; age at appointment 298–303; and Catholic League 359–64; and choice of coadjutors 23–4, 306–8; and diplomacy 287; and experience of cure of souls 269–71; and humanist learning 213; and letters 210, 546–7; and priestly orders 74, 247; and tenure of dioceses **293–333**; and university studies 210–12, 225–44; as beneficiaries of pensions 157; as *seigneurs* 98–102, 208; clerical status of at nomination 248–9, 251–7; colleges attended by 219–25; commoners among 186, 187, 189, 206, 410–12; consecrations of 73–6; criticism of ignorance among 241; deaths of 57; degrees taken by 225–44; deposed for rebellion 462–5; destinations of 168, 176–8; determinants of career durations of 303; dominate French church 547–51; drawn from cathedral chapters 271–7; drawn from religious orders 265–6, 269, 547–8; education of **208–44**; elder sons among 259; elections of 366, 370, 553–4; expenditure by 132; fiscal obligations of 136; foreign universities attended by 231; foreigners among 178–83, 186; geographical origins of 167–83 (*see* Parisians); holders of benefices *in commendam* 291; *in sacris* 246, 248, 251, 252, 254, 255; Italians among 178–9, 180, 181. (*See* Italians); journey to Rome 70; lengths of careers 296–7, 303–4; letters of nomination 60–1; limited mobility of 423; making of **46–89**; mechanisms of nomination 18; mendicants among 266, 268; minimum age for 50, 248, 264; nominations of revoked 59–60; number of 26; oath of

fidelity to king 71, 72, 79; of monastic origins 265, 268; orders taken before nomination 254–7; origins of 12, 167–207, 220, 224, 237, 242; pluralism among 358; powers of 45; pre-episcopal careers of 13, 245–92; preaching as preparation for 283; professional origins of 201–7; promoted to archdioceses 316; related to other bishops 330–2; reputation as preachers 280–4; resignations under Henri IV 391; response to Reformation 337–9; responsibility for *confidences* 357–9; retirement of 297, 317–18, 418; rival nominations during League 366–7; secular careers followed by 261–2, 263, 286; social profile of 167–8, 183–202, 252, 543–4; suspected of Protestant sympathies 338–9; total figures of 309; transfers of 423–4, 462, 554–6; types of nobility among 185–8, 189–202; university professors among 244; unrelated to other bishops 328–9; without orders on nomination 259, 250; without university degrees 229; younger sons among 263

bishoprics. *See* Dioceses, Episcopate
Blois 53, 191, 353, 468
Bluche, François, historian 7
Boivin, François de, coadj of Avranches 424
Boivin de Péricard, Henri de, coadj of Avranches 24, 424
Bologna, Concordat of 8, 58, 65, 185, 271, 294, 335, 336, 337, 341, 384, 408, 414, 557; and annates 65; and minimum age of bishops 73, 246, 264, 300, 302; and royal episcopal patronage 48–52, 347; and university degrees 210–11, 212–13, 215, 233, 239; provinces excluded from 50, 369, 370; terms of 48–52, 55–6
Bologne, Antoine de, bp of Digne 150, 394
Bologne, Etienne de 150, 394
Bologne, Louis de, bp of Digne 425
Bologne, Raphaël de, bp of Digne 425
Bolognetti, Giorgio, papal nuncio 459
Boniface VIII, pope 357–8
Bonnechose, Jean de 349
Bonsi, family 180, 182, 221, 323, 324, 326, 425, 470
Bonsi, Clement de, bp of Béziers 260, 456
Bonsi, Dominique de, coadj of Béziers 250, 260, 425, 434
Bonsi, Francesco 533
Bonsi, Jean de, Cardinal, bp of Béziers 250–1, 260, 394, 425, 427, 434
Bonsi, Pierre de, Cardinal, bp of Béziers, abp of Toulouse, Narbonne 326, 530
Bonsi, Thomas I de, bp of Béziers 394
Bonsi, Thomas II de, bp of Béziers 251, 260, 261, 425, 426
bonus pastor 209, 294
Bordeaux 29, 119, 169, 170, 173, 175, 244,
535; abp of 34, 249; college of 220, 221, 224; council of 42; parlement of 199, 229; see of 40, 64–5, 93–4, 110, 115, 117, 152, 239, 275, 361, 377, 389, 421, 423, 443, 446, 456, 471, 472, 475, 481, 486, 497, 498; Univ of 228, 229, 231, 233, 237, 238
Borromeo, Carlo, Cardinal 4, 8, 209, 280
Bosquet, François, bp of Lodève, Montpellier 5, 85, 288, 282–3, 447, 501, 502, 506, 511, 520
Bossuet, Jacques-Bénigne 193, 281, 281, 546
Boucher, Jean 367–8
Boucicault, Etienne le Meingre de, bp of Grasse 196, 207
Bouillon La Marck, house of 192, 193, 376
Bouillon, Alexandre de La Marck de 375, 376
Bouillon, duc de 104, 124, 304, 376, 441, 464
Boulogne bp of 223, 325, 397, 456, 473; see of 32, 36, 110, 119, 136, 157, 171, 176, 423, 468, 473, 497. *See* Dormy, Bouthillier, Olce, Perrochel
Bourbon, Charles de, Cardinal ('Charles X') 190, 343, 352, 360
Bourbon, college of 224
Bourbon house of 189, 341
Bourbon succession 359–64, 365
Bourbon-Navarre, Charles, abp of Rouen 145, 319, 345, 358, 378, 382, 403
Bourbon-Vendôme, Charles de, Cardinal 145, 190, 363, 381
Bourbon-Verneuil, Henri de, bp of Metz 4, 37, 190, 301
Bourbonnais 53
Bourdeille, family 80, 81, 151, 156, 284, 411, 429
Bourdeille, André de 80
Bourdeille, François de, bp of Périgueux 80. *See* Brantôme
Bourdeille, Henri, vicomte de 80, 378
Bourdeille, Marguerite de 328
Bourges, abp of 5, 218, 284, 286, 297, 304, 348, 358, 364, 422, 448; council of 357; see of 30, 40, 41, 100, 100, 110, 115, 119, 151, 238, 317, 358, 376, 394, 422, 444, 522; Univ of 219, 226, 228. *See* Beaune, Frémiot, Hardivilliers, Hébert, Ventadour
Bourgneuf, Charles de, bp of Saint-Malo, Nantes 319
Bourgogne, duc de 96
Bourgoing, Nicolas, bp of Coutances 273
Bourlemont, Charles d'Anglure de, bp of Aire, Castres, Toulouse 182, 231
Bourlon, family 536
Bourlon, Mathieu, bp of Soissons 279
Boutault, Gilles, bp of Aire, Evreux 219, 473, 518, 519, 531
Bouthillier de Chavigny, Léon 85, 478, 500, 503
Bouthillier, family 197, 473, 474
Bouthillier, Claude 77, 92, 197, 477, 478, 483

Index

Bouthillier, Denis 197
Bouthillier, Sébastien, bp of Aire 53, 274–5, 279, 451, 473
Bouthillier, Victor, bp of Boulogne, abp of Tours 157, 279, 317, 322, 423, 456, 463, 468, 472, 473
Boylesve, Claude de, financier 535
Boylesve, Gabriel de, bp of Avranches 256, 531, 535, 542
Bragelongne, Emery de, bp of Luçon 421, 465
Brandon, Philibert de, bp of Périgueux 262, 505, 514, 520, 523
Brantôme, Pierre de Bourdeille, abbé de 80
Breslay, René de, bp of Troyes 215, 216, 230
Bretel, Louis, abp of Aix 470
Breton. *See* Brittany
brevets de nomination 19, 57, 59–61, 140, 222, 327, 350, 351–2, 353, 367, 381, 397–8, 466, 479, 481, 442, 522, 525, 536
brevets de réserve 420
Brézé, family 328, 376
Brézé, Louis de, bp of Meaux 376
Brienne, Henri-Louis de Loménie, comte de 58, 59
Briroy, Nicolas de, bp of Coutances 269–70, 373, 411, 439, 353
Brittany 40, 42, 47, 173, 177, 462. (*See* Medici, Marie de', Mercoeur); autonomy of 361, 371; bishops in 67, 356, 379; dioceses in 31, 35, 52, 92, 93, 115, 117, 147, 171, 393, 450–1, 456, 466, 467–9, 482, 483, 497, 521, 531; estates of 288; outside terms of Concordat of Bologna 369
Broc, Pierre de, bp of Auxerre 328, 474
Broutin, Paul, historian 7
Brûlart, family 162
Brussels 367
Bruyères, Antoine de 355, 383
Budos, Balthasar de, coadj of Castres, bp of Agde 192, 424, 429, 447
Buffalo, Innocenzo del 409
Bullion, Claude de 474
bulls 155, 407. *See* provisions
buon governo 544
bureaux des décimes 137
bureaux des finances 199
Burgundy 32, 42, 150, 171, 191, 321, 361, 373, 380, 398, 519

cabale des importants 501, 507
Cadillac 171
Caetani, Enrico, papal legate 367, 371, 372
cahier de doléances, of clergy 436
Cahors, bp of 4, 135, 140, 159, 233, 237, 512, 513–15; see of 29, 40, 79, 101, 110, 116, 117, 247, 340, 348, 426, 467, 513, 515, 516–17, 523; Univ of 79, 228, 229, 233, 236, 237, 238. *See* Habert, Popian, Sévin, Solminihac

Calvinism 338, 339, 341; hostility to episcopacy 338
Cámara de Castilla 95
Cambrai, see of 36
Camus, family 170, 396
Camus de Pontcarré, abbé 521
Camus de Pontcarré, Jacques, bp of Séez 169, 283, 467
Camus de Saint-Bonnet, Jean-Pierre, bp of Belley 36, 37, 280, 297, 397, 546
Canigiani, Alexander, abp of Aix 361
canon law 211, 212, 216, 227, 229, 230, 233, 234, 235, 238, 239, 294, 347, 387, 388, 412
canons regular of St Augustine 266, 467
Capuchins 265
Caracciolo, Antonio, bp of Troyes 338
Carcassonne, bp of 260, 285, 382, 402, 405, 407, 438; see of 86–8, 89, 93, 110, 117, 149, 151, 153, 192, 317, 353, 536, 382, 383, 402, 537–8. *See* La Valette, Lestang, Rucellaï
cardinals: and diocesan revenues 157; free to select episcopal successors 286, 421–2; involvement in *confidences* 358
caretaker bishops 323, 353. *See also confidences, confidentiaires*
Carmelites 76, 240, 265, 401, 500
Carpentras 38
Carthusians 84, 230, 231, 240, 444, 474
Caset de Vautorte, Louis, bp of Lectoure, Vannes 199
Castelnau de Clermont. *See* Clermont
Castile. *See* Philip II, *Patronato Real*, Spain
Castres, bp of 363, 424, 429, 446, 447; see of 110, 113, 153, 356, 359. *See* Bourlemont, Budos, Fossé, Tubeuf
Catalonia 86, 501
Cathars 31, 32
cathedral chapters 339; bishops recruited from 271–7, 353; damage to during wars 135; and episcopal elections 46, 294; in Catholic Europe 548–9; loss of influence in France 548–9
Catholic League 9, 32, 35, 47, 78, 125, 128, 145, 151, 169, 280, 287, 321, **359–64**, 365–7, 374, 380, 382, 383, 386, 389, 393, 394, 400, 401, 407, 423, 518; agents in Rome 367; causes crisis in episcopate 360–4; collapse of 371; episcopal vacancies during 365–2; episcopal wavering over 392; in cities 367, 378, 379–80, 396; papal support for 371–2, 383
Catholic Reformation 10, 245, 280
Caulet, Etienne, bp of Alet 68, 270, 487, 505
Cavelesi, Raymond, bp of Nîmes 356, 401, 403
cessio regiminis 297
Chalon-sur-Saône, bp of 538; see of 30, 110, 398, 536. *See* Maupeou, Neuchèze, Thyard
Châlons-sur-Marne, see of 42, 110, 121–4, 171, 362, 466. *See* Clausse, Vialart

Chambéry 38
chambre des comptes 71–2, 95, 199
Champagne 115, 205, 361
Champigny, abbé de 483, 500
Champion, Guy, bp of Tréguier 199
Chandenier, Louis de, abbé 521, 522, 523
Chapelain, Jean 482, 492, 493
charges anoblissantes 197–200
charges ordinaires 134, 135, 137, 138, 143
Charles IX 55, 72, 143, 144, 148, 157, 186, 190, 201, 318, 323, 420, 340, 344, 348, 350, 351, 352, 354, 359, 557
Charles V, Emperor 142, 212
Charles X, (Cardinal Bourbon) 366
Charton, Jacques 507, 508, 524–5
Chartrain 173
Chartres 363, 378, 379, 468; bp of 54, 126, 157, 364, 472, 546; see of 30, 41, 53, 54, 110, 115, 116, 218, 270, 312, 469, 492, 502, 538. *See* Etampes, Hurault, Lescot, Neufville de Villeroy, Thou
Chasteignier de la Rocheposay, Henri-Louis, bp of Poitiers 218, 233, 420, 526
Châteauneuf, Charles de Laubespine, marquis de 524, 529
Châtelet 534
Châtillon, family 192, 341
Châtillon, Odet de, Cardinal 338, 351
Chavagnac, Jean de 393
Chavigny. *See* Bouthillier de Chavigny
Chéry, Eustache, bp of Nevers 490
Cheverny. *See* Hurault
Choart de Buzenval, Nicolas, bp of Beauvais 522, 541
Choiseul, Gilbert de, bp of Comminges, Tournai 76–7, 223, 243, 505, 509
Chrysostom, St John 208
Cinq-Mars, Henri Coeffier de Ruzé, marquis de 85
Cistercians (Cîteaux) 268, 465, 547
Cîteaux, abbot general of 354, 465
civil law 211, 227, 230, 231, 233, 234
Claret, Louis de, bp of Saint-Papoul 445
Clausse, family 199
Clausse, Cosme, bp of Châlons-sur-Marne 121, 362
Clausse, Henri, bp of Châlons-sur-Marne 121, 122
claveries 107
Clement VII, pope 8
Clement VIII, pope 39, 78, 146, 216, 302, 361, 364, 389, 402, 406, 409, 554; and Catholic League 369, 370; and Henri IV 370; defends papal rights 407–8; fears about episcopal nominations 372; reduces annates for French bishops 408, 432
Clérambault, Gilbert de, bp of Poitiers 220, 285, 532, 533, 535, 539
Clérambault, Marshal 532

Clergé de France 28, 37, 289
clerics 246–8, 250–1
Clermont, bp of 25, 99, 102, 108, 213, 319, 372, 399, 430, 521; see of 30, 31, 52, 104, 110, 120, 270, 319, 362, 430, 450, 468, 520–2, 537. *See* Estaing, La Rochefoucauld, Rose
Clermont, college of 76, 221, 222–4, 229, 239, 327
Clermont, comté of 102, 348
Clermont, Gabriel de, bp of Gap 338–9
Clermont de Castelnau, family 428–9
Clermont de Castelnau, Monsieur de 150, 446
Clermont-Tonnerre, François de, bp of Noyon 264, 543
cloche, noblesse de 197, 200
Cluny, abbey of 266, 268; abbot of 368; order of 440–1, 547
Coadjutor(ship)s 23, 56, 73, 84, 88, 90, 92, 93, 121, 129, 147, 148, 155, 156, 158, 161, 198, 222, 243, 247, 250, 253, 263, 272, 276, 283, 284, 288, 297, 300, 301, 310, 322, 323, 327, 332, 344, 387, 391, 393, 395, 399, 419, 423, 424, 425, 426, 427, 429–30, 430–1, 432, 434, 443–4, 446, 447, 461, 463, 465, 468, 471, 472, 475, 486, 490–1, 492, 496, 499, 500, 503, 509, 511, 522, 523, 524, 528, 531, 536, 554, 557; attempts to impose from above 491–2; consecrations of 308; crown views of 58; decline of 309, 438, 465, 489–91; die before succession 424; efforts to reform nominations of 437–9; form of episcopal nepotism 428; justifications of need for 308, 439; nominated to archdioceses 317; orders taken by 308; papal criticism of 431–5, 458; pattern of nominations of 306–9; reduce episcopal vacancies 435, 527; return of under Mazarin 496–7, 498–500, 502, 522; role in French church 23; unconsecrated 24, 425; under Henri IV 391, 394; under Louis XIII 419, 422, 428, 435, 443, 461
Coëffeteau, Nicolas, suffragan bp of Metz 25, 158, 424
Coeuvres. *See* Estrées
Cohon, Anthime-Denis, bp of Nîmes, Dol 207, 218, 283, 317–18, 320, 321, 497, 498, 501, 508, 518, 524, 530, 539
Colbert, family 331, 536
Colbert, Charles 99
Colbert, Jean-Baptiste 5, 87–8, 96, 109, 162, 198, 203, 517, 537, 539
Colbert, Nicolas, bp of Luçon 162, 529, 539, 542–3
Coligny, Admiral 338
Collège Royal 266
collèges de plein exercise 241; curricula of 219. *See* Jesuits
collegiate chapters, canons of 272–3
Collegium Germanicum 244
commende. See benefices, *in commendam*

Comminges, bp of 405, 424, 486, 509; see of 39, 41, 110, 113, 157, 320–1, 413, 420, 423, 424, 444, 466, 503, 509. *See* Choiseul, Donadieu, Labatut, Saint-Gelais, Souvré
Como, Cardinal 353
Compagnie du Saint-Sacrement 77, 222, 327, 460–1, 505
Comtat Venaissin 180, 181
Concini, Concino 22, 82, 179, 426, 430–1, 436, 437. *See* Galigaï
Condé, Charlotte de Montmorency, princess of 479, 519
Condé, Henri, prince of 100, 190–1, 284, 305, 316, 422, 444, 475, 494
Condé, Louis de Bourbon, prince of II 77, 475, 517, 521, 522, 525, 526, 531
Condom, bp of 21, 191, 195; see of 52, 110, 113, 348, 356, 393–4, 413, 457, 481, 504, 514. *See* Cous, Estrades, Lorraine-Guise
Condren, Charles de 254, 268, 466, 467, 486
conférences de mardi 486, 487, 491, 505
confidences 148, 156, 343, 346–7, 351–7, 381, 385, 387, 410, 412, 414, 449, 458, 557; terms of 80
confidentiaires (caretaker bishops) 78, 81, 89, 156, 215, 349, 372, 381, 384, 389, 397, 401–11, 444, 446–7, 543
Congregation of the Mission 76, 486
consecrations, of bishops 73, 246, 262, 280, 308, 425, 545
conseil de conscience 95, 243, 437, 439, 453, 461, 476, 485, 501, 510, 513, 524, 525, 540, 541, 544, 552. (*See* de Paul, La Rochefoucauld, Mazarin); after Fronde 529; beginnings of 495, 505–6; changes to during Fronde 523–4; decline of 514; early suggestions of 436; membership of 507, 508; Richelieu uninterested in 479; role of 508–9, 544; tensions within 508
conseil privé 378, 412
conseillers d'état 262, 263, 475
Conserans, bp of 84–6, 263, 305, 368, 380–1; see of 30, 84–6, 110, 113, 321, 369, 370, 380, 381, 430, 500. *See* Bellegarde, Bonard, Lingua, Marca, Marmiesse, Ruade
Consistory, papal 69
Constantin, Robert 243
Conty, Armand de Bourbon, prince of 77, 191, 284, 479, 482, 522, 526, 532
Conty, François de Bourbon 247
Conty, Françoise de Bonnétable, princess of 357
Cordeliers 267, 534, 535
Corneilhan, family 398, 399
Corneilhan, François de, bp of Rodez 319
Corsini, Ottavio, papal nuncio 62, 458
Cosnac, Daniel de, bp of Valence, Aix 284, 532
Cospeau, Philippe, bp of Aire, Nantes, Lisieux 66, 146, 155, 178, 182, 237, 285, 318, 411, 451, 455, 472, 473, 507, 508; influence of 484–5
Cossé, Artus de, bp of Coutances 100, 352, 353
Coton, Pierre, Jesuit, royal confessor 267, 393
council for ecclesiastical affairs: suggested in 1625 453
Counter-Reformation 7
coupe extraordinaire 98
coupe ordinaire 98
cour des aides 169, 199
Coutances, bp of 60, 93, 231, 269, 273, 352–3, 439; see of 66, 92, 100, 110, 117, 173, 177, 344, 351, 352–3, 371, 375, 407, 424, 444, 498, 534. *See* Auvry, Bourgoing, Briroy, Cossé, Le Blanc, Le Clerc de Lesseville, Lesley, Matignon
Coutras 359
Créqui, family 162
Crillon, Louis de Bertons de 145, 146, 147, 148, 149, 154, 316, 378, 404, 413
Cristin 372
Cros, Antoine de, bp of Saint-Paul-Trois-Châteaux 326, 327
Crown. *See* Charles IX, François I, Henri II, Henri III, Henri IV, Louis XIII, Louis XIV, Mazarin, Richelieu; alienates its episcopal patronage 349–53; and Concordat of Bologna 48–51, 335–7; and creation of new dioceses 32–4, 35; and episcopal elections 47–8; and lack of nomination procedures 56, 58; and nature of episcopal patronage after 1516 49–51, 55–6, 89; creates pensions off bishoprics 138–64; diminished power of during religious wars 351–4; grants bishoprics to Italian prelates 342; grants of apanages by 52–4, 347–9; growth of its episcopal patronage 32, 47–8; limitations of patronage of 296; patronage traditions of 347–8
Cum Occasione, papal bull 540
Cupif, Robert, bp of Saint-Pol-de-Léon, Dol 35, 60, 87, 140, 141, 142, 153, 155, 464, 469, 498, 501, 518, 519, 521, 534
Cuppis, Antoine, bp of Sisteron 361
Curia 179, 215, 287, 339, 341, 350, 352, 374, 383, 386, 406, 544. (*See* papacy, provisions, Rome); and annates 65, 92; critical of episcopal nominations 408–9, 431–3; crown builds party in 179, 355, 406, 413; search for provisions in 64–5
Cusance 79

Daffis, family 199
Daffis, Bernard, bp of Lombez 229, 237, 446
Daffis, Jean II, bp of Lombez 229, 230, 453–4, 456
Daillon du Lude, Gaspard, bp of Agen, Albi 231, 321, 463, 475, 519
Daillon du Lude, René, bp of Bayeux 152, 373, 376, 378, 406
Dandino, Anselmo, papal nuncio 356–7

Danès de Marly, Jacques, bp of Toulon 253, 475
Danès, Pierre, bp of Lavaur 213
Dauphiné 29, 42, 50, 222, 324, 326, 340
Dax, bp of 240; see of 66, 78, 110, 115, 239, 378, 469. *See* Desclaux, du Sault, Le Boux, Noailles
de non vacando in curia, papal brief 51
De Paul, Vincent 76, 541, 543, 553. (*See conseil de conscience, dévots*, Solminihac); as mentor of bishops 260, 270, 486, 487, 491, 497, 504, 505, 521; influence of 254, 486, 543; removed from *conseil de conscience* 529; role in *conseil de conscience* 509; role in making bishops 506–10, 511–17, 524, 552–3
De Sales, François, bp of Geneva 4, 8, 181, 280, 282, 209, 404, 545
de vita et moribus, enquiry 19, 61–2, 216, 298, 432, 434, 443, 431, 459
décimes 96, 107, 133, 134, 136, 137, 138, 143
Delbène bishops 520
Delbène, Alphonse I, bp of Albi 382, 401–2, 404
Delbène, Alphonse II, bp of Albi 304, 463, 464, 498, 502
Delbène, Alphonse III, bp of Orléans 502
Deschaux, Bertrand, bp of Bayonne, Tours 157, 249, 325, 393, 423, 468, 473
Desclaux, Jacques, bp of Dax 474
Desclaux, Pierre 474
Deslandes, Noël, bp of Tréguier 158, 240, 475, 477, 481
Desportes, Philippe 375, 381
Despruets, Bernard, bp of Saint-Papoul 71, 273, 484
Destrappes, Léonard, abp of Auch 207, 388, 412–13
dévots 33, 513, 553. (*See conseil de conscience*, de Paul, Medici, Mazarin, Richelieu, Solminihac); and *conseil de conscience* 243, 495, 505, 510; and educated episcopate 242–4; and nobility 504–5; and orthodoxy of bishops 512, 541; and Richelieu 417–18, 455, 460–1, 475; conceptions of episcopate of 159–60, 278, 499, 505, 512; entering episcopate 456, 497, 505; growth of influence of 232, 252, 418, 437, 460, 467, 469, 501; influence of in Richelieu entourage 487–8; loss of influence in Fronde 523–4; networks of 327, 417, 439–40, 470, 471, 484, 491; refuse episcopal office 466; relations with Mazarin 501, 512, 523–4
Die, see of 34, 50
Dieppe 98
Digne bp of 58–9, 531; see of 30, 40, 102, 110, 150, 171, 394, 425. *See* Bologne, Forbin-Janson
Dijon 32, 33, 175, 199, 221, 222
Dinet, Gaspard, bp of Mâcon 240, 393
Dinet, Jacques, Jesuit, royal confessor 506

Dinet, Pierre 425–6
Dioceses. *See* Bishops, Episcopate; admininstration of temporalities 98, 105–8, 121–32; attitudes of families towards 327–8; attractiveness of 138, 176–8, 312, 316; *charges ordinaires* of 133; contemporary views of revenues of 91–4; crown and revenues of 94–5; delays in filling 318; dynastic tenure of 317, 322–6, 330–1, 332; enclaves within 31; exchanges of 56, 312, 424, 473, 497; financial attractions of 89, 93–4; grouped into provinces 40; hierarchy of revenues of 113–20; included in apanages 348–9; movements of bishops between 312–22; new additions to 36; number of 28; numbers of bishops holding 309 12; occupied by Huguenots 339–40; partitions of 31–4; pensions payable by 138–64; refusals of 425, 465–6; regional variations in revenues of 103, 115–20; reserved in advance of vacancy 420; revenues of 79, 108–37; size of 29; spiritual revenues of 103–4; subdivisions of 31; tables of revenues of 110–12; temporalities of sold 100–1, 129, 340, 351; temporalities of 97–105; tithes belonging to 102–3, 122, 128, 131, 133; unions of 34–5; vacancies under Henri III/IV 343–5, 366–9, 390; variations in status of 41–2
Diou, Jacques de 367
Dissay 99
Doctrinaires 219, 241
Dol, bp of 218; see of 30, 35, 92–3, 111, 171, 318, 370, 375, 396, 456, 482, 497, 498, 531, 534. *See* Cohon, Cupif, Douvrier, Révol, Thoreau
Dominicans 76, 182, 240, 266, 267, 356, 401, 403, 424, 481, 501, 547
Don Antonio, Portuguese pretender 178
don gratuit 96, 136, 520
Donadieu, François de, bp of Saint-Papoul 150, 157, 398
Donadieu, François de, bp of Auxerre 150, 157, 231, 320, 398, 424
Donadieu, Pierre de 150
Donnaud, Pierre de, bp of Mirepoix 424, 444
Donnaud, Pierre de, coadj of Mirepoix 270, 424
Dony d'Attichy, Louis, bp of Riez, Autun 93, 106, 180, 194, 240, 321, 456, 518, 519, 534
Dormy, Claude, bp of Boulogne 397
Douai 257
Douvrier, Hector, bp of Dol, Nîmes 230, 497–8
droit annuel 435, 556
Du Bec, Jean, bp of Saint-Malo 149, 394, 413
Du Bec, Philippe, bp of Nantes, Reims 21, 149, 151, 319, 362, 364, 368, 371, 376, 377, 394, 406, 410, 413
Du Bois, Olivier 431
Du Laurens, André 206, 395
Du Laurens, Gaspard, abp of Arles 206, 266,

395
Du Laurens, Honoré, abp of Embrun 206, 233, 395
Du Louet, René, bp of Quimper 93
Du Molinet, Claude, bp of Séez 393
Du Perron, Jacques, Cardinal, bp of Evreux, Sens 152, 230, 169, 206, 249, 262, 274, 277, 280, 284, 319, 369, 376, 378, 384, 393, 411, 419, 436
Du Perron, Jean Davy, abp of Sens 206
Du Plessis de Richelieu, Jacques, bp of Luçon 355
Du Puy, Bernard, bp of Agde 356, 446
Du Sault, family 396
Du Sault, Jean-Jacques, bp of Dax 78
Du Serre, Charles-Salomon, bp of Gap 147
Du Vair, family 396
Du Vair, Guillaume, bp of Lisieux 81–2, 262, 274, 430
Du Vair, Pierre, bp of Vence 24, 35
Du Val, André 283, 441
Duchaine, Louis, bp of Senez 430
Dupes, day of 460, 461
Duprat, Antoine, chancellor of France 212

économats/économes 72, 377, 380, 384, 385, 387, 418; and *confidences* 356; and lay control of dioceses 343, 346, 356, 374, 375, 377, 388; criticism of 356, 357; papal hostility towards 350, 357; role of upper clergy in 346, 358
Edelstein, Marilyn, historian 8, 185, 186
Education: cost of 224
Effiat, Antoine Coeffier, marquis d' 92, 476
Elne, see of 39
Embrun, abp of 206, 233, 428; see of 29, 38, 40, 111, 119, 160, 317, 340, 395, 396, 398, 427, 428, 520. *See* Aubusson de la Feuillade, Du Laurens, Hugues
Empire, Holy Roman, churches of 25, 339, 553. (*See Reichskirche*); bishops in 21; churches of 37, 226; elections of bishops in 553
England 30, 92, 95, 107, 226, 244, 484; bishops in 132, 545–6, 554; dioceses in 28. *See* Gifford
Entragues, Henriette d' 395, 502
epée, noblesse d' 194, 241
Epernon, house of 192, 448, 454. *See* La Valette
Epernon, Bernard de Nogart de la Valette, duc d' 503, 516
Epernon, Jean-Louis de Nogart de la Valette, duc d' 23, 66, 67, 88, 128, 146, 149, 155, 171, 221, 237, 285, 377, 382, 404, 411, 422, 440, 444, 445–6, 485
Epinac, Pierre d', abp of Lyon 360, 367, 386, 396
Episcopate. *See* Bishops, Coadjutors, Dioceses. attractiveness of 45, 551; composition of in 1589 342–45; de-territorialisation of 178;

demographic factors in composition of 297–8; elections to 46, 48, 56; experience needed for 543; family networks in 326–332; Gallican views of 294, 545; historiography of 3–10, 185–6, 337; ideals of 544–6; improvement in nominations to 457–8; low mobility levels in 318–21; nobility and changes in 543–4; noble dynasties among 325–6; pattern of transfers among 317, 320, 321–2; pluralism in 307, 340–1; pool of candidates for 480–2; social character of 183-202, 543; stability of 555; turnover within 337, 340, 390–1
equivalent, tax 130. *See* Serres, Jacques de 130
Erasmus 545
Esparbès de Lussan, Jean-Paul d' 357
Essarts, Charlotte des 21
Estaing, Joachim d', bp of Clermont 25, 108, 430, 521
Estaing, Louis d', bp of Clermont 521, 531, 537
Estaing, Jean d', vicomte d' 521–2
Estates, provincial 472
Estates General 47, 81, 186, 212, 213, 284, 288, 290, 360, 364, 435, 436, 437, 453, 526; and episcopal elections 47, 435–6
Este, family 104, 192, 342. *See* Nemours
Este, Alessandro, Cardinal d' 405
Este, Luigi, Cardinal d', abp of Auch 358, 372
Este, Rinaldo, Cardinal d' 83, 179
Estrades, family 195
Estrades, Jean d', bp of Condom 504, 514
Estrées, family 193
Estrées, Annibal, marquis de Coeuvres, Marshal d' 375, 376
Estrées, César d', Cardinal, bp of Laon 223, 287, 301, 532, 543
Estrées, Gabrielle d' 259, 395
Etampes, Léonor d', bp of Chartres, Reims 22, 124, 126, 237, 464–5, 472, 475, 482, 488, 502, 546
Evreux, see of 111, 117, 131, 274, 312, 368, 369, 376, 378, 384, 400, 478, 479, 482, 531. *See* Boutault, du Perron, Maupas, Péricard
expectatives 347

fabriques 97
Farnese, family 192, 342
Faure, François, bp of Glandèves, Amiens 321, 205, 267, 282, 521, 533, 534–5, 539
Fay-Peyraud, Paul-Antoine de, bp of Uzès 156, 285, 463
Fénélon. *See* Salignac
Fenouillet, Pierre, bp of Montpellier 71, 181, 182, 189, 207, 217, 220, 282, 404, 411
fermes générales 107–8, 122, 123, 125, 126, 131, 134
fermiers généraux 107–8, 125
Fervacques, Guillaume de Hautemer, Marshal 349, 379

Feuillants 67, 76
feuille des bénéfices 19, 506, 529
financiers: relatives become bishops 536–7. *See* Boylesve, Tubeuf, Zamet
Fisquet, Henri, historian 6
Fizes, Simon 356
Flanders 40, 462
Fleyres, family 429
Fleyres, Jean-Jacques de, bp of Saint-Pons 429
Fleyres, Pierre de, bp of Saint-Pons 428–9, 463
Florence 178, 180, 221, 324
Foix 192
Foix, Paul de, abp of Toulouse 285
Foix-Albret, house of 39
Foix-Candale, François de, bp of Aire 377
Folembray, edict of 383, 400–1, 402
Fontainebleau, colloquy of 393
Fontenay-le-Comte 34
Forbin, family 444
Forbin-Janson, Toussaint de, Cardinal, bp of Digne, Marseille, Beauvais 59, 238, 287, 301, 531, 543
Forez 53
Fossé, Jean I, bp of Castres 446
Fouquet de la Varenne, Guillaume 193
Fouquet de la Varenne, Guillaume, bp of Angers 193, 427
Fouquet, family 474, 536
Fouquet, Basile 161–2, 536
Fouquet, François 473
Fouquet, François, bp of Bayonne, Agde, Narbonne 75, 87–8, 161–2, 223, 235, 259, 260, 301, 317, 318, 322, 470, 471, 473, 486, 497, 500, 528, 536
Fouquet, Louis, bp of Agde 75, 161–2, 223, 235, 254, 260, 262, 301, 528, 536, 541, 542, 553
Fouquet, Nicolas 528, 536
Franche-Comté 212
Franciscans 240, 266, 267, 282, 394, 428, 521, 534, 547
François I 8, 26, 49, 58, 65, 121, 141, 179, 185, 186, 187, 189, 197, 200, 201, 212, 213, 291, 335, 337, 341, 342, 350, 358, 556; and Concordat of Bologna 49, 337
Fréjus, bp of 17, 370; see of 17, 111, 115, 146, 154, 175, 378, 380, 407, 413, 525, 535, 536. *See* Bellenger, Camelin, Ondedei
Frémiot, André, abp of Bourges 199, 218, 231, 297, 304, 394, 422, 435
Frémiot, family 394, 396
French ambassadors in Rome 64, 67, 69, 70, 94, 153, 154, 267, 428, 432, 434
French church. *See* Assemblies of Clergy, bishops, crown, dioceses, episcopate; problems in defining size of 27; territorial evolution of 29; financial autonomy of 96
Fronde 22, 23, 24, 35, 55, 77, 83, 88, 123, 159, 160, 161, 162, 163, 168, 195, 201, 255, 267, 279, 282, 287, 290, 304, 321, 376, 445, 447, 461, 463, 471, 494, 495, 496, 497, 498, 501, 502, 504, 508, 509, 517, 518, 519, 521, 523, 527, 528, 530, 531, 532, 533, 534, 535, 536, 537, 538, 539, 540, 542, 551. *See* Mazarin
Fulbert of Chartres 546
Fumée, Nicolas, bp of Beauvais 362, 367

Galigaï, Léonora 43–1
Galigaï-Dori, Sébastien 22, 179, 431
Gallia Christiana 5, 6, 218
Gallia Christiana Novissima 6
Gallia Narbonnensis 29
Gallican 86, 263, 423, 454–5, 458; attitudes 42, 63, 72, 243, 417, 423, 455, 458, 512, 545, 553; church 26, 49; liberties 28, 338, 339, 408
Gams, P B 6
Gap, bp of 147, 195, 338, 492, 520; see of 95, 111, 148, 160, 181, 195, 263, 332, 339, 474, 492, 538. *See* Clermont, Du Serre, Lionne, Paparin
Garnier, Jean, bp of Montpellier 67, 282, 404, 407, 409, 411
Gascony 29, 97, 107, 113, 146, 340, 345, 356, 471, 503
Gassendi, Pierre 425
Gassion, Jean de, Marshal 503
Gassion, Pierre de, bp of Lescar 503
Gaul 29
Gault Jean-Baptiste, bp of Marseille 4, 22, 239, 268, 467, 475, 486, 505
Gault, Eustache 22, 268, 475, 486, 492, 505
Gazette 77, 243, 481, 485, 503, 544
Gelas de Léberon, family 398
Gelas, Claude, bp of Agen 275, 399
Génébrard, Gilbert, abp of Aix 74, 266, 370, 371, 380, 386, 387, 393, 407
Geneva 4, 181
Genoulhac, Jean-Richard de, bp of Tulle 400
German church. *See* Empire, *Reichskirche*
Germanic Concordat 37
Gerson, Jean 209, 337
Gévaudan 42
Gifford, William, abp of Reims 21, 124, 178, 257–8, 441, 442
Givry, Anne d'Escars de, Cardinal, bp of Lisieux, Metz, coadj of Langres 319, 322, 363–4, 379, 387, 389, 399, 419
Glandèves bp of 368, 397; see of 40, 101, 111, 134, 168, 321, 369, 387, 399, 534, 535, 539. *See* Faure, Isnard, Ithier, Le Clerc
Godeau, Antoine, bp of Grasse and Vence 4, 5, 6, 24, 35, 66, 76, 139, 159, 161, 255, 259, 262, 280, 426, 472, 475, 480, 486
Gondi, family 54, 194, 317, 323, 324, 394, 430, 443; episcopal members of 15, 120, 152, 259
Gondi, Albert, duc de Retz 194
Gondi, Henri, duc de Retz 440

Gondi, Henri, Cardinal de Retz, bp of Paris 53–4, 180, 394, 397, 436, 437, 438, 439
Gondi, Jean-François de, abp of Paris 41, 222, 488
Gondi, Jean-François-Paul de, Cardinal de Retz, abp of Paris, 4, 8, 23–4, 41, 86, 191, 222, 223, 242, 243, 245, 253, 268, 270, 290, 487, 304, 324, 463, 495, 498–9, 499–500, 502, 505, 518, 527, 528, 553
Gondi, Pierre, Cardinal, bp of Paris 324, 362, 381, 385, 388, 394
Gondrin, Henri-Louis de Pardailhan de, abp of Sens 239, 301, 499, 502, 541
Gonzaga, Ferdinando, Cardinal 420
Grammont, family 162, 192
Grammont, Antoine de 325
Grancey, Raoul Rouxel de Médavy, comte de 521
Grand Almoner of France 71, 436, 439, 476. See Beaune, Du Perron, La Rochefoucauld, Richelieu, Barberini
grand conseil 67, 376, 384, 385, 406; bans search for papal provisions 374; regulates administration of benefices 374
grands 247, 284, 387–8, 494, 500. (*See* nobility); and changes in episcopate 543; during Fronde 532; eclipsed after 1630 477
Granvelle, Antoine Perrenot, Cardinal 212
Grasse, bp of 4, 24, 196, 207, 280, 380, 480; see of 29, 34–5, 111, 115, 159, 161, 171, 175, 255, 344, 370, 373, 426, 469, 470, 472. *See* Bernage, Godeau, Grasse, Guerin, Le Blanc, Boucicault, Villeneuve
Grasse, family 444
Grasse de Cabris, Jean de, bp of Grasse 276
Great Schism 48
Gregory XIII, Pope 348, 349, 353
Gregory XIV, Pope 61, 216, 217, 361, 367
Grenoble, bp of 57, 169; parlement of 197, 263; see of 29, 38, 60, 111, 119, 140, 173, 175, 426. *See* La Croix de Chevrières, Scarron
Grignan, family 326–7, 498
Grignan, François d'Adhémar de, bp of Saint-Paul-Trois-Châteaux, Arles 222–3, 327, 498, 500, 505
Grignan, Louis-François d'Adhémar, comte de 327
Grignan, Jacques d'Adhémar de, bp of Saint-Paul-Trois-Châteaux, Uzès 223, 322, 327, 505, 538
Grillié, Nicolas, bp of Bazas, Uzès 283, 308, 321, 456, 463, 481–2, 484, 485
Grimaldi, family 15
Grimaldi, Domenico, legate in Avignon 370
Grimaldi, Jérôme, Cardinal, abp of Aix 52, 83, 179, 520, 526, 534
Guenée, Bernard, historian 210
Guise, house of 15, 259, 344, 362, 373, 398, 440, 472. (*See* Lorraine-Guise (for ecclesiastical members)); and see of Reims 21–2, 124–6, 156–7, 372, 440–2, 443, 464–5, 472; clients of 24, 247, 284, 368, 372, 441, 443, 446, 454, 470; ecclesiastical interests of 37, 124–6, 191, 317, 341, 361, 371–2, 378
Guise, Catherine de Clèves, duchesse de 371–2
Guise, Charles de Lorraine, duc de 382, 421, 440–1, 470
Guise, Claude de, abbot of Cluny 368
Guise, François de Lorraine, duc de 342, 372
Guise, Henri de Lorraine, duc de (*le Balafré*) 360
Guise, Henri, duc de. *See* Lorraine-Guise
Guise, Henriette-Catherine de Joyeuse, duchesse de Guise 156, 441, 446
Guron de Rechignevoisin, Louis de, bp of Tulle 526, 533, 535, 539
Guyenne 128, 169, 171, 276, 324, 445, 469, 471, 515. *See* Bordeaux

Habert, Isaac, bp of Vabres 511
Habert, Pierre, bp of Cahors 218, 247, 426
Harcourt, college of 223
Hardivilliers, Pierre, abp of Bourges 174, 284
Harlay, family 317, 525
Harlay de Beaumont, abbé 544
Harlay de Sancy, Achille de, bp of Saint-Malo 170, 268, 397, 455, 468, 469, 482, 485, 499
Harlay, François I de, abp of Rouen 422, 488
Harlay, François II de, abp of Rouen, Paris 193, 524, 525, 531, 534
Haute Marche 53
Hayden, J Michael, historian 186, 188
Hébert, Roland, abp of Bourges 284, 444
Hémery, Michel Particelli d' 496
Hennequin, Aymar, bp of Rennes 363, 368
Hennequin, Dreux, coadj of Soissons 24, 425
Hennequin, Jeanne 67
Hennequin, Jérôme, bp of Soissons 24, 425
Henri II 36, 121, 187, 188, 213, 337, 341, 342, 344, 351, 396
Henri III 50, 52, 53, 61, 78, 84, 109, 146, 170, 171, 192, 195, 198, 201, 207, 217, 275, 318, 320, 340, 341, 362, 365, 372, 379, 385, 396, 401, 407, 410, 420, 421, 422, 429, 467, 475, 481, 542, 549; and grants of apanages 52, 348, 349; assassination of 26, 360–1; *confidences* under 215, 323, 346, 352–7; criticised by clergy 343, 345, 360, 412; episcopal nominations made by 26–7, 343–5, 346, 370; generosity towards prelates 358–9, 373, 402; grants episcopal presentation rights to nobles 55, 80, 81, 143, 144, 145, 350, 352, 355, 373, 378, 395, 428; last episcopal nominations by 365–6; papal indult for 50, 369; pensions under 148, 154; social profile of episcopate under 186, 188
Henri IV 4, 16, 19, 21, 31, 35, 37, 38, 39, 51, 52, 55, 59, 61, 67, 76, 116, 128, 129, 161, 170, 174, 175, 176, 178, 182, 189, 190, 193,

196, 198, 199, 201, 206, 215, 217, 229, 231, 232, 240, 251, 252, 253, 257, 259, 261, 262, 267, 272, 273, 274, 276, 277, 278, 281, 282, 283, 284, 286, 287, 288, 289, 304, 309, 310, 323, 328, 329, 331, 335, 336, 337, 338, 340, 341, 348, **359–415**, 416, 417, 418, 421, 423, 425, 427, 429, 431, 432, 435, 442, 449, 450, 481, 530, 542, 549, 556, 557; age of bishops nominated by 299–300, 301, 302; and bishops in Provence 398; and bishops nominated by rivals 380–1; and Breton dioceses 398; and coadjutorships 307, 419–20, 427, 446; and Concordat of Bologna 384; and *confidences* 346, 354, 410; and disputed episcopal nominations 380–2; and episcopal resignations 405; and grants of pensions 83, 141, 145–55, 156, 157, 163, 164, 388, 412, 413; and Italians in episcopate 404–5; and Languedoc bishoprics 383, 400–4; and nobility in episcopate 395–99; and noble control of bishoprics 77–81, 388; and reform demands 414–5; and royalist bishops 394; attitude towards League bishops 379; beneficiaries of pensions granted by 149–52; bishops chosen from household of 392–3; bishops nominated by 220; cancels episcopal nominations 57, 60; coadjutors nominated by 391; commoner bishops under 410–12; concessions to noble families 80, 375, 377 (*see confidences, économes*); conversion of 363–4; determined to nominate own bishops 372–3, 378; early episcopal nominations of 26–7, 368, 370, 374–5; early episcopal views of 361–4; ecclesiastical advisors of 365; episcopal dynasties under 323, 325, 327–7; episcopal mobility under 318–20; episcopal nominations under 390–2; episcopal support for 364–5; grants pensions off bishoprics 145–55; limited generosity towards favourites 395; nominates bishops without orders 249; nominates outsiders to bishoprics 398; nominates own episcopal candidates 373–4; nominates regulars to bishoprics 266, 268; papal reserve towards 369; patronises Jesuit college 221–2; praised for episcopal choices 435; renews presentation rights to wife 348; restores relations with Rome 384–5; rewards supporters 376, 392–4; social profile of bishops under 186–8; suspicions of conversion 365; treatment of *ligueurs* 379, 381–2, 399–400
Henrietta Maria 484
Henry VIII 545
Heurtelou, Adam de, bp of Mende 358
Hierarchia Catholica 20, 21, 23, 227
Holy Roman Empire. *See* Empire, *Reichskirche*
Huguenots 32, 71, 88, 92, 135, 199, 215, 338, 340, 356, 360, 401, 404, 407, 415, 417, 441, 465, 546 *See* Protestant(ism)
Hugues Guillaume d', abp of Embrun 267, 428, 486
Hurault de Cheverny, family 152
Hurault de Cheverny, Philippe chancellor of France 260, 385, 396, 542
Hurault de Maisse, André 377, 380, 393
Hurault, Paul, abp of Aix 380, 393, 407
Hurault, Philippe, bp of Chartres 396
Hyver, François, bp of Luçon 270, 304, 376, 411

Iharse, family 399
Ile de France 174
in commendam (benefices held) 124, 143, 153, 224, 245, 264, 265, 266, 291, 292, 458, 528, 529, 539, 549
in sacris 246, 248, 251, 252, 253, 257
in utroque jure 211, 227
indult, papal 50, 370; for episcopal nominations 369
Innocent X, pope 52, 520, 534, 540
Innocent XI 545
Inquisition 547
intendants des finances 77, 206
Intolerabilis, papal bull 357
Ireland 60, 534
Irenaeus 546
Isnard, family 399
Isnard, Clement, bp of Glandèves 181, 380
Isnard, Octave, bp of Glandèves 181
Italian Cardinals: and French bishoprics 83, 185, 192, 337; and French pensions 141, 142, 143
Italians 169, 194, 231, 342, 417: among French episcopate 178–80, 182–3, 342, 361, 394, 405–6, 501, 533
Italy 70, 179, 194, 231, 280, 393, 463, 472; dioceses in 28, 29; pensions off bishoprics in 142; power of bishops in 544–5; religious orders in 547; transfers of bishops in 554
Ithier, Dominique, bp of Glandèves 267, 282, 533, 535, 539
ius spolii 550
Ivo of Chartres 546

Jansenism 63, 123, 244, 268, 290, 499, 512, 516, 540–1, 546
Jars, commandeur de 215
Jeannin, Pierre 392
Jesuits 267–8, 425, 506, 508, 522, 547; colleges run by 76, 100, 219, 221–3, 239, 241, 250, 267, 268, 327, 376; hostility towards 223; recalled to France 393. *See also* royal confessors (Annat, Arnoux, Coton, Dinet, Paulin, Ségueran, Suffren); Clermont, La Flèche, Tournon (colleges); Ventadour churches of 75, 76
John XXII, pope 31, 35, 40
Joyeuse, house of 86, 181, 192, 316, 340, 356, 400–404, 446; and Folembray edict 402;

clients in episcopate 355, 402, 403, 429, 446; disappearance of influence of 448; ecclesiastical patronage of 356, 359, 402–4; power in Languedoc 361, 382–3, 400–3, 445, 446; rivalry with Montmorency 382–383, 401–5

Joyeuse, Ange, duc de 383, 400, 401, 402

Joyeuse, François, Cardinal, abp of Narbonne, Toulouse, Rouen 113, 128, 149, 152, 156, 157, 237, 284, 285, 316, 319, 341, 343, 359, 361, 367, 382, 383, 384, 385, 400, 401, 402, 411, 413, 430, 431, 440, 445, 446, 470; ecclesiastical movements of 403; resignation of sees by 421–2

Killala, see of 60, 534
King's confessor. *See* royal confessor

L'Estoile, Pierre de 3
L'Hôpital Nicolas de, Marshal 76, 375, 382
L'Hôtel, Jean de, bp of Viviers 355
La Barde, Denis de, bp of Saint-Brieuc 474
La Baume de Suze, François, comte de 355
La Baume de Suze, family 429
La Baume de Suze, Louis de, bp of Viviers 310, 312, 439
La Baume, Pierre de, bp of Saint-Flour 78, 79
La Baume, Prosper de 78
La Béraudière, François de, bp of Périgueux 489
La Croix de Chevrières, family 396
La Croix de Chevrières, Alphonse de, bp of Grenoble 426
La Fayette, François de, bp of Limoges 147
La Fère, governorship of 532
La Ferté, Emeric Marc de, bp of Le Mans 288
La Feuillade. *See* Aubusson
La Flèche, college of 221, 222, 223, 224, 229, 240
La Force, Jacques Nompar de Caumont, duc de 379
La Guesle, family 152, 396
La Madeleine de Ragny, Claude, bp of Autun 73
La Marck. *See* Bouillon
La Meilleraye, Charles de la Porte, Marshal 532
La Mothe-Houdancourt, Daniel, bp of Mende 474
La Mothe-Houdancourt, Henri de, bp of Rennes, Auch 253, 243, 474, 500, 532, 533
La Noue, François de 215
La Porte, Amador de 71
La Rivière. *See* Barbier
La Rochefoucauld, abbé 544
La Rochefoucauld, Alexandre de 372, 383, 401
La Rochefoucauld, Antoine de, bp of Angoulême 155, 405
La Rochefoucauld, François de, Cardinal, bp of Clermont, Senlis 120, 213, 319, 372, 399, 430, 436–7, 438–9, 440–1, 442, 447, 454–5, 476–7. *See conseil de conscience*, grand almoner of France

La Rochefoucauld, François, duc de 503, 509, 533
La Rochefoucauld, Louis de, bp of Lectoure 503, 504
La Rochelle 287, 447, 482, 484, 490; see of 33–4, 111, 287, 497. *See* Raoul
La Valette. *See* Epernon
La Valette, Louis de, bp of Mirepoix 88–9, 444, 445, 516
La Valette, Louis de, Cardinal, abp of Toulouse 23, 128, 146, 157, 221, 237, 285, 422
La Vieuville, Charles de, bp of Rennes 220
La Voulte 169
Labatut, Hugues de, bp of Comminges 486
Labbé, Pierre 96
Lagny, abbey of 538
Langres bp of 33, 363, 399, 420, 445; see of 32–3, 42, 111, 117, 119, 121, 189, 284, 324, 387, 395, 419–20, 445, 532, 534, 538. *See* Barbier, Escars, Zamet
Languedoc 29, 42, 103, 107, 113, 115, 117, 119, 130, 132, 136, 149, 150, 151, 163, 169, 171, 175, 177, 181, 182, 270, 283, 321, 324, 340, 345, 352, 356, 361, 362, 421, 428, 443, 445, 446, 447, 448, 463, 470, 472, 475, 506; bishops after Fronde 530; bishops in 448, 469, 488, 519, 536; bishoprics of 382, 383, 400, 445–7; estates of 42; Estates of 362, 446; political settlement in 1596 382–3; revolt in 1632 304, 462; struggles over bishoprics in 382–3, 400–4. *See* Joyeuse, Montmorency
Lansac, family 413
Laon, see of 42, 111, 119, 171, 369, 375, 400, 532. *See* Billy, Brichantau, Estrées
Larchiver, François, bp of Tréguier 405
Laubespine, family 171, 199, 396
Laubespine, Gabriel de, bp of Orléans 453
Laubespine, Guillaume de 73
Laubespine, Jean de, bp of Orléans 363, 378–9
Laubespine, Madeleine de 396
Laval-Boisdauphin, Henri de, bp of Saint-Pol-de-Léon 239, 531
Lavaur, bp of 283, 361, 478, 525, 546; see of 38, 111, 182, 397, 467, 471, 501. *See* Birague, Du Vergier, Raconis, Tulles
law 227, 230, 231, 244; character of degrees in 233; faculties of 226, 241
Le Blanc, Guillaume, bp of Vence 35, 370, 380, 386
Le Blanc, Guillaume, canon of Agen 424
Le Boux, Guillaume, bp of Dax, Périgueux 239, 240, 268
Le Breton, Jean 377
Le Clerc de Lesseville, family 536
Le Clerc de Lesseville, Eustache, bp of Coutances 200, 231, 279
Le Clerc, René, bp of Glandèves 168–9
Le Mans 218, 221; bp of 4, 364, 398; see of

111, 115, 398, 513. *See* Angennes, Beaumanoir de Lavardin, La Ferté
Le Masuyer, Gilles 490
Le Prestre, Guillaume, bp of Quimper 276
Le Puy, bp of 479; see of 40, 99, 102, 104, 108, 111, 129–32, 171, 362, 363, 383, 401, 446, 482. *See* Maupas, Senneterre, Serres
Le Tellier Charles-Maurice, abp of Reims 126, 442
Le Tellier, Michel 517, 525, 537
leases. *See fermes, femiers-généraux*
Lectoure, see of 30, 111, 345, 377, 503. *See* Caset, Esdresses, La Rochefoucauld, Plas
Lenoncourt, Robert de, Cardinal 192, 363
Lerma, duke of 409
Lescar, bp of 393; see of 39, 111, 151, 175, 178, 273, 274, 391, 393, 503. *See* Abbadie, Salette, Salies
Lescot, Jacques, bp of Chartres 474, 492, 502, 538, 546
Lesdiguières, duc de 398
lèse-majesté 463
Lesley, John 371
Lestang, Christophe de, bp of Alet, Carcassonne 86, 260, 317, 319, 383, 402, 403, 436, 438, 446
Lestang, Vital de, bp of Carcassonne 86, 446
letters of nomination 64, 85, 350, 397, 432, 442
lettres d'économat 377, 408, 410
Liège, see of 553
Ligny, Dominique de, bp of Meaux 253, 262, 289, 536
ligueurs 145, 250, 319, 368, 378, 379, 380, 386, 394, 396, 397, 398, 399, 365, 367, 392, 397, 400, 401, 415
Lille 257
Limoges bp of 147, 379; see of 30, 31, 111, 117, 175. *See* La Fayette, La Marthonie
Limousin 173
Lingendes, Jean de, bp of Sarlat, Mâcon 66, 196, 280, 282, 284, 318, 471, 475, 489, 514, 521, 522
Lingua, Jérôme de, bp of Conserans 380–1, 430
Lionne, family 196, 256, 262
Lionne, Artus de, bp of Gap 195, 160, 262–3, 295, 332, 474, 489, 492
Lionne, Charles de 538
Lionne, Hugues de 95, 120, 295, 509, 520, 524, 525, 538
Lisieux, bp of 101, 400; see of 81–3, 98, 101, 111, 120, 177, 312, 319, 321, 349, 350, 378, 387, 389, 399, 411, 424, 430, 469, 478, 498, 507. *See* Aleaume, Cospeau, Du Vair, Givry, Matignon, Rouxel
Litolfi-Moroni, family 194
Litolfi-Moroni, Henri de, bp of Bazas 279, 471
Lodève, bp of 5, 169, 282, 383, 402, 511; see of 111, 149, 151, 153, 158, 317, 319, 321, 382, 383, 402, 403, 446 447–8, 476. *See* Robin,

Bosquet, Plantavit
Lombez, bp of 229; see of 30, 111, 113, 116, 446, 536. *See* Daffis
Longueville, Henri d'Orléans, duc de 501, 518, 521, 531
Lopis de la Fare, François, bp of Riez, 83
Lorraine 37, 122, 482
Lorraine-Guise, Cardinal Louis II de 360. *See* Guise
Lorraine-Guise, Cardinal Louis III de 151, 372, 421, 410, 440, 514
Lorraine-Guise, Henri de, abp of Reims, duc de Guise 21, 24, 125, 260, 304, 305, 441–2, 462, 464–5, 466, 482, 553
Lorraine-Guise, Louis bp of Condom 21, 513, 514
Loudun 205
Louis XII 8, 49, 185
Louis XIII 10, 16, 19, 20, 28, 33, 37, 38, 41, 51, 53–4, 59, 60, 76, 81, 93, 125, 156, 157, 182, 188, 200, 229, 231, 240, 243, 253, 277, 278, 279, 281, 286, 300, 305, 329, 337, 338, **416–93**, 494, 495, 498, 499, 500, 502, 505, 507, 508, 509, 514, 540, 546; and coadjutorships 490, 499–500; and *confidences* 429, 444, 447; and *dévots* 417, 437; and Jesuits 221; and pensions off bishoprics 155, 158–160, 538; episcopal mobility under 319–21; episcopal nominations under 155–6, 187, 251, 252, 272, 276, 307, 319–20, 323, 328, 335–6, **416–93**, 506; favourites of 55, 82, 84, 416, 431, 445, 454; patron of individual bishops 279–80; relations with Richelieu 448–50, 452–4, 457, 476–80, 493
Louis XIV 5, 8, 10, 12, 19, 26, 27, 35, 36, 37, 40, 41, 43, 47, 50–1, 71, 72, 96, 99, 104, 108, 120, 160, 178, 184, 186, 193, 195, 196, 198, 199, 201, 203, 206, 232, 234, 243, 244, 257, 267, 270, 276, 278, 279, 287, 290, 300, 304, 309, 318, 325, 327, 331, 336, 390, 417, 442, 467, 468, 474, 489, 494, 498, 499, 501, 506, 508, 514, 515, 524, 525, 526, 529, 533, 541, 555
Louis XVI 201
Loyac, abbé de 19, 479
Loyseau, Charles 184
Luçon, bp of 162, 304, 328, 411, 465; see of 31, 55, 111, 117, 150, 157, 159, 171, 257, 270, 274, 295, 346, 355, 376, 421, 450, 539, 543. *See* Bragelongne, Colbert, du Plessis, Hyver, Nivelle, Richelieu
Luxembourg, house of 192
Luynes, Charles d'Albert, duc de 82, 416, 417, 431, 436, 440, 443, 444
Lyon 143, 169, 170, 175, 197, 220, 221, 222, 324, 399; abp of 102, 260, 286–7, 305, 309, 367,423, 428, 451; cathdral of 74; chapter of 275, 548; see of 25, 41, 51–2, 102, 111, 113, 115, 116, 117, 119, 158, 295, 306, 310,

316, 321, 386, 396, 423, 427, 428, 455, 456, 471, 472, 474, 529, 532, 533, 538. *See* Bellièvre, Epinac, Marquemont, Miron, Neufville de Villeroy, Richelieu
Lyonnais 222, 275

Mâcon, bp of 196, 240, 361, 379, 521; see of 30, 111, 119, 318, 393, 425, 520–1, 522, 523. *See* Alemanni, Dinet, Lingendes
Madrid 409
Maillezais, bp of 177; see of 31, 33–4, 9–4, 111, 113, 116, 117, 312, 318, 423, 456, 481–2, 498. *See* Sourdis
Maine 40, 173
mainlevée des saisies 71
maître de chambre 68
maîtres des requêtes 206, 247, 262
Malier, family 171
Malier du Houssay, Claude, bp of Tarbes 475, 520
Malier du Houssay, François, bp of Troyes 474, 490, 491
Malines, see of 36
Malta 144
mandements 102, 107
Mantes 363
Marca, Pierre de, bp of Conserans, Toulouse, Paris 85–6, 128, 129, 163, 253, 263, 287, 321, 500, 501, 512, 516, 529, 530, 539, 541
Marconnay, Melchior de, bp of Saint-Brieuc 400
Marguerite de Valois 349; episcopal presentation rights granted to 348
Marillac, Michel de 180, 240, 440, 455–6, 457, 483, 492
Marillac, Octavien de 455–6, 482
Marmiesse, Bernard de, bp of Conserans 76, 77, 84, 85, 86, 229
Marmiesse, Pierre de 84, 85, 86
Marquemont, Denis Simon de, abp of Lyon 51, 287, 427–8, 435, 438
Marseille 531; bp of 4, 22, 59, 98, 105, 144, 179; Catholic League in 363, 371, 379, 380; see of 25, 40, 111, 116–17, 394, 424, 469, 471, 486, 492. *See* Coëffetau, Epinay, Gault, Loménie, Puget, Raguenau, Turicella
Marsillac, Sylvestre de, bp of Mende 42, 456, 474, 488, 519
Martin, Jacques, bp of Vannes 397
Martin, Jean 356
Martin, Jean, bp of Périgueux 80–1, 89, 284, 411, 429
Massillon, Jean-Baptiste 281
Matha, comte de 537
Matignon, family 60, 100, 151, 177, 217, 444, 454
Matignon, Lancelot de 352
Matignon, Léonor de, bp of Coutances, Lisieux 177, 230, 444, 498, 518, 531
Matignon, Jacques de, Marshal 207, 352, 353, 375, 411
Mauléon, abbey of 64
Maupas du Tour, Henri de, bp of Le Puy, Evreux 131–2, 279, 475, 479, 482
Maupeou, family 196, 331, 536
Maupeou, Jean de, bp of Chalon-sur-Saône 536
Maurists 6
Mayenne, Charles de Lorraine, duc de 145, 266, 372, 374, 378, 380, 398, 414. (*See* Catholic League, Henri IV); challenged by Henri IV 378; clients of 490; creates pensions 145; exercises crown's episcopal patronage 366–9, 382, 383, 400; limited episcopal success of 368, 369
Mazarin 10, 12, 16, 26, 35, 52, 53, 58, 74, 86, 92, 93, 131, 136, 174, 186, 193, 197, 201, 232, 240, 243, 252, 253, 254, 261, 262, 271, 274, 282, 284, 285, 291, 301, 302, 309, 310, 323, 325, 417, 418, 466, 475, 476, **494–540**, 557; and Assemblies of Clergy 29, 464, 520, 528, 551; and clerical orders 246–7; and *conseil de conscience* 508–11; and *dévots* 501, 504–5; and episcopal patronage after Fronde 87–8, 527–8, 530, 533, 537, 538; and episcopal patronage during Fronde 519–22, 524–6; and episcopal transfers 319–20; and Italians in episcopate 38, 83, 179–80, 182–3, 342; and nobles entering episcopate 187, 255, 476, 531–3, 537; and pensions off bishoprics 128, 160, 161, 162–3, 538–9; attacked for ingratitude 533–5, 539; attitudes towards episcopal office 513; benefices held by 529–30, 539; clientèle of 17, 68, 160, 163, 182, 205, 260, 279, 282, 286, 287, 301, 321, 495, 501–2, 504, 515, 519, 535, 542, 543; episcopal nominations made by 27, 36, 38, 66, 251, 268, 272, 276, 318, 328–9, 331, 461–2, **494–540**; episcopal supporters of in Fronde 518–19; relations with nobility 176, 502, 532; use of church benefices by 290, 537–8, 551
Mazarin, Michele, Cardinal, abp of Aix 38, 52, 501, 520, 534
Mazarinades 519
Meaux 30, 98, 376; coadj bp of 536; see of 30, 41, 111, 171, 177, 218, 308, 382, 375, 382, 474. *See* Belleau, Brézé, Ligny, Vieuxpont, Séguier
Medici, family 342
Medici, Alessandro de', Cardinal 152, 153, 366, 385–97, 401, 406, 407, 410; and restoration of episcopate 386–9; changes views of French church 386; dealings with nobility 387–8; pragmatism criticised by Fr clergy 388; rejects criticisms 388
Medici, Catherine de' 342, 349, 350, 351, 355, 543
Medici, Marie de' 22, 84, 283, 416, 417, 442, 453, 469, 472, 475, 484, 543; and *dévots*

439–40, 460; as regent 53, 416, 417, 426–7, 431–2, 436, 450; exile of 60, 454, 462, 470; entourage of 417; household of 278–9, 394, 474, 497–8 presentation rights to bishoprics 52–4, 348–9, 430, 450–1, 467–8
Medici, Giuliano de' 355
Melun 143, 382
Mende, bp of 42, 348; see of 38, 40, 111, 117, 119, 154, 158, 163, 171, 182, 267, 340, 358, 362, 394, 501. *See* Heurtelou, La Mothe-Houdancourt, Marsillac, Rousseau, Serroni
Mercoeur, Philippe-Emmanuel de Lorraine, duc de 370, 372, 382; claims episcopal patronage in Brittany 369–70
Metz, see of 25, 36, 37, 40, 190, 301, 395, 399, 424, 495, 529; suffragan bp of 479. *See* Bourbon-Verneuil, Coëffeteau, Puget
Milan 4
Minims 240, 265, 267, 393
Miossens, Jean de, bp of Oloron 195
Mirebeau 205
Mirepoix, bp of 88, 163, 448; see of 30, 111, 268, 270, 321, 424, 522. *See* Donnaud, La Valette, Ventadour
Miron, Charles, bp of Angers, Lyon 51, 309, 317, 423, 436, 451, 453, 456, 542
Molé, Edouard, bp of Bayeux 87, 161, 239, 259–60, 504
Molé, François 87, 161
Molé, Mathieu 161
Molé, Mathieu, keeper of the seals 87, 88, 260, 504
Monistrol 129
Monluc, family 413
Monluc, Blaise de 215
Mons 178
Mont-Saint-Martin, abbey of 104
Montaigne, Raymond de, bp of Bayonne 94, 230, 233, 262, 457, 473, 481
Montauban 444; bp of 24, 107, 135, 368, 400, 490–1; see of 98, 103, 111, 198, 243, 369, 375, 382, 490–1. *See* Bertier, Murviel
Montchal, Charles de, abp of Toulouse 128, 157, 207, 285, 456, 506, 507, 516, 526
Montigny, abbé de 26
Montmorency, house of 181, 190, 192, 285, 429, 446, 454, 500; governors of Languedoc 382. *See* Languedoc
Montmorency, Charlotte, 190
Montmorency, Henri duc de 462–3, 469–70
Montmorency, Marguerite de, duchesse de Ventadour 77
Montmorency-Châtillon, house of 192
Montmorency-Damville, Henri de, constable of France 146, 149, 153, 154, 156, 340, 351, 352, 356, 362, 382, 383, 400, 401, 403, 404, 421, 424, 429, 446; and see of Carcassonne 402; dioceses controlled by 346,

402; episcopal patronage of 352, 356–7; power in Languedoc 362, 383, 403, 446–7; temporalities usurped by 153
Montpellier 230, 429; bp of 182, 356, 404; cathedral 463; see of 71, 83, 111, 115, 179, 282, 351, 404, 407, 409, 534. *See* Bosquet, Fenouillet, Garnier, Ratte, Subject
Montpensier, Henri de Bourbon, duc de 319, 403, 404
Montrésor, Claude de Bourdeille, comte de 156
Montrouge, Jacques de, bp of Saint-Flour 279, 288, 502, 515
Morenne, Claude de, bp of Séez 393, 394
Moret, comte de 284
Morgues, Mathieu de 158, 454, 455
motu proprio 51, 408
Mozun 99
Munier, Jean 368, 378
Murviel, Anne de, bp of Montauban 24, 75, 369, 382, 400, 490–1

Nantes bp of 21, 151, 182, 362, 368; edict of 365, 393; *ligueur* parlement at 371; see of 111, 115, 312, 321, 376, 394, 413, 451, 455, 469, 473, 507; vicar-general of 371. *See* Beauvau, Bourgneuf, Cospeau, Du Bec
Naples 550
Narbonne abp of 85, 161, 222, 240, 341, 411, 443, 446, 470, 528; see of 29, 39, 42, 111, 113, 117, 149, 156, 161, 284, 326, 341, 343, 356, 358, 359, 383, 403, 470, 500, 509, 523, 528. *See* Joyeuse, Fouquet, Rebé, Vervins
Nassau-Orange 38
Navarre 39, 175
Navarre, college of 75, 76, 219, 223, 240, 393
Navarre, Henri de. *See* Henri IV
Nemours. *See also* Este
Nemours, house of 104, 146, 375, 382, 388
Nemours, Anna d'Este, duchesse de Guise and 342, 372, 388
Nemours, Henri de Savoie, marquis de Saint-Sorlin, duc de 149, 152, 182, 372, 388, 412–13
Nemours, Henri de, duc d'Aumale and 22, 23, 124–125, 531–2
Nesmond, family 197, 331
Netherlands 32, 36, 39, 178, 391, 553
Netz, Nicolas de, bp of Orléans 54, 169
Neuchèze, Jacques de, bp of Chalon-sur-Saône 73
Neufville de Villeroy, family 170, 198, 499
Neufville de Villeroy, Camille, abp of Lyon, 169, 170, 223, 275, 286, 287, 456, 484, 529, 532–3, 538
Neufville de Villeroy, Ferdinand, bp of Saint-Malo, Chartres 169, 170, 223, 499, 502
Neufville de Villeroy, Nicolas de, secretary of state 59, 67, 70, 170, 384, 392, 396, 426–7, 427–8, 430, 432

Nevers 207; see of 111, 119. *See* Chéry, Du Lis
Nevers, Charles de Gonzague, duc de 420
Nîmes 490; bp of 304, 320, 465, 488; see of 34, 111, 317, 321, 356, 382, 401, 404, 470, 498, 530–1. *See* Cavalesi, Cohon, Douvrier, Saint-Bonnet, Valernod
Nivelle, Pierre de, bp of Luçon 465
Noailles, family 78, 193, 398
Noailles, Charles de, bp of Saint-Flour, Rodez 79, 80, 81, 463, 498, 512, 515
Noailles, François de, bp of Dax 78
Noailles, Gilles de, bp of Dax 78
Noailles, Henri de, comte d'Ayen 78–9, 81, 377–8, 411
Nobility. *See confidences, économes, grands*, Henri III, Henri IV, Mazarin, pensions, Richelieu; age when nominated bishops 299; and changes in episcopate 543; and coadjutorships 429; and pensions off bishoprics 146; and university studies 210, 213, 242, 244; attitudes to education 213–14, 224; attitudes to episcopal office 445; attitudes towards dioceses 324–5; bénéfices held by during wars 387; eclipse of after 1630 475, 477; in episcopal office 396–7, 430, 531; occupy dioceses during religious wars 340; purchase of episcopal properties 351; types of 184–6, 189, 194–9, 200; young bishops from ranks of 264
Normandy 30, 31, 53, 117, 173, 177, 217, 224, 288, 319, 352, 361, 378, 393, 403; bishops in/after Fronde 531
Noyon, bp of 218, 273, 368, 434; see of 42, 55, 111, 119, 151, 171, 264, 368, 375, 376, 378, 395, 434, 445, 523. *See* Balsac, Baradat, Clermont-Tonnerre, Munier

official 271, 275, 276
Olce Jean d', bp of Boulogne, Bayonne 223, 325, 473, 497
Olier, Jean-Jacques 243, 254, 270, 466, 467, 499, 505, 509, 513
Olivier-Razali, Séraphim 405
Oloron, bp of 237, 532; see of 38, 39, 40, 111, 151, 175, 178, 195, 391, 503. *See* Gassion, Maytie, Miossens
Ondedei, Zongo, bp of Fréjus 17, 254, 533, 535, 543
Orange, bp of 267, 501; see of 182. *See* Tulles, Serroni
Oratory 76, 219, 239, 240, 241, 265, 267, 268, 397, 466, 475, 484, 486
Orléans 363, 468; bp of 169; see of 41, 53, 54, 73, 111, 171, 173, 177, 475–6, 477, 502; Univ of 224, 226, 228, 234, 236. *See* Delbène, Laubespine, Netz
Orléans, Gaston, duc d' 441; and episcopal nominations 54, 457, 477, 502, 517, 521, 522–3, 526; apanage of 53, 349, 468, 502; clients of 55, 218, 247, 278–9, 284, 445,
505, 509, 521, 532
Orléans, Philippe, duc d' 76, 77, 278
Ormée 535
Ossat, Arnaud d', Cardinal, bp of Rennes, Bayeux 152, 249, 285, 287, 319, 384, 385, 391, 393, 399, 405, 408, 411
Oxbridge 244

Paleotti, Gabriele 280
Pamiers, bp of 357; see of 68, 111, 157, 288, 356, 455, 490, 502, 506, 515. *See* Caulet, Esparbès, Sponde
Papacy 20, 45, 92, 251, 282, 287, 441, 472, 522, 527, 537, 550. *See* curia, *de vita et moribus*, papal legates, papal nuncios, provisions, Rome; and bishops under Henri IV 406–8; and coadjutorships 307–8, 432; and *confidences* 346, 349, 357; and cost of provisions 68; and demands over annates 432–3; and education of bishops 215–17, 242; and episcopal nomination indults 50; and episcopal nominations during League 367, 370–2, 385, 386; and pensions 130, 142, 152–154, 155–6, 388, 414; and underaged bishops 246, 301–2, 409–10, 434; condemns certain French bishops 338; critical of episcopal nominations 415, 431–3, 435; defends incumbent bishops 407; enquiries about bishops/dioceses 20, 92, 135, 298; episcopal nomination rights of 51, 501; fears of Protestant bishops 339; makes demands on incoming bishops 458–9; secondary role in making bishops 336; suspicions of episcopal resignations 297; suspicions of unorthodox bishops 407; undermines episcopal elections 46; welcomes better nominations 458
papal bulls. *See* provisions
papal legates: under Henri IV 371–2. *See* Sega, Caetani, Medici
papal nuncios 163, 281, 339, 431, 437, 458; activities of 408–9; role of 443. *See* Silingardi, Dandino, Barberini, Ubaldini, Bentivoglio, Corsini, Spada, Bolognetti, Spada
Paparin, Pierre, bp of Gap 147
Parabère, abbé de 526
Parabère, Henri de Baudéan, comte de 513
Pardailhan, family 162. *See* Gondrin
Paris 30, 106, 109, 168, 170–1, 173–4, 181, 197, 198, 199–200, 362, 367, 378, 379, 387, 523, 535; abp/bp of 23, 180, 316, 317, 323–4, 362, 457, 486, 487, 498, 499; 394, 443, 457, 481, 515, 527, 528. (*See* Gondi, Marca); becomes an archdiocese 40–1; episcopal consecrations in 74–7; parlement of 43, 49, 60, 87, 121, 161, 206, 214, 219, 220, 221, 222, 223, 224, 226, 228, 229, 230, 231, 234, 235, 236, 237, 238, 239, 240, 241, 243, 244, 247, 259, 260, 262, 368, 371, 379, 385, 388, 399, 425, 434, 438, 504, 518; see of 4, 24,

30, 40–1, 105, 111, 113, 115, 120, 129, 173, 290, 498; theology faculty in 235–6, 237–9, 270, 407, 487; Univ of 49, 219, 221, 223–4, 226, 227, 228, 229, 230, 231, 235, 241, 257, 285, 308, 487; vicar-general of 308
Parisians 169, 170–171; in episcopate 168–9, 170–1, 173–5, 176, 177, 223, 275, 469
Patronage: language of 350, 442; study of 13–18
Patronato Real 18, 19, 95
Pau, parlement of 85
Paul V, pope 154, 415, 431, 432, 554; and coadjutorial nominations 434–5; and pensions 414; and underaged bishops 434
Paulin, Charles, Jesuit, king's confessor 508, 529, 532–3, 535
Pavillon, Etienne, bp of Alet 270, 467, 475, 486, 541
pays d'états 321, 471; role of bishops in 42, 288, 471
pays d'obédience 50. *See* Brittany, Provence
Peiresc, Nicolas Fabri de 58, 292, 423, 462, 492
Pellevé, Nicolas de, Cardinal, abp of Sens, Reims 367, 368, 372
pensions. *See* crown, dioceses, papacy; and control of dioceses 149–51; aristocracy and 151, 156, 161–2; as proportion of episcopal revenues 142–3, 154–5; criticism of 141, 152; dioceses escaping 151, 163; for clerics only 156; for retiring bishops 148; geography of 164; given to bishops' families 150; given to laymen 143, 152; litigation over 149; nature and evolution of 139–43; personal nature of 164; practice of redeeming 147; problems of payment of 143; return during and after Fronde 160–1; sociology of holders of 151; under Henri IV 145–55, 387–9, 412–13; under Mazarin 536; uses in Rome 83; virtual disappearance of in 1630s 158
Père Joseph (François Le Clerc du Tremblay) 486
Péréfixe, Hardouin de, bp of Rodez, Paris 500, 508, 515, 519, 520, 524, 529
peregrinatio academica 220, 231
Péricard, family 24
Péricard, François, bp of Angoulême 239
Péricard, François, bp of Avranches 24, 309, 368–9, 371, 424
Péricard, Georges, bp of Avranches 441
Péricard, Guillaume, bp of Evreux 400
Périgueux, bp of 284, 411, 516; see of 31, 80, 111, 156, 378, 427, 477, 481, 489, 492, 514. *See* Bourdeille, Brandon, La Béraudière, Le Boux, Martin, Villers-la-Faye
Péronnet, Michel, historian 8, 9, 186
Perpignan, see of 39
Perrochel, François, bp of Boulogne 270, 487, 497, 505
Philip II 36, 40. *See Patronato Real*, Spain.

ecclesiastical policies of 32, 39, 552, 554; papal praise for 409
Philip III 409
Philip IV 554
Philip the Fair 47
Picardy 30, 115, 174, 263, 361
Piedmont 180, 181; bishops from 342
Pingré, family 536
Plantavit de la Pause, Jean, bp of Lodève, 5, 447, 463
Plutarch 213
Pluvinel, Antoine de 57
Poitiers 170, 197, 205; bp of 99, 218, 233, 420, 517, 526, 536; see of 23, 30, 31, 33, 111, 117, 119, 175, 179, 182, 285, 396, 420, 427, 450, 518, 526–7, 532, 535 ; Univ of 228
Poitou 171, 173, 348, 396, 535
politiques 361, 362, 392
Polverel, Etienne, bp of Alet 250, 260, 403
Polverel, Pierre 250, 260, 285, 383, 403
Pont à Mousson 231
Pontoise 76
Port-Royal 75
Potier, family 161, 396, 430, 431
Potier, Augustin, bp of Beauvais 134, 507–8, 522
Potier, René, bp of Beauvais, 250, 388, 430
Pouillé royal 96, 109, 116, 123, 126, 129
Pourcelet, *banquier expéditionnaire* 109, 113, 120, 121, 129
Pragmatic Sanction 32, 48, 49, 50, 65
Preachers. *See* royal court preachers; entering episcopate 284; suitability for episcopate 367
prédicateurs ordinaires. *See* royal court preachers
prête-noms 154, 162
Prévost, Charles 60
priesthood, ideal of 545
prise de possession 77
procureur 204, 206
promoteur 271, 275, 510
Protector of France 341, 383, 385, 400, 404, 412, 421. *See* Bentivoglio, Joyeuse
Protestant Reformation 32, 39, 208, 245
Protestantism 32, 41, 192, 230, 274, 282, 283, 337–8, 339, 341, 356, 359, 380, 397, 545
Protestants 33, 34, 169, 192, 206, 280, 407, 490
Provençal 101, 103, 179, 205, 471, 472, 512, 534
Provence 6, 24, 29, 30, 34, 35, 50, 58, 82, 93, 115, 117, 119, 120, 144, 150, 159, 160, 168, 171, 175, 177, 179, 181, 205, 282, 310, 324, 340, 356, 361, 369, 371, 380, 393, 394, 430, 444, 469, 472, 480, 518; bishops in/after Fronde 531; bishops of 470; estates of 394; nobility and episcopate 382; outside terms of concordat 369; pacification of 382
provinces, ecclesiastical: councils of 42; shape

and creation of 40
Provisions, papal 109, 146, 211, 216, 250, 285, 294, 295, 310, 318, 339, 343, 367, 401, 402, 409, 411, 419, 447, 456, 459, 465, 475, 482, 489, 502; age at which granted 246, 298, 299–302; ban on search for 374; bishops' quest for 60, 64; concerning pensions 140, 153–4, 413, 414; cost of 64–8, 318, 549; criticisms of papacy over 431; delays in despatch of 307, 344, 346, 434, 543; denials of 406–7, 469; during Catholic League 367, 368, 378, 381; failure to seek 136; grant of 69–70; restoration of 385–6, 387, 388, 389, 390
Puget, Etienne, bp of Marseille 25, 69
Puysieux, Pierre Brûlart, marquis de 59, 82–3, 427–8

Quercy 79
Quimper, bp of 276, 469; see of 93, 112, 177–8, 288, 469. *See* Du Louet, Le Prestre, Visdelou

Raconis, Charles-François d'Abra de, bp of Lavaur 279, 283, 471, 546
Ragny, Léonor de la Madeleine, marquis de. *See* La Madeleine 430. *See* La Madeleine
Ragueneau, Fréderic, bp of Marseille 363
Rastelles, Eleazar de', bp of Riez 394
Ratte, Guichard de, bp of Montpellier 404
Ravitch, Norman, historian 8
Raymond, Jean de, bp of Saint-Papoul 146–7
Rebé, Claude de, abp of Narbonne 443, 446, 470, 528, 534, 536
recherches de noblesse 184, 196
Récollets 267
régale 72–3, 79, 95
Regress, right of 307, 317, 423
Reichskirche 25, 190, 273, 326, 547. *See* Empire
Reims abp of 21, 149, 178, 260, 304, 410, 482, 488, 531; see of 36, 41, 42, 104, 112, 115, 116, 119, 120, 121, 124–7, 151, 173, 179, 191, 231, 257–8, 268, 305, 316, 317, 368, 372, 376, 378, 382, 394, 413, 421, 440–2, 443, 444, 465, 466, 472, 475, 502, 523, 524, 532. *See* Barberini, Du Bec, Etampes, Lorraine-Guise, Le Tellier
Religious orders 438; and university degrees 212, 239, 240, 241; members entering episcopate 169, 256, 265–9, 353
Renaudot, Théophraste 77
Rennes, bp of 368, 450; parlement of 199; see of 112, 115, 175, 243, 312, 370, 393, 405, 424, 450–1, 469, 474, 500. *See* Cornulier, Hennequin, La Mothe-Houdancourt, Larchiver, La Vieuville, Ossat
rentes 101, 121, 122, 351
resignatio in favorem 56
Resignations, episcopal 128, 283, 297, 307, 319, 389, 404, 410, 412, 462, 512, 522, 527; and co-option of succesors 421; as retirement 305–6; decline of 465; during 1610s 420–2; forced upon bishops 304–5; *in favorem* 56, 420, 473; limited numbers of 304; suspicion of 294, 305; under Henri IV 391
Retz. *See* Gondi
Revol, family 396
Revol, Antoine, bp of Dol 67, 396
Revol, Ennemond 375, 376, 396
Revol, Louis 396
Ribier, Jacques 24, 426
Richelieu, family 55, 305, 355, 376, 411, 474, 532
Richelieu, Alphonse de, Cardinal, abp of Aix, Lyon 25, 230, 240, 316, 321, 423, 456, 474, 476, 501, 532
Richelieu, Armand-Jean du Plessis de, Cardinal 16, 54, 67, 84, 85, 136, 171, 177, 182, 191, 243, 281, 295, 306, 448–57, 460–93, 494, 495, 497, 501, 503, 507, 514, 540, 543; accusations against 285–6, 289; and *agents-généraux* 290–1; and Assemblies of Clergy 289–90, 504, 551; and Breton dioceses 468–9; and church reform 485; and *dévots* 33, 160, 417, 455, 460–1, 485–6; and king's conscience 453, 479; and Marie de' Medici's patronage 467–8; and nobility 454, 475–6, 502; and pensions 157, 159; and *régale* 72; and Rome 62; and royal favourites 454; and search for episcopal candidates 480; as bishop 70, 150, 155, 257, 258, 264, 280, 302, 331, 398; blocks episcopal candidates 257, 267, 305, 498–9; clients of in episcopate 126, 262, 421, 473–4, 488, 515; concern at state of dioceses 488; *créatures* of 473–5; criticises individual bishops 488; demands special episcopal commission 488–9; entourage as brokers 483; episcopal patronage of 456–7, 467–9, 471–6; extended entourage of 475–6; household servants of 285, 286, 287, 328, 474; influence on bishops' studies 242; ministerial position of 417, 418, 540; number of nominations during ministry of 462; on careful choice of bishops 479; patron of bishops 24, 35, 66, 68, 255, 282, 284, 301, 500; places clients in bishoprics 253, 274, 278–9, 288, 328, 451, 455–7, 468, 473–4, 491; pre-ministerial experience of episcopal patronage 449–50; pursues negligent bishops 489; relations with Louis XIII 54, 448, 476–9, 493, 506; resignation as bishop 157, 159, 421; role in making bishops 457–93; studies followed by 219, 220, 237; sub-ministerial clients of 474; success of clients after death of 500–2; view of role in making bishops 452–3; views about episcopal office 188–9, 546; warns royal confessor 453–4
Richelieu, François de 203, 355, 398

Richelieu, town of 486
Ridolfi, family 342
Rieux, family 100
Rieux, René de, bp of Saint-Pol-de-Léon 60, 100, 221, 304, 317, 427–8, 462–3, 464, 465, 466, 469, 498
Rieux, René de, comte de Sourdéac 100
Rieux, bp of 269; see of 30, 112, 149–50, 198, 325, 348, 393. *See* Bertier
Riez, bp of 93, 106, 160, 180, 240, 430, 532; see of 30, 82–3, 112, 171, 179, 205, 310, 321, 394, 424, 512. *See* Aleaume, Bentivoglio, Dony, Lopis, Rastelles, Saint-Sixte, Valavoire
robe, noblesse de 197, 200, 201, 325, 326, 430
Robert, Claude 5
Robin, Gérard de, bp of Lodève 169, 403, 447
Rodez 363, 429; bp of 101, 319, 392; see of 29, 40, 48, 112, 117, 171, 175, 394, 399, 498, 512, 515. *See* Corneilhan, Noailles, Péréfixe
Rohan, family 192, 193
Roman Empire 30
Rome. *See* curia, papacy, provisions; and creation of new dioceses 33; bishops consecrated in 70; careers in 287; suspicious of episcopal nominees 17; French relations with 65, 82
Rosa, Mario, historian 142
Rose, Antoine, bp of Senlis, Clermont 319, 320, 399, 430
Rose, Guillaume, bp of Senlis 74, 106, 319, 379, 399
Rosmadec, Charles de, bp of Vannes, Tours 239
Rouchon, Raymond, bp of Saint-Flour 79–80, 81, 89, 411
Rouen 437; abp of 145, 190, 524; college at 221, 224; see of 30, 98, 112, 113, 115, 120, 145, 152, 173, 175, 273, 288, 316, 317, 319, 341, 375, 378, 381, 403, 404, 421–2, 531. *See* Bourbon, Harlay, Joyeuse
Rousse, Jean 377
Roussel, Gérard, bp of Oloron 39
Roussillon 39
Rouxel de Médavy, François, bp of Lisieux 400
Rouxel de Médavy, François, bp de Séez, Rouen 230, 521, 531
royal almoners 76, 203, 259, 277, 278, 279, 282, 283, 394
royal confessor 87, 267, 393, 437, 440, 500, 506, 529, 534, 547; attack on role of 453. *See* Annat, Arnoux, Benoist, Coton, Dinet, Paulin, Ségueran, Suffren
royal council 239, 262, 280, 326, 354, 412, 413, 436, 438, 439, 450, 455, 470, 475, 511, 534; and pensions 144, 150
royal court preachers 277, 280–1, 393, 404, 407; dioceses given to 282–3; modest social origins of 282
royal favourites. *See* Henri IV, Louis XIII, and episcopal office 444–5

Ruade, Bruno, bp of Conserans 84–6, 231, 240, 305, 306, 445, 475
Rucellaï, Annibale, bp of Carcassonne 373, 382, 402, 405
Rucellaï, Orazio 373, 402
Rueil, Claude de, bp of Bayonne, Angers 282
Ruffier, Claude, bp of Saint-Paul-Trois-Châteaux 268

Sacre. See consecrations
Saint Augustine 4
Saint Paul 4
Saint Peter's 260
Saint-André-des-Arts 393
Saint-Bonnet-de-Toiras, Claude de, bp of Nîmes 304, 445, 446, 463, 497
Saint-Brieuc, bp of 400, 466; see of 112, 370, 469. *See* La Barde, Le Porc de la Porte, Marconnay, Villazel
Saint-Cloud 43
Saint-Cyran, Jean Duvergier, abbé de 254, 456, 466, 467, 484, 541, 545
Saint-Denis-en-France, 379; abbey of 80, 266
Saint-Denis-de-Reims, abbot of 478, 479. *See* Maupas du Tour, Henri de
Saint-Esprit, order of 437
Saint-Flour, bp of 78–80, 88, 141; see of 31, 52, 73, 78–80, 112, 378, 411, 450, 468, 498, 502, 515. *See* La Baume, Noailles, Montrouge, Rouchon,
Saint-Gelais, Urbain, bp of Comminges 379
Saint-Germain-des-Prés 76
Saint-Germain, treaty of 338
Saint-Jean, Léon de, Carmelite 500
Saint-Jean-les-Sens, abbey of 104
Saint-Lazare 270, 486, 543
Saint-Lô 100, 352
Saint-Louis-des-Français, Rome 405
Saint-Magloire, abbey of 105
Saint-Malo 362; bp of 149, 170, 261, 263, 379; see of 112, 119, 257, 319, 321, 413, 455, 468, 469, 482, 535–6. *See* Du Bec, Harlay de Sancy, Le Gouverneur, Neufville de Villeroy, Villemontée
Saint-Martin of Tours 273
Saint-Maur-les-Fossés, abbey of 105
Saint-Nicolas-du-Chardonnet 270
Saint-Omer 36
Saint-Papoul, bp of 71, 146, 151, 320, 398, 480; see of 30, 112, 146, 273, 378. *See* Claret, Despruets, Donadieu, Montpezat, Raymond
Saint-Paul-Trois-Châteaux, see of 30, 112, 222–3, 326–7, 498, 505. *See* Cros, Gaume, Grignan, Ruffier
Saint-Pol-de-Léon, bp of 100, 239, 304; see of 35, 60, 112, 239, 317, 351, 427, 462, 464, 465, 466, 469, 498, 521. *See* Cupif, Laval de Boisdauphin, Rieux, Visdelou
Saint-Pons, bp of 428–9, 446; see of 30, 112,

Index 759

163, 356, 428–9, 538. *See* Fleyres, Tubeuf
Saint-Rémy-de-Reims, abbey of 104, 116, 124–5, 126, 441
Saint-Sixte, Charles de, bp of Riez 394
Saint-Sorlin. *See* Nemours
Saint-Sulpice 245, 270, 271, 466, 499, 505, 509, 543
Saint-Thierry, abbey of 104, 126
Saint-Victor, abbey of 76
Sainte Chapelle 72, 73, 79, 95, 273
Sainte Quiterie 205
Sainte-Geneviève, abbey of 76
Sainte-Marthe, brothers 6
Saintes 262; bp of 34; see of 112, 273, 484, 503. *See* Bassompierre, La Rochelle, Raoul
Salette, Jean de, bp of Lescar 274, 393
Salies, Jean du Haut de, bp of Lescar 237
Salignac, family 229, 323, 324, 332, 398, 399, 491–2
Salignac, François de La Mothe-Fénélon, bp of Sarlat 256, 270, 324, 515
Salignac, François de La Mothe-Fénélon, abp of Cambrai 324, 546
Salignac, Louis II de La Mothe-Fénélon, bp of Sarlat 489, 491
Salla, René de 355
Sanguin, Nicolas, bp of Senlis 106
Santacroce, Prospero, Cardinal, abp of Arles 144
Santacroce, Silvio, abp of Arles 144
Santarelli, Antonio, Jesuit 458
Sariac, Bernard de, bp of Aire 289
Sarlat, bp of 135, 196, 229, 305, 514, 521; see of 31, 112, 256, 318, 323, 324, 332, 399, 471, 489, 491, 492, 514, 515. *See* Lingendes, Salignac
Sarpi, Paolo 141
Sauve, barony of 356
Savoy 37–8, 180; bishops originating from 342; dioceses in 38; duke of 380
Scaliger 218
Scarron, Pierre, bp of Grenoble 169
Schomberg, Charles de, Marshal 463, 470
Schomberg, Gaspard de, Marshal 388
Scotti, Ranuccio, papal nuncio 459
secrétaire du roi 198, 200, 201
secretaries of state: role in making bishops 59, 433, 438
Sedan 125, 441, 464
Séez, bp of 169, 207, 217; see of 112, 283, 393, 394, 427, 520–1. *See* Bertaut, Camus, Du Molinet, Morenne, Rouxel, Suarez
Sega, Filippo, papal legate 74, 371, 372
Seguéran, Gaspar de, Jesuit, royal confessor 453
Séguier, family 221, 474
Séguier, Dominique, bp of Auxerre, Meaux 177, 308, 463, 472, 482, 536
Séguier, Jacques 536
Séguier, Louis 73, 375
Séguier, Pierre, chancellor of France 85, 253, 474, 500, 507, 514, 529, 536
Senez, bp of 430; see of 30, 40, 112, 146
Senlis bp of 98, 319, 320; see of 30, 41, 106, 112, 120, 171, 319, 321, 379, 399. *See* La Rochefoucauld, Rose, Sanguin
Senneterre, Antoine de, bp of Le Puy 363
Senneterre, Henri de 85
Sens, abp of 84, 104–5, 239, 301, 368, 372, 499; see of 30, 40–1, 104, 112, 117, 173, 191, 274, 312, 376, 394, 396, 406, 423, 444, 499. *See* Beaune, Bellegarde, Gondrin, du Perron, Pellevé
Serres, family 129–30, 196
Serres, Jacques de, bp of Le Puy 401
Serres, Jean de 401
Serres, Juste de, bp of Le Puy 266
Serres, Olivier de 401
Serroni, Hyacinthe, bp of Orange and Mende 38, 163, 182, 267, 287, 501, 539
Servien, Abel 87, 263, 474, 492, 525, 536, 542
Servien, François, bp of Bayeux 87, 161, 220, 332, 525, 531, 536, 542
Sévigné, Mme de 3
Sévin, Nicolas, bp of Sarlat, Cahors 171, 322, 505, 514, 515, 516
Sidonius 546
Silingardi, Gasparo, papal nuncio 408
Silly, François de 149
Simon. *See* Marquemont
Simony 140, 294, 340, 354, 357, 414, 442, 458
Sisteron 205; bp of 361; see of 30, 112, 160, 512
Sixteen (Paris) 379, 454. *See* Catholic League
Sixtus IV, Pope 38
Sixtus V, Pope 69, 144, 360; and *confidences* 346
Soissons, bp of 24, 425; see of 112, 119, 158, 171. *See* Bourlon, Hacqueville, Hennequin, Le Gras
Soissons, Louis de Bourbon, comte de 304
Solminihac, Alain de, bp of Cahors 4, 101, 467, 489 233, 266, 467, 489, 514–7, 520, 523, 541; advisor to de Paul 513–17
Sorbonne 75, 76, 77, 231, 239, 242, 441, 474, 491, 499. *See* Paris, Theology Faculty
Sorèze, abbé de 87, 88
Sourdis, family 152, 230
Sourdis, François de, Cardinal, abp of Bordeaux 75, 249, 259, 260, 389, 395, 419, 421, 443
Sourdis, Henri de, bp of Maillezais, Bordeaux 93–4, 421, 423, 446, 456, 471, 472, 475, 481, 485, 486, 488, 489, 491–2, 497
Souvré, family 259, 454
Souvré, Gilles de, bp of Comminges and Auxerre 219, 420, 424, 434
Souvré, Gilles de 320–1, 377
Spada, Bernadino, papal nuncio 458
Spain 226, 269, 408, 470. (*See* also *Càmara de Castilla*, *Patronato Real*, Philip II); age of bishops in 554; bishops in 28, 136, 217, 263, 316, 321, 545; cathedral chapters in 548–9;

church in 29, 276; crown patronage in 549; dioceses in 39, 296, 316; episcopal transfers in 554–5; fiscal pressure on bishops in 550; mendicant orders and episcopate in 547–8; monarchy in 18, 40, 68, 554–5; pensions off bishoprics in 95, 142–3, 154; pliancy of episcopate in 550, 555
Sponde, Henri de, bp of Pamiers 455, 490
Sponde, Jean de, bp of Pamiers 490
Strozzi, family 342
Strozzi, Filippo 355
Stuart, Mary 348
Suarez, Jacopo, bp of Séez 178, 283, 427
Subject, Antoine, bp of Montpellier 356
Sublet des Noyers, François 474, 480, 483, 499, 500
suffragan bishops 424; contemporary views of 25; presence in French church 25–6, 257, 306, 340, 439
Suffren, Jean de, Jesuit, royal confessor 453–4
Sully, Maximilien de Béthune, duc de 71, 93, 145, 182, 381, 396, 404, 420, 450
survivance 307, 429
Swiss Leagues 204

taille 194, 199
Tallemant des Réaux 3, 195
Talleyrand-Périgord, Charles-Maurice de 245
Talon, Charles-François 60, 466
Talon, Omer 60, 466, 469
Tarbes, bp of 475; see of 112, 356, 399, 513, 520. *See* Iharse, Malier
Tarragona 39
Tende-Savoie, Henri, comte de 144
Testament Politique: and nobility in episcopate 189, 476; as clue to Richelieu's ideas 449, 546. *See* Richelieu
théologal 272, 273
Theology 231, 244. (*See* Nobility, University); bishops and study of 235–44; degrees in 211, 212, 216, 229, 230, 231; duration of studies in 235–6; examinations in 235–6; faculties 214, 226, 236; inflation of degrees, 236–7; limited demand for graduates in 241; nobility and study of 213
Thérouanne 32
Thoreau, family 536
Thoreau, Mathieu, bp of Dol 197
Thou, Augustin de 158
Thou, Nicolas de, bp of Chartres 364, 396
Thyard, Héliodore de, sgr de Bissy 373
Thyard, Cyrus de, bp of Chalon-sur-Saône 373, 398
Thyard, Pontus de, bp of Chalon-sur-Saône 213, 373, 381
Tilenus 218
Toiras, Jean de Saint-Bonnet, Marshal 445, 454. *See also* Saint-Bonnet
tonsure 246, 247, 248, 249, 273

Torigny, comte de 375
Toul, bp of 482; see of 36–7, 121, 257, 482
Toulon, bp of 454, 475; see of 19, 40, 112, 146, 370, 377, 378, 471, 479. *See* Danès, Forbin, Le Blanc, Pingre, Seytres
Toulouse 197, 361, 363, 429; abp of 23, 163, 207, 422, 445, 470; colleges in 220, 221; Catholic league in 379; parlement of 198, 199, 229, 317, 383, 392, 403, 404, 490, 516, 519, 530; see of 29, 40, 74, 84, 86, 96, 98, 112, 113, 116, 117, 127–9, 133, 134, 137, 157, 175, 199, 237, 270, 285, 319, 321, 326, 341, 343, 356, 359, 421–2, 427, 445, 456, 516, 526, 539; Univ of 219, 228, 229, 230, 237, 238. *See* Joyeuse, La Valette, Marca, Montchal
Touraine, duchy of 348
Tournon, college of 222, 223
Tournon, family 192
Tournon, François de, Cardinal 286–7, 341
Tours 169, 363; abp of 22, 325, 414, 456, 473; royalist parlement of 379; see of 40, 112, 119, 157, 179, 268, 273, 377, 396, 423, 431, 468, 472, 481. *See* Bouthillier, Deschaux, La Guesle
Treaty of Lyon 37
Tréguier, bp of 240; see of 112, 147–8, 393, 395, 424, 469, 477, 481. *See* Amboise, Champion, Cornulier, Deslandes, Grangier
Trent, council of 42, 63, 140–1, 192, 208–10, 215, 216, 22, 239, 246, 248, 280, 384, 408, 420, 423, 435, 544, 557; against pluralism 341; attacks aspects of benefice-holding 347; and coadjutorships 306–7; and education of bishops 211, 212; and enquiries on new bishops 61; and episcopal power 293; and university studies 233; model of bishops 4
Trente-Trois, seminary of 507
Tresnel, François des Ursins, ambassador in Rome 434
trésoriers de France 197
trésoriers de l'Epargne 206
Trier 37
Trivulzio 192
Trois-Evêchés 36, 50. *See* Metz, Toul, Verdun
Troyes, bp of 215–16, 230, 338, 368, 475, 490; see of 112, 115, 119, 339, 368, 371, 375, 376, 393, 406. *See* Benoist, Breslay, Caracciolo, Malier
Tubeuf, family 536
Tubeuf, Jacques 542
Tubeuf, Michel, bp of Saint-Pons 163, 256, 542
Tulle, bp of 400; see of 5, 31, 112, 515, 535. *See* Genoulhac, Guron
Tulles, family 38
Tulles, Jean-Vincent de, bp of Orange, Lavaur 38, 182, 501, 518, 519, 534
Turicella, Jacopo, bp of Marseille 105, 394

Ubaldini, Roberto, papal nuncio 417, 431–2
Ultramontane 365, 423
University 210, 211, 212, 213, 214, 216, 219, 220, 221, 223, 224, 225, 226, 227, 228, 229, 230, 231, 233, 234, 235, 238, 240, 241, 242, 243, 244; attitudes to study at 225; degrees taken by incoming bishops 298; higher degrees granted by 233; nobility and 505; posts reserved for graduates of 214; professors as bishops 546;
Urban VIII 51, 61, 153, 154, 182, 216, 281, 441, 458, 488, 554
Uzès, bp of 240, 268, 463, 308, 429, 446; see of 112, 115, 156, 283, 285, 321, 327, 377, 382, 401, 463, 465, 470, 472, 482. *See* Fay-Peyraud, Grillié, Grignan, Vigne

Vabres, see of 30, 112, 117, 344, 482, 503, 511. *See* Corneilhan, Delauro, Habert, La Valette de Cornusson
Vaillan, Thomas Bonsi, comte de 251. *See* Bonsi
Vaison, see of 38
Valavoire, Nicolas, bp of Riez 160, 205, 512, 513, 531, 533
Valavoire, Pierre 205
Valence 326; bp of 546; see of 34, 112, 284, 532; Univ of 228, 236, 238, 241. *See* Cosnac, Gelas de Léberon
Valentinois 50
Valernod, Pierre, bp of Nîmes 401, 404, 438–9, 446
Valladier, André 267
Valois, Louis-Emmanuel de, comte d'Alais, bp of Agde 100, 190, 230, 260, 305, 446–7, 501, 502–3, 512
Valois-Angoulême, house of 217
Valois-Auvergne, house of 192
Valois, Marguerite de 52, 373, 393
Vannes 112, 239; bp of 47; see of 370, 371, 397. *See* Aradon, Martin, Rosmadec
Vassé, Jean de 349
Vaudémont, Charles de Lorraine, Cardinal de 359
Vautier, François 456
Velay 401
Vence, bp of 4, 24; see of 29, 34–5, 112, 115, 161, 171, 370, 426, 481. *See* Du Vair, Godeau, Le Blanc, Ribier
Vendôme, house of 185, 189, 485
Vendôme, César de Bourbon, duc de 76
Venice 141, 520; bishops in 549; Erastian attitudes of 553
Ventadour, Anne de Lévy, duc de I 149, 383, 401, 402, 403, 404, 432
Ventadour, Anne de, abp of Bourges 223, 286, 287, 447–8, 500, 503, 522, 526, 531, 532
Ventadour, duc de 432, 446, 447
Ventadour, house of 158, 181, 192, 400, 403, 447–8, 475–6, 503, 403, 446
Ventadour, Charles de Lévy de 447
Ventadour, François de Lévy de 447
Ventadour, Henri de Lévy de, duc de 327
Ventadour, Louis-Hercule de Lévy, bp of Mirepoix, Carcassonne 163, 267–8, 448, 522
Verdun 36, 37, 121
Verfeil 128
Verneuil, Catherine-Henriette de Balsac, marquise de 395
Versailles 168
Vervins, Louis de, abp of Narbonne 156, 240, 401, 403, 411
Vialart, Charles, bp of Avranches 67, 474
Vialart, Félix, bp of Châlons-sur-Marne 121, 122, 123–4, 270, 474, 487, 489
Vic, family 199, 221
Vic, Dominique de, abp of Auch 62, 443
Vic, Méric de 443
Vicars-general 271, 274, 275, 276, 284, 272, 289, 515
Vienne 324; abp of 38, 218, 275, 399, 414; chapter of 308; see of 112, 119, 175, 317, 323, 344. *See* Villars
Vieuxpont, Jean de, bp of Meaux 218
Vigne, Louis de, bp of Uzès 240, 401
Villars, family 195, 196, 275, 317, 323, 324, 326, 399
Villars, Jérôme de, abp of Vienne 399, 435
Villars, Nicolas de, bp of Agen 218, 275, 399
Villars, Pierre II, abp of Vienne 386
Villars, Pierre III de, abp of Vienne 218, 308, 399
Villars-Brancas, Georges de 381, 403
Villazel, Etienne, bp of Saint-Brieuc 279, 485
Villefranche 38
Villemontée, François, bp of Saint-Malo 235, 261, 263
Villeneuve, family 444
Villeneuve, Scipion, bp of Grasse 471
Villers la Faye, Cyrus, bp of Périgueux 516
Visdelou, François, bp of Quimper, Saint-Pol-de-Léon 288
Visitation, order of nuns 76
Viviers bp of 42, 439; see of 112, 171, 310, 346, 355, 362, 429, 446. *See* La Baume de Suze, l'Hôtel

Wars of religion 12, 121, 169; and episcopate 335–64, 415; and loss of church temporalities 99–100
Wales 28, 95

Younger sons: and episcopate 245

Zamet, Sébastien 395, 542
Zamet, Sébastien, bp of Langres 33, 189, 221, 397, 399, 419–20, 434, 486